blacking top pg edges 11-09 CIRCUL

Let's go: In
915.4 Let

P9-DWY-701

Silver City Public Library

LET'S GO

■ THE RESOURCE

"The guides are aimed ... at young budget travelers but at the independent traveler; a sort of streetwise cookbook for traveling alone."

—*The New York Times*

"Unbeatable; good sight-seeing advice; up-to-date info on restaurants, hotels, and inns; a commitment to money-saving travel; and a wry style that brightens nearly every page."

—*The Washington Post*

"Lighthearted and sophisticated, informative and fun to read. [Let's Go] helps the novice traveler navigate like a knowledgeable old hand."

—*Atlanta Journal-Constitution*

"A world-wise traveling companion—always ready with friendly advice and helpful hints, all sprinkled with a bit of wit."

—*The Philadelphia Inquirer*

■ THE BEST TRAVEL BARGAINS IN YOUR PRICE RANGE

"All the dirt, dirt cheap."

—*People*

"Anything you need to know about budget traveling is detailed in this book."

—*The Chicago Sun-Times*

"Let's Go follows the creed that you don't have to toss your life's savings to the wind to travel—unless you want to."

—*The Salt Lake Tribune*

■ REAL ADVICE FOR REAL EXPERIENCES

"The writers seem to have experienced every rooster-packed bus and lunar-surfaced mattress about which they write."

—*The New York Times*

"A guide should tell you what to expect from a destination. Here Let's Go shines."

—*The Chicago Tribune*

"[Let's Go's] devoted updaters really walk the walk (and thumb the ride, and trek the trail). Learn how to fish, haggle, find work—anywhere."

—*Food & Wine*

LET'S GO PUBLICATIONS

TRAVEL GUIDES

Alaska 1st edition **NEW TITLE**
Australia 2004
Austria & Switzerland 2004
Brazil 1st edition **NEW TITLE**
Britain & Ireland 2004
California 2004
Central America 8th edition
Chile 1st edition
China 4th edition
Costa Rica 1st edition
Eastern Europe 2004
Egypt 2nd edition
Europe 2004
France 2004
Germany 2004
Greece 2004
Hawaii 2004
India & Nepal 8th edition
Ireland 2004
Israel 4th edition
Italy 2004
Japan 1st edition **NEW TITLE**
Mexico 20th edition
Middle East 4th edition
New Zealand 6th edition
Pacific Northwest 1st edition **NEW TITLE**
Peru, Ecuador & Bolivia 3rd edition
Puerto Rico 1st edition **NEW TITLE**
South Africa 5th edition
Southeast Asia 8th edition
Southwest USA 3rd edition
Spain & Portugal 2004
Thailand 1st edition
Turkey 5th edition
USA 2004
Western Europe 2004

CITY GUIDES

Amsterdam 3rd edition
Barcelona 3rd edition
Boston 4th edition
London 2004
New York City 2004
Paris 2004
Rome 12th edition
San Francisco 4th edition
Washington, D.C. 13th edition

MAP GUIDES

Amsterdam
Berlin
Boston
Chicago
Dublin
Florence
Hong Kong
London
Los Angeles
Madrid
New Orleans
New York City
Paris
Prague
Rome
San Francisco
Seattle
Sydney
Venice
Washington, D.C.

COMING SOON:
Road Trip USA

LET'S GO

SILVER CITY PUBLIC LIBRARY
515 W. COLLEGE AVE.
SILVER CITY, NM 88061

INDIA &
NEPAL

JANE YANG EDITOR
DANIEL HOYOS ASSOCIATE EDITOR
MEREDITH SCHWEIG ASSOCIATE EDITOR

RESEARCHER-WRITERS

JOHN BACHMAN
NEERAJ "RICHIE" BANERJI
KELZIE E. BEEBE
KEVIN CONNOR
PAUL GUILIANELLI
DAVID HUYSSEN
MIN LIESKOVSKY

FRAN MOORE
D.K. OSSEO-ASSARE
CATHY PHAM
NARESH RAMARAJAN
ROONA RAY
NATALIA A. JOSÉ TRUSZKOWSKA

ELIZABETH H. PETERSON MAP EDITOR
NITIN SHAH MANAGING EDITOR

915.4
Let

ST. MARTIN'S PRESS ✹ NEW YORK

0242587
$ 23   11/09

HELPING LET'S GO
If you want to share your discoveries, suggestions, or corrections, please drop us a line. We read every piece of correspondence, whether a postcard, a 10-page email, or a coconut. **Address mail to:**

> **Let's Go: India & Nepal**
> **67 Mount Auburn Street**
> **Cambridge, MA 02138**
> **USA**

Visit Let's Go at **http://www.letsgo.com,** or send email to:

> **feedback@letsgo.com**
> **Subject: "Let's Go: India & Nepal"**

In addition to the invaluable travel advice our readers share with us, many are kind enough to offer their services as researchers or editors. Unfortunately, our charter enables us to employ only currently enrolled Harvard students.

Maps by David Lindroth copyright © 2004 by St. Martin's Press.

Distributed outside the USA and Canada by Macmillan.

Let's Go: India & Nepal Copyright © 2004 by Let's Go, Inc. All rights reserved. Printed in the United States of America. No part of this book may be used or reproduced in any manner whatsoever without written permission except in the case of brief quotations embodied in critical articles or reviews. Let's Go is available for purchase in bulk by institutions and authorized resellers. For information, address St. Martin's Press, 175 Fifth Avenue, New York, NY 10010, USA.

ISBN: 0-312-32006-X

First edition
10 9 8 7 6 5 4 3 2 1

Let's Go: India & Nepal is written by Let's Go Publications, 67 Mount Auburn Street, Cambridge, MA 02138, USA.

Let's Go® and the LG logo are trademarks of Let's Go, Inc.
Printed in the USA.

ADVERTISING DISCLAIMER
All advertisements appearing in Let's Go publications are sold by an independent agency not affiliated with the editorial production of the guides. Advertisers are never given preferential treatment, and the guides are researched, written, and published independent of advertising. Advertisements do not imply endorsement of products or services by Let's Go, and Let's Go does not vouch for the accuracy of information provided in advertisements.

If you are interested in purchasing advertising space in a Let's Go publication, contact: Let's Go Advertising Sales, 67 Mount Auburn St., Cambridge, MA 02138, USA.

HOW TO USE THIS BOOK

PLANNING YOUR TRIP. Need ideas for where to go? **Discover** provides an at-a-glance look at India and Nepal's many possibilities. Culture student? History buff? Study up on these two South Asian countries in **Life and Times**. Ready to plan a trip? Get all the facts in **Essentials,** chock full of stuff you'll need to know about everything from visas to packing, transportation to health and safety. If you'd like to study abroad, teach English, or volunteer in India or Nepal, **Alternatives to Tourism** can serve as a jumping-off point for planning your adventure.

ORGANIZATION. The India section of *Let's Go: India and Nepal* is organized in alphabetical order by state. In Nepal, coverage starts in the Kathmandu Valley, moves through the Western Hills, the lowland Terai, and the Eastern Hills before culminating at the highest point on earth in the Trekking in Nepal and Rafting in Nepal chapters. The black tabs on the side of the book should help you navigate.

In each chapter, coverage begins in the capital of that region, moving clockwise outward from there. Large cities have more complex coverage, with separate Orientation, Practical Information, Transportation, Accommodations, Food, and Sights sections, while small towns, villages, and transport hubs have all the same information presented in paragraph form.

Within the Accommodations and Food sections, listings are ranked in decreasing order of value and quality. While on the road, Let's Go researchers seek out the best options for a budget traveler, evaluating quality while keeping an eye on price. We give the Let's Go ✦thumb to outstanding establishments that are the best of both worlds. For those times when you just can't bear to eat at another roadside *dhaba*, or when you want to splurge on a hotel with A/C and room service, each listing is also marked with a price diversity symbol ranging from ❶ to ❺. For a full breakdown of our price diversity rankings, see the detailed chart in the book's front matter.

TRANSPORTATION INFO. Within each city, the Transportation section gives general information on destinations reachable from that city. Information is presented in the following format: destination city name (duration of the trip, departure time(s), ticket price). All prices are individual ticket prices for 2nd class travel. In India, the train ticket prices we quote are for 3A class, and for 2nd class sleeper cars where available.

PHONE CODES AND PHONE NUMBERS. The phone code for each region, city, or town appears opposite the name of that region, city, or town, and is denoted by the ☎. Phone numbers are also marked with a ☎. In India and Nepal, the number of digits in a phone number depends on the size of the city or town. Since India is now in the process of expanding its telephone service, some phone numbers we list will have lengthened by one digit (usually a 2 or a 4 at the beginning of a number) by the time of publication. If a phone number does not seem current, ask a local if any digits have been added.

SCHOLARLY ARTICLES. *Let's Go: India and Nepal* features articles written by scholars and experts on the geological reasons for the rise of the Himalayas (p. 794) and the experience of musical study in India (p. 93).

A NOTE TO OUR READERS The information for this book was gathered by *Let's Go* researchers from May through August of 2003. Each listing is based on one researcher's opinion, formed during his or her visit at a particular time. Those traveling at other times may have different experiences since prices, dates, hours, and conditions are always subject to change. You are urged to check the facts presented in this book beforehand to avoid inconvenience and surprises.

SEE YOURSELF HERE?

Experience a whole new world

Volunteer on SPW's 4-9 months Health Education and Community Resource Programs in Asia and Africa.

To contact us

tel (603) 356-2765   email spw@worldpath.net   web www.spw.org

SPW is a registered charity no 292492

CONTENTS

MAP INDEX

RESEARCHER-WRITERS

John Bachman   *Western Nepal, Trekking, Sikkim, West Bengal*

We were privileged to have this veteran of *Let's Go: India and Nepal* and *Let's Go: Turkey* on our team. John trekked through Nepal's stunning Annapurna region and climbed the verdant slopes of Sikkim to send us coverage that made us dream of being there. From his writing on West Bengal to Western Nepal, John's passion for the Sub-continent shines through every word.

Neeraj "Richie" Banerji   *West Bengal, Orissa, Andhra Pradesh*

We waited all summer long for Richie's lovingly written prose on his native India, all the while hearing his Indian accent grow stronger and stronger. On the road, no *thali* went untasted and no *lassi* went unsipped. While adding loads of new listings to this year's edition, Richie experienced India as he never had before: *Let's Go* style.

Kelzie Beebe   *Patan, Gorkha, Everest Trek, and Garhwal*

Sometimes we wonder if the lack of oxygen has gone to her head. After writing for *Let's Go: South Africa*, this veteran RW suited up to conquer the world's tallest peak. She took on the mountains of India and Nepal, and, as if that wasn't enough, still managed to find time to sample the city life in Patan. After taking a well-deserved deep breath, she delivered some of the best coverage we've seen.

Kevin Connor   *Delhi, Kumaon, Punjab and Haryana, and Uttar Pradesh*

Kevin heated up the Subcontinent when he arrived in Delhi, and things haven't cooled down since. A veteran RW for *Let's Go: Greece*, he traded in his *souvalaki* for *palak paneer* and made some new friends along the way. After spotting the Dalai Lama, Kevin wrestled both monsoons and bad stomachaches to trek his way across India to the Pindari Glacier and beyond.

Paul Guilianelli   *Gujarat, Rajasthan*

This veteran researcher worked previously as a mapper for *Let's Go: India and Nepal* and as an RW for *Let's Go: Southeast Asia* and *Let's Go: Italy* before making his way to the Subcontinent. Now that he's met up with Mr. Desert, visited the Rat Temple, and traveled to the westernmost point of Hinduism's holy compass, Paul can officially say he's done it all.

David Huyssen   *Goa, Kerala*

This sexy-voiced former associate editor for *Let's Go: Peru, Ecuador, and Bolivia* and editor of *Let's Go: Austria and Switzerland* broke out of the office to "research" surf-side raves and glistening white sand beaches in Goa and Kerala. It was tough work, but we're glad this stellar RW was willing to help us out.

Min Lieskovsky   *Madhya Pradesh, Maharashtra*

Always up for a challenge, Min took on extreme heat, rats, and many bad *samosas* in India. Catwalking her way down the streets of Mumbai, she shouldered her 80 lb. backpack with grace and style. When Min wasn't sneaking into restricted areas or getting run out of towns, she managed to send back sparkling prose that made us want to go on an adventure, too.

RESEARCHER-WRITERS

Fran Moore *Andhra Pradesh, Karnataka, Maharashtra, Tamil Nadu*

From temple towns to high-tech cities, our British *dahling* dodged hippies, auto-rickshaws, and camera thieves on her turn in India. But Fran did it all between sips of Tata tea and fresh strawberries. This first-time RW regaled us with her beautifully written tales of giant *ghee*-covered statues, fantastic turn-of-the-century trains, and some of the most glorious scenery on earth.

D.K. Osseo-Assare *Andamans, Bihar, National Parks, Northeast India*

After many close encounters of the fanged, winged, and hooved kind, this former *Let's Go* map editor delivered meticulous prose on India's national parks in carefully penned script. In spite of millions of mosquito bites, D.K. still managed to jet-set from Bihar to the Andamans for some days of sun and sand and more frequent flier miles than he'll ever know what to do with.

Cathy Pham *Delhi*

Cathy's immaculate, handwritten copy glowed with the excitement of one returning to a place she adores. Whether making sense of Delhi's tangled avenues or bringing the Red Fort to life, she put her best foot forward and delivered a city's worth of genuinely Phamtastic coverage. Keep on keepin' on, Cathy.

Naresh Ramarajan *Himachal Pradesh*

After researching for *Let's Go: Spain, Portugal, and Morocco*, Naresh made his way to Kinnaur-Spiti for some hearty adventure. This resident of Chennai dodged landslides and washed-out bridges for us, proving that the perils of the monsoon are no match for a determined RW. We never doubted him for a second—up against Naresh, the monsoon didn't stand a chance.

Roona Ray *Munnar, Tamil Nadu, Himachal Pradesh*

With a rudimentary slingshot constructed from a glue stick and several rubber bands, Roona battled pesky primates and testy bus drivers in India. Her extensive coverage of numerous temple towns was nothing to laugh at, while her hilarious roadside commentary did nothing *but* make us laugh. A true team player, Roona's amazing attitude and sense of humor was the secret of our success.

Natalia A. José Truszkowska *Kathmandu Valley, Eastern Hills, Rafting*

After two tours researching for *Let's Go: Eastern Europe* and *Let's Go: Costa Rica*, Natalia globetrotted over to Nepal for a taste of Kathmandu and heaping platefuls of *dal bhat*. Unfazed by the machismo of her overeager rickshaw-*wallah*, she donned the latest Nepali garb and convinced more than one local that she could handle both Class IV rapids and all too many bumpy bus rides.

CONTRIBUTING WRITERS

Wang-Ping Chen is a geophysics professor at the University of Illinois at Urbana-Champaign. He published his first scientific article on seismic waves over Tibet in 1975. He is currently coordinating Project Hi-CLIMB, a large-scale research endeavor in the Himalayas and Tibet, involving eight institutions in five countries.

Joanna O'Leary is a *Let's Go* managing editor and former editor of *Let's Go: Austria and Switzerland*. She was a volunteer in a rural village in northern India, where she worked at a daycare center and researched health issues. She is preparing for a career in medicine.

Sharmila Sen is Assistant Professor of English and American Literature and Language at Harvard University. She is currently writing about the line of control between India and Pakistan in Bollywood cinema and working on a book on consumption and representations of India in anglophone texts.

Richard K. Wolf is the Harris K. Weston Associate Professor of the Humanities at Harvard University, where he teaches in the music department. He has conducted ethnomusicological fieldwork in India and Pakistan for more than six years, and is the author of publications on various aspects of South Asian classical, folk, ritual, and tribal musical traditions.

Katie Heller	*Southern Gujarat*
Adam Kampf	*Jammu and Kashmir*
Matt Kutcher	*Jammu and Kashmir*

ACKNOWLEDGMENTS

LET'S GO

TEAM I&N THANKS: Prod, especially Thomas. Nitin and all the MEs. Elizabeth, our mapper. www.dictionary.com, Roka (on Mass Ave.), Toscanini's, the word "bustling," and many pushy *pandas*. To our dazzling team of RWs—congrats, you made it!

JANE THANKS: Mer and Dan, for the hard work and quality words, on and off the page, and for the daily serenades. Nitin, friend and ME extraordinaire. Damaris for the typing, the typos, and the smiles. Joanna and Podmate Jesse for always being there to help. Nick, John, and Paul for helping the homeless. And mom, for everything, especially for making sure I always had a good lunch.

MEREDITH THANKS: The bookteam (Jane, Dan, Nitin, Elizabeth, and the RWs) for all the laughs, evil laughs, generosity, and, of course, love. Jesse, Joanna, and Ganesh for answering every question I could have had. Damaris for being my typist soulmate. Ruby and Burnett for wasting hours of their lives watching Fox with me. Andres and my funny, lovable family for being the best.

DANIEL THANKS: Fellow Indophiles Jane, Mer, and Nitin for helping me realize every dream I ever dreamed about India. The RWs for their blood, sweat, and *ghee*. Damaris for Kornatala. Elizabeth, Joanna, Jesse, and Scrobee-doowopbop. The roomies at Dane Street for putting up with my food experiments. Eric, Sarah, Tiffany, PJ, and my family. I'd also like to thank the Academy.

ELIZABETH THANKS: Jane, Dan, and Meredith, for being great editors. Nathaniel, for being an awesome boss. And all my fellow mappers, especially my sister Christine.

Editor
Jane Yang
Associate Editors
Daniel Hoyos, Meredith Schweig
Managing Editor
Nitin Shah
Map Editor
Elizabeth H. Peterson
Typesetter
Thomas Bechtold

Publishing Director
Julie A. Stephens
Editor-in-Chief
Jeffrey Dubner
Production Manager
Dusty Lewis
Cartography Manager
Nathaniel Brooks
Design Manager
Caleb Beyers
Editorial Managers
Lauren Bonner, Ariel Fox,
Matthew K. Hudson, Emma Nothmann,
Joanna Shawn Brigid O'Leary,
Sarah Robinson
Financial Manager
Suzanne Siu
Marketing & Publicity Managers
Megan Brumagim, Nitin Shah
Personnel Manager
Jesse Reid Andrews
Researcher Manager
Jennifer O'Brien
Web Manager
Jesse Tov
Web Content Director
Abigail Burger
Production Associates
Thomas Bechtold, Jeffrey Hoffman Yip
IT Directors
Travis Good, E. Peyton Sherwood
Financial Assistant
R. Kirkie Maswoswe
Associate Web Manager
Robert Dubbin
Office Coordinators
Abigail Burger, Angelina L. Fryer,
Liz Glynn

Director of Advertising Sales
Daniel Ramsey
Senior Advertising Associates
Sara Barnett, Daniella Boston
Advertising Artwork Editor
Julia Davidson

President
Abhishek Gupta
General Manager
Robert B. Rombauer
Assistant General Manager
Anne E. Chisholm

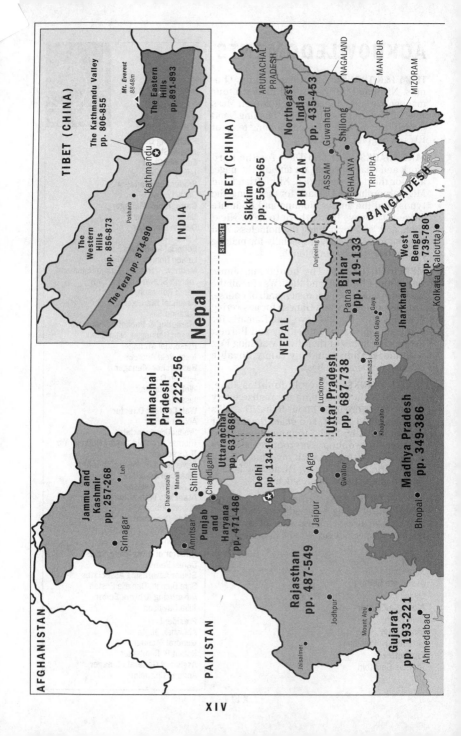

XIV

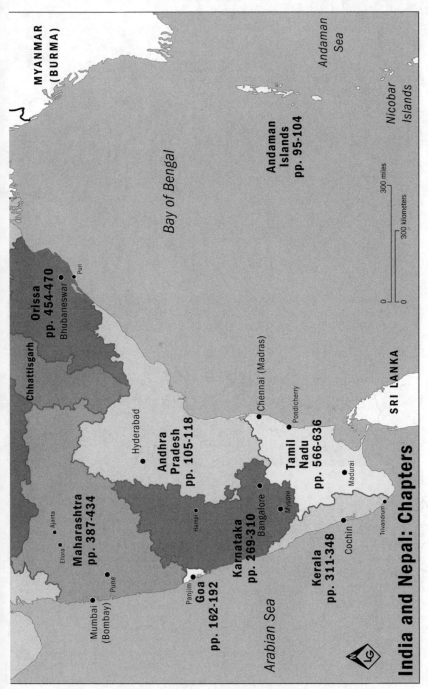

India and Nepal: Chapters

MYANMAR (BURMA)

Andaman Sea

Nicobar Islands

Bay of Bengal

Andaman Islands pp. 95-104

Orissa pp. 454-470
Puri
Bhubaneswar

Chhattisgarh

Maharashtra pp. 387-434
Ajanta
Ellora
Pune
Mumbai (Bombay)

Hyderabad

Andhra Pradesh pp. 105-118

Chennai (Madras)
Pondicherry

Tamil Nadu pp. 566-636
Madurai

SRI LANKA

Karnataka pp. 269-310
Hampi
Bangalore
Mysore

Panjim
Goa pp. 162-192

Kerala pp. 311-348
Cochin
Trivandrum

Arabian Sea

300 miles
300 kilometers

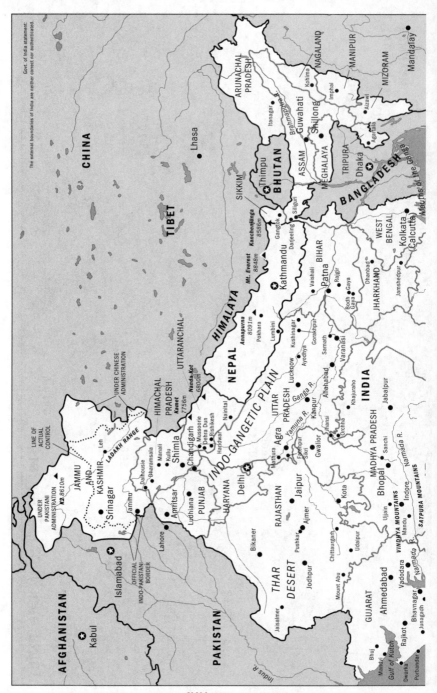

Govt. of India statement:
The external boundaries of India are neither correct nor authenticated.

XVI

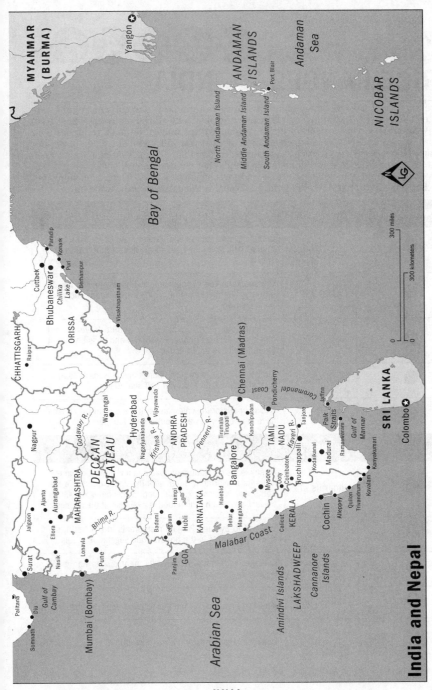

India and Nepal

1 2 3 4 5

PRICE RANGES >> INDIA

Our researchers list establishments in order of value from best to worst; our favorites are denoted by the Let's Go thumbs-up (☝). Since the best value does not always translate to the lowest price, we have incorporated a system of price ranges for quick reference. Our price ranges are based on a rough calculation of what you will spend at a given place. For **accommodations,** we base our price range on the least amount of money a single traveler can spend for a single night's stay. For **restaurants** and other dining establishments, we estimate the average amount you can expect to spend for a snack or a meal. The tables below tell you what you will *typically* find in India and Nepal at the corresponding price range.

ACCOMMODATIONS	RANGE	WHAT YOU'RE *LIKELY* TO FIND
❶	under Rs150	Camping; most dorm beds. Expect bunk beds and a communal bath; you may have to provide or rent towels and sheets.
❷	Rs150-350	Upper-end hostels or small hotels. You may have a private bathroom, or there may be a sink in your room and communal shower.
❸	Rs350-600	A small room with private bath. Should have decent amenities, such as phone, TV, shower and possibly a seat toilet. May have an air cooler.
❹	Rs600-800	Similar to 3, but may have more amenities such as A/C. Almost always with a shower and seat toilet.
❺	above Rs800	Classy hotels or upscale chains. If it's a 5 and it doesn't have the perks you want, you've paid too much.
FOOD	RANGE	WHAT YOU'RE *LIKELY* TO FIND
❶	under Rs30	Mostly roadside stands, dhabas and low-end sit-down restaurants in Northern India; slightly higher quality in the South. For instance, Punjabi food in this category will be basic; good South Indian food is available at these prices.
❷	Rs30-60	Low-end to average Punjabi restaurants in the North, sit-down restaurants in the South. Good vegetarian meals.
❸	Rs60-100	Average restaurants, mid-quality meat dishes and great vegetarian meals.
❹	Rs100-150	A relatively fancy restaurant with waitstaff and a full menu.
❺	above Rs150	Quality foreign foods and luxury restaurant.

PRICE RANGES >> NEPAL

1 2 3 4 5

ACCOMMODATIONS	RANGE	WHAT YOU'RE *LIKELY* TO FIND
❶	under Rs150	Camping; most dorm beds. Expect bunk beds and a communal bath; you may have to provide or rent towels and sheets.
❷	Rs150-350	Upper-end hostels or small hotels. You may have a private bathroom, or there may be a sink in your room and communal shower.
❸	Rs350-550	A small room with private bath. Should have decent amenities, such as phone, TV, shower and possibly a seat toilet. May have an air cooler.
❹	Rs550-800	Similar to 3, but may have more amenities such as A/C. Almost always with a shower and seat toilet.
❺	above Rs800	Classy hotels or upscale chains. If it's a 5 and it doesn't have the perks you want, you've paid too much.

FOOD	RANGE	WHAT YOU'RE *LIKELY* TO FIND
❶	under Rs60	Mostly roadside stands, dhabas and low-end sit-down restaurants.
❷	Rs60-125	Low-end sit-down restaurants. Mid-range vegetarian dishes and low-end meat dishes fall in this category.
❸	Rs125-200	Average restaurants, mid-quality meat dishes and great vegetarian meals.
❹	Rs200-300	A relatively fancy restaurant with waitstaff and a full menu.
❺	above 300	Quality foreign foods and luxury restaurant.

ABOUT LET'S GO

GUIDES FOR THE INDEPENDENT TRAVELER

Budget travel is more than a vacation. At *Let's Go*, we see every trip as the chance of a lifetime. If your dream is to grab a knapsack and a machete and forge through the jungles of Brazil, we can take you there. Or, if you'd rather enjoy the Riviera sun at a beachside cafe, we'll set you a table. If you know what you're doing, you can have any experience you want—whether it's camping among lions or sampling Tuscan desserts—without maxing out your credit card. We'll show you just how far your coins can go, and prove that the greatest limitation on your adventure is not your wallet, but your imagination. That said, we understand that you may want the occasional indulgence after a week of hostels and kebab stands, so we've added "Big Splurges" to let you know which establishments are worth those extra euros, as well as price ranges to help you quickly determine whether an accommodation or restaurant will break the bank. While we may have diversified, our emphasis will always be on finding the best values for your budget, giving you all the info you need to spend six days in London or six months in Tasmania.

BEYOND THE TOURIST EXPERIENCE

We write for travelers who know there's more to a vacation than riding double-deckers with tourists. Our researchers give you the heads-up on both world-renowned and lesser-known attractions, on the best local eats and the hottest nightclub beats. In our travels, we talk to everybody; we provide a snapshot of real life in the places you visit with our sidebars on topics like regional cuisine, local festivals, and hot political issues. We've opened our pages to respected writers and scholars to show you their take on a given destination, and turned to lifelong residents to learn the little things that make their city worth calling home. And we've even given you Alternatives to Tourism—ideas for how to give back to local communities through responsible travel and volunteering.

OVER FORTY YEARS OF WISDOM

When we started, way back in 1960, Let's Go consisted of a small group of well-traveled friends who compiled their budget travel tips into a 20-page packet for students on charter flights to Europe. Since then, we've expanded to suit all kinds of travelers, now publishing guides to six continents, including our newest guides: *Let's Go: Japan* and *Let's Go: Brazil*. Our guides are still annually researched and written entirely by students on shoe-string budgets, adventurous travelers who know that train strikes, stolen luggage, food poisoning, and marriage proposals are all part of a day's work. Even as you read this, work on next year's editions is well underway. Whether you're reading one of our new titles, like *Let's Go: Puerto Rico* or *Let's Go Adventure Guide: Alaska*, or our original best-seller, *Let's Go: Europe*, you'll find the same spirit of adventure that has made *Let's Go* the guide of choice for travelers the world over since 1960.

GETTING IN TOUCH

The best discoveries are often those you make yourself; on the road, when you find something worth sharing, please drop us a line. We're Let's Go Publications, 67 Mt. Auburn St., Cambridge, MA 02138, USA (feedback@letsgo.com).

For more info, visit our website: www.letsgo.com.

DISCOVER
INDIA & NEPAL

For the daring traveler, India and Nepal are both as challenging—and as threatening—as they are rewarding and unforgettable. This is not a region where you can sit back and observe; it demands reaction. After a few weeks here, many people are all too happy to escape back to a safer world, a world where things move at a different pace. But nobody leaves the Subcontinent completely unchanged.

Birthplace of three of the world's oldest religions—Hinduism, Buddhism, and Jainism—**India** today accommodates countless others and struggles to maintain its secular facade as the world's largest democracy. The sublime beauty of India's natural scenery and towering temples are as likely to overwhelm as the ubiquitous smells of dirt, dust, and dung. *Paan* stains the city streets, *tilak* powder dusts the temple walls, and the traffic horns will honk you out of your senses. But the magical swirl of color and life, the mosques and the minarets, the quick and spicy meal at a roadside *dhaba*, and the early-morning echoes of prayer chants make the Subcontinent quite unlike anywhere you've ever been before.

Hidden among the world's highest peaks, **Nepal** is a country shaped by its geography. Ancient temple towns and palace squares help to bring true every romantic dream you ever dreamed about the Kathmandu Valley. The rice fields of the Terai share the land with the rare wildlife that roams about its natural habitat. Soaring high above the valleys and farms, of course, are the mighty Himalayas, which offer some of the best hiking and most spectacular scenery on the planet.

INDIA	NEPAL
☆ **Population (people):** 1 billion	☆ **Population:** 23 million
☆ **Population (cows):** 200 million	☆ **Average annual ascents of Everest during the 1990s:** 67.2
☆ **Annual mango production:** 11 million tons	☆ **National Motto:** "The Motherland is worth more than the Kingdom of Heaven."
☆ **Spit produced per annum by paan chewers:** 1.5 million tons	☆ **Number of toes on a yeti's foot:** 4
☆ **Average Income Per Capita:** US$350	☆ **Average Income Per Capita:** US$165
☆ **Literacy:** 66% male, 38% female	☆ **Literacy:** 41% male, 14% female

WHEN TO GO

Both India and Nepal have high and low periods for tourism. The high season (roughly November to March) brings higher prices and a flood of tourists. Low season (June through August—monsoon season across most of the Subcontinent) means reduced services and reduced traffic at reduced prices. Some tourist towns close down altogether during this time. Peak seasons vary by location. It is worth timing your trip to coincide with one or more of the many festivals that take place every year throughout India and Nepal (see **Holidays and Festivals,** p. 89).

INDIA

Because the geography of this huge country is so diverse, different regions have vastly different weather, even at the same time of year. The mountain valleys of the Himalayan foothills have intensely cold winter nights (November-January). Fall asleep in the wrong place here, and you might find yourself chipped out of the ice and put in a museum in three thousand years. Daytime temperatures are comfortable all year. In northern India, some mountain roads are only accessible during the summer months (June-September), generally the best time to visit the hills. The northern reaches of Himachal Pradesh and Ladakh are in rain-shadow and are not hit by the monsoonal torrents. The rest of India, however, relies heavily on the mighty **monsoon.**

The first of the country's two major monsoons sweeps across Western India in late May or early June sloshing into Rajasthan and Gujarat. The second wave hits the East and South, pouring water over Tamil Nadu and southern Andhra Pradesh from October to November. During the monsoon season it rains most days, generally in the late afternoon towards sunset. Getting caught in a monsoonal downpour is a little like taking a shower with all your clothes on—probably not a treat you will want to indulge in on a daily basis. Storms are generally intense and short: after thirty minutes or so of torrential rain, the sun will emerge and steam things up again—mountain views, however, remain perpetually obscured. The monsoons can be extremely destructive, causing mudslides and floods, cutting communications and transportation lines, and causing power outages and widespread loss of temper. The mountains of Northeast India are especially hard-hit in July and August, and deadly landslides are common.

The monsoon lets up in September, when India's **cool season** begins. It takes a few months more for the Deccan plateau to dry out completely. December and January are cool, even cold, at night. Tropical ovens like Mumbai and Chennai go from being unbearably hot to merely uncomfortably hot, and many travelers head south to the beaches of Goa and Kerala. **Winter** (September-January) is probably the best time to visit India. By February, the heat starts to build up across the plains. April, May, and June are all very cruel months indeed, with temperatures of over 45°C (110°F). And then come the rains, and the cycle repeats itself.

NEPAL

Most tourists visit Nepal in October and November, when the countryside is fresh, the temperatures mild, the air clear, and the views breathtaking. The dry, clean air makes this the best time of year for trekking. March and April are also good months to visit: huge rhododendrons are in bloom on the hillsides and the days are long and warm without being too hot. Winter (December-February) is probably the worst time to visit: snow covers anything higher than 2000-3000m, and even Kathmandu gets damp and cold. The monsoon descends from late June to September. Most of the country is beset with downpours at this time, but western Nepal is largely in the rain-shadow, and tends to be drier. Although the land turns noticeably greener during the monsoon, there are drawbacks: roads get washed out, flights get canceled, and leeches become your closest companions on trekking routes.

THINGS TO DO

From scaling the world's highest mountains to spelunking its ancient caves, from racing on a camel to raving on a beach, you can do it all in India and Nepal. For a more detailed list of the best things to see and do, refer to the **Let's Go Picks** below and the **Highlights** box at the beginning of each chapter.

HOLY PLACES

Visit some of the Subcontinent's most sacred sites and witness the rituals and traditions that have remained intact for thousands of years. Hinduism's holiest city, **Varanasi** (p. 721), is the chosen home of Lord Shiva himself, and the place where many pious Hindus come to spend their last moments of earthly existence. Trace the footsteps of the 9th-century saint, Shankara, who established India's four major *dhams* (divine abodes): **Badrinath** (p. 664) in the north, **Dwarka** (p. 214) in the west, **Rameswaram** (p. 617) in the south, and **Puri** (p. 464) in the east. Take in some of the finest Hindu temple architecture in India at **Bhubaneswar** (p. 454), or sing songs of praise to Lord Krishna in his playground, **Vrindaban** (p. 703). The holiest city for Sikhs, **Amritsar** (p. 477) houses the beautiful Golden Temple. Free yourself from all worldly desires in **Bodh Gaya** (p. 127), where the Buddha attained enlightenment, or circumambulate Nepal's most important *stupa* in **Boudha** (p. 839). Jains head to **Mount Abu** (p. 526) and its gorgeous Dilwara temples or to the foot of the 17m-high Jain saint Bahubali in **Sravanabelagola** (p. 290). Worshippers flock to the Har-ki-Pairi *ghat* in **Haridwar** (p. 648) to bathe at sunrise, while followers of the sun god watch the sunset at the Sun Temple in **Konark** (p. 461). The Meenakshi Amman Temple in **Madurai** (p. 610) amazes visitors with over 30 million sculptures. Finally, those with iron stomachs can witness animal sacrifices to the goddess Kali at **Dakshinkali** (p. 854) in Nepal and in **Kalighat** (p. 757) south of Kolkata.

OLDIES BUT GOODIES

It shouldn't come as much of a shock that one of the world's oldest civilizations also has some of its most fascinating monuments. Delhi's **Red Fort** and **Jama Masjid** (p. 150) are an impressive introduction to the relics of India's Mughal rulers. The abandoned city of **Fatehpur Sikri** (p. 700) is an architectural time-machine that will whisk you back to the Mughal era faster than you can say Shah Jahan. The erotic sculptures of **Khajuraho** (p. 369) allure and enchant, while carvings in the caves at **Ellora** and **Ajanta** (p. 427) are equally seductive, if somewhat less racy. Patan's **Durbar Square** (p. 831) is full of ancient temples. The skeletons of such holy spaces are all that remain at Hampi's breathtaking **Vijayanagar ruins** (p. 300). The **Lake Palace** in Udaipur (p. 518) encapsulates the romantic allure of Rajasthan, but it is just one of many famous forts and palaces in India, including **Gwalior Fort** (p. 382), Jaipur's **City Palace** (p. 497), the windswept **Jaisalmer Fort** (p. 540), Hyderabad's **Golconda Fort** (p. 111), and Mysore's **Maharaja's Palace** (p. 283). Oh, and don't forget the **Taj Mahal** (p. 696).

WAVES 'N' RAVES

For some serious beach action, nothing beats Goa. From the tourist-trafficked shores of **Anjuna** (p. 176) to the less-crowded strands of **Benaulim** (p. 189) and **Palolem** (p. 190), Goa has more sand than you can shake a coconut at. Party your way north to **Dwarka** (p. 214), whose shores are lapped by the waves of the Arabian Sea. Pretend you're in the south of France on the beaches of **Pondicherry** (p. 590) in Tamil Nadu. The white sands of **Kovalam** (p. 318) and **Puri** (p. 464) are outdone only by the pristine shores of **Varkala** (p. 325) and temple-studded **Mahabalipuram** (p. 585). The **Andaman Islands** (p. 95), 1000km off shore in the Bay of Bengal, have been attracting greater numbers of tourists in recent years, but are still far off the beaten track. If you've traversed both coasts and still haven't gotten enough sun or sand, leave the waves behind and catch the next camel out to Rajasthan's **Thar Desert** (p. 487).

TREKKING, RAFTING, AND TIGER-SPOTTING

Adventure-seekers and trail-blazers already know that the best trekking in the world is in the Himalayas. Journey past **Mount Everest**, the **Annapurna Range,** and the **Langtang Valley,** and watch tiny Nepali villages become even tinier Tibetan hamlets against a backdrop of rock, water, and ice (p. 894). The **Kinnaur-Spiti Road** (p. 250) in Himachal Pradesh passes through the most remote regions of India, with some great hikes along the way, particularly near **Kalpa** (p. 252) and **Kaza** (p. 255). Trek through **Western Sikkim** (p. 558), wander across the desert plateau of **Leh** (p. 259), or marvel at Kashmir's **Nubra Valley** (p. 264). Coast your way down the Himalayas on the white water rapids of the **Karnali River** or battle Jaws as you zip down **Sun Kosi** (p. 922). Get up close and personal with rhinos in **Kaziranga National Park** (p. 444) or with bears in Nepal's **Chitwan National Park** (p. 880). Elephants rumble and trumpet their way through **Jaldapara Wildlife Sanctuary** (p. 763). Tiger enthusiasts can enjoy the **Periyar Tiger Reserve** (p. 328) and **Corbett National Park** (p. 666), and birders will get an eyeful at the world-renowned **Keoladeo Ghana National Park** (p. 503). Estuarine crocodiles slink along the muddy shores of **Sunderbans National Park** (p. 764).

OUT OF SIGHT

The best way to avoid the crowds is to travel off-season, but some fascinating places see surprisingly little traffic regardless of the season. **Kausani** (p. 677) in Uttaranchal, **Ayodhya** (p. 715) in Uttar Pradesh, **Chamba** (p. 238) in Himachal Pradesh, **Bikaner** (p. 544) in Rajasthan, **Mandvi** (p. 220) and **Bhuj** (p. 216) in Gujarat, **Mandu** (p. 359) in Madhya Pradesh, **Rameswaram** (p. 617) in Tamil Nadu, and **Kirtipur** (p. 836), **Manakamana** (p. 859), and **Tansen** (p. 860) in Nepal, stay serene no matter the time of year. If political volatility and the occasional bomb aren't enough to get you ruffled, nothing beats a night on a houseboat in **Kashmir** (p. 257) or watching the closing of the Indo-Pakistani border at **Wagah** (p. 485). If safety is what you crave, breath easy in the eucalyptus- and *kurinji* blossom-scented air of **Kodaikanal** (p. 624), Tamil Nadu.

OUT OF MIND

Whether you seek New Age enlightenment at **Osho** (p. 417) and **Auroville** (p. 596), or centuries-old secrets in **Boudha** (p. 839) and **Bodh Gaya** (p. 127), count on getting earloads of advice about the lastest path to enlightenment from your fellow travelers. Swap travel yarns, drink tea, and make arrangements for the next leg of your journey alongside them at the backpacker meccas of **Manali** (p. 244) and **Dharamsala** (p. 229) in Himachal Pradesh, **Pushkar** (p. 510) in Rajasthan, **Anjuna** (p. 176) in Goa, **Kovalam** (p. 318) in Kerala, **Mahabalipuram** (p. 585) in Tamil Nadu, **Puri** (p. 464) in Orissa, **Darjeeling** (p. 764) in West Bengal, **Pokhara** (p. 864) in Nepal's Western Hills, and **Kathmandu's** Thamel district (p. 815), to just name a select few. After a couple of days, you'll know all the newest yoga positions, herbal remedies, and enough meditations to be your own travel guru.

🕮 LET'S GO PICKS

BEST PLACES FOR PACKRATS: If you've ever thought twice about tossing your elephant-shaped foot scrubbers, a visit to the Raja Kelkar Museum (p. 417) in Pune or the Jai Vilas Palace (p. 385) in Gwalior will remind you that you're not alone. Better still, slurp up the sacred spit of the thousands of holy rats that pack the Karni Mata Temple (p. 549) in Deshnok, Rajasthan.

BEST MOUNTAIN HIGH: Grass and hippies grow wild in the Himachal hilltop town of Manali (p. 244), at the base of the Himalayas. For a milder buzz, head to the Happy Valley Tea Estate (p. 772) in the hill station retreat of Darjeeling, and watch workers pluck those world-famous leaves before your eyes.

BEST REASONS TO GET OUT OF BED IN THE MORNING: Rise at dawn to have buckets of holy water dumped over your head at the Ramanathaswamy Temple (p. 618), a once-in-a-lifetime experience sure to clear your head and absolve you of the sins of the night before. Keep dry and watch the sun crawl above Mt. Everest from the Nepalese town of Nagarkot (p. 852), or trace its ascent over the ancient *ghats* of Varanasi (p. 721), with the chime of temple bells providing the mood music.

BEST CHANCE OF GETTING BITTEN: Prowl close to endangered (though still extremely ferocious) tigers at the Chitwan National Park (p. 880) in Nepal or the Periyar Tiger Reserve (p. 328) in Kerala. If they don't get you, head to Kashmir, where *lha-ba* healers will open wide and suck evil spirits out of your soul.

BEST KEPT SECRET: Artists and pretty people commune in the calm glow of candlelight at the Villa River Cat in the secluded beach town of Mandrem (p. 185) in Goa. Be sure to find it before it gets found out.

BEST PARTIES IN TOWN: The largest event of its kind in the world, the International Kite Festival kicks off the month of January (p. 200) in Ahmedabad. Pack it in at Pushkar in November, when 50,000 hump-backs and 200,000 humans squeeze into one square kilometer for the Pushkar Camel Festival (p. 513).

BEST BENDERS: Freak out at the full-moon raves on Anjuna beach, Goa (p. 176), an experience sure to turn your mind inside out. Or be like the Beatles and join thousands of other body benders for the world-renowned International Yoga Festival along the banks of the Ganga in Rishikesh (p. 653). Twist and wind through vibrant valleys, dry, sandstone plateaux, and breathtaking Himalayan peaks along the Manali-Leh Road (p. 258), one of the highest highways in the world.

BEST WAYS TO GET A BLISTER: Wander through mind-blowing mountainscapes and past meditative monasteries on the Local Trek in Sikkim (p. 561)—a 3-4 day hike that includes a visit to the holy Khechopalri Lake, where all your wishes are guaranteed to come true. Carouse through the lush Langtang Region (p. 903), the least crowded and least clichéd of Nepal's classic trinity of treks.

BEST PLACE TO FLAUNT YOUR MOUSTACHE: Compete for the crown of Mr. Desert (p. 540) in Jaisalmer if you're the man who best embodies Rajasthani masculinity with your full-bodied bristles.

BEST PLACES TO GET DOWN: Groove and gyrate into the wee hours at The Ghetto (p. 408), one of Mumbai's hippest discos, and at The Club in Bangalore (p. 279), site of MTV's South Asia launch. Or plunge into the coral-studded depths of the Bay of Bengal—teeming with angelfish, sea anemones, silver jacks, and hammerhead sharks—at the Mahatma Gandhi National Marine Park (p. 101) in the Andaman Islands.

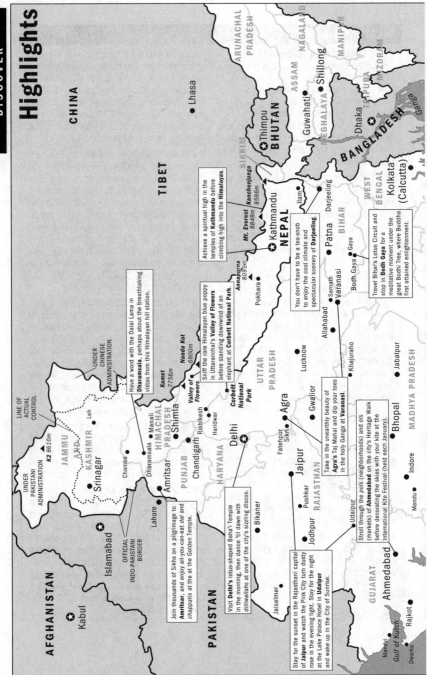

Highlights

CHINA

TIBET

• Lhasa

AFGHANISTAN

✪ Kabul

✪ Islamabad

Lahore

PAKISTAN

K2 8610m ▲

UNDER
PAKISTANI
ADMINISTRATION

LINE OF
ACTUAL
CONTROL

UNDER
CHINESE
ADMINISTRATION

**JAMMU
AND
KASHMIR**

Leh

Srinagar

OFFICIAL
INDO-PAKISTANI
BORDER

Join thousands of Sikhs on a pilgrimage to **Amritsar**, and enjoy all-you-can-eat *dal* and *chappatis* at the at the Golden Temple.

Amritsar

Chamba

Dharamsala • Manali

**HIMACHAL
PRADESH**

Shimla

Chandigarh

PUNJAB

Have a word with the Dalai Lama in **Dharamsala**, perhaps about the breathtaking vistas from this Himalayan hill station.

Kamet
7756m

Nanda Kot
6800m

Valley of
Flowers ■

Sniff the rare Himalayan blue poppy in Uttaranchal's **Valley of Flowers** before standing downwind of an elephant at **Corbett National Park**.

Corbett
National
Park

Rishikesh

Haridwar

HARYANA

Delhi ✪

Visit **Delhi's** lotus-shaped Bahá'í Temple in the morning, then dance 'til dawn with *dilliwallahs* at one of the city's sizzling discos.

**ARUNACHAL
PRADESH**

NAGALAND

ASSAM

MANIPUR

MEGHALAYA • Shillong

Guwahati •

MIZORAM

TRIPURA

✪ Thimpu

BHUTAN

Dhaka ✪

BANGLADESH

Ganga

SIKKIM

Mt. Everest
8848m

Kanchenjunga
8586m

Ilam •

✪ Kathmandu

NEPAL

Achieve a spiritual high in the temples of **Kathmandu** before climbing high into the **Himalayas**.

Annapurna
8091m ▲

Pokhara •

Darjeeling •

**WEST
BENGAL**

Kolkata
(Calcutta) ✪

You don't have to be a tea-snob to enjoy the cool climate and spectacular scenery of **Darjeeling**.

Patna •

BIHAR

Gaya •
Bodh Gaya •

Travel Bihar's Lotus Circuit and stop in **Bodh Gaya** for a meditative moment under the great Bodhi Tree, where Buddha first attained enlightenment.

Allahabad •

Samath •
Varanasi •

Lucknow •

**UTTAR
PRADESH**

Take in the unearthly beauty of **Agra's** Taj Mahal and dip your toes in the holy Ganga at **Varanasi**.

Khajuraho •

Gwalior •

Agra •

Fatehpur
Sikri •

Jaipur

RAJASTHAN

Pushkar •

Bikaner •

Stay for the sunset in the Rajasthani capital of **Jaipur** and watch the Pink City turn dusty rose in the evening light. Stay for the night at the Lake Palace Hotel in **Udaipur** and wake up in the City of Sunrise.

Jodhpur •

Jaisalmer •

Udaipur •

Stroll through the *pols* (markets) of **Ahmedabad** on the city's Heritage Walk before decorating the skies with your kite at the International Kite Festival (held each January).

GUJARAT

Ahmedabad •

Indore •

Mandu •

Bhopal •

Jabalpur •

MADHYA PRADESH

Rajkot •

Mandvi •

Gulf of Kutch

Dwarka •

MYANMAR (BURMA)

Port Blair

Andaman Sea

Go wild in the **Kanha National Park**, home to India's largest tiger population, and inspiration for Rudyard Kipling's *The Jungle Book*.

Send your wishes for a monsoon-free afternoon to the sun god Surya at **Konark's** Sun Temple.

Hop over to **Havelock Island** and snorkel in the sapphire sea before stretching out on a white sand beach.

Bay of Bengal

Bhubaneswar

ORISSA

Konark

Puri

Raipur

At **Hyderabad's** Golconda Fort, try to imagine the headquarters of the Qutb Shah kingdom during its 16th and 17th century glory days.

Receive *darshan* at **Trupati** and **Tirumala's** Sri Venkateshwara Temple and then take a moment to view its dazzling gold-covered *vimana* and sculpted columns.

If you spend 1 second with each sculpture at the Meenakshi Amman Temple in **Madurai**, it would take you just under a year of round-the-clock viewing to see all 30 million.

Nagpur

Hyderabad

Chennai (Madras)

Pondicherry

ANDHRA PRADESH

Tirumala,
Tirupati

Kanchipuram

TAMIL NADU

Bangalore

Mysore

Madurai

SRI LANKA

Palk Straits

Rameswaram

Gulf of Mannar

Kanyakumari

INDIA

Ajanta

Ellora

Aurangabad

MAHARASHTRA

Pune

Anjuna

GOA

Panjim

Benaulim

Hampi
(Vijayanagar)

KARNATAKA

Mangalore

Tiruchirappalli

KERALA

Cochin

Alleppey

Kovalam

Stroll through the Gateway of India as you enter frenetic and fabulous **Mumbai**.

Mumbai (Bombay)

Gulf of Cambay

Diu

Take in some sun on the palm-bedecked beaches of **Anjuna**, and follow up all that relaxation with a party under the full moon.

Play a tune on the musical pillars of the Vittala Temple in **Hampi**, home to the UNESCO-certified Vijayanagar Ruins.

Backwater cruise through the green canals of **Alleppey** while getting a taste of local life with a traditional Keralite meal served to you on a banana leaf.

Arabian Sea

Mouths of the

N

0   300 miles

0   300 kilometers

ESSENTIALS

FACTS FOR THE TRAVELER

ENTRANCE REQUIREMENTS

Passport (p. 9). Required for all travelers to India and Nepal.

Visa (p. 10). Required for all travelers except citizens of India traveling to Nepal and vice versa. Visas for Nepal are issued on arrival.

Immunizations (p. 20). Visitors who have been in Africa, South America, or Trinidad and Tobago within six days of their arrival in India must have a certificate of vaccination against yellow fever.

Special Permits (p. 10). India's island territories and parts of the Northeast States require special permits in addition to an Indian visa.

Work Permit (p. 11). Required for all foreigners planning to work in India or Nepal.

Driving Permit (p. 46). Required for all those planning to drive.

EMBASSIES & CONSULATES

INDIAN CONSULAR SERVICES ABROAD

Australia: 3-5 Moonah Pl., Yarralumla, **Canberra,** ACT 2600 (☎02 6273 3999). **Consulates:** 25 Bligh St., Level 27, **Sydney,** NSW 2000 (☎02 9223 9500); 195 Adelaide Terrace, Level 1, **East Perth,** WA 6004 (☎08 9221 1485); 15 Munro St., First Floor, **Coburg,** Victoria 3058 (☎03 9384 0141).

Canada: 10 Springfield Rd., **Ottawa,** Ontario K1M 1C9 (☎613-744-3751). **Consulates:** 1835 Yonge St., 4th fl., **Toronto,** Ontario M4S 1X8 (☎416-960-0751); 325 Howe St., Second Floor, **Vancouver,** BC V6C 1Z7 (☎604-662-8811).

Ireland: 6 Leeson Park, **Dublin** 6 (☎01 497 0843).

New Zealand: 180 Molesworth St., P.O. Box 4045, **Wellington** (☎04 473 6390).

South Africa: 852 Schoeman St., P.O. Box 40216, Arcadia, **Pretoria** 0007 (☎012 342 5392). **Consulates:** Old Station Building, 160 Pine Road, 4th fl., P.O. Box 3276, **Durban** 4000 (☎031 304 7020); 1 Eton Road, Corner Jan Smuts Ave., P.O. Box 6805, Parktown 2193, **Johannesburg** 2000 (☎011 482 8487; www.indconjoburg.co.za).

UK: India House, Aldwych, **London,** WC2 B 4NA (☎020 7836 8484; www.hcilondon.net). **Consulates:** 20 Augusta St., Jewelry Quarter, Hockley, **Birmingham** B18 6JL (☎0121 212 2778); 17 Rutland Sq., **Edinburgh** EH1 2BB (☎0131 229 2144).

US: 2536 Massachusetts Ave. NW, **Washington, D.C.** 20008 (☎202-939-9806; www.indianembassy.org). **Consulates:** 3 East 64th St., **New York,** NY 10021 (☎212-774-0600); 540 Arguello Blvd., **San Francisco,** CA 94118 (☎415-668-0662); 455 North Cityfront Plaza Dr., #850, **Chicago,** IL 60611 (☎312-595-0405); 1990 Post Oak Blvd., #600, **Houston,** TX 77056 (☎713-626-2355).

NEPALESE CONSULAR MISSIONS

Tourist visas are available upon arrival in Nepal. Don't go through the trouble of arranging a visa in advance unless you need something besides a tourist visa. Travelers from Ireland should contact the London embassy. The Sydney consul serves New Zealanders. There is no embassy in South Africa.

Australia: 3rd Level, 441 Kent St., **Sydney,** NSW (☎02 264 5909). Level 1, 72 Lincoln Rd., **Essendon** 3040, Victoria (☎03 9379 0666). AMP Palace, 10 Eagle St., Level 21, Ste. 44, **Brisbane,** Queensland 4000 (☎07 232 0336). Ste. 2, 16 Robinson St., **Nedlands** 6009, WA (☎09 368 2102).

Canada: Royal Bank Plaza, 200 Bay St., **Toronto,** Ontario M5R 1V9 (☎416-865-0110).

UK: 12a Kensington Palace Gardens, **London** W8 4QU (☎020 229 1594; www.nepembassy.org.uk).

US: 2131 Leroy Pl. NW, **Washington, D.C.** 20008 (☎202-667-4550; www.nepalembassyusa.org). **Consulates:** 820 Second Ave., #17B, **New York,** NY 10017 (☎212-370-3988); 1500 Lakehorse Dr., **Chicago,** IL 60610 (☎312-263-1250); 909 Montgomery St., #400, **San Francisco,** CA 94133 (☎415-434-1111); 16250 Dallas Pkwy., #110, **Dallas,** TX 75248 (☎214-931-1212).

CONSULAR SERVICES IN INDIA AND NEPAL

Most countries have embassies in **Delhi** (see p. 142). Many have consulates in **Mumbai** (see p. 395), and a few in **Chennai** (see p. 574) and **Kolkata** (see p. 747). In Nepal, all foreign diplomatic missions are in **Kathmandu** (see p. 812).

TOURIST OFFICES

The **Tourist Information Department** has its main offices in New Delhi (see p. 140) and branches in most major cities. There are also independent **Tourist Development Corporations,** offering information on local sights, transportation, guided tours, hotel bookings, etc. *Let's Go* lists details for both Government of India and state-run tourist information offices in the **Practical Information** listings for each town.

Australia: Level 2, Piccadilly, 210 Pitt St., **Sydney,** NSW 2000 (☎ 02 9264 4855).

Canada: 60 Bloor St. (West), Ste. 1003, **Toronto,** Ontario M4W 3B8 (☎416-962-3787).

UK: 7 Cork St., **London** W1X 2LW (☎0044 454 1048).

US: 3550 Wilshire Blvd., Rm. 204, **Los Angeles,** CA 90010 (☎213-380-8855); 1270 Ave. of the Americas, Ste. 1808, **New York,** NY 10020. (☎212-586-4901).

DOCUMENTS & FORMALITIES

PASSPORTS

REQUIREMENTS. Citizens of Australia, Canada, Ireland, New Zealand, South Africa, the UK, and the US need valid passports to enter India and Nepal and to re-enter their home countries. India and Nepal do not allow entrance if the holder's passport expires in under six months; returning home with an expired passport is illegal, and may result in a fine.

NEW PASSPORTS. Citizens of Australia, Canada, Ireland, New Zealand, the United Kingdom, and the United States can apply for a passport at any post office, passport office, or court of law. Citizens of South Africa can apply for a

ESSENTIALS

passport at any Home Affairs office. Any new passport or renewal applications must be filed well in advance of the departure date, although most passport offices offer rush services for a very steep fee.

PASSPORT MAINTENANCE. Be sure to photocopy the page of your passport with your photo, as well as your visas, traveler's check serial numbers and any other important documents. Carry one set of copies in a safe place, apart from the originals, and leave another set at home. Consulates also recommend that you carry an expired passport or an official copy of your birth certificate in a part of your baggage separate from other documents.

If you lose your passport, immediately notify the local police and the nearest embassy or consulate of your home government. To expedite its replacement, you will need to know all information previously recorded and show ID and proof of citizenship. In some cases, a replacement may take weeks to process, and it may be valid only for a limited time. Any visas stamped in your old passport will be irretrievably lost. In an emergency, ask for immediate temporary traveling papers that will permit you to re-enter your home country.

VISAS, SPECIAL PERMITS & WORK PERMITS

VISAS. All travelers to India and Nepal need visas. Indian visas must be arranged in advance through your nearest embassy or consulate. Nepalese visas are issued on arrival and must be bought with US dollars. Entering India or Nepal to study or work requires a special visa. For more information, see **Studying Abroad,** p. 57.

Double-check entrance requirements at the nearest embassy or consulate (listed under **Embassies & Consulates Abroad,** on p. 8) for up-to-date visa information before departure. US citizens can also consult the website at www.pueblo.gsa.gov/cic_text/travel/foreign/foreignentryreqs.html.

INDIA. Indian tourist visas permit stays of six months or one year and typically allow for multiple entries. When applying for a visa, make sure your passport is valid six months beyond the date of intended return. Other options include a one-year visa for students, journalists, or business travelers. Foreign citizens planning to stay for more than 180 days are required to register at the nearest Foreigners Registration Office within 14 days of arrival.

It is fastest to apply through the embassy in your home country. You'll need to fill out an application form and provide your current passport, at least two passport photos, and a visa processing fee, which varies by country. The process can take anywhere between a few hours and a few weeks. While tourist visas requested ahead of a trip to India are usually processed within a few weeks, other types of visas can take several months. **Contact your nearest embassy well in advance of your trip** for more information. Once in India, it is often possible to extend tourist visas at government offices in major cities, but the process can take up to a week.

SPECIAL PERMITS. Certain areas require a special permit in addition to an Indian visa. Be sure to check your country's latest travel advisories before entering restricted areas of India. Travelers to the following areas must obtain **special permits: Andaman Islands,** permits issued on arrival (see The Andaman Islands, p. 97); **Arunachal Pradesh, Nagaland, Manipur,** and **Mizoram** in the Northeast, contact the Ministry of Home Affairs in New Delhi (see p. 141); **Sikkim,** (see Sikkim Permits, p. 552); and certain areas around **Darjeeling** in West Bengal, contact the Home Department of West Bengal in Kolkata. Certain areas require **special per-**

mission from the Indian government to travel: parts of the **Kullu** and **Spiti** districts of Himachal Pradesh, some areas of **Uttar Pradesh,** the Indo-Pakistani border areas in **Jammu** and **Kashmir,** and west of National Hwy. 15 in **Rajasthan.** For more information on travel to these areas, consult your local embassy or consulate.

NEPAL. You may buy a Nepalese visa upon arrival at the airport in Kathmandu or at any of the land border crossings. The fee is US$30 for a 60-day, single-entry visa, more for multiple-entry visas. **This fee must be paid in US dollars.** Any Nepalese consulate or embassy can issue visas for up to 60 days, although this can often be extended once you're in Nepal. The Department of Immigration, Tridevi Marg, Thamel, Kathmandu (☎01 470650 or 494273), grants extensions for up to four months. Apply for a visa extension a day or two before you really need it. Extensions are no longer granted while you wait.

WORK PERMITS. Admission as a visitor does not include the right to work, which is authorized only by a work permit. Entering India and Nepal to study requires a special visa. For more information, see **Alternatives to Tourism** (p. 51).

SURROUNDING COUNTRIES. Several of the countries surrounding India and Nepal are politically volatile; it's always a good idea to check for up-to-date information before packing your bags and setting out for the border.

Bangladesh: Passengers arriving in Dhaka by air can get a 15-day visa at the airport. Single-entry visas are valid for 90 days. Visa rules change frequently. For the latest contact a Bangladesh embassy.

Myanmar (Burma): Visas are valid for a single entry of up to 28 days. For visa information, contact a Myanmar embassy.

China: To travel to **Tibet** from Nepal, you need a Chinese visa. These are almost impossible to obtain in Kathmandu but are easily available through the embassy in Delhi. Visas are valid for 30 days and can sometimes be extended. In Kathmandu, contact one of the many agencies specializing in tours to Tibet. Permits take between a few hr. and several days to process. The usual trip includes a 5-day drive to Lhasa and all the necessary permits. Once in Lhasa, you are allowed to stay for a maximum for 7 days. Reserve your return ticket when you book. **Do not attempt to enter Tibet on your own.**

Pakistan: A visa is required to enter Pakistan. These are normally valid for one month.

Sri Lanka: For stays of up to 30 days, citizens of most European countries, the US, Canada, and Australia will be granted free visas on arrival with a confirmed ticket on a flight out of the country and enough funds to support themselves during their stay.

Thailand: Citizens from most European countries and the US, Canada, and Australia do not need visas if they plan to be in Thailand for less than 30 days.

IDENTIFICATION

When you travel, always carry at least two forms of identification on your person, including at least one photo ID. A passport combined with a driver's license or birth certificate is usually adequate. Never carry all of your IDs together.

TEACHER, STUDENT & YOUTH IDENTIFICATION. The **International Student Identity Card (ISIC),** the most widely accepted form of student ID, provides travel discounts, access to a 24hr. emergency helpline (call US collect ☎715-345-0505), and insurance benefits for US cardholders (see **Insurance,** p. 18). The **International Teacher Identity Card (ITIC)** offers teachers the same insurance coverage as well as similar but limited discounts. For travelers who are 25 years old or under but are not students, the **International Youth Travel Card** (**IYTC**) also offers many of the same benefits as the ISIC. Similarly, the **International Student Exchange ID Card (ISE)** provides discounts, medical benefits, and the ability to purchase student airfares. For information, contact the **International Student Travel Confederation (ISTC)**, Herengracht 479, 1017 BS Amsterdam, The Netherlands (☎ 20 4212800; www.istc.org).

CUSTOMS

Upon entering India and Nepal, you must declare certain items you are bringing in from abroad and pay a duty on the value of those articles if they exceed the allowance established by the Indian or Nepalese customs service. Note that goods and gifts purchased at **duty-free** shops abroad are not exempt from duty or sales tax; "duty-free" merely means that you need not pay a tax in the country of purchase. Upon returning home, you must likewise declare all articles acquired abroad and pay a duty on the value of articles in excess of your home country's allowance.

MONEY

CURRENCY & EXCHANGE

The currency charts below are based on August 2003 exchange rates between local currency and Australian dollars (AUS$), Canadian dollars (CDN$), European Union euros (EUR€), New Zealand dollars (NZ$), South African rand (ZAR), British pounds (UK£), and US dollars (US$). For the latest exchange rates, check a major newspaper or a financial website such as www.bloomberg.com.

THE INDIAN RUPEE

The Indian rupee (Rs, IRs in the Nepal section of the book), is divided into 100 paise (p.). Coins are issued in denominations of p.10, 25, 50, Rs1, 2, and 5. Bills come in values of Rs1, 2, 5, 10, 20, 50, 100, and 500.

INDIAN RUPEE (Rs)		
AUS$1 = Rs29.55		Rs100 = AUS$3.38
CDN$1 = Rs32.93		Rs100 = CDN$3.04
EUR€1 = Rs49.87		Rs100 = EUR€2.01
NRs1 = Rs0.63		Rs100 = NRs159.03
NZ$1 = Rs26.38		Rs100 = NZ$3.79
SAR1 = Rs6.25		Rs100 = SAR15.99
UK£1 = Rs72.00		Rs100 = UK£1.39
US$1 = Rs45.87		Rs100 = US$2.18

THE NEPALESE RUPEE

The Nepalese rupee (Rs, NRs in the India section of the book), is divided into 100 paise (p.). Money comes in the following shapes and sizes. Coins: p.1, 2, 5, 10, 25, 50, Rs1, and 2. Bills: Rs1, 2, 5, 10, 25, 50, 100, 500, and 1000.

Neither the Indian nor the Nepalese rupee may be exported. There are 24hr. branches of the national banks at international airports. British pounds and US dollars are the best currencies to bring with you; others will not always be easy to exchange. In smaller towns it can be particularly difficult to find any bank set up to deal with foreign currency. Since changing money takes a long time and requires great reserves of patience, you should aim to take part in this farce as seldom as possible. In India, get an **encashment certificate** as proof of the transaction whenever you change money. This is sometimes demanded

NEPALESE RUPEE (Rs)		
AUS$1 = Rs47.00	Rs100 = AUS$2.13
CDN$1 = Rs52.37	Rs100 = CDN$1.91
EUR€1 = Rs79.31	Rs100 = EUR€1.26
IRs1 = Rs1.59	Rs100 = IRs62.88
NZ$1 = Rs41.95	Rs100 = NZ$2.38
SAR1 =Rs9.95	Rs100 = SAR10.05
UK£1 = Rs114.50	Rs100 = UK£0.87
US$1 = Rs72.95	Rs100 = US$1.37

when paying for plane and train tickets or large bills in rupees, and you will need it if you want to change any leftover rupees back into hard currency before you leave.

TRAVELER'S CHECKS

American Express and **Thomas Cook** traveler's checks are the most widely recognized in India and Nepal and are one of the safest and least troublesome means of carrying funds. Check issuers provide refunds if the checks are lost or stolen, and many provide additional services, such as toll-free refund hotlines abroad, emergency message services, and stolen credit card assistance. Banks in some smaller towns may not be able to change traveler's checks.

While traveling, keep check receipts and a record of which checks you've cashed separate from the checks themselves. Also leave a list of check numbers with someone at home. Never countersign checks until you're ready to cash them, and always bring your passport with you to cash them. If your checks are lost or stolen, immediately contact a refund center (of the company that issued your checks) to be reimbursed. They may require a police report verifying the loss or theft. Less-touristed areas may not have refund centers, in which case you might have to wait to be reimbursed.

American Express: Checks available with commission at select banks and all AmEx offices. US residents can also buy checks by phone (☎888-887-8986) or online (www.aexp.com). AAA (see p. 46) offers commission-free checks to its members. Checks available in many different currencies. *Cheques for Two* can be signed by either of 2 people traveling together. For more information contact AmEx's service centers: In the US and Canada (☎800-221-7282); in the UK (☎0800-521-313); in Australia (☎800 25 19 02); in New Zealand (☎0800 441 068); in India (☎011 614 5920); elsewhere US collect (☎801-964-6665).

Visa: Checks available (generally with commission) at banks worldwide. To find the nearest issuing location call Visa's service centers: In the US (☎800-227-6811); in the UK (☎0800-89-50-78); elsewhere UK collect (☎020-7937-8091). Checks available in US, British, Canadian, Japanese, and Euro currencies.

Travelex/Thomas Cook In the US and Canada (☎800-287-7362); in the UK (☎0800 62 21 01); in India (☎011 335 6571); elsewhere call collect (☎+44 733 31 89 50).

CREDIT CARDS

Credit cards are gaining acceptance in South Asia, but they are still hardly recognized outside the big cities. In places like Delhi and Mumbai, many expensive hotels and restaurants accept payment by card, but budget hotels will want cash. Where they are accepted, credit cards offer superior exchange rates—up to 5% better than the retail rate used by banks. **American Express, MasterCard** (a.k.a. **EuroCard** or **Access** in Europe), and **Visa** (a.k.a. **Carte Bleue** or **Barclaycard**) are the cards most likely to be accepted in the Subcontinent.

Credit cards are also useful for **cash advances,** which allow you to withdraw rupees from associated banks and ATMs in major cities. However, transaction fees for all credit card advances (up to US$10 per advance, plus 2-3% extra on foreign transactions after conversion, plus possible foreign transaction fees) tend to make credit cards a more costly way of withdrawing cash than ATMs or traveler's checks. To be eligible for an advance, you'll need to get a **Personal Identification Number (PIN)** from your credit card company (see **Cash Cards (ATM Cards),** below).

Credit card scams are common in India and Nepal. Be cautious when purchasing items with a credit card. Make sure that the card remains in view at all times to ensure that the vendor does not make extra imprints. Also, if you're planning to ship goods through a shop owner, don't believe him when he says he won't forward the credit slip for payment until you've received the goods.

ATM CARDS (CASH CARDS)

ATMs are scattered throughout major cities in India and Nepal and are beginning to pop up in smaller towns as well. The two major international money networks are **Cirrus** (to locate ATMs US ☎ 800-424-7787 or www.mastercard.com) and **Visa/PLUS** (US ☎ 800-843-7587 or www.visa.com). Cirrus is not available in Nepal. Most ATMs charge a small transaction fee. **Visa TravelMoney** allows you to access money from any ATM on the Visa/PLUS network. TravelMoney cards are available at Travelex/Interpayment locations worldwide; US residents may also obtain them through AAA offices (see p. 46) or by calling ☎ 877-394-2247. **American Express Express Cash** allows AmEx cardholders to withdraw money from American Express ATMs worldwide. To enroll, US cardholders may call ☎ 800-227-4669.

GETTING MONEY FROM HOME

This is not something you want to do. The easiest and cheapest solution is to have someone back home make a deposit to your credit card or cash (ATM) card. Failing that, consider one of the following options.

WIRING MONEY. It is possible to arrange a **bank money transfer**, which means asking a bank back home to wire money to a bank in India or Nepal. This is the cheapest way to transfer cash, but it's also the slowest (at least two working days). Note that some banks only release your funds in local currency, potentially sticking you with a poor exchange rate. Wiring money to India and Nepal can be a bureaucratic fuss. Foreign banks such as Citibank and ANZ Grindlays are the most reliable; be precise about the branch you want the money sent to. Money transfer services like **Western Union** are faster and more convenient but pricier. Visit www.westernunion.com, or call in the **US** ☎ 800-325-6000, in **Canada** ☎ 800-235-0000, in the **UK** ☎ 0800 83 38 33, in **Australia** ☎ 800 501 500, in **New Zealand** ☎ 800 27 0000, in **South Africa** ☎ 0860 100031, in **India** ☎ 01 336 8771, and in **Nepal** ☎ 01 418738. Money transfer services are also available at **American Express** and **Thomas Cook** offices.

US STATE DEPARTMENT (US CITIZENS ONLY). In dire emergencies only, the US State Department will forward money within hours to the nearest consular office, which will then disburse it according to instructions for a US$15 fee. If you wish to use this service, you must contact the Overseas Citizens Service division of the US State Department (☎ 202-647-5225; nights, Sundays, and holidays ☎ 202-647-4000).

ESSENTIALS

COSTS

The single biggest cost of your trip will probably be your round-trip **airfare** to India or Nepal (see **Getting to India and Nepal: By Plane,** p. 39). Once you get there, travel in India or Nepal is fairly cheap. Depending on where you visit and your definition of comfort, budget between US$5-20 per person per day. Accommodations start at about US$2-3 per night for a grim room with shared bathroom and squat toilet. For US$10 you can normally find a decent-sized, clean, well-aired room, often with extra little luxuries such as clean sheets, seat toilets, and toilet paper. International-standard five-star luxury hotels can be found in major cities. A basic **meal** costs under US$1, but quality increases dramatically if you spend a little more.

TIPPING, BARGAINING, AND BAKSHEESH

"Baksheesh" is usually translated as a "tip," but this broad concept includes everything from simple gifts to outright bribes. Baksheesh can be a bribe given to a railway porter to find a seat on a "full" train; it can also be the small change given to a beggar. **Small tips** are expected for restaurant service, porter service, and unofficial tour guides. There is no need to tip taxi or rickshaw drivers. Tips depend on your level of satisfaction and usually run between Rs1 and Rs20, not following any particular percentage rule. Most Indians and Nepalis expect great tips from foreigners, but don't be swayed by pleading groans. If your first offer is met with a quick roll of the head signifying "OK," then you have done well.

TOUTS, MIDDLEMEN, AND SCAMS

Touts surround travelers at airports, bus stands and train stations, or accost them on the streets of the tourist ghettos, offering deals on transportation, currency exchange, drugs, or any other service rupees can buy. They are pushy and will try to convince you to buy something you don't want. They count on foreigners to be too naive or too polite to refuse. Many touts are equipped with a guilt-trip line tailored to your demographic group: "My friend, one question: Why don't you white Americans like to talk to us Indians?" Don't let these guilt trips get to you—touts are only interested in your money.

It's hard to find a hotel without a tout getting involved; you'll usually be approached as soon as you get off the plane, bus, or train. Hotels pay touts, taxi drivers, and rickshaw-*wallahs*, commission to gather tourists and then add commission to your hotel bill. If the hotel doesn't pay commission, touts will tell you it's full, closed, or burnt down. Don't believe them. Be firm—decide on your hotel before you arrive in town and have a taxi or rickshaw-*wallah* take you there directly.

Many **travel agents** near train stations are little more than touts behind desks. They are notorious for giving out false information, charging hefty commissions, and selling tickets for trains that don't exist. You will save money and time if you **eliminate the middleman** and purchase directly from the train station.

Another annoyance at many monuments and temples are the unofficial **guides** who spout drivel at you, refuse to leave you alone, and then have the cheek to demand *baksheesh* for their unwanted services. If you stay calm and say clearly, "No thank you, I do not want a guide," exactly once, then they will leave you alone when you begin to ignore them. It is best to book a guide through a tourist office or other government organization than wait to be approached.

Be cautious about accepting **food or drinks** from a stranger. Con men have drugged travelers and then robbed them. Bear in mind, however, that offers of food and drink are one of the primary forms of Indian hospitality. If you don't feel comfortable accepting food or drink from strangers, a gracious "the doctor told me I shouldn't have that" is a good way to turn down an offer.

ESSENTIALS

THE ART OF THE DEAL

In India and Nepal, bargaining isn't just practical knowledge, it's an art form. With a little practice, you may leave the country a master. Vendors and drivers will automatically quote you a price that is much too high; it's up to you to get them down to a reasonable rate. With the following tips and a bit of finesse, you might be able to impress even the most hardened of hawkers:

1. Bargaining needn't be a fierce struggle. Quite the opposite: good-natured wrangling with a cheerful smile may prove your biggest weapon.

2. Use your poker face. The less your face betrays your interest in an item, the better. If you touch an item to inspect it, the vendor will be sure to "encourage" you to name a price or make a purchase. Cooing over that plastic elephant or coming back again and again to admire that marvellous mother-of-pearl Taj Mahal are good ways to ensure that you pay a higher price. Be cool.

3. Know when to bargain. In most cases, it's quite clear when it's appropriate to bargain. Taxi and auto-rickshaw fares and things for sale in outdoor markets are all fair game. Don't bargain on prepared or pre-packaged foods on the street or in restaurants. In some stores, signs will indicate whether fixed prices prevail. When in doubt, ask tactfully, "Is that your lowest price?" or whether there are discounts.

4. Never underestimate the power of peer pressure. Bargaining with more than one person at a time—particularly rickshaw-*wallahs*—always leads to higher prices. Bargaining in the company of other travelers—especially travelers who are discouraging you from buying—can drop a price dramatically.

5. Know when to turn away. Refuse any vendor or rickshaw driver who bargains rudely, and move to another vendor if the one you are dealing with will not be reasonable. However, bargaining without an intention to buy is a major *faux pas*. It is extraordinarily rude to agree on a price and then decline. If you are given a high price, turn away slowly with a smile and a "thank you." The price may plummet.

6. Start low. Never feel guilty starting with a ridiculously low price.

 WARNING. Locals in Delhi, Jaipur, Agra, and Kathmandu sometimes accost travelers to chat about tourism, their city, and cricket. Having thus established themselves as friends, they offer their hospitality: "You're a guest in my country. The least I can do is invite you to my place for some food." Nine times out of ten, their "place" is a jewelry, gems, or carpet shop. Eventually, travelers are offered the opportunity to carry US$500 to US$10,000 worth of jewelry abroad to be handed over to an "overseas partner." In return, these dealers offer a 100% commission. The scheme is straightforward. Export laws impose a 250% tariff on gems and jewelry, but foreigners with tourist visas may carry a certain amount of gems and jewelry out of the country. So, by having tourists do their exporting for them at 100% commission, gem dealers save a lot of money. First, however, they will insist you give them your **credit card** number for "insurance purposes," since corrupt customs officials sometimes confiscate valuables. The gem dealers call it "couriering," and insist that it's done all the time. As soon as you hand over your card, they charge hundreds of dollars to your account. **Export schemes** sound too good to be true because they are—stay away from them. If you ever feel uncomfortable in a store, just leave, even if it seems rude or awkward. (Also see **Credit Cards,** p. 13.)

BEGGING

Thirty rupees is more than many Indians see in a week. **Carry coins and one- or two-rupee bills**—these are appropriate baksheesh for beggars. For children, give food instead of money—a gift of biscuits is more likely to benefit the child than cash, which often goes straight into the hands of a ringleader. It is customary to give to beggars at pilgrimage sites, to *sadhus* (wandering Hindu holy men who survive by begging), and to transvestites (*hijras*) on trains. Don't give to cute, healthy kids who approach with requests for rupees, coins, or pens. These are not beggars, but regular schoolchildren trying their luck. You can recognize them by their shoes—no legitimate Indian beggar has shoes. Today, many Indians are concerned that foreigner's handouts are creating a culture of laziness and low self-esteem. A more responsible way to distribute you charity is to donate to a local aid organization.

SAFETY & SECURITY

PERSONAL SAFETY

India and Nepal have low rates of crime, especially violent crime. The sheer mass of people means that you will almost always be surrounded, and Indians and Nepalis are often willing to go out of their way to help a foreigner in trouble.

BLENDING IN. Unless you look South Asian, your chances of blending in are approximately zero. The best you can do is to pretend you know what you're doing and to try not to stand out too much. **Dress modestly.** Don't flaunt money or jewelry in public. Knowing the words for "hello," "thank you," "yes/no," and "where" in the **local language** (see **Appendix,** p. 927), may gain the aid of someone who would not help you otherwise. Also, see **Customs and Etiquette,** p. 82.

The gawking camera-toter is a more obvious target for robbery than the low-profile traveler. Familiarize yourself with your surroundings before setting out; if you must check a map on the street, duck into a shop or restaurant first. If you are traveling alone, be sure someone at home knows your itinerary. If you are female, never admit that you're traveling alone.

EXPLORING. Find out about unsafe neighborhoods from tourist offices, from the manager of your hotel, or from a trustworthy local. Whenever possible, *Let's Go* warns of unsafe areas, but only your eyes can tell you for sure when you've wandered into one. When walking at night, stick to busy, well-lit streets and avoid dark alleyways. Do not cross through parks, parking lots, or other large, deserted areas. Look for children playing, women walking in the open, and other signs of an active community. If you feel uncomfortable, leave quickly and directly, but don't allow fear of the unknown to turn you into a hermit. Careful exploration will build confidence and make your trip more rewarding.

SELF DEFENSE. A good self-defense course will give you concrete ways to react to unwanted advances. **Impact, Prepare, and Model Mugging** can refer you to local self-defense courses in the US (☎800-345-542; www.impactsafety.org). Workshops (2-3hr.) start at US$50; full courses run US$350-500.

TRANSPORTATION. Planes and trains are the safest way to travel in the Subcontinent. Although the railways are extensive, they don't run to some of the smaller towns, and they don't exist at all in Nepal. Buses are the only alternative in these situations. However, road rules are nonexistent, and bus accidents are common, particularly in hilly or mountainous regions. Getting on a bus is the most dangerous thing many tourists do in India. **Take trains whenever possible.** Indian bus drivers, who drive sometimes drunk and always recklessly, are guys who have a hard

ESSENTIALS

time getting a life insurance policy. Minibuses are deadliest of all and almost never worth the money you'll save over a full-sized bus. When on foot, be very careful of the traffic, which is generally chaotic—most vehicles will not stop for pedestrians.

WILDLIFE. Rabies (see p. 25) is far more prevalent in India and Nepal than in Western countries. The rhesus **monkeys** that hover in the treetops above temples are aggressive, and they snatch food and bite. If a stray **dog** growls at you, pick up a stone and act like you're about to throw it. Even if you can't find a stone, just pretending to pick one up usually scares them away. Also be wary of **rats,** both indoors and out. Since rats are attracted to crumbs, keep food away from your bed. India's larger wildlife—**buffalo, elephants, tigers**—can gore, trample, and maul.

TERRORISM AND POLITICAL INSTABILITY. Most governments advise their citizens not to travel to Jammu and Kashmir even in times of relative peace. Since 2002, a number of terrorist attacks by violent secessionist groups **have killed over 1,000 civilians.** Extremist groups based in Pakistan attacked American interests in Kolkata and Karachi in 2002, and travelers are advised to avoid border regions in Gujarat, Punjab, and Rajasthan. **Do not linger outside US consulates** (see p. 72). A deadly terrorist attack in Mumbai in August 2003 was aimed at tourist and financial targets, underscoring the potential danger at popular, crowded sights. Hindu-Muslim violence led to 1000 deaths in Gujarat in early 2002 (see p. 71). The situation remains unstable, and travelers are advised to avoid Gujarat and areas around the contested holy city of Ayodhya in Uttar Pradesh, until tensions subside. Banditry and organized thuggery continue to make parts of Bihar dangerous. The **ongoing Maoist rebellion in Nepal** makes many areas outside the Kathmandu Valley a less popular destination for safety-conscious travelers, although tourists have not yet been targeted. The box on **travel advisories** (p. 18) lists offices to contact and webpages to visit for an up-to-date list of government travel advisories.

TRAVEL ADVISORIES. The following government offices provide travel information and advisories by telephone, by fax, or via the web:

Australian Department of Foreign Affairs and Trade: ☎ 1300 55 51 35; fax-back service 02 6261 1299; www.dfat.gov.au.

Canadian Department of Foreign Affairs and International Trade (DFAIT): In the US call 800-267-6788, in Canada collect +1 613-944-6788; www.dfait-maeci.gc.ca. Call for their free booklet, *Bon Voyage...But.*

New Zealand Ministry of Foreign Affairs: ☎ 04 494 8500; fax 494 8506; www.mft.govt.nz/trav.html.

United Kingdom Foreign and Commonwealth Office: ☎ 020 7008 0232; fax 7008 0155; www.fco.gov.uk.

US Department of State: ☎ 202-647-5225, faxback service 202-647-3000; http://travel.state.gov. For *A Safe Trip Abroad,* call 202-512-1800.

FINANCIAL SECURITY

PROTECTING YOUR VALUABLES. There are a few steps you can take to minimize the financial risk associated with traveling. First, **bring as little with you as possible.** Leave expensive watches, jewelry, cameras, and electronic equipment (like your Discman) at home. Chances are you'd only break them, lose them, or get sick of lugging them around anyway. Second, buy a few combination **padlocks** to secure your belongings either in your pack—which you should **never leave**

unattended—or in a hostel or train station locker. Third, **carry as little cash as possible.** Instead carry traveler's checks and ATM/credit cards, keeping them in a **money belt**—not a "fanny pack" or "bum bag"—along with your passport and ID cards. Fourth, **keep a small cash reserve separate from your primary stash.** This should consist of about US$150 in hard currency (US dollars or UK pounds) sewn into or stored in the depths of your pack, along with your traveler's check numbers and important photocopies. Keep a small amount of money in your pockets so that you don't need to sift through a thick wad of cash every time you buy a bottle of Thums Up.

CON ARTISTS & PICKPOCKETS. Con artists often work in groups. Children are among the most effective. They possess innumerable ruses. Beware of certain classics: sob stories that require money, rolls of bills "found" on the street, mustard spilled (or saliva spit) onto your shoulder to distract you while they snatch your bag. Don't hand your passport to someone whose authority you question (ask to accompany them to a police station if they insist), and **be careful when your passport is out of your sight.** Don't let your bag out of sight; never trust a "station-porter" who insists on carrying your bag or stowing it in the baggage compartment or a "new friend" who offers to guard your bag while you buy a train ticket or use the restroom. Beware of **pickpockets** in city crowds, especially on public transportation. For the low-down on low-lifes, see **Touts, Middlemen, and Scams,** p. 15.

ACCOMMODATION & TRANSPORTATION. Most **hotels** have locks on the doors, but this doesn't mean you will be the only one with access to your room. Hotel staff can get into your room, and some make a good living by looting backpacks while guests are away. Avoid leaving valuables in your hotel room, even if it's locked. If you are going on a trek, you might want to leave your luggage at a guest house, but think twice about leaving your valuables. If you leave anything, make sure it is securely locked. Many travelers bring their own locks for extra security. Western locks are many times stronger than the ones you can get in India.

Be particularly careful on **buses.** Carry your backpack in front of you where you can see it and don't trust anyone to "watch your bag for a second." If your bag is going on a bus roof rack, make sure it's tied down so that it doesn't fall or get taken off. Thieves thrive on **trains;** professionals wait for tourists to fall asleep and then carry off whatever they can. When alone, **lock and chain** your pack to the bunk. Keep important documents and other valuables on your person and try to sleep on top bunks with your luggage stored above you (if not in bed with you).

If your belongings are stolen in India or Nepal, you can go to the police although it is doubtful that they will be much help. There is virtually no chance you will ever see your camera again, but you can at least get an official **police report,** which you will need for an insurance claim.

DRUGS & ALCOHOL

Marijuana (*ganja*) and hashish (*charas*) are grown throughout the Himalayas and are extremely cheap, but **they are illegal** and considered socially unacceptable by most Indians and Nepalis. An exception is made for *sadhus* (holy men), since *ganja* is associated with the worship of Shiva. A few ethnic groups in the Himalayas also use *ganja* and *charas* with no stigma. These indulgences do not extend to tourists, however. In fact, penalties are sometimes harsher for foreigners.

India has a 10-year minimum sentence for drug possession or trafficking. If charged with drug possession, you are likely to find yourself required to prove your innocence in an often-corrupt justice system whose rules you won't understand. **This will be a horrible experience.** Those who attempt to influence a police officer must do so discreetly and indirectly. Drug law enforcement in Nepal is more relaxed,

ESSENTIALS

but sentences are still stiff. If you do get into trouble with the law, police are required to contact your country's diplomatic mission. If you are arrested, diplomats can visit you and provide a list of lawyers, but they cannot get you out of jail.

In the more touristy places, alcohol is easy to come by. Beer is popular, and India and Nepal produce drinkable vodka, gin, rum, whisky, and other liquors. In India, these are classified as IMFL (Indian-Made Foreign Liquor). Beware of home-brewed concoctions, however, as dodgy batches of toddy have killed dozens. The state of Gujarat is officially dry, and its mildly successful prohibitive efforts have recently been copied by Haryana and Manipur. Other areas (Tamil Nadu, Mumbai, and Delhi) have dry days. There is no standard drinking age in India or Nepal.

HEALTH

Travelers complain most often about their feet and their stomach, so take precautionary measures. Drink three liters of water per day to prevent dehydration and constipation, and wear sturdy, broken-in shoes with clean socks. During the hot season, take extra precautions against heatstroke and sunburn.

BEFORE YOU GO

In your **passport,** write the names of any people you wish to contact in case of a medical emergency, and also list any allergies or medical conditions. Matching a prescription to a foreign equivalent is not always easy, safe, or possible, so carry up-to-date, legible prescriptions or a statement from your doctor stating the medication's trade name, manufacturer, generic name, and dosage. While traveling, be sure to keep all medication with you in your carry-on luggage. For tips on packing a basic **first-aid kit** and other health essentials, see p. 28.

IMMUNIZATIONS & PRECAUTIONS

In some cases, no inoculations are required for entry into India or Nepal, but most travelers get a number of recommended inoculations (see box below). Visit a doctor at least 4-6 weeks before your departure to allow time for the series of vaccinations. For immunizations and prophylaxis, consult the CDC (see below) in the US or the equivalent in your home country, and check with a doctor.

INOCULATION REQUIREMENTS & RECOMMENDATIONS
The US Centers for Disease Control (CDC) recommends immunizations for:
Hepatitis A: Immune globulin (IG).
Hepatitis B: If you might be exposed to blood, have sexual contact, stay longer than 6 months, or undergo medical treatment. Hepatitis B vaccine is recommended for infants and for children who did not receive the series as infants.
Japanese encephalitis: If you plan to be in a rural area for over 4 weeks.
Rabies: If you plan to see Indian animals or wildlife.
Typhoid: Vaccination is particularly important because strains in India and Nepal are resistant to multiple antibiotics.
Others: Vaccines for tetanus-diphtheria, measles, mumps, and rubella. One-time dose of polio for adults, and haemophilus influenza B (meningitis).

Travelers over two years old should make sure that the following vaccines are up to date: MMR (for measles, mumps, and rubella); DTaP or Td (for diptheria, tetanus, and pertussis); OPV (for polio); HbCV (for haemophilus influenza B); and HBV (for B). Adults traveling for more than four weeks should consider the following additional immunizations: Hepatitis A vaccine and/or immune globulin (IG), an additional dose of Polio vaccine, and typhoid and cholera vaccines, particularly if traveling off the beaten path. Visitors who have been in Africa, South America, or Trinidad and Tobago within six days of their arrival in India must have a certificate of vaccination against yellow fever.

USEFUL ORGANIZATIONS & PUBLICATIONS

The US **Centers for Disease Control and Prevention** (☎877-FYI-TRIP/394-8747; toll-free fax 888-232-3299; www.cdc.gov/travel) maintains an international travelers' hotline and an informative website. The CDC's comprehensive booklet *Health Information for International Travel*, an annual rundown of disease, immunization, and general health advice, is free online or US$30 via the Public Health Foundation (☎877-252-1200). Consult the appropriate government agency of your home country for info sheets on health, entry requirements, and other issues for various countries (see the listings in the box on **Travel Advisories,** p. 18). For quick information on health and other travel warnings, call the **Overseas Citizens Services** (☎202-647-5225; after-hours 202-647-4000), or contact a passport agency, embassy, or consulate abroad. US citizens can send a self-addressed, stamped envelope to the Overseas Citizens Services, Bureau of Consular Affairs, #4811, US Department of State, Washington, D.C. 20520. For info on medical evacuation services and travel insurance firms, see the US government's website at http://travel.state.gov/medical.html or the **British Foreign and Commonwealth Office** (www.fco.gov.uk).

For detailed information on travel health, including a country-by-country overview of diseases (and a list of travel clinics in the USA), try the **International Travel Health Guide,** by Stuart Rose, MD (US$25; www.travmed.com). For general health info, contact the **American Red Cross** (☎800-564-1234; www.redcross.org).

MEDICAL ASSISTANCE ON THE ROAD

Tourist centers are full of pharmacies, and many pharmacists (called chemists in India) speak enough English to understand what you need. Most pharmacies sell prescription medicines as over-the-counter drugs. Only a few are open 24hr. In an emergency, head to the nearest major hospital that is open all night and has an in-house pharmacy. Outside the major tourist centers, the going is a bit rougher, although every major town should have at least one pharmacy.

India and Nepal suffer from a lack of doctors and medical equipment. **Public hospitals** are overcrowded, short on staff and supplies, and rarely have English-speaking staff. In many places in India, "hospitals" function essentially as hospices—homes for the dying. Most foreign visitors in India go to more expensive **private hospitals.** These are mainly in the big cities; elsewhere, they are usually known as nursing homes. Small private clinics, usually operated by a single physician, are also widespread and reliable. In Kathmandu, a number of tourist-oriented clinics offer care up to Western standards. For serious medical problems, however, those who can afford it have themselves evacuated to facilities in Singapore or Europe.

You can also contact your **diplomatic mission** and ask for **list of doctors.** Carry these names with your other medical documents. If a **blood transfusion** is necessary, ask whether someone from your diplomatic mission can donate blood or whether family members at home can send blood by air. Also ask whether your diplomatic mission can arrange emergency evacuation.

Travel insurance (such as ISIC and ITIC) will cover most **medical expenses** in India or Nepal. Even for long-term stays and major surgery at top hospitals, costs are much lower than back home. Nevertheless, it's a good idea to carry a credit card for immediate payment. Unfortunately, Westerners do not have good reputations for paying their bills fairly and squarely; many hospitals are hesitant to trust them with late payments.

Several companies also offer special medical support services to travelers. The *MedPass* from **GlobalCare, Inc.**, 6875 Shiloh Rd. East, Alpharetta, GA 30005, USA (☎800-860-1111; www.globalems.com), provides 24hr. international medical assistance, support, and medical evacuation resources. The **International Association for Medical Assistance to Travelers** (**IAMAT;** US ☎716-754-4883, Canada ☎519-836-0102; www.cybermall.co.nz/NZ/IAMAT) has free membership, lists English-speaking doctors worldwide, and offers detailed info on immunization requirements. If your regular **insurance** policy does not cover travel abroad, you may wish to purchase additional coverage (see p. 18).

Those with medical conditions (diabetes, allergies to antibiotics, epilepsy, heart conditions) may want to obtain a **Medic Alert** membership (first year US$35, annually thereafter US$20), which includes a stainless steel ID tag, a 24hr. collect-call number, and other benefits. Contact the Medic Alert Foundation, 2323 Colorado Ave, Turlock, CA 95382, USA (☎888-633-4298; outside US collect 209-668-3333; www.medicalert.org).

ONCE IN INDIA AND NEPAL

ENVIRONMENTAL HAZARDS

Air Quality: Some of the world's most polluted cities are on the Subcontinent. The exhaust fumes and high industrial emissions affect big and small cities alike. These may aggravate respiratory problems and create new problems for previously healthy travelers. If you suffer from allergies or asthma, take inhalers and/or prescription medication with you, and consult your doctor before you leave.

Heat exhaustion and dehydration: Heat exhaustion leads to nausea, excessive thirst, headaches, and dizziness. Avoid it by drinking plenty of fluids, eating salty foods, and avoiding dehydrating beverages (e.g., alcohol and caffeinated beverages). Continuous heat stress leads to heatstroke, characterized by a rising temperature, severe headache, delirium and cessation of sweating. In the event of heat exhaustion, victims should be cooled off with wet towels and taken to a doctor.

Sunburn: If you're prone to sunburn, bring sunscreen (it's more expensive and hard to find when traveling), apply it liberally, and also protect yourself with sunglasses and a hat. Sunburn can be particularly severe if you're on snow or ice. Because of the angle of reflected light, it can also show up in the strangest places, like under your chin or even inside your mouth. You can never have too much sunblock. A good pair of sunglasses with wraparound protection can help prevent snow blindness, a condition caused by the reflection of UV light off snow or ice. If you get sunburned, drink more fluids and apply an aloe-based lotion. Severe sunburn can lead to sun poisoning, a condition that affects the entire body, causing fever, chills, nausea, and vomiting. Sun poisoning should always be treated by a doctor. Note that UV light is stronger at higher altitudes.

Heat rashes: For some travelers, a visit to India and Nepal will mean an introduction to **prickly heat,** a rash that develops when sweat is trapped under the skin. Men are susceptible to developing this rash in the groin area. To alleviate itch, shower regularly and dry your skin thoroughly. Wear loose-fitting clothes made of absorbent fibers like cotton.

Hypothermia and frostbite: A rapid drop in body temperature is the clearest sign of overexposure to the cold. Victims may shiver, feel exhausted, have poor coordination or slurred speech, hallucinate, or suffer amnesia. *Do not let hypothermia victims fall* *asleep.* To avoid hypothermia, keep dry, wear layers, and stay out of the wind. When the temperature is below freezing, watch out for frostbite. If skin turns white, waxy, and cold, do not rub the area. Drink warm beverages, get dry, and slowly warm the area with dry fabric or steady body contact until a doctor can be found.

High altitude: Travelers to high altitudes such as the Himalayas should ascend at a gradual rate, less than 1000 meters per day, to let their bodies adjust to the lower oxygen levels in the air. High elevations can cause insomnia, headaches, nausea and **Acute Mountain Sickness** (AMS; see p. 35). At high altitudes, alcohol is more potent and UV rays are stronger.

INSECT-BORNE DISEASES

Many diseases are transmitted by insects—mainly mosquitoes, fleas, ticks, and lice. Be aware of insects in wet or forested areas, especially while hiking and camping. **Mosquitoes** are most active from dusk to dawn. Wear long pants and long sleeves (preferably light-colored) and try tucking your pants (and your vanity) into your socks. Some travelers also bring along a mosquito net, but this can add extra weight to your pack. Use insect repellents containing DEET, and soak or spray your gear with permethrin (licensed in the US for use on clothing). Consider natural repellents like vitamin B-12 or garlic pills, which make you too smelly for some insects. To stop the itch once you've been bitten, try Calamine lotion or topical cortisones (like Cortaid), or take a bath with a half-cup of baking soda or oatmeal.

Malaria: Transmitted by *Anopheles* mosquitoes that bite at night, malaria is the most serious disease travelers to India and Nepal stand a chance of contracting. The incubation period varies from 6-8 days to several months. Early symptoms include fever, chills, aches, and fatigue, followed by high fever, sometimes with vomiting and diarrhea. See a doctor for any flu-like sickness that occurs after travel in a risk area. Left untreated, malaria can cause anemia, kidney failure, coma, and death. It is an especially serious threat to pregnant women. To reduce the risk of malaria, use mosquito repellent, particularly in the evenings and when visiting forested areas, and take oral prophylactics, like **mefloquine** (Lariam) or **doxycycline** (ask your doctor for a prescription). These drugs can have serious side effects, including slowed heart rate and nightmares.

Dengue fever: An "urban viral infection" transmitted by *Aedes* mosquitoes, which bite during the day. Dengue has flu-like symptoms and rash 3-4 days after the onset of fever. Symptoms for the first 2-4 days include chills, high fever, headaches, swollen lymph nodes, muscle aches, and in some instances, a pink rash on the face. If you experience these symptoms, see a doctor, drink plenty of liquids, and take a fever-reducer such as acetaminophen (Tylenol). *Never take aspirin to treat dengue fever.*

Japanese encephalitis: Another mosquito-borne disease, most prevalent during the rainy season in rural areas near rice fields and livestock pens. Aside from delirium, most symptoms are flu-like: chills, headache, fever, vomiting, muscle fatigue. Since the disease carries a high mortality rate, it's essential to go to a hospital as soon as symptoms appear. The JE-VAX vaccine, usually given in 3 shots over a 30-day period, is effective for a year, but it has been associated with serious side effects. According to the CDC, there is little chance of being infected if proper precautions are taken, such as using mosquito repellents containing DEET and sleeping under mosquito nets.

Yellow Fever: Yellow fever occurs only in areas of South America and Africa, but many countries require a certificate of vaccination for travelers arriving from affected regions. **(See Immunizations and Precautions, p. 20.)**

Other insect-borne diseases: Filariasis is a roundworm infestation transmitted by mosquitoes. Infection causes enlargement of extremities and has no vaccine. **Leishmaniasis,** a parasite transmitted by sand-flies, can occur in the Subcontinent. Common

ESSENTIALS

symptoms are fever, weakness, and swelling of the spleen. There is a treatment, but no vaccine. The **plague** and **relapsing fever,** both transmitted through fleas and ticks, still occur. Treatment is available for both.

FOOD- & WATER-BORNE DISEASES

Food- and water-borne diseases are the biggest cause of illness among travelers to India and Nepal. Prevention is the best cure: be sure that the water you drink is clean and that everything you eat is cooked properly. **Avoid ice and drink only boiled water.** If you're a staunch purist, keep your mouth shut in the shower and don't brush your teeth with tap water or rinse your toothbrush under the faucet. To purify your own water, bring it to a rolling boil for five minutes or filter it with a portable water filter (available at camping goods stores) and treat it with **iodine tablets.** Bottled mineral water is sold everywhere in India. Beware of unsealed bottles—these have probably been refilled with tap water. **Carbonated drinks** ("cold drinks") are also safe as long as they are fizzy. **Coffee** and *chai*, which are boiled are usually safe. As tasty as they may be, avoid *lassis* or *nimbu pani* (lemonade) except in the ritziest restaurants; these are often made with ice water. Insist on drinks without ice, even if means quenching your thirst with a lukewarm Limca. It's riskier to drink water or eat seafood during **monsoon.**

Street vendors and juice stands are rarely sanitary, and although *pani puri* may please a parched palate, the equipment used to make it is open to disease-carrying flies. If possible, eat in restaurants that serve local food and are popular with locals. Touristy restaurants that serve shoddy imitations of Western food are often less clean than *dhabas* that dish out *dal bhat* to truckers all day. Your body will adapt better if you eat at regular times and eat the same sort of foods daily.

The biggest risk to travelers usually comes from **fruit, vegetables,** and **dairy products.** With fruits and vegetables, if you can peel it, you can eat it. Beware of watermelon, which is sometimes injected with impure water, and vegetables like lettuce. Stick to pasteurized dairy products. It might take your stomach time to adjust to the spiciness of the food and the variability of ingredients. Adjust to the food slowly, and have high-energy, non-sugary foods with you to keep your strength up; you'll need plenty of protein and carbohydrates. **Wash your hands before you eat.** Since sinks and soap may not always be available, bring a few packs of baby wipes or a liquid hand sanitizer. Your stomach will thank you.

Traveler's diarrhea: Results from drinking **untreated water** or eating **uncooked foods;** a temporary (and fairly common) reaction to the bacteria in new food ingredients. Symptoms include nausea, bloating, urgency, and malaise. Try quick-energy, non-sugary foods with protein and carbohydrates to keep your strength up. Over-the-counter anti-diarrheals (e.g., Imodium) may counteract the problems, but can complicate serious infections. The most dangerous side effect is dehydration; drink 8 oz. of water with ½ tsp. of sugar or honey and a pinch of salt, try uncaffeinated soft drinks, or munch on salted crackers. If you develop a fever or your symptoms don't go away after 4-5 days, consult a doctor. Also consult a doctor for treatment of diarrhea in children.

Dysentery: Results from a serious intestinal infection caused by certain bacteria. The most common type is bacillary dysentery, also called shigellosis. Symptoms include bloody diarrhea (sometimes mixed with mucus), fever, and abdominal pain and tenderness. Bacillary dysentery generally only lasts a week, but it is highly contagious. Amoebic dysentery, which develops more slowly, is a more serious disease and may cause long-term damage if left untreated. A stool test can determine which kind you have;

seek medical help immediately. Dysentery can be treated with the drugs norfloxacin or ciprofloxacin (commonly known as Cipro). If you are traveling in high-risk (especially rural) regions, consider obtaining a prescription before you leave home.

Cholera: An intestinal disease caused by bacteria in contaminated food. Symptoms include diarrhea, dehydration, vomiting, and muscle cramps. See a doctor immediately; if left untreated, it may be deadly, even within a few hours. Antibiotics are available, but the most important treatment is rehydration. Consider getting a (50% effective) vaccine if you have stomach problems (e.g., ulcers) or will be living where water is unreliable.

Hepatitis A: A viral infection of the liver acquired primarily through contaminated water and food. Symptoms include fatigue, fever, loss of appetite, nausea, dark urine, jaundice, vomiting, aches and pains, and light stools. The risk is highest in rural areas and the countryside, but it is also present in cities. Ask your doctor about the vaccine (Havrix or Vaqta) or an injection of immune globulin (IG; formerly called gamma globulin).

Parasites: Microbes, tapeworms, etc. that hide in unsafe water and food. **Giardiasis,** for example, is acquired by drinking untreated water from streams or lakes. Symptoms include swollen glands or lymph nodes, fever, rashes or itchiness, digestive problems, eye problems, and anemia. Boil water, wear shoes, avoid bugs, and eat only cooked food.

Schistosomiasis: Also known as bilharzia; a parasitic disease caused when the larvae of flatworm penetrate unbroken skin. Symptoms include an itchy localized rash, followed in 4-6 weeks by fever, fatigue, painful urination, diarrhea, loss of appetite, night sweats, and a hive-like rash on the body. If exposed to untreated water, rub the area vigorously with a towel and apply rubbing alcohol. Schistosomiasis can be treated with prescription drugs. In general, swimming in fresh water should be avoided.

Typhoid fever: Caused by the salmonella bacteria; **common in villages and rural areas.** While mostly transmitted through contaminated food and water, it may also be acquired by direct contact with another person. Early symptoms include fever, headaches, fatigue, loss of appetite, constipation, and sometimes a rash on the abdomen or chest. Antibiotics can treat typhoid, but a vaccination (70-90% effective) is recommended.

OTHER INFECTIOUS DISEASES

Rabies: Transmitted through the saliva of infected animals; fatal if untreated. By the time symptoms appear (thirst and muscle spasms), the disease is in its terminal stage. If you are bitten, wash the wound thoroughly, seek immediate medical care, and try to locate the animal. A rabies vaccine, which consists of 3 shots given over a 21-day period, is available but is only semi-effective.

Hepatitis B: A viral infection of the liver transmitted via bodily fluids or needle-sharing. Symptoms may not surface for years. Vaccinations are recommended for health-care workers, sexually active travelers, and anyone planning to seek medical treatment abroad. The 3-shot vaccination series must begin 6 months before traveling.

AIDS, HIV, & STDS

According to estimates by the World Health Organization, over 4 million cases of HIV/AIDS have been reported in India and Nepal. For detailed information on **Acquired Immune Deficiency Syndrome (AIDS)** in India and Nepal, contact the **Joint United Nations Programme on HIV/AIDS (UNAIDS),** 20, ave. Appia, CH-1211 Geneva 27, Switzerland (☎ 22 791 3666; fax 22 791 4187) or call the **US Centers for Disease Control's** 24hr. hotline at ☎ 800-342-2437.

Incoming travelers planning extended stays in India are required to register at the nearest Foreigners' Registration Office within 14 days of arrival and provide HIV test results from an approved laboratory. The Indian government may likely deny a stay of longer than 6 months to a visitor who tests positive for HIV or AIDS. If you are a traveler with HIV or AIDS, contact your Indian and Nepalese embassy or consulate for more information.

Sexually transmitted diseases (STDs) such as gonorrhea, chlamydia, genital warts, syphilis, and herpes are easier to catch than HIV. **Hepatitis B** can also be transmitted sexually (see p. 25). Though condoms may protect you from some STDs, oral or even tactile contact can lead to transmission.

WOMEN'S HEALTH

Women traveling in unsanitary or extremely hot conditions are vulnerable to **urinary tract** and **bladder infections,** common and very uncomfortable bacterial conditions that cause a burning sensation and painful, frequent urination. Try to avoid these infections by drinking plenty of water and urinating frequently, especially right after sexual intercourse. Doctors advise that eating yogurt may help to prevent UTIs. Over-the-counter medicines can sometimes alleviate symptoms, but if they persist, see a doctor. If left untreated, UTIs can lead to more serious medical conditions, especially kidney infections. **Vaginal yeast infections** may flare up in hot and humid climates. Wearing loosely fitting trousers or a skirt and cotton underwear will help, as will over-the-counter remedies like Monostat or Gynelotrimin. Bring supplies from home if you are prone to infection, as they may be difficult to find on the road. Also, since **tampons, pads,** and reliable **contraceptive devices** are sometimes hard to find when traveling, bring those supplies with you as well.

INSURANCE

Travel insurance covers four basic areas: medical/health problems, property loss, trip cancellation/interruption, and emergency evacuation. Although your regular insurance policies may well extend to travel-related accidents, you may consider purchasing travel insurance if the cost of potential trip cancellation/ interruption or emergency medical evacuation is greater than you can absorb. Prices for travel insurance bought separately run about US$50 per week for full coverage. Trip cancellation/interruption may be purchased separately at about US$5.50 per US$100 of coverage.

Medical insurance (especially university policies) often covers costs incurred abroad; check with your provider. **US Medicare** does not cover foreign travel. Americans can consult the U.S. Department of State's Bureau of Consular Affairs Overseas Citizens Services webpage (http://travel.state.gov/medical.html) for further information. **Canadians** are protected by their home province's health insurance plan for up to 90 days after leaving the country; check with the provincial Ministry of Health or Health Plan Headquarters for details. **Homeowners' insurance** (or your family's coverage) often covers theft during travel and loss of travel documents (passport, plane ticket, railpass, etc.) up to US$500.

ISIC and **ITIC** (see p. 11) provide basic insurance benefits, including US$100 per day of in-hospital sickness for up to 60 days, US$3000 of accident-related medical reimbursement, and US$25,000 for emergency medical transport. Cardholders have access to a toll-free 24hr. helpline (run by the insurance provider **TravelGuard**) for medical, legal, and financial emergencies overseas (US and Canada ☎877-370-4742, elsewhere call US collect 715-345-0505). **American**

Express (US ☎ 800-528-4800) grants most cardholders automatic car rental insurance (collision and theft, but not liability) and ground travel accident coverage of US$100,000 on flight purchases made with the card.

INSURANCE PROVIDERS. STA (see p. 40) offers plans that can supplement your basic coverage. Other private insurance providers in the US and Canada include: **Access America** (☎ 800-284-8300); **Berkely Group/Carefree Travel Insurance** (☎ 800-323-3149; www.berkely.com); **Globalcare Travel Insurance** (☎ 800-821-2488; www.globalcare-cocco.com); and **Travel Assistance International** (☎ 800-821-2828; www.europ-assistance.com). Providers in the **UK** include **Columbus Direct** (☎ 0845 330 8518; www.columbusdirect.co.uk). In **Australia**, try **AFTA** (☎ 02 9264 3299; www.afta.com.au).

PACKING

One of Indian Railways' sternly comic admonitions sums it up: **Less Luggage, More Comfort.** As a general rule, pack only what you absolutely need, then take half of the clothes and twice the money. The less you have, the less you have to lose (or to store or carry on your back).

LUGGAGE. If you plan to cover most of your itinerary by foot, a sturdy **backpack** is unbeatable. (For the basics on buying a pack, see p. 34.) Toting a **suitcase** or **trunk** is fine if you plan to live in one or two cities and explore from there, but a very bad idea if you're going to be moving around a lot. In addition to your main piece of luggage, a **daypack** (a small backpack or courier bag) is a must.

CLOTHING. Bring lightweight clothing that you can wear in layers; avoid jeans in favor of cotton and linen pants. Women should leave the miniskirts and tank tops at home. Wearing shorts is considered disrespectful for women and juvenile for men. Even if you're in the middle of a trek, shorts are still a bad idea—you'll make yourself vulnerable to insects and leeches. Comfortable walking shoes are essential. For heavy-duty trekking, don't leave home without a pair of sturdy lace-up **hiking boots**. A double pair of socks—light polypropylene inside and thick wool outside—will cushion feet and keep them dry. **Flip-flops** or waterproof sandals are must-haves for grubby hostel showers, although these can be easily purchased once in India. **Rain gear** is a necessity in cooler climates. During the monsoon, a good **rain jacket** (Gore-Tex is both waterproof and breathable) and backpack cover (or even plastic garbage bags) will take care of you and your gear at a moment's notice, which is often all you'll get. No matter when you're traveling, it's a good idea to bring a **warm jacket** or wool sweater. If you plan to **trek**, see p. 30. Remember that you will need to be respectfully dressed to visit religious sites and government offices. See **Customs and Etiquette**, p. 82.

SLEEPSACK. Most hotels provide sheets and pillows, but it is still a good idea to bring along a sleepsack. To make your own, fold a full-size sheet in half lengthwise, and then sew it closed.

CONVERTERS & ADAPTERS. In India and Nepal, electricity is 240 volts AC, enough to fry any 120V American or Canadian appliances. Visit a hardware store for an adapter (which changes the shape of the plug) and a converter (which changes the voltage). Don't make the mistake of using only an adapter (unless appliance instructions state otherwise—many portable electronic devices have built-in converters). New Zealanders (230V) and South Africans (220V/230V) as well as Australians (230V) won't need a converter, but will need

ESSENTIALS

a set of adapters to use anything electrical. Don't count on electricity to be regular or dependable, especially in rural areas. For more on all things adaptable, check out http://kropla.com/electric.htm.

TOILETRIES. Toothbrushes, towels, cold-water soap, talcum powder, deodorant, razors, tampons, and condoms are often available, but may be difficult to find, so bring extras along. **Contact lenses** may also be expensive and difficult to find, so bring enough solution and extra pairs for your entire trip. Also bring your glasses and a copy of your prescription. If you use heat-disinfection, either switch temporarily to a chemical disinfection system (check first to make sure it's safe with your brand of lenses), or buy a converter to 220/240V.

CELLULAR PHONES. A cell phone can be a lifesaver (literally) on the road; if you own a cell phone and are traveling abroad, it most likely will not work when you arrive at your destination. Let's Go has partnered with Cellular Abroad to create **Let's Go Cellular,** offering international cell service and budget short- and long-term cellular solutions for travelers. Visit http://letsgo.cellularabroad.com for more.

FIRST-AID KIT. For a basic first-aid kit, pack: bandages, pain reliever, antibiotic cream, a thermometer, a Swiss Army knife, tweezers, moleskin, decongestant, motion-sickness remedy, diarrhea or upset-stomach medication (Pepto Bismol or Imodium), an antihistamine, sunscreen, insect repellent, burn ointment, and a syringe for emergencies (get an explanatory letter from your doctor).

FILM. Photo film in India and Nepal generally costs US$3-4 for a roll of 24 color exposures, and the quality is usually good. Developing costs under $1, but you might not be thrilled with the results. Less serious photographers may want to bring a **disposable camera** or two rather than an expensive permanent one. Despite disclaimers, airport security X-rays *can* fog film, so buy a lead-lined pouch at a camera store or ask security to hand-inspect it. Always pack film in your carry-on luggage, since higher-intensity X-rays are used on checked luggage.

IMPORTANT DOCUMENTS. Don't forget your passport, traveler's checks, ATM and/or credit cards, adequate ID, and photocopies of all of the aforementioned in case these documents are lost or stolen (see p. 11).

OTHER USEFUL ITEMS. For safety purposes, you should bring a **money belt** and a strong **padlock** (some hotels don't have locks on room doors, and on trains it's a good idea to lock your bag to something). Other useful items include: sealable plastic bags (for damp clothes, soap, food, shampoo, etc.), an alarm clock, waterproof matches, sun hat, needle and thread, safety pins, sunglasses, compass, flashlight (torch), soap, earplugs, umbrella, electrical tape (for patching tears in your pack), garbage bags, and a small calculator.

ACCOMMODATIONS

Cheap accommodation is everywhere in India and Nepal. Wherever you go, it should be possible to find a place to stay without spending more than Rs100-200 per night, as long as you don't mind life without air-conditioning. Even upscale hotels are much cheaper than at home. There can be drawbacks: some hostels close during certain daytime "lockout" hours, have a curfew, don't accept reservations, impose a maximum stay, or, less frequently, require that you do chores. In India and Nepal, a dorm bed in a hostel will average around Rs100 and a private room around Rs200. **Prices fluctuate wildly according to season, and the sea-**

sons are very different from destination to destination. Most foreign tourists come to India during the winter months (Nov.-Feb.), so places that draw mostly foreigners have "high season" (and correspondingly high prices) during these months. Indian tourists head for the hills during the sweltering pre-monsoon months (May-July), causing rates to head higher too.

BUDGET HOTELS

The main travelers' centers have **tourist districts,** enclaves of shabby, bare-bones hotels with hard beds and a ceiling fan on overdrive. Managers are usually happy to provide any service rupees can buy. Where tourist districts have developed and the clientele is foreign, competition has made hotels much cheaper, cleaner, and more comfortable. It is rarely necessary to make **reservations,** except at major peak times (such as festivals). However, it can be difficult to find a place to stay in big cities that see few foreign tourists, where the hotels may be full of businessmen or might lack the paperwork to accept foreigners. Budget hotels frequently have **restaurants** attached and sometimes Star TV and air-conditioning. Another attractive feature is **room service,** which usually costs no more than food in the restaurant. If you are a lazy **launderer,** you can surrender your clothes to the local *dhobi* (most hotels have their own and store-front laundries are everywhere).

One thing to look out for when choosing a hotel is the **check-out time**—many cheap hotels have a 24hr. rule, which means if you arrive in the morning after an overnight train you'll be expected to leave as early when you check out. **Don't let touts or rickshaw-*wallahs* make your lodging plans for you.** These shady characters cart tourists off to whichever hotel offers the biggest commission. For more information, see **Touts, Middlemen, and Scams,** p. 15.

Many budget travelers prefer to bring their own **padlock** for budget hotels; the locally made padlocks are easy to break. You should also carry sheets, towels, soap, and **toilet paper.** Many places have **hot water** only at certain hours of the day or only in buckets. Since the power supply is erratic everywhere in India, **generators** provide a very noisy solution. **Air-cooling,** a system by which air is blown by a fan over a surface of water, is common.

Some hotels have built reputations as places for foreign travelers to hang out and share stories. Some places have even instituted discriminatory **no-Indians policies** to create foreigners-only environments for their guests.

Nepal's budget scene is the result of a recent boom, and foreigners are its main targets. Major tourist districts, unlike anything in India, have grown up in Pokhara and Kathmandu, where fierce competition has led to rock-bottom prices and generally better hotels than in India.

HOSTELS

Youth hostels are scattered throughout India, especially in the far north and south. They are extremely cheap and popular with foreign visitors. **YMCAs** and **YWCAs** are only in the big cities and are usually quite expensive, although the women-only policy of YWCAs makes them a good option for women traveling alone. Hostels in India rarely exclude nonmembers or charge them extra. **Hostels in Nepal are nonexistent.** In India, the state tourism development corporations have set up large **tourist bungalows** in both popular and less-touristed areas. Combining hotel with tourist office, these places are convenient, but the slight improvement over budget hotels is seldom worth the price.

BOOKING HOSTELS ONLINE. One of the cheapest and easiest ways to ensure a bed for a night is by reserving online. Our website features the Hostelworld booking engine; access it at www.letsgo.com/resources/accommodations. Hostelworld offers bargain accommodations everywhere from Argentina to Zimbabwe with no added commission.

UPSCALE HOTELS

Nicer hotels offer an escape from life on the road and can help you maintain sanity. Pricier accommodations are available almost anywhere in India, with A/C, 24hr. hot water, and TVs. The rates will seem exorbitant compared to the budget hotels. However, many expensive hotels are all show: a spacious, carpeted lobby disguises rooms that are only marginally better than those in budget hotels. Across central and western India, former **palaces** of rajas and maharajas have been turned into mid-range hotels and offer travelers the decadence of a bygone era at a more or less affordable price. Large, expensive hotels such as the Taj, Sheraton, and Oberoi chains and the ITDC's line of Ashoks are in the main cities and tourist centers. In Nepal, more expensive hotels are only in Kathmandu and Pokhara. Even if a night's stay is beyond your budget, the bookstores, restaurants, and pools at these places are still great resources. Larger hotels require payment in **foreign currency;** this rule extends even farther down the price scale in Nepal.

OTHER TYPES OF ACCOMMODATIONS

RELIGIOUS REST HOUSES

Traditional rest houses for Hindu pilgrims known as *dharamsalas* sometimes provide foreign guests spartan accommodation free of charge. You will be expected to give a donation. Sikh *gurudwaras* also have a tradition of hospitality. Be on your best behavior if you stay in these religious places. They are not hotels; many have curfews or other restrictions. Smoking and drinking are not allowed.

HOMESTAYS

Homestays with Indian families provide the paying guest with an opportunity to experience the daily life of the country at first-hand; the Government of India's Tourist Department is promoting the concept aggressively. The **Paying Guest Scheme** is a relatively new phenomenon in India, but it is gaining momentum in a number of states, particularly Tamil Nadu and Rajasthan. Government of India Tourist Offices publish a list of host families and information about the rooms, facilities, and meals provided. Homestays are more expensive than budget hotels, but cheaper than starred hotels. They are rare in Nepal.

TREKKING

Trekking is neither mountaineering nor backpacking. It is simply a journey on foot through the hills that can take a day, a week, a month, or if it suits you, a lifetime. You might be walking from village to village along ancient highways or striking off into more remote areas where accommodation is sparse and a tent the only place to sleep. However you do it, you'll be living off the land, eating local food and meeting local people. A classic "day" involves five to six hours on the trail with frequent stops for tea and photo-taking. Most treks go through populated country, but some venture over high passes and along trails used only by herders on their way to high-altitude pastures. Keep in mind that the Himalayas are the tallest mountains in the world, and even the foothills provide plenty of tough walking. At the end of the day, while you are putting bandages on your blisters, admire the magnificent views; a few aching muscles are a small price to pay.

WHEN TO GO

In India, the pre-monsoon (May-June) and post-monsoon (Sept.-Oct.) seasons afford the best hiking in the hill regions of **Kangra, Kullu** (see p. 240), **Shimla** (see p. 222), and **Uttaranchal** (see p. 637). The areas of **Upper Kinnaur** (see p. 249), **Lahaul** (see p. 256), **Spiti** (see p. 250), and **Ladakh** (see p. 259) are in the rain-shadow and get none of the monsoon. The post-monsoon reprieve (Oct.-Nov.) is the most popular season for trekking in **Nepal** (see p. 894), and the more popular routes teem with hikers. March to May is Nepal's second and less crowded trekking season. From December to February, it is too cold for trekking at high altitudes, and snow blocks many passes. The temperatures rise in March and April and make trekking more feasible. The air is usually dusty and dry, but rhododendra, magnolias, and orchids are impressive compensation. With the monsoon just around the corner in May—the hottest and least predictable of months—most trekking activities taper off as trekkers retreat to higher regions. Despite the stunning views in places like the Valley of Flowers, few choose to endure the cloud-bound, slippery, and leech-beleaguered trail conditions of the monsoon. For the persistent and enterprising, however, trekking during the summer season has at least one benefit—the virtual absence of foreign tourists.

PLANNING A TREK

There are two ways of organizing a trek in the Himalayas. Trekking independently saves money and allows you to set the pace, choose companions, and plan rest days and side trips of personal interest. However, arranging your own trek also entails obtaining your own permits, renting equipment, buying supplies, and hiring porters and guides. If you would rather not deal with these details, a trekking agency can take care of the preparations for you, and their expertise might make it possible to trek through more remote back country, though this is done at a price.

Trekking in India requires more self-sufficiency than trekking in Nepal. Because you will need more equipment in India, you'll need porters more often. Population tends to be a lot thinner in the Indian Himalayas than in Nepal, and trekkers often see no one for days, so it is important to go with someone who knows the trails. On the other hand, villages along Nepal's most popular routes have outdone themselves to accommodate foreigners, and they are lined with tea houses and small hotels offering meals and a place to sleep. In Nepal, English signs advertise **lodging** and **food** at bargain prices (usually under NRs20), and often an English-speaking manager greets the guests. The tea house social scene can be lively, and these lodges are full of potential trekking companions.

PORTERS AND GUIDES

One variation on trekking alone is to hire your own porters and guides. You will have a knowledgeable local with you, you won't need to carry as much, and you'll be supporting the local economy. **Porters** carry most of your gear, allowing you the comfort of walking with just a small pack containing the items you will need dur-

TREKKING PERMITS AND OTHER FEES. Permits are no longer required for the Everest, Langtang, and Annapurna trekking areas in Nepal. Permits for other areas can be obtained at immigration offices in Kathmandu (for more information see **Kathmandu, Practical Information: Immigration Office,** p. 811). You can normally complete the process in one day, though long lines at the height of the season can extend the process to 2-3 days. **Your permit will be checked regularly (and stamped) at police check-posts.** If your trek enters a national park, you will have to pay a fee. Trekking permits are not required in India, except in **North Sikkim** (see p. 10), although you will need a permit merely to enter certain regions considered to be "defense areas," such as parts of **Northeast India** (see p. 10) and regions bordering Tibet. **Camping is not allowed in national parks or wildlife sanctuaries.**

ing the day. Of course, you'll have to make sure that your porter understands what you want him to do and where you want to go. There is always a small chance that your porter will disappear, leaving you with just a pair of sunglasses and a pack of playing cards. Choose your porter carefully; the expense entailed in hiring a porter through a recognized trekking agency is a sound investment.

Guides, who usually speak English, are not necessary on the better-known routes, where it is easy to find your way. Having someone who knows English might prove helpful in negotiations and pre-trek planning, however. A guide can color your experience with his knowledge, and often, guides will take trekkers on unusual side trips to visit friends and family. Guides will not carry anything (that's what porters are for).

In general, porters and guides are easy to find, but you will want to investigate their honesty and experience. You can be almost certain to get reputable workers through a guest house or trekking agency. Ask to see **letters of recommendation** from previous trekkers. Guides and porters hired through companies are slightly more expensive but are usually more reliable and better qualified, with the added security of a company to hold responsible if your guide is no good. If you do hire your own guides and porters, make sure you know exactly what services are covered, where you will go, and what supplies you will need to provide along the way. Most agreements stipulate that guides and porters pay for their own food and housing. As a responsible employer, you should make sure that porters and guides are adequately clothed when trekking at high altitudes by outfitting them with good shoes, a parka, sunglasses, mittens, and a sleeping bag. Establish beforehand if you expect them to return anything. (For more information on porters' living conditions and responsible trekking, consult the **International Porter Protection Group,** www.ippg.net, which has representatives across the world.)

The standard salary for a porter carrying 20kg. is about US$10 per day in Nepal, US$5 per day in India; the salary for guides is higher (US$12-20 per day in India). In addition to these fees, your staff will expect a generous tip at the end of a trek.

ORGANIZED TREKKING

Many people do not want to spend precious vacation time planning their trek, buying equipment, and hiring porters and guides. You can book treks through a large, international adventure travel company in your home country, in which case everything is arranged before you even leave for the airport. If you wait until you arrive, you can book through a local trekking agency, which usually requires one week's notice. The agent makes reservations for hotels and transportation and provides a complete staff—guide, porters, and cooks—for the trek. You will have to commit to the prearranged itinerary, and you might also be trekking with smelly people you have never met before. Organized treks often veer off into more remote areas. The group carries its own food, prepared by cooks skilled in the art of kerosene cuisine. The comforts of trekking through an agency can also include tables, chairs, dining tents, and toilet tents. All this comfort and convenience usually costs US$15 to US$150 (usually US$40-50) per person per day.

PACKING AND EQUIPMENT

What you carry with you on your trek will depend greatly on where you go, the style of trekking you choose, and—if you have arranged a trek through an agency—what they provide. For the most part, outfitting yourself for a trek is easier in Nepal than in India. In India, it might be necessary to bring your own gear. In some areas, there might be an occasional rest house, but these are often out of the way, and food supplies are unreliable. Tents are essential for shelter, and the supplies and equipment you will need to carry are much greater. Nepalese tea houses relieve you of the need to carry food, cooking supplies, and tents—unless you're going to high altitudes beyond the reach of tea house culture. For more information on packing, see p. 27. A quick checklist of items to carry along on a trek:

CLOTHING	EQUIPMENT
boots or running shoes	sleeping bag
camp shoes or flip-flops	water bottle
lots of socks (polypropylene and wool)	flashlight, batteries
down jacket	insulated mat, if camping
woolen shirt	backpack and daypack
shorts/skirt	toilet paper and hand towel
long trousers	lighter, stove, fuel
rainwear and umbrella	sunblock and lip balm
cotton T-shirts or blouses	towel
thermal underwear	water purification system
gloves	sewing kit with safety pins
sun hat and wool hat	small knife
snow gaiters	first-aid kit (see p. 28)
snow goggles/sunglasses	Zip-Loc bags

IF YOU PLAN TO BUY...

Good camping equipment is sturdy and light. Here are some shopping guidelines:

Sleeping Bag: Most sleeping bags are rated by season ("summer" means 30-40°F at night; "four-season" or "winter" often means below 0°F). They are made either of **down** (warmer and lighter, but more expensive and miserable when wet) or of **synthetic** material (heavier, more durable, and warmer when wet). Prices range US$70-210 for a summer synthetic to US$250-300 for a good down winter bag. **Sleeping bag pads** include foam pads (US$10-30), air mattresses (US$15-50), and Therm-A-Rest self-inflating pads (US$45-120). Bring a **stuff sack** to store your bag and keep it dry.

Tent: The best tents are free-standing (with their own frames and suspension systems), set up quickly, and require staking only in high winds. Low-profile dome tents are the best all-around. Good 2-person tents start at US$90, 4-person at US$300. Seal the seams of your tent with waterproofer, and make sure it has a rain fly. Other tent accessories include a **battery-operated lantern,** a **plastic groundcloth,** and a **nylon tarp.**

Backpack: Internal-frame packs mold better to your back, keep a lower center of gravity, and flex adequately to allow you to hike difficult trails. **External-frame packs** are more comfortable for long hikes over even terrain, as they keep weight higher and distribute it more evenly. Make sure your pack has a strong, padded hip-belt to transfer weight to your legs. Any serious backpacking requires a pack of at least 4000 in^3 (16,000cc), plus 500 in^3 for sleeping bags in internal-frame packs. Sturdy backpacks cost anywhere from US$125-420—this is one area in which it doesn't pay to economize. Fill up any pack with something heavy and walk around the store with it to get a sense of how it distributes weight before buying it. Either buy a **waterproof backpack cover,** or store all of your belongings in plastic bags inside your pack. This is important.

Boots: Be sure to wear hiking boots with good **ankle support.** They should fit snugly and comfortably over 1-2 pairs of wool socks and thin liner socks. Break in boots over several weeks first in order to spare yourself painful and debilitating blisters.

Other Necessities: Synthetic layers, like those made of polypropylene, and a pile jacket will keep you warm even when wet. A **space blanket** will help you retain your body heat and can double as a groundcloth (US$5-15). Plastic **water bottles** are virtually shatter- and leak-proof. Bring **water-purification tablets** for when you can't boil water. If you're trekking without a cook and no decent food option presents itself, you'll need a **camp stove** (the classic MSR WhisperLite starts at US$60) and fuel. (Gas stations and supply stores are few and far between in the mountains, so have adequate fuel before hitting the trail.) Also don't forget a **first-aid kit, pocketknife, insect repellent, calamine lotion,** and **waterproof matches** or a **lighter.**

HEALTH AND SAFETY

Trekking is hard work, so don't overdo it. Go at a comfortable pace and take rest days when necessary. Make sure your water is safe; boiling is often impractical (and ineffective at high altitudes where water boils at a lower temperature). Chemical treatment is the best option. Iodine solution or iodine-water purification tablets will do the job. Use Tang orange-juice powder or chewable vitamin C tablets to mask the flavor. If you're eating in local inns, go vegetarian and stick to fried food—a good dose of hot oil does wonders for even the most resilient of nasties, and given the rate at which calories burn as you toil uphill, the forbidden delights of the frying pan can be consumed guilt-free. The popular Nepalese trekking routes witness a lot of diarrhea and nausea-induced misery. For more information, see **Health,** p. 20.

Women should not trek alone. It is better to find a group, either on your own, through notice boards, or through a trekking agency. Some agencies now specialize in providing female porters and guides for women.

Knee and ankle sprains: These are common trekking injuries. Knees in particular can become painfully inflamed. If you are susceptible to knee injuries, bind your knees with a cloth bandage as a preventive measure. Sprained ankles can keep you from walking for days. Good footwear with ankle support is the best prevention.

Blisters: These have potential to ruin your trek. If you feel a "hot-spot" coming on, cover it with moleskin. Keep your feet dry; take your boots and socks off at every rest stop, and change your socks regularly. Once you've got a blister, drain the fluid using a needle sterilized in a metal flame and then dress it.

Cuts: External injuries like cuts to the skin should be cleaned with water and covered with Betadine and a firm bandage. Clean and dress the wound daily. If the wound becomes infected, apply an antibiotic ointment. Although trekkers do not often need serious medical attention, trekking mishaps do occur. If urgent medical attention is needed, **emergency rescue** request messages can be sent by radio at police, army, national park, and other official offices. Helicopter rescue is very expensive (usually US$1000-2000). In Nepal, money must be deposited or guaranteed in Kathmandu before the helicopter will fly. For people on agency treks, the agency will often advance the money. This process is a lot easier if you are registered with your embassy, which you can do quickly and easily at your embassy in Kathmandu.

Acute Mountain Sickness (AMS): If you are trekking to altitudes above 3500m, you will probably experience mild symptoms of altitude sickness, which can worsen into Acute Mountain Sickness (AMS). AMS is the body's reaction to the low oxygen environment of high altitudes, and it can kill you if left untreated. Since the rate of acclimatization is so variable and unpredictable, budget plenty of time for high-altitude portions of your trek. If you're trekking in Nepal, having a trekking permit valid for a week longer than you anticipate is a good idea. Trekkers who fly directly to high altitudes are more likely to be affected by AMS than those who walk up gradually. Susceptibility to AMS is almost impossible to predict—some people have no problems acclimatizing; others take a long time. Despite what you might have read, there are no prescriptions for avoiding AMS. The best advice is to **drink lots of water, take it slow,** and to **sleep low, go high.** Once you're at about 3000m, try to sleep no more than 300m higher than the previous night. If you have to cross a high pass, sleep at the bottom and make it a long day up and over. **Drink lots of fluids.** It's always sensible to be well hydrated, but the need for hydration is especially important at higher altitudes. Note that alcohol impedes acclimatization. **Watch for symptoms.** Typically the first symptom is a mild headache, but there's a whole suite of other symptoms: dizziness, nausea, insomnia, racing heart, fatigue. If you experience any of these, do not sleep at higher altitudes. Don't ascend, and the symptoms will probably pass within 24hr. If your condition continues to deteriorate, you *must* descend. Even a descent of just a few hundred meters can make all the difference. **Most AMS fatalities occur in groups,** since badly affected trekkers don't want to hold up others in the group. Ensure that this does not happen by gaining altitude at a rate suited to the slowest acclimatizer. For more information on AMS and other trekking illnesses visit the **High Altitude Medicine Guide** website at www.high-altitude-medicine.com.

Hypothermia and Frostbite: Hypothermia and frostbite might seem a long way away when you're sweating in sunny valleys, but they're an ever-present danger at high altitudes. All too often people run into problems because they are determined to press on through bad conditions. If the weather turns against you, get to shelter as soon as you can, even if it means retracing your steps. For tips on preventing and combating these conditions, see p. 22.

Sunburn: See **Environmental Hazards,** p. 22.

Leeches: Leeches are rampant during monsoon season. Trekkers often get them on their legs or in their boots. Carry salt with you in a small container for chemical attack on them. Carefully applying a lit cigarette is another effective way of removing them. Unlike ticks, they do not leave any part of themselves behind, so it is safe to pull them off; disinfect the bite anyway. A leech bite isn't painful, and leeches do not transmit diseases. The effect is mostly psychological.

Water: Sanitary drinking water is a must. Although it is possible to purchase bottled water along major trekking routes, there will be times when you have to treat your own water. **Iodine**-treated water tastes awful, but iodine is both widely available and effective; add five drops per liter. Adding Tang flavor crystals will usually help with taste. A pricier, but easier, alternative is iodine tablets (e.g. **Potable Aqua**), available in bottles of 50; add two tablets per liter.

RESPONSIBLE TREKKING

Trekking can help the local economy, but it can hurt the environment. Cultivate respect for the land you are trampling. The ecological balance in the Himalayas is at risk as a result of overgrazing, pollution, and, most importantly, **deforestation.** Never cut vegetation or clear new campsites. Loss of vegetation is the beginning of an ecological spiral that leads to **erosion** and **landslides.** Whenever possible, ask for kerosene or gas to be used for cooking and heating water; blazing campfire hearths are taboo where deforestation is a problem. Even in regions with plentiful trees, gather only dead branches and brush for burning. Limit hot showers to those heated by electricity, solar energy, or back-boilers. Industrious and innovative shower suppliers deserve encouragement.

Trekkers and their waste also contribute to litter, sanitation, and water pollution problems. The rule to follow is: **burn it, bury it, or carry it out.** Toilet paper is generally burned, biodegradables such as food wastes are buried, and non-disposables (plastics, aluminum foil, batteries, glass, cans, etc.) are packed up and carried. Make sure your campsite is at least 150 ft. (50m) from water supplies or bodies of water. If there are no toilet facilities, bury human waste (*not* paper) at least four inches (10cm) deep and above the high-water line, and 150 ft. or more from any water supplies, campsites, village compounds, and crop fields. Use biodegradable soap and shampoo, and don't rinse directly in streams. If you can't leave the area clean, don't go. On organized treks, make sure that a person from your team is the last to leave camp; guided tour operators seldom do what they promise about garbage disposal.

FURTHER RESOURCES

Himalayan Rescue Association (HRA), P.O. Box 4944, Jyatha, Thamel, Kathmandu (☎01 440292; www.himalayanrescue.com). Just off Jyatha, south of Thamel, in Kathmandu. A volunteer non-profit organization that provides info for trekkers on where and how to trek, hazards, altitude sickness, and how to protect the environment. They also have in-season clinics with volunteer Western doctors during the trekking season in Pheriche on the Everest trek and in Marang on the Annapurna Circuit. Open Su-F 10am-5pm.

Kathmandu Environmental Education Project (KEEP), PO Box 9178, Jyatha, Thamel, Kathmandu (☎01 259567; www.keepnepal.org). Also off Jyatha, close to the HRA. A non-profit organization that promotes "soft trekking," which minimizes impact on the environment and culture. They offer free advice to trekkers and trekking staff. During the trekking season (Oct.-Dec. and Feb.-May) they have a free talk on eco-tourism at their office at 4pm every Friday. A good place to find trekking companies and a source of up-to-date information. Open Su-F 10am-5pm.

Annapurna Conservation Area Project (ACAP), c/o King Mahendra Trust, P.O. Box 3712, Kathmandu (☎01 526571; www.kmtnc.org.np/acap.html), in the King Mahendra Trust Office, near Grindlay's bank in Jawalakhel or in the Natural History Museum on Pokhara's Prithvi Narayan campus. Authoritative source on the Annapurna region of Nepal; promotes environmentally sound trekking. Open M-F 9am-5pm.

Nepal Mountaineering Association (NMA), (☎01 434525; www.nma.com.np), south of Nag Pokhari in Naxal, in Kathmandu. Issues permits for the Nepalese Himalayas.

Indian Mountaineering Foundation, 6 Benito Juarez Marg, New Delhi 110021 (☎011 4677935 or 4671211; www.indmount.org). Information on treks above 6000m.

KEEPING IN TOUCH

BY MAIL

SENDING MAIL HOME

Airmail is the best way to send mail home. Allow two weeks for mail delivery from South Asia. Write "Air Mail" or "SpeedPost" on the front. **Surface mail** is by far the cheapest and slowest way to send mail. It takes one to three months to cross the Atlantic and two to four to cross the Pacific. Standard rates for unregistered air mail to Australia, Canada, Ireland, New Zealand, the UK and the US are:

Postcards/aerogrammes: Rs 8.50

Letters up to 30g: Rs 24

Parcels up to 0.5kg: Rs 465

Parcels up to 2kg: Rs 1,005

Registered mail costs an additional Rs 15.

Sending a **parcel** home will involve getting it cleared by customs, getting it wrapped in cloth and sealed in wax, going to the post office to fill out the customs forms, buying stamps, and finally, seeing it processed. It might take months or even years by surface mail. All packages run the risk of being X-rayed or searched.

SENDING MAIL TO INDIA AND NEPAL

Mark envelopes "air mail," or your letter or postcard may never arrive. In addition to the standard postage system, express mail services such as the following will deliver mail in 3-7 days, though the speed comes at a hefty price: **Federal Express** (Australia ☎ 13-26-10; US and Canada ☎ 800-247-4747; New Zealand ☎ 0800 73 33 39; UK ☎ 0800 12 38 00; www.fedex.com); **US Express Mail** (www.usps.gov); **DHL** (Australia ☎ 13 14 06; UK ☎ 087 0110 0300; US ☎ 800-225-5345; www.dhl.com).

Standard airmail services usually take 7-14 days to reach India and Nepal. For more information, consult your national postal service: **Australia** (www.auspost.com.au.); **Canada** (www.canadapost.ca); **Ireland** (www.anpost.ie); **New Zealand** (www.nzpost.co.nz); **UK** (www.royalmail.co.uk); **US** (www.usps.gov).

RECEIVING MAIL

There are several ways to arrange pick-up of letters sent to you by friends and relatives while you are abroad. Mail can be sent via **Poste Restante** (General Delivery) to almost any city or town in India or Nepal with a post office, but it is unreliable. Address *Poste Restante* letters like so:

Napoleon BONAPARTE

Poste Restante, GPO

Delhi, 110001

India

The mail will go to a special desk in the central post office, unless you specify a post office by street address or postal code. It's best to use the largest post office, since mail may be sent there regardless of what is written on the envelope. If you need to receive a package from abroad, have it registered—this will reduce the chance that your goods will get stolen. Bring your passport (or other photo ID) for pick-up. If the clerks insist that there is nothing for you, have them check under your first name as well. *Let's Go* lists post offices in the **Practical Information** section for each city and most towns.

ESSENTIALS

American Express travel offices throughout the world offer a free **Client Letter Service** (mail held up to 30 days and forwarded upon request) for cardholders who contact them in advance. Address the letter in the same way shown above. Some offices will offer these services to non-cardholders (especially AmEx Travelers Cheque holders), but call ahead to make sure. *Let's Go* lists AmEx office locations for most large cities in **Practical Information** sections; for a complete, free list, call ☎ 800-528-4800.

BY TELEPHONE

CALLING HOME

Phones are almost everywhere in India and Nepal. The STD/ISD sign (Standard Trunk Dialing/International Subscriber Dialing) means that there's a phone nearby. Some STD/ISD booths are open 24hr. and offer fax services. Incoming calls often cost Rs5 per min., so it's a good idea to have someone call you back. Check with the booth operator before you try it; sometimes they charge a per-minute rate for incoming calls, or don't allow them at all.

A **calling card** is another (often futile) alternative. Calls are billed either col-

PLACING INTERNATIONAL CALLS. To call India or Nepal from home or to place an international call from India or Nepal dial:

1. The **international dialing prefix.** To call out of **Australia**, dial 0011; **Canada** or the **US**, 011; the **Republic of Ireland, New Zealand,** or the **UK,** 00; **South Africa,** 09; **India** or **Nepal,** 00.

2. The **country code** of the country you want to call. To call **Australia,** dial 61; **Canada** or the **US,** 1; the **Republic of Ireland,** 353; **New Zealand,** 64; **South Africa,** 27; the **UK,** 44; **India,** 91; **Nepal,** 977.

3. The **city** or **area code.** *Let's Go* lists phone codes opposite the city or town's name, alongside the following icon: ☎. If the first digit is a zero (e.g. 020 for London), omit it when calling from abroad.

4. The **local number.**

lect or to your account. Though calling cards often work in the major tourist centers of India and Nepal, the STD/ISD booths in many smaller cities and villages do not have access to international operators. And even those cards that might potentially work are often disallowed by booth owners, who don't profit on these calls. International **collect calls** cannot be made from India or Nepal to some countries, and booth owners often won't let you try.

Let's Go has recently partnered with eKit.com to provide the Let's Go Phonecard, a calling card that offers a variety of services, including email and voice messaging. For more info, visit www.letsgo.ekit.com.

CALLING WITHIN INDIA AND NEPAL

To call within India or Nepal, dial the city code and then the number. Long-distance calls are either full price (M-Sa 8am-7pm); half-price (M-Sa 7-8am and 7-8:30pm, Su 7am-8:30pm); one-third price (daily 6-7am and 8:30-11pm); or one-quarter price (daily 11pm-6am).

INDIA PHONE CODES	
Agra	0562
Ahmedabad	079
Amritsar	0183
Bangalore	080
Bhopal	0755
Bhubaneswar	0674
Mumbai (Bombay)	022
Chandigarh	0172
Delhi	011
Dharamsala	01892
Guwahati	0361
Hyderabad	040
Jaipur	0141

Khajuraho	07686
Kolkata	033
Leh	01982
Chennai (Madras)	044
Manali	01902
Patna	0612
Panjim (Panaji)	0832
Shimla	0177
Trivandrum	0471
Varanasi	0542
NEPAL PHONE CODES	
Kathmandu	01
Chitwan	056
Pokhara	061

TIME DIFFERENCES

India is 5½hr. ahead of Greenwich Mean Time (GMT), 4½ hr. behind Sydney, 13½ hr. ahead of Vancouver and San Francisco, 10½ hr. ahead of New York, 4½ hr. ahead of Johannesburg. Summer puts the northern countries an hour closer to India. Nepal is 15min. ahead of India.

BY EMAIL AND INTERNET

Thousands of **cybercafes** can be found all over India and Nepal. Outside the major cities, connections are slow, and cybercafes tend to get crowded, so don't count on being able to send digital copies of your holiday snaps home every night unless you have patience and time.

Though in some places it's possible to forge a remote link with your home server, in most cases this is a much slower (and thus more expensive) option than taking advantage of free web-based email accounts (e.g., www.hotmail.com and http://mail.yahoo.com). Travelers with laptops can call an Internet service provider via a modem. Long-distance phone cards specifically intended for such calls can defray normally high phone charges; check with your long-distance phone provider to see if it offers this option. Internet cafes and the occasional free Internet terminal at a public library or university are listed in the Practical Information sections of major cities.

GETTING TO INDIA AND NEPAL

BY PLANE

When it comes to airfare, a little effort can save you a bundle. If your plans are flexible enough to deal with the restrictions, courier fares are the cheapest. Tickets bought from consolidators and standby seating are also good deals, but last-minute specials, airfare wars, and charter flights often beat these fares. The key is to hunt around, to be flexible, and to ask persistently about discounts. Students, seniors, and those under 26 should never have to pay full price for a ticket.

AIRFARES

Airfares to India and Nepal peak between mid-June and early September; holidays are also expensive. Midweek (M-Th morning) round-trip flights run US$40-50 cheaper than weekend flights. Traveling with an "open return" ticket can be pricier than fixing a return date when buying the ticket. Round-trip flights are by far the cheapest; "open-jaw" (arriving in and departing from different cities, e.g. London-Delhi and Kathmandu-London) tickets tend to be pricier. Patching one-way flights together is the most expensive way to travel. Flights between capital cities and regional hubs offer the most competitive fares.

If India or Nepal is just one stop on a more extensive globe-trotting trip, consider a round-the-world (RTW) ticket. Tickets usually include at least 5 stops and are valid for about a year (US$1200-5000). Try **Northwest Airlines/KLM** (US ☎800-447-4747; www.nwa.com) or **Star Alliance,** a consortium of 22 airlines including United (US ☎800-241-6522; www.star-alliance.com).

Fares for roundtrip flights to **Delhi** or **Mumbai** from the **US** or **Canada** cost US$900-1200 during the low season/US$1200-1700 during the summer; from **London,** UK£450-750/UK£500-900; From **Australia** and **New Zealand,** peak-season fares (late Nov. to late Jan.) are between AUS$2000-3000 round-trip from the east coast of Australia to Delhi, Kolkata, or Kathmandu. Low-season fares are AUS$1500-2200. Flying from Perth is usually about AUS$150 cheaper than flying from the east coast.

BUDGET & STUDENT TRAVEL AGENCIES

While knowledgeable agents specializing in flights to India and Nepal can make your life easy and help you save, they may not spend the time to find you the lowest possible fare—they get paid on commission. Travelers holding **ISIC and IYTC cards** (see p. 11) qualify for big discounts from student travel agencies. Most flights from budget agencies are on major airlines, but in peak season some may sell seats on less reliable chartered aircraft.

USIT, 19-21 Aston Quay, Dublin 2, Ireland (☎01 602 1600; www.usitworld.com) Ireland's leading student/budget travel agency has 22 offices throughout Northern Ireland and the Republic of Ireland. Offers programs to work in North America.

CTS Travel, 30 Rathbone Pl., London W1T 1GQ, UK (☎020 7290 0630; www.ctstravel.co.uk). A British student travel agent with offices in 39 countries including the US, Empire State Building, 350 Fifth Ave., Ste. 7813, New York, NY 10118 (☎877-287-6665; www.ctstravelusa.com).

STA Travel, 7890 S. Hardy Dr., Ste. 110, Tempe AZ 85284, USA (24hr. reservations and info ☎800-781-4040; www.sta-travel.com). A student and youth travel organization with over 150 offices worldwide (check their website for a listing of all their offices), including US offices in Boston, Chicago, L.A., New York, San Francisco, Seattle, and Washington, D.C. Ticket booking, travel insurance, railpasses, and more. In the UK, walk-in office 11 Goodge St., **London** W1T 2PF or call 0207 436 7779. In New Zealand, Shop 2B, 182 Queen St., **Auckland** (☎09 309 0458). In Australia, 366 Lygon St., **Carlton,** Victoria 3053 (☎03 9349 4344).

Travel CUTS (Canadian Universities Travel Services Limited), 187 College St., Toronto, ON M5T 1P7 (☎416-979-2406; www.travelcuts.com). Offices across Canada and the United States in Seattle, San Francisco, Los Angeles, New York and elsewhere. In the UK, 295-A Regent St., London W1B 2H9 (☎0207 255 2191).

Travel CUTS (Canadian Universities Travel Services Limited), 187 College St., **Toronto,** ON M5T 1P7 (☎416-979-2406; www.travelcuts.com). 60 offices across Canada. In the UK, 295-A Regent St., **London** W1R 7YA (☎0207 255 1944)

FLIGHT PLANNING ON THE INTERNET. Many airline sites offer special last-minute deals on the Web. Other sites do the legwork and compile the deals for you—try www.bestfares.com, www.flights.com, www.lowestfare.com, www.onetravel.com, and www.travelzoo.com.

StudentUniverse (www.studentuniverse.com), **STA** (www.sta-travel.com and **Orbitz.com** provide quotes on student tickets, while **Expedia** (www.expedia.com) and **Travelocity** (www.travelocity.com) offer full travel services. **Priceline** (www.priceline.com) allows you to specify a price, and obligates you to buy any ticket that meets or beats it; be prepared for antisocial hours and odd routes. **Skyauction** (www.skyauction.com) allows you to bid on both last-minute and advance-purchase tickets.

An indispensable resource on the Internet is the *Air Traveler's Handbook* (www.cs.cmu.edu/afs/cs/user/mkant/Public/Travel/airfare.html), a comprehensive listing of links to everything you need to know before you board a plane.

BORDER CROSSINGS

India-Nepal: There are 6 crossings: Mahendranagar, Dhangadi, Nepalganj, **Sunauli** (see p. 875), **Raxaul/Birganj** (see p. 133), and **Kakarbhitta** (see p. 890). Sunauli is a 3hr. bus ride from Gorakhpur in Uttar Pradesh; from there you can catch a 10hr. bus to Pokhara or a 11hr. bus to Kathmandu. Raxaul is a 6hr. bus ride from Patna in Bihar; from Birganj, across the border, it's a 10-12hr. bus ride to Kathmandu. The Kakarbhitta crossing, at the eastern end of Nepal, is easily accessible from **Siliguri,** which is a transit point for Darjeeling. It is unnecessary to get a Nepalese visa before you arrive at the border. You must have an Indian visa ahead of time if you are going from Nepal to India. You can also drive across the border if you have an international *carnet* (see p. 44).

India-Bangladesh: Trains and buses run from Kolkata to **Bangaon** in West Bengal. From there a rickshaw ride can take you to **Benapol, Bangladesh,** with connections via Khulna or Jessore to Dhaka. The northern border, from Jalpaiguri to Haldibari, is only periodically open and requires an exit permit. The border from Agartala, Tripura, to Akhaura, Bangladesh, sees little traffic.

India-Myanmar (Burma): No land frontier open.

India-Bhutan: If you are lucky enough to get a Bhutanese visa, you must cross the border at **Puntsholing,** a 3-4hr. bus ride from **Siliguri** in West Bengal. Make sure you also have a "transit permit" from the Indian Ministry of External Affairs.

India-China: No land frontier open.

India-Pakistan: Only one road crossing is open along the entire length of the 2000km border. Trains between Amritsar in Indian Punjab and Lahore in Pakistan stopped running in January 2002, as the result of increased tensions between the two countries. The direct bus service between Delhi and Lahore was reinstated in July 2003. The road crossing at **Wagah** is open and accessible by bus, van, or auto-rickshaw. For more information, see **Wagah,** p. 485.

India-Sri Lanka: The boat service from Rameswaram in Tamil Nadu to Talaimannar in Sri Lanka has been indefinitely suspended because of the war in northern Sri Lanka. Travelers must fly to Colombo, Sri Lanka.

Nepal-China: The Arniko Rajmarg (Kathmandu-Kodari Highway) links Kathmandu with the Tibet Autonomous Region of China via the exit point of Kodari. The border is open only to travelers on organized tours. Before crossing into Tibet, check in with your

ESSENTIALS

embassy in Kathmandu to make sure that the border situation is stable, as there have occasionally been difficulties for tourists crossing overland into Tibet. For more information on requirements for travel to Tibet, see **Surrounding Countries**, p. 11.

GETTING AROUND

BY PLANE

India and Nepal both have relatively safe and extensive air networks. However, air travel is far more expensive than ground travel. Waiting in airport-office queues, traveling to and from airports (often far from town), and checking-in can all slow you down. Airports in South Asia sometimes subject passengers to purgatorial delays. Fly only to escape unbearable cross-country bus or train rides. In the mountains, where the roads are poor—and bus rides therefore dangerous and interminable—the balance may be shifted slightly in favor of air travel.

 AIRCRAFT SAFETY. The airlines of developing world nations do not always meet safety standards. The *Official Airline Guide* (www.oag.com) and many travel agencies can tell you the type and age of aircraft on a particular route. This can be especially useful in India and Nepal, where less reliable equipment is often used for internal flights. n India and Nepal, private carriers, especially Jet Airways (see below), use newer aircraft and better trained crew than state-run Indian Airlines and its affiliate, Alliance Air. The **International Airline Passengers Association** (US ☎ 800-821-4272, UK ☎ 020 8681 6555) provides region-specific safety information. The **Federal Aviation Administration** (www.faa.gov) reviews the airline authorities for countries whose airlines enter the US. **US State Department** travel advisories (☎ 202-647-5225; http:// travel.state.gov/travel_warnings.html) sometimes involve foreign carriers, especially when terrorist bombings or hijackings may be a threat.

IN INDIA

Though government-run **Indian Airlines** (http://indian-airlines.nic.in/) still maintains the largest flight network, private companies are challenging its former monopoly. **Jet Airways** (www.jetairways.com) is the second largest domestic airline and is far ahead of Indian Airlines in quality and service. **Sahara Airlines** (www.airsahara.net) is the third major domestic carrier. **Reservations** are essential on nearly all flights and must be made well in advance, especially during peak season (Nov.-Mar.), when flights are almost always full. Book through airline offices or travel agencies.

Indian Airlines and Jet Airways offer 25% discount off Economy Class fares for passengers aged 12 to 30. Children under 12 pay 50%, and infants under 2 pay 10%. Both airlines sell package deals for foreign tourists called **"Discover India"** (Indian Airlines) and **"India Pass"** (Jet Airways) that give 21 days of unlimited air travel for US$750, 15 days for US$500, or 7 days (Jet Airways only) for US$300. There is a nominal fee for booking each flight. No destination can be visited more than once, except the first and last points, and itineraries must be structured in one continuous direction. A limited number of seats is allotted to these programs.

IN NEPAL

Air travel is essential to Nepal's economy. It provides access to the mountainous regions of the north where there are no roads. Travelers should opt for air travel to avoid long, hellish bus rides. Government-operated **Royal Nepal Airlines Corporation**

(RNAC; www.royalnepal.com) operates flights to 35 airports and airstrips in Nepal, though it is suffering financially, and its planes are constantly filled to capacity. Privatization has recently given birth to several new airlines: **Everest Air, Gorkha Airlines** (www.gorkhaairlines.com.np), **Necon Air** (www.neconair.com), and Nepal Airways. All airlines' prices are the same, but the new private companies are generally thought to have better service. **Foreigners must pay for flights with foreign currency.** Domestic flight prices range from US$50-160. On the whole, air travel in Nepal is unpredictable. Bad weather prevents take-offs and landings; long delays are the norm. During the high trekking season it may be difficult to get tickets for popular destinations. Book through a travel agent.

BY TRAIN

The Indian rail network is extensive. For budget travelers, rail through **Indian Railways** (www.indianrailways.com) is *the* way to go in India. Because of its mountains (and freedom from colonization), Nepal has no trains, except for one that runs across the Indian border to Janakpur.

TYPES OF TRAINS. The two main kinds of trains are **express** (or mail) and **passenger.** The express trains are much faster and a bit more expensive than passenger trains. The extra-special **"super-fast"** trains—*Shatabdi Express, Rajdhani Express,* and *Taj Express*—cover routes between the major cities. These luxury trains come with full air-conditioning and meals, and cost at least four times as much as standard second class fares. A few scenic hill stations, such as Darjeeling, Ooty, and Shimla, are reached by **"toy trains,"** narrow-gauge machines that chug along at a snail's pace and gush billowing clouds of steam.

CLASSES OF COMFORT. Second class unreserved (previously known simply as Third class) is generally the cheapest fare available, but it is crowded, uncomfortable, and sometimes risky (pickpockets have easy access to your things). The 2nd class unreserved car is usually at the front or back of the train. You will probably have to stand for your entire trip. Ride in this class only if you want a goat in your lap and your face squashed against the window grille. Much better is the **second class sleeper** (requires a reservation; see "Buying a Ticket" below), featuring guaranteed seats and modest three-tiered berths for overnight trips. This is the most popular class among budget travelers. The lack of air conditioning is tempered by the cool breeze that streams through the open windows, though it would be a stretch to say that the air is always cool during the summer. **First class,** three to four times the price of 2nd class sleeper, is less crowded and offers a more "protected" experience, with views of the countryside through scratched, amber-tinted windows and private compartments made up of three to four berths. For air-conditioned travel, there are **chair cars** (with reclining seats) built into the "superfast" trains. **A/C 2nd class sleepers** and **A/C 1st class** round out the options at prices ranging from ½-2½ times 1st class. Women traveling on their own or with children should inquire about ladies' compartments, available on many overnight mail and express trains. Some locals advise women to opt for the open berths in 2nd class reserved (where there are always kind-but-tough older women) rather than the private compartment cars.

BUYING A TICKET. For overnight trips, any travel during the high season (Nov.-Mar.), and all reserved trains (all classes mentioned above, except 2nd class unreserved), make **reservations** and purchase your ticket at least a day or two before traveling (seats on popular trains can sell out a week ahead of time). At computerized stations, you can make a reservation up to 60 days before your date of travel. It is safest to do this at the station (look for the **reservation office**), though travel agents can also get you train tickets for a commission. Expect long delays and anarchic queues at big stations. At the biggest stations, you can pay in US dollars, pounds sterling, or in rupees (with an encashment certificate or ATM receipt). A **tourist quota** is often set aside for foreigners, and at stations in the major tourist cities there are even separate lines for tourists. Some stations have **ladies' queues** or allow women to jump to the front of the line to avoid the pushing and shoving.

When you arrive at the office, get a reservation slip from the window, and scribble down the train you want. Each route has a name and a number; for route information, arm yourself with a copy of the indispensable *Trains at a Glance* (Rs25), which contains **schedules** for all express and mail trains. The staff at most train station **enquiry counters** are well-informed. A 21st-century alternative to the trusty old *Trains at a Glance* has recently appeared, in the form of two excellent **Web sites** run by the major rail companies. The official websites of Indian Railways (www.indianrailways.com) and Southern Railway (www.srailway.com) tell you more than you will ever need to know—train names, numbers, and timetables. You can also make on-line reservations.

Foreign passport holders can buy **Indrail Passes,** available for half day, two-day, four-day, and longer periods up to 90 days in a variety of classes (paid for in US Dollars, British Pounds, and other currencies). They include all fares, reservation charges, and supplementary charges, but prices are high, and it's hard to get your money's worth. Indrail Passes can save you some hassle—on super-fast trains, pass holders are exempt from reservation fees and extra charges and don't need tickets on shorter journeys. Reservations are still necessary for longer trips.

If you have a reservation, you'll be fine getting to the station just a few minutes before the train arrives. If you're leaving from a major station, check the computer-printed list (usually on the platform or the side of each train car) for your last name and seat number, and listen for announcements. Don't be surprised if your train is delayed—find a waiting room and ask a coolie (porter)—preferably more than one—when he thinks your train will arrive. Railway **retiring rooms,** cheaper than most budget hotels, are available to anyone with a valid ticket or Indrail pass. They operate on a 24hr. basis, and most also rent for 12 hours at a time.

If you fail to get a reservation, you can still get on the waiting list (ask about the tourist quota) and hope. If you cancel your reservation more than 24hr. before your trip, you can still get a refund, but you'll be charged Rs10-50 depending on the class; up to four hours before, you'll get 75% back, and after that (sometimes even 12hr. after the train has left), you can still get a refund of up to 50%.

BY BUS

In trainless Nepal, buses are *the* mode of long-distance transportation. In India, they come a close second. Buses are often almost as fast as trains, or even faster. They can climb the hilly areas of India, where trains cannot go, and generally involve far less pre-departure hassle. Seats are narrow, with very little cushioning and no leg room. There are (more often than not) more passengers than seats, and many pass the trip standing up. You will often lose your seat if you get up. But then, you might find yourself unable to stand up at all if you go a whole journey without at least one stroll. At scheduled stops, women have a hard time finding a toilet and should ask the conductor to wait longer for them as they search.

Road conditions are bad—expect to hear gears grinding and horns blaring, and to feel sudden lurches as the bus bumps its way along potholed roads. The bigger and newer the bus, the more likely you'll arrive alive. No one ever sur-

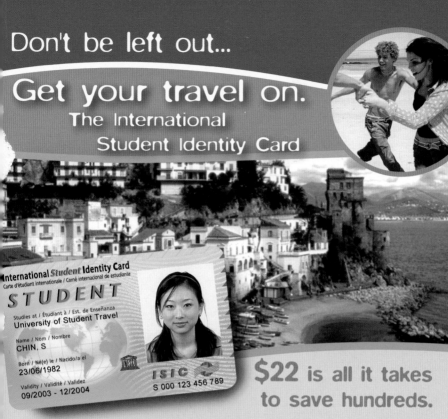

Don't be left out...

Get your travel on.
The International
Student Identity Card

$22 is all it takes to save hundreds.

Accepted worldwide for awesome discounts!

The International Student Identity Card (ISIC) is a great way to take advantage of discounts and benefits such as airfare, accommodations, transportation, attractions, theme parks, hotels, theaters, car rentals and more!

visit **www.ISICus.com** to find out about discounts and the benefits of carrying your ISIC.

Call or visit STA Travel online to find the nearest issuing office and purchase your card today:

www.ISICus.com   **(800) 474.8214**

enough already...
Get a room.

Book your next hotel with the people who know what you want.

» hostels
» budget hotels
» hip hotels
» airport transfers
» city tours
» adventure packages
» and more!

(800) 777.0112
www.statravel.com/hotels

STA TRAVEL

WE'VE BEEN THERE.

Exciting things are happening at www.statravel.com.

vives **minibus** crashes, so avoid minibuses whenever possible. Riding in the mountains at night is suicidal. **Never ride on the roof of a bus.** It is illegal and very, very dangerous.

INTERCITY BUSES. Express buses are the norm. They have thinly padded seats, are jam-packed, and stop for anyone and everyone at any point along the route. **Tourist buses** or **"superdeluxe" buses,** usually available only on popular tourist routes on the west coast, have cushioned seats and more space; although they are certainly not luxurious by Greyhound standards, they seat four passengers to an aisle rather than five (or six or seven). They often have fans and sometimes even air-conditioning. In Nepal, and some places in India, there are special **night buses,** which have reclining seats and a bit more leg room, though you shouldn't count on getting any sleep. They stop for *chai* endlessly (just be glad the driver is getting his caffeine). Avoid **video coaches** unless you enjoy being subjected to black-and-white Hindi films for five hours (or more) at ear-splitting levels. **Luggage** on the roof rack of a bus is usually safe, but bags have been known to disappear at intermediate stops in a flurry of untraceable movement. Make sure your pack is tied down, or ask if you can put it somewhere else—in a compartment at the back, or at the front where you can keep an eye on it. If your luggage goes on the roof, give some *baksheesh* to the person who put it up there.

IN INDIA

In this guide, **bus stands** and **bus stations** are where state (and sometimes private) buses roll in and out; private buses often leave from the particular company's office. **Government buses** are often crowded, so get to the bus stand at least 30min. before departure. For longer trips (over 8hr.) it may be necessary to book a day ahead; do this at the bus stand rather than through an agent. Some **private bus companies** offer excellent service; others don't deserve to be licensed at all. There are so many private bus companies that it is difficult to know the quality of an operation until you're already screaming down the highway. As with train tickets, it is unwise to buy bus tickets from random travel agencies.

 WARNING. Both Indian and Nepalese buses have extremely high rates of accident. When there is a train, take it.

IN NEPAL

Bus travel is widely used in Nepal, although road conditions are poor and the hilly terrain increases travel time. Almost all buses are private, but look out for the **government Sajha buses,** which are generally safer and much more comfortable. For these, you'll probably have to book tickets a day in advance from the bus stand. Booking bus tickets from Kathmandu or Pokhara can be a hassle since the bus stands are so far from the tourist centers; it may be easier to book through a travel agent. Avoid package deals for bus journeys with connections; these are often scams. It's best to buy your second ticket once you arrive.

BY CAR

Driving a car (better yet, a VW Microbus) across Asia was a classic 1960s hippie expedition. Today, it's a nightmare. Besides swerving to avoid cars, motorcycles, rickshaws, people, and cows, there is also a general disregard for traffic regulations. Drivers are reckless and aggressive, constrained only by potholes and the vehicles they drive. Many pedestrians who have just arrived from villages lack basic traffic sense. Not surprisingly, India and Nepal have high rates of road accidents. If you get into a traffic accident in India or Nepal, **leave the scene of the accident immediately and go to the nearest police station.** A quarter of the world's cows reside in India, where they are considered sacred, so if you plan to drive be extremely careful to avoid them on the road: killing a cow in India and Nepal, even by accident, is often punishable by law.

RENTING

A car is utterly unnecessary in a large city, where buses, rickshaws, and taxis can get you anywhere cheaply. The cost of renting a four-door sedan is many times the cost of a night's stay at a guest house. Also, some rental companies do not offer insurance; a serious accident can mean spending time in jail or the hospital and shelling out a large sum of money to cover damages. If you absolutely must have a car, keep your **international driving permit** (see below) handy, as well as a lot of money. A safer alternative is to hire a car with a **driver.**

DRIVING PRECAUTIONS. When traveling in the summer or in the desert, bring substantial amounts of **water** (a suggested 5 liters of water per person per day) for drinking and for the radiator. For long drives to unpopulated areas, register with police before leaving, and again upon arrival at the destination. Check with the local automobile club for details. When traveling long distances, make sure tires are in good repair and have enough air, and get good maps. A **compass** and a **car manual** can also be very useful. You should always carry a **spare tire** and **jack, jumper cables, extra oil, flares, a torch (flashlight)**, and **blankets**. If you don't know how to **change a tire,** learn before heading out, especially if you are planning on traveling in deserted areas. Blowouts on dirt roads are exceedingly common. If you do have a breakdown, **stay with your car;** if you wander off, there's less of a chance you'll be found.

DRIVING PERMITS & CAR INSURANCE

INTERNATIONAL DRIVING PERMIT (IDP). Renting a **car, motor-scooter,** or **motorcycle** usually requires an International Driving Permit (IDP). You must be over 18 and have a driver's license from your own country. Your IDP, valid for one year, must be issued in your own country before you depart. An application usually requires one or two photos, a current local license, an additional form of identification, and a fee. Contact your local automobile association for more information.

CAR INSURANCE. Most credit cards cover standard insurance. If you rent, lease, or borrow a car, you will need a **green card,** or **International Insurance Certificate,** to certify that you have liability insurance and that it applies abroad. Green cards can be obtained at car rental agencies, car dealers (for those leasing cars), some travel agents, and some border crossings. Rental agencies may require you to purchase theft insurance. Ask at your rental agency.

BY LOCAL TRANSPORTATION

BUSES. Getting around by **local buses** can be chaotic and confusing. Bus schedules are difficult to decipher, and figuring out which bus goes where takes years of patient trial and error. Smile at locals waiting at bus stops and hope they know what they're talking about. In a hurry to wedge themselves into city traffic, bus drivers roll-start, so you might want to learn the skill of leaping on and off the back stairs. Once safely inside, sit or stand until the bus-*wallah*, with his little satchel, comes by and clicks a small metal contraption in your face. That means pay up—ask how much it is to your destination, since prices vary by distance. Women get preferential seating; men are expected to give up their seats. Women (and men) should watch out for groping hands in crowded buses.

AUTO-RICKSHAWS AND TEMPOS. To some, these podlike three-wheelers are a powerful symbol of the South Asian experience; to others, they are just dirty diesel fume-belching beasts. Auto-rickshaws seat one to three adults. Drivers will often say that it's "broken," but insist that they use the **meter** if you're unsure of the regular cost of going to your destination. Avoid pushy drivers. If you can't find one who will go by the meter, aim to bargain at least 30-40% off his original price. **In many cities, it is illegal for rickshaw-wallahs to overcharge for local, daytime service.** Asking a local shop-keeper or consulting Let's Go about the normal price of a given trip will give you greater confidence in your bargaining. A threat to report them to the police can sometimes help to squeeze out a more reasonable fare. And never be afraid to walk away if a driver refuses to be reasonable. Depending on the town, drivers may add a surcharge to the meter or display a government-issued "fare adjustment card" to compensate for outdated meters. **Nighttime fares** can be up to double the standard rate. Also, **make sure your rickshaw-wallah is not drunk or stoned**—odd behavior may be a sign that he is under the influence. Also, see **Touts, Middlemen, and Scams,** (p. 15) for more information on shady rickshaw-*wallahs.*

Tempos seat about six people, follow fixed routes, and have low fares; they are of limited use to foreigners, however, because their destinations are never marked, and they are usually over-packed anyway.

CYCLE-RICKSHAWS. Ubiquitous in most medium-sized-and-smaller cities, cycle-rickshaws are the environmentally-friendly but human labor-intensive alternative to auto-rickshaws. The driver pedals in front and his trusting passengers sit on a cushioned box above the rear axle. If your rickshaw-*wallah* jumps out to push up a hill that's too steep to pedal, get out and lend a hand. The **price,** as always, is highly negotiable. Foreigners often pay around Rs10 per km—more in touristy places, less in villages—but will pay much more unless you haggle energetically.

TAXIS. You will find taxis in the larger cities of India and Nepal. India's international airports offer reliable **pre-paid taxi services**—you pay at an official counter and give your receipt to a driver in the waiting queue, who takes you where you need to go. Taxis are supposed to have meters, but since these are sometimes out of date, the driver will sometimes add a percentage or wave about an official-looking "fare adjustment card" with up-to-date prices. All this varies from city to city; there are no hard-and-fast rules, but in general you should use the meter rather than negotiate a price. Private companies rent out taxis and **drivers** for longer hours, short trips, or even days; inquire at train stations, airports, tourist offices, or travel agents. In mountainous regions, **jeeps** (sometimes called Gypsies or Mahindras) and **Sumos** function as taxis or mini-buses.

SPECIFIC CONCERNS

WOMEN TRAVELERS

In Bihar and eastern Uttar Pradesh, where the maintenance of law and order is a constant problem, foreign women have been raped. The Himalayan regions, however, from Himachal Pradesh to Nepal to Sikkim, are among the safest areas; attitudes toward women are much more liberal among many mountain ethnic groups. In the cosmopolitan circles in major cities (especially in Mumbai), women can usually feel as comfortable as they would in any big city anywhere in the world.

Incidents of **sexual harassment** are not uncommon, especially in northern India, but seldom more serious than verbal advances or groping. Many Indians and Nepalis believe that foreign women are indiscriminately promiscuous. This belief is due partly to stereotypes picked up from American television and movies and partly to the fact that many foreign women do things that Indians and Nepalis do not.

Look as if you know where you're going (even when you don't) and approach other women (or couples) if you need help or directions. **Dress conservatively, covering legs and shoulders, and always wear a bra.** Don't jump to the conclusion that since Indian women wearing saris reveal their lower backs and stomachs, it's OK to wear shorts—it's definitely not. And don't automatically assume that a T-shirt, which appears to cover the same vital areas as a sari, if not more, is appropriate. The shape of the breast should be left a mystery—most women's chests are covered by more than one layer of clothing. Consider wearing a *salwar kameez*, baggy pants with a loose long-sleeved shirt. Wearing a conspicuous **wedding band** can also help prevent unwanted overtures. Some women find that carrying pictures of a "husband" or "children" can be useful in helping to back up marital status. Even a brief mention of a husband waiting back at the hotel is enough in some places to counteract your potentially vulnerable, unattached appearance. Remember that **non-verbal communication** is different from what you're used to back home—making eye contact, responding when asked a question, even smiling can be perceived as a come-on by South Asian men. Invest in secure accommodation, particularly family-run guest houses with doors that lock from the inside. Stay in central locations and avoid late-night walks. **Hitchhiking** is never safe for women. Trains often have separate **ladies' compartments** and stations may have **ladies' waiting rooms.** On buses, you should be allowed to sit near the front.

The slightest bit of resistance usually stops most harassers, who have generally encountered few foreign women before. Your best answer to harassment is no answer at all; feigned deafness, sitting motionless and staring straight ahead at nothing in particular can do a world of good. The extremely persistent can sometimes be dissuaded by exactly one firm, loud, and very public *"Mujhe chod dho!"* ("Leave me alone!" in Hindi). If need be, turn to an older woman for help in an uncomfortable situation; her stern rebukes will usually embarrass even the most persistent jerk. Don't hesitate to get the attention of passersby and point at your harasser, as there is a strong sense of public morality. Seek out a policeman if you need one, but don't place all your trust in them, particularly in untouristed areas. Emergency numbers (uniform across India and Nepal) are listed on the inside back cover of this book, as well as in the Practical Information listings of cities. A **self-defense course** (see p. 17) will not only prepare you for a potential attack, but will also raise your confidence and your awareness of your surroundings. Also be aware of the health concerns that women face when traveling (see p. 26).

TRAVELING ALONE

There are many benefits to traveling alone, including independence and greater interaction with locals. On the other hand, any solo traveler is a more vulnerable target of harassment and street theft. Lone travelers need to be well-organized. Spread good will and smile; locals will help you and watch out for you. Maintain regular contact with someone at home who knows your itinerary.

Alternatively, several services link solo travelers with companions who have similar travel habits and interests; for a bi-monthly newsletter for single travelers seeking a travel partner (subscription US$48), contact the **Travel Companion Exchange**, P.O. Box 833, Amityville, NY 11701, USA (☎ 631-454-0880 or 800-392-1256 in the US; www.whytravelalone.com; US$48).

BGLT TRAVELERS

ESSENTIALS

Homosexuality is taboo in India and Nepal, and most people choose to keep their sexual orientation private. In India homosexual intercourse is illegal, and harassment by police of gay and lesbians still occurs. Male friends may hold hands or hug in public, but these gestures are not considered sexual. Most gay and lesbian organizations in India and Nepal remain underground, but in the past decade, some groups have gained recognition for their work on sex and gender issues. In 1990, three gay men in Mumbai started **Bombay Dost** (www.bombay-dost.com), a quarterly magazine that addresses issues such as sexual health and hygiene, attitudes toward sexuality, and gay activism. *Bombay Dost* can be purchased from select newsstands and can be ordered directly from Pride Publications Pvt. Ltd., 105 Veena Beena Shopping Centre, Bandra Station Road, Bandra (West), Mumbai 400 050. The success of Bombay Dost inspired the founding of **The Humsafar Trust** (www.humsafar.org), an organization dedicated to activism, outreach, research, and advocacy for gay men in India. The Internet is a good place to find up-to-date city-specific information on gay happenings and events. **http://members.tripod.com/gaydelhi** and **www.gaybombay.com** have links to a number of sites.

Trikone, P.O. Box 21354, San Jose, CA 95151, USA (☎415-789-7322; www.trikone.org), is a US-based organization for gay and lesbian South Asians.

Footprints Travel, 506 Church St., Ste. 200, Toronto, ON Canada M4Y 2C8 (☎888-962-6211 or 416-962-8111; www.footprintstravel.com) offers gay and lesbian travel packages to India and Nepal.

Out and About (www.planetout.com) offers a bi-weekly newsletter and a comprehensive site addressing gay travel concerns.

Gay's the Word, 66 Marchmont St., London WC1N 1AB, UK (☎20 7278 7654; www.gaystheword.co.uk). The largest gay and lesbian bookshop in the UK, with both fiction and non-fiction titles. Mail-order service available.

Giovanni's Room, 1145 Pine St., Philadelphia, PA 19107, USA (☎215-923-2960; www.queerbooks.com). An international lesbian/feminist and gay bookstore with mail-order service (carries many of the publications listed below).

International Lesbian and Gay Association (ILGA), 81 rue Marché-au-Charbon, B-1000 Brussels, Belgium (☎2 502 2471; www.ilga.org). Provides political information, such as homosexuality laws of individual countries.

OTHER RESOURCES

Let's Go tries to cover all aspects of budget travel, but we can't put *everything* in our guides. Listed below are books and websites that can serve as starting points for your own research.

TRAVEL PUBLISHERS & BOOKSTORES

Hippocrene Books, Inc., 171 Madison Ave., New York, NY 10016, USA (☎718-454-2366; www.hippocrenebooks.com). Publishes foreign language dictionaries and language learning guides.

Hunter Publishing, 470 W. Broadway, Fl. 2, South Boston, MA 02127, USA (☎617-269-0700; www.hunterpublishing.com). Has an extensive catalog of travel guides and diving and adventure travel books.

Rand McNally, P.O. Box 7600, Chicago, IL 60680, USA (☎847-329-8100; www.randmcnally.com), publishes road atlases.

Adventurous Traveler Bookstore, P.O. Box 2221, Williston, VT 05495, USA (www.adventuroustraveler.com).

Travel Books & Language Center, Inc., 4437 Wisconsin Ave. NW, Washington, D.C. 20016, USA (☎800-220-2665; www.bookweb.org/bookstore/travelbks/). Over 60,000 titles from around the world.

WORLD WIDE WEB

Listed here are some budget travel sites to start off your surfing; other relevant web sites are listed throughout the book. Because website turnover is high, use search engines (such as www.google.com) to strike out on your own.

WWW.LETSGO.COM We are proud to announce that our brand-new website now features sample content from our guides, additional articles, and trial versions of Let's Go City Guides for download on Palm OS™ PDAs. As always, our website also has photos and streaming video, online ordering of all our titles, info about our books, a travel forum buzzing with stories and tips, a newsletter, and links that will help you find everything you ever wanted to know about India and Nepal.

BUDGET TRAVEL

How to See the World: www.artoftravel.com. A compendium of great travel tips, from cheap flights to self defense to interacting with local culture.

Rec. Travel Library: www.travel-library.com. A fantastic set of links for general information and personal travelogues.

Lycos: http://cityguide.lycos.com. General city and region introductions throughout India and Nepal, accompanied by links to history, news, and local tourism sites.

INFORMATION ON INDIA AND NEPAL

Bollywood World: www.bollywoodworld.com. News and gossip from the world of Indian cinema.

Cricket Info: www-ind.cricket.org. Comprehensive cricket news site, with daily updates on all the games and players. Essential reading for bluffers and old-hands alike.

Indian Railways: www.indianrail.gov.in. Online timetables and ticket reservation service.

Music India: www.musicindiaonline.com. A first-class resource, featuring hundreds of articles, reviews, and recordings covering all genres of Indian music.

My Travel Guide: www.mytravelguide.com. Country overviews, with everything from history to transportation to live Web cam coverage.

Nepal Homepage: www.info-nepal.com. Cultural, business, and tourism resources.

Nepal News: www.nepalnews.com. An online English newspaper detailing current events in Nepal.

Samachar: www.samachar.com provides a digest of articles, updated daily, culled from all the major English-language papers in India.

Times of India: www.timesofindia.com. India's premier English-language newspaper.

Tour India: www.tourindia.com. A useful site on Indian tourism, providing links to the Indian airlines and tourist offices throughout the Subcontinent.

Webguide India: www.webguideindia.com. Provides city directories as well as lists of everything from freebies and shopping to schools and cricket in India.

ALTERNATIVES TO TOURISM IN INDIA & NEPAL

Going abroad presents an enticing personal challenge that can be among life's most rewarding experiences. Unfortunately, even as most travelers enjoy exploring new places, commercial travel has the capacity to inhibit local economies and damage the environment. In India, the tourism industry has led, in some places, to increased air and water pollution, as well as the accelerated decay of ancient and sacred religious sites. In Nepal, the yearly income generated by rafting expeditions has deterred efforts to dam the country's many raging rivers for energy-efficient hydroelectric power. But travelers are not limited to simply perpetuating these problems. Numerous opportunities exist for you to learn more about these issues and to work toward alleviating them in ways that are both exciting and enriching.

There is a great need for enthusiastic and able-bodied volunteers of all ages to aid organizations specializing in everything from protecting the environment to fighting for human rights. India and Nepal face a number of difficulties characteristic of developing nations, including extreme poverty, disease, social conflict, inequality, hunger, political instability and lack of sufficient educational opportunities. There are opportunities to suit every level of ability and every kind of educational or professional background. If your passion is medicine, you can help to provide healthcare to rural populations or underprivileged children. If you are interested in expanding your own understanding of Indian or Nepalese culture, you may choose to explore the Subcontinent's spiritual traditions by living on a commune or studying in a monastery.

Alternatives to tourism can translate into a longer, more meaningful experience than that of the average budget traveler's. Some programs enable foreigners to live, study, and volunteer abroad for periods of up to two years. There are many resources and programs available for those seeking non-tourist experiences in India and Nepal, and this chapter outlines some ways to plan such experiences. The listings on the following pages can serve as a starting point for your search. A surprising number of alternatives can be arranged informally, especially if you're willing to work for room and board. If you choose this option, make sure you have the correct documentation, valid visas, etc. We list out-of-the-way opportunities in the specific city sections when we can, but the best advice we can give you is to keep your eyes open and ask around

A PHILOSOPHY FOR TRAVELERS

When we started out in 1961, about 1.7 million people in the world were traveling internationally each year; in 2002, nearly 700 million trips were made, projected to be up to a billion by 2010. The dramatic rise in tourism has created an interdependence between the economy, environment, and culture of many destinations and the tourists they host. With approximately 2 million foreign visitors each year, India is no exception to this rule. The tourism industry provides powerful stimulation for India's growing economy, but this is often to the detriment of the country's cultural and physical environments.

We at *Let's Go* look to improve the traveler-destination interchange. We've watched the growth of the 'ignorant tourist' stereotype with dismay, knowing that the majority of travelers care passionately about the communities and environments they explore—but also knowing that even conscientious tourists can inadvertently damage natural wonders and cultural enclaves. We believe the philosophy of **sustainable travel** is among the most important travel tips we could pass on to our readers, to help guide fellow backpackers and on-the-road philanthropists. Through sensitivity to the local community, today's travelers can be a powerful force in preserving and restoring this fragile world.

Two rising trends in sustainable travel are ecotourism and community-based tourism. **Ecotourism** focuses on the conservation of natural habitats and using them to build up the economy without exploitation or overdevelopment. **Community-based tourism** aims to channel tourist revenue into the local economy by emphasizing tours and cultural programs that are run by members of the host community and that often benefit disadvantaged groups.

VOLUNTEERING

Volunteering can be one of life's most fulfilling experiences, especially if it is combined with the thrill of traveling in a new place. India and Nepal, while rich in culture and history, currently have many significant concerns that demand attention. As a result, there are numerous opportunities for travelers to make a contribution as they explore. Many volunteer services charge participation fees. These costs can be surprisingly hefty, and although they frequently cover living expenses, they rarely cover airfare. Most people choose to go through a parent organization that takes care of logistical details and frequently provides a group environment and support system. Many programs also offer insurance through this option. If you choose to design your own program through an organization in India or Nepal, ask for help in planning your accommodations before arriving, as you will have to research many logistical details (such as insurance) on your own. There are two main types of organizations, religious and non-sectarian, although there are rarely restrictions on participation for either.

The experience of volunteering in India or Nepal can sometimes be dangerous rather than rewarding. Don't be afraid to ask for testimonials from past volunteers, as some programs may be more structured than others. Different programs are geared toward people of different ages and levels of experience, so make sure that you are not taking on too much.

VOLUNTEERING DATABASES

Idealist (www.idealist.org), has a database with many excellent service opportunities.

ServeNet (www.servenet.org), is a database of service opportunities. You can search within 10 miles of the place you'd like to volunteer with added stipulations of dates, duration, community, and activity preferences.

VOLUNTEER OPPORTUNITIES

Action Aid (www.actionaid.org) offers an entirely new way to travel through a region. They provide adventure tours, for which volunteers pay and raise money. Their cause is worldwide poverty. Check the website for specific listings.

Action Zone (www.actionzone.cc) is an ideal resource for backpackers who want to make a difference. In addition to providing a wealth of information about local issues, it also provides listings of shelters, community centers and organizations which fight against HIV/AIDS and poverty and hunger.

A NEW PHILOSOPHY OF TRAVEL

We at *Let's Go* have watched the growth of the 'ignorant tourist' stereotype with dismay, knowing that the majority of travelers care passionately about the state of the communities and environments they explore—but also knowing that even conscientious tourists can inadvertently damage natural wonders, rich cultures, and impoverished communities. We believe the philosophy of **sustainable travel** is among the most important travel tips we can impart to our readers, to help guide fellow backpackers and on-the-road philanthropists. By staying aware of the needs and troubles of local communities, today's travelers can be a powerful force in preserving and restoring this fragile world.

Working against the negative consequences of irresponsible tourism is much simpler than it might seem; it is often self-awareness, rather than self-sacrifice, that makes the biggest difference. Simply by trying to spend responsibly and conserve local resources, all travelers can positively impact the places they visit. Let's Go has partnered with **BEST (Business Enterprises for Sustainable Travel,** an affiliate of the Conference Board; see www.sustainabletravel.org), which recognizes businesses that operate based on the principles of sustainable travel. Below, they provide advice on how ordinary visitors can practice this philosophy in their daily travels, no matter where they are.

TIPS FOR CIVIC TRAVEL: HOW TO MAKE A DIFFERENCE

Travel by train when feasible. Rail travel requires only half the energy per passenger mile that planes do. On average, each of the 40,000 daily domestic air flights releases more than 1700 pounds of greenhouse gas emissions.

Use public mass transportation whenever possible; outside of cities, take advantage of group taxis or vans. Bicycles are an attractive way of seeing a community firsthand. And enjoy walking—purchase good maps of your destination and ask about on-foot touring opportunities.

When renting a car, ask whether fuel-efficient vehicles are available. Honda and Toyota produce cars that use hybrid engines powered by electricity and gasoline, thus reducing emissions of carbon dioxide. Ford Motor Company plans to introduce a hybrid fuel model by the end of 2004.

Reduce, reuse, recycle—use electronic tickets, recycle papers and bottles wherever possible, and avoid using containers made of styrofoam. Refillable water bottles and rechargable batteries both efficiently conserve expendable resources.

Be thoughtful in your purchases. Take care not to buy souvenir objects made from trees in old-growth or endangered forests, such as teak, or items made from endangered species, like ivory or tortoise jewelry. Ask whether products are made from renewable resources.

Buy from local enterprises, such as casual street vendors. In developing countries and low-income neighborhoods, many people depend on the "informal economy" to make a living.

Be on-the-road-philanthropists. If you are inspired by the natural environment of a destination or enriched by its culture, join in preserving their integrity by making a charitable contribution to a local organization.

Spread the word. Upon your return home, tell friends and colleagues about places to visit that will benefit greatly from their tourist dollars, and reward sustainable enterprises by recommending their services. Travelers can not only introduce friends to particular vendors but also to local causes and charities that they might choose to support when they travel.

GIVING BACK

TOUR NO MORE

India's influence on American pop culture in the form of yoga, *bindis*, and *samosas*, sparked a generation of visitors eager for an "alternative" vacation on the Subcontinent. I was among the many caught up in this frenzy and made the journey to India after my freshman year at college. I toured Andhra Pradesh and Maharashtra for two weeks, shopping for fabric, photographing temples, and adjusting to what seemed like life as the only white person around. And although my travels were incredible, I longed to do something more meaningful in India. I returned the next year as a volunteer in a rural Himalayan village on a mission to make a difference, change lives, and satisfy the other naïve clichés of most first-time volunteers. I expected some fulfilling experiences but no major surprises, since I was confident that my knowledge of India from my previous travels was complete.

I was still shocked the first day when I entered the village daycare. The tiny shack, with its crumbling concrete floor and two drab posters, was definitely not child-friendly. My six charges filed in and sat on the floor, peering at me expectantly; I was to teach the alphabet and animal names in English and Hindi. Soon after starting, I saw that my lessons were not challenging enough. Although the kids were very young, the alacrity and accuracy with which they learned was amazing. These were not the intellectually deprived children I thought I would encounter, but rather quite precocious young-

Amizade, 920 William Pitt Union, University of Pittsburgh, Pittsburgh, PA 15260, USA (☎888-973-4443; www.amizade.org). Sends individuals (over age 18) or groups to work on either short-term or long-term community-oriented projects in Nepal, such as building schools and health centers, giving vocational training to children, etc. Cost of participation US$500-2500.

Asha (www.ashanet.org), undertakes projects to improve and provide education to children. Their projects are located all over India, and they seek volunteers for various locations and projects.

Center for Science and Environment, 41, Tughlakabad Institutional Area, New Delhi, 110062; (☎299 55124; www.cseindia.org). This research institution analyzes environmental impact and pollution problems. It takes volunteers at its Delhi office. Volunteers are given a Rs100 daily stipend.

Child Family Health International, 953 Mission St., Ste. 220, San Francisco, CA 94103, USA (☎415-957-9000; www.cfhi.org). Sends pre-med undergraduate and medical students to work with physicians in India, although the focus is more on working with the community and learning about healthcare rather than actually providing medical assistance. Program fees are around US$1500, airfare not included.

Children and Women's Promotion Center, Royal Chitwan National Park, Nepal (☎580158; cwpcenter@hotmail.com or childrenwpc@wlink.com.np), a 10 minute walk north of Sauraha, on the road to Chitrasari. This center provides education for underprivileged children and vocational training for women. They seek volunteers and English language instructors.

Child Workers in Nepal (CWIN), P.O. Box 24073, Rabi Bhawan, Kathmandu, Nepal (☎977 1 278064; www.cwin-nepal.org). A non-governmental organization of activists seeking to improve and protect children's rights. CWIN works to eliminate the use of child labor and human rights violations against children. They accept volunteers through the CWIN Voluntary Service program.

Cross-Cultural Solutions, 47 Potter Ave., New Rochelle, NY 10801, USA (☎800-380-4777 or 914-632-0022; www.crossculturalsolutions.org). Operates short- and long-term humanitarian work in health care, education, and social development. Fees are US$2300-4300.

Dakshinayan, c/o Siddarth Sanyal, F-1169, Ground Floor, Chittaranjan Park, New Delhi 110019, India (☎2627 6645; www.linkindia.com/dax). Places volunteers in short or long-term work projects in India

Earthwatch, 3 Clocktower Pl. Ste. 100, Box 75, Maynard, MA 01754, USA (☎800-776-0188 or 978-461-0081; www.earthwatch.org). Arranges 1- to 3-week programs in India and Nepal designed to promote conservation of natural resources. Fees vary based on program location and duration; costs average US$1800 plus airfare.

Global Vision International (www.gvi.co.uk), offers opportunities in conservation, wildlife expeditions, and teaching.

Global Volunteers (www.globalvolunteers.org), sponsors "volunteer vacations," which are short-term service programs, usually lasting 2-3 weeks. Programs run US$1000-3000.

Habitat for Humanity International, 121 Habitat St., Americus, GA 31709, USA (☎229-924-6935 ext. 2551; www.habitat.org). Volunteers build houses in over 83 countries for anywhere from 2 weeks to 3 years. Short-term program costs are US$1200-4000.

Hands for Help, P.O. Box 9012, Samakhusi, Kathmandu, Nepal (☎981050178; www.handsforhelp.org.np). Provides volunteer placements in Nepal teaching English and environmental awareness. Assists with training volunteers upon arrival and with arranging accommodations. Program costs US$150-$900 for 1 week to 5 months.

Hanuman-dhoka Durbar Square Conservation Program (☎1268969), offers volunteer opportunities in conserving the Hanuman-dhoka Durbar Square UNESCO World Heritage Site in Nepal (see p. 818).

International Cultural Youth Exchange (ICYE) (www.icye.org), offers voluntary work placements throughout India and Nepal.

International Volunteer Welfare Project of Nepal, P.O. Box 4832, Kathmandu, Nepal (☎1 528413; www.ivwpnepal.org/ivwpn.htm). A Nepali organization that places volunteers into positions in the fields of education, medicine, environmental protection and social work with orphanages. Volunteers stay with a Nepali host family. Application online.

The Joint Assistance Center, Attn: Prof. P.L. Govil, G17/3 DLF Qutab Enclave Phase I, Gurgaon 122022, Haryana, India (☎0124 352141), places volunteers directly in India or Nepal. **Friends of JAC in the Americas,** P.O. Box 6082, San Pablo, CA 94806, USA (☎510-464-1100; jacusa@juno.com), assists with placement.

Peace Corps, Paul D. Coverdell Peace Corps Headquarters, 1111 20th St., NW, Washington, D.C., 20526, USA (☎800-424-8580; www.peacecorps.gov). Opportunities in 70 developing nations, including Nepal.

SCI International Voluntary Service, (www.sci-ivs.org) Similar to work camps, these programs are for two weeks or more, with long-term positions available. Room and board is often provided, but there is a fee, which varies according to age and location.

sters. I left feeling silly for presuming that impoverished conditions would somehow affect their cognitive capacity.

Working at the village hospital was equally eye opening. After touring the facility and talking with physicians, I realized that I was not there to inform them about how American doctors worked but instead learn about Indian medicine, an institution free from the trials of insurance companies and malpractice lawsuits. Though Indian technology was limited (X-rays were dried on the hospital's front lawn), the practitioners' knowledge was not. In fact, their raw diagnostic skills were arguably better than those of American doctors. Their medical prowess earned them prestige bordering on divinity, because their healing powers made them godly for some patients.

And I was never without reminder that I was in a culture far different from my own. The patient forms that I helped the nurses file still had space for caste information, and female doctors wore traditional saris under their white coats. The occasional case of tuberculosis or goiter reminded me that I was in a place where malnutrition and lack of vaccinations were an everyday reality.

I often think about all the activities that India made so thrilling, exasperating, and wonderful: stumbling down a mountain to brush my teeth, listening to a child switch from English to Hindi to Nepali without blinking, and fighting off aggressive monkeys. When I accepted such mundane activities as routine, I was no longer a tourist, rather someone privileged to better a country she was, albeit briefly, calling home.

-Joanna O'Leary, 2003

Service Civil International Voluntary Service (SCI-IVS), US Applicants: SCI USA, 5474 Walnut Level Road, Crozet, VA 22932, USA (☎/fax 206-350-6585; www.sci-ivs.org). Canadian applicants: International Volunteer Service Canada, 110 George Street South, Unit 909, Toronto, Ontario M514P9, Canada (☎416-216-0914; fax 209-391-2257). Arranges placement in work camps in India and Nepal for those 21 and over. Registration fee US$65-175.

United Nations Volunteers (www.unv.org), has opportunities to work in nearly every facet of humanitarianism, from direct service to administration. Direct service opportunities usually require a 12 month commitment.

Voluntary Service Overseas (www.vsocanada.org) is a placement program that is Canada's answer to the American Peace Corps. Most programs are 2 years, though there are some for 6 months.

Volunteers for Peace, 1034 Tiffany Rd., Belmont., VT 05730, USA (☎802-259-2759; www.vfp.org). Arranges placement in work camps in India and Nepal. Membership required for registration. Annual *International Workcamp Directory* US$20. Programs average US$200-500 for 2-3 weeks.

Volunteer International (www.volunteerinternational.org). A search engine for volunteer opportunities in every country in every field.

Voluntourist (www.voluntourist.com), has a limited, though decent, listing of volunteer opportunities around the world.

TEACHING ENGLISH

Teaching jobs abroad are rarely well-paid. Volunteering as a teacher in lieu of getting paid is a popular option; in those cases, teachers often get some sort of a daily stipend to help with living expenses. In most developing countries, teacher's stipends may seem meager, though they are most likely fairly generous compared to the salary of a native. In addition, the low cost of living in a country such as India or Nepal means that teachers do not need much money to get by. In almost all cases, you must have at least a bachelor's degree to be a full-fledged teacher, although college undergraduates can often get summer positions teaching or tutoring. In both India and Nepal, opportunities abound for native English speakers to teach not only students, but workers and professionals as well. Oftentimes these positions are found through Non-Governmental Organizations (NGOs) and other groups who place teachers where there is need. Teaching positions also frequently come with assistance in locating accommodations.

Many schools require teachers to have a **Teaching English as a Foreign Language (TEFL)** certificate. This does not necessarily exclude you from finding a teaching job, but certified teachers often find higher paying jobs. Native English speakers working in private schools are most often hired for English-immersion classrooms where no native languages are spoken. Those volunteering or teaching in poorer public schools are more likely to be working in both English and Nepali, Hindi, or another local dialect. Placement agencies or university fellowship programs are the best resources for finding teaching jobs in India and Nepal. The alternative is to make contacts directly with schools or just to try your luck once you get there. If you are going to try the latter, the best time of the year is several weeks before the start of the school year. The **International Schools Services (ISS),** 15 Roszel Rd., P.O. Box 5910, Princeton, NJ 08543-5910, USA (☎609-452-0990; www.iss.edu), is extremely helpful in placing teachers in India and Nepal. It hires teachers for more than 200 overseas schools, including schools in Chennai, Mumbai, New Delhi, and Kathmandu; candidates should have experience teaching or with international affairs, 2-year commitment expected.

Additional opportunities are listed under the location of the school. English language schools in places such as Uttar Pradesh (see p. 714) often accept foreign volunteers.

STUDYING ABROAD

VISA INFORMATION
Student visas for Nepal are issued upon arrival. Student visas for India are required and must be obtained prior to departure from your home country. Once in India, students and anyone over 18 planning to stay over one year must register within 14 days at the nearest Foreigners' Registration Office. HIV test results from an accepted laboratory must accompany registration.

Study abroad programs range from basic language and culture courses to college-level classes, often for credit. In order to choose a program that best fits your needs, you will want to research all you can before making your decision—determine costs and duration, as well as what kind of students participate in the program and what sort of accommodations are provided. Most programs in Nepal are in Kathmandu, while most programs in India base you in a specific city with some time alloted for individual or group travel across the Subcontinent.

In programs that have large groups of students who speak the same language, there is an important trade-off. You may feel more comfortable in the community, but you will not have the same opportunity to practice a foreign language or to befriend international students from other countries. For accommodations, dorm life provides a better opportunity to mingle with fellow students, but there is less of a chance to experience the local scene. If you live with a family, there is a potential to build lifelong friendships with natives and to experience day-to-day life in more depth, but conditions can vary greatly from family to family.

Some American schools still require students to pay them for credits obtained elsewhere. Most university-level study-abroad programs are meant as language and culture enrichment opportunities, and while some courses may be conducted in English, concurrent or previous study of Hindi, Nepali, or other languages may be required. Those relatively fluent in Indian languages or Nepali, on the other hand, may find it cheaper to enroll directly in a university abroad, although getting college credit may be more difficult. The following is a list of organizations that can help place students in university programs abroad, or have their own branch in India or Nepal.

UNIVERSITY AND LANGUAGE PROGRAMS

For semester- or year-long programs for college credit, most American undergraduates usually enroll in programs sponsored by US universities. Many programs offer classes in English and beginner- and lower-level language courses; ask around. For **language study,** *Let's Go* recommends traditional university study-abroad programs, both for summer-study and during the regular school year. Unlike American universities, language schools are frequently independently-run international or local organizations or divisions of foreign universities that rarely offer college credit. Language schools are a good alternative to university study if you desire a deeper focus on the language or a slightly less-rigorous courseload.

A good resource for finding programs that cater to your particular interests is **www.studyabroad.com,** which has links to a huge number of study-abroad programs in the Subcontinent. The following is a list of organizations that can help place students in university programs abroad.

American Institute of Indian Studies, 1130 East 59th St., Chicago, IL 60637, USA (☎773-702-8638; www.indiastudies.org). Offers language courses to advanced-level students enrolled at American colleges and universities at various locations throughout India. Fees are around US$2000 for summer programs and US$6000 for one-year courses, not including airfare.

Antioch Education Abroad, Antioch College, 795 Livermore St., Yellow Springs, OH 45387, USA (☎800-874-7986; www.antioch-college.edu/aea/in_prog.html). Offers Buddhist Studies program in Bodh Gaya, Bihar, from Sept.-Dec. Course offerings include Buddhist meditation, philosophy, history and culture, as well as language instruction in Hindi and Tibetan. Applicants must have completed at least 2 years of undergraduate study. US$14,285 includes airfare from London—where the program begins—to Delhi.

Applied Hindi Course: Faculty of Asian Studies, National University of Australia, Canberra ACT 0200, Australia (☎2 6249; www.anu.edu.au/asianstudies). Runs intensive study of Hindi, Sanskrit, and Urdu designed for students with the equivalent of at least a year's previous study.

Association of Commonwealth Universities (ACU), John Foster House, 36 Gordon Sq., London WC1H OPF, UK (☎020 7380 6700; www.acu.ac.uk). Publishes information about Commonwealth universities in India and Nepal.

Brethren Colleges Abroad (BCA), P.O. Box 407, 50 Alpha Drive, Elizabethtown, PA 17022, USA (☎866-222-6188; www.bcanet.org). Organizes study-abroad programs for American college students at the Cochin University of Science and Technology in Kerala. Study costs roughly the same as tuition, room, and board at your home college or university.

Council on International Educational Exchange (CIEE), 633 3rd Ave., 20th floor, New York, NY 10017, USA (☎800-407-8839; www.ciee.org/study) sponsors study abroad at University of Hyderabad in Andhra Pradesh. Costs US$8700 per semester, $15,250 for the academic year, not including airfare.

Elderhostel, Inc., 11 Ave. de Lafayette, Boston, MA 02111-1746, USA (☎877-426-8056; outside the US or Canada ☎978-323-4141; www.elderhostel.org). A non-profit organization that sends adults age 55 and over around the world to engage in learning and adventure. Programs in both India and Nepal. Costs average US$4000 and generally include airfare, accommodations, lectures, and other program fees.

International Partnership for Service Learning, 815 Second Ave., #315, New York, NY 10017, USA (☎212-986-0989; www.ipsl.org), offers 3-week and semester-long study beginning in Jan. or Aug. Programs combine volunteer social work at Mother Teresa's homes with language and cultural study in Kolkata. Student homestays during the semester include trips to Agra and Delhi or Konark. 3-week program US$6,800 (airfare included); semester-long program US$10,800 (including airfare and intercession).

Naropa Institute, 2130 Arapahoe Ave., Boulder, CO 80302, USA (☎303-546-3594; www.naropa.edu/studyabroad/). Runs programs in Sikkim as well as in Mysore and Auroville; students take classes in art and culture, language, culture, and religion. Open to both undergraduate and graduate students. Approx. US$10,900 for tuition, room, and board; does not include international airfare.

Pitzer College, External Studies, 1050 N. Mills Ave., Claremont, CA 91711, USA (☎909-621-8104; www.pitzer.edu/academics/ilcenter/external_studies). Semester-long program (fall and spring) on Nepali language and culture. Family homestays just outside Kathmandu, with treks in Annapurna Conservation Area and Chitwan National Park. US$6,965 includes airfare, tuition, room and board, and field trip. Financial aid usually transferable.

Rutgers Study Abroad, Rutgers, The State University of New Jersey, 102 College Ave., New Brunswick, NJ 08903, USA (☎732-932-7787; http://studyabroad.rutgers.edu/india.htm). Runs fall term and academic year study-abroad programs for college-level students at St. Stephen's College, Delhi. Costs are around US$8000 per semester for NJ residents, $10,000 out-of-state. Does not include travel and food costs.

School for International Training, College Semester Abroad, Admissions, Kipling Rd., P.O. Box 676, Brattleboro, VT 05302, USA (☎800-336-1616 or 802-257-7751; www.sit.edu). Semester-long programs in India and Nepal run around US$1000-3700.

Thamel Nepali Language Institute, Thamel, Kathmandu, Nepal (☎4442949; www.geocities.com/n_language), across the street from the Kathmandu Guest House, on the 2nd fl. Run by the friendly and experienced teacher Nabin Karki, the Institute's one-on-one Nepali courses are excellent for volunteers, trekkers or anyone else hoping to pick up the local language quickly. Courses can be as short as 10 days or as long as one year, and prices are negotiable. Classes are up to six days a week for 1 1/2 hours, though schedules are very flexible.

University of Iowa, International Programs, 120 International Center, Iowa City, IA 52242, USA (☎319-335-0353; www.uiowa.edu/~uiabroad), offers semester-long program from mid-Aug. to mid-Dec. in Mysore, Karnataka, with time for independent travel, research, and internship.

University of Minnesota, 230 Heller Hall, 271 19th Ave. S., Minneapolis, MN 55455, USA (☎612-626-9000; www.umabroad.umn.edu). Offers academic-year and semester-long study of international development and social issues in Jaipur, Rajasthan. US$7500-$7900 per semester, $10,500 for the academic year. Additional programs in India and Nepal are available for University of Minnesota students.

University of Wisconsin-Madison, International Academic Programs, 261 Bascom Hall, 500 Lincoln Dr., Madison, WI 53706, USA (☎608-262-2782; www.wisc.edu/studyabroad). Has college-year programs in Hyderabad, Madurai, Varanasi, and Kathmandu. The college-year programs concentrate on field work, with a year-long local language class and independently-chosen tutorial. One year of local language study is required. Fees cover academic expenses, administrative costs, a one-way plane ticket to India from the West Coast, room, meals, and pocket expenses: US$13,500 for India and Nepal. A summer performing arts program in Kerala is also offered for US$4500 (Wisconsin residents pay only US$1400).

Vishwa Bhasa Campus, Exhibition Road, Kathmandu, Nepal (☎ 4258132 or 4226713; www.yomari.net/nepali-language/message.html). The international language campus of Nepal's Tribhuvan University, Vishwa Bhasa offers six-month and one-year courses in Nepali, Newari, Tibetan, and Sanskrit. Classes meet every weekday for two hours; tuition is US$400 for six months or US$650 for one year, not including visa fees. Courses begin February 15 and July 15th, with application deadlines of December 30 and May 30, respectively. Vishwa Bhasa's courses are a good option for those looking for in-depth language study or who need to extend their stay in Nepal beyond the 150-day tourist visa limit.

SPIRITUAL INTERESTS

Although many people journey to South Asia to catch sight of the region's legendary spiritual landmarks, some pilgrims go in search of a more involved and comprehensive religious experience. With tens of thousands of retreats, temples, communes, and missions, India and Nepal offer numerous opportunities for those with spiritual interests. Aside from the mainstream traditions in India and Nepal (see **India: Religion,** p. 75, and **Nepal: Religion,** p. 787), the following kinds of religious communities—organized here by faith—are generally open to initiates from abroad. As with all of *Let's Go's* Alternatives To Tourism listings, be sure to check each establishment's references and, if at all possible, speak to someone who has visited there prior to making your travel arrangements.

HINDUISM

India and Nepal boast an abundance of *ashrams*, religious or spiritual retreats that call for widely varying degrees of spiritual and financial investment. Many of these are under the leadership of a modern-day guru—those who have attracted particularly large numbers of foreign devotees are sometimes referred to as "export gurus." Some of the most famous ashrams in India include that of the late **Sri Aurobindo** in Pondicherry (see p. 594), the **Osho Commune** in Pune (see p. 417), and **Sai Baba's** ashrams in Andhra Pradesh and Karnataka. **Rishikesh** (see p. 653) in Uttaranchal is a major center for gurus and students of yoga. If you stay in an ashram, you will usually be required to stay clean and quiet and to avoid meat, alcohol, tobacco, *paan* (betel), and drugs.

BUDDHISM

Since the 1959 Chinese crackdown in Tibet, India and Nepal have become the most accessible places in the world to study **Tibetan Buddhism. Dharamsala** (see p. 229) in India, the home of the Dalai Lama and the Tibetan government-in-exile, is a popular place to learn about Tibetan culture. There are opportunities for volunteer work among the Tibetan community here (see **Volunteer Opportunities,** p. 235). In Nepal (the Buddha's birthplace), the foremost Tibetan Buddhist center is located at **Boudha** (see **Study and Volunteer Opportunities,** p. 842), just outside Kathmandu. Unlike *lamas* (monks), Western students of Tibetan Buddhism do not usually live in monasteries, though they are expected to live austerely. Public lectures and meditation courses are offered at major Buddhist centers, including **Bodh Gaya** in Bihar (see **Buddhism and Volunteer Opportunities,** p. 131), the site of the Buddha's Enlightenment. The **Panditarama Center** (☎580118) in Lumbini, Nepal, offers instruction in the Pandita technique. The **Dhamma Janani** offers 10-day courses starting on the 15th of each month (see p. 876). The **Jamyang Foundation** (www.jamyang.org/index.html) for Himalayan Women educates women with Tibetan Buddhist backgrounds. It accepts volunteers for many of its programs. The **Dzogchen Monastery** (www.dzogchenmonastery.net/help) also places volunteers interested in Tibetan Buddhism in positions throughout the world.

CHRISTIANITY

Christianity is India's third largest religion. There are long traditions of faith and missionary work in the Subcontinent. Many hospitals, schools, and NGOs are run or supported by local or international Christian organizations. The **Missionaries of Charity,** founded by Mother Teresa, is the most famous of these organizations (see p. 760). Volunteers interested in other Christian service options should contact their local church.

FOR FURTHER READING ON ALTERNATIVES TO TOURISM

Alternatives to the Peace Corps: A directory of third world and U.S. Volunteer Opportunities, by Joan Powell. Food First Books, 2000 (US$10).

How to Live Your Dream of Volunteering Oversees, by Collins, DeZerega, and Heckscher. Penguin Books, 2002 (US$17).

International Directory of Voluntary Work, by Whetter and Pybus. Peterson's Guides and Vacation Work, 2000 (US$16).

International Jobs, by Kocher and Segal. Perseus Books, 1999 (US$18).

Overseas Summer Jobs 2002, by Collier and Woodworth. Peterson's Guides and Vacation Work, 2002 (US$18).

Work Abroad: The Complete Guide to Finding a Job Overseas, by Hubbs, Griffith, and Nolting. Transitions Abroad Publishing, 2000 ($16).

Work Your Way Around the World, by Susan Griffith. Worldview Publishing Services, 2001 (US$18).

Invest Yourself: The Catalogue of Volunteer Opportunities, published by the Commission on Voluntary Service and Action (☎ 718-638-8487).

ALTERNATIVES TO TOURISM

Find (Our Student Airfares are cheap, flexible & exclusive) great Student Airfares everywhere at StudentUniverse.com and Get lost.

StudentUniverse.com

Student Airfares everywhere

INDIA
LIFE AND TIMES

LAND

The colors of the Indian flag symbolize the country's terrain: green tropical jungle, white Himalayan snow, and saffron-colored Deccan earth. The **Himalayas** (Sanskrit for "abode of snow") crown the country and form a barrier between India and Central Asia, Tibet, and China. The world's highest mountain range, the Himalayas are the source of the Subcontinent's three great rivers, the **Indus**, the **Ganga**, and the **Brahmaputra**. These rivers and their tributaries nourish the densely-populated **Indo-Gangetic Plain**, which stretches from Rajasthan in the west to Bengal in the east.

The **Vindhyas**, a belt of stepped hills, divide the Indo-Gangetic Plain from the **Deccan Plateau** (Maharashtra, Karnataka, and Andhra Pradesh). The **Arabian Sea** washes the continent to the west, the **Bay of Bengal** is on the east, and the southern tip, Kanyakumari, borders the Indian Ocean. Flanking the **Malabar Coast** of Kerala, Karnataka, and Goa, the **Western Ghats** (a north-south chain of mountains and hills) are separated from the coast by a narrow strip of richly forested coastal plain. The **Coromandel Coast** of Tamil Nadu and Andhra Pradesh is bounded by the **Eastern Ghats**. The Ghats converge at the **Nilgiri Hills** of Kerala and Tamil Nadu. The **Lakshadweep Islands**, in the Arabian Sea, and the **Andaman and Nicobar Islands**, in the Bay of Bengal, are also Indian territories. For information on India's climate, see **When To Go** (p. 1). For a chart of **average temperatures and rainfall**, see **p. 927**.

FLORA & FAUNA

India is home to more than 500 species of mammals, 1000 species of birds, and 6% of the world's reptile species, including 250 kinds of snakes. One of India's national symbols is the majestic (and endangered) **Bengal tiger.** Poachers brought tigers close to extinction in the years after Independence, but more recently the establishment of national parks, reserves, and conservation projects—notably **Project Tiger** (see p. 328)—have reversed the slide. Other Indian felines include leopards, panthers, and jungle cats. Also endangered is the **one-horned rhinoceros,** which once roamed across the Subcontinent but now survives in only two places: **Kaziranga National Park** in Assam (see box below) and the **Royal Chitwan National Park** in Nepal (see p. 880). Other mammals include bear, buffalo, bison, mongoose, and dozens of species of antelope, deer, and gazelle. India also offers some of the best bird-watching spots in the world, including the **Keoladeo Ghana National Park,** near Bharatpur in Rajasthan (see below). Even outside the parks and reserves, colorful species such as peacocks, parrots, mynahs, bee-eaters, and hoopoes are common throughout the country. Dozens of species of monkey inhabit India, and not just its jungles and forests; the small, long-tailed *langurs* are common in cities and towns, especially in temple precincts, where they are revered as sacred. These beasts are aggressive, scavengers and are best avoided. Elephants are used as work animals, and can also be seen in several national parks.

PARK	LOCATION	BEST TIME TO VISIT	WHAT YOU MIGHT FIND
Bandhavgarh National Park	Jabalpur, Madhya Pradesh (p. 368)	Nov. - Jun.	Highest-density tiger population
Corbett National Park	Uttaranchal (p. 666)	Nov. - Jun.	Tiger, elephant, leopard
Eravikulam National Park	Munnar, Kerala (p. 342)	Sept. - May	Nilgiri *tahr*, jungle cat, mongoose
Gibbon Wildlife Sanctuary	Jorhat, Assam (p. 447)	Nov. - Apr.	Home to the Indo-US Primate Project
Kanha National Park	Jabalpur, Madhya Pradesh (p. 367)	Nov. - Jun.	Setting for Kipling's *Jungle Book;* tiger, leopard, boar, bear
Kaziranga National Park	Assam (p. 444)	Nov. - Apr.	Rhino, elephant
Keoladeo Ghana National Park	Bharatpur, Rajasthan (p. 503)	Nov. - Jan.	400-plus species of birds
Mahatma Gandhi Marine National Park	Andaman Islands (p. 101)	Nov. - May	Diving, snorkeling, fish-watching
Nameri National Park	Assam (p. 443)	Nov. - Mar.	Elephants, orchids, rare duck, and tiger
Nandankan Zoological Park	Bhubaneswar, Orissa (p. 461)	Year-round	Zoo; rare breeds squeezed into tiny cages
Orang Wildlife Sanctuary	Assam (p. 443)	Nov. - Mar.	Rhino, elephant
Periyar Tiger Reserve	Kerala (p. 328)	Sept. - Mar.	Elephant, tiger, boating
Sundarbans National Park	West Bengal (p. 764)	Nov. - Mar.	Tiger, crocodile, deer

ECOLOGY

Air and water pollution in India have gone unchecked for decades. In a country where 300 million people live in poverty, green issues are often an afterthought. However, the vast majority of India's one billion people live in rural areas and depend on nature for their livelihood. Cash crops such as cotton, paper, rubber, tobacco, and spices account for a huge portion of the country's GDP. Illegal logging continues to destroy forests, the natural habitat of species such as the **Bengal tiger** and the one-horned rhino, already threatened by poaching. Mines, highways, and hydroelectric dams have also disrupted India's ecological equilibrium. In the 1970s and 1980s, resistance to the destruction of India's forests was organized into what became known as the Chipko Movement. The movement's success led in 1980 to a moratorium on logging in the Himalayan forests of Uttar Pradesh. Recently in Madhya Pradesh and Gujarat, a well-organized grass-roots movement has opposed government plans for dams along the River Narmada because the dams may damage the environment and displace as many as half a million people. Booker Prize winning novelist Arundhati Roy has been a prominent part of the protest and served a night in jail for contempt in March 2002. A recent Supreme Court mandate that all buses and auto-rickshaws in Delhi convert to more efficient gas-burning engines has been abided slowly and sporadically.

HISTORY

ANCIENT HISTORY (3500-1500 BC). India gets its name from the Indus River, along whose banks the first significant civilization on the Subcontinent flourished 4000 years ago. During the 1920s, the remains of huge cities were unearthed at

Harappa and **Mohenjo-Daro** (both in Pakistan). The Indus Valley civilization prospered for more than a thousand years and comprised perhaps 100 cities, stretching out across half a million square miles. The population of its metropolitan centers—like the one at Harappa—was as high as 35,000. Unearthed artifacts indicate that the Indus people traded by land and sea with Mesopotamia, Egypt, and Assyria. Little else is known about the everyday life of these people. Unearthed seals feature humans, gods, and animals, and suggest that the Indus people worshipped a mother-goddess and another deity similar to the Hindu god Shiva. Environmental changes were probably what killed the Indus civilization: tectonic plate movements around 1800 BC changed the river's course, flooding the carefully irrigated farmland that had nourished the valley for more than a thousand years.

THE ARYANS (1500-300 BC). As the Indus civilization declined, a new group entered the Subcontinent. The Aryans were Indo-European nomads who had been raping and pillaging their way across the continent since being kicked out of the Caucasus around 2000 BC. They spread out in all directions, and a group of them came to the Subcontinent by 1500 BC. The language of the Aryans was **Sanskrit**, a member of the same Indo-European family that spawned Latin and Greek and is the root of the modern North Indian languages. Aryans worshipped the forces of nature: they performed fire-sacrifices to guarantee the continued sponsorship of **Agni**, the fire god, and **Indra**, god of war and an embodiment of the monsoon.

They brought to the Subcontinent not only their language and religion but also a new social order. Aryan society was divided into three classes or *varna*, probably originally based on race, and forming the basis for the caste system (see p. 76).

THE MAURYA EMPIRE (300-200 BC). By the 6th century BC, Aryans occupied the whole of northern India, where 16 separate Aryan kingdoms vied for supremacy. Having finished his conquest of Persia and the Mediterranean, **Alexander the Great** proceeded toward India's northwest frontier in 326 BC. But his troops had already had enough empire-building, and Alexander was forced to turn back when they mutinied. Shortly after Alexander's retreat, **Chandragupta Maurya**, an adventurer from eastern India, seized control of the kingdom of Magadha, the most powerful Aryan state, in Bihar. Chandragupta moved quickly to subdue the area around the Ganga Valley. Over the next 100 years, the Mauryan Empire came to control the whole of the Subcontinent except its southern tip—the closest anyone would come to wielding power over all of India until modern times.

The Mauryan Empire abandoned its policies of violent military expansion at the height of its power, after the invasion of the Kalinga Kingdom in Orissa, during which more than 100,000 people were killed. This bloody battle horrified the great Mauryan emperor **Ashoka** (r. 269-232 BC) so much that he renounced violence forever and became a Buddhist. With the last of his enemies (conveniently) dead, Ashoka preached the virtues of peaceful government. Edicts promoting Buddhism to the status of official creed were inscribed on pillars and stones, and the emperor passed rules to ensure that the vast lands under Mauryan control would be governed according to "moral law." The Mauryan Empire collapsed soon after Ashoka's death, but many of his edict-inscribed pillars still stand.

THE GUPTAS: A GOLDEN AGE (AD 300-500). In AD 319 another Chandragupta came to power in the eastern kingdom of Magadha. No relation to the founder of the Maurya dynasty, **Chandragupta II** (r. 375-415) followed in his namesake's illustrious footsteps and launched an empire of his own. At the peak of its power, the Gupta empire ruled over all of North India.

Today, the Guptas are remembered for the cultural refinement and religious tolerance that marked their rule, often referred to as India's "Golden Age." They were great patrons of the arts and sciences, into which they funneled their wealth from

LIFE AND TIMES

overseas trade. Engineers built India's first stone dams and temples, artisans carved the cave-sculptures at **Ajanta** out of a sheer cliff face (see p. 429), and **Kalidasa,** India's greatest lyric poet, served at the court of Chandragupta II.

REGIONALISM (AD 500-1192). The Gupta Empire disintegrated in the 5th century, when the Huns of Central Asia invaded. North India fractured into small kingdoms again and remained divided for most of the next 700 years.

The strongest kingdom in India at the time was the **Chola** dynasty of Tamil Nadu, which conquered most of the southern peninsula and sent forces to the Maldives, Sri Lanka, and Malaysia. After the 8th century, a group of warriors known as the **Rajputs** dominated northwest India. They set up several small kingdoms from their base in the **Thar Desert** in Rajasthan and developed a culture distinguished by chivalric values and a proud architectural and literary tradition.

THE ARRIVAL OF ISLAM (1192-1526). Islam, spread eastward from its birthplace in Arabia to the northwest fringes of the Indian Subcontinent. Although Muslims traded with India by sea, and many settled along the west coast, Islam made little impression on the Subcontinent until the raids of **Mahmud of Ghazni,** the king of a Turkish dynasty in Afghanistan. Between 997 and 1030, Mahmud's armies plundered North India on an almost annual basis, though they never made any attempt at a more permanent invasion.

But at the end of the 12th century, another Turko-Afghan king, **Mohammed of Ghur,** had conquest on his mind. In 1192 he defeated a loose coalition of Rajput armies and conquered the Ganga Valley. Though Mohammed himself soon headed home to Afghanistan, he left his slave-general **Qutb-al-Din Aibak** behind in Delhi to govern on his behalf (see **Qutb Minar,** p. 152). When Mohammed died in 1206, Qutb-al-Din succeeded him, and proclaimed the birth of the **Delhi Sultanate,** India's first Muslim kingdom. The Sultanate ruled most of North India for 300 years. By the early 15th century, independent Muslim kingdoms had emerged in Bengal, Gujarat, and Central India. The palace was in constant turmoil, and the sultans' habit of financing their extravagant life at court with taxes paid by the Hindu masses caused frequent revolts and widespread unhappiness. In 1398, the Central Asian conqueror **Tamerlane** overtook Delhi and burned the city to ashes.

Islam won huge numbers of converts, but ultimately, religious fragmentation undermined the centralized political authority of the **Lodis,** the last dynasty of the Delhi Sultanate. Provincial governors seceded in Bihar, Portuguese ships landed in Goa, and in central India the one-eyed, one-armed Rajput leader Rana Sanaga called for foreign intervention to vanquish the Delhi Sultanate.

THE MUGHALS (1526-1700). Rana Sanaga's call was heeded by the Central Asian warlord **Babur** (1483-1530), who counted both Tamerlane and Genghis Khan among his ancestors. In the Battle of Panipat, fought outside Delhi in 1526, Babur prevailed against numerically superior forces and crushed the Lodi dynasty. When Babur died in 1530, his son **Humayun** was proclaimed emperor over a kingdom that stretched from Bihar to Kabul. In 1540 the Afghan warlord **Sher Shah** deposed Humayun. Sher Shah banished Humayun to the sand dunes of the Sindh desert while he worked to secure his position, but when the warlord was killed during a siege of a Rajput stronghold in 1545, Humayun retook Delhi, though he died just four months later. His son **Akbar** (1542-1605) took the throne in 1555 at the age of 13.

Akbar quickly squashed rebellions and cemented Mughal dominion by conquering Rajasthan, Gujarat, Orissa, Kashmir, and Bengal. He also worked to create a **centralized imperial bureaucracy.** To win Hindu support, Akbar married a Rajput princess and appointed Hindus to government posts. He also stopped the bulldozing of Hindu temples and eliminated the *jizya*, a despised tax on non-Muslims.

Akbar's successors **Jehangir** (r. 1605-27) and **Shah Jahan** (r. 1628-57) built on Akbar's work. Together, their reigns were a golden era for the Mughals. This period also saw the construction of stunningly beautiful buildings, including the marble **Taj Mahal** in Agra (p. 696) and the sandstone **Red Fort** in Delhi (p. 150). But when Shah Jahan fell ill in 1657, his sons went to war, **Aurangzeb** eventually emerging victorious, having murdered his brother and imprisoned his father.

Aurangzeb's rule lasted 48 years. Fanatically pious, he undid a century of tolerance. He banned the repair of Hindu temples and reinstated the *jizya*. By the time Aurangzeb died, the Mughal empire was already disintegrating. For the next half-century, the Mughals ruled in name only.

THE BEGINNINGS OF BRITISH INTERFERENCE (1700-1757). European ships had been sailing the seas for hundreds of years in search of the riches of the East, but they didn't reach India until the 17th century, when the English, Portuguese, Dutch, and French governments chartered trading companies. The gradual decline of Portuguese sea power, and a Dutch decision to focus on Indonesia, paved the way for the **British East India Company** to assert control over South Asia's resources. From Calcutta and Madras, the Company ran a highly profitable trade, exchanging gold and silver for Indian finished goods, especially hand-crafted textiles.

The Company recruited small Indian armies to defend its warehouses with European weapons. These mercenary armies allowed the Company to dominate Bengal in the mid-18th century. Led by Robert Clive, the Company allied itself with a coalition of Muslims and Hindus, and after a series of battles culminating at **Plassey** in 1757 established unrivalled authority over much of Eastern India.

EAST INDIA COMPANY RULE (1757-1857). During the late 18th century the Company, led first by Warren Hastings and then by Lord Cornwallis, developed a British-dominated bureaucracy to administer its rule in Indian territories.

Between the late 1820s and 1857, the Company attempted to recast Indian society in a European mold. It introduced railways, textile mills, and telegraphs, and outlawed **sati,** in which widows burned themselves on their husbands' funeral pyres, and **thugi,** in which devotees of the goddess Kali committed ritual robbery and murder. British authorities changed the official language of state from Persian to English in 1847 and funded the development of secondary schools, medical colleges, and universities. In all of these, both the curriculum and language of instruction were English. Millions of Indians resented the British influence, and in the 1850s, the situation turned violent.

SEPOY MUTINY AND AFTERMATH (1857-1858). In 1857, the Company outfitted its 200,000 *sepoys* (Indian soldiers) with the Lee-Enfield rifle, whose ammunition cartridges were rumored to be lubricated with pig and cow fat. Hindus (for whom cows are sacred) and Muslims (for whom pigs are impure) were incensed when they learned that soldiers had to bite the tip off these cartridges with their teeth before loading them. In the **Sepoy Mutiny** of May 1857, Indian soldiers raised the Mughal flag over Delhi, indiscriminately massacring Europeans as they took control of the city; similar bloodshed occurred in several other cities, most famously in Lucknow (see p. 707). The victory was short-lived: backed by Sikh regiments, British troops retaliated four months later, recapturing Delhi and Lucknow, and killing thousands. By March of 1858, the British had suppressed the Mutiny (the War of Independence, as Indian nationalists call it today).

The revolt alarmed the British and triggered dramatic changes in the way they governed India. An 1858 Act of Parliament stripped the East India Company of its rule; within a year, the Crown was administering India directly as a full-fledged colony. The **Raj Era** had begun. To ensure tight control over India, Crown authori-

LIFE AND TIMES

ties increased the number of British troops stationed in South Asia, banned Indians from becoming officers in the army, and staffed the upper echelons of the burgeoning Indian Civil Service with British bureaucrats. The British tended to withdraw from Indian society, setting up hill stations remote from the cities and for the most part abandoning their quest to westernize South Asia.

RAJ VS. SWARAJ (1858-1915). A group of 70 wealthy Indians met in Bombay in 1885 to form the **Indian National Congress,** a political association that demanded reform and independence. As it grew, the Party split into two wings: the moderates, who advocated reform, and the extremists, who wanted to put an end to British meddling once and for all. The extremist view began to win widespread support after 1905, when the British viceroy partitioned Bengal into two provinces: one with a Hindu majority, the other Muslim.

The terms of the debate had shifted, and self-rule, or **swaraj,** became the ultimate objective. In the next decade, Indians actively resisted British rule by whatever means possible. Millions of Indians boycotted British-made textiles, opting instead for the rougher, homespun *swadeshi* cloth. Muslims concerned about Hindu domination of Congress founded the **All-India Muslim League** in 1906. Indian nationalists cooperated with the British during World War I in the hope that their loyalty would be rewarded with greater freedom. Instead, the British suspended civil liberties and imposed martial law. In 1919, British soldiers massacred over 300 unarmed who had assembled in **Amritsar** to protest.

It was to this atmosphere of violence and unrest that **Mohandas Karamchand Gandhi** (later proclaimed the Mahatma, or "Great Soul," by Bengali poet Rabindranath Tagore) returned in 1915. Born into a Gujarati family in 1869, Gandhi had gone abroad to study law. After studying in England, Gandhi spent 20 years in South Africa, where he devoted his energies to ending racial discrimination against Indians living in that country. Upon his return, he developed *satyagraha*, a kind of non-violent resistance he described as "soul force."

THE STRUGGLE FOR FREEDOM (1915-1947). Gandhi enjoyed amazing popularity throughout the 1920s. His religious tolerance earned him support from both Hindus and Muslims, and his rejection of Western products in favor of *swadeshi* goods made him popular among the peasant masses. This popularity paved the way for his leadership of Congress, and he seized the opportunity and reshaped the elite party into a populist one supported by millions of ordinary Indians.

Millions participated in non-violent civil disobedience throughout the 1920s. In 1930 **Jawaharlal Nehru,** the charismatic young leader of the Congress Party's radical wing, audaciously declared the 26th of January to be Indian Independence Day. Seven weeks later, Gandhi embarked on his famous **salt march,** an open defiance of the law prohibiting Indians from making their own salt. British authorities responded by arresting 60,000 people, but there was little they could do to control the rising tide of nationalism. In 1932, the army granted its first commissions to Indian officers, and in 1935, the Government of India Act was passed, giving elected Indian representatives authority over provincial government.

At the end of WWII, Britain's new Labour government agreed to grant India full independence. Vicious religious conflicts wracked Calcutta, the Punjab, and the Ganga Valley in 1946 and encouraged the division of India into two sovereign states—one Hindu, one Muslim. Defying geography, the government carved the new state of Pakistan out of Muslim-majority areas in both the east and the west. Independence for India arrived at the same time as **Partition,** division of the vast territory that had been the "jewel in the crown" of the British Empire. The independent nation of **Pakistan** was born on August 14, 1947, and **India** followed suit 24 hours later. The last British viceroy, Lord Mountbatten, stayed on to oversee the exchange of power. Hours before **Independence,** Nehru made one of the most famous speeches of the 20th century to the Constituent Assembly in New Delhi: "At the stroke of the midnight hour, when the world sleeps, India will awake to life and freedom. A moment comes, which comes but rarely in history, when...the soul of a nation, long suppressed, finds utterance."

PARTITION AND AFTER (1947-1964). As countries were created, so were refugees: millions of desperate Sikhs and Hindus streamed into India, fearing for their lives, while millions of Muslims fled to Pakistan. These massive migrations, one of the largest movements of people in history, touched off violence on a horrific scale. Well over 500,000 were killed. Five months later, Mahatma Gandhi was assassinated on his way to evening prayers by **Nathuram Godse,** a Hindu extremist angered by Gandhi's cordial relations with the Muslim League.

Nehru's India faced innumerable economic problems. The vast majority of Indians lived in poverty, and huge economic rifts separated the urban middle classes from the village-based majority. Nehru embarked on a series of **five-year plans** and successfully solicited foreign aid, but sluggish economic growth failed to keep pace with the needs of an ever-expanding population.

Foreign policy problems plagued Nehru's administration. Independence forced **Kashmir,** a formerly independent kingdom in the Himalayas with a Hindu maharaja and a population that was 75% Muslim, to choose to be part of either India or Pakistan. Border skirmishes with Pakistan led the maharaja to choose India, with Nehru promising a fair plebiscite soon. A brief, undeclared war between India and Pakistan ended in 1949 with a UN cease-fire. The war established a still-disputed "line of control" between Pakistani and Indian Kashmir, but did nothing to solve the problems at the root of the conflict (see **Jammu and Kashmir,** p. 257). At the same time, the new nation bickered about Kashmir's borders with China. They went to war in 1962.

INDIRA'S INDIA (1964-1984). After Nehru's death in 1962, **Lal Bahadur Shastri** became prime minister, but died shortly after a victory in a war against Pakistan. Shastri was succeeded by Nehru's daughter, Indira Gandhi. As soon as she came to power, Mrs. Gandhi fought with the Congress "old guard" and aligned India with the Soviet Union. Pakistan aligned with the U.S.

In 1971, East Pakistan broke away from West Pakistan, prompting a swift invasion by West Pakistan. The flood of millions of refugees into India inflicted a heavy burden on India's already-strained treasury. India started arming and training Bengali guerrillas, and in December, Pakistani planes attacked Indian airfields. The next day, Indira Gandhi sent troops into both East and West Pakistan. Less than two weeks later, Pakistan surrendered; the result was the creation of the country of **Bangladesh.**

After the **oil crisis** of 1973, India faced runaway inflation and the threat of famine. Millions slipped toward starvation, but the corrupt and nepotistic government did little to help. In 1975, Mrs. Gandhi was found guilty of election fraud. Rather than step down, she declared a **national emergency** and suspended all civil rights. She imposed sterilization on families with more than two children, aggressively censored the press, converted India's intelligence agencies into her own private police force, and locked up her political opponents.

The state of emergency ended in January 1977, by which time Mrs. Gandhi was confident that she would be re-elected legitimately. She wasn't. The **Janata Dal,** an anti-Indira coalition led by **Morarji Desai,** came to power in March that year. The party crumbled, however, Mrs. Gandhi was reelected in 1980.

Regional problems plagued her second term. In 1984 she ordered the dismissal of Kashmir's popular Chief Minister, Farooq Abdullah. Soon afterward, she gave another order to the governor of Andhra Pradesh, demanding the removal of the state's popular Chief Minister, **N.T. Rama Rao,** a former film star and leader of a major opposition party. She also confronted separatist **Sikh militants,** who had launched a terrorist campaign calling for a sovereign Sikh nation in **Punjab and Haryana.** In 1984, when armed Sikh militants occupied the Golden Temple in Amritsar—the Sikhs' holiest site—Mrs. Gandhi sent in troops (see p. 482). Thousands died during the ensuing four-day battle dubbed **Operation Bluestar,** but for Mrs. Gandhi the worst was yet to come. By desecrating the temple, Mrs. Gandhi incurred the wrath of the militants, and on October 31, 1984, two Sikh bodyguards shot her to death in her home. Her murder sparked enormous riots throughout the capital and widespread massacres of Sikhs by Hindu thugs.

THE RISE OF THE BJP (1984-2000). A sympathy vote in the elections that followed Indira's assassination gave an impressive majority to Rajiv Gandhi's Congress party. Rajiv's term as prime minister began inauspiciously with a gas leak from the Union Carbide chemical plant that killed nearly 3000 people in **Bhopal** in December 1984. He had mixed success with foreign policy. He improved relations with the US without moving away from the Soviet Union, but he made several ill-advised decisions in the case of **Sri Lanka,** only 35km off the south coast of India. The **Tamil Tigers,** a guerrilla group fighting for an independent Tamil state on the island, had been surreptitiously armed and trained in India during Mrs. Gandhi's administration. Rajiv sent the Indian Peace Keeping Force (IPKF) to Sri Lanka to join the fight against the Tigers, and the Sri Lankan government was only too happy to withdraw its troops from the fray. The Tigers routed the government forces—by the time the IPKF withdrew, there were 100 Indian soldiers dead for every Tiger killed.

The 1989 elections transferred power to a fragile coalition of parties led by the Hindu Nationalist **Bharatiya Janata Party (BJP),** and Prime Minister V.P. Singh of the Janata Dal. The situation in Kashmir worsened, even as Singh struggled to put an end to the crisis in Punjab. Muslim militants, trained and armed by Pakistan, attacked Indian government offices. The state capital of **Srinagar,** once a popular tourist destination, turned into a war zone.

The elections of 1991 reinstated Congress power, thanks largely to another sympathy vote following the assassination of Rajiv Gandhi, who was killed by a **Tamil Tiger** suicide bomber. The new prime minister, **P.V. Narasimha Rao,** won widespread support for instituting drastic economic reforms that cut government expenditure and opened India to foreign investment. Late 1991 saw the renewal of a long-running dispute over the **Babri Masjid** in Ayodhya. In December 1992, with the BJP in power in Uttar Pradesh, Hindu nationalists called for volunteers to build a Hindu temple in place of the mosque that stood on the site of Rama's birthplace. Devotees from all over India converged on Ayodhya with bricks in hand and tore down the mosque. Hindu-Muslim violence erupted across the country.

Though considerably weakened, the Rao government clung to power and continued its economic liberalization. But by the mid-nineties, the Hindu nationalists had made a comeback. In 1995, the radical nationalist party **Shiv Sena** took control of **Maharashtra,** which includes the financial powerhouse of Mumbai. Kashmir continued to be a problem, and the response by the government to local insurrections brought international condemnation for human rights violations.

The BJP's bad luck in the 1996 elections enabled a coalition government of low-caste, populist, and socialist parties called the United Front to rise to power, with **H.D. Deve Gowda** as prime minister. Between 1996 and 1998, India stumbled from one teetering coalition government to another. The Hindu

Nationalist BJP won elections in 1998. In May that year, a series of nuclear weapons tests by India and Pakistan brought Prime Minister **Atal Bihari Vajpayee** into the international spotlight and intensified the subcontinental arms race. Later that year, Indian and Pakistani troops exchanged shelling across Kashmir's Line of Control, and more than 90 soldiers and civilians were killed. In May 1999, Indian jets attacked Muslim guerrilla forces that had advanced beyond the Line of Control marking the disputed border with Pakistan. The battle killed hundreds.

In April 1999, the government collapsed after the southern **AIADMK** party withdrew its support from the ruling coalition. The opposition, headed by Congress leader **Sonia Gandhi** (widow of former PM Rajiv Gandhi) was unable to form a majority in parliament, and India went to the polls for the third time in three years. The **New Democratic Alliance,** dominated by Prime Minister Vajpayee and his BJP won nearly 300 of the 536 parliamentary seats up for grabs. Their victory came on the back of success in that summer's military tussles with arch-rival Pakistan in the Kargil region of disputed Kashmir. In October 1999, a series of **cyclones** ripped through **Orissa,** killing more than 10,000 people and causing untold damage across one of the poorest parts of the country. Bill Clinton's final year as US president brought him to India in March 2000—the first visit by an American head of state in over 20 years. A devastating **earthquake** measuring 7.9 on the Richter scale rocked the western state of Gujarat on Republic Day, January 26 2001, causing unprecedented damage and killing an estimated 40,000 people. Many thousands more lost their homes.

TODAY

RECENT NEWS

In October 2001, Kashmiri separatists set off a car bomb outside the State Legislature building in Srinagar, Kashmir, leaving dozens dead and many more injured. In December, gunmen shot up the Indian Parliament in New Delhi, and a bomber killed 20 people by blowing himself up as legislators left the building. In January 2002, Pakistani President Pervez Musharraf outlawed Lashkar-e-Taiba and Jaish-e-Mohammed, two militant groups suspected of involvement in the attack, but this did little to ease tension between the two countries. In early 2002, both nations tested ballistic missiles capable of carrying nuclear warheads. India and Pakistan amassed troops along the border throughout early 2002. India recalled its senior diplomat from Islamabad and suspended transport links with Pakistan in January 2002. India expelled Pakistan's high commissioner in May 2002 after an attack on an Indian army base in Jammu killed 34, many of them women and children.

Hindu-Muslim violence broke out in Gujarat in February 2002, when a train carrying Hindu activists to a contested holy site in Ayodhya, Uttar Pradesh was set on fire, killing 50. Retaliatory violence claimed many more lives across the country, and a Muslim section of the city of Ahmedabad in Gujarat was torched later the same month, leaving dozens dead and thousands homeless. At least 1000 people died in sectarian violence in 2002, and tensions remain high in many parts of the country. A twin set of car bombings in Mumbai in August 2003 killed dozens; authorities quickly blamed Muslim militants, although no groups stepped forward.

GOVERNMENT AND POLITICS

That India's frenzied politics have managed to plod along more or less successfully despite persistent secessionist threats, extreme malnutrition and human suffering has astonished political scientists for much of the 55 years since Independence. Somehow, the parliamentary system has stayed afloat.

Ongoing violence makes much of **Jammu and Kashmir** off-limits for travelers; separatists in Kashmir have kidnapped and killed several tourists. Tensions with neighboring Pakistan remain high, so it is best to avoid traveling in border areas. The presence of US troops has led to a rise in anti-Western sentiment in that country. Five people, including a US diplomat and her daughter, were killed in a church bombing in Islamabad in March 2002. In May 2002, a suicide attack on a bus in Karachi killed 15 people, including 11 French nationals. **Pakistan-based extremist groups have been blamed for several attacks on Indian soil, including a shoot-out at an American Cultural Center in Kolkata that left five dead in January 2002.**

The country's **constitution,** adopted in 1950, is the longest in the world, with 395 articles legislating, among other things, universal suffrage and fundamental rights. The Indian constitution is distinctive in combining traditional liberal rights—freedom of press, free speech, and free association—with **Directive Principles** designed to deal with the social and economic reforms essential for a poor democracy. The framers of the constitution sought to create a **federal system** that would reflect India's diversity, but they also wanted a central government strong enough to handle poverty and religious conflict. The result has been a highly centralized form of federalism, with the national government holding the power to dismiss state governments in an emergency, an option known as **"President's Rule."**

The vice-president, a council of ministers, and the prime minister head India's government. The president (currently A.P.J. Abdul Kalam), appointed for a five-year term, is a figurehead. The prime minister (currently Atal Bihari Vajpayee of the BJP), chosen by the majority party in the **Lok Sabha** (House of the People), the lower house, holds executive power. The Lok Sabha and the **Rajya Sabha** (Council of States), chosen by the state governments, together make up the Indian parliament. Each of India's states has a legislative assembly, or **Vidhan Sabha.** The states have jurisdiction over education, agriculture, welfare, and the police. India's **Supreme Court** is remarkably independent and often asserts its right to make decisions on controversial issues that others would rather avoid.

India may be a working democracy, but one family and their party, the **Nehrus** and **Congress,** dominated for most of the first 50 years after Independence. Despite Congress' inclusiveness, it has found it difficult to unite the conflicting interests of ideology, caste, region, and religion. As a result, politics have become highly regionalized, with parties such as the **DMK** (in Tamil Nadu), the **Communist Party of India** (in Bengal), and the **Akali Dal** (in Punjab) often earning more votes in state elections than Congress. In the 1996 national elections, no single party won a majority of seats in the Lok Sabha, leading to the formation of piecemeal left-wing coalitions such as the Janata Dal and the Communist Party of India. The party that burst the Congress bubble, the **Bharatiya Janata Party (BJP),** won a majority of the Lok Sabha seats in 1999 elections under the leadership of Atal Bihari Vajpayee, the current prime minister.

Caste politics are increasingly influential, as lower castes begin to translate their demographic strength into political clout, particularly in Bihar and Uttar Pradesh. Corruption scandals have brought down numerous state and national governments, and groups in some regions regularly use violence and bribery to intimidate voters.

LIFE AND TIMES

ECONOMICS

In his famous "Tryst with Destiny" speech, delivered on the eve of Independence, Prime Minister Jawaharlal Nehru promised "the ending of poverty and ignorance and disease and inequality of opportunity" in the new nation. Nehru drew inspiration from the Soviet Union and advocated heavy industrialization and state ownership of major companies. The aim of Nehruvian socialism was self-sufficiency in the tradition of the *swadeshi* movement. In a sense, this isolationist scheme worked: direct foreign investment was virtually nil throughout the 1950s and 1960s, and stringent licensing requirements, known as the **"license-permit raj,"** restricted private enterprise. The outcome was anything but self-sufficiency, however; the economy puttered along at a growth rate of 5% per annum, a figure derisively referred to as the **"Hindu rate of growth."**

In 1991, a shortfall in foreign exchange reserves resulted in a **financial crisis** that almost forced the Indian government to default on foreign debt. India made dramatic changes in its economic policies. The immediate result of these efforts was increasing growth and investment by foreign companies. In recent years, high-tech industries (especially in Bangalore and Hyderabad, Microsoft's Asian headquarters) have made India a major player in international IT markets.

Economic liberalization still has a long way to go. The government has delayed the sale of money-losing public sector industries for fear of massive lay-offs, and the rise of a Hindu nationalist government has scared off some foreign investors. And rapid economic growth has yet to benefit the poorest segments of Indian society. Slums continue to proliferate in the cities, and 53% of children under five are malnourished. The national per capita is a mere US$500, half of the population is illiterate, and average life expectancy is 63 years.

MEDIA

Hundreds of newspapers are published every day in Hindi and dozens of other languages. Major English-language dailies include *The Times of India*, *The Indian Express*, and *The Hindu*. All are excellent, if a little dry and sober in style, and provide solid, up-to-date India-specific news coverage via their comprehensive Web sites (http://timesofindia.indiatimes.com; www.indianexpress.com; www.thehindu.com). **www.samachar.com** provides a digest of articles, updated daily. Glossy news weeklies such as *India Today* and *Outlook* provide more in-depth analysis and coverage; both put a strong emphasis on domestic politics and economics. Slightly less cerebral (and much more popular) are specialist movie magazines like *Filmfare*, which bring the latest Bollywood gossip to hundreds of thousands of readers every month. Poverty and illiteracy mean that only one-third of the population reads the press; many more (over 50%) watch TV. Doordarshan is the national TV channel; over the past decade or so, Rupert Murdoch's Star TV network has provided a more popular alternative, bringing soap operas and live cricket broadcasts to all but the most remote and impoverished parts of the country. All India Radio is the government public station (and the only one officially allowed to broadcast the news), and often acts as a government mouthpiece. The press and other media enjoy a good degree of freedom and autonomy, although the Official Secrets Act allows government censorship "in the interests of national security," and this option is occasionally used to limit criticism, as well as to curb the influence of the often-hostile Pakistani media. India is estimated to have 25 million Internet users by 2005.

EDUCATION

The state governments control education, and policy varies greatly from one state to another. Although the Indian Constitution guarantees every citizen's right to complete primary education, in 20 of 28 states there is no compulsory education at all. Currently only around 3.8% of government spending is dedicated to education. Almost 50% of India's adult population (15 years and older) is illiterate, and less than 3% complete tertiary education. Literacy rates vary by state: in Kerala, 90% of the population is literate; in Rajasthan, only about 40% can read and write. Throughout the country, women and members of lower castes have the lowest literacy rates. Across South Asia, 20% more boys than girls are enrolled in primary education. In most states the local language is the primary language of instruction. Hindi is also compulsory in most states (Tamil Nadu is a notable exception), and English is compulsory in every state but Bihar.

PEOPLE

DEMOGRAPHICS

India is not a country; it's a world. Six major religions (see p. 75), 18 major languages, and countless racial and ethnic groups coexist (often harmoniously, sometimes not). Seventy-five percent of the population lives in rural areas. The inhabitants of India's four largest cities (Mumbai, Kolkata, Delhi, and Chennai) make up only 4% of the country's population. The most densely packed areas are in the valley and delta of the Ganga River and in the extreme south (Tamil Nadu and Kerala). Population growth is a major concern; 20 million people are born each year, putting ever more pressure on the already depleted natural resources. UN studies project that India will top 1.5 billion within 50 years, overtaking China as the most populous country on earth.

India's ethnic make-up reflects a mixture of **Aryan** peoples (see p. 65), who live mostly in the north, and **Dravidian** peoples of the south. Numerous smaller groups of **adivasi** (aboriginal peoples) are concentrated in Madhya Pradesh, Orissa, and Gujarat, though they also live in other parts of the Subcontinent. The *adivasi* pre-date the arrival of the Aryans and Dravidians in India; many of them have been subject to exploitation and have been pushed off their lands.

LANGUAGE

The people of India speak 1600 dialects of at least 18 different languages. North Indian languages such as **Hindi** and **Bengali** descended from Sanskrit, the language spoken by the Aryan invaders who wandered into the area around 1500 BC. These languages are part of the Indo-European family; it's not unusual to find North Indian words that resemble their counterparts in English or other European languages. **Urdu,** spoken by many Muslims in India, is similar to Hindi, but borrows heavily from Persian and Arabic. The major **South Indian languages,** Kannada, Telugu, Malayalam, and Tamil, belong to the Dravidian family and are unrelated to the North Indian languages. English is more prevalent in the South than in the North—partly the result of resentment over the designation of Hindi as the national language.

The 1950s reorganization of India into new states according to linguistic boundaries recognized 18 official languages—Assamese, Bengali, Gujarati, Hindi, Kannada, Kashmiri, Konkani, Malayalam, Manipuri, Marathi, Nepali, Oriya, Punjabi, Sanskrit, Sindhi, Tamil, Telugu, and Urdu. For basic vocabularies, see the **Phrasebook,** p. 933.

RELIGION

India's politics, society, and culture are all marked by religion. India's major faiths are Hinduism, Islam, Christianity, Sikhism, Buddhism, and Jainism, although a number of other religions are practiced by smaller numbers of adherents. A panoply of believers, from Agnostics to Zoroastrians, call India home.

HINDUISM

Hinduism is one of the oldest of the world's religions and has approximately 800 million followers in India alone. Worship and ritual are critical to its practice; street-side shrines and temples attract constant crowds and form the centerpiece of most cities and villages. Hinduism eludes easy definition. Unlike other religions, it has no founding figure, no single central text, and no fixed regimen of formalized practice. Instead, it is a kaleidoscope of local and regional religions, all integrated into an ever-shifting whole that manages somehow to accommodate them all.

CENTRAL HINDU BELIEFS. The doctrine of Hinduism is based on an absolute, unchanging, and omnipresent reality called **Brahman.** As the universal spirit, *Brahman* is in every individual in the form of **Atman,** the self or soul. The goal of life is to overcome the illusory separation between *Brahman* and *Atman* (known as **maya**) and achieve supreme bliss. The individual is trapped in **samsara,** the continual cycle of birth, death, and rebirth. A person is bound to the cycle of reincarnation by **karma,** the moral law of cause and effect, where present conditions are the result of past deeds. One is reborn into the world again and again until one's karmic debt has been paid. The attainment of **moksha** (liberation) for the immortal human soul is still possible, and the *Bhagavad Gita* describes four paths for making the first steps toward *moksha:* action, devotion, knowledge, and psychic exercises. Dying in the holy city of Varanasi will also grant *moksha.*

In addition to the attainment of *moksha,* there are three other aims in life. **Dharma** has several meanings, but it most commonly refers to an individual's duty to maintain social, and ultimately, cosmic order. There is also room for **kama** (sensual enjoyment) and **aartha** (wealth). Hindu thought traditionally divides life into four stages. The first 25 or so years of one's life should be devoted to the acquisition of knowledge; the second 25 to maintaining a household and fulfilling the duties to raise a family; the third stage rounds out the householder's life and is preparatory to the fourth, ascetic stage—detachment from worldly connections and complete renunciation in preparation for death.

GODS AND GODDESSES. Traditional estimates have put the number of Hindu gods and goddesses at 333 million, but no one really knows how many there are. From the central trinity of **Brahma** (Creator), **Vishnu** (Preserver), and **Shiva** (Destroyer) emerge the countless hundreds of other gods and goddesses, each one embodying an attribute of the eternal soul. The popularity of a god can vary from region to region, village to village, and family to family.

HINDU RITUALS. Hindu ritual appeals to all five senses. Contrary to appearances, the idols and images *(murti)* worshipped in temples and household prayer rooms are merely the vessels in which the deities reside. *Puja* (loosely translated as "worship") centers on these images, and acts of reverence to a god are made through offerings of food, flowers, and incense. Different ritual offerings are traditionally made to different deities, depending on each god's tastes.

In the temple, priests *(pujari)* pamper the gods by performing more elaborate *puja* services. Beginning at dawn, they bathe the image *(abhisheka)* in yogurt, milk, and *ghee.* After the bath, the deity is dressed in new clothes and adorned

A HINDU WHO'S WHO (PART ONE)

Brahma: Four-faced god, often pictured sitting on a lotus growing from Vishnu's navel. Despite his role as creator of the human world, Brahma is rarely worshipped, and only a single temple in Pushkar, Rajasthan (see p. 513) is dedicated to him.

Devi: Many Hindus worship a vast array of female deities, referred to collectively as the Devi (the Great Goddess). Goddesses embody **shakti,** the female force that drives the universe. The goddess cult probably predates worship of male gods, though specific goddesses are now incorporated into the male-dominated pantheon as consorts.

Durga: This beautiful heroine was created by the combined powers of male deities too weak to destroy the demon **Mahisha.** Durga charged forth with her trusty tiger (occasionally a lion), clutching a weapon in each of her 10 hands, and emerged victorious to save the world from destruction. Most popular in Kolkata, **Durga Puja** (see p. 757) marks this cosmic event with animal sacrifices and rites of fertility.

Ganesh: Beloved by many Hindus, this chubby, elephant-headed god, also known as **Ganpati,** is revered as the "remover of obstacles." He is often the first to be worshipped in religious ceremonies, and his image adorns the thresholds of many homes and temples. He holds various weapons in his four hands, as well as a bowl of *laddoo,* his favorite sweet. Ganesh's vehicle of choice is a mouse.

Hanuman: The flying monkey-god enjoys celebrity status in the **Ramayana** (see p. 620) as Rama's faithful sidekick. Hanuman is also a favorite of Indian wrestlers.

Kali: Although Kali is sometimes considered a consort of Shiva, she is an independent goddess of destruction in her own right. Kali is easily recognized by her terrifying appearance: long, tangled hair, dark skin, protruding red tongue, serpent bracelets, and a long necklace of freshly cut heads. She is often depicted on the battlefield as a combatant who gets drunk on her victims' blood.

with fancy accessories behind a curtain. Finally, the climactic moment arrives when the curtain is drawn back and devotees clamor for a glimpse of the deity. Bells ring out through the temple, and mantras are sung as *darshan* the auspicious eye contact between deity and worshipper, communicates divine blessing. Before leaving the temple, worshippers have their foreheads marked with ash, sandalwood paste *(sandana),* or red turmeric powder *(kumkum).* Priests also pour holy water and drop *prasad* (blessed food) into the hands of devotees.

In addition to temple rituals, Hindu ceremonies mark human rites of passage such as marriage and cremation. Festivals *(utsava)* punctuate the Hindu calendar (see **Festivals and Holidays,** p. 89). Pilgrimages *(tirtha yatra)* to the sacred points of India are also important. People travel to these holy places to seek the fulfillment of a wish, to spread the ashes of a relative in a holy river, or to boost personal health and spiritual merit. There are seven especially sacred pilgrimage destinations: Ayodhya, Mathura, Haridwar, Varanasi, Ujjain, Dwarka, and Kanchipuram.

The practice of Hinduism relies on the caste system. Ancient codes divided Hindu society into four ranks, each of which was supposed to have emerged from a different part of the primordial person, **Purusha.** The brahmin, the priestly and scholarly caste, came from his mouth; the *kshatriya,* the warrior-ruler caste, from his arms; the *vaishya,* or merchants, from his thighs; and the *shudra,* or laborers, from his feet. The group of people traditionally treated as **Untouchables,** now officially referred to as **Dalits** (the Oppressed), includes those involved in occupations like toilet-cleaning, leather tanning, and other professions considered so highly polluted that they aren't even considered *part* of the caste system. Efforts at reform and the demands of city life have done much to reduce the pernicious influence of the caste system. The notion of untouchability is on the wane, and caste in general is less likely than it once was to determine a person's social position.

A HINDU WHO'S WHO (PART TWO)

Krishna: Krishna is worshipped by followers in a variety of guises. As a young man, Krishna is adored as a cowherder who jams on his flute and cavorts in the Yamuna River. He is also respected as the philosophical charioteer of the Bhagavad Gita.

Lakshmi: A benign, feminine goddess, Lakshmi has a reputation as a bringer of luck, wealth, fertility, and general well-being. The autumn holiday of **Diwali** is an especially auspicious time of year when Hindus look to Lakshmi to bring prosperity during the new year. She is a wife of Vishnu, and is also associated with elephants.

Saraswati: Saraswati's existence can be traced back to the *Vedas,* when she was identified with the Saraswati River. Later, Saraswati's talents brought her into her current role as goddess of speech, poetry, music, culture, and learning. This pure and transcendent goddess is often depicted seated on a lotus flower, holding various objects in her four hands: a book, a rosary, a pot, and a *veena* (a stringed instrument).

Shiva: Terrifying yet compassionate, Shiva, the Destroyer, is portrayed as an uncouth ascetic who adorns himself with live cobras and leopard skins, wields a trident, and rides his bull **Nandi.** From his dreadlocked head flows the mighty **Ganga.** He is worshipped through the **linga,** a simple, phallus-shaped stone shaft fixed in a circular base called the *yoni.*

Vishnu: Though sometimes spotted relaxing upon a serpent afloat in a sea of milk, Vishnu is on call 24hr. as Preserver of the Cosmos. Time and again he has stepped in to save the universe from calamity, in the form of one of his 11 *avatars* (manifestations), which include **Rama,** the hero of the *Ramayana* (see p. 620), **Krishna,** and the **Buddha.** Vishnu, recognizable by his blue skin and four arms, travels via a man-bird named **Garuda,** and carries a discus.

LIFE AND TIMES

Politically, caste has been an increasingly important issue in recent years. Lower castes have managed to turn their strength-in-numbers into political clout, although the sheer size of the groups involved makes internal cohesion almost impossible. Lower-caste parties have gained a following in many states; the one with real nationwide appeal is the **Janata Party.** Affirmative action programs for lower-caste Hindus have also been implemented recently, and large numbers of university places and civil service jobs are now set aside for them.

ISLAM

Around 11% of India's population is Muslim, the fourth-largest Muslim population of any country in the world. Brought to India by the Afghans in the 12th century, Islam has had a profound influence on Indian culture. Religious violence between Muslims and Hindus has repeatedly been the cause of death and disruption across the nation.

HISTORY. Islam was founded by the **Prophet Mohammed,** who lived in Mecca (in what is now Saudi Arabia) during the 7th century. Between AD 610 and 622, Mohammed received a series of revelations from the angel Gabriel about the true nature of God. His teachings were received coolly in polytheistic Arabia, and he and his followers were driven from Mecca in 622; this **Hijra** (flight) to Medina marks the start of the Muslim calendar. The people of Medina were the first to embrace the new faith, and after building up an army, Mohammed returned in triumph to Mecca in 630, establishing himself as the spiritual leader of a new Muslim state. After Mohammed's death, the Muslims conquered Arabia and adjacent lands at an incredible rate, and by 711, Islam had extended its rule from Spain to Sindh (in eastern Pakistan).

Islam trickled into India slowly at first; its messengers were Arabian traders, Sufi mystics from Persia, and the armies of **Mahmud of Ghazni.** Under the **Delhi Sultanate** and then the **Mughal Empire,** Islamic influence became stronger, and after 1192, India was ruled by Muslims for more than 500 years (see **The Arrival of Islam,** p. 66). Some converted to Islam to join the new elite; many low-caste Hindus converted to escape the caste system. But the vast majority of the population always remained Hindu. Only on the eastern and western frontiers of South Asia, modern-day Pakistan and Bangladesh, did large scale conversions take place. Before the British left in 1947, they carved out the nation of Pakistan, a Muslim nation with one wing on the west and one wing on the east of India. A sizable minority of Muslims remained in India.

BELIEFS. All Muslims believe in one supreme god, **Allah,** and express their devotion to Him through the five pillars of Islam: declaration of one's faith; praying five times daily; the giving of alms *(zakat)* to the poor; fasting during the holy month of Ramadan; and making the *Hajj* (pilgrimage to Mecca) at least once in a lifetime, barring physical or financial hardship. A single holy book, the **Qur'an,** is believed to be the direct word of God as recorded by His Prophet.

Friday is Islam's holy day, when special prayers are said at the mosque. The ninth month of the Muslim calendar marks the celebration of **Ramadan,** a holiday commemorating the Prophet's receipt of the Qur'an from God, during which all Muslims (with the exception of the very young and the very sick) abstain from food and drink during daylight hours. **Muharam** memorializes the death of the Prophet's grandson, and is of particular importance to Shi'ite community, who observe Muharram with 12 days of song and prayer.

ISLAM IN INDIA. Unlike the Arab practice of Islam, often marked by doctrinal austerity, Islam in India tends to be much more devotionally and aesthetically oriented. While orthodox Islam frowns upon the notion of worshiping anyone but God, Indian Muslims have a tradition of *pir* (saint) worship, and both Muslims and Hindus make pilgrimages to *pir* shrines to pray. Art and architecture flourished under the Mughals, who often ignored the Islamic injunction against painting human and animal figures. Sufi mystics were responsible for the introduction of the **qawwali,** a melancholy devotional song akin to the Hindu *bhajan,* and the **ghazal,** poetic songs developed by Persian Muslims in India.

Islam considers all people equal and prohibits any discrimination on the basis of race, but many Muslim women stay secluded in their homes according to the custom of *purdah.* Muslims are required by the Qur'an to avoid alcohol, pork, and shellfish. Unlike Hindus, however, they do eat beef, as long as the cow has been slaughtered according to religious prescription and is *halal.* At noon on Fridays, men gather for communal prayers at the *masjid;* women usually pray at home. Most Indian Muslims speak Urdu, which is linguistically similar to Hindi.

Muslims and Hindus have coexisted in a tense sort of peace for most of their time together, but this peace has been repeatedly shattered by incidents of communal violence. As the British divided and conquered India, they inflamed tensions between the two groups. Recently, relations have worsened with the rise of Hindu nationalist groups who claim that India is a Hindu country. In December 1992, events came to a head when militant Hindus destroyed the **Babri Masjid,** a mosque in Ayodhya that was allegedly built on the site of the birthplace of Lord Rama. Hindu extremists have repeatedly demanded the right to build a Hindu temple on the site. In February 2002, a group of Hindu campaigners on their way to Ayodhya died when their train was set alight by Muslim protesters. Hindu retributions soon followed, and thousands lost their homes when Hindu extremists torched Muslim areas of the city of Ahmedabad in Gujarat.

CHRISTIANITY

Since Independence, Christianity has become increasingly visible in India, attracting followers and increasing its political relevance with a speed that would have pleased the **Apostle Thomas.** In the apocryphal *Acts of Thomas,* Thomas was chosen to spread the Gospel to India. Thomas is said to have arrived on the coast of

Kerala as early as AD 52, where he was able to attract a number of converts before being martyred near modern-day Chennai, where his remains were interred in the church that bears his name today (see p. 578).

In the 16th century, Portuguese missionaries led by the Jesuit St. Francis Xavier sought to spread Catholicism along the Konkan coast; their conversions left behind the strong Catholic enclave of modern-day Goa. The last years of British rule were marked by an increase in missionary activity, which concentrated on building schools and hospitals. Grand churches were built as well, mainly to serve the spiritual needs of the ruling Brits.

There are about 25 million Christians in India today, 50% more than there were in 1970. Most of India's Christians are Protestant; the largest denominations are the Church of South India and the Church of North India, both members of the worldwide Anglican church. There are also sizable Catholic populations, particularly in Goa. In recent years, Christians have fallen victim to a surge of Hindu nationalism, and killings and forced conversions have taken place.

SIKHISM

Guru Nanak (1469-1539), a philosopher-poet born into a *kshatriya* family in what is now Pakistan, is the venerated founder of Sikhism. After traveling to Mecca, Bengal, and many places in between, Nanak proclaimed a religious faith that fused elements of Hinduism and Islam. He followed the Islamic rejection of image-worship, borrowed Hinduism's use of music in worship, and rejected Islam's reliance on a holy book. He also discarded caste distinctions, sexual discrimination, and ancestor worship. Nanak proclaimed that the one God was **Sat** (Truth), and asserted that liberation from *samsara* was possible for those who embraced God, known to people through **gurus.** Nanak taught that bathing, the giving of alms to charity, and meditation would help to clear the way for individuals to accept God's truth.

After Nanak's death in 1539, the spiritual leadership over his *sikhs* (disciples) passed to another guru, **Angad.** Guru Angad wrote down his own, and Guru Nanak's hymns into a new script, called **Gurumukhi** (*gurmukh* means "God"), now used as the modern Punjabi script. The third guru, **Amar Das** (1509-74), encouraged Sikhs to worship publicly in temples called **gurudwaras;** the fifth guru, **Arjun Dev** (1563-1606), collected more than 5000 hymns into a book called the **Adi Granth** and founded the magnificent **Golden Temple** at Amritsar (see p. 481). During Mughal rule, there was much Mughal-Sikh tension, and the Mughal Emperor Jehangir executed Guru Arjun, ushering in an era of Mughal repression. By the time the tenth and final guru, Gobind Singh, was assassinated in 1708, raids and skirmishes had become a sad fact of life throughout Punjab, the Siwalik Hills, and other parts of northern India where large numbers of Sikhs made their homes.

Under the leadership of the tenth guru, **Guru Gobind Singh** (1666-1708), Sikhism underwent a series of changes that gave the faith a more cohesive identity. These changes and the military tradition they encouraged were an attempt to defend Sikhs against persecution. Sikh men now had to undergo a kind of "baptism": they had to pledge not to smoke tobacco, not to eat *halal* meat, and not to have sexual relations with Muslim women. They also had to renounce their caste names; men took the name **Singh** (Lion) and women took the name **Kaur** (Princess). The Khalsa also required its members to carry with them at all times the **five kakkars:** *kangah* (wooden comb), *kirpan* (sword), *kara* (steel bracelet), *kachch* (shorts), and *kesh* (uncut hair). Sikh men are identifiable by the turbans with which they wrap their long hair. Gobind Singh added new hymns to the *Adi Granth* and renamed it the **Guru Granth Sahib.** Since Gobind Singh's death, the *Guru Granth Sahib* has been the spiritual guide and holy book of the Sikhs.

LIFE AND TIMES

Although Sikhs have a strong military tradition, they also have strong traditions of equality, hospitality, and community service *(seva)*. Sikh services include *kirtan*, or hymn singing, where verses from the *Adi Granth* are sung to rhythmical clapping, after which, Sikhs gather for a meal where everybody sits at the same level and eats the same food cooked in the *gurudwara's* kitchen. Strong believers in hospitality and kindness, Sikhs offer shelter and food to those who come to their *gurudwaras*. Sikh militants and members of separatist Sikh parties of Punjab, still struggle for an independent Sikh homeland, Khalistan.

JAINISM

Jainism began as one of the alternatives to established brahmin authority that came to prominence around 500 BC. The most important element in all these new developments was the doctrine of **samsara,** the cycle of death and rebirth. People are bound to go through this cycle, birth after birth, by their **karma,** or past actions. Release from the influence of karma can be gained through the practice of austerities and meditation: Jainism, Buddhism, and the Upanishads all prescribe this sort of individual effort toward liberation. Of these three, Jainism has perhaps the most radical approach. It begins with the belief that all life is sacred and that every living being (human, animal, plant, or insect) possesses an immortal soul *(jiva)*. The obligation of **ahimsa** (non-violence) toward all living beings is therefore fundamental to Jain belief. They are strict vegetarians, and the most orthodox monks wear nets over their mouths and nostrils to prevent the possibility of killing any insects that might fly in. Agriculture is avoided, since pulling a plow through the soil would murder millions of tiny creatures. Their conscientiousness is an attempt to avoid the karmic consequences of taking life, even by accident. Monks and nuns also undertake severe austerities *(tapas)*, under which death by starvation would actually be the lofty goal.

Jainism was founded by the *kshatriya* prince Vardhamana, or **Mahavira** (Great Hero). At the age of 30, he renounced the world, plucked out all his hair, and began a new life as a wandering ascetic. Mahavira's disciples were called **Jains,** meaning "followers of the *jina* (conqueror)," and Mahavira is revered as the 24th and last of a line of **tirthankaras,** or "ford-makers," those who lead the way to another side of existence. There are two sects within Jainism: the **Digambara** (Sky-Clad) and the **Shvetambara** (White-Clad). The Digambaras are more orthodox than the Shvetambaras, and more distinctively, they do not wear any clothes.

Ornate Jain temples are found throughout India, primarily in Gujarat and along the west coast. The two most famous sites are at **Palitana** in Gujarat and **Sravanabelagola** in Karnataka (see p. 290). Today there are between four and five million Jains in India, most of them in Gujarat.

BUDDHISM

Despite of its origins in the Ganga Valley, few traces of Buddhism remain in India today. **Siddhartha Gautama,** who would come to be called the Buddha (Enlightened One), was born around 560 BC in Lumbini, just within the modern borders of Nepal (see p. 875). Gautama was born a *kshatriya* (prince), but at his birth, where he emerged from between his mother's ribs, an astrologer foretold that Siddhartha would become either a *chakravartin* (universal monarch) or an enlightened sage. In response, his father denied him freedom and lavished him with comforts and luxuries in the hope that Siddhartha would learn to appreciate life in the palace. Eventually, Siddhartha persuaded his charioteer to take him on a trip out into the world beyond the palace walls. Legend tells of his encounters with a sick man, an old man, a dead man, and a wandering ascetic.

He renounced his royal lifestyle at 29, leaving his wife, child, and kingdom to join a band of ascetics and wander the forests of India. He meditated and practiced severe austerities until he found himself on the brink of death. Realizing that neither abundant wealth nor punishing self-denial could offer release from suffering, he resolved to follow a Middle Path between the two extremes. He sat and meditated under a pipal tree in Bodh Gaya, Bihar (see p. 127), where he achieved **nirvana,** and successfully resisted the temptations offered to him by the demon **Mara.** He set off to preach the truth about suffering, and gave his first sermon in a deer park in **Sarnath** (see p. 731).

The Buddha advocated total detachment from the world. All misery stems from desire; by eliminating desire, it is possible to eliminate suffering too. Central to Buddhist doctrine is the idea of the **Four Noble Truths.** All life is suffering, and all suffering is caused by desire for physical and mental comfort. There is a way out, and that way out is the **Eightfold Path:** Right Understanding, Right Thought, Right Speech, Right Action, Right Livelihood, Right Effort, Right Mindfulness, and Right Concentration. The Buddha rejected Hinduism's gods, rituals, and its concept of an enduring soul, but he kept its doctrine of karma and rebirth. The Buddha also spoke against the caste system, and, as part of the Eightfold Path, Buddhists became advocates of **ahimsa** (non-violence).

This idea that followers should abandon all desire and worldly life put Buddhism beyond the reach of most people, and the first Buddhists tended to band together in small monastic communities. In the 3rd century BC the Mauryan Emperor **Ashoka** converted to Buddhism, and his state patronage helped to make Buddhism a major religion in India and throughout Asia. Although Buddhism had more or less died out in India by the 1st century AD, there are about 7 million Buddhists in India today, mostly in Ladakh and Sikkim, on the fringes of the Hindu world. Since the Chinese invasion of Tibet in 1959, there has been an influx of refugees, and an increased Tibetan Buddhist presence, especially in **Dharamsala** (see p. 229), home to the exiled Dalai Lama. In 1956, the champion of the Hindu Untouchables, Dr. B.R. Ambedkar, publicly converted to Buddhism as a political protest against caste discrimination; he was followed by another 200,000 Untouchables (mainly in Maharashtra). Sacred Buddhist sites like Sarnath (see p. 731) and Bodh Gaya (see p. 127) are among the most important pilgrimage centers for Buddhists, and attract millions of pilgrims every year from all over the world.

ZOROASTRIANISM

Zoroastrianism was founded in Persia between 700 and 500 BC by Zarathustra (also known as Zoroaster). The central tenet of the faith is that the world is divided between pure good (represented by the god **Ahura Mazda**) and pure evil (represented by the god **Angra Mainyu**). According to Zoroastrian belief, **Saoshyant,** an immaculately conceived messiah, will one day come to establish Ahura Mazda's reign of goodness on earth. Zoroastrians believe that burial and cremation pollute the sacred elements of earth, fire, and air, and leave their dead in specially designed **Towers of Silence,** where vultures have easy access to the bodies.

Zoroastrianism came to India in the middle of the 10th century, when Persian Zoroastrians, fleeing the advance of Islam, arrived on the Gujarati coast. Called **Parsis** because of their ancient roots in Persia, today's dwindling numbers of Indian Zoroastrians—about 95,000 are left—are concentrated in western India, especially in Mumbai. Though few in number, the Parsis are known for their great wealth. One Parsi family, the Tatas, is renowned throughout India for its manufacturing industries, and for its early support of the Independence movement.

CULTURE

CUSTOMS & ETIQUETTE

CLOTHING. Dress modestly and respectably. Only young boys wear shorts in public. Women should keep their legs covered, at least to the knee. Bare shoulders are another sign of immorality (not to mention a surefire way to get sunburned). How you dress affects the way people respond to you. In India, women will often be treated with more respect if they wear a *salwar kameez*. Men's clothing is typically more "internationalized," but men may still want to buy a thin cotton *kurta pajama*. Try to look clean and presentable. In the eyes of Indians, foreign tourists are an affluent and privileged group, and many Indians find it hard to understand why Westerners choose to dress like the poorest of India's poor. (See also **Blending In,** p. 17.)

COMMUNICATION AND BODY LANGUAGE. A quick **tilt of the head,** a sort of wobbly sideways nod, means "OK," or "I understand." Many foreigners are baffled by this gesture, thinking their hosts are answering their most innocent comments and requests with a firm "no." **Indian English,** especially when written, is full of antique civilities. You will often hear people address you as "madame" or "good gentleman," and read letters asking you to "kindly do the needful" and signed "your most humble servant."

Many foreigners have trouble adjusting to the constant **stares** they receive in India. There is no taboo against staring in South Asia and no harm is intended, but be sure not to send mixed signals. Meeting someone's gaze is often tantamount to expressing a desire for further contact. Meeting new people and talking to them about their way of life is one of the things that makes travel worthwhile, but it can be hard to sustain interest and patience if you are tired and you feel you have already answered all the same questions hundreds of times already. Remember that it is sometimes both acceptable and appropriate to ignore attempts at conversation.

FOOD. Most Indians eat with their hands, though many restaurants give cutlery to foreigners. The most important thing is to **eat with your right hand only.** The left hand is used for cleaning after defecation and is seen as polluted. You can use your left hand to hold a fork or to pass a dish, but it should never touch food or your lips directly. Any food or drink that comes into contact with one person's saliva is unclean for anyone else. Indians and Nepalis will not usually take bites of each other's food or drink from the same cup; watch how locals drink from water bottles, pouring the drink in without touching their lips. In Hindu houses, the family **hearth** is sacred. If food is cooked before you on a fire (as it frequently is in trekking lodges) never play with the fire or throw trash into it.

All Jains and many Hindus (especially in South India) are **vegetarian,** and even for non-vegetarians, meat is an expensive luxury. Because of the cow's sacred status in Hinduism, beef is scarce. Muslims don't eat pork and are supposed to shun alcohol. In many place it's considered offensive for women to drink alcohol in public.

HYGIENE. All **bodily secretions** are considered polluted. The people who come into contact with them—laundrymen, barbers, latrine cleaners—have historically formed the lowest ranks of the caste system. The **head** is the most sacred part of the body, and purity decreases all the way down to the toes. To **touch something with your feet** is a grave insult; you should never touch a person with your feet, step over a seated person's legs, or point at someone with your foot. Never put your feet on a table or any other surface. Conversely, to touch somebody else's feet is an act of veneration. If you accidentally touch someone else with your foot, touch your eyes and then their knee or foot, whichever is more accessible. The **left hand** is polluted. Always use your right hand to eat, give, take, or point.

WOMEN AND MEN. Displays of physical affection between women and men are rare. Same-sex affection, on the other hand, is considered completely natural and acceptable, and you will often see men walking down the street clasping hands. Many Indian and Nepali women are meek and quiet in public, and it is considered inappropriate for strange men to talk to them. Women travelers might find it hard to meet Indian and Nepali women, though women should always try to find other women to assist in emergencies (see **Women Travelers**, p. 47).

PLACES OF WORSHIP. Be especially sensitive about etiquette in places of worship. **Dress conservatively,** keeping legs and shoulders covered, and **take off your shoes** before entering any mosque, *gurudwara*, or temple. Visitors to Sikh *gurudwaras* and women entering Muslim mosques should cover their heads as well—handkerchiefs may be provided. At the entrance to popular temples, shoe-*wallahs* will guard your shoes for a few coins. Ask before taking **photographs** in places of worship. Taking pictures of the deities in Hindu temples is normally not allowed. Many Hindu temples, especially those in Kerala, Nepal, and in pilgrimage sites such as Puri and Varanasi, ban non-Hindus from entering. In practice this rule excludes anyone who doesn't look sufficiently South Asian. Purity laws dictate that menstruating women are forbidden to enter some Hindu and Jain temples.

It is common practice in Hindu temples to partake of offerings of consecrated fruit and water called **prasad,** which is received with the right hand over the left (and no one takes seconds). It is customary to leave a small donation at the entrance to the temple sanctuary. This can cause dilemmas when temple priests aggressively force *prasad* into your hands, expecting large amounts of cash in return. Usually a donation of one or two rupees will suffice. Hinduism and Buddhism consider the right-hand side auspicious and the left-hand side inauspicious; it is customary to walk around Hindu temples and Buddhist *stupas* **clockwise,** with your right side toward the shrine.

FOOD AND DRINK

Once upon a time, protracted Vedic prose prescribed every dash and pinch of every spice and herb, and every plate was placed to provide the therapeutic and medicinal benefits of sustenance in just the right way. Today, the main worry for many travelers is avoiding overexposure to the intense flavors of the Subcontinent's famously uncompromising cuisine. Most people in India begin the day with a small breakfast, eat lunch between noon and 2pm, enjoy sweet tea and salty snacks in the late afternoon, and eat dinner between 7 and 10pm.

Meals in India begin with the staple: usually whole wheat flatbread in the north, rice in the south and east. Since most Indians eat with their hands, the bread and rice replace cutlery and are used to scoop food from the plate into the mouth. In a typical North Indian meal, the bread is accompanied by one or two spicy vegetable dishes, a lentil soup called **dal,** and sometimes by rice and curd. The most basic bread, the **chappati** (or **roti**), is thin and round like a tortilla. Though flat when served, the *chappati* fills with hot air when cooked over an open fire. Elaborate variations on the theme include: **paratha,** a two-layered bread usually stuffed with vegetables such as onions, radishes, and potatoes, and eaten with curds at breakfast; **naan,** a chewier kind of bread made of white flour and baked in a *tandoor*, or clay oven; and **puri,** a fried version of the standard *chappati* that is generally eaten with potatoes. Common Indian rice dishes such as **biryani** or **pulao** come mixed with vegetables and occasionally meat. Most non-vegetarian options involve chicken or lamb, as beef is off-limits to Hindus and pork is unclean for Muslims.

South Indian cuisine uses rice and rice flour much more than northern dishes, with **dosas** (thin pancakes) and **idlis** (thick steamed cakes) taking center stage. These are accompanied by broths such as **sambar** (a thick and spicy lentil soup), rasam (thinner, with tomatoes and tamarind), and **kozhambu** (sour), which are poured onto the rice and mixed in with it. *Dosas* are often stuffed with spiced potatoes to make *masala dosa.* Less meat is eaten in the south, though seafood is common along the coast. A standard South Indian meal is often served on a banana leaf, or else comes in the form of a **thali,** a steel plate filled with *chappati,* rice, *sambar,* fresh yogurt, *dal,* and vegetable dishes.

Condiments like **achar** (pickles) and **papadum,** a thin, crunchy wafer that is roasted or fried serve to spice up an already spicy meal. Popular snacks include **samosa,** a spicy, fried potato turnover served with tamarind and mint sauces, and **bhel puri,** a sweet and sour mixture of fresh sprouts, potatoes, and yogurt. Desserts are often made of boiled milk, fried, and are drowned in heavy cream or whole milk flavored with pounds of sugar. For a lightweight alternative, try **paan,** the after-dinner chew that is the cause of the crimson-colored spatterings that stain every street you walk down. A *paan* leaf can be filled with everything from coconut to sweetened rose petals to flavored betel nut and tobacco.

Unfortunately, those afraid of illness often avoid many of India's delicious drinks because they contain ice cubes made of untreated water. **Lassi,** made with yogurt and sugar, salt, or fruit, and the widely sold sugarcane juice are good for cooling off. Besides the famous **chai** (tea), coffee is also popular, especially in South India.

Drinking alcohol is an accepted practice in some parts of the country, but it is frowned upon in other regions and may be hard to find (see **Drugs and Alcohol,** p. 19). Popular brands of beer include Taj Mahal and Kingfisher. Be careful when ordering difficult or obscure mixed drinks—what gets called Kahlua could taste a bit like fermented Ovaltine, and is probably an example of Indian-Made Foreign Liquor (IMFL). Imported brands are available in big cities, and not-so-good domestic wines are available at expensive restaurants.

THE ARTS

India is a country with a rich artistic tradition heavily influenced by cultural interaction with other civilizations, and diversified by numerous regional styles. Many Indian art forms originally served a religious function—for centuries, almost all art was used to decorate sacred buildings or to illustrate sacred stories. Today, art remains an important means of spiritual expression for Indians of all religions, but has also moved into the realm of the purely aesthetic, as well as providing a popular form of entertainment.

ARCHITECTURE

The typical **Hindu temple** is the result of thousands of years of evolution. Temples originally consisted of little more than a small, dark, square sanctum referred to as the *garbhagriha* ("womb chamber"), which housed the deity. A tall pyramid-shaped spire, or *shikhara,* was later added to symbolize the connection between heaven and earth. As temple architecture grew more elaborate, distinctive North Indian and South Indian styles began to emerge. In a typical northern temple, a series of four rooms leads to the sanctum. This row of spires resembles a mountain range and perhaps symbolizes the Himalayan peaks where the gods live. Some of the most stellar examples remain in **Orissa** (see p. 454) and in **Khajuraho** (see p. 369). In **South India,** the sanctum was expanded and surrounded by four rectangular entrance towers, or *gopurams,* which had *shikharas* of their own, topped by barrel-vaults. These *gopurams* eventually grew to dwarf the central *shikhara,* creating grand temple-city complexes such as the one in **Madurai** (see p. 610) in Tamil Nadu.

The conquest of India by Muslim forces in the 12th century brought the Islamic styles of Persia and Central Asia to India. Since Islam forbids the depiction of human and animal images, Muslim artists concentrated instead on pure mosque-building, dotting the landscape with gorgeous domes, arches, geometric patterns, and calligraphic inscriptions. The biggest and brightest of these Muslim jewels are the **Qutb Minar** complex in Mughal stronghold Delhi (see p. 152), the pink and red post-and-lintel buildings of the city of **Fatehpur Sikri** (see p. 700), and a little marble ditty in Agra called the **Taj Mahal** (see p. 696).

SCULPTURE

The people of the Indus Valley civilization left behind them simple terracotta figurines and seals decorated with pictures of animals and marked with a script that has still not been deciphered. Little else remains of Indian sculpture prior to the 3rd century BC, when the Mauryan emperor **Ashoka** set up stone columns all over India as a symbol of his rule (see p. 65). These columns were often topped with elaborate animal sculptures like those found at the **Lion Capital** in **Sarnath** in Uttar Pradesh (see p. 731).

The next two centuries saw the development of two-dimensional **bas-relief sculpture**, which was often used to decorate the railings of *stupas* and which usually told stories from the life of the Buddha or myths about gods and goddesses. The beginnings of classical Indian sculpture can be traced to the 1st century AD, when artists in **Mathura**, Uttar Pradesh, began to carve three-dimensional images of the Buddha (see p. 703). Influenced by Greek sculpture, Gandharan artists produced ornate images of the Buddha, emphasizing intricate folds of clothing and other details.

During the Gupta period (4th-6th centuries AD), sculpture in Mathura reached its peak. Spreading throughout North India, sculptors applied principles borrowed from Buddhist imagery to depictions of Hindu gods. Distinct regional styles developed from the Mathura style, contributing to the architectural wonders at **Sarnath** (see p. 731) and in the cave temples of **Ajanta** in Maharashtra (see p. 429).

In North India, the sensuous and voluminous figures of the Mathura style of sculpture gave way to more elegant, rhythmic forms. This style climaxed in the 10th century, when it was used to adorn the exteriors of North Indian temples. A distinctively **South Indian style** produced the 7th-century bas-reliefs of **Mahabalipuram** (see p. 585), and the miniature sculptures used to decorate temples in Tamil Nadu during the 9th century. **Bronze sculpture** in South India peaked during the 9th and 10th centuries producing images like that of Shiva as **Nataraja** (Dance King) surrounded by a ring of fire. This image is common throughout Tamil Nadu, but the one at the **Brihadishwara Temple** in Thanjavur (see p. 603) is the most famous. Regional traditions developed in other areas, such as Maharashtra, where sculptors created large, stocky figures; the **Kailasa Temple** in **Ellora** (see p. 427) is a good example.

PAINTING

The history of painting in India reaches far back to the nation's ancient history, when palm leaves served as the first canvases. The only ancient paintings that have survived are those there were sheltered by rock, like the **Buddhist wall paintings at Ajanta** in Maharashtra, dating from the 2nd century BC to the 5th century AD (see p. 429). The style of Indian painting best known today began in western India during the medieval period. Colorful, cluttered scenes with figures shown in profile were made to illustrate **Jain manuscripts.** This style gradually spread throughout the country, and was used for a wide variety of religious paintings.

The Delhi sultans and Mughal emperors who began to arrive in India after the 12th century brought with them a taste for Persian art and radically altered the course of Indian painting. **Emperor Akbar** (r. 1556-1605), a great patron of the arts, played a decisive part in the development of the Mughal school of painting. He supervised his painters closely as they produced beautiful miniature illustrations for written histories, myths, and fables. Among other works, his court artists illuminated a magnificent Persian edition of the *Mahabharata*, now kept in the City

Palace in Jaipur. As the Mughals settled in India, some Muslim artists began to disregard the Islamic injunction against the representation of human forms, and during the reign of **Jehangir** (r. 1605-27), artistic emphasis shifted to portraiture.

The delicate, detailed Mughal style influenced Hindu painting as well. Under the patronage of Hindu Rajput kings in the 16th and 17th centuries, the **Rajasthani School** emerged, combining the abstract forms of the western Indian style with some of the naturalism of Mughal art. Rajput paintings usually depicted religious subjects, especially myths about Krishna cavorting with his *gopis* (milkmaid consorts) or pining for Radha, his favorite.

The Mughal and Rajasthani styles had fallen into decline by the 18th and 19th centuries, when European art became influential. The first Indian attempts to copy European styles, known collectively as the **Company School,** were mostly lifeless engravings and watercolors. In the late 19th and early 20th centuries, artists of the Calcutta-based **Bengal School,** led by Rabindranath Tagore, combined older Indian styles with modern Western art. Twentieth century artists like Jamini Roy and M.F. Hussain combine Eastern and Western influences.

FILM

India's obsession with the movies began in 1912, when Dadasaheb Phalke produced the first Indian feature film, *Raja Harishchandra.* Referred to as "Bollywood," the Indian film industry, based in Mumbai (Bombay) is by far the most prolific in the world today (see **Bollywood Beat,** below), producing more than 800 films a year and attracting annual audiences of more than a billion people worldwide. Chennai in Tamil Nadu is home to its own booming movie industry and its own galaxy of stars (many of whom go on to play star roles in local politics after their retirement from the big screen). The appearance of the first talkie *(Alam Ara)* in 1931 split the movie-going audience along linguistic lines, but it wasn't long before directors hit on a solution, by incorporating into their films a language that nearly everyone could understand and enjoy—music. A tradition was born. Since then, some films have managed to squeeze in nearly 70 songs. By the 1940s, the introduction of pre-recorded songs and playback singing meant that actors no longer had to be singers. The most successful playback singer, **Lata Mangeshkar,** holds the world record for most songs ever recorded, having put out more than 25,000 songs during her career. Today, a film's soundtrack is almost as important for its chances of success as its plot or its big-name stars. Most of the music you hear as you travel will come from one of the latest blockbuster smashes; don't be surprised if you find yourself humming along by the end of your trip.

During the 1930s and 1940s, the **social film** served as a useful way of addressing the concerns of contemporary life. It also introduced the preference for loudness—gaudy costumes, flighty and capricious music, exciting choreography, and, wink-wink, nudge-nudge, sex—that continues to be the hallmark of Indian film to this day. The masterpieces of serious film-makers like Satyajit Ray *(Pather Panchali,* 1955) have long been acclaimed by critics around the world as some of the finest films ever made. More popular films have had to wait longer for international acceptance, but in 2002 Ashutosh Gowariker's Raj-era epic *Lagaan* was the first Indian film ever to win an Oscar nomination (for Best Foreign Film; it didn't win), and in June 2002 a major exhibit at the Victoria and Albert Museum in London brought Bollywood and its colorful history to a whole new audience. In recent years pictures such as Mira Nair's *Monsoon Wedding* have shown to huge audiences around the globe. Perhaps the world is learning to dance to the Bollywood Beat at last. For all the latest Bollywood news, consult the online edition of India's favorite *filmi* magazine, *Filmfare* (www.filmfare.indiatimes.com).

BOLLYWOOD BEAT She emerges against the backdrop of a lush green Alpine landscape, singing a love song as her sari-clad hips swing in time to the beat. Hearing her voice, he rushes in to hold her in a rapturous embrace, only to be rudely interrupted by his evil nemesis and a band of thugs sent by her panicky parents to tear the two lovers apart. A brief but boisterous scuffle ensues and our hero emerges, not a hair out of place, to return to the embrace. This utopia of romance, chivalry, and cheap thrills is available to millions in the form of the ultimate modern day kitsch, the *masala* movie, named for the cheap-but-effective spice mixture used in Indian cooking.

No city in the world produces more action, comedy, romance, and trash than Mumbai, playfully known as Bollywood. Playing to millions of people every day, churning out 800 formula flicks a year in 23 languages, and grossing more than US$850 million each year, Bollywood movie-making is big business. Popular film tabloids such as **Stardust, Filmfare,** and **Cineblitz** (available at any newsstand, and now on the web) sell thousands of copies throughout India and all over the world. Movie stars almost eclipse the gods with the size of their fan following—you'll probably run into more posters of Shahrukh than of Shiva. Until recently, however, movie-making was not considered a legitimate industry by government authorities, and film producers were forced to seek other sources of "informal" capital (i.e., the mob) to finance their projects. Bollywood bigwigs are now also starting to form alliances with studios in Hollywood in an attempt to wriggle free of the entanglements that have come to endanger their businesses and their lives.

Sometimes ridiculed for their formulaic story lines—quality typically loses out to quantity in a crushing first-round knockout—Bollywood flicks offer an easy and affordable means of escape for the average person in India, who typically wants to ignore reality or a couple of hours, not to see it re-created on the silver screen in gory technicolor. Stumble into a theater anywhere in India and you're guaranteed a good three hours or so of escapism and entertainment such as you'll find nowhere else in the world. *Let's Go* particularly recommends movies starring our mascot **Hrithik Roshan,** and no traveler to Tamil Nadu should miss the opportunity to join the masses in cheering on the Tamil people's favorite action-hero, the incomparable **Rajnikanth.**

MUSIC

The art of making music is not just entertainment in India; it is a spiritual undertaking. A piece of classical Indian music is based on a *raga* and a *tala*, which form the melodic and rhythmical framework for the piece of music respectively. In the Hindu tradition, each *raga* is associated with a different moment of the day or season of the year. *Ragas* differ from one another in scale and in *rasa* (mood). Unlike Western music with its fixed-pitch scales, the Indian musician is free to place the tonic note wherever he wishes. Once the musician has established the tone for the *raga*, he improvises within the constraints of the chosen *raga*, exploring its potential to be created anew with each performance. Opportunities for improvisation likewise exist between the fixed beats of the *tala* and its repeated rhythmical cycle.

Modern Indian classical music, often divided into northern **Hindustani** and southern **Carnatic** systems, has its origins in ancient chants. Musical form is first discussed in the *Bharata Natyashastra*, a textual source of music written between 2 BC and AD 4 by the sage Bharat. North Indian music was particularly influenced by the styles of Persia and Turkey, where court patronage of musicians from the Middle East encouraged the development of an elaborate musical culture.

Many Indian musicians have gained worldwide followings. **Ravi Shankar,** who introduced Hindustani music to Western ears during the 1960s and attracted the attention of The Beatles, is a master of the sitar, a fretted, 20-stringed instrument with a long teak neck fixed to a gourd. **Ali Akbar Khan** has amazed audiences with the strains of the sarod, a stringed instrument similar to a sitar. **Allah Rakha** and his son, **Zakir Hussain,** mesmerize audiences with their virtuosity on the tabla, two drums played together and capable of producing an incredible range of tones, and musicians like **"Mandolin" U. Srinivasan** and the legendary singer **M.S. Subbulakshmi** have ensured Carnatic music's place in Indian music history.

Folk music is linked closely to folk dance and varies from region to region. From Punjabi *bhangra* to Rajasthani *langa*, folk tunes remain close to the hearts of Indians, and have recently gained an even larger audience through the international releases of **Ila Arun** and *bhangra*-rap performers in the UK. Bengali musicians have produced their own unique genre, *Rabindrasangit*, in which the poetic words of Rabindranath Tagore are set to quasi-classical song.

Popular music ranges from the "filmi" love songs of **Lata Mangeshkar** to the disco-hybrid-pop of vocal diva, **Alisha**, whose album *Made in India* sold over one million copies in 1995. Popular vocalists include the playful and prolific **Kishore Kumar,** whose versatile voice has filled in the melodic blanks for more actors than anybody can remember, and Punjabi crooner **Daler Mehndi,** whose 1996 hit, "*Bolo Ta Ra Ra*," brought *bhangra* out of the North Indian countryside and onto satellite television, launching Indipop's international career.

DANCE

The Hindu god Nataraja, King of the Dance, has made his influence felt in every sphere of Indian life. Indian dance forms, both classical and folk styles, evolved as acts of worship that dramatized myths and legends. Technique and philosophy, passed down from gurus to students, have carried the "visual poetry" described in the *Natya Shastra* (dating from between the 2nd century BC and the 2nd century AD), into modern times. **Bharatnatyam,** India's most ancient dance form, originated in the temples of Tamil Nadu where dancers performed intricate, fluid combinations of eye movements, facial expressions, hand gestures, and strong, rhythmic steps. It was originally studied as a form of worship, and performed by *devadasis*, women who lived in temples and devoted their lives to the temple's deity. **Kathak,** first performed by *nautch* (dancing courtesans) against the opulent backdrop of North India's Mughal courts, is remarkable for the dizzying speed of its characteristic footwork and hand gestures (see **Nrityagram Dance Village,** Bangalore, p. 280 and **Lucknow,** p. 707). Developed from a rigorous system of yoga, **Kathakali,** an elaborately costumed form of dance-drama unique to Kerala, presents mythological stories of heroes, lovers, gods, and battles (see **Cochin,** p. 331). The dancers, all male, must study for a minimum of 15 years before they are considered ready to come out and strut their stuff.

SPORT

Cricket isn't just a game in India—it's a national obsession. Indians turn out in their thousands to watch the big games, and an informal game or two seems to be constantly underway on every street corner in the country, often played by young boys using sticks for bats and bricks for wickets. Like many other former colonies, India regularly beats England at its own game these days. One of the few occasions when India is able to forget its internal conflicts and come together as one nation comes whenever the Indian cricket team plays against arch-rival, Pakistan. **Test matches** are watched by millions of people across India—huge crowds gather wherever there's a game being shown on TV. The gentleman's game had its reputation dragged through the dirt as the new millennium began, when allegations of dodgy dealings with shady betting syndicates brought many of India's national heroes out of the dressing room and into court to answer charges of game-fixing and bribe-taking.

India is also a consistent Olympic medal-winner at field hockey. Soccer and horse racing are especially popular in the east and in urban areas. **Kabbadi,** a breathless game of tag, is popular throughout the north.

HOLIDAYS AND FESTIVALS

Hindu, Muslim, Sikh, Buddhist, and Jain festivals correspond to the lunar calendar, so the dates vary from year to year with respect to the Gregorian calendar; the dates given are approximate. Secular holidays in India are dated according to the Gregorian calendar. The dates given here are for 2004.

LIFE AND TIMES

DATE	HOLIDAYS AND FESTIVALS
January 1	**New Year's Day.** This Indian festival culminates in drunken revelry at midnight. Held annually.
January 5	**Guru Gobind Singh's Birthday,** celebrated by Sikhs everywhere; particularly important in the Punjab.
January 26	**Republic Day,** one of India's four national public holidays; highlights include a military parade in New Delhi.
January - February	**Kite Festival, Rajasthan**
February 18	**Maha Shivaratri,** an all-day, all-night Hindu festival dedicated to Shiva, whose creation dance took place on this day.
February 22	**Muharram** commemorates the martyrdom of the Prophet Mohammed's grandson; especially important for Lucknow Muslims.
March 6	**Holi,** a rowdy Hindu festival of color celebrated by throwing colored water and powder at each other.
April 13	**Vaisaki,** the Sikh festival celebrating the day Guru Gobind Singh founded the Khalsa; features readings of the Guru Granth Sahib, besides major feasting.
Late April (approx.)	**Mahavira Jayanti,** Jainism's major festival, celebrates the birthday of its founder.
May 2	**Milad-un-Nabi (Eid-ul-Mulad),** the Prophet Mohammed's birthday.
May 4	**Buddha Jayanti** honors the Buddha's birthday and his attainment of *nirvana.*
June 23	**Rath Yatra,** commemorates the journey Krishna made to Mathura; Hindus throng the Jagannath's Temple in Puri and cities in the South.
August 15	**Independence Day,** India's biggest national holiday.
August 21	**Zoroastrian New Year's Day,** celebrated by Parsis in India.
August 30	**Raksha Bandhan** celebrates the Hindu sea god Varuna; the holiday is associated with brother and sisters.
September 6	**Krishna Jayanti,** Krishna's birthday.
September 17	**Ganesh Chaturthi** is when Hindus venerate the chubby elephant-headed god of obstacles with spectacular processions, especially in Mumbai and Rajasthan.
October 15	**Ramadan** begins. A 28-day period
October 22	**Dussehra** (also known in some parts as **Navaratri**), a 9-10-day festival, celebrates the vanquishing of demons and honors Durga, the demon-slaying goddess. Known as **Durga Puja** in West Bengal.
November 5-8	**Pushkar Mela (Pushkar Camel Fair),** held at the sacred lake at Pushkar, Rajasthan. Camels and pilgrims galore.
November 12	**Diwali (Deepavali),** a five-day festival of lights celebrating Rama and Sita's homecoming as per the *Ramayana.*
November 14	End of **Ramadan,** a 28-day period when Muslims fast. Fasting ends with **Eid-ul-Fitr,** a three-day feast celebrating the Prophet's recording of the word of God in the Holy Koran.
November 23-26	**Pushkar Mela (Pushkar Camel Fair),** held at the sacred lake at Pushkar, Rajasthan. Camels and pilgrims galore.
November 26	**Guru Nanak Jayanti,** the birthday of the founder of Sikhism.

ADDITIONAL RESOURCES

For a list of useful India-related websites, see **World Wide Web,** p. 50

For a list of useful India-related websites, see **World Wide Web,** p. 50

GENERAL

Scoop-Wallah, by Justine Hardy (2000). Young English journalist's engaging account of a year spent working on *The Indian Express* in Delhi. Full of self-deprecating humor and minutely observed vignettes.

Travels On My Elephant, by Mark Shand (paperback reprint 1998). Hilarious and often touching memoir of a British writer's trek across India on the back of an elephant. The sequel, *The Queen of the Elephants,* is also worth a read.

Tropical Classical, by Pico Iyer (1997). Essays and articles culled from the last 10 years of the journalist's career. Always entertaining, and the history of the Raj is solid, as are the pieces set in Mumbai and Nepal.

In Light of India, by Octavio Paz (1997). Nobel laureate's perceptions of India based upon his time as Mexico's man in New Delhi.

Culture Shock! India, by Gitanjali Kolanad (2001). A guide to Indian customs and etiquette for those planning to live and work in India, with useful advice for dealing with all sorts of social situations and bureaucratic hassles.

The Great Railway Bazaar, by Paul Theroux (1975). A classic, worth reading for descriptions of a snooty Westerner jammed on a train with hundreds of others.

HISTORY

Modern South Asia: History, Culture, and Political Economy, by Sugata Bose and Ayesha Jalal (1998). A controversial volume by two of the most prominent historians of South Asia that questions the traditional dichotomy between India's "democracy" and Pakistan's "authoritarianism."

A Traveller's History of India, by Sinharaja Tammita-Delgoda (2002). A clear and readable introduction to Indian history, with references to sites that can be visited today.

Sources of Indian Tradition, by Ainslie Thomas Embree and Stephen Haye (1988). This comprehensive sourcebook of Indian history follows the country's important texts from pre-historic times to the mid-eighteenth century, with valuable commentary and introductions to the country's major religions.

The Discovery of India, by Jawaharlal Nehru (1946). Indian history as seen by the founder of modern India—a classic.

An Autobiography, or, the Story of My Experiments with Truth, by Mohandas K. Gandhi (1927). Gandhi's personal account of the development of his beliefs, with surprisingly little commentary on the political events of the time.

POLITICS AND ECONOMICS

India: Government and Politics in a Developing Nation, by Robert L. Hardgrave, Jr. and Stanley A. Kochanek (1996). The best summary of recent Indian political issues and the government of modern India.

India: Economic Development and Social Opportunity, by Jean Drèze and Amartya Sen (1995). Analyzes the economic development of India from a social perspective and with empathy for the underprivileged.

LIFE AND TIMES

No Full Stops in India, by Mark Tully (1992). Thoughtful collection of essays by former BBC correspondent, focusing on contemporary politics and current affairs.

A Million Mutinies Now, by V.S. Naipaul (1991). Nobel Prize-winner's examination of how individuals from different backgrounds cope with the tensions threatening to crack the peaceful veneer of modern India apart. Insightful, ambitious, and beautifully written.

RELIGION

The Sikhs: Their Religious Beliefs and Practices, by W. Owen Cole and Piara Singh Sambhi (1998). A good, succinct survey of the Sikh religious tradition.

Islam: The Straight Path, by John L. Esposito (1998). An excellent introduction. Esposito traces the development of Islam from its beginnings down to the present day.

Hinduism: A Cultural Perspective, by David R. Kinsley (1993). A comprehensive, thematic introduction to Hindu beliefs, practices, and culture.

Karma Cola, by Gita Mehta (1979). A cynical journalistic satire about Western infatuation with "spiritual" India.

What The Buddha Taught, by Walpola Rahula (1959). A Sri Lankan monk's authoritative and easy-to-follow explanation of Theravada Buddhist philosophy.

GENDER ISSUES

Neither Man Nor Woman: The Hijras of India, by Serena Nanda (1998). A well-researched ethnography of India's transvestite *hijra* community.

May You Be the Mother of a Hundred Sons, by Elizabeth Bumiller (1990). A British journalist's exploration of *sati,* sex-selective abortion, and dowry deaths, this is a good introduction to Indian society and politics, with a great chapter on Hindi film actresses.

FICTION

The Vintage Book of Indian Writing, edited by Salman Rushdie and Elizabeth West (1998). Superb anthology of Indian prose writing in English, published to celebrate 50 years of independence.

Love and Longing in Bombay, by Vikram Chandra (1997). Seven very different stories, all superbly told. Ghosts, soldiers, society ladies, and computer programmers are all brought to life in lean, perfectly chiselled prose.

The God of Small Things, by Arundhati Roy (1997). An exquisitely woven story of love, betrayal, and tragedy set against the backdrop Kerala's social and political landscape.

A Suitable Boy, by Vikram Seth (1994). If you're only going to take one book with you, it may as well be this one. Huge, sprawling, vividly imagined novel set in 1950s UP. Long enough for coast-to-coast train journeys, and heavy enough to swat rats with.

Such a Long Journey, by Rohinton Mistry (1992). A humanely written tale of Mumbai Parsis (Zoroastrians) who inadvertently become involved in Indira Gandhi's government corruption; a great read with an introduction to Parsi culture and India in the 1970s.

A Strange and Sublime Address, by Amit Chaudhuri (1991). Masterful evocation of boyhood memories of Bombay and Calcutta, marked by richly poetic language and telling attention to detail.

Malgudi Days, by R.K. Narayan (1986). One of India's first English-language writers as well as one of its best, Narayan spent most of his long career in the Indian South. No post-colonial angst here, just subtle, wry, and charming stories set in a fictional village in Tamil Nadu.

Midnight's Children, by Salman Rushdie (1980). Rushdie's masterpiece tells the magical tale of children born at midnight on the eve of Independence, and how the country's life and theirs evolve together.

A Passage to India, by E.M. Forster (1924). This classic novel tells the story of a friendship between an Englishman and an Indian during the British Raj. An honest, sensitive account whose observations about culture shock still hold true today.

POETRY

Sanskrit Poetry From Vidyakara's "Treasury", by Daniel Ingalls (paperback reprint 2000). Beautifully translated selections from an 11-century anthology of the best of classical Sanskrit verse.

Gitanjali, by Rabindranath Tagore (1913). Nobel prize-winning work of the great Bengali poet, it uses images from Indian love poetry to discuss a relationship with God.

FILMS

Monsoon Wedding, by Mira Nair (2002). Winner of the Lion d'Or at the Venice Film Festival, a poignant and dramatic look at middle-class family life in contemporary Delhi.

Lagaan, by Ashutosh Gowariker (2001). Heroic story of a team of poor villagers who defeat their British rulers in a game of cricket and win immunity from crippling land taxes. Much more fun than it sounds.

Fire, by Deepa Mehta (1996). The story of two women bound by culture and longing for love who eventually find consolation with each other. The film was banned in India for its depiction of lesbianism and is the first of an Earth, Fire, Air trilogy by Mehta.

Muthu, by A.R. Rahman (1995). A heroic man of the people, a beautiful princess, and lots of dark family secrets...and that's just the start of it! A light-hearted, thrill-a-minute epic that never takes itself too seriously, this is an example of the mass-market Indian blockbuster at its best. Tamil folk hero Rajnikanth shines in the title role.

Bandit Queen, by Shekhar Kapur (1994). The story of Phoolan Devi, a low-caste bandit-turned-politician. A horrifyingly graphic, true-life portrayal of caste oppression in UP.

Salaam Bombay, by Mira Nair (1988). A disturbing tale of Bombay's street children. This fictional story told in documentary style is somewhat exploitative, but it's a moving and well-acted film.

Pather Panchali, by Satyajit Ray (1955). The first film by the late master of Indian cinema. Produced on weekends with a borrowed camera and unpaid actors. Its visuals capture the beauty of the Bengali landscape and the isolation of the village where Apu and Durga, the hero and heroine, live. Musical accompaniment by Ravi Shankar.

When I paid my first visit to Karaikkudi Veena Lakshmi Ammal of Madurai, Tamil Nadu, in 1982, the prominent music teacher eyed me with reserve. In earlier times, masters of note would choose their disciples; not vice-versa. I fervently hoped that Laskmi Ammal would teach me to play the veena, a lute-type South Indian classical instrument, and I needed to win my future guruji's respect. The veena's rich, mellow sounds had piqued my musical interest, steering me away from what I had heard, growing up, of North Indian music—mostly the swelling overtones and exciting attacks of the sitar in Beatles' songs and Ravi Shankar records.

A veena is four feet in length with a scalloped fingerboard fashioned of wax; its carved belly on one end is balanced by a painted, gourd-shaped resonator on the other. The Hindu god Siva was inspired to create the veena, one myth recounts, when he observed his divine consort Parvati lying with her arm draped across her breasts. The image of her curled hand became the pegboard upon which the four main playing strings are fastened. The veena's notable ornament is the carved head of the mythical Yali, craned away from the frets in a display of the toothy beast's submission to the instrument's charming melodies. The veena is also said to embody Sarasvati, the goddess of music and learning in whose arms the instrument is depicted in Indian iconography.

Accepting a student in South Indian classical (Karnatak) music is a sacred trust, in part because the melodies and rhythms of Indian music are considered perfect forms, the improper treatment of which is considered almost sinful. Celestial beings are believed to physically suffer when a raga (a melodic framework for improvising or composing) is improperly rendered. One's first lesson and first performance, then, are marked by special rituals, and well-known artists formally acknowledge their gurus on stage. Bharata Natyam dancers, for example, execute a choreographed obeisance to the teacher at the beginning of each class and virtually every recital. Even people who are not religious regard performing and listening to Karnatak music in all its aspects—sounds, instruments, and texts—as a spiritual exercise

A similar spiritual association adheres to many of the Indian subcontinent's panoply of musical traditions, including types of melodic recitation that would not locally be termed "musical," such as Muslim praise—poems in honor of the Prophet Muhammad. Even popular film music provides a setting for symbolic narratives of the undying earthly and spiritual quests of the lover for the beloved.

Classical North and South Indian music continues to be taught in ways that resemble those of the old days. However, students may now learn from a variety of teachers rather than just one; they partake of an intellectual, musicological tradition of representing music that is thousands of years old in India, but was not always as accessible as it is today. Such institutional study constitutes a move away from the orientation of some traditional teachers who emphasize "practice" over "theory." True knowledge, to many musicians, lies in the ability to actually play music well. My teacher was fond of saying that music is more difficult than other subjects: in other subjects, one can study hard and memorize the relevant material the night before (especially true in Indian schools which focus on rote learning); if one has not practiced regularly, however, no amount of practice on a single day can give the student the skill and musicianship to deliver a convincing performance.

The texture of the teacher-student (guru-shishya) relationship has changed noticeably in much Indian music instruction. In earlier times, students would perform household chores and run errands for their teachers, and even live with them. Money was less important than the work and devotion a student demonstrated for the guru. While a small minority cling on to this way of teaching, most private teachers accept monetary payments, usually according to the means of the family or individual paying. Music colleges charge tuition, adhere to admissions dates, administer examinations, and schedule classes just like other colleges.

Yet it would be too much to assume from this that something essential has been lost in the social and cultural life of music making in South India. In line with what Lakshmi Ammal used to say, the most important things are still "affection" between teacher and student, and respect for the tradition. My own story, which ends with a beginning, illustrates this. Lakshmi Ammal did agree to take me on as a student. I overcame a few initial gaffes, such as deciding to jump across the veena (and thus inadvertently sullying the instrument by raising my feet over it) rather than navigate around it. I also managed to hold my characteristic impatience at bay long enough to learn a discipline that can only be acquired over time. Twenty-one years later, I may still have much to learn, but have certainly been known to bark at any student of mine who might casually step over her instrument.

Richard K. Wolf is a professor in the Music Department at Harvard University. He specializes in South Asian musical traditions.

Find (Our Student Airfares are cheap, flexible & exclusive) great Student Airfares everywhere at StudentUniverse.com and **Get lost.**

 StudentUniverse.com

Student Airfares everywhere

ANDAMAN ISLANDS

अंदमान द्वीपसमूह

Mobs of backpackers and Indian tourists have made the Andaman dream of secluded beaches and pristine coral little more than wishful thinking. Much of the natural splendor and marine wildlife remain as breathtaking as ever, but be prepared to see more wild Israelis than wild sea turtles. During colonial times, the British built a penal colony here to imprison agitators against colonial rule. Since Independence, the Indian government has developed an anthropological interest in the indigenous inhabitants. Because the Andaman and Nicobar Islands (the latter being off-limits to foreigners) are administered directly from Delhi, the quality of the roads and infrastructure here is far above the Indian average. The population is a mishmash of ethnic groups from around the Subcontinent; Telugu and Bengali speakers are the most numerous. Rising awareness of the islands' natural wealth has led to increased efforts to make sure that they survive. Temperatures hover around 30°C (86°F) all year. The monsoon lasts from late May to September.

HIGHLIGHTS OF THE ANDAMAN ISLANDS

The stunning underwater scenery of **Mahatma Gandhi National Marine Park** (p. 101) will have you jumping overboard to cavort with the fish.

Ritchie's Archipelago (p. 101) is a paradise of white sand, wild jungle, and a few isolated villages, with abundant tropical fruit for beach picnics.

PORT BLAIR ᴾ पोर्ट ब्लैअर   ☎ 03192

Port Blair hasn't changed much since its days as a British penal colony, leaving nothing much to see or do in the capital. Corbyn's Cove, the one beach, is crowded, remote, and not that beautiful. But since Port Blair is the only town approaching city status on the Andamans, it is an important place to buy a hammock and stock up on camping, snorkeling, and diving supplies.

▐▔ TRANSPORTATION

Flights: The **airport** is on Jungleghat Rd., 3km south of Aberdeen Bazaar. Public buses leave from the bus stand (every 30min. 5am-8:30pm, Rs3). Auto-rickshaws to the airport cost Rs40. **Indian Airlines** (☎ 233108), across from the tourist office, flies to **Chennai** (2hr.; M, W, F, Su 8:05am; US$205) and **Kolkata** (2hr., 7:30am, US$205). Open M-Sa 9am-1pm and 2-4pm. **Jet Airways** flies to **Chennai** (2hr., 9:15am, US$205).

Ships: Enhance your Andaman experience with a voyage across the Bay of Bengal. Four sailings per month connect the Islands to **Kolkata** (90hr.); three sailings head to **Chennai** (65hr.). Prices are the same for all crossings (bunk Rs1272; 2nd-class cabin Rs3112; 1st-class cabin Rs3932). It's worth shelling out a bit of extra cash to get a cabin since rough seas and weak stomachs make the toilet-less bunks a less-than-pleasant option. The **Directorate of Shipping Services** (☎ 234299), in the Phoenix Bay Jetty, sells tickets for Chennai at its computerized ticketing center. The **Shipping Corporation of India** office (☎ 233590; fax 233778), in Aberdeen Bazaar, sells for Kolkata. Open daily 9am-12:30pm. **Note:** tickets go on sale 3 days before departure and Oct.-Mar. sell out within a day. However, to accommodate teachers who leave the Andamans for holiday at the

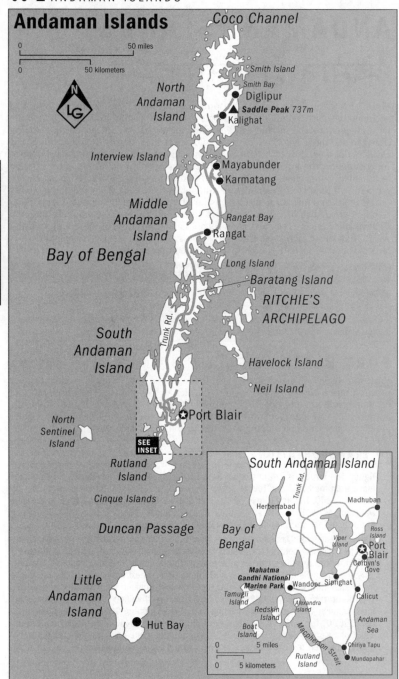

Andaman Islands

Coco Channel

0 _____ 50 miles
0 _____ 50 kilometers

Smith Island

North
Andaman
Island

Smith Bay

● Diglipur
▲ **Saddle Peak** 737m
● Kalighat

Interview Island

● Mayabunder
● Karmatang

Middle
Andaman
Island

Rangat Bay

● Rangat

Bay of Bengal

Long Island

Baratang Island

RITCHIE'S
ARCHIPELAGO

South
Andaman
Island

Trunk Rd.

Havelock Island

Neil Island

North
Sentinel
Island

★ Port Blair

SEE INSET

Rutland
Island

Cinque Islands

Duncan Passage

Little
Andaman
Island

● Hut Bay

Inset: South Andaman Island

Trunk Rd.

Herbertabad

Madhuban

Ross
Island

Bay of
Bengal

Viper
Island

★ Port
Blair
Corbyn's Cove

**Mahatma
Gandhi National
Marine Park**

Wandoor ● Sippighat

Tamugli
Island

Alexandra
Island

Redskin
Island

Calicut

Andaman
Sea

Boat
Island

Macpherson Strait

Rutland
Island

Chiriya Tapu
● Mundapahar

0 ___ 5 miles
0 ___ 5 kilometers

ANDAMAN ISLANDS

end of the term, a 2-month advance booking policy is in effect Apr.-June, on a competitive first-come, first-serve basis. If the official avenues inform you that all ships are sold out, it is often still possible to dredge up a ticket from the travel agents in the Bazaar, for an extra Rs500-600 on top of the actual price. The tourist office sometimes posts current sailing details on the bulletin board, but you are better off checking the schedules published in the *Daily Telegram,* available at newsstands. The Inter Island Ticketing Counter at **Phoenix Bay Jetty,** a short walk west of the bus stand, sells tickets for destinations within the Andamans a day prior to departure (if there is still space). Open daily 9am-noon. Tickets can also be bought on board for double the price. Andaman ferry schedules vary greatly, so its best to check at the jetty first when planning. Speed boat to: **Havelock** (2hr.; most days 7am; chair Rs39, cabin Rs117) via **Neil Island** (3hr., Rs16). Some days the boat continues on to **Rangat** (4hr., Rs74). Slow boat to: **Diglipur** via **Mayabunder** (14hr., Tu morning and F afternoon, Rs74); **Havelock** (9hr., Rs45) via **Long Island** (7hr., Rs45); **Hut Bay** (8½hr.; M, W, F 6:30am; chair Rs43, cabin Rs139); **Ross Island** (20min., Th-Tu 4 per day, Rs20). Sightseeing boats to **Mahatma Gandhi National Marine Park** leave from **Wandoor Jetty,** 36km from the city (5hr.; Tu-Su 10am; Rs125 for Jolly Buoy, Rs90 for Red Skin Island).

Buses: Government bone-shakers leave from the bus station (☎232278) in Aberdeen Bazaar for: **Mayabunder** (9hr., 5am, Rs95) via **Rangat** (6hr., Rs65) and **Wandoor** (1½hr.; 5:30, 8:30am, 9am-4:30pm; Rs9). Private coaches depart from the lot next door. Ask the ticket-*wallahs* on the buses for route information. **Dolphin Travels** (☎240116), at the rear of the non-government bus stand, runs luxury service to **Rangat** (6hr., 11:25pm, Rs130) and **Mayabunder** (8hr., 4:35am, Rs160). The ferry connects with the bus in Mayabunder for **Diglipur** (2hr., Rs20). Buses are less comfortable than ferries, but you may see indigenous Jarawa tribesmen on northbound routes.

ENTRY REQUIREMENTS. For those arriving by air, a permit issued on arrival covers all of the Andaman Islands except the indigenous Jarawa reserve and several wildlife sanctuaries (such as Smith Island). The latter require a special permit issued by the Forest Ranger Office in Diglipur. Almost all travelers will receive 30-day permits if they request them. Those arriving by sea should contact the **Deputy Commissioner** (☎33089), next to the ADN Tourism Office. Extensions are rarely issued. Travelers report that minor overstays go unpunished, but don't press your luck. **The Nicobar Islands are off-limits to foreigners.**

Local Transportation: Most distances are walkable, though the terrain is hilly. **Auto-rickshaws** go anywhere in central Port Blair for Rs10-20, but a trip to Corbyn's Cove costs Rs60. **Jagganath Guest House** rents **motorbikes** (Rs150 per day). **TSG Autos,** Aberdeen Bazaar, also rents motorbikes. (☎232894. Rs150 per day, Rs500 deposit; mopeds Rs100.) **Patel Cycle Center,** behind the bus stand, has the best bicycles for hire in town (Rs35 per day). Open M-Sa 9am-7pm.

▦ 🔂 ORIENTATION AND PRACTICAL INFORMATION

Aberdeen Bazaar, at the north end of Port Blair, is the city's main commercial district. Downhill to the west are the **bus stand** and **Phoenix Bay Jetty.** The level road leads east to **Netaji Stadium,** and curves along the coast for 5km to **Corbyn's Cove.**

Tourist Office: The **A&N Islands Tourism Office** (☎232747 or 232694; fax 230933), in the tall, spiffy-looking building at the top of a hill, near the Secretariat. Bookings for all government accommodations *must* be made through this office or through the branch at the airport. Most of the major islands have government rest houses; fewer have private accommodations. Open M-F 8:30am-4:45pm, Sa 8:30am-12:30pm.

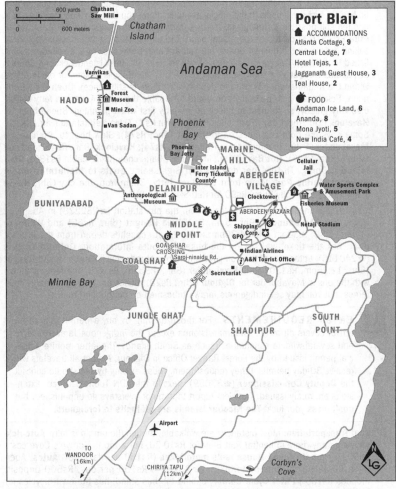

Port Blair

▲ ACCOMMODATIONS
Atlanta Cottage, **9**
Central Lodge, **7**
Hotel Tejas, **1**
Jagganath Guest House, **3**
Teal House, **2**

🍴 FOOD
Andaman Ice Land, **6**
Ananda, **8**
Mona Jyoti, **5**
New India Café, **4**

Currency Exchange: The **State Bank of India,** opposite the bus stand. Open M-F 10am-2pm, Sa 10am-noon. **Island Travels** (☎233358), 60m east of the clock tower, is a better bet. Open daily 9am-6:30pm; off-season 3-4pm. **ICICI Bank,** one block east of the State bank has a **24hr. ATM** that accepts MC/V.

Police: Aberdeen Bazaar (☎232400). **Superintendent of Police** (☎233077), behind the Tourist Office.

Pharmacy: Devraj Medical Store, Hosptial Rd. (☎234344), in the bazaar, opposite the stadium. Open daily 8am-1pm and 2-8pm.

Hospital: G.B. Panth Hospital (☎232102), has ambulance service.

Post Office: GPO (☎232226). From the tourist office, go downhill and turn right at the 1st intersection. Open M-Sa 9am-12:30pm and 1-3pm. **Postal Code:** 744101.

░ ACCOMMODATIONS

Hotels in Port Blair, crowded around Aberdeen Bazaar, are a far cry from the cheap tranquility that awaits only a ferry ride away. The ocean front options are both more peaceful and expensive. All hotels have 7 or 8am check-out policies; most offer a 25% discount from May to September. All government accommodations on the islands require prior booking, either in-person or over the phone, through the tourism offices in Port Blair.

Central Lodge (☎233634), in Goalghar. The ultimate budget guest house. Clean and comfy rooms are barely divided by wooden slats. Common bath. A great place to socialize with other travelers. Camping Rs50; singles Rs70; doubles Rs100-120. ❶

Teal House, J. Nehru Rd. (☎234060 or 234061), a 15min. walk up Moulana Azad Rd. from the bus station. Sweet-smelling, carpeted rooms with a wonderful hilltop view. Telephones, bamboo furniture, mosquito nets, and big bathrooms with hot showers. Book in advance with the tourist office. Doubles Rs400, with A/C Rs600. ❸

Jagganath Guest House, Moulana Azad Rd. (☎232148). Well-kept rooms have balconies, bathrooms, and free filtered water. Snorkeling equipment (Rs50 per day) and attached motor bikes (Rs150 per day) available. Singles Rs200; doubles Rs300. ❷

Hotel Tejas, J. Nehru Rd. (☎237760 or 230360), 1km past Teal House, just after the Forest Museum. Rooms have ocean views over the relaxed neighborhood of Haddo, cable TV, and attached bathrooms. Internet access downstairs. Singles Rs300; doubles Rs550, with A/C Rs750. ❷

Atlanta Cottage, Medical Rd. (☎241449), overlooking Netaji stadium. Meticulous rooms with TV and attached baths—those in front are light and open to ocean breezes. Multi-windowed 2nd fl. restaurant ensures you won't miss the ocean view, even if your room does. Curfew 10pm. Doubles Rs350, with ocean view Rs500; triples Rs650. ❸

▟ FOOD

China Room. From the *jama masjid* (mosque) near Aberdeen Bazaar, walk uphill, turn left in front of the government middle school, then continue a few blocks. Fresh seafood in an intimate garden away from the Aberdeen Bazaar bustle. Succulent shark and barracuda Rs100. Open daily 6-10pm. ❸

Andaman Ice Land, 1 block north of Goalghar Crossing. A dazzling array of Arun brand ice cream and confections. Everything from the kulfi classic (Rs28) to ice-cream cake (Rs38) and a vanilla party pack (1000ml tub Rs134). Open daily 9am-10pm. ❶

Ananda, Aberdeen Bazaar, 50m uphill from the clock tower, opposite the police station. Crabs, prawns, fish, chickens, all recently killed and spiced with a thousand seasonings. Ginger chicken Rs50, fish *pakora* Rs32. Open daily 6:30am-10:30pm. ❷

New India Cafe, near the bus stand, 40m before Jagganath Guest House. Frequented by Indian sailors at lunch and a foreign crowd during the evenings. This is the place to go to pick up hand-drawn maps of treasure islands and hear accounts of stormy sailings. Fish *thali* Rs45, prawn coconut curry Rs40. Open daily 6am-11pm.❷

Mona Jyoti Rubber Stamp Shop and Eatery, 20m down the road from New India Cafe. One tiny room packed with locals gulping down egg curries and fried fish along with *sambar*-soaked *dosas* and *sabzi*-laden rice. Meals Rs25. Open daily 6am-11pm. ❶

◉ SIGHTS

CELLULAR JAIL AND MUSEUM. The British locked up political dissidents in the Andamans Cellular Jail. If exile from the mainland didn't stifle a dissident, he was led to the gallows, now visible in the central courtyard. Since then, the jail has been transformed into a monument to India's struggle for independence. The museum's ground floor galleries chart the history of the prison and document Indian resistance to colonialism. *(From the clock tower, walk toward the ocean; bear left and head uphill. ☎230117. Jail open daily 9am-5pm; museum open Tu-Su 9am-noon and 2-5pm. Sound and light show Tu-Su 7:15pm, weather permitting. Free.)*

OTHER SIGHTS. The one-room **Zonal Anthropological Museum** displays photos and artifacts taken from the Islands' indigenous peoples. *(Open Tu-Su 9:30am-12:30pm and 1-4pm. Free.)* A better bet for getting information about the indigenous cultures of the Andaman and Nicobar Islands would be the Tourism Department's **free documentary screenings.** *(M-F 5:30pm; information at the Teal House.)* A 15min. bike ride along the coast from the Netaji Stadium leads to **Corbyn's Cove**, a beach surrounded by palms. The cove is more beautiful than any other spot in Port Blair, but packed with tourists. Port Blair's **Water Sports Complex and Amusement Park** makes for a fun evening. *(Open M-Sa 4-8pm.)*

NEAR PORT BLAIR

SOUTH ANDAMAN ISLAND

On the northeast side of South Andaman, **Ross Island** was once the center of operations for the British penal colony. The ruins are a surreal place to wander around for the day. **Ferries** leave from Phoenix Bay Jetty (2hr.; Tu-Th 8:30, 10am, 12:30, 2pm; Rs15). The last ferry back to Port Blair leaves at 5:30pm. **Viper Island** is also dominated by the haunting, overgrown ruins of the British penal project. You can reach Viper on the **Harbour Cruise,** which leaves daily from Phoenix Bay Jetty (2hr., Th-Tu 3pm, Rs25). **Chiriya Tapu** is a fishing village at the south end of South Andaman, 30km from Port Blair. The road winds through countryside and jungle until it reaches mangroves and wooded mountains that rise from the sea. Most people come on a day trip from Port Blair to the **Mundapahar beach and wildlife area,** 2km past the village. In the **Forest Department Guest House ❸,** you can find two A/C rooms overlooking the bay; get permission from the Chief Wildlife Warden, Van Sadan, Haddo, Port Blair. (☎2233549. Open M-F 8:30am-4:30pm. Rs400.) This is an excellent snorkeling area; get equipment in Port Blair and hire a motorboat in Chiriya Tapu to take you to the reefs.

LITTLE ANDAMAN

Sparsely settled by Bangladeshis and Nicobarese and Onges tribes, this is the southernmost point open to foreign tourists. Boats from Port Blair sail to Hut Bay (9hr.; M, W, F 6:30am; chair Rs43, cabin Rs139; return ferries depart at 8pm). **Forest Corporation Guest House ❷,** in Hut Bay (doubles Rs200), and **Butler Bay Beach Resort ❷,** 14km north along the road from Hut Bay Jetty (huts Rs200, cottages Rs400) provide a place to stay. Booking for both should be done in Port Blair at the **Vanvikas Eco Tourism** section of the Forest Development Corporation, 36 J. Nehru Rd., Haddo. (☎233212. Open M-F 8:30am-5pm.) Don't forget mosquito repellent.

MAHATMA GANDHI NATIONAL MARINE PARK

Mahatma Gandhi National Marine Park is something out of Jacques Cousteau's wildest dreams. A fantastic kaleidoscope of living coral, the marine park is also home to colorful marine life, including angel fish, clown fish, starfish, butterfly fish, parrot fish, sea anemones, and sharks. The only problem is that without special arrangements the only two places open to visitors are **Jolly Buoy** or **Red Skin Island,** where much of the coral has fallen victim to boatloads of touchy-feely tourists. Snorkel equipment rental costs Rs50, but is hard to find during high season— bring your own or rent it from a Port Blair hotel. For **scuba diving,** ask at any of the larger Port Blair hotels or try **Safety Stop Dive Center** (☎280120 or 231215), on the beach. (US$60 for 2 dives with equipment). Glass-bottomed boats are available for sightseeing, although collecting coral and shells is forbidden (1hr. plus 2½hr. on the island, 2pm). After the bend at the pier, the road continues 2km to New Wandoor Beach. From the Port Blair bus stand, the 8:30am **bus** to Wandoor (1½hr., Rs8) connects with the 10am boat to either Jolly Buoy (Rs125) or Red Skin Island (Rs90). You have to buy a boat ticket from any one of the many agents around the pier (Shumpen Travels has a boat with a bathroom) before you can buy a park permit (Rs500; camera fee Rs25). The last bus from Wandoor to Port Blair leaves at 5pm, usually 5min. early. There is a Rs100 deposit per water bottle, refundable on return of the bottle; the islands have no food or drinking water. The best place to stay the night is **Sanctuary ❶,** a well-crafted eco-resort with cottage huts on a hill near Safety Stop Dive Center. The resort just opened in 2003 but seems destined to become a classic. (☎280143. Rs50 to pitch your own hammock, Rs75-100 for a rental; singles Rs150; doubles Rs300-1200.) The resort also arranges boat trips for coral sightseeing. (40min. Rs300-350 with groups of 4-5. Mask Rs50; fins Rs100.) **Safety Stop Dive Center** (see above) has a **restaurant** (fish curry Rs35).

RITCHIE'S ARCHIPELAGO

Havelock Island is the most popular tourist getaway on Ritchie's Archipelago. **Neil Island, Long Island,** and **North Passage** are also open for overnight stays. Ferries from Phoenix Bay Jetty stop at Neil Island (3-4 per week 6:15am, Rs16) and Long Island (2 per week 6:15am, Rs45). Ferries from Havelock to Rangat sometimes stop at Long Island. Officials check tourists' permit validity at most ferry stops.

HAVELOCK ISLAND

Havelock Island has white sand and an occasional dolphin leaping up out of the sapphire blue water. Jungle covers most of the island, but clears in the north to make room for a few villages surrounded by fruit and coconut plantations.

◼ TRANSPORTATION

Ferries leaving Port Blair for Havelock Island (4hr., 3-4 per week 6:15am, Rs16-39) arrive at the **jetty** (also known as Govindanagar or Village #1) and return from Havelock the next day. It's a bumpy ride, so have motion sickness pills handy. Ferries from Havelock sail to **Port Blair** (10:30am) and **Rangat** (Tu, W, F, Sa 11:30am). Check with the guards on the dock for exact times and to find out if the ship stops at Long or Neil Islands. An unpredictable **bus** chugs between the jetty and Beach #7. Your best bet is to hire a **bicycle** (Rs50 per day) or **moped** (Rs150 per day) in the jetty market. Many guest houses rent mopeds, but only a few have bicycles. For gas, ask at the shops in Village #3.

ANDAMAN ISLANDS

ANDAMAN ISLANDS

✴ 🔖 ORIENTATION AND PRACTICAL INFORMATION

The island's main **bazaar,** on the jetty, holds several restaurants and a **post office.** (Open M-F 10am-5pm.) A road extends 3km to **Village #3,** referred to as "the capital" by islanders. This metropolis has the only **STD/ISD** booth on Havelock plus the Andaman and Nicobar Cooperative **Bank,** the only place to exchange foreign currency on the island. (Open M-Sa 9am-1pm.) In #3, the road forks 2km to the left and leads to **Beach #5,** spoiled only by a government lodge. The road to the right winds for another 11km to reach **Village** (and Beach) **#7,** Havelock's nicest but most remote beach.

🔖 🔖 ACCOMMODATIONS AND FOOD

Every inhabited area of Havelock has a few decent guest houses. The cheapest and most comfortable way to sleep is to bring a hammock and pay a small camping fee at a beachside resort. Hidden in the jungle off Beach #7 is the **Jungle Lodge ❷,** managed by a Port Blair native who returned from Switzerland to pioneer eco-awareness in the Andamans. Forty percent of profit goes into island development projects. Jeep transportation to and from the jetty is complimentary. Reservations must be made through **Travel World** (☎ 237656; fax 237657), in Port Blair. (Simple straw huts Rs200; huge luxurious huts Rs1800.) **Eco Villa ❶,** on Beach #2, has helpful management and serves an excellent buffet dinner for Rs100. (☎282336. Camping Rs30; huts Rs100-150.) Most resorts are similar, with simple huts and mosquito nets, but the vibe can change dramatically with the current clientele. **Pristine Beach Resort ❷,** at #3, offers exceptional service, good food, and one of the area's few bars. (☎282344. Huts Rs150 per person). **Orient Beach Resort ❷,** 200m down the road, occupies an expansive clean-swept area set back from the beach and sheltered by tall trees. (Huts Rs150 per person). **Tent Resorts ❷** is a government-run lodge on Beaches #5 and 7. (Singles Rs150; doubles Rs500.) **Dolphin Resort ❸,** another government place, has the only concrete buildings on Beach #5. (☎282411. Doubles with showers Rs500, with A/C Rs1000, VIP Rs1500). Both government hotels must be booked through the tourist office in Port Blair. **Greenwood Resort ❶,** the last in this string of beachfront resorts, has a slightly more secluded beach. (Huts Rs100-150.) Food is cheap and tasty at the jetty. **Anjana Restaurant ❷,** in the bazaar, serves ginger prawns (Rs45), garlic crabs (Rs50), and fish curry with *parathas* for Rs15. (Open daily 6am-1:30pm and 4:30-9pm.) The **market,** under the trees, is the best place to buy delicious mangos (Rs20 per kg) and other fruit.

🔖 WATERSPORTS

The best place for snorkeling is **Elephant Beach.** Take the road toward Beach #7 until you pass a school. Leave your bike by the road, turn left onto the path through the woods, and walk 45min. to the coral. To go further, you will have to arrange a *dungee* with your hotel manager. Many guest houses rent snorkeling equipment (Rs50). An afternoon fishing trip on a local *dungee* costs about Rs1000. Fishing is best in early morning. There are only a few **dive shops,** as it is difficult for foreign dive instructors to obtain permission to stay in the Andamans. **Samudra Manavi Thakker,** on Neil Island, is an Indian woman who teaches a 4-day introductory course to groups of at least four people, but she can be hard to find.

NEIL ISLAND

Speed boats going to Havelock from Port Blair usually stop by Neil Island (3hr.; most days 7am; Rs16). Little Neil can be circumnavigated by foot in part of an afternoon. **Shanti Guest House ❷** has doubles with private balconies and common bathrooms (Rs150). **Hanabill Nest ❶** is a government-run accommodation. (☎ 282630. Dorms Rs75; doubles with shower Rs400, with A/C Rs600.)

MIDDLE ANDAMAN

🐚 RANGAT

Though Rangat mainly serves as a transit point on the way to the wild north, there are a few decent beaches. **Ships** sail from Rangat to **Port Blair** via **Havelock** (W, Th, Sa, Su; Rs45-74), sometimes stopping at Neil and Long Islands (Th, Su). **Buses** run to: **Port Blair** (6hr.; 7am-noon; Rs65, deluxe Rs130) and **Mayabunder** (3hr., 5:30am-5pm, Rs16). Rangat Bay is 8km from the town itself; minibuses run back and forth. **Hotel Avis ❶**, on Church Rd., has tiny rooms with snow-white sheets. If you arrive after dark, look for the neon red crucifix and grail-shaped beacon 100m from the main road; the tiny hotel is next to it. (☎274554. Singles Rs70; doubles Rs120.) The deserted **Hawksbill Nest ❶** is on the beach, 15km from Rangat, on the road to Mayabunder. (Dorms Rs75; doubles Rs250.)

🐚 MAYABUNDER

Mayabunder is a dull little transit town useful only for its ferry to **Kalighat** on North Andaman (2hr., 8am and 2:30pm, Rs20). From Kalighat, a bus connects to **Diglipur** (30min., Rs3) and **Aerial Bay** (40min., Rs16). Karmatang Beach is 7km from town. Mayabunder has **pharmacies, STD phones,** and a **post office.** The **Swiflet Nest ❶** is the local government's bid to bring you bliss. (Dorms Rs75; doubles Rs250.)

NORTH ANDAMAN

As you get farther from Port Blair, the tourist crowds thin out and conditions become increasingly rustic. North Island, the most remote of the major islands, is blanketed with deep jungle and has a beautiful skyline dominated by **Saddle Peak** (741m). North Andaman's main town is **Diglipur**. The main port is **Aerial Bay**.

AERIAL BAY

ENTRY REQUIREMENTS. The **Forest Ranger Office** (open M-Sa 6am-2pm) in Aerial Bay grants **permits** for Smith, Ross, and other islands (Rs10). Just show your passport and Andaman permit. Smith Island permits are good for a one day visit, but longer stays can be approved by the ranger on Smith.

🚍 TRANSPORTATION

Ships sail for **Port Blair** (14hr., W 6am and Sa 4pm, Rs74). Tickets can be bought from the Tehsil office in the Diglipur Bazaar (open M-F 9-11am), from the jetty ticket office, or aboard ship for double the price. The bus from Aerial Bay to **Kalighat** (1hr., 3am, Rs6) connects with the 5am ferry to Mayabunder, which is greeted by Port Blair-bound buses. The only other ferry leaves at noon, and gets into Mayabunder too late to catch anything going farther than Rangat. **Buses** also run to **Diglipur** (30min., 9am-8pm, Rs3) and **Kalipur** (30min.; 6 per day 6:30am-5:30pm, last bus back at 6pm; Rs2). Irregular boats go to **Havelock** (9½hr., Rs50).

✈ ⓘ ORIENTATION AND PRACTICAL INFORMATION

Aerial Bay, the fishing village that acts as Diglipur's port, is 12km from the town. In the **bazaar** at Aerial Bay, you will find mosquito nets, plastic sheets, strings, kerosene, pots, rice, fruit and vegetables, Beatles wigs, and a 24hr. **STD booth** to contact the outside world. The closest place to buy a hammock is Diglipur. The nearest doctor and **pharmacies** are in Diglipur.

🛏 🍴 ACCOMMODATIONS AND FOOD

To get a good night's sleep in Aerial Bay, you may need to jump through a few hoops. The rooms on the main road are bland and filled with blaring music from the street. A better bet is the Power and Water Department's **PWD Guest House ❶,** on a high hill overlooking the bay. The PWD's two rooms exist to house visiting employees; you'll have to get special permission from the Aerial Bay Junior Engineer to sleep there. If she isn't at the guest house, go bang on her door; she lives in a rickety duplex 50m from the main road near the fruit market. (Doubles Rs100.) Several shops on the main drag serve meals at good prices.

Twelve kilometers from Aerial Bay, in the shadow of Saddle Peak, **Kalipur** has walks along the craggy shore and a passable beach. Government-run **Turtle Resort ❶** features hot showers and balconies. (Dorms Rs125; doubles Rs400, with A/C Rs600.) A bus runs between Kalipur and Diglipur during the day. Otherwise, the 3hr. walk back to Aerial Bay passes through mango plantations and Bengali villages.

🏝 ISLANDS

Smith and **Ross Islands** are as close to Robinson Crusoe as you're likely to get. Wild dogs, hermit crabs, two friendly fishing families, and one forest ranger are the island's only permanent inhabitants. Waves break on beautiful coral reefs and white sand beaches, empty except for the rare skinny-dipping tourist. Free camping and the chance to live the primitive life for a few days have lured many a foreign traveler. For now, the numbers remain small enough to preserve the islands' natural beauty, but the hype among backpackers threatens to end the golden age of free camping and tropical solitude. Environmentalists worry that campfires and litter are ruining wildlife habitats, and developers plan to open a guest house.

A thin strip of sand connects Smith with its tinier sibling, Ross. You can take a **boat** to **Aerial Bay** and **Smith** (30min., 9am and 11am, Rs50), or hire a local *dungee* (Rs150-200) and split the cost with as many as 12 other travelers. Bring hammocks, food, cooking supplies, and a machete with you; water is available at two wells, but you must bring containers to carry it back to your campsite. The families who live on the island might sell you some produce. Dogs and monkeys will steal any food left out overnight. **Campfires are illegal,** so buy a cheap stove.

ANDHRA PRADESH

अडफद ध्इक्छ्ाउउ

The state of Andhra Pradesh occupies a large chunk of southeastern India, from the dry Deccan Plateau to the coast of the Bay of Bengal. The state is named for the kingdom of the Hindu Andhra kings, who ruled most of the Deccan from the 2nd century BC until the 3rd century AD. As part of Emperor Ashoka's vast kingdom, the region was also a major Buddhist center. Beginning in the 16th century, Andhra Pradesh was ruled by Muslims, first under the Golconda Sultanate, then as part of the Mughal Empire, and finally under the Nizams, who ruled the region of the princely state of Hyderabad under British protection from 1723 until 1948. When India gained independence in 1947, the Nizam of Hyderabad refused to cede his lands. He demanded that, as a Muslim ruler, he be allowed to join the newly created Muslim theocracy of Pakistan. After a year-long standoff, the Indian government forcibly annexed the territory, which was later merged with other Telugu-speaking areas to form Andhra Pradesh. In spite of their religious differences, the people of Andhra are bound together by their language, Telugu, distinctive cuisine and customs, and the legacy of centuries of peaceful coexistence. Though one of the least touristed destinations in India, the state is home to a number of superb attractions, ranging from the fabulous ruins of majestic forts to ancient temples. Forests, hills, 34 rivers including the holy Krishna and Godavari, waterfalls, lakes, and a 1000km coastline enhance the state's natural splendor.

HIGHLIGHTS OF ANDHRA PRADESH

Hyderabad's bazaars and monuments (below) complement the nearby spooky ruins of **Golconda Fort** (p. 111) and the gorgeous marble **Birla Mandir** (p. 112).

A visit to **Tirupati's** hilltop temple frenzy (p. 116) provides insight into contemporary Hinduism, and then thrills with a harrowing bus ride down to calmer climes.

Wander the centuries-old ruins of **Nagarjunakonda** (p. 115) and picnic at the picturesque **Ethipothala Waterfall** (p. 115).

HYDERABAD ్ద౦౯౦దు   ☎ 040

Let millions of men and women of all castes, creeds, and religions make it their abode, like fish in the ocean.
    —Muhammad Quli Qutb Shah, upon laying Hyderabad's foundation

Standing testament to the transcendent power of love, the city of Hyderabad was founded in the late 16th century by Muhammad Quli Qutb Shah, Sultan of Golconda, poet, art-lover and heir to Golconda's Persian Shah dynasty. Though he was to ascend to the throne of one of the greatest kingdoms in India, Muhammad had fallen in love too hard and too fast to heed religious and caste barriers. His love, Bhagmati, was a beautiful dancer and singer, but she was a commoner and a Hindu. Risking his inheritance and his neck, he made midnight journeys on horseback from Golconda Fort, then the capital, to a village on the banks of the Musi River to court her. Upon discovering the depths of his son's infatuation, Muhammad's father relented and allowed his son to marry her. The prince planted a new city on the banks of the Musi, which he named Bhagnagar after his lover Bhagmati, and when he became king, he erected great monuments in the city to honor her. Because Bhagmati took the name Hyder Mahal when she married, Bhagnagar soon became Hyderabad. The Qutb Shah Dynasty was decimated by Mughal Emperor Aurangzeb in 1687, and after a brief period of Mughal control, when Aurangzeb died in 1707, his viceroy, Nizam Asaf Jah, proclaimed himself ruler of the region, and his descendants ruled the princely state of Hyderabad under the protection of the British from the city itself rather than Golconda Fort. The last ruling Nizam was ousted by independent India in 1948.

A legacy of tolerance has honeyed the tongues of this comfortably polyglot (and "multicuisine") metropolis of nearly six million inhabitants. In the streets, Urdu blends with Hindi and Telugu as Muslims, settled more densely here than in any other city in the south, work and worship side by side with Hindus. The wealth of the Nizams, displayed in the city's impressive examples of Indo-Saracenic architecture, has returned in hi-tech fashion to this new capital of information technology. Progressive governments have successfully transformed Hi-Tech City, to the north of Hyderabad, into a research center for many multi-national corporations. The New City is clean, efficient, and one of corporate India's most comfortable residences. In just over two years, 25 overpasses were constructed to facilitate traffic. Meanwhile, women draped head-to-toe in black burqas haggle away in the bazaars of the Old City across the Musi, whose many Muslim monuments shine resolutely through the dust.

▐▀ TRANSPORTATION

Flights: Begumpet Airport (☎ 140, flight info 142), on the north side of Husain Sagar, off Sardar Patel Rd., 8km north of Abids. Auto-rickshaws go to Abids (Rs60-70). Private taxis cost twice as much. **Air Canada, Air France** (☎ 23230947), **Bangladesh Biman, Gulf Air** (☎ 23240870), **Kuwait Airways** (☎ 23234344), and **Royal Jordanian** (☎ 23298774) are all in the same bldg., Flat 202, Gupta Estate, 500m north of Basheer Bagh. **Lufthansa,** 3-5-823 Hyderguda Rd. (☎ 23235537), to the right, off Basheer Bagh Circle. **Delta Airlines** and **Jet Airways** (☎ 23401222) are in the Navbharat Chambers, Raj Bhavan Rd., Somajiguda. **Air Sahara,** Sahara Manzil (☎ 23212767, airport office 27901315), opp. Secretariat, Saifabad. Open daily 10am-6pm. **Air India,** 5-9-193 HACA Bhavan (☎ 23389713), opposite the Public Gardens. Open M-Sa 9:30am-1pm and 1:45-5:30pm. **Indian Airlines,** Secretariat Rd. (☎ 23299333 or 141), opposite Ravindra Bharati. Open daily 10am-1pm and 2-5:15pm. Daily flights to: **Ahmedabad** (2hr., US$165); **Bangalore** (1hr., US$105); **Bhubaneshwar** (1½hr., US$105); **Chennai** (1hr., US$105); **Delhi** (2hr., US$215); **Kolkata** (2hr., US$210); **Mumbai** (1hr., US$120); **Nagpur** (1hr., US$105); **Tirupati** (1hr., US$85); **Vishakhapatnam** (1hr., US$105).

Trains: There are tourist quotas at each of the three stations (inquiry ☎ 131): **Secunderabad, Nampally** (in Abids), and **Kachiguda** (east side of Sultan Bazaar). Reservations open M-Sa 8am-8pm, Su 8am-2pm. To: **Bangalore** (13½hr.; leaves Secunderabad 5:40pm, leaves Kachiguda 5:58pm; Rs255); **Chennai** (13½hr., 3:50 and 7pm, Rs255); **Delhi** (26hr., 6:40am and 9:30pm, Rs200); **Mumbai** (15½hr., 2:30 and 8:40pm, Rs255); **Tirupati** (13½hr., 5 per day 5:30am-7pm, Rs245).

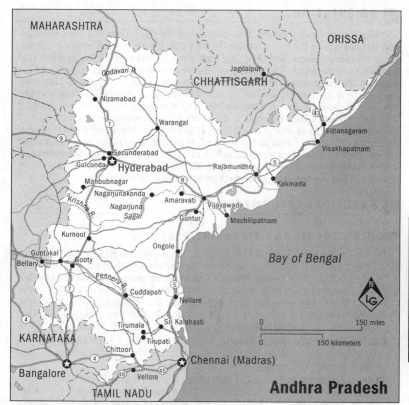

Andhra Pradesh

Buses: The **Imlibun Central Bus Stand** (inquiry ☎ 24614406), across the river in Malakpet, east of the Salar Jung Museum, proclaims itself Asia's largest. Open 24hr. Deluxe service to: **Bangalore** (12hr., every 30min. 4:30am-9pm, Rs294); **Chennai** (14hr., 4:30pm, Rs344); **Hospet** (8hr., 5:30pm, Rs230); **Mumbai** (16hr., 10:30am and 9:30pm, Rs360); **Nagarjunakonda** (4hr., every hr., Rs90); **Tirupati** (14hr., 6 per day 4:30-10pm, Rs294).

Local Transportation: Since **buses** may not come to a full stop, you'll need turbo-*chappals* to catch one. The orange-and-white **city buses** stop (or at least slow down) anywhere if you wave to them. The grey **Metro Express** buses are much quicker, more expensive, and stop only at designated locations. Terminals at **Nampally, Koti, Afzalgunj,** near the **Charminar,** and **Secunderabad Railway Station.** The Nampally terminal is north of the railway station on Public Garden Rd., at the entrance to the Public Gardens. City buses **#2** and **8A** run from Secunderabad Station to Nampally. City buses **#119** and **142N** and Metro **Express #66** run from Nampally to Golconda Fort via Charminar and Salar Jung. At Rs4 per km, **auto-rickshaws** are by far the most convenient and quickest way to get around the city. Minimum fare of Rs8. Drivers charge 1½ times the meter between 10pm and 5:30am, and there are no waiting charges factored in. Mention your exact destination at the outset and insist that the driver use his meter. **Private taxis** and hired cars are unmetered and twice as expensive.

ORIENTATION

The Musi River divides the **Old City**—containing the Charminar, the Mecca Masjid, and the bazaars in the south—from the **New City,** which has government offices, glitzy downtown shops and shopping malls, and glimmering Birla-commissioned landmarks to the north. The **Abids** area, the heart of the New City, is about 1.5km south of the gargantuan, Buddha-guarded **Husain Sagar,** the artificial lake built back in the days of the Golconda Empire. Abids adjoins **Hyderabad (Nampally) Station.** The business district of **Lakdi-Ka-Pul** ("The Wooden Bridge") lies just north of Nampally. West of Husain Sagar is the posh residential and commercial area of **Banjara Hills,** north of which lies the Raj Bhavan in the commercial hub of **Somajiguda.** North of the Sagar is the area of **Begumpet** and the airport. Begumpet adjoins the other main transportation hub in Hyderabad's twin city, **Secunderabad,** to the northeast of Husain Sagar, basically a part of greater Hyderabad itself, where a major railway station sends travelers in and out of the area.

PRACTICAL INFORMATION

TOURIST, LOCAL, AND FINANCIAL SERVICES

Tourist Office: India Tourism Office, 1st fl., 3-6-140 Himayatnagar Main Rd. From Basheer Bagh, the office is 1km down the road, on the right. Free city map. Open M-F 9:30am-5:30pm. The **Andhra Pradesh Tourism Development Corporation (APTDC)** has its booking office next to Lumbini Park, Tank Bund Rd. (☎23453036, 24hr. 1901334033; www.aptourism.com). Open daily 6:30am-8:30pm. It offers local **sightseeing tours** (daily 8am-5:45pm, Rs160), and tours to Nagarjunasagar (daily 7am-9.30pm, Rs260), Tirupati-Tirumala, and other South Indian destinations.

Budget Travel: Sita World Travel, 3-5-874 Hyderguda Rd. (☎23233629; fax 23234223), next to Apollo Hospital. Turn right coming from Abids Circle to Basheer Bagh. Open M-F 9:30am-6pm, Sa 9:30am-1:30pm.

Currency Exchange: State Bank of Hyderabad, MG Rd. (☎23201594), north of Abids Circle. Open M-F 10:30am-2:30pm, Sa 10am-noon. **Thomas Cook,** 6-1-57/A Nasir Arcade, Saifabad (☎23231988), at the intersection of Secretariat and Public Gardens Rd. Both change cash, traveler's checks. Open M-F 9:30am-5:30pm, Sa 9:30am-5pm.

Bookstore: Walden, 6-3-871 Greenlands Rd., Begumpet (☎23413434), between Abids and the airport, in the Vivekananda Hospital complex. Open daily 9am-9pm.

EMERGENCY AND COMMUNICATIONS

Police: Abids Circle Police Station (☎23230191, emergency 100). To the right as you face the GPO.

Pharmacy: Apollo Pharmacy (☎23231380), in the Apollo Hospital Complex (see below). Also opposite Mehdipatnam bus stop (☎23516107). Open 24hr. **Medwin Hospital Pharmacy** (☎23202909), off Station Rd., on Chirag Ali Ln., in a tall bldg. visible even from the Nampally Railway Station, inside the lobby to your left. Open 24hr.

Hospital: Medwin Hospital (☎23202902), Nampally, near the station. **Apollo Hospital Medical Center** (☎23607777), Jubilee Hills, 8km northwest of Abids. Open 24hr.

Internet: Yahoo Citi The Hangout Point, 5-9-88 Fateh Maidan, 3rd fl., on your right as you turn onto Chapel Rd. from the Public Gardens Rd. Rs30 per hr. Open daily 9:30am-1am. **Netplanet** (☎23205594), 150m down Abids St. #2. Rs30 per hr. Open daily 11am-11pm. **Pragnya Infotech,** 5-4-435/1 Station Rd. (☎24732044) next to Hotel Sai Prakash. Rs25 per hr. Open daily 10am-9:45pm.

Post Office: GPO (☎24745978). Open M-Sa 8am-8:30pm. **Postal Code:** 500001.

ANDHRA PRADESH

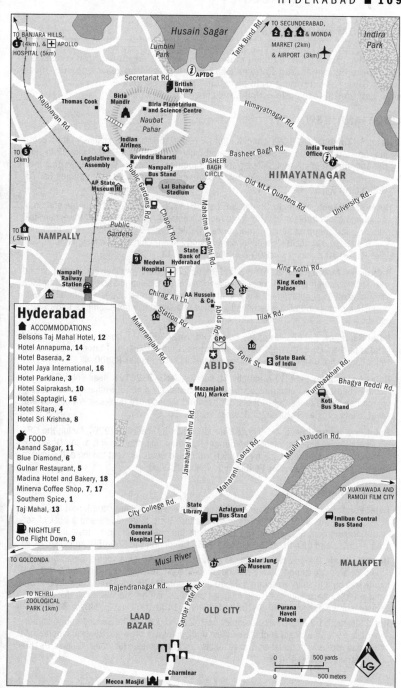

ANDHRA PRADESH

TO BANJARA HILLS,
1 (4km), & ✚ APOLLO
HOSPITAL (5km)

Husain Sagar

*Lumbini
Park*

TO SECUNDERABAD,
2 3 4 & MONDA
MARKET (2km)
& AIRPORT (3km)

*Indira
Park*

Tank Bund Rd.

Secretariat Rd.

i APTDC

British
Library

Rajbhavan Rd.

Thomas Cook

Birla
Mandir

Birla Planetarium
and Science Centre

*Naubat
Pahar*

Himayatnagar Rd.

TO **5**
(2km)

Indian
Airlines

Legislative ■
Assembly

Ravindra Bharati

Nampally
Bus Stand

BASHEER
BAGH
CIRCLE

Basheer Bagh Rd.

Old MLA Quarters Rd.

India Tourism
Office *i* **7**

HIMAYATNAGAR

University Rd.

AP State
Museum

Lal Bahadur
Stadium **6**

Mahatma Gandhi Rd.

TO **8**
(.5km)

NAMPALLY

*Public
Gardens*

Public Gardens Rd.

Chapel Rd.

King Kothi Rd.

King Kothi
Palace

Nampally
Railway
Station

10

9 Medwin
Hospital ✚

State
Bank of
Hyderabad

11

Chirag Ali Ln.

AA Hussein
& Co.

12 **13**

Tilak Rd.

Station Rd.

14

15

Abids Rd.

GPO
✉

16

State Bank
of India

Mukarramjahi Rd.

ABIDS

Bank St.

Turrebazkhan Rd.

Bhagya Reddi Rd.

Koti
Bus Stand

Hyderabad

🛏 **ACCOMMODATIONS**
Belsons Taj Mahal Hotel, **12**
Hotel Annapurna, **14**
Hotel Baseraa, **2**
Hotel Jaya International, **16**
Hotel Parklane, **3**
Hotel Saiprakash, **10**
Hotel Saptagiri, **16**
Hotel Sitara, **4**
Hotel Sri Krishna, **8**

🍴 **FOOD**
Aanand Sagar, **11**
Blue Diamond, **6**
Gulnar Restaurant, **5**
Madina Hotel and Bakery, **18**
Minerva Coffee Shop, **7, 17**
Southern Spice, **1**
Taj Mahal, **13**

🎷 **NIGHTLIFE**
One Flight Down, **9**

Mozamjahi
(MJ) Market

Jawaharlal Nehru Rd.

Maharani Jhansi Rd.

Maulvi Alauddin Rd.

TO VIJAYAWADA AND
RAMOJI FILM CITY

TO GOLCONDA

City College Rd.

State
Library

Azfalgunj
Bus Stand

Osmania
General
Hospital ✚

Imlibun Central
Bus Stand

Musi River

17

Salar Jung
Museum

MALAKPET

TO NEHRU
ZOOLOGICAL
PARK (1km)

Rajendranagar Rd.

Sardar Patel Rd.

18

OLD CITY

Purana
Haveli
Palace ■

LAAD
BAZAR

0   500 yards
0   500 meters

N

Charminar

Mecca Masjid

ACCOMMODATIONS

Budget dives are a rupee a dozen in the commercial Abids area. A few lodges are around the Secunderabad Railway Station, but there's no reason to stay there unless you have a morning train to catch. The fanciest places are located in the ritzy Banjara Hills area. Almost all hotels have 24hr. check-out.

ABIDS AND NEW CITY

Hotel Sri Krishna, 6-1-1081 Lakdi-Ka-Pul (☎23230156; badam_krishna@yahoo.com), just 5min. from Nampally Station. Situated close to the Husain Sagar Lake, Birla Temple and other touristy spots. Clean, spacious rooms with cable TV, phones, a doctor on call, and an efficient travel desk. 24hr. room service. Singles Rs290; doubles Rs375-550; suites Rs750. ❷

Hotel Saiprakash, Nampally Station Rd. (☎24611726), about 2min. from the station. A plush and comfortable place with large rooms, central A/C, and a host of travel services, laundry, and shopping at unbeatable prices. Cable TV and 24hr. room service. The multicuisine restaurant, Rich-'n'-Famous, serves good Indian, Chinese and Mughlai food. Singles Rs700-800; doubles Rs800-900. AmEx/MC/V. ❹

Belsons Taj Mahal Hotel, 82 Main Guard Rd. (☎27810810; www.belsontaj.com), behind the MCH Swimming Pool. Located between the airport, Secunderabad Station and the shopping malls of Abids, the Taj is one of Hyderabad's reputed hotels. Comfortable, well-furnished rooms and all the bells and whistles of a smart city hotel. Singles Rs695-895; doubles Rs795-995; suites Rs1200. AmEx/MC/V. ❹

Hotel Saptagiri, 5-4-651 Nampally Station Rd. (☎24603601), down a narrow dirt road opposite the CLS Bookshop. Scrubbed and polished through and through. Balconies, telephones, hot water, and seat toilets. Singles Rs250; doubles Rs300. ❷

Hotel Annapurna, 5-4-730 Nampally Station Rd. (☎24732612), near Hotel Saptagiri, sandwiched between electronics stores. Overwhelmingly pink (but otherwise unexciting) place has TVs, phones, and towels. Star-shaped rooms have faux-leather couches and seat toilets. Singles Rs250-275; doubles Rs300-550. ❷

Hotel Jaya International, 4-1-37/A&B Reddy Hostel Rd. (☎24752929), facing the GPO in Abids Circle, bear left along Mahipatram Rd., then take the first left at the Dhanalakshmi Bank. Really good value for its price, with huge windows, seat toilets, and showers. Singles Rs300-600; doubles Rs400-750. AmEx/MC/V. ❷

SECUNDERABAD

Hotel Parklane, 115 Parklane (☎27840466; parklanehotel@yahoo.com), next to Chenoy Trade Center, about 5min. down from the station. Neat, large rooms and a host of services ranging from a doctor on call to a decent but small multicuisine restaurant. 24hr. room service and friendly staff. Singles Rs475-750; doubles Rs650-950. AmEx/MC/V. ❸

Hotel Baseraa, 9-1-167 S.D. Rd. (☎27703200; reserve@baseraa.com), 5min. down the road towards the airport from Secunderabad Station. Its elegance and central A/C are quite welcome in sultry Hyderabad. Piped music, satellite TV, telephone, safe deposit box and a fridge make your spacious room as plush as can be. Helpful travel desk and in-house laundry. Singles Rs1200-1350; doubles Rs1400-1600. AmEx/MC/V. ❺

Hotel Sitara, 7-1-2 SPG Church Complex (☎26219402). From the Secunderabad station, veer left. By far the cleanest and friendliest budget hotel in the area. Spacious rooms with tiled bathrooms with squat and seat toilets, and balconies. Hot water. Singles Rs150-300; doubles Rs250-400. ❷

🍴 FOOD

For incendiary Andhra cuisine, gourmets make their way to the upscale terraces of Banjara Hills. The hard-working Hyderabadi plows into the *biryani* that built this town, but you can cool it down at one of the ubiquitous juice stands, bakeries, or softy joints lining the alleys.

Southern Spice, 8-2-350/3/2, Rd. #3, Banjara Hills (☎ 23353802). The most authentic Andhra food in the city, this place is an Indian Cuisine Award-winner, and for good reason. The cool and classy surrounds belie the fiery Andhra dishes available. Brave the Chicken Chettinad or pick from a host of spicy veg. dishes. A full meal for Rs200-270. ❷

Gulnar Multicuisine Family Restaurant, Masab Tank Rd. (☎ 23370074), opposite the Polytechnic and beside Satya Apartments. This is a favorite haunt of Hyderabad's middle-class families, especially on the weekends, and also serves some good Hyderabadi cuisine. Also offers a passable attempt at "authentic" Chinese and tandoori specialties. The takeaway has awesome portions. Meals around Rs200 per person. ❺

Madina Hotel & Bakery, at the 1st major intersection south of the river on Sardar Patel Rd. Famous for its Hyderabadi *biryani,* different from the kind available in other parts of India. Topped with egg, the half-order of mutton *biryani* (Rs45) is delicious. Fast, friendly service on the breezy mezzanine overlooking the bakery. Open Sa-Th 11am-11pm. ❷

Taj Mahal, in the Taj Mahal Hotel, King Kothi Rd. off MG Rd. A family favorite, and with good reason: it's cheap, comfortable, and generous with mostly veg. South and North Indian favorites (Rs32-65). *Chhola bhatura* Rs39, extensive *thali* Rs50. Packed tiffin 7am-9:30pm. Open daily 11am-3:30pm and 7-10:30pm. ❷

Blue Diamond (☎ 23230612), Fateh Maidan, 100m south of Basheer Bagh Circle. An excellent Szechwan and Manchurian selection that caters to Hyderabad's spicy tastes. Chicken Szechwan Rs125, Manchurian prawns Rs125, Hong Kong Chicken Rs110 and sweet-and-sour pork Rs80. Open daily 11am-3:30pm and 6-10:30pm. ❸

Minerva Coffee Shop, 22-8-290 Hamad Plaza, 1st fl. On the river, just to the left of the main bridge entering the Old City. Servers weave between the rows of potted plants as locals gossip away. Rava *dosa* Rs23, huge *puris* Rs20. "Love of California," a fluffy lime-green ice cream fantasia, only Rs20. Open daily 7am-11pm. ❶

Aanand Sagar, 50 Unity House, about 2min. down Dhirag Ali Lane by Medwin Hospital. Excellent double *pav bhaji* (Rs25), *puris,* pizzas, and juices. Open daily 9:30am-11pm. ❶

👁 SIGHTS

GOLCONDA

8km west of the city. From the Nampally bus stand, take bus #119, 142, or Metro Express #66.

QUTB SHAHI TOMBS. Containing the remains of seven of the dynasty's patri-archs, the Qutb Shahi tombs play an undeserved second fiddle to the Golconda Fort, the latter having a steep climb and a slightly steeper entrance fee. The tombs are magnificent buildings set in the midst of gardens flush with bougainvillea. Each tomb is capped with an Islamic-style onion dome and adorned with Hindu motifs. All the domes were originally overlaid with blue and green tiles of which now only a few pieces remain. The cenotaph in the center of the tomb covers the crypt below. Though the tombs all have a similar shape, each bears the distinctive mark of its designer. The grandest tomb, surrounded by gardens and criss-crossed by waterways, is that of Sultan Muhammed Quli Qutb Shah. Farthest from the entrance, the tall tomb of Jamshid Qutb Shah commands views of Golconda from its terrace. Next door, a small museum displays artifacts from Qutb Shahi times: ceramics, weapons, handwritten texts, and portraits of the kings who have their tombs here. *(1km north of Golconda Fort. Open 9am-4:30pm. Rs5. Museum open Sa-Th 9:30am-1pm and 2-4:30pm. Rs5; camera fee Rs5, video fee Rs25.)*

GOLCONDA FORT. Headquarters of the Qutb Shah kingdom from 1512 to 1687, the fort is Hyderabad's most popular attraction. It was originally built by the region's Hindu rulers, the Kakatiyas, but became the center of power for the Shahs, who greatly expanded the modest bastion into a granite fortress expanding 7km in circumference, in the early 16th century. The kingdom was a thriving center for the arts and learning and a bastion of religious tolerance, until it was crushed and annexed after two sieges by the Mughal emperor Aurangzeb. The 1000-step ascent to Durbar Hall takes about 30min. At the top is a panoramic view over the ramparts below, and if you squint hard enough, you should be able to make out the Birla Mandir and the Charminar to the east. If you can pass up the vista and the exercise, your Rs25 ticket to the sound and light show will get you into the fort's ground-level attractions from 5:30pm onwards, after the official visiting hours. AP Tourism does an hour-long and highly informative guided tour (Rs150-250).

On the way up, visitors follow the winding counter-clockwise path used by commoners and visitors during the fort's active days. The steep descent leads down a route once used exclusively by the king and his attendants. You first pass through the heavily studded **Balahisar Gate,** which served as the first line of defense against invaders. Ahead is the **Grand Portico,** where guides are often seen clapping to demonstrate the fort's acoustics. Golconda was engineered so that a clap at the summit of Durbar Hall would reverberate at five places along the inside perimeter of the fortress wall. A clap at the center of the Grand Portico can be heard at the summit, 1.5km away. This built-in communication system was used to notify the king of any visitors while they were still far away. Straight ahead are the covered **bodyguard barracks.** Ahead and to the right is the **Nagina Bagh,** a royal garden. From the gardens, a stone staircase begins the ascent to the summit. At the foot of the steps, on the right, you can see the 12m-deep **water tank,** one of three within the fort. The water came from a natural spring hundreds of feet below the forts ground level and was transported by a complex system of Persian wheels and limestone pipes, the stumps of which can still be seen today.

Durbar Hall commands spectacular views of Hyderabad and Secunderabad. The summit is also home to the 12th-century Hindu **Sri Jagadamba Temple,** which has stayed intact despite intervening generations of Muslim rule, as a testament to the region's communal harmony. From Durbar Hall, you have to go almost all the way down the king's staircase before you get to the next site. At the foot of the hill is a water tank. Around the corner are the **Rani Mahals,** a series of buildings once occupied by the king's harem. A modest fountain is in the central courtyard, where the sound and light show is held daily. Once decorated with curtains, mirrored glass, and jewels, the main building is now occupied by bats. The gardens and manicured lawns are still painstakingly preserved. Passing through the Rani Mahals takes you past the **Taramati Mosque** to the three-story **arsenal,** which houses huge dusty guns and cannon balls and is in the process of being converted into a museum, due to open in 2005. *(Open daily 7am-5pm. US$5 or equivalent; video fee Rs25. 1hr. English sound and light show daily Mar.-Oct. 7pm, Nov.-Feb. 6:30pm; Rs30.)*

HUSAIN SAGAR AREA

BIRLA MANDIR. The spectacular Birla Mandir, dedicated to Lord Venkateshwara, crowns Naubat Pahar Hill. Commissioned by the industrial kings of India and built over 10 years, it has awesome views of Hyderabad and Secunderabad, especially at sunset. The pure white Rajasthani marble against the blue of Husain Sagar combine to paint quite a sublime picture. For once, the serenity is unmarred by shoe-touts or alms-driven priests. At night, the structure is illuminated. *(Open daily 7am-noon and 2-9pm.)* The **B.M. Birla Science Centre and Archaeological Museum** is opposite the temple. Downstairs is an archaeological section, with excavations from Vadd-amanu dated between 100 BC and AD 200, sculptures, paintings, and a Dinosau-rium. *(Open daily 10:30am-7:45pm, closed last Tu of each month. Rs12.)* Exit to the right and climb the stairs to the domed **Birla Planetarium**. *(☎ 2241067. 3 English shows per day. Closed last Th of each month. Rs15; combined ticket to planetarium and museum Rs25.)*

HUSAIN SAGAR. Visitors to Hyderabad are drawn ineluctably to Husain Sagar, the 6.5km by 800m tank whose blue waters provide a pleasant backdrop to the cityscape. Historians say that the tank was constructed during the days of the Gol-conda Empire, and dedicated in 1562 by Ibrahim Quli Qutb Shah to Husain Shah Wali, who cured him of a debilitating illness. However, legend has it that the tank was promised hundreds of years ago by a *sadhu* who collected large sums of money from the thirsty populace. Weeks passed, and no construction had begun, prompting the people to confront the *sadhu*, who then promised to undertake the project or return their money. The next morning, a shimmering tank was in place, and the *sadhu* had disappeared. The magic continued in the 1980s, when a mono-lithic **Buddha statue** was built and placed on a barge for transport across the artifi-cial lake. It sank into the water, dragging down seven people with it. Several years ago, the statue was retrieved from the bottom intact, no damage having been inflicted by the accident. The only real park near the lake is **Lumbini Park,** which is small but nicely landscaped and well maintained. Boats are available for tours or do-it-yourself jaunts. A musical fountain chimes three times every night. *(Just off Secretariat Rd., near Public Gardens Rd. Open Tu-Sa 9am-9pm. Rs2. Boats available Tu-Su 9am-6pm; paddleboats Rs20 per person, speedboats Rs100, water scooters Rs45.)*

OLD CITY

The back streets of the Old City, with their distinctive Muslim flavor, are arguably the most Hyderabadi part of town. During Ramzan, the Islamic holy month (Dec.-Jan.), the action begins at sunset as burqa-clad women flood the bazaars. Fueled on cheap *haleem*, a shredded mutton delicacy, the party continues into the night. Along these streets are several pilgrimage sites sacred to Shi'a Muslims, each one housing a revered *alam*, a banner into which gold, gemstones, and precious objects are woven. If you're near the Madina Hotel, ask a local to show you the **Bibi ka alawa,** which protects a green shrine within its walls. The *alam* contains pieces of a wooden plank upon which the Prophet Muhammad's daughter is believed to have bathed. Not far away is the **Sar tauq ka alawa,** which houses an *alam* contain-ing portions of the shackles and chains which bound the fourth *imam*.

CHARMINAR. The four-minaret Charminar (literally "four minarets") is Hydera-bad's oldest and most recognizable landmark. The edifice was built by Muhammed Quli Qutb Shah in 1591 to celebrate the end of an epidemic that had been plaguing the city. An image of the four towers even graces every pack of Charminar ciga-rettes. It is said that the last Nizam of Hyderabad refused to smoke any other brand. There's not much to see in the building, since you're no longer allowed to climb the 149 steps to the mosque on top, but a prime bazaar area ideal for a typi-cally Hyderabadi souvenir of jewelry or *attar* surrounds the towers. The **Laad Bazaar** (see **Shopping,** p. 115) stretches west and south from the Charminar.

MECCA MASJID. Like the Charminar, the Mecca Masjid was built during the sul-tanate of Muhammad Quli Qutb Shah. After Golconda's fall in 1687, Aurangzeb completed the mosque. It took 1400 bulls to haul the granite slabs that form the entrance. Named for the few bricks from Mecca embedded in its central arch, the

ANDHRA PRADESH

mosque is the largest in Hyderabad, accommodating up to 10,000 people at Friday prayers. Before entering the mosque, check your *chappals* at the podium on the left and walk through a pavilion containing the tombs of various Nizams of Hyderabad. *(2km south of the Musi River off Sardar Patel Rd., just southeast of Charminar.)*

SALAR JUNG MUSEUM. The impressive Salar Jung Museum is hailed as one of the world's largest collections amassed by a single individual, but it is actually the work of three generations of Salar Jungs, each of whom served as the Nizam's *wazir* (prime minister). The huge museum is stocked with everything from Bronze Age Chola sculptures to mediocre 18th and 19th century European oil paintings. The Western Wing has a 200-year-old copy of the Mona Lisa, and a Clock Room where over a hundred clocks chime the hour together. Room 14, the Ivory Room, displays a some solid ivory chairs given to Tipu Sultan by Louis XVI, apart from some fabulous richly carved elephant tusks. The Armory next door has 12 ft. swords and blunderbusses. Room 12 has some modern paintings by premier Indian artists such as Ravi Varma and K. Hebbar. In Room 13, next door, you can trace the chronological and regional evolution of Indian miniature painting. Check out a copy of King Tut's throne in the Egyptian Room (25A) and entire dinner services of Dresden and Spode in the European Porcelain section (29). But the collection's *piece de resistance* is undoubtedly the beautiful Italian marble statue in Room 9 of the Veiled Rebecca dated 1876, by G.B. Benzoni. *(CL Badari, Malakpet, south of the Musi River. Open Sa-Th 10am-5pm. Rs150.)*

🔲 🎵 NIGHTLIFE AND ENTERTAINMENT

Hyderabad hosts countless dance programs, *ghazal* sessions, and plays. **Ravindra Bharati** (☎23233672), across from the Public Gardens, stages about four events per week. **Bharatiya Vindya Bhavati** (☎23237825), off Basheer Bagh Circle, holds classical and popular dance and music concerts, often for free. Hyderabad claims to have more than 100 cinemas. The best English theaters are **Sangeet**, 23 Sardar Patel Rd., Secunderabad (☎27703864), and **Skyline**, 3-6-64 Basheer Bagh Rd., (☎23231633). There are usually 3-5 shows per day. Balcony seats Rs30-70. The **Alliance Française de Hyderabad** (☎27700734; afhyd@sol.net.in), now in West Marredpally, Secunderabad, screens two flicks per week: one in French, the other in German or English. The **Hyderabad Film Club** (☎23373265) has weekly screenings at the Sarathi Studio Preview Theatre in Ameerpet, north of Banjara Hills. Those looking for a more behind-the-scenes exposure to Telugu film should go to **Ramoji Film City**, 35km to the north-west past Jubilee Hills. Guided tours are the best ticket to get there; ask at the APTDC. (Daily 7:45am-6:30pm, Rs360.) The **Ravindra Bharati** (☎23233672) on Public Garden Rd. and **SPIC Macay** (☎27534374) organize regular theatre and cultural shows. *Channel 6 Magazine* and *Primetime Prism*, monthly publications available at hotels and bookstores are the best sources of information for upcoming events.

It's been several years since Andhra Pradesh repealed its prohibition laws, and the bar scene is coming of age. If it's a Guinness or a Bushmills you want, saunter across to its Irish-themed **Dublin Pub** (☎23400132). **One Flight Down** (☎23204060), in the Residency on Public Garden Rd., across from the Asian Lodge, draws a fun crowd and offers mugs of Kingfisher for Rs45. A plusher theme restaurant pub (yet not too posh to offer a third-drink-free special) is the **Hare and Hound** (☎23243095) in the Hotel Amrutha Castle, the building that looks like a castle on Secretariat Rd. All bars close at 11pm. For a different kind of liquid refreshment, try the **Ritz Hotel,** Hill Fort St., Basheer Bagh, where you can swim in the same **pool** as the Nizam's privileged guests. (☎23233570. Open daily 3-7pm. Rs60 per hr.) If you can't handle the sultry mid-mornings, there is also a pool at the **Taj Residency**, Rd. #1, Banjara Hills. (☎23399999. Rs150 per hr. Open daily 7am-7pm.) Hang out with the city's hippest at one of Hyderabad's only discotheques, **Tunnel 2** (☎23392323), at the Taj Krishna, Rd. #1, Banjara Hills.

▐ SHOPPING

Hone your bargaining skills at the bazaars around the Charminar in the Old City. The **Laad Bazaar,** extending west and south from the Charminar, is renowned for its wedding fashions, pearls and *attar* (perfume), luring people from all over India for pre-nuptial purchases. Step into a shop and take a look at the heavily embroidered *kamdani* dresses for women or the sultan-esque caps for men. If you're not into buying jewelry (strands of imperfect pearls Rs100-5000) and armfuls of bangles (Rs25 per set), you can always just stroll around and look into the stalls. Most of the shops in the Old City are open 10am-7pm; some observe Friday as a holiday. One of the twin cities' most famous bazaars is the **Monda Market** just outside Secunderabad Station. While shopping for groceries, flowers, fruits and vegetables, jostle for space with cows and goats. (Open daily 7am-9pm.) Emporiums and large shopping arcades line the roads in the Abids area. **MPM Mall** near the Abids GPO is one of Asia's largest malls with boutiques, galleries and shopping galore. On a slightly smaller scale is the **Lifestyle Mall** near Somajiguda. **Kalanjali Arts and Crafts,** Hill Fort Rd., opposite the Air India office, is not too expensive. (☎23231147. Open daily 9:30am-1pm and 2-8:30pm.)

NAGARJUNAKONDA పఃఝవ్ప్రోడ   ☎08680

One hundred and fifty kilometers southeast of Hyderabad and about 20m underwater lie the ruins of one of the largest Buddhist monasteries and learning centers in South India. Excavations in 1926 first revealed evidence of *stupas, chaityas,* and other artifacts dating back to the 2nd century BC. One *stupa,* known as the Mahachaitya, houses an inscription stating that the sacred relics of Lord Buddha lay within. In the 1950s, plans to build a dam on the Krishna River adjacent to the site spurred government archaeologists to resume digging. The most important ruins were evacuated, brick by brick, to a nearby hill before the dam was finished in 1966. Today, an immense artificial lake submerges the original site, and the island of Nagarjunakonda supports the rebuilt structures and a museum. Nagarjuna, the great 1st century AD Buddhist scholar said to have founded the university here, had no problem meditating in the sleepy village of Nagarjunasagar nearby. Today, the town is little more than a hydroelectric project. Most visitors take in the region on an APTDC daytrip from Hyderabad (see p. 105).

The nearest **train station** is in Miryaiguda, about 30km from town, but Vijayawada has better service. **Buses** leave from **Nagarjunasagar,** 14km from the ruins in Nagarjunakonda, bound for: **Hyderabad** (4hr., every hr., Rs69); **Tirupati** (13hr., 7:30am and 1:30pm, Rs150); **Vijayawada** (4hr., 7am and 1pm, Rs71). Buses into town will drop you off (on request) at the boat launch on the opposite end of the dam at Vijayapuri South. An **auto-rickshaw** costs Rs5.

The **Nagarjunasagar Dam** separates the lake to the west and the **Krishna River** to the east. To the north is **Hill Colony,** where you'll find the bus stand and the better hotels. The APTDC **tourist office** (☎277364) is opposite the bus stand in Project House (Sagara Paryataka Vihar). They operate guided minivan tours to Nagarjunakonda, the dam, the museum, and Ethipothala Waterfall for Rs150 per person. (☎276634. Open Sa-Th 9am-6pm. Museum closed F.) APTDC bus tours from Hyderabad visit the same sites; they leave Hyderabad at 7am, returning at 9:30pm (adults Rs260, children Rs210). The **police station** (☎276533) and **post office** are on the main road from Hill Colony to the dam. **Postal Code:** 508202.

The best rooms in town are those in Hill Colony run by the APTDC. **Punnami Hill Colony ❶** is attached to the acceptable **Amruta Bar and Restaurant ❷,** and offers large, clean, and airy doubles. (☎276540. Check-out 24hr. Non-A/C rooms Rs150-300, A/C rooms Rs500; 6-person dorms Rs100.) Ferries, or "launches," shuttle visi-

ANDHRA PRADESH

tors to the island and back. (45min. every hr. Sa-Th 9:30am-2:30pm. Ordinary ferry Rs40; A/C cruise Rs150.) The **museum** features a range of sculpture, friezes, and other artifacts, some from the Paleolithic and Neolithic eras. (Open Sa-Th 9am-4pm. Rs5.) The rebuilt ruins are somewhat disappointing, considering the richness of South Indian architecture, but these ruins are over 2000 years old. The **Ethipothala Waterfall,** a popular picnic spot 11km away from the boat launch, is reachable by shared auto-rickshaw (Rs200). The area lacks accommodation, so don't plan to stay the night unless you've brought your own camping gear. If you want to use the spot as a campsite, you will need permission from the APTDC in Hyderabad or, preferably, Nagarjunakonda.

TIRUPATI AND TIRUMALA౹ తిరుపతి AND
తిరుమల ☎08574

Rock hills covered with greenery enfold the temple of Sri Venkateshwara, known to his devotees as Lord Balaji, the most popular pilgrimage site in South India. Built in the 11th century by the founder of the Sri Vaishnava sect, the temple draws over 20,000 pilgrims every day who wait up to ten hours for a brief **darshan** with the god. The task of housing, feeding, and moving the masses falls to Tirupati, the little boomtown 20km down the hill. The temple allows non-Hindus into the inner sanctum but is rarely visited by foreigners. Wading through the masses of devotees can be exhausting. If you're not a devout Hindu, make your trip on a weekday, preferably Tuesday, in order to avoid the weekend rush. In early June and September, and on public holidays waiting times often double.

⬛ TRANSPORTATION. Tirupati's **airport** is 12km from the city. To reach **Indian Airlines,** turn right out of the railway station and walk for 2min. down and to the left. (☎2283992. Open daily 9am-6pm.) To: **Hyderabad** (1hr., Th and Sa 7:45 and 9:20am, US$85). The **railway station** (☎131) is in the busiest part of town near the bus stand. The reservations counter is opposite the station. (☎2225850. Open M-Sa 8am-8pm, Su 8am-2pm.) **Trains** run to: **Chennai** (3hr.; 6:45, 9:45am, 5:20pm; Rs120); **Hyderabad** (15hr.; 5:30am, 5, 6:50, 7:15pm; Rs230); **Mysore** via **Bangalore** (10-13hr., 10:30pm, Rs111); **Mumbai** (24hr.; Th and Su 9:40pm; Rs220; 4 trains per day also leave from nearby **Renigunta** station); **Trichy** (11hr., 3:40pm, Rs194). The **APSRTC bus stand** (☎2222333) is 500m from the center of Tirupati. To get there, turn right as you exit the station and follow that road around to the left, past the police station. Bear right when you reach the Gandhi statue; it will be on your left. **Buses** travel to: **Bangalore** (5½hr., every hr. 6:30am-11:30am, Rs150); **Chennai** (4hr., every 30min. 5am-11:15pm, Rs63); **Hyderabad** (12hr., 6 per day 2-8:45pm, Rs250); **Nagarjunasagar** (12hr., 5:30pm, Rs199); **Pondicherry** (7hr., 8am and 9pm, Rs85); **Vijayawada** (10hr., 8 per day 4:30am-11:30pm, Rs211). Buses for **Tirumala** leave from two bus stations in Tirupati. One terminal is next door to the APSRTC bus stand, the other 250m from the railway station, 2min. down on the left. Buses leave every 10min. (50min., Rs22), but there can be a long wait to buy a ticket. Get a round-trip ticket to avoid waiting again. Shared **taxis** also go up the hill from in front of the bus stands (Rs60 per person). Buses back to Tirupati leave from in front of the CRU Office or from the long-distance bus stand if it's busy. For the truly devoted, walking up 4,200 steps takes at least 6hr. Free buses leave from in front of the train station.

⬛⬛ ORIENTATION AND PRACTICAL INFORMATION. The **train station** and the **RTC bus stand** and **Tirumala bus stand** are clustered together in the south of Tirupati. Most of the restaurants and hotels are nearby. **G-Car Street** runs north from in front of the train station past the **Govindarajaswamy Temple** and the post

ANDHRA PRADESH

office. **Gandhi Road** crosses it from east to west. The road and footpath to **Tirumala** begin at Alipuri gate in the north-west of town. The **tourist office** (☎2252062), next door to the Tirumala bus stand, offers daily tours of temples around Tirupati (Rs250. Open daily 6am-9pm.) Branches at the Tirumala bus stand and at the temple Central Reservations Office are open 24hr. The **State Bank of India** takes major traveler's checks. Follow the road opposite the Bhimas Deluxe Hotel and take the first right. (☎2220699. Open M-F 10am-4pm, Sa 10am-1pm.) There is also a **24hr. ATM** at ICICI Bank which takes MC/V. Turn left out of the railway station and walk 2min. down on the left. **East Palace Station** (☎22253010) is on the road from the train to the bus station. The **post office** is 500m down G-Car St., in front of the train station. (☎2222103. Open M-F 10am-5pm, Sa 10am-2pm.) **Postal Code:** 517501

DARSHAN. Tickets are available at all the town bus stands. It's best to get them as soon as you arrive as times are usually for 12-24hr. in advance. Free *darshan* tickets are only available in Tirupati. Special darshan tickets are sold at Tirumala at the Central Reservation Office and at the Rambagicha Guesthouse. There's no difference in the waiting time between the Rs40, Rs50, and Rs60 tickets.

⚆⚆ ACCOMMODATIONS AND FOOD. Staying in clean, quiet Tirumala is pleasant and more convenient for *darshan*. The **Tirumala Tirupati Devasthamam (TTD)** has cheap but basic rooms at rock-bottom prices as well as free dormitory accommodation for over 4000 pilgrims. Most families make reservations well in advance but your can try your luck at the Central Reservations Office opposite the bus stand in Tirumala. The tourist office also has a guest house in Tirumala, past the Rambagicha Guesthouse. (Triples Rs300. Check availability at the tourist office at the Tirumala bus stand in Tirupati.) Reservations for pilgrim guest houses can be made at the TTD counter in nearby cities; Hyderabad's counter is on Himayatnagar Rd. (☎040 3220852) and Vellore's on Arni Rd., near the regional bus stand. (See www.tirumala.org for details.)

Tirupati has more options with the cheapest ones near the bus stand. The **Bhimas Hotel ❶**, 42 G-Car St., about a block from the railway station, is popular with Indian pilgrims because of its reasonable price and prime location, though it's often full. (☎2225744. Singles Rs75; doubles Rs225-350; triples Rs375.) A clutch of mediocre three-star hotels are clustered around the bus station. Turning left out the bus stand and walking 10min. takes you to **Hotel Bliss ❸**, Reni-

THE LOCAL LEGEND

LORD VENKATESWARA

This living Hindu deity's life is renowned for the miracles he performs for devotees. Two legends explain why he sits at Tirumala.

The first describes a contest of strength between the king of serpents, Lord Adisesha, and the wind god Vayu. Vayu tried to blow away a holy mountain but was stopped by Adisesha, who wrapped himself around it. Opening his mouth all the wider, Vayu was able to blow off the peak, which landed at Tiripati. The snake king, utterly humiliated, turned himself into a hill and invited Lord Vishnu to live on his head. The seven hills around Tirumala represent the seven heads of the giant serpent.

A different legend tells of a group of priests who could not decide to which god they should dedicate a sacrifice. They sent the sage Bhrigu to consult Brahma, Shiva, and Vishnu. But Brahma and Shiva were too busy with their consorts to be bothered. When Vishnu, too, ignored his arrival, the infuriated sage kicked him in the chest. Vishnu appeased Brighu by attending to his injured goat, but Lakshmi was angered by the sage's disrespect for her husband and left for Kolhupar. Vishnu took to wandering the earth and eventually settled down at Tirumala.

The ancient text known as the *Venkatachalamahatmyan* describes more legends of Tirupati and Tirumala.

gunta Rd. (☎ 2237770; fax 2237774. Singles Rs525-925; doubles Rs950-1075. AmEx/ MC/V.) Few restaurants stand above the huddled crowd of *dosa* and *thali* joints. Most of the nicer hotels around the bus station have similar quality restaurants attached **Woodside Restaurant ❶,** opposite the Bhimes on G-Car St., has enormous *thalis* (Rs25-50) as well as the standard range of snacks and curries (Rs10-50). Open daily 5am-11pm. **Hotel Lakshmi Priya ❷,** opposite the train station, is better and cleaner than most. (Open daily 3am-midnight.) **Bhimes Residency ❶,** near the Hotel Bliss, keeps a 24hr. coffeeshop.

◙ **SIGHTS.** Receiving the *darshan* of Lord Venkateshwara (Balaji) at the **Sri Venkateshwara Temple** in Tirumala is something a devout Hindu would hope to experience at least once during his or her lifetime. It is believed that any wish made at the temple will be granted by Lord Venkateshwara, an avatar of Vishnu. Visits to the temple begin in Tirupati, where buses shuttle passengers along a mountainside road to Tirumala and deposit them at the top of the hill. From there, you can float with the crowds through broad, clean, bazaar-lined paths to the temple. Don't be surprised to see a lot of shaved heads; pilgrims often offer up their hair in a sort of barber-barter deal with the god. If you want to lose your locks, 100 barbers are standing by day and night at the tonsuring station on the way to the "Q" complexes (Turapiti is also home to a flourishing wig industry.)

Receiving **darshan** requires getting a ticket from one of 14 *sudarshan* counters in Tirupati and Tirumala. There are two types of ticket. Free *darshan* tickets are usually timed for about 24hr. in advance and involve a wait of 6hr. or more. Special *darshan* tickets cost Rs40-60. Times are usually earlier and the wait is cut to about 3hr. Get in the line at least 1hr. before the time on your ticket. Be sure to leave your shoes at one of the shoe counters and to leave any cameras or leather goods at your hotel as you won't be allowed to enter the temple with them. The long wait begins at the Vaikuntam Queue Complex off to the left from the main route to the temple. The wait to enter the temple—even in the "special *darshan*" line—involves pressing through a network of narrow wire cages and constricted passageways with thousands of other pilgrims. Once you've entered the line, you'll have little idea of where you're going or how much farther you have to inch along.

As you approach the home stretch, the crowd becomes increasingly crushed and frenzied until you're finally swept along into the temple interior. Non-Hindu foreigners can avoid the crowd (and the experience) by going straight to the Deputy Executive Officer in the Vaikuntam Queue Complex. Here an "express *darshan*" taking one or two hours can be arranged upon presentation of your passport and Rs100. (☎ 2277199. Open daily 9-10am, 4-8pm, and 8-10pm.)

Entry to the temple is through a pair of silver doors, with a *vimana* fully covered in gold. The dazzling brilliance is testimony to the wealth of the richest temple in India—pilgrims pour Rs250,000 into temple coffers every day. Donations help relieve Lord Balaji of his debt, borrowed from Lord Kubera when he married.

After the long wait, *darshan* will seem exceptionally short. At the moment of truth, bare heads crane toward the holy image for one transcendent glimpse, while temple workers yank your arm to force your exit. The impressive image is made of gold and inlaid with precious stones. It is always covered with flowers so that not much is visible, apart from the mask of Vishnu drawn clearly on its forehead. The last leg of the visit takes you to the *prasad* line, where workers dish out free *laddus* consecrated by Lord Venkateshwara. Opposite the temple is a small and unremarkable **museum.** *(Open M-F 8am-8pm. Rs3. Temple open daily 24hr.)*

BIHAR बिहार

> ⚠️ **WARNING.** Women should not travel alone, and **no one should travel at night** in Bihar. Physical violence against tourists is rare, but *dacoits* still terrorize Bihar's countryside.

Many of India's formative events took place in the once-lush forests of Bihar, which is today the poorest and least urbanized state in India. The state gets its name from *vihara* (monastery), which refers to the secluded centers of Buddhist learning that flourished here more than a thousand years ago. The Buddha attained enlightenment under a tree in Bodh Gaya, and the Mauryan and Gupta Empires both grew from the city of Pataliputra (modern-day Patna).

Few traces are left of Bihar's past glories. Bihari politics have seen unending controversy and periodic caste-based violence over the years. Bihar's government is now under the notoriously corrupt control of the husband-and-wife combo Laloo Prasad Yadav and Rabri Devi: Devi, thanks to some scandals and abbreviated jail time, has accepted the official title of Chief Minister, which Laloo bestowed upon her. However, as head of his RJD party, Laloo remains an unchecked power in the state. While opposition groups protest the lack of development and the brazen ties between Laloo and the underworld, and more than once the Centre (national government) has intervened with special police units to help restore law and order, the decade-long dynasty is yet to be toppled.

In November 2000, Bihar was divided into two states: Bihar in the north and **Jharkhand** in the south. Jharkhand is a mineral-rich region with little else but mines and industrial plants. The Bihari countryside is mostly ruled by *goondas* (thugs) with connections to politicians, and *dacoits* (bandits) still roam Bihari streets.

Traveling in Bihar can be frustrating: conditions are bare, electricity cuts are frequent, and journeys of a few kilometers can take most of the day. Partly because of these inconveniences and the state's lawlessness, Bihar draws few tourists. Some, however, put up with Bihar's many hassles in the interests of experiencing the insight it offers into India, outside the *baksheesh* cocoon of the tourist circuit.

HIGHLIGHTS OF BIHAR

The so-called **Lotus Circuit** traces the Buddha's footsteps through several of Bihar's towns: **Bodh Gaya** (p. 127), where the Buddha attained enlightenment; **Rajgir** (p. 123), where his teachings were first compiled; **Nalanda** (p. 124), a major center of learning and philosophy; and **Vaishali** (p. 132), where some of his ashes are interred.

PATNA पटना ☎ 0612

As the capital of Bihar, Patna is simultaneously the state at its best and its worst. Many of the city's streets are buried beneath layers of foul fumes, plastic bags, and rotting muck. Hour-long rickshaw rides connect unimpressive attractions, and as the sun sets, blood-alcohol levels rise, making clashes with the police a nightly occurrence. The few tourists who linger more than a day before proceeding on the Buddhist pilgrimage circuit may find some interest in seeing a major Indian city almost totally unaffected by foreign tourism. For those willing to dig through the modern grit, there are traces of historical interest in Patna. The Mauryan empire had its center here, and the Guptas also made this their capital. Pataliputra, as it was called then, was abandoned after the Guptas' decline, but it rose again during the 17th century to become a regional center for the Mughals. The birth of the last Sikh guru, Gobind Singh, turned a narrow lane in the north of the city into a major Sikh pilgrimage destination. The East India Company had its largest opium warehouses here, now converted (vice for vice) into a state government printing office.

▐ TRANSPORTATION

Flights: Patna Airport, 6km from the railway station (taxi Rs150, auto-rickshaw Rs50, cycle-rickshaw Rs25). **Indian Airlines,** Gandhi Maidan (☎2222554). Open daily 10am-1pm and 2-4:30pm. To: **Kolkata** (1hr., 9:25pm, US$75); **Delhi** (2hr., 1-3 per day 11:35am-3:50pm, US$155); **Mumbai** (4hr., 3:50pm, US$225).

Trains: To: **Kolkata** (7-13hr., 7-10per day 2:15am-9:55pm, Rs154); **Delhi** (13-24hr., 11-12 per day 4:31am-11:55pm, Rs320); **Gaya** (2½hr., 4 per day 9:55am-10:45pm, Rs30); **Guwahati** (15-24hr., 2-4 per day 2:35am-10:20pm, Rs370); **Mumbai** (33hr., 2-3 per day 1-11:20pm, Rs409); **Rajgir** (2½hr., 3:40-9:15am, Rs16); **Varanasi** (3-6hr., 6-9 per day 2:30am-10:01pm, Rs135).

Buses: You can get anywhere in Bihar from **Harding Road bus stand,** 500m west of the railway station. To: **Bihar Sharif** (3hr., every 10min. 4:30am-8pm, Rs35); **Gaya** (3hr., 4 per day 5:30am-2:30pm, Rs40); **Raxaul** (6hr., every 1½hr. 6am-noon and 11:30pm, Rs120). Buses run frequently to **Hajipur,** where connections to Vaishali and Raxaul are available throughout the day.

Local Transportation: Shared **tempos** ply the main city arteries (Rs2-5 per ride) between the railway station, Patna Junction, Gandhi Maidan, and along Ashok Raj Path and Kankar Bagh Rd.

✦ ▐ ORIENTATION AND PRACTICAL INFORMATION

Patna sprawls along the south bank of the mighty Ganga. Getting from east to west across the city is a road trip in itself. Budget a minimum of two hours at peak traffic times. **Ashok Raj Path** is the main thoroughfare, sticking close to the river the whole way. **Kankar Bagh Road (Old Bypass Road)** covers the same distance on the south side of the city, just south of the railroad tracks. The east end of town is Old Patna. Most trains stop at **Patna Junction Station,** in the west. **Fraser Road,** where Patna's hotels, restaurants, and other conveniences are concentrated, runs straight north from the station. **Gandhi Maidan,** a large park north of Fraser Rd. (touching Ashok Raj Path), is a major landmark and local transportation hub. Next to the railway station, **Station Road** leads west to the **bus stand** and various government buildings.

Tourist Office: Bihar Tourist Office, Fraser Rd. (☎2225295), on the 2nd fl. of the blue-green Chowda Family Restaurant. Likely locked and abandoned, but officially open M-Sa 10am-5pm. Similarly, there is a "24hr." branch at the railway station, with brochures but no English speakers. The **Government of India Tourism Office** (☎2345776), Kankar Bagh Rd., is on the 3rd floor of Sudama Palace, opp. the railroad overbridge.

Currency Exchange: State Bank of India, Gandhi Maidan (☎2226134), on the left coming from Fraser Rd. Open M-F 10:30am-4pm, Sa 10:30am-12:30pm.

Library: Khuda Baksh Oriental Library, Ashok Raj Path. Houses intricate Mughal paintings, rare texts from Muslim Cordoba and a 1 in. Koran.

Police: Control Room, N. Gandhi Maidan (☎2223131), next to the futuristic, flattened white dome of the Shri Krishna Memorial Hall.

Hospital: Raj Lakshmi Nursing Home, Kankarbagh Rd. (☎2352225 or 2354320), 4km east of the Government of India Tourist Office.

Bihar

NEPAL

SIKKIM

0   60 miles
0   60 kilometers

Birganj
Raxaul (28A)
Gorakhpur
(28) Motihari Sitamarhi Jaynagar
Gandak R. Madhubani Nirmali Kishanganj
Muzaffarpur Kishanpur (57)
Vaishali
UTTAR Lalganj (28) Purnia (34)
PRADESH Sonepur (31)
(29) Maner Hajipur Ganga R.
Arrah Patna
Buxar Munger
Nalanda Bihar Sharif Bhagalpur
(30) Jahanabad Rajgir Pawapuri Rajmahal
Barabar
Caves
Sasaram Gaya
Son R. Bodh Simaltala
Gaya (31)
(2) Devghar
Kodarma Madhupur Dumka
Tilaiya Masanjor
JHARKHAND Parasnath
Hazaribag Dhanbad
Damodar R. Sindri (2)
Betla (Palamau)
National Park
Netarhat Ranchi WEST
(23) BENGAL
Gumla Jamshedpur
CHHATTISGARH (6)
Govt. of India statement:
The external boundaries (6)
of India are neither correct
nor authenticated.

BIHAR

Internet: Microgate, (☎2206009), Exhibition Rd., 150m from Station Rd. Call ahead evenings to reserve a slot. Cheap at Rs10-15 per hr. Open 9:30am-9pm. **Rendezvous Internet Cafe,** in the trendy nearby Windsor Hotel, has fast separate connections for each computer. Rs25 per hr. Open 10am-9pm.

Post Office: GPO, Station Rd., 500m west of the railway station. Open M-Sa 10am-4pm, Su 10am-1pm. **Postal Code:** 800001.

ACCOMMODATIONS AND FOOD

The hotel situation in Patna exemplifies how poorly the city accommodates (foreign) tourists: only the few upscale hotels around Fraser Rd.—and no budget ones—are authorized to accept foreign tourists. **Hotel Anand Regency ❷,**

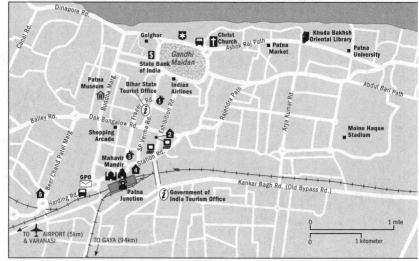

Station Rd. (☎2223960), the tall, white building beside the railway station, is the cheapest (legal) option. The rooms are equally large with huge windows that let in the blaring train whistles and announcements, day and night. (Doubles with attached baths Rs250-400. MC/V.) **Kautilya Vihar ❶**, Beer Chand Patel Path, (☎2225411) is Bihar State Tourism's typical labyrinth concrete megablock. More information for tourists here than elsewhere. Rooms are big and only a little bit gloomy. (6-bed dorms Rs80; doubles with attached bath Rs428-750. MC/V.) The **Windsor Hotel ❹**, Exhibition Rd. (☎2203250), offers professional luxury at one-third the price of its competition. (Singles Rs600-800 and doubles Rs750-1000 with attached bath. MC/V.) If you are persuasive or an IYH member, you may be able to stay (for free) at the **Patna Youth Hostel,** Fraser Rd., next to the Maurya Hotel.

Restaurants include **Anand Restaurant ❺**, on the 2nd fl. of the building at the intersection of Fraser and S.P. Verma Rd., which has a good Indian, Chinese, and Continental menu, plush seating, A/C, and bold geometric decor. Chicken steak sizzler RS100. (Open daily 10am-11pm.) **Mayfair Ice Cream Parlor and Restaurant ❶**, Fraser Rd., opposite the Bansi Vihar, 5min. north of the railway station. With the charm of a subterranean mess hall, the Mayfair overflows with people slurping ice cream (Rs12). Veg. and non-veg. fare Rs18-60. (Open daily 8am-10:30pm.)

👁 SIGHTS

PATNA MUSEUM. The Patna Museum contains a superb collection of stone and bronze sculpture, much of it dating from the Mauryan (3rd century BC) and Gupta (4th-6th centuries AD) periods. The most famous piece is the Chauri Bearer, in the second chamber on the left. *(Buddha Marg. Open Tu-Su 10:30am-4:40pm. Rs2.)*

HAR MANDIR. In the twisting lanes of Old Patna is Har Mandir, a Sikh *gurudwara* that marks the birthplace of the 10th and last Sikh guru, Gobind Singh (b. 1666). The second-most important throne of the Sikh religion (after the Golden Temple in Amritsar) and the only beautiful edifice in Patna, Har Mandir is a white-domed building set among the busy bustle of the old town's *chowk*. The present building was constructed after a 1954 earthquake destroyed the original. There is a

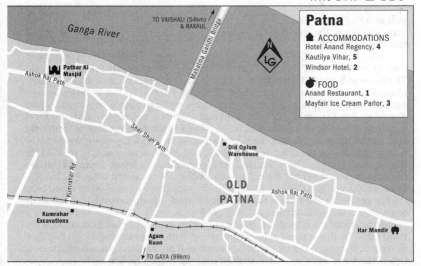

Patna

♠ ACCOMMODATIONS
Hotel Anand Regency, **4**
Kautilya Vihar, **5**
Windsor Hotel, **2**

🍎 FOOD
Anand Restaurant, **1**
Mayfair Ice Cream Parlor, **3**

Ganga River

TO VAISHALI (54km) ↗
& RAXAUL

Mahatma Gandhi Bridge

Pathar Ki Masjid
Ashok Raj Path

Sher Shah Path

Kumrahar Rd.

Old Opium Warehouse

OLD
PATNA

Ashok Raj Path

Kumrahar Excavations

Agam Kuan

Har Mandir

↓ TO GAYA (98km)

one-room museum upstairs with exhibits on the history of Sikhism. *(Share a tempo from Sri Krishna Hall on Gandhi Maidan (Rs6). Budget 2hr. for the ride in bad traffic. Visitors must cover their heads. Open daily 5am-9pm; museum open daily 8am-noon and 3-8pm. Free.)*

GOLGHAR. One of Patna's most bizarre landmarks is the Golghar, an egg-shaped grain storage bin. Built in 1786 to protect against famine, it was never used and now sits like a great stone space helmet just left of Gandhi Maidan. The two staircases that spiral high above the street represent the quickest way to get away from the smog and dirt; hence this sight's otherwise inexplicable popularity.

RAJGIR राजगीर ☎ 06112

Bodh Gaya will always be first in the hearts of Bihar's Buddhist pilgrims, but for the truly devoted, Rajgir is a close second. The capital of the once powerful Magadha Kingdom now lies in rubble with a few worthy sights on its mountainous outskirts. Pilgrims flock here during the winter months to climb Vulture Peak, where the Buddha delivered many of his most famous sermons. The first Buddhist Council took place in Rajgir, and the ruins of the university at Nalanda nearby show the success and scale of Buddhist learning that thrived here for nearly a thousand years. Jain influence in Rajgir was also strong; Jain temples dot the low hills around the town center, commemorating the 14 seasons that Mahavira spent in this tranquil valley. Surrounded by mountains and scattered with ruins, Rajgir is the most scenic and most relaxed of all Bihar's Buddhist towns.

Trains go to **Patna** (3-5hr., 5 per day 5:30am-3:40pm, Rs20-24). **Jeeps** and buses from Bihar Sharif pass Nalanda and arrive at the bus stand in Rajgir 15km later. From here, **buses** run to: **Gaya** (3hr., every 30min. 6:30am-6pm, Rs30); **Nalanda** (every 10min., Rs4); **Patna** (4hr., 3 and 6pm, Rs35). For Patna, you can also take a jeep or bus to **Bihar Sharif** (1hr., frequent 5am-7pm, Rs10) and then catch a bus from there (3hr., Rs25). From the bus stand, the **train station** is 400m down National Highway 82 towards Nalanda, on the left. In the opposite direction, towards Gaya, NH 82 passes the hot springs and other pilgrimage sites. A dirt street lined with shops leads east from the bus stand, and after 200m hits the **main street,** which connects with NH 82 near the hot springs. The

BIHAR

post office is here. **Postal Code:** 803116. To the right of its intersection with the main street are the **New Popular Pharmacy** (open daily 6am-9pm) and the **police station** (☎ 2255228).

Two monasteries offer flawless **lodging** around the ruined ramparts of an ancient fort. In January and February, Burmese travelers occasionally fill these places. The **Burmese Buddhist Temple ❶**, at the end of the main road, is a pleasant, friendly place, with views of the fields and hills. Managing Priest U Za Yan Ta, to the annoyance of visiting Burmese government officials, displays photos of Aung San and Aung San Suu Kyi. (☎ 2255024. Beds in single, double, and triple rooms are Rs60 each if you use the clean common baths.) The **Bengali Buddhist Society Temple ❶**, next to the Burmese temple, lacks views but features hot geyser-equipped bathrooms capable of pleasing *bodhisattvas* and backpackers alike. (☎ 2255116. Rooms Rs100-200.) There's always the government's **Hotel Gautam Vihar ❶**, between the bus stand and the railway station, next to the **tourist office.** (☎ 2255273. Dorms Rs50; doubles Rs450, with bath Rs525.) Another option is **Green Hotel,** near the hot springs, a few meters past the bypass road, which cooks the best *thali* in town. (Open daily 8am-10pm.)

Rajgir's **sights** are spread out over a 5km long stretch of road best covered by *tonga* (Rs30-50 if you share; otherwise Rs150-200 during peak season and half that the rest of the year). Centers of Buddhist interest are on **Ratnagiri,** a scenic mountain at the far end of the road. A **chairlift** leads up to the top, where the huge Japanese-built **Vishva Shanti Stupa** (world peace *stupa*) casts its shadow over the valley below. The chairlift (Rs25) is open daily 8am-1pm and 2-5pm, but only when there are at least five passengers. If you don't trust this aerial contraption, there is also a 1km footpath. From the *stupa*, the small path winds around the side of the mountain back down to the road; take the first left onto a series of stony steps that leads up and down until it arrives at **Gridhrakuta,** or "Vulture's Peak." Once a favorite rainy season retreat of the Buddha, Gridhrakuta marks the site of two caves where the Buddha gave sermons. The remains of a monastery from the Gupta period are also here. At the foot of Ratnagiri are the remains of **Jivakamra Vana,** an early monastery built in the mango garden which was another of the Buddha's favorite haunts.

Near the intersection with Gaya Rd. is **King Bimbisara's jail,** where the Buddhist convert-king was imprisoned and eventually executed by his son and successor, Ajatasatru. Legend says that the king chose the site of his incarceration; from here he could look out from his cell and watch the Buddha as he meditated and taught on the mountain. Today the rubble of the prison is unimpressive. Along the dirt road that passes the *math* are two chambers carved out of the cliff face known as the **Swarna Bhandar,** which are said to mark the location of Bimbisara's treasury.

At the foot of Vaibhara Hill, on the outskirts of town, is **Brahma Kunj,** where a half-dozen hot springs have been incorporated into a Hindu temple. A stone stairway past the baths leads up to **Pippala Cave,** a rectangular piece of rock that was once a hermitage. The stairway continues to **Saptaparni Cave,** where 500 of the Buddha's disciples held the first Buddhist Council. The surrounding hills are home to over 40 Jain shrines, most of them connected by stone paths. Visiting the temples on the five principle mountains of the area—in clockwise direction, Vipulachal, Ratnagiri, Udaxgiri, Savrangiri, and Vaibhargiri—is an arduous but worthwhile task. Bring coins to leave with the temple keepers.

NALANDA नालन्दा

Built by the Guptas during the 5th century AD and boasting a reputation as a center of learning that dates back to the 1st millennium BC, Nalanda is the site of one of the oldest universities in the world as well as a major pilgrimage destination for Sri Lankan and Japanese Buddhists. By the time the Buddha visited Nalanda, the town was a teeming and prosperous population center. Other religious VIPs also sojourned in Nalanda: Jainism's founder Mahavira used it as a retreat from the monsoon, and Sariputra, the Buddha's earliest disciple, was born and died here. Legendary Chinese traveler Xuanzang, known for his detailed accounts of the places he visited on his sutra-collecting journeys around India, studied at the university during the 7th century along with 4000 other students studying everything from Buddhist and Vedic philosophy to logic, grammar, chemistry, and medicine. As Nalanda's fame grew during the centuries that followed, so did its size. New buildings soared to the height of nine stories, and with the aid of King Harsha of Kannauj, Nalanda amassed a library of 9 million manuscripts. By the 13th century, though, successive waves of Muslim invaders had chased out all the students and reduced the library's collection to cinders.

Frequent **jeeps** and **buses** leave for **Nalanda** from the bus stand at **Rajgir** (Rs4). From Nalanda's bus stand, you can share a *tonga* (Rs5) or walk 2km to the site. Although it makes sense to visit Nalanda as a daytrip, you can stay at the modest **Chinese Temple ❶**, by the bus stand (Rs50-100 per person), or the **PWD Guest House ❶**, near the park (doubles Rs100).

In the tranquil, well-kept **park** run by the Archaeological Survey of India, visitors can stroll through the excavated remains of a dozen monastery buildings. There is a one-room **museum** opposite the entrance, 200m down the road, containing stone and bronze Pala sculptures. (Park open daily 7:30am-5pm. Rs230 or US$5. Museum open Sa-Th 10am-4:40pm. Rs2.)

GAYA गया ☎ 0631

The city of Gaya takes its name from the demon Gayasura, who purified himself through a rigorous series of yoga poses and received this sacred tract of land along the River Phalgu as a reward. As an additional reward, Gaya also received the power to absolve ancestral sins—it is said that one *shraddha* (funeral rite) in Gaya is equivalent to 11 *shraddhas* anywhere else. Hindu pilgrims visit each of the 45 shrines in Gaya (including the Bodhi Tree in Bodh Gaya), offering prayers for the dead and rupees for the *gayaval* (attending priests). The high season begins in September when the Phalgu swells with the monsoon rains and thousands of pilgrims descend upon the *ghats* to perform their ritual ablutions. While Gaya is slightly less important to devout Hindus than Bodh Gaya is to Buddhists, it manages to surpass its sister city in its levels of grime and poverty. Thirty-six kilometers north are the **Barabar Caves,** a series of rock-hewn Jain temples dating from the 3rd century BC, that were featured as the "Marabar Caves" in E.M. Forster's *A Passage to India*.

▐ TRANSPORTATION

Trains: Trains leave from **Gaya Junction Station.** The railway **reservation office** is to the right of the station. Open M-Sa 8am-8pm, Su 8am-2pm. To: **Kolkata** (3½-8hr., 5-8 per day 3:59am-11:15pm, Rs203); **Delhi** (15-18hr., 3-6 per day 1:39am-9:25pm, Rs258-360); **Patna** (2½hr., 4am and midnight, Rs121; frequent unreserved "passenger trains," 3-4hr., 5:15am-10pm, Rs19); **Varanasi** (3½-5½hr., 3-7 per day 2:35am-9:15pm, Rs128). From Bela to the **Barabar Caves,** it's a 12km *tempo* or *tonga* ride (Rs20-25) plus a 5km walk.

Buses: From the **Zila School Bus Stand** to **Bodh Gaya** (30min.-1hr., frequent, Rs6). Shared **tempos** leave almost continuously from both sides of the school (Rs8-10). The **Manpur Bus Stand,** across the Phalgu River, near the bridge, has buses to **Nalanda** and **Rajgir** (3hr., every hr. 6am-6pm, Rs30). Drivers congregate outside the train station and ferry passengers directly to Bodh Gaya at slightly inflated prices.

Local Transportation: Rickshaws go to: the Zila School Bus Stand, the Vishnupad Temple, and the Mangla Gouri Temple (Rs10-15). Shared **tempos** run between the railway station, Gandhi Chowk, and the Manpur Bus Stand (Rs6).

■ ⁊ ORIENTATION AND PRACTICAL INFORMATION

Gaya is on the west bank of the Phalgu River. From **Gaya Junction Station**, temple-topped Ram Silad Hill to the left marks the north edge of town. To the right, **Station Road** runs south for several blocks; **Swarajpuri Road** continues on to **Gandhi Chowk.** A left turn at the end of Station Rd. leads east to the main bazaar, **Gautama Buddha (GB) Road,** and the bridge. GB Rd. extends south to **Vishnupad Temple, Brahmyoni Hill.** GB Rd. turns into **Gaya Road** and extends 10km more to **Bodh Gaya.**

Tourist Office: Inside the railway station. Has a dated wall map of Gaya, some relic posters and a Buddhist Circuit pamphlet (Rs5). Open M-Sa 10am-5pm.

Currency Exchange: The nearest banks that change currency are in Bodh Gaya. In emergencies, **Hotel Saluja** (☎2436243) changes major currencies and traveler's checks.

Police: Control Room (☎2223131 or 2223132). **Superintendent of Police** (☎2420004), two blocks north of the Zila School.

Hospital: The **Magadh Medical College** (☎2222410), west of Gandhi Chowk, is a government hospital, and an awful place to be sick.

Internet: Cyber City, on Station Rd., opposite the Station View Hotel. Has a generator and printer (Rs20 per page). Rs20 per hr. Open daily 10am-10pm.

Post Office: GPO, GB Rd., one block north of the Zila School. Open M-Sa 10am-4pm. There is a smaller post office on Station Rd., 150m right of the station, on the left. **Postal Code: 823001.**

⌂ ACCOMMODATIONS

All of Gaya's hotels are unfortunately on Station Rd., closest to the train whistle blasts. Check-out is 24hr.

Hotel Buddha, Laxman Sahay Ln. (☎2423428), at the end of the small road, left of the Ajatsatru Hotel. Doubles have comfortable mattresses, TVs, and both filtered water and electric anti-mosquito units available on request. Second-floor, Western-style rooms open onto a roofed garden terrace. Singles Rs165; doubles Rs250; triples Rs300. ❷

Pal Rest House, Station Rd. (☎2229042). Turn right out of the station; the rest house is 250m down on the left-hand side, after the post office. Simple rooms around a central stairwell. Clean, cheap, and quiet. Singles Rs70-100; doubles Rs135; triples Rs250. ❶

Ajatsatru Hotel, Station Rd. (☎2434584). Opposite the railway station. Orderly rooms with TVs, local phones and attached bathrooms. Complete with porters ready to carry business travelers' luggage to the elevator. Singles Rs187; doubles Rs268-375. ❷

◖ FOOD

Haji Market, a block south of Gandhi Chowk, next to Chatta Masjid, is the place to sample the local speciality of *bakharkhani,* a sweet, round, Muslim bread. Except for some hotel restaurants and roadside joints, Gaya has slim pickings for food. The **Sujata Restaurant ❶,** in the Ajatsatru Hotel, serves the best meals in town. Zesty fish curry Rs24, creamy stuffed capsicum Rs60. (Open daily 7am-10pm.)

👁 SIGHTS

Though Gaya is one of the most sacred cities in the Hindu religion, its temples lack the splendor of those in other large pilgrimage sites. Non-Hindus may be disappointed. The shrines listed below are within walking distance of each other.

BRAHMYONI HILL. The hill is sacred to Buddhists, who associate it with Gayasirsan, the mountain where the Buddha delivered several important sermons. One thousand steep stones twist up to the Shiva temple at the top of the hill, and a handful of smaller Hanuman and Goddess shrines are scattered along the way. Prepare to encounter persistent requests from Hindu priests asking for money as you head for the summit's panorama, which is worth the long walk up. *(1km southwest of the Vishnupad Temple, by rickshaw Rs20.)*

VISHNUPAD TEMPLE. Perched on the bank of the Phalga River, this expansive temple complex houses a footprint of Vishnu in the form of the Buddha under a spire capped by a 50kg gold ornament. The footprint is embedded in stone and enshrined in a 2m-long silver basin. Non-Hindus may not enter the main shrine, but they can try to get a closer look at the sanctum (but not the footprint) by climbing the stairs of the raised area near the temple's entrance. *(5km from the train station, by rickshaw Rs10-15.)*

DURGA TEMPLE. In this rather mundane temple, non-Hindus can observe and even participate in the *shraddhas* (funeral rites). Pilgrims wishing to perform the *shraddha* at Gaya must first circumambulate their own village five times. *(1km east of the Vishnupad Temple.)*

MANGLA GOURI TEMPLE. Also referred to as Shaktipith since Sati's breast fell here after she was cut to pieces (see **Local Legend**, p. 440.) Images of the goddess are housed in a squat, cave-like mausoleum, inscribed with the epic verse of Sati's destruction. *(On the same road to Brahmyoni, 500m closer to town.)*

BODH GAYA बोध गया ☎ 0631

Bodh Gaya is the holiest site in the Buddhist religion and the only Bihari pilgrimage site that attracts non-Buddhist tourism. One of the most significant events in the history of Asia took place here in the 6th century BC, when Prince Siddhartha Gautama attained enlightenment under the famous pipal tree, a descendent of which stands on the same spot today (see **The Tree of Knowledge,** below).

> ## THE TREE OF KNOWLEDGE The Bodhi Tree at Bodh Gaya
> has been the subject of countless legends. Central to the mystique and holiness of this particular pipal tree is the belief that it is a direct descendent of the one under which the Buddha meditated more than 2500 years ago. Some believe that Emperor Ashoka cut down the original tree before his famous conversion to Buddhism. The tree miraculously sprang back to life, only to be hacked down again by Ashoka's wife, jealous of the attention and respect her husband had started to pay the tree since its remarkable recovery. However, the tree once again sprang up from its roots. Unnerved and impressed by its hardiness, Ashoka and his wife sent a sapling from the original tree to Sri Lanka, where it is believed to still prosper today. The centuries to come witnessed a series of attacks on the tree at Bodh Gaya, which weakened it to such an extent that it finally fell to a storm in 1876. The revered incarnation of the original tree that stands today grew from a seedling taken from the original tree's offspring in Sri Lanka.

BIHAR

Buddhism in Bodh Gaya, however, is new and mostly foreign. Although Buddhist monasteries thrived here long ago, they were left to sink into the mud after Buddhism faded out of India in the 12th century. It wasn't until the 19th century that Bodh Gaya was reborn as an important religious center, when British-led archaeological teams persuaded monks from Sri Lanka and Burma to raise the funds necessary to restore the Mahabodhi Temple to its former glory.

The steady flow of wealthy tourists has elevated Bodh Gaya to a level of economic prosperity unmatched in Bihar. The state's usual problems of robbery and violence mostly end within the city limits, although bandits have boarded buses at night between Gaya and Bodh Gaya. The winter (Dec.-Feb.) is the busiest time to visit, when students, pilgrims, and monks (the Dalai Lama included) congregate here. The monasteries fill up, visiting teachers offer meditation courses, tent restaurants abound, and monks from around the world intone *sutras* in monasteries and temples built in their own national styles. By April, however, the crowds thin out, many of the restaurants and hotels close down, and the streets of Bodh Gaya resume the air of meditative tranquility that has reigned for thousands of years.

▐ TRANSPORTATION

The nearest **train station** is in Gaya, but there is a **railway reservation counter** at the corner of the Bihar State Tourism Complex, though the computer connection is not always reliable. Open M-Sa 10am-4:30pm. **Buses** leave for **Gaya** from the stand near the Burmese Temple (every 30min. 5am-6pm, Rs6), with the bus stopping every 10m for passengers to embark, disembark, and sometimes just bark. Shared *tempos* and **jeeps** ply the route in less time (Rs8-10). Buses also run to **Patna** (7am and 2pm) from the Bihar State Tourism Complex, and to **Varanasi** (6-7hr., 6am, Rs100) from next to the Gaden Phelgyeling Monastery.

✺ ? ORIENTATION AND PRACTICAL INFORMATION

It would require real effort to get lost in Bodh Gaya. The main road through town is interrupted only by a pedestrian strip-mall in front of the **Mahabodhi Temple.** The market, museum, Thai Temple, and Roof Institute—as well as just about every notable sight and hotel in the city—lie on this rickshaw and *tonga* path.

Tourist Office: (☎23400672), first block west of the Thai temple. Packaged with hotels and restaurants as the **Bihar State Tourism Complex.** Open M-Sa 10am-5pm.

Currency Exchange: State Bank of India, Bodh Gaya Rd. (☎2200746), next to the Chinese temple. Open M-F 8:30am-2:30pm, Sa 10:30am-12:30pm.

Police, Gaya Rd.(☎2200741), 200m south of the Burmese Temple.

Hospital: Conditions at the **government hospital,** on the left on the way to town, are not ideal. Doctors at **Indosan Nipponji Temple's clinic** will see tourists with emergencies.

Internet Access: Internet cafes by the Thai Temple are twice as expensive as the kiosks opposite the Mahabodhi Temple (Rs20 per hr.)

Post Office: Gaya Rd. (☎2200471), on the left just after Bodh Gaya Rd. Open M-Sa 10:30am-5pm. **Postal Code:** 842231.

▐ ACCOMMODATIONS

Bodh Gaya is full of hotels, but the temple- and monastery-run guest houses are best. During the winter months, they fill up quickly. Remember to respect the rules of the religious community—no drinking, smoking, or "improper sexual conduct."

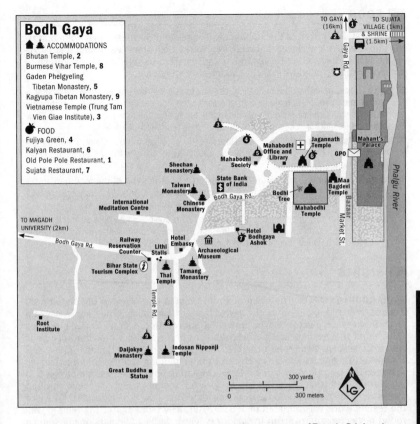

Bodh Gaya

🏠 🏕 ACCOMMODATIONS
Bhutan Temple, 2
Burmese Vihar Temple, 8
Gaden Phelgyeling
  Tibetan Monastery, 5
Kagyupa Tibetan Monastery, 9
Vietnamese Temple (Trung Tam
  Vien Giae Institute), 3

🍴 FOOD
Fujiya Green, 4
Kalyan Restaurant, 6
Old Pole Pole Restaurant, 1
Sujata Restaurant, 7

TO GAYA (16km)
TO SUJATA VILLAGE (1km) & SHRINE (1.5km)
Gaya Rd.
Jagannath Temple
Mahant's Palace
Mahabodhi Office and Library
GPO
Mahabodhi Society
Phalgu River
Shechan Monastery
State Bank of India
Taiwan Monastery
Bodhi Tree
Maa Bagdevi Temple
Chinese Monastery
Bodh Gaya Rd.
Mahabodhi Temple
International Meditation Centre
Bazaar Market St.
TO MAGADH UNIVERSITY (2km)
Bodh Gaya Rd.
Railway Reservation Counter
Hotel Embassy
Lithi Stalls
Archaeological Museum
Hotel Bodhgaya Ashok
Bihar State Tourism Complex
Thal Temple
Tamang Monastery
Temple Rd.
Root Institute
Daijokyo Monastery
Indosan Nipponji Temple
Great Buddha Statue

0   300 yards
0   300 meters

🏛 **Bhutan Temple** (☎ 2200710). Entrance gate on the street east of Temple Rd. In a beautiful garden dominated by a colorful Bhutanese temple. Rooms are clean and spacious and have mosquito nets. Gates close 10pm. Fills up Nov.-Dec. Doubles Rs100-200. ❶

Vietnamese Temple (☎ 2220237), past the end of the road beside the Gaden Phelgyeling Monastery. Exquisitely-furnished sitting areas and a quarry full of marble. Coal doubles with hot water and an air of luxury. Rs200 per person. ❷

Gaden Phelgyeling Tibetan Monastery (☎ 2200722), next to the Mahabodhi Society. An ever-expanding universe overrun by Tibetan monks Oct.-Feb. Gates close 9:30pm. Small singles with attached bath Rs150; larger rooms with hot water Rs200. ❷

Kagyupa Tibetan Monastery, Temple Rd. (☎ 2200795). The more remote and peaceful of the two Tibetan temples, Kagyupa is less likely to be full during the packed winter months. Clean common bath with hot water. Doubles Rs150, Nov.-Jan. Rs250. ❷

Burmese Vihar Temple, Gaya Rd. (☎ 2200721), opposite the bridge to Sujata Village. High rises and bazaar festivity. Simple rooms with mosquito coils and nets look out onto quiet fields and rice paddies on one side and the busy Gaya road on the other. Packed Nov.-Jan. Common bath. Gates close 9:30pm. Dorms Rs45; doubles Rs80. ❶

◨ FOOD

Seasonal stalls in front of the Mahabodhi Temple and Burmese Vihar whip up *lassis* and cakes. A few places in the market lane sizzle fritters year-round. The *lithis* in the family-operated tea stalls in front of the Thai temple have been known to transport hungry pilgrims to higher states of contentment.

▨ **Fujiya Green,** near the Tibetan Temple. Leaving the pedestrian precinct with the Mahabodhi Temple to your left, make a right and follow the signs around to the left. Lamps-and-shades shack serves up simple dishes to the lamas from the monastery next door. *Thukpas* Rs10, vegetable chop suey Rs25. Open daily 7am-9pm. ❶

▨ **Old Pole Pole Restaurant,** Gaya Rd. Opposite the Burmese Temple. Quirky menu ranges from spinach spaghetti (Rs30) to Japanese *okonomi-yaki* (Rs30). All excellent. Open daily 6:30am-10:30pm. ❷

Sujata Restaurant, inside Hotel Bodh Gaya Ashok, at the end of the road next to the museum. This is the best but most expensive in town. Offers A/C atmosphere with Indian veg. and non-veg. dishes (Rs125-165). Open daily 8am-10pm. ❹

Kalyan Restaurant, opposite the main temple, 70m down a small lane on the left-hand side. Simple, open-air place serves the usual range of dishes as well as vegetable *gyoza* for Rs25. Open daily 7am-10pm. ❶

◉ SIGHTS

MAHABODHI TEMPLE. The town of Bodh Gaya is built around the Mahabodhi Temple, referred to simply as the *stupa* by most Buddhists. The temple rises up from flowery gardens to tower above the sacred Bodhi Tree. Smaller shrines throughout the grounds mark different stages in the Buddha's meditations; he is said to have spent 49 days here, deep in thought after deciding that extreme asceticism was bringing him no closer to a true understanding of life's suffering than his previous life as a playboy-prince. Emperor Ashoka built the first temple on this site during the 3rd century BC, but the present temple, which has been through layers and layers of restorations, probably dates from the 6th century AD. Much of the rescue work was initiated in 1882 by Burmese monks after the temple was found neglected and overrun by squatters. Over the last 30 years, many statues have been stolen from the temple's circular niches. The oldest structure left on the site is a stone railing built in the 1st century AD to keep out wild animals; a quarter of it, however, has been whisked away to museums in London and Kolkata.

At the back of the temple is the sacred **Bodhi Tree** (see p. 127), a direct descendent of the tree under which the Buddha attained enlightenment. Throngs of pilgrims gather around the tree during all seasons to pay respects to the enshrined plant. The **Vajrasana,** or "diamond throne," between the tree and the temple, is thought to be where the Buddha sat. A gilded image of the Buddha is behind glass in the temple, and another is on the first floor, which is open in the evenings for meditation. A part of the first floor is permanently closed due to one depraved tree surgeon's attempt to saw off a branch of the sacred tree as a souvenir. *(Temple compound open daily 5am-9pm. Free; camera fee Rs20.)*

SUJATA VILLAGE. In the winter, you can cross the dry river bed from the Mahant's palace in Bodh Gaya to the peaceful village on the other side (in summer, use the bridge 200m downstream). Here, 500m through the eastern fields, grows a descendant of the banyan tree under which the Buddha feasted on *kheer* (sweet rice milk) offered by Sujata, a local woman who has since become perhaps the most famous beverage vendor in history. This was his first meal after six years spent in ascetic solitude. The tree has been converted into a shrine. The **Matang Rishi Ashram** is the banyan's neighbor. In the middle of the village is a grass mound believed to mark the site of Sujata's house.

MAHAKALA CAVES. The Buddha and five companions undertook six years of ascetic meditation in these two caves on Dungeswari Mountain. A tiny Tibetan monastery marks the spot. On the summit, six *stupas* commemorate the six mendicants. From Bodh Gaya, walk the 6.5km to the mountains northeast of Sujata Village (2hr.) The temple is the small white block on the Gaya end of the range, near Pragbodhi Village. Hop on a motorbike to cover the longer, uneven road via Gaya (45min., Rs250) more efficiently than auto-rickshaw or taxi (1½hr., Rs300-600).

OTHER TEMPLES AND MONASTERIES. Throw a stone in any direction and you'll hit two temples and half a dozen monks. A 1hr. walk around Bodh Gaya will show you all the major temples. The chapel walls of the **Gaden Phelgyeling Tibetan Monastery,** next to the Mahabodhi Society, are painted with *thanka*-style clouds, wheels, and *bodhisattvas*. East along Bodh Gaya Rd., the **Chinese Temple** and **Shechen Monastery,** down a lane just in front, are also impressive. The **Thai Temple,** Bodh Gaya's second most prominent landmark, is 500m after the main road takes a sharp left. A large *wat* with classic claw-like tips on its orange roof, the temple opened in 1957 (year 2500 in the Buddhist calendar). Side-roads branch off the main road on either side of the Thai Temple. To the left are the **Bhutan Monastery** and the Japanese **Indosan Nipponji Temple.** The lane on the right side of the Thai Temple leads to the **Kagyupa Tibetan Monastery,** which contains brightly colored, larger-than-life murals depicting the life of the Buddha. Next door is the **Daijokyo Temple,** another Japanese construction with an oppressive concrete exterior. Just up the road is the 25m **Giant Buddha Statue,** which was built by Japanese monks, to second the original at Nagoya, and inaugurated by the Dalai Lama in 1989.

The **Mahant's Palace,** on the left just before you reach the center of town, has morphed into a Hindu temple and offers views of the Niranjana River and the mountains beyond. *(Most temples open daily 7 or 8am-noon and 2-5pm.)* The Archaeological Survey of India has a small **museum,** just off the main road, which contains statues unearthed nearby. *(Open M-Th and Sa-Su 10am-5pm. Rs2.)*

BUDDHISM AND VOLUNTEER OPPORTUNITIES

During the high season, meditation courses are a major industry in Bodh Gaya. Teachers from all over the world jet (or rickshaw) in to train Buddhists and aspiring Buddhists in this temple town. A few permanent institutions in Bodh Gaya also conduct courses; though the peak season runs from October to March, a couple of places remain open and active throughout the summer. **The Root Institute for Wisdom Culture** (☎2200714; www.rootinstitute.com), at the edge of town down a dirt path south from the main road, offers 10-day Tibetan Buddhism courses during the winter with guest lamas and Western teachers in a quiet, intimate compound that doubles as a hospital for lepers and polio victims. (Rs2900-5300; includes room and board.) Daily meditation sessions which are open to outsiders on a walk-in basis are also held during the winter. Room and board is available for non-meditators, and although they don't provide instruction in the off season, visitors are welcome all year. **The International Meditation Center** (☎2200707), opposite the Thai monastery, offers free instruction in the Vipassana Method year-round. Participants can stay as long as they want; a donation of Rs75-100 per day will defray the costs of a dorm bed in a double or triple and three meals. The **Vipassana Meditation Center** (☎2200437), behind the university, has 10-day courses twice every month except May and June. They will house and feed you for a donation.

There are a number of charitable organizations in Bodh Gaya. It may be more worthwhile to give money to these organizations than to the children begging on the streets, whose actual need can be tough to determine. The **Root Institute,** which runs one of the area's major clinics always welcomes donations and volunteers with experience in medicine or physical therapy. Anyone can ride along on the mobile clinic trips to nearby villages (9am departure) if you schedule the day before. The **Mahabodhi Society,** set back from the road, across the street from the Mahabodhi Temple, runs a number of charitable programs including a free pharmacy, a primary school, an ambulance service, and a rehabilitation center. The **Buddha Handicap Development Society** (☎2200047), in the RBM Guest House, near the Bhuta Temple, provides specialized training and mobility aids for persons with physical disabilities.

VAISHALI वैशाली

Fifty-five kilometers north of Patna, Vaishali is a tiny, one-cow town, surrounded by rice paddies and home to a handful of farming families, several sites of interest to religious pilgrims, and the ruined remains of the world's first republic. As the capital of the Licchavis during the 6th century BC, Vaishali was renowned for its peace, prosperity, and elected system of government. The town is also the birthplace and hometown of Jainism's founder, Mahavir, and the site at which the Buddha preached his last sermon before announcing his approaching *parinirvana.* During the in season (Oct.-Feb.), the town occasionally attracts tourists of Bihar's Buddhist sites; off-season, you will almost certainly have the place to yourself.

▐ TRANSPORTATION

Direct **buses** go to Vaishali from the main bus stand in Patna (2hr., up to 4 per day in-season 6am-2pm, Rs30). From Harding Rd. in Patna, hop on one of the frequent buses to **Hajipur** (Rs12) and get on another bus to **Lalganj** (Rs10), where shared **taxis** and **jeeps** and buses headed to Muzaffarpur all ply the road through Vaishali (Rs10). Ask to be let off at the Government's Tourist Lodge. In practice, you'll just have to show up at the bus stand and repeatedly scream and holler your destination. Erratic direct buses to **Patna** (4-6 per day 6:30am-4pm, Rs35) pass by the Tourist Lodge, and will stop if aggressively flagged down; also there are regular jeeps and trucks to Lalganj, where connections to Patna are frequent. To get to **Raxaul** from Vaishali take a jeep or bus north to **Muzaffarpur** (2hr., Rs20), and switch to one of the Raxaul-bound buses (4hr., Rs50) that depart from the bus stand across the tracks; the Muzaffarpur train station is a fetid madhouse but does have trains to Raxaul (4hr., 4 per day, Rs44).

▐▌ ACCOMMODATIONS AND FOOD

Despite throngs of pilgrims, the **Sri Lanka Buddhist Guest House ❶,** on the road that leads to the *stupa,* has spotless rooms and terraces; the friendly monks will even gladly cook up mountains of Sri Lankan food (doubles Rs100-200).

The **Tourist Hotel ❷,** past the Sri Lanka Guest House, alongside the Coronation Tank, offers threadbare luxury. (Doubles Rs350.) On the north side of Coronation Tank is the **Youth Hostel ❶.** (☎29425. Dorms Rs40; doubles Rs150.)

◉ SIGHTS

Vaishali's proud beginnings as the earliest republic have been reduced to a humble group of grassy mounds behind the Tourist Lodge. Farther down the main road, a gateway leads 1km to the **Coronation Tank,** a large rectangular pond at the center of Vaishali's tourist area, once used to anoint the town's leaders during inaugural ceremonies. To the left of the tank is the Japanese Temple and the magnificent crowned white dome of the Japanese-sponsored **Vishwa Shanti Peace Stupa,** consecrated here in 1996. (*Stupa* and temple open dawn-dusk.) A small **museum** on the other side of the tank showcases some of the stone and terracotta pieces dug up from nearby sites. (Open M-Th and Sa-Su 10am-5pm. Rs2.) Down a small lane to the right of the Tourist Hotel, a well-maintained garden encloses the **relics stupa,** thought to contain a portion of Buddha's ashes, which were divided up after his cremation and distributed among the leaders of the eight major kingdoms of northern India. Today, a shallow circle of stones covered by a conical green tin roof is all that remains of the *stupa.*

This same lane zig-zags another 5km through fields and villages to the walled compound containing the **Ashokan Pillar** (locally known as **Kolhua Lat**); a more direct route is north via the main highway, turning left at the gate, away from the tourist lodge, and left at the fork in the road 50m later. The lion capital that tops the pillar is cut from a single piece of limestone and is where the Buddha died. In the pillar's shadow, an age-withered **stupa** and a small tank commemorate the spot where a monkey once presented honey to the Buddha. Ongoing excavations and brick-laying are Bihar Tourism's effort to unearth (or "reconstruct") a more extensive complex, on par with attractions like Nalanda. (Open dawn-dusk. US$5.) On the other side of the main road, a 10min. walk through the village, is the ancient **Chaumukhi Mahadev Mandir,** a four-faced Shiva *linga.*

 BORDER CROSSING: RAXAUL रक्सौल

Raxaul ain't pretty. Mercifully, trains are ready to whisk you away. **Trains** run from Raxaul to: **Kolkata** (19hr., 10:20am, Rs288); **Delhi** (26-29hr., 2 per day 12:45 and 9:55am, Rs335); **Muzaffarpur** (4hr., 5 per day 5:30-12:45am, Rs44) where more train connections are available. Whenever deemed full enough, **buses** to **Patna** leave from the Old Bus Stand just off the main road by the railroad tracks (9hr., every hr. 4am-10pm, Rs120), via Muzaffarpur (4hr., Rs50). Raxaul's main street leads straight over the bridge into **Birganj** in Nepal, cutting through the market area and the tangle of alleyways to the east and west. **There is no currency exchange in Raxaul**—Birganj and Patna are the closest places. A row of money changers by the railroad tracks will do the job at emergency-only rates. The **police station** (☎ 062552 21021) is on the main street, next to the Sun Temple.

 BORDER PATROL. Whether you are coming from India or Nepal, make sure you stop at *both* immigration offices. You need a Nepal departure stamp to be allowed into India and an India departure stamp to get into Nepal. The **Indian Immigration Office** is hidden below the bridge, to the left when coming from Raxaul. (Open daily 6am-8pm.) **Indian visas are not issued here.** The closest place to get one is Kathmandu. If you are leaving India and your visa has expired, you will be sent to the closest Superintendent of Police (in Motihari), who will fine and reprimand you. The Nepalese Immigration Office is next to the gate and is open daily 6am-7pm. You will need **one passport-size photo and US$30 for a single-entry (30-day) visa.** The only other visa this office is authorized to issue is a 60-day multiple-entry visa for US$80, which can be extended for two more periods of 30 days (US$30 each time) and a third, only in Kathmandu, for a total of 150 days. Only US dollars are accepted; bring correct change. The cheapest way of getting across the border is to take a rickshaw from the main market in Raxaul to the Indian Immigration Office (Rs3-5), and then walk 200m across the bridge to Nepalese Immigration. From here, you can share a *tonga* to Birganj bus station (NRs8-10). Alternatively, you can hire a rickshaw to take you the whole way, but all the "waiting" causes the price to jump to NRs50. The whole border crossing ritual should be over in 30min.

BIHAR

DELHI दिल्ली

All of the contrasts familiar to travelers in India are in full force here in the nation's capital: rich and poor, old and new, chaos and order. Delhi maintains a dignified front as a proud metropolitan center of government and commerce, with its official-looking edifices spanning the broad green blocks that provide clean air and empty spaces to the city's south-central districts. Behind this facade of order and control are Delhi's other streets, crammed with the city's legendary slow-churning traffic and threaded by careening auto-rickshaws. The large majority of people populate these streets, and you'll find turbaned Sikhs, dreadlocked *sadhus*, and down-and-out pavement-dwellers all rubbing shoulders and sharing space, if not conversation. It is in these streets that North India's heat and humidity are refracted through layers of polluted air only worsened by the generators and air conditioners that provide electricity and cool relief for the city's wealthy elite.

Although Hindu mythology records a settlement along the banks of the Yamuna River as far back as 1000 BC, the history of Delhi begins in AD 736, with the founding of Lal Kot by the Tomara clan of Rajputs. Their tumultuous and gory rule was abruptly ended in 1192 by Mohammed Gauri and his slave general Qutb-ud-din Aibak, who swept in from Central Asia and conquered great stretches of North India, introducing Islam and founding the Delhi Sultanate. For the next 300 years, Delhi was wracked by political instability, especially in 1398, when Timur, another Central Asian warlord, attacked the city. By the early 16th century, the ruling Lodi dynasty had made its share of enemies in the region. Too meek to challenge the Sultanate on their own, they requested help from Timur's great-grandson, Babur. Babur beat the Lodis into submission and launched the Mughal Empire, which would unite much of South Asia for the next two centuries. The Mughals repeatedly shifted their capital between Delhi and Agra, leaving both cities with monumental tombs, palaces, and forts. Old Delhi's grandest edifices were built during the 17th century by Mughal emperor Shah Jahan. However, Mughal strength began to wane during the 18th century and the British moved in to fill the void. In 1911, the British announced that the capital was to be moved here from Kolkata, but it was not until 1931 that Delhi was finally inaugurated. For the next 16 years the city served as a focal point of the independence movement, and Indian nationalists vowed that the flag o f an Indian Republic would one day fly from the Red Fort. Every year since 1947, modern Delhi has fulfilled the nationalists' hopes, as Independence Day is celebrated with a speech by the Prime Minister delivered from the Red Fort and a tremendous parade in front of the city's most important British buildings.

HIGHLIGHTS OF DELHI

Old Delhi is packed with bazaars and monuments, including the **Red Fort** (p. 150) and the **Jama Masjid** (p. 152), the largest mosque in India.

South of the city center, emperor **Humayan's Tomb** (p. 154), the prototype for the Taj Mahal, and the Mughal ruins at the **Qutb Minar** complex (p. 152), have been inspiring awe for centuries.

Delhi's lotus shaped, garden-ringed **Baha'i Temple** (p. 153) is one of India's most beautiful modern structures.

Complete with massive marble sundials, the immense, uniquely structured **Jantar Mantar** (p. 154) is an 18th-century astronomical observatory.

With a population of 14.1 million, Delhi is an enormous microcosm of India's religious and social diversity; here Hindus, Muslims, and Sikhs (not to mention Buddhists, Christians, and Jews) live side by side in relative harmony. Modern Delhi has become the nation's cosmopolitan hub, celebrating multiple faiths and cultural backgrounds while serving as a major gateway for travelers. In many ways, this concentrated mix of colors, creeds, and classes is where today's India begins.

■ INTERCITY TRANSPORTATION

INTERNATIONAL FLIGHTS

 WARNING. You may be tired from your flight, but keep your wits about you, even in the airport. If you don't understand what's going on or feel pressured or herded in a particular direction, stop to collect yourself—there's really no hurry. When paying at a counter, **count out your cash as you hand it over.** Switch-the-bill schemes are common. **Never** let a cab driver convince you that the hotel you ask for is full or closed. And remember, **the more assertive someone is with offers of help, the more likely it is that there's something in it for him.** If you need help or have a question, ask someone who hasn't approached you first.

Indira Gandhi International Airport (☎25652011 or 25652021) serves as the main entry and departure point for international flights. There is a 24hr. **State Bank of India** office and a **Thomas Cook Foreign Exchange** counter in the arrivals hall, next to the **Government of India Tourism** and the **Delhi Tourism** information desks. This is the place to pay for a **prepaid taxi,** the most hassle-free way to get into the city (Rs200-250 to the city center). Once you pay, you'll receive a receipt with your destination and a taxi number written on it—make sure that the driver takes you where *you* want to go. Delhi Transport Corporation (DTC; ☎23868836) and EATS (☎23316530) run frequent **buses** to Connaught Pl. from the airport (Rs50, Rs10 per bag). DTC buses also stop at New Delhi Railway Station and the Interstate Bus Terminal (ISBT) at Kashmiri Gate. **Auto-rickshaws** shuttle from the airport to downtown at cheaper rates (Rs100–160) than taxis but without the security of the pre-payment system. The government **railway booking office,** on the right after the arrivals hall, provides info about train tickets. (Open M-Sa 8am-8pm, Su 8am-2pm.) To get to the airport (international and domestic terminals), pick up the DTC bus from the Super Bazaar in Connaught Place (every 30min.) or the EATS bus near the Indian Airlines office on Janpath (6am and 2:45pm).

INTERNATIONAL AIRLINES. Aeroflot, Tolstoy House (☎23312843), Tolstoy Marg; **Air Canada,** 56 Alps Bldg. (☎23720014), Janpath; **Air France,** 7 Scindia House (☎23738004), Janpath; **Air India,** Jeevan Bharati Building (☎23736446), Sansad Marg; **Alitalia,** DCM building, 16 Barakhamba Rd. (☎23329551); **British Airways,** Gopal Das Bhawan, 28 Barakhamba Rd. (☎23328298); **Cathay Pacific,** 24 Barakhamba Rd. (☎23323332); **Delta,** 66 Janpath (☎23352257); **KLM/Northwest,** Prakash Deep Bldg., 7 Tolstoy Marg (☎23357747); **Lufthansa,** 56 Janpath (☎2332310); **RNAC (Royal Nepal Airlines),** 44 Janpath (☎23321164); **United Airlines,** Ambadeep Bldg., 14 KG Marg (☎23353377). Indian Airlines flies to **Dhaka, Bangladesh** via Kolkata and **Kathmandu, Nepal** (2hr., 1 per day, US$142).

DOMESTIC FLIGHTS

The airport's **domestic terminal** (☎25675126) is 8km from the international terminal. **Prepaid taxis, buses,** and **rickshaws** run to and from downtown (see **Indira Gandhi International Airport,** above). Youth fares generally offer a 25% discount to anyone under 30. Domestic airlines include: **Archana** (☎26842001); **Jagson** (☎23721594); **Jet** (☎26853700); **Sahara** (☎23320013). **Indian Airlines** (☎24620566

DELHI

or 23310517) flies to: **Agra** (35min.; M, W, F; US$65); **Ahmedabad** (1½hr., 2 per day, US$145); **Amritsar** (1½hr., M and F, US$110); **Aurangabad** (3½hr., 1 per day, US$185); **Bangalore** (2½hr., 4 per day, US$265); **Bhopal** (1hr., 1 per day, US$130); **Bhubaneswar** (2hr., 1 per day, US$225); **Kolkata** (2hr., 3 per day, US$210); **Chandigarh** (40min., 1 per day, US$85); **Chennai** (2½hr., 3-4 per day, US$270); **Cochin** (4hr., 1 per day, US$340); **Goa** (2½hr., 1-2 per day, US$245); **Guwahati** (2½hr., 1 per day, US$220); **Hyderabad** (2hr., 2 per day, US$215); **Jaipur** (40min., 2 per day, US$65); **Jammu** (1hr., 2 per day, US$115); **Khajuraho** (2hr.; M, W, F; US$110); **Leh** (1½hr.; T, Th, Sa, Su; US$115); **Lucknow** (1hr., 3-5 per day, US$100); **Mumbai** (2hr., 9-10 per day, US$185); **Nagpur** (1½hr., M-Sa, US$160); **Patna** (3hr., 1-3 per day, US$155); **Srinagar** (2½hr., 2 per day, US$125); **Trivandrum** (4½hr., 1 per day, US$340); **Udaipur** (3hr., 1 per day, US$115); **Varanasi** (2hr., 1-2 per day, US$135).

TRAINS

STATIONS. New Delhi Railway Station, the main depot for trains in Delhi, is north of Connaught Pl., at the east end of Paharganj Main Bazaar. Be prepared to push your way around and beware of theft. Your best bet is to get tickets from the **International Tourist Bureau** (☎23705156), a large, A/C room upstairs at Platform 1. The office books reservations on tourist-quota seats which come in handy when normal seats are fully booked. Tickets from here must be bought in foreign currency or in rupees with encashment certificates. (Open M-Sa 8am-8pm, Su 8am-2pm.) You can also book tickets at the Current Reservations windows in the station (for general booking) or the **Computerized Reservation Terminal,** one block south of the station on Chelmsford Rd. Book as much as a week ahead for some of the more popular trains. **Do not go to the tourist offices around the railway station, as few are legitimate.** Train schedules, fares, and availability are posted online at www.indianrailways.com and book online at www.irctc.co.in.

Delhi has three other railway stations: **Delhi Station,** in Old Delhi; **Hazrat Nizamuddin Station,** in the southeast part of the city; and **Sarai Rohilla,** in the northwest. Trains leaving from all stations can be booked at the International Tourist Bureau. Some important phone numbers are: **general enquiry and reservations** (☎131) and **arrivals/departures** (☎1330, 1331, or 1335).

DEPARTURES. You can make a reservation for any domestic train from Delhi. **Timetables** for major destinations are posted in the International Tourist Bureau. The invaluable *Trains at a Glance* booklet can be bought at bookstalls (Rs25). Air-conditioned *Shatabdi Express* and *Rajdhani Express* trains cost 3-4 times more than standard 2nd-class tickets, but they're much faster and provide food and comfy seats. The listings that follow represent a tiny selection of the many trains available from **New Delhi Railway Station.** *Shatabdi Express* trains to: **Ajmer** (#2015, 6½hr., Tu-Su 6:10am, Rs580) via **Jaipur** (4½hr., Rs465); **Amritsar** (#2013, 5½hr., 4:30pm, Rs595); **Bhopal** (#2002, 8hr., 6am, Rs860) via **Agra** (2hr., Rs390); **Chandigarh** (#2005, 3hr., 5:15pm, Rs415); **Chennai,** from H. Nizamuddin (#2434, 28½hr., W and F 3:30pm, Rs2050); **Dehra Dun** (#2017, 5½hr., 7am, Rs465); **Lucknow** (#2004, 6hr., 6:20am, Rs700) via **Kanpur** (5hr., Rs620). 3-tier *Rajdhani Express* trains to: **Ahmedabad** (#2958, 14½hr.; M, W, F 7:35pm; Rs1200); **Allahabad** (#2306, 2302, and 2310; 7hr.; 5pm; Rs1035); **Bangalore,** from H. Nizamuddin (#2430, 34hr., M-Tu and F-Sa 8:50pm, Rs2095); **Kolkata** (#2302, 2306, and 2314; 17hr.; 5pm; Rs1510); **Mumbai** (#2952, 16½hr., 4pm, Rs1485).

BUSES

TERMINALS. Delhi has three **interstate bus terminals (ISBTs):** the new **Anand Vihar ISBT** (☎22152431), east of the Yamuna River about 12km from downtown Delhi; **Sarai Kale Khan ISBT** (☎24358092), two blocks east of Nizamuddin Railway Station; and **Kashmiri Gate ISBT** (☎23865181), north of Old Delhi Railway Station. Each ISBT serves specific cities, and there is limited overlap. Make sure to go to the correct bus station for your destination; call ahead if you don't know where to go. For information on ordinary and deluxe bus prices and schedules, call one of the bus companies: government-run **Delhi Transport Corporation** (☎23868836 or 23865181), **Haryana Roadways** (☎23861262), **Himachal Roadways** (☎23863473), **Punjab Roadways** (☎23867842), **Rajasthan Roadways** (☎23861246), or **UP Roadways** (☎23868709). Many private bus companies have booths or offices in the Kashmiri Gate ISBT. Shop around for the best price and **avoid touts offering implausibly low rates.**

DEPARTURES. The following just a sampling of bus destinations. **Kashmiri Gate ISBT** runs daily buses to: **Amritsar** (10hr., Rs205); **Chandigarh** (5hr., Rs116); **Dehra Dun** (6hr., Rs120); **Dharamsala** (13hr., Rs265); **Haridwar** (5½hr., Rs97); **Jammu** (12hr., Rs226); **Kullu** (15hr., Rs300); **Manali** (17hr., Rs334); **Mandi** (12hr., Rs244); **Mussoorie** (8hr., Rs178); **Rishikesh** (6hr., Rs113); **Shimla** (9hr., Rs200).

 Anand Vihar ISBT runs daily buses to: **Allahabad** (15hr., Rs277); **Almora** (12hr., Rs228); **Gorakhpur** (20hr., Rs349); **Lucknow** (12hr., Rs230); **Nainital** (8hr., Rs153); **Ramnagar** (6½hr., Rs119); **Ranikhet** (12hr., Rs207); **Varanasi** (20hr., Rs331).

 Sarai Kale Khan ISBT runs daily buses to: **Agra** (4½hr., Rs100); **Ajmer** (8½hr., Rs175); **Chittaurgarh** (10hr., Rs225); **Gwalior** (8½hr., Rs153); **Jaipur** (6hr., Rs121); **Mathura** (4hr., Rs71); **Udaipur** (15hr., Rs291); **Vrindaban** (3hr., Rs68).

■ ORIENTATION

Situated west of the Yamuna River, Delhi stretches 30km from north to south and 10km from east to west. Just west of the **New Delhi Railway Station** is **Paharganj,** Delhi's backpacker ghetto, crammed with budget hotels, dreadlocked Europeans, and shops full of handicrafts and hippie wear. The area north of the station is **Old Delhi.** Built by Shah Jahan (and also called Shahjahanabad), Old Delhi is a delightfully tatty tangle of streets and bazaars. The busiest road in this area is the **Chandni Chowk,** which runs from west to east across the old city, terminating at the **Red Fort.**

 South of New Delhi Station, the center of **New Delhi** radiates out from **Connaught Place,** a circular hub of two-story colonnaded buildings. Connaught Pl. is the heart (and capitalist soul) of New Delhi. Of course, with tourists come touts and tricksters—Connaught Pl.'s hustlers are aggressive and exceptionally savvy; ignore them. Off the radial roads to the south of Connaught Pl. sprout the high-rise office buildings of India's most powerful banks, airlines, and international corporations. The inner and outer circles were given new names in 1995 **(Rajiv Chowk and Indira Chowk)** but everyone still calls them collectively Connaught Pl.

 Of the streets that radiate from Connaught Pl., **Sansad Marg** and **Janpath** are the most crowded; Sansad Marg leads to the Raj-era parliamentary buildings on the end of **Rajpath,** which runs 2km straight east to **India Gate,** bisected by Janpath along the way. One kilometer southwest of the parliamentary buildings is **Chanakyapuri,** home to many foreign embassies. **South Delhi** begins just south of Chanakyapuri. Except for **Ring Road** and **Mehrauli Badarpur Road,** South Delhi's major thoroughfares run north-south. The central thoroughfare, **Aurobindo Marg,** connects Safdarjung's Tomb with the **Qutb Minar Complex.** In the east, **Mathura Road** slices through **Nizamuddin** and turns into **Dr. Zakir Hussain Road** as it proceeds northwest back up to India Gate.

DELHI

Delhi

🍎 FOOD
Sagar, 3

♪ NIGHTLIFE
Djinn's, 2
Dublin, 1
Float, 5
Mirage, 4

SHADARA

Grand Trunk Rd.

MAYUR VIHAR

TO ANAND VIHAR
ISBT (4km)

Vikas Marg

National Highway 24 (Guru Samrat Mihirbhol Marg)

Geeta Colony Rd.

Marginal Bandh Rd.

Yamuna River

Vikas Marg

Ring Rd.

Vijay Ghat
Shanti Vana
Raj Ghat

Grand Trunk Rd.

MG Rd.

Delhi Gate

Red Fort

Netaji Subhash Marg
Jawaharlal Nehru Marg

Supreme Court

Crafts Museum

National Stadium

Purana Qila
Sher Mandal

National Gallery of Modern Art

Zoological Park

Humayun's Tomb

Golf Course

Dr. Zakir Hussain Rd.

Lothian Rd.
GPO
Old Delhi

Kashmiri Gate

Interstate Bus Terminal

Delhi Railway Station

SP Mukherji Rd.

Chandni Chowk

OLD DELHI

Jama Masjid

Ajmeri Gate

Mathura Rd.

Tilak Marg

Barakhamba Rd.

Nepal

Kasturba Gandhi Marg

India Gate

Rajpath

National Museum

NEW DELHI

European Commission

Akbar Rd.

Aurangzeb Rd.

Prithviraj Rd.

MG Rd.

Shamnath Marg

Mutiny Memorial

Rani Jhansi Marg

TO CHANDIGARH (245km) & AMRITSAR (475km)

Grand Trunk Rd.

Swami Narain Marg

SEE CENTRAL DELHI MAP

New Delhi Railway Station

Qutb Rd.

SADAR BAZAR

PAHARGANJ

Main Bazar

Panchkuian Marg

Desh Bandhu Gupta Rd.

CONNAUGHT PLACE

Jantar Mantar

Ashoka Rd.

Janpath

Sansad Bhavan

pesues

GPO

Talkatora Rd.

Rashtrapati Bhavan

Nehru Memorial Museum and Planetarium

United Kingdom

Panchsheel

Sardar Patel Marg

Pusa Rd.

KAROL BAGH

Shankar Rd.

Lakshmi Narayan Temple (Birla Mandir)

Mandir Marg

Willingdon Crescent

Vandematram Marg

Buddha Jayanti Park

Sarai Rohilla Railway Station

Guru Govind Singh Marg

Patel Rd.

Ring Rd.

DELHI

DELHI

TO AGRA
(204km)

Ma Anandmayee Marg

Tughluqabad

Guru Ravidas Marg

OKHLA

Apollo
Hospital

Mathura Rd. (NH 2)

Crowne
Plaza Surya
4

NEHRU
PLACE

Bahai
Temple

Park Royal

KALKAJI

Ashokan
Edict

Sarai
Kale
Khan ISBT

Nizamuddin
Station

Mathura Rd.

LAJPAT
NAGAR

Ring Rd.

Lala Lajpat Rai Path
5

GREATER
KAILASH I

Ho Chi Minh Marg

Hazrat
Katarie
Nursery

Nizamuddin
Hazrat

NIZAMUDDIN

Hazrat
Nizamuddin Dargah

Lala Lajpat Rai Path

Bangladesh

Kailash
Temple

Tibet House

DEFENCE
COLONY
3

Bishan Pratap Marg

Ansal
Plaza

ANDREWS
GANJ

Josip Broz Tito Marg

Outer Ring Rd.

Lodi Rd.

Lodi
Gardens

Ireland

SOUTH
EXTENSION

All India Institute
of Medical Sciences

SOUTH
DELHI

August Kranti Marg

Khel Gaon Marg

Press Enclave Rd.

Mehrauli Badarpur Rd.

TO GURGAON
(11km)

Safdarjung's
Tomb

Safdarjung
Airport

Aurobindo Marg

Dilli
Haat

Ina
Market

SAROJINI
NAGAR

Ring Rd.

Foreigners
Registration
Office

Hauz
Khas
Village

Aurobindo Marg

Vinay Marg

CHANAKYAPURI

Australia

Shanti Path

Canada

New Zealand

RAMAKRISHNAPURAM

Africa Avenue

Gamal Abdel Nassar Marg

Qutb Minar
Complex

United
States

Maurya
Sheraton

National
Rail Museum

Hyatt Regency

Vivekanand Marg

1 mile

1 kilometer

Taj
Palace
Hotel

ANAND
NIKETAN

Rao Tularam Marg

Benito Juarez Marg

Olof Palme Marg

Paschimi Marg

South
Africa

Vasant Marg

Poorvi Marg

VASANT VIHAR

Nelson Mandela Marg

JAWAHARLAL
NEHRU
UNIVERSITY

Indian
Mountaineering
Foundation

Swarn Jayanti Marg

Gurgaon Rd. (NH 8)

TO AIRPORT (2km),
GURGAON (11km),
& JAIPUR (270km)

1

2

▐ LOCAL TRANSPORTATION

RICKSHAWS

Auto-rickshaw drivers have a knack for driving around in circles and *then* over-charging at the end of the trip. All auto-rickshaws in Delhi have meters, but most drivers will not use them. If you do find a meter-friendly auto-*wallah*, expect to pay three times the readout. It is usually better to set the auto-rickshaw price in advance if you don't know your way around Delhi—insisting on use of the meter can provoke the drivers into adding a few extra kilometers to the journey. **Prepaid auto-rickshaws** are available at the airports, train stations, bus stations, and at the Delhi Traffic Police Booths on Janpath near the Government of India Tourist Office (open M-Sa 11am-6pm) and at Palika Bazaar, along the inner circle (open M-Sa 10am-7pm). The maximum reasonable non-prepaid fares are: Airport to Connaught Pl. or Paharganj Rs100-160; Paharganj to Connaught Pl. Rs15-20; Paharganj to Old Delhi Railway Rs40-50; Connaught Pl. to Old Delhi Rs35-50; Connaught Pl. to Chanakyapuri Rs35-40. **Cycle-rickshaws** can't go through parts of New Delhi like Connaught Pl., but they are ideal in the narrow streets of Old Delhi. A rickshaw fares from Old Delhi to New Delhi Station should cost about Rs30; from Paharganj to Connaught Pl. Rs5-10.

BUSES

City buses are extremely cheap (Rs5-10), but using them involves a whole host of difficulties. First of all, there is the problem of over-crowding: drivers stop every five seconds to pick up passengers from the side of the road, making trips irritatingly long and uncomfortable. And then there's the problem of figuring out which bus goes where. Not even the managers of **Delhi Transport Corp (DTC)** are helpful when it comes to pointing you toward the correct bus. The staff at the tourist office is just as clueless. Drivers sometimes post a sign on the side of the bus with a number, the origin, and destination of the bus; more often they don't. And these signs are usually only written in Hindi anyway. For a theoretically up-to-date city bus schedule, pick up a blue-cover-copy of *Delhi Road Map* (Rs15). Good luck.

BICYCLES

Cycling in Delhi can be harrowing, but is also the source of some adrenaline- and leg-pumping fun. Old Delhi is congested and slow, New Delhi fast and frantic. Try **Mehta Cycles** (also known as Adaya Shakti Handicrafts), at the entrance to a small alley known as Gali Chandekar Waliat, at the west end of Paharganj's Main Bazaar, just past Jacksons Books. Bell and lock are included with bike rentals, but the store doesn't stock helmets, claiming that they are "completely unnecessary" in Delhi. (☎ 23585892. Bikes Rs45 per day, Rs8 per hr., Rs10 overnight charge; Rs600 deposit. Open daily 10am-7:30pm.)

▐ PRACTICAL INFORMATION

TOURIST AND FINANCIAL SERVICES

Tourist Office: Government of India Tourist Office, 88 Janpath (☎23320005), just south of Connaught Circus and Scindia House, next to Kapoor Lamps and Delhi Photo Company. Great place to go for help getting around the city and in easing those first-arrival jitters. Open M-F 9am-6pm, Sa 9am-2pm. 2 other government-sponsored agencies provide information and bookings. **India Tourism Development**

WARNING. Delhi is full of "tourist offices" claiming to provide booking assistance, free maps, and other "information" and services. Several of these offices are near the railway. Their bookings are likely to be overpriced, if not fraudulent. Stick to the main government tourist office on Janpath and, for train tickets, to the International Tourist Bureau in the New Delhi Railway Station and government-sponsored travel bureaus. **Delhi is a haven of subversive activity.** Con-artists are as common as flies, particularly in Paharganj and other tourist hot-beds. If you realize that you've been cheated, contact the Government of India Tourist Office. They can at least put you in touch with the authorities.

Corporation (ITDC), Connaught Pl., at the corner of Middle Circle and Radial Rd. 6. (☎23412336), is also called India Tourism or Ashok Travels. Open daily 7am-9pm. **Delhi Tourism (DTTDC),** Connaught Pl., N-block, Middle Circle (☎23365358 or 23315322). Open daily 7am-9pm. All 3 government agencies have branches in the international and domestic airport terminals. The different states of India all run offices in Delhi; many are located in Kanishka Shopping Plaza, 19 Ashok Rd., between the Indraprastha and Kanishka Hotels, or around the state emporia on Baba Kharak Singh Marg. The back of the Chandralok Bldg., 36 Janpath, south of the Central Cottage Industries Emporium, houses the offices for **Uttar Pradesh** (☎23741296 or 23322254; open M-Sa 10am-5pm), **Himachal Pradesh** (☎23325320 or 23324764; open M-Sa 10am-5pm), and **Haryana** (☎23324911; open M-F 9am-5pm). **Indian Mountaineering Foundation,** 6 Benito Juarez Marg, Anand Niketan (☎26883412), provides information and services for trekkers. Open M-Sa 10am-5pm. **Survey of India Map Sales Office,** 124-A Janpath Barracks (☎23322288), sells city and trekking maps. Open M-F 9:30am-5pm.

Immigration Office: Getting a visa extension is not easy, and the process brings many travelers back to Delhi again and again. For an extension (15 days max.) on a simple **tourist visa,** first head to the **Ministry of Home Affairs Foreigners Division,** 1st floor Lok Nayak Bhawan (☎24693334), behind Khan Market, off Subramaniya Bharati Marg around Lodi Estate. They're only open M-F 10am-noon, so arrive early with 4 passport photos and a letter stating your grounds for extension. If they process your application, head over to the **Foreigners Regional Registration Office** (FRRO), East Block 8, Level 2, RK Puram (☎26711348), behind the Hyatt Regency Hotel. Open M-F 9:30am-1:30pm and 2-4pm. The FRRO is also the place to get **student visas** (with a bona fide student ID issued by a recognized school/university, a bank remittance certificate, and an extension application in duplicate with 4 photos and proof of stay), as well as **permits** for restricted areas of India. The FRRO can issue **exit visas** in 20min.

Currency Exchange: American Express, A-block, Connaught Pl. (☎23324119 or 23712513) sells and changes AmEx traveler's checks. Other brands cashed with no commission. There's a counter for lost and stolen cards, but the main office for 24hr. check replacement is in Gurgaon (☎95124 2801234). The A-block office issues and receives AmEx moneygrams and offers the usual cardholder services (see p. 13). Open M-F 9:30am-5:30pm, Sa 9:30am-2:30pm. **S.P. Securities Ltd.,** M-96, Middle Circle, Connaught Pl. (☎23417070). Open M-Sa 9:30am-8pm, Su 11:30am-2pm. **Bank of Baroda,** Sansad Marg (☎23321882), in the tall, white building just beyond the Outer Circle, gives MC/V cash advances and cashes traveler's checks. Open M-F 10am-3:45pm, Sa 10am-12:30pm. **Standard Chartered Bank,** opposite the Bank of Baroda and in E-block, Connaught Pl., has 24hr., Cirrus ATMs. **HSBC** has 24 ATMS dotted around Delhi, most conveniently at Ele House, on the corner of Connaught Circus and KG Marg. The main branch of **The State Bank of India,** Sansad Marg (☎51502400) changes currency and traveler's checks. Open M-F 10am-4pm, Sa 10am-1pm. Another branch is in the international terminal of the airport. (Open

24hr.) **Western Union Money Transfer,** 1st fl. Sita World Travel office, F-12 Connaught Pl. (☎23353203), charges a 5% commission to transfer money from abroad. Open M-F 9:30am-11pm, Sa 9:30am-9:30pm, Su 10am-2pm. **Citibank,** Jeevan Bharati Bldg., 124 Connaught Circus (☎95124 2542484), near Paharganj in the red stone-and-mirrored, modern high-rise before the Bank of Baroda, has a 24hr. Cirrus ATM. Another 24hr. Citibank ATM, as well as a **Thomas Cook Foreign Exchange** booth, are located at the New Delhi Railway Station (☎23211819). Open 24hr. **Hotel Gold Regency,** Main Bazaar (☎23562101), 300m from the New Delhi Railway Station, changes all major currencies and traveler's checks. In truly desperate situations, some use the **illegal money changers** along Main Bazaar in Paharganj. Don't let them go off with your money promising to return with rupees, even if they leave a "friend" with you while you wait.

EMBASSIES

Australia, 1/50-G Shantipath (☎26888223; fax 26885199). Open M-F 8:30am-1pm and 2-4:30pm. **Bangladesh,** EP-39, Dr. S. Radhakrishnan Marg (☎26878948; fax 26878953). Open M-F 9:30am-5:30pm. **Bhutan,** Chandragupta Marg (☎26889809; fax 26876710). Open M-F 9am-5pm. **Canada,** 7/8 Shantipath (☎26876500; fax 26876579). Open M-Th 8:30am-5pm, F 8:30am-1pm. **European Commission,** 65 Golf Links (☎24629237; fax 24629206). Open M-F 9am-5pm. **Ireland,** 230 Jor Bagh (☎24626733; fax 24697053). Open M-Tu and Th-F 9:30am-1:30pm and 2:30-5pm. **Israel,** 3 Aurangzeb Rd. (☎23013238; fax 23014298). Open M-Th 9am-5pm, F 9am-3pm. **Nepal,** Barakhamba Rd. (☎23327361 or 23329218; fax 23326857). Open M-F 9am-1pm and 2-5pm. **New Zealand,** 50-N Nyaya Marg (☎26883170; fax 26872317). Open M-Th 8:30am-5pm, F 8:30am-1pm. **South Africa,** B-18 Vasant Marg, Vasant Vihar (☎26149411; fax 26143605). Open M-F 9am-5pm. **Sri Lanka,** 27 Kautilya Marg (☎23010201; fax 23793604). Open M-F 9am-5pm. **UK,** Shantipath (☎26872161; fax 6872882). Open M-F 9am-1pm and 2-5pm. **US,** Shantipath (☎24198000; fax 24190017). Open M-F 8:30am-1pm and 2-5:30pm.

LOCAL SERVICES

Luggage Storage: Many hotels store luggage at a nominal charge (Rs2-5), but only for guests. The railway stations also have luggage storage (Rs7-10 per day) for anyone holding a valid train ticket; just be sure to lock your bags.

Bookstores: There are several well-stocked bookstores on the Inner Circle of Connaught Pl., including **Bookworm** (☎23322260; open M-Sa 10:30am-7:30pm); **New Book Depot** (☎23320020; open M-Sa 10:30am-7:30pm); **E.D. Galgotia and Sons** (☎23322876; open M-Sa 10:30am-7:30pm). All on B-block. Many bookstores along the Main Bazaar in Paharganj buy and sell new and used books. **Jackson's Books** is opposite Medikos Opticians on Main Bazaar (☎23520801; open daily 10am-11pm).

Bi-Gay-Lesbian Organization: Humrahi and **Sangini,** Andrews Ganj (☎26563929 or 26567049). Counseling services and support group meetings. Call M-F 10am-6pm.

Cultural Centers: The American Center and British Council (see above) have regular lectures and film screenings. **Max Mueller Bhavan,** 3 Kasturba Gandhi Marg (☎23329506), has a library and shows films in Siddhartha Hall. Indian cultural centers include **Indian Council for Cultural Relations,** Azad Bhavan, I.P. Estate (☎23379309); **India International Centre,** 40 Lodi Estate (☎24619431); **Indira Gandhi National Centre for the Arts,** CV Mess, Janpath (☎23389216). **Sangeet Natak Akademi,** Rabindra Bhavan (☎23387246), has information on classical music concerts.

EMERGENCY AND COMMUNICATIONS

Police: Emergency (☎100); central control (☎23270000 or 23362229). Branches all over—look for Delhi Traffic and Tourist Police kiosks at major intersections. Stations at Chandni Chowk, next to Bahrandi Mandir, and Paharganj, opposite the railway station.

Pharmacy: The multi-story **Super Bazaar** (☎23413833 or 23413170), outside the M-block of Connaught Pl., has a 24hr. pharmacy. Several pharmacies along Paharganj Main Bazaar sell tampons, contact lens solution, and toilet paper, as well as the usual bandages and medicine.

Hospital/Medical Services: Ambulance (☎102). Dr. Sharwan Kumar Gupta's **Care Clinic and Laboratory,** 1468 Gali Sangatrashan (☎23587841, home 29213088, emergency mobile 9811128179). Heading west down the Paharganj Main Bazaar, take a right onto Gali Sangatrashan before Hotel Vivek; the clinic is 100m down on the left. English-speaking staff is used to dealing with foreign insurance companies. Recommended by IAMAT. Open M-Sa 8:30am-8:30pm, Su 8:30am-2pm. The **East-West Medical Clinic,** B-28 Greater Kailash 1 (☎26293701), is recommended by many embassies. Expensive by local standards, the clean and efficient clinic runs a 24hr. emergency room with a fully stocked 24hr. pharmacy. Other hospitals include **Apollo,** Mathura Rd., considered to provide quality medical care (☎26925801; open 24hr.), and the **All India Institute for Medical Services (A.I.I.M.S.),** Aurobindo Marg, known in the country as an excellent government-run hospital (☎26561123).

Internet: In Paharganj, Internet shops are everywhere and generally cheaper than in Connaught Pl. **Hotel Gold Regency,** Main Bazaar (☎23562101), has a "Cyber Bar-Be-Que" with full restaurant service. There may be a wait for one of their 60 computers, though. Rs10 per hr. Open 24hr. Closer to the center of Paharganj in the same alley, just opposite the Hare Rama Guesthouse, is **Bholenath Travels,** 419 Main Bazaar (☎23588992), where you can get both laundry service and a decent Internet connection. Rs20 per hr. Open 24hr. In Connaught Pl., **The Hub,** B-block, above Volga Restaurant, offers Internet (Rs30 per hr.) and cappuccinos (Rs10). Open daily 9am-9pm.

Post Offices: Branches everywhere in Delhi. **New Delhi GPO,** Gole Dakhana on Ashoka Rd. and Baba Kharak Singh Marg (☎23364111). Bring a passport to claim mail. Open M-Sa 10am-5pm. Speedpost available 24hr. To receive mail at **Old Delhi GPO,** Lothian Rd. (☎23869771), near the Red Fort and ISBT, use this address: GPO, Delhi, 110006. **Overnite Express**

THE LOCAL LEGEND

LORD VENKATESWARA

This living Hindu deity's life is renowned for the miracles he performs for devotees. Two legends explain why he sits at Tirumala.

The first describes a contest of strength between the king of serpents, Lord Adisesha, and the wind god Vayu. Vayu tried to blow away a holy mountain but was stopped by Adisesha, who wrapped himself around it. Opening his mouth all the wider, Vayu was able to blow off the peak, which landed at Tiripati. The snake king, utterly humiliated, turned himself into a hill and invited Lord Vishnu to live on his head. The seven hills around Tirumala represent the seven heads of the giant serpent.

A different legend tells of a group of priests who could not decide to which god they should dedicate a sacrifice. They sent the sage Bhrigu to consult Brahma, Shiva, and Vishnu. But Brahma and Shiva were too busy with their consorts to be bothered. When Vishnu, too, ignored his arrival, the infuriated sage kicked him in the chest. Vishnu appeased Brighu by attending to his injured goat, but Lakshmi was angered by the sage's disrespect for her husband and left for Kolhupar. Vishnu took to wandering the earth and eventually settled down at Tirumala.

The ancient text known as the *Venkatachalamahatmyan* describes more legends of Tirupati and Tirumala.

(☎25714512; open daily 7am-10pm) is at Gupta Market in Karo Bagh. Or try **Blue Dart,** 597 Gandhi Cloth Market (☎23987128), in Chandni Chowk, Old Delhi. Connected with FedEx. Open M-Sa noon-8pm. **Belair Travel and Cargo,** 10-B Scindia House (☎23313440), ships bulky luggage and boxes overseas. Open M-F 9:30am-6pm, Sa 9:30am-2pm. **DHL Express,** 11 Tolstoy Marg (☎23737587), offers express mail. Open M-F 9:30am-8pm, Sa 9:30am-6pm. **Postal Code:** 110001.

♔ ACCOMMODATIONS

Staying in Delhi can be frustratingly expensive. Prices have been driven up so much that it is hard to find anything acceptable for less than Rs100. **Paharganj** (Main Bazaar) is Delhi's main tourist enclave. Though it has adapted to travelers' needs, it still retains its legendary seediness and can be dangerous, especially for women traveling alone. If you've just arrived in India or are simply not into grime, head to **Connaught Place** for its own collection of nicer, though more expensive, guest houses and hotels. On the other hand, if you really want to get a feel for Delhi, there's always **Old Delhi,** the purist's retreat.

ACCOMMODATIONS BY PRICE

UNDER RS150(❶)		RS150-350 (❷) (CONT'D)	
Sunny Guest House (p. 147)	CP	Hotel Vishal (p. 146)	PJ
Ringo Guest House (p. 147)	CP	Hotel Palace Heights (p. 147)	CP
Khush-Dil Hotel (p. 147)	OD	Hotel New City Palace (p. 147)	OD
RS150-350 (❷)		Hotel Ambar (p. 147)	OD
⚑ Hotel Rak International (p. 144)	PJ	Vaishnaw Hotel (p. 147)	OD
⚑ Major's Den Guest House (p. 144)	PJ	**RS350-600 (❸)**	
Anoop Hotel (p. 145)	PJ	Hotel Prince Palace (p. 145)	PJ
Hotel Karlo Kastle (p. 145)	PJ	⚑ H.K. Choudhary Guesthouse (p. 146)	CP
Yes Please Guest House (p. 145)	PJ		
Hotel Shelton (p. 145)	PJ		
Hotel Namaskar (p. 145)	PJ		

PJ Paharganj **CP** Connaught Place **OD** Old Delhi

PAHARGANJ

Paharganj is one long, messy line of cheap hotels and restaurants. Unless otherwise noted, check-out is at noon. Most of the better places have rooftop restaurants and generators for Delhi's all-too-frequent power outages. Rooms vary greatly based on whether they have A/C. All of the following directions (right, left) are given as you walk west on Main Bazaar from the New Delhi Railway Station.

⚑ **Hotel Rak International** (☎23586508), Chowk Bowli, down an alley to the right off Main Bazaar before 6 Tooti Chowk. Peaceful, slightly upscale place where you'll almost forget you're in grungy Paharganj. Part of *Holy Smoke,* starring Kate Winslet, was filmed on the rooftop terrace. Comfortable, newly painted rooms have small couches, octagonal glass tables, and clean white sheets. Singles Rs250-550; doubles Rs350-650. ❷

⚑ **Major's Den Guest House,** Lakshmi Narayan St. (☎23584163), at the west end of Main Bazaar. Turn right at Metropolis Tourist Home, then take another right after Imperial Cinema; Major's is at the end of the street on the right. Tucked away from all the noise, this den is the perfect retreat from the impersonal tourist bungalows of the main bazaar. Meet the Major himself whose motto is "Treat the guest as God." Friendly family staff

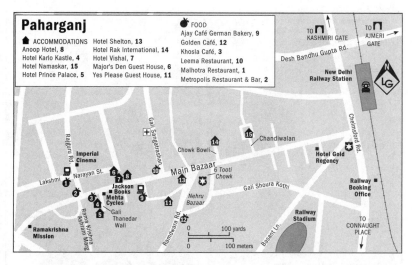

Paharganj

🏠 ACCOMMODATIONS
Anoop Hotel, **8**
Hotel Karlo Kastle, **4**
Hotel Namaskar, **15**
Hotel Prince Palace, **5**

Hotel Shelton, **13**
Hotel Rak International, **14**
Hotel Vishal, **7**
Major's Den Guest House, **6**
Yes Please Guest House, **11**

🍴 FOOD
Ajay Café German Bakery, **9**
Golden Café, **12**
Khosla Café, **3**
Leema Restaurant, **10**
Malhotra Restaurant, **1**
Metropolis Restaurant & Bar, **2**

lives downstairs. Feeling of security, comfortable and clean rooms, peaceful rooftop patio. Singles Rs250-350; doubles Rs450-500. ❷

Anoop Hotel (☎23589366), Main Bazaar. Popular, multi-storied backpackers' hotel with one of the best 24hr. rooftop restaurants in Paharganj. Spacious, well-kept rooms cooled by powerful fans and a small balcony on each floor. Check-out 24hr. Singles Rs180-350; doubles Rs250-400. ❷

Hotel Prince Palace (☎23588873), Gali Thanedar Wali, down an alley on the left just past Appetite Restaurant. Sandwiched between Hotel Karlo Kastle and Hotel Prince Palace Deluxe, 2 slightly lesser clones whose rooms are at least Rs100-150 less, this hotel has a bit more panache with an open lobby, mixed marble interior, and elevator. Supertidy rooms have attached bath and TV; some even have fridges and balconies. 24hr. rooftop restaurant. Singles Rs350-750; doubles Rs450-850. ❸

Hotel Karlo Kastle (☎23582821), Gali Thanedar Wali, next to Hotel Prince Palace. Relaxed and clean with marble-lined hallways. Spacious rooms with attached bath and TV. Rooftop restaurant. Singles Rs250-500; doubles Rs300-550. ❷

Yes Please Guest House (☎23588688). From Main Bazaar, turn left down the alley for Ajay Guest House and take a left after Hare Rama Guest House; Yes Please is on the right. Newly remodeled, clean, comfortable rooms with effective A/C are a great value. Not to be confused with Hotel Yes Please. Singles Rs160-170; doubles Rs200-300. ❷

Hotel Shelton (☎23580575), Main Bazaar, on the left after 6 Tooti Chowk. This 5-story hotel has perhaps one of the biggest and brightest signs in Delhi, visible from the railway station. Provides clean towels and soap as well as tidy rooms with spotless, tiled bathrooms. Singles Rs250-500; doubles Rs300-550. ❷

Hotel Namaskar (☎23582233), Chandiwalan, down an alley 300m on the right, off Main Bazaar. Turn before Camran lodge. Basic rooms with sparkling clean bathrooms set back from the Main Bazaar hubbub. Helpful staff. Singles and doubles Rs200-450. ❷

DELHI

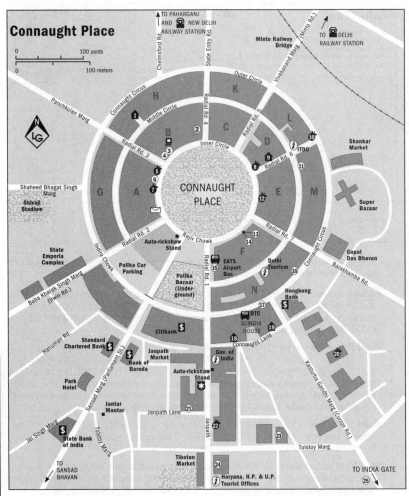

Connaught Place

0 [____] 100 yards

0 [____] 100 meters

TO PAHARGANJ AND ■ NEW DELHI RAILWAY STATION

Minto Railway Bridge

TO ■ DELHI RAILWAY STATION

Shankar Market

Super Bazaar

Gopal Das Bhavan

CONNAUGHT PLACE

Shaheed Bhagat Singh Marg

Shivaji Stadium

State Emporia Complex

Palika Car Parking

Palika Bazaar (Underground)

Auto-rickshaw Stand

Rajiv Chowk

EATS Airport Bus

Delhi Tourism

Hongkong Bank

SCINDIA HOUSE

DTC

Citibank

Standard Chartered Bank

Janpath Market

Bank of Baroda

Gov. of India

Auto-rickshaw Stand

Park Hotel

Jantar Mantar

Janpath Lane

State Bank of India

Tibetan Market

TO SANSAD BHAVAN

Haryana, H.P. & U.P. Tourist Offices

TO INDIA GATE

Hotel Vishal (☎23562123), Main Bazaar, west end, after Hare Krishna Guest House. More mellow than other backpacker hangouts. Bathrooms cleaner than the bedrooms. Great rooftop for relaxation. Singles Rs150-400; doubles Rs200-400. ❷

CONNAUGHT PLACE

Connaught Pl. is less chaotic Paharganj, though some travelers might find it *too* quiet, especially at night.

▨ **H.K. Choudhary Guesthouse,** H-35/3, H-block, Middle Circle (☎23322043). Excellent service. Rooms are exceptionally clean and nicely decorated. Follow the tree growing through the building to the rooftop terrace. Discounted rates for longer stays. Singles Rs450-550; doubles Rs550-770. ❸

Connaught Place

♠ ACCOMMODATIONS

H.K. Choudhary Guesthouse, **1**
Hotel Palace Heights, **9**
Ringo Guest House, **18**
Sunny Guest House, **19**

♥ FOOD

Embassy Restaurant, **8**
Hotel Saravana Bhavan, **22**
Nirula's, **10**
Parikrama, **20**
Rodeo, **7**
United Coffee House, **12**
Wenger & Co. Pastry Shop, **5**

○ SERVICES

American Express, **6**
Belair Travel, **17**
Bookworm, **2**
Central Cottage
   Industries Emporium, **24**
DHL Express, **23**
E.D. Galgotia & Sons, **4**
Indian Airlines, **15**
Jet Airways, **16**
Max Mueller Bhavan, **25**
New Book Depot, **3**
S.P. Securities, **11**
Sita World Travel, **13**
Survey of India Map Sales
   Office, **21**
Western Union Money Transfer, **14**

Hotel Palace Heights, Radial Rd. 6, D-block, on the top floor (☎23415419). High above the streets, this hotel's rooms are a bit drab, but the wide, breezy terrace provides a welcome break from the bustling city below. Singles Rs300-475; doubles Rs350-735. ❷

Sunny Guest House, Scindia House, Connaught Ln. (☎23312909), off Janpath beyond Connaught Circus. Standard backpacker grotto. Dorm room is like a military barracks, but more spacious than Ringo's (see below). Basic rooms face a pleasant central courtyard. Dorms Rs90; singles Rs125-170; doubles Rs250-400. ❶

Ringo Guest House (☎23310605), Scindia House, near Sunny Guest House. A little hideaway above the waves of cars and people. Staggeringly popular backpackers' retreat is overcrowded and overpriced, but has a pleasant garden area and a relaxed atmosphere. Dorms Rs90; singles Rs150; doubles Rs250-400. ❶

OLD DELHI

This is the chicken-squawking, dung-slathered real thing. While prices are cheaper and people are less likely to try to cheat you, it can be hard to find anyone who speaks English. **Western women should exercise caution.** Stereotypes about foreigners—Western women in particular—are stronger here than elsewhere in the city. Many men will assume that solo female travelers are willing to give sexual favors, so women should avoid dressing provocatively or going out alone after dark.

Hotel New City Palace (☎23279548 or 23255820), west of the Jama Masjid. Excellent views of the mosque. Clean rooms have attached baths with seat toilets and balconies with rooftop access. Check-out 24hr. Singles with bath Rs200; doubles Rs250-650. ❷

Hotel Ambar, Katra Banyan (☎23965081 or 23925692), south of Fatehpuri Corner. A sun-lit foyer with purple tile walls provides a nice introduction to colorful, air-cooled rooms with comfortable beds. Doubles Rs325. ❷

Vaishnaw Hotel (☎23978925 or 23960354), north of Fatehpuri Corner. Look for the bright yellow sign. Four floors of recently renovated, spacious rooms off a garden courtyard. Check-out 24hr. Singles Rs150-350. ❷

Khush-Dil Hotel, Chandni Chowk (☎23952110), at the west end, just south of the mosque on Fatehpuri Corner. Small rooms with narrow beds and good views of the hectic street below. Check-out 24hr. Singles with common bath Rs100; doubles Rs150-200. ❶

◻ FOOD

It's worth shelling out a little cash for some of Delhi's fantastic meals. There are restaurants in every price range: Western-style fast food, decent Chinese and Middle Eastern cuisine, a couple of Mexican restaurants, and, of course, excellent Indian food. For a real splurge (up to Rs300-400 per entree), head to one of the five-star hotels, such as the Maurya Sheraton or the Ashok Frontier.

DELHI

FOOD BY TYPE

CONTINENTAL	
Golden Cafe (p. 148)	PJ ❶
Ajay Cafe German Bakery (p. 149)	PJ ❶
Metropolis Restaurant and Bar (p. 149)	PJ ❺
Embassy Restaurant (p. 149)	CP ❹
Rodeo (p. 149)	CP ❺
Nirula's (p. 149)	CP ❸
United Coffee House (p. 149)	CP ❸
Rinkey Restaurant (p. 150)	OD ❷
The Yellow Brick Road (p. 150)	ND ❺

EAST ASIAN	
Malhotra Restaurant (p. 148)	PJ ❶
Golden Cafe (p. 148)	PJ ❶
Ajay Cafe and German Bakery (p. 149)	PJ ❶
Metropolis Restaurant and Bar (p. 149)	PJ ❺
Nirula's (p. 149)	CP ❸
Parikrama (p. 149)	CP ❺
United Coffee House (p. 149)	CP ❸
🏚 Sagar (p. 150)	ND ❷
The Yellow Brick Road (p. 150)	ND ❺

NORTH INDIAN	
Malhotra Restaurant (p. 148)	PJ ❶
Leema Restaurant (p. 148)	PJ ❷
Metropolis Restaurant and Bar (p. 149)	PJ ❺
Embassy Restaurant (p. 149)	CP ❹
Parikrama (p. 149)	CP ❺
United Coffee House (p. 149)	CP ❸
🏚 Karim (p. 149)	OD ❸

NORTH INDIAN (CONT'D)	
Moti Mahal Restaurant (p. 150)	OD ❸
Rinkey Restaurant (p. 150)	CD ❷
🏚 Sagar (p. 150)	ND ❷

SOUTH INDIAN	
Hotel Saravana Bhavan (p. 149)	CP ❷
United Coffee House (p. 149)	CP ❸
🏚 Sagar (p. 150)	ND ❷

BREAKFAST	
Khosla Cafe (p. 149)	PJ ❶

BAKERY	
Ajay Cafe German Bakery (p. 149)	PJ ❶
Nirula's (p. 149)	CP ❸
Wenger and Co. Pastry Shop (p. 149)	CP ❶

DESSERT	
Nirula's (p. 149)	CP ❸
United Coffee House (p. 149)	CP ❸
The Yellow Brick Road (p. 150)	ND ❺

FAST FOOD	
Nirula's (p. 149)	CP ❸

CAFE	
Golden Cafe (p. 148)	PJ ❶
Khosla Cafe (p. 149)	PJ ❶
Ajay Cafe German Bakery (p. 149)	PJ ❶
United Coffee House (p. 149)	CP ❸
The Yellow Brick Road (p. 150)	ND ❺

PJ Paharganj **CP** Connaught Place **OD** Old Delhi **ND** New Delhi

PAHARGANJ

This backpackers' district has developed several hot spots for hanging out; most of them are five stories up. None of these places serves exceptional food, but the rooftops are the place to find Paharganj's backpack-rats sipping tea and slurping curd after hours. It's best to get off the Main Bazaar for food—most of the main strip's restaurants cater to the jaded palates and fragile digestive systems of backpackers. Wander the streets north of Paharganj to see where the locals are eating.

Malhotra Restaurant, 1833 Lakshmi Narayan St. Walk to the west end of Main Bazaar, turn right on Rajguru Rd. at the Metropolis, then take the first left. A simple place packed with a mix of locals and tourists. Quick, efficient service and good Indian and Chinese food from Rs25. Best deal on the block—succulent, full-sized tandoori baby chicken Rs65. A/C comfort upstairs. Open daily 11am-11pm. ❶

Leema Restaurant, Main Bazaar, next to Hotel Vivek. Perhaps the best budget-hotel restaurant in Paharganj. Clean bright interior, A/C, attentive staff, and scrumptious veg. *thalis* with all the fixings Rs60. Open daily 7:30am-11pm. ❷

Golden Cafe, Nehru Bazaar. From Main Bazaar turn left at 6 Tooti Chowk and walk 100m; it's on the left. Small joint with window front seating specializing in East Asian cuisine. Enjoy watching the vegetable market over Veg. Manchurian (Rs25) or "Om Rice" (Rs25). Open daily 8am-11pm. ❶

Khosla Cafe, Main Bazaar, on the left 30m before Rajguru Rd. Start the morning with tasty fruit curd (Rs20). Shaded outdoor seating is pleasant for people-watching. ❶

Ajay Cafe German Bakery, Main Bazaar, inside Ajay guest House opposite Hare Rama Guest House. Great place to satisfy late-night munchies and play a game of pool. Or come early for cinnamon rolls (Rs15) fresh out of the oven. ❶

Metropolis Restaurant & Bar, at the west end of Main Bazaar, in Metropolis Tourist Home. Sit-down dining with A/C, full bar, and dim lighting. Large selection of Chinese, Indian, and continental dishes. "Le Steak Minute Diane" (Rs200) is served with vegetables. Open daily 8am-11pm. ❺

CONNAUGHT PLACE

Catering to the elite, restaurants in Connaught Pl. serve Indian and international cuisine several times better than the usual fare served down the road in backpackers' paradise. Dishes are priced accordingly.

Embassy Restaurant, D-block (☎23415163). Semi-formal dining, attentive service, and fine Indian and continental food at "oh-why-not" prices. Try the Mutton Chop Masala (Rs142), patties of minced meat marinated with fresh herbs cooked in thick almond and cream gravy. Open daily 10am-11pm. ❹

Rodeo, A-block, near the AmEx office. Step into a saloon and get a taste of the Wild West lassoed into the New Delhi East. Cowboy-Indian waiters shoot up an array of cocktails, beer, and rather authentic Tex-Mex food. Nachos Rs60-160, chicken enchiladas Rs275. Happy Hour 3:30-7:30pm, 50% off selected beverages. Open daily noon-midnight. ❺

Nirula's, L-block (☎23417419). Huge multi-restaurant the size of a multi-story car garage to accommodate any taste or budget. Head to **21 Ice Creams** to try Indian flavors like Zafrani Badaam Pista, 21 Love, and Delhi Delight (Rs29 per scoop). Hit the family eatery **Potpourri** upstairs (open daily 7am-midnight) for Western fare, or sip drinks in the popular, pricey **Pegasus Bar.** Open daily 11am-midnight. Step into oriental decadence at the **Chinese room** for scrumptious stir-fry. Open daily 12:30-4pm and 7-11pm. For food on the go, try **Hot Shoppe's** SubZ burger (Rs10). Open daily 11am-11pm. **The Pastry Shop** has a 50% discount on bread after 8pm. Open 9am-10pm. ❸

Parikrama, 22 Kasturba Gandhi Marg. Delhi's revolving 24th fl. restaurant takes 1½hr. to go round, and you probably won't want to finish in less. Amazing, labeled views are complimented by delicious but expensive Indian and Chinese entrees (Rs150-410). Beer Rs125. A feast for your eyes and your stomach. Open daily noon-11:30pm. ❺

Hotel Saravana Bhavan, 46 Janpath, just before Tolstoy Marg. This popular chain restaurant originating from Tamil Nadu serves 2 ft. *dosas* (Rs30), South Indian *thalis* on a banana leaf (Rs60), and fresh blended juices (Rs20-45). Always packed but has comfortable seating. Open daily 8am-11pm. ❷

Wenger & Co. Pastry Shop, A-block, Inner Circle, next to the AmEx office. Gourmet take-out bakery and patisserie (most Rs22). Open daily 10:30am-8pm. ❶

United Coffee House, E-block. Victorian-Era flashback with high ceilings, ornately carved walls, crystal chandeliers, and plush vinyl seats. Veg. and non-veg. dishes Rs75-295. Coffee with ice cream Rs52. Open daily 9:30am-11:30pm. Last order at 11:30pm. ❸

OLD DELHI

Old Delhi offers everything from *dal bhat* to pizza, although most of the restaurants here are frequented only by locals.

▨ Karim, in a small courtyard off Matya Mahal, about 8 shops down from the Jama Masjid (not visible from the road). One of the city's most popular and famous restaurants, Karim has been run by descendants of the cooks of Mughal royalty since 1913. Menu full of rich, meaty meals. Half dishes (at half-price) fit the bill for the budget traveler. Half chicken *biryani* Rs75, full mutton stew Rs90. Open daily 7am-midnight. ❸

Moti Mahal Restaurant, Netaji Subhash Marg. Delicious *tandoori* cuisine served in an air-conditioned dining room with sparkling chandeliers. Kebabs from Rs105, veg. curries Rs50-90. Live music some nights 8pm-midnight. Open daily 11am-midnight. ❸

Rinkey Restaurant, Bara Bazaar. From the Kashmiri Gate ISBT, turn left on Lothian Rd. and then right on Bara Bazaar. One of the few sit-down places near the bus station. Lots of choices. Fresh pizza Rs70, onion *uttappam* Rs30. Open daily 9:30am-9:30pm. ❷

NEW DELHI

Many of Delhi's newest and best eating options hide in the south, at the posh arcades of Defence Colony Market and greater Kailash, away from tourist centers. These hip, popular, and sometimes affordable restaurants make a great night out or a well-deserved break after touring.

▩ **Sagar,** 18 Defence Colony Market. Winner of the "Times Food Award" for Best South Indian Restaurant in Delhi. Lightning-quick service brings tasty *thalis* (Rs45), *idli vadas* (Rs26), *uttappams* (Rs30-45), and 30 different flavors of meal-capping ice cream. North Indian and Chinese branch a few doors down. Open daily 8am-11pm. ❷

The Yellow Brick Road, Ambassador Hotel, Sujan Singh Park, near Khan Market, 1km south of India Gate. Follow the yellow brick road and take your taste buds to new heights. Listed as one of New Delhi's "Top 20 Restaurants," this festive coffee shop with a garden patio prepares excellent dishes ranging from the mouth-tingling Bangkok vegetable curry (Rs 280) to extra virgin pasta (Rs285). Leave room for the infamous "Bull's Eye" dessert (Rs145). Open daily 6am-4am. ❺

SIGHTS

Like any capital city, Delhi has a vast number of things to see. There are a whopping 1376 monuments, two of which are UNESCO World Heritage sites (Qutb Minar and Humayun's Tomb). If you're spending only a couple of days in Delhi, budget your time wisely. The must-sees are the Qutb Minar Complex (p. 152) and the sights of Old Delhi (p. 150)—Lal Qila (Red Fort), the Jama Masjid (Friday Mosque), and the bazaars. Round out your time by having a look at Rashtrapati Bhavan and Humayun's Tomb.

Several agencies offer **guided tours** of Delhi (about Rs210-230). If you only have a short amount of time in Delhi, guided tours are helpful, but the experience will depend greatly on the quality of the tour guide and tour bus. Another option is to ditch the tourist bus and hire a guide and/or vehicle for 8-12hr. stints. Standard taxis cost about Rs625-650 for 8hr. Book through ITDC or Delhi Tourism (see **Tourist and Financial Services,** above).

OLD DELHI

RED FORT (LAL QILA)

Enter through Lahore Gate. Fort open Tu-Su 7:30am-7pm. Rs100. Video camera fee Rs25. Mumtaz Mahal museum open Tu-F 10am-5pm; Naubat Khana and Sanghralaya museums open Tu-Su 10am-5pm. Museums Rs2 each. English sound and light shows Nov.-Jan. 7:30-8:30pm; Feb.-Apr. 8:30-9:30pm; May-Aug. 9-10pm; Sept.-Oct. 8:30-9:30pm. Rs50, under 12 Rs10. Reservations ☎ 23274580.

Shortly after moving the capital from Agra to Delhi in 1639, Mughal emperor Shah Jahan began construction on the Red Fort. Work started on April 16 and was completed nine years later to the day. Soaring to a height of 33.5m, the fort's red sandstone ramparts form a 2km perimeter. They are surrounded by a moat into which the Yamuna once flowed. Military occupation now renders two-thirds of the fort inaccessible, and many of the fort's more resplendent features are gone—the famed Peacock Throne was snatched away in 1739, the gems that adorned the palaces were removed long ago, and the canals where the Stream of Paradise once gurgled now run dry. But the Red Fort remains what it has always been—an architectural marvel and an incredible monument to Mughal power.

LAHORE GATE AND NAUBAT KHANA. The entrance to the fort is toward the middle of its west wall at the three-story Lahore Gate, and it was through this gate that the Mughal emperors would leave for the Jama Masjid. Lahore Gate leads to **Chatta Chowk,** the covered passageway filled with shops that nowadays peddle souvenirs, but that during the Mughal era provided nobles with silks, jewelry, and fine cloth. Chatta Chowk opens onto the rectangular, three-storied Naubat Khana (Drum House). Musicians played here five times a day in tribute to the emperor. The floral carvings adorning the walls of Naubat Khana were once painted with gold.

DIWAN-I-AM. Naubat Khana leads into the palace area. Across the courtyard stands the Diwan-i-Am (Hall of Public Audience), where the early Mughal emperors used to sit (everyone else stood) for two hours a day, chatting with nobles, deciding criminal cases, and generally having a royal time. The throne used to sit on top of the nearby canopied, white-marble platform. At the back is a series of panels adorned with flowers, birds, trees, and lions. Presiding over the entire scene is the Greek musician Orpheus. Scholars speculate that the panels, which were returned from the British Museum in 1903, were crafted in Florence. The low marble platform in front of the emperor's platform was reserved for the prime minister, who, within earshot of the emperor, would entertain grievances.

PRIVATE PALACES. Beyond Diwan-i-Am were the private palaces of the Mughal emperor. Of the original six palaces, five remain; each was connected to its neighbor by a canal called **Nahir-i-Bihisht** (Stream of Paradise). The palaces were set in spacious, formal *charbagh* gardens. The southernmost of the palaces (the one farthest to the right when coming from Diwan-i-Am), **Mumtaz Mahal** (Palace of Jewels), originally housed the harem. These days, it houses a museum (see below). North of Mumtaz Mahal is the **Rang Mahal** (Palace of Colors), a white marble pavilion where the emperor ate his meals. During the Mughal heyday, the ceilings were decorated with silver; other parts of the ceiling are embedded with tiny mirrors that reflected the light from the emperor's candle-lit banquet tables. Just north of the Rang Mahal is the **Khas Mahal** (Private Palace); each of the apartments here was decorated in silk. The southernmost of these is the **Baithak** (Sitting Room). The emperor used to sleep in the center apartment, or **Khwabagh** (Sleeping Chamber). Attached to the outer wall of the Khwabagh is a tower called the **Musamman Burj** (Octagonal Tower), where the emperor would greet his subjects or watch animal fights staged below. King George V and Queen Mary sat here before thousands in 1911, when the announcement was made amidst much rejoicing that the imperial capital would be moved to Delhi from Kolkata. North of the Khwabagh is the **Tasbih Khana** (Chamber for Telling Beads), where the emperor prayed.

DIWAN-I-KHAS AND MOTI MASJID. Just north of Khas-Mahal is the Diwan-i-Khas (Hall of Private Audience), constructed entirely of white marble. Here, the emperor would make crucial political decisions, consult privately with advisors, and speak with VIPs. Attempting to rekindle the old spark, Bahadur Shah II, the last Mughal emperor, held court here during the Mutiny of 1857; in retaliation, the British tried him in the Diwan-i-Am and then exiled him to then-Burma. To the north is the **Hammam** (bath), composed of four large rooms (cold water, hot water, rosewater, and makeup). West of the Hammam is the delicate **Moti Masjid** (Pearl Mosque), built in 1662 by Emperor Aurangzeb for his personal use. The black marble outlines on the floor were designed to help with the proper placement of *musallas* (prayer mats).

MUSEUMS. There are three museums inside the Red Fort complex. **Mumtaz Mahal** is the best of the three, displaying astrolabes, royal *hookahs*, and other artifacts from the Mughal reign. The arms and weapons museum in the **Naubat Khana** concentrates on military history and displays various implements of war from the past 200 years. The **Sanghralaya Museum** traces the development of the Indian independence movement with some life-sized dioramas.

DELHI

JAMA MASJID

1km southwest of the Red Fort. Open to tourists 30min. after dawn until 12:15pm (noon on F), 1:30pm until 20min. before prayer call, and again after prayers until 20min. before sunset. No shoes, shorts, or sleeveless shirts allowed. Camera fee Rs100.

Built between 1650 and 1656 by Emperor Shah Jahan, the Jama Masjid is the largest active mosque in India. Set on a high platform on top of a low hill, the Jama Masjid dominates the tangle of surrounding streets, with soaring minarets and bulky walls of red sandstone. The east gate was once reserved for the emperor and his family; now it is open to all worshippers on Fridays and Muslim holidays. The huge courtyard packs in 25,000 worshippers during Friday prayers. As in most South Asian mosques, a *hauz* (tank) at the center of the courtyard is used for cleansing feet and hands before prayer, and each rectangle designates the space for one worshipper. Prayers are sung from the *imam's* platform, under the center arch at the westernmost point of the mosque. Just west of the mosque is the official residence of the *imam;* the Muslim priests have lived here since the time of Shah Jahan, and you can still see them before prayers. It's worth climbing one of the minarets for the superb views of the city (Rs10). Foreigners should go in groups of two or more, as lone tourists in the claustrophobic stairwell have encountered thieves.

OTHER SIGHTS

RAJ GHAT. Here, a perpetually burning flame and a simple black slab set in a grassy courtyard offer a memorial to Mahatma Gandhi, cremated at this spot after his 1948 assassination by a Hindu extremist. Gandhi's name is notably missing from the monument—the only inscription bears his last words, "Hai Ram" ("Oh God"). Hundreds of visitors come each day to cast flower petals and pray. Just south of the monument is a park full of plants bestowed by dignitaries: flowers from Eisenhower, a pine from Queen Elizabeth II, and a tree planted by Nasser. To the north of the monument, a large park with grassy meadows and a few stands of trees contains memorials to the men and women who have earned a place in India's pantheon of political heroes, including an effusive monument to slain Prime Minister Rajiv Gandhi. An adjacent memorial to his older brother Sanjay was taken down after critics reminded the government that this particular Gandhi never served in office or ever accomplished much at all. Sanjay's admirers continued to leave flowers at the spot, however, and eventually the monument returned. The grassy mound that marks the life and death of Jawaharlal Nehru mentions only his wish to have his ashes thrown in the Ganga. Still farther north is **Shanti Vana**, a pleasant wooded area where many amorous couples can be seen enjoying quiet time together. *(Off Ring Rd, 1km east of Delhi Gate and 2km southwest of the Red Fort. Open dawn-dusk. Free.)*

SOUTH DELHI

QUTB MINAR COMPLEX

At the intersection of Aurobindo Marg and Mehrauli Badarpur Rd., 14km southwest of Connaught Pl. Take bus #505 from New Delhi Railway Station or Janpath. Open daily dawn-dusk. Rs250. Video camera Rs25.

The ruins of the **Qutb Minar** complex boast the tallest stone tower in India. Construction on the complex began in AD 1199 after the Turkish ex-slave Qutb-ud-din Aibak swept into North India and demolished the Rajput empire. Qutb-ud-din Aibak installed himself at Lal Kot, the site of an old Rajput city, founding what was to become India's first Muslim kingdom in 1206. The events that led to the building of the complex were epoch-making, and the Qutb Minar serves as a 72.5m high exclamation point.

The red sandstone Qutb Minar was designed as a celebration of Qutb-ud-din Aibak's triumphs in Northern India and as a monument marking the eastern frontier of the Muslim world. As an inscription on one tower notes, "the tower was erected to cast the shadow of God over both East and West." Modeled on the brick victory towers in Central Asia, the Qutb Minar also served as the minaret for the Quwwat-ul-Islam Masjid (see below). Before dying, Qutb-ud-din Aibak was able to complete only the first story of the tower. His son-in-law Iltutmish added the next three stories. Firoz Shah Tughluq incorporated marble into the mix to offset the monotony of the red sand-tone and completed the tower with a fifth story while repairing damage caused by a 1368 lightning strike. The cupola erected by Firoz was felled by an 1803 earthquake and replaced by British major Robert Smith; Smith's Mughal-style cupola now sits in the gardens, having been removed from the Qutb Minar because it was so awkward. Visitors have been forbidden to climb the 379 steps of the minaret since 1981, when more than 30 panicked school children were trampled to death during a power outage. Most of the calligraphy carved on the minaret displays Arabic passages from the Qur'an, though a few Devanagari inscriptions provide some evidence of Indian influence in its design.

QUWWAT-UL-ISLAM MASJID. Just to the right of the Qutb Minar is the Quwwat-ul-Islam Masjid (Might of Islam Mosque), India's oldest mosque outside of western Gujarat. Begun in AD 1193 and completed in AD 1197 (extensions were added over the next two centuries), the mosque was built from the remains of 21 Hindu and Jain temples destroyed by Qutb-ud-din Aibak. At the center of the courtyard is the 98% pure iron **Gupta Pillar** that was built in the 5th century and has remained rust-free for the last 1500 years. According to the Sanskrit inscription, the pillar was erected in honor of Vishnu and in memory of Chandra, believed to be the Gupta emperor Chandragupta II (r. AD 375-415). Tradition holds that Anangpal, the founder of Lal Kot, brought the pillar here. It is said that those who can stand with their backs against the pillar and wrap their arms around it are blessed with super-human strength; these days, a fence defies any attempt to do so.

ALA'I DARWAZA. Just south of Qutb Minar is the red sandstone Ala'i Darwaza, built in AD 1311 to serve as the southern entrance to the mosque. Immediately east of Ala'i Darwaza is a domed tomb with *jali*, decorative screens characteristic of the Lodi period. The tomb holds the body of Imam Zamin, a Central Asian Sufi saint who reigned from 1489 to 1517.

ALA'I MINAR. North of the Quwwat-ul-Islam Masjid is a massive, unfinished minaret, Ala'i Minar, a monument to grandiose ambitions and plans gone awry. Expansion had doubled the size of the mosque, and Ala'i Minar was designed to be twice as tall as Qutb Minar. After its first 24.5m high story was completed around AD 1300, construction stopped and the madly ambitious project was abandoned.

TOMB OF ILTUTMISH. West of Quwwat-ul-Islam Masjid is the Tomb of Iltutmish, which the sultan himself erected in 1235. Iltutmish's red sandstone tomb isn't particularly interesting from the outside, but the artfully decorated interior is well worth a look, with its mingling of Hindu and Jain themes (wheels, lotuses, and bells) and Muslim motifs (calligraphic inscriptions, geometric patterns, and alcoves facing Mecca built into the west wall). Directly south of Iltutmish's tomb are the ruins of a *madrasa*, an institution of Islamic learning. In keeping with Seljuk Turkish traditions, the tomb of the *madrasa's* founder, Ala-ud-din Khalji, has been placed within.

BAHA'I TEMPLE

Kalkaji, 4km north of Tughluqabad. Open Tu-Su Apr.-Sept. 9am-7pm; Oct.-Mar. 9:30am-5:30pm. Free.

DELHI

Over the past three decades, members of the Baha'i faith have donated millions of dollars toward the construction of seven Baha'i Temples in locations as varied as Uganda, Samoa, and the midwestern United States. The latest addition to this series was finished in 1986 and is situated in South Delhi on a 26-acre expanse of cropped grass and elegant pools. The temple, which invites comparisons to the Sydney Opera House, is built from white marble in the shape of an opening lotus flower, symbolizing purity and equality of all religions. Followers of any faith are free to visit the temple and pray or meditate. Silence is requested of all visitors.

OTHER SIGHTS. Perched on a lonely outcropping is **Tughlaqabad,** a fortified city built by Ghiyas-ud-din Tughlaq, who ruled the Delhi Sultanate from AD 1321 until his murder in 1325. Shortly after Tughlaq was killed, Tughlaqabad was abandoned, having been occupied for only five years. Legend has it that Tughlaqabad became a ghost city after the Sufi saint, Azam-ud-din, put a curse on it. Nowadays, the still-abandoned fort has been conquered by weeds, monkeys, and a general air of desolation. Massive walls run along the 6.5km circumference of the fort and provide expansive views of the Delhi skyline. Thirteen separate gates once led through the walls, but now the only access is on the southern side. (*Mehrauli Badrapur Rd., 9km east of the Qutb Minar and 16km southeast of Connaught Pl. Open dawn-dusk. Rs100.*) Across from the entrance is the red sandstone and white marble **Tomb of Ghiyas-ud-din Tughlaq.**

CENTRAL NEW DELHI

JANTAR MANTAR. This Mughal astronomical observatory looks like an M.C. Escher lithograph rendered as a red-and-white, brick-and-limestone diorama, its stairs twisting around tight bends and soaring upward to the heavens. Charged by emperor Mohammed Shah with the task of revising the Indian calendar accordance to modern astronomy, Maharaja Jai Singh of Jaipur built Jantar Mantar in 1725 after studying European and Asian science and spending years observing Delhi's skies. The result is as scientifically impressive as it is visually striking: the massive instruments keep accurate time (in Delhi, London, and Japan), predict eclipses, and chart the movement of the stars. (*Connaught Pl., 200m down Sansad Marg from the outer circle, on the left, opposite Park Hotel. Open daily sunrise-sunset. Rs100. Video camera Rs25.*)

HUMAYUN'S TOMB. A smorgasbord of red sandstone and black-and-white marble, Humayun's Tomb is set amid geometrical gardens and rows of palm trees. Humayun was the second Mughal emperor, ruling from 1530 until 1540, when he was vanquished by Sher Shah. He ruled again from 1555 until 1556, but an accident cut short his reign. While walking down the stairs of his library in the Old Fort, Humayun heard the *azan.* He quickly sat down on the nearest step, but, upon rising, tripped and slid down the stairs, incurring fatal injuries. His tomb was built nine years later by his widow, Queen haji Begum, who is said to have spent 1.5 million rupees on the monument. Later, many other prominent Mughals were buried at the site, including Dara Shikoh (Shah Jahan's favorite son) and Bahadur Shah II, the last of the Mughal emperors, who was captured here by the British during the Mutiny of 1857. Humayun's Tomb is at the center of a rectangular, quartered garden laced with channels and paths. In 2003, over 1 million rupees were donated to restore water flow to the garden's channels. A pioneering work of Mughal architecture and predecessor to the Taj Mahal, the octagonal tomb sits alone in a central hall, whose double dome rises to a height of 40m and is home to hordes of squealing bats, birds, and bees. (*2.5km southeast of India Gate, at the end of Lodi Rd. Open daily dawn-dusk. Rs250.*)

HAZRAT NIZAMUDDIN DARGAH. One of Sufism's greatest shrines, Hazrat Nizamuddin Dargah was originally built in AD 1325, the year its occupant, the great mystic Sheikh Nizamuddin Aulia, died. The complex was refurbished in the 16th century by Shah Jahan, one of Nizamuddin's many devotees. Its marble verandas and delicate latticework are radiant at dawn and dusk. At twilight, people gather here to sing *qawwali*, Sufi songs of spiritual ecstasy. To reach the shrine, head down the street behind the police station opposite Kataria Nursery, through the market, and into the small, marble courtyard. On the way, you will pass the grave of the great Urdu poet, Mirza Ghalib. Visitors are requested to remove their shoes before entering the courtyard and women should wear a head covering before entering the shrine. *(A short walk southwest of Humayun's tomb, across Mathura Rd., 6km from Connaught Pl.)*

LODI GARDENS. The leafy Lodi Gardens provide a beautiful, blissful place to stroll on the rolling green carpet of grass or take an afternoon nap in the cool shade. In addition to the wide variety of trees and birds, the well-maintained gardens also contain a few parrots, a jogging trail, and a steamy greenhouse. A few ruined buildings rise from the closely cropped grass. One hundred meters to the right of the Gate 1 entrance is the **National Bonsai Park.** Toward the center of the garden is the late 15th-century **Bara Gumbad**, a tomb of red, gray, and black stone topped by a massive dome. Scholars have no idea who is buried here. Attached to the tomb is a mosque built in AD 1494. The square tomb just north of Bara Gumbad is the early 16th-century **Shish Gumbad** (Glass Dome), decorated with remnants of the blue-tiled friezes that once covered it. About 200m north of Shish Gumbad is the **Tomb of Sikandar Lodi** (1517-18). Less than 50m east of the tomb is a 16th-century bridge with seven arches. Also in the Lodi Gardens, 200m southwest of Bara Gumbad, is **Mohammed Shah's Tomb**, a high-domed octagonal building built in the mid-15th century. *(Gate 1, Lodi Rd. Gardens open daily dawn-dusk. Free.)*

SAFDARJUNG'S TOMB. Built in 1753-54 for Safdarjung, prime minister to Mughal emperor Mohammed Shah, the tomb is the last piece of great Mughal architecture built in Delhi. The centerpiece of expansive *charbagh* gardens, the tall, domed edifice was constructed of white marble inlays. Respectable dress is requested in keeping with the character of the monument. *(West of the Lodi Gardens, at the end of Lodi Rd. Open daily dawn-dusk. Rs100. Video fee Rs25.)*

PURANA QILA. The Purana Qila (Old Fort) marks a spot that has been continuously inhabited since the Mauryan period (324-184 BC). The discovery of ceramic shards dating back to 1000 BC vindicated bearers of local tradition, who have long claimed that the fort was built on the site of Indraprastha, the capital city of the Pandava heroes of the *Mahabharata* (commemorated in a nightly sound and light show). In the 16th century, the Purana Qila's massive walls, towering gates, finely preserved mosque, and ruined library formed the centerpiece of Humayun's Delhi. Built in AD 1541 by Sher Shah, the **Qila-i-Kuhna Masjid** (Mosque of the Old Fort) is an ornate tangle of arabesque Qur'anic inscriptions and red sandstone with oriel windows and eaves supported by brackets. Humayun died in AD 1556 after a fatal fall from the steps of his nearby library (see Humayun's Tomb, p. 154). A small, free museum on the premises showcases some of the artifacts discovered in and around Purana Qila. To get a good sense of the incredible height of the fort's ramparts, climb onto the top of the walls and admire the panoramic view of Delhi. A pleasant **exercise trail** winds pleasantly around a small lake where paddleboats can be rented for Rs40 per 30min. *(Off Mathura Rd., 1km east of India Gate. Open daily dawn-dusk. US$5. Sound and light show Tu, Th, Sa, Su Nov.-Jan. 7:30pm; Feb.-Apr. and Sept.-Oct. 8:30pm; May-Aug. 9pm. Rs40.)*

Next to Purana Qila is the **National Zoological Park,** which houses over 1200 animals on 176 acres of land. *(Open Sa-Th Apr. 1-Oct. 15 9am-4pm; Oct. 16-Mar. 31 9:30am-4pm. Rs40. Video fee Rs50.)*

DELHI

DELHI

Central Delhi

▲ ACCOMMODATIONS
Hotel Ambar, 4
Hotel New City Palace, 5
Khush-dil Hotel, 3
Vaishnaw Hotel, 2

● FOOD
Karim, 6
Moti Mahal Restaurant, 7
Rinkey Restaurant, 1

Yamuna River

Shanti Vana
Vijay Ghat
Ring Rd.

Vir Bhumi
Rajiv Gandhi's Memorial
Raj Ghat
Mahatma Gandhi's Memorial
Gandhi Darshan
Gandhi National Museum
Ashoka's Pillar
Kotla Firoz Shah
Dolls Museum
Vikas Marg

DARYA GANJ

Biba Music Emporium

Delhi Gate

Gandhi Smarak Sangrahalya

Bhadurshah Zafar Marg

Red Fort (Lal Qila)

Mirdard Marg

Deen Dayal Upadhyaya Marg

Supreme Court

Sikandra Rd.

Sangeet Natak Akademi

Old Delhi GPO

Mahatma Gandhi Rd.

Lothian Rd.

Netaji Subhash Marg

Ticket Office & Entry Gate

Jama Masjid

Karim

Bazar Chitli Qabar Marg

Nepal

Firoz Shah Rd.

Kashmiri Gate

Delhi Railway Station

Shyma Prasad Mukherji Marg

Delhi Public Library

Chandni Chowk

Chawri Bazar

OLD DELHI

Sitaram Bazar Rd.

Asaf Ali Rd.

Jawaharlal Nehru Marg

Vivekanand Marg

Barakhamba Rd.

Kasturba Gandhi Marg

Zorawar Singh Marg

Fatehpuri Corner
Town Hall

Lalkuan Bazar Rd.

Ajmeri Gate

CONNAUGHT PLACE

Lala Hafeez Sahal Marg

Fatehpuri Mosque

Lahori Gate

Shardhanand Marg

New Delhi Railway Station

Chelmsford Rd.

SEE CONNAUGHT PLACE MAP

Janpath

Jantar Mantar

Sansad Marg

Qutab Rd.

SEE PAHARGANJ MAP

PAHARGANJ

Main Bazar

Desh Bandhu Gupta Rd.

Panchkuian Marg

Shaheed Bhagat Singh Marg

Babar Rd.

Bhai Nayak Singh

Ashoka Rd.

GPO

Pandit Pan

SADAR BAZAR

MOTIA KHAN

Rani Jhansi Rd.

Idgah Rd.

Mandir Marg

Ramakrishna Ashram Marg

Link Rd.

Faiz Rd.

KAROL BAGH

Desh Bandhu Gupta Rd. (Pusa Rd.)

Lakshmi Narayan Temple (Birla Mandir)

Vandemataram Marg

Park St.

Rohtak Rd.

Sarai Rohilla Station

Guru Ravi Das Marg

Sadhu Vaswani Marg (Pusa Rd.)

Shankar Rd.

Shankar Rd.

Vandemataram Marg

N

LG

DELHI

NEW DELHI

Ring Rd.

Sarai Kale Kahn ISBT

Hazrat Nizamuddin Station

LAJPAT NAGAR

Humayun's Tomb

NIZAMUDDIN

Mathura Rd.

SUNDAR NAGAR

Zoological Park

Pragati Maidan (Exhibition Grounds)

Crafts Museum

Purana Qila (Old Fort)

Bhairon Marg

Mathura Rd.

Khairul Manzil Masjid

Hazrat Nizamuddin Dargh

Lala Lajpat Rai Path

Link Marg

DEFENCE COLONY

National Gallery of Modern Art

Dr. Zakir Hussain Rd.

Delhi Golf Course

National Stadium

Tilak Marg

Purana Qila Rd.

Bikaner House

India Gate

Children's Park

Shah Jahan Rd.

Bhisham Pitamah Marg

Jawaharlal Nehru Stadium

GOLF LINKS

Maharishi Raman Marg

SOUTH EXTENSION

Indira Gandhi National Centre for Arts

Kanishka Shopping Plaza

Ashok Rd.

European Commission

Khan Market, Ministry of Home Affairs

Max Mueller Marg

LODI ESTATE

Tibet House

LODI COLONY

Janpath

National Museum

Archeological Survey of India

Israel

Sikandar Lodi's Tomb

India Intl. Centre

National Bonsai Park

JOR BAGH

National Philatelic Museum

Rajpath

Maulana Azad Rd.

M. Nehru Marg

Shish Gumbad

Bara Gumbad

Lodi Gardens

Ireland

Parliament St.

Sansad Bhavan

Aurangzeb Rd.

Prithviraj Rd.

Md. Shah's Tomb

Lodi Rd.

Aurobindo Marg

Talkatora Rd.

Vijay Chowk

Secretariats

Kamal Ataturk Rd.

Safdarjung's Tomb

Gurudwara Rakab Ganj Rd.

Ashoka Rd.

Akbar Rd.

Rajaji Marg

Indira Gandhi Memorial

Safdarjung Rd.

Church of the Redemption

Rashtrapati Bhavan

Dalhousie Rd.

Kushak Rd.

Rajaji Marg

Kamal Ataturk Rd.

Safdarjung Airport

Mughal Gardens

President's Estate

Teen Murti Marg

Nehru Memorial Museum and Planetarium

Santushti Shopping Palace

Racecourse

Willingdon Crescent

Dandi Yatra Statue

Ashok Frontier

Nehru Park

SAROJINI NAGAR

Raisina Rd.

Sri Lanka

Indonesia

China

Norway

United Kingdom

Australia

Pakistan

Yugoslavia

Japan

Germany

Shanti Path

Ethiopia

Sander Patel Marg

Panchsheel Marg

United States

France

Russia

Netherlands

Canada

Satya Marg

Vinay Marg

Buddha Jayanti Park

Raidon Rd.

Switzerland

Sweden

Nyaya Marg

Chandra Gupta Marg

Italy

Thailand

New Zealand

Bhutan

National Rail Museum

Mahavir Jayanti Park

CHANAKYAPURI

Rao Tularam Rd.

1 mile

1 kilometer

0

DELHI

SANSAD AND RASHTRAPATI BHAVANS. Of the scores of buildings built by the British when they moved their capital from Kolkata to Delhi in 1911, the Rashtrapati Bhavan **(President's Residence)** and the Sansad Bhavan **(Parliament House)** are the most impressive. Designed by the renowned architect Edwin Lutyens, the buildings possess a massive grandeur intended to communicate the British determination to keep India as the jewel of the imperial crown. The effort backfired—the aesthetic anomaly of European-style buildings in the heart of an Indian city only further angered Indian nationalists.

Sansad Bhavan, at the end of Sansad Marg, 1.5km southwest of Connaught Pl., is an imposing, circular, colonnaded building that vaguely resembles a flying saucer. Because India's parliament, the Lok Sabha and Rajya Sabha, meet here (see **Government and Politics,** p. 72), it is often difficult to get close to the building. On December 13, 2001, terrorists attacked the parliament building, killing 13 people inside and heightening tensions between the two countries. (*To get inside, you will have to obtain a letter from your embassy.)* To reach **Rashtrapati Bhavan,** head down to Rajpath and walk between the Secretariats to the entrance; or walk 2km west from India Gate down Rajpath. Once the residence of the viceroy, the pinkish Rashtrapati Bhavan now houses India's president. *(To visit Rashtrapati Bhavan, you'll need to apply at the reception office at least 2 days in advance. Tours are offered M, W, F. Bring your passport.)* The 45m high pillar between the gate and the residence was donated by the Maharaja of Jaipur and is known as the **Jaipur Column.** The pillar is capped with a bronze lotus and a six-pointed Star of India.

SECRETARIATS. Flanking Raisina Hill are the symmetrical Secretariats, which now house government ministries. The buildings are adorned with various slogans praising enlightened imperial rule. For some shade (and fresh air), pass under the slogans and into the **Great Hall,** a dark and airy room adorned with medallions and crowned by a baroque dome. Try to visit **Raisina Hill,** the area between the two Secretariats, on a Saturday, when troops march in front of Rashtrapati Bhavan. (*Ceremonial changing of the guard in summer 8:30-9:15am; in winter 10:35-11am.)* As you look east from the Secretariats, the 42m high arch in the distance is **India Gate,** a memorial to the 90,000 Indian soldiers killed in WWI and the Afghan War of 1919. A memorial beneath the arch commemorates those who were killed in the 1971 Indo-Pakistani War; An eternal flame has been burning since then.

BIRLA MANDIR. Built in 1938 by the wealthy Birlas in honor of Lakshmi, the goddess of material well-being, the Lakshmi Narayan Temple is a marvel of Orissan-style temple architecture and opulent extravagance. The room of mirrors at the back of the temple allows you to see yourself together with reflections of a flute-playing Krishna. The gardens contain a colorful fountain in the shape of a pile of cobras, gaily painted sculptures of tigers and elephants, and a plaster cave that can be entered through the mouth of a giant plastic boar. The temple was inaugurated by Mahatma Gandhi. People of all faiths are welcome to worship at the temple. *(Mandir Marg, 2km west of Connaught Pl. Open daily 4:30am-9pm. Free.)*

🏛 MUSEUMS

NATIONAL MUSEUM. This museum's ambitious mission is to provide an overview of Indian life and culture from prehistoric times to the present. Exhibits are all built around a circular courtyard and the ground-floor galleries showcase some of the museum's most popular items. Other displays trace the development of Indian scripts, iconography, and coins over the past 16 centuries. An enormous vault houses the museum's impressive jewelry collection, which includes gaudy gilded earrings, necklaces, and bracelets dating from the 1st century AD. Remarkable works of decorative art and a collection of Neolithic stone artifacts (3000-1500

BC) fill the remaining ground floor galleries. Upstairs, the maritime heritage gallery charts Indian naval progress since ancient times. In the adjacent room, there are replicas of the cave murals and ceiling paintings from Ajanta. The top-notch collection of musical instruments in the Sharan Rani Gallery, donated in 1980 by renowned *sarod* player Sharan Rani, is remarkably comprehensive; instruments include handcrafted *sarangis* and sitars as well as a glass tabla. *(Janpath, just south of Rajpath. ☎ 23019272. Open Tu-Su 10am-5pm. Rs150; students with ID Rs1. Camera fee Rs300. Guided tours begin at the enquiry counter at 10:30, 11:30am, noon, 2, 3:30pm.)*

CRAFTS MUSEUM. Built in 1991, the Crafts Museum has a collection of 22,000 objects originating from nearly every state in the country. The museum is divided into three sections. Near the entrance, an open-air, live demonstration area provides an opportunity to glimpse artisans casting metal for sculptures, stringing jewelry, and weaving baskets from straw. Also outdoors is a complex filled with life-size reproductions of rural huts and houses brought to Delhi from around the country. Inside, impressive displays showcase the diversity of traditional Indian crafts, including 18th-century wood carvings from Karnataka, string puppets from Rajasthan, a myriad of textiles, and a model of a Bihari wedding chamber. *(Pragati Maidan, Bhairon Marg, off Mathura Rd. Open Tu-Su 10am-5pm. Craft demonstrations and outdoor displays open daily 10am-7pm. Outdoor displays partially closed July 1-Oct. 1. Free.)*

NATIONAL GALLERY OF MODERN ART. Once the mansion of the Maharaja of Jaipur, this gallery houses a diverse collection of Indian art produced over the last 150 years. The paintings range from European landscapes to finger paintings and Cubist abstractions, though most were produced after Independence. Some provocative sculptures linger precariously in the middle of the gallery halls. Highlights include the bold designs of Jamini Roy, the paintings of the turn-of-the-century Bengal School, which were inspired by South Asian folk art and East Asian high art, and Badrinath Arya's *Khoj*, a painting of subterranean stalactite-like staircases. Affordable reproductions are available (Rs30-50) at the entrance lobby. *(Jaipur House, southeast of India Gate. ☎ 23382835. Open Tu-Su 10am-5pm. Rs150.)*

NEHRU MEMORIAL MUSEUM AND PLANETARIUM. Built inside the estate of India's first prime minister, the museum has as much to say about the independence movement as a whole as it does about Nehru himself. Between peeks into Nehru's study, office, and living room, visitors are guided past shots of Nehru as a dour youth, as a student at Harrow and Cambridge, and as the humble, generous leader of India. Adjacent to the museum is the Nehru Planetarium, where you can visualize a pulsar or find out what your weight would be on Jupiter. *(Teen Murti Bhawan, Teen Murti Rd., 400m northeast of Chanakyapuri. Open Tu-Su 9am-5pm. Free. Planetarium open 11am-5pm. Rs2. Planetarium showings in English Tu-Su 11:30am and 3pm. Rs15.)*

OTHER MUSEUMS. The **Indira Gandhi Memorial** exhibits a sentimental collection of photos and quotations honoring India's two fallen prime minsters, all arrayed in Rajiv and Indira's former residence. Indira Gandhi's last few steps outside her home, where she was assassinated on Oct. 31, 1984, are covered with sheets of glass crystal. *(1 Safdarjang. Open Tu-Su 9:30am-4:45pm. Free.)* The **National Rail Museum** has indoor and outdoor exhibits on the history of Indian Railways and a miniature "joy train" (Rs10) you can ride. *(Chanakyapuri, near the NZ and Bhutan embassies. Open Tu-Su Apr.-Sept. 9:30am-7:30pm; Oct.-Mar. 9:30am-5:30pm. Rs10. Video fee Rs100.)*

⬛ ENTERTAINMENT

Delhi Diary (Rs10) comes out every Friday and details weekly musical and cultural events. **Dances of India** is a nightly performance of Indian dance and music, including *kathak* and *bharatnatyam*. (Parsi Anjuman Hall, opposite the Ambedkar Football Stadium, Delhi Gate. ☎ 26234689 or 26429170. Shows 6:45pm. Rs200.) Many **movie theaters** in Delhi show Hindi movies. **PVR Priya 1,** Basant Lok, Vasant

DELHI

Vihar (☎26140048), and **PVR Saket,** Saket Community Centre (☎26865999), show English-language films for Rs45-130. Most theatres showing Hindi films will have one English-dubbed or subtitled showing in the morning. Check daily papers for movie listings. Various cultural centers (see p. 142) screen foreign films and Indian "art" films not shown elsewhere.

The Red Fort's nightly **sound and light show,** focusing on the city's Mughal heritage, is unexpectedly entertaining. (see **Lal Qila,** p. 150). The Old Fort has a sound and light show 4 times per week on the *Mahabharata* (see **Purana Qila,** p. 155).

▣ SHOPPING

Although it's usually better to buy goods directly from the region where they are produced, Delhi is a fantastic place to shop for popular handicrafts from all over the country. Markets and stores range from the grimy and cheap to the glitzy and prohibitively expensive. Right in backpacker haven, **Paharganj's Main Bazaar** can satisfy all of your kitschy paraphernalia cravings. To the northwest of Paharganj, **Karol Bagh** contains shops of all sizes and kinds. (Open Tu-Su.) If fluorescent "Om" iron-on patches aren't your style, the priciest of Delhi's boutiques are concentrated in **Connaught Place,** where armed guards stand in front of jewelry shops and tailors sell saris made from the finest silk. (Open M-Sa.) Literally under Connaught Pl. is the **Palika Bazaar,** an underground, A/C maze of stores selling anything and everything, mostly to locals. (Open daily 10am-8pm.) Down Janpath from Connaught Pl. is the **Central Cottage Industries Emporium,** a multi-floored mini-mall selling high-quality, pricey handicrafts from all over India including carved metal boxes, Mughal-style paintings, wooden elephants, and oriental rugs. (☎23321617. Open M-Sa 10am-7pm.) Opposite the emporium is the tourist-targeted stretch of **Tibetan Market,** which sells cheap Kashmiri crafts. (Most shops open M-F 10am-7:30pm.) Several states also have their own emporia selling unique, non-local fare on **Baba Kharak Singh Marg.** (Most open M-Sa 10am-6:30pm.) **Dilli Haat,** off Aurobindo Marg, across from Ina Market in South Delhi, features a changing cast of craftsmen and a food stall from each of India's states. (Entrance Rs10. Open M-Sa 10am-10:30pm.) For more expensive souvenirs, head to the boutiques of **Hauz Khas Village** (open W-M) or the antiques market of **Sunder Nagar** (open M-Sa).

Many of Delhi residents shop among the rows of name-brand and generic stores in South Delhi's markets, such as **Ansal Plaza** (open W-M), **South Extension** (open Tu-Su), **Sarojini Nagar** (open Tu-Su), **Lajpat Nagar** (open Tu-Su) and, for the tragically trendy, **M and N blocks of Greater Kailash** (open W-M). Alternatively, Old Delhi's **Chandni Chowk** (open M-Sa), which runs from the Fatehpuri Masjid to the Red Fort, and all of its south-leading alleys are one enormous bazaar with old world atmosphere; the road buzzes with the sound of haggling throughout the day. Many of the products sold here are household items, but plenty of shops also stock clothes, jewelry, and musical instruments of varying quality and price. **Netaji Subhash Marg,** which runs south from the Red Fort to Delhi Gate, is lined with music stores. **Biba Music Emporium,** 500m north of Delhi Gate, has an extensive collection of sitars (Rs1200-15,000), including some beautiful antique instruments, tablas for Rs700-6000, and harmoniums for Rs1500-6000. (☎23284558. Open M-Sa 10am-7:30pm.)

▨ NIGHTLIFE

Despite what the shadowy and deserted streets of Connaught Place might imply, Delhi's nightlife is not confined to lounging with the *chai*-sipping crowd on Paharganj rooftops. The clubs of the capital thump and flash with the same techno and whirling lights as the best clubs anywhere. But like the luxury hotels that house them, Delhi's discos cater to the elite, and cover charges may seem forbiddingly steep to budget travelers. Interestingly, Irish pubs with dance floors have recently been sprouting all over town with increasing popularity. If you want to get down and dirty with the jet-set of India, you'll have to cough up some serious cash and dig down deep into your pack to find the necessary clothes to fit in. Most of the clubs listed below are 21+ (although the strict legal drinking age is 25), require men to be accompanied (women, however, can often get in alone), and prohibit torn clothing, sneakers, and uncool insophisticates of all kinds.

Dublin (☎26112233), at the Maurya Sheraton, Chanakyapuri. A 106 ft. bar takes you through 11 distinct "zones," or theme lounges, in this trendy Irish pub. Try one of the 100 types of whiskey in "The Great Whisky Library" or dance to the hottest beats in the "Ghungroo," a sunken dance floor where a packed crowd of locals and foreigners strut their stuff to 138 decibels of techno, hip-hop, and Punjabi music. Su-Th no cover; M Ladies' Night; F-Sa Rs500 per couple. Open daily 6pm-2am. Bar closes at 12:45am.

Float (☎26223344), at Park Royal Hotel, Nehru Place. Considered by many to be Delhi's hottest nightclub, Float pulls off the futuristic look with finesse. Sleek, ultra-modern furniture fills the huge lounge area, while the space between the live band stage and octagonal island bar becomes the dance floor. The DJ plays everything under the sun. Happy Hour 6-8pm (50% off selected beverages). No cover. Couple entry only. Open daily 6pm-1am.

Djinn's (☎26702334), at Hyatt Regency, Bhikaiji Cama Place, Ring Rd. Delhi's top trendsetter in the Irish pub scene has everything from a model biplane and massive swordfish hanging from the ceiling to an elegant vintage bar, a red telephone booth, and wooden barrel tables imported from the UK. A billiards table in the side alcove and a small dance space in front of the DJ console provide ample entertainment. The resident DJs play techno and pop favorites. Happy Hour 6-9pm (50% off drinks). W-M live music. W Ladies' Night. No cover. Couple entry only. Open daily 6pm-1am.

Mirage (☎26835070), at Crowne Plaza Surya, New Friends Colony. A swanky club with a subdued Egyptian theme, Mirage's flashing neon lights hang in profusion over the dance floor and the wrought-iron railings surrounding it. The DJ usually spins techno, hip-hop, Hindi pop, and a bit of reggae. W Ladies' Night. Sa Diplomats' and Theme Night. Cover Rs500 per couple. Open W-Su 9pm-1:30am.

DELHI

GOA
गोवा

Sun-bathed white beaches, elegantly crumbling Portuguese manors, and an easy-going spirit have long made Goa a prime destination for travelers. However, continuing waves of an invading tourist culture have splashed Goa's shores with red Coca-Cola umbrellas, stubbornly persistent sarong peddlers, and hordes of leather-skinned package-tourists. Resort complexes and the middle-aged sun worshippers who populate them compete for space on the beach with European and Israeli vacationers taking an extended break from reality. Still, despite the development, you are never far from an unspoiled beach, where you can revel in the simple splendor of drinking from freshly fallen coconuts and watching fishermen fold their nets. The revelry and insanity have calmed down a bit under the influence of tightening regional authority, but the sweet-smelling breeze blowing in off the ocean suggests that Goa is still a good place to come for an exhilarating natural high.

Europeans have come to Goa since 1498, when Portuguese explorer Vasco da Gama landed on the Keralan coast in search of spices. Portugal was looking to establish a foothold in India, and in 1510, Goa became a Portuguese colony. During the 16th century, the region developed as a commercial center where Portuguese soldiers and adventurers mixed with and married the locals, many of whom converted to Catholicism. Thanks to the additional "encouragement" of the Jesuit Inquisition, Goa became a stronghold of Catholicism in India and remains so to this day. The Portuguese made sure that Goa never became a part of the British Raj, and held on here until 1961, when Indian troops annexed the region. The state thus holds the dubious distinction of being both the first piece of subcontinental soil clutched by Europeans and the last to be returned to Indian control. It first became a Union Territory, and eventually, in 1987, an official state.

After five centuries of Portuguese rule, Goa is unique among Indian states: about 30% of Goa's inhabitants are Christian, so Portuguese-speaking Roman Catholics dressed in jeans and muscle shirts live side-by-side with *lungi*-clad fishermen shouldering the day's catch. The state has literacy and income levels among the highest in India. Goa is small enough to explore thoroughly during a stay of moderate length, and locals are often eager to share their paradise with visitors.

HIGHLIGHTS OF GOA

India's most legendary (and most decadent) nightlife scene raves away all winter on the northern beaches of **Anjuna** (p. 176) and **Chapora and Vagator** (p. 180).

Time stands still in **Old Goa** (p. 170), home to Portuguese monuments, cathedrals, and the mortal remains of **St. Francis Xavier** (p. 171).

The northernmost and southernmost Goan beaches, **Arambol** (p. 183) and **Palolem** (p. 190), will do their best to seduce you into staying longer than you ever planned to.

WHEN TO GO(A)

Goa's northern beaches are hopping from early November to late March, when hot and cloudless skies draw sun-worshippers in droves. Beach fever is intense in the weeks before and after Goa's Christmas; the months of December and January are considered peak season. Almost everything closes down during the monsoon

Goa

MAHARASHTRA

KARNATAKA

Terekol Fort
Querim
Pernem
Alorna Fort
Arambol
Mandrem
Chopdem
Thivim
Chapora
Siolim
Bicholim
Sri Brahma Carambolim
Vagator
Anjuna
Baga
Mapusa
Mayem Lake
Valpoi
Calangute
17
Candolim
Old Goa
Karmali
Bondla Wildlife Sanctuary
Fort Aguada
Panjim(Panaji)
Sri Manguesh
Tambdi Surla
Dona Paula
Siridao
Cortalim
Sri Nagesh
Sri Mahalsa
Farmagudi
Sancordem
Mormugao
Sri Shantadurga
Ponda
4A
Molen
Vasco da Gama
Dabolim Airport
Molen Wildlife Sanctuary
Bogmalo
Rachol
Dudhsagar Falls
Colva
Margao (Madgaon)
Benaulim
Sanguem

Arabian Sea

Sri Chandreshwar Bhutnath

N
LG

Betul

Cabo de Rama
Agonda
Sri Malikarjun
Cotigao Wildlife Sanctuary
Palolem
Chaudi

0   10 miles
0   10 kilometers

(June-Sept.), and guest house prices bottom out as tourists head north to the green fields of Manali (p. 244). The monsoon cools Goa down, but the showers often cease for long sunny stretches. Other holidays well worth the trip are the **Carnival,** Panjim's pre-Lent revelry, and the more solemn festivities in honor of Goa's favorite saint, Francis Xavier, held in Old Goa on December 3 every year.

■ INTERCITY TRANSPORTATION

Most travelers reach Goa from Mumbai, 600km to the north.

FLIGHTS

Dabolim Airport (info ☎ 0854 2512644), 29km south of Panjim. **Indian Airlines** and **Jet Airways** offer flights to and from: **Bangalore** (1½hr., 3pm, US$89-115); **Delhi** (2½hr., 7:25am, US$245); **Mumbai** (1hr., 4 per day, US$80-103). During late Dec. and early Jan., seats on the Mumbai-Goa flight can be difficult to obtain, but flights are normally available mid-week; call a few days in advance.

Dabolim's prepaid **taxi** counter, outside the airport's main entrance, will ferry you just about anywhere in Goa. A board to the left of the counter lists fares (to Panjim Rs400-450). Off season (May-Sept.), touts clutter the main exit. **Local buses** run to **Vasco da Gama** (8am-8pm; Rs5), with connections to **Panjim** and **Margao.**

GOA

TRAINS

Traveling south from Mumbai on the **Konkan Railway** is efficient and comfortable. The only drawback is that the tracks were laid 15-20km outside city stations, so the railway only skirts major towns. Two trains from **Mumbai** head to Goa daily: the Mumbai-Madgaon Mandovi Express (7:05am) and the Mumbai-Madgaon Konkan Kanya Express (10:55pm). These trains stop at several stations in Goa, including: **Tivim,** 20km east of Vagator beach (10¼hr.); **Karmali,** 12km east of Panjim (10½hr.); **Margao,** in the south, 5km outside the city of Benaulim (12hr.). All Mumbai fares are Rs796 for 3-tier A/C sleepers. The Mandovi Express (10:30pm) and the overnight Konkan Express (6pm) make the return trip for the same fares. Trains for **Delhi** leave daily from the coastal town of **Vasco da Gama,** near the airport (41 hr., 2pm, Rs1750).

GOOD TO GOA Since word got out that Goa is an earthly paradise, huge resorts and small guest houses alike have been falling all over themselves to house and bathe legions of visitors. But laundering all those sweaty tourists has taken its toll, draining some village wells dry or contaminating them with salty sea water. You can help preserve Goa's glory by taking bucket baths, turning off the shower as you suds up, and having a *dhobi* wash your clothes instead of washing them in the sink. The Ghost of Tourists Past litters beaches with bottles; think about the future of tiny Goa and put your junk in a garbage can. After all, you're eating fish from just off shore. If you are considering a long stay, volunteering for one of Goa's Non-Governmental Organizations (NGOs) allow you to help on a local level. ECOFORUM in Mapusa publishes a book, *Fish Curry & Rice* (Rs200), which has a listing of Goa's activist groups.

BUSES

Buses are the cheapest way to reach Goa from: **Bangalore** (14hr., Rs330); **Mangalore** (10hr., 2 per day, Rs153); **Miraj** (10hr., 2 per day, Rs225); **Mumbai** (16hr., 1 per day, Rs315); **Mysore** (15hr., Rs250); **Pune** (12hr., Rs230). In most cities, you can buy your ticket on the bus. **Private carriers** offer more extensive services and more comfort (except for the infamous "video coaches," see p. 45). Book private coaches through a travel agency or at one of the shacks near the bus terminals. Prices for: **Bangalore** (Rs200-330); **Mangalore** (Rs143-182); **Miraj** (Rs120-133); **Mumbai** (Rs255-366); **Mysore** (Rs222-247); **Pune** (Rs230-286). Check the individual town listings for more bus information.

▐ LOCAL TRANSPORTATION

Traveling by bus along Goa's narrow roads is not as stomach-wrenching as in other parts of the country; the popular routes are generally packed but short.

BUSES

Intrastate buses go between the **Kadamba Bus Terminals** in the transport hubs of Panjim, Mapusa, and Margao. **Express buses** are the fastest; other buses stop in every village and rice paddy. There are few bus stops in the state, and most locals simply flag down non-express buses as they pass by. For more details on interstate bus travel, see listings for **Margao** (p. 185), **Mapusa** (p. 172), and **Panjim** (p. 165).

TAXIS AND RICKSHAWS

Tourist vehicles (expensive minivans) and **taxis** are available for short jaunts or longer-term rentals (Rs8 per km). **Auto-rickshaws** disinclined to set their meters zip between beaches or herd passengers in at rickshaw stands in town (Rs8 1st km,

Rs5 each additional km). Fares tend to be a little more than half of what taxis charge. During the off-season and when heading to more remote areas, all auto-rickshaws require return fares. The distinctly Goan **motorcycle-rickshaws** (Rs5 1st km, Rs3 each additional km) or **pilot taxis** are the cheapest options.

MOTORCYCLES

The simplest, riskiest, and sexiest transportation method employed by many visitors is an automatic Enfield, Honda Kinetic, or Yamaha **motorcycle,** which can be rented by the day or month through most hotels and guest houses in virtually every town and beach. Prices fluctuate by season (Rs150-300 per day). Technically, you must obtain an Indian or international driver's license in order to drive one. **Helmets** can be hard to come by, but some official bike rental places might be able to find you one. Or pick up a helmet (with a visor to block dust) in Panjim or Mumbai.

BICYCLES

Bicycles (Rs4-6 per hr., Rs40-60 per day) can be hired from hotels and guest houses. You can pedal along the whole of Colva Beach when the tide is out; plan to get wet, and bring plastic bags for cameras and valuables. Cycling long distances is tough since rental bikes have only one gear and there are many hills.

NORTH GOA

PANJIM (PANAJI) पणजी   ☎ 0832

Red-tiled Portuguese mansions, Hindu shrines, and Catholic icons all jostle for space in Goa's capital, Panjim (pop. 100,000), but a slow and friendly pace prevails nonetheless. Many of the town's crumbling buildings date from around 1759, when the viceroy moved his residence from Old Goa to Yusuf Adil Shah's old palace in Panjim (today's Secretariat). Panjim's Church Square and waterfront bustle with activity and have plenty of amenities for the beach-bound traveler. The city deserves more than just a quick stocking-up stop, thanks to its proximity to lovely Old Goa and the hidden Hindu temples farther inland.

▐ TRANSPORTATION

Flights: Indian Airlines (☎ 2223826 or 2237821), DB Marg, at the northwestern edge. Open M-Sa 10am-1pm and 2-5pm. **Jet Airways** (☎ 2438792), Patto Plaza, just south of the Department of Tourism. Open M-F 9:30am-1pm and 2-5pm. **Jet Air** (☎ 2222438), 102 Rizvi Chambers, 1st fl., at the corner of Gen. Bernarado Guedes and Heliodoro Salgado Rd., is an agent for **American Airlines, Austrian Airlines, Gulf Air,** and **Royal Jordanian.** Open M-F 9:30am-1pm and 2-5:30pm, Sa 9:30am-1pm. **Thakkers Travel Service** (☎ 2436678), Mahalaxmi Chambers, on 18th June Rd. and up 4 flights of stairs, is an agent for **KLM.** Open M-F 9:30am-1pm and 2-5:30pm, Sa 9am-1pm.

Trains: Karmali, 12km east of town, is the nearest station on the Konkan Railway (see **Getting There,** p. 163). Reservation office for **Konkan Railway** is upstairs at the **Kadamba Bus Terminal,** Patto. Open M-Sa 8am-2pm and 2:15-8pm. You can also buy tickets at Karmali Station 8am-2pm. Buses and tourist taxis shuttle to Panjim.

Buses: Kadamba Bus Terminal, Patto. **Interstate buses** to: **Bangalore** (14hr., 3:30pm, Rs330); **Mangalore** (10hr., 6:15am and 1:30pm, Rs153); **Miraj** (10hr., 10 and 10:30am, Rs225); **Mumbai** (16hr., 5pm, Rs315); **Mysore** (15hr., 3pm, Rs250); **Pune** (12hr., 3 per day 6:15am-7pm, Rs230). Advance reservations can be made at the

booking office. Most counters are open 9am-6pm, but try to show up before 4pm, as some close early. **Private buses** departing for the same destinations can be booked at many hotels and travel agents, or just show up at the bus stand along the river and hunt out a bus going the right way. **Intrastate buses** zip to destinations throughout Goa from 6am-7:30pm. To: **Calangute** (40min., every 15min., Rs7); **Mapusa** (regular 30min., express 15min.; every 5min.; Rs5-6); **Margao** (regular 45min., express 30min.; every 5-10min.; Rs15); **Ponda** (every 15min., Rs12); **Vasco Da Gama** (every 15min., Rs15).

Local Transportation: Taxis officially gather in front of the Hotel Mandovi, the Tourist Hostel, and at stands along 18th June Rd., but are unofficially everywhere, and universally insistent about your need for them. **Auto-rickshaws** line up near the Municipal Market and the Municipal Gardens. In good weather, budding capitalists hawk **motorbikes** across the street from the GPO. It's inadvisable to rent in Panjim without an international driver's license. One-speed **bikes** are available at **Daud M. Aga** (☎2222670), opposite the Cinema National entrance. Bikes Rs4 per hr. Open M-Sa 9am-1pm and 2-7pm, Su 9am-noon.

■ ■ ORIENTATION AND PRACTICAL INFORMATION

Panjim, located at the confluence of the **Mandovi** and **Ourem Rivers,** is easy to get around on foot. On the east bank of the Ourem is the **Patto** area and its chaotic **bus terminal. Emidio Gracia Road.** leads west uphill from the Ourem to **Church Square.,** dominated by the towering white **Mary Immaculate Conception Church.** From here, **18th June Road,** featuring many hotels, restaurants, and shops, leads southwest. **Dayanand Bandodkar (DB) Marg (Avenida Dom Joao Castro)** follows the bank of the Mandovi River. The best budget guest houses are in the old Portuguese quarter, **Fontainhas,** south of Emidio Garcia Rd. by the Ourem River.

Tourist Office: Government of India Tourist Office, Communidade Bldg., Church Sq. (☎2223412 or 25641653). Open M-F 9:30am-1pm and 2-6pm, Sa 9:30am-1pm. **Dept. of Tourism, Government of Goa** (☎2438753; goatour@goatelecom.com), between the traffic bridge and the footbridge on the Patto side of the Ourem River. Offers the useful Goa Tourist Directory. Open M-F 9:30am-1:15pm and 2-5:45pm, Sa 9:30am-1pm. **Goa Tourism Development Corporation (GTDC)** (☎2226515; www.goacom.com/goatourism), Trionora Apartments, Dr. Alvares Costa Rd.; turn into the driveway and make a right. Arranges accommodations, tours around Goa, and sunset cruises. Open M-F 9am-1pm and 2-5pm, Sa 9am-1pm. Branch: on the ground floor of the Dept. of Tourism, Government of Goa building.

Currency Exchange: State Bank of India (☎2426125), DB Marg, opposite the Hotel Mandovi. Open for exchange on the 2nd fl. M-F 10am-1:30pm, Sa 10am-noon. **Thomas Cook,** DB Marg (☎2221312), exchanges cash and all traveler's checks, usually at better-than-bank rates. Open M-Sa 9:30am-6pm; Oct.-Mar. also Su 10am-5pm. **AmEx** is right next door.

Pharmacy: Farmacia Salcete (☎2225959), 18th June Rd., just beyond the Municipal Gardens. Open M-Sa 9am-7:30pm.

Hospital: Dr. Bhandare Hospital (☎2224966), Fontainhas, go south on 31st January Rd., passing the Panjim Inn; bear left where the road forks, turn right at the People's High School, and take the first left.

Police: Headquarters (☎2224486 or 2223266), Malaca Rd., on the west edge of the Azad Maidan gardens.

Telephones: STD/ISD signs are everywhere.

Internet: Cosy Nook, 18th June Rd., beyond the Municipal Garden, is one of many options that provides fast connections. Rs20 per 30min., Rs35 per hr. Open daily 8:30am-9pm.

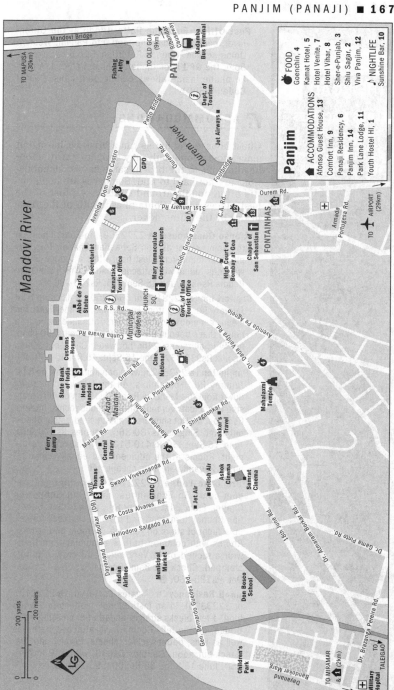

Panjim

FOOD
Goenchin, 4
Kamat Hotel, 5
Hotel Venite, 7
Hotel Vihar, 8
Sher-e-Punjab, 3
Shiu Sagar, 2
Viva Panjim, 12

NIGHTLIFE
Sunshine Bar, 10

ACCOMMODATIONS
Afonso Guest House, 13
Comfort Inn, 9
Panaji Residency, 6
Panjim Inn, 14
Park Lane Lodge, 11
Youth Hostel HI, 1

GOA

FROM THE ROAD

MARVELOUS MACHINES

Tthe auto-rickshaw is ubiquitous in India. Hundreds cluster at each intersection, with the black and yellow coloring of a swarm of angry bees. Fast, yet super compact, the auto-rickshaw can zip through narrow gaps, leaving lumbering cars and buses behind. For the traveler, it is an unparalleled mode of transport. But beware: there are traps lying in wait for the inexperienced customer.

First, choosing a rickshaw is not to be done impulsively. One must examine each driver for a devilish glint of the eye—the presence of such a glint identifies the *wallah* most likely to put pedal-to-the-metal when the lights turn green. Bumper stickers—like "Keep Distance" and "STOP!"—are also good signs. Finally, the odd idol never hurts: having divine providence on your side can't hurt as you engage in that most perilous of things, the rickshaw ride.

As you blast off into the terrifying merry-go-round that is the Indian road system, there will finally be time to relish the excitement. Feel the tension as you wait for the light to turn. Now, the throb of the engine is a battle-drum! The blaring horn is a trumpet-call! For one brief moment, all is chaos. And then you jet off and speed along the open road with the wind in your hair and other lesser rickshaws eating your dust.

-Fran Moore, 2004

Post Office: From the Patto Bridge at the Ourem River, continue along the road into Panjim. Western Union service. Open M-F 9:30am-5:30pm, Sa 9am-5pm. The **GPO** is on the left behind a garden. A public phone inside allows calling card calls. **Postal Code:** 403001.

⚑ ACCOMMODATIONS

Guest houses and hotels run a brisk business, but since most people only stay a night or two before heading out to the beach, same-day accommodations are not hard to find. Standards are high; tariffs often double around Christmas. Most of the best places are in Fontainhas, south of the footbridge by the Ourem River.

Afonso Guesthouse (☎ 2222359), in Fontainhas, on the same street as San Sebastian Chapel. This very pleasant family-run guest house has a terrace and 8 spacious rooms with attached baths. Check-out 9am. Rooms Rs450. June 15-Sept. 15: Rs250-280. ❸

Comfort Inn (☎ 2228145 or 5642250), walking up 31st January Rd. away from Fontainhas, on the right. Ten clean, generous doubles, 7 with attached bath, in a house that's been in the family for 120 years. 50-channel TV in all rooms. 24hr. hot water. Check-out 10am. Rooms Rs232-332; June 15-Sept. 15 Rs150-200. ❷

Panjim Inn (☎ 2226523; www.panjiminn.com), on 31st January Rd., Fontainhas, on the left when heading down from the Mandovi River. This 18th-century mansion has a leafy veranda and gorgeous rooms. Internet Rs50 per hr. Hot showers in all attached baths. Check-out 9am. Singles Rs730-865, doubles Rs770-990; June 16-Sept. 30 Rs410-510. A/C Rs360 extra per night. Rooms at the adjacent and equally beautiful annex **Pousada** are 10% cheaper. ❹

Park Lane Lodge (☎ 2227154; pklaldg@goatelecom.com), in Fontainhas, near San Sebastian Chapel. From 31st January Rd., walk to San Sebastian Chapel, turn right, and it's about a block farther, up a flight of stairs on your left. TV room and terrace. Rooms with common baths are roomier than those with attached bath. Very quiet and cozy, if mildly cramped. Check-out 8am. Rooms Rs305-441; Apr.-Oct. Rs185-260. ❷

Panaji Residency Dr. Alvares Costa Rd. (☎ 2227103 or 2223396), in an institutional, multi-storied white bldg. a few blocks straight ahead after crossing Patto Bridge, on the left. Rooms have attached baths as well as fans, phones, clean sheets, towels, and TVs. Check-out noon. Doubles Rs630, with A/C Rs750-850; June 16-Sept. 30 Rs500/550-750. ❸

Youth Hostel HI (☎ 2225433), in suburban Miramar, a 45min. walk from the town center off DB Marg. Worth the hike if you want to pinch rupees, but it's often full even weeks in advance. Buses from town head out here; ask for Miramar. Meals Rs18. Check-out 8am. Dorms Rs40, HI members Rs20. ❶

🍴 FOOD

Panjim's restaurants are a good reason to stay in the city longer. Visitors can pick from chow mein, lasagna, biryani, Punjabi *dal*, and Goan fish curry.

Hotel Venite, on 31st January Rd., near the river. An unassuming sign on the right when facing the river will direct you up a narrow staircase to this mellow and airy space. Try the prawn curry (Rs85) and nightly specials (Rs60-100). Beer Rs45, coconut or cashew *feni* Rs20. Open M-Sa 8:30am-3pm and 7-10pm. ❸

Shiu Sagar, MG Rd. (☎ 2436348), in Shiu Sagar Hotel, near the small, white Immaculate Conception Chapel. This veg. joint serves up *dal Makhali* (Rs50) and naan (Rs13) just like your mother never made, but should have. Entrees Rs35-60. Open daily 8am-11pm. ❷

Viva Panjim, in Fontainhas, around the corner from Afonso Guesthouse. The wait is long, but the tasty Goan and Chinese specialties merit patience in this quiet alleyway spot. Prawns fried rice Rs55. Open M-Sa 8am-11pm. ❷

Goenchin, Dr. Dada Vaidya Rd. (☎ 2227614 or 2434877), on the left as you come from Church Sq. Look for a sign pointing uphill. Delicious Chinese food (only slightly Indianized) in a refined setting; worth the extra rupees. Veg. and non-veg. entrees Rs85-195. Open daily 12:30-3pm and 7:30-11pm. ❸

Sher-e-Punjab (☎ 2227204), on 18th June Rd., on the right as you walk away from the river, with a garden patio in back. Beer Rs25-50. Entrees under Rs60. Open daily 10:30am-midnight. ❷

Kamat Hotel, 18th June Rd., next to the Municipal Gardens, busily serves up *samosas* (Rs13) and generous *thalis* (Rs23) to loyal local customers. Open daily 8am-9pm. ❶

Hotel Vihar, MG Rd., around the corner from Hotel Venite. This popular veg. stainless steel and formica joint deals meal-sized *dosas* (Rs15) and banana omelettes (Rs15). Open M-Sa 7am-9pm. ❶

👁 SIGHTS

While Panjim isn't known for its breathtaking sights, it's a pleasant enough place for idle meandering, particularly in the Fontainhas area on the west bank of the Ourem. The blindingly white **Chapel of San Sebastian,** dating from 1818, stands at the end of a short street opening off 31st January Rd. The statue of Christ on the cross that used to hang in the Palace of the Inquisition in Old Goa now hangs here. Towering over Church Sq. is the **Mary Immaculate Conception Church (Igreja Maria Immaculada Conceição),** the top tier of a stack of white and blue criss-crossing staircases. The original chapel, consecrated in 1541 and renovated in the 17th century, was a first stop for Portuguese sailors. The musty, dark interior broods with silence and prayer. *(Open Su and holy days 11am-12:30pm and 3:30-5pm, other days 9am-12:30pm and 3:30-5:30pm.)*

For a less spiritual but equally authoritative experience, mount the 140 staggered steps on the left side of Emidio Gracia Rd. to the aptly named **High Court of Bombay at Goa.** Manicured palm and flower gardens, crumbling colonial mansions, and the High Court itself—a magnificent building with grand pointed-arch windows—await above. The court may not deliver redemptive judgements, but the views over Panjim undoubtedly vindicate the climb.

GOA

The **Secretariat,** constructed in the 16th century as a palace and fortress for Yusuf Adil Shah of Bijapur, sits unassumingly on the banks of the River Mandovi. The Portuguese rebuilt it in 1615, and in 1759 it became the palace of the Portuguese viceroy.

🎵 🎭 ENTERTAINMENT AND NIGHTLIFE

Panjim's nightlife is fairly tame, though not for lack of alcohol. Local brews are sold in small shops, and tiny bars dot the city, especially in Fontainhas. Try hole-in-the-wall **Sunshine Bar,** pumping music and laughter from the corner of Emidio Gracia Rd. and 31st January Rd. **Viva Panjim** (see **Food,** above) also serves up frothy Kingfishers and cashew *feni* in bulk. Government-run and private companies organize **evening cruises** on the Mandovi River. The cruises feature traditional dancing—*denki, fijddi*, Portuguese, and *corredmino* styles—and stunning views of the sunset at sea. Book at the Panaji Residency (see **Accommodations**), or just show up at the pier and look for the boat. (1hr.; daily 6, 7:15, and 8:30pm; Rs100.)

OLD GOA ओल्ड गोवा

The cavernous churches of Old Goa, 9km east of Panjim, prove that Europeans flocked to Goa long before Calangute's 1970s hippie blowouts. Old Goa's colonial days began in 1510, when Alfonso de Albuquerque trounced the Bijapur Sultan and seized the city on the Mandovi, then known as Ela. The virtual monopoly on regional trade, as well as sailors' epic debauchery, attracted the Inquisition's Jesuit priests. Their zeal for preaching and proselytizing inspired the construction of Old Goa's most ornate cathedrals. Old Goa declined as Portuguese power faded, the Mandovi River filled with silt, and malaria ran rampant. By the 18th century, the government seat had moved to Panjim. The churches remain as reminders of the city's former glory.

🚍 TRANSPORTATION

Auto-rickshaws (Rs70-100), **motorcycle taxis,** and **bicycles** (available for rent in Panjim) make the scenic 9km trip along the Mandovi riverbank from Panjim to Old Goa. **Buses** also shuttle from Panjim's bus terminal (15min., every 15min. 7am-7pm, Rs4). If you bike, avoid the main road; continue past the traffic circle beyond the Kadamba bus stand in Patto (the left fork goes directly to Old Goa) and go straight; take the smaller left-hand road parallel to the main road, then take the first fork to the left and follow the road through a village. Take a left at the first chapel and the road will meet up with NH4 again. Finally, turn right into Old Goa. Stands and "tourist restaurants" huddle at both ends of the Basilica de Bom Jesus.

👁 SIGHTS

As you arrive from Panjim, the **Basilica de Bom Jesus** will be on your right, the **Se Cathedral** on your left. Unofficial guides frequenting the churches in search of earthly reward expect to be tipped in return for their knowledge.

BASILICA DE BOM JESUS. Built between 1594 and 1605 to house the remains of St. Francis Xavier, the Basilica de Bom Jesus is Old Goa's legendary site. Resplendent with gold, the Basilica, with its 3m statue of St. Ignatius presiding over all comings and goings, attracts Sikh tourists, beach-bound revels, and

Sisters of Charity alike. Off to the right of the altar and behind a curtain of stars lies St. Francis Xavier's mausoleum, containing the saint's dried-out body inside a windowed silver casket. The casket was "donated" by Cosimo III de Medici in exchange for a pillow on which the saint's head had rested. Though St. Francis looks sadly shrunken now, his body refused to decay for months after his death. He's still unrotted and intact (though his baptizing arm now lays in state in Rome). A doorway to the left of the mausoleum leads to a small room with historical tidbits and photographs of the relic. Stairs lead to an **art gallery.** On the way out is a lovely cloister. *(Opposite the Se Cathedral. Open M-Sa 9am-6:30pm, Su 10:30am-6:30pm. Gallery open M and W-Sa 9:30am-12:30pm and 2-5:30pm, Su 10:30am-12:30pm and 2-5:30pm.)*

AROUND THE BASILICA DE BOM JESUS. Up the hill from the basilica are the romantic ruins of the **Church of St. Augustine.** The 46m tower has been standing since 1602. Barely legible grave markers pave the floor, and knobby alcoves hint at carvings that have long since eroded. Below the church is the massive **Church and Convent of St. Monica Christon,** built in 1636. Its "miracle cross" was once well known for its tendency to open its eyes, bleed from its wounds, and speak. Inside the Convent is the **Museum of Christian Art,** relocated from Margao, the first museum of its kind in Asia. The museum reflects the blend of Hindu and Christian traditions in Goan art. *(As you exit the basilica, make a left at the first street, then take an immediate right. Rs10, students Rs5, under 12 free. Open daily 9:30am-5pm.)*

SÉ CATHEDRAL. On the left, along the main road from Panjim, the sun-bleached yellow Sé Cathedral complex presides over an expanse of lawn. After the Chapel of St. Catherine on your left is the **Convent and Church of St. Francis of Assisi.** The frescoed ceiling arches over a gravestone floor, paved with coats of arms from the 17th century on. There is gold leaf detail on the walls, along with floral patterns, and delicate woodwork. The attached convent is now the mildly interesting **Archaeological Museum,** which exhibits portraits of the viceroys, currency from "India Portuguesa," Christian icons, and Goan Hindu sculpture dating from as early as the 9th century. *(Convent and Church open daily 8:30am-5:30pm. Free. Museum open Sa-Th 10am-5pm. Rs5.)*

Beyond the museum is the **Sé Cathedral** dedicated to St. Catherine. Erected by the viceroy in 1564, the vast, three-naved cathedral took 80 years to build. One of the twin towers was destroyed by lightning in 1775. The other houses the mellow-toned **Sino du Ouro (Golden Bell),** said to be the largest bell in Asia. Sepulchres of expensive imported stone line the floor. Scenes from the life of St. Catherine are carved into the grand golden altar, and 14 smaller altars are set within the cavernous church. *(Open daily 8:30am-5:30pm.)*

AROUND THE SÉ CATHEDRAL. Signs point you to the nearby **Church of St. Cajetan.** According to local lore, Italian friars of the Order of Theatines built the church on top of an ancient Hindu temple in the 17th century. Today, the church is known for its dome (modeled after St. Peter's in Rome) and the woodwork of its interior. A tiny wooden trap door in the raised stone dais gives evidence of a secret well once used to funnel water across the town for the baths of Goan royalty. The ruined **gate** to Yusuf Adil Shah's collapsed palace, by the entrance to the church grounds, rises in forlorn tribute to pre-Portuguese Goa. Farther up the road toward the Mandovi River is the modest **Viceroy's Arch,** whose gate bears an inscription left by Governor Francisco da Gama (r. 1597-1600) in memory of his great-grandfather, Vasco. There is a path from the arch to the Mandovi River. *(From the Cathedral's grand entrance, head straight out to the road (if the gates are open) and make a left. Church open daily 9am-5:30pm.)*

GOA

▶ DAYTRIPS FROM OLD GOA

A handful of Hindu temples near the Portuguese ruins of Old Goa are worth a look. Although far from India's finest, they remind daytrippers of the massive Hindu majority that always remained just behind the Portuguese-controlled coast.

Most of the temples hide along NH4, conveniently becoming less interesting toward drab **Ponda**. When you get tired of the temples, just hop on a bus back to **Panjim** (45min., every 15-20min. 6am-7:30pm, Rs12). Buses from Panjim are often full—tell the conductor where you want to get off, and be sure to stand near a door so you can fight your way out. The first temple is at **Mangeshi** (also called Priol) village (30min., Rs7). Head down the palm-lined path to the colorful arch that leads to the **Sri Mangesh** temple. Like most of the temples in this area, it was built in the 18th century to house deities that had been smuggled inland in the 16th century from the Inquisition-ravaged coast. Muslim architectural influence shows itself in several minaret-esque turrets, and the silver guards of Shiva on either side of his sanctuary sparkle in the reflecting light. Less than a 15min. walk south (1km) leads to the cool-tiled **Sri Mahalsa**, acclaimed for the stunning wood carvings on the facades of its *mandapam* (sloping roof). It deserves near-equal praise for the serene respite it offers from the highway.

From Sri Mahalsa or the Mangeshi bus stop, get on a bus to Ponda, where you can transfer onto a bus heading for **Nageshi** village (Rs4). To reach **Sri Nagesh** after getting off at Nageshi, head right and then left down the road for about 5min. The entrance to the grounds is on your left. Colorful woodcarvings in the entrance hall depict scenes from the *Ramayana* (see p. 620), though it's difficult to piece together the narrative. Blue swan-gargoyles regard your entrance and exit solemnly. Ambling back along the path of the bus for about 20min. will not only provide gorgeous views of rice paddies framed by palm forests, but will also bring you to the red-roofed **Sri Shantadurga** temple (don't confuse it with the more modern temple on the way). You'll know you've arrived when you spot the tourist taxis and the rows of stands hawking religious kitsch. Head back uphill to catch the bus back to Panjim.

MAPUSA म्हापुसा　　　☎ 0832

The North Goan transit hub town of Mapusa lies on a hillside, 30km north of Panjim and 10km inland from the hopping beaches at Anjuna, Calangute, and Baga. Mostly of use to travelers for its bus terminal, beach bums from Mumbai or Bangalore jump off the bus at Mapusa and flee straight for the sand. Friday's labyrinthine market lures a handful back to sample spices and fondle fabrics.

▤ TRANSPORTATION. Buses shuttle frequently from the **Kadamba Bus Terminal** to a variety of sinful locations. Most intrastate buses run from 7:30am to 7:30pm and travel to: **Anjuna** (20min., every 5min., Rs5); **Arambol** (1hr., every hour, Rs10); **Baga** and **Calangute** (30min., every 30min., Rs5-6); **Panjim** (every 5min.; local 40min., express 20min.; Rs5); **Siolim** (15min., every 15min., Rs5). If you're leaving Goa, the area around Kadamba teems with private coach operators. State-run buses also make the trip. The long-distance booking office is opposite bus stall 8. (Open daily 6am-1pm and 2-8pm.) Buses go to: **Miraj** (8hr., 10:45am, Rs115); **Pune** (12hr., 6:15am, Rs215). **Motorcycle rentals** are hard to come by, thanks to Mapusa's police crackdown on foreigners without papers.

▤▶ ORIENTATION AND PRACTICAL INFORMATION. The **State Bank of India** changes money and does cash advances. Turn right out of the bus station and walk toward the roundabout decorated alarmingly with cannons. Take the last right before the roundabout, go straight for two blocks, take another right, and you'll see it on the left. (Open M-F 10am-2pm, Sa 10am-noon.) For cash advances, head back uphill from State Bank of India, take a right, and go about one block farther to **Bank of Baroda.** (Open M-F 9:30am-2:30pm, Sa 9:30am-noon.) **Internet** access (Rs 40 per hr.) is available opposite the main entrance to the market, on the corner. The **police station** (☎2262231) and the **GPO** (1st fl.; open M-F 9am-5pm, Sa 9am-1pm) are two blocks west of the roundabout. **Postal Code: 403507.**

⌂ ▢ ACCOMMODATIONS AND FOOD. Staying in Mapusa should not be necessary. It's worth taking a taxi to Calangute or Panjim rather than hanging around here. If you must stay, try the well-staffed **Hotel Satyaheera ❸,** on the cannon roundabout, with spacious rooms, spectacular views (on the upper floors), phones, and even an antiquated TV. (☎2262849 or 2262949; satya@goatele-com.com. Check-out 9am. Doubles Rs420. June 15-Sept. 15 Rs300.) For more bare-bones accommodations, check out any number of dormitories around the market area, but don't expect cleanliness. **Ruchira ❷,** the Hotel Satyaheera's rooftop restaurant, serves Goan, Chinese, and standard Indian dishes in a breezy setting. (Entrees Rs30-65, beer Rs27-50. Open daily 7-11am and 11:30am-10:45pm.) Food stalls around the bus terminal serve the standard greasy fare, but Mapusa's **market,** southeast of the bus terminal, is for the more adventurous. It's a more authentic version of the Anjuna flea market, so if you've been craving coconuts, searching for 30cm springs, or needing a brace of live roosters, you've come to the right place. It's at its busiest every Friday (early morning through late afternoon), but there's almost always something going on.

CALANGUTE AND BAGA कालंगुड़ AND बागा

☎ 0832

The twin villages of Calangute and Baga have seen their popularity wane in the past few years, but if you're looking for some peace and quiet, that might be the best argument for staying here. The sugary sand and warm sea remain gorgeous, so lie back with a *lassi,* let the waves drown out the sound of the ubiquitous vendors hawking wooden elephants and mirrored purses, and wait for the package tourists to trickle home. By late afternoon, you'll be left alone with the cows to watch the sun go down.

▭ TRANSPORTATION

Buses: Every 15min., buses from Mapusa stop at **Calangute market** (Rs5-6) and at the main roundabout en route to **Baga** (Rs3) and back to **Mapusa** (Rs7). Buses to and from **Panjim** (Rs7) stop at the market and beyond the roundabout before the beach.

Local Transportation: Tourist taxis go between Calangute and Baga for Rs40-50. **Rickshaws** and **motorbikes** make the same trip for about Rs20-30, and to Panjim (Rs70-150) and Anjuna (Rs50-100). **Motorcycle** rental is common in season (Rs150 per day). Off season, inquire near the gas station west of the market. For **bicycle** rental, ask along the main road (Rs50-60 per day).

▰▰ ORIENTATION AND PRACTICAL INFORMATION

Most buses smoke their way into **Calangute market** at the bottom of the main road that heads west to the **beach.** They also stop at the roundabout about halfway down the main east-west road before heading back to Panjim. From the market stop, continue in

GOA

the same direction as the bus until you come to the roundabout and Rama Books. Turn right (north) onto the main north-south road that runs between Calangute and Baga; the entire length of this road is lined with guest houses, restaurants, and souvenir stalls, with innumerable side-streets offering more of the same. The main east-west road leads from the **market** to the **beach** and comprises Calangute proper.

Budget Travel: MGM Travels (☎ 2276601), on the Calangute roundabout. Sells plane, bus, and train tickets. Open M-Sa 9:30am-1:30pm and 2:30-6pm.

Currency Exchange: State Bank of India (☎ 2276032), at Calangute market. Open M-F 10am-4pm, Sa 10am-1pm. **Thomas Cook** is inside the bank. Open M-F 10am-5pm, Sa 10am-1pm. If you don't see them, ask any of the market vendors for directions.

Pharmacy: Walsons & Walsons Chemist and Druggist (☎ 2276366), next door to Fatima Clinic, in the same bldg. as the State Bank of India. Open daily 8:30am-2pm and 3:30-9pm.

Post Office: In a pink bldg. south of the market. Head east from the roundabout, turn right at the market, and then take the first left. Open M-Sa 9am-2pm and 2:30-5pm. **Postal Code:** 403516.

▟ ACCOMMODATIONS

Head north toward Baga for more pleasant surroundings, though most of the places between the villages are a fair distance from the beach. In season (Dec.-Jan.), prices can double. As usual, the taxi- and rickshaw-*wallahs* who claim a hotel is full are usually receiving commission from other places; insist on going to your first choice. Flats and houses for longer stays are usually still available in early December—the best of them are just north of Baga. Ask around.

Villa Fatima (☎ 2277418; villa.fatima@sympatico.ca), on the main north-south strip, closer to Baga. Look for the sign on the left when coming from Calangute. A cheerful family runs this lush, 40-room complex, draped with colored lights and plants. Spacious rooms with attached bath, hot water, and refrigerators surround a courtyard restaurant. Rooms without hot water that are just as big cost Rs100 less. Safe deposit box. Check-out 10am. Rs300-400; June-Sept. Rs200-300. ❸

Hallmark Guest House (☎ 2275030), just off the east-west road that leads to Tito's, between Joaquim's and La Fontana. Absurdly large rooms in a prime beach location offer hot water with sparkling attached baths, lockers in the rooms, and mosquito nets over the bed. Check-out 11:30am. Rs300; June-Sept. Rs200. ❷

Nani's and Rani's (☎ 2277014), at the northern tip of Baga, across the river. From the main road, bear right on the dirt path to the covered bridge. A bit far, but worth it for a tranquil, backpacker-friendly spot. Splendid doubles with bath cluster around the popular restaurant. Check-out noon. Doubles with bath and fan Rs300; May-Oct. Rs250. ❷

Joaquim's (☎ 2281064), off the east-west road that leads to Tito's, just beyond Hallmark Guest House. Follow the sign on your right to La Fontana, and continue straight. Seconds from the beach. Clean rooms with attached baths and 24hr. hot water. Check-out 10am. Rs350; June-Sept. Rs200. ❷

Alidia Cottages (☎ 2279041 or 2276835; alidia@rediffmail.com), just beyond Villa Fatima along the road to Baga, behind a white church on the left. Ritzy, family-run establishment with phenomenal rooms, all with attached bath. Wander through the back gate, past the tiny fishing village, and out to the beach. Safety deposit box. Check-out 11am. In Sept., rates begin to rise, reaching Rs600-800 by Dec.-Jan. Apr.-Oct. doubles drop to Rs100-150. ❸

Stay Longer Guest House (☎ 2277460), on the inland side of the Calangute-Baga road. Decent rooms in a low price range. Paise-pinchers can snag the windowless ground-floor rooms with shared bath. Those who intend to stay true to the guest house's name should opt for the spacious rooms with attached baths upstairs. A pair of rooftop chairs are primed for sunset watching. Checkout 8am. Rs200-300; June-Sept. Rs100-150. ❷

West Horizon (☎ 2276489). Follow the main east-west road to the beach, and turn right just before the beach. Follow signs from the next east-west road. Clean, small rooms with attached bath. Practically on the beach. Doubles Rs175; Family room Rs450. May-Oct. Rs100-300. ❷

Tourist Dormitories, in the Calangute Resort Annex. Take the main road west toward the beach; you'll see a giant sign on your right. Dorms Rs90. June 15-Sept. 15 Rs70. ❶

⌷ FOOD

Numerous seafood shacks in Calangute and Baga with copycat menus offer mediocre renditions of regional delights and favorites from home. If you're just looking for a good spot to meet fellow travelers over a cold beer and a sunset, try the popular **Britto's** or **St. Anthony's,** side by side on the Baga beachfront.

Calangute and Baga

🏠 ACCOMMODATIONS
Alidia Cottages, 2
Hallmark Guest House, 5
Joaquim's, 4
Nani's and Rani's, 1
Stay Longer Guest House, 10
Tourist Dormitories, 14
Villa Fatima, 3
West Horizon, 13

🍎 FOOD
Anand Restaurant, 15
Clisher's, 12
German Bakery, 11
Indian Cafe, 9
La Fontana, 6
♪ ENTERTAINMENT
Mambo, 7
Tito's, 8

BAGA

Arabian Sea

■ Goan Bananas
■ Atlantis

CALANGUTE

Rama Books & Jewelry   MGM Travels   Market

TO ANJUNA (9km)
TO MAPUSA (10km)
TO (100m)

German Bakery, just past the Stay Longer Guest House on the way to Calangute. Linger in the shade over a fresh fruit juice (Rs30-40) and delicious homemade pastries (Rs8-40). Cinnamon rolls Rs18, omelettes Rs15-30. Open daily 8am-11pm. ❶

Indian Cafe, on the main north-south road midway between the two towns; look on the inland side for the Milky Way. This excellent, quiet lunchtime retreat serves delicious *masala dosa* (Rs25) and fruit shakes. The best and cheapest Indian food in town. Open daily 8am-5pm. ❶

Nani and Rani's Bar and Restaurant, neighboring their hotel north of Baga. Goan specialties, breezy tropical drinks, and chill card games make it worth the hike. Open daily 8am-3:30pm and 6:30-10:30pm. ❶

Clisher's, just west of the West Horizon Guest House. From the Calangute tourist complex, follow the large, fish-shaped sign. Excellent seafood and fresh juices (Rs25-30) in surroundings so quiet you can hear the waves on the shore. Indian dishes Rs30-65, seafood Rs80-340. Open daily 9am-11pm. Closed Jun. 1-Aug. 31. ❸

La Fontana (☎ 2275027), next to Joachim, across the street from Tito's. Seafood, pasta, and the chef's special steak provide a taste of the West in a pleasantly low-lit atmosphere. Entrees Rs50-135. Open daily 8:30am-midnight. ❸

Anand Restaurant (☎ 2276259), at the inland Calangute bus stop, on the way to the Post Office. Popular with local kids and the occasional tourist, this greasy spoon serves Indian staples for peanuts. Entrees Rs20-65. Open 6am-10:30pm. ❶

G O A

BEACHES

> **WARNING.** The water on some beaches is off-limits during the monsoon season (roughly mid-June to late Aug.) because of rough waves and dangerous undertow. Ask before taking a dip, and watch for boulders and steep drop-offs.

It's hard to complain about the beach between Calangute and Baga. Despite all the development, the sand is still quiet in the morning, and the water always seems to be at an ideal temperature. But as the sun starts to climb higher in the sky, leather-skinned men in Speedos waddle out onto the sand. As you head north, the bodies get slightly younger, as a small backpacker crowd strives to work up a credible tan before heading off to the beaches farther north.

South of Baga, a strip of beach has been set aside for water sports. **Goan Bananas** has a fleet of boats ready for just about anything. (☎ 2276362. Parasailing Rs1000.) Next door, **Atlantis** will take you water-skiing (Rs600 for 10min.), set up wind-surfing lessons, rent surfboards (Rs300 per hr.), or drag you behind a boat on an inflatable banana (Rs350 for 15min.). When you see the sign for German Bakery turn onto the road to the beach; Atlantis is to the right of Sea Breeze Restaurant. In season, fishing boats, chartered by numerous companies, make the wet-'n-wild journey to the Anjuna flea market every Wednesday and offer dolphin-, crocodile-, and hippie-spotting tours for Rs350-1300 per day.

NIGHTLIFE

Despite a raucous past, nightlife in Calangute and Baga tends to wind down early and errs on the side of resort-area hokeyness. The more upscale hotels pack their bar-restaurants with live "musicians" who'd be confined to street performing back home though there could be worse places for a night of drunken revelry.

As far as a nightclub scene goes, there's only one real after-hours game in town: **Tito's,** a gigantic bar-restaurant complex on the Baga beach with multiple dance floors, DJ's, and even a pair of pool tables in its offshoot bar closer to the beach, **Mambo.** Get revved up with drinks (Rs30-100) at Mambo starting around 11pm, then head to Tito's proper to party until the break of dawn. If Tito's wears you out, stumble back toward the main road; there are plenty of bars on the way.

DAYTRIPS FROM CALANGUTE

The hillside south of the Taj Holiday Village in package-touristy **Candolim** hides the impressive remains of the massive 17th-century **Fort Aguada,** which guards the mouth of the Mandovi. Over the years, the Fort has served variously as a stop for Portuguese merchant ships, a prison for Indian freedom fighters during the last days of the British Raj, and a signature book for thousands of thoughtless tourists. From the Calangute market, take the Mapusa bus to Sinquerim (Rs3), where the north-south road ends. Then take the road to the left and turn right before the chapel; a series of dirt paths bearing left winds to the top of the hill. The citadel commands an impressive view of the Mandovi and the southern coast. Behind you lies Calangute and Baga beach; before you, the Goan coastline stretches south, visible all the way to Mormugao.

ANJUNA अंजुना ☎ 0832

For many a budget traveler, Anjuna remains the Goan ideal: long, lazy days on the beach, wild, raving nights, and liberal doses of inexpensive drugs to smooth the transition between the two. Each day is tagged by a beautiful sunset, each week

GOA

brings free-market madness in the form of Anjuna's famous flea market (closed off-season), and each month is marked by the world-renowned full-moon rave; the town has something for everyone. Just don't come hoping for peace and quiet. From freaks to fishermen, package tourists to backpackers, and Euro-yuppies to Kashmiri handicraft hawkers, Anjuna's crazy cast of characters will keep you on your toes at all hours of day and night.

> **WARNING. Theft occurs frequently in Anjuna,** particularly on party nights. Carry important documents and valuables with you or lock them somewhere safe.

TRANSPORTATION

Buses: Buses to **Mapusa** (20min., Rs5) stop at the main intersection in town and at the end of the road above the beach. Buses to **Vagator** and **Chapora** leave from the main intersection (10min., every 30-40min., Rs3). You can also flag buses down as they trundle along the road from the beach. If your bus doesn't appear, hop on one to Mapusa and make your connection there.

Local Transportation: Motorcycles (Rs150-200 per day) and **bicycles** (Rs50-75 per day) can be rented along the main road.

ORIENTATION AND PRACTICAL INFORMATION

From the main intersection (crowned by the **Starco Restaurant**), roads lead west to the beachfront and bus stand, east to Mapusa and most banking facilities, south to the flea market and restaurants, and north to Vagator. For a small town, Anjuna sprawls over a surprisingly large area. Most get around by motor bike; it's possible to negotiate it on foot, but be prepared for distances to be longer than you expect.

Budget Travel: MGM Travels (☎ 2274317). Deals with bus, train, and plane tickets, reconfirmations, and car rentals. Western Union service. Open M-Sa 9:30am-6pm. June-Sept.: closed 1:30-2:30pm.

Currency Exchange: Bank of Baroda, straight inland of the main intersection on the left. Cashes traveler's checks and gives MC/V cash advances. Open M-F 9:30am-1:30pm and Sa 9-11am. **Orchard Food Stores** (☎ 2273231). From the main intersection head east, take the first right after Coutinho's Nest, and then the first left. Cashes traveler's checks. Open daily 8:30am-9pm.

Bookstore: Walk About Books (☎ 2273946). In the Oxford Stores. Open M-Sa 9am-9pm.

Internet: There are tons of email places in Anjuna. Try **Nehal Communications,** near the bus stand by the beach. Rs1 per min., minimum 10min. Open daily 9am-11pm.

Post Office: 2km up the road from the beach on the right. Open M-Sa 9am-2pm and 3-5pm. **Postal Code:** 403509.

ACCOMMODATIONS

You can normally secure a room somewhere in Anjuna just by showing up; if your first choice is full, the owner will usually give you an honest recommendation. Guest houses hug the beachfront and the main east-west road, and "Room To Let" signs are everywhere. South of the flea market is a veritable colony of long-term tourists, making that area a good place to look for bare-bones lodgings for stays ranging from a week to several months. As usual, bargain away off-season.

Mary's Holiday Home (☎ 2273216), next to the beachfront bus stand. Clean, quiet, and equidistant from the craziness and the exit route. Simple rooms with attached bath face inland. Check-out 10am. Doubles Rs150-250. ❷

Cabin Disco's (☎ 2273254), on the south side of the road, just east of the main intersection. Nice rooms with bar-restaurant out front providing a low-key, communal alternative to beach madness. Check-out noon. Singles Rs100-200; doubles Rs300-500. June-Sept.: rates go as low as Rs150. ❶

Arjun Villa (☎ 2274590), toward the beach from the main intersection, 100m down the street across from the Oasis cafe. Owner Godfrey offers guaranteed security, gorgeous rooms with spacious attached bath, and a little distance from the raucous party crowd. Laundry next door. Check-out 10am. Rooms Rs400-500. ❸

Manali Guest House (☎ 2273477). Just south off the main intersection. This friendly spot in a central location offers email and a convenience store. All rooms have shared bath. Rs175-200. Mar.-Oct. Rs80-125. ❷

Day's Guest House (☎ 2273289). Just north of the Orchard Store, 20min. from the beach, run by a lovely couple. Immaculate doubles with bath, fridge, cable TV, and sound systems. Call ahead. Dec.-Jan.: Rs450-500. May-Oct.: 50% off. ❸

Guru Bar-Restaurant and Guest House (☎ 2273319). One of the many spartan but aromatic cliffside options. Bare rooms are serviceable, but the outdoor common shower can get a bit muddy. Rooms Rs100, with attached bath Rs250. ❶

◖ FOOD

The food served up at most of Anjuna's seaside restaurants is fast, cheap, greasy, and plentiful. Those seeking culinary variety, however, will be better off at the restaurants that line the roads farther inland. There are several vegan restaurants and falafel stands to frequent. On Wednesdays, an army of food vendors materializes out of nowhere to make up the **flea market,** Anjuna's premier spot for lunch or early dinner. The atmosphere is unbeatable. These places and some of those listed below are closed off-season.

▨ German Bakery. Watch carefully for the sign; from the flea market road, cross the paved road and follow a worn dirt path east, or take the paved road east of Mario's. Not to be confused with the German Bakery at the Paradise Restaurant on the main road. Communal seating comes complete with savory baked goodies every morning (Rs15-40). Veg. and North Indian food at night (Rs35-75). Open daily 8am-11pm. ❷

Mango Shade, just west of the German Bakery. This often-packed, chalkboard-menu spot offers cheaper food but has less atmosphere. Still, it's hard to argue with Nutella. Fresh fruit juices and *lassis* Rs20-40, sandwiches and toasts with delicious spreads (including avocado) Rs30-50. Open daily 8am-5pm. ❷

Temptations Bar & Restaurant. Head south from the main east-west road past the Arjun Villa and take your first left and second right to find this tiny, classy, couple-run establishment a world away from the beach bums. Perfect for a quiet breakfast with a book or a friend. Veg. omelette Rs25. Open 8am-11pm. No dinner served. ❶

Paradise Bar & Restaurant, down the Mapusa road away from the beach; look for the sign on the right. This place sports an open kitchen firing up mainly Chinese and Indian specialties. Tender chicken masala Rs50, banana lassi Rs25. Open 9am-11pm. ❷

Whole Bean, along the road between town and the flea market. Vegan tofu and tempeh shop with botanical murals pours out soy milkshakes and fresh juice in a variety of flavors (Rs25-50). Eggs and omelettes Rs20-40. Open daily 8am-5:30pm. ❷

Green Palms, on the Mapusa road, about 1.5km inland. Delicious, crunchy falafel sandwiches with fresh veggies Rs50, banana *lassis* Rs25. Don't let the melancholy Israeli pop music get you down. Open M-Sa 9am-11pm. ❷

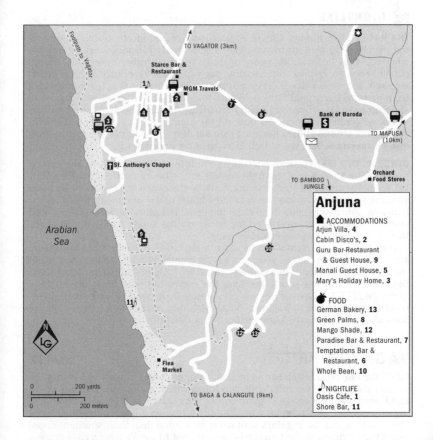

Anjuna

🏠 ACCOMMODATIONS
Arjun Villa, **4**
Cabin Disco's, **2**
Guru Bar-Restaurant
 & Guest House, **9**
Manali Guest House, **5**
Mary's Holiday Home, **3**

🍎 FOOD
German Bakery, **13**
Green Palms, **8**
Mango Shade, **12**
Paradise Bar & Restaurant, **7**
Temptations Bar &
 Restaurant, **6**
Whole Bean, **10**

🎵 NIGHTLIFE
Oasis Cafe, **1**
Shore Bar, **11**

🌊 BEACHES

While Anjuna's sands are shimmeringly beautiful, the hawkers making tracks in them are annoyingly persistent; practically the only things not for sale are tranquility and solitude. Still, there's no other beach in North Goa with quite the daytime scene of tanned and toned ravers in various states of inebriation crashed along the strip. Wednesdays are popular.

🛍 SHOPPING

"Like something?" If you've been eyeing the sarongs, *bindis*, bracelets, and magic boxes that clutter roadside stands, a trip to the **Anjuna flea market** will show you endless permutations of these tourist staples. Every Wednesday in season, the abandoned stalls and wooden poles of the market transform into a wilderness of colored fabrics and bargaining people. You'll even be able to check out those rave pants before you buy them.

GOA

▣ NIGHTLIFE

THE RAVES. The sloping hills of Anjuna have gained international renown in the past decade as a hip rave venue. The monthly full moon brings out the werewolf that lurks inside many of Goa's tourists, transforming them from placid beach-goers into wild, snarling party-animals, especially during Christmas and New Year's Eve. Every night the roads are full of people motorcycling from party to party, and huge fields are flooded by rivers of ravers. Domestic and European DJs of varying quality broadcast the rave's techno soundtrack to a core of gyrating dancers. To find out the location of any given night's main events, ask around at **Guru Bar** and **Shore Bar** during the day, or head up to **Primrose Restaurant & Bar** (see p. 182) in Vagator for pre-partying.

OTHER NIGHTLIFE. If there isn't any scheduled action, most of the crowd heads to the **Shore Bar,** right in the middle of the beach north of the Flea Market area. The terraced steps leading down to the beach are layered with beer-guzzling sunbathers or stargazers at most hours of day and night. Upstairs, the indispensable black lights flicker and imported DJs pilot the gargantuan sound system, while techno ravers go for broke on the small, sandy dance floor. Hours vary wildly by season and evening.

Oasis Cafe, on the right when heading to the beach from the main bus stand, attracts intimate groups of young ravers for a small bite or several beers while they plan their nights of debauchery. (☎2273957. Open daily 24hr. Small Kingfisher Rs25.) Farther south, the **Guru Bar** serves tall cold ones late into the night. (☎2273319. Open 8am-late.) If Anjuna feels dead on any given night, head down the road to Vagator; those with motorbikes make the commute back and forth regularly to get the best of both worlds.

VAGATOR वागातोर ☎0832

Of all the northern beach towns in Goa, Vagator comes closest to striking the perfect balance between hotspot and hideaway. Popular but not over-populated, scenic but not seedy, Vagator suns all day and raves all night without losing its cheerful, down-home vibe. The town houses a large number of long-term visitors, but the regulars here seem less jaded than their southern counterparts; the rigors of the tourism boom have yet to sap Vagator's easy grace.

▣ TRANSPORTATION

Buses stop at the crossroads about 1km inland, where the road forks for Chapora and Ozran, and run to: **Anjuna** (every 30min. 7am-7pm, Rs3); **Chapora** (every 15min. 6:30am-8pm, Rs5); **Mapusa** (every 30min. 6:45am-7pm, Rs5). **Prakash Motors,** on the main road, rents and repairs **motorcycles** at good rates. (Rs150-200 per day. Open daily 8am-8:30pm.) Vendors along the road from Ozran Beach rent motor bikes at similar rates. This area is also a good place for **bicycle rentals** (Rs50-75 per day). From behind Big Vagator Beach, **taxis** run to **Anjuna** (Rs50), **Arambol** (Rs250), **Chapora** (Rs30), and **Mapusa** (Rs150).

▣▣ ORIENTATION AND PRACTICAL INFORMATION

Most resources for the budget traveler line the street that runs east-west from Big Vagator Beach. The **Rainbow Bookshop,** opposite the Primrose Bar and south of the main east-west road, sells and swaps used **books.** A **police booth** looks out over the Big and Little Vagator beaches from atop the stairs that connect them. (Officer present M-F 10am-7pm in-season.) **Eddie's Cyberzone,** on the east-west road close to Jaws Restaurant, has **Internet** (Rs50 per hr.), **currency exchange,** and a wine store. (Open daily 8:30am-midnight.) **Lalita Communications,** just inland, offers **currency exchange,** provides bus bookings, and has Internet-connected computers. (☎2274481. Internet Rs50 per hr. Open daily 9am-11:30pm.) Follow the signs from the main road. The nearest **post office** is in **Anjuna.**

⚓ ACCOMMODATIONS

Vagator has some top-notch lodging compared with its neighbors to the north and south, both budget and mid-range; it's just a question of getting in past the long-term visitors. Guest houses line the main east-west road and the path to Ozran Beach, to the south. Off season, many guest houses close.

Dolrina (☎/fax 2273382). Follow the yellow signs north of Big Vagator Road to this large and popular guest house. Library, in-house convenience store, the communal backyard garden. The friendly family who runs it will tempt you to stay longer than planned. Book well in advance Dec.-Mar. Doubles with common bath Rs250; deluxe with balcony and hot water bath Rs450. ❷

Reshma Guesthouse (☎2273568). On the south side of the road from Big Vagator Beach, has two clean shared bathrooms and bare but excellent rooms. Check-out 11am. Rooms Rs250-300. Closed Apr.-Sept. ❷

Jolly Jolly Roma (☎2274897). Just past Reshma down the hill from the main east-west road. Offers immaculate rooms, soft pillows, hot water, sparkling showers, and fresh towels. Quite a respite for the beach-weary. Check-out 10am. Doubles Rs500-700. ❸

Jolly Jolly Lester (☎2273620), is Roma's older counterpart across the way. Beautiful sheets, a little garden cafe with a TV, and a safe for valuables. Check-out 10am. Singles Rs400; doubles Rs500. ❷

🍴 FOOD

Le Bluebird (☎2273695), near the seashore along the Ozran Beach road. Particularly mellow and comfy lounge with cushioned wicker chairs and a Van Gogh replica on the back wall. Enjoy delicious, reasonably priced French entrees (Rs80-150). Open daily 9am-2pm and 6:30-10:30pm. ❷

Jaws Restaurant, at the inland intersection on the main east-west road. Down some mouth-watering BBQ as you watch screenings of bootleg Hollywood movies (7:30pm). The pool table in back adds to the Western atmosphere. Tandoor BBQ Rs70. ❸

Alien Beans (☎2273578), past the Vagator Parish Youth Sports Club on the cliffside above Ozran Beach. Enjoy a quiet breakfast in the company of the birds, the sea, and perhaps a couple of German tourists. Chinese, Continental, Indian, Italian, and veg. entrees Rs30-90. Open 8:30am-11pm. ❷

Snackataria de World Peace (also Shawn's Juicy Joint), at the end of the left fork of Big Vagator Road; overlooking Big and Little Vagator beaches. A great place to grab a Punjabi samosa (Rs5), an icy drink, and a cool clifftop breeze. Open daily 8am-8pm. ❶

Garden Villa, toward the beach from Jaws, dishes up Goan, Punjabi, Chinese, and Italian food in the company of a large, noisy TV. Bootlegged American movies aired nightly at 7:30pm. Entrees Rs25-70. Chicken masala Rs50. Open daily 7:30am-11:30pm. ❶

◉ ♋ SIGHTS AND BEACHES

The southern **Ozran Beach** reigns as Vagator's most pleasant strip of sand—coconut palms, tranquil beach-shacks, and minimal vendor-fuss or daytrippers. At the southern tip of Ozran is a small bay—deep, calm, and perfect for lazy swimming. Farther north, Vagator's distinctive, gently terraced hills lead, like giant steps, to the crowded shore at **Little Vagator Beach.** This rocky bit is separated from the hills by a large, grassy field—an enviable spot for a seaside picnic. A white stairway leads from Little Vagator past the Snackataria de World Peace down to Big Vagator Beach, the biggest (and usually the most crowded) beach. Head toward the distant northern end of the beach if the bronzing vacationers and package-tourists cramp your style. To the northeast are the expansive ruins of the 17th-century **Portuguese Fort** that separates Chapora from Vagator. Although visited only by the occasional errant cow or the more enterprising traveler, the ruins reward the willing with a spectacular view of the Goa scene—beach-blanket bingo to the south, fishermen hauling in their nets to the east, and lush, unspoiled territory looming across the Chapora River to the north. The southern scramble from Vagator to Anjuna, along rocky beaches and a pleasant path, is another enjoyable walk.

◗ NIGHTLIFE

Vagator's official party scene has lost intensity over the last few years, but a few bars still bump and jive all night long in December and January. The **Primrose Bar and Restaurant,** with psychedelic lighting, techno/trance/acid house DJs, cheap beer (Rs30), and a perpetually good crowd, is the place to go in Vagator, and a good source of information on other parties. Heading inland on the main east-west road, follow signs to Rainbow Books; it's right across the street. (☎2273210. Entrees around Rs80. Open 9am-3am.) If you're itching to get out early, the **Nine Bar** above Ozran Beach is good spot to pre-party, pumping trance before 10pm. Parties often break out between Vagator and Anjuna, with partiers commuting back and forth in search of the hippest scene. The cafes around Chapora market are usually also a good source of info on where the next party will be.

NEAR VAGATOR

◗ CHAPORA

To get to the main market area, follow the turn-off for Chapora along the main road and bear right at the fork; the teeming bazaar is just up the road on the right. On foot, follow the road that continues from the end of Big Vagator Road for 5min.; when you reach another paved road, stay on the middle track. You'll end up squarely in Chapora market.

Just a few hundred meters (and one old ruined fort) away from Vagator, Chapora isn't blessed with a beach, but it makes up for it with its hippie-chic aesthetic. Tattooed and tanned backpackers suck down fresh juices in crowded cafes and muse about where to bring the party next. **Taxi drivers** huddle under the banyan tree on Chapora's main street when they're not hustling for fares to: **Anjuna** (Rs50); **Mapusa** (Rs120-150); **Panjim** (Rs250); **Vagator** (Rs20). **Buses** head to **Mapusa,** via **Vagator** (every 20min., Rs5). **Soniya Travels,** in the market area, deals with **bus and plane reservations** and has **email, phone, currency exchange,** and **Western Union** services. (☎2273344. Open daily 9am-midnight. Off season 9am-10pm.) **Guest houses** line the main road. One good option is **Helinda's ❷,** just north of the market, which has spacious, clean rooms and a welcoming restaurant. (☎2274345. Checkout

10am. Rs100-300.) **Private rooms ❶** are a good alternative (inquire at the restaurants); two can sleep well for under Rs150-200 per night. **Yak Restaurant ❷**, opposite Soniya Travel, has delicious fresh juices and generous veg. and non-veg. *thalis* (Rs45-65) as well as standard Indian, Continental, Thai, and Chinese delights. (Open daily 8:30am-2am.) **Tai Ganesh Fruit Juice Center ❶**, right next to Yak, dishes out mango *lassis* (Rs25) and fresh juices (Rs15-50). (Open daily 8:30am-11pm.)

ARAMBOL (HARMAL) आरामबोल

Pleasant and friendly, Arambol might just be the best North Goa has to offer. Its pristine beaches, freshwater lake, and lines of coconut palms are mainly populated by easygoing travelers who come in search of some tranquility, a few rays, and a little patch of the Arabian Sea to splash around in. Arambol's secret has gotten out recently, adding flesh to the main beach and filling out the restaurant and cafe crowds, but isolation still exists nearby, if that's what you're here for. A casual stroll down to Mandrem or a quick bus ride to Querim will land you on stretches of sun-swept beach with only sand crabs for company.

E TRANSPORTATION. The simplest route to Arambol is the **bus** from Mapusa (1hr., every hr., Rs10). Buses arrive at **Arambol Junction** from Chopdem in the south. From the junction, backtrack south and take the first right; a sign points the way. The narrow road winds about 1km to the beach. If you're coming from another coastal town, however, and don't want to trek back to Mapusa, you can take a rickshaw or taxi to **Siolem** (Rs80-150) and catch the Mapusa-Arambol bus en route (Rs5), or simply take the ride all the way to Arambol (from Vagator, Chapora, or Anjuna Rs250-350). A third option is to take the **boat** from Anjuna during the Wednesday flea market (one-way from Anjuna Rs100).

Many visitors to Arambol rent **motorcycles** or **mopeds** from vendors along the beach road (Rs100-150 per day). The region's only **petrol station** is to the north along the main road. Fill up here before heading north to Querim or Terekol.

⊠🛈 ORIENTATION AND PRACTICAL INFORMATION. Tara Travels, at the corner where the beach road makes its final turn toward the beach, handles transport bookings and reconfirmations, does **currency exchange**, gives cash advances on MC and V, has **Internet** access, and a **book exchange**. (☎2292442. Internet Rs40 per hr. Open daily 9am-11pm.) There is a **police station** on the north side of the beach road, and a tiny **post office** at the beginning of the beach road. (Post office open M-Sa 10am-1pm and 2-6pm.) **Postal Code:** 403524.

🛏🍴 ACCOMMODATIONS AND FOOD. Guest houses lining the beach road are available for short-term stays, and even during peak season, accommodations can be arranged with a little legwork. Expect to pay around Rs100 for a room without shower or toilet, and up to Rs300 for a spacious, toilet-endowed room. During the monsoon, most lodges and restaurants are closed. **Houses** can be rented for Rs200 per night or for Rs3000-5000 per month. Sizes and facilities vary as widely as the prices; many houses have no toilets or running water, just access to nearby bushes and wells. The most spectacular lodgings are perched at the north end of the main beach off a cliffside footpath. The cheapest beds are in rooms along the road to the beach. **Relax Inn ❷**, on the beach a bit north of the beach road, has few amenities, but rooms are big and the crashing of the waves will lull you to sleep. (☎2207711. Rs200-300. Closed Jun. 15-Aug. 15.) **Vasu Tourist Guest House ❶**, behind Double Dutch Cafe heading inland, has clean, large rooms with attached baths, terraces, and mosquito nets. (☎2292452. Rs100-150).

G O A

Restaurants line the road and beach front, but the cream of the crop is ■**Fellini ❷**, an absolutely scrumptious Italian spot just inland on the beach road. Imported extra virgin olive oil and tomatoes make for a meal you'll remember and pine for long after it's done. Crowds of travelers pack the rooftop terrace for generous pizzas (Rs80-115), sandwiches (Rs30-80), live music on weekend nights, and movie screenings. (Open M-Tu and Th-Sa 10am-11pm, W 7:30-11pm, Su 2-11pm.) Lounge at the ■**Double Dutch Cafe ❸** over a cup of tea (Rs15) and a slice of pie (Rs35); follow the signs toward the Om Ganesh Guesthouse on the beach road. Meat-lovers will relish the garlic steak (Rs130) as much as music-lovers will the Sunday morning coffee concerts of classical Indian. (Open daily 7am-11pm.) **21 Coconuts Inn ❷**, one shack south of where the road intersects with the sand, serves excellent Indian food. Attentive waiters serve up rice dishes (Rs20-70), Goan specialities (Rs60-70), and tasty banana pancakes (Rs25). (Open daily 8am-late.)

◨▣ BEACHES AND ENTERTAINMENT. Arambol's gorgeous main beach stretches several kilometers to the south, perfect for a lazy amble. Fishing boats and sunbathers spread out over its wide expanse, which becomes more sparse the farther south you venture. North of the main beach, along a rocky path negotiable only by foot, lies the smaller, more secluded **Paradise Beach**, behind which is a resplendent **freshwater lagoon**. Despite the fact that sunbathers and hawkers are slightly more concentrated here than elsewhere on the beach, it's still one of the most beautiful natural formations in Goa.

On Wednesdays, a fun and popular daytrip can be had by catching a boat to Anjuna for the **flea market**. The **Welcome Restaurant** and other shacks near the beach send boats there every Wednesday morning (45min., 9:30am, Rs150 roundtrip). The northernmost boat on the main beach usually makes the trip. A jazz band composed of fellow travelers plays every Friday night to a packed house at **Fellini** (see above). The dozen or so bars along the main road pour great fizzies.

❷ DAYTRIPS FROM ARAMBOL: QUERIM BEACH AND TEREKOL FORT. North of Arambol Junction, virtually every trace of backpacker culture disappears. A couple of places stand out, though, beyond the pale of hippie settlement. The first is **Querim** or **Keri Beach**, a fir-backed strip of white sand where you can lounge from Noel to New Year's with not a Kodak or a dreadlock to disturb you. Querim Beach is a 45min. walk north from Paradise Beach in Arambol, but the beach route heads over a rocky embankment for which shoes are a must. Alternatively, you can head north from Arambol Junction by taxi, moped, or bus, following the signs to Keri (about 10km). White writing on the road will point you to the beach.

Past Querim, you can take a ferry across the Terekol River and continue up the road to **Terekol Fort**, at the northern tip of Goa (15-20min. on foot, 5min. by motorbike). The fort itself, although owned by the government, has been longterm leased to a hotel-owner who has exacted a twisted revenge on the Portuguese for years of colonial oppression: he turned their battle-station into a mustard-yellow, incredibly overpriced hotel and restaurant (coffee Rs55). The ambience may lack the grandeur and gravity of most 400-year-old military installations, but if you arrive just before sunset, the view of sparkling lines of waves rolling in onto the Subcontinent from miles away will leave you utterly speechless. **Buses** also make the trip from Chopdem/Arambol to Querim (20min., every 15min., Rs4), stopping at the Terekol ferry. **Ferries** cross the Terekol from Querim (5min., every 30min. 6am-9:30pm, free for passengers, Rs4 for motorbikes). From there it's just a few kilometers west—a 15min. hike or Rs50 taxi ride—to the fort. (Open daily 9am-6pm.)

NEAR ARAMBOL

MANDREM

*Mandrem village lies on a short stretch of road that branches off from the main thorough-fare between Arambol and Chopdem, or a brisk 30min. walk south from Arambol. **Nikita Travels,** just over the river and some distance south after End of the World Restaurant when coming from the beach, arranges bus, train, and plane reservations, has **currency exchange,** gives MC/V **cash advances,** and offers **Internet** access. (☎ 2297956. Internet Rs40 per hr. Open 9am-10pm.) **Rickshaws** from Chopdem (Rs80) and the **bus** to Arambol will stop at Mandrem.*

"Beach" is a bit of a misnomer for Mandrem's seaside landscape of stately palm trees, green rivers, and windswept white sand—it's more like a desert vista. At its widest point, the expanses of sand stretch over 100 unspoiled meters, and it's rare to see more than a dozen beachcombers sauntering about, even on the busiest days. Mandrem's solitude will probably be lost someday soon, but for now there are enough other beaches nearby to keep people away from this hidden gem.

Accommodations, both short- and long-term, are sprouting up apace in Mandrem. They're equally visible from the road or the beach, and you should have little trouble dropping in unannounced. At the very end of the road or beach lies an exception to this—and nearly every other—rule of Indian accommodation: the spectacular and unique ▨**River Cat Villa** ❸. If you are on a bike, take the Junuswaddo Junction road to the very end. If you are walking on the beach south from Arambol, after about 40min. you'll pass a cluster of beach shacks and a creek heading inland. About 3min. past the large concrete building with two towers, head inland between the tiny huts crowning the sand dunes. The sign to the Oasis Restaurant will point you in the right direction. More of a communal retreat than a guest house, this sprawling, beautiful home just off the beach might be the best accommodation on the whole Goan coast. The mellow owner encourages an international group of residents to light candles and bask in the riverbank paradise, cooking and eating together in the guest kitchen. Yoga instruction and Ayurvedic massage treatment available. Reserve well in advance by email. If you arrive without a reservation and there's no room, you get a free hammock for the night. (☎ 2297928; www.rivercatvilla.com. Singles Rs450; doubles Rs650-850; swanky triples with spotless shared bath Rs1000-1500. 25% discount for "artists.") The **Miau Restaurant** ❺, is the River Cat Villa's back porch, but non-guests are welcome to join in the fantastic family-style meals. (Rs150-200. Breakfast 8-11am. Dinner served around 8pm. Book in person.) The **beach shacks** ❸, a few hundred meters north of the Villa, serve standard shack fare. (Meals Rs 60-80.)

SOUTH GOA

MARGAO (MADGAON) मारगाँव ☎ 0834

Capped with a shaking arterial highway, bounded by the Konkan railway, and fed by the constant streams oozing from the dusty maw of the gigantic KTC bus terminal, Margao is very much a transport hub. Most travelers spend only enough time here to catch their next connection, hurrying away as soon as possible. Tourist-hungry accommodations lie less than 30min. away in Colva and Benaulim. Margao doesn't exactly teem with attractions, but the bustling streets come as a possibly necessary reality check for anyone who has spent too many moons hopping from one other-worldly beach to the next.

GOA

◖ TRANSPORTATION

Trains: Margao Railway Station, 4km southeast of the municipal gardens and 2km east of the old railway station, along Station Rd.—a brisk 15min. walk from the gardens. The Konkan Railway's major station has service to: **Cochin** (16hr., 7:35am); **Mangalore** (7hr.; 12:20am, 2:10, 4:10, and 11:10pm; Rs167-468); **Mumbai** (11hr., 10:30am and 6pm, Rs293-796); **Trivandrum** (24hr., 7:35am, 12:30, and 10:30pm, Rs313-379). Helpful info-desk (open 24hr.) and reservation desk (open M-Sa 8am-8pm, Su 8am-2pm).

Buses: KTC Bus Stand, 2km north along the road to Panjim, discharges government buses bound for: **Bangalore** (14½hr., 6:30pm, Rs300); **Hubli** (6hr., every hr. 6:15am-7pm, Rs70); **Mangalore** (8hr., 7am and 2:30pm, Rs165); **Pune** (15hr., 5:30pm, Rs300). Travel agents around the tourist hostels book frequent **private buses** to the same destinations. **Intrastate buses** depart from KTC for **Chaudi** (30min., every 10min. 6am-7pm, Rs12) and **Panjim** (every 5min. 6am-8:40pm, Rs15). Buses to and from **Colva** via **Benaulim** (30min., every 30min. 7am-8pm, Rs5) also stop on both sides of the Municipal Gardens. Buses to other intrastate destinations stop on the western side of the Municipal Gardens, in front of the police station.

◣◪ ORIENTATION AND PRACTICAL INFORMATION

The city's center, the **Municipal Gardens,** is bounded on the west side by **National Highway 17.** The bustling **Station Road,** the middle of three roads heading south, originates from the southeast corner of the gardens, diagonally opposite the Bank of India. The main railway station is southeast of the gardens.

Currency Exchange: State Bank of India (☎2715155), west of the Municipal Gardens, also has a **24hr. ATM.** Bank open M-F 10am-2pm, Sa 10am-noon.

Police: Margao police station (☎2705095), just north of the State Bank of India, behind the bus depot. On duty 24hr.

Pharmacy: Farmacia Molio (☎2706123), around the corner from Rukrish Hotel, toward the Municipal Gardens. Open 8:30am-9pm. **Raikar Medical Stores,** Station Rd. (☎2732924). Open M-Sa 8am-8pm.

Hospital: (☎2735766). 5min. up Station Rd. from Municipal Gardens, on the right. 24hr. emergency.

Internet: Tokina Cyber Cafe (☎2711739). Head up the west side of the Municipal Gardens and turn left after Bharat Petroleum. Follow signs upstairs. Internet Rs25 per hr. Open 24hr.

Post Office: GPO, at the northern border of the Municipal Gardens. Open M-Sa 7am-6:30pm. **Postal Code:** 403601.

◖ ACCOMMODATIONS

Most foreigners stay one night at most in Margao; the steady influx from the trains and buses ensures that most hotels along Station Rd. see continual turnover.

Rukrish Hotel, Station Rd. (☎2715046). In a tall, yellow bldg. diagonally opposite the Bank of India, just south of the Municipal Gardens. Offers decent, spacious rooms, some with a terrace. Singles Rs125; doubles Rs237. ❶

Margao Residency (☎2715096), just south of the Municipal Garden. Huge, and a good bet if you haven't reserved ahead. The cushioned chairs and attached bath in all the rooms (with hot water) will look pretty luxurious if you're coming from a spell on the beach-shack circuit. Check-out noon. Single-occupancy Rs447; doubles Rs525. Prices drop June 15-Sept. 15. ❸

Milan Lodge (☎2705815), off Station Rd. Take the first left after Janata Hotel heading toward the train station. Show up early or call ahead. Singles Rs135-150; doubles Rs225-250. ❶

⬛ FOOD

Cafe Tato (☎2736014), one block east of the Municipal Gardens off the north-south Valaulikar Rd. in the dead-end Apna Bazaar Complex. Excellent, cheap veg. food in A/C comfort and function-over-form ambience. *Thalis* Rs27. Open M-Sa 7am-10pm. ❶

Longuinhos (☎2739908), opposite the Tourist Hotel. This breezy, high-ceilinged ex-pat joint dishes out cheap Goan meals (Rs35-80), breakfast (Rs2-30), and copious cocktails (Rs8-50), one of which bears the promising title, "The Booze Master." Open daily 8am-10:45pm. ❷

Kamat, in the Milan hotel. Very good special *dosa* (Rs16) in a hole-in-the-wall atmosphere. Samosas Rs12, *thalis* Rs23. Open daily 7:30am-9:30pm. ❶

⬛ SIGHTS

Margao's sights, more pleasant than impressive, can be seen at leisure within a couple hours. The central **Municipal Gardens** constitute a wonderland of flowers, children, bronze busts of Portuguese dignitaries, fountains run dry, and reclining bums. Almost 1km north of the Gardens, at Largo de Igreja, stands the **Church of the Holy Spirit,** a classic Goan cathedral with carvings of the apostles and a history of religious conflict; it was built on the ruins of a Hindu temple sacked by Muslims and rebuilt by Catholics. Open daily 6-9am. To the east is a narrow road leading up Monte Hill to **Our Lady of the Mount Chapel,** a 15min. hike or quick drive leading to a few stone benches and expansive views of Margao's hills. In plain view to the north lies the mammoth **football stadium,** the largest in Goa, which can hold 40,000. Consult a daily paper or ask around for upcoming games, but be prepared to fight your way to the ticket windows.

⬛ DAYTRIPS FROM MARGAO

Margao's immediate vicinity suffered a major cultural setback recently, when the **Museum of Christian Art,** formerly located in **Rachol,** just 7km from Margao, was moved lock, stock, and barrel to the Convent of Santa Monica in Old Goa. The town of Rachol itself provides little else of interest beyond a pleasant walk alongside rice paddies and a rather grand seminary building to which tourists are not allowed access.

On the cheekier, but remarkably entertaining side, **Ancestral Goa** (follow signs to Big Foot), in **Loutilim** (10km east of Margao; buses 30min., every 30min., Rs5), offers a presentation of Goan village life as it was in the good old days, the Limca Book of World Records' longest laterite (a ferrous product of rock decay) sculpture, a garden full of carefully labeled fruits and spices, and a surprisingly interesting and informative tour that somehow ties these wildly disparate elements together. One point in the tour is devoted to telling the mythological story of "Big Foot," in which a Hindu Job-esque character donates all his wealth to the poor, becomes destitute, and when offered a chance at restitution by Vishnu, asks only for a spot of land to pray for mankind for the rest of his days. Vishnu playfully assents by giving him a scalding rock to stand on with one foot. The vaguely foot-like "impression" left on the rock accounts for the alternate name of the museum. (Open daily 9am-6pm. Rs20.) You can arrange at the reception to tour **Casa Araujo Alvares,** an old Portuguese villa. (Open daily 10am-12:30pm and

GOA

3-6pm. Rs100.) If the return bus from Loutilim is being shy, head from the bus stand toward Ancestral Goa, taking the right fork. In 20min., you should hit the main road where there is a constant stream of buses heading to Margao (Rs3).

COLVA कोल्वा ☎ 0832

Myriad gawking Indian men, hordes of daytripping Mumbaites, and rosy-cheeked package tourists all descend on Colva's beach for a piece of resort-town action. This overdeveloped and still developing mass of concrete pavement, garish resorts, and skeletal construction sights silently urges backpackers to flee with haste. But with a rented bike and a bottle of water, you can escape the beachfront mob and stake out your own private paradise a few kilometers away.

🔳 **TRANSPORTATION. Buses** from **Margao** stop at the crossroads and at the beachfront roundabout. Buses leave from the crossroads on their way back to **Margao,** via **Benaulim** (every 30min., Rs3). For other destinations in Goa it is necessary to travel first to Margao. From the beach and the main road, **auto-rickshaws** go to **Benaulim** (Rs50), **Margao** (Rs60-70), and **Palolem** (Rs300-400). **Taxis** charge almost twice as much. **Bicycles** (Rs60 per day) and **motorbikes** (Rs150-250 per day) can be rented at many shops and resorts, including **Maria Joanna Cycle Shop,** west of the crossroads. (Open daily 9am-6pm.)

🔳🔳 **ORIENTATION AND PRACTICAL INFORMATION.** Colva's main strip, **Madgaon Road,** begins at a beachfront restaurant **roundabout** and heads 2km east into **Colva Village.** Midway between the roundabout and the village, Madgaon Rd. intersects a major north-south street at a **crossroads.** From this fateful spot, you can head north to Vasco da Gama, south to Benaulim, or you can catch the bus to Margao. The beach road housing most resorts heads north off Madgaon Rd. about 300m inland of the roundabout. West of the church in the village, the **Bank of Baroda** gives cash advances on Visa. (☎2780528. Open M-F 9am-1pm, Sa 9-11am.) **Weizmann Forex Ltd.,** across from the football field between the crossroads and the beach road, **exchanges currency** and gives MC/V cash advances. (☎2780186. Open 9:30am-7pm.) Inland of the roundabout on the north side of Madgaon Rd. is the **tourist police** station. (☎2788396. On duty 24hr.) **Colva Medical Stores,** towards the crossroads from the beach, on the right, stocks all sorts of pharmaceutical goodies. (☎2788591. Open 9:15am-1pm and 4:15-8:30pm.) Swap a dog-eared paperback at **Damodar's Books,** just inland off the roundabout on the left side. (Open daily 9:30am-9:30pm.) **Internet** services are available along the east-west road. Try **World Linkers,** west of the crossroads on the main road. (☎2788064. Rs50 per hr. Open 8:30am-midnight.) A small **post office** is right behind the church in the village. (Open M-F 9am-noon and 2-4pm.) **Postal Code:** 403708.

🔳🔳 **ACCOMMODATIONS AND FOOD.** Transients holing up in Colva after a tour of duty in the north may be pleasantly surprised by the quality of the digs down here, even if they find character to be a bit lacking. Outside Christmas week, only the most popular lodges fill up—bargain hard! The **Tourist Nest Hotel ❶,** off the road north from the crossroads (follow the signs), offers some a homey locale with soft beds and spacious rooms, all a goodly distance from the package-tourists. (☎2788624. Check-out noon. Rooms Rs100-200; 2-bedroom cottage Rs350.) From east of the roundabout, follow signs to Longuinhos on the beach road to find **Lucky Star ❸,** just before it on the left. Fourteen spotless attached rooms on the second floor above the eponymous **bar and restaurant ❸** offer a terrace with a sea view. (☎2788071. Seafood Rs85-120. Restaurant open daily 7:30am-3pm and 6-11pm. Check-out noon. Doubles Rs350-450. Off-season Rs150-250.) **Fisherman's**

Cottages ❷, Lucky Star's neighbor to the south, has similar rooms in view of the rolling surf. All rooms have attached bath. Just be prepared for the smell of fish in the afternoon. (☎2788054. Check-out noon. Doubles Rs200. Mar.-Sept. Rs50-150.) From the crossroads, head west toward the beach and follow signs opposite William's Beach Resort to the quiet area known as the **4th Ward,** where **Vinson's Cottages ❷** has spacious, newly renovated doubles with big attached bath and hot water on request. (☎2788202. Doubles Rs200-300.) Look for signs on the right when heading up the beach road for **Clinton Guest House ❷,** yet another option not so far from the beach with spacious doubles. (☎2788085. Check-out noon. Rs200-250.) **The Sea Pearl ❷,** north on the road east of the roundabout leading to Fisherman's Cottages, draws crowds of tourists with fresh seafood specials in both outdoor and indoor gardens. (Entrees Rs45-95. Open daily 8:30am-2pm, 6-11pm.)

🖭🎐 NIGHTLIFE AND BEACHES. Colva by night is far quieter than its neighbors. **Boomerang Bar,** also known as the **Malibu Beach House,** on the beach north of the roundabout, hosts an easygoing international mix of alcohol-appreciators. Peter the owner and Brian the bartender will regale you with tales of Colva's past. (☎2788149. Beer Rs45-50, cocktails Rs60-80. Open 9am-late.) **Lucky Star** (see above) has live music Th-F, and a few other nondescript bars pepper Madgaon Rd. Beach shacks, as always, are plentiful.

Colva village and its **beach** lie midway along the longest strip of sand in Goa state. Decked out with 26km of sparkling white and sapphire blue, the beach is long enough to make bicycles the best way of getting about. At low tide, it's possible to **cycle** on wet, packed sand along the whole length of the beach (bike rental Rs60 per day). Even when the beach gets crowded around Colva—that is, every day—solitude awaits those willing to venture 1km north or south. Between Colva and Benaulim, the relatively quiet water makes for pleasant swimming. Balmy breezes and mild tides make **boogie boarding** and **windsurfing** popular here. Shacks south of Colva beach lease equipment (boogie board Rs30-100 per hr.; sailboard Rs200-300 per hr.). **Colva Residency,** on the roundabout, arranges tours and cruises (Rs100-140).

BENAULIM बेनावलीम ☎ 0832

The miles-long glory of Colva's beach continues to Benaulim, a 20min. walk south of Colva, but the daytripping often don't make it this far. Resorts-in-training are in the nascent stages, but for now, the guest house rooms are cheap and plentiful, and the long walk or bike ride to the beach along a road bordered by rice paddies still affords pleasant encounters with agrarian local life. A bike rental will let you rattle south, down the beach, away from any excess sunbathers and beach shacks.

🗐 TRANSPORTATION. Buses stop at the eastern (Maria Hall) crossroads. Benaulim is on both the Margao-Mobor and Margao-Colva routes (every 30min. 7:30am-8:30pm), and from Benaulim buses head to: **Colva** (15min., Rs5-6); **Margao** (25min., Rs5); **Varca** (10min., Rs4). **Taxis** and **auto-rickshaws** wait at the drop spot to whisk you off to the shimmering sands 2km away (Rs20 by rickshaw), to **Colva** (Rs50-75 by taxi), or to **Margao** (Rs150 by taxi). Benaulim is a 50min. taxi ride from Dabolim **airport** (Rs350). At the western crossroads, the north-south road faces the majority of guest houses and is cluttered with signs and entrepreneurs touting **bicycle** (Rs50) and **motorcycle** (Rs150-250) rentals.

🗐🎐 ORIENTATION AND PRACTICAL INFORMATION. Two parallel north-south roads comprise the heart of Benaulim Village; they intersect the east-west Margao Rd. as it heads west toward the beach. Travel agents, whose offices line

G O A

the western crossroads, do **currency exchange. GK Tourist Centre,** at the northwest corner of the western crossroads has good rates and **Internet.** (☎2771221. Rs40 per hr. Open daily 9am-10pm.) The **Benaulim Medical Store**, just west of the Maria Hall crossroads on the Margao road, has medications, toiletries, mobile phone cards, and cheap film developing (☎2770619. Open M-Sa 9am-1pm and 4-9pm, Su 10am-1:30pm.) To get to the **post office,** walk south from the eastern crossroads 2km and turn right (west) just past the Holy Trinity Church in Trinity Hall. (Open M-Sa 8am-1pm and 2-4pm.) **Postal Code:** 403716.

▐▐ ACCOMMODATIONS AND FOOD. Lodging and dining in Benaulim beats Colva easily. Try one of the cheap and comfortable guest houses that line Margao Rd. and the two north-south streets for accommodation. Since there are so many guest houses in town, it's easy to get a room without reserving ahead. Head south from the western crossroads and watch for signs to **Diogo Con ❶,** on the dirt road 100m east of the Meridian Restaurant. One of Benaulim's best-kept secrets, here you'll find small, simple rooms with baths and a large, welcoming family. (☎2733749. Rs100-150.) Along the east-west beach road, the pleasant **Caroline Guest House ❷** has a second-floor terrace, which provides a nice hangout area. Most rooms have attached bath, but there are two without if you're pinching rupees. (☎2770590. Rooms Rs150-200. June-Sept. Rs100-150.) **Cacy Rose ❶,** on the main east-west road between the two crossroads, is a centrally located house that has rooms with shared baths. (☎2721813. Singles Rs50-80; doubles Rs150. Off season Rs30-100.)

Palmira's Breakfast Garden ❶ is a choice breakfast spot. Sip your *chai* (Rs5) under bright streamers in this transplanted section of beach, west of the western crossroads on the main road. The banana pancakes (Rs15) are heavenly with a little honey. **Sea View Restaurant ❷,** on the beachfront south of the road, is particularly friendly and serves fresh seafood (Rs50-150) and Indian or Chinese standards for Rs30-60. (☎2771679. Open daily 8am-midnight.) Follow the road to the beach and take a right past Johncy to reach **Coco's Bar & Restaurant ❷,** a sprawling beach restaurant with specialty Tandoor BBQ, Chinese, Thai, Indian, and Goan—the menu is as endless as the sea in front of you. (Entrees Rs35-90. Open 7am-late. Closed May-Sept.) **Johncy Restaurant ❷,** Coco's older and more down-home neighbor, fires up the *tandoor* with the best of 'em. The mussels *amotik* (Rs50), with its fiery chilies, is mercilessly mouth-watering. (Open daily 7:30am-late.) **Pedro's ❸,** right next door to Johncy on the inland side, cooks breakfast (French toast Rs20) as well as Chinese and *tandoori* dishes for Rs65-150 in beach shack surroundings transplanted to the road. (☎2771308. Open daily 8am-midnight.) After dark, a few beach shacks south of the road play host to people loafing around, playing cards, and chatting—Benaulim isn't a party town, but you can certainly enjoy a few late-night drinks in the restaurant's bars, or at a table under the stars.

PALOLEM पालोलेम ☎0832

When overworked desk jockeys daydream of quitting the rat race and starting life anew in a tropical paradise, the place they have in mind often looks a lot like Palolem. A kilometer-long, gently sloping crescent of white sand flanked by forested hillocks, black rocks, and unobtrusive groups of palm huts certainly makes the outside world seem a long way away. Hammocks strung between densely packed palm trees shelter mainly young backpackers and the tide recedes to connect the northern end of the beach with an island inhabited by monkeys. The crowds here are mellower and more content than any to the north: Palolem has plenty of paradise for everybody, so very few are angling for more.

☞ TRANSPORTATION. Compared to the rest of Goa's beach towns, Palolem is fairly isolated. **Buses** run regularly to and from **Margao** (every 30-90min. 6:30am-4:30pm, Rs15). Buses pick up and drop off where the road to Chaudi turns to the beach. Fortunately, most guest house owners double as accurate bus timetables. If you miss the direct services, the bus from nearby **Chaudi** to Margao (1½hr., every hr. 8am-6:30pm, Rs10) is a viable option. If you are continuing on to **Gokarna**, take the bus toward Margao and get off in Canacona. Here you can pick up the Gokarna Express (1½hr., 2:30pm, Rs19). The Canacona **train** station is just outside Chaudi on the road to Margao. To **Margao** (40min., 7:45pm). From Chaudi to Palolem, you can take a **rickshaw** (Rs30) or **taxi** (Rs80-100) or take advantage of **motorcycle rental** (Rs120-200 per day).

▰▱ ORIENTATION AND PRACTICAL INFORMATION. The road from **Chaudi** zigzags 4km northwest to Palolem, running parallel to the surf midway along and intersecting the beach road halfway along the half-moon of sand. If you're on foot, it's generally more direct to reach places by walking on the beach than on the circuitous road. There's a small **library** at **Ciaran's Camp,** on the beach south of the beach road with a decent selection of English beaching-reading staples like *Cosmo* and *Elle.* (Rs20 deposit, Rs20 per day. Open 9am-5:30pm.) The **Sun-N-Moon** on the main road parallel to the beach offers **currency exchange** at decent rates as well as **Internet** access. (☎2645219. Rs40 per hr. Open daily 7am-midnight.) The nearest **post office** is in Chaudi.

▰▱ ACCOMMODATIONS AND FOOD. Compared to Colva and Benaulim, Palolem's accommodations are overpriced and underkept—expect to pay Rs200 in season for the privilege of crashing in a charmless double and using a common bathroom outside. A stay in one of the **straw hut colonies ❷** on the beachfront provides a more picturesque alternative. (On-the-ground huts Rs150-250; up-on-stilts huts Rs 250-500.) Just head south on the beach from the road, and pick among the cluster of huts. ▨**Bridge & Tunnel ❷,** over a bridge at the extreme southern end of the beach and extending onto the hills above it, offers a total backpacker community package: bar, restaurant, and 18 huts in a unique locale overlooking all of Palolem to the north. The sunsets from the upper huts are uncontrollably beautiful. Just don't come home drunk, or the other guests will be picking up your pieces the next morning from the rocks below. (☎2642237. Rs200-500. Price rises with elevation.) Midway down the beach, south of where the road lets out, the **Deena Bar and Restaurant ❷,** often known by its restaurant's name, **Cuba,** rents ample huts with nice mattresses, fans, and mosquito nets. Four toilets and three showers for 14 rooms, laundry and safe lockers available. (☎2643449. Restaurant open 8am-11pm. Rooms Rs200-300. Closed May-Sept.) For a slightly more luxurious beach experience, **Cozy Nook ❷,** at the far northern end of the beach, offers 10 huts with attached bath and a relaxed restaurant out front (see below for restaurant details). (Huts Rs300-500.) Just south of Deena, **Island View Cottages ❷** offers standard huts with mosquito nets, plus bonus hammocks tied between palm trees. (☎2634258. Rs150-350.) For the good old-fashioned, four-solid-walls treatment, **New La Alegro ❷,** right next to Blue Jays Restaurant on the main road toward Chaudi, offers basic, clean rooms with attached bath and beach access around the back. (☎2644261. Doubles Rs300.)

Restaurant fare and prices are pretty standard, so look for atmosphere and a good crowd, since most serve the same food. The restaurant at **Cozy Nook ❷** (see above), is an oasis of good karma, with soft purple and yellow cushions, tree-trunk tabletops, and a lolling crowd to match. (Entrees Rs40-86. Open daily 8am-11pm.) **Blue Jays ❸** and its neighbor, **Sun n' Moon ❸,** are both popular, the latter with a TV

G O A

that gets BBC. (Seafood Rs65-95, breakfast Rs10-30. Both open daily 7:30am-11pm.) Folks can be found blowin' in the wind at **Dylan's** ❷, fairly far south along the beach, in a slightly more relaxed environment than most. (Indian standards Rs40-80. Open 6am-late.)

🖈 DAYTRIPS FROM PALOLEM. Those who are looking for a truly isolated beach getaway can wind their way northwest from Palolem to the as-yet-undiscovered **Agonda Beach** (Rs3 by bus from Chaudi), populated by greater numbers of cows than people. A cove almost as picturesque as Palolem's (although it doesn't match it palm-for-palm), Agonda shows some tiny signs of development behind the treeline, including a couple restaurants and at least one hotel with beach huts. **Dersy Bar, Restaurant, & Rooms** ❷, south down the road from the intersection with the beach, offers the whole package, with both beach huts and four-wall treatment (and a wraparound terrace) separated only by the empty road. (☎ 2647503. Rice entrees Rs25-70, Goan Rs50-150. Check-out noon. Huts Rs150-200, rooms Rs250-500.) Supplies (petrol, cold snacks) are available from the garage-like complex of stores on the left as you head toward the beach (most close at 7pm).

Farther northwest (1hr. by scooter, available in Palolem for Rs150-200 per day), the immense ruins of a Portuguese fort wait for the invasion that never happened in **Cabo de Rama,** a town consisting only of a name, a fort, and a few bars scattered along the one and only road. The ruins overlook a crescent of jutting rocks and strips of empty beach embracing the aqua waves as they roll in and break on the shore. It's inconvenient at best to visit Cabo de Rama by any means other than motorbike—taxis are expensive (Rs250-300 from Palolem), and the daily buses to Cabo de Rama from Margao and Agonda take 2hr.

GUJARAT ગુજરાત

One of India's richest industrial regions, Gujarat boasts savory cuisine, august mosques, and impressive wildlife, all of which remain for the most part underappreciated. Perhaps due to its statewide prohibition laws and a tourism infrastructure aimed at domestic travelers, Gujarat sees far fewer travelers than its neighbors, Rajasthan and Maharashtra. Westerners are still a curiosity in much of the region, and the touts that swarm neighboring Rajasthan have yet to congregate here. The honest friendliness experienced in Gujarat is reason enough to forgo booze and rooftop restaurants in exchange for a few weeks of dozing on pristine beaches, mingling with pilgrims, and lion-gazing in Sasan Gir.

Originally settled as part of the Indus Valley civilization around 2500 BC, Gujarat prospered under several empires, including the Solanki dynasty in the 11th and 12th centuries, which imbued the region with a blend of Jainism and Hinduism. In AD 1299, the area was conquered by Muslims, who formed the Sultanate of Gujarat. The Portuguese stormed onto the scene in the 16th century, capturing the ports of Diu and Daman. During India's struggle for Independence, Gujarat came to prominence as the birthplace of Mahatma Gandhi, and as the home of Mohammed Ali Jinnah, a well-known architect from Pakistan.

Gujarat can be divided into three vastly different geographical regions. The eastern region, containing the capital Gandhinagar, the metropolis Ahmedabad, and the commercial cities of the mainland strip, is a modern industrial center. The northwestern quasi-island of Kutch is a dry and isolated area known for its traditional villages and handicrafts. The Kathiawar Peninsula (also known as Saurashtra) features breathtaking beaches, forts, palaces, and all things Gandhi.

On January 26, 2001, Gujarat was rocked by one of the most disastrous earthquakes ever to hit India. The 7.9-magnitude quake, whose epicenter was located in the Kutch region, created considerable tremors as far away as Chennai, Tamil Nadu. Death estimates ran from 20,000 to 50,000, and up to one million people have been made homeless by the disaster. The earthquake destroyed significant portions of the state's infrastructure and prompted groups around the globe to aid in disaster-relief efforts. Their efforts have restored transportation links and basic infrastructure all over the state, reopening every corner of this region to the wandering traveler.

HIGHLIGHTS OF GUJARAT

Gandhi and gingham combine in **Ahmedabad** (p. 193), at the Mahatma's **Sabarmati Ashram** (p. 200) and the **Calico Museum of Textiles** (p. 201).

India sets its western compass point at **Dwarka** (p. 214), where pilgrims congregate and antique lighthouses afford sublime sunset vistas.

One of India's most isolated regions, beautiful **Kutch** (p. 216) is home to unique tribal cultures and the labyrinthine port of **Mandvi** (p. 220).

AHMEDABAD અમદાવાદ ☎079

Ahmedabad, the largest city in Gujarat, is one of Asia's most eccentric and fascinating cities. It is also one of its most polluted and congested. Much of Ahmedabad's appeal is well-hidden these days, covered up by billboards and signs advertising its booming businesses. For those willing to dig a little deeper, much beauty still remains within the *pols* (self-contained neighborhoods) of the old city,

GUJARAT

where spectacular mosques, temples, and *havelis* await on nearly every corner. Wandering the streets of the old city, you can expect to see craftsmen adding the finishing touches to batiks put out to dry in the sun.

Across the river lies the new city and its expansive web of shopping arcades and cinemas, interrupted by the occasional wandering camel or stray ox cart. Though not of much interest to tourists, the new city operates at a more relaxed pace than the old city and offers all the modern conveniences available in Delhi or Mumbai.

Founded in 1411 by Sultan Ahmed Shah, the city expanded rapidly, attracting large numbers of traders, craftsmen, and artisans. The construction of numerous mosques in the Indo-Saracenic style gave the city the Muslim character that it retains today. Ahmedabad's prosperity waxed and waned over the centuries, and its growth was periodically impeded by famines. Ahmedabad has always been known for its textiles and handicrafts, and Gandhi's *swadeshi* movement was started in an ashram here. Today, Ahmedabad has the second largest textile industry in the country.

▜ TRANSPORTATION

Flights: Ahmedabad International Airport (international terminal ☎2869283, domestic 2869233). 10km northeast of the city center. Taxis into the city Rs250, auto-rickshaws Rs150. Buses run to Lal Darwaja Bus Stand (every hr., Rs7). Bus #102 goes to the airport from Lal Darwaja; bus #18 goes to the airport from the railway station, both during flight times. **Air India** (☎6585633 or 6585644; fax 6585900), behind the High Court off Ashram Rd., north of the tourist office. Open M-F 10am-1:15pm and 2-5:15pm, Sa 10am-1:30pm. **Jet Airways,** Ashram Rd. (☎7543304), 1km north of Gujarat Tourism. Open M-F 10am-6:30pm, Sa-Su 10am-4pm. The Ahmedabad edition of the *Times of India* has up-to-date flight and train information. **Indian Airlines,** Lal Darwaja (☎5503061; fax 5505599). Near the east end of Nehru Bridge. Open daily 10am-1pm and 2-5:15pm. To: **Bangalore** (3hr., 6:50pm, US$230); **Delhi** (1½hr., 8:05am and 8:50pm, US$145); **Hyderabad** (1½hr.; M and F 7:50am, Tu, Th, Su 5:25am; US$175); **Jaipur** (1hr.; Tu, Th, Sa 6:20pm; US$65); **Mumbai** (1hr.; 7:10am, 6:50, 8:55pm; US$85).

Trains: Ahmedabad Railway Station (☎131 or 1331). **Reservation Office** (☎135). In the bldg. to the right as you face the station. Open M-Sa 8am-8pm, Su 8am-2pm. To: **Abu Road** (4½hr., 7 per day 6am-1:50am, Rs53); **Bhopal** (14hr., 6:45pm, Rs221); **Chennai** (35hr., 6:30am, Rs445); **Delhi** (14-20hr., 4 per day 9:50am-5:45pm, Rs286); **Dwarka** (13hr., 5:35am, Rs182); **Jaipur** (12-14hr; 3-4 per day 6, 9:50am, 5:45pm; Rs218); **Kolkata** (43hr., 9:25am, Rs467); **Mumbai** (7-9hr., 9 per day 3:50am-10:45pm, Rs182); **Rajkot** (4-5hr., 7per day 5:35am-2:30am, Rs107); **Udaipur** (9hr., 11:15pm, Rs124); **Varanasi** (39hr.; Tu, Th, Sa 8:30pm; Rs349); **Veraval** (12hr., 9:45 and 11pm, Rs173).

Buses: The **ST Bus Stand** (☎2214764) is near Astodia Darwaja (rickshaw Rs15 from Lal Darwaja). To: **Abu Road** (5hr., every hr. 5am-midnight, Rs82); **Bhuj** (8hr., 12 per day 8am-11pm, Rs112; semi-deluxe 3:30 and 8:10pm, Rs120); **Chittaurgarh** (10hr., 9am, Rs155); **Diu** (10hr., 8am, Rs120); **Dwarka** (11hr., 3 per day 6:15am-11pm, Rs120); **Jaipur** (15hr., 4:30 and 9:30pm, Rs280); **Mt. Abu** (6hr., 3 per day 7-11am, Rs90); **Mumbai** (12hr., 5 per day 2-8pm, Rs220); **Rajkot** (5hr., every 30min., Rs84); **Udaipur** (6hr., 11 per day 5am-11:30pm, Rs107; deluxe 7 per day 11:30am and 10:30pm, Rs118); **Una** (10hr., 3 per day 8am-8pm, Rs90); **Veraval** (12hr., 5 per day 6:15am-8:45pm, Rs121). There are dozens of private bus company stalls opposite the ST Bus Stand, but most are ticket agents only; most private buses depart from the main company office. Two good companies are **Punjab Travels,** Embassy Market, off Ashram Rd., north of the tourist office (☎6589200; open daily 7am-9:30pm), and **Shrinath Travels,** Shahi Bagh, near the police commissioner's (☎5625351; open daily 6am-midnight).

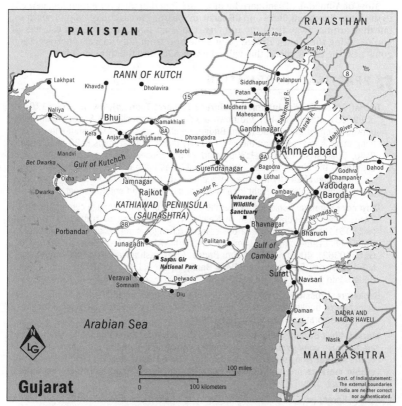

Local Transportation: Auto-rickshaws are the most convenient local transport. Insist on the meter and ask to see the fare card. **Local buses** are cheap, and go just about everywhere. The **Lal Darwaja Bus Stand** (☎5507739) is the local bus stand. Buses ending in 0-5 are based at Lal Darwaja; those ending in 6-9 are based near the railway station; #82 and 84 cross the river and run north up Ashram Rd.; #52 hits Panchwati Circle; #32 runs to the ST Bus Stand and southeast to Kankaria Lake; #34 and 112 run past the Civil Hospital; #131 and 133-135 run to the railway station. Fares run Rs3-12. It's best to go to the counter at platform O, tell them your destination and have them direct you to the correct platform and bus. A/C Ambassador **taxis** can be found at Lal Darwaja, the 2 bus stands, the airport, the railway station, and the V.S. Hospital.

✦ ORIENTATION

Ahmedabad is divided in two by the **Sabarmati River,** which runs north-south between the old and new sections of the city (the riverbed is usually dry and filled with grazing water buffalo). The **Lal Darwaja (Red Gate)** opens into the old city on the east side of the river; the newer industrial and urban centers are to the west. The two parts of the city are connected by a series of five bridges.

GUJARAT

Most of Ahmedabad's modern facilities are found in the ever-expanding **new city** to the west. **Panchwati Circle** and **CG Road** are bustling areas full of helpful services, but they are far away from the old city, the most interesting area to tourists. If you're taking the Nehru Bridge (that's the one from Lal Darwaja) across, keep going past the **Law Gardens;** this will take you right into the thick of things.

🛈 PRACTICAL INFORMATION

Tourist Office: Tourist Information Bureau (Gujarat Tourism), HK House (☎ 1364 or 6589683), off Ashram Rd. and down a side street opposite the South Indian Bank, between Gandhi Bridge and Nehru Bridge. Helpful English-speaking staff knows everything there is to know about the city. Free city maps, Gujarat maps Rs20, road atlases Rs40. Open M-Sa 10:30am-1:30pm and 2-6pm. Closed 2nd and 4th Sa. The **tourist counter** at the airport is open at fight arrival times but has limited information. Check out the **Ahmedabad city website** (www.ahmedabadcity.com) for everything from emergency phone numbers to flight information to city tours and entertainment.

Currency Exchange: Banks are all over the city. Many of them exchange currency and have 24hr. ATMs, especially those in New City. **State Bank of India,** Lal Darwaja (☎5506116), near Lal Darwaja bus stand, exchanges currency and traveler's checks. Open M-F 11am-4pm, Sa 11am-1:30pm. 24hr. ATM. **Bank of Baroda,** Ashram Rd. (☎6580362), 400m north of Nehru Bridge. Gives cash advances on MC and V. Open M-F 11am-2pm, Sa 11am-noon. **Dena Bank,** Ashram Rd. (☎6584292), north of Nehru Bridge, 2nd fl. Open M-F 10am-2:30pm.

Bookstore: Crossword (☎6430238), basement of Shree Krishna Center, Mithikali. Huge selection of books, tapes, CDs, VHS, and VCDs. Best selection of English language books in Gujarat and Rajasthan. Open daily.

Market: Khas Bazaar, Relief Road, Gandhi Road, Sardar Patel Road, and **Ashram Road** are the main commercial areas. Most stores open daily 9am-9:30pm. There is a **handicrafts market** along the western edge of the **Law Gardens** daily 6-11pm. The main **vegetable markets** are near the railway station on **Relief Road** and **Kasturba Gandhi Road.** Open daily 7am-7pm.

Police: Karanj (☎5507580), in Teen Darwaja; **Shaherkotada** (☎2125338), behind the railway station; and **Ellis Bridge** (☎6578202) at the intersection with Ashram Rd.

Hospital: One of the best private hospitals is **Chaturbhuj Lajpatrai Hospital,** also known as **Rajasthan Hospital** Dr. Tankeria Rd. (☎2866311), south of the Police Commissioner's Office. English-speaking, modern, efficient. Well-stocked **24hr. pharmacy.**

Internet: Interscope White House, Panchwati Circle, Ambavadi Rd. (☎6404131). Rs30 per hr. Open 24hr. **Cyber Valley,** Sri Krishna Shopping Centre, Mithakali (☎6409200). Rs30 per hr. Open daily 8am-11pm.

Post Office: GPO, Mirzapar Rd. (☎5500977), near Lal Darwaja. Open M-Sa 10:30am-6pm, Su 10:30am-3pm. Branches at the airport, Gandhi Ashram, and opposite the railway station. Open M-Sa 10am-5pm. **Postal Code:** 380001.

🏠 ACCOMMODATIONS

The best budget hotels are conveniently scattered around the western half of the city center. None of them cater to the Western tourist, a testament to Ahmedabad's off-the-beaten-track status, so don't come expecting rooftop restaurants, station pickup, or a travel desk. Luxury hotels cluster around Khanpur Darwaja, between Gandhi Bridge and Nehru Bridge on the east side of the river. All hotels add 10-15% luxury tax.

Hotel Sohel, Lal Darwaja (☎5505465 or 5505466), on a side street off Advance Cinema Rd. Well-kept, modern, and smack in the middle of Lal Darwaja. 24hr. hot water, TVs, and room service. Check-out 24hr. Singles Rs180-400; doubles Rs340-400. ❷

Gandhi Ashram Guest House (☎7559342), opposite Gandhi Ashram. This guest house catches some of the peaceful vibes that emanate from the ashram across the street. Grecian busts, phones, TVs, and hot showers. Breakfast included. Good veg. restaurant. Check-out 9am. Singles Rs325-550; doubles Rs500-750. ❷

Hotel Shakunt (☎2144615), opposite the railway station. A marble staircase lined with Rajasthani art leads up to this modern hotel, featuring a pleasant rooftop terrace. Rooms are slightly stuffy but have TVs, phones, and baths. STD service in the lobby. Check-out 24hr. Singles Rs220-600; doubles Rs380-700. ❷

Hotel Diamond, Gujarat Samachar Rd., Khanpur (☎5503699). Decent value for the facilities. Wall-to-wall carpeted rooms with baths, TVs, and phones, are well-insulated from the noise (and air) outside. Check-out 24hr. Singles Rs190-353; doubles Rs270-433. ❷

Hotel Natraj (☎5506048), next to Ahmed Shah's Mosque south of the local bus stand. Rooms with balconies overlooking the gardens of the mosque next door offer the best budget view in the city proper. Rooms are large but aging. All have attached baths. Check-out 24hr. Singles Rs130; doubles Rs220. ❶

⚑ FOOD

Ahmedabad has some of the best restaurants in Gujarat, and they are often very reasonably priced. Gujarati *thalis* blend several local specialties in a delightful, frequently sweet, mix. For quick and spicy stall food, **Khas Bazaar** can't be beat. The **Havmor** outlet near Roopum cinema on Relief Rd. (Open daily 10am-10pm) and **Sidewalk Restaurant** past the Xavier Ladies Hostel near Swastik Crossroads in the new city (Open daily 10am-midnight) offer a variety of flavors.

▓ **Chetna Dining Hall,** Relief Rd., directly north of the Jama Masjid. High-quality *thali* house. South Indian dishes (*dosas* Rs23-38) downstairs noon-10pm; *thalis* (Rs60) upstairs. Every *samosa* and *sabil* spiced evocatively, and topped off with unlimited *shrikhand.* Open daily 10:30am-3pm and 6:30-10pm. ❷

▓ **Gopi Dining Hall,** off Ashram Rd. near V.S. Hospital on the west side of the river; look for the sign above the bldg. This packed little den of a place serves up excellent, enormous sweet Gujarati (Rs50) and spicy Kathiawadi *thalis* (Rs60). Come early, or be prepared to wait. Great service. Open daily 10:30am-3pm and 6:30-10:30pm. ❷

Agashiye, on the roof of the red-and-white mansion opposite the Sidi Sayid Mosque. Scented candles and flower-filled fountains welcome you to this exquisitely decorated rooftop paradise. Incredible Gujarati *thalis* (lunch Rs150-170, dinner Rs195-220). Open 11am-3pm and 7-11pm. ❹ Downstairs, the **Greenhouse Restaurant** serves juices, ice cream, and *lassis* (Rs25-35) as well as South Indian snacks (Rs45-70). Open daily noon-3pm and 7-11pm. ❷

Colours of Spice, just off Swastik Crossroads in the new city. The only place in town serving authentic East Indian dishes. Huge menu includes Chinese (Rs110-135), Indonesian, Thai (Rs120-150), continental (Rs135-195), kebabs, and regional Indian cuisine (Rs70-150). Great seafood. Open daily 12:30-3pm and 7:30-11pm. AmEx/MC/V. ❹

Sunrise Restaurant, MG Rd., opposite the railway stations near Hotel Shakunt. A 2m-high waterfall helps to drown out all the outside railroad noise in this busy diner where the *dosas* (Rs20-30) are salty and the cold coffee ice cream floats (Rs35) are a bittersweet end to the meal. Packed lunches are available, convenient for those daytime train journeys to Mumbai and Rajasthan (Rs48). Open daily 7am-midnight. ❷

G U J A R A T

Ahmedabad

🏠 ACCOMMODATIONS

Gandhi Ashram Guest House, 1
Hotel Diamond, 5
Hotel Natraj, 9
Hotel Shakunt, 12
Hotel Sohel, 7

🍎 FOOD

Agashiye, 6
Cellad Eatery, 2
Chetna Dining Hall, 10
Colours of Spice, 3
Gopi Dining Hall, 4
Kalapi Restaurant, 8
Sunrise Restaurant, 11

TO GANDHINAGAR
(35km)

N
LG

0   400 yards
0   400 meters

Naranpura Rd.

Ravjikaka Rd.

Sabarmati

Tribal Research
and Training
Museum

Ashram Rd.

Jet
Airways

Saardar
Patel
Stadium

Ghandhi
Statue

Gandhi
Bridge

Air
India

Punjab
Travels

ⓘ

Navrangpura

CG Rd.

2
3

Crossword
Bookstore

University Rd.

Mehta Museum &
L.D. Museum of
Indology

Shri C. Chinai Rd.

MITHAKALI

Gandhigram
Railway
Station

Ashram Rd.

Law
Garden

Satellite Rd.

Parimal
Garden

V.S.
Hospital

Dr. H. Desai Rd.

Netaji Marg

Shreya's
Folk Museum

PALDI

New Sharda Mandir Rd.

Saneevani Rd.

TO VISHALLA

GUJARAT

TO ✈ (4km)

Sabarmati (Gandhi) Ashram

Subhash Bridge

SHAHIBAG

Shahibag Rd.

City Rd.

Civil Hospital

Dada Hari Vav

Ashram Rd.

Vadaj Low Level Bridge

DUDHESWAR

Calico Museum of Textiles

Police Commissioner's Office

River

Chamanpura Rd.

HARIPURA

Mehta Rd.

Balvantri Mehta Rd.

Naroda Rd.

Hatheesingh Temple

Jagivan Ram Rd.

Kasturba Gandhi Rd.

Shahpur Darwaja

Delhi Darwaja

Dariapur Darwaja

Lady Vidyagauri Rd.

Rani Rupmati's Mosque

Peer Mohammedshah Rd.

Dr. Tankeria Rd.

Dr. Bapisa Rd.

Kalupur Darwaja

Swaminarayan Temple

Khanpur Darwaja

Indian Airlines

5

GPO

KHAS BAZAAR

Ramanlal Sheth Rd.

Ahmedabad Railway Station

Tilak (Relief) Rd.

10

Nehru Bridge

Lal Darwaja

Sidi Salyad's Mosque

6

7

8

12

11

Arjun Lala Rd.

Mahatma Gandhi Rd. (MG Rd.)

Shaking Minarets & Sidi Bashir's Mosque

Local Bus Stand

SBI

9

Akhandanand Rd.

Panchkuva Darwaja

Ellis Bridge

Teen Darwaja

Jama Masjid

KT Desai Rd.

Sarangpur Darwaja

Ahmed Shah's Mosque

Victoria Garden

Bhadra Fort & Azamkhan's Palace

RM Rd.

Anandshankar Dhruv Rd.

Sadar Patel Rd.

Rani Sipri's Mosque

RAIPUR DARWAJA

Astodia Darwaja

Vivekananda Rd.

Sardar Bridge

Jamalpur Rd.

S.T. Bus Stand

Dayanand Rd.

Picnic Garden

Jagannathji Rd.

JAMALPUR

Kankaria Lake

Zoo

Nehru Kids Park

Cellad Eatery, on a side street across from Colours of Spice, just off Swastik Cross-roads. This unique restaurant specializes in soups and salads. The unlimited salad bar includes *daal*, rice, fresh fruit, two soups, and 15 salad options (Rs118). Open daily 11am-3:30pm and 7-11pm. ❹

Kalapi Restaurant, opposite Advance Cinema, Lal Darwaja. Superior service and meticulous preparation distinguish this veg. restaurant from its many look-a-like neighbors. ❷

LET'S GO FLY A KITE
For three nights in January, the skies of Ahmedabad are speckled with kites of all styles, colors, and sizes. Enthusiasts from all over the world descend upon the city for the **International Kite Festival,** also known as **Uttarayan,** the largest kite-related event in the world. For the weeks leading up to the event, local shops and stalls sell an enormous variety of kites and kite-flying equipment, and experts roam the streets offering lessons on the finer points of the craft. In the festival itself there are competitions for kite size, originality, and beauty. At night, the skies light up with kites' illuminated tails. Dancing, singing, shows, parades, and general merriment round out the festival, which ends with a highly competitive contest in which kite strings are coated with adhesive and ground glass, turning them into razor-sharp lines. Kites are then sent flying into one another to slash at each other's lines until one kite emerges victorious.

◎ ♫ SIGHTS AND ENTERTAINMENT

■ **HERITAGE WALK.** Because Ahmedabad was built to thwart and confuse invaders the Ahmedabad Municipal Corporation decided that Ahmedabad needed a walking tour to "unveil" the city to tourists and residents alike. The guided tour takes you through the numerous *pols* (neighborhoods) and *ols* (markets) that make up the old city and explains the rationale behind Ahmedabad's design and architecture while outlining the city's history. It winds through narrow streets and secret passageways, takes you under 400-year-old, carved wooden gates, and goes past ornamented temples, community squares, and **chabutras** (bird feeders) that were once the focal point of daily life. The Heritage Walk takes you to parts of the city you would never see otherwise. *(2hr. walk starts at the Swaminarayan Temple, up the stairs to the right of the main gate. 8am. Rs50.)*

SABARMATI (GANDHI) ASHRAM. Every year thousands of admirers and followers of Mahatma Gandhi descend upon Ahmedabad to visit this ashram, from which much of Gandhi's spiritual and political influence emanated. Gandhi founded the original ashram in the middle of the city in 1915, upon his return from South Africa. However, a city-wide plague two years later forced him to relocate to a plot of donated land on the banks of the Sabarmati River. Gandhi lived here until 1930, along with his wife, Kasturba, and 600 other residents. The Mahatma's simple living quarters, several of his personal objects, and an exhibition of his achievements are on display. The display touches not only on the political and spiritual sides of his life, but also on the role that he played in the revitalization of the Ahmedabad textile industry. Don't miss the series of moving portraits next to the ashram office. The museum library, open to visitors, holds a mammoth collection of over 36,000 of Gandhi's letters. Beyond **Vinoba/Mira Kutir,** the modest abode of two particularly fervent devotees, is a large building referred to as **the "hostel,"** which was the first part of the ashram to be built. The room on the riverside was Gandhi's original dwelling and work room for three months. The building is now home to 2,000 orphans and children from impoverished families living in nearby slums, as well as a few NGOs. Also of interest is **Pasana Mandir,** a small plot of land over-looking the river where Gandhi and his fellow ashram mates recited their daily prayers. The ashram's current inhabitants hold their evening prayer sessions at the same spot *(6:30pm)*. Gandhi's main residence lies to the right as you face the *mandir*. Those interested in volunteering at the ashram should contact Jayesh Patel (☎7560002; manavsadhna@icenet.net), next door to the ashram. The Department of Gandhian Studies of Gujarat Vidyapith offers classes struc-tured after Gandhian principles. *(Ashram Rd., north of the Gandhi Bridge; take local bus #81, 83, 84. ☎7551102. Open daily 8:30am-6:30pm. Free. 1hr.-long sound and light show Nov. 1-June 30 daily 8:30pm. Rs5.)*

CALICO MUSEUM OF TEXTILES. Housed in the *haveli* of the city's richest fam-ily, India's premier textile museum is worth a visit simply for the building itself, which is split into two sections surrounded by peacock- and fountain-filled gar-dens. The first section displays non-religious textiles, and features an enormous collection of items made from every possible fabric, in every possible style, for every possible purpose, and from every part of India. The white-on-white translu-cent shadow work is remarkable, as are the lavish silk embroideries. Other high-lights include beautiful saris (valued at Rs80,000 and up) made according to a highly complex method—one tiny mistake in the sewing ruins the entire piece—and clothes so heavily laden with gold lace that their weight exceeds 9kg. *(Shahi Bagh, 3km north of Delhi Gate; take local bus #101, 102, or 106. ☎2868172. Open Th-Tu. Two guided tours daily, the textile collection 10:30am; the Sarabhai collection, with religious-themed textiles and artifacts, 2:45pm. Entry permitted up to 3omin. after tours begin; both last 2hr. Free. Photography permitted only in the gardens.)*

JAMA MASJID. Built in 1424 by Sultan Ahmed Shah I, the Jama Masjid centers on a large marble courtyard and a small pool that is often surrounded by devo-tees. The 15 domes of the mosque are supported by 256 pillars with detailed carvings, most of which are Hindu-themed. The curious black slab by the main massive archway is said to be an inverted Jain image. The twin minarets, which once towered over the main structure, collapsed in an 18th-century earthquake and the broken stubs are all that remain. The names of the prophets are written on the **north wall** so that mothers can bring their newborns here to pick a name. Through the left gate of the courtyard is the tomb of **Ahmed Shah** and the **Rani-ka-Hazira,** the tomb of his queens. The cenotaphs, in vast pillared chambers, are covered with fancy gold-laced cloths. A guard can lift one for you to reveal the fine stonework underneath. *(Gandhi Rd. Jama Masjid is the only mosque in town that allows women inside. Even so, there are restrictions: Women are allowed to enter the main hall, except during prayer times, but are prohibited from entering the chambers that hold tombs of male members of the family. Open sunrise-sunset.)*

SIDI SAIYAD'S MOSQUE. Constructed in 1573 by one of Ahmed Shah's slaves, Sidi Saiyad's Mosque, in Lal Darwaja, graces at least half of Gujarat Tourism's propaganda pamphlets. The interior is impressive, with elaborately carved ceilings and domes, but the highlight is the delicate latticework on the screens of the upper walls. *(Women are not allowed to enter, but can view the screens from the gardens. Open sunrise-sunset.)*

▷ DAYTRIPS FROM AHMEDABAD

VISHALLA. The Gujarati village mock-up of Vishalla, 4km south of Ahmeda-bad, offers a night of earthy village dining and rustic entertainment. Eat plenti-ful, spicy food from leaf plates and drink from clay cups while musicians play and attendants dressed in traditional village garb fan scented insect-repelling

GUJARAT

smoke in your face. The adjoining utensils museum in a well-maintained open *haveli* has an impressive collection of nut crackers, *puja* jars, pressure cookers, teaspoons, and toys among its many utensils from various eras and locations around India. The oldest item is an 1000 year-old copper pot (Rs8). Allow 2-3hr. for the meal, pre-meal, and post-meal entertainment. Buffet *bapora* (lunch) Rs71. Buffet dinner Rs188. *(Open daily 11am-3pm and 7-11pm. Bus #31 from Lal Darwaja and #64 from the railway station run near Vishalla. The stop is on the Ahmedabad-Sarkhej highway, a 2min. walk from the village. Look for the sign.)*

ADALAJ VAV. Nineteen kilometers north of Ahmedabad is the step well at Adalaj Vav, one of the most impressive in the state. Built in 1499 by Rani Rudabai as a summer retreat, it now serves as a popular relaxation spot for locals. The gardens around it are pleasant, but the carvings on the well are the main attraction. Intricate lattices and detailed carvings of mythological scenes adorn the walls, pillars, and platforms of the five-story well. The best time to visit is just before noon, when sunlight illuminates the stonework all the way to the bottom. *(Buses going to Mehesana Kalol from the ST Bus Stand pass Adalaj Vav: 30min., every 30min. 6am-10pm, Rs9. The well is 1km west of the bus stop.)*

MODHERA. The ordinary town of Modhera, 84km northwest of Ahmedabad, is home to an extraordinary Jain-influenced **Sun Temple.** Built in 1026 by the Solanki King Bhimdev I, the temple was constructed and positioned so that, at the time of the equinoxes, sunlight will fall directly on the image of Surya, the sun god, in the sanctuary. Many worshippers come to watch this sacred event. The main entry hall is adorned with 12 *adityas* representing the sun's phases through the year. A multitude of sexy Kama Sutra-style carvings cover the inner sanctum and outer walls. The step-well in front of the temple contains over 100 smaller shrines. *(Open daily sunrise to sunset. Rs100; video fee Rs25.)* Stop for a cup of *chai* (Rs5) at the GTDC-run **Torah Garden Restaurant ❶,** in front of the temple. *(Open daily 9am-6pm. Buses run frequently to Mesehana from the ST Bus Stand. 2hr., 9:30am-4pm, Rs25. From Mehesana catch one of the frequent buses to Modhera. 30min., Rs11. The temple is on the opposite side of town from the bus stand, a 10min. walk west.)*

LOTHAL. The discovery in 1945 of the archaeological site at Lothal ("place of the dead" in Gujarati), 90km southwest of Ahmedabad, was a major event. Lothal is all that remains of an ancient Indus Valley civilization city, dating from 2400 to 1900 BC, and the objects unearthed here have helped historians piece together a picture of what life was like in India's earliest civilizations. Lying in ruin are old roads, houses, shops, a bathhouse, and a sewer; the discovery of a dock and a cargo warehouse suggest that Lothal was a major port city. A **museum** showcases the findings of years of excavation. *(Open Sa-Th 10am-5pm. Free. To reach Lothal, take the bus headed toward Bhavnagar but get off at Dholka: 2hr. every 30min. 7am-1am, Rs33. From Dholka, and take one of the frequent buses to Lothal. Alternatively, some of the trains headed to Bhavnagar stop at Lothal-Burkhi station. Train tickets Rs33. From here motorbike trailers (Rs5) will take you to Lothal.*

BARODA (VADODARA) ☎0265

The sophisticated greenery and wealth that once marked this former state capital has not completely deserted the sprawling urban center. Today, the remaining pockets of green and tucked away palaces serve as reminders of Baroda's royal past, even though the administrative splendor of the Gaekwad dynasty has all but given way to a new hierarchy of cows, pigs, and the occasional donkey. Regardless, the largely well-heeled city is still home to a teeming moped-riding college crowd and a collection of pleasant and eclectic museums.

⊑ TRANSPORTATION. Baroda is accessible by bus, train, and plane from locations throughout India. **Trains** go to: **Ahmedabad** (2hr., 20 per day); **Delhi** (17hr., 9:53pm); **Mumbai** (6-7hr., 18 per day). **Buses** go to: **Ahmedabad** (every 15min. 5am-10pm, Rs50) and **Mumbai** (5:30pm, Rs170). **Indian Airlines** runs flights to **Mumbai** (daily) and **Delhi** (daily 7:45am). **Jet Airways** flies to **Delhi** (daily 8:10pm) and **Mumbai** (daily 7:10am and 7:20pm). **Gujarat Airways** flies to **Ahmedabad** (daily 7:30am); **Pune** (daily 7:30am); **Mumbai** (M, W, F 8:30pm). Auto-rickshaws are ubiquitous in Baroda, but taxis are rare. As always, insist that drivers use the meter, although fares are seldom what the meter reads, so when in doubt, demand to see the "official" fare card. Government and some private buses departing from the **Kirti Stumb bus stand** head to outlying towns and villages near Baroda.

◧⑦ ORIENTATION AND PRACTICAL INFORMATION. The **Vishramitri River** bisects Baroda. To the west lies the ritzier **Alkapuri, Sayajigunj,** and **Fategunj** districts, to the east the **Sur Sagar Lake** with its imposing Shiva statue, and the labyrinthine **Old City.** From the train station, **Tilak Road** crosses the river by the **Sayaji Bagh Park,** while **Chhori Road** leads north to the **Bus Station.** The **Tourist Office** is in **Narmada Bhavan,** on Jail Road, just opposite the **Police Bhavan.** (☎2437489. Open daily 10:15am-6:10pm, closed 2nd and 4th Sa and holidays.) **Pharmacies** and **Internet Cafes** are on almost every corner. **Thomas Cook Travel Agents,** 25/26 Shiram Chambers, opposite Circuit House on RC Dutt Road, exchanges traveler's checks. (☎2350469. Open daily 9:30am-5:30pm.) The **post office** can be found at Alkapuri Society, Alkapuri. (Open daily 10:30am-3:30pm.)

⑤◲ ACCOMMODATIONS AND FOOD. Hotels cluster around the train station; for more upscale digs at slightly higher prices, head to Alkapuri or Sayajigunj. **Hotel Kalyan ❷,** Sayajigunj, offers elegantly furnished modern rooms, some with balcony and TV, at the top of a steep white staircase. (☎2362211. Non-A/C singles Rs200-450; doubles Rs300-400.) **Hotel Surya Sayajigunj ❸** has tasteful rooms with TV and cable. (☎2361361. Breakfast included. Singles Rs500; doubles Rs750.) For truly budget accomodation, **R.V. Dongre's Traveller's Lodge ❶,** Kadak Bazar Corner, opposite the railway station, has spartan rooms and squat toilets. (☎2363621 or 2225080; vivekdongre@hotmail.com. Singles Rs80; doubles Rs125, each additional person Rs25.)

The **Crispy Crème ❶,** GEB Cir., at the end of RC Dutt Rd. on the right in Alkapuri, serves western baked goods, including flaky French croissants, olive oil and garlic focaccia, melt-in-your-mouth chocolate chip cookies, and calzones. (☎5909560. Open daily 7:30am-10pm.) The **New Alka Restaurant ❸,** Sandeep Apartment, RC Dutt Rd., across from Siddharth Complex, specializes in South Indian cuisine, but also offers Chinese food, excellent *dosas*, and mixed fruit juices. (☎2332315. Open daily 8am-11pm.) Join Baroda's collegiate hipsters for Mexican, Indian, Chinese, and Italian food at **Kalyan Restaurant ❶,** Sayajigunj. (☎2332315. Entrees Rs10-40. Open daily 7am-11pm.) **Hotel Surya Restaurant ❸,** Sayajigunj, has attentive waiters who dish out excellent unlimited veg. *thali* options (Rs70). (☎2361361. Open 11am-2:30pm, 7:30-11pm.) Guard against Gujarat's heat at **Janta Ice Cream Parlor ❷,** Helixraj Trade Center, Sayajigunj, serving Baroda's best and cheapest ice cream. (Dishes Rs50.)

◔ SIGHTS. At **Laxmi Vilas Palace,** on the sprawling grounds of the Gaekwad Maharaja's familial home, the cries of quails and the occasional lawnmower replace Baroda's usual auditory wallpaper of car horns and rickshaw engines. The palace itself is intricately decorated with stained glass and mosaics, a welcome respite from Baroda's semi-urban chaos. Walk down the long dirt road

GUJARAT

and through the narrow path barely marked entry, before crossing the leafy courtyard. Murano tile mosaics line the inner and outer facades, between elaborate carvings, portraits, and taxidermied trophies. An enormous ballroom hints at the grandeur that clearly remains undiminished in this upscale urbania of Baroda. Baroda's reputation as once a city of parks and greenery lives on in the lawns and paths of the **Sayajibagh park.** Families picnic and schoolgroups wander between the park's several attractions. **The Baroda Museum of Art,** in the center of the park, has a smidgeon of everything—from Chinese, Japanese, and Indian art to displays on the ethnic origins' many turban styles. There is also a an entire section on whales and a copper urn that once contained Mahatma Gandhi's ashes. (Open daily 10:30am-5pm. Indians Rs10, foreigners Rs150.) Other diversions within the park include a **planetarium.** (Open daily. 35min. shows in Gujarati 4pm, English 5pm, Hindi 6pm. Rs5.) The **Health Museum** will frighten you into hygiene with its dioramas on good health and illness. (Open daily 11am-6pm. Free.) A small **zoo** rounds out the park. One gate down from the Laxmi Vilas Palace entrance, and well-hidden down along the lane lined with crumbling but inhabited palace outbuildings, the **Maharaja Fatesingh Museum** pays homage to the Barodan maharajas. The museum's elegant furnishings and brightly painted rooms provide the paintings a setting befitting their royal subjects. Friendly guides demonstrate some of the quirkier tricks of the eye in the central first floor room. From one doorway, the white horses on either side of the room seem to face each other; from the other, they stare stonily ahead. The museum also has a small collection of unremarkable European art, some beautiful glass work, and a reconstructed French sitting room. (Open Tu-Su 10:30am-5:30pm. Adults Rs15, children Rs10, foreigners Rs100.)

▶ DAYTRIP FROM BARODA: CHAMPANER AND PAVAGADH. Several forts and the remains of temples are all that is left of the glorious medieval capital of Gujarat. After great conflict over control of the Champaner-Pavagadh area, it rose to the pinnacle of medieval Gujarati society. Champaner was displaced as the capital in the 16th century, however, when the state seat was moved back to Ahmedabad. The city never regained its former stature. Today, fragments of the past are visible in the outer fort walls of Champaner and the mosques remaining are scattered throughout the town, earning the sight a place on the World Monuments Fund's list of the 100 most endangered heritage sights. Scaling the hill across the street, the hillside area of Machi leads up to the fortifications atop Pavagadh Hill and the still-functioning mosque at its peak.

Cross from the bus stand through the fort gates to meander through the temples and small villages. The Rs100 entrance fee for the **Shakri Masjid** will also cover entrance to the elaborate **Jami Masjid.** Bear right from Shakri Masjid through the town and head down to the minarets. Jami Masjid's elegant cloisters enclose serene gardens and romantic archways, under the watch of imposing minarets and the protective web of windows with stone tracery. Across the street from the Champaner fort, just down from the bus stand, a winding road leads up **Pavagadh Hill** toward the hilltop forts. Municipal buses and jeeps head up and down frequently (Rs7). From the weigh station mid-way up, start climbing along the wide, cobbled path to enlightenment, through the small villages, past countless *saddhus* and *pakhora* vendors, and the tourist area stands lining the way. At the top, pilgrims line up to pay their respects in the highest hilltop temple, which commands excellent views of the valley below. Heading right at the small temples in the last village, cross the plain to the remains of a simple but many-domed stone temple, more secluded but consequently used as a hangout for fieldtripping kids. *(Champaner is most easily accessed by bus from Baroda. 1½hr., every 30min., Rs25.)*

RAJKOT રાજકોટ ☎ 0281

Rajkot is a clean, relaxed, typical Gujarati town, primarily of interest to travelers as a gateway to the Kathiawar Peninsula. Founded in the 16th century, it was the capital of the state of Saurashtra and an important administrative center for the Raj. Its recent fame is mostly due to its connection to Mahatma Gandhi, who spent his youth in Rajkot. Here Gandhi went to school, got married, and received permission from his mother to go to England. The rest, as they say, is history.

▐ TRANSPORTATION

Flights: Rajkot Airport (☎2454533), 4km northwest of town. **Indian Airlines,** Dhebar Rd. (☎2234122), near the circle. Open daily 10am-1pm and 2-8pm. Purchase tickets before 4:30pm for flights to **Mumbai** (2hr., daily 5:50pm, US$76. 25% discount for passengers under 30). **Jet Airways,** 78 Bilkha Plaza, Kasturba Rd. (☎2479623 or 2479624), opposite Lord's Banquet Restaurant. Open M-Sa 9:30am-7pm, Su 9:30am-6:30pm. Also offers flights to **Mumbai** (1hr., daily 11:25am and 8:30pm, US$79).

Trains: Rajkot Railway Station (☎131 or 2443535), 2km north of city center. To: **Ahmedabad** (5hr., 6-8 per day 6:25am-12:40am, Rs67-107); **Bhuj** (6½hr., 7:05am, Rs71-113); **Dwarka** (5½hr., 1-3 per day, Rs63-100); **Veraval** (5½hr., 10:55am, Rs54) via **Junagadh** (3½hr., Rs35).

Buses: Main Bus Stand (☎2235025). To: **Ahmedabad** (5hr., hourly 5am-10pm, Rs84); **Bhuj** (7hr., 15 per day 4:45am-11:30pm, Rs80); **Diu** (6hr., 5 per day 6:45am-2:30pm, Rs110); **Dwarka** (6hr., 13 per day 4:45am-12:30pm, Rs85); **Junagadh** (2hr., every 30min. 6am-midnight, Rs43); **Somnath** and **Veraval** (4hr., every hr. 6am-midnight, Rs75.) **Private bus companies,** opposite the bus stand, go to cities in Gujarat and Rajasthan.

Local Transportation: Auto-rickshaws buzz to the airport (Rs20-25). **Local buses** can take you anywhere in the city (Rs5), though "anywhere" might not be where you wanted to go. **Chakka-rickshaws** (*tempo*-motorcycle hybrids) go most places (Rs5-10).

▟ ▐ ORIENTATION AND PRACTICAL INFORMATION

Everything of interest in Rajkot is sandwiched between the **railway station** to the north and the **bus stand** to the south. The bus stand is on **Dhebar Road,** which darts north to **Trikonbaug,** a major circle that marks the city center. East of the circle is **Lakhajiraj Road;** west is an intersection at the eastern edge of the **Playing Fields.** To the left, **Dr. Yagnik Road** heads south and circles the fields; to the right, **Jawahar Road** runs north past Jubilee Gardens to the Civil Hospital and **Junction Road.** A right at Junction Rd. and a left onto **Station Road** takes you to the railway station. From the Civil Hospital, **Kasturba Road** leads to the **race course,** west of the Playing Fields.

Tourist Office: Tourist Information Bureau (☎2234507). Behind the State Bank of Saurashtra at the south end of Jawahar Rd.; ground fl. in the yellow brick bldg. Open M-Sa 10:30am-6pm; closed 2nd and 4th Sa.

Currency Exchange: Bank of Baroda, MG Rd. (☎2227404). Exchanges currency and traveler's checks. Open daily M-S 11am-3pm. **24hr. ATM** for ICI Bank, opposite statue in Trikonbaug.

Police: Police Commissioner's Office (☎2477220), opposite the race course next to Galaxy Cinema. The **control room** (☎100) is open 24hr.

Hospital: Civil Hospital (☎2440298), at the intersection of Kasturba Rd. and Jawahar Rd. Clean facilities, English-speaking staff, and **24hr. pharmacy.**

GUJARAT

Internet: Interlink Cyber Cafe, just off Lakhajiraj Rd. The first major right as you walk away from the statue. Look for the sign on the left. Rs20 per hr. Open daily 10am-12:30am.

Post Office: GPO, MG Rd. (☎2228611), west of Jawahar Rd., opposite Jubilee Gardens. Open M-Sa 10am-6pm. **Postal Code:** 360001.

▐▀ ACCOMMODATIONS

Budget hotels dot the railway station area and Lakhajiraj Rd. Business hotels surround the Playing Fields. There are plenty of both behind the bus stand.

Vishram Guest House, Lakhajiraj Rd. (☎2230555 or 2229208), the blue-and-white bldg. opposite Rainbow Restaurant. The best deal in town, with spotless rooms, attached baths, and TVs. Check-out 4pm. Reservations recommended, even in the off-season. Singles Rs150-190; doubles Rs275-325. ❷

R.R. Hotels, Dhebar Rd. (☎2236811), between Jawahar Rd. and Para Bazaar. A decent choice if Vishram is full. All rooms have picture windows with views of the city and hot showers in tiny, but clean bathrooms. Singles Rs322-430; doubles Rs400-645. ❷

Hotel Moon Guest House (☎225522). Behind the bus stand, look up. Don't be deterred by the betel-stained walls in the stairwell. Plain rooms similar to the ones you'd find in the countless hotels in the vicinity, but with clean bathrooms and great views from the terrace. All rooms have phones. Singles and doubles Rs150-200. ❶

The Galaxy Hotel, Jawahar Rd. (☎2222904; galaxyhotel@wilnetonline.net), just north of the Playing Fields. Rajkot's biggest, oldest hotel has a wide range of rooms, all spacious and decorated with local children's artwork. The autographed bats of the West Indies cricket team are on display in the lobby. The team stayed here for its 2002 tour. Singles Rs440-990; doubles Rs660-1485; suites Rs1760-2640. Add 10-15% tax. ❸

▐▘ FOOD

An abundance of food stalls and fast food patios crowd the street behind the bus stand. Fruit vendors can be found on MG Rd. and Lakhajiraj Rd. by the bazaar.

Lord's Banquet Restaurant, Kasturba Rd. Flowers on every table, attentive service, cushy A/C booths, and an enormous selection of Chinese, continental, and Indian veg. specialties (Rs45-98) elevate this restaurant above the pack. Open daily 12:30am-3pm and 7:30-11:30pm. ❸

Rainbow Restaurant, Lakhajiraj Rd., under the Himalaya Guest House. Cheap South Indian veg. snacks (Rs15-30), Punjabi and Chinese dishes, and 40 novelty ice cream confections. Dodge the flies and head upstairs for the A/C. Open daily 9am-11pm. ❶

Chalks 'n' Cues Sugar 'n' Spice, Kasturba Rd., ground floor of Bilkha Plaza across from Lord's Banquet Restaurant. Tasty Gujarati approximations of Western diner grub. A nice break from the Punjabi/Chinese restaurants. Billiards next door Rs50 per game. Pizza Rs70-140. "Loaded" *parathas* Rs65. Open daily 11am-11pm. ❸

Jai Ganga Restaurant, Jawahar Rd., across from the Galaxy Hotel. A wrap-around, textured mural of pastoral Indian scenes whisks patrons away from the noise and grit just outside. Gujarati *thalis* Rs45. Chinese and Punjabi dishes Rs35-80. Open daily 11am-3pm and 6:30-11pm. ❷

◉ SIGHTS

Flanked by stone lions, the **Watson Museum** is dedicated to Colonel John Watson, a 19th-century British political agent. The museum houses artifacts from the ancient Indus Valley civilization, exquisite miniature paintings, Gujarati handicrafts and metalwork, and classical Indian musical instruments. (In the Jubilee Gardens. Open M-Sa 9am-1pm and 2-6pm; closed 2nd and 4th Sa. Rs50.) The **Kabo Gandhi no Delo** on Ghitaka Rd. was the Gandhi family's residence when they moved to Rajkot in 1881. It now features a small collection of photographs and memorabilia. Friendly caretaker gives a comprehensive tour. (Open M-Sa 9am-noon and 3-6pm. Small donations appreciated. Walk east down Lakhajiraj Rd. into the bazaar and start asking for directions.)

DIU દીવ ☎ 02875

Local life on the small island of Diu, off the southern coast of Gujarat, revolves around the pursuit of fish and alcohol. For tourists, it revolves around the pursuit of sun, sand, and, well, alcohol. A Portuguese colony until 1961, when India reclaimed it, Diu is now considered part of Union Territory rather than part of Gujarat. As a result, Gujarat's alcohol prohibition laws don't apply here, making it prime party ground for the thousands of Gujaratis who descend upon the island every weekend. Despite this weekly migration, Diu's streets are quiet, its beaches serene, and its people accommodating.

▄ TRANSPORTATION

Flights: Diu Airport, 5km west of Diu Town, north of Nagoa Beach (auto-rickshaw Rs30). **Goa Travels** (☎ 252180), off Bunder Rd., next to the GPO. Books domestic and international flights. Open daily 9am-1pm and 3-7pm. Jet Airways flights to **Mumbai** via **Porbander** (3hr., daily 12:15pm, US$100). Departures are often delayed or canceled.

Trains: Delwada Railway Station (☎ 222226), between Una and Goghla, 8km from Diu Town (auto-rickshaw Rs100). To: **Junagadh** (7hr., 1:30pm, Rs35) via **Sasan Gir** (5hr., Rs20) and **Veraval** (4½hr., 6:30am, Rs23).

Buses: ST Bus Stand, just outside the city's northern gate. To: **Ahmedabad** (10hr., 7:30am, Rs100); **Rajkot** (6½hr., 6 per day 5am-2:30pm, Rs80); **Una** (30min., every 30min. 6am-10pm, Rs7); **Veraval** (2½hr.; 4, 5am, 2:15pm; Rs25). The **Una Bus Stand** (☎ 221600) services: **Ahmedabad** (9½hr., 9 per day 6am-10:30pm, Rs95); **Junagadh** (5½hr., 6 per day 4am-7:45pm, Rs50); **Rajkot** (6hr., every hr. 5am-7:45pm, Rs70); **Veraval** (2hr., every 30min. 5:30am-8pm, Rs20). **Private bus companies** surround the Main Sq. and send buses to destinations around Gujarat and to Mumbai. **Reshma Travels** (☎ 252383), near the mosque, opposite Nilech Guest House, books private bus, train, and airline tickets. Open M-Sa 9am-8:30pm and 9:30-11pm, Su 9:30am-1pm and 6-10pm.

Local Transportation: Auto-rickshaws travel within Diu Town (Rs5-10) and go to Nagoa Beach (Rs30-40) and Una (Rs100). A 3hr. tour costs about Rs150. Night travel out of Diu Town costs an extra Rs20. **Local buses,** departing from the Main Sq., service **Nagoa Beach** (departs 8, 11am, 4pm, returns 30min. later; Rs5). **Private buses,** departing from the ST Bus Stand, go to **Delwada** (every hr. 6am-7pm, 9:30pm; Rs8-10). Buses from ST Bus Stand to Una (see above) also stop at Delwada (Rs5-10). **Bikes** or **mopeds** are the best bet for getting around. **A to Z Travel Center,** Mota Ishwar Temple, Vania Sheri (☎ 254080), behind the high school, rents mopeds (Rs100 per day), scooters (Rs150 per day), and bicycles (Rs20 per day); also offers roadside assistance. **Kismat Cycle Store** (☎ 252971), behind Main Sq. near the high school, also rents bikes (Rs15 per day) and mopeds (Rs100 per day). Open M-Sa 9am-8pm, Su 9am-1pm.

GUJARAT

✳ 🛈 ORIENTATION AND PRACTICAL INFORMATION

Diu town occupies the small eastern tip of the island. **Bunder Road** runs from the bridge into town through the northern gate, along the coast to the rickshaw stand in the Main Square. Bunder Rd. continues east, becomes **Fort Road** and terminates at **Diu Fort,** which marks the extreme eastern tip of the town and island. The main **Bazaar** runs parallel to Bunder Rd., from the southern end of the bus stand through the middle gate, past the mosque, high school, and vegetable market before angling toward **St. Paul's Church.** The main road in the southern part of town runs east along the coast past **Sunset Point, Chakratirth,** and **Jallandhar Beaches,** bending past the hospital and St. Thomas' Church to Bunder Rd. **Nagoa Beach** and the **Diu Airport** are near the middle of the island, and are most easily reached by rickshaw.

Tourist Office: Tourist Information Bureau, Bunder Rd. (☎252653), near Main Sq., has maps (Rs10) and information. Open M-Sa 9-1:30pm and 2:30-6pm.

Currency Exchange: State Bank of Saurashtra (☎252135), around the corner from the GPO. Open M-F 10am-2pm, Sa 10am-noon. The authorized changers offer better rates and faster service. **Mayur Suitings** (☎253686), opposite Nilesh Guest House, is a reliable changer. Open M-Sa 8:45am-1:15pm and 3:30-7:30pm, Su 8:45am-1:15pm.

Market: Most markets and stores are closed M-Sa 1-3pm and Su. The **fish market** is behind the Main Sq.; the **vegetable market** is farther down Bunder Rd., 200m past the Main Sq. Open daily 8am-noon.

Police: Fort Rd. (☎252133), past the Collectorate on the left. 24hr.

Pharmacy: Manesh Medical Stores, Dr. Ragaram Kelkar Rd. (☎252253), up the road from Nilech Guest House. Open M-Sa 8am-1pm and 2:30-8pm, Su 8:30am-12:30pm.

Hospital: Government Hospital (☎102), in St. Francis of Assisi Church, 200m north of Jallandhar Beach. English-speaking. Emergency room open 24hr.

Internet: Deepee Communications, Bunder Rd., below the GPO. Open 9am-11pm. **A to Z Travel Center** (see. local transportation above). Both charge Rs40 per hr. Connections on the island are notoriously sluggish.

Post Office: GPO, Bunder Rd. (☎252122), in Main Sq. Open M-Sa 9am-noon and 2-5pm. **Postal Code:** 362520.

🏠 ACCOMMODATIONS

Considering that most visitors to Diu are only looking for a place to pass out after a night of drinking, most hotels in Diu Town have no real incentive to impress. The best accommodations are located near the island's various beaches. In the off season (roughly Feb.-Oct.), discounts can be substantial, but you'll need to bargain. Avoid the island during Diwali, Holi, Christmas, and New Year's when the hotel prices skyrocket due to the massive holiday demand. Free-standing bars are prohibited, so they masquerade as restaurants, offering only the minimum amount of food required by law. For an actual meal, hotels are your best bet.

▨ The Resort Hoka (☎253036), near Nagoa Beach, 200m from the ocean. Breezy, palm-shaded Hoka is the best value here. Wordly Aditya and his laid-back staff make guests feel at home. New pool. Clean, comfortable doubles, most with bath Rs250-950. ❷

Jay Shankar Guest House, Jallandhar Beach (☎252424 or 252050). Caters to backpackers. Aging rooms, but peaceful location. Restaurant serves Indian and Western dishes. French toast Rs15, excellent seafood Rs50-75. Dorms Rs80; singles Rs100-200; doubles Rs150-250. Off-season Rs50/80-130/100-150. ❶

Hotel Samrat, Old Collectorate Rd. (☎252354 or 254554; fax 252754), near the vegetable market. Shiny tiled floors, large attached bathrooms and attentive management separates this hotel from the rest of the pack in town. TVs and phone in every room. Restaurant and bar downstairs. Doubles Rs500-1200; off-season Rs250-1000. ❸

Hotel Prince, Main Bazaar (☎252265), northwest of the Main Sq. Clean but lacks character. Attached restaurant. Doubles Rs300-800; off-season Rs200-600. ❸

◖ FOOD

Rio Restaurant (☎252209), in the Kohinoor Hotel in Fudam. A little out of the way, One of Diu's two luxury hotels has a good restaurant serving Indian and Chinese food (Rs45-190) and beer (Rs35-45). Open daily 7am-11pm. ❸

Local Thali House, the unmarked yellow bldg. with arched veranda, opposite the circular planting 200m up the road from Jay Shankar Guest House. Escape the tourist fare in town and join locals at this private home-turned-restaurant. *Thalis* Rs35. Open daily noon-2pm and 7:30-8:30pm. Bring your own mineral water. ❷

Ram Vijay, just off the main square, near the GPO and bank. It's unclear whether Gujaratis flock to Diu for the alcoholic beverages or Ram Vijay's sinfully sweet drinks. Try the "hand-made" drinks and ice cream (Rs5-20). Sweet fresh lemon soda (Rs7) is fantastic. Open 8am-1pm and 3-10pm. ❶

◉ ◖ SIGHTS AND BEACHES

The massive **Diu Fort,** built between 1535 and 1541, is guarded by a tidal moat, which once made it virtually impenetrable. There is little to do here except wander through the cannons and cannonballs and catch the beautiful views over the sea and town. (At the end of Bunder Rd. Open daily 8am-6pm.) From the fort, you can also see the **Fortress of Panikota,** a stone structure that now floats in the middle of the sea and was used as a prison by the Portuguese.

Wandering through the labyrinthine streets is the best way to see the Portuguese-influenced old city. **Nagar Seth's Haveli** is the most impressive and distinctively Portuguese building in Diu Town (near A to Z Tourist Center; ask for directions once you're in the old city). **St. Paul's Church** is badly weathered but still has grand ceilings and arches, excellent paintings, and a beautiful organ. Mass is still spoken here every Sunday. (Open daily 8am-9pm.) Nearby, St. Thomas' Church houses the Diu Museum, with its Catholic paintings and statues. (Open daily 8am-9pm. Free.) The **Naida caves** make for an intriguing spelunk and cool refuge from the mid-day heat. (North of Chakratirth Beach just outside city walls.) **The Seashell Museum** displays a retired sailor's collection of shells from around the world. The captain is friendly and quick with an explanation about his pieces. (Rs10. Near Diu Airport, 1km from Nagoa Beach. Open.)

Travelers sick of (or from) drinking might enjoy one of Diu's excellent beaches. The island's most famous is **Nagoa Beach,** 7km west of town. Secluded **Gomti Mata Beach** is 2km past Nagoa and features bigger surf and no crowds or vendors (but also no shade). On the southern side of Diu Town, **Jallandhar Beach** is rocky but great for wading. **Chakratirth Beach,** to the west of Diu Town, is better for swimming, and nearby **Sunset Point** is a favorite local hangout. Across the bridge from Diu Town, **Goghla's** long beach is great for swimming and has fewer tourists—but less shade—than Nagoa Beach. **Auto-rickshaws** shuttle from the bazaar to Jallandhar Beach and Chakratirth (Rs20), Goghla Beach (Rs20), and Nagoa Beach (Rs30).

GUJARAT

VERAVAL વેરાવળ AND SOMNATH સોમનાથ

☎ **02876**

The busy city of Veraval is Saurashtra's most important port, home to a thriving *dhow*-building industry, and harboring over 1000 boats. The docks are a fascinating area through which to stroll—if you can stomach the foul stench—but Veraval is more important to travelers as a stepping stone to nearby Somnath, just 5km away. Somnath, known for its once-magnificent temple, is a popular vacation spot.

TRANSPORTATION. From **ST bus stand** (☎221666), **buses** go to: **Ahmedabad** (10hr., every 2hr. 6:45am-11pm, Rs120); **Diu** (2½hr., 4 per day 7:30am-5:15pm, Rs45); **Dwarka** (7hr.; 7:30, 10:30am, and 4pm; Rs80); **Junagadh** (2hr., every hr. 5am-midnight, Rs40); **Rajkot** (5hr., every hr. 6:30am-10:30pm, Rs70). **Local buses** run from the clocktower to **Somnath** and back (every 30min. 6am-11pm, Rs2). **Auto-rickshaws** make the same trip for Rs30. **Veraval Railway Station** (☎220660; reservation office open M-Sa 8am-8pm, Su 8am-2pm). To: **Ahmedabad** (11hr., 5 and 7:25pm, Rs180); **Junagadh** (2hr., 6 per day 7:10am-3:40am, Rs32); **Rajkot** (5½hr., 6 per day 7:10am-3:40am, Rs95).

ORIENTATION AND PRACTICAL INFORMATION. ST Road, Veraval's main thoroughfare, runs roughly northwest-southeast past the **ST bus stand,** through the center of town, past the **clock tower,** and to a dead-end at the port. At the clock tower, Somnath Rd. heads northeast, past the first left that heads toward the **GPO** (☎221255, open M-Sa 10am-6pm), before bending around the railroad sidings. A left off Somnath Rd. where it bends right heads to the **railway station.** After the bend the road passes the noxious harbor on its way to Somanth. The **State Bank of Saurashtra,** Shubash Rd., past the clock tower toward the port, exchanges currency and traveler's checks. (Open M-F 11am-3pm, Sa 11am-1pm.) A branch of the **police station** is to the right of the tower. (☎272037. Open 24hr.) **Magic Cyber Point,** on ST Rd. across from Sagar Restaurant, is pleasantly surfable. (Open daily 10am-1:30am. Rs25.) The **bus stand** in **Somnath** is within view of the temple in the heart of the small town. **Postal Code:** 362265.

ACCOMMODATIONS AND FOOD. Hotels line the route between the bus stand and the railway station. Although staying in Veraval is more convenient, the hotels in Somnath are cheaper and far more peaceful, if slightly spartan. **Hotel Kaveri ❷,** Akar complex, 2nd floor, is on the first side street on the left to the left after you exit the Veraval bus station. Offers upscale hotel luxuries for budget hotel prices. The rooms here come with TVs and 24hr. hot water. The hotel also has laundry service and 24hr. room service. (☎220842 or 243842. Singles Rs200-550; doubles Rs350-650.) **Hotel Ajanta ❶,** on the right as you exit the Veraval bus stand, has very basic rooms in a central location. Laundry and 24hr. room service. (☎223202. Singles Rs100-300; doubles Rs150-350.) In Somnath, **Hotel Shivam ❷** is conveniently located to the right of the bus stand as you face the temple. Clean, airy rooms some with carpeting, TV, and balconies, all with attached bath. (☎231451 or 233086. Singles Rs150-450. Doubles Rs300-550.) Most restaurants in Veraval are between the bus stand and the clock tower. Somnath has many food stalls but few real restaurants. Though Veraval is a fishing town, pious Gujarati culture relegates seafood to a handful of hotels and Muslim restaurants. Meat is nowhere to be found in Somnath. **Sagar Restaurant ❸,** off ST Rd. across from Hotel Kaveri, serves standard Punjabi, Chinese, and Continental fare (Rs30-90) amidst flashing Christmas lights and a rock garden. (Open daily 9am-3:30pm and 5-11pm.) For delectable unlimited *thalis*, head over to **Prakash Dining Hall ❷**, ST Rd., top floor of the building to the left of the Swastik Building. (Open daily 10:30am-3pm and 6:30-10:30pm. Closed Su evening. *Thalis* Rs40.)

🔲 **SIGHTS.** Somnath is renowned throughout Gujarat for the **Temple of Somnath,** a beautiful tableau cut against the sea. Also known as **Prabhas Pratan Mandir,** it holds one of India's 12 *jyotirlingas.* According to popular myth, the temple site was dedicated to *soma,* a hallucinogenic plant that appears in the *Vedas* (see **Vedic Literature,** p. 75). People say the temple was built first of pure gold by Samraj, the moon god, then of silver by Ravana, the sun god, then of wood by Krishna, and finally of stone by the Pandava brother, Bhima (of *Mahabharata* fame). Boring old historians, however, contend that the temple was built in the early 10th century AD, and that it has always been made of stone. The temple was once staffed by hundreds of dancers and musicians and was so rich that its coffers were stuffed with gold and jewelry. The notorious Mahmud of Ghazni put an end to all that when he raided and destroyed the temple in the early 11th century, starting a cycle of pillaging and rebuilding that persisted until Aurangzeb's final plundering in 1706. Sardar Patel, the philanthropist who funded the temple's reconstruction in 1950, is commemorated with a statue that stands outside the temple. The history of the temple is more interesting than the building itself; very little of the original structure remains. The stonework is quite elaborate in places, but the sea winds have worn down the carving on the ocean-side walls. (Open daily 6am-9:30pm; *puja* 7am, noon, 7pm. No cameras allowed inside.) The **Prabhas Pratan Museum,** a 5min. walk down the road to the right of the temple, holds the varied remains of the temple's past glories, including paintings, latticework, stone sculptures, and pottery. (Open M-Sa 9am-noon and 3-6pm; closed 2nd and 4th Sa.)

JUNAGADH જૂનાગઢ ☎0285

Less than 100km north of Diu, the lively town of Junagadh, also known as Junagarh, is refreshingly free of large numbers of foreign tourists. Situated at the base of Mount Girnar, Junagadh's wealth of temples, *havelis*, mosques, and vibrant bazaars makes it one of Gujarat's most compelling cities as well as a fascinating place to get lost. From the 4th century BC until Emperor Ashoka's death, Junagadh was the capital of Mauryan Gujarat. Control of the town then passed through several hands before falling under Muslim rule, where it remained until Independence. Although its leaders wanted to unite Junagadh with Pakistan, the town's Hindu majority insisted on joining India. While the town is typically less than packed, expect crowds when the town hosts a wild, four-day party replete with naked *sadhus* during **Shivaratri** (late Feb. or early Mar.).

🔲 **TRANSPORTATION.** From the **ST Bus Stand** (☎2630303), buses go to: **Ahmedabad** (7hr., every hr. 4:30am-1am, Rs100); **Bhuj** (7hr., 6 per day 8:30am-10pm, Rs85); **Dwarka** (6hr., 5 per day 6:45am-4pm, Rs75); **Rajkot** (2hr., every 30min. 4:30am-1am, Rs43); **Una** for **Diu** (4hr., 13 per day 6am-11pm, Rs63); **Veraval** (2hr., every 30min. 6am-11pm, Rs42). **Private bus companies** along Dhal Rd. run comfortable minibuses and buses to **Mumbai,** direct to Diu, and elsewhere in Gujarat. **Junagadh Railway Station** (☎131) is on Station Rd. Reservation office open M-Sa 8am-8pm, Su 8am-2pm. The Junagadh line is undergoing a change from meter gauge to broad gauge. Travel times should reduce when the change is complete. Trains run to: **Ahmedabad** (9hr., 7:06 and 9:23pm, Rs157); **Rajkot** (3hr., 1:35pm, Rs35); **Veraval** (2hr.; 3 per day 6:15, 8:59am, 2:13pm; Rs32). You can walk just about anywhere in 15min., or **auto-rickshaws** can toot you around town for Rs5-10. **Rickshaws** to Mt. Girnar cost Rs35. **Bikes** (Rs5 per hr., Rs30 per day) can be rented around Chittakhana Chowk.

GUJARAT

▉ ▌ ORIENTATION AND PRACTICAL INFORMATION. From the **ST Bus Stand, Dhal Road,** the main thoroughfare, runs east, crossing the tracks and through **Chittakhana Chowk** (marked by twin minarets) on its way up to **Uperkot Fort.** Just after the tracks **Rajkot Road** runs north to the train station. At Chittakhana Chowk, **Mahatma Gandhi (MG) Road** branches south, passing the **Government Hospital** (☎ 2620652, open 24hr.), and **Azad Chowk,** where the **local bus stand,** a branch of the **GPO** (☎ 2623701; open M-Sa 9:30am-6pm, Speedpost counter M-F 10am-3:30pm, Sa 10am-1:30pm), and the main **police station** (☎ 2655778), cluster on its way to **Kalwa Chowk,** another market area. **Internet** can be found on Jayshree Talkies Rd., a right off MG Rd. at Kalwa Chowk. (Rs20 per hr. Open daily 10am-1am.) Halfway between Chittakhana Chowk and Uperkot Fort, **Jhalorapa Road** branches south off Dhal Rd. through Diwan Chowk, near the **State Bank of India.** (☎ 2621094. Open M-F 11am-4pm, Sa 11am-2pm.) **Pharmacies** are in Kalwa and Chittakhana Chowk near the Government Hospital. **Shree Medical Stores,** Dhal Rd., is just west of the railway crossing. (☎ 2631818. Open 24hr.) **Postal Code:** 362001.

▐ ACCOMMODATIONS. Most hotels are on Dhal Rd. in and around Chittakhana and Kalwa Chowks, but there are also a few near the ST Bus Stand and the railway station. Reserve well in advance during Shivaratri.

▉ Hotel Relief, Chittakhana Chowk (☎ 2620280). The gracious and helpful staff has unofficially assumed the role of the town's tourist information center. Above-average rooms with baths. The hotel has a great city map on the wall, and dispenses information on sights and bus and train departure times. Singles Rs150; doubles Rs200-400. ❷

Hotel Somnath, Rajkot Rd. (☎ 2624645), on the right as you exit the railway station, is on the quieter outskirts of the town center. Somnath has bright, well-furnished rooms and clean attached baths with hot water. Popular with the business crowd. Singles Rs200-600; doubles Rs300-700. ❷

Hotel Anand, Dhal Rd. (☎ 2630657 or 2631228), between the ST Bus Stand and Chittakhana Chowk. Dimly lit, clean rooms with attached baths in a somewhat noisy area. All with TVs. Singles Rs100-200; doubles Rs250-700. ❶

Lion Hills Resorts, Girnar Rd. (☎ 2652844; lhresort_ad1@sacharnet.in), east of Uperkot Fort on the road to Mt. Girnar. Despite the fun fair appearance with its go-karts and min-golf facilities, the resort offers huge, comfortable, rooms all with attached bath, TV and 24hr. room service. Swimming pool, health club, steam and sauna room and billiards available as well. Singles Rs800-1050; doubles Rs950-1200.❺

▐ FOOD. Although there are food stalls and *dhabas* in Chittakhana and Kalwa Chowks, they're your only dining option between 3-5pm. You'll find better fare at the hotel restaurants in town.

Sagar Restaurant, Jayshree Talkies Rd., near Kalwa Chowk. Serves excellent food in its dimly lit, A/C dining room. Try anything off the Sagar top ten list. Huge portions. Entrees Rs30-95. Open daily 9am-3pm and 5-10:45pm. ❷

Swati Restaurant, Jayshree Rd., near Jayshree Cinema. Hindi pop fills the chilly air as friendly waiters serve deliciously spiced entrees (Rs25-70) in this crowded veg. restaurant. Open daily 11am-3pm and 5:30-10:30pm. ❷

Santoor Restaurant, MG Rd., before Kalwa Chowk. The culinary tour of Junagadh's dimly lit, A/C restaurants concludes with Santoor. Popular spot with locals. Veg. dishes from Rs30-55. Open daily 9:45am-3pm and 5-11pm. ❷

Poonam Daining Hall, Dhal Rd., west of Chittakhana Chowk. Look for the sign across the street pointing down a side alley. Entrance is the yellow stairwell on the left. No-frills joint with never-ending *thalis* (Rs30). Open daily 11am-3pm and 6:30-10:30pm. ❶

◙ **SIGHTS.** The impressive **Uperkot Fort,** on top of a mini-plateau in the middle of the town, is one of the best in the state. Built in 319 BC, it was ignored for almost 1300 years until it was rediscovered in AD 976. Over the next 800 years, the fort was besieged 16 times; one ultimately unsuccessful siege lasted 12 years. A high stone *tripolia* gate marks the entrance to the fort and the start of the road that loops through the fort. A clockwise circuit on this road covers all the sights in the fort. First stop is to the **Jama Masjid,** built on top of a Hindu temple. Once an impressive edifice with 140 pillars supporting its high ceiling, the mosque has suffered from years of neglect. Next, 100m past the masjid, are the **Buddhist Caves.** Allegedly dating back to the 2nd century BC, two levels are open to the public. (Open daily 8am-6pm. Rs100.) Two step-wells burrow into the east side of the fort. The first, the **Adi Chadi Vav** has 170 steps, and the second, the extraordinary **Navghan Kuva,** with its unique 11th-century circular staircase, winds down 50m into the ground. On the way back out, the stairs on the left lead up to a shaded but poorly maintained park, and the fort walls protected by a 5m canon cast in Egypt in 1531. (Fort open daily 7am-7pm. Rs1.) From the fort, down the road and to the left through the double arched gate, is the **Durbar Hall Museum.** (Open Tu-Th 10:30am-5:30pm. Rs2.) The **Khapra Kodia Caves,** north of the fort—ask locals for directions—are also popular. (Open sunrise-sunset. Rs100.)

North of Chittakhana Chowk, on MG Rd., is the **striking Baha-ud-din-Bhar Maqbara,** with its spiraling minarets, grand arches, and numerous domes. The mausoleum's complex design and opulent interior make it unlike any other in Gujarat. The pastel **Jama Masjid** is next door. (Both open sunrise-sunset. Free.) On the way to Mt. Girnar is a granite boulder inscribed with **Ashokan edicts.** Dating from the 3rd century BC, these edicts teach moral lessons of *dharma,* tolerance, equality, love, peace, and harmony. The Sanskrit inscriptions, which refer to flooding in nearby areas, were added by later rulers. (Open daily 8am-6pm. Rs100.)

Mount Girnar, 4km east of Junagadh, is an 1100m extinct volcano that has been sacred to several religions for over 2000 years. Over 5000 steps wind through forest and past sun-scorched stone outcroppings to the summit. At about 4500 steps (1½-2hr.), you'll come upon a cluster of intricately decorated Jain temples. The marble **Neminath Temple** is dedicated to the 22nd *tirthankara* who, according to legend, died on Mt. Girnar. Its black marble image sits amid finely carved pillars, domes, and arches. Another 2000 steps take you to the mountain's peak, where the small **Amba Mata Temple** and several other shrines offer a breathtaking view. Since a visit to the temple is said to guarantee a happy marriage, the summit sees many newlyweds. Another 1000 steps, down then up, lead to the Gorakshnath Temple on the second peak, and yet another 1000 steps yields the Thethatri Temple on the third peak. It is possible to spend the night on the second, third, or fourth peak at the temples with the *yogis.* Bring enough fruit, biscuits, and water to last the night. The hike to the first peak takes approximately 5-6hr. round-trip, so begin your hike before 7am to avoid the heat. There are drink stalls along the way, but they are overpriced. If you plan to stay on the mountain, leave your pack in Junagadh. A daypack will suffice for the hike and your thighs will thank you.

NEAR JUNAGADH

▓ **SASAN GIR NATIONAL PARK**

*The park is accessible by **train** (Delwara Local 352, 3hr., 6:10am, Rs15) and **bus** (2hr., every hr. 6:30am-9pm, Rs28) from Junagadh. Buses run between Sasan and Veraval in both directions (2hr. every hr. 7am-6pm, Rs23). **Shared jeeps** are required to tour the park (Rs500 for up to six people; departures 6:30-9:30am and 3-5:30pm. Sanctuary* *open Oct. 16-Feb. 15 7am-noon and 3pm-sunset, Feb. 16-June 15 6:30-11am and 4pm-sunset). Entry fee Rs100. The fees can add up for the solo traveler, US$22 all told. The total price per person for a group of four is a more reasonable US$12. A knowledgeable local guide like **Raju** can help figure out these and other budget shortcuts. (Ask for him at any guest house in town. Tip as you like.) An average trip through the park takes about 3hr., during which you are likely to catch a glimpse of at least one of the lions, although there are no guarantees, especially in the afternoon. Wear earth tones, dark green is best. Visitors will have a better chance to glimpse the lions at the **Gir Interpretation Zone** in nearby Devalia, 15km northwest of Sasan. The Zone is an enclosure that houses 4-5 of the animals and while not a true safari experience, it offers a more certain photo opportunity. Same hours and fees as the sanctuary.*

Sasan Gir, 65km from Junagadh, is the last stronghold of the **Asiatic lion.** These great cats once roamed forests and grasslands all the way from Greece to Bengal, but by the turn of the 20th century, there were only 239 left on the planet. In 1900, the Nawab of Junagadh invited Lord Curzon, then Viceroy of India, to a lion hunt on his land, the only place outside Africa where wild lions could still be found. The two met a barrage of criticism for further endangering the threatened species, and Lord Curzon canceled the hunt, advising the Nawab to protect the lions. The forest became a wildlife sanctuary in 1969, and it now covers over 250 sq. km. The lion population (today more than 300) is increasing at a healthy rate. The park's forests and grasslands are also a sanctuary for peacocks, hyenas, panthers, and several varieties of deer.

There are a few cheap guest houses near the main park entrance. The government forest lodge near the reception office is terribly overpriced, especially for foreigners. **Hotel Annapurna ❶,** across from the bus stop and near the park reception offers clean, basic rooms with attached bath and lots of natural light. (☎ 02877 285569. Singles Rs100-200; doubles Rs200-350.) **Gumalbar Restaurant ❷** dishes unlimited *thalis* (Rs40). (Open daily 9am-3:30pm and 6:30-11pm.)

DWARKA द्वारका ☎ 02892

Most Hindu legends agree on the subject of Dwarka's holiness. The *Puranas* designate it as one of the seven holy cities in which pilgrims can attain *moksha.* Krishna set up his capital here, on the westernmost point of the Kathiawar peninsula, after being forced to flee Mathura in Uttar Pradesh. Vishnu descended to Dwarka in the form of a fish to battle local demons, and the 9th-century saint Shankara established a monastery here, marking it as India's western *dham.* Few tourists come here, so Dwarka is remarkable for its sense of peace, active temple, sea breezes, and mystical remoteness.

▐ TRANSPORTATION. Trains head from the railway station (☎ 234044; reservations office open M-Sa 8am-8pm, Su 8am-2pm). To: **Ahmedabad** (10hr., Rs176); **Mumbai** (20hr., 12:15pm, Rs292) via **Rajkot** (5hr., Rs63-100). **Intercity buses** run from the main bus stand (☎ 234204). To: **Ahmedabad** (10hr., 6 per day 7am-8:45pm, Rs127); **Bhuj** (10hr., 7:30am and 9:30pm, Rs120); **Junagadh** (7hr., 5 per day 9:30am-2:45pm, Rs71); **Mandvi** (10½hr., 7:30am, Rs130); **Rajkot** (5hr., 14 per day 4:45am-9:45am, Rs80); **Veraval** (6hr., 7 per day 5:45am-7:45pm, Rs82). **Local buses** shuttle to **Okha** (45min., every 30min. 6am-10pm, Rs13). Shared jeeps leave from the front of the bus stand when full (45min., Rs15).

▐▶▐ ORIENTATION AND PRACTICAL INFORMATION. The national highway approaches the town from the southeast and marks the town's eastern border. The highway bends left on the north side of town passing the two main gates. A right turn at the highway bend leads to the train station. The bus station is just past the GPO and the second main gate, where the highway heads out of town toward Okha, the port for **Bet Dwarka**. **Bhadrakali Road** begins as you pass through the second main gate and runs past **Hospital Road** to **Teen Batti Chowk**, the center of the Old City marked by the multicolored oversize candle-shaped monument. A right at the Chowk leads to the best hospital in town, **Navajyot Hospital** (☎234419), 50m down the road that eventually terminates at the Dwarka lighthouse. A left at the Chowk passes the **pharmacy** (open daily 9am-1pm and 4:30-8:30pm, 24hr. for emergencies) and **Shrejee Cyber Cafe** (open 24hr., Rs40 per hr.). The oldest section of town is the maze of tiny streets around the Dwarkadish Temple, between Teen Batti Chowk and the southern coast. The main **police station** (☎234523) is next door to the temple. **Postal Code:** 361335.

⌂ ACCOMMODATIONS AND FOOD. Hotel Rajdhani ❷, Hospital Rd. Look for the sign off Bhadrakali Rd. Spacious rooms with balconies, color TVs, and room service. (☎234070 or 234679. Check-out 3pm. Doubles Rs250-500.) **Hotel Meera ❶,** on the highway near the first main gate into the old city, has spotless, whitewashed rooms and a whole family of friendly staff members. The best valued rooms are on the top floor. (☎234031. Check-out 24hr. Singles Rs120; doubles Rs200-1000.) The **Toran Tourist Guest House ❶,** near the coast, the first right as you walk into town from the bus stand (follow the signs), has big, well-kept rooms with attached baths and hot water. Mosquito coils and toilet paper provided. (☎234013. Check-out 9am. Dorms Rs50; doubles Rs200-400.) **Sharanam Restaurant ❷,** Bhadrakali Rd., dishes out pizzas (Rs30-50), sandwiches (Rs12-30), Punjabi, Chinese, and South Indian fare (Rs15-75) in a bright, A/C dining room. (Open daily 11am-3:30pm and 8-11pm.) **Milan Dining Hall ❷,** Hospital Rd., opposite Hotel Rajdhani, serves delicious Punjabi dishes in a dining hall atmosphere that's all the rage in town (Rs30-50). (Open daily 10:30am-3pm and 7-11pm.) The **Meera Dining Hall ❶** serves delicious, never-ending *thalis* for Rs30. (Open daily 10:30am-3pm and 7-11pm).

◪ SIGHTS. Dwarka's principal attraction is the staggering **Dwarkadish Temple,** also known as Jagat Mandir, or "Temple of the World," which marks the center of town with its 6-story main spire. The temple was allegedly constructed over 1,400 years ago, and, although the spiky exterior stonework looks a bit weathered these days, the elaborate carvings of various incarnations of Vishnu are still visible on the temple's inner walls. Sixty columns support the main structure, which houses a black marble image of Krishna in a silver-plated chamber. Smaller shrines decorate the edges of the complex. (Temple open daily 7am-1pm and 5-9:30pm. Non-Hindus must sign a release form to enter, declaring their faith and respect in the Hindu religion. Bags must be left at storage area Rs2, with camera Rs5.) The **Dwarka Lighthouse** offers spectacular views of the sunset over the Arabian Sea, though no cameras are allowed inside the lighthouse. (Open daily 4:30pm-sunset. Rs5.) The long, clean **beach** nearby is rarely crowded (except Su), and is great for wading past the small beach temples.

No pilgrimage to Dwarka would be complete without a visit to the tiny island of **Bet Dwarka,** where Vishnu slayed the demon Shankasura. Right on the tip of the peninsula, Bet Dwarka has a number of Krishna temples, where devotees come for *prasad* and *puja*. The main temple, which marks the spot of Krishna's death, has a central well that is said to bring up sweet-tasting water, although it apparently draws from the surrounding ocean. Bet Dwarka's real appeal, however, is its eery quietude. The island is accessible via the port at Okha, 45min. north of Dwarka. Pastel-colored boats make the crossing (15min., every 30min., Rs5).

GUJARAT

KUTCH કચ્છ

One of the most isolated regions in India, Kutch is bordered on the south by the Gulf of Kutch and the Arabian Sea, and on the north by the Rann of Kutch, a perfectly flat and often featureless salt marsh in the Thar desert that is home to pink flamingoes and wild ass. The sultans who ruled Gujarat made repeated attempts to cross into Kutch, but it managed to remain independent and develop its own customs, laws, and a thriving maritime trade with Muscat, Malabar, and the African coast. Kutch was absorbed into the Indian Union in 1948. During the monsoon season, floods in the Rann of Kutch cut the region off from its neighbors Saurashtra (Gujarat) and Sindh (Pakistan), causing varying degrees of damage every year. The Rann is a scenic place during the rest of the year. The dry northern part of Kutch is useless for agriculture, but the southern district of Banni used to be one of India's most fertile regions. Though drier today, Banni still produces cotton, castor-oil plants, sunflowers, and wheat. When the people of Kutch abandoned agriculture because of climactic changes, they turned to handicrafts. The region suffered a terrible earthquake on January 26, 2001. Thousands were crushed by the concrete rubble that alone will take years to clear; many thousands more have been displaced, living in roadside cities of tents and shipping containers. Relief and reconstruction efforts are directed by UNICEF.

BHUJ ભુજ ☎ 02832

In the center of the region of Kutch, Bhuj is mainly used by tourists as a base for exploring outlying villages, now more than ever. Bhuj was rocked by the earthquake in 2001 and many of its intriguing sights remain under renovation. Services are up and running and the handicraft villages that drew tourists in the first place have already bounced back. It seems that the earthquake failed to shake the honest hospitality and open smiles of the people of Bhuj. The city is still the gateway to Kutch, founded in the 16th century as the capital of Kutch by Rao Khengarji, a Jadeja Rajput. It remained the region's center of economic activity until the establishment of the city of Gandhidam and the port of Kandla to the east. Be sure to inquire about the sights as many could open shortly. Unfortunately, Bhuj was also near the epicenter of the earthquake that hit Gujarat in January 2001, and services listed may not be running for awhile. The old city was hit especially hard.

▐ TRANSPORTATION

Flights: Bhuj Airport, 5km north of town (auto-rickshaw Rs50, taxi Rs100-150). **Indian Airlines,** at the airport (☎250204 or 21433). Open daily 10am-5:30pm. **Jet Airways,** Station Rd. near ST Rd. (☎253671 or 253674). Open daily 9am-6pm. **H.M. Memon and Sons,** ST Rd., opposite V.R.P Guest House (☎252285), is an agent for both IA and Jet. Open daily 9am-1:30pm and 2:30-8pm. Flights to **Mumbai** (1hr., 12:35pm, US$115).

Trains: New Bhuj Railway Station (☎20950), 1km north of town (auto-rickshaw Rs20). Reservations office (☎131 or 132). Open M-Sa 8am-8pm, Su 8am-2pm. To **Ahmedabad** (7-8hr.; 5am, 6:30pm; Rs150); **Gandhidham** (1hr.; 5am, 3pm, 6:30pm; Rs26); **Mumbai** (17½hr., 6:30pm, Rs280); **Rajkot** (7hr., 3pm, Rs120).

Buses: ST Bus Stand, ST Rd. (☎220002). To: **Ahmedabad** (8hr., 12 per day 5am-10:30pm, Rs100-130); **Dwarka** (10hr.; 10:45am, 8:45pm; Rs130); **Junagadh** (8hr., 7 per day 5am-9:30pm, Rs107); **Mandvi** (1½hr., every 30min. 6am-11pm, Rs19-27); **Rajkot** (every hr. 6am-9pm, Rs85). **Private bus companies** line ST Rd. **Ashapura Travels** (☎255661), opposite the bus stand, has buses to Rajasthan. Open daily 6am-9pm.

GUJARAT

Local Transportation: Auto-rickshaws around town cost Rs5-10. **Taxis** congregate around the bus stand (Rs3 per km).

◄ 🛈 ORIENTATION AND PRACTICAL INFORMATION

Bhuj's main **bus stand** is in the center of **ST Road,** which runs roughly east-west along the southern edge of the old city. From **Mahadev Gate** at the west end of ST Rd., **Uplipad Road** runs along the edge of Hamirsar Lake, past the Swaminarayan Temple and the walled complex of the Prag and Aina Mahals. **College Road** leads south from the Kutch Museum, past the **police station,** and the Folk Art Museum. Near the eastern end of ST Rd., **Waniawad Road** leads north to **Shroff Bazaar.** From the northern edge of the old city, roads lead to the **railway station** and the **airport,** 6km away. **Station Road** borders the old city to the east and turns into **Hospital Road** as it runs south. The oldest section of the old city, between Shroff Bazaar and the northern city wall, is still largely in shambles, particularly northeast of Aina Mahal.

Tourist Office: Aina Mahal Trust in Aina Mahal (☎220004). Very helpful in planning rural tours. Updated maps and informative guidebook on the region Rs50. Guide service on Su. Open M-Sa 9am-noon and 3-6pm.

Currency Exchange: State Bank of India, Hospital Rd. (☎256100). Exchanges currency and travelers checks. Open M-F 10am-3pm. Across the street the **ICI Bank** has a **24hr. ATM.**

Police: The main **police station** (☎253050), on the east side of College Rd., has English-speaking officers. To get permits for the sensitive border area north of Bhuj, go to the **District Superintendent of Police** (☎253593, ext. 132), east of College Rd., down the road opposite the Collector's Office. Bring a copy of your passport and visa. Open M-Sa 10:30am-1:30pm and 3-6pm; closed 2nd and 4th Sa.

Hospital: General (☎222850), on the road to Gandhidam. Clean and ultra modern with English-speaking doctors. Completely rebuilt after it was leveled in the quake. Also has a **24hr. pharmacy.**

Post Office: GPO (☎222952), off Station Rd., south of ST Rd. Open M-Sa 10am-5pm. Small branch on Langa Rd., opposite the City Guest House (☎222650). Open M-Sa 9am-5pm. **Postal Code:** 370001.

🏠 ACCOMMODATIONS

🏠 **Hotel Annapurna,** Bhid Pol (☎220831), at the top of Station Rd. Popular with the backpacking crowd, Annapurna offers 12 well-decorated rooms with TVs and balconies. The owner, Vinod, is knowledgeable. Outstanding restaurant downstairs. Check-out 24hr. Singles Rs150; doubles Rs250. ❷

Hotel Gangaram, Darbargarh Chowk (☎224231), near Aina Mahal, look for the signs. This is a self-sufficient fortress on the fringe of the old city's rubble-desert. An alarming, life-sized clown portrait stands guard over the minty-fresh doubles (Rs300). ❷

Hotel Abha, ST Rd. (☎2544513). While its slightly cheaper next-door neighbor is gutted, at Abha, there remain several clean rooms with attached baths, hot water, 24hr. room service, phones, and TVs. Singles Rs200-800; doubles Rs400-1100. ❷

V.R.P. Guest House, ST Rd. (☎221388 or 222777). Centrally located and cheap, but you get what you pay for. The rooms are uninspiring but functional. Singles Rs75, with attached bath Rs130; doubles Rs130-190. ❶

GUJARAT

Hotel Prince, Station Rd. (2203702; fax 250373; princad1@sancharnet.in). Currently the nicest place to stay in Bhuj. All rooms are carpeted with TV, phone, attached hot water bath, and regional artwork. Two restaurants on the premises (see below), and an alcohol permit shop. Standard singles Rs550, with A/C Rs1380, deluxe Rs2000; doubles Rs1840/2000/2300. ❸

🍴 FOOD

Most restaurants in Bhuj open only for lunch and dinner, with a hefty break between the two, making three square meals a day a virtual impossibility. Instead, take advantage of the abundance of food stalls and have a meal in the street. Try the local Kutch favorite, double *roti*, a small bread roll stuffed with potato and chutney (Rs5). Look for vendors along ST Rd. and Darbargarh Square.

🍴 Annapurna Restaurant, Bhid Pol, in Hotel Annapurna. Popular dinette with make-your-own *thalis*, veg. dishes, sweets, rice, and *chappatis*. Gujarati *thalis* are served in the dining room on the right. Punjabi dishes in the dining room on (Rs20-40). Open M-Sa 10:30am-3:30pm and 7-11:30pm, Su 10:30am-3:30pm. ❶

Hotel Noorani Palace, near the vegetable market as you walk through the main bazaar from Aina Mahal. One of the few spots in Gujarat where meat is consumed without remorse. Roasted chicken (half-order Rs60), mutton *biryani* (Rs25). Open daily 11am-3:30pm and 7:30-10pm. ❷

Hotel Nilam, Station Rd., opposite Hotel Prince. Comfortable padded booths and a bright, open interior separates this place from the rest of the pack. Try a refreshingly sweet lime soda (Rs20). Punjabi and Chinese cuisine, pizza, and sizzlers (Rs35-65) served daily 11am-3pm and 7-11pm. South Indian snacks available 8am-9pm. ❷

Jesal, Station Rd., in Hotel Prince. If the omelette center by the bus stand doesn't do breakfast as you would like, then this place will. Lavish spreads Rs70-125 and *murghi chetti nad* Rs110. Open daily 11am-3pm and 6-10:30pm. ❸

📷 SIGHTS

AINA MAHAL (PALACE OF MIRRORS). Maharao Lakhad (r. 1741-60) was renowned for his love of Kutch regional art. His palace is a small, fortified structure in the old city. A raised platform here was once surrounded by a pool of water and fountains, where the maharao would sit as musicians entertained him. Inside the Aina Mahal, the beautifully designed **Maharao Madansinji Museum** is filled with artifacts and memorabilia, and the maharao's bedroom has remained untouched. His *chakri* slippers still sit by the bed; they were designed to produce an olfactory warning of his proximity—with each step a flower at the toe of the slippers opens to release scented powder. Miraculously, about 90% of the museum's collection survived the quake. Nevertheless the palace and museum are still undergoing renovations and are closed to the public. If you're visiting the tourist office however, curator Pramod Jethi might let you poke around.

PRAG MAHAL (NEW PALACE). The soaring sandstone clocktower seems a lot taller these days standing sentry over the beleaguered old city. A spiral staircase leads to the top of the bell tower which affords fantastic views. Marble stairs ascend to the main hall beneath the curving arches and sandstone columns of the palace, built in 1816. The main hall is a macabre monument to death, as well as a taxidermist's nightmare—the floor is covered with the decaying heads of lions, tigers, leopards, deer, and wild cows. *(Open M-Sa 9-11:45am and 3-5:45pm. Rs10; camera fee Rs30; video fee Rs100.)*

SHARAD BAGH MUSEUM. This beautifully-kept museum at the southwestern corner of Hamirsar Tank was the residence of the last maharao of Kutch until his death in 1991. Built in the mid-19th century and styled after an Italian villa, the palace is much as the maharao left it, with his TV and VCR set among his hunting trophies. *(Closed indefinitely for renovations as of July 2003.)*

OTHER MUSEUMS. Bhuj's museums are an excellent place to learn about Kutch culture before heading out to the villages. The **Kutch Museum,** the oldest in the state, has excellent anthropological and archaeological exhibits on the region. *(Closed indefinitely for renovations as of July 2003.)* The **Bharatiya Sanskriti Darshan,** also called the **Folk Museum,** contains a small collection of local textiles, embroideries, paintings, and bead work, as well as a library. The highlight of the museum is its reproduction of Rabari *bhungas* (huts) with their decorated inner walls. *(Mandvi Rd., at the south end of College Rd. Open M-Sa 9am-noon and 3-6pm. Rs10; camera fee Rs50.)*

OTHER SIGHTS. On the way to Harmirsar Tank from the Darbargadh complex lies the **Swaminarayan Temple.** This early 19th-century technicolor temple housed the town's major shrines before the earthquake and retains the most vibrant architecture in Bhuj. *(Open daily 7-11am and 4-8pm.)* South of Hamirsar Tank, in the midst of a sandy, deserted plain, the eerie **Memorial Chattris** commemorate some of the previous maharaos of Kutch and their wives who committed *sati*. The red sandstone memorial to Maharao Shri Lakhpatji (1710-61) and his 15 wives, formerly the largest of the lot, was yet another casualty to the earthquake and now lies in ruins.

 # DAYTRIPS FROM BHUJ

VILLAGE TOURS

Tours can be made by taxi (Rs900 for up to four people for a full day tour to several villages) or, more slowly, by bus from Bhuj. Contact the tourist office for more information on arranging village tours. Permits are needed to visit some of the villages. These can be obtained for free by bringing a copy of your passport and visa to the District Superintendent of Police Office (see p. 196). As of July 2003, permits were needed for Khavda and Lilpur among a number of other villages. For the latest info inquire at the Police Superintendent's Office.

Most tourists use Bhuj as a base from which to explore the nearby villages. These tours offer a glimpse of village life and provide opportunities for you to spend your money on local handicrafts. While the earthquake decimated many of the villages, relief efforts have rebuilt the rural infrastructure and economy and virtually all of the villages have recovered from the disaster. The only aspect of the local economy that hasn't recovered is tourism. Because of the dearth of visitors, a buyers market reigns. Villagers are genuinely excited by any tourist traffic and enjoy showing visitors around, sale or no sale.

The village of Sumrasar, 21km north of Bhuj, is home to Kala Raksha (☎02808 277238), a research institute and women artists' cooperative dedicated to the "preservation of traditional arts." Founded in 1993, the center has a large collection of embroidered textiles from Kutch. A small store sells local work; the items are of excellent quality, prices are reasonable, and profits go directly to the artists. For information on research opportunities and accom-

GUJARAT

modations at Kala Raksha, contact Judy Frater, Project Coordinator (☎ 253697; fax 255500; info@kala-raksha.org). Buses to Sumrasar leave hourly 6am-6pm (Rs10). Alternatively, hop in one of the jeeps (Rs10) that leave from outside the bus stand.

Kera, 22km south of Bhuj, is home to a Shiva temple thought to have been built in the 10th century (buses 45min., every hr. 6am-8:30pm, Rs7). Farther south is the Rabari village of **Tundawadh** (best reached by car or by bus from Mandvi), famed for its exquisite embroideries. **Anjar,** 40km southeast of Bhuj, is a major center for handicraft enthusiasts and specializes in weapons, nutcrackers, jewelry, and textiles (buses 1½hr., every hr. 5am-11pm, Rs22). For block printing galore, head to **Dhamanka,** 50km east of Bhuj (buses 1½hr., 7 per day 6am-5:30pm, Rs20). The village of **Khavda,** 60km north of Bhuj, specializes in pottery and has some block printing (buses 2hr., 7 per day 7:30am-7:45pm, Rs30). **Bhirandiyari,** on the way to Khavda, is known for its embroidery and leather work (1hr., Rs16). **Zura,** home of the copper bell, and **Nirona,** specializing in Rogan painting, are accessible by the same bus (1½hr., 7 per day 8am-6pm, Rs20).

If you get sick of handicrafts, head 60km northwest of Bhuj to the remote **Than Monastery** on the slopes of the oldest hills in Kutch. It's possible to stay overnight at the monastery (donation as you like), which is a great base for trekking in the dormant volcanic hills. Glimpses of the Great Rann are available from some peaks. (bus 3hr., 5am, Rs20). The ruins of **Dholavira,** 250km by road from Bhuj, one of the largest sites uncovered in the Indus Valley, dates to 2500 BC (bus 6hr., 2pm, Rs67). Tourists are not allowed to stay in the village of Dholavira. The Gandhi Ashram in **Lilpur,** 150km east of Bhuj has rooms for a nominal fee. The town is a 2km walk west of the road. Lilpur is accessible by any Rahpar-bound bus (4hr., 6 per day 7am-5pm, Rs50).

MANDVI માંડવી ☎ 02834

Established by Maharao Khengarji in 1588, Mandvi rose to prominence as an important port, trading with South Africa, the Middle East, China, and Japan. The Arab and European traders who settled here in the 18th century left behind grand mansions in the winding lanes of the old city, along with a dwindling boat-building industry. Pushcarts and auto-rickshaws almost seem to be propelled by the breeze, and hand-built wooden *dhows* lean lazily against the docks, and their beautifully rusted anchors beached by the tide. Shop-owners rest quietly on the steps of medieval buildings, while blacksmiths and welders send dust and sparks into the salty evening air. Bordered by vast stretches of untainted shore and surrounded by a horizon studded with palm trees, Mandvi is the ideal place to sit back and do a whole lot of nothing.

▐ **TRANSPORTATION.** From the **ST Bus Stand** (☎ 220004), buses travel to: **Ahmedabad** (12hr.; 6:45, 8:45am, 6:30pm; Rs130); **Bhuj** (1hr., every 30min. 7am-9pm, Rs19-25); **Dwarka** (10hr; 9:30am, 7:30pm; Rs130); **Rajkot** (8hr.; 4 per day 6, 7:45am, 2, 9pm; Rs99).

▓▜ **ORIENTATION AND PRACTICAL INFORMATION.** From the bridge that stretches over the salt flats, a left turn takes you down **ST Road** past the main police station (☎ 223008, open 24hr.) and the ST Bus Stand, coming to a dead-end at Bandar Road. The small road straight ahead from the bridge leads to the Rukmavati Guest House. The **Shree Gokul Hospital** (☎ 223361), next door, is a clean, modern facility with an English-speaking staff. (Open M-F 9am-1:30pm and 4-6:30pm for consultations, 24hr. for emergencies.) There are many pharmacies near the hospital. (Open M-Sa 9am-9pm.) A right turn from the bridge takes you along the northern city wall and leads eventually to Vijay Vilas Palace, 8km away. A left on Bandar Road leads past the **State Bank of India** (☎220031; open M-F 11am-3pm, Sa 11am-1pm; exchanges currency in emergencies) and terminates at the port. A right on Bandar Rd. leads into the town center toward Bhid Chowk, which is the central market area. **Internet** is cheapest at Sanghui Communications, (Rs40) just north of the market. The **GPO** is 1km to the right away from the bridge. (☎222266. Open M-Sa 10am-6pm.) **Postal Code:** 370465.

ACCOMMODATIONS AND FOOD. The best place to stay in Mandvi is the ▦**Rukmavati Guest House ❶**, near the bridge. Enormous, well-furnished rooms open onto a plant-filled terrace with a porch swing. Hot water, laundry service, and kitchen available for guest use. (☎220557. Check-out 24hr. Dorms Rs100; singles Rs150-750; doubles Rs250-990.) The **Maitri Guest House ❶**, Kanthawalo Gate, has bright, clean rooms in the heart of the old city. (☎232583. Check-out noon. Dorms Rs70; singles Rs150-200; doubles Rs200-250.) ▦**Hotel Nayna ❷**, Azad Chowk, serves the best lunchtime *thalis* in town (Rs40), and standard Punjabi and Chinese fare in the evening (under Rs50). (☎231007. Open daily 11am-3pm and 6-11pm.) The restaurant in the Osho Hotel, **Zorba the Buddha ❷**, dishes out unlimited *thalis* (Rs40) to a constant stream of locals. Don't let the grungy atmosphere fool you; the food is fresh and delicious, and the service extends beyond the call of duty, go ahead, try them. (Open daily 11:30am-4pm and 7-10pm.)

SIGHTS AND BEACHES. Mandvi is blessed with many beautiful haunts—the old city walls, the port with its wooden ships moored on the salt flats, the canyon-like streets with their stone mansions, and the temples and mosques that crowd the eastern side of the salt flats. But the **Vijay Vilas Palace,** 9km west of town, is Mandvi's biggest draw. A domed, latticed mansion set on 692 acres, the palace was built in 1927 as a summer home for the Maharao of Kutch. Spotless marble floors, walls delicately inlaid with floral patterns, and gorgeous carved rosewood and teak furniture decorate the inside. From the third floor, a rusting spiral staircase leads to a domed terrace with a view of the Arabian Sea and the coconut trees and windmills of the flat, green Kutch. Perhaps the highlight of the palace, though, is its private **beach,** 1km away. The nearly 2km stretch of sand is litter-free and blissfully unpopulated. Follow the road past the GPO and veer left at all three forks. (Open daily 9am-1pm and 2-6pm. Rs15; camera fee Rs50; video fee Rs200. Bike Rs5, rickshaw Rs15. They'll ask for Rs15 for beach access, but it's just around to the right as you leave the palace.) Fresh coconut milk at the Palace Rs5. Be sure to bring food and water if you're going to make a day of it at the beach. Mandvi's seemingly endless shoreline draws many visitors. The town's main beach, called **Windfarm** because of the numerous windmills that line it, can get a bit crowded, but the farther west you go, the more isolated it becomes. **Kashivishvanath Beach** is quieter and lies on the opposite side of the port. Cross the bridge and take your first right, the immediate left fork and then a right at the next crossroads. Follow this road to the ocean (15min. walk from town.)

HIMACHAL PRADESH

हिमाचल प्रदेश

Travel through Himachal Pradesh is an experience of complete detachment from the urban world. You'll walk through apple orchards, cross rivers swollen with glacial run-off, and gaze in wonder at the breathless scenery of diverse worlds that exist alongside each other in Himachal Pradesh. The rain-drenched forests of Manali give way to the rock and ice of the Lahaul Valley and the vast emptiness of Spiti. From Shimla to Kaza, Hindu temples are replaced by Buddhist prayer flags and *gompas*. The road from Manali to Leh, in Kashmir, defies description.

With the unpredictable situation in Kashmir, more foreign tourists have been going to Himachal; the three main towns in HP are both backpacker retreats and gateways to the lands beyond. Dharamsala has a strong Tibetan population and is the base for treks into the Dhauladar and the Pir Panjal ranges. Manali and Shimla are favorite vacation spots with both Indian and foreign travelers. The less touristed rain-shadow areas—Lahaul, Spiti, and Upper Kinnaur—can be reached from Manali via the Rohtang La or from Shimla via Kaza, but routes that should be open from June to September can close at any time due to avalanches and floods. The main tourist season in most of HP runs from May to June and from September to October, but winter—when roads to Shimla, Manali, and Dharamsala and from Shimla to Chamba remain open—is also an ideal time to visit.

HIGHLIGHTS OF HIMACHAL PRADESH

The Kullu Valley towns of **Manali** (p. 244), **Kullu** (p. 240), and **Naggar** (p. 241) are famous for green pastures, apple orchards, and great views of the Western Himalayas.

Dharamsala (p. 229) is where the mythic East meets and mixes with the equally mythic West, to the delight of hippies, pop stars, and Buddhist saints alike.

From its green forests to its icy mountain tops, HP has some of the most beautiful **trekking** in India, particularly in **Kinnaur** and **Spiti** (p. 250).

SHIMLA सिमला
☎ 0177

With its cool air, magnificent views, and lingering spirit of the Raj, Shimla can leave visitors spellbound. A stroll along the Ridge can be a daunting experience; Indians, foreigners, and monkeys all vie for space along broad streets lined with Highland-esque houses. Once the summer capital of the British Empire, today's Shimla is a good place to stopover before heading to busier (or rougher) parts of the state. It is connected by a road to Kullu and Lahaul in the north, Kangra and

Chamba in the west, and the Kinnaur in the east. During May, June, Sept., and Oct., times when the town is free from snow and monsoonal downpours, the mountain quiet disappears, and the area is flooded with Indian tourists and backpackers.

⌐ TRANSPORTATION

Flights: Jubbarhatti Airport, 22km from town. Rs420 cab ride. Flights to **Delhi** (1hr.; M, W, F 10:20am; US$120) via **Kullu** (30min., US$75). Book **Jagson Airlines** flights and taxis to the airport at Bandbox Travels (see p. 223).

Trains: Shimla is connected to **Kalka** via the narrow-gauge railway (5hr.; 10:45am from Town Rail Station, 2:30 and 5:30pm from Main Rail Station; Rs40). From Kalka, connections can be made to: **Ambala** (2hr.; 7am, and 5:30 and 9pm; Rs40); **Amritsar** (9hr., 4pm, Rs140); **Delhi** (8hr., 4:45 and 11:30pm, Rs130).

> **WARNING.** Foreigners planning to travel between Jangi and Sumdo, in the eastern regions of Kinnaur, must obtain an all-inclusive **inner-line permit** from the sub-divisional magistrate, as these areas are sensitive border regions. In Shimla, see the **Additional District Magistrate,** on the 2nd fl. of the left side of the green colonial building just south of The Mall, beneath the telegraph office (open M-Sa 10am-1pm and 2-5pm). Fill out an application and have a local travel agent sign on as a sponsor and submit the form for you—regulations require that an agency submit the form. **Band Box Heights and Valleys** (see **Budget Travel,** p. 223) does all this for Rs200. As of Aug. 2003, there is no charge for the permit itself.

Buses: There are two bus stands in Shimla. **Main Station** sends buses to: **Chamba** (15hr.; 4am, 5 and 6:40pm; Rs268); **Chandigarh** (4hr., every 15min. 3:30am-10pm, Rs90); **Delhi** (10hr., 10 per day 6am-10:30pm, Rs242; deluxe 3 per day 8:25am-9:40pm, Rs405); **Dharamsala** (10hr., 7 per day 6:50am-10:15pm, Rs184); **Haridwar** via **Dehra Dun** (10hr., 4 per day 5am-4pm, Rs182); **Manali** via **Kullu** (10hr., 5 per day 8am-8:15pm, Rs197); **Pathankot** (12hr., 4 per day 5am-8:20pm, Rs200). **Rivoli Bus Stand** sends buses to: **Kalpa** via **Rampur, Jeuri, and Rekong-Peo** (13hr., 6am, Rs203); **Rampur** (6hr., 4 and 9am, Rs90).

◪ ? ORIENTATION AND PRACTICAL INFORMATION

Shimla stretches from Himachal Pradesh University in the West across a ridge to **Lakkar Bazaar,** where many of the town's Tibetan refugees live. Most major streets run from parallel to Mall Road from east to west, each at a different elevation. Trains and most buses arrive on **Cart Road.** Above Cart Rd. is the bazaar, and above the bazaar is Shimla's main drag, **The Mall,** which is off-limits to motorized vehicles. The easiest (and laziest) way to get up and down is to take the **tourist elevator** on Cart Rd., just after the street turns south. (Open in summer 8am-10pm, in winter 9am-8pm. Rs5.) For a workout, take any path or stairway leading up. At **Scandal Corner,** directly above the main bus stand, The Mall divides into a lower section and an upper section known as **the Ridge,** which becomes Lakkar Bazaar as it curves left beyond **Christ Church.**

Tourist Office: Himachal Tourism Marketing Office (☎2252561), on the left, next to Scandal Corner. Open M-Sa 10am-6pm. Two doors down is the **Road Transport Booth,** which gives information on bus schedules and road conditions. The office also arranges helicopter tours of the Shimla area (20min.-1½hr., Rs1500-5000). Open 9am-5pm.

Budget Travel: Travel agents are on every corner of The Mall; most give both transport and trekking assistance. **Band Box Heights and Valleys** (☎2258157), on Scandal Corner, arranges **inner-line permits** (Rs200 commission), 9-10 day jeep tours of Kinnaur-Spiti (Rs1600 per day), and will put together groups of travelers wishing to share the cost of the jeeps. Open 9am-9pm daily.

Himachal Pradesh

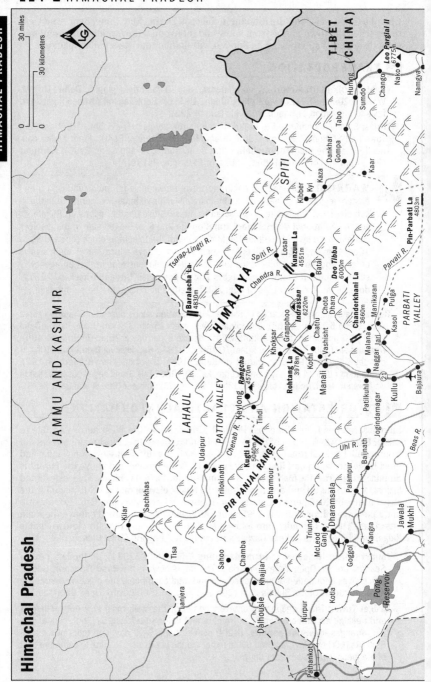

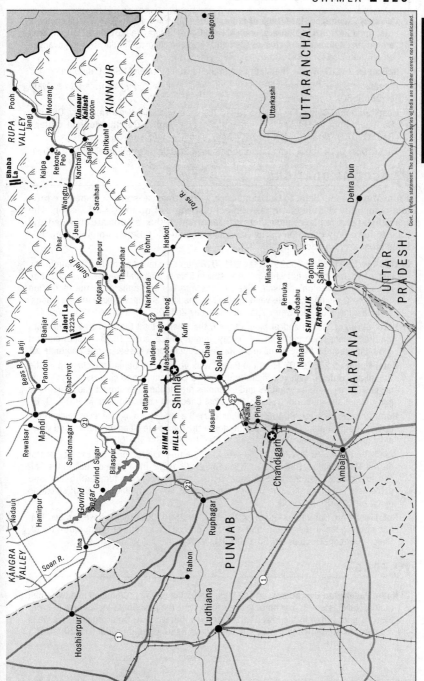

Govt. of India statement: The external boundaries of India are neither correct nor authenticated.

HIMACHAL PRADESH

Currency Exchange: State Bank of India, interior open M-F 10am-2pm, Sa 10am-noon; ATM open 24hr. **ANZ Grindlays,** open M-F 9:30am-2:30pm, Sa 9:30am-12:30pm. Both are on The Mall, and both change cash and traveler's checks. Grindlays gives advances on MC and Visa for a Rs100 fee.

Police: (☎2812344). On The Mall, next to the town hall. Open M-Sa 10am-5pm.

Pharmacy: Several are along The Mall and Lower Mall, including **Vohra's** (Lower Mall) (☎2805530). Open daily 9am-8pm.

Hospital: Nehru Clinic, The Mall (☎2801596). Women only. Down a side alley. Open M-Sa 10am-2pm and 4-6pm. In emergencies, call **Indira Gandhi Medical College** (☎2803073). **Tara Hospital** (☎2803275), also has 24hr. service.

Post Office: GPO, above Scandal Corner. Open M-Sa 10am-6pm. **Postal Code:** 171001.

ACCOMMODATIONS

From May to June, Sept. to Oct., and during Christmas season, vacancies are rare, and come only at inflated prices. Expect discounts of up to 50% off season. The really inexpensive places near Victory Tunnel and the bus station are crowded and tend to have only common baths (in-season Rs200-250). Better hotels are up The Mall. Most levy an additional 10% tax.

YMCA (☎2804085 or 2652375; fax 2811016), up the stairs behind Christ Church. The last affordable, truly worthwhile place to stay in Shimla. Colonial grandeur blends seamlessly with postcolonial kitsch. Clean rooms and TVs and billiards in the recreation areas. Rs40 membership fee valid for 1 week. The staff arranges treks and jeep safaris. Breakfast included. Hot water 7pm-9am. Singles Rs400-500; doubles Rs250-600. ❸

Hotel Shringar, at the end of Mall Rd. near the Oberoi Hotel Clarke. Large rooms with mirrored ceilings can make for a fun stay. Room service, cable TV, clean showers and central location on Mall Rd. make the Rs1200 double room in-season rate palatable. ❺

Hotel Uphar (☎2657670). From the Ridge, walk up the path behind the clock, past the Dreamland Hotel; it's on your right. Rooms of varying quality and size. Hanuman's temple is close by, and the windows and balconies are all barred to protect guests from the god's curious retinue. Hot water in all rooms. Check-out noon. Doubles Rs300-400. ❷

Hotel Amar Palace (☎2804055), farther along the street running one level below Hotel Uphar. Though outside looks mildly run down, the rooms are clean and have good views of valley. Rooms have color TV and hot water. Doubles Rs450-900. ❸

Woodville Palace (☎2823919), 2km south of the town center, past the tourist elevator on The Mall. Built in 1938 for Raja Rana Bhagat Chandra, the Prince of Jubbal, the Palace exudes colonial charm. Spacious rooms, good views, nice furniture, baths, and cable color TV make this one of the best splurges in HP. Doubles Rs1800; suites as much as Rs8000. MC/V. ❺

Hotel Mehman, Daisy Bank Estate (☎2813692 or 2804390). Rooms have carpets, TVs, hot water, heat in the winter, and a doctor on call. Nice terrace restaurant on roof. Check-out noon. Doubles Rs550-1100. MC/V. ❸

FOOD

Nalini Vegetarian Restaurant, on The Mall, before the elevator. Crammed into two small rooms, Nalini is well known among locals for serving the best South Indian food in town. Steeper prices than in the lower bazaar *dhabas,* but worth it. Oddly enough, the walls are covered with a mural of Olde England. *Thalis* Rs80. Open daily 9am-10:30pm. ❸

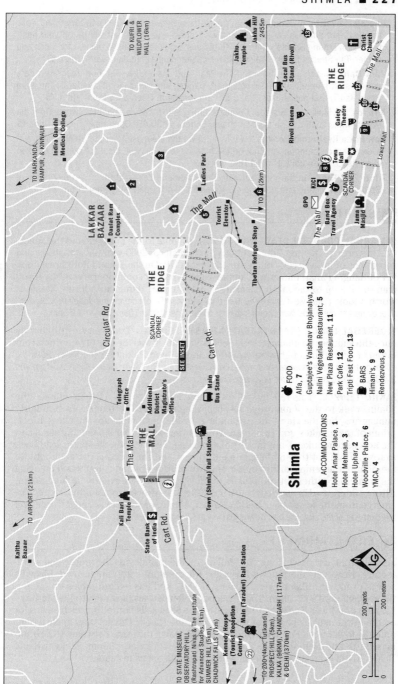

HIMACHAL PRADESH

TO KUFRI &
WILDFLOWER
HALL (16km)

Jakhu Hill
2455m

Jakhu
Temple

Local Bus
Stand (Rivoli)

Christ
Church

THE
RIDGE

The Mall

Rivoli Cinema

TO NARKANDA,
RAMPUR, & KINNAUR

Indira Gandhi
Medical College

Galety
Theatre

Town
Hall

3

Lower Mall

Ladies Park

1

2

LAKKAR
BAZAAR

Daulat Ram
Complex

4

The Mall

5

Tourist
Elevator

TO 6 (2km)

The Mall

GPO

KICI

Band Box
Travel Agency

SCANDAL
CORNER

Jama
Masjid

Tibetan Refugee Shop

THE
RIDGE

SCANDAL
CORNER

Circular Rd.

Cart Rd.

SEE INSET

TO STATE MUSEUM,
OBSERVATORY HILL
(Rashtrapati Niwas & The Institute
for Advanced Studies, 1km)
SUMMER HILL (5km),
CHADWICK FALLS (7km)

TO ZOO (4km, Tutikandi),
PROSPECT HILL (5km),
KALKA (96KM), CHANDIGARH (117km),
& DELHI (370km)

Kennedy House
(Tourist Reception
Center)

Main (Taradevi) Rail Station

Telegraph
Office

Additional
District
Magistrate's
Office

Main
Bus Stand

The Mall

THE
MALL

TUNNEL

Town (Shimla) Rail Station

Kali Bari
Temple

State Bank
of India

Cart Rd.

Kaithu
Bazaar

TO AIRPORT (21km)

200 yards

200 meters

Shimla

▲ ACCOMMODATIONS

Hotel Amar Palace, **1**
Hotel Mehman, **3**
Hotel Uphar, **2**
Woodville Palace, **6**
YMCA, **4**

🍴 FOOD

Alfa, **7**
Guptajee's Vaishnav Bhojanalya, **10**
Nalini Vegetarian Restaurant, **5**
New Plaza Restaurant, **11**
Park Cafe, **12**
Tripti Fast Food, **13**

🍺 BARS

Himani's, **9**
Rendezvous, **8**

Guptajee's Vaishnav Bhojanalya, on the stairway between The Mall and lower mall. Take the first right after Gaiety Theatre and walk down—the restaurant will be on your right. Local gem among Shimla's eateries, Guptajees' small restaurant is packed for lunch and dinner. The Special Deluxe *thali* (Rs45) is outstanding. Open daily 9am-10pm. ❷

Park Cafe, on the slope between The Mall and the Ridge. Bamboo-decorated cafe enthralls with American classic rock, daily papers, and foreign food standards. The pizza (from Rs45) and milkshakes (Rs25-50) are excellent. Open daily 8am-10pm. ❷

Alfa, on The Mall, near Scandal Corner. Patrons enjoy *masala chai* and sweets from the bakery while seated in soft brown chairs. Entrees Rs30-45. Open daily 11am-10pm. ❷

New Plaza Restaurant, on the lower Mall, down the staircase from the Gaiety Theatre. A wide selection of Indian and not-quite-Chinese meat and veg. dishes. Excellent chicken curry Rs55. Open daily 10am-11pm. ❷

Tripti Fast Food, on the right between the Ridge and Lakkar Bazaar. A wide variety of South Indian *dosas* and *utthapams*. Meals Rs25-40. Open daily 9am-10pm. ❶

◖ SIGHTS

HIMACHAL PRADESH STATE MUSEUM. It's a hike to the museum, but the collection is worth it. The first floor contains the remains of 2000-year-old sculptures and specimens of Indo-Greek coinage unearthed in HP. On the second floor are a number of Kangra Pahari miniature paintings and works by contemporary artists. If you plan to hike up to the **Jakhu Temple** (see below), the "Hanuman Adoring Rama" is worth a look. *(Walk west along The Mall until you reach a concrete ramp labeled "Museum," directly next to the Ambedkar Chowk sub-post office. Open Tu-Su 10am-1pm and 2-5pm.)*

VICEREGAL LODGE (RASHTRAPATI NIVAS). This neo-Tudor style lodge was once the summer headquarters of the Raj. In 1945, it was the site of important (but failed) negotiations between would-be Indian and Pakistani leaders. *(Pass the entrance to the state museum and walk 10min. west along The Mall. Open daily 10am-1pm and 2-4:30pm. Rs10 admission includes a guide.)*

JAKHU TEMPLE. This red-and-yellow temple is at the top of a 2455m hill and the 20min. walk to the summit can be surprisingly steep. The temple itself is fairly uninspiring, but the views are astounding. Inside the temple are the alleged footprints of the monkey god Hanuman. You may see some tourists feeding snacks to the hordes of monkeys, but this is not advisable. Two networks of paths lead back to town. Both cut through magnificent forests, but the sinuous paths directly to the right of the temple afford better opportunities for taking detours and enjoying the scenery. Neither set of paths is marked, but they all eventually lead down. Allow 45min. to 1hr. to reach town on the way down from Jakhu. Expect to emerge from the forest near Lakkar Bazaar, 15min. or so from Scandal Corner. *(At the east end of the city. The trail begins just left of Christ Church.)*

◖ ENTERTAINMENT

Most visitors just stroll along The Mall or the Ridge, enjoying the breeze and architecture. However, there are a few pubs for the non-teetotaling crowd. **Himani's** serves drinks at inflated prices (beer Rs75-80), and has billiard tables on the top floor. Open until 9 or 10pm. There is a bar at **Rendezvous,** just next to the statue of Lalalajpatrai (beer Rs75), and **The English Wine Shop** sells bottled spirits from a spot on the lower mall. Take the fourth right after the Gaiety Theater, and make a right onto the lower mall. For **movies,** head to **Rivoli,** down the ramp between ANZ Grindlays Bank and Rendezvous. English-language flicks at 4:30pm. Tickets Rs50. Below Rivoli is an **ice-skating rink,** which typically opens in January.

HIMACHAL PRADESH

🛍 SHOPPING

There are extraordinary handicrafts in Himachal: fine woodwork, engraved metal-work, patterned carpets, and traditional woolen shawls. **Kashmir Craft Emporium,** 92 The Mall, has an impressive collection of shawls (Rs150-5000) and silk saris (Rs250-4000). **Maria Brothers,** 78 The Mall, just below the church, specializes in bizarre and beautiful old books. (Open daily 10:30am-1pm and 3:30-8pm.) Much of the **bazaar** is closed on Sundays.

DHARAMSALA धर्मशाला ☎01892

After China's occupation of Tibet began in 1959, the 14th Dalai Lama and his Bud-dhist government were given asylum in Dharamsala. Since then, a steady stream of Tibetan exiles has relocated here, some of them walking across the Himalayas to escape oppression and be near the man they regard as their religious and political leader. Today, Upper Dharamsala, also called McLeod Ganj—named after David McLeod, a former governor of the Punjab—attracts students, tourists, hippies, and devotees of Buddhism to its monasteries, meditation centers, and Tibetan shops, giving this refugee community the feel of an energetic international crossroads.

Embraced by the craggy Dhauladar mountains, and covered with pine and deo-dar forests, Dharamsala commands fantastic views of Himalayan peaks and the Kangra Valley. Several easy hikes from McLeod Ganj lead to the slopes, while more rigorous treks head up and over the snowy passes. In early summer, daily fog and rain are a constant bother, but in July and August the flowers blossom and infuse the mountain air with a sweet-smelling freshness.

🚋 TRANSPORTATION

Flights: Goggol Airport, 9km from town. Flights to **Delhi** (1hr.; M, W, F 3pm; US$150). During the summer, book in advance.

Buses: Most intercity government buses depart from the **bus circle** in McLeod Ganj, making a stop at the **New Bus Stand** in Lower Dharamsal 30min. to 1hr. later. To **Chandigarh** (8hr., 17 per day 5am-7:30pm, Rs140); **Dalhousie** (6hr., 8:30am, Rs100); **Delhi** (12hr., 5 per day 4:30-7:30am, Rs281-390); **Pathankot** (4hr., 5 per day 10am-3:45pm, Rs75). The only buses that depart from Lower Dharamsala without stopping in McLeod Ganj are those that go to: **Chamba** (10hr., 2 per day 7:10 and 8:30am, Rs131); **Haridwar** (13hr., 3pm, Rs263); and **Shimla** (10hr., 6 per day 5:30am-9:30pm, Rs191). **McLeod Ganj booking office** (☎221750. Open daily 10am-5:30pm. **Lower Dharamsala booking office** (☎224903). Roads are sometimes blocked by landslides during monsoon and winter.

Local Transportation: Buses run between the New Bus Stand and McLeod Ganj (every 30min. 6:30am-8:30pm, Rs4). The **shared jeeps** that run between Kotwali Bazaar and McLeod Ganj (Rs6-7) are cramped but faster. You can hike along Jogibara Rd. (1hr. up, 45min. down). The **Taxi Union Stand** beside the bus circle has high fixed rates (Rs120 from Lower to Upper Dharamsala); they're only worth it if you're heading up to Dharamkot or Bhagsu at night or sharing with a few others.

🏔 ORIENTATION

Dharamsala is split into two sections differing by 500m in altitude; this is a result of a massive earthquake in 1905 that destroyed all of the town's build-ings and killed 900 people in the Kangra Valley. Alarmed by the destruction, the British administration established **Lower Dharamsala,** which now houses mostly offices, banks, and the Indian population. The largely Tibetan enclave of **Upper Dharamsala (McLeod Ganj)** attracts the most tourists. Seven roads branch off the **main bus circle** in McLeod Ganj. The first is **Cantonment Road,** the route used by buses to travel to and from Lower Dharamsala. As you go clockwise, the next road is **Taxi Stand Road,** which leads to the Tibetan Children's Village. Next is a steep road leading to **Dharamkot,** 50min. away. The fourth spoke off the bus circle is **TIPA Road,** which also leads to Dharamkot, passing the Tibetan Institute of Performing Arts (TIPA) on its way. Next, **Bhagsu Road** leads to Bhagsu (20min.) after passing many restaurants and hotels. The sixth road is **Jogibara Road,** and finally, **Temple Road** leads to the Dalai Lama's residence, Tsuglagkhang (Main Temple), and Namgyal Monastery. As you walk along Temple Rd., you will encounter a fork; both routes lead to Namgyal, but the lower one (to your right) is quicker and has a better view. Bear left and head uphill to reach the **Himachal Tourism Office** and more expensive hotels. A 30min. walk down either Jogibara or Temple Rd. lands you in Gangchen Kyishong, the location of the Tibetan government-in-exile.

⚠ PRACTICAL INFORMATION

TOURIST AND FINANCIAL SERVICES

Tourist Office: Himachal Tourism Marketing Office (☎224212), 50m below Kotwali Bazaar in Lower Dharamsala, before the Bank of Baroda. Open daily 9am-1:30pm, 2-7pm. The **McLeod Ganj Office** (☎221232), off Temple Rd. behind the State Bank of India, is less helpful. Open M-Sa 10am-1:30pm and 2-5pm. Both offices are closed on official holidays and the 2nd Sa. of each month.

Budget Travel and Trekking: Most agencies in McLeod Ganj do bus and plane tickets; a few organize treks. For airline, train, and deluxe bus bookings, **Dhauladar Travel,** Temple Rd., accepts AmEx/MC/V for charges over Rs500. Open M-Sa 9:30am-5:30pm. For more info on **Trekking,** see p. 30.

Currency Exchange: Punjab National Bank, Temple Rd., in McLeod Ganj, a few steps from the bus circle. Changes currency and traveler's checks. Open M-F 10am-2pm, Sa 10-noon. **Western Union** money transfers and **DHL** service are available at **Paul Merchants** (☎221421), to the right after Temple Rd. splits. Open M-Sa 9:30am-8:30pm. **Bank of Baroda** (☎223175), Lower Dharamsala, opposite the Museum of Kangra Art, changes money and gives MC/V cash advances. Cash advances require 24hr. for processing. Open M-F 10am-2pm, Sa 10am-noon.

LOCAL SERVICES

Bookstore: Bookworm, on Temple Rd. At the fork, bear left; it's 10m up on the right. Carries the standard books on Tibet and Buddhism, as well as English-language classics. Buys books as well. Open Tu-Su 9:30am-7pm. **Namgyal Bookshop,** Namgyal Monastery, next to the Tsuglaghang. All proceeds go to the government-in-exile. Open M-Sa 9am-noon and 1:30-5pm.

EMERGENCY AND COMMUNICATIONS

Police: The main police station (☎221483) is in Lower Dharamsala, below the GPO.

Hospital: The Tibetan **Delek Hospital,** Jogibara Rd. (24hr. ☎222053), 2km. from McLeod Ganj, just before Gangchen Kyishong. Has a good walk-in clinic. Open M-Sa 10am-1pm and 2-5pm. They have a branch in McLeod Ganj on Bhagsu Rd., just before the Green Cyberspace Cafe.

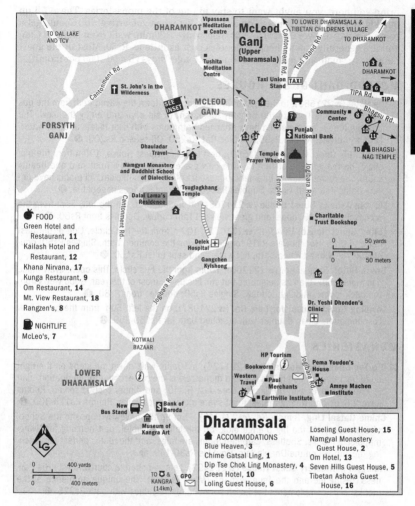

Dharamsala

🏠 ACCOMMODATIONS
Blue Heaven, **3**
Chime Gatsal Ling, **1**
Dip Tse Chok Ling Monastery, **4**
Green Hotel, **10**
Loling Guest House, **6**

Loseling Guest House, **15**
Namgyal Monastery
 Guest House, **2**
Om Hotel, **13**
Seven Hills Guest House, **5**
Tibetan Ashoka Guest
 House, **16**

🍴 FOOD
Green Hotel and
 Restaurant, **11**
Kailash Hotel and
 Restaurant, **12**
Khana Nirvana, **17**
Kunga Restaurant, **9**
Om Restaurant, **14**
Mt. View Restaurant, **18**
Rangzen's, **8**

🍺 NIGHTLIFE
McLeo's, **7**

Internet: Everywhere in McLeod Ganj. The connections are fast, and the standard price is Rs30 per hr. The **Green Cyberspace Cafe,** Bhagsu Rd., in Green Hotel, has more than 10 computers. Rs30 per hr. Open daily 9am-10pm.

Post Office: GPO, Lower Dharamsala, 1km south of Kotwali Bazaar. Another branch is along Jogibara Rd., past the State Bank. Both open M-F 9am-2pm and 3-5pm. **Postal Code:** McLeod Ganj 176219; Lower Dharamsala 176215.

🏠 ACCOMMODATIONS

Dharamsala is usually packed in spring and autumn; even in summer it can be hard to find a room. Most tourists stay in McLeod Ganj, and guest houses continue to spring up along Jogibara, Temple, and Bhagsu roads. If spiritual interests are what bring you here, you might want to stay in one of the monasteries. These fill up quickly, but if you put yourself on a waiting list when you arrive, you should get a room in a day or two. **Bhagsu** and **Dharamkot** are a 20min. walk from McLeod Ganj and are generally much cheaper; doubles cost as little as Rs50. Most of the guest houses are small, and many rent rooms for longer stays (Rs500-1000 per month).

MCLEOD GANJ GUEST HOUSES

Om Hotel (☎221580), to the right of Temple Rd., just down the paved path from the bus stand. Travelers flock to the balcony restaurant to sip *chai* and enjoy the view. The upscale rooms are large and have attached bathrooms with seat toilets and hot water. Laundry service. Rooms Rs80; doubles Rs150-250. Off-season Rs200. ●

Seven Hills Guest House (☎221580), next to Loling Guest House, 100m from the bus circle, on the left side of TIPA Rd. The only place in town with a front yard and beauty salon. The restaurant and Internet lab make it entirely self-sufficient. All rooms have private baths and great views. Doubles Rs100-200. Winter prices negotiable. ●

Tibetan Ashoka Guest House (☎221763), off Jogibara Rd., on the left, 75m from the bus circle. Over 40 rooms and great views. 11pm curfew. Doubles from Rs60. ●

Loling Guest House, TIPA Rd. (☎221072), 100m from the bus circle. One of the best deals in town. Hot showers Rs10 for guests using the common bath. Singles Rs50; doubles Rs75, with attached bath, hot water, and seat toilet Rs150. ●

Green Hotel, Bhagsu Rd. (☎221200), 150m from the bus circle. This open, lively place has more rooms than its neighbors but still fills up for most of the year. Good views from the back rooms. Midnight curfew. Singles Rs60; doubles from Rs80. ●

Loseling Guest House, Jogibara Rd. (☎221087), on the left, 50m from the bus circle. Loseling offers clean doubles with attached bath for Rs150-250. ●

MONASTERIES

🏯 **Dip Tse Chok Ling Monastery** (☎221726), a 10min. walk down the steps on the right ridge past the Om hotel. This isolated monastery is the perfect spot for meditation. Join in evening prayer with the *lamas*. Breakfast (Rs40) and dinner (Rs60) served. Rooms have 2 beds and writing tables; most share a clean, tiled toilet. Rooms Rs125-300. ●

Chime Gatsal Ling, Temple Rd. (☎221340), 75m up the driveway opposite the School of Dialectics; it's the big orange bldg. on the left. Part hotel, part housing for Nyingmapa-sect monks. Spotless, carpeted rooms are huge, and the roof is perfect for watching the sun set on the Dhauladars. Doubles Rs80-140. ●

Namgyal Monastery Guest House (☎221492). Lets you share a courtyard with His Holiness' residence and the Tsuglagkhang (Main Temple). The unique ambience of the monks' cells complements the lavish surroundings. Doubles with bath Rs225. ●

BHAGSU AND DHARAMKOT

Blue Heaven (☎221005), just below Dharamkot, a 25min. walk up TIPA Rd. or Rs40 in a rickshaw. Turn right on the forest path. This most tranquil of places has enormous doubles with or without cushy carpet and tiled bathrooms. Doubles Rs150-200. ●

◖ FOOD

The heavy, flat noodles and hunks of mutton should remind you that you're in Tibetan culinary territory. Yet the apple pie on the dessert menu leaves no doubt that Dharamsala is, at the same time, both tourist trap and traveler's heaven.

🍴 **Khana Nirvana,** Temple Rd., above Western Travels. Has possibly the best burritos in Asia; guitars and drums flirt in the background as you sit on comfortably cushioned chairs. This happenin' joint features a "Sunday at Sunset" lecture series, jam sessions M, and an interfaith Shabbat F. Inquire here for volunteer opportunities in Dharamsala. Entrees Rs30-60. Open Su-F 10am-10pm. ❶

Kunga Restaurant and Nick's Italian Kitchen, Bhagsu Rd., before the Green Hotel. A native New Yorker once taught his Bologna-acquired art to Tibetan chefs who have taken the skill to the requisite *bodhisattva* level of perfection. The pasta is homemade, and the Parmesan is flown in fresh from the Apennines. Open daily 6:30am-9:30pm.

Om Restaurant, near the bus circle. Good food and even better prices. A delightful spot to enjoy the sunset over a cup of tea (Rs3). Dishes Rs25-30. Open daily 8am-10pm. ❶

Rangzen's, Bhagsu Rd., just before Nick's Italian Kitchen. This comfortable place has great valley views and serves up Tibetan specialities. Nothing beats the *tsampa* (barley porridge), a Tibetan staple cooked here according to a *Bonpo* shaman's magic formula. Most dishes Rs25-60. Open daily 8am-10pm. ❶

Mt. View Restaurant, Jogibara Rd. On the left, past the post office. The owners toss up authentic Amdo cuisine from the northeastern region of Tibet. Try the hand-pulled noodles *(thankthuk)* and Szechuan hot sauce. Meals Rs20-45. ❶

Green Hotel and Restaurant, Bhagsu Rd. Western hangout and restaurant, this place serves carefully prepared Tibetan and Chinese dishes. Cappuccino (Rs18) makes clear why this is a traveler's favorite. Most dishes Rs25-50. Open daily 7:30am-10pm. ❶

Kailash Hotel and Restaurant, Temple Rd., near the bus circle. Owned by a Tibetan family, Kailash dishes out spicy *momos* to a mostly local crowd; wash 'em down with a cup of mild jasmine tea. Dishes Rs20-75. Open daily 8am-9pm. ❶

📷 SIGHTS

TSUGLAGKHANG TEMPLE. This temple, whose Tibetan name simply means "Main Temple," houses images of the Buddha, Padmasambhava, and Avalokiteshvara ("Chenresig" in Tibetan). This last image, representing the *bodhisattva* of whom the Dalai Lama is an incarnation, was rescued from the Tokhang Temple in Lhasa and brought here during the Chinese Cultural Revolution. On the days of the Buddha's birth, death, and enlightenment, hundreds of monks circumambulate the temple three times on their hands and knees, giving money to the hundreds of beggars who flock to this path during the ceremony. **Remember always to walk clockwise on this path, spin the prayer wheels clockwise, and remove footwear before entering the temple.** Monks from the School of Dialectics come to debate—snapping, clapping, and shouting at each other—in the temple's courtyard in the afternoons. Each snap, clap, and stomp corresponds to a specific point in the argument being advanced. The debates are one of the features of the Gelugpa sect's teachings and are governed by an immensely complex system of logic. *(Behind the Buddhist School of Dialectics; a 10min. walk from the bus circle in McLeod Ganj. Open daily sunrise to sunset.)*

THE BHAGSU-NAG TEMPLE. This temple rests beside several cool *kunds* (pools) where Hindus and monks bathe. According to legend, 9000 years ago, there was a drought in the kingdom of Ajmer, in present-day Rajasthan. To save his realm, King Bhagsu headed to a 5400m high peak nearby, discovered two lakes, and trapped their waters in his bowl. Just as the king lay down to sleep, Nag, the cobra who owned the lakes, challenged him to a fight. Mortally wounded in the ensuing struggle, the king made a dying request for the people of Ajmer to be rid of the drought. Impressed by Bhagsu's devotion to his people, Nag granted him his wish. The fruit of his efforts is today known as the Indira Gandhi Canal, which irrigates most of Rajasthan. The **Bhagsu Waterfall** beyond the temple becomes 10m of cascades during the monsoon season. There are small cafes around the falls. The lower cafe has cold drinks, snacks, and crowds of Indian bathers. The upper one, Shiva Cafe, has hot meals and chess. Above the path to the falls, there are caves where monks meditate for extended periods. *(At the northern end of Bhagsu; a 25min. walk from McLeod Ganj. The waterfall is 15min. beyond the temple; follow signs to the path.)*

NORBU LINGKA. To see Tibetan art head to Norbu Lingka, a compound 10km from Dharamsala. Its bamboo groves enclose a display of Tibetan architecture designed to resemble the symmetries of a *bodhisattva*. The **Norbu Lingka Institute**, dedicated to preserving Tibetan culture, is located here, and it offers an opportunity to watch *thanka* masters, woodcarvers, metal-workers, and their pupils at work. The **Losel Doll Museum** exhibits costumes from Tibet. *(Take a jeep or bus to Lower Dharamsala (Rs5). From there, take the Palampur bus, and get off at Sacred Heart High School (Rs3). From the school, it's a 20min. walk up the road to the left. Open M-Sa 9am-6pm; arrive before 4pm to see the workshops or catch a guided tour. Doll Museum Rs25.)*

THE TIBETAN CHILDREN'S HANDICRAFT AND VOCATIONAL CENTER. The vocational center instructs refugees in the arts of *thanka* painting, carpet weaving, and capitalist marketing. Under the Dalai Lama's patronage, the Tibetan Children's Village School (TCV) has been housing and educating more than 2400 orphaned Tibetan children since 1960. Foreigners are welcome to visit the school. You can volunteer here for a few months or sponsor a child (US$30 per month). Donations are welcome. *(The center is a 30min. walk up the hill from the McLeod Ganj taxi stand. The TCV is a 10min. walk farther uphill, past Dal Lake on the right. School open M-F 9am-4pm.)*

SO YOU SAY YOU'RE RICHARD GERE... To

schedule a private audience with His Holiness the Dalai Lama, send your request four months in advance and start praying. Private audiences are rare but not unheard of, particularly if your reason is truly specific to the Dalai Lama. Much more common are public audiences of 300 people or so, held once or twice a month for foreigners and recent arrivals from Tibet. At a public audience, the crowd files slowly past His Holiness, who takes time to speak and laugh with each person (despite his aides' attempts to speed things up). You need to bring your passport a few days ahead to be cleared for the audience. You can contact the Office of His Holiness the Dalai Lama by mail, phone, or email. (Thekchen Choeling, McLeod Ganj, Dharamsala, HP, 176219; ☎/fax 221492; ohhdl@cta.unv.ernet.in.) Check with the security branch office near Hotel Tibet on Bhagsu Rd. to see when the Dalai Lama will next be in town.

OTHER SIGHTS. The **Dip-Tse-Chok-Ling Monastery** is home to a small (and young) community of monks who built the monastery after the destruction of their own in Tibet. *(A 10min. walk from the bus circle down a stone path that begins just past Om Hotel. Open daily 7am-7pm.)* The original monastery once lay south of Lhasa, and has become functional in recent years. Some of the monks alternate between the two locations. The church of **St. John's in the Wilderness** is a functioning relic of the bygone British era. Lord Elgin, an ex-Viceroy of India, is buried in the church cemetery. *(Follow the narrow road from the Dip-Tse-Chok-Ling monastery guest house up to Cantonment Rd.; from there it's a 15min. walk downhill toward Lower Dharamsala. Open daily 9am-5pm. Sunday services in English 11:30am. Candle-light services on Christmas.)* The **Amnye Machen Institute** aims to bring Tibetan culture into the 21st century. The institute gathers contemporary writers and scholars, translates classical works into Tibetan, publishes journals on history and culture, and serves as the main cartographic center for Tibet. The institute has film festivals, lectures, and other Tibet-related events;

details are on their website. *(On Jogibara Rd., just past the post office. ☎ 220173; www.amnyemachen.org.)* The **Museum of Kangra Art,** opposite the Bank of Baroda in Lower Dharamsala, has nice exhibits of old carpets, Pahari miniatures, and archaeological artifacts from the Kangra region. *(Open Tu-Su 10am-1:30pm and 2-4pm; closed on local and national holidays. Free.)* A pleasant day-hike from Dharamkot takes you to the grassy ridge-top of **Triund.** There's a small rest house here, and a second, more basic rest house 5km up the trail. Resist the urge to climb higher unless you have mountaineering experience. Be prepared for rain in the early afternoon.

GANGCHEN KYISHONG

On Jogibara Rd., halfway between McLeod Ganj and Lower Dharamsala; turn left through the archway. ☎ 222467. Monastery open M-Sa 10am-1pm and 2-5pm, closed 2nd and 4th Sa of each month and on Buddhist holidays. Free. Tibetan center open daily 9am-1pm and 2-5pm. Library reading membership Rs50 per month. 9-month courses in Buddhist philosophy: M-Sa 9 and 11am, except 2nd and 4th Sa of each month; Rs150 per month, plus Rs50 registration fee. Tibetan language courses: spring, summer, and fall daily 10am; Rs250 per month. Rooms available to students enrolled in 2 or more classes: Rs1000-3000 per month.

The site of the administrative offices of the **Tibetan government-in-exile,** Gangchen Kyishong also houses several non-governmental organizations (NGOs), including the **Tibetan Center for Human Rights and Democracy,** on the top floor. Stop by the Ministry of Information for an update on Tibet's political situation. The **Library of Tibetan Works and Archives,** at the far end of Gangchen Kyishong, has 10,000 volumes in English and other languages on Buddhism, Tibet, and related subjects, and 70,000 texts and scrolls in Tibetan. The books and scholarly periodicals are available for general use in the reading room. Language and philosophy courses taught by renowned *lamas* are also offered. You can attend a session or two for free, although the Tibetan government would appreciate the registration fee. Arrive on time for opening prayers, behave respectfully during class hours, remove your shoes before entering the hall, and for philosophy sessions, don't stand up until the *lama* has left. The **museum** has beautiful *thankas,* Tibetan coins, and several rooms rescued from the Cultural Revolution (Rs10). The **Nechung Monastery,** next to the library, is a peaceful spot for meditation.

🎭 ENTERTAINMENT

The market section of Jogibara Rd. is home to two **movie houses** showing a random assortment of American blockbusters, cult classics, and low-grade flicks. The wooden benches are only slightly more comfortable than the seats on a bus, but the big TV screens have good reception. (Check schedule outside theaters for show times; Rs30.) **McLeo's** third-floor bar, on the bus circle, with its Hawaiian decor and haphazard mix of the Beatles, techno, and reggae, is a surreal place to swill beer (Rs75). Young Tibetans gather here to mingle with the mobs of foreigners. Occasional Godfather beer-infused **dance parties** last until the 95%-male dance floor clears around midnight to 2am. The **Tibetan Institute of Performing Arts (TIPA)** has cultural shows, performs a Tibetan opera for the New Year, and usually has shows on Tibetan holidays. Stop in for more details. (A 10min. walk up TIPA Rd. toward Dharamkot. Stop by to check the schedule; if you want to see the theater, be persistent. Open M-Sa 10am-5pm, closed 2nd and 4th Sa.)

VOLUNTEER OPPORTUNITIES

In its struggle for freedom, the Tibetan community has deemed the ability to speak English a priority; therefore, English teachers and simple conversationalists are welcome. The enthusiastic monks and Tibetan students, mostly McLeod Ganj regulars, often agree to exchange regular language lessons with foreigners. Ask around at the various monasteries to see if they would be willing to take on short- or long-term English teachers. The **Tibetan Children's Village** is always interested in committed, long-term English, math, and science teachers.

The **Earthville Institute,** Temple Rd., at the Khana Nirvana Restaurant, serves as a community center, non-profit educational society, and clearing house for info about volunteer opportunities in and around Dharamsala. (☎220073; contactmagazine2003@yahoo.co.in. Write to Khana Nirvana Cafe, Temple Rd., the McLeod Ganj, Dharamsala, HP.) The official **Community Center,** near Rangzen's on Bhagsu Rd., has postings on local events. The **Green Shop,** part of the Center, employs a squad of dedicated workers who operate the recycling unit and teach volunteers how to make paper or bind books. Contact the Tibetan Welfare Office, Environmental Desk (☎221059).

Those interested in short-term projects should consider the **Yong Ling Creche** (☎221028), opposite the nunnery on Jogibara Rd. Yong Ling also organizes home-stays (Rs200 per day including meals). Many Tibetan organizations want to put their message online, so volunteers with web-designing skills are in high demand. Try the **Amnye Machen Institute** (see **Other Sights,** p. 234). Finally, there may be opportunities at the **Tibetan Centre for Human Rights and Democracy,** Gangchen Kyishong, northern building (☎223363; www.tchrd.org); the **Tibetan Youth Congress,** Bhagsu Rd., opposite the Green Shop; the **Tibetan Women's Association** (☎221528; twa19842001@yahoo.com); and the **Tibetan Medical Institute** (☎222618), in the Delek Hospital. All have English publications that need proofreading. You can contact any of the above institutions in writing: name of the institution, P.O. McLeod Ganj, Dharamsala, 176219. Other volunteer opportunities can be found at www.tibet.org.

MEDITATION

Everyone in Dharamsala seems to be involved in some sort of mind and body twisting activity, be it Thai massage, Reiki, yoga, or meditation. If you're interested in joining the fun, ask people who are already involved for recommendations or check the postings around in McLeod Ganj. The **Tushita Meditation Centre** offers 10-day or shorter residential courses that provide a good introduction to Tibetan Buddhism and analytical meditation. The classes are taught by a Tibetan *lama* and a Western monk. Register by phone or email two months in advance. (☎221866; tushita@ndf.vsnl.net.in. Classes Mar.-June and Sept.-Nov. Open M-Sa 10am-noon and 1-4pm; registration M-Sa 1-3pm.) The center also has a **library** with a selection of books on Buddhism, which anyone can borrow after depositing a passport. (Rs10 per book per week. Open M-Sa 10am-4pm.) Also check out the community newsletter *Contact* for info on courses. Another option is the **Vipassana Meditation Centre,** next door, which runs residential courses in single point meditation. Vipassana has centers all over the world, so you can continue your course after leaving Dharamsala. Register by mail and send a brief resume. Registrations are not accepted over the phone, so register in person M-Sa 4-5pm. Both meditation centers operate on expected donations. For professional **acupuncture** or **Thai massage,** head to the third floor of the **Mount View Hotel,** on Jogipurn Rd., past the post office. (☎221309. Open 9am-6:30pm. Reserve one or two days in advance. Massage Rs350 per hr.; acupuncture Rs250 per hr.)

DALHOUSIE डलहौजी ☎01899

Built along the edge of the Dhauladar mountain range, Dalhousie was named for Lord James Ramsey, Marquis of Dalhousie, who became Governor General of India in 1848. The hill station was founded in 1854, when the British rented the land from the largely autonomous Chamba raja in order to expand vacation

options for their increasingly stressed-out administrators and bureaucrats. Designed as a colonial retreat, Dalhousie also played a part in the drama that led to Indian Independence; Subhash Chandra Bose came here during the 1940s to cook up anti-British strategies for the Indian National Army. Cool air and mountainside strolls make Dalhousie a pleasant summer stop, that is, if you can stand the cooing honeymooners and frolicking families that come to town during high season (roughly Apr. 1-Jul. 15). Because of the higher prices and lack of sights and temples, many foreigners skip Dalhousie and head straight for nearby Chamba.

Buses depart from the main bus stand to: **Chamba** (2hr., 4 per day 7am-3:30pm, Rs35); **Dharamsala** (5hr., 3 per day 7am-8:30pm, Rs85); **Pathankot** (3½hr., frequent 5am-4:30pm, Rs50); **Shimla** (12hr., 12:45pm, Rs185); **Khajjiar** (1hr., 2-3 per day 9-10am, Rs50). All Dharsamsala and Pathankot buses stop in **Baniket,** where there are many more connections. Pathankot has more connections, including to **Amritsar** and **Jammu.**

All of Dalhousie can be covered on foot. Facing the taxi counter, the narrow road that heads to the right from the **bus stand** leads to **Subhash Chowk** (10min. walk). The steps to the left climb up to **Gandhi Chowk.** The *chowks* are round plazas connected by two horizontal roads, **Mall Road** on the northern side of the ridge and **Garam Sarak** to the south. Most of the hotels and restaurants are on these two streets. **Treks 'n' Travels,** at Gandhi Chowk, makes ticket reservations, and organizes treks. (Open daily 9am-10pm.) **Broad Street** leads down the hill from Subhash Chowk to **Punjab National Bank,** which changes cash and traveler's checks. (Open M-F 10am-2pm, Sa 10am-noon.) Across the street is the **police station.** (☎242126. Open 24hr.) **Dalhousie Medical Hall Pharmacy.** (Open M-Sa 8am-6pm, Su 8am-2pm.) Across the street is the **Civil Hospital.** (☎242125. Open 24hr.) The **post office** is also at Gandhi Chowk (open M-Sa 9am-5pm). **Postal Code: 176304.**

There are plenty of hotels in Dalhousie, and during the low season you can get a sizeable room with a view and private bath for Rs200 (plus Rs100 for a heater). In-season (Apr. 15-July 1 and Sept. 15-Nov. 15), prices are usually at least double. Dalhousie has a water shortage problem, and running water is often limited or unavailable. The friendly **Hotel Crags ❸,** Garam Sarak, a 5-minute walk from Subhash Chowk, has some of the best views on the ridge. Most rooms are equipped with wood-framed beds, mirrors, and TV. (☎242124. Rooms Rs400-700. Off-season 50% discount.) If you are short on cash, walk up the road opposite State Bank of India to the **Youth Hostel ❶.** The squat toilets are not exactly sparkling, but are still bearable. Check-in 7-10am and 5-9pm. Doors lock at 10pm, lights out by 11pm. (☎242189. Dorms Rs50; rooms Rs100.) At Subhash Chowk, **Friends Punjabi Dhaba ❷** is well known for its good food. The service is slow, but the view makes up for it. (Entrees Rs30-150. Open daily 8:30am-10:30pm.) **Amritsari Dhaba ❶,** just beyond Friends Punjabi, is a well-furnished place with quick service. *Dal mah* fried (Rs18). (Open daily 8am-11pm.)

Most people come to Dalhousie to stroll the tree-lined streets, breathe the pine-fresh air, and enjoy the mountain views. The **Garam Sarak walk** is especially pleasant, since no cars are allowed on the road. Along the road, Tibetan refugees have painted reliefs of Chenresig (of whom the Dalai Lama is an incarnation) and other Tibetan notables onto the stone cliffs. Panch Pulla Rd., off Gandhi Chowk, leads to a dried-up **water spring,** notable because Ajit Singh, a supporter of Subhash Chandra Bose, died here on Independence Day. **Khajjiar,** a pristine meadow 22km from Dalhousie, is trumpeted by the local tourist industry as "the Switzerland of the East." The scenery is beautiful, but be prepared to share it with hundreds of yodeling tourists, who arrive by the busload. **Horseback riding** is Rs50 per hr.

CHAMBA चम्बा ☎01899

Locked in between four major mountain ranges (Shivalik, Dhauladhar, Pir Panjal, and the Greater Himalayas), the region of Chamba is often referred to as the lap of the Himalayas. At an altitude of 990m, Chamba is high enough to escape the scorching Punjabi heat, but remains warmer and drier than Dalhousie or Dharamsala. The town, filled with porticoed houses and hidden temples, stretches along the slopes that rise above the Sal and Ravi Rivers. It was founded in AD 940 as the new capital of an older princely state administered from Bharmour. Mountain ridges, isolation, altitude, and wily diplomacy have kept the Chamba Valley pretty much independent ever since. The Mughals never managed to reach this far, and Chamba's temples were spared the miserable fate of so many Hindu shrines in other parts of the country. Improved roads have brought new residents, but Chamba has maintained its individuality. The trademark styles of cooking, handicrafts, and art that developed over the centuries can be seen in the town's restaurants, craft shops, and museum. Town spirit peaks in early August, when residents celebrate a riotous week-long harvest festival, **Minjar**.

⫶ TRANSPORTATION

Buses go to: **Bharmour** (3½hr., 9 per day 5am-4:10pm, Rs50); **Dalhousie** (2½hr., 9 per day 6am-6:30pm); **Dharamsala** (8hr., 6 per day 6am-9:30pm, Rs140); **Manali** (14hr., 11:30am, Rs3100); **Pathankot** (5hr., 7 per day 5:30am-midnight, Rs80); **Khajjian** (1½hr, 3 per day 7:30am-5:15pm, Rs19). With the exception of Bharmour buses, all buses stop in **Baniket**.

✴ 🛈 ORIENTATION AND PRACTICAL INFORMATION

Most businesses are concentrated around **Court Road,** which runs from the crowded **bus stand** area in the south of town along the eastern side of the **Chaugan,** Chamba's grassy mall and cricket ground. Court Rd. becomes **Hospital Road** and then loops back through chicken shacks and liquor counters as **Museum Road** Uphill from Court Rd., past the Chaugan, is **Temple Road,** which leads to the **Laxmi Narayan Temple** and into alleys packed with ancient shrines. **Mani Mahesh Travels** (☎222507), next to the entrance to Laxmi Narayan Temple, is very helpful with train reservations, treks, and temple info. Farther down, on Hospital Rd., the **Punjab National Bank** changes traveler's checks. (Open M-F 10am-2pm, Sa 10am-noon.) **Pharmacies** line Hospital Rd. There is a **District Hospital,** Hospital Rd. (☎222392. Open 24hr.) There are also a few private clinics. The **police station** is on Hospital Rd. (☎222226). There is **Internet** access at **Mani Mahesh Travels.** On the Chaugan, 20m past Hotel Inavati, is the antediluvian **post office.** (Open M-Sa 9:30am-4pm.) **Postal Code:** 176310.

⫶ ⫶ ACCOMMODATIONS AND FOOD

Chamba's accommodations scene ain't spectacular. An exception is the ▓**Orchard Hut** ❶, a wood-and-clay guest house and restaurant high up on the slope away from the Sal River, 12km from Chamba in the Panj-La Valley. Everything you eat, from the plum preserves served with crisp *parathas*, to the fresh vegetables, is organically grown around the hut. Call ahead or stop by Mani Mahesh Travels (see p. 238), run by the same family. To get to the hut, take the Chamba-Sahoo bus from the Chamba bus stand and get off at the Chaminu stop. Walk across the river and hike 20min. uphill; ask in the Chaminu store for directions. Cooking lessons (Rs100), Hindi lessons (Rs100),

and organic farming workshops are available. Ask about hiking to the family's mountain-top cottage, 4hr. uphill from the hut. (☎222607. Rs380-650 per person per day. Includes feasts of delectable local and Indian food.) Another decent stop is **Rishi Hotel and Restaurant ❶**, up Temple Rd., on the right. Rooms are small but clean, with seat toilets and cable TV. Some rooms have views of the temple interior. (Singles Rs150; doubles Rs300.) **Jimmy's Inn ❶**, right across from the bus station, has small rooms with seat toilets and hot water, but with its proximity to the bus station, you may wake up to the sound of Tata horns blaring. (☎224748. Check-out noon. Dorms Rs50; doubles Rs300.)

Chamba is well-known for its sweet-but-fiery chili sauce, *chukh*, which the bold can sample on fried chicken at shops along Museum Rd. Two floors above the shops, the **Park View Restaurant and Milk Bar ❶**, serves up the local specialty, *madhara*, kidney beans and curry cooked in *ghee* (Rs50). (Open daily 9am-10pm.)

◉ SIGHTS

BHURI SINGH MUSEUM. To learn about Chamba's royal and military past, head north on Museum Rd. to the Bhuri Singh Museum. Named for Raja Bhuri Singh, ruler of the Chamba district from 1904-1919, the museum displays his collection of small weaponry, musical instruments, *rumals* (a form of silk embroidery native to the valley), and a collection of *pahari* miniatures. *(Open Tu-Su 10am-5pm. Free.)*

LAXMI NARAYAN TEMPLE. The largest temple complex in Chamba is the Laxmi Narayan Temple, up Temple Rd., opposite the Akhand Chandi Palace. The shrines in the complex date from the 9th to the 10th centuries, when Chamba's founder commissioned the main temple and the statue of Laxmi Narayan (Vishnu asleep on the cosmic ocean) inside it. The copper statue of Gauri Shankar is an excellent example of metal work in Chamba. *(Open daily 5am-noon and 2-8pm.)* The **Hari Rai Temple,** on Museum Rd., next to the red gate, was built in the *shikhara* style during the 9th century and is covered with Kama Sutra carvings.

DURGA TEMPLES. A walk along the outskirts of town will take you past several other important holy sites. From the bus stand, a short climb south and east leads to the long staircase up to Chamunda Devi Temple. Chamunda Devi is a form of the goddess Durga in a wrathful temper; the brass bells are meant to clear your head of worldly scheming. At the northern edge of Chamba, above the road to Sahoo, is the ancient temple of Vajreshwari. Tradition has it that this is the oldest temple in Chamba, a thank-you gift from Raja Sahil Varman to the family who donated the land for the town. Although a number of stone carvings have been looted from the sides of the main shrine, finely crafted images of Durga, Undavi (the goddess of food), and other deities grace its walls. Look for the Tibetan-style demonic faces at the back of the main shrine—their presence here is a mystery.

RANG MAHAL AND HIMACHAL EMPORIUM. When they weren't trying to keep the gods happy, Chamba's 18th-century elite retired to the Mughal-style corridors of the **Rang Mahal** ("Old Palace"). Dominating the upper center of Chamba, the palace houses the **Himachal Emporium,** a shop selling *rumals*, hand-woven shawls, candle holders, and brass plates. Ask the shopkeeper to see the workshop upstairs.

▶ DAYTRIPS FROM CHAMBA

BHARMOUR
Bharmour is a bumpy, sometimes harrowing, 3½hr. bus ride (Rs50) away from Chamba.

The capital of the Chamba Valley from the 6th to the early 10th centuries, Bharmour's temple square encloses 84 separate shrines, most only a few feet tall, and some dating back to the 7th century. The most famous of these is the Narsingha Temple with its half-lion, half-man statue dedicated to the incarnation of Vishnu who descended to earth to destroy an evil spirit who could not be killed. Once Narsingha tasted blood, however, he just kept on killing. Realizing his demonic powers, he went up into the mountains where there was less to kill. The temple is supposedly built on the site where he secluded himself. Aside from the temples, Bharmour is in a very peaceful spot far away from the onslaught of tourism.

Bharmour is the trailhead for **treks** over the Dhauladhar and Pir Panjal ranges. In the summer, you're likely to meet some of the nomadic shepherds who make seasonal migrations up and down the valley. It is also the starting point of the **Manimahesh Yatra,** a devotional procession that winds its way 34km up to the lake at Manimahesh, where people worship and bathe in the icy waters. The procession takes place in September, 15 days after Krishna's birthday. There are no restaurants in town, but food stalls line the main streets.

SAHOO
A 1hr. bus ride from Chamba or a gorgeous 20min. bike ride from the Orchard Hut.

The quiet farming village of Sahoo is in the opposite direction from Bharmour, up the Sal River valley. It has an 11th-century temple and breathtaking views of the Pir Panjal range. The **Chandra Shekhar** (moon-crowned Shiva) temple houses an ancient Shiva *linga*, apparently given to spurts of rapid and inexplicable growth—a hole had to be cut into the temple's stone ceiling to accommodate the *linga's* sky-high ambitions until a visiting priest was able to bring it back down to size. The ceiling has since been removed and now stands in front of the temple, where worshippers crawl through it for luck and strength. Opposite the *linga* is a particularly fine stone sculpture of Nandi. In earlier times, when the temple bell was struck, the ball around Nandi's neck would resonate. These days, devotees coat the image with a thick layer of *ghee*, muffling the sound.

KULLU कुल्लू ☎ 01902
Kullu is tucked between two green mountains at the southern end of the Kullu Valley. Tourists often pass through on their way to the beautiful Parbati Valley and nearby Naggar and Manali, missing the lively pedestrian market and shawl shopping (mostly outside of town) that the bustling town has to offer. Every year in early October, however, tourists and Indians crowd Kullu for **Dussehra,** a huge festival celebrating the 360 gods of the Himachal Valley.

Bhuntar Airport is 10km to the south of town. Most local buses heading to points south along Route 21 stop at the airport (Rs12); ask before boarding to be certain. There are also 10 buses per day in each direction that connect Kullu's main bus stand to Bhuntar (Rs8). Taxis cost Rs100-125 and auto-rickshaws are around Rs75. **Ambassador Travel** has an office a short walk off the maidan on the road to Manali. They book flights from Bhuntar and for Indian Airlines in general. **Flights** go to Delhi (M, W, F 11:10am; US$130). **Buses** can be booked at the **booking office** (☎ 222728), open daily 4am-9pm, and go to: **Amritsar** (12hr., 4 and 5:30pm, Rs237-257); **Delhi** (12hr., 9 per day 4am-7pm, Rs302-526); **Dharamsala** (9hr, 3 per day 9:30am-8:30pm, Rs165); **Jammu** (13hr., 4:30 and 6pm, Rs252); **Manali** (2hr., every 15min. 4am-6pm, Rs30); **Manikaran** (2½hr., 5 per day, 6:30a,-1:30pm, Rs35); **Naggar** (1½hr., every hr, Rs20); **Shimla** (10hr., 5 per day, 4:15am-8:45pm, Rs167-175).

The main **bus station** is at the north end of town, next to the river. Above the bus station, across the footbridge and to the left, extends the **market street,** leading to the **maidan,** Kullu's main square and cricket ground. The **State Bank of India,** 1km from the center of town, is the nearest place to exchange currency and traveler's checks. (Open M-F 10am-2pm, Sa 10am-noon.) Vipasha Guest House, in the pedestrian market, has **Internet access** (Rs70 per hr.). The **post office** is on the road that branches to the left of the National Hwy. as you walk north from the maidan, 20m after the split on the left. Open M-Sa 10am-5pm. **Postal Code:** 175101.

   The Madhu Chandrika Guest House ● has balconies that look out over the town, the Beas River, and surrounding mountains. (☎224395. Dorms Rs50; doubles Rs150-300. Off-season 50% discount.) Turn right at the top of the pedestrian market, and walk 50m past the post office to reach **Shishamati Resort,** which has large carpeted rooms with TVs and amazing views. (☎224133. Doubles Rs110-550.) Most of the food in Kullu is of the street-stall variety. Kill your hankering for samosas and *pakoras* at the pedestrian market across the river from the bus stand. **Hotstuff ●** dishes up excellent pizzas (Rs45 and up) and burgers (Rs40).

⚄ DAYTRIP FROM KULLU: BIJLI MAHADEV TEMPLE. A daytrip from Kullu takes you up to the **Bijli Mahadev** (God of Electricity) **Temple** where, legend has it, lightning strikes each year and breaks the massive *linga*, which then has to be reassembled by a priest. Take a bus from town (Rs8) to the Chan Sari stop; from there, hike 3km uphill to the temple, where you can observe the pilgrimage rites.

NAGGAR नाग्गर   ☎01902

Halfway between Kullu and Manali, on the eastern side of the Beas River, rests the hillside village of Naggar, blanketed by pine forests, apple orchards, and fields of cannabis. The regional capital until the mid-1600s, Naggar is now a serene town with slate-shingled roofs, delicate temples, and a mountain-top art gallery. While Manali has been overrun by hash-smoking tourists and Kullu is frantic, Naggar is a peaceful haven to begin or end some fine trekking.

◨⚄ ORIENTATION AND PRACTICAL INFORMATION. Buses arrive and depart by the shops on the highway 1km below the **castle.** Buses to **Kullu** (1½hr., every hr. 6am-6pm, Rs20), **Manali** (1½hr., every hr. 6am-6pm, Rs15) and other destinations such as Dharamsala and Chandigarh are more frequent at **Patilkahl,** across the river. To get to the castle from Patilkahl, walk across the bridge, and take the shortcut path along the creek in front of you (a 45min. walk up). Or, take a taxi or rickshaw (Rs50-80). To get to the castle from Naggar's bus stop, walk (10min.) or take an auto rickshaw (Rs20). There is a small **hospital** opposite Hotel Alliance, 2km. above the bus stand. (Open M-F 9:30am-4pm.) The **post office** is on the narrow road below the castle. (Open M-Sa 10am-4pm.) **Postal Code:** 175130.

◩◪ ACCOMMODATIONS AND FOOD. Hotel Alliance ● is up the hill toward the Roerich Gallery. The attached restaurant offers excellent French and local cuisine. (☎248263. Rooms Rs120-250; room rates often negotiable.) **Poonam Mountain Lodge ●,** 50m below the castle, blends with the traditional village architecture. Poonan also rents a fully equipped cottage, 1km above the village, and has an attached vegetarian restaurant. (☎248248. Rooms Rs150-250.) **Sheetal Guest House ❷,** next to the castle, has rooms ranging from a dark double with common bath to a spacious single with shower and magnificent views. (☎248250. Rooms Rs200-550.) Also near the Castle, **Ragini Hotel ❷** has large rooms, hot water, balconies in most rooms, and a rooftop garden. (☎248185. Rooms Rs330-600.) **La Purezza Cafe ●,** on the road above the Tripuri temple, loads you with fresh pasta (Rs50-80) and other carbs. (Open 10:30am-10:30pm.) The patio at **Rag Cafe ●,** before the gallery entrance, serves tea (from Rs3) as you bask.

◙ SIGHTS. Naggar's 507-year-old castle, 1km up from the highway, houses an expensive hotel and a sacred slab of stone called **Jagti Patt.** Local legend has it that the valley's gods were "transformed into honey bees endowed with great strength" to cut the hefty block and fly it up. On top of the hill, past the Castle Hotel, the **Tripuri Sundri Temple,** with its three-tiered pagoda roof, is the site of a local *mela* in mid-May. Farther up the pine-lined road, past the Alliance Hotel, stands the **Nikolai Roerich Art Gallery,** named for the early 20th-century Russian artist who settled there with his family. The house displays paintings which capture the spirit of the Himalayas. Roerich was also highly respected by the Indian government: letters from state authorities and a portrait of Indira Gandhi, done by Roerich's son, adorn the gallery. The Roerich-founded **Urusvati Institute,** 200m farther, once had a faculty of leading scholars of Himalayan culture. *Urusvati* means "Light of the Morning Star," and the Institute was said to "radiate" the sacred knowledge revealed by the mountains. Now, it is the site of the **Himalayan Folk and Tribal Gallery,** which holds collections of traditional North Indian dress and metalwork. The gallery upstairs has some of Nikolai's earlier mystic paintings, a few works by his son Sviatoslav, and a number of paintings by local Kullu artists influenced by Roerich. *(Both galleries open Tu-Sa 10am-1pm and 1:30-6pm. Rs20 ticket covers both.)*

◙ TREKKING

Naggar is an ideal base for treks up the slopes of the Valley of Gods. **Himalayan Mountain Treks,** at Poonam Lodge, is a reliable trekking agency. They organize treks all over Himachal Pradesh, as well as paragliding, fishing, and jeep safari expeditions. (☎248248. Fully organized treks Rs1000 per person per day; treks with only a guide and a tent Rs500; prices are negotiable for groups of 2 or more.)

A two-day hike over the **Chandrakhani La** (3660m) takes you to **Malana,** a mountain village whose inhabitants claim to be descendants of Greek soldiers under Alexander the Great. Malana has never come under the patronage of the Government of India Tourism Department, and visitors are not allowed to touch the villagers or the holy stones. The fine for violating this law is Rs1000. Tents and sleeping bags are recommended as there are only 1 or 2 guest houses in Malana. From here, you can continue to **Manikaran, Jari,** or **Kasol,** in the Parbati Valley (see below). Manikaran is a base for treks over the Pin-Parbati Pass (see **Treks around Kaza,** p. 255). Streams in both the Kullu and Parbati Valleys have trout. Many trekking agencies offer fishing trips and equipment rentals.

JARI ☎01902

From the road, Jari appears to be just a collection of shops perched high on the edge of the Parbati Valley, halfway between Bhuntar and Manikaran. A 10min. walk up through cornfields, sunflowers, and apple trees, however, brings you to Jari's quiet village, home to a handful of *"shanti* places," guest houses where peace-loving foreigners come to gaze at the mountains on long holidays. Owing to the 5-year-old hydroelectric power project 2km up the river, many tourists have been scared away from Jari, leaving the village a scenic hideout for travelers in need of respite from the hippie, hash-smoking, trekking masses.

Buses bound for **Manikaran** (1hr., Rs10) and **Bhuntar** (1½hr., Rs25) stop in front of the Village Photostat every 30min. With the river at your back and Village Photostat (**Internet** Rs80 per hr.) in front of you, the **police station** (☎276074) is 2km to the left, up the road near the power project. There is a small **hospital,** 150m to your right, on the other side of the road. (☎276257. Open 24hr.) Just across the street from the hospital is the very clean and pleasant **Om Shira Guesthouse,** with views of the valley. (☎276202. Rooms Rs100-150.) A 10min. hike left and up the paved path beside the Village Photstat takes

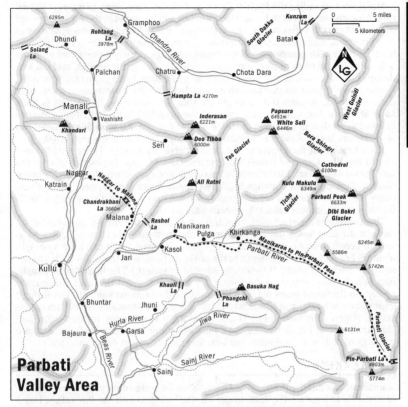

Parbati Valley Area

you to the village, where there are many lovely, quality guest houses. Another good option is the **Village Guesthouse,** set among cornfields and gardens. (☎276070. Rooms Rs75-100.) All of the guest houses have **cafes.** There are **no currency exchange** services in Jari.

MANIKARAN ☎01902

The town of Manikaran is situated in the beautiful Parbati Valley. With its ancient temples, famous hot springs, which are a Sikh pilgrimage site, and plentiful supply of the valley's most renowned cash-crop, Manikaran draws trekkers, hippies, and travelers looking for some rest and relaxation. A good alternative to Manali's tourist glut, many visitors to Manikaran have decided to turn short stays into long ones. The town's hot springs are the centerpiece of the modern village. According to local lore, Naga, the serpent god, stole Parvati's earrings, returned to his subterranean lair, and sequestered the jewelry inside his nostrils. When Parvati's lover, Mahadeva, threatened the thief, Naga became so angry that he snorted out the earrings with such force that they tore through the earth, creating the hot springs.

Buses leave for **Bhuntar** (2½hr., every 30min., Rs25) and stop at the Parbati villages along the valley road, including **Kasol** and **Jari.** From Bhuntar, there are many connections to **Kullu, Manali, Shimla,** and other major destinations.

Manikaran straddles the Parbati River, and almost everything of interest to visitors is located on the north bank. There is a **bus and taxi stand** at the far eastern end of town where the valley road ends on the south bank. A bridge crosses the river at the bus stand, and a footbridge straddles the river near the western end of town, leading to the **Sikh gurudwara** and the famous **springs.** Between these two crossing points is a pedestrian market, crowded with *dhabas*, guest houses, and trinket-dealers. There is no Internet access here, so you'll have to go to Jari for your e-fix.

Manikaran's guest houses tend to be squished into the pedestrian market along the north bank. A noisy but clean choice that almost always has rooms is **Hotel Amar ❶,** at the bus stand. Some rooms have attached bath. (☎273740. Doubles Rs100-200.) A decent option in the thick of the market is **Paradise Guest House** with some rooms overlooking the river and hot springs. (☎273075. Rooms Rs100.)

The **dhabas** near the center of Manikaran serve cheap eats. There are also several Indian, Western, and Israeli food places. The one upscale place in town is the **Holy Palace Restaurant,** identifiable by its ornate and carved wooden exterior in the market. Porridge with bananas Rs25. **Hot Spring Restaurant ❶,** near the springs, plays Western music and serves pizza (Rs30-80) and burgers. Other dishes Rs25-90. They also organize **treks.** (Open daily 8am-midnight.)

The **hot springs** are the highlight of the town. To see the springs you must enter through the **Guru Nanak Dev Ji Gurudwara,** at the western end of town. (Ask permission to enter. Remove your shoes and cover your head.) You can take a complimentary hot bath here. The men's baths are open pools and the women's baths are separate enclosed pools. (Open daily sunrise to sunset.) The **Ram Mandir Temple,** between the two bridges on the north bank road, is also worth a visit. Some parts are over a thousand years old, and the intricate decorations highlight the spring's importance as a Sikh and Hindu pilgrimage site. Small donations (Rs10) are appreciated. (Open daily 8am-9pm.) The wooden **Naini Devi Temple,** located near Ram Mandir, is not as big as its neighbor, but the temple's interior features intricate carvings of deities and religious symbols and motifs. (Open daily 9am-7pm.)

◤ TREKKING

Manikaran and nearby Kasol are popular bases for treks of varying degrees of difficulty. It is at least a 6-day hike to the Pin-Parbati Pass into the Pin Valley. Day 1 (9-10km) brings you to **Khirkanga** and a tea stall. Day 2 (11-12km) takes you across the river suspended in a cable car to **Tantapuj,** where there is shelter and another tea stall. On day 3, you'll find yourself at **Takarkua,** at which point you'll need a **stove** because there is no wood to be found anywhere. There is a shelter here. On Day 4, you'll cross back over the river to **Pandupul,** with a cave and **Mantalai.** You'll have to pick your way across rocks to the **Base Camp** on Day 5, where the glacier begins. Glacial conditions vary considerably. **Be sure to consult with a trekking agency, and bring a guide before you set off on this trek.** Finally, on Day 6, you'll make it up through the Pin Pass and into the Pin Valley. From here, it's another 2 days to the village of **Mud,** where there is a road and you can bus or taxi to **Kaza** in the **Spiti Valley** (see p. 255). One trekking agent in Manikaran can be found at Hot Spring Restaurant (see above, Rs250-300 per day for a porter). Another excellent guide to the region is at Himalayan Mountain Treks in Naggar (see p. 242).

MANALI मनाली ☎ 01902

At once both Indian honeymooner's paradise and Himalayan backpacker's base camp, Manali boasts a range of activities. Romantic treks, handicraft shopping, rugged mountain biking, and night long raves entice some visitors into month-long stays, but a day or two resting up in Manali should suffice for the traveler heading to the north in Ladakh or to the east in Lahaul and Spiti. The Mall and the Model Town in Manali are the headquarters of the Indian tourist invasion, but choice guest houses and restaurants make Old Manali a more mellow and inviting option.

HASHISH IN MANALI. Manali, where cannabis grows wild, has been touted as the cool place to hang out and smoke hash, but stories of local use have been greatly exaggerated. It is used by locals only in times of duress or during cold weather. A number of foreigners every year are searched and arrested for hash possession, resulting in hefty fines of Rs1000-10,000. Saying that you were feeling cold or under duress will get you nowhere. However painful it might be to see a wild hash plant and not smoke it, **hashish is illegal, even in Manali.**

TRANSPORTATION

Flights: The nearest airport is the **Kullu-Manali Airport** in Bhuntar, 52km from Manali (see **Kullu,** p. 240). **Matkon Travel** (☎ 252838), at the intersection of Old Manali Rd. and The Mall, is the agent for Jagson Airlines. To **Delhi** (M, W, F 11:10am; under 30 US$130, over 30 $170).

Buses: The **bus stand** is right in the center of the Mall. To: **Amritsar** (15hr., 2pm and 7pm, Rs290); **Chamba** (15hr., 7pm, Rs310); **Dehra Dun** (17½hr., 6:30pm, Rs340); **Delhi** (16hr., 6 per day 11:30am-5pm, Rs335; deluxe 14hr., 5pm, Rs565); **Dharamsala** (10hr.; 8:10am, 6 and 7pm; Rs196); **Haridwar** (19hr., 10am and 12:40pm, Rs335); **Jammu** (16hr., 4 and 10pm, Rs285); **Keylong** (6hr., every 45min. 5:30am-6pm, Rs95); **Kullu** (2hr., every 15min. 5am-6:30pm, Rs35); **Leh** (48hr., noon, Rs430); **Naggar** (1½hr., every 30min. 5am-6:30pm, Rs25); **Shimla** (10hr., 6:10 and 7am, Rs200; semi-deluxe (with fan) 9hr., 6 and 7:15pm, Rs208). Government deluxe buses can be booked at the **Himachal Tourism Marketing Office,** The Mall (☎ 253531). The deluxe bus stand is at the southern end of town, a 300m walk down along The Mall. Confirm where your bus departs from. Private deluxe buses operated by agencies like **Matkon Travel** are usually cheaper and can be booked at any travel agency around town. To: **Delhi** (15hr.; 3:30 and 4pm; in-season Rs500, off-season Rs350); **Dharamsala** (10hr., 7:30pm, Rs300/250); **Shimla** (10hr., 7:30 and 8:30am, Rs300/200); **Leh** via shared taxi (17½hr., 3:30am) or deluxe bus (48hr., 6am, Rs800-900). For info on the **Manali-Leh Road,** see p. 258.

ORIENTATION AND PRACTICAL INFORMATION

Manali is built in a rough "Y" shape. **The Mall** makes up the trunk, where you'll find a **bus stand** and most other tourist services. Off to either side are alleys lined with gift shops, *dhabas,* and provision stores. The latter are particularly common just behind and north of the bus stand. The Mall splits at the Nehru Statue, and the left fork leads uphill 1km on the **Old Manali Road,** separating **Model Town** on the left from the **Great Himalayan National Park** on the right before making a descent to the bridge over the Manalsu River. Across the bridge, **Old Manali** spreads out along the uphill road to your left. Taking the right fork at the Nehru statue leads you across the **Beas River bridge.** Continue 2km upstream along the road and turn right for the steep 1km ascent that leads to the village of **Vashisht.**

Tourist Office: Government of India Tourist Office, The Mall (☎ 252175), close to the Nehru Statue next to Hotel Kunzam. Open M-Sa 10am-5pm. **HPTDC Marketing Office,** The Mall (☎ 252116), in a white bldg. next door to the govt. tourist office, books trains and buses. Open M-Sa 8am-8pm; 9am-5pm during winter (Nov-Mar).

Budget Travel: Plenty of travel agents offer treks (US$30 per person per day, all inclusive) and rafting trips (starting at Rs900 per day). Two reliable companies are **Dragon Tours** (☎ 252790; fax 252769), in Old Manali, open from 10am-9pm, which also organizes shared taxis and exchanges currency, and **Himalayan Journeys** (☎ 252365; www.himalayanjourneysindia.com), just past the bus stand, open 9am-9pm, which also doubles as an Airtel cellphone agent.

Currency Exchange: State Bank of India, Old Manali Rd., just past the Mall. Speedy service for all the usual currency needs. Open M-F 10am-2pm, Sa 10am-1pm.

Police: The police station (☎ 252326) is next to the deluxe bus stand.

Hospital: Mission Hospital, School Rd. (☎ 252379). A block west of the mall. **Khana's Clinic,** Old Manali Rd. Open M-Sa 8am-2pm and 4-8pm, Su 10am-2pm.

Internet: Nirvana Cybercafe, on the road between Model Town and Old Manali offers convenient access and good rates (Rs45 per hr.) for Manali. Open daily 10am-8pm. **Cyberia,** to the left of the Manalsu bridge, is email central but the wait can be long. Rs60 per hr. Open daily 9am-10pm.

Post Office: Down the alley opposite the bus stand and to the right of Monal Himalayan Travels. Open M-Sa 10am-5pm. **Postal Code:** 175131.

◤ ACCOMMODATIONS

Most travelers trek to Old Manali, where guest houses can't be told apart from village houses. The farther up the hill, the quieter the lodgings and the better the views. To avoid the crowds and enjoy a soak in some hot springs, head down to **Vashisht** (rickshaw from Manali Rs60 up, Rs30-40 down), where most guest houses are around the temple and have hot baths. The area between the Old Manali Rd. and the Hadimba Temple, known as the **Model Town,** is an agglomeration of large hotels inundated by Indian tourists and honeymooners. Remember, almost all guest house rates are negotiable, especially in off-season or if you are willing to shop around, so bargain away.

OLD MANALI

▒ **Monal Guest House** (☎ 253848). On the top of the hill, Monal is the last house in the village. The astounding views of the river and the mountains, and location at a popular trailhead into the valley make the climb and search for the tough-to-find guest house well worth it. Make the first trip in daylight, and bring a good flashlight to find your way back at night. Front rooms Rs150; back Rs80. ❶

Raj Guest House (☎ 253570). Follow the dirt trail from the end of the tarred Old Manali Rd. The older rooms share a clean bathroom and a porch with gorgeous views. The new rooms in the back all have tiled baths but lack views. Filled with hippies, backpackers and long term Old-Manali *firangis*, Raj Guest house is more lively than places farther up the hill. Rooms Rs80-200. Off-season Rs50-150. ❶

Hotel Splendour, up the hill in Old Manali; look for the small beat-up "endour" (the "Spl" worn out) sign on your right, or ask a local to point you to the small side path that takes you 5min. through apple orchards and cornfields to the guest house. Perched farther out than most accommodations, Splendour offers a remote feel and magnificent views. Each room has a water heater and seat toilet. Singles Rs150; doubles Rs250; pitch your own tent Rs75; 2-person tent rental Rs200. Off-season discounts. ❷

John Banon's Guest House (☎ 252335 or 252388), a 5min. walk up Old Manali Rd. from the Mall. One of the oldest, best-maintained hotels in Manali, with its own private apple orchard. Spacious, carpeted rooms with huge windows and working fireplaces. Doubles Rs450-550. Make reservations 1 month in advance during in season. ❸

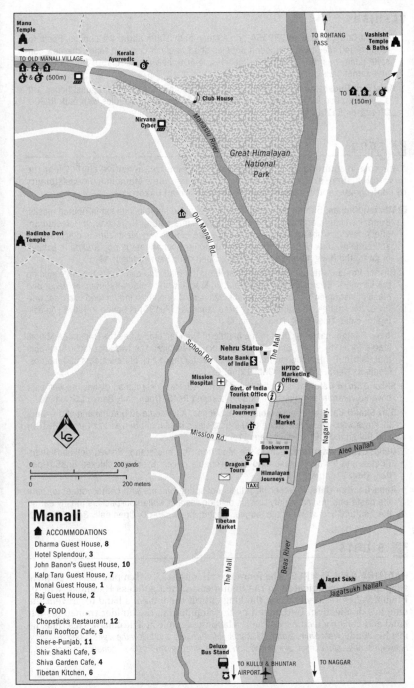

Manu Temple

TO OLD MANALI VILLAGE,

Kerala Ayurvedic

Club House

Nirvana Cyber

Manaslu River

Great Himalayan National Park

TO ROHTANG PASS

Vashisht Temple & Baths

TO (150m)

Hadimba Devi Temple

Old Manali Rd.

School Rd.

Nehru Statue

State Bank of India

The Mall

HPTDC Marketing Office

Mission Hospital

Govt. of India Tourist Office

Himalayan Journeys

New Market

Nagar Hwy.

Aleo Nallah

Mission Rd.

Bookworm

Dragon Tours

Chopsticks

Himalayan Journeys

TAXI

Tibetan Market

The Mall

Beas River

Jagat Sukh

Jagatsukh Nallah

N

0   200 yards
0   200 meters

Manali

♠ ACCOMMODATIONS

Dharma Guest House, 8
Hotel Splendour, 3
John Banon's Guest House, 10
Kalp Taru Guest House, 7
Monal Guest House, 1
Raj Guest House, 2

🍎 FOOD

Chopsticks Restaurant, 12
Ranu Rooftop Cafe, 9
Sher-e-Punjab, 11
Shiv Shakti Cafe, 5
Shiva Garden Cafe, 4
Tibetan Kitchen, 6

Deluxe Bus Stand

TO KULLU & BHUNTAR AIRPORT

TO NAGGAR

VASHISHT

Dharma Guest House (☎252354), on a steep path 100m above the springs. Porch for reading and meditation. Wooden doubles share a clean common toilet; the new concrete annex has rooms with extra facilities. Rs100; new rooms Rs350. The owners run an Internet cafe in a nearby building. ❶

Kalp Taru Guest House (☎253443), right next to the baths. Standard guest house with a great location for those planning long soaks in the baths. Doubles with bath Rs200. Off-season Rs100. ❷

🞑 FOOD

Numerous restaurants in Old Manali have imaginative, inventive chefs. Near the bus station, there's at least one *dhaba* down every alley. Manali also boasts plenty of falafel joints and several strudel-serving "German bakeries."

Tibetan Kitchen, 50m to the right of the bridge in Old Manali. With small Tibetan masks, Buddhist chants and a picture of the Dalai Lama setting the scene, this restaurant offers delicious Tibetan, Japanese and Chinese food in very clean surroundings. Try the authentic *gyathuk* (Rs45) here before attempting second rate *dhaba thukpa* in Lahaul, or go for the Hong Kong chicken (Rs65). Open daily 8am-midnight. ❷

Khyber Restaurant, near the Nehru Statue on The Mall. You can't miss the large sign on the first floor. One of the few restaurants in Manali with traditional Himachali decor and musical instruments adorning the walls, Khyber's divine north Indian food is a treat worthy of the splurge. The regal *paneer tikka lababdar* (Rs135) is bound to leave you asking for more. Open daily 9am-11pm. ❹

Sher-e-Punjab, has one outlet in the middle of The Mall marked as the Original. A Manali staple for many years, Sher-e-Punjab's success inspired the two knockoff restaurants that flank it. Punjabi food at reasonable prices for those sick of Italian eats and *momos*. Meals Rs30-65. Open daily 9am-11pm. ❷

Shiva Garden Cafe, after the first bend in Hill Rd. Has tasty Italian dishes, as well as a covered veranda and pleasant garden. Lasagna Rs45. Open daily 8am-11:30pm. ❷

Shiv Shakti Cafe, just below Monal Guest House. A welcome stop at the end of the road, its glass walls showcase some of the best views in Manali. Serves fresh trout (Rs100) and Italian food. Open daily 9am-11pm. ❸

Chopsticks Restaurant, across the Mall from the bus stand. Serves delicious Indo-Tibetan and Indian Chinese food at reasonable prices. Szechuan chicken Rs85. Open daily 8am-11pm. ❸

Ranu Rooftop Cafe, in Vashisht, refuels hot-spring bathers with carbohydrates of both the pasta and *thukpa* variety. Locals dine downstairs while backpackers mostly eat on the "rooftop" with views of the temple. Most dishes Rs25-60. Open daily 8am-10pm. ❶

🞑 SIGHTS

HADIMBA DEVI TEMPLE. The four-tiered Hadimba Devi Temple, with its pagoda-shaped roof, is dedicated to the demoness-turned-goddess Hadimba, wife of Bhima. Valley residents claim the king cut off the builder's hand to prevent the temple's duplication. Undaunted by the amputation, the builder trained his left hand and constructed an even more elaborate temple at Tritoknath. This time, he lost his head. *(Walk 5min. along Old Manali Rd., turn left, and follow the signs. Open to visitors between sunrise and sunset; ask permission before entering. An Rs10-50 donation is expected.)*

HIMACHAL PRADESH

MANU TEMPLE. The Manu Temple, a 30min. walk uphill from Old Manali, is reputedly where Manu first stepped onto the earth after a flood. Manu, the first man to possess knowledge, and his wife Shatrupa, had a series of thoughtful children who developed the world's religions. The temple was rebuilt in 1992 with vaulted ceilings and marble floors. Wear dresses covering the knees and shoulders while in the temple. *(Open 9am-6pm. An Rs10-50 donations expected.)*

GREAT HIMALAYAN NATIONAL PARK. The park shows visitors what the towering pine forests might have looked like before the modern architectural invasion. *(Entrance at the Wildlife Information, Education, and Awareness Center, Old Manali Rd. Open daily 10am-5pm. Rs20 for foreigners. Camera fee Rs5.)*

🎵 📷 ENTERTAINMENT AND SHOPPING

The Himachal Tourism-run **Club House,** to the right after the bridge in Old Manali, offers sundry attractions, not the least of which is a fully stocked bar (beer Rs80). Try your hand at billiards (Rs100 per hr.) or badminton (Rs70 per hr.), or just kick back in the plush lounge with one of the books from the small library. (☎252141. Open daily 10am-9pm. Rs10.) **All-night raves** are frequent in Manali. Check the German Bakery and Cafe in Old Manali for notices. In addition to all the shawl shops on the Mall and Old Manali Rd., the **Tibetan Market,** at the southern end of town, provides good opportunities for good old-fashioned hard bargaining. But be forewarned—there are better deals to be had in Dharamsala. (Open daily 8am-10pm.)

📍 DAYTRIPS FROM MANALI

The temple in Vashisht has a natural **hot springs bath.** There is a medium sized small tank filled with hot spring water where men can bathe, and a small cubicle nearby with a door where women can bathe (although the latter is mostly used to wash clothes). Men should wear bathing shorts, not swimsuits, while in the tank since it is a public space near the temple. (Open daily 5am-9pm. Free) The **Mountaineering Institute** (☎252206 or 253788; fax 253509), 2km south of the bridge over the Beas River, offers courses in mountaineering, skiing, and water sports throughout the year, with fees ranging from US$190 (skiing) to US$250 and up (for a 4-week mountaineering course). The institute can also organize expeditions for large groups. For info, write to: Mountaineering Institute, Manali, HP 175131. Farther south is **Jagat Suk** and its tiny-yet-glorious Shiva temple. The regular bus from Manali (30min., every 15min. 5am-6:30pm, Rs3) will drop you in Jagat Suk, where you can check out the temple and drink *chai* with the locals. The **Rohtang La** (3998m), open erratically between June and September, is the only motorable way into the Lahaul-Spiti area from Manali (see **Kinnaur-Spiti Road,** below). Although it's best described as a polar dump (the place is a mess of tea tents and scattered debris), Rohtang can still make for a decent trip if you're looking for high-altitude scenery. Buses, as well as HPTDC tours (Rs150), will take you here. Check out the creative HPPWD road advice on the way up, including slogans like "Divorce speed" and "Peep, peep, don't go to sleep."

KINNAUR-SPITI

One of the most incredible routes in the world, the road from Shimla cuts through mountains of solid rock and traverses Kinnaur, Spiti, and Lahaul, eventually crossing the Rohtang La and winding down into Manali. The ride can be harrowing, but the reward for accepting the risks of travel is the chance to see some of the most awe-inspiring natural beauty in all of India. Each of the three regions that the road cuts across presents a distinct landscape. The deep Sutlej Valley connects fertile valleys inhabited by the Kinnauri, round-hut dwellers who share the surname "Negi." The greenery is quickly replaced by mountains of mud resembling giant piles of tea leaves. The Spiti River cuts through these mountain deserts dotted by oases of barley fields and enclaves of Tibetan culture. After crossing the Kunzum La, it enters the Lahaul Valley, a lunar landscape of grey-white mountain rock topped with glaciers and moss-covered granite that can only sustain fields of lichen, nomadic shepherds and their flocks.

When the road was opened to outsiders in 1992, the only accommodations were Public Works Department (PWD) rest houses. Today, lodges, hotels, and guest houses line the major towns along the route, and you will be able to find many four-bed truck stops along the way if stranded between two major towns. The road is open between June and October, but it is unlikely that you will make it through without encountering at least one road-block or delay (mudslides, stone avalanches, washed out bridges, etc.). Road conditions change in minutes, and bus drivers rely on updates from passing vehicles. If it rains, especially in the drier Spiti Valley, the roads can become treacherous. The rain-softened ground tends to loosen large boulders, and you might get stuck until the roads clear. If you're traveling by bus, you can usually get off, cross the obstacle on foot (which can be quite physically demanding and risky, especially in August and September when it pours), hike to the next town, and then catch another bus from there. If you're prone to altitude sickness, it's best to start in Shimla, where the climb is more gradual. Non-Indians traveling between Jangi and Sumdo must obtain an **inner-line permit** (available from the sub-divisional magistrates in Shimla, Rampur, Peo, Kaza, Chamba, Kullu, Keylong, and the home office in Delhi; for more information, see **Warning**, p. 223). The **Kaza-Manali Road** should be open from mid-June to mid-September, but weather makes it unreliable as well. **There are no facilities for currency exchange along the route.**

THE KINNAUR-SPITI ROAD

SUTLEJ VALLEY. From Shimla, the road climbs to **Narkanda** (60km, 2½hr. by bus) and then descends to **Rampur** (120km, 3½hr. by bus) and **Jeuri** (143km, 4hr. by bus) from where you can reach the Kinnauri village of **Sarahan** (see p. 251), site of the Bhima-Kali Temple. The green concrete building by the road in Jeuri has simple beds (Rs40)—an option if you get stranded. Two hrs. up the road a path takes you to **Wangtu**, the trailhead for treks over the Bhaba La. Another hr. gets you to Karcham, where you can catch a bus to **Sangla** in the Lower Sangla Valley (see p. 251). Beds are available in one of the shacks across the bridge over the Baspa River (Rs50). From Karcham, it's 1hr. to **Rekong-Peo** (see p. 252), the district headquarters of Kinnaur, and **Kalpa** (see p. 252), Shiva's winter residence. From Peo, the landscape becomes drier, and military bases increase nearer the Tibetan border. You will need to show your permit and passport in Jangi. At **Khab** (or Kabo), 70km from Peo (5hr. by bus), the road climbs to the plateau above. In the middle of this muddy brown plain is the village of **Kah.** Farther down from Yang Thang, you can take a detour to see the Tibetan village of **Nako** (see p. 253) and its green lake. Nako has the only guest houses around (a 2km uphill hike or 10km bus ride). If you get stranded in Yang Thang, there are beds available (Rs50). You may also stay in **Chango,** 100km (3½hr.) from Peo, where there is a 13th-century temple that was supposedly hewn out of a single stone in one day.

SPITI VALLEY. The bus then proceeds through **Shalkar,** the check-post at **Sumdo** (the Spiti boundary), and the truck-stop of **Hurling** (beds Rs50) on its way to the thousand year-old *gompa* at **Tabo** (see p. 254). The 47km Tabo-Kaza stretch passes the villages of **Poh** and **Shichling.** Near Shichling, a road branches off to **Dhankar Gompa.** One kilometer down, a bridge leads to the **Pim Valley.** Between Hurling and Tabo and between Poh and Shichling, the road passes under mountains of mud. **Do not attempt to walk this route in the rain.** From **Kaza** (see p. 255), the road gets even bumpier as it winds 50km up to the village of **Losar** (5hr.). Losar has two guest houses and is the access point for the **Kunzum La** (4500m), 18km (1½hr.) away.

LAHAUL VALLEY. After the pass, the road drops steeply to the four tents that make up **Batal,** in the Lahaul Valley (see p. 256); beds are available here. An 18km hike takes you to **Chandratal Lake.** After Batal, there is a *dhaba* in **Chota Dhara** (12km) and tented accommodations in **Chatru** (16km) before the route turns back onto a main road at **Gramphoo** (17km). From here, it's a 4hr. ride over Rohtang La to **Manali** (64km). The opening of the segment between Losar and Gramphoo is dependent on how long the snow takes to melt, but it is usually open from mid-June to mid-September.

SARAHAN सराहान ☎ 01782

Eight hundred meters above the Sutlej River Valley, the Kinnauri village of Sara-han is notable for its impressive wooden **Bhima-Kali Temple** complex. The temple used to be the site of human sacrifice, until the practice was banned by the British. Inside the Durga shrine, there is a council of marble Buddhas, mountain deities, and Hindu gods, showcasing the rich mingling of beliefs and traditions in the Kin-nauri region. No leather is allowed inside the temple, so leave your wallet and belt in your hotel room. Hats are provided at the temple as covered heads are man-dated by Kinnauri tradition. A donation of Rs50-100 might induce the priest to give you an extended tour of the temple while anything less might limit you to the main shrine. The views of the snow-clad Shrikand Peak, endless fruit orchards, and groves of jacaranda pine make this a perfect setting for walks through the area. **Buses** from Jeuri go to Sarahan (1hr., every hr. 6am-5pm, Rs20). The **Temple Rest House ❶,** in front of the temple, has both a dorm and several private rooms. (☎274248. Dorms Rs50; rooms Rs200-350.) The huge **Shrikand Hotel ❶** run by HPTDC is expensive, but the 8-bed dorm is a good deal, with pleasant views and large bathrooms (beds Rs75). Doubles Rs660-1320). **Ajay Chinese Food ❶,** next to the temple entrance, serves delicious noodles and Shanghai *momos.*

LOWER SANGLA VALLEY संगला

After a perilous 17km bus ride on a road carved out of the mountain face, the deep canyon widens, and the fertile Sangla Valley unfolds in all its splendor. For centu-ries, the natural barriers of the wild river and the snow-capped peaks were enough to keep this area isolated from the rest of the world, and its distinct vegetative and cultural features developed largely free from outside influences. The scenery between **Sangla** and the last village of **Chitkuhl** is unforgettable. The landscape and vegetation change almost every hundred meters—the day-long hike, which passes villages of peak-roofed houses, is well worth it. The valley was not open to outsid-ers (including Indians) until 1992, so **be very careful where you wander.**

From Sangla, the 2km road that turns left past the police station leads to the vil-lage of **Kamru,** former capital of the Baspa kingdom. On top of a rock overlooking the entrance into the valley are a Buddhist temple with rich Tibetan wall paintings and a Hindu shrine adorned with exquisite woodcarving. High above all of this is a temple dedicated to one of the mountain deities and guarded by a legion of lizards; ask permission before entering. From Chitkuhl it's another week farther up the valley and over a pass to the holy town of **Gangotri** in UP. You must be fully self-sufficient for this trek; there are no settlements of any type on the way.

The **bus** from Karcham (1hr., 7 and 9:30am, Rs12) drops you off in **Sangla**. Buses from Sangla go to **Peo** (3hr.; 7, 8am, 2pm; Rs25) and **Rampur** (5hr., noon, Rs60). In the market in Sangla, there are a few restaurants, guest houses, and a **National Travelers** branch (☎ 242358), which organizes treks. The **Mount Kailash Guest House ❶**, just off the road in Sangla, has a clean, four-bed dorm (beds Rs75) and several doubles (Rs250-450). On the first floor, there is a restaurant and an **STD/ISD** telephone. Six kilometers along the route before you reach Rakchham village, the **Fayal Guest House ❷** has doubles (Rs150-300), a dorm, and a restaurant serving local specialties. Down the path past Fayal, in an apple orchard, is the **Ganga Gardenview Guest House ❸**, which has doubles (Rs250), and cooks local cuisine. In Chitkul, the **Chiranjan Guest House ❷** offers doubles (Rs150-300).

REKONG-PEO (PEO) पिओ ☎ 017852

Halfway between Shimla and Tabo, Peo serves as the district headquarters of Kinnaur. Just off the main road, the town is a small collection of concrete military barracks, *dhabas*, and market stalls, ordinarily not meriting more than a few hours' visit. However, the **Lavi Fair**, during the first week of November, draws tourists and locals from all over Himachal Pradesh. Pashmina wool, dried fruits, horses, and other goods are traded on the grounds near the District Commissioner's office. Peo is also famous for its nearby forests (10min. walk up from the bus station, toward Kalpa). Twenty minutes uphill from Peo is the *gompa* that was the site of the *kalachakra* ceremony performed by the Dalai Lama in 1992 (see p. 254). The village of Kalpa (see below) is only 3km away from Peo. Although **buses** also stop in the market, it is better to catch them at the bus stand (10min. uphill) since they are almost always packed when they reach the market. Buses run to: **Chandigarh** (15hr.; 6:15 and 7:15am, and 3:30pm; Rs220); **Kalpa** (30min., 5 per day 7:30am-5pm, Rs10); **Kaza** (13hr., 7:30am, Rs135); **Nako** (6hr.; 7:30am and 1pm; Rs65); **Rampur** (3hr., every hr. 4am-1:30pm, Rs40); **Sangla** (2hr., 9:30am and 4:30pm, Rs25) and **Shimla** (12 hr., 4 per day, 7:40am-6:30pm, Rs150). The **police station** is in the administrative complex near the market. The Additional District Magistrate is in the same building on the first floor and issues **inner-line permits** (see p. 223) for the road between Jangi and Sundo (open M-F 9am-5pm). To get a permit you must go through a travel agent such as **National Travellers** (☎ 222830), down the steps before Fairyland Guest House. Ask for Bhagwan Singh Negi. National Travellers can also help with treks. The **district hospital** is 2km uphill from town, on the road to Kalpa. The **post office** is next to the bus stand (open M-Sa 9am-1pm and 2-5pm). **Postal Code:** 172107.

The **Fairyland Hotel ❷**, above the market, has clean rooms and a restaurant. (☎ 222477. Doubles Rs300-450.) **Mayur Guest House ❶**, next door, is another option. (☎ 222771. Dorms Rs50; rooms Rs225.) The **Shivling View Guest House ❶**, on the road from the bus stand towards the market to your right, has rooms with hot showers, large-screen TVs, and mountain views. Located conveniently for those with early buses to catch. (☎ 222421. Simple bed Rs80-120; doubles Rs200-300.)

KALPA कल्पा ☎ 017852

The village of Kalpa is noteworthy for its proximity to **Kimmer Kailash**, which is Shiva's winter residence, according to Hindu mythology. Aside from this, there are many festivals held here, reflecting the influences of Hinduism, Buddhism, and various other mountain religions. **Fullaich**, in September, is the most famous. Ask any local to point out the *Shivling* atop Kimmer Kailash. This 74 ft.-tall rock outcropping looks like a tiny finger atop a small peak from Kalpa. It is believed to be the symbol of Shiva, and several miraculous qualities are ascribed to it. Shiva's winter residence, Kimmer Kailash is believed to remain snowless when the entire town of Kalpa is covered in snow and ice. Furthermore, the rock itself is held to change color several times a day. Once a year in September, a team of priests and locals climb Kimmer Kailash to worship and pay homage to the *Shivling*.

The center of Kalpa is a handful of wood and stone houses and Kinnauri shrines crammed onto an outcrop overlooking the valley. The rest of the village stretches up the ridge; getting from one place to another can be a small trek in itself. There are apricots, apples, plums, and blackberries everywhere, as well as spectacular views. To reach Kalpa, walk from the bus stand along the road to the left until you reach Shivling View Guest House. Behind the guest house is the 3km path that takes you through pine woods and past village houses (see below). Buses leave from the market and the bus stand to: **Peo** (5 per day, Rs10) and **Shimla** (12hr., 7am, Rs160). More connections can be made from Rekong-Peo, farther down the hill. From the market, a stone path leads steeply uphill to a paved road; turn right and walk 400m to reach **Aucktong Guest House ❷**, with its bright flowers out front. (☎226019. Doubles Rs250.) The family prepares meals. The **Shivalik Guest House ❷**, just to the left of where the stone path reaches the road, is frequented by Bengali tourists and offers varying rooms. (☎226158. Singles Rs150; doubles Rs400.) For a real treat, head 1km farther down to the left to **Kimmer Villa ❸**, which has luxurious rooms with terraces. (☎226079. Rs1000.) Food is available in the hotels and in the **Snow White Coffee House** in the market. The **sub-post office** is next to the temple (open M-Sa 9am-5pm). **Postal Code:** 172108.

◪ TREKS AROUND KALPA

The most popular trek within Kalpa is to **Chaka** (5-6km, a 2hr. hike one-way), a plateau above the village that makes an ideal picnic spot. Kalpa can also serve as a starting point for longer treks. The famed **Parikrama trek** begins at **Thangi** (60km from Kalpa, approachable by road) and ends 3-4 days later in Chitkul. The descent to Chitkul is extremely steep, so walk in the opposite direction only if you really want to challenge your knees. There are villages and shepherd huts on the way, making it possible to leave tents and food supplies at home. Sleeping bags and good shoes are a must, for you reach altitudes of over 5000m. The climb can be done in August and September without mountaineering equipment. **Timberline Tent Camps** (☎226006), in Kimmer Villa, can arrange guides for Rs600 per day (negotiable). The most difficult route in this region—one that should only be attempted by seasoned trekkers—is the trail leading up **Kinnaur Kailash** (6050m). The base of the mountain is in **Powari**, 20km from Kalpa. The best time to do this trek is in July and August. Expect the trek to take two days each way.

NAKO नाको

At the fringe of a small green lake in a high-altitude bowl, this village of stone walls and mud-roof houses is one of the first fully Tibetan settlements along the way; the surrounding ridges are dotted with mud *gompas*, prayer flags, and piles of *mani* stones. This region has a distinct landscape, with barren hills, the deep Spiti Canyon, and distant white mountains. A daily **bus** runs from Peo to Nako (6hr., 1pm, Rs55). You can also reach Nako by taking the **Kaza** (6hr., 7:15am, Rs55) or Shalkar-bound bus and getting off at **Yang Thang**. From there it is a steep 2km walk. A bus runs back from Nako to Peo at 6am (Rs60). To continue from

Nako to Spiti, walk down and catch the one Kaza bus that passes through Yang Thang (anytime after 11am). **Loulan Guest House ❶**, next to the bus stand, has dorm beds (Rs50) and doubles with baths (Rs200-300). It also has the only *dhaba* in town, serving *dal*, rice, and the local barley brew (upon request). Another **guest house ❷**, 100m up the path to the left, has rooms (Rs200) and a porch where you can snooze (Rs25) if everything else is full.

TABO ताबो ☎ 01906

The hamlet of Tabo is home to fewer than 400 intensely devout people, whose houses surround the 1000-year-old Tabo *gompa* near the river. Tabo remained in virtual isolation until the border disputes with China during the 1950s, when the geopolitical importance of this region brought it to center stage. Today, the area is home to several Indian military outposts, and **foreigners must obtain a permit before visiting.** A visit to Tabo can bring peace to the mind of the most rushed traveller, and the 1000-year-old paintings in the *gompa* alone are worth a trip into Spiti from Shimla or Manali.

▐▚ TRANSPORTATION AND PRACTICAL INFORMATION. The **bus** to Peo arrives anytime after 10am (9hr., Rs125), and two buses go to Kaza, one after 9am and another after 4pm (2hr., Rs35). Tabo's **Primary Health Center,** at the edge of town, provides treatment and medicine and operates on donations. (☎ 233325. Open M-Sa 9am-1pm and 3-5pm.) The closest **police** assistance is in Sumdo or Kaza. The **post office** is farther down the cow path in a barn (open M-Sa 10am-3pm). If the postmaster isn't there (most of the time he isn't), ask around; he is usually in a nearby *dhaba*. There is one **STD/ISD** booth at the back side of the Tenzin Restaurant behind the Monastery Guest House. **Postal Code:** 172113.

▐▐ ACCOMMODATIONS AND FOOD. The **Monastery Guest House ❶** has a number of doubles with both private and sparkling common baths and a spacious dorm. (☎ 233315. Dorms Rs50; doubles Rs150-250.) Ask the receptionist to let you into the well maintained library, where you can read up on Buddhism or Tibetan *thankas* (open M-F 10-12am and 1-4pm). The Belgian Librarian who lives nearby opens the library outside regular hours for those who make special requests, and helps beginners to Buddhism choose books. Donations of any amount to the library are encouraged, but are by no means necessary. **Ajanta Guest House ❷,** also near the temple, has carpeted doubles. (☎ 233312. Rs150-200.) There are two food options: the restaurant in the monastery guest house, and the Tenzin *dhaba* across the street. Their menus include Tibetan bread, *thukpa*s, and *momo*s (both open 5:30am-9:30pm). The **Banjara Resort ❸** near the bus stop on the main road offers a restaurant serving some North Indian food for those seeking a change from Tibetan cuisine. (Side dishes Rs45, Double rooms Rs2600.)

◙ SIGHTS. According to an ancient inscription, Tabo was founded in AD 996. The **Tabo Gompa** is the largest monastic complex in the Spiti Valley, and one of the holiest Buddhist sites anywhere in the Himalayas. Following the massive cultural purges of Tibet by the Chinese government, Tabo assumed a role as treasury of Tibetan art. On the *gompa's* 1000th birthday, the Dalai Lama came to perform the sacred **Kalachakra** ceremony, a rite of initiation, rejuvenation, and prayer offered once every four years. The monastery consists of five temples from the original settlement and four shrines that were added at a later date. At the core of the complex is the Temple of the Enlightened Gods, otherwise known as the **Assembly Hall.** At the center is a statue of the four-fold Vairocana, the Divine Being regarded by

Vajrayana Buddhism as one of the spiritual sons of Adibuddha, the self-creative primordial Buddha. Vainocana is depicted turning the wheel of law. Along the wall are images of the other 33 deities of the pantheon. Hidden in darkness, the sanctum behind Vainocana is adorned with wall paintings depicting the life of the Buddha. In the ante-room, ask the lama to show you the **Gom-khang,** the Temple of Wrathful Gods. Twice a day, a lama shielded by protective meditation performs a secret ceremony to appease the fierce deities. Daily prayers are performed in the hall every morning at 6am. To the right of the Assembly Hall is the **Maitreya Temple,** with a 6m high statue of the Buddha of the Future. To the left is the **Mystic Mandala Temple,** where the initiation to monkhood takes place. On the sheer cliff face overlooking the town is a series of **caves** that once functioned as monastic dwellings. With a flashlight, you can see traces of the paintings that once adorned these walls. *(To visit the temples, ask at the reception of the monastery guest house for the temple keeper, and make sure to bring your own flashlight.)*

KAZA काज़ा   ☎ 01906

Strategically situated in the middle of the valley, Kaza continues to be the trading center of Spiti. An old village and a government post, Kaza is also a major base for travelers visiting this long-forbidden land. The millennial Kalachakra ceremony was held in the nearby Kyi Gompa. New hotels spring up around Kaza every year.

⌷ TRANSPORTATION. Bus service to **Manali** (12hr., 4am, Rs100) begins sometime around early June and mid-August, and continues until October. Buses also go to: **Kibber** (1½hr., 2pm, Rs12) via **Kyi; Lasar** (3½hr., 9am, Rs45); **Mikim** in the Pin Valley (2hr., 8am, Rs25); **Peo** (12hr., 8am, Rs120) via **Tabo** (2hr., Rs30). As always in the mountains, bus schedules depend on the whims of weather and drivers.

⊞ 🛈 ORIENTATION AND PRACTICAL INFORMATION. Both **Old Kaza** and **New Kaza** lie between the main road and the river—a small, often dry stream separates the two. New Kaza can be reached by following the road that goes up above the bus stand. The **bazaar, STD/ISD,** and restaurants are all in Old Kaza; the **hospital, police station,** and government buildings are in the new town. The **bus stand** is just off the main road in Old Kaza. The **hospital** (☎ 222218), in a big shed, runs an ambulance service. The Sub-Divisional Magistrate's office, which grants **permits** for the journey onward to Kinnaur, is in New Kaza. The **post office** is 2min. from the road (open M-F 10am-5pm). **Postal Code:** 172114.

🛏 🍴 ACCOMMODATIONS AND FOOD. Lodging in Kaza is available from April to November, when the town is not covered with snow. **Mahabaudha ❷,** at the top end of the market road in Old Kaza, has the cleanest rooms, common bath with hot water, and a traditional Tibetan kitchen. However, spots fill up quickly so go early in the morning. (☎ 222232. Doubles Rs200.) **Sakya's Abode ❶,** across the stream in New Kaza, has a beautiful garden area and tiled rooms, and is popular with Indian tour groups. (☎ 222254. Dorm beds Rs100; singles with bath Rs150; doubles with hot shower Rs450-650.) Next door, **Milarepa Guest House ❷** offers a simple bed and bathroom for Rs250 a night. If you need to catch an early bus, **Art Guest House ❷,** below the bus stand, has clean rooms, all with common bath. (Doubles Rs250-350.) *Dhabas* along the market serve *dal* and noodles; the one on the second floor near the bus station is the best source for road information.

🗹 TREKS AROUND KAZA. The most popular trek takes you through the Pin Valley National Park and over the Pin-Parbati La to **Manikaran** (6 days), where there are soothing hot springs and bus connections to Kullu and Manali. From

Kaza, take a bus to **Mikim** (2hr., 8am, Rs25), where a *jula* will transport you on a rope across the river to the trailhead at Kaar village—ask for Chine Dorge, who can arrange guides for your trek. Instead of turning west over Pin-Parbati, you can continue south over the Bhaba La to **Wangtu** on the Shimla-Peo road (5 days).

DAYTRIPS FROM KAZA

KYI. The largest fort monastery in Spiti, Kyi rests on the top of a cliff 12km from Kaza. The monastery, home to 1000 lamas, has a superb collection of *thankas*. The *gompa* received a major face-lift in preparation for the **Kalachakra** ceremony: a road was cut through sand and stone to connect the new monastery guest house to the village, a large assembly hall was constructed on the hill, solar panels were installed, and repairs were made to the temples. To get to Kyi, many travelers put their faith in the erratic **bus** from Kaza (2pm).

KIBBER. On a hilltop, Kibber is a Tibetan village of white mud houses surrounded by barley fields. At an altitude of 4250m, Kibber is one of the highest villages in the world reachable by motor vehicle. Kibber and the adjoining wildlife sanctuary offer amazing treks and a feeling of remoteness. A daily **bus** leaves Kaza (1½hr., 2pm, Rs12) and loops around at Kibber. If the bus driver is having a bad day, though, you might have to hike the 18km stretch or take a taxi (Rs250). The **Resang Hotel ❶,** at the village entrance, has doubles with baths and a kitchen (Rs150). Farther down the road, the **Pasang La Guest House ❷** charges inflated prices for its rather bleak rooms (doubles Rs300-500). **Village houses ❶** are known to provide pleasant stays to many travelers. (Rs60-100 per night; ask around.) In the village, there is a huge prayer wheel, a *gompa* for curing spiritual afflictions, and a local healer for bodily ones (open M-Sa 9am-1pm and 3-5pm).

DHANKAR GOMPA. Named for its precarious location (*dhankar* means "cliff"), Dhankar Gompa was one of the first fort monasteries incorporated into Spiti's defense system. The *gompa* is an 8km hike up from the road near Shichling, about 20km from Kaza. You can take the **Peo** bus (1hr., 7:30am, Rs15). The views are amazing, and the **gompa ❶** provides beds (Rs50).

LAHAUL VALLEY

With glaciers within reach, the Chandra River Valley is watered by fresh water springs and melted snow, and its grassy pastures are grazed upon by wild horses. Above, the **Chandrathal Lake** is the jewel of the valley.

When road conditions permit, the Kullu-Kaza **bus** runs through the valley between **Gramphoo** and **Batal**. Situated on the Manali-Keylong road, Gramphoo's two *dhabas* have beds (Rs50). Expect shepherds or family members to join you at any time. It is 17km to **Chatru,** where food and tents (Rs200 for rental, Rs30 if you bring your own tent) are available; bring a sleeping bag unless you want to freeze. Chatru is the trailhead for a trek over the Hamta La to Manali. The hike takes two days on the way down and three days on the way back. From Chatru, another 16km takes you to **Chota Dhada,** where there is rice and *dal* and a campground. In Batal, 12km away, there are tents and bowls of *thukpa* (Rs25). After the bridge in Batal, the road forks: the right branch scales the Kunzum La, while the left goes 18km until it reaches Chandrathal Lake. There is a campground nearby. Alternatively, you can descend to Chandrathal on a path that starts at the *gompa* on the Kunzum La. From Chandrathal, it is another three days of walking to the **Baralacha La** on the Manali-Leh road (p. 258). There is no accommodation available between Batal and Baralacha La, and the closest medical assistance is in Keylong.

JAMMU जम्मु AND KASHMIR کشمیر

> **NOTE.** Due to safety concerns, *Let's Go* has not updated coverage for Jammu and Kashmir since 2001.

For centuries travelers have been drawn to Kashmir, India's northernmost state. Until the late 1980s, it was one of the most popular tourist destinations in Asia, and many a Bollywood starlet has been filmed against the backdrop of Kashmir's stunning mountainscapes. But despite the undeniable beauty of its scenery, Jammu and Kashmir is also volatile, and since 1989, the western half of the state has been wracked by an armed insurgency. So far, the violence has been confined to the Kashmir Valley, which is predominantly Muslim, and Jammu, which has a large population of Dogra Hindus. **The lake-rimmed capital, Srinagar, is dominated by the military, and most foreign state departments advise against traveling here or anywhere in the western part of the state.** The eastern part of the state, consisting of the Tibetan Buddhist regions of Ladakh and Zanskar, is somewhat safer, but travelers should check the latest news and information before finalizing their plans.

Kashmir's troubles began at Partition in 1947. Although the population was predominantly Muslim, the Hindu raja did not want his kingdom to become part of Pakistan *or* India, and most Kashmiri Muslim leaders agreed with him. Later that year, Pathan tribesmen entered the region and attempted to force Kashmir into Pakistan. Desperate, the maharaja asked India for help. The Indian government accepted the offer, and agreed to hold a plebiscite to determine whether the Kashmiri people wanted to join India. In other words, a common vote would allow the residents of the region to vote for or against the proposal. After violent clashes, however, Pakistan still held large chunks of Kashmir. India and Pakistan went to war over Kashmir again in 1965, but no territory changed hands. The 1948 cease-fire line, called the Line of Control (LOC), remains the *de facto* India-Pakistan border, but the plebiscite promised by India has never materialized.

At the end of the 1980s, many Kashmiris who had fought against the Soviet invasion of Afghanistan returned home with better guns and training. This, together with Kashmiri fears of absorption into India, led to an outbreak of violence in 1989. The violence hasn't stopped since and has claimed as many as 100,000 lives over the past 13 years. In 1995, five foreign tourists were taken hostage in Kashmir; one of them was beheaded. In July 2000, a German backpacker was kidnapped and killed in the Zanskar Valley. Hundreds are killed in Kashmir every year, and the continued rise of militant groups makes peace seem increasingly unlikely. Large-scale intrusions across the line of control at Kargil in 1999 nearly escalated into another Indo-Pakistani war. Bombings and guerrilla activity are routine in many areas of the state, and Kashmir's future is uncertain. Relations between India and Pakistan reached their lowest point for more than 20 years in early 2002, when both countries tested nuclear-capable missiles and massed their troops along the border as part of open preparations for another war. **As of August 2003, most governments strongly advise their citizens to avoid all travel anywhere within the state.** Think long and hard about your priorities in life before you decide to travel anywhere in Jammu and Kashmir.

JAMMU & KASHMIR

HIGHLIGHTS OF JAMMU AND KASHMIR

The beautiful, medieval town of **Leh** (p. 259), at 3500m, is a base for treks through the surrounding mountain ranges and to the *gompas* which dot the Indus Valley.

Approached by the highest motorable pass in the world, the radiant **Nubra Valley** (p. 267) features flower-filled villages, sand dunes, wild camels, and stunning views of the Karakoram.

THE MANALI-LEH ROAD

Two routes connect Leh to the rest of the world: the Manali-Leh Road and the Srinagar-Leh Road. Each is a two-day-plus haul requiring you to cross several passes well over 5000m. These roads are theoretically open from mid-June to mid-September, but they can be washed out for weeks by rains and mudslides. Travel is often delayed by accidents, herds of goats, and military check-points. If you're on a tight schedule you might want to fly to Leh, but you'd be missing out on a lot.

 WARNING. Following the large-scale Pakistani intrusion across the Line Of Control (LOC) in spring 1999, India has cemented its position in the Dras-Kargil area, leading to increased militant activity in northern and western Kashmir. Traveling along the **Srinagar-Leh Road** can get hairy at times. Stay within the limits of the road, where a strong military presence reduces the risks.

The **Manali-Leh Road,** the second-highest motorable road in the world, is one of the most beautiful overland journeys on the planet, winding its bumpy way through green mountains, roaring streams, and across the stunning, high-altitude desert of Ladakh. The Manali-Leh road crosses the Rohtang La (3980m) and then twists through the Baralacha La (4892m) and Taglang La (5325m) passes before descending to Upshi and into Leh. **Bring warm clothes:** it can get below freezing at the high passes. And try to get a seat at the front: you'll need a crash helmet, or at least kneepads, if you get stuck in the back. Local and deluxe buses leave Manali daily (10am, Rs405/800-1000), but if you can make some friends, hire a shared jeep (Rs900 per person; the same jeeps from Leh to Manali cost Rs1300). This will let you stop along the way and get you to Leh quicker. It rarely rains along this road, but when it does, the road can become treacherous. You might have to get off the bus and trudge through the mud past obstructions.

Small settlements line the road from Manali to Leh, and there are places to stay all along the road. The trip can take anywhere from 30hr. to two or more days, depending on weather conditions, accidents, and the number of military check-points. Where you stop is determined by where you happen to be when it starts to get dark. The bus first descends into the Lahaul Valley, where it might stop in Keylong, Lahaul's administrative center, and leave the next morning (4am). At sunrise, the bus reaches **Darcha** (1hr.; tents Rs35), the trailhead for treks into the **Zanskar Valley.** Over the next two to three hours, the bus climbs the main Himalayan ridge, crossing it at **Baralacha La** (4892m). The three-day trail for **Chandratal Lake** begins here (see p. 251). The first tea stop is in **Bharatpur** (tents Rs35), 3km below Baralacha La. A descent into a vast plain brings you to **Sarchu** (4hr.; tents Rs150), after which the road makes 27 turns, climbing 1000m to cross the Zanskar range at **Lunga-lacha La** (5059m). From here, it's "badlands" territory. You first hit the village of **Pang** (8hr.; tents Rs30-50), and after crossing a pass, the road enters the plains of **Rupshu.** At the end

AFGHANISTAN

CHINA

Disteghil Sar
7785m

UNDER
PAKISTANI
ADMINISTRATION

Rakaposhi
7788m

K2
8611m

Gilgit

Masherbrum
7821m

BALTISTAN

Shyok River

UNDER
CHINESE
ADMINISTRATION

Nanga Parbat
8126m

LINE OF ACTUAL CONTROL

Dha   Hunder Diskit

Zoji-La
3529m

Kargil

Mulbekh

Khalsi

LADAKH

Khardung
La 5606m

Baramula

Sonamarg

Dras

Lamayuru

Spitok Leh

Gulmarg

Srinagar

Alchi

Tikse

Khilanmarg

Pahalgam

Hemis

Nun Kun
7135m

TIBET
(CHINA)

Anantnag

ZANSKAR

PIRPANJAL RANGE

Kishtwar

Padum

Taglang
La

Indus River

RUPSHU

Batoti

Kud

Jammu

OFFICIAL
INDO-PAKISTANI
BORDER

Kathua

Chamba

Keylong

Rhotang
La 3955m

Manali

UNDER
CHINESE
ADMINISTRATION

PAKISTAN

Govt. of India statement:
The external boundaries of India are
neither correct nor authenticated.

PUNJAB

HIMACHAL
PRADESH

Jammu and Kashmir

of the plains, below the glacier-lined **Taglang La** (5325m) pass (12hr.), there are thousands of sheep and goats, and views of the Karakoram range and the Great Himalayas. The bus then descends into the Ladakhi village of **Rumtse** (14hr.), screeching through villages and *gompas* before reaching **Upshi** (16hr.). From then on, it's smooth cruising down the main road to **Leh** (18hr.).

LEH   ☎ 01982

The capital of the old kingdom of Ladakh, Leh is remarkably distinct from cities farther south in Kashmir. Its location on a 3500m desert plateau in the middle of the Indus Valley, halfway between Punjab and Yarkand on the "southern" silk route, has made it a crossroads between Tibetan Buddhist culture from the east and Islamic influences from the west. While Old Leh, with its maze of narrow lanes winding up to the ruins of the Namgyal Palace, seems to be stuck in a time warp, New Leh thrives on tourism. If Kashmiri traders and the clicking of tourists' cameras get to be too much, you can seek refuge in one of the many *gompas* and deserted mountain trails near the city. Some of these follow the same routes used for centuries by traders hauling goods from Western Tibet over the Chang La (5547m) and Khardung La (5602m) into the bustling bazaars of the ancient city.

WARNING. When you make the road journey, **carry your passport with you at all times.** The routes to Leh come close to areas under Pakistani and Chinese control. When arriving by plane, remember that Leh is 3505m above sea level. **Rest for at least one day** (that means not even walking around and definitely not consuming alcohol) before undertaking anything strenuous, and **watch for any signs of Acute Mountain Sickness (AMS).** The symptoms—headaches, breathlessness, and nausea—normally develop during the first 36hr. (see **Trekking: Health and Safety,** p. 34). Leh has an emergency facility for dealing with AMS. (24hr. ☎52012 or 52360.) Several seats are reserved on every plane out of town for people needing to leave because of AMS.

⌐ TRANSPORTATION

Flights: Airport (☎52255), 4km from Leh, down Fort Rd. **Jet Airways,** main bazaar (open daily 9am-1pm and 2-4pm), has daily flights to **Delhi** (7am, US$112). Book a few weeks in advance during the summer. **Indian Airlines,** Fort Rd. (open daily 9am-1pm and 2-4pm), flies to more destinations, but you must still book ahead. Flights are often delayed or canceled due to bad weather. To: **Chandigarh** (1hr., W 7:50am, US$75); **Delhi** (1½hr., daily, US$105); **Jammu** (1hr., M and F 7:30am, US$70); **Srinagar** (1hr., Su 7:50am, US$60). Security is tight on flights to Jammu or Srinagar. Persons under 25 are eligible for a discount.

 NOTE. The impulsive traveler arriving in Leh without a reserved return ticket—and unwilling to take the two-day shared jeep ride back to Manali—will not necessarily have to stay in Leh until a flight is available. Due to the unpredictable nature of flights out of Leh (flight capacity is determined just prior to take-off and is contingent on cloud cover, temperature, and the pilot's mood), many tickets are sold on a waiting list. These can usually be purchased a day before travel, at which time you can get the ticket "confirmed" by having the airline manager sign it. This can be costly (Rs2000), but talk to local travel agents to make arrangements.

Buses: The **Tourist Information Office,** Fort Rd., by the taxi stand, has up-to-date schedules and prices. To: **Diskit** (8hr.; Tu, Th, Sa 6am; Rs65); **Hemis** (1hr., daily 9:30am and 4:30pm, Rs25); **Kargil** (12hr., daily 5:30am, Rs143) via **Lamayuru; Matho** (2hr., 3 per day 7:30am-5pm, Rs15); **Manali** (48hr.; daily 4am; semi-deluxe Rs400, deluxe Rs525); **Panamik** (8hr., Tu 6am, Rs85); **Phyang** (30min.; daily 8am, 1:30, 5pm; Rs12); **Shey, Tikse,** and **Spituk** (every 30min., 8am-7pm, Rs15); **Srinagar** (48hr.; 5:30am; Rs220, deluxe M-Tu and Th-Sa Rs300); **Stok** (45min.; daily 8am, 2, 5pm; Rs10). **Minibuses** go to **Alchi, Saspul, Likir,** and **Bagso** (all 4pm).

Local Transportation: The **taxi union** is near the top of Fort Rd. There is a fixed rate of Rs8 per km for all destinations during the tourist season (July-Aug.).

■✈🛈 ORIENTATION AND PRACTICAL INFORMATION

The **main bazaar** marks the western edge of the **Old City.** Running west from the center of the main bazaar is **Fort Road,** which is lined with restaurants, travel agents, and carpet shops. **Zangsty Road,** beginning at the north end of the main bazaar, connects to Fort Rd. via **Library Road,** and then runs north into two lanes, **Changspa** and **Karzoo,** which pass several small guest houses. Buses arrive in the south on **Airport Road,** a 10min. walk from the bazaar.

JAMMU & KASHMIR

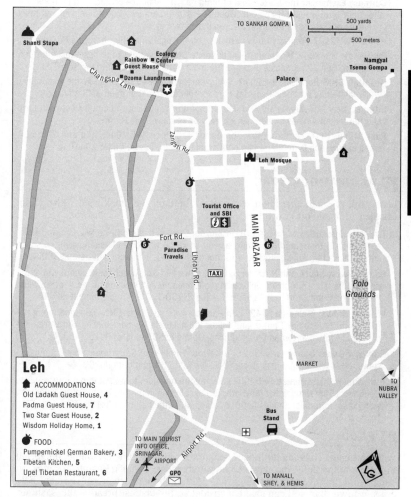

Leh

♠ ACCOMMODATIONS
Old Ladakh Guest House, **4**
Padma Guest House, **7**
Two Star Guest House, **2**
Wisdom Holiday Home, **1**

● FOOD
Pumpernickel German Bakery, **3**
Tibetan Kitchen, **5**
Upel Tibetan Restaurant, **6**

Tourist Office: Tourist Information Office, Fort Rd. (☎53462). Open May-Sept. M-Sa 8am-7pm. Closed off season. Information counter at the airport open all year.

Trekking Agents: Fort Rd. is full of trekking agents. Not all are trustworthy; ask around before putting your life in the hands of a stranger. **Dreamland Trek&Tour,** Fort Rd. (☎53128, 52089, or 53616; www.dreamladakh.com), on the left walking away from the bazaar. An affordable agency with years of experience in putting together well-organized and worry-free treks. Credit cards accepted only for groups of several people. **Virgo Adventure** (☎52250; www.geocities.com/virgoadventure). Operated through the Two Star Guest House, this new agency has been making a name for itself, with perfectly arranged treks and great prices.

JAMMU & KASHMIR

Currency Exchange: The **State Bank of India** has an exchange counter in their branch at the main bazaar just off Fort Rd. Open M-F 10am-2pm, Sa 10am-noon. Many travel agencies and shops in town will also exchange money.

Police: (☎52167), halfway up Zangsty Rd., on the right after the Changspa Rd. turn off.

Pharmacy: Himalaya Medical Store, opposite SNM Hospital, is the best-stocked. Open daily 9am-6pm. Pharmacies also line the main bazaar; most open daily 8am-7pm.

Hospital: SNM Hospital (☎52012, 24hr. emergency ☎52360), below the bus stand. Well maintained and has a special ward for tourists (most of them AMS-afflicted).

Internet: Very slow. **Gypsy's World,** Fort Rd., in the White House complex between town and the Indian Airlines office. Rs3 per min. Open daily 9am-10pm.

Post Office: GPO, 2km from town on Airport Rd. Open M-F 10am-1pm and 2-5pm. A small sub-branch is in the middle of the main bazaar. **Postal Code:** 194101.

ACCOMMODATIONS

Leh is full of small guest houses, most of them on the outskirts of town along Changspa Rd. and off Fort Rd.

Two Star Guest House (☎52250), in Karzoo, 20m past the path to Wisdom and Rainbow. You will be treated like family as you sit in the windowed kitchen gazing at snow-clad Stok Kangri. Singles Rs100-150; doubles Rs250, with attached bath Rs350. ❶

Padma Guest House and Hotel (☎52630), down Fort Rd.; watch for a sign pointing to a path on the left. 15-room complex with rooftop restaurant, new rooms, and hot showers. Well-kept grounds add to the charm. Rooms Rs250-1200. Bargain mercilessly. ❷

Wisdom Holiday Home (☎52427), in Karzoo. Walk up Zangsty Rd., continue along the road from the Ecology Centre, and follow the signs. In a wheat patch, with views of a bleached-white *chorten* and rugged cliffs. Dorms Rs50; doubles Rs150-350. ❶

Rainbow Guest House (☎52332), in Karzoo. Family-run. Some rooms have mountain views. Near Wisdom Holiday Home. Doubles with attached bath Rs200. ❷

Old Ladakh Guest House (☎52951). Facing the mosque, turn right into a narrow alley. Continue 150m through the labyrinth. The best option in the Old Town. Centrally located with pleasant rooms. Singles Rs80; doubles with attached bath Rs150. ❶

FOOD

With authentic Tibetan and Indian restaurants, not-so-authentic Italian ones, and Punjabi *dhabas* in the bazaar, Leh can satisfy most cravings. Head to Dzomsa, on Zangsty Rd., for eco-safe drinking water. Although there are more "German" bakeries in town than you can shake a strüdel at, the tastiest bread is the Kashmiri *naan* sold in the bakeries behind the mosque.

Summer Harvest Restaurant, just above Dreamland Trek&Tour on Fort Rd. Delicious Tibetan, Kashmiri, and Chinese food (most meals Rs45-80). The pan-fried *momos* (Rs30) and *rishta* (Rs80) are both astounding. Open daily May-Sept. 7am-10:30pm. ❷

Upel Tibetan Restaurant, in the middle of the Main Bazaar, 3rd fl. The Darjeeling cooks seem to have mastered the culinary arts of Tibet and China. Great views of the bazaar. Most dishes Rs30-80. Open daily 7:30am-9:30pm. ❷

Tibetan Kitchen, 5min. down Fort Rd., just before the White House. Clean tablecloths and artistic decor. Tibetan specialties like *shaba-gleb* (meat bread Rs40) and Amdo bean stew (Rs60). Open daily 8am-3pm and 6-11pm. ❷

Pumpernickel German Bakery, between Fort Rd. and Zangsty Rd. As much an expat community center as an eatery. Board posts bulletins about taxis to Manali and ads for trekking partners. Excellent yak-cheese and tomato sandwiches Rs30, huge breakfasts Rs55-70, and a range of breads Rs45-55. Open daily 7am-9pm. ❷

🅒 SIGHTS

SENGGE NAMGYAL PALACE. Towering above the Old Town, this nine-story palace was built during the 1630s to show Leh's ascendancy over Shey as the Ladakhi capital. It is said to have inspired the Potala Palace in Lhasa. The opening of the East Gate used to be marked by the roar of a caged lion; nowadays the gate serves as the entrance. *(Open daily 8am-5pm. Rs20 for Indian nationals, US$5 for everyone else.)*

SHANTI STUPA. Referred to by locals as the **Japan Stupa,** the Shanti Stupa in Changspa village sits at the top of 560 steps. Feast your eyes on the legacy of Fujii Guraji, a Japanese Buddhist who moved to India in 1931. One of many Japanese-built *stupas* in the region, this Peace Pagoda, built in 1983, features gilt panels depicting episodes from the life of the Buddha. *(3km west of the bazaar; walk to Changspa and follow a direct line to the stupa. Open 24hr.)*

NAMGYAL TSEMO GOMPA. High above the palace, the red Namgyal Tsemo Gompa is distinguished by its *gon-khang*, which features sculptures of wrathful deities and wall-paintings of benign *Bodhisattvas*. *(Open briefly in the morning and evening when a lama climbs up from Samkar to light the butter lamps. The lama's movements are hard to predict. The inside is dark—bring a flashlight.)*

OTHER SIGHTS. The imposing **mosque** at the end of the main bazaar was built in 1666 by the Ladakhi king Deldan Namgyal as an offering to the Mughal emperor. The mosque is built in a style more Ladakhi than Islamic, but the *namaaz* prayer calls can be heard five times a day from every corner of Leh. The **polo grounds** above the Old Town see annual tournaments and occasional games between locals and soldiers. The **Sankar Gompa,** the official local residence of the reformist Gelug-pa ("Yellow Hat") sect, houses a hundred-headed, thousand-armed image of Avalokitesvara, the *Bodhisattva* of Compassion. *(Walk along the footpath across the fields from the Ecological Centre. Open daily 8-11am and 3-6pm. Rs25 donation expected.)*

🛍 SHOPPING

There are many opportunities to shop in Leh; masks, carpets, jewelry, shawls, and so-called "antiques" fill the shops along Fort Rd., but prices are often higher than those in Delhi or Dharamsala. The **Tibetan Children's Village Handicrafts Centre,** on the road toward Choglamsar, sells crafts made at the Tibetan Children's Village. (Open M-Sa 9:30am-5pm.) The **Tibetan Handicraft Emporium,** in the main market, is approved by the Dalai Lama. (Open M-Sa 9am-1pm and 2-7pm.) The **Ecology Centre's** handicraft store sells local Ladakhi goods (open M-Sa 11am-5pm), and the **Co-operative store,** in the Galdan Hotel complex just off Fort Rd., sells similar items. These places support the local community and have fixed prices. **Cashmere Ladakh Arts,** on Zangsty Rd., is a private shop that prides itself on its fixed prices and no-hassle salesmanship. **Kpleasure Arts,** on Fort Rd., specializes in pashmina and in Ladakhi art. Shopping elsewhere is much like a sophisticated mugging.

VOLUNTEER OPPORTUNITIES

Travelers who would like to volunteer either with the **Leh Women's Alliance** or the **Ecology Centre,** or those wishing to arrange homestays at a Ladakhi farm (1 month minimum) should contact **The International Society for Ecology and Culture (ISEC),** Apple Barn, Week, Totnes, Devon TQ9 6JP, UK—preferably a year ahead. The center has ongoing projects that need volunteers, and can also refer would-be volunteers to other local organizations. (☎441803 868650; www.isec.org.uk. Open M-Sa 10am-4pm.) The **Student Educational and Cultural Movement of Ladakh** (SECMOL), at the Rid-zong Labrang Complex in Old Leh (☎52421; fax 53012), between the bazaar and the polo grounds, has volunteer positions at its camp for Ladakhi youth in Choglamsar.

◪ DAYTRIPS FROM LEH

Fifteen kilometers up the main road from Leh is the ancient Ladakhi capital of **Shey.** The hillsides are home to the famous giant twin images of Sakyamuni. The one of gilt copper is a part of a palace temple; the other is in a temple past a group of *chortens* 300m from the palace. (Open daily 8am-8pm. Rs20.) Four kilometers farther up the road, on a craggy bluff, is **Tikse,** the most photographed *gompa* in Ladakh. A few kilometers above Tikse, you can get off the bus and cross the Indus to reach the **Stakma Gompa,** which rises dramatically on a 60m high rock from the flat Indus Valley. The *gompa*'s three temples are small but well maintained, and the views from their windows are superb. (Admission Rs20.)

From Stakma, you can make out the **Matho Gompa** to the southwest, set on a hill at the foot of the mountain. Separated from the Stakma *gompa* by 7km of mead-ows and barley fields, Matho, the only monastery in Ladakh that belongs to the Saskya-pa sect, is famous for the oracles delivered here. Lamas are chosen every three years and then spend several months fasting and praying until they are able to deliver prophecies and perform miraculous feats. The tiny *gon-khang* at the top of the *gompa* contains fierce images of deities. Unlike in most other *gon-khangs*, the ferocious faces are not covered. (Women are not allowed to enter.)

From Matho, descend to the left and follow the path at the foot of the ridge for 12km until you reach **Stok,** the residence of the Namgyal dynasty. There is a museum displaying family heirlooms; the turquoise-inlaid crown once belonged to a Chinese princess of the Tang dynasty who married a Tibetan king. Curiously enough, this is China's oldest claim to Tibet. (Open daily 8am-6pm. Rs25.)

Four kilometers from Saspol (up the Indus Valley from Leh) and across the river is Ladakh's oldest and most precious *gompa*, **Alchi,** a village founded in the 11th century. Bring a strong flashlight; the *gompa* is unlit. **Lotsava Guest House ❶,** 50m to the left of where the taxis stop, has a quiet garden. (Singles Rs80; doubles Rs150.)

◪ TREKKING AROUND LEH

WARNING. Allow several days to acclimatize before setting out on a trek; altitude sickness is very common among visitors. Consult one of the many **trekking agents** in town (see p. 261). In case of accidents, the only available rescue is the military helicopter that operates at a cost of at least Rs40,000 per hr. and flies out only if there is a guarantee that the cost will be met. Before setting out, whether alone or with an organized group, be sure to leave the following with your guest house owner in Leh: detailed itinerary, photocopies of your passport, visa, and insurance policy, 3 filled-out forms guaranteeing payment, acceptance certif-icate, and indemnity bond. All are available from any travel agent in town.

Set between the world's two highest mountain ranges, Ladakh is a favorite destina-tion for trekkers, who come for the scenery and for the (relatively) reliable weather. During the trekking season (June-Oct.), the days are hot and the nights

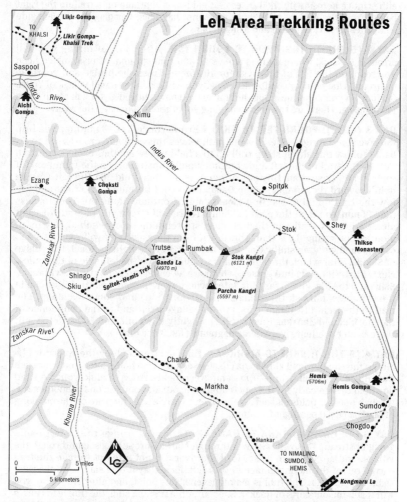

Leh Area Trekking Routes

bitterly cold. You should not attempt treks deep into the mountains with fewer than three people, and you may want to hire a guide. You can rent and buy equipment (tent Rs100 per day, stove Rs20 per day) in the **White House,** Fort Rd. (☎ 53048).

MARKHA VALLEY TREK

*The **Markha Valley Trek,** starting in **Spitok** and ending in **Hemis,** is one of the best routes for solo trekking and lasts 7-9 days. The landscape is varied, going through isolated villages, and the passes are high enough to brag about. There are supplies along the way and no tough river crossings, but the Stok La (4900m) is a challenge.*

DAY 1 (4-5HR.): SPITOK TO JING CHON. The trek starts in **Spitok.** The first stage is particularly barren and exposed. Turn right, and after about 1hr., follow the steep path to your left up to another jeep road. About 30min. later, you will reach a small ford. After the crossing, there is a wider stretch of river; you can either move across with the horses and guides or continue on a trail up the right bank. From the bridge, it is 20min. to camp. **Jing Chon Camping** has stream-side campsites (Rs40 per night) and a snack bar.

DAY 2 (5-6HR.): JING CHON TO YOURN TSO. After 3hr. of hiking you will arrive in **Rumbak,** where there is a tea stall and campground. After Rumbak, head upstream on the left of the river for 10-15min. Cross the bridge and continue upstream. One hour or so after Rumbak, you will reach the small village of **Yrutse** (4180m). If you continue along the trail carved into a hillside, you will reach **Yourn Tso Camping.** There are two more camping spots about 30min. up the river.

DAY 3 (6HR.): YOURN TSO TO SKIU. From Yourn Tso Camping, head up the river on the right side. A small path leaves this trail and crosses the river-bank; follow this short, steep trail up to a field where another camp is located. Follow the trail to the left and continue uphill (upstream) on the right bank of the stream. Less than 1hr. out of camp is another field. To the left (facing uphill toward the summit) is the **Ganda La** itself. Continue to the right and fol-low the trail uphill to the first **mountaintop.** Continue along this trail for less than 30min. to reach the pass (4900m). There will be a medium-grade descent along a narrow trail and then an easy stretch along a streambed, dry in all months but spring. Less than 1hr. down from the pass, you will reach a small **campground** with tea stalls. Continue on the trail for 30min. to reach the village of **Shingo,** after which the path climbs to a hillside on the left side of the valley. Next, the trail heads into **gorges,** which are awesome to behold. You will reach **Skiu** (and the Markha River) 4hr. later, where there is a *gompa* (usually open in the evenings, but ask the villagers; Rs10 donation) and some tea stalls. The trail to the right (10-15min.) goes to the village itself and to the confluence of the Markha and Zanskar Rivers (3hr.). Slightly downhill, and 100m to the left, there is an excellent riverside **campground** (Rs60 per night).

DAY 4 (5-7HR.): SKIU TO MARKHA. Hike upstream along the river for 2½-3hr. to the campground at **Homurja** (Rs50 to camp). Two hours later, you will reach the village of **Chaluk** with *stupas* and green fields. After Chaluk, you can head downhill to stop early for the day (camping Rs50), or continue on for another 2hr. through boulder fields and across the river, to arrive at a campsite on the outskirts of **Markha** (Rs50 per night to camp).

DAY 5 (4-5HR.): MARKHA TO HANKAR. Cross the bridge to the left bank, going upstream; this will take you through Markha proper. Descend through the village, and after 30min. or so, ford the river. Do not attempt to take the trail carved out of the mountain face to your left; locals say it is unsafe. Ford the river again 45min. later. The trail is mainly level at this point, and after 1hr. or so, you will reach the outskirts of **Hankar.** Soon after the first tea stall, the trail leads into a gorge on the left of the Markha. Follow it up the steep switchbacks. As you come over this dry "mini-pass," the village of Hankar (2030m) comes into view.

DAY 6 (3-5HR.): HANKAR TO NIMALING. This stage is short and should be used to acclimatize for the next pass. After leaving camp, you will cross a broad stream on stepping stones. The trail becomes steep and curves left into the hillside above a small stream. After about 1hr., you'll reach a lakeside tea stall. Less than 1hr. after the stall is the camp at **Nimaling** (4850m), which costs Rs40 per day.

DAY 7 (7-8HR.): NIMALING TO SUMDO. With a pass over 5000m, a steep descent, and 7-8hr. of walking, this is the most difficult stage of the trek. Start by crossing the river on the birch-trunk bridge. The steep trail eventually becomes switchbacks until it reaches the **Kongmaru La** (5030m) after 1-1½hr. The initial descent is steep and difficult for horses and most humans. The trail soon drops into a **gorge** with walls of changing hue. This section is a challenge since it alternates between stone fields and gorge-side trails. However, the hillside sections of trail become much easier, and after about 1½hr., you will arrive in **Sumdo**. Shang Sumdo is the farthest and smallest camp, but is cheap (Rs50 per day).

DAY 8 (4-5HR.): SUMDO TO HEMIS. After leaving camp, a moderately difficult ford leads to a jeep track. Follow this for 4-5hr. to reach the Manali-Leh road at Hemis. Buses to Leh cost Rs18 and can be hailed beside the road.

OTHER TREKS

Also known as the "Baby Trek," the **Likir-Khalse** (2-4 days) leads over moderate passes to remote villages and *gompas*. The demanding **Lamayuru-Padum-Darcha** trek (19 days), which crosses both the Zanskar range and the Himalayas, is one of the most traveled in the Western Himalayas. Provisions are sold along the way. The **Karzok-Kibber** trek starts at **Tso-Morari Lake**, one day from Leh by car (you need a **permit** to reach Tso-Morari; see p. 267), and takes you through **Rupshu**, inhabited by the nomadic Changpas. On day four, you will cross the Ohirsta Phu River, which usually flows from Tibet to Tso-Morari but reverses flow seasonally. This crossing requires proper equipment. The trek climbs to the **Parang La**, where it descends to the village of **Kibber** in Spiti (see **Trekking Around Kaza**, p. 255).

THE NUBRA VALLEY

For centuries, caravans have trekked across Khardung La on the road between Punjab and Yarkand. Surrounded by the mighty mountains of Ladakh, the Nubra ("green") Valley has a varied landscape, covering long stretches of barren desert as well areas of lush greenery. Recent conflicts have reduced the passage of caravans, and only a small section of the valley (between Panamik and Hunder) is now open to the latest sources of foreign exchange: tourists. A new road has made Khardung La the highest motorable pass in the world, traveled along daily (in one direction per day) by military and tourist convoys and the occasional camel.

 WARNING. Four newly opened areas in Ladakh—Drok-pa, Nubra Valley, Pangong Lake, and Tso-Morari Lake—require a **special permit**, issued by the Deputy Commissioner in Leh. The 7-day permit can be obtained only through a travel agent; bring a photocopy of your passport and visa. Officially, you need 5 people to get the permit. Most travel agencies will have photocopies recently taken from other travelers' passports. These will be provided at a cost; expect to pay Rs100 each. The permit takes a day to arrange. You will be asked to leave a copy of your permit at every check-post; bring at least 5 photocopies with you.

DISKIT

Diskit is the administrative headquarters of the Nubra Valley. The western part of Diskit is an unimpressive collection of ugly concrete buildings while the eastern half is a jumble of village houses and barley fields. There are paths on both sides of the *chortens*, but you should not use the ones on the left, since the prayer-wheels should only be turned clockwise. From the prayer wheel on the main road, it's a 30min. climb up to the *gompa* along the path to the left, over a hill covered in *chortens*. There are great views from the new *du-khang* (assembly hall). You can also visit the protective deities in the *gon-khang*. Their fierce faces are unmasked on only one day of the year; their veils make it safe for women to enter (Rs20).

Buses from Leh go to Diskit (8hr.; Tu, Th, Sa 5am; Rs50), and return to Leh the next day. Guest houses line the *mani* wall, and most serve good, cheap food. When coming from the *gompa* and the main road, **Sunrise Guest House ❷** is on your right. (☎20011. Doubles Rs150.) **D. Khangsar Guest House ❶**, farther down a path to the right, is probably the best place to experience village life—you'll be shacking up with the cows. The rooms are clean, carpeted, and dirt cheap. (☎20014. Rooms Rs50. Breakfast Rs15; dinner Rs25.) Follow the road for 10min. to New Diskit, near the bus stand, where the only restaurant in town serves rice and *dal* (Rs25).

HUNDER

At the end of New Diskit, a dirt road turns off to the right, continuing along past pastures and sand dunes for 7km until it reaches Hunder. This walk is one of the most picturesque in the whole valley. Your permit allows you to go to the *gompa* near the bridge on the main road. Most sights lie outside the *gompa*; the paintings inside the biggest *chorten* are 50m below it; the temples are on the ridge above.

Once in Hunder, walk with the military barracks on your left until you see a sign for the **Snow Leopard Guest House ❶**, on the right. (Singles Rs60; doubles Rs150.) **Moon Land (Nerchungpa) Guest House ❶**, deeper inside the village, is hard to find, but the rooms (Rs75) are spacious and meals (Rs40) can be taken in the garden. There are also **campsites ❶**, in Hunder (Rs100-150), but it gets cold at night.

SUMUR

Sumur is a large village lined by *chortens* and a *mani* wall. Keeping these always on your right, walk up to **Sampan Ling Gompa**. Almost as big as Diskit Gompa, it has spectacular views and a school for young monks. A daily **bus** runs from Diskit to Sumur (2¼hr., evenings, Rs7) and returns the next morning. There are a number of guest houses along the way. **Stakrey Guest House ❷**, farther to the right, is the best—ask locals for directions. Doubles with semi-private, almost-clean bathrooms are Rs200. **Tashis Khahgsar Guest House ❶**, next to the school, 30m off the main road, has new rooms with common baths (doubles Rs150) and a shaded garden.

KARNATAKA

ಕರ್ನಾಟಕ

With beautiful beaches, ancient ruins, and fabulous palaces, Karnataka embodies just about every romantic dream ever had about South India. It is one of India's most progressive states, with an attitude that is neither staunchly traditional nor irritatingly mellow. The region has been dominated for centuries by the city of Mysore, which rose to political and architectural prominence during long years of Muslim rule. Karnataka first prospered under the Muslim Sultanate, and was ruled by Haider Ali and his son Tipu Sultan until the British took direct control of Mysore State in 1831. In 1956, Kannada-speaking regions in the north were added to Mysore State, renamed Karnataka in 1973.

Karnataka's coastline is dominated by the jagged Western Ghats, which shield the Deccan Plateau from coastal monsoons. On the plateau, red earth gives way to green fields and streams. The area upland from the Ghats is covered in dense teak and sandalwood forests. The mines around the Ghats provided the material for some of India's architectural masterpieces: in the north, Chalukyan temples and the Vijayanagar ruins at Hampi; in the south, the temples at Somnathpur.

HIGHLIGHTS OF KARNATAKA

India's technology capital, **Bangalore** (below) brims with pubs, gardens, unbelievable shopping, and all things cyber.

The **Maharaja's Palace** (p. 283) is a fairy-tale vision set amid the laid-back, sweet-smelling chaos of **Mysore** (p. 280).

Hippie-tested and UNESCO-certified, **Hampi's** extensive **ruins** (p. 298) are enough to make you happy to be in the middle of nowhere.

Party hardy on **Gokarna's** gorgeous beaches (p. 308) with the holy town's hip set.

BANGALORE ಬೆಂಗಳೂರು ☎ 080

The West makes its cameo on the Deccan Plateau in Bangalore. Here, American and Indian executives down *dosas* streetside, families open cybercafes in their front yards, and rickshaw-*wallahs* post web addresses in their rear windows. Founded in 1537 as the cool summer retreat from the state capital of Mysore, Bangalore has since left its erstwhile rival in the Deccan dust. With its booming economy and unprecedented expansion, Bangalore is now India's fifth-largest city and mission headquarters for the country's technological revolution. Like many Indian cities, Bangalore is noisy, dirty, crowded, and has few sights. Its biggest draw is the best nightlife south of Mumbai, which just about makes life bearable if you're stuck here for transportation or administrative purposes.

✈ INTERCITY TRANSPORTATION

FLIGHTS

The airport is 8km southeast of the city from the MG Rd. area (auto-rickshaw Rs60, or local bus #333). 24hr. pre-paid taxi booth (Rs250 to the city center).

INTERNATIONAL AIRLINES. Air India, JC Rd., Unity Bldg. (☎ 2277747; fax 2273300), a block from Corporation Bldg. **Air France** (☎ 5589397), **Kuwait Airways** (☎ 5589021), **Gulf Air** (☎ 5584702), **American Airlines** (☎ 5594240), and **Royal Jordanian** are located in Sunrise Chambers, 22 Ulsoor Rd., 1 block north of MG Rd., behind Taj Residency. **British Airways,** 7 St. Marks Rd. (☎ 2271205; fax 2241503). **KLM,** Taj Residency, Race Course Rd. (☎ 2268703). **Lufthansa,** 42-2 Dickenson Rd. (☎ 5588791), near Manipal Center. **Qantas,** 13 Westminster Cunningham Rd. (☎ 2264719), near Wockhardt Hospital. **Sabena, Singapore Airlines** (☎ 2867868), and **Swissair** (☎ 2867873) share Park View, 17 Curve Rd., off Richmond Rd. **Thai Airways, Air Nippon,** and **Royal Nepal** are in Imperial Court, Cunningham Rd. (☎ 2256194 or 2256195). **United Airlines,** 12 Richmond Rd. (☎ 2244625).

DOMESTIC AIRLINES. Indian Airlines, Cauvery Bhavan, Kempegowda Rd. (☎ 2211914). Open M-Sa 6am-5:30pm. Airport office (☎ 5266233). Open daily 8:30am-8:30pm. **Jet Airways,** 22 Ulsoor Rd., Unity Bldg. (☎ 227661720), behind the Taj Residency. Open M-F 8:30am-7pm, Sa 9am-5pm. **Sahara,** 35 Church St. (☎ 5583897 or 5584507). Open M-F 8am-8pm, Sa 10am-5pm. Airport branch (☎ 5271286 or 5271287). To: **Ahmedabad** (2hr., 1 per day, US$230); **Kolkata** (2½hr., 4 per day, US$275); **Chennai** (45min., 11 per day, US$75); **Cochin** (1hr., 2 per day, US$90); **Delhi** (2½hr., 8 per day, US$265); **Goa** (1hr., 2 per day, US$115); **Hyderabad** (1hr., 6 per day, US$115); **Mumbai** (1½hr., 14 per day, US$150); **Pune** (1½hr., 2 per day, US$155); **Trivandrum** (1hr., 1 per day, US$140).

TRAINS

City Railway Station is right next to the KSRTC Bus Stand and the City Bus Stand west of Cubbon Park. The **reservations counter** (☎ 2876464) is in the bldg. on your left as you face the station. Open M-Sa 8am-8pm, Su 8am-2pm. The **inquiries** counter (☎ 131, 132 or 1361) is in the main bldg. Open daily 7am-10:30pm. Trains are often booked weeks in advance—there are also *tatkal* (immediate) and tourist quotas for some trains to major cities. To get these, go to the reservation counter the day or morning before you want to leave. To: **Kolkata** (37hr., W and F 11pm, Rs397); **Chennai** (5-7hr., 6-7 per day 6:30am-11pm, Rs118); **Coimbatore** (7-8hr., 6:15am and 9pm, Rs181); **Delhi** (42hr., 6:25pm, Rs561; express 35hr.; M, W, Th, Su; Rs2205); **Hospet** (15hr., 10pm, Rs212); **Mumbai** (26hr., 12:45 and 8pm, Rs381); **Mysore** (2-3hr., 8 per day 5:30am-11:45pm, Rs41).

BUSES

KSRTC Bus Stand, Bhashyam Rd. (☎ 2870099). **Reservation and inquiries counter** open 7am-11pm. To: **Badami** (10hr.; 5:30, 6:30am, every hr. 5:30-9:30pm; Rs198); **Bijapur** (12hr., 8am and every hr. 4-9pm, Rs260); **Chennai** (8hr.; 9:30, 9:45, 11:15am, every 30min. 8:30-11:30pm; Rs151); **Cochin** (12hr., 7 per day 1-8pm, Rs360); **Hassan** (4hr., every hr. 6am-11:30pm, Rs63); **Hospet** (8hr.; 5, 9:30, 11:30am, noon, every hr. 4-10pm; Rs120); **Hyderabad** (12hr., 6:30am and every hr. 4:30-8:30pm, Rs317); **Kodaikanal** (10hr., 9:15pm, Rs160); **Mangalore** (8hr., every hr. 5am-11:40pm, Rs150); **Mumbai** (24hr., 3 and 4pm, Rs450-800); **Mysore** (3hr., every 15min. 5am-9pm, Rs46); **Ooty** (8hr.; every 30min. 8:30-10:30am, 9, 10pm; Rs190); **Panjim** (12hr.; 3:30, 5, 7pm; Rs395); **Trivandrum** (16hr., 1 and 4pm, Rs560). **Private buses** to Mumbai, Mysore, Ooty, and other destinations are near the KSRTC bus stand.

▣ ORIENTATION

Bangalore's throbbing commercial heart is the intersection of **Mahatma Gandhi (MG) Road** and **Brigade Road.** The business district is west on MG Rd. where most of the large bank offices are located. South of MG Rd. are **Church Street** and **Residency Road,** home to hi-tech pubs, high-class hotels, and high-price shops. Bangalore's museums sit in **Cubbon Park** to the north of MG Rd. Further north are most of

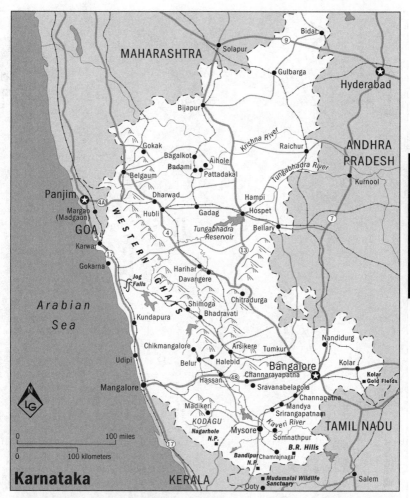

Karnataka

the government offices as well as the bustling market district of **Shivajinagar.** The local and long-distance bus stands and the railway station are all to the west of Cubbon Park. The oldest and busiest part of the city is the frenetic **City Market** area (also called Krishnarajendra or KR Market), with its unpaved narrow roads, bullock carts, temples, and mosques. Lots of Bangalore's main roads are one-way, which means rickshaws often make a number of detours.

🚌 LOCAL TRANSPORTATION

Insist that **auto-rickshaws** use their meters—it's the law and common practice. It's Rs10 for any ride under 2km. From 10pm-6am, expect to pay 1½ times the meter charge or negotiate with the driver. The biggest **local bus** stand is the Majestic (City) Bus Stand west of Cubbon Park. From here buses leave from platform 17 for MG Rd. and Ulsor Lake and from platforms 11 and 12 for Lalbagh Gardens. Bus

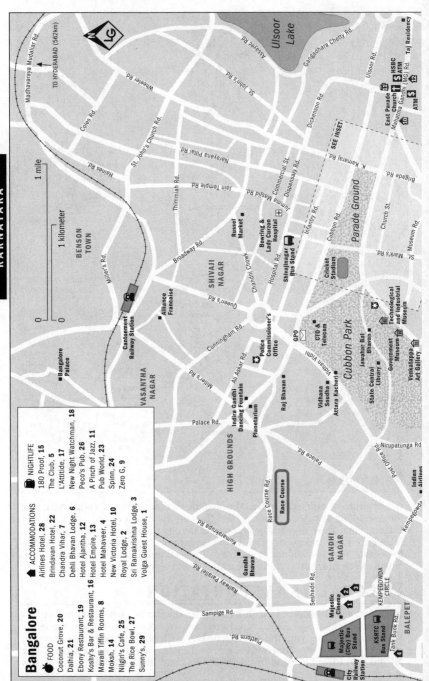

Bangalore

● FOOD
Coconut Grove, **20**
Dalhia, **21**
Ebony Restaurant, **19**
Koshy's Bar & Restaurant, **16**
Mavalli Tiffin Rooms, **8**
Moksh, **14**
Nilgiri's Cafe, **25**
The Rice Bowl, **27**
Sunny's, **29**

▲ ACCOMMODATIONS
Airlines Hotel, **28**
Brindavan Hotel, **22**
Chandra Vihar, **7**
Dehli Bhavan Lodge, **6**
Hotel Ajantha, **12**
Hotel Empire, **13**
Hotel Mahaveer, **4**
New Victoria Hotel, **10**
Royal Lodge, **2**
Sri Ramakrishna Lodge, **3**
Volga Guest House, **1**

🛏 NIGHTLIFE
180 Proof, **15**
The Club, **5**
L'Attitide, **17**
New Night Watchman, **18**
Peco's Pub, **26**
A Pinch of Jazz, **11**
Pub World, **23**
Spinn, **24**
Zero G, **9**

TO HYDERABAD (562km)

Ulsoor Lake

KARNATAKA

BENSON TOWN

SHIVAJI NAGAR

VASANTHA NAGAR

HIGH GROUNDS

GANDHI NAGAR

BALEPET

Cubbon Park

Parade Ground

Race Course

KEMPEGOWDA CIRCLE

1 mile

1 kilometer

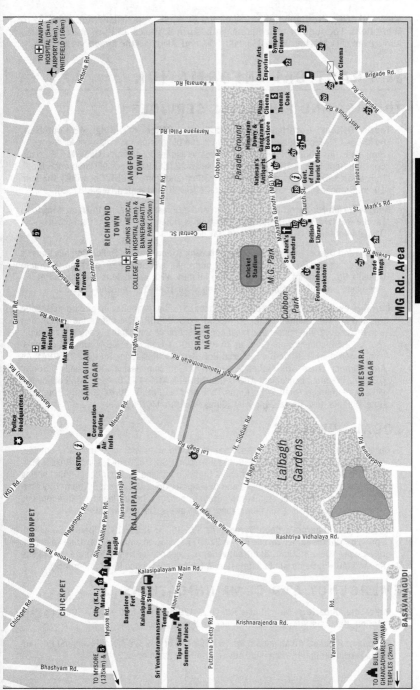

KARNATAKA

MG Rd. Area

TO MANIPAL HOSPITAL (5km), AIRPORT (6km), & WHITEFIELD (16km)

Victoria Rd.

LANGFORD TOWN

RICHMOND TOWN

Marco Polo Travels

Richmond Rd.

TO ST. JOHNS MEDICAL COLLEGE AND HOSPITAL (3km) & BANNERGHATTA NATIONAL PARK (20km)

Grant Rd.

Lavelle Rd.

Residency Rd.

Mallya Hospital

Max Mueller Bhavan

Kasturba (Gandhi) Rd. (KG) Rd.

Police Headquarters

SAMPAGIRAM NAGAR

Corporation Building

Air India

KSTDC

CUBBONPET

Naggarthpet Rd.

Avenue Rd.

Silver Jubilee Park Rd.

Narasimharaja Rd.

Mission Rd.

KALASIPALAYAM

Lal Bagh Rd.

Langford Ave.

Infantry Rd.

K. Kamaraj Rd.

Narayana Pillei Rd.

Cubbon Rd.

Parade Ground

Cauvery Arts Emporium

Symphony Cinema

Rex Cinema

Brigade Rd.

Rest House Rd.

Residency Rd.

Himalayan Dowry & Gangaram's Bookstore

Plaza Cinema

Thomas Cook

Natesan's Antiquarts

Govt. of India Tourist Office

Museum Rd.

Mahama Gandhi (MG) Rd.

Church St.

St. Mark's Rd.

Central St.

St. Mark's Cathedral

British Library

Lavelle Rd.

M.G. Park

Cricket Stadium

Cubbon Park

Fountainhead Bookstore

Trade Wings

SHANTI NAGAR

Kengal Hanumanthaiah Rd.

SOMESWARA NAGAR

H. Siddiah Rd.

Lal Bagh Fort Rd.

Jachamaraja Wodeyar Rd.

Lalbagh Gardens

Siddapura Rd.

Rashtriya Vidhalaya Rd.

CHICKPET

Chickpet Rd.

Mysore Rd.

TO MYSORE (135km) &

Bhashyam Rd.

City (K.R.) Market

Jama Masjid

Bangalore Fort

Kalasipalayam Bus Stand

Sri Venkataramanaswamy Temple

Tipu Sultan's Summer Palace

Albert Victor Rd.

Kalasipalayam Main Rd.

Puttanna Chetty Rd.

Krishnarajendra Rd.

Vanivilas Rd.

BASAVANAGUDI

TO BULL & GAVI GHANGADHARESHWARA TEMPLES (2km)

#365 and 366 go to Bannerghatta National Park, #253 to Nrityagram and #334 to Whitefield. The inquiry office is near platform 2. Buses and private buses also leave from City Market. Bus #333, 303, 304, and 305 go to the **airport** via MG Rd.

⁊ PRACTICAL INFORMATION

TOURIST AND FINANCIAL SERVICES

Tourist Offices: Government of India Tourist Office, KFC Bldg., 48 Church St. (☎5585417). From Brigade Rd., turn right; the bldg. is on the right. Ask for a copy of *Bangalore This Fortnight,* which has complete listings for the city. Open M-F 9:30am-6pm, Sa 9am-1pm. **KSTDC,** Badami House (☎2275869), opposite Corporation Bldg., N.R. Square. Daily tours of Bangalore (7:30am and 2pm, Rs85). Open daily 6:30am-10pm. Branches in the railway station (☎2870068) and airport (☎5228753).

Budget Travel: For car rental, bus, rail, air, and tour reservations, go to **Trade Wings,** 48 Lavelle Rd. (☎2214595), opposite the Airlines Hotel. Open M-F 9:30am-6:30pm, Sa 9:30am-4pm. Also changes cash and traveler's checks.

Immigration Office: The **Foreigners Registration Office** is at the **Police Commissioner's Office,** 1 Infantry Rd. (☎2942186). Go north along Cubbon Park past the GPO onto Queen's Rd., then left 1 block later onto Infantry. **Visa extensions** are granted at the same desk and take one or two days. Open M-Sa 10am-1:30pm and 3-5:30pm.

Currency Exchange: There are plenty of places to exchange money up and down Brigade Rd. and MG Rd. **Thomas Cook,** 55 MG Rd. (☎5594168), just before the intersection with Brigade Rd. The fastest and most convenient place to exchange cash and traveler's checks, Rs50 commission. Gives up to Rs20,000 advance on MC/V with 1% commission. Open daily 9:30am-6pm. **Marco Polo Travels,** Residency Rd. (☎2215984). An AmEx branch office. Will exchange money with no commission. Open daily 9:30am-6:30pm. The most convenient ATM is the **Citibank ATM,** 171 Brigade Rd., outside Nilgiri's Supermarket. Open 24hr. Cirrus/Citibank/MC/Plus/V. **HSBC,** MG Rd., opposite Hotel Ajantha, also has a 24hr. ATM. Cirrus/Maestro/MC/Plus/V.

LOCAL SERVICES

Market: Nilgiri's, 171 Brigade Rd. Popular supermarket with veg. and dairy outside, everything else inside. Open M-F 9:30am-9:30pm, Sa 10:30am-1:30pm. **Russel Market,** 1.5km north of MG Rd., off Chandni Chowk, Shivajinagar. An indoor market selling fruit, flowers, veg., meat, antiques, and bric-a-brac. Open M-Sa 5am-9:30pm. **City Market,** 1.5km southwest of City Railway Station, near the Jama Masjid, is an enormous wholesale bazaar selling silk fabric, food, and flowers. Open dawn-dusk.

Bookstore: Gangaram's Book Bureau, 72 MG Rd. (☎5581618). Open M-Sa 10am-8pm. **Fountainhead,** 41 Lavelle Rd. (☎2219777), has an amazing magazine selection. Open daily 10am-8:30pm. **Sidewalk vendors** (cheaper for bestsellers) are on Brigade Rd. and MG Rd. Some will be interested in taking your second-hand paperback.

EMERGENCY AND COMMUNICATIONS

Police: Headquarters, Nirupatunga Rd. (☎2942999), next to the YMCA. **Cubbon Park station,** Kasturba Rd. (☎2942591), next to the aquarium.

Pharmacy: Hosmat, 45 Maganath Rd. (☎5593796 or 5593797), off Richmond Rd. **Janatha Bazaar** in the Bowring and Lady Curzon Hospital is open 24hr.

Hospitals: St. John's Medical College and Hospital, Sarjapar Rd. (☎2065000 or 5530720), 4km south of Cubbon Park, is an enormous complex. The two private hospitals, **Mallya Hospital,** 2 Vittal Mallya Rd. (☎2277979) and **Monipal Hospital,** 98 Rustumbagh Rd. (☎5266646), provide the best private care money can buy. The government's **Bowring and Lady Curzon Hospital** (☎5591362) is just off Hospital Rd.

Internet: It's hard to go far in Bangalore without finding an Internet place. **Cafe Coffee Day,** 13 Brigade Rd. (☎5591602), Bangalore's first cybercafe, is still the best place to grab a coffee and surf (Rs60 per hr.). Open daily 7am-11pm. Almost every major office or commercial bldg. has at least 1 shop; the **Brigade Gardens** bldg., 19 Church St., stands out with five (Rs10-20 per hr.).

Post Office: The **GPO** (☎2866772) is a stone colossus on the corner of Raj Bhavan and Ambedkar Rd. in Cubbon Park. Open M-Sa 9am-8pm, Su 10am-5pm. *Post Restante* at the inquiries desk. There is also a branch on Brigade Rd., between Church St. and Rest House Rd., and another on Avenue Rd. south of Kempegowda Rd. Both open M-Sa 10am-6pm. **Postal Code:** 560001.

⌂ ACCOMMODATIONS

Rooms in the center of the city in the hip, hi-tech, and happening **MG Road** area are often pricey and usually full. Make reservations about a week in advance. The area around the bus stand and railway stations has plenty of cheap places to stay—5km from the action. The lodges in **City Market** are cheap but smack-dab in the middle of one of the busiest, noisiest parts of the city. Most have 24hr. check-out.

MG ROAD AREA

Hotel Ajantha, 22-A MG Rd. (☎5584321; fax 5584780), 10min. from Brigade Rd. The best deal in the MG Road area. Clean rooms, seat toilets, cable TVs, and phones. Reserve in advance. Singles Rs275; doubles Rs425. ❷

Hotel Empire, 78 Central St. (☎5592821), a 5min. walk north on St. Mark's Rd., after the cricket stadium and just past Cubbon Rd. This pleasant, friendly hotel is in a slightly quieter area, tucked away on a quiet, tree-lined block. Rooms have soft mattresses, Star TV, towels, and hot water. Attached restaurant. The hotel has a dedicated following, so book in advance. Singles Rs475-650; doubles Rs650-750. ❸

Brindavan Hotel, 108 MG Rd. (☎5584000). This large, institutional hotel lacks anything resembling charm, but its rooms are some of the cheapest on MG Rd. Reserve in advance. Singles Rs230-350; doubles Rs520. ❷

Airlines Hotel, 4 Madras Bank Rd. (☎2273783 or 2273786), just east of Lavelle Rd., 5min. from MG Rd. Rooms are plain, but they're well-furnished: towels, seat toilets, and hot water until 11am. A vast complex with Internet parlor, bakery, hair salon, and drive-in diner. Singles Rs360; doubles Rs450-550. AmEx/MC/V. ❸

New Victoria Hotel, 47-48 Residency Rd. (☎5584076 or 5585028). Lost in trees and wildflowers, the Victoria's cozy, quirky rooms with attached bathrooms sport canopy beds with antique furniture and Star TV. Service charge 10%. Singles Rs490; doubles Rs1360. Credit cards and traveler's checks accepted. ❸

RAILWAY STATION AND BUS STAND AREA

Sri Ramakrishna Lodge, SC Rd. (☎2263041), next to Kapali Theater. Reasonable rooms have squat toilets and bucket showers. Morning hot water, laundry, room service, travel counter, and restaurant. Singles Rs165; doubles Rs270-310. ❷

Royal Lodge, 251 SC Rd. (☎2266951), near Kapali Theatre. Basic rooms with dirty bathrooms. Squat or seat toilets, hot water 6:30-9am. Doubles with common bath Rs175, with attached bath Rs280-340. ❷

Volga Guest House, 41/2 S.C. Rd. (☎2870040), opposite Kapali Theatre. Dorm beds in clean but crowded rooms. Lockers available. Men only. Rs100. ❶

Hotel Mahaveer, 8/1 Tankbund Rd. (☎2873670). South of the station near the KSRTC bus stand. Pleasant, clean rooms with sheets, seat toilets, and a downstairs travel desk. Laundry service. Singles Rs300; doubles Rs400-650. MC/V. ❷

CITY MARKET

Chandra Vihar, MRR Ln. (☎2224146), across Avenue Rd. from KR Market, west of Jama Masjid. Fifty modern rooms with desks, cable TV, and phones. Reserve a day in advance. Hot showers 6-10am. Attached restaurant open 8am-9pm. Singles Rs200; doubles Rs300-500. ❷

Delhi Bhavan Lodge, Avenue Rd. (☎2875045), just north of the market area. Rooms are cheap but dire. Hot water 6-9am. Singles Rs115-165; doubles Rs175-210; triples Rs390; dorm beds for men only Rs45. ❶

◘ FOOD

Bangalore is packed full of trendy bistros and upmarket restaurants, which leave the stomach full and the wallet running on empty. The city's international flavor means you can find everything from *aloo* to ziti. The culinary melting-pot of Brigade Rd. might just leave you yearning for a decent curry. For those who've partied down to the last petty paise, cheap *paratha* joints at City Market stay open past midnight, and there are plenty of *thali* shacks around the station.

▨ Mavalli Tiffin Rooms, 11 Lal Bagh Rd. (☎2222022). A legend since it opened way back in 1924. Barefoot waiters in *lungis* serve Bangalore's best *dosas* (Rs18) and never-ending "full meals" (Rs75), leaving other restaurants 10 courses in the dust. Expect to wait on weekends. Open Tu-Su 6:30am-9:30pm, lunch 12:30-2:30pm, dinner 8-9:30pm. ❸

Koshy's Bar and Restaurant, St. Marks Rd. near MG Rd. Koshy's was started by a Keralan baker in the 1940s and is still owned by the same family. Serves MG Rd.'s only budget curries (Rs45-120) in a buzzing hall. Open daily 9am-11:30pm. ❷

Coconut Grove, 86 Church St. Huge servings of culinary curiosities presented beneath the palms, in a traditional Keralan bungalow. Entrees Rs60-130, tempting desserts Rs35-60 and Coorg coffee Rs25. Open daily 12:30-5:30pm and 7-11pm. ❸

Dalhia, G-37/38 Brigade Gardens, 19 Church St. (☎5580958). Packed with Japanese businessmen every night. *Udon* or *soba* Rs230-300. Sushi and sashimi M, W, F, Rs300-450. *Tekka domburi* Rs300. Open M-Sa noon-3pm and 6:30-9:30pm. AmEx/MC/V. ❺

Moksh, Chancery Hotel, Lavell Rd. (☎2276767), near MG Rd. Quite simply the last word in elegant Indian dining, Moksh serves some of Bangalore's best vegetarian dishes in a stylish setting. Friendly staff have good suggestions for entrees Rs135-175), but leave room for dessert (Rs70-90). Open daily 11am-3pm and 7-11:30pm. AmEx/MC/V. ❹

The Rice Bowl, 24 Residency Rd. One of the oldest and most popular Chinese restaurants. Ginger chicken Rs76. Open daily noon-3:30pm and 7-11pm. ❸

Sunny's, 35/2 Kasturba Cross (☎2243642), off Lavelle Rd., near Trade Wings travel agency. A multi-floor Mediterranean bistro topped with an open-air terrace. Optimal for leisurely lunch deals. Desserts Rs65-105. 10% service charge. Open daily noon-3:30pm and 6:30-11pm. AmEx/MC/V. ❺

Ebony Restaurant, 84 MG Rd. (☎5589333). Open-air terrace on the magnificent 14th fl. of the Barton Centre. Tandoori, Balti, Parsi, and French cuisine. A great deal for the buffet lunch, M-Sa Rs155, women Rs110. Open daily 12:30-3pm and 7:30-11:30pm. Reservations needed for dinner. AmEx/MC/V. ➎

Nilgiri's Cafe, 171 Brigade Rd. Hefty grilled sandwiches Rs38-60, doughy pizzas Rs65-90, hazelnut milkshakes Rs30, French toast Rs25. Open daily 9am-9pm. ➌

◉ SIGHTS

CUBBON PARK AND MUSEUMS. Founded in 1864 and named for the former Viceroy of India, Lord Cubbon, the park contains 300 acres of rather sparse greenery and the freshest air you're likely to find in central Bangalore. The highlight is the children's park, **Jawahar Bal Bhavan,** complete with boat, pony, and toy train rides, a doll museum, and a children's theater. *(Open daily 9:30am-6:30pm. Free.)* There are several museums along the south side of the park later on Kasturba Rd. The **Government Museum,** one of India's oldest, is a fine example of monumental neoclassical architecture. Objects include Harappan artifacts from the Indus Valley, stone Haysala sculptures, and cannons of the Tipu Sultan. Next door is the **K. Venkatappa Art Gallery,** which exhibits watercolor landscapes by K. Venkatappa, the court artist who painted much of the Maharaja's Palace in Mysore. The second floor displays rotating exhibitions of contemporary Karnatakan artists. *(Museum and gallery open Tu-Su 10am-5pm. Rs4.)* Next door, the **Visveswaraya Industrial and Technological Museum** delights grandparents and grandchildren with interactive and educational exhibits. *(Open daily 10am-6pm. Rs15.)*

VIDHANA SOUDHA. The great, grey bulk of the Vidhana Soudha is Bangalore's most recognizable landmark. In the early 1950s, a visiting Russian delegation pointed out the abundance of European architecture in Bangalore. Spurred to action by these remarks, the Chief Minister decided to build this spectacular neo-Dravidian structure. The Vidhana Soudha became not only an affirmation of Indian sovereignty, but also an assertion of Bangalore's new legislative power. It was built out of pure granite by craftsmen from Andhra Pradesh. Statues of Jawaharlal Nehru and B.R. Ambedkar stand in the front lawn, gesticulating at each other beneath the self-congratulatory inscription, "Government Work is God's Work." No visitors are allowed, but you can gaze from afar at the hefty domes and columns, which now house Karnataka's equally weighty bureaucracy. The building is lit up every Sunday evening. Across the street from the Vidhana Soudha stands its architectural nemesis, the neo-classical *Altara Kacheve,* which houses the High Court offices. *(Vidhana Vidi, north of Cubbon Park. Lights Su 7-8pm.)*

BULL TEMPLE. The Bull Temple's 5m high black Nandi was built in the 16th century. Legend has it that a raging bull used to torment local farmers by ravaging their fields at night. The frustrated farmers finally hired a night watchman to kill the bull with a crowbar. The next morning, they discovered that the carcass had transformed into a solid granite bull. At the foot of the same hill is the **Dodda Ganapathi** temple, one of the oldest and most popular in Bangalore. *(Bull Temple Rd., 2km south of the Summer Palace. Temples open daily 8am-8pm.)*

LALBAGH GARDENS. Though smaller than Cubbon Park, these gardens are older and more elegant. They were laid out by artisans brought back from Haider Ali's campaigns in Tamil Nadu. His son Tipu Sultan expanded the 16-hectare gardens to 96 hectares and added the mango grove. After Tipu's demise in 1799, the British took over. Prince Albert Victor of Wales built the

Glass House in the late 1800s to resemble the Crystal Palace in London. The gardens are home to over 150 different varieties of roses, a giant floral clock, a lotus pond, and a deer park. One of Kempegowda's four watchtowers, built in 1537 to mark Bangalore's city limits, can still be seen here. *(Lalbagh Font Rd., south of Cubbon Park. Open daily 9am-7pm. Rs5.)*

ULSOOR LAKE. Ulsoor Lake spreads over northeastern Bangalore, its 1.5 sq. km of water speckled with tiny, picturesque islands. Enjoy a boat ride or swim at the Ulsoor Boat Club (see **Other Diversions,** p. 279). During the annual Ganesh Festival (Aug.-Sept.), devotees dunk an elephantine statue, decked out in ceremonial regalia, into the lake. *(2 blocks north of MG Rd., on Gangadhana Chetty and Kensington Rd., near the Taj Hotel and Cottage Emporium. Open daily dawn-dusk.)*

OTHER SIGHTS. One kilometer south of the Bull Temple, the **Sri Gavi Gangadareshwara Temple** is formed from a natural rock cave. On the morning of the Makara Sakrantic Festival, sunlight passes through the Nandi's horns to hit the *linga* inside the sanctum. *(Bull Temple Rd. Open daily 7am-8pm.)* The **Jawaharlal Nehru Planetarium** was built to commemorate the 100th birthday of the freedom fighter and prime minister who called Bangalore "India's city of the future." *(T. Chowdiak Rd., opposite Raj Bhavan.* ☎ *2266084. Open Tu-Su; closed 2nd Tu. English shows Tu-Sa at 4:30pm, Su 12:45pm. Rs15.)* Just across the street and open the same days, the **Indira Gandhi Musical Dancing Fountain** puts on a kitschy little show *(7 and 8pm, Rs10).* The **Gandhi Picture Gallery,** on the second floor of **Gandhi Bhavan,** has grainy, enlarged photographs and a few of Gandhi's letters and possessions, though most of the information is in Kannada. *(Kumara Krupa Rd.* ☎ *2261967. Open M-Sa noon-6pm. Free.)* The mighty **Bangalore Palace** was built by the Wodeyars and is modelled on Windsor Castle. Although it appears in plenty of tourist brochures, it's not worth visiting as it is private property—the closest you'll get is a fence 100m away.

▣ NIGHTLIFE

BARS

Though plagued by water shortages, Bangalore is never truly dry. Its burgeoning pub culture has earned the city the name "Bar Galore." Most pubs are clustered around Brigade Rd., with classier establishments up and down Residency Rd. Pubs may serve alcohol only from 11am to 11pm. The police visit around midnight, suggesting that "good people sleep early." Most accept major credit cards.

180 Proof, 40 St. Mark's Rd., south of MG Rd. The "heppest" meeting place for Bangalore's sophisticated set, complete with black-blazered bouncers standing guard. This colonial armory-turned-loft is the place to see and be seen on F and Sa nights. Beer per bottle Rs75-180, per pint Rs80. Cover F-Sa Rs100. Open daily noon-11:30pm.

New Night Watchman, 46/1 Church St. Pumping music and a relaxed crowd give this place a pleasant atmosphere. Beer per pint Rs70. Open daily 11am-11:30pm.

A Pinch of Jazz, 47 Dickenson Rd, in The Central Park Hotel. Bangalore's most stylish chill-out spot. Give the vinyl menus a spin for Cajun standards (Rs60-140) as you kick back to Getz, Mingus, and one of India's only frosted margaritas (Rs100). A 4-piece combo plays live nightly 8:30-11:30pm. Open daily noon-3pm and 7-11:30pm.

Pub World, 65 Lakmi Plaza, Residency Rd. A British pub, German beer hall, Hollywood bar, and Wild West Saloon under one roof, but they could all blend into one after a few drinks. Beer Rs50-120. Open daily 11:30am-11:30pm.

Zero G, 10th floor, Prestige Towers. Come to cool down in this bar with a view and an open-air feel. Open M-Th noon-midnight, F and Sa noon-2:30am.

Peco's Pub, 34 Rest House Rd., off Brigade Rd, south of Church St. Garcia, Marley, Joplin, and Zeppelin grace the walls. Packed with a college-age crowd imbibing mugfuls (Rs30), and Cajun cooking (Rs100-170). Relaxing rooftop. Open daily 11am-11pm.

DISCOTHEQUES

Another much-loved city ordinance, the one against the late operation of discos, prevents a proper club scene from taking root. Most places are couples only. The city's hippest dance floor is at **Spinn,** 83 Residency Rd., which packs in the young and wealthy on Wednesdays and weekends. New-age decor and classy open-air terrace. (Open daily 7:30pm-12:30am. Dance floor open W, F, and Sa; Rs300 cover per couple.) At **The Club,** Mysore Rd., outside of town, DJs spin the latest techno, trance, and hip-hop. Site of MTV's South Asia launch, The Club draws up to 6000 revelers for its live gigs and sports a swimming pool, squash, tennis, and basketball courts, and a 24hr. coffee shop. (☎8600669 or 8600768. Open W-Sa 8pm-5am. Cover Rs350 per couple. Taxis Rs300 for a one-way ride. Be wary of traveling alone or in rickshaws.) The decor may be dated (red and black faux leather) and the music may be cheesy, but its early morning closing time makes **L'Attitude,** 80/1 MG Rd., the place for late-night revelers. (Open M-Tu, Th 5pm-1am. No cover. Dance floor W, F-Sa 5pm-5am. Cover Rs250.)

OTHER DIVERSIONS

A lot happens in Bangalore, so check the weekly listings in papers available at magazine stands; www.bangalorebest.com also has up-to-date information on current cultural events. Several cinemas in the MG Rd. area show English-language flicks. **The Plaza,** 74 MG Rd. (☎5587682), **The Rex,** Brigade Rd. (☎5587350), and **The Symphony,** 51 MG Rd. (☎5585988), all show not-too-old American movies (showtimes noon, 3:30, 6:30, 9:30pm; Rs40-80). Buy tickets at least 1hr. in advance, especially for evening and weekend performances. Celebrate India's favorite sport at the **Chinaswamy Cricket Stadium,** near Cubbon Park. Check at the stadium office for dates and times. You can rent boats or go for a swim at **Utsoor Boat Club,** Kensington Rd. (Swimming Rs10 per hr. Open Th-Tu 6:30-10am and 12:30-4pm.) Every month or two, **Bangalore Palace** hosts large rock concerts, often featuring Western groups. Check *Bangalore This Fortnight* for listings.

▗ SHOPPING

Bangalore's arts and crafts emporiums, with handpainted or inlaid tables, saris fit for a *rani*, and life-size sandalwood Krishnas, merit a shopping expedition. Many emporiums, most of them flogging the same collection of pashmina shows, silk cushion covers, and Kashmiri carpets, line MG Rd. and Infantry Rd. Most are hideously overpriced, so be prepared to bargain hard. Most accept credit cards and can arrange international shipping. **Natesan's Antiqarts,** 76 MG Rd., sells art pieces of their own design. (☎5588344. Open M-Sa 10am-7:30pm.) **Himalayan Dowry,** 72 MG Rd., sells Kashmiri and Tibetan handicrafts and donates a portion of its proceeds to anti-dowry campaigns. The owner, Mr. Zaffar Shawl, is a Himalayan crystal healer and would be happy to rid you of your negative energy. (☎5597366. Open M-Sa 10am-9pm.) On **Commercial Street,** you'll find *salwar kameez* and saris in all permutations of style, color, and price, while Brigade Rd. has shopping malls with Western brand names.

⚡ DAYTRIPS FROM BANGALORE

NRITYAGRAM DANCE VILLAGE

Buses run regularly from Bangalore (#253, 253A, 253D, 253E, 266 from City Market or #253 from platform 21 of Majestic Bus Stand) to Nrityagram, but the village is 5km from the bus stand. Rickshaws are Rs90 for a return trip and waiting time. You can also book through KSTDC, Cosmopole Travels (☎ 2281591), or Cox and Kings Travel (☎ 2239258). The village closes in the summer when the dancers go on tour, so call ahead to check if it's open (☎ 8466313 or 8466314).

Dancers from all over India come to Hessaraghatta to train at the Nrityagram Dance Village. Thirty-five kilometers from the city on the Bangalore-Pune Highway, the village was established by the late Protima Gauri, one of the most respected *odissi* dancers of the 20th century. Tours of the village include an hour-long lecture demonstration of *odissi* and *kathak* dance, a lecture on Indian philosophy and culture, and an organically grown lunch. (Casual tours Rs20 per person.) During the first week of February the village conducts an all-night dance and music festival. The festival is free, featuring performances by students as well as musical favorites Zakir Hussain and Amjad Ali Khan. Get there by 3:30pm if you want a seat. (Dance performance Rs1100, minimum 10 people; advance booking required. Village open Sept.-May Tu-Su 10am-5pm.)

BANNERGHATTA NATIONAL PARK

Bus #366 runs from Majestic Bus Stand to Bannerghatta (50min., every 15min., Rs10).

This 105 sq. km national park is a popular getaway and picnic spot 22km from the city. The park's biggest draws are the 23 tigers, including several of the rare white tigers, and 7 lions which roam semi-wild through natural habitat. The entrance fee includes a 30min. "safari" in an overcrowded minibus through the tiger and lion enclosures. There is also an attached zoo with cobras, elephants, and zebras. The park is packed on weekends with Bangalore day-trippers. (☎ 7828425. Open daily except Tu 9am-5:30pm. Rs 200; camera fee Rs15.)

MYSORE ಮೈಸೂರು ☎ 0821

Calm, graceful, and magisterial, Mysore welcomes visitors with the friendly charm of a small town. The Wodiyars, who ruled here from the 15th century until Independence, lavished money on the city. They left behind them acres of tree-lined avenues, elegant, classical buildings, and an air of dignified grandeur. Forts, palaces, and temples all call for a piece of your time and attention. The city comes to life at the beginning of October during the annual 10-day Dussehra Festival.

⬛ TRANSPORTATION

Trains: The **railway station** is the pink collonaded building at the intersection of JCB Rd. and Irwin Rd. Relatively few trains run from Mysore. For most connections, head to Bangalore. The inquiry and reservations desks (☎ 131 or 2422103) are open M-Sa 8am-8pm, Su 8am-2pm. To: **Bangalore** (3hr., 10-12 per day 6am-11:30pm, Rs46); **Chennai** (7-10½hr., 2:20 and 6pm, Rs215); **Hassan** (2-3hr.; 7:30, 10:15am, 6pm; Rs23).

Buses: Long-distance buses leave from the **Central Bus Stand** (☎ 2520853), on BN Rd., near Wesley Cathedral. Reservations desk open daily 7:30am-8pm. Buses run to: **Bangalore**, via **Sriringapatam** (3½hr., every 10min. 5am-9pm, Rs55); **Belur** (5hr., every hr. 6am-10:30pm, Rs60); **Bijapur** (18hr., 1pm, Rs211); **Chennai** (12hr.; 5, 7, 8pm; Rs280); **Coimbatore** (6hr., 11 per day 6am-11:30pm, Rs55); **Hassan** (3hr., every

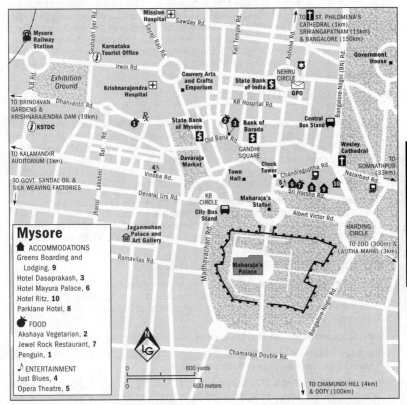

Mysore

🏠 ACCOMMODATIONS
Greens Boarding and
Lodging, **9**
Hotel Dasaprakash, **3**
Hotel Mayura Palace, **6**
Hotel Ritz, **10**
Parklane Hotel, **8**

🍴 FOOD
Akshaya Vegetarian, **2**
Jewel Rock Restaurant, **7**
Penguin, **1**

♪ ENTERTAINMENT
Just Blues, **4**
Opera Theatre, **5**

30min. 5:30am-11pm, Rs50); **Madikeri** (3hr., every 30min. 5:30am-11pm, Rs50);
Mangalore (7hr., every hr. 6am-2pm and 9-11pm, Rs140); **Ooty** (6hr., every hr. 6am-
11pm, Rs60). **Private buses** and **maxicabs** crowd the street between the cathedral and
Gandhi Sq. It can be an effort finding one going in your direction.

Local Transportation: Local buses leave from the **City Bus Stand,** off KR Cir. Fares are
Rs3-8; signs are in Kannada. To: **Somnathpur** via **Bannur** (platform 7, 45min., every
20min.); **Brindavan Gardens** (#303 and #304, platform 6, 30min., every 30min.);
Chamundi Hill (#201, platform 7, 20min., every 20min.); **Srirangapatnam** (#313 and
316, platform 6, 45min., every 20min.). **Taxis** cluster in Gandhi Sq. Make sure **auto-
rickshaw** drivers use their meters. Minimum fare is Rs9, Rs4.5 for each additional km.

◼ ORIENTATION

Though the center of Mysore is small, it's easy to become hopelessly disoriented.
Navigation isn't helped by the fact that most of the shady boulevards and elegant
intersections are indistinguishable from one another. The **Central Bus Stand** sits
on the busy north-south thoroughfare, **Bangalore-Nilgiri (BN) Road.** Parallel to and

west of BN Rd. is **Sayaji Rao Road,** which runs into KR Circle. Running north-south, Sayaji Rao Road bisects Mysore into roughly equal halves, cutting through **KR Circle,** the true center of the city. The **City Bus Stand** is in the southeast quadrant of KR Cir., sitting before the gates of the gigantic **Maharaja's Palace.** Restaurants and hotels cluster along **Sri Harsha Road,** north of the palace. The **Train Station** is in the northwest corner of town on the east-west running **Irurin Road.** The summit of **Chamundir Road** is 4km to the south of town.

🛈 PRACTICAL INFORMATION

Tourist Office: Karnataka Tourist Office, Old Exhibition Bldg. (☎2442096), at the corner of Irwin and Seshadri Iyer Rd., 1 block east of the railway station. Open M-Sa 10am-5:30pm; closed 2nd Sa of each month. **KSTDC,** on JLB Rd. (☎2423652), adjacent to the Hotel Mayura Hoysala has day tours of Mysore including Somnathpur and Srirangapatnam. Open 6:30am-9pm. Tours 7:30am-9pm daily, Rs230. Tours can be booked through branch offices at the train and central bus stations.

Currency Exchange: The **State Bank of Mysore** (☎2443866) has foreign exchange branches at the junction of Sayaji Rao and Old Bank Rd. and on Nehru Cir. Open M-F 10:30am-2:30pm, Sa 10:30am-12:30pm. **Bank of Baroda,** at the northeast corner of Gandhi Sq., exchanges cash in US dollars, euros, and pounds. Open M-F 10:30am-2:30pm and 3-4pm, Sa 10:30am-1pm.

ATM: At the train station, takes Plus and Visa. Open 24hr.

Market: Devaraja Market, tucked behind the glitzy sari shops on Sayaji Rao Rd. and the sandalwood shops on Dhanvantri Rd. Crammed with the full spectrum of brightly colored vegetables and fruit, and *kum-kum* powder, as well as the ubiquitous incense. Open daily dawn-dusk.

Police: Laskash Police Station, on Nehru Cir. (☎2520762), opposite the GPO.

Pharmacy: Janatha Bazaar Drug Unit, Dhanvantri Rd. (☎2427678), on KR Hospital grounds opposite Indra Bhavan Hotel. Open 24hr.

Hospital: Krishnarajendra (KR) Hospital (☎2443300), at the corner of Sayaji Rao Rd. and Irwin Rd., opposite Cauvery Emporium. This enormous complex of yellow and white buildings is crowded and dirty. The private **Holdsworth Memorial (Mission) Hospital,** Sawday Rd. (☎2446544), is marginally better.

Internet: Take advantage of early morning connections at **Internet World,** on Chandraguptha Rd., between the Clock Tower and Wesley Cathedral in the Chamundi Vasathi Gruha lodge. Rs30 per hr. Open daily 6am-11:30pm.

Post Office: GPO, Nehru Circle (☎2520052). Open M-Sa 10am-6pm, Su 10am-3pm. Post-restante counter #6. **Postal Code:** 570001.

🛏 ACCOMMODATIONS

Mysore is full of reasonably priced, centrally located hotels. The nicest places to stay are in the central area north of the Maharaja's Palace. Many of the best hotels have a devoted following, so reservations (a week ahead Nov.-Feb.) are a good idea. 5-10% state tax on rooms Rs150 and up.

📽 **Hotel Ritz,** 5 BN Rd. (☎2422668), 100m south of the Central Bus Stand, on your right as you exit. High quality, batik-blanketed rooms with armchairs, tiled bathrooms, and seat toilets. Take lunch or dinner from the excellent restaurant in the private sitting room upstairs (see **Food**). It's often booked solid, so make reservations well in advance. Doubles Rs400; quads Rs530. Check-out noon. AmEX/MC/V. ❸

Greens Boarding and Lodging, 2722/2 Sri Harsha Rd. (☎2422415). Large rooms with desks, chairs, seat toilets, and showers (bucket hot water) come super-cheap. Some rooms even open onto a balcony. Attached restaurant and bar open daily 10:30am-2:30pm and 5:30-11pm. Singles Rs70; doubles Rs100. ❶

Parklane Hotel, 2720 Sri Harsha Rd. (☎2430400). Clean, smallish rooms with mosquito nets. Popular restaurant and nightly music give it a lively atmosphere. Hot water 6-10am. Singles Rs125; doubles Rs125-150. AmEx/MC/V. ❶

Hotel Dasaprakash (☎2442444 or 444455), on the corner of Gandhi Sq. and Old Bank Rd. Spacious and airy. Palm-fringed courtyard meets all your needs—an ice cream parlor, an astropalmist, and a travel agency. Towels and soap provided. Seat or squat toilets, and veg. restaurant. Singles Rs185-415; doubles Rs325-775. ❷

Hotel Mayura Palace, 2716 Sri Harsha Rd. (☎2435913). A range of comfortable rooms, all with armchairs, cable TV, phone, seat toilets, and showers. Morning hot water and 24hr. room service. Check-out noon. Doubles Rs450-640, with A/C Rs920. ❸

🍴 FOOD

Mysore's traditional sweet **pak** is melt-in-your-mouth delicious and can be found at most of the sweet shops in the city. Vendors between Wesley cathedral and the Central Bus Station sell every type of fruit imaginable.

▩ **Parklane Hotel,** Sri Harsha Rd. This leafy garden terrace is jumping every evening. Candlelight and live music make it perfect for wining and dining. Sa and Su nights are the extra-special BBQ-night. Chinese and Indian dishes Rs45-80. Beer Rs50-70. Open daily 10:30am-3:30pm and 6:30-11:30pm. Live music 7:30-10:30pm. AmEx/MC/V. ❸

Hotel Ritz, 5 BN Rd. Another great restaurant featuring gardens, candlelight, and friendly service. Chicken dinners from Rs60, *Rumali* rolls Rs35-60, kebab platter Rs75, veg. dishes Rs36-55. Open daily 7am-11pm. Bar open daily 11am-11pm. ❸

Penguin, Dhanvantri Rd., just west of Hotel Indra Bhavan. It's no mirage: this rooftop oasis serves fresh fruit juices (Rs10-15), milkshakes (Rs15-25), homemade ice cream (Rs15), and 9 types of *dosas* (Rs15). A perfect getaway from busy and ugly Dhanvantri Rd. Open daily 9:30am-11pm, roof garden open after 4:30pm. ❶

Akshaya Vegetarian Restaurant, in the Hotel Dasaprakash. Serves brimming bottomless *thalis* (Rs30-45) and thick Nilgiri coffee (Rs6) to hordes of locals and travelers. Open daily 6am-10pm, lunch noon-3pm, dinner 7:30-10pm. ❷

Jewel Rock Restaurant, 2716 Sri Harsha Rd., at Hotel Maurya Palace. A friendly staff recommends delicious tandoori, *tikkas,* and *biryanis* made-to-order (Rs40-100). Classy atmosphere with dim lighting and jazz. Open daily 11am-3:30pm and 7-11:30pm. ❷

📷 SIGHTS

THE MAHARAJA'S PALACE. The opulence and workmanship of the Maharaja's Palace will astound even the most jaded of temple-hopping tourists. Built in 1897 after the original burned down in a fire, it took 15 years to complete and cost 4.2 million rupees. The vast majority of the palace as seen on the visit was used for only two weeks of the year, during the annual Dussehra Festival in Oct. The first room exhibits objects used in the festival, including the **80kg solid-gold howdah** and the Durga idol that now rides in it, in place of the maharaja. Twenty-six murals showing the 1934 festival lead you on into the enormous **Marriage Hall,** still used for family celebrations by the maharaja's family. The best artistry from around the

KARNATAKA

world is brought together here: magnificent stained glass from Belgium, cast-iron pillars from Scotland, tiles from England, and a chandelier from the former Czechoslovakia. A marble staircase leads up to the pillared **Durbar Hall** where the king addressed his subjects and watched the ceremonies on each of the ten days of the festival. Here, gilded mirrors, a carved teak ceiling, marble inlay-work, and paintings of gods and goddesses create the ultimate in good gaudy opulence. The **Conference Hall** behind was used for the day-to-day running of the kingdom. The solid silver doors at the far end show the life of Krishna and the ten incarnations of Vishnu. Visible from the exit, the tattered **Residential Museum** is slightly disappointing. Something of a box-room for maharaja memorabilia, the museum has toys, toiletries and clothes, and furniture of the royal family. At 7pm on Sundays and government holidays the palace is illuminated with 80,000 light bulbs. *(Entrance from southern gate. Open daily 10am-5:30pm. Maharaja's Palace and Residential Museum, Rs15 each. Approved guides Rs235 for 1-4 people.)*

CHAMUNDI HILL. Even if you're not religious, a visit to Chamundi Hill can be a spiritual experience. The ride affords a divine view of the Deccan plain, with its squares of saffron and green, and of Mysore city—even at a distance, you can see the Maharaja's Palace and the twin spires of Philomena's Church. At the top of the hill, the 5m-high **Mahishasura,** the buffalo demon who plagued Mysore (and from whom the city takes its name), greets you in all his god-awful gaudiness. The **Sri Chamundeswari Temple,** with its 40m *gopuram,* derives its name from Chamundi, an incarnation of the goddess Durga who brought Mahishasura down to size. The hill is one of the holiest in Karnataka, and can be a bit of a madhouse. Over 10,000 free meals are provided to visitors each week by a private campaign. *(Temple open 7:30am-2pm and 4-8pm.)* One thousand steps lead up Chamundi Hill to the temple. Ascending or descending can give you a case of "My-sore" feet (2hr.). On the plus side though, the hike is said to wipe away sins. Three hundred steps from the summit, the enormous granite **Nandi Bull** at the entrance to the Shiva temple is worth a visit. Nandi protects the temple, and it's rumored that he grows by about a centimeter each year. *(Shiva temple open 7:30am-2pm and 3:30-9pm. Chamundi Hill is southeast of town. Local bus #201 leaves every 20min. from platform 7 of the City Bus Stand, Rs5. Autorickshaws Rs80-100 round-trip.)*

ST. PHILOMENA'S CATHEDRAL. Mysore's very own piece of "medieval" Europe rises incongruously from the palm trees and rickshaw stands that surround it. Built in 1933 but modeled on the Cologne Cathedral, Philomena's is certainly one of the more extraordinary churches in South India. French-made stained glass windows show scenes from the life of Christ. Exit through the small catacombs where generations of Mysore's Christians are buried. *(Open daily 8am-6pm. Free.)*

OTHER SIGHTS. The crumbling **Jaganmohan Palace** is a fitting home for the jumble of ill-assorted **objects d'art** collected in the **Jayachamrajendra Art Gallery** inside. Objects from India, England, Japan, and Persia vie for space in the pillared and painted halls. Highlights include Rabindranath Tagore watercolors and Raja Ravi Varma oils, a collection of tablas, sitars, and veenas, and a series of Buddhas carved onto an elephant tusk. *(2 blocks west of the Maharaja's Palace. Open daily 8:30am-5pm. Rs15.)* Indian tourists flock to the **Brindavan Gardens** and **Krishnarajendra Dam** on the weekends. The vast, severely tended gardens lack flowers, but the fountains are let loose at night in a sound and light show. The dam was built across the Kaveri River at the turn of the century. *(City bus #303 or 304 from platform 6 of the City Bus Stand. 30min., every 30min., Rs7-10. Gardens open daily 7:30am-9pm. Fountains M-F 7-8pm, Sa-Su 7-9pm.)* As Indian zoos go, the **Mysore Zoo** is rather pleasant. Tigers (including the endangered white tiger), elephants, rhinos, and India's only gorilla roam the open-air enclosures. Efforts to house animals in their most natural habitats led to the 1994 escape of two vagrant crocodiles into rural Karnataka. *(Open W-M 8:30am-5:30pm. Rs15; camera fee Rs10; video fee Rs15.)*

🎵 📷 ENTERTAINMENT AND SHOPPING

Opera Theatre, Sri Marsha Rd. has English language films. (Rs25-35. Showtimes 10:30am, 1:30, 4:30, and 7:30pm.) **Just Blues: The Blues Concept Pub,** in the Balaji Palace Hotel, is not a blues pub, but Mysore's only club. Bask in the violet glow at the bar (mugs of beer Rs30, pitchers Rs140) as the DJ spins upstairs and the dance floor pumps fresh hip-hop (open daily 11am-11:30pm). **GRS Fantasy Water Park** is a 15 min. bus ride northwest of the city. It boasts a range of wet and dry rides and amusements. (Bus #133, 121, or 4 from City Bus Stand. Open M-Sa 10:30am-6pm, Su 10:30am-8pm. Adults Rs200, children Rs125; after 4pm Rs100/75.) Check *The Hindu* or *New Indian Express* for cultural programs at **Kalamandir,** Vinoba Rd.

Mysore hosts the country's most spectacular **Dussehra Festival** at the beginning of October. Ten days of dance, drama, and music celebrate the victory of Durga over the water buffalo demon. The festival climaxes on the last day with a procession from the royal palace. Shopping in Mysore revolves, almost exclusively, around **silks** and **sandalwood.** Mini-emporiums crowd Dhanvantri Rd. near its intersection with Sayaji Rao Rd. Fend off hoardes of incense and oil vendors around Devaraja Market. Farther down Sayaji Rao Rd., near KR Cir., silk stores sell enough saris to clothe an army of elephants. The **KSIC Government Silk Weaving Factory** in Vidyaranyapuram allows tours. Here, you can watch your silk being woven and buy it later at mill prices. (☎2481803. Open M-Sa 10am-noon and 2-4pm.) Next door is the **Government Sandal Oil Factory,** which will give you a quick tour. (☎2483651. Open M-Sa 9-11am and 2-4pm.) Take the bus (# 3, 8, 9, 11, 13, 14, or 44; 15min., every 10min.) to Vidyaranyapuram.

🔳 DAYTRIPS FROM MYSORE

SOMNATHPUR

Few buses go directly to Somnathpur. The quickest route is to go to Bannur from either the private bus stand near Wesley Cathedral or platform 7 of the city bus stand (45min., every 40min., Rs8-10). From there, buses run regularly to Somnathpur (20min., every 20min., Rs5). Temple open daily 9am-5:30pm. Rs100; video fee Rs25.

A small, sleepy village 38km east of Mysore, Somnathpur is the site of the beautiful **Keshava Temple.** Built in 1268 by the Maysala general Somanatha, the incredible carvings are unparalleled examples of the Maysala style. Legend has it that when the temple was completed, the gods deemed it too beautiful and too grand for this earth and wanted to transport it to heaven. The temple quaked and began to levitate. In horror, the chief sculptor mutilated some images on the outside wall to avert such a catastrophe. The slightly disfigured temple came crashing back down to earth. These events explain why the *garudagamba* (stone pillar symbolizing the divine mount, the eagle Garuda) is not opposite the entrance, as is traditional, but skewed to the northeast. The numerous carved friezes of the temple base show elephant processions, flower scrolls, scenes from the epics, and no less than 193 deities. Look out for the names of individual sculptors carved at the bases. Inside, three shrines to Vishnu, Krishna, and Keshava face north, south, and west respectively. Each of the 16 elaborately carved roof panels is unique.

SRIRANGAPATNAM

Take bus #3134 or 316 from platform 6 of the city bus stand or one of the private buses that crowd Chandraguptha Rd. (30min, every 20min. 6am-8pm, Rs7-11). Last bus returns to Mysore at 9pm. A rickshaw will take you around all the sights for Rs100.

Srirangapatnam, 16km from Mysore, was the site of Tipu Sultan's island fort and the seat of his vast kingdom until the fourth Anglo-Mysore war in 1799. Tipu's father, Haider Ali, defeated Mysore's Hindu maharaja in 1761. In 1782, Tipu inherited the throne, along with the problem of growing British power in South India. After roundly defeating the British and their Mahrathi and Hyderabadi allies in 1782, Tipu's subcontinental conquest was brought to an end in 1799. The British stormed the fortress and firmly established their presence in South India. Tipu's elaborate summer palace, the **Daria Daulat**, is 1km east of the bus stand. The palace was built in 1784 to commemorate Tipu's victory over the British. After the fall of the city, the palace was used by Arthur Wellesley, future duke of Wellington and nemesis of Napoleon. Every inch of the palace is covered in paintings. One wall, showing frightened redcoats and a dashing Tipu, records the memorable victory; the opposite portrait wall shows various royalty and dignitaries of Tipu's time. Inside is a **museum** housing some pictures from the time, including a striking, full-length portrait of Tipu himself. *(Auto-rickshaw Rs15. To walk, turn right out of the bus stand platform and take an immediate left; the palace is on the left. Open daily 9am-5pm. Rs100.)* Beyond Daria Daulat, another 1.5km down the road, lies **Gumbaz**, the onion-domed mausoleum where Tipu, also known as the "Tiger of Mysore," rests alongside his parents. The tomb-chamber is decorated in Tipu's signature tiger-stripes. His tomb is covered in tiger skin. *(Open daily 8am-6:30pm. Free.)*

In the opposite direction from the bus stand (left, then left again) sit the remains of the Sriringapatnam fort. Three successive gates take you through the crumbling fortifications. Immediately on your right is the **Jama Masjid,** the mosque Tipu built on the grounds of an old Hindu temple. The tombs to the left of the entrance are those of Tipu's tutor and his family. About 500m further down the main road, the **Sri Ramganatha Temple** is a mish-mash of Haysala, Vijayanagar, and Wadiyar styles. The main shrine contains a colossal Vishnu reclining on a five-headed serpent. *(Open daily 7:30am-1pm and 4-8pm.)* A left out of the temple takes you to Tipu's **dungeon,** where 11 of the 24 British officers imprisoned here met their grisly deaths. The cannon fell through the roof in 1799 and has never been removed. Turning left out of the dungeon takes you along the city walls and eventually back to the main gate. After 750m, you'll pass the **Water Gate** and obelisk commemorating the spot where Tipu's body was found after the storming of 1799. It is rumored that the ghost of Tipu still wanders in search of his stolen belt buckle. For those looking to learn more about the feathered residents of Karnataka, the **Srirangapatnam Bird Sanctuary** is 7km south of the town.

MADIKERI   ☎ 08272

The small, quiet town of Madikeri is the capital of the tiny coffee-growing district of Kodagu (Coorg). The area has been dubbed the "Scotland of India" for its hilly terrain, damp climate, and independent spirit. The region had its own government from 1952 to 1955 when it was merged with Karnataka. The residents still retain a Kordava culture and identity distinct from their neighbors. The town itself is set in the middle of lush tropical hills which offer unrivaled trekking opportunities. The best time to visit is from October to May, when crisp nights follow temperate days. In summer, rain pounds the hills. Though the town is still somewhat off the beaten path, word about this beautiful destination has begun to spread in recent years.

■ **TRANSPORTATION.** The steep road by the private bus stand on GT Rd. leads to the long-distance KSRTC bus stand. To: **Bangalore** (8hr., every hr. 5:30am-11pm, Rs110) via **Hassan** (4hr., every 30-60min. 6:30am-7:30pm, Rs45) and **Kushalnagar** (1hr., Rs13); **Mangalore** (4hr.; every 30-60min. 5:30am-8:30pm, 7 night buses after 10:45pm; Rs43-56); **Mysore** (3½hr., every 30min. 5:30am-9:30pm, Rs55); **Ooty** (9hr., 7:30am). Unmetered **auto-rickshaws** charge at least Rs12 for a trip around town.

■ ? **ORIENTATION AND PRACTICAL INFORMATION.** Spread out over several hillsides and with numerous dead ends and curving lines, Madikeri can be somewhat difficult to navigate. **Main Road,** also called General Thimmaya (GT) Rd., runs north from GT Circle past the fort and private bus stand in the center of town to the Raiga tombs, 1km to the north. **Race Course (MA) Road** runs west from the fort past Raja Seat and makes a big loop to rejoin Main Rd. as **College Road.** Opposite Race Course Rd., **Temple Road** runs east looping past the Omkoreshwara Temple to become **Junior College Road.** It rejoins Main Road at the **private bus stand.** The **Tourist Office** is in the PWD Inspection Bungalow by GT Circle (☎228580. Open M-Sa 10am-1:15pm and 2:15-5:30pm), but it's pretty useless. **Mr. Ganesh Aiyanna,** at the Hotel Cauvery is a powerful force in the burgeoning tourist industry and can arrange anything you might want, from working on a coffee plantation to serving a traditional Kordava wedding, as well as 1-3 day treks. **Coorg Travels** (☎225274, MG road near Raya Seat) and the **Hotel Chitra** can also arrange treks. **Canara Bank,** Main Rd. on the bazaar by the Bata Shop, handles currency exchange and traveler's checks and gives $500 advances on AmEx/MC/V. (Open M-Sa 10:30am-2:30pm.) The **police station** (☎229333) is on Main Rd. opposite the fort. Several **pharmacies** cluster around GT Circle; **Gautham Pharma** is the cleanest and friendliest of the bunch. (☎255768. Open M-Sa 8:30am-8:45pm.) The **Government Headquarters Hospital** (☎223444) is the huge grey fortress-style building 50m south of GT circle. Superfast **Internet** access comes surprisingly cheap at **Netraiders.com,** a couple steps past Chowk from the main road. (Rs30 per hr. Open M-Sa 9:30am-8:30pm.) The **Head Post Office** is on General Thimaya Rd., just up the hill from the private bus stand. (☎225413. Open M-Sa 9:30am-5:30pm.) **Postal Code:** 571201.

■ ■ **ACCOMMODATIONS AND FOOD.** Hotels in Madikeri tend to be on the pricier side. Prices fall slightly in the off-season (June-Aug.). The **Hotel Cau-**

THE HIDDEN DEAL

THE PALACE ESTATE

Because miles of lush, dramatic scenery are visible from nearly every street in Madikeri, a peaceful getaway often seems tantalizingly close. The town itself is busy and noisy, hardly the rural idyll that visitors to Kodayu might be expecting. But the tranquil paradise of your dreams *does* exist and it's only 1hr. away, in the thick of some of the most beautiful scenery in Karnataka.

The Palace Estate is set on the edges of the Western Ghats, 1.5km from the village of Kakkabe. Parts of the Estate date to the 1860s, and it has been inhabited by the current owners for four generations.

Although the traditional Kerala-style house is elegant and comfortable, the real draw is the beautiful countryside that surrounds it. The Estate is a superb base for a series of day hikes. A 1½hr. walk takes you to the summit of Mt. Tadiyendamal, the highest peak in Kodagu.

The rooms themselves are pleasant, if basic, with shared bathrooms and bucket showers.

(Palace Estate, Kakkabe Village, Kodagu. ☎08272 238446. Take one of three morning buses from Kakkabe (6:45-8:15am), or a taxi (Rs400). Singles Rs210; doubles Rs375, with attached bath Rs450. Home-cooked breakfast Rs65, lunch and dinner Rs100. Organic coffee grown on the surrounding land Rs5. The Palace Estate does not take bookings, so call a few days before you arrive to check availability.)

very ❷, School Rd. below Capital Restaurant, near the private bus stand, has clean, lilac painted rooms and accommodating staff who will arrange anything. (☎225492. Singles Rs210; doubles Rs375.) The nearby **Hotel Chitra ❷** has similar reasonably priced rooms. (☎225191. Singles Rs250; doubles Rs400. Off-season Rs200/275.) **Viniyaka Lodge ❷,** next to the bus stand, is the cheapest place in town. (☎229830. Singles Rs150; doubles Rs300. Off-season Rs125/Rs225.) Slightly nicer rooms are available at the **Hotel Amrita ❸,** Junior College Rd., behind the Cauvery. (☎222706. Singles Rs350; doubles Rs500; quad Rs1000. Off-season Rs250/400/800.) The Hotel Cauvery can also arrange stays at the **Capital Village Resort ❷,** a pleasant lodge on a plantation 5km from town. Rooms are very clean, have private baths with seat toilets, mosquito nets, hot water, and balconies. Book ahead through the Cauvery (☎225492) in-season. (Dormitory Rs250; singles Rs500; doubles Rs750.)

Compared to the crowd of stainless steel, garish "meals" hotels, **Red Fern Bar & Grill ❸,** Sudarshan Rd. behind the hospital, might as well have dropped from the heavens. This elegant roadhouse prepares chicken (Rs45-60) and stocks whiskey (Rs25-90 per 60ml) in a variety of flavors. (Open daily 10am-11:30pm.) **Hotel Capital ❷,** Main Rd. by the private bus stand, serves the local Kodava specialties of *pandi* (pork) curry, *koli* (chicken) curry, and *aki* (rice roti). (Open daily 8am-11pm.) **Santrupti ❷,** 116/2 MG Rd., in the Hotel Rajdarshan, is one of the nicer restaurants in town. (Indian and Chinese dishes Rs38-120. Open daily 7:30am-3pm and 4:30-11pm.) **Hotel Veglands ❶,** near the police station, stands out for its small-town prices. (Meals Rs12-17. Open M-Sa 7am-9pm.)

◙ **SIGHTS.** A favorite of the long-gone kings, the views from **Raja's Seat,** on MG Rd., are now popular with tourists, especially at sunset. The **fort** at the center of town houses a pair of rather alarmed-looking life-sized elephant statues. The neighboring **St. Mark's Church** has a hodge-podge of archeological objects. (Open Tu-Su 9am-5pm, closed 2nd Sa.) Accessible from the steps leading down from the police station, the **Omkareshwara Shiva Temple,** Temple Rd., is an unusual blend of Hindu, colonial British, and Islamic architectural styles. Atypical of Hindu monarchs, the rajas of Madikeri were buried rather than cremated. Their domed **tombs** lie at the north end of Main Rd., 1km from the bazaar. The path, well-labeled with signposts, continues 7km through coffee plantations and cardamom estates to **Abbi Falls,** a popular place for rowing. The walk is pleasant, but auto-rickshaws will take you there and back for about Rs150.

NEAR MADIKERI

BYALAKUPPE AND SERA JE

The area around Kushalnagar, 22km east of Madikeri, is dotted with Tibetan settlements, collectively known as **Bylakuppe,** one of the largest expatriate Tibetan communities in the world. Some 10,000 refugees relocated here during the 1960s and early 1970s after subsisting for 4-5 years in a former British internment camp in the jungles of Assam. Within this group were about 200 monks who had escaped when Lhasa's Sera Je Monastery was destroyed in 1959. They set about rebuilding it 6km southwest of Kushalnagar. Today the new **Sera Je Monastery** serves as a university for more than 3000 monks who came from throughout the world to study Buddhist philosophy. The Tibetan architecture, prayer flags, and, most of all, peace and quiet, create an extraordinary contrast with the nearby Indian town. On the road to Sera Je is the **Nyingmapa Monastery,** which houses the **Golden Temple.** The three towering gilded statues and wall paneling of the prayer hall are an amazing sight.

Kushalnagar is an easy day trip from Madikeri. **Buses** and **maxicabs** run regularly between the towns (1hr., Rs12-13). From Kushalnagar, **auto-rickshaws** charge Rs30 to go to Sera Je, but you can probably share one with some monks. The **Sera Je Guest House ❶,** established to raise money for the monastery, is the only place to stay in town. The manager is friendly and speaks good English. The attached restaurant is always filled. Follow the signs for the health clinic. (☎698672. Doubles Rs125.) Another monastic fave is the **Norling Hotel ❶,** opposite the monastery, serving only chow mein (Rs15), *parathas*, and eggs *du jour*. Kushalnagar has more accommodation options, but no gems. **Ganesh Lodge ❶,** Bus Stand Circle, has basic rooms with attached bathrooms and 24hr. check-out. (☎674528. Singles Rs80; doubles Rs140.) The **Kannika International ❸** has better, nicer, but overpriced rooms. Turn left out of the bus stand and follow the signs. (☎674728. Doubles Rs500-600.) The attached **restaurant ❷** has *thalis* (Rs20) and curries (Rs30-70).

HASSAN ಹಸನ ☎08172

The industrial city of Hassan has little tourist appeal and no sights of its own. Even an enthusiastic tourist office can promote it only as a "gateway" to other, more exciting destinations. Easily accessible and only 40km from the Haysala sites of Helbid and Belur, Hassan is a good place to sleep while exploring the nearby area.

▛ TRANSPORTATION

Trains: The **railway station** serves **Arsikere** (1½hr.; 10:15am, 2:20, 3:30, 9pm; Rs10) and **Mysore** (3hr.; 6:20am, 1:30, 6:30pm; Rs23). Head to Mysore for **Banglore.**

Buses: To: **Bangalore** (4hr., every 15min. 4:30am-2am, Rs62) via **Channarayapatna** (1hr., Rs13); **Belur** (1½hr., every 15min. 7am-8:30pm, Rs13); **Halebid** (30min., frequent 7am-8:30pm, Rs11); **Mangalore** (4hr., frequent 5:30am-6:30pm, Rs50); **Mysore** (3½hr., frequent 5:30am-8:30pm, Rs40). For **Hospet/Hampi,** head to **Shimoga** (3½hr., frequent 5:30am-11pm, Rs45) and transfer. Hordes of **private bus** companies go to Bangalore (Rs70). **Tempos** also service Belur and Halebid (frequent; Rs8 and 10, respectively). They leave from the road north of the Maharaja Park. Turn left out of the bus stand and go straight through the park.

➔✷ 🛈 ORIENTATION AND PRACTICAL INFORMATION

The **bus stand** is in the center of town on the southwest corner of the intersection of **Bus Stand Road** (north-south) and **College Road** (east-west), also known as **Park Road.** At the other end of Bus Stand Rd. is the other east-west running **Bangalore-Mangalore (BM) Road.** Parallel to Bus Stand Rd. is **Race Course Road,** 200m to the east. The **railway station** is 2km from the bus stand on BM road.

Tourist Office: Regional Tourist Office, College Rd. (☎268862), east of the bus stand at the intersection with Race Course Rd. Open M-Sa 10am-5:30pm.

Currency Exchange: Shenoy Tours and Travel, Picture Palace Building, Bus Stand Rd. (☎269729). Changes cash and traveler's checks in most currencies. Open M-Sa 9:30am-1:30pm and 4-8pm.

Police: City Police Station (☎268333), at the corner of Bus Stand Rd. and BM Rd.

Pharmacy: Gopal Medicines, Bus Stand Rd. (☎268678). Open M-Sa 9am-9:30pm and Su 9am-8pm.

Hospital: The Government Hospital, Race Course Rd., but a better bet is the private **CSI Redfern Memorial Hospital,** Race Course Rd. (☎267653), 2 blocks north of the intersection with Church Rd.

Internet: Cyber Park above Vaishnavi Lodging. Not too speedy but an unbeatable Rs15 per hr. Open daily 9:30am-11pm. Faster is Cyber Net next to Hotel Suvarna Regency. Open daily 7:30am-10:30pm. Rs30 per hr.

Post Office: Bus Stand Rd. Open M-Sa 10am-6pm. **Postal Code:** 573201.

ACCOMMODATIONS

Most hotels are within 500m of the bus station with a series of very basic "lodges" right next door. Most rooms are taxed at a rate of 10-12%.

Sri Ganesha Lodge, Devaraj Market, Subhash Sq. Exit the bus stand by the alley next to Hotel Ashraya. Walk straight down the market then take a right at the sign. Friendly and family-run with spotless rooms, seat toilets, and showers. Hot water 6-9am. Singles Rs125; doubles Rs225; triples Rs300. ❶

Vaishnavi Lodging, Harsha Mahal Rd. (☎2638859). Take a left out of the bus stand, a right onto Church Rd., and the first left. Clean sheets, fluffy pillows, phones, and big attached baths. Hot water 6-9am. Singles Rs130; doubles Rs190. ❶

Hotel Suvarna Regency (☎264006 or 266774), BM Rd. From Bus Stand Rd., turn right after the police station and follow BM Rd. to where it turns south. Very nice rooms with TVs, phones, and showers. Single Rs275; double Rs400; triple Rs500. AmEx/MC/V. ❷

Hotel Hassan Ashok, BM Rd. (☎268731). An upscale option. Pleasant rooms overlook a garden. Attached bar and restaurant. Single Rs700-1000; double 1000-1500. ❹

FOOD

🍴 **Suvarna Sagar,** BM Rd., attached to Hotel Survarna. Tasty *thalis* (Rs30), snacks (Rs5-15), and North and South Indian dishes. A *paneer* is so fresh, it melts in your mouth. Ice cream Rs9-35. 10% surcharge to sit in the A/C. Open daily 7am-10:30pm. ❷

Hotel Sanman, MO Rd. From the bus stand, head south on Bus Stand Rd. and turn right after the Picture Plaza building. Popular eatery for its *dosas* (Rs10), *puri* (Rs5), and *thalis* (Rs15). Open daily 6am-9:45pm. *Thalis* served 11:30am-4pm and 7-9:45pm. ❶

Blue Diamond, behind Suvarna Sagar. For those who can't handle another "meals" joint. Tandoori/Mughlai Rs60-140, Chinese Rs35-80. Open 11:30am-11:30. ❸

Hotel GRR, Bus Stand Rd., opposite the bus stand. Excellent cheap and quick banana-leaf *thalis* (Rs15). Open daily 11:30am-4:30pm and 7:30-11pm. ❶

SRAVANABELAGOLA ಶ್ರವಣಬೆಳಗೊಲ ☎08176

As the site of the world's tallest monolithic statue and some of the oldest Jain temples, Sravanabelagola is one of the most important Jain pilgrimage sites in India. The 17m-high statue of the saint Bahubali stands high on a hill overlooking the pleasant, tiny town. Sravanabelagola's streets are clean and empty, its air is suffused with calm, and its touts are less aggressive than their postcard-pushing buddies in other temple towns. Close to Hassan, the town makes a pleasant daytrip.

⊟⚡ TRANSPORTATION AND PRACTICAL INFORMATION. The **bus stand** is on **Bangalore (CR Patna) Road,** opposite the *bastis* on Chandarigi Hill. **Buses** to: **Bangalore** (3hr., 4 per day 6:45am-3pm, Rs49); **Channayapatna** (15min., every 15min. 6am-9pm, Rs4); **Mysore** (2½hr., 8pm, Rs29). For Hassan, change at Channayapatna. In Sravanabelagola, make a right from the station onto Bangalore Rd. and continue as it bends right. Ahead is the Mohagiri with the Bahubali statue at the summit. The KSTDC **tourist office** is at the base. (☎ 657254. Open M-Sa 10am-5:30pm.)

▐▌⬚ ACCOMMODATIONS. Most visitors make Sravanabelagola a daytrip, but the town has plenty of places to stay. Nicest are the **Jain lodging houses ❶** which must be reserved through the **Accommodation Office** (☎ 657258) in the center of the guest house complex. Largest of the guest houses is **Yatri Nivas ❷**, which has quiet, clean rooms with attached bath and seat toilet. (Doubles Rs150; triples Rs250; quad Rs300.) From the bus station, turn left; it's the green-pillared building further down on the right. Visitors should respect Jain prohibitions on meat and alcohol.

◪ SIGHTS. Built around AD 981, the **Bahubali statue,** on top of Indragiri Hill, is a relatively recent fixture in Sravanabelagola. Son of the first Jain *tirthankara* and a saint in his own right, Bahubali wears an enlightened smile and not much else. The simple statue gazing over the town is the image of serenity while the surrounding temple with its magnificent view over the plain is calm and peaceful. Vines creep up his legs, snakes coil around his feet, and anthills fester at his ankles, all symbolizing his detachment from the world of the senses. The 620 steps leading up to the statue require about 15-20min. of dedicated climbing. Wear a pair of thick socks as the stairs are burning hot. A group of old men can carry you up in a chair for Rs85. *(The temple housing the statue is open daily sunrise-sunset. Puja 8am. Visit in the morning to avoid the crowds and the heat.)*

Every 12 years, the Bahubali statue forms the center of the **Mahamastakabhisheka ceremony,** or "anointing of the head ceremony." On the eve of the ceremony, scaffolding is erected behind the monument and 1008 pots of sacred colored water are placed in front of the statue. Priests and wealthy devotees chant mantras as they anoint Bahubali with water, milk, dates, bananas, curds, sugar, almonds, and gold and silver flowers. Flowing down the face of the statue, they are believed to become spiritually

NO WORK, ALL PLAY

MAHAMASTA-KABISHEKA

The 17m-tall statue of the saint Bahubali towers over the town of Sravanabelagola. A rendering of Ardinatha, the son of the first of 24 Jain saints, the statue was built in 981 AD. Usually, an air of tranquility prevails on the hilltop, but every 12 years, Bahubali's serenity gives way to frenetic excitement as it becomes the focus of the Mahamastakabisheka celebration. For the duration of this festival (which translates to "anointing of the head"), Sravanabelagola is India's most important Jain pilgrimage site.

On the night before the festival, 1008 jars, each containing water and a coconut, are emptied at the foot of the statue. *Puja* ceremonies are performed atop specially constructed scaffolding. At the climax, the head of the statue is first anointed with water, and then with thousands of gallons of sugar cane juice, coconut milk, and *ghee*. Finally, a series of sandalwood pastes is applied to the statue to color it brown, red, and yellow.

In 1993, over one million people came from all over the world for the event. The next Mahamastakabisheka is scheduled for 2005. Ten to fifteen days of continuous celebration follow the anointing of the statue, including music and cultural events. Festivities then continue for up to a year in the form of first weekly, then monthly ceremonies.

charged. They are afterwards given to the waiting pilgrims and believed to help on the road to enlightenment. Last time over a million people attended, crowding Chandarigi Hill in pin-drop silence.

Though the tall naked holy man gets much of the attention, the hills surrounding him have been a Jain pilgrimage site since before the statue was carved. The Mauryan emperor Chandragupta came to Sravanabelagola in 300 BC, when he abdicated his throne to become an ascetic. His guru Bhadrabahu attained enlightenment here and passed away in a cave on Chandragiri Hill. Chandragupta faithfully spent days inside the cave worshipping the footprints of his deceased teacher until he, too, died of starvation. The site still attracts pilgrims who believe that viewing the prints can cure all illness. Fourteen other Jain temples crowd the top of the hill, dating from as early as 300 BC.

MANGALORE ಮಂಗಳೂರು ☎ 0824

An important trading port for centuries and a major shipbuilding center during the 1700s, Mangalore today retains much of its mercantile feel down its alleyways and in its traffic-clogged streets. The city derives its current fame from its status as India's biggest cashew and coffee processor and as a major *bidi-*production center. Mangalore is not exactly a tourist magnet, but it makes a decent urban stopover and stock-up point between Goa and Kerala.

⌐ TRANSPORTATION

Flights: Bajpe Airport (info ☎ 253434 or 252709), 22km from town, can be reached by local buses #47B and 47C, or by taxi (Rs275). **Indian Airlines** (☎ 451045) is on Hat Hill. Head west from Lalbagh Circle, and take the first right (rickshaw Rs12 from KS Rao Rd.). Open daily 10am-6pm. **Jet Airways,** KS Rao Rd. (☎ 441181). Open M-Sa 9:30am-1pm and 2-6pm. To: **Chennai** (2hr., daily 12:20pm, US$115) via **Bangalore** (1hr., US$90); **Mumbai** (1hr., 2 per day 11:30am and 3pm, US$125).

Trains: Railway station (info ☎ 131), 500m south of the intersection of KS Rao and Lighthouse Rd. From Hampankatta, take the road going south between Maidan. and Falnir Rd. Reservations open 8am-8pm. To: **Chennai** (18hr., 11:15am and 8:10pm, Rs250); **Ernakulam** (10hr., 4:15am and 5:50pm, Rs102-170) via **Calicut** (5hr., Rs65-124); **Margao** (5hr., 2:30pm, Rs53-200).

Buses: KSRTC Bus Stand, in Bijai, 3km from the center of town (Rs15 by auto-rickshaw from Hampankatta). Reservations open daily 7am-9:30pm. To: **Bangalore** (8hr., 30-40 per day 6am-11pm, Rs130); **Hassan** (4hr., every 30min., Rs68); **Mysore** (7hr., 15 per day 6am-11pm, Rs94); **Panjim** (10hr., 8:30am and 9:30pm, Rs143). **Private buses,** at the new bus stand near the intersection of Maidan and Maidan Cross Rd., run more frequently and are closer to the city center. Many companies have offices at the old bus stand, in the alley near the intersection of Lighthouse Hill and KS Rao Rd. **Ganesh Travels** (☎ 441277; open daily 5am-11pm), sends buses to: **Bangalore** (8hr., 9 per day, Rs170-350); **Cochin** (10hr., 8 and 9pm, Rs310); **Margao** (9hr., 9pm, Rs200); **Mumbai** (22hr., 7:15am and 11:15pm, Rs450); **Mysore** (7hr., 10:30pm, Rs200); **Panjim** (9hr., Rs200); **Udipi** (1¼hr., frequent, Rs21).

Local Transportation: Most **local buses** stop on Dr. UP Maliya Rd., west of Town Hall. In general, buses are numbered in front or on the side, and many stands list the buses that stop there. **Auto-rickshaws** are the easiest way to get around.

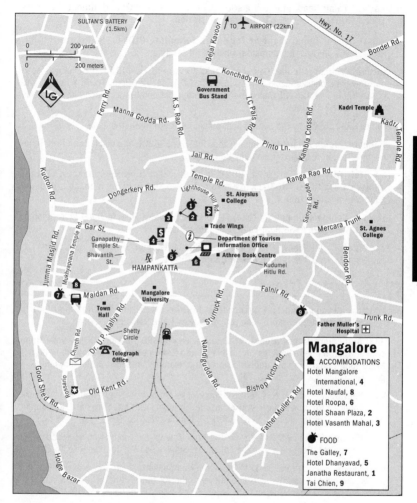

KARNATAKA

Mangalore

🛖 ACCOMMODATIONS
Hotel Mangalore
  International, **4**
Hotel Naufal, **8**
Hotel Roopa, **6**
Hotel Shaan Plaza, **2**
Hotel Vasanth Mahal, **3**

🍎 FOOD
The Galley, **7**
Hotel Dhanyavad, **5**
Janatha Restaurant, **1**
Tai Chien, **9**

⚡ 🛈 ORIENTATION AND PRACTICAL INFORMATION

Mangalore's mangled street plan can make navigation tricky. The monthly *Mangalore Today* (Rs10), available at newsstands, usually includes a map. **Hampankatta** is the central, chaotic traffic circle from which six major thoroughfares radiate. Heading northeast and uphill from Hampankatta is **Lighthouse Hill Road.** Forking east off Lighthouse Hill Rd. is **Balmatta Road.** Just west of Lighthouse Hill Rd., **KS Rao Road** heads due north and is cluttered with budget hotels and restaurants. To the southwest, **Maidan Cross Road** passes south of the **Town Hall** and heads to **Shetty**

Circle. Branching west off Maidan Cross Rd. is **Maidan Road.** Due east off Hampankatta is **Falnir Road,** and going southeast between Falnir and Maidan Cross, is the road leading 500m south to the **railway station.**

Tourist Office: Department of Tourism Information Office, Lighthouse Hill Rd. (☎442926). In Hotel Indraprastha. Open M-Sa 10:30am-1:30pm and 2:30-5:30pm.

Currency Exchange: Indian Overseas Bank, KS Rao Rd. (☎440701). Exchanges cash and traveler's checks. Open M-F 10am-3pm, Sa 10am-12:30pm. **Trade Wings,** Lighthouse Hill Rd. (☎426225), also exchanges money at good rates. Open M-Sa 9:30am-1:15pm and 2-5:30pm.

Police: (☎426426), by the central post office, just beyond Shetty Circle.

Pharmacy: Indian Medicals, Maidan Cross Rd. (☎869820), one block down from Hampankankatta, on the right. Open daily 8am-10pm.

Hospital: City Hospital (☎217902), in Kadri, 3km from Hampankatta. **Father Muller's Hospital** (☎436301), in Kankanady, also 3km from Hampankatta. Both are good and privately run.

Internet: Kohinoor Computer Zone, Lighthouse Hill Rd., close to Hotel Indraprastha. Rs25 per hr. Open M-Sa 8am-2am, Su 10am-2am.

Post Office: Dr. UP Mallya Rd. (☎423053). Southwest from Town Hall, past Shetty Circle. Open M-Sa 8:30am-6pm. **Postal Code:** 575001.

ACCOMMODATIONS

Weary travelers need look no farther than KS Rao Rd., where the hotels are fairly cheap, clean, and dependable. The places below have 24hr. check-out.

Hotel Mangalore International, KS Rao Rd. (☎444860), about 100m above Hampankatta, on the left. Doubles with cable TV and 24hr. hot water in attached bath, not to mention papers on your doorstep and complimentary breakfast in the morning. Single occupancy doubles Rs600. ❹

Hotel Naufal, Maidan Rd. (☎428085). Two blocks down on the right from the main exit of the Maidan Rd. bus station. Very clean, well-lit rooms with attached bath. Restaurant downstairs serves basic fare. Singles Rs150; doubles Rs225. ❷

Hotel Vasanth Mahal, KS Rao Rd. (☎441310). Cheap, big rooms with attached baths with seat toilets. Some rooms have balconies. Singles Rs135; doubles Rs200. ❶

Hotel Roopa, Balmatta Rd. (☎421271). From Hampankatta, head toward Falnir Rd. and it's on the right. A good, cheap alternative to the KS Rao Rd. hotels, Roopa has spacious rooms with telephone and hot water. Singles Rs150; doubles Rs200-450. ❷

Hotel Shaan Plaza, KS Rao Rd. (☎440312). Large hotel with terraced rooms and a terrific restaurant. Phones, seat toilets, and movies. Singles Rs320; doubles Rs435. ❷

FOOD

While in Mangalore, don't miss the town staple, cashews, available in countless grades and flavor permutations at dried fruit and nut shops everywhere.

Janatha Restaurant (☎426889). In the Hotel Shaan Plaza, this busy restaurant serves up marvelous North and South Indian dishes (*thalis* Rs20-35) and ice cream treats (Rs8-28) in a lively environment. Open daily noon-3pm and 7-10:30pm. ❶

Tai Chien, Fahir Rd. (☎441441), in Hotel Moti Mahal just beyond Milagres Church. Fantastic Chinese cuisine, perfect table-setting, international pop and house music, and first-rate imported liquor. The Jade Chicken with garlic and ginger (Rs95) will make your mouth water. Open daily 11am-3pm, 7pm-midnight. ❸

Hotel Dhanyavad, on the corner of KS Rao and Lighthouse Hill Rd., below street level. No-frills, dirt-cheap South Indian, and the only place in town for an early-morning breakfast. Two large, fresh buns Rs10. Entrees Rs12-50. Open daily 5:30am-10:30pm. ❶

The Galley, in Manjarun Hotel. Don whatever you have approaching business attire, and head west from Shetty Circle to Mangalore's fanciest address. All-you-can-eat lunch buffet Rs220. Entrees Rs100-250. Open daily 12:30-3pm and 7:30-11pm. ❹

👁 SIGHTS

KARNATAKA

KADRI TEMPLE. Once a center for the Shiva and tantric Natha-Pantha cult, the temple is notable for its bronze figures, including a 10th-century seated Lokeshvara, considered among India's finest. A steep staircase, opposite the temple entrance, leads to several shrines and the **Shriyogishwar Math,** whose tantric *sadhus* are depicted contemplating Kala Bhairawa (a terrifying aspect of Shiva), Agni, and Durga. *(2km northeast of the city center, at the bottom of Kadri Hill. City buses #14 and 19; rickshaws Rs35 round-trip. Open daily 6am-1pm and 4-8pm.)*

LIGHTHOUSE HILL. The **Lighthouse** itself fails to justify the walk up the hill, but it is surrounded by lovely public gardens with fine views of the city—a fair reward for a bit of sweat. The water tank dwarfing the lighthouse to its right has a suspiciously rusty ladder leading to what is probably the highest point in Mangalore. Climb it at your own risk. *(Public gardens open daily 4-9pm.)*

ST. ALOYSIUS COLLEGE CHAPEL. Just beyond the lighthouse, off the road to the left, is the Jesuit **St. Aloysius College Chapel,** whose lovely painted walls and ceilings date back to 1899. Portraits of Christ's journey to Calvary include certain scenes that betray more than a little Impressionist influence over the artist. *(Chapel open M-Sa 8:30-10am, noon-1:30pm, and 2-6pm. English mass M-Sa 6:30am and 7am, Su 6:30am and 8am. Saturday confession 5-6pm. Ceiling-oglers not welcome during Sa-Su services.)*

SULTAN'S BATTERY. The fort was constructed by Tipu Sultan on the headlands of the old port. Besides the modest ruins of the tiny fortress, there's not much to see here but a peaceful river scene and a few fishermen going about their work. *(5km northwest of the city center. Take the #14, 16, or 16A bus or a rickshaw for about Rs40.)*

HOSPET ಹೊಸಪೇಟ್   ☎08394

The Vijayanagar king Krishnadevaraya built Hospet between 1509 and 1520, and it became one of his favorite haunts. The last traces of the Vijayanagar Empire were long ago trampled into the dust, and Hospet today is typical of humdrum Karnataka, treading the line between heavy industrialization—blaring trucks transporting the products of a burgeoning steel industry—and village life. Hospet has no sights of its own and the only reason to visit is its proximity to Hampi, 12km away. Regular buses run from here to the ruins of Hampi. Although food and lodging can also be found in Hampi, Hospet offers a modicum of luxury unavailable in Hampi.

▄ TRANSPORTATION

Trains: Hospet Junction Station (☎131), 1km from the bus stand, at the end of Station Rd. Reservation counter open daily 8am-8pm. To: **Bangalore** (11hr., 8:10pm, Rs210); **Bijapur** via **Gadag** (2hr.; 5:15, 8, 8:50am, 4pm; Rs30); **Delhi** and **Mumbai** via **Guntakal** (2½hr.; 4, 8:10, 11pm).

Buses: Bus station, Station Rd. (☎28802), opposite Hotel Vishwa. To: **Badami** (5hr.; 7, 9am, 4pm; Rs60); **Bangalore** (9hr.; 8 per day 9am-2pm, then every hr. 8-11pm; Rs150); **Bijapur** (4hr.; 8, 11am, 4pm; Rs80); **Hassan** (10hr.; 11am, 3, 6:30pm; Rs100); **Hyderabad** (11hr.; 10am, 2, 7pm; Rs130); **Mangalore** (13hr., 2 and 10pm, Rs180); **Mysore** (10hr., 11am and 7pm, Rs130). Deluxe **KSTDC** tourist buses to **Bangalore** (7½hr., 10pm, Rs200).

Local Transportation: Auto-rickshaws to Hampi cost Rs80-100. **Cycle-rickshaws** cost Rs10 to the railway station. **Local buses** go to **Hampi** from platform 10 (30min., every 30min. 5:30am-7:30pm, Rs4). **Khizer Cycle Market,** at the circle where Station Rd. turns into the bazaar, rents **bikes** (Rs3 per hr.). Open daily 7:30am-8:30pm.

▄ ▄ ORIENTATION AND PRACTICAL INFORMATION

Life in Hospet revolves around **Station Road** (occasionally called MG Rd.), which runs south from the **railway station,** passes the **bus station** at the intersection with College Rd., and grows increasingly congested as it turns into **Main Bazaar Road** in Hospet's commercial area. Station Rd. bridges two canals in the process and encounters northeast-running **Hampi Road** and **Tungabhadra (TB) Dam Road,** which runs west and skirts the market area.

Tourist Office: KSTDC office (☎428537), at the corner of College and Old Bus Stand Rd. **Tours** of Hampi and the Tungabhadra Dam (9:30am, return 5:30pm; Rs95). KSTDC open M-Sa 10am-5:30pm; open daily for tour reservations 7am-8pm.

Currency Exchange: Andhra Bank, Station Rd. (☎424918), just before the bazaar and above the cycle shop. Exchanges traveler's checks, US$, and UK£. Open M-F 10:30am-2:30pm and 3-4pm. **Hampi Travels,** Saudri Buildings, Station Rd. (☎420564), exchanges cash and travelers checks and makes train and bus reservations. Open daily 9am-9pm.

Police (☎426100), Old Bus Stand Rd., 2min. down from the tourist office.

Hospital: Government General Hospital, Hospital Rd. (☎4231099), 1km south of the bazaar. Open 24hr.

Pharmacy: The Government Hospital has a 24hr. pharmacy. There are also many along Station Rd., to the north of the bus station.

Internet: Cyber Net, Shivananda Lodge Complex, College Rd. Turn left from the bus stand; it's on the left. Fairly slow access at Rs60 per hr. Open daily 8:45am-11pm.

Post Office (☎428210), Station Rd., 400m south of the bus stand; take the left fork. Open M-Sa 8am-6pm. **Postal Code:** 583201.

▄ ACCOMMODATIONS

There's a much wider range of standards in Hospet than in Hampi. Most of the larger hotels have everything from plain budget rooms to fancy deluxe rooms.

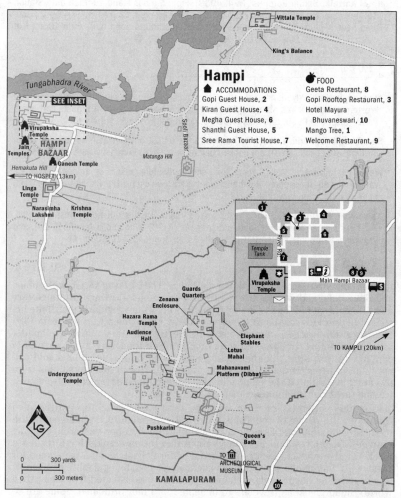

Malligi, JN Rd. (☎428101), 250m south of the bus stand. Turn left at the first intersection then follow the signs up the dirt road. Little luxuries can make a lot of difference and the budget rooms here have plenty—fresh towels, phone, complimentary soap, and a shower so powerful it blasts the dirt right off. The deluxe rooms are superb and the nicest in Hospet. Pool open Tu-Su 7am-7p, Rs25 per hr. for non-deluxe room guests. Singles Rs140; doubles Rs200; deluxe Rs600-2250. AmEx/MC/V. ❶

Hotel Priyadarshini, V/45 Station Rd. (☎428838), 150m north of the bus station. Spacious rooms with balconies, seat toilets, TV and phones. Two good attached restaurants. Singles Rs150-200; doubles Rs250-700, triples Rs395. MC/V. ❷

Hotel Shalini, Station Rd. (☎428910), 300m south of the railway station. This place may not be the cleanest, but it's cheap. Singles Rs50; doubles Rs75; quads Rs100. ❶

Hotel Karthik, Sardar Patel Rd. (☎424938). From the bus stand, turn left onto Station Rd.; take the first left onto College Rd., then the next right. Singles are very basic; doubles have slightly more amenities. Attached restaurants open daily 6am-10pm. Hot water 5:30-11am. Singles Rs100; doubles Rs250-500. ❶

☕ FOOD

Manasa, in Hotel Priyadarshini, Station Rd. Popular restaurant with Indian, Chinese, and Western selections in a shady, open-air setting. Shepherd's pie Rs80, pasta carbonara Rs80, gazpacho Rs25, and beer Rs55-65. Open daily noon-11:40pm. ❸

Shanbhag Fast Food, College Rd., opposite the tourist office. Watch as your *idli* (Rs5) and *masala dosas* (Rs10) are cooked before your eyes. Open daily 6am-11pm. ❶

Waves Restaurant, in Malligi. Tasty North and South Indian dishes on an open-air terrace with a relaxed atmosphere. Kashmiri *pulao* Rs50, chicken *tikka* Rs55, pancakes with honey Rs30. Open daily 6:30am-11:30pm. ❷

Naivedyam Restaurant, also in Hotel Priyadarshini. Dishes out huge, fresh portions. Offerings include North and South Indian *thalis* (Rs20), *aloo* and *palak* (Rs18-24), and veg. pizza and burgers (Rs45). Open daily 11am-3pm and 7-10:30pm. ❶

HAMPI ಹಂಪೆ   ☎08394

It is said that gold once rained down on Hampi. The city was awash with rubies and diamonds, and wealth dripped from its rooftops, flowing into its gutters and filling its sacred tanks. The Vijayanagar king would regularly distribute his weight in precious metals to the area's needy. Five dynasties ruled from 1336 and the state reached its peak early in the 16th century under Krishnade-varaya, becoming the largest Hindu empire of all time. The kings paved the capital city with their wealth, creating temples, pavilions, aqueducts, and palaces, but riches eventually led to ruin. A confederacy of Muslim sultans from the north annihilated the empire in 1565 and looted Vijayanagar's treasures, leaving the thriving capital desolate.

After the Christmas raves in Goa, the loud parties pack up and head to Hampi on the banks of the Tungabhadra River, much to the chagrin of the town's residents. Hampi's high season runs from October to March, peaking between December and February. More than a few expats have turned a week's stay into years. Best remembered is the Belgian woman who came for two weeks, fell in love with a holy man and stayed on, living the life of a *sadhu* in a cave in the north bank of the river for 24 years. Isolated from the urban world, Hampi beckons travelers to imagine its former brilliance. Some are so dazzled, they never leave.

📞📄 TRANSPORTATION AND PRACTICAL INFORMATION

The road from **Hospet** skirts 13km of unexceptional scenery before reaching **Hampi Bazaar,** a clump of guest houses, restaurants, and bauble shops clustered between the **Virupaksha Temple** and the **Tunghabadra River.** The ruins of Vijayanagar spread across 26 sq. km and are concentrated into three distinct groups: the **Virupaksha Temple,** ruins of the **Krishna Temple,** and many other shrines directly above the bazaar on Hemakuta Hill make up the **Sacred Center;** the **Royal Center** includes the **Palace Area** and the **Zenana Enclosure,** 3km southeast of Hampi, along the paved road to Kamalapuram. About 2km to the northeast of the bazaar lies the other major area of ruins, including the **Vittala Temple.**

WARNING. There have been reports of muggings and rapes on Matanga Hill, near the Vittala Temple and along the foot path leading from there to the Royal Center. **These roads should not be traveled alone or at night. Foreigners are asked to register with the police** when they arrive in Hampi.

Local Transportation: Buses to Hospet depart from the intersection of Hampi Bazaar and the road to **Hospet** (30min., every 30min. 6:15am-8:15pm, Rs4). **Auto-rickshaws** run between Hampi Bazaar and Kamalapuram (Rs5) and Hospet (Rs50). Prices double at night. Another way to get around is to rent a **bike** at Rayo Bicycle Shop, 20m behind the tourist office (Rs5 per hr. or Rs30 for the day). Open daily 7am-7pm.

Tourist Office: (☎441339), 100m toward the Virupaksha Temple from the bus stop. Detailed maps of the ruins. Approved guides (half-day Rs300, full-day Rs500). Open Sa-Th 10am-5:30pm.

Currency Exchange: Canara Bank (☎441243), exchanges AmEx and Thomas Cook traveler's checks and gives advances on Visa. Open M-Tu, Th-F 11am-2pm, Sa 11am-12pm. In season, travel agencies exchange currency—try **Modi,** next to the tourist office.

Bookstores: There is a 2-for-1 paperback book exchange in the **Prasanth Library** opposite Shanthi Guest House. **Aspirations** on Main Hampi Buzzer near the Virupaksha Temple has new books and postcards.

Police: (☎441241), inside the Virupaksha Temple, immediately to your right. Registering here when you get in town takes 2min. Open 24hr. There's also a branch in Kamalapuram (☎441240), 4km southeast of the bus stand.

Hospital: The nearest medical services are in the Government Hospital in Hospet.

Internet: Hampi boasts many Internet cafes but only one server, which means access can be dreadfully slow. Speeds tend to pick up in evening and early morning. **Shambu Internet** (☎441383), is next to the tourist office (Rs60 per hr.). Open daily 2am-11pm.

Post Office: (☎441242), just outside the temple, beside the *gopuram*. Open M-Sa 9am-2:30pm. **Postal Code:** 583239.

ACCOMMODATIONS

It seems as though every home in Hampi has been converted into a tourist guest house, most offering the standard combination of basic, dirty rooms and squat toilets. Prices drop in the off-season. Outside of peak season, you shouldn't have to pay more than Rs40-60 for a room. The guest houses listed below (the best in town) are open all year. Many others open only during the tourist season.

 Shanthi Guest House (☎441568), from the bus stand, walk toward the Virupaksha Temple, turn right, and go around Sree Rama. Don't let the common baths put you off. A host of amenities means this is the best in town. Enclosed garden and cheerful exterior make it a wellspring of tourist camaraderie. Check-out 10:30am. Singles Rs120; doubles Rs150. Mar.-Dec. Rs60/80. ❶

Sree Rama Tourist House (☎441219). The beds and rooms are decent. Sree Rama offers attached bathrooms with squat toilets and showers. Internet and phone access available. Check-out 24hr. Singles Rs100; doubles Rs120. ❶

Kiran Guest House, Janata Plot (☎441479). Six rooms overlooking the river, some with attached bath. Rs100; with bath Rs150; off-season Rs40-50. ❶

Gopi Guest House (☎441695). Ordinary rooms, friendly management, and a great rooftop restaurant. Singles Rs150; doubles Rs250. Off-season Rs60/80. ❷

Megha Guest House (☎441398). This cheerful green and yellow guest house proudly features what have to be the only seat toilets in Hampi. Large, clean rooms come with private bath and mosquito nets. Enter through the attached Shiva Restaurant down the road from the tourist office. Singles Rs100; doubles Rs150. Off-season Rs75/100. ❶

🍴 FOOD

To 15th-century traveler Domingo Paes, the Hampi Bazaar was "a broad and beautiful street, full of rows of fine houses and *mantapas*...[where] you will find all sorts of rubies, and diamonds, and emeralds, and pearls, and every other sort of thing there is on earth that you wish to buy." To this list, modern tourists have added pancakes, spaghetti, and hash—all of which are indulged to excess.

Mango Tree, behind Virupaksha Temple. Follow the path around the temple past Shanthi Guest House. Walk 5min. along the river, then turn right along the dirt track before the white gates. Set under a stand of mango trees, you can't get more sedate than this. Banana *parathas* Rs30, pancakes Rs20-25, *momos* Rs35-40, pasta Rs25. Service is slow, but the food is worth the wait. Great riverside view, but bring a flashlight if you plan on staying late. Open daily 7am-10pm. ❷

Gopi Rooftop Restaurant, above Gopi Guest House, with a view over Virupaksha Temple. Special *thalis* Rs35 and *dal makhani* Rs30. Open daily 7am-10pm. ❷

Welcome Restaurant, Hampi Bazaar. Popular for its pasta (Rs30-40) and falafel (Rs30). Rice pudding Rs20, espresso Rs35. Open daily 7am-9:30pm. ❷

Geeta Restaurant, Hampi Bazaar. A good place to sit and watch the world go by. Lunch and dinner options Rs20-45. Open daily 6am-10pm. ❷

Hotel Mayura Bhuvaneswari, Kamalapuram. Take the road toward Kampli. The only enclosed restaurant in the whole area, it has *thalis* (Rs25-37) and veg. (Rs18-32) and chicken (Rs40-48) curries. Beer Rs55-60. Open daily 6:30am-10pm. ❷

👁 SIGHTS

THE VIJAYANAGAR RUINS

Though it won't enable you to see every sacred centimeter of the 26 sq. km of ruins, you can squeeze most of the major sights into one foot-sore, back-aching day. Renting a bike in Hospet, Kamalapuram, or Hampi Bazaar will help you squeeze everything in. Hampi's quiet, flat roads make biking ideal. Alternatively, the rickshaw-*wallahs* waiting outside the bus station are happy to take you around the sights. Rs350 for 4-5hr.; off-season Rs250.

THE SACRED CENTER. At the west end of Hampi Bazaar is the imposing **Virupaksha Temple,** once the king's personal temple. The eleven story, 50m high tower dominates the town. The temple is one of Hampi's earliest, possibly founded by Harihora, the founder of the Vijayanagar state. To the rear is a small room where the pin-hole camera effect is used to project an upside-down image of the *gorpuram* outside. *(Open daily 6:30-noon and 2-8:30pm. Rs2.)* Turning right after leaving the temple leads to the **Jain Temples** and a rocky hill with views of Hampi from the top. Most of the sights are along the main road from the bus stand. First on the left is the **Kalu Gonapati Temple** containing an enormous and striking statue of Ganesh in the shrine. Continuing on the left fork of the road leads to the run-down **Krishna Temple.** Make a right on the dirt path to reach the **Narasimha Lakshmi statue.** When

Muslim sultans sacked the city, they sliced open Narasimha's belly to see if the 7m-high monolith had eaten any gems, but they found nothing. Although the statue is disfigured, it is one of Hampi's most striking and popular sites. Beside the statue is the **Bavadi Linga Temple,** containing the second-largest *linga* in India, usually submerged in three-feet of water.

THE ROYAL CENTER. From the main road, continue on to the Royal Center until you see a large dirt road off to the left. You should be able to see the top of the **Underground Temple** from the road. Take a left and the entrance is on your right. The temple fills up with rainwater and fish during the monsoon season and has small canals flowing around the base. Follow the signs to the Lotus Mahal at the end of the road. Make a left past the pink Archaeological Camp House. Here you'll see the **Zenana Enclosure,** a stone wall where the ladies of the court used to live, protected from male ogling. Twelve meter-high walls, three watch towers and four false gates ensured correct behavior. *(Open daily 8:30am-6:30pm. US$5. If you visit both on the same day, this ticket will also get you into the Vittala Temple.)* To the right is the elegant pink stucco pavilion, the **Lotus Mahal,** a fine example of Indo-Saracenic architecture. Just outside the Zenana are the **Guard's Quarters.** Next door are the 11 domed **Elephant Stables,** decorated with elephant heads (appropriately enough), some with original paint. Backtrack to the sign pointing to the Mahanavami Dibba and take that road south; on your right will be the **Hazara Rama Temple,** or the Temple of One Thousand Ramas. The enclosure walls are carved with 108 panels showing the entire *Ramayana* on the inside and with a parade of horses, elephants, dancing girls, and soldiers on the outside.

Continue on the road and just as the path veers to your left, you will see the **Royal Enclosure.** The large platform in front of you was once the **Audience Hall** and foundations for other palaces are nearby. Further on, the 3-story **Mahanavami Dibba** is the throne platform and center for the 10-day Dussehva Festival that takes place here. The base is carved with scenes of hunting, processions, and festivals. South of the platform is the recently excavated **Pushkarini,** a deep, sacred water tank. On the left, just before the dirt road joins the main paved road to Kamalapuram, you will see the **Queen's Bath,** a graceful stone enclosure surrounded by a moat. Inside is a huge pool where the queen used to kick back after a hard day.

Kamalapuram is 600m further down the main road. The **Archeological Museum** is better than the average and has an interesting collection of sculptures as well as a stone model of Hampi. *(Take the first turn on your left. Open Sa-Th 10am-5pm. Rs5.)*

VITTALA TEMPLE. It's worth coming to Hampi just to see this building. The single most lavish temple in Hampi, it epitomizes the distinct Vijayanagar style. There is a wealth of detail on every column, and ornate carvings drip from the ceiling. Even the crowds of tour groups cannot spoil the magical atmosphere. Construction of the temple, which was never finished or consecrated, was begun around 1513, and the work was halted when the city was destroyed in 1565. A competing bit of lore has it that Vittala, an incarnation of Vishnu, came to look at the temple, found it too grand for him, and hightailed it back to his humbler home in Maharashtra. If you see people apparently trying to listen to the pillars, don't worry, you haven't cracked–each of the 56 pillars imitates a different Indian instrument when tapped. With the original roof, the sound would echo around the chamber (and no, they're not hollow; the British checked in 1856 by sawing one in half). The room behind the musical pillars is older, dating from 1422. In the courtyard in front, sits the **stone chariot,** subject of many-a-postcard. It sits there, in place of the traditional pillar, as the vehicle of Vishnu. Inside is an image of the eagle god Garuda, who Vishnu traditionally rides. *(Open daily 8am-6:30pm. US$5.)* Just before the temple sits the fabled **King's Balance,** the arch from which the potentate's weight in gold, gems, grain, or—in leaner times—happy thoughts, would be measured and meted out to his subjects. A paved road runs 5km from Kamalpuran to the complex or a footpath winds 2km from Hampi Bazaar. Though they are fine during the day, **these roads are dangerous at night.** If alone, use the river footpath.

▓ DAYTRIP FROM HAMPI: ANEGUNDI

The city of Anegundi, across from Hampi on the north bank of the Tungabhadra River, was once the capital of the area. It later became a suburb of Hampi, after the capital was moved. Though most of the ancient city has disappeared, there are still several interesting and active temples to visit. The Archaeological Survey of India isn't in charge here, and getting to the caves is an adventure in itself. Because there are no signs, it is best to solicit the assistance of a certified **guide** at Hampi's tourist office. Rs300 for half a day. To get around all the sights you'll also need a **bicycle** (Rs30) or a **motorbike** (Rs200).

From the Vittala Temple, continue on the main road along the Tungabhadra River. At the river bank, two boats shuttle people and bikes to and from Anegundi. Once you reach the other side, walk straight up a small slope and you'll see the village. A left turn at the first opportunity and then a left at the next fork will lead you past the Andhra Bank and under a small gate. After the gate, turn left onto the paved road that cuts through the rice paddies. A dirt path veers off to the left; take it and you'll be at the base of a rocky hill. Midway up the hill is the **Durga Temple,** supposedly the site where Rama killed the monkey king Vali, and the place Vijayanagar kings would pray before battle. On the other side of the hill is the **Laxmi Temple.** Here, Sita prayed for Rama's forgiveness after she had been banished, demonstrating her devotion to her husband as well as the purity of her mind, body, and soul. The nearby **Pampasarovara Pond** is believed to be the site where Parvati prayed for a husband—the reward was Shiva himself, who came here to bathe. Further west along the main road, 585 steps climb up to the Hanuman Temple, which marks the birthplace of the monkey god. There are incredible views from the top, but watch out for the monkeys. From here, the most convenient crossing point for bicycles is 2km further west, opposite the Virupaksha Temple. A small 7th-century temple marks **Hanuman Hill.**

BADAMI ಬಾದಮಿ   ☎08357

Badami, an unassuming little town in the middle of nowhere, was the capital of the mighty Chalukyan Empire from AD 543 to 757. Its main attraction is the ancient cave temples carved into the imposing red-rock mountains surrounding an ancient Chalukyan tank. Badami is also good for exploring the temples of Pattadakal, 20km away, where Chalukyan kings were crowned, and Aihole, 44km away on the Malaprabha River, the first Chalukyan capital. Together, these three towns are a fascinating study in the development of Indian temple architecture.

▐ TRANSPORTATION

Buses run from Badami to: **Aihole** (2hr., 7 per day 7:15am-4pm, Rs10) via **Pattadakal; Bagalkot** (2hr., every hr. 6am-10:15pm, Rs12); **Bangalore** (10hr., 5:30, 7:30, 8:30pm; Rs175); **Bijapur** (4hr., 6 per day 6:30am-3:45pm, Rs60); **Gadag** (2hr., every hr. 5am-8:30pm, Rs30); **Pattadakal** (45min., 7 per day 8:35am-6:30pm, Rs6.50); **Solapur** (7hr., 6 per day 6am-8pm, Rs90) for train connections to **Mumbai.** There is **super-deluxe bus** service to **Bangalore** (11hr., 7:30pm, Rs320); book through Hotel Mookambika

Deluxe (☎720067). Private **maxicabs** run on local routes, including Pattadakal (Rs8). **Trains** run north to **Bijapur** and **Solapur** for connections to **Mumbai** and south to **Gadag** for connections to **Hospet** and **Bangalore** every 2-3hr.

■ ⚡ ORIENTATION AND PRACTICAL INFORMATION

Station Road is Badami's main road. From the **railway station** in the north, it runs 5km south to the **bus stand**, which is roughly in the center of town. From the southern end of Station Rd. **College (Ramdurg) Road** runs west from Station Rd., south of the bus stand, and winds around to the KSTDC hotel and **Tourist Information Center** 1km later who will provide maps for Rs1. (☎720414. Open M-Sa 10am-5:30pm; closed second Sa.) There is no currency exchange in Badami. Heading north (left) out of the bus station along Station Rd., **Mexacom Internet,** on the right side, has slow and unreliable Internet access. (☎721036. Rs60 per hr. Open M-Sa 8am-9pm, Su 10am-4pm.) Further up on the left is a small private **hospital**. (☎720256. Open daily 9:30am-2:30pm, 6-9pm.) In the opposite direction from the bus stand, the **police station** (☎720133) is on the left. Opposite that is the well-stocked **Shrimanju Pharmacy.** (☎120630. Open daily 7am-10:30pm.) A 2min. walk further down, the **Post Office** is on the left. (Open M-Sa 9am-5pm.) **Postal Code:** 587201.

⚡ ▢ ACCOMMODATIONS AND FOOD

Compared to Aihole and Pattadakal, Badami has plenty of places to stay; most are near the bus stand. Prices drop in the off season (June-Sept.). Expect to pay about Rs100 less. The best choice is the **Hotel Mookambika Deluxe ❷,** Station Rd., opposite bus stand. Rooms are reasonable and have seat toilets and showers. Some windows look out upon the Chalukyan hills. (☎720067. Singles Rs300; doubles Rs350.) Cheaper, but not so nice is the **Hotel Satkar ❷,** a few doors north on Station Rd. Ordinary rooms have squat toilets and showers. A newly renovated first floor has the nicest rooms in town, complete with cable TV, balcony, and complimentary soap. (☎720417. Singles Rs200; doubles Rs275, first floor doubles Rs500.) The rooms at **Hotel Anand ❶,** across the street, aren't as nice but are cheaper than Satkar. (☎720074. Doubles Rs150-500.) For nice rooms and a quiet atmosphere farther out from town, try the KSTDC's **Hotel Mayura Chalukya ❷,** College Rd. Turn right from the bus stand, walk 500m, and turn right onto the first wide paved road; the hotel is 1km down on the right, next to the PWD Inspection Bungalow. The large rooms look out onto an overgrown garden and palm trees. Attached restaurant has standard dishes (Rs30-50). Plenty of small, basic "hotel" restaurants crowd the intersection of Station and College Rd. Better quality restaurants all come attached to hotels. (☎720046. Doubles Rs200.) Probably the best restaurant in town is attached to the **Hotel Moohambeka ❷,** which offers standard curry dishes (Rs25-55) and an open-air terrace. For cheaper food, try the no-nonsense, **Geeta Darshini ❶,** just south of the bus stand, where nothing on the menu (*dosas* and *idlis*) costs more than Rs7. (Open M-Sa 6:30am-9pm.)

◉ SIGHTS

SOUTH FORT TEMPLE COMPLEX. High on the cliff face overlooking Badami are four of the most important cave temples in India. Built by the Chalukyan dynasty between AD 550 and 700 to grace their capital, the caves are a marvelous collection of elaborate and imaginative carvings. The three earliest temples are Hindu, but both Jain and Buddhist influence is evident. **Cave 1,** the oldest, is dedicated to Shiva in his different guises. On the right front wall is the complex's most famous statue. The striking group to the right inside the entrance shows an Amdanarishwa figure, half Shiva (axe, bull, tiger skin, snake earring) and half his consort Parvati (lotus flower, bangles, big earrings). The goddess cursed him so he lost all flesh and blood and became a skeleton. Opposite is a Marihara statue, half Shiva, half Vishnu (crown and conch shell). A *linga* protected by granite cobras is in the back of the cave. **Caves 2 and 3** are both dedicated to Vishnu. In the first, to the right of the entrance, he is shown in his fifth incarnation as a Lord of Heaven and Earth. Opposite that is the third incarnation as wild boar. Inside, the column capitals are decorated with scenes of **Mituna** (platonic) couples. Between caves two and three is a natural rock cave with a defaced Buddhist image. **Cave 3**, the largest and best-sculpted of the group, dating from AD 578. The front of the steps are carved with 33 images of dancing demon-dwarves. In the scene to the left, in one scene, Vishnu is depicted as Narayan, reclining on the serpent Sesa's lap at the dawn of creation. The path up to Cave 3 leads past a natural cave once used as a Buddhist temple. The smooth graves on the threshold to the hall were used to grind the herbs used for paint. *(From the bus stand, head right on Station Rd.; 15m past the intersection with College Rd. turn left and follow that road to the end. Temples open daily 7am-6:30pm. Rs100. Official guides Rs200 for a 2-3hr. tour, Rs350 for a full day. Up to 4 people per tour.)*

OTHER TEMPLES. Visible across the 6th-century Agastyatirtha Tank is the Upper **Shivalaya Temple** with carvings depicting scenes from the life of Krishna. From on top of the hill are magnificent views of the surrounding countryside. To get there from the caves, walk along the tank, past the peaceful Butanatha Temples and the Archaeological Museum. It's on the opposite side of the hill, so follow the lane by the Police Station to the end. Turn right and take the first left. In town to the west of the tank the **Jambulinga Temple** is the oldest of the free-standing temples and the only one still active. It was the first in Karnataka to be dedicated to the Hindu trinity, Brahma, Shiva, and Vishnu, and their images are on the ceiling of the entrance. On the first pillar to your right as you enter, a Sanskrit inscription records the temple's founding in AD 699. *(Museum open Sa-Th 10am-5pm. Rs2.)*

DAYTRIPS FROM BADAMI

PATTADAKAL

Pattadakal makes a nice daytrip from Badami or Aihole. Buses (45min., every 45min. 6am-7pm, Rs7) and private maxicabs (Rs5-8) make the trip to Badami.

Pattadakal was the Chalukyan capital in the 8th century. Its free-standing temples are the most stylistically advanced in the region, and have some of the best and most detailed carvings. All the most important temples sit in a complex, now a Unesco World Heritage Site, at the base of a pink sandstone hill. Pattadakal's only active temple, the **Virupaksha (Lokeshvara) Temple,** built in AD 720, has a three-story spire with a huge stone Nandi sitting in front of it. Passages lead around the shrine past carvings depicting episodes from the *Ramayana* (see p. 620) and *Mahabharata*, and scenes of Chalukyan martial triumphs. Inscriptions on the temple and eastern gate record the names of the artists responsible for the carvings. Other prominent temples in the compound include the **Mallikarjuna Temple,** with elephants covering the columns, the **Papanatha Temple,** which has a Nandi bull inside the temple, and the unfinished **Sangemeshwara Temple,** which has carvings in various stages of completion. The **Jain Temple** is 1km south of the compound, and has an upper-story sanctuary guarded by a crocodile-carved gate. *(Temple compound open daily 6am-6pm. US$5. Guides Rs50.)*

AIHOLE ಐಹೊಳ

Buses run between Aihole and Badami (2hr., 7 per day 7:15am-4pm, Rs10-11). Occasionally, and completely unpredictably, only 2 buses will run (7:45am and 1:45pm). In this case, you can take the bus to Godur (via Pattadakal, Rs8) and take a local bus to Aihole from there.

The narrow streets of Aihole, 44km northeast of Badami on the banks of the Malaprabha River, are chock-full of over 100 temples. The beautiful, half-finished temples here were once the playground of a civilization determined to build the greatest architecture around. The most famous and impressive temple is the **Durga Temple,** dedicated to Vishnu. The elaborate entranceway shows scenes of courting couples and larger carvings of the gods are around the outside. Next door is the two-story **Ladh Khan Temple,** named after a 19th-century Muslim who set up house in the sanctuary. This temple is believed to have been built between the late 6th and the early 8th centuries. *(Compound open daily 6am-6pm. Rs100.)* A 10min. walk from the compound is the Ravan Phadi Cave, which echoes many of the best sculptures of Badami on a smaller scale. To the left of the entrance is an extremely well preserved Denang Shiva, complete with wife Pavarti, two sons Ganesh and Kortikuya, and devotee Bringi. Take the road to the right of the compound then the first left to double-back to the rock outcrop. Apart from some good views, little is left at the **Jain Meguti Temple** but a stone inscription that has been dated to AD 634—which makes it one of the oldest dated temples in India. On the road from the compound, take the second left. It's the temple on the right.

The ■KSTDC Tourist Home ❶ is the only place for non-locals to lay their weary heads, but you're in luck. The manager is gracious, the food is cooked to order (*thalis* Rs20-25), and there are no postcard touts hanging around. Huge, clean rooms cost half of what they would in Badami. (☎08851 34541. Doubles Rs60-75.)

BIJAPUR ☎08352

Among the many mausoleums, minarets, and museums that crowd the city, Bijapur has some of India's most remarkable Muslim architecture, most of which dates from the 15th to the 17th centuries. Ruled from 1482 by the Adil Shahi kings, Bijapur was the capital of one of five splinter states of the Muslim sultanate of Delhi, conquered in 1688 by the Mughal emperor Aurangzeb. Modern Bijapur reflects its Muslim heritage and the call of the *muzzein* echoes throughout the city at sunset. Today, only the Golgumbaz receives attention, but with 50 mosques and almost 20 tombs, the city has many more sights worth visiting.

▉ TRANSPORTATION

Trains: The **railway station** is just beyond the eastern city walls, north of Station Rd. A small, slow meter-gauge line serves **Gadag** (5hr., 5 per day 4am-6:25pm, Rs32) via **Badami** (3hr., Rs23) and a normal line goes to **Solapur** (2½hr.; 5:05, 11:30am, 5:05pm; Rs22). All other destinations require a transfer at Gadag or Solapur.

Buses: The **KSRTC bus stand** is in the center of town, at the intersection of Bagalkot and Bus Stand Rd. Reservation counter open daily 7am-1:30pm and 2-8pm. To: **Aurangabad** (14hr.; 5:30am, 7:30, 9, 10pm; Rs180); **Badami** (4hr.; 5:30, 10am, 4:45pm; Rs43-47); **Bangalore** (12hr., 9 per day, Rs232); **Gadag** (6½hr., 5 per day 11am-8:30pm, Rs90); **Hospet** (6hr., every hr., Rs93); **Hyderabad** (12hr., 7 and 8:31pm, Rs191); **Mumbai** via **Pune** (11hr.; 7:31, 9:31am, and every hr. 6-10pm; Rs215); **Solapur** (2hr., every 30min., Rs50). **VRL Vijayanand Travels,** Padmashri Complex,

Bagalkot Cross Rd. (☎35220), south of the bus stand, with branches at Station Rd. at Gandhi Chaute, runs luxury buses to: **Bangalore** (every 30min. 7-9:30pm, Rs220-240); **Mangalore** (4pm, Rs280); **Mumbai** (8:30pm, Rs300).

Local transportation: Bijapur's light traffic and simple layout make **biking** an ideal way to get around. Bicycles can be rented to the left of the bus stand, opposite Golgumbaz, and at Gandhi Chowk. (Rs2 per hr. plus outrageous deposit, up to Rs1500). Unmetered **auto-rickshaws** are readily available (Rs10-20). Horse-drawn **tongas** and 2-wheeled buggies are more scarce and more expensive. A local **bus** (Rs2) runs along Station Rd. from the train station to the western walls on the other side of town.

✦✷ 🛈 ORIENTATION AND PRACTICAL INFORMATION

The Adil Shahis built 10km of massive fortified walls around their capital, and much of modern Bijapur is still contained within these walls. The train station is just outside the eastern city walls. From there, **Station Road** runs past the Galgumbaz Mausoleum to the center of town and the market at **Gandhi Chowk.** Here it becomes **MG Road** and continues past the western walls to the **Ibrahim Rauza. Jama Masjid Road** runs parallel to Station Rd. to the south. The citadel sits between Station and Jama Masjid Rd. The bus stand is at the southwest corner of the citadel. Turning left as you exit takes you north to Station Rd., while a right takes you to **Balgalkot Road,** which runs to the southern walls.

Tourist Office: KSTDC, Indi Rd., off Station Rd. (☎250359), behind the KSTDC Mayura Adil Shahi Annex. Has maps of the city showing all the major sights. Open M-Sa 10am-5:30pm; closed 2nd Sa of each month.

Currency Exchange: Girikand Tours and Travels, 1st fl., Ram Mandir Rd. (☎220510). Behind the Upli Burji in the market area to the north of Gandhi Chowk, on the 1st fl. of the bldg. opposite the Union Bank of India. Exchanges 32 currencies and traveler's checks for a Rs25 fee. Open M-Sa 9am-2pm and 4-8pm.

Police: Gandhi Chowk Police Station (☎250033), on the south side of MG Rd., just before Gandhi Chowk.

Pharmacy: Pharmacies are all along Station Rd. Most close by 9pm.

Hospital: City Hospital, Hospital Rd. (☎270009), beyond Atke Gate, 2km west of town.

Internet: Cyber Park (☎220273), opposite the GPO on MG Rd. It's in a cloth shop, but the connection is reasonably fast. Rs30 per hr. Open daily 9:30am-1:30am.

Post Office: GPO, MG Rd. (☎250041), 50m west of the citadel. Open M-F 8am-6pm, Sa 8am-1pm. **Postal Code:** 586101.

▮◖ ACCOMMODATIONS AND FOOD

Most hotels sit along Station Rd. with budget places at the Gandhi Chowk end and more upscale hotels nearer the Golgumbaz. Standards of quality tend toward the shabby; insist on seeing rooms before booking. Unless otherwise noted, hotels have 24hr. check-out. The most pleasant budget option is the KSTDC's **Hotel Mayura Adil Shahi ❶,** Anand Mahal Rd., off the south side of Station Rd. to the north of the citadel. Large rooms with clean private bath overlook a garden courtyard. (☎250934. Singles Rs135; doubles Rs185.) Further down Station Rd. is **Hotel Samrat ❷,** Station Rd., halfway to the Golgumbaz. Huge attached baths with squat toilets and showers. (☎251620. Singles Rs150; doubles Rs250.) The **Hotel Kanishka ❸,** Station Rd., on the south side of Station Rd. about 1km from the Golgumbaz, has good value mid-range rooms, some with balconies and attached restaurant. (☎223788.

Doubles Rs450, with A/C Rs750.) The nicest and priciest place is the brand new **Hotel Pearl ❹**, Station Rd., near the Kanishka. Classy rooms have showers, phones, balconies, and cable TV. (☎ 256002. Singles Rs700; doubles Rs900-1400.)

The only restaurants in town come attached to the hotels and the nicest ones are with the best hotels near the Golgumbaz end of Station Rd. The **Hotel Samrat Restaurant ❶** is popular with local families. Eat *thalis* (Rs17-40) or one of 12 kinds of *dosas* (Rs6-15) in an open-air courtyard that is very pleasant when the generator isn't running. Most dishes Rs20-45. Also popular is the **Hotel Madhuvan Restaurant ❶**, Station Rd. (☎ 255571), down a side street 150m east of Hotel Samrat; look for the signs. The wide-ranging veg. menu includes *thalis* (Rs20-50) and North Indian and Chinese dishes (Rs25-45). Open daily 8am-11pm. *Thalis* served 11am-4pm.

◉ SIGHTS

Robust souls with resilient soles see all the sights on foot in one strenuous day; everyone else rents bicycles.

GOLGUMBAZ. Towering over low-rise Bijapur is the Golgumbaz mausoleum, the first sign of the city for travelers approaching from the plains. The cubic structure is reinforced by four octagonal minarets and crowned by an enormous dome, 38m across, said to be the second-largest in the world after St. Peter's in the Vatican. The tomb was built by the seventh Adil Shahi ruler, Mohammed. It took 20 years to build and was finally finished in 1659. The outside is decorated with ornate carvings, an elaborate cornice, and the lotus-petal motif that is a hallmark of Bijapur architecture. The more austere interior contains the gravestones of Mohammed Adil' Shah, several of his family members, and his favorite court dancer and mistress, Rambha. Seven stories above the hall, at the base of the dome, is the famous Whispering Gallery, where sounds are said to echo over ten times. Predictably, many visitors love to test this aspect of the acoustics; when the clapping gets to you, step outside for some stunning views of Bijapur and the Deccan plains. The large building obscuring the entrance to the mausoleum is an **Archaeological Museum**—one of the country's finest—featuring Jain *tirthankaras*, ancient stone inscriptions, 17th-century copies of the Qur'an, and Chinese porcelain. The entire complex is set on several acres of elegant park-land. *(Open daily 6am-6pm. Rs100; video fee Rs25; bike parking Rs1. Museum open Sa-Th 10am-5pm. Rs2.)*

▨ IBRAHIM RAUZA. Built by Ibrahim Adil Shah II, this graceful mausoleum is the last resting place of the sultan himself, his queen, Taj Sultana, his mother, and three of his children. The shaded archways, soaring gateway, and intricate arabic inscriptions give this tomb an elegance that is lacking in the simply massive Golgumbaz. Across the courtyard is the equally wonderful mosque. Together, the two structures compose one of the most beautiful examples of Islamic architecture in India. The Persian architect of the tomb (which is said to have inspired the Taj Mahal) is buried in the enclosed courtyard. Compared to Golgumbaz, the Ibrahim Rauza is fairly quiet, so you could have this glorious place all to yourself. *(1km beyond the western walls, 500m south of Station Rd. Open daily 6am-6pm. Rs100.)*

JAMA MASJID. One of the finest mosques in India, the Jama Masjid was built by Ali Adil Shah I to commemorate his victory over the Vijayanagars in 1565. It is the earliest and largest mosque in Bijapur. The cavernous prayer hall is etched and painted with more than 2200 rectangular spaces for individual prayer mats. The Mughal emperor Aurangzeb added these, apparently to atone for hauling away the velvet carpet and other valuables that originally covered the hall. He also extended the mosque, adding the Aurangzeb gate opposite the prayer hall. The Jama Masjid still functions as a religious place so dress appropriately. *(Directly opposite the Golgumbaz, Shanmukharudh Mahadwar Rd. leads under a large arch 500m to Jama Masjid Rd. Turn right toward the town center; the Jama Masjid is another 500m down on the left. Free.)*

OTHER SIGHTS. Just north of the Shivaji statue is the **Barakaman**. This monument, begun by Mohammed Adil Shah, is one story of a tower designed to match Golgumbaz in height. Though it's in a ruinous condition, the empty archways have a haunting and eerie grace to them. Along the western walls, 1.5km west of the citadel is a gigantic cannon, aptly named **Malik-I-Maidan**, or "Lord of the Plains." The cannon was cast around 1550. It took 10 elephants, 400 oxen, and hundreds of men to haul it up to its place on top of the ramparts. The muzzle is fearsomely carved in the form of a tiger crushing two elephants in its jaws. Visible just behind Malik-I-Maidan to the northeast, the circular tower of **Upli Burji** features more enormous cannons and views of the city and sights. The walls and moat of the **citadel** are in the center of town between Station and Jama Masjid Rd. The citadel is just to the west. Most of the buildings have collapsed, but the ruins of **Gagan Mahal** and **Sat Manzil,** the sultan's durbar hall and pleasure quarters, respectively, still stand.

GOKARNA ಗೋಕರ್ಣ ☎ 08386

Gokarna is your typical South Indian village, independent and blissfully removed from the tourist resorts of Goa and Kerala. The streets are filled with vendors selling kitchenware, bangles, and bright skirts, and the temple to Shiva draws pilgrims and worshippers daily. Foreigners are barred from the temples, but Gokarna's beaches are open territory and well worth a visit. The definition of tranquility, a string of unspoiled coves hugged by sea-washed cliffs stretches six kilometers from town. A few hipsters snooze in hammocks while *chai* shops provide them with caffeinated sustenance. The occasional party breaks out as well, adding a bit of excitement to this dream-like paradise.

▐ TRANSPORTATION

From Gokarna station, 10km out of town, **trains** run north to **Canacona/Chaudi,** in Goa (2hr., 7:25am and 10:40pm, Rs19) and south to **Mangalore** (4hr., 2am, Rs46). For other train destinations take a bus to **Kumta** (see below). **Buses** from Gokarna run to: **Bangalore** (13hr., 7pm, Rs297); **Hampi** (9hr., 2:45pm, Rs122); **Hospet** (13hr., 7am, Rs122); **Hubli** (3hr., 2:45 and 4pm, Rs67); **Kumta** (1-2hr., every 30-60min. 6am-5:15pm, Rs12); **Margao** (4hr., 8:15am, Rs50); **Mysore** (13hr., 6:45am, Rs645); **Panjim** (5hr., 8:15am, Rs60). Many **buses** pass through Kumta, but check first with the station master in Gokarna to be sure yours does. To: **Bangalore** (5 per day 6:45am-8:45pm); **Hyderabad** (7:30am, 8:15am, 9:45pm); **Mangalore** (every hr.); **Mumbai** (11am and 2:30pm); **Panjim** (4 per day 9am-1:30am); **Pune** (4pm). If you're heading to Gokarna from **Palolem,** take a rickshaw to the Canacona railway station (Rs20) to catch the train to Gokarna (1.5hr., 2:30pm, Rs19). In Gokarna, Vaibhav Nivas (see below) can help book train and private bus tickets. **Minibuses** shuttle backpackers from the train station to town (Rs25). **Local buses** depart from in front of the bus station parking lot and head to the railway crossing (15min.).

▐▌ ▐ ORIENTATION AND PRACTICAL INFORMATION

Gokarna's **Main Street** runs north-south on the east side of the bus station. **New Bus Stand Road** runs north-south on the west side of the bus station. Main St. heads north to the post office, and, after narrowing a bit, goes south to the giant temple bathing tank. **Car Street** begins at the southern narrowing of Main St. and heads west to the **Mahabaleshwara Temple** and the **town beach.** New Bus Stand Rd. also intersects Car St., west of the intersection with Main St. A footpath beside the temple at the bathing tank leads to the **beaches** at Kudle, Om, Half-Moon, and Paradise.

Vaibhav Nivas, on the right side of Main St. when heading north from the bus station, **exchanges currency** at decent rates. (Open 7:30am-11:30pm.) The **police station** (☎ 2656133; 24hr.) is up a hill on a road heading east off Main St., south of the bus station. **Hegde Medical Stores,** on the right side of Main St. heading south toward the intersection with Car St., can fulfill your pharmaceutical needs. (☎ 2656394. Open daily 8:30am-2pm and 4pm-9:30pm.) **Shet's Cyber Zone,** north on Main St. from the bus station, has decent **Internet** connections. (Rs40 per hr. Open 9am-11pm.) The main **post office** is 5min. north of the bus station along Main St.; bear right at the fork. Mail international packages before 3pm. **Western Union** money transfers also available. (☎ 2656130. Open M-Sa 9am-5pm.) **Postal Code:** 581326.

ACCOMMODATIONS AND FOOD

Although there are several more comfortable places to stay in town, most people prefer to flop down in huts on the beach. In town, **Vaibhav Nivas ●,** just east off Main St., north of the bus station, has small, clean rooms with common bath and a restaurant downstairs. Take a left out of the front of the bus station, then follow the signs. They take care of nearly every tourist need: currency exchange, travel arrangements, Internet access, safe locker deposit, convenience store. (☎ 2656714. Singles Rs50; doubles Rs100; family room Rs150. June-Oct. Rs50-100.) Snazzier lodging is available at the **Hotel Gokarna International ❷,** along Main St. north of the bus station. Immaculate rooms have balconies, hot water on request, and room service. (☎ 2656622. Check-out 4pm. Doubles Rs250-400.) If you are staying for a while, it might make sense to settle down in a **beach hut,** though you should check out how many and what kind of people are on the beach before committing to a specific strip of sand. Accommodations on Kudle Beach run the gamut—an unmarked **chai shop ●,** just south of the German Bakery has basic, decently spaced huts for Rs50. The hippest crowd gravitates towards Om Beach, either stringing up **hammocks** (Rs150 along Main St. in Gokarna) or renting thatched **huts** (Rs50-75) from a row of various *chai* huts and cafes. **Namaste Cafe ●,** on the extreme northern end of Om Beach, has Internet, a restaurant, and a community of simple huts, rooms, and even a bamboo house. (☎ 2657141. Restaurant open 7am-11pm. Huts Rs50; rooms Rs100; bamboo house Rs300.) For truly isolated bliss, make the trek to Paradise Beach, about 6km from town—several cliffside accommodations await to reward your perseverance.

On Kudle and Om beach, **chai huts ●,** turn out snacks (Rs10-25) and the usual range of *thalis* (Rs30), eggs, and sandwiches. **Vaibhav Nivas ●,** in town (see above), serves standard Goan cuisine in a fluorescent-lighted communal atmosphere. (Breakfast Rs5-50, entrees Rs15-50. Open 7:30-11:30am.) The **Downtown Bar and Restaurant ❷,** in the Hotel Gokarna International, serves up tangy *tandoori* specialties (Rs40-80), and a variety of other Indian standards. (Entrees around Rs50. Open 10am-3:30pm and 6pm-midnight.)

SIGHTS AND BEACHES

Gokarna is packed with temples, although they're a bit of a false temptation since foreigners aren't allowed inside. Still, Car St., the main east-west road on which most temples lie, is a sight in and of itself, with countless little shops selling everything from baked goods to religious iconography in all colors of the rainbow. Car St. also leads to the **Mahabeleshwara Temple,** where two massive chariots sit outside, waiting to be dragged through Gokarna's streets for *shivaratri*, Shiva's birthday. The massive **bathing tank,** south on Main St. past Car St., also merits a visit, looking somewhat like a displaced, drowned Venetian piazza.

The road to the temple continues straight to the **town beach,** which is pretty but unremarkable. From here you can catch a **boat taxi** to Om Beach, which is the fastest and most painless way to get there. Those who feel like a bit of exercise can **hike** to the beaches. Depending on which beach you choose, the hike can take anywhere from 20min. (Kudle Beach) to 2hr. (Paradise Beach), covering between one and four ascents and descents of various terrain and steadily increasing difficulty. The sweat pours freely, but the stunning and continual bird's-eye view of sugary sand and black rock stretching to the horizon is unavailable from the boat taxi.

The first beach worthy of mention is **Kudle Beach,** to the south, amiably populated by a few dozen sunbathers and fringed by widely-spaced restaurants and *chai* shops. From the bathing tank, take the cowpath beside the tankside temple; it quickly climbs uphill to a rocky, barren landscape and follows a string of telephone poles before heading to the sand. When the road forks, bear right and cut left through a *chai* shop to the beach. From the beach, it's another 20-min. hike over a cliff to the more picturesque **Om Beach,** two narrow, semi-circular beaches lined with trees and *chai* shops. You can also take a **boat taxi** or **rickshaw** (Rs200) to Om; a paved road connects it to town. Behind the last *chai* shop, a narrow path leads up along the ridge of the black cliffs to **Half-Moon Beach** (20min.), where there is a restaurant and not much else. The beach itself is miniscule, and only opens onto the sea between the rocks at a few places. If you are scared of heights, you might want to turn back at this point. Otherwise, a 15min. dirty, rocky scramble brings you to **Paradise Beach,** the emptiest and most peaceful location in Gokarna. Two cliffside *chai* shops play host to some of the most easygoing people in India, playing chess and sipping drinks contentedly as time slips quietly by.

NEAR GOKARNA

JOG FALLS

Jog Falls are the highest waterfalls in India. The Sharavathi River falls in four separate cascades known as the Rani, Raja, Roarer, and Rocket, the tallest of which plummets 253m. The Linganamakki Dam limits the amount of water that can be released, but to please daytrippers, more water is occasionally let through on the weekends. The falls are most dramatic after monsoon. Pleasant (if indistinct and garbage-strewn) trails twist throughout the area. The comfortable government-run **Hotel Mayura ❷,** offering gigantic room-suites, is one of several places to stay in Jog Falls. Its **restaurant ❷** on the main road might be the only sit-down place in town. (☎08186 2344732. Restaurant open 8am-10pm. Doubles Rs220-330.)

The **hike** into the falls (2hr.) is 4km down and back. Those who make it across the striated, irregularly placed boulders will be treated to vivid upward views: glistening cliff faces painted with rainbows reflecting the sun, a fairy-dust mist spraying, and tiny birds flitting back and forth between the reddish-brown cliff faces. A pair of shimmering pools awaits the eager swimmer.

From Gokarna, take a bus to **Kumta** (1-2hr., every hr. 6am-6:15pm, Rs12), where buses go onward to **Jog Falls** (4hr., Rs31), or to further connections at **Honavar** (45min., Rs8) and **Talguppa** (4hr., 7am and 10:45am, Rs32).

KERALA കേരളം

The locals call it "God's own country," and there is no denying that Kerala is spectacular. Lined with palm trees and golden beaches, the state's famous backwaters are quite stunning. Forty lazy rivers run through canals and rice paddies from the Western Ghats down to the sea, channeling their way through tiny fishing villages and islands of palm groves. Beautiful beaches have made the state second only to Goa as a haven for coconut-oiled sun-worshippers and beach bums from around the world. Renowned for its unique *kathakali* dance, Ayurvedic medicine, and beautiful scenery, Kerala's growing popularity with tourists is well-deserved.

Legend has it that when Parashoram, an incarnation of Vishnu, threw his axe into the sea at Gokarna, the oceans retreated to reveal the land that is now Kerala. As early as the 3rd century BC, travelers from China and the Middle East had set up trade routes with Kerala, and people from around the ancient world came here in search of spices, ivory, and sandalwood. Jews fleeing Roman persecution in Palestine landed here 2000 years ago, and many believe that St. Thomas the Apostle was the first to bring the Christian gospel to Kerala, less than 20 years after the death of Jesus. Arabs dominated the spice trade for centuries, spreading Islam throughout the region, until the Portuguese landed at Calicut in 1498 and gunboated their way to exclusive trading rights. Rivalry between the port cities of Cochin and Calicut weakened both, and Dutch and British forces ejected the Portuguese from their forts early in the 17th century. Kerala became a part of the British Raj during the 18th century.

After Independence, the princely states of Cochin and Travancore were combined to form the state of Kerala. In 1956 Kerala's boundaries were redrawn along linguistic (Malayalam) lines to include Malabar. A year later, Kerala became the first state in the world to elect a communist government. The state's leftist tradition has brought many advantages to its citizens: reforms have given Kerala the most equitable land distribution in India, and Kerala's literacy rate—around 90%—is the highest in the country. Vestiges of ancient matrilineal, polyandrous systems, such as those still practiced by the Nayar people, have given women a somewhat higher status in Kerala than elsewhere in India, and the UN has commended the state for its exemplary women's rights record.

Kerala's biggest festival is Onam, held in September to celebrate the harvest, when carnivals, elephant processions, and dance performances take place all over the state. Kerala is renowned for its elephant pageants; the most famous is the Trichur Pooram in May. The Nehru Trophy Boat Race is the most popular of the many backwater boat races, and is held on the second Saturday in August.

HIGHLIGHTS OF KERALA

Through the tourist melee that has overtaken the town, **Kovalam** (p. 318) remains a haven for beach-seekers and offers all the luxuries of Indian resort-style life—boogie boarding, massage, boat cruises, and *kathakali* performances.

No troubled waters here: **backwater cruises** that run out of Alleppey (p. 326) will certainly ease your mind as they float through green canals and past tranquil villages.

The influence of foreign immigrants from St. Thomas the Apostle to Portuguese sailors has blessed **Cochin** (p. 331) with a mixture of architectural styles, spices, religions, and traditions that are to sure to fascinate any traveler.

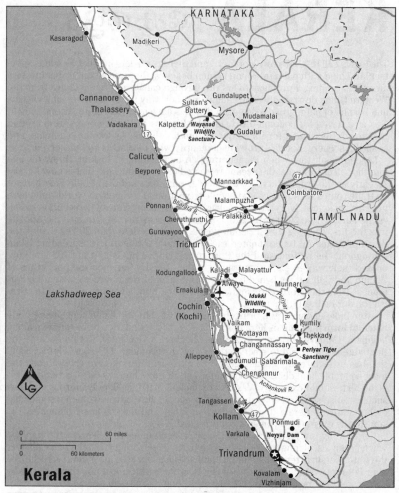

Kerala

TRIVANDRUM (THIRUVANATHAPURAM)
തിരുവനന്തപുരം   ☎ 0471

Although many travelers may overlook Trivandrum on their way to the balmy beaches of Kovalam or the backwaters of Alleppey, Kerala's state capital merits a closer look. Speckled with parks, palaces, monuments, and museums, it is a good place to gain some insight into Kerala's culture. Trivandrum had already been the capital of Travancore for two centuries when the city became the capital of Kerala in 1956, and today it retains the trademark red-tiled, pagoda-roofed houses that are common throughout the state. The city differentiates itself with its endlessly intertwined streets, beautiful gardens, and a museum complex housing several exhibits of both master opuses and mysteri-

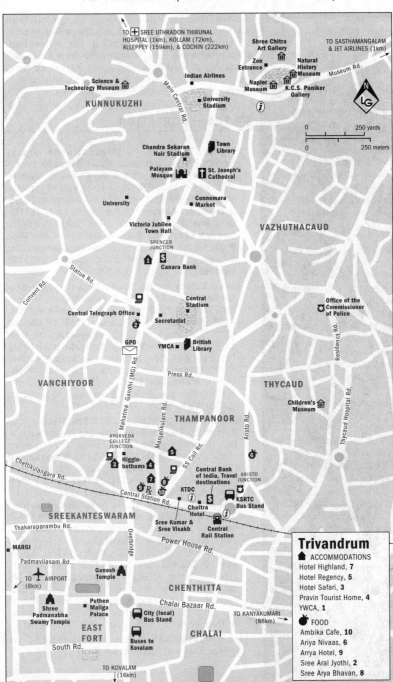

KERALA

TO ✚ SREE UTHRADON THIRUNAL HOSPITAL (1km), KOLLAM (72km), ALLEPPEY (159km), & COCHIN (222km)

TO SASTHAMANGALAM & JET AIRLINES (1km)

Shree Chitra Art Gallery

Zoo Entrance

Natural History Museum

Indian Airlines

Napier Museum

K.C.S. Paniker Gallery

Museum Rd.

Science & Technology Museum

KUNNUKUZHI

University Stadium

Main Central Rd.

Chandra Sekaran Nair Stadium

Town Library

Palayam Mosque

St. Joseph's Cathedral

University

Connemara Market

Victoria Jubilee Town Hall

SPENCER JUNCTION

Canara Bank

VAZHUTHACAUD

Statue Rd.

Convent Rd.

Central Telegraph Office

Central Stadium

Office of the Commissioner of Police

Secretariat

GPO

YMCA

British Library

Press Rd.

VANCHIYOOR

THYCAUD

Mahatma Gandhi (MG) Rd.

Manjalikulam Rd.

THAMPANOOR

Children's Museum

AYURVEDA COLLEGE JUNCTION

Higginbothams

S.S. Coil Rd.

Aristo Rd.

Residency Rd.

Thycaud Hospital Rd.

Chettikulangara Rd.

Central Bank of India, Travel destinations

ARISTO JUNCTION

KTDC

KSRTC Bus Stand

Central Station Rd.

Chaitra Hotel

SREEKANTESWARAM

Sree Kumar & Sree Visakh

Central Rail Station

Thakaraparambu Rd.

MARGI

Power House Rd.

Padmavilasam Rd.

TO ✈ AIRPORT (8km)

Ganesh Temple

CHENTHITTA

Shree Padmanabha Swamy Temple

Puthen Maliga Palace

Chalai Bazaar Rd.

TO KANYAKUMARI (88km)

City (local) Bus Stand

EAST FORT

CHALAI

Buses to Kovalam

South Rd.

TO KOVALAM (16km)

N

0   250 yards
0   250 meters

Trivandrum

⌂ ACCOMMODATIONS
Hotel Highland, 7
Hotel Regency, 5
Hotel Safari, 3
Pravin Tourist Home, 4
YWCA, 1

🍴 FOOD
Ambika Cafe, 10
Ariya Nivaas, 6
Arrya Hotel, 9
Sree Aral Jyothi, 2
Sree Arya Bhavan, 8

GIVING BACK

MITRANIKETAN: RURAL DEVELOPMENT IN KERALA

Established in 1956 by K. Viswanathan in his hometown of Vellanad, Kerala, Mitraniketan was inspired by the efforts of American Arthur Morgan, Dane N.F.S. Grundtvig, and Indians Mohandas Gandhi and Rabindranath Tagore to "promote rural development with a human face."

The 75-acre campus, located outside Trivandrum, is home to a "People's College" and a host of other educational facilities. Today, it promotes "educational tourism" and development education through its community-based center. It also invites volunteers from around the world to work in either an agricultural capacity or at the Rural Technology Center, which aims to replicate "appropriate technologies," develop technologies suitable for rural people, upgrade the technical skills of local artisans, and provide vocational training for rural youth.

Remarkably, the NGO also runs a number of other outreach organizations, among them a school for the hearing impaired, a women's silk weaving training center, and carpentry, metal, and leather workshops. Many of the products manufactured at Mitraniketan are sold to generate income for the organization. Contact the center for opportunities. (☎472 882045l or ☎471 451566; www.mitraniketan.org. Mitraniketan PO, Vellanad, Thiruvahanthapuram, Kerala 695543, or Mitraniketan City Centre, West Fort, Trivandrum, Kerala 695008.)

ous oddities. The city's Malayalam name refers to Anantha, the serpent that holds the reclining Lord Vishnu (Lord Padmanabha) in the Shree Padmanabha Swami Temple—a major draw for Indian tourists. A welcome and edifying break from beach-hopping, Trivandrum is a good place to begin or end any South Indian trip.

TRANSPORTATION

Flights: Trivandrum's **international airport** (☎2500710) is 8km outside town. Buses for the airport leave from the city bus station **Indian Airlines,** Museum Rd. (☎2396942), 1 block west of the intersection with MG Rd. Open M-Sa 10am-1pm and 1:35-5:35pm. **Jet Airways,** Akshay Towers (☎2721018), Sasthamamgalam Junction, about 1.5km east of the museum compound along Museum Rd. Open M-Sa 9:30am-6pm, Su 9:30am-1:30pm. To: **Chennai** (2hr., 8:10am, US$115); **Delhi** (5½hr., 1:35pm, US$370); **Mumbai** (2hr., 1:35pm, US$205).

Trains: Railway station, Station Rd., a few min. east of MG Rd. Reservations open M-Sa 8am-8pm, Su 8am-2pm. To: **Alleppey** (3½hr., 3-9 per day 12:30am-10pm, Rs48); **Bangalore** (20hr., 9:20am, Rs301); **Chennai** (20hr., 2:30 and 4pm, Rs345); **Ernakulam** (5hr., 6 per day 5am-9:20pm, Rs65); **Kanyakumari** (2hr., 11:10am and 3:10pm, Rs85) via **Kollam** (1½hr., Rs29); **Madurai** (8hr.; 4:30am, 4:10, and 8:40pm; Rs79); **Mangalore** (6hr., 6:10am and 6:20pm, Rs138); **Mumbai** (46hr., 3-5 per day 3:45am-10am, Rs402); **Varkala** (1hr., every hr., Rs24).

Buses: The long-distance **KSRTC Bus Station** is on Station Rd. (☎2323886), opposite the railway station. To: **Alleppey** (4hr., every 15min., Rs74); **Cochin** (5½hr., every 15min., Rs102-120); **Kanyakumari** (2½hr., 9 per day 4:30am-12:30am, Rs32); **Kollam** (2hr., every 15min., Rs34); **Thekkady** for Periyar (8hr., 8:45am, Rs150); **Varkala** (2hr., every hr. 7:15am-9:30pm, Rs26). The **Tamil Nadu Transport Office** (☎2327756), at the far east end of the KSRTC bus station, runs buses to cities in Tamil Nadu. Open daily 10am-6pm. To: **Chennai** (17hr., 9 per day 11:30am-8pm, Rs297-348); **Madurai** (7hr., 12 per day 10:30am-10:30pm, Rs109); **Pondicherry** (16hr., 3:30pm, Rs261). The **local bus stand,** MG Rd., is a few min. south of the train tracks at East Fort. Buses to **Kovalam** (25min., every 20min. 5:50am-8:30pm, Rs5.50) depart from the bus stand on Overbridge Rd., 100m south of the local stand.

Local Transportation: Auto-rickshaws should use meters. Base Rs6. Rs150 to Kovalam.

⚡ ORIENTATION AND PRACTICAL INFORMATION

The streets tangle over 74 sq. km of coastal hills, but navigation is easy if you stick to the few main roads. The north-south **MG Road** dumps all its traffic onto **Museum Road**, at the north end of town. To the south, MG Rd. cruises downhill to a hectic intersection with the city's other main drag, **(Central) Station Road.** One hundred meters east on Station Rd. from MG Rd., **Manjalikulam Road** leads north to the budget hotel district. Farther down Station Rd., the long-distance **KSRTC Bus Station** is on the left, opposite the **railway station.** MG Rd. becomes **Overbridge Road** when it heads south over the railway tracks to the **East Fort** area. A great white gate marks the entrance to **Shree Padmanabha Swamy Temple,** opposite the **local bus stand.** Behind the stand, **Chalai Bazaar Road** leads east through the bazaar.

TOURIST, FINANCIAL, AND LOCAL SERVICES

Tourist Office: Tourist Facilitation Centre (☎ 2321132), in the Directorate of Tourism on Museum Rd., opposite the museum compound. Ask for the useful *Kerala Companion* and the list of festivals. Open daily 10am-5pm. Smaller branches at the **KSRTC Bus Stand** (☎ 2327224) and the **train station** (☎ 2334470) also have maps. Both open M-Sa 8am-8pm, Su 10am-5pm. **KTDC Reception Centre** (☎ 2330031), on Station Rd. in front of Chaitram Hotel, next to the bus stand. Promotes KTDC tours. Open daily 6:30am-9:30pm.

Immigration Office: Foreigners Registration Office, Residency Rd. (☎ 2321399), in the Office of the Commissioner of Police. Extensions for student and entry visas "with proper documents." The process takes a minimum of 2 weeks. Open M-Sa 10:15am-1:15pm and 2-5:15pm. Closed 2nd Sa of each month.

Currency Exchange: Central Bank of India (☎ 2330359), in the Chaitram Hotel lobby. Exchanges foreign currency and traveler's checks. Open M-F 10am-5pm, Sa 10am-noon. **Canara Bank,** MG Rd. (☎ 2331536), at Spencer Junction just north of the Secretariat, gives cash advances on Visa and exchanges cash and traveler's checks. Open M-F 10am-5pm, Sa 10am-2pm.

Market: Chalai Bazaar Road, which intersects MG Rd. at the local bus station. The smaller and more sedate **Connemara Market** is north of Spencer Junction on MG Rd.

EMERGENCY AND COMMUNICATIONS

Police: Thampanoor Police Station, Station Rd. (☎ 2326543), near the KSRTC bus station, before Aristo Junction. **Museum police** inside museum compound (☎ 2315096).

Pharmacy: Darsana Medicals, Station Rd. (☎ 2331398), just west of Manjalikalam Rd. Open daily 8:45am-9:45pm.

Hospital: Shree Uthradon Thirunal Hospital (☎ 2446220), in Pattom, north of the city center (Rs40-50 rickshaw from Station Rd.). Considered the best private hospital here.

Internet: Peak Internet Cafe, MG Rd. (☎ 2478793), opposite the Secretariat. Rs15 per hr. Open M-Sa 8:30am-10pm, Su 10am-10pm. **Omkar Communications,** Old Shree Kanteswaram Rd. (☎ 2451803), south of Ayurveda College Junction, is also good. Rs15 per hr. Open daily 7am-11pm.

Post Office: GPO, MG Rd., south of the Secretariat. Open M-Sa 8am-8pm, Su 10am-4pm. **Postal Code:** 695001.

🏠 ACCOMMODATIONS

Manjalikulam Rd. is the real budget hotel district, though MG and Station Rd. also have plenty of large hotels.

Pravin Tourist Home, Manjalikulam Rd. (☎2330443). A 3min. walk north from Central Station Rd., across from a dirt cricket field. Rooms have big windows and attached bathrooms (seat and squat toilets). Check-out 24hr. Singles Rs135; doubles Rs210. ❶

Hotel Highland, Manjalikulam Rd. (☎2333200 or 2333421), near Central Station Rd., on the left. Large, posh, and popular hotel has big airy rooms with TV. Retreat from street life to the 2nd fl. restaurant. Seat toilets. Check-out 24hr. Singles Rs360-800; doubles Rs405-1000. ❸

Hotel Regency, (☎2330377). Follow Manjalikulam Rd. to the first cross-street, then turn right. Classy joint with big, clean, disinfected rooms with TV. Several restaurants (including one on the roof open for dinner only). Currency exchange. Check-out 24hr. Singles Rs450-750; doubles Rs550-800. MC/V. ❸

Hotel Safari, MG Rd. (☎2477202), a few min. north of Central Station Rd. Fifteen spacious rooms with big windows and seat toilets, 10 of which have TVs. Restaurant has city views, although lone women might want to steer clear of the hotel bar. Singles Rs250; doubles Rs300. ❷

YWCA, 4th fl., Indian Overseas Bank Building, (☎2477308), near the Secretariat. Well-lit, clean, expansive rooms with attached baths. Best to call ahead, since it's slightly out of the way. No unmarried couples allowed. Singles Rs250; doubles Rs350-600; family room Rs450. ❷

▐ FOOD

Travelers coming from the beach will be relieved to escape the yoke of banana pancakes and spaghetti: in Trivandrum it's authentic Indian all the way, mostly a mix of Keralan and Tamil cuisine.

▨ **Sree Arya Bhavan,** on the corner of SS Coil and Station Rd., 100m west of Hotel Chaitram. This tiny hole-in-the-wall serves terrific North Indian veg. food, and its toasty-fresh wheat *parathas* (Rs2) are not to be missed. Excellent menu changes daily (entrees Rs13-21). Open daily 8:30am-3pm and 7-11pm. ❶

▨ **Sree Aral Jyothi,** MG Rd., (☎2470240), opposite the Secretariat. Crowded, real-deal local restaurant serves authentic Keralan "raw rice meals" (Rs23) and *masala dosas* (Rs16). Windowless A/C space in the back, or heart-of-town street views in front. Open daily 6:30am-10pm. Meals served 11:30am-3:30pm and 7-10pm. ❶

Aarrya Hotel, Central Station Rd., between Manjalikulam and the intersection with MG Rd. Simple, smashing South Indian fare. Good *masala dosa* (Rs13) and Keralan meals (Rs20). Open daily 6:30am-11pm. ❶

Ambika Cafe, MG Rd., where Manjalikulam and SS Coil meet. Turns out good veg. and non-veg. meals at unbeatable prices (Rs12; *paratha* Rs2). Open daily 6am-1am. ❶

Ariya Nivaas, around the corner from the station, toward Aristo Junction. The flashing neon sign in the sky calls to middle-class families like a siren's song; pristine ambience and carefully prepared dishes make them stay. Fancy *thalis* served on a banana leaf (Rs55 in the A/C upstairs). Open daily 7:30am-10:30pm. ❷

◉ SIGHTS

MUSEUM COMPOUND. A big red gate marks the entrance to the lovely, 20-hectare public gardens, with its two museums and galleries, zoo, and crowds of mooneyed couples. The **Natural History Museum** features polymer dioramas of natural history, a model of a traditional upper-class house in Travancore, dolls dressed in traditional styles from all over India, and a life-sized, ivory model of a human skeleton made for Marthandavarma Maharaja in 1853. Don't miss the invertebrates preserved in jars. To the left as you come out of the Natural History Museum is the **K.C.S. Paniker Gallery,** which features mainly modern and abstract paintings by the 20th-century Indian artist in a mildly moldy room. Better maintained is the **Shree Chitra Art Gallery,** across the grounds, decked with Western-style portraits by the famed Raja Ravi Varma (1848-1906); Tibetan *thangas;* Japanese, Chinese, and Balinese paintings; 400-year-old Rajasthani miniatures; and modern Indian works. The eclectic exhibit can make wading through some cramped rooms well worth it.

In the center of the grounds is the **Napier Museum,** an architectural cross between a giant mausoleum and a Walt Disney spin-off—the building is done in heavy red, black, and pink bricks and tiles. The inside doesn't get much more sedate. It is striped in yellow, pink, red, and turquoise, while the shade and high ceilings lend it a weird solemnity. In fact, the building is an Indo-Saracenic experiment by Robert Fellowes Chisholm, who attempted to combine traditional Keralan and colonial architectural styles (hence the contradictions). The museum, along with the mandatory *kathakali* figures, includes a bizarre collection of Southeast Asian and Balinese art. Some of the choice pieces of kitsch on display, including an engraved plate to mark Kuwait Airlines' inaugural flight to Trivandrum, were gifts from foreign rulers to First Ministers of Kerala. *(Museum Rd., about 2.5km from Station Rd. Follow MG Rd. north until it comes to a dead end, then go right (east). The complex will be on your left. Galleries open Tu and Th-Su 10am-4:45pm, W 1-4:45pm. Rs5 for all four museums. Purchase tickets at the Natural History Museum 10am-4pm.)*

The compound also contains a **zoo** housing a wide assortment of birds and beasts. Though some animals are kept in depressingly small cages, the zoo may be worth a visit for its pleasantly wandering walkways. *(Open Tu-Su 9am-5:15pm. Rs5, children Rs3. Camera fee Rs10; video fee Rs500. Tickets sold until 5pm.)*

PUTHEN MALIGA PALACE (KUTHIRAMALIKA OR HORSE PALACE). Every inch of this palace of Prince Swati Tirunal Ramavarma, also a famed musician, singer, and court composer, is decorated exquisitely. Its beautiful wooden carvings took four years to complete, after which the surly Swati Tirunal occupied the palace for just one year before he left in a huff. The Puthen Maliga Palace or "Horse Palace," named for the 122 smiling horse sculptures beneath its eaves, provides some fascinating insight into how the lucky few once lived. The palace also functions as a museum (i.e. "repository of old stuff"), featuring life-size *kathakali* figures in full regalia, paintings of the rajas and ranis of Travancore, weapons, and thrones in ivory and Bohemian crystal. *(Open Tu-Su 8:30am-1pm and 3-5:30pm. Rs20. Camera fee Rs15. Photography prohibited inside. Official museum guides must accompany visitors.)*

SHREE PADMANABHA SWAMY TEMPLE. Marked by a large white gate and a gigantic, intricately carved facade of white stone, the Shree Padmanabha Swamy Temple features a 6m-high statue of a reclining Vishnu. The whole of the god's body is made visible by the opening of three doors—one at the head, one at the midsection, and one at the feet. The *gopuram* was built in 1566, but the structure was not completed until 1733. The temple itself is open only to Hindus, but non-Hindus can climb the steps and peek in at some of the less sacred images. The lane leading up to the temple, through a thicket of handicraft sellers, houses a large green **tank** used by bathing pilgrims.

◘ FESTIVALS

The Attukal Bhagavathy Temple, 2km south of East Fort, holds the **Festival of Attukal Pongala** in late February or early March, corresponding to the day of the Makom star. Thousands of women converge on Trivandrum during this time, each one setting up a miniature kitchen on the streets in the center of town. The women offer *pongala*, a sweet rice porridge, considered the goddess's favorite food, which they cook in earthenware pots over sanctified fires from the temple. Men are not permitted in the vicinity of the temple during the festival. Trivandrum's center is closed to traffic and takes on an uncharacteristically peaceful air as the smoke from thousands of cooling fires drifts up into the heavens. The **Swati Music Festival** (late Jan.-early Feb.) brings performances of classical music on the lawn of the Puthen Maliga Palace in the evenings. The annual **Nishagandhi Dance Festival,** with outdoor classical performances, takes place during the last week of February. Contact the Tourist Facilitation Centre for a complete festival schedule.

🎵 DANCE AND THEATER

MARGI (☎2478806). Follow MG Rd. south over the train tracks, turn right at the corner temple, and walk 10min. into West Fort. When the street comes to a final "T," turn right. MARGI is behind Fort High School on your left—look for the big banyan tree. Look for the image of a dancer on the sign. This school at West Fort occasionally performs **kathakali dance drama** and **kutiyattum theater** (Keralan martial arts) in the evenings. Performances are free, but they are not regularly scheduled and often take place in local temples; call in advance for details.

KOVALAM കോവളം ☎0471

The pounding of hammers and the pouring of concrete have forever altered the calm landscape of Kovalam's black sands and turquoise waters. Since the arrival of the first sun-seekers back in the 1930s, Kovalam has become Kerala's most touristed beach resort and probably the most popular in India. The busy beachfront has been consumed by hotels, swallowed by touts, and spat out again by thieves dressed up as tailors and handicraft sellers. Enjoy the carnivalesque atmosphere created just for you. Beyond the tourist enclave, fishing boats still prowl the bays and life continues as it always has, amid thatched huts and rice paddies.

▐ TRANSPORTATION

Buses: The **bus stand,** at the top of the path from the north end of Eve's Beach, has no ticket office, but the Tourist Facilitation Centre (see below) can give bus schedules. To: **Cochin** (5½hr.; 6, 6:30am, and 3:30pm; Rs82) via **Alleppey** (4hr., Rs55.50) and **Kollam** (2hr., 6 and 6:30am, Rs40); **Kanyakumari** (2½hr., 4 per day 6:30am-6:30pm, Rs40) via **Nagercoil** (1½hr., Rs25); **Trivandrum** (20min., frequent 5:30am-10pm, Rs7).

Local Transportation: Auto-rickshaws and **taxis** hover at the bottom of Lighthouse Rd., the bus stand, and Kovalam Junction. A rickshaw to Trivandrum should cost Rs80-100, one to the airport Rs150-175.

▐ ☷ ORIENTATION AND PRACTICAL INFORMATION

Kovalam Beach is made up of three coves divided by rocky promontories. A lighthouse marks the southernmost **Lighthouse Beach.** From here, **Lighthouse Road,** crawling with seafood restaurants, leads down to the water and the budget hotels favored by foreign tourists. **Eve's Beach** is north of a rocky promontory. The headland is home to the **Kovalam Ashok Beach Resort,** north of which is **Samudra Beach.** A road leads steeply uphill from Eve's Beach past several travel offices, handicraft shops, and tailors to the **bus stand** at the entrance to the Ashok Beach Resort. From there, the road that leads southeast goes first to **Kovalam Junction,** 2km away, where a left turn at the fork brings you to the **post office,** and 14km later to Trivandrum. Between Lighthouse Rd. and the road to the bus stand, paths twist through the palm trees, connecting the beach to some of the quieter restaurants and hotels. The power shuts down at 8 or 8:30pm every night for 30min. Some hotels have back-up generators, but don't count on it.

Tourist Office: Tourist Facilitation Centre (☎2480085), near the bus stand toward Ashok Beach Resort. Arranges tickets for the backwater cruises (see p. 321). Keeps current copies of int'l. newspapers. Open daily 10am-5pm; off-season closed Su.

Budget Travel: Western Travels (☎2481334), next to the bus stand. Organizes a variety of **sightseeing tours** in season, ranging from 3hr. to full-day affairs (Rs225-4000). Currency exchange and cash advances on credit cards. Taxis for hire. Open daily 7am-10pm. AmEx/MC/V.

Currency Exchange: Several shops on the beach exchange currency. The reception desk at **Wilson's Tourist Home,** behind Hotel Neelakanta, offers bank rates. Open M-Sa 9am-5pm. The **Central Bank of India** has a small branch in the Kovalam Hotel shopping complex. Open M-Sa 9am-4pm.

Police: (☎2480255). Left off the road to Kovalam Junction, 10min. from the bus station on the left. In-season, the **Tourist Aid Post** is on the beach. Open daily 24hr.

Hospital: Upasana Hospital (☎2480632), a right off the road to Kovalam Junction, 10min. on foot from the bus stand. **Pharmacy** open M-Sa 9am-10pm, Su 9am-1pm. In an emergency, you can call Dr. Chandrasenan (☎2457357).

Internet: There are lots of places; almost all charge Rs40-60 and are relatively fast. **Surfers Cove** (☎2485788), close to the top of the road leading uphill to the bus stand, on the right. Rs40 per hr. Open daily 9am-9pm. **Alpha Internet Services,** right on Lighthouse Beach, close to the southern end. Rs60 per hr. Open daily 9:30am-11pm.

Post Office: Branch next to Tourist Facilitation Center. Open M-Sa 9am-3pm. The **main office** can be reached by taking a left at Kovalam Junction. Open M-Sa 9am-1pm and 1:30-5pm. **Postal Code:** 695527.

ACCOMMODATIONS

Prices peak in December and January. Off-season and during the monsoon, bargain hard—don't let touts determine where you stay. In general, room quality is high. All the places listed below are on (or a short distance behind) Lighthouse Beach and include attached bathrooms and (usually) hot water. The off season is May-October unless otherwise noted.

THE LOCAL LEGEND

GOOD HUMOR

The predominant medical tradition in Hindu culture is associated with *ayurveda*, which translates as the "knowledge of long life." Practitioners of ayurvedic medicine are called *vaidyas*. Ayurvedic medicine takes a holistic approach to diagnosis (a broken heart is as much an ailment as a broken leg) and to treatment (a combination of herbal potions and worthy notions). The earliest known prescriptions date back to the *Atharva Veda* (c. 1000 BC), when *vaidyas* were performing surgery on wounds. Ayurvedic medicine, however, is mainly associated with maintaining balance between the three bodily essences or *doshas: vatta* (wind), *pitta* (bile), and *kapha* (phlegm). *Vatta*, associated with the nervous system and movement, represents kinetic energy. *Kapha*, potential energy, is associated with lymph and mucus, opposes *vatta*. Finally, *pitta* mediates between these two forces, governing digestive and metabolic processes. Balance between the *doshas* is essential to good health.

■ **Green Valley Cottages** (☎2480636). From the beach, walk straight past Hotel Neptune and follow signs away from the beach. Forsaking the beachfront has its advantages—lower prices, spotless sheets, and dreamy views of lush greenery, for instance. Each immaculate room (renovated yearly) has a private balcony and chairs to loll around in. A sales counter with a book selection ensures no desire goes unfulfilled. Doubles Rs200-400. Off-season Rs200. The same friendly folks run **Silent Valley Inn** (☎2487928) right behind Green Valley Cottages. Gorgeous, larger rooms with balconies from which you can see the sea. Doubles Rs200-400. Off-season Rs150-250. ❷

Sandy Beach Resort (☎2480012; sandybeach@vsnl.com), opposite Hotel Neptune, about 75m in from the beach. Sparkling and spacious rooms with balconies around a courtyard. Singles Rs350; doubles Rs550. Off-season Rs200-300. ❸

Wilson's Tourist Home (☎2480051). From the beach, turn inland at the Palm Beach Restaurant and take your first right, close to Hotel Neelakanta. Rooms with big beds and balconies. Doubles Rs200-600. Off-season Rs150-400. MC/V. ❷

Pappukutty Beach Resort (☎2480235; nadarajan@hotmail.com). Walk through the Nirvana Restaurant in the middle of the beach to find this luxurious option. Balconies overlooking the waves, cool green walls, marble floors, hot water, fridge, towels, and seat toilet: no expense spared. Check-out noon. Cottage Rs500; doubles Rs800-1000. ❸

Hawah Beach Restaurant (☎2485862), behind the restaurant. Tony the manager offers the cheapest rooms on the beach. Digs are basic, but you can buy decorations galore with the money you'll save. Doubles Rs100-150; family rooms Rs350-500. ❶

Hotel Jeevan House (☎2480662), on the sand halfway down the cove, next to the Coral Reef Cafe. Pleasant, airy rooms with balconies, fridge, hot water, and safety deposit. Doubles Rs500-750. Off-season Rs300-500. ❸

Hotel Surya (☎2481012). From the beach, turn inland between the Coconut Grove Restaurant and the Coral Reef Cafe, near the Hotel Jeevan House. A little back from the beach, but the price is right, rooms are clean and spacious, and the tiling is hot pink. Doubles Rs300-350; with fridge and TV Rs500-700. Off-season Rs150-350. ❷

◖ FOOD

Restaurants stretch in an almost uninterrupted sweep all the way along the beaches. What little Indian food there is has been largely de-spiced to appease Western palates. Alcohol is served at many beachfront places (beer Rs70).

■ **Red Star Restaurant.** This is the best place in Kovalam to get a feel for the old days, not to mention an unparalleled tomato-onion-garlic omelette (Rs15). So small that you get to hang out and chat with the owner, Mani. *Masala dosa* Rs20, excellent Keralan meal Rs20, and tasty fried fish Rs34. Open daily 6am-11pm. ❶

■ **German Bakery,** toward the south end of Lighthouse Beach. There's always a breeze (and usually a crowd) at this rooftop spot. Though you're a long way from home, you wouldn't know it after a bite of that cinnamon-apple crumble (Rs25). Open daily 7:30am-11pm. ❶

Leo's Restaurant, toward the north end of Lighthouse Beach. This popular, amiable spot makes a mean cheese-tomato-onion-garlic omelette (Rs45). Tasty fish and chips with salad Rs140, spaghetti with mussels Rs90. Open 7am-11pm. ❷

Cafe Spice Garden, near the north end of Lighthouse Beach. Formerly "Swiss Cafe," this brick-floor locale has returned to its roots (at least outwardly) with traditional Keralan art on the wall and potted spice plants peppered between tables. The menu covers all major European and subcontinental cuisines. Entrees mostly Rs100-200. ❹

Coconut Grove Restaurant, in the middle of Lighthouse Beach. Come here for the unadulterated tourist experience: the open tandoori oven commands rapt gazes, as do nightly movie screenings in the back room. Chicken *biryani* with pineapple chunks Rs70 (reconfirm the "boneless" status when ordering). Open 7am-11pm. ❸

Beatles: The Food and Music Club, on the northern end of Lighthouse Beach. A picture of this restaurant's namesake band hangs on the wall and there's BBC broadcast in the morning. Entrees Rs50-175. Open 8am-midnight. ❷

🔍 🎵 SIGHTS AND ENTERTAINMENT

BEACHES. Well, you're here for the sand—no two ways about it. The most popular beach among foreign tourists is **Lighthouse Beach,** the southernmost. Here you can rent beach chairs (Rs50), beach beds (Rs100), and boogie boards (Rs50 per hr.) in front of Hotel Jeevan House, while fending off hawkers of edibles and durables. Always swim near the lifeguard. Almost as popular is **Eve Beach.** North of the headland is **Samudra Beach,** delightful but largely ignored by the crowds. **The undertow and rip currents in Kovalam can be very strong. Follow the warnings of the signs, flags, and lifeguards.**

MASSAGE AND YOGA. Tired of the waves? Kiss your aches and pains good-bye with an **Ayurvedic massage.** Kerala is touted as an Ayurvedic haven, and there are numerous establishments in Kovalam providing treatment. **Wilson's Tourist Home** has a *masseur* for men and a *masseuse* for women. (☎2480051. Open daily 9am-6pm. Rs500 per hr.) **Medicus,** adjoining Hotel Neptune, does a 1hr. full body massage from Rs500. (☎2480596. Open daily 8:30am-6pm.) Peak season also means that **yoga** is in full swing at many hotels and private institutions. Hotel Neptune offers classes (2hr. session Rs300).

NIGHTLIFE. During peak season, "cultural nights" featuring *kathakali* dance take place at the Hotel Ashok (☎2480101; Tu and F Rs150) and Hotel Neptune. (☎2480222. M, W, and Su Rs150. Make-up starts at 5pm; the dance program begins at 6:45pm.) Pirated movies, complete with laughter from the original audience, are shown nightly at several restaurants, including the Coconut Grove Restaurant (☎2485047) and the Hawah Beach Restaurant (☎2485862).

BACKWATER CRUISES. The Tourist Facilitation Centre arranges **backwater cruises** around an island 5km from Kovalam. The Rs350 fee (Rs400 if you're alone) covers transportation to the boat, 3hr. of cruising time, and the return trip to Kovalam. Unlike on the Alleppey-Kollam tour, the boat used in season is a traditional, non-motorized vessel with a rattan shade; off-season, an uncovered boat is used. The Tourist Facilitation Centre can book tickets for the Kollam-Alleppey backwater cruise as well (Rs300). Western Travels (see p. 319) offers many varieties of cruise, including a 4hr. backwater cruise along some of the Alleppey-Kollam canals. (7am-6pm, Rs550.)

OTHER SIGHTS. It's worth wandering up to the landscaped grounds around the Tourist Facilitation Centre and the Kovalam Ashok Beach Resort, part of which is housed in the 250-year-old **castle** that was once the Maharaja's summer retreat. The views are gorgeous, and if you're lucky, no one will try to sell you anything. Stop to rest in the living room made of rock overlooking the sea. If, after spending too much time in Kovalam, you've forgotten that you're in India, take the 20min. stroll along the coastal road to the ramshackle village of **Vizhinjam** (VEER-in-yam). Only ruins of some small shrines remain in this former capital of the Ay Kings. Brightly painted fishing boats fill the harbor, crowned at the north end by a dizzying pink-and-yellow **mosque.** A magnificent view of the entire Kovalam scene—resorts to the right, Vizhinjam to the left, the sea stretching to infinity ahead—is available on the **Lighthouse Hill,** a short climb over rocks and through underbrush from the southern end of Lighthouse Beach.

KERALA

FESTIVALS

Kovalam's biggest to-do is **Gramam** (Jan. 14-23) when a Keralan village is recreated on Eve's Beach, complete with the traditional *nalukettu* (square house with courtyard), where an arts and crafts fair is held. Countless festivals celebrating various gods, goddesses, heroes, and imps (well, maybe not) occur practically every weekend in season. Get the program of events published annually in November from the Tourist Facilitation Center.

KOLLAM (QUILON) കൊല്ലം ☎0474

Kollam is one of the oldest ports on the Malabar Coast. Called "Kaulam" Mall by ancient Arabs, and "Coilum" by Marco Polo in the 13th century, the town was the center of the "heroic rebellion" against British rule led by Veluthambi Dalava. Today, the prosperous city is the center of the country's cashew trade, and its location on the sprawling Ashtamudi Lake makes it an excellent base for exploring the backwaters. Whether it's only for a few hours on a pole-boat village tour, or on the perennially popular full-day route to Alleppey, the backwater tours are not to be missed. Little remains from Kollam's glory days, as shopping malls and storefronts have largely obliterated palaces and temples, but it is worth staying a night or two in the lovely Government Guest House and sampling some cashews before hopping into a boat or heading to the coast.

TRANSPORTATION

Trains: The station is about 1km southeast of the center of town. Fares listed are sleeper class. To: **Alleppey** (1½hr., 7 per day 6:20am-10:20pm, Rs61); **Bangalore** (5hr., 10:40am, Rs189); **Chennai** (16hr., 3:30pm, Rs330); **Ernakulam** (3hr., every hr. 6:20am-12:05am, Rs81); **Kanyakumari** (4hr., 9:30am and 1:10pm, Rs80); **Mangalore** (14hr., 7:30am and 7:15pm, Rs145); **Trivandrum** (1½hr., every hr. 7:30am-8:30pm, Rs54).

Buses: KRSTC bus station, Jetty Rd. (☎2752008), north toward the river and the boat jetty. To: **Alleppey** (2hr., every 20min., Rs40); **Ernakulam** (3½hr., every 20min., Rs70); **Trivandrum** (1½hr., every 10min., Rs34); **Varkala** (1½hr., 7 per day 7:30am-6:40pm, Rs16). The 6:40pm Varkala bus usually scoops up most passengers disembarking the backwater cruise from Alleppey.

ORIENTATION AND PRACTICAL INFORMATION

Kollam's streets follow the bends of the canals and turn at confusing angles—try to pick up a map at a tourist office. **National Highway (NH) 47** runs southeast-northwest through town. Beginning in the southeast edge of town, NH47 passes the **railway station** before crossing the tracks to the congested center of town. At the junction of Chinnakkada, marked by the **clock tower,** it intersects with the nearly-parallel, southeast-northwest **Main Road.** Just beyond on the right is the large junction of NH47 with the wide northeast-southwest **Tourist Bungalow Road.** From there NH47 twists in a northern direction past the **post office,** and the sprawling **Bishop Jerome Nagar Shopping Centre,** before curving northwest again past the wild Shrine of Our Lady of Velankanni. The next junction is with **Jetty Road,** which leads to the right (northeast) to the **KSRTC bus station** and the **ferry jetty,** 100m away. A 10min. walk to the left (southwest) leads to the fruit and vegetable **market.**

Tourist Office: District Tourism Promotion Council (DTPC) has outposts at the railway station. Open M-Sa 9am-5pm. The bus station branch (☎2745625; open daily 9am-6pm) is especially helpful for backwater tour booking and hotel reservations.

Currency Exchange: State Bank of Travancore, in the Bishop Nagar Shopping Centre, changes currency and traveler's checks. Open M-F 10am-3:30pm, Sa 10am-12:30pm. Toward the jetty, **Bank of Baroda** does cash advances. Open M-F 9:45am-3:30pm, Sa 10am-12:30pm.

Police Station: (☎2742072). Turn right from the railway station, next to the large temple.

Pharmacy: Kochappally Medicals, Tourist Bungalow Rd. (☎2749286). Just southwest of the main intersection with NH47 and Main Rd. Open daily 8am-9:30pm.

Hospital: Nair's Hospital (☎2749411). 1.5km northeast of the jetty.

Internet: Net4you (☎2767450). 2nd fl. in the Bishop Jerome Nagar Shopping Centre. Six terminals, Rs20 per hr. Open daily 9am-8:30pm. **SilverNet,** on the ground floor, is not as posh but does the job. Rs20 per hr. Open M-Sa 9:45am-8:30pm.

Post Office: Head Post Office, NH47, northeast of the intersection with Tourist Bungalow Rd., on the left. Open M-Sa 7am-8pm. **Postal Code:** 691001.

ACCOMMODATIONS

The Tourist Bungalow (Government Guest House), Tourist Bungalow Rd. (☎2743620), a few km outside of town (rickshaw Rs25). This beautiful, old British mansion sports a huge, echoing ballroom hall and airy, pink-and-yellow rooms with 4m high ceilings. The antique furniture adds a romantic touch—come for a look around even if you can't get a room. Attached bathrooms (seat toilets). Only government officials can make reservations, but call ahead to see if there are rooms available. Singles and doubles Rs220. ❷

Yatri Nivas (☎2745538), on the lake opposite the boat jetty. Phone ahead for a pickup from the jetty in their speedboat (Rs20). Otherwise, hire a rickshaw (Rs10). Standard rooms in a stacked motel layout have attached baths and balconies with great views over the water. Singles Rs220; doubles Rs275. ❷

Hotel Sea Bee (☎2744696; hotelseabee@satyam.net.in), just off the intersection of Jetty Rd. and NH47. This mammoth, cookie-cutter hotel just 200m from the bus stand offers spic-and-span singles and spacious doubles with attached baths and cable TV. Check-out 24hr. Singles Rs200-250; doubles Rs400-450. ❷

Hotel Shah International (☎2742362), on Tourist Bungalow Rd. 100m from NH47. Convenient to rail arrivals, this impressive sloping structure provides giant rooms with balconies and attached bath, including seat toilets, towels, and soap. Peeling paint in the hallways rebukes initial impressions of grandeur, but so do the low prices. Singles Rs210; doubles Rs333. ❷

FOOD

Mysore Cafe, Jetty Rd., directly opposite the bus stand. Truck-stop feel and first-rate food. Delicious veg. meals (Rs15) for all who enter. Open 6am-11pm. ❶

Supreme Bakers, from the post office, turn right onto NH47, then take an immediate right; it's on the left. Sumptuously laid-out cakes, fresh breads, and pastries for a mere Rs4-22. Cold drinks and A/C offer relief from the heat. Open M-Sa 9am-8pm. ❶

👁 🎵 SIGHTS AND ENTERTAINMENT

The highlight of Kollam's calendar is the **Ashtamudi Craft and Art Festival** in late December and early January (Dec. 26-Jan. 7), when craftsmen from all over India come to demonstrate their skills. There are also demonstrations of traditional dance and music.

BACKWATER CRUISES

Backwater cruises depart at 10:30am from the DTPC office near the KSRTC bus stand and the boat jetty, and arrive in Alleppey at 6:30pm. Report to the office by 10am. Rs300, Rs100 for ISIC holders. Village tour departures daily from KDTC 9am and 2pm; 3hr.; Rs300, Rs50 discount for students and seniors. Book online at www.dptc-quilontourism.com or by contacting the DTPC directly. Prices start at Rs1000-8000 for two people for the 24hr. Kollam-Alleppey Starnight Cruise (Nov.-Jan.).

The backwater cruises to Alleppey are the main attraction in Kollam. The boat can take both you and your luggage, making this a convenient and beautiful mode of transport north up the Keralan coast. Many of the cruises make several stops along the way, including one at the Mata Amrithanandamayi Ashram (see below). Cruises are run by the District Tourism Promotion Council (DTPC); though others offer similar service, discounts are available by booking through the DTPC. (For more information, see p. 327.) The KDTC office at the bus station organizes additional backwater tours, including a justifiably popular 4hr. **village tour** that winds through barely 3m wide canals, prawn farms, and fishing communities in Manroe Island in a traditional wooden boat. This tour offers an up-close examination of traditional Keralan village life. Professions are few and divided by gender; the men make boats and dive for mussels, while the women produce coconut-husk rope. There is also a range of cheap **houseboat tours.**

MATA AMRITHANANDAMAYI ASHRAM

☎ 0476 897578 or 897678. Rs250-1000 per day in a room with attached bath and 1 or 2 roommates; meals included.

Backwater cruises frequently stop to pick up and drop off passengers at the ashram of one of India's few female gurus, Mata Amrithanandamayi, usually known as Amma, the Hugging Mother. Particularly popular with Westerners, the ashram houses hundreds of residents and visitors in pink skyscrapers that look somewhat incongruous against the surrounding backwaters. There are many amenities at the ashram including a general store, a hospital, an Ayurvedic massage center, and 24hr. STD/ISD phones. Ask in Alleppey or Kollam, or call the ashram to see if Amma is in residence and not on tour. The backwater cruise boats honor partially-used tickets—a single ticket will take you from Kollam to the ashram and, a few days later, on to Alleppey (or vice versa).

SHRINE OF OUR LADY OF VELANKANNI

NH47, near Jetty Rd., across from Hotel Sea Bee. Mass W 8am and noon; 5pm mass usually in Malayalam.

This towering, pink, polygonal shrine, visible on the horizon from the south end of town, pales slightly when examined close-up. The altar, festooned with bright plastic flowers and housing a silver-sequin-caped Mother and Babe icon, occupies a central place in Kollam's religious life. Although a mere 15 years old, the shrine has already gained a reputation for healing and performing miracles. On Wednesdays, crowds line up inside, fingering rosaries and praying for hours.

VARKALA ☎ 0470

Varkala's quiet beach and towering cliffs just might rescue South India's reputation for over-commercialized coastal resort-towns. Though the beach-side businesses and hotels have developed more of an affinity for tourist dollars of late, the distance between town and seashore still ensures a measure of the beauty and tranquility for which Kovalam was once famed.

⌐ TRANSPORTATION. Buses stop at the temple junction, a short walk from the beach. To: **Kollam** (1-2hr., 6-7 per day 8am-5pm, Rs25) and **Trivandrum** (1½hr., 5 per day 6am-6:30pm, Rs25.50). A direct bus heads to **Kovalam** (2hr., 4:30pm, Rs20) from **Trivandrum. Trains** are faster and more reliable, if less conveniently located; the **railway station** is a couple of kilometers from the temple junction (auto-rickshaw ride Rs15-20). Trains run to: **Kollam** (40min., 7 per day 7:32am-6:48pm, Rs21) and **Trivandrum** (1hr., 7 per day 4:10am-9pm, Rs25).

🔃 PRACTICAL INFORMATION. Venus Travels/JK Tours and Travels, located opposite the temple staircase at the temple junction, has train and bus schedules, books backwater cruises, and **exchanges currency.** (☎2600164. Open daily 8am-9:30pm.) The same office offers **Internet** facilities (Rs50 per hr). Email at the Seaview Restaurant is available 24hr. (Rs40 per hr.) The tiny Janardhanapuram **post office** is at the temple junction. (Open M-Sa 10am-2pm.) Varkala's Head Post Office is on Maidan Rd., in town. (Open M-Sa 8am-5pm.) **Postal Code:** 695141.

🍴🛏 ACCOMMODATIONS AND FOOD. The cliff-top overlooking the beach is crowded with hotels; follow Beach Rd. west and head north uphill for a sweaty 15min., or take a more circuitous rickshaw route from the temple junction (Rs15-20). Views usually cost money in Varkala, so wander inland if your budget is tight. Turn east from the cliff road at the Virgin Vegetarian Restaurant or take a bumpy rickshaw ride to find the pleasant **Greenhouse ❶.** Look for the purple walls with the name painted sporadically along several buildings. Not many plants here, despite the name, but the big, clean rooms with attached baths are just in from the cliff. (☎2604659. Doubles Rs100-125, with attached bath Rs250; off-season Rs150.) The **Clafouti Bakery ❷,** lets rooms and bungalows at the north end of the cliff, and their bakery-cum-restaurant (see below) overlooking the ocean provides a tranquil spot for pastry-munching. Slightly inland rooms with bath are larger, cleaner, and pricier than the pleasantly self-contained bungalows. (☎2601414. Rs250-500; off-season Rs100-200). On the cliff, the aptly named **Seaview Restaurant and Cliff House ❸,** has views of the sea. (☎2602050. Doubles Rs450-800; off-season Rs200.)

Varkala's restaurants, which open early and close late, have lengthy menus featuring everything from hash browns to *pad thai.* 🍴 **Clafouti Bakery ❶,** specializes in delicious muffins of various flavors (Rs15-35), brownies (Rs20), and assorted fresh breads, as well as the usual array of eggs, *dosas,* rice, and noodles. The idyllic location on the edge of the cliff makes it all taste that much better. (Open daily 8am-midnight.) At the south end of the cliff the popular **Sunset Restaurant ❸,** does several *prix fixe* breakfasts (Continental Rs60, God's Own Country Rs70, American Rs80) to save you the arduous task of choosing individual items a la carte. Extensive lunch and dinner menus make your job slightly harder, but worthwhile. (Entrees Rs25-150. Open daily from 7:30am-midnight.)

📷🎭 SIGHTS AND ENTERTAINMENT. The town's only real **beach,** Papanasham, lies at the base of a cliff that shoulders the burden of most of Varkala's tourist infrastructure. From the cliff, steep narrow paths pick their way down to the sand. There are dangerous riptides; always swim near the lifeguard and ask about conditions. The cliff-top **path** winds north for quite a distance, with superb views of the rocky coastline.

KERALA

Beach Rd. leads west from the **Sree Janardhana Swami Temple,** a Hindu pilgrimage site—one of the seven most important Vaishnavite shrines in India. The temple was built around what is now a massive ficus tree, and although non-Hindus are prohibited from entering, it's still worth hiking up the short staircase for the external view. From the beach, rickety bridges lead up the cliff to the **Kerala Kathakali Centre,** which stages **kathakali dance** performances. (Daily shows. Make-up 5pm, show 6:30pm. Rs100-150.) Operations all along the beach specialize in Ayurvedic treatments and assorted curative programs. Other places on the cliff-top north of the beach, including the **Scientific School of Yoga and Massage** (1¾hr. massage Rs400), promise a combination of spiritual and physical rejuvenation, and offer yoga classes (Rs100 per class, Rs1000 per 14-class course).

ALLEPPEY (ALAPPUZHA) ആലപ്പുഴ ☎0477

The two main canals that run through Alleppey were once the major arteries of a great shipping center. Today, however, tangles of water lilies fill the waterways, and most of the town's activity revolves around all the local *coir* (woven coconut fiber) trade. Partly because of its fading economic importance, Alleppey itself offers very little to see and do. Instead, it serves travelers mainly as an embarkation point for the justifiably popular Alleppey-Kollam backwater cruises. Unless you're here during the second Saturday in August, when the town's snake-boats (traditional Keralite battle vessels) compete in the annual Nehru Trophy Boat Race, you'll probably want to hop on a boat and float away as soon as possible.

█ TRANSPORTATION. The **railway station** is near the beach, 4km southwest of the town center. Trains go to **Ernakulam** (1-1½hr., 8 per day 6am-7pm, Rs14) and **Trivandrum** (3hr., 4 per day, 7:20am-12:45am, Rs42). An **auto-rickshaw** from the train station to the boat jetty or bus station will cost you Rs25. Privately operated **local buses** leave from the street directly opposite the most eastern footbridge over the North Canal to the train station (Rs4). The **KSRTC bus station** is at the east end of **Boat Jetty Road,** which runs along the south bank of North Canal. (Inquiries ☎2252501.) Buses go to: **Cochin** (1½hr., every 20min., Rs27); **Kollam** (2hr., every 20min., Rs47); **Trivandrum** (4hr., every 30min., Rs78). Buses run from Kottayam to **Kumily** and **Periyar** (3hr., Rs44). Public and private **boats** leave from the **jetties** 200m west of the bus station, just before the Mullackal Rd., the large street that bridges the North Canal. Boats to **Kollam** (8hr., daily 10:30am, Rs300).

█ ▐ ORIENTATION AND PRACTICAL INFORMATION. The town is sandwiched between two east-west canals: the **North Canal** and the **South Canal,** about a 10min. walk apart. The streets between the two canals are laid out in a grid. The **bus station** is at the east end of the North Canal; boat jetties are farther west, near the **DTPC** office. **Mullackal Road** runs north-south, bridging the North Canal at the western edge of the boat jetties.

The helpful **District Tourism Promotion Council (DTPC),** on Boat Jetty Rd. (☎2251211), next to the boat jetties, sells tickets for boat rides (Rs300) and the Nehru Trophy Boat Race. (Open M-Sa 9am-6pm.) To get to the equally helpful **ATDC Tourist Office** (☎2243462), take Mullackal Rd. north, turn right immediately after crossing the canal, and then turn left; the office will be on your left. (Open daily 8am-8pm.) **Canara Bank,** across from the DTPC on the south bank of the North Canal, gives cash advances on MC and V and cashes traveler's checks. (Open M-F 10am-2pm and 2:30-3pm, Sa 10am-1pm.) A **market** lines Mullackal Rd., both north and south of North Canal. To get to **Medical College Hospital** (☎2251611), head south along the road one block west of Mullackal Rd., continue south across the Iron Bridge and the South Canal, and take the third left after the canal. **Haifa Medicals** is just south of the North

Canal on Mullackal Rd. (Open daily 8:30am-9pm.) Take the street opposite the foot-bridge to **Cyber Graphix** for Internet access. (Open 9am-9pm. Rs30 per hr.) Just past Cyber Graphix, you'll spot **N&G Communications,** with three terminals. (Open 11:30am-11pm. Rs25 per hr.) Take Mullackal Rd. south until it ends at the South Canal, then turn right to reach a branch of the **post office.** (Open M-Sa 9am-5pm.) For the **Head Post Office,** continue to the west and take the second right on Exchange Rd. (Open M-Sa 9:30am-5:30pm.) **Postal Code: 688001.**

ACCOMMODATIONS AND FOOD. Hotels line Boat Jetty Rd., the stretch of road that runs west from the bus station along the North Canal. **Hotel Raiban Annexe ❶,** just east of the boat jetty and 400m west of the bus station, is in a quiet courtyard complex off the road, and the price is right. (☎ 2261017. Attached baths, some with squat toilets, some with seat toilets. Singles Rs108; doubles Rs172-440.) The **Arcadia Hotel ❷,** just west of the bus station, has a good location but is a bit more costly than other spots. It offers comfortable rooms with seat toilets and a popular restaurant and bar. (☎ 2251354. Doubles Rs300-750.) **Mutteal Holiday Inn ❸,** Nehru Trophy Rd., on the northern side of North Canal and east of the footbridge, has double rooms and private, quiet rooms which surround a garden; each room has its own patio. (☎ 2242365. Doubles Rs300.) The **Karthika Tourist Home ❶,** 50m north over the North Canal traffic bridge, has great prices for plain rooms. Attached baths with squat toilets. (☎ 2245524. Singles Rs80; doubles Rs150.)

Hotel Annapoorna ❶, Boat Jetty Rd., across from the boat jetty, next to Hotel Raiban Annexe, serves standard South Indian veg. fare in a roadside diner atmo-sphere. *Thalis* Rs16-22, *masala dosa* Rs12. (Open daily 7:30am-10:30pm. Meals noon-2:45pm.) **Cafe Venice ❷,** next to the DPTC, is named for its location overlook-ing the picturesque, fetid canal. For a giant, tasty lunch, ask for the Kerala meal (Rs30). Cafe Venice is also a convenient breakfast stop for departing backwater trippers. (☎ 2254256. Open daily 8am-9:30pm.) Ruffle-clad waiters at the **Indian Coffee House ❶,** Mullackal Rd., a few blocks south of the North Canal, serve the stan-dard snacks and coffee. (☎ 2253862. Open daily 8am-9pm.) **Bakeries** line Boat Jetty Rd. Most of Alleppey's hotels also have restaurants.

SIGHTS AND ENTERTAINMENT. The highlight of Alleppey's tourist calen-dar is the annual **Nehru Trophy Boat Race,** which finds hundreds of oarsmen rowing 65m-long snake-boats. The first race was held in honor of Prime Minister Jawaha-rlal Nehru during his visit here in 1952. Nehru was so flattered and fascinated by the race that he awarded the winners a trophy; the event soon developed into an Alleppey institution. (Tickets are available from the ATDC and DTPC and may be pur-chased up to one week in advance or on the day. Rs50-1000.) Other races are held throughout the year, including the **Moolam Boat Race** at Champakulam in July. The ATDC runs boat rides to the race (Rs100 round-trip).

BACKWATER TRIPS. Daily **backwater cruises** run the 80km of green canals that separate Alleppey from Kollam. From the boat, you can see an 11th-century statue of the Buddha, temples, churches, *coir*-producing villages, and an ashram. A traditional Keralite meal is served on a banana leaf for lunch (Rs20-30) and drinks are sold aboard the boats. The ATDC and DTPC both operate cruises. (10:30am departure, 6:30pm arrival; tours operate in both directions. Make reser-vations one day in advance or on the day, before 10am. During June and July, trips with fewer than 10 people will be canceled. Both the ATDC and DTPC charge Rs300 and give a Rs50 discount to children under 12. If you decide to stop for a few days at the ashram, your ticket will be honored whenever you resume your jour-ney.) The ATDC, DTPC, and private agencies along Boat Jetty Rd., including **Penguin Tourist Service** (☎ 2261522. Open daily 8am-6pm.), west of Mullackal Rd., arrange shorter trips around Alleppey's rice fields and Kuttanad.

Private agencies, including Penguin Tourist Service, also arrange stays on traditional cargo boats—converted **houseboats** with tiny bedrooms, bathrooms, dining areas, and two fellows to pilot the boat. (Rs5000 for 2 people for 24hr.; Rs7500 for 4 people.) The budget backwater cruise is the public **ferry ride** to and from Kottayam (3hr., 4-5 per day 7am-5:30pm, Rs15). Most Kottayam ferries stick to the wide canals, but those going to Nedumudi (2hr., frequent, Rs5) and Changanssherry (3hr., 4:45pm, Rs15), cruise along the narrow canals and capture more local flavor. (From Kottayam a 2:30pm ferry goes to Munnar; get off at Nedumudi and catch a local bus for the 30min. ride to Alleppey.)

PERIYAR TIGER RESERVE AND KUMILY

☎ 0486

The misty forest highlands of Periyar Tiger Reserve shelter herds of wild boar and elephants, 140 species of orchid, a turtle-friendly lake, countless birds, and a few predatory tigers. Set aside as reserved forests in 1899, these woods on the edge of Tamil Nadu became the Nellikkampatty Sanctuary in 1934 and were incorporated into Project Tiger in 1979 (see p. 367). Tigers are elusive, but a twilight boat cruise usually turns up herds of wild elephants munching grass or taking a dip in the lake.

Surrounded by spice plantations, Kumily, where most tourists stay, is suffused with the sweet smells of cardamom, cinnamon, cloves, and nutmeg. The town's religious fervor makes it a lively contrast to Thekkady, the cluster of hotels within the park; the mosque and temple keep up a steady stream of chanting, singing, and bell-tolling, which is blasted all over town by a network of loudspeakers; don't plan on sleeping late.

▐ TRANSPORTATION

Buses: Both private and state buses operate out of **Kumily Bus Stand** at the northern edge of town. From Kumily to: **Ernakulam** (6hr., 10 per day 3:10am-11:45pm, Rs74); **Kottayam** (4hr., every 30min., Rs44); **Munnar** (5hr., 1:30pm, Rs55.50); **Thekkady** (15min., 4 per day noon-9:50pm, Rs3). A **Tamil Nadu Bus Stand** a bit farther north sends buses to **Madurai** (4hr., every 15min., Rs38.50). From Thekkady to: **Ernakulam** (6:30am and 2:30pm, Rs75); **Theni**, for transferring to other Tamil Nadu destinations (every 30min. 6am-7pm, Rs50); **Trivandrum** (8hr., 4 per day 8am-8:30pm, Rs150).

Local Transportation: Taxis, jeeps, and **auto-rickshaws** to the boat jetty in Periyar (Rs40-100) are available from the Kumily bus stand. A **park bus** runs between the bus stand in Kumily and the Periyar boat landing about every 30min., but waits for a full bus (first bus from Kumily 8:30am; last bus to Kumily waits for the boat tour at 6pm; Rs10). Any bus to Kottayam can drop you at the Spring Valley Spice Garden for a truly budget tour (Rs50).

▐ ORIENTATION AND PRACTICAL INFORMATION

Periyar's borders contain the reserve, a boat dock, information office, and a few expensive hotels that form the hamlet of **Thekkady.** Most tourists stay in **Kumily,** the town that lies on the northwest border of the park. The cheap hotels are along **Thekkady Road,** which runs from the Kumily bus station on the border of Tamil Nadu to the Thekkady boat jetty (bearing left at the fork and right at Hotel Ambadi). The entrance to the reserve is about 1.5km from the bus stand; it's another 3km to the boat jetty. Walking through the park is permitted as long as you stay on the road, but you may not enter the forest without a guide. **Unless otherwise noted, the following listings are for Kumily.**

Tourist Office: When you step off the bus in town, grab a map and some friendly advice from the **tourist police** booth at the station. Open daily 8am-6:30pm. For more detailed info, visit the larger **Idukki District Tourism Information Office, Dept. of Tourism Govt. of Kerala** (☎9322620), 10min. from the bus station toward the reserve. It's on the left, away from the road, up the stairs in a yellow bldg. Arranges various private tours of local spice plantations (2-3hr., Rs450-600 for 2-3 people). Open M-Sa 10am-5pm. **Rickshaw drivers** also offer tours of spice plantations; it should cost Rs300-450 for 3hr. For information on activities in Periyar, see the **Wildlife Information Centre** (☎9322028) at the boat jetty in Thekkady. Open daily 6:30am-6pm.

Currency Exchange: The State Bank of Travancore, behind the bus station, exchanges foreign currency and traveler's checks. Open M-F 10am-3:30pm, Sa 10am-12:30pm.

Bookstore: DC Books (☎9322548), a bit beyond the tourist office on the left. Lovely collection of fiction and literature. Open daily 9:30am-9:30pm.

Police: (☎9322049). Past the bus station toward the border. **Tourist Police Office,** at the bus station and also on Thekkady Rd. Open daily 8am-6:30pm.

Pharmacy: High Range Drug House (☎9322043). About 5min. away from the bus stand toward the reserve. Open M-Sa 9am-8:30pm.

Hospital: St. Augustine Hospital, Spring Valley (☎9322042). 3km from the town center. Take a rickshaw (Rs35) or any bus toward Kottayam. The smaller **Kumily Central Hospital** (☎9322045) is on the road to the reserve.

Internet: Rissas Communication, Thekkady Rd. (☎9322752), on the left at the fork toward Thekkady. Open 8am-11:30pm. Rs60 per hr.

Post Office: Next to the Kerala bus stand. Open M-Sa 9am-5pm. **Postal Code:** 685509. There is also a Thekkady branch at the park entrance. Open M-Sa 9am-5pm. **Postal Code:** 685536.

ACCOMMODATIONS

There are only three hotels inside the reserve, all run by the KTDC. Expect to pay high prices and be locked in at 6pm every night. Stay in Kumily for cheaper and less restrictive accommodations.

Hotel Regent Tower, Thekkady Rd. (☎9322570), fifty meters from the bus stand on the left. Big rooms with tree-trunk coffee tables and access to balconies overlooking the bus station, the music-broadcasting temple, and the mountains. Attached baths with seat toilets, some with bathtubs. Buckets of hot water. Soap and towels included. Singles Rs150; doubles Rs200-450. ❷

Coffee Inn/Wild Huts (coffeeinn@satyam.net.in). Reception is in the Coffee Inn, 500m before the park entrance, and offers 12 rooms (6 with attached bath, 6 with common bath) set around a lovingly maintained spice-and-flower garden. A common observation tower overlooks part of the wildlife refuge. Singles Rs100; doubles Rs200-400. ❶

Hotel Ambadi (☎9322193), one kilometer from the bus stand. Carved wooden doors, balconies, shiny fixtures, and countless amenities tip you off to the price. Worth it for the luxury and relative proximity to the park entrance. Attached baths with towels and toilet paper. Check-out noon. Cottages Rs1075; rooms Rs1400-1935. MC/V. ❺

Hotel Revathy International, Thekkady Rd. (☎9322434). This seven-story building 70m from the bus station offers small, tidy rooms with TV and attached bath. Check-out noon. Singles Rs268; doubles Rs484-753. ❷

Rissas Rooms (☎9311402). Enquire at Rissas Communications (see **Internet,** above). A family runs these 4 spacious rooms with attached or private bath in their home off the main road. Campfire facilities and horseback riding (Rs100 per 30min.) available. Rooms Rs150 per person. ❷

KERALA

Periyar House (☎9322026), 2km inside the reserve. The cheapest option within the park. High-ceilinged rooms with attached baths, seat toilets, and blue carpeting in the deluxe rooms. Breakfast and dinner included. No check-in (or leaving the bldg.) after 6pm. Singles Rs911; doubles Rs1083-1620. MC/V. ❺

 FOOD

Coffee Inn, 500m before the park entrance. Try teas from cardamom to hibiscus (Rs10-15) in this pleasant garden patio shop. Newspapers and magazines available on request; nice view of the surrounding hills complimentary. Live *tabla* performances Nov.-Jan., M-F 6:15-7:15pm. Open 7am-9:30pm. ❶

Hotel Lake Shore (☎9322302), opposite Rissas Communications. Artificial plants and flower-print curtains give color to this non-veg. family restaurant. Generous and tasty Kerala *thalis* Rs40. Most entrees Rs25-75. Open 6:30am-10pm. ❶

Hotel Ambadi Restaurant, in the hotel of the same name. Offers all the standards and many variations (Rs25-140). Check out the encouragingly multi-religious wall decor. The "Kerala meal" (Rs25) is delicious. Open daily 6:30am-10:30pm. ❶

Hotel Maharani, on the 1st fl. of the Regent Tower Hotel, packs them in for the midday Keralite meal (Rs20; with an excellent fish curry Rs32). Speedy service, solid eats. Egg breakfasts Rs15-25. Open daily 7am-10pm. ❶

Cafe Periyarenis, near the Thekkady jetty. Run by the park staff cooperative society, Periyarenis, a food stand, is the only non-hotel food option in the reserve. Snacks, drinks in biodegradable containers, and *dosas* (Rs10) served beside the Periyar River. Internet Rs60 per hr. Open daily 7:30am-5:30pm. ❶

THE RESERVE

Open daily 6am-6pm. Rs50 per multiple-entry day. KDTC Boat Tours (7, 9:30, 11:30am, 2, and 4pm; Rs100 top deck, Rs50 lower deck). Park boats (9:30, 11:30am, 2, and 4pm; Rs15). Boat rides last 2hr. Purchase tickets at Wildlife Information Centre for their smaller, cheaper boats, or at the KTDC ticket booth at the boat jetty, just up the stairs toward Aranya Nivas. Only same-day advance bookings. If a boat cruise is sold out, inquire about extra tickets at the reception desk of the Aranya Nivas Hotel, up the steps behind the jetty. Also available: Group jungle walks (3hr., 7am, 11am, and 2pm, Rs70); special trekking (3hr., depending on availability of tribal guides, Rs260); elephant rides (30min., every 30min. 11am-5pm, Rs30). Book jungle walks and elephant rides at the Wildlife Information Center; special treks can be booked at the Forest Range Office or the Wildlife Information Center.

The reserve is home to a wide variety of animals, including wild boar, monkeys, the Nilgiri Langur, Malabar giant squirrels, barking deer, and gaur. Most people, however, come to Periyar to see its main attractions: wild elephants and rarely-spotted tigers. Periyar claims to be home to at least 46 of the world's 3700 remaining wild tigers, but you would have to be very lucky to see a tiger. At a cool and breezy 900m above sea level, Periyar is a good place to relax, take a leisurely boat cruise, and watch herds of wild elephants bathe. September to March is the best time to visit; January through April are the dry months, when animals come down to the lake to drink. During the monsoon, come prepared to encounter leeches.

 WARNING. So-called "official" guides often approach tourists with offers of jungle walks and jeep tours. Contracting them is illegal, and you may be fined.

The two main ways of exploring the reserve are by **boat tour** and 🚶**trekking**. Early morning and evening are the best times to see the animals. Jungle-walking groups allow you the closest look you'll get at the park's flora and fauna. During the morning trek you might startle herds of wild boar or catch elephants eating their breakfasts. Regardless of the fauna sightings, the flora is gorgeous and untainted by the usual roadside garbage—taking a trek is worth it if only for the infectious tranquility of the forest. To get the most out of your Rs50 daily entrance fee, take the morning jungle walk and the tranquil late-afternoon cruise. If you want more variety, some of the fancier hotels—including the KTDC hotels in the park and Hotel Ambadi—have government permission to lead jungle treks. The Wildlife Information Center can also organize additional walks for small groups. On both the walk and the boat rides, you are likely to see elephants, herds of boar, and tons of birds.

Elephant rides are purely for entertainment, so you probably won't see very much. One of the best ways to see the wildlife is to spend a night in one of two observation towers. The Wildlife Information Centre handles the necessary reservations. The tower houses two people (minimum *and* maximum), who must provide their own food, water, and bedding. The center will arrange transportation by boat (Rs50 per person, park boat fee Rs15). Try to reserve in advance, as demand can be high for these coveted spots.

COCHIN (KOCHI) കൊാമ്പി ☎ 0484

The pungent scent of fresh pepper has lured explorers to Cochin from as far away as King Solomon's Israel, ancient Rome, Kublai Khan's pleasure dome, and colony-hungry Portugal, Holland, and England. Cochin's magnificent eclecticism is legendary: Chinese fishing nets line the harbor's mouth, Dutch-style houses cram narrow streets, and sacks of spices fill the air with the same evocative smells that intoxicated merchants and journeymen. Across the water from Fort Cochin, Ernakulam plays the part of the modern alter-ego; its frantic, brash streets contrast with the slow, vaguely Mediterranean quality of Cochin.

KERALA

▐ TRANSPORTATION

Flights: Airport, 30km northeast of the city. Taxis run from here to Ernakulam (Rs300-350) and Fort Cochin (Rs450-500). From the Indian Airlines office in town, a private shuttle transports passengers to the airport (Rs125). **Air India,** MG Rd. (☎2351260), north of Thomas Cook. Open M-F 9:30am-1pm and 2-5pm, Sa 9:30am-1pm. **Indian Airlines,** DH Rd., Ernakulam (☎2371141), near the Foreshore Rd. intersection. Open daily 9:45am-1pm and 1:45-5:20pm. **Jet Airways,** MG Rd. (☎2293231), across the street and just south of Thomas Cook. Open M-Sa 9am-5:30pm, Su 9am-4pm. To: **Bangalore** (1hr., 8am, US$90); **Chennai** (1hr., 2:40pm, US$130); **Delhi** (4hr., 8:30am, US$335); **Mumbai** (2hr., 3 per day 1:30-3:35pm, US$160).

Trains: Cochin has 3 stations. **Ernakulam Junction Railway Station,** 2 blocks east of Jos Junction, handles most traffic (24hr. inquiries ☎2375131). To: **Alleppey** (1½hr., 7 per day 6:15am-11:50pm, Rs39); **Delhi** (59hr., 4 per day noon-midnight, Rs569); **Hyderabad** (26hr., 10:10am, Rs401); **Mumbai** (26hr., 1:30 and 2:50pm, Rs441); **Trivandrum** (4½hr., 6 per day 5:50am-5:15pm, Rs95). **Ernakulam Town Railway Station,** 2km north of the Junction Station along Banerji Rd., is far from MG Rd. Sleeper class to: **Bangalore** (13hr., 2:35pm, Rs261); **Calicut** (4½hr., 4-5 per day 10:55am-2:10am, Rs83); **Chennai** (13hr., 7:10pm and midnight, Rs221); **Kanyakumari** (15hr., 6 and 9:15am, Rs120). **Cochin Harbour Railway Station,** on Willingdon Island, is serviced by few trains.

Buses: KSRTC Bus Stand (☎2372033), central Ernakulam, 2 blocks east of Shenoys Junction. Reservations 9am-1pm and 2-5pm. To: **Alleppey** (1½hr., every 30min., Rs30); **Bangalore** (14hr., 4 per day 6am-9:30pm, Rs242); **Calicut** (5hr., 3:20pm, Rs98) via **Coimbatore** (4½hr., Rs91); **Kollam** (3½hr., every 30min., Rs70); **Madurai** (10hr., 7:45pm, Rs140); **Mangalore** (10hr., 6:30pm, Rs212); **Munnar** (5hr.; 6, 6:30am, noon; Rs51); **Mysore** (10hr., 3 per day 6am-9:30pm, Rs192); **Trivandrum** (5hr., frequent, Rs102). **Tamil Nadu State Transportation** services, around the corner from the main KSRTC enquiry desk services, has buses to **Chennai** (15hr., 2pm, Rs310) and **Madurai** (10hr., 8:15am, Rs144) via **Kumily** (6hr., Rs100). Private bus companies also run long-distance buses from several terminals in Cochin: **Ernakulam South,** opposite the Ernakulam Junction Railway Station, and **High Court Junction,** at the end of Shanmugham Rd. Several agencies have offices around Jos Junction, Ernakulam. *Hello Cochin* lists departure times.

Ferries: Water transport is the most scenic—and often only—way to move from one island to another. Ferries are cheap (usually around Rs2.50), generally run 5:50am-9:30pm, and hop between islands along a variety of routes. Vypeen Island is the center of water traffic and ferries go to and from this jetty frequently. Routes from **Ernakulam: Main Jetty** are listed below. To: **Embarkation Jetty,** Willingdon Island (frequent 6am-9:50pm, Rs2); **Fort Cochin** (frequent 6am-noon and 1-9:50pm; buy tickets at the SWTD counter); **Mattancherry Jetty** (9 per day 6am-6:30pm, Rs3.50); **Vypeen Island** (frequent 5am-10pm, Rs2).

Other Local Transportation: Local buses are generally under Rs6. In Ernakulam, local buses leave the KRSTC bus station and can also be boarded throughout town. Buses to Ft. Cochin leave from the east side of MG Rd., just south of Jos Junction (last bus 9pm, Rs5.50). In Ft. Cochin, local buses run from the bus stand (opposite the Vypeen Island jetty), over the bridge to Willingdon Island, past the airport, across the bridge to Ernakulam, and up MG Rd. In Ernakulam, **auto-rickshaws** are plentiful. Most in-town auto-rickshaw fares should be under Rs20. For rickshaws from Ernakulam to Fort Cochin you will be charged round-trip fare for a one-way trip (at least Rs80; twice that after dark). **Bike** rentals are available from the **Vasco Hospitality Center** (Rs5 per hr., Rs35 per day).

ORIENTATION

Wider Cochin consists of a bunch of islands around **Lake Vembanad** and the mainland city of **Ernakulam. Fort Cochin** and **Mattancherry** occupy a peninsula that juts into the Arabian Sea; nearby islands include **Vypeen Island** and the smaller islands of Willingdon, Vallarpadam, Gundy, and Bolghatty. The central railway, bus stations, and many hotels are in Ernakulam, but tourists generally devote their waking hours (if not their whole stay) to Fort Cochin and the peninsula.

Ernakulam's three main streets, **Shanmugham, Mahatma Gandhi (MG),** and **Chittoor Road,** run north-south, parallel to the shore. Three major cross-streets intersect MG Rd. and lead to the lakeshore: **Convent Road** intersects at **Shenoys Junction,** a couple of blocks west of the **central bus station;** three blocks south of Shenoys Junction, **Hospital Road** runs to the lake-front; farther south, **Jos Junction** marks the intersection with **Durbar Hall (DH) Road.** The **Main Jetty** is midway between **Press Club Road** and **Hospital Road.**

The north-south **Princess Street** is Fort Cochin's main drag. It begins at **Calvathy Road** (called River Rd. in the west and Bazaar Rd. in the east), which curves along the shoreline. **Mattancherry, Jew Town,** and the Dutch Palace, are south of Fort Cochin, on the eastern side of the peninsula. In the early 20th century, a mammoth dredging project created **Willingdon Island,** sandwiched between Ernakulam and the peninsula.

KERALA

TO AIRPORT (30km)

Azad Rd.

KP Vallon Rd.

Cochin

▲ ACCOMMODATIONS
Basoto Lodge, **1**
Hotel Aiswarya, **7**
Hotel Luciya, **3**

◆ FOOD
Bimbi's, **5**
Chinese Garden, **9**
Hot Breads, **10**
Ice Magic, **8**

ERNAKULAM

Ernakulam Town Railway Station

Ernakulam Junction Railway Station

Paramhithara Rd.

Veekshanam Rd.

KSRTC Bus Stand

Amman Kovil Rd.

Chittoor Rd.

Ernakulam South Bus Stand

Warriam Rd. (Sahodaran Ayappan Rd.)

Mankathi Rd.

Banerji Rd.

Jews St

Mahatma Gandhi Rd.

Buses to Fort Cochin

Bank of Baroda

Medical Trust Hospital

TD Rd.

Gopalaprabhu Rd.

Press Club Rd.

Convent Rd.

Durbar Hall Rd.

JOS JUNCTION

Church Landing Rd.

Air India

Rayuram Rd.

Market Rd.

GPO

Hospital Rd.

Park Ave.

Foreshore Rd.

Broadway

Sealord Hotel

State Bank of India

Tourist Desk

Shanmugham Rd.

KTDC Tourist Reception Center

Main Jetty

High Court Junction Bus Station

Police Commissioner's Office

Marine Dr. Walkway

Sealord Jetty

High Court Jetties

Mathai Manjooran Rd.

Bolghatty Island

Lake Vembanad

Vypeen Island Jetty

Customs Jetty

Taj Malabar Hotel Embarkation Jetty

Milne Rd.

ITDC

Malabar Hotel Jetty

Indira Gandhi Rd.

Mattancherry Terminus Jetty

Cochin Harbour Railway Station

Bristow Rd.

Willingdon Island

Gundy Island

Vypeen Island

Arabian Sea

Calvathy Rd.

Mohamed Rd

Bastian St.

Fosse St.

Ridsdel Rd

Nadar St.

TM Jacob Rd

Bazaar Rd.

Dutch Palace

Pardesi Synagogue

Mattancherry Jetty

Nehru Memorial Town Hall

Padinara Mosque

Jain Temple

Palace Rd.

Santo Gopalan Rd.

Moulana Azad Rd.

MATTANCHERRY

TO GANTHAM HOSPITAL (3km)

FORT COCHIN

SEE FORT COCHIN MAP

Beach Rd.

N

300 yards

300 meters

● SITES AND SERVICES
Chavara Cultural Centre, **4**
Cochin Cultural Center, **13**
Current Books, **2**
Indian Airlines, **6**
Indo World Tours & Travel, **16**
Jet Airways, **15**
Kerala Ayurveda Pharmacy, **11**
See India Foundation, **12**
Thomas Cook, **14**

ⓘ PRACTICAL INFORMATION

Tourist Office: There is a privately run **Tourist Desk** in Ernakulam (☎2371761), at the dock-side ticket office of the Main Jetty. For information on their **Backwater Cruises,** see p. 331. Open daily 8am-6:30pm. **KTDC Tourist Reception Centre,** Shanmugham Rd., Ernakulam (☎2353234), next to the State Bank of India, just northwest of the end of Press Club Rd., offers backwater tours. Open daily 8am-7pm. There are a number of private tourist offices in and around Princess St., Ft. Cochin, including the helpful **Vasco Information Centre** (☎2216262), which distributes the informative map and brochure *Walking Through Ft. Cochin.* Open daily 9:30am-8pm.

Budget Travel: Indo World Tours and Travels, MG Rd. (☎2370127). At the intersection with Ravipuram Rd. in Ernakulam. Arranges backwater tours (Rs300-800), trips throughout Kerala, and wildlife tours. Open M-Sa 8am-8pm, Su 9am-2:30pm.

Currency Exchange: Thomas Cook, MG Rd., Ernakulam (☎2369729). Near the Air India bldg. There's also a branch at the **airport** (☎2610052). Both open M-Sa 9:30am-6pm. **State Bank of India,** at the west end of Press Club Rd. (☎2351403). Exchanges currency and does cash advances. Open M-F 10am-4pm and Sa 10am-1pm. In Ft. Cochin, **Canara Bank,** TM Mohammed Rd. (☎2215467). At Kunnumpuram Junction, one block east of where Bastian and KB Jacob Rd. meet. Gives cash advances and changes traveler's checks. Open M-F 10am-2pm, Sa 10am-noon.

Bookstore: Current Books, Press Club Rd., Ernakulam (☎2215467), has a wide selection. Open M-Sa 9:30am-7:30pm. **Idiom Books** has two locations—one in Ft. Cochin (☎2217075) at Bastian and Quirose St.—(open daily 10am-6pm), and one in Mattancherry (☎2224028), opposite the Pardesi Synagogue (open daily 10am-6pm). Idiom has a good selection of Keralan authors.

Police: For the Ernakulam central **police station** (☎2394500), head inland from Shanmugham Rd. and take the first left onto Erg Rd. Then, turn right onto Banerji Rd. **Fort Cochin Police** (☎2224055) is behind the bus station opposite the Vypeen Island Jetty.

Hospital: Medical Trust Hospital, MG Rd., Ernakulam (☎2371852). Three blocks south of Jos Junction. The **pharmacy** inside is open 24hr. **Gautham Hospital** (☎2223055) is 3km from Ft. Cochin, to the southeast, in Chullickal.

Pharmacy: In Ft. Cochin, **Jeny Medicals,** Kunnumpuram Junction (☎2224253), at the intersection of TM Mohammed and Fosse St. Open daily 8:15am-10pm.

Internet: In Ernakulam, try **Blitz Internet Cafe** (☎2383262), at the corner of Press Club and Market Rd. Rs15 per hr. Open daily 8:30am-11pm. In Ft. Cochin, email is omnipresent but costs a bit more. **Cafe de Net** (☎2383262), opposite Hotel Park Avenue, has a cool airy upstairs room with multiple terminals. Rs30 per hr. Open daily 9am-11pm.

Post Office: Kochi Head Post Office, Ft. Cochin. Open M-Sa 9am-5pm. Ernakulam's **GPO,** Hospital Rd., between Foreshore and MG Rd, is open M-Sa 10:30am-7pm. **Postal Code:** 682011 (Ernakulam) and 682001 (Cochin).

🏠 ACCOMMODATIONS

FORT COCHIN

The tranquility of Ft. Cochin is preferable to craziness of Ernakulam. During high-season (Dec.-Jan.), accommodations can fill up fast, though it would be unusual not to find somewhere to stay. Most hotels double as tourist offices, offering backwater cruises, Ayurvedic massages, and tickets for dance shows. Prices drop in the off-season (roughly late Mar.-Nov.).

▨ Spencer's Tourist Home, Parade St. (☎ 2215049). Spencer's is the handsome, rambling old house on the left with the *"Let's Go* recommends" plaque on the doorway, at Parade Rd. and Lilly St. Big common room with cable TV, couch, and reading materials. Large, clean rooms with huge soft beds. Hang out in the backyard garden. Singles Rs100-150; doubles with bath Rs250-400. ❶ The owner of Spencer's has also recently opened another guest house on Burgher St. opposite the Kashi Art Cafe called **Oy's Homestay,** for those craving cheaper doubles or A/C. Doubles 250-300; with A/C Rs800. ❷

▨ Chiramel Residency, Lilly St. (☎2217310; chiramel@rediff.com), close to the intersection with Parade St. A small, plush, family-run guest house with rich teakwood panelling and an inner courtyard garden. Mosquito-proof, shoe-free, and beautifully furnished; if you request in advance, you can get home-cooked meals. Internet Rs60 per hr. Check-out noon. Rooms Rs200-600. Off-season 25% discount. ❷

Delight Tourist Resort, Ridsdale Rd. (☎2217658; flowery@spectrum.net.in), at the southeast corner of the parade ground. Overhanging vines and fir branches presage high-ceilinged rooms with attached baths, set in a lovely house with a large library. Internet access available. Owner David handles travel arrangements and runs private tours of South India. Check-out noon. Rooms Rs450-900. Off-season 50% discount. ❸

Tharavadu Tourist Home, Quirose St. (☎2216897). From the south end of Princess St., turn right, then left. In a 400-year-old Dutch row-house with 8 clean, small rooms, 2 with common bath (seat toilet and shower). Singles Rs200; doubles Rs300. ❷

Elite Hotel, Princess St. (☎2215733), has 14 rooms ranging from basic to spacious with tiled floors. All rooms have attached bath, and the restaurant is a neighborhood social center. Check-out noon. Singles Rs250; doubles Rs350. ❷

Vasco Homestay (☎2216267), on the corner of Bastian and Rose St. Offers 4 basic rooms in a tired old house. Local legend has it that Vasco da Gama spent his last moments here on Christmas Eve, 1524. Provides tourist information, foreign exchange, film developing services, bike rentals (Rs5 per hr., Rs40 per day), and Internet access (Rs40 per hr.). Singles Rs100-200; doubles with bath Rs200. Aug.-Oct.: Rs75-150. ❶

Hotel Park Avenue (☎2212671), at the hopping intersection of Princess and Bastian St. A marble-faced sore thumb that is nevertheless a convenient place to stay. Modest-sized rooms have attached baths. Rooftop restaurant. Check-out noon. Add 7-15% tax. Singles Rs269-690; doubles Rs430-920. Off-season 30% discount. ❷

Fort House Hotel, Calvathy Rd. (☎2217103), just west of Seagull Restaurant, toward the jetty. This more upscale waterside option offers spacious rooms with stone floors, mosquito nets, hot water, and seat toilets in attached bath. Breakfast included in the fantastic, down-home restaurant. Internet access available. Check-out noon. Rooms Rs950. ❺

ERNAKULAM

Ernakulam's rooms tend to be characterless, but they're convenient.

Hotel Luciya (☎2381177), behind the KRSTC bus station on Stadium Rd. Its expansiveness almost guarantees room availability. Check-out 24hr. Singles with squat toilet Rs162; doubles with seat toilet and balcony Rs325. ❷

Hotel Aiswarya, Warriam Rd. (☎2364454), south off DH Rd. Cool marble floors and solid furnishings add a touch of class. All rooms have TV, bath, hot water, and seat toilets. Check-out 24hr. Singles Rs350; doubles Rs400-450. Add 7.5% tax. MC/V. ❸

Basoto Lodge, Press Club Rd. (☎2352140), close to Market Rd. Comfortable and popular with foreigners, Basoto has basic facilities and an in-house tourist desk. Check-out 24hr. Singles Rs70; doubles with bath (squat toilets) Rs140. ❶

KERALA

FOOD

FORT COCHIN

Sea-front shacks and restaurants grill fish to order and serve the usual fried snacks. The restaurants here tend to be expensive and prefer to serve Western, rather than Indian food. Bakeries and vegetable stores cluster at the intersection of Bastian St. and TM Mohammed (one block east and parallel to KB Jacob), and fruit is sold near the bus stand. There are also some bakeries along Fosse and Pullupalam Rd., the eastern extensions of Bastian Rd.

Kashi Art Cafe, Burgher St., one block from Princess St. A little pretentious and overpriced perhaps, but *real* coffee (Rs30) and the sun-dappled courtyard make the pretension worthwhile. A menu of Euro meals changes daily (Rs55-60). For Rs5, fill up your water bottle with boiled and purified water and spare the street another piece of plastic. Open daily 7:30am-8:30pm. ❶

Fort House Restaurant, Calvathy Rd. (☎2217103), in the Fort House Hotel. Drop a few extra rupees on good old, down-home Keralan cooking (seer fish Kerala Rs150) under delicate paper lanterns in pleasant, open-air surroundings. Entrees Rs125-350. Open noon-3pm and 7-10:30pm. ❹

Elite Hotel Restaurant, Princess St. (☎2215733), on the ground floor of the hotel. Locals and long-termers congregate here, catching up on the latest news from Goa and trying the seafood of the day with finger chips (Rs50). *Dosas* (Rs15) served after 5pm. Egg breakfasts Rs15-25. Entrees Rs50-150. Open daily from 8am until the crowd trickles out (10 or 11pm). ❶

KATHAKALI DANCE

Kathakali, which means "story play," is one of India's four major schools of classical dance. Transformed into gods and demons with wildly colored make-up, massive golden headdresses, and skirts bright and full enough to put any ballerina to shame, the performers blink, bound, and flap expressively to tell their tale. Usually male, the actors study scripture, Kalaripayatu, Ayurvedic massage, and music for eight years, beginning at age 10 or 12. They then train in dance for four years. Emphasis is given to proper lifestyle and the deep understanding of archetypes portrayed in the *Vedas*. The dancers communicate ideas and feelings through 24 *mudras*, hand gestures combined with convulsive eye and face movements and the pounding of *ghungroo*-laden feet. By using combinations of these *mudras*—signifying things like "love," "sarcasm," "bee drinking from a lotus flower," etc.—the dancers depict stories from the *Ramayana* and *Mahabharata* while piercing drums and classical vocals provide narration. Although traditional *kathakali* was—and still is on special holy days—performed as part of a temple ritual, modern-day shows last only an hour or so and are performed for tourists who come to "watch the Gods dance."

Hotel Seagull Restaurant, Calvathy Rd. (☎2217172), on the waterfront about half a kilometer east of the jetty. Seafood fresh from the water and cold beer (Rs60) to wash it down, served on a patio overhanging the sea. A crowded aviary on the wall ensures birdsong throughout the meal. Entrees Rs70-120. Open daily 7:45am-10pm. ❸

Rooftop Restaurant (☎2212671), perched above the Hotel Park Avenue. Quiet and calm, with views over red-tiled roofs and a tree-fringed horizon. Serves affordable Keralite seafood dishes. Entrees Rs35-150. Open daily 7am-11:30pm. ❶

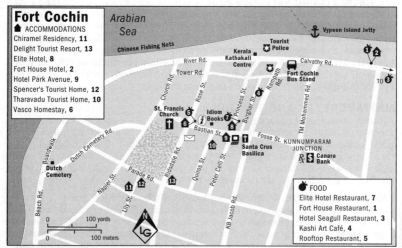

Fort Cochin

▲ ACCOMMODATIONS
Chiramel Residency, **11**
Delight Tourist Resort, **13**
Elite Hotel, **8**
Fort House Hotel, **2**
Hotel Park Avenue, **9**
Spencer's Tourist Home, **12**
Tharavadu Tourist Home, **10**
Vasco Homestay, **6**

Arabian Sea

♣ FOOD
Elite Hotel Restaurant, **7**
Fort House Restaurant, **1**
Hotel Seagull Restaurant, **3**
Kashi Art Café, **4**
Rooftop Restaurant, **5**

KERALA

ERNAKULAM

Ernakulam's eateries serve both international foodstuffs and Indian food (somewhat rare in Fort Cochin). Try local foods like *appam* (a thick *dosa* served with fish stew), and dishes prepared with coconut. Excellent bakeries and tempting juice bars (no water, no ice) line the streets.

Bimbi's, Jos Junction (☎2376457). The chaotic ambience of this local landmark is mesmerizing, and its food is good and cheap. Pay at the register, claim your food at the counter, then sit down and watch the world whiz by. Excellent *masala dosa* Rs15. North Indian *thali* Rs40. Huge selection of sweets and a primo milkshake counter at the front. Open daily 8am-10pm. ❷

Ice Magic, South Railway Station Rd., toward MG Rd. from the station—one in a row of enticing juice bars. Various blended fruits (Rs10-20) and mean mango milkshakes (Rs25) provide quick and delicious coolants for the overheated backpacker's motor. Open daily 9am-10pm. ❶

Hot Breads, Warriam Rd. Follow MG Rd. south from Jos Junction and turn right; it's on the right. Fresh pastries and cakes, including chocolate danishes (Rs11) and brownies (Rs10). Pizza, burgers, and *samosas,* too (Rs8-19). Fantastic aroma of baking is absolutely free. Open daily 9am-9pm. ❶

Chinese Garden, Warriam Rd. (☎2363710). This restaurant might win a prize for garishness (Chinese lanterns, blinking colored lights, a huge aquarium, and wildly painted columns), but its 5-course Executive Lunch is a steal at Rs65. Entrees Rs65-150. Open daily 11am-11pm. ❸

SIGHTS

FORT COCHIN

As the heavy orange sun sinks into the Arabian sea, fishermen haul up Chinese fishing nets while ancient church bells toll. All the romantic fantasies of colonial, cosmopolitan India come true in Fort Cochin. The brochure *Walking Through Fort Cochin,* available at tourist offices, offers details about the area in a walking-tour format.

■ **CHINESE FISHING NETS.** Like giant spiders, Cochin's Chinese fishing nets surround the northern edge of the peninsula, and are commonly used in the deeper backwaters of Vypeen Island as well. The first of these nets was set up between 1350 and 1450 when Kublai Khan's traders brought the design to Kerala. As massive cargo ships pull into the harbor, fishermen in their canoe-like boats return from the sea with the day's catch. Stick around to watch teams of men pull up the nets; high tide is the time to see them in action. Keep an eye out for dolphins, who feast on the fish near the nets.

MATTANCHERRY AND JEW TOWN

A 45min. stroll from Ft. Cochin (or a 5min. Rs20 auto-rickshaw ride) brings you to the heart of Mattancherry, one of the historic centers of the international spice trade, and a former center of India's Jewish community. Follow Calvathy Rd. to the Customs Jetty and keep going as it turns into Bazaar Rd.—it's a pleasant walk past rows of export warehouses, where rich smells of tea, pepper, and spices waft out from every alley. The shops are most lively M-F 9am-5pm.

PARDESI SYNAGOGUE. Originally built in 1568 (though the current structure dates from 1664), the synagogue is lit by 19th-century oil-burning chandeliers suspended over a floor of blue-and-white **Cantonese tiles** given in 1762. The 1100 hand-painted tiles vary subtly from each other, using three scenes (a river landscape, a rosebush, and a willow tree) to create endless variations. Spending a little time silently picking out the minute differences in the tiles can be quite therapeutic after the commercial assault of the streets outside.

The synagogue's Torah is written on sheepskin scrolls and stored in ornate metal canisters, one of them a gift from the Raja of Cochin. A Helnas-inscribed stone set into the outside wall of the synagogue comes from a now-defunct synagogue built in 1344 in Kochangadi. Gravestones with Hebrew inscriptions are propped around the outside of the synagogue. The synagogue in **Jew Town** is tucked in an alleyway parallel to Bazaar Rd. The area is teeming with stores selling curios and antiques—bargain hard. *(5min. from the Dutch Palace. Walk away from Ft. Cochin until the road makes a right turn and make a sharp right there; the synagogue is at the end of the street on the left. Open M-F and Su 10am-noon and 3-5pm. Rs2. Services held F 6:30pm and Sa 8:30am if enough people arrive.)*

ST. FRANCIS CHURCH. Believed to be the first church built by Europeans in India, St. Francis Church (locally called the Vasco da Gama Church), was built around 1500 by Franciscan friars from Portugal. The stone version, constructed a few years later, still stands among the houses built by British traders and Dutch farmers. When **Vasco da Gama** died in Cochin in 1524, he was buried beneath the church floor, remaining until his relatives moved his body to Lisbon fourteen years later, leaving behind his worn, empty tomb. Cochin fell to the Dutch in 1663, and the church was Protestantized in 1779. Although the British occupied Cochin in 1795, the church remained a Dutch stronghold, and extremely worn Dutch gravestones bearing coats of arms cover the walls. The church became Anglican in 1864; the Church of South India has since dedicated it to St. Francis. Pre-electricity fans hang from the ceilings; a very sweaty crew had to pull constantly at the cords to keep the breeze blowing down on the worshipers below. Behind the church, local kids play cricket on the wide **Parade Ground,** which was once the site of colonial-era demonstrations. *(Open M-F 9:30am-1pm and 2:30-5:30pm.)*

THE DUTCH PALACE. The **Mattancherry Palace** (a.k.a. the Dutch Palace) was built by the Portuguese in 1555 for Raja Virakerala Varma. Its construction was a "goodwill gesture," probably made in exchange for trading rights. During their

ANY MATZOH WITH THAT PALAK PANEER?

Jews probably first came to Kerala during the 10th century BC as traders from King Solomon's Israel; 1000 years later, the Romans destroyed the Temple in Jerusalem, dispersing Jews throughout Europe. A few landed in Shingly (30km north of Cochin, now known as Cranganore) a few years later. Their descendants still live in Cochin today. In AD 379, Joseph Rabban, was made a prince of Anjuvanam and established a Jewish Kingdom. Around AD 500, another large group of Jews immigrated here from Iraq and Iran. During the Portuguese Inquisition in the 16th century, the Jews were expelled from Shingly. Legend has it that Joseph Azar, the last surviving Jewish prince, swam to Cochin with his wife on his shoulders. The Jewish Keralans placed themselves under the protection of the Raja of Cochin, who gave them a parcel of land for a synagogue next to his palace (see p. 338).

Emigration to Mumbai and Israel has significantly pared down Cochin's Jewish population, but you'll still see menorahs in some of the windows. There has been no rabbi here for several years, so the elders of the synagogue conduct ceremonies and make decisions regarding Jewish law. Happy to discuss their future with visitors, the remaining Jews seem unconcerned about the survival of their community. Sixty or seventy Jews remain in Kerala, along with some four to five thousand in India as a whole, most of whom live in Mumbai.

occupation in 1663, the Dutch renovated and renamed the palace. Three **temples,** one dedicated to Krishna, one to Shiva, and one to Laxmi were built on the palace grounds, but only Hindus may enter. Beautiful, detailed **murals** depicting scenes from the *Ramayana*, the *Mahabharata*, and the *Puranas*, painted by locals in distinct Keralite style, cover nearly 300 sq. m of the palace walls. Downstairs, a number of less detailed paintings show divine sexual scenes set in a beautiful forest. Rooms without murals make up a **museum** and house oil portraits of Cochin rajas with their palanquins, robes, weapons, Dutch drawings, and umbrellas. *(Palace open Sa-Th 10am-5pm. Rs2. No photography permitted.)*

VYPEEN ISLAND

Miles of **beaches** roll along the Arabian Sea on Vypeen Island, passing a **Lighthouse** at Ochanthuruth (1.5km west of the main road; open daily 3-5pm) and the early 16th-century **Pallipuran Fort** (open Th 10am-5pm). The beaches are empty most of the year, except for herds of sunbathing cows and a few fishing boats, but the in-season brings Indian and foreign tourists en masse. Men come from the nearby villages to see the show—women are advised to swim in a t-shirt and shorts or pants. **Cherai Beach,** just a few kilometers shy of the northern tip of the island, is frequented by more foreigners and may be safer for women than the others. From Vypeen Island, catch one of the frequent buses (50min., Rs7) to Cherai Junction. From there, continue away from Vypeen and bear left (west) onto Cherai Beach Rd. for a scenic walk to the beach (15min.; Rs20 by rickshaw), passing between inland backwaters where Chinese fishing nets dip and pull all the live-long day. Sprinkled along the main road are bakeries and produce stands; just before Cherai Beach, the tranquil **Kadaloram** serves the usual snacks for Rs10-40 and Chinese and Indian cuisine for Rs40-180. (Open daily 9am-9:30pm.) **Ferries** run between Vypeen Island and Ernakulam's Main Jetty (every 20min. 5:30am-10:30pm). Ferries from Ft. Cochin to Vypeen (6:30am-9pm) depart from the launch opposite the bus stand.

ENTERTAINMENT

KATHAKALI DANCE

Cochin offers spectacular nightly performances of ▨**kathakali dance,** Kerala's startling and gorgeous brand of traditional music and movement (see p. 336). Frequently geared toward tourists, these performances are usually prefaced by elaborate make-up demonstrations, an explanation of the music and hand-symbols, and a synopsis of the tale to be enacted. Performances last from one hour to 90min., or, in true form, a whopping eight hours.

Kerala Kathakali Centre (☎2215827), near the Ft. Cochin bus stand and the Chinese fishing nets, has a young troupe of artists who perform in a dockside version of a blackbox theater. Lively and fun. Make-up 5pm, performance 6:30-8pm; Rs100.

See India Foundation (☎2376471). From MG Rd. in Ernakulam, head east on Warriam Rd. for 2 blocks; the Foundation is on the right under the painted face. Director Devan has been performing here for 30 years. Make-up 6pm, performance 6:45pm; Rs100.

Cochin Cultural Centre (☎2380366). From Jos Junction in Ernakulam, head south on MG Rd., turn left on Sahodaran Ayappan Rd., right on Chittoor Rd., and finally, left onto Manikath Rd. Make-up 5:30pm, performance 6:30pm; Rs125.

AYURVEDIC BLISS

The **Kerala Ayurveda Pharmacy,** on Warriam Rd. (or A.M. Thomas Rd.) in Ernakulam, 30m east of MG Rd., is one of many places in Cochin that offers **Ayurvedic massage.** (☎2375292. Open M-Sa 8am-7pm, Su 8am-4pm; men only M-Sa 4-7pm. Rs400, with steam wash Rs500.) The **Sree Narayana Holistic Clinic,** on Vypeen Island, offers a full body Ayurvedic massage and steam bath as well as an excellent home-cooked Keralite meal for Rs500. (☎2502362. Open for appointments daily 9am-5pm. Book one day in advance and the doctor will pick you up from the Vypeen ferry jetty. Many guest houses also set up appointments.) Since it's an important component of *kathakali,* several dance centers also offer Ayurvedic massage by appointment, including the **Cochin Cultural Centre** (☎2380366) and the **Chavara Cultural Centre** (☎2368443).

BACKWATER CRUISES

Beyond the city lie magical emerald fields, towering palms, and lazy backwaters—some of India's most remarkably green and pleasant landscapes. Kerala's tourist industry has capitalized on all this, offering ▨**backwater tours** on both motorized and non-motorized boats through the maze of lagoons, lakes, canals, and streams. A guide paddles the vessel, which can hold four to eight people, for several enchanting hours, stopping for a fresh coconut break and a stroll through paddy fields. The whole scene is enthralling, especially for bird-watchers. The tours also offer a unique opportunity to see Keralite village life up close without the feeling of being an invasive tourist. Some tours provide a traditional lunch on banana leaves. Moonlight cruises on full-moon nights are offered in season. The Tourist Desk, Main Jetty, Ernakulam, charters daily tours. In season, reserve at least one day in advance; off-season, show up 30min. before departure. (☎2371761. Tours 9am-noon and 2-5pm; Rs275.) The KTDC also provides backwater tours on country boats (8:30am-1pm or 2:30-7pm; Rs315, minimum two people), and water tours of Cochin from the Sealord Jetty (day cruise 9am-12:30pm and 2-5pm, Rs70; sunset cruise 5:30 and 7pm, Rs40). Most hotels also arrange cruises and offer a 6hr. cruise that includes a tasty traditional lunch (Rs800; inquire at any hotel).

MUNNAR വുന്നാർ ☎ 04865

Smaller and more intimate than Ooty or Kodaikanal, litter- and crowd-free Munnar handles tourism with grace. This hill station's soaring mountain peaks and miles of rolling tea plantations are unmatched, inviting long hikes and longer vistas. The scruffy little town has friendly inhabitants who slow down their jeeps to inquire if travelers need help. Not even the rickshaw-*wallahs* will try to scam you here.

It was a Scotsman, J.D. Munro, who kicked off the town's development during the 1870s, creating a fiefdom for generations of Scottish tea-planters. When Munro and friends finally left in the 1970s, they left their rolling oceans of tea to Tata Tea Ltd., an offshoot of the same Parsi-owned mega-company that built the bus that brought you into town. Today, the precisely manicured tea plantations continue to dominate every aspect of life in Munnar, though the burgeoning tourist industry contributes more and more to the local economy every year. Get to Munnar while you still can; its unique mix of hospitality, agreeable climate, and scenery will not go unnoticed for long.

⟨ TRANSPORTATION. Buses depart from the KSRTC bus station, 2km south of New Munnar; most buses also stop by the main bazaar in the center of New Munnar. To: **Cochin** (4½hr., 8 per day 6am-2:40pm, Rs51); **Chinnar** (2¾hr., 7 per day, Rs26.50); **Theni** (3¾hr., 6 per day, Rs33.50). **Bicycles** can be rented from City Cycles, a little stall across from Tata Tea sports grounds on the road between Old and New Munnar (Rs 10 per hr).

Rickshaws (Rs10 from New Munnar to JSRTC bus station) are hard to miss. Ask a rickshaw-*wallah* to see his copy of the list of standardized rickshaw tour fares to the mountains and waterfalls around Munnar (Rs150-750, depending on the tour you choose).

⟨ ORIENTATION AND PRACTICAL INFORMATION. In Tamil, Munnar means "Three Rivers," and the heart of the town centers on the point where the three rivers meet. The road from Cochin enters the relatively flat valley alongside the main river 3km south of Munnar's town center. It passes the **KSRTC bus station** after 1km, Old Munnar after another 1km, and finally reaches happening New Munnar Town after yet another 1km. The road to Chinnar leads north out of town. Several budget hotels, restaurants, tourist offices, and local bus stands are packed into the bazaar here, overlooked by the **Tata Tea Regional Headquarters** on Cochin Rd. Joseph Iype, in his tiny **Tourist Information Centre** in the main bazaar, is Munnar's local tourist action hero. Keen to share the delights of the region, he can provide bus times, tours, and hiking maps. He also offers lodging in his cottage and will find you a doctor if you need one. (☎231136, or at home 230349. Open daily 9am-1pm and 3-6pm.) There is also a government-run tourist information centre 10m to the left of Ipye's shop and an excellent **DPTC Information Centre** in Old Munnar, 1km south of the bazaar. They run full day tours (10am-6pm, Rs250) which include all of Munnar's major attractions, including visits to Rajamala Gap, Mattupetty Dam, Echo Point, and Top Station, among others. You can change money at the **Federal Bank,** a short walk from the main bazaar with the temple on your right. (Open M-F 10am-2pm, Sa 10am-noon.) Or, a little farther down the same road on your right is the **State Bank of India.** Farther along the same road is the town **Tata Hospital** (☎230270). **Ramm Communications** close to Krishna Lodge and the Chicken Corner Restaurant in the bazaar has Internet access (Rs50 per hr.; open daily 8:30am-9:30pm), but so do many other places around town. The **post office** is across the river from Tata Tea. (Open M-Sa 9am-5pm.) **Postal Code:** 685612.

KERALA

⚑🏠 ACCOMMODATIONS AND FOOD. Most of the cheap eating and sleeping options are in the center of town, but the short auto-rickshaw ride to the edges of town and the slightly higher prices are well worth the effort; the lodgings on the outskirts of town provide tranquility and a view of the country side. ▨**Zina Cottage ❸**, a snug cottage up in the hills owned by Joe Iype, is a short ride through the tea plantations. Comfortable rooms, hot water, and seat toilets. (☎231136 or 230349. Doubles Rs400-600.) **Royal Retreat ❺**, on NH-49 between the KSRTC bus station and Blossom Park, has clean rooms along a perfectly manicured garden and attached restaurant. (☎230240. Regular Rs950, deluxe Rs1150. Check-out noon.) For a pricier stay with the hoity-toitiest of India's tourists, try the **Copper Castle ❺**. Its location on Potnumedu Rd., overlooking a river valley, provides breathtaking views. (☎231201, 230633. Singles Rs1700, doubles Rs2900.) In town, **Krishna Lodge ❶**, on the opposite side of the river, has singles with shared bath or doubles with clean, attached bath and seat toilets. (☎230669. Singles Rs100; doubles Rs250.)

The best place to eat in the center of town is the **Silver Spoon Restaurant ❶**, in the Munnar Inn next to the bus stand—a brand new shiny place serving a wide range of Indian and Western dishes such as chilli fish (Rs100), lemon rice (Rs40), and cardamom tea (Rs15). (Open daily 8:30am-9:30pm.) Another good mid-range option is **Greens ❷**, in the East End Hotel, a short walk from the main bazaar. It's a big, wide, airy place with an extensive menu that ranges from fish curry (Rs45) to fried chicken (Rs75), plus *aloo mutter* (Rs40) and *navratan korma* (Rs40). (Open daily 7:30am-9:30pm.) In the bazaar itself, **Rapsy Restaurant ❷**, also called **Chicken Corner**, is a nifty little place deservedly popular for its efficient service and excellent spicy chicken dishes. They offer chicken (Rs50), egg roast (Rs10), and veg. *biryani* (Rs25). (Open daily 9am-8pm.) For "meals" and all other fall-back favorites, the **Hotel Plaza ❶**, attached to the Hill Top Lodge, tempts with egg *biryani* (Rs28) and fish curry (Rs15). (Open daily 7am-9pm.)

◼️📷 SIGHTS AND HIKING. The best way to experience Munnar is to stroll through the tea fields and splash around in the waterfalls. Be sure to spend a few extra *paise* to bus or rickshaw out to some of Munnar's vistas. The cascades of **Athukad Falls** can be found near **Pullivasal Tea Estate,** just off Cochin Rd. They are accessible by foot with the option of returning by local bus. There is a lake with boating and (land-bound) elephants 15km away. For more information on these places and other scenic walks around Munnar, see Joe Iype in his tourist information shop in the bazaar. The Kerala government's District Tourism Promotion Council office (☎231516) in Old Munnar, 1km south of the bazaar, offers full day **Tea Valley Tours** to all the major sights in Munnar. (Open daily 10am-6pm, Rs250.)

Munnar's biggest attraction is the ▨**Eravikulam National Park,** 15km away, established in 1978 to protect the spectacular Mt. Anaimundi (2694m), the highest Indian peak south of the Himalayas. The mountain and its surroundings are home to the endangered mountain goat, the Nilgiri tahr, of which only 2500 are estimated to remain. The park's ecosystem also supports gaur, wild dogs, jungle cats, mongoose, and barking deer. Surrounded by beautiful tea fields, visitors can stroll past waterfalls and through fields of grass along the mountainside to where the wild goats are. Take an auto-rickshaw from town to the second forest check-point (one-way Rs100, with 1hr. wait Rs150), the farthest a rickshaw can go. From there, it is a 2km walk up to **Rajamalai Gap** on the mountain's shoulder and then another 4km down to a tea factory. Unless you have a rickshaw waiting for you, walk 4km back down the hill from the check-point to catch a local bus on Munnar Rd. *(Park admission Rs50 for foreigners, Rs10 for Indians; rickshaw fee Rs5.)*

Lockhart Mountain offers another superb mountain ridge hike. Take a bus (Rs3) or a rickshaw (Rs120) to Lockhart Gap. The round-trip hike takes about 3hr. and offers some spectacular views. A lazier way to soak in the scenery is to bus it to **Top Station.** The first bus of the day (1½hr., 7:15am) should get you there before the clouds come down and the haze comes up. The last bus returning to town from Top Station is at 3pm.

In case you're curious about just what they do with all that tea, you can try your hand at a **tea factory tour.** Tata Tea isn't exactly keen on conducting **tours** of its factories, but a word with Joe Iype may prove fruitful.

🎵📷 **ENTERTAINMENT AND NIGHTLIFE.** Munnar doesn't exactly have a happening club scene, but the closest you'll get is trying to get yourself admitted to the exclusive members-only **High Range Club,** where the old world atmosphere of the planters' social world still lives on in the gentlemen's bar, lined with hunting trophies and a collection of venerable headwear. Call first to speak to the club secretary (☎230253) and be prepared to dig around at the bottom of your pack for clean clothes.

COCO-LOCO The coconut tree, or *kalpa vrishka* ("heaven-gifted tree" in Malayalam), and its products are everywhere in Kerala, from the rug beneath your feet to the bed you sleep in at night. Coconut trees mature in 7-8 years. Every 40 days, a flower bud pops out among the leaves, containing a sticky liquid which ferments into toddy, the sweet local booze that gets stronger as the day goes on. Each bud blossoms into 10-12 tender coconuts within three months; the sweet water inside will mellow even the meanest toddy hangover. In a year, the water inside dries and condenses into white coconut meat, which is grated and used in cooking. The drying coconuts you see along the roadside are squashed for coconut oil, which is used in cooking, Ayurvedic massages, and Kathakali make-up. The fibrous husks of the coconut shells are spun into *coir* ropes and woven into mats. The shells are used to make spoons, cups, bowls, and vases, and as charcoal for cooking sweets. Dried palm fronds thatch roofs and are woven into hut walls and fences; stems are used as brooms. After 80 years this hard-working tree is felled and sculpted into furniture.

TRICHUR (THRISSUR) തൃശ്ശൂർ ☎0487

Though Trichur bills itself as the "cultural capital of Kerala," its only real draw is the annual **Puram Festival,** next scheduled for May 1, 2004. During Puram, deity-bearing revelers from neighboring villages descend on the town, heralded by musicians and brightly decorated elephants. Trichur hardly merits a lengthy detour during the rest of the year, but its rolling central park and zoo-art museum complex make it a fine stopover.

▐ TRANSPORTATION

Trains: The **railway station** (info ☎131 or ☎2423150) is on Railway Station Rd. Fares listed are 2nd class. To: **Bangalore** (12hr., 4:15pm, Rs121); **Calicut** (3hr., 8 per day 3am-1am, Rs40); **Chennai** (12hr., 4 per day, Rs235); **Delhi** (43hr., 2:10 and 5:10pm, Rs500); **Ernakulam** (1½hr., frequent, Rs32); **Kanyakumari** (11hr., 4 and 7:50am, Rs100); **Mangalore** (10hr., 12:45pm and 1am, Rs287); **Margao** (12hr., 2-3 per day 11:35am-7:55pm, Rs200); **Mumbai** (26hr., 1-2 per day, Rs450); **Trivandrum** (6hr., 10-12 per day, Rs84).

Buses: The **KSRTC bus stand,** Masjid Rd. (☎ 2421150), is near the railway station, south of Railway Station Rd. Reservations noon-8pm. To: **Alleppey** (3½hr., frequent, Rs66); **Calicut** (3hr., frequent, Rs57); **Chennai** (14hr., 2:50 and 5:30pm, Rs260); **Coimbatore** (2½hr., frequent, Rs55); **Ernakulam** (2hr., frequent, Rs38); **Mangalore** (12hr., 9:30pm and 1:30am, Rs178); **Trivandrum** (7hr., frequent, Rs140).

Local Transportation: Most of Trichur's sights and accommodations are within walking distance. **Auto-rickshaws** are plentiful. Rs7 first km, Rs4 per km thereafter.

ORIENTATION AND PRACTICAL INFORMATION

Trichur is laid out like a wheel. The hubcap is the vast, green **Swaraj Round,** the site of the **Vadakkumnathan Temple.** The major roads, moving clockwise from the western edge, are **Mahatma Gandhi (MG), Shornur, Palace, College, High, Municipal Office (MO), Chembottil, Kurrapam,** and **Marar Roads.** Most hotels and restaurants are on these thoroughfares, near the Round. **Railway Station Road** runs east-west, 500m south of the Round; to get to the KSRTC **bus stand** and **railway station,** head south down Kurrapam Rd. from the Round to Railway Station Rd. and follow the signs.

Tourist Office: KTDC (☎ 2320800), near the corner of Palace and Museum Rd., across from the Town Hall, provides advice about Trichur and travel throughout Kerala. Open M-Sa 10am-5pm.

Currency Exchange: State Bank of India, (☎ 2322796), on the northeastern edge of the park. Changes cash and traveler's checks. Open M-F 10am-4pm, Sa 10am-1pm.

Pharmacy: Girija Medical Stores, Round South (☎ 2445010). Open daily 8:45am-8:45pm.

Hospital: Jubilee Mission Hospital (☎ 2420361), East Fort, northeast of the city center. The best private hospital. Auto-rickshaw from city center Rs10.

Police: East Police Station (☎ 2421400), off MO Rd., just south of Railway Station Rd. and to the right.

Internet: IRS Computers (☎ 2425560), on Round West, past MG Road, 2nd fl. Dozens of terminals, Rs30 per hr. Open 7am-8pm.

Post Office: Trichur City Post Office, Railway Station Rd. at MO Rd. Open M-Sa 9:30am-5:30pm. **Postal Code:** 680001.

ACCOMMODATIONS

During Puram, the room rates listed below often quadruple. Check-out 24hr. Backpackers are scarce in Trichur, so be prepared to discuss world politics with middle-aged businessmen.

Alukkas Tourist Home (☎ 2424067), just north off Railway Station Rd., opposite the bus station. The best option for those arriving on late-night buses, this hotel welcomes you with blaring Keralite TV, then proceeds to shower you with soap, towels, and seat toilets. Hot water in deluxe doubles. Singles Rs215-400; doubles Rs270-430. ❷

Chandy's Tourist Hotel, Railway Station Rd. (☎ 2421167), between the bus and train stations. Simple rooms with attached bath at this cheap and convenient place. Singles Rs113; doubles Rs204. ❶

Hotel Elite International, Chembottil Ln. (☎ 2421033), off the Round South, between Kurrappam and Municipal Office Rd. The premier hotel in town, with hot water, phones, seat toilets, balconies with expansive city views, and a laundry service that will turn your white clothes blue. Attached restaurant. Singles Rs256-366; doubles Rs366-452. ❷

FOOD

◈ **Delite Sweet Parlour,** Round South (☎2424029), at the corner of Chembottil Ln., turns out excellent sweet and savory snacks (Rs3-10) with a moist yet crumbly Mysore *pak* (a type of peanut maple sugar candy, Rs7). Open daily 9am-8:30pm. ❶

Hotel Bharath Restaurant, Chembottil Ln. (☎2421720), between Round South and Railway Station Rd. Cheap South Indian (*thalis* Rs19, special Rs27) and North Indian veg. fare (*aloo gobhi* Rs21). Big airy doors and big airy windows await satisfied customers. Packed at mealtimes and justifiably popular. Open daily 6am-10:30pm. ❶

Ming Palace (☎2422203), around the corner from the Hotel Elite, 1st fl. of the Pathans bldg. Chinese and Thai dishes (Rs25-70) served under red lamps and Japanese lanterns, occasionally to the tune of country music. Open daily 11am-10pm. ❷

SIGHTS AND ENTERTAINMENT

Featuring a multitude of elephants, onlookers, and noisy bands, the annual **Puram Festival** is Indian pageantry at its very best. Hotels fill up fast and charge exorbitant rates during the festival, so plan well in advance, or better yet, just make a daytrip from Cochin. It is held on the grounds of the **Vadakkumnathan Temple,** the oldest and largest temple complex in the state, which lies at the center of the Swaraj Round in the heart of town. Dedicated to Shiva, the temple sits on the site where Nandi, Shiva's bull, is said to have rested. The temple is closed to non-Hindus.

Outside of Puram, you'll be hard-pressed to have a rip-roaring good time in Trichur. Check out the exterior of the **Vadakkumnathan Temple** at the center of the Round, since you probably won't be allowed inside. In the northeast corner of Trichur, 2km from the Round, you'll find a zoo and museum complex. Though the **zoo** is small, and usually full of school kids (and sometimes grown people) teasing and gawking at depressed animals in tiny cages, the **art museum** on the same grounds has a fantastically eclectic collection. Indian, Chinese, Japanese, Hindu, Buddhist, Christian, sculpture, painting, vase-work, and historical artifacts ranging from centuries BC to photography of the late 19th century—the lack of organization makes it that much more fun. There is also a "multipurpose" museum that contains an extensive geological rock display, an armory, dried butterflies, and what are presumably the stuffed remains of erstwhile zoo occupants. (Zoo and art museum open Tu-Su 9am-5:15pm. Rs5. Multipurpose museum open Tu-Su 10am-5pm. Free.) You'll find more carvings and models of many famous temples at the **Archaeological Museum,** 100m farther along Museum Rd. Murals upstairs depict scenes from the *Ramayana,* mostly of Lord Ram killing enemies. (Open Tu-Su 9:30am-5pm. Free.)

The market area behind Municipal Office Rd. is worth exploring; colorful vegetable and spice stands pack the narrow streets. The pretty Puttanpalli Church, just off High Rd., is also worth a look. The flashing blue, red, and yellow neon cross will make you see the light(s). (Open M-Sa 9am-5:30pm, Su 2-4pm.)

CALICUT (KOZHIKODE) കോഴിക്കോട്☎0495

Chinese and Middle Eastern spice traders visited Calicut as early as the 7th century, and Vasco da Gama arrived on the Subcontinent just north of here in 1498. Tipu Sultan pillaged the region in 1789, but the British soon put Calicut back on the map when they dubbed the locally produced fabric "calico" and began exporting it to Europe. These days, heaping piles of mangoes and brimming sacks of dried chili peppers add charm to an otherwise unremarkable city that serves mainly as a stopover for tourists between Cochin and Mysore.

KERALA

⌐ TRANSPORTATION

Flights: The **airport** is in Karipur, 28km from Calicut. Taxis cost Rs300. **Air India,** Eroh Centre, Bank Rd., 1st fl. (☎2766714). Open M-Sa 9:30am-5:30pm. To **Mumbai** (1½hr., 5 per week, US$80). **Indian Airlines** (☎2766243), is next door. Open M-Sa 10am-5:35pm. To: **Chennai** (1½-2hr., 4 per week, US$100); **Mumbai** (1½hr., 2 per day, US$150).

Trains: The **railway station** (☎2701234) is 1km south of the park; follow Town Hall Rd. To: **Chennai** (18hr., 1:40am and 4:30pm, Rs268); **Delhi** (36hr., 5:40pm, Rs59); **Ernakulam** (5hr., 6 per day 6:40am-11:45pm, Rs58); **Mangalore** (5hr., 5 per day 12:55am-6pm, Rs65); **Trivandrum** (9hr., 5 per day 8:50am-11:40pm, Rs190).

Buses: KSRTC Bus Stand, Mavoor Rd. (☎2723796), is not far from the intersection with Bank Rd. Reservation desk open 8am-noon. To: **Bangalore** (8½hr., 9 per day 7am-11:45pm, Rs144-210) via **Mysore** (5½-6½hr., Rs94); **Cochin** (5½hr., 15 per day, Rs98-150); **Mangalore** (7hr., 4 per day, Rs97); **Mysore** (5½-6½hr., 19 per day 6am-11:30pm, Rs81); **Trivandrum** (10½hr., 10 per day 1am-9pm, Rs195). Cheaper **private buses** run from the bus stand farther down Mavoor Rd., at the intersection with Stadium Rd. To: **Cochin** (6hr., 6 per day, Rs73); **Devala** for Ooty (10hr., 3:30pm, Rs56); **Mangalore** (6hr., 5 per day, Rs73); **Mysore** (6hr., 8am, Rs73).

Local Transportation: Auto-rickshaws are your best bet (Rs7 for the first km, Rs4 for each successive). **Taxis** are unmetered and everywhere. **Local buses** run around town, to Beypore and to the beach.

▉✴ ⚡ ORIENTATION AND PRACTICAL INFORMATION

Calicut's layout is a confused mess; it's easiest to get around by the cheap and omnipresent auto-rickshaws. The KTDC office (see below) can also help out with the *Kerala Road Atlas* (Rs50) which includes detailed maps of every major tourist destination in Kerala, including Calicut. At the center of town is **Ansari Park,** which is flanked to the west by **Town Hall Road** and to the east by **Bank Road,** which turns into **GH Road. SM Road** begins at the south end of the park and runs between Town Hall Rd. and GH Rd. **Mavoor Road (Indira Gandhi Road)** veers east off Bank Rd., leading to the KSRTC and private **bus stations.** To the south, GH Rd. intersects with east-west **MM Ali Road,** which leads east to an older part of the city, and west to the beach as **Palayam Road.** The **railway station** is on Town Hall Rd., south of the park. The **beach,** 2km west of the town center, is unsafe at night.

Tourist Office: The **KTDC** office (☎2722392) is at the reception desk of the Malabar Mansion, on the south side of the park. Open 24hr. The **Kerala Tourism Information Booth** (☎2702606) is at the railway station. Open M-Sa 10am-1pm and 2-5pm.

Budget Travel: PL Worldways, Lakhotia Computer Centre, 3rd fl. (☎2722564), at the intersection of Mavoor and Bank Rd. Books airline reservations and processes foreign visas. Open M-F 9:30am-1pm and 2-5:30pm, Sa 9:30am-1:30pm.

Currency Exchange: State Bank of India, Bank Rd. (☎2721321). Changes currency and traveler's checks. Open M-F 10am-4pm, Sa 10am-1pm. **PL Worldways** (see above) also changes currency and cashes traveler's checks.

Police: Manachira (☎2722673). On the east edge of the park.

Hospital: National Hospital, Mavoor Rd. (☎2723061 or 2723062), near the intersection with Bank Rd. on the north side of the street. The best in town. Its **pharmacy** is open daily 8am-midnight.

Internet: Shell Technologies Internet Zone, on the south side of the park, next to the library. Rs30 per hr. Open 9:30am-10pm.

Post Office (☎2722663), on the west edge of the park. Open M-Sa 8am-8pm, Su 2-4:45pm. **Postal Code:** 673001.

♔ ACCOMMODATIONS

A legion of (mostly) high-quality tourist homes vies for your business in Calicut.

Metro Tourist Home (☎2766029), at the junction of Mavoor and Bank Rd., close to the KSRTC bus stand. Huge rooms have forest green wall-to-wall carpeting, soft bedspreads, and seat toilets in attached bath. Singles Rs140-190; doubles Rs200-380. ❶

Hotel Sasthapuri (☎2723281), down MM Ali Rd. from GH Rd., on the left. A quiet nook in the wildly colorful market area of town. Cozy rooms with attached bath. Don't miss the fern-filled rooftop and its lovely restaurant (open 5-10pm). Check-out 24hr. Singles Rs120; doubles Rs180-250. ❶

Malabar Mansion (☎2722391), on the south side of the park. KTDC-run and smack-dab in the center of town, with a tourist desk, restaurant, and beer parlor. All rooms have TV, phone, and bath. Check-out 24hr. Singles Rs215-450; doubles Rs269-550. ❷

Kalpaka Tourist Home, Town Hall Rd. (☎2720223), just south of the park. Fresh towels, hot water, and a TV for a few extra rupees make the spartan seem scenic. Check-out 24hr. Singles Rs160-269; doubles Rs269-377. MC/V. ❶

♘ FOOD

Woodlands Restaurant, in the Hotel Whitelines on GH Rd. (☎2701608), not far from the intersection with MM Ali Rd. Pretty curtains fluttering under fans and A/C cast a cool shade over stone tables in this excellent veg. restaurant. Deliciously crispy *paneer* Manchurian, Rs50. Entrees Rs20-50. Open daily 8am-10:30pm. ❶

Dakshin-The Veg, Mavoor Rd. (☎2722648), near the intersection with Bank Rd. Burgers, pizzas, South Indian *thalis* (Rs25), and North Indian veg. (Rs32-43). Self-service downstairs; A/C and non-A/C restaurants upstairs. Open daily 6am-11pm. ❶

Cochin Bakery (☎2727777), opposite the State Bank of India. Specializes in spicy snacks, cold drinks, and tasty pastries (from Rs4). Open daily 9am-9:30pm. ❶

Malabar Mansion Restaurant, in KTDC hotel, 1st fl., serves up a small assortment of dishes (Rs18-45) and has eggs for breakfast (Rs12-15). A raised TV provides a little entertainment with your meal. Open daily 7am-9:45pm. ❶

◉ ♪ SIGHTS AND ENTERTAINMENT

ANSARI PARK. Ansari Park, also known as **Manchira Maidan,** gives a splash of well-maintained and desperately needed green to Calicut's center. Join the locals for a midday nap in the shade of the trees fringing the outer fence. The **tank** on the western edge of the park is all that remains of a palace built by one of the local rulers, the Zamorin king Manavikrama. The public **library** on the south edge of the park is a good example of traditional Keralite architecture: stacked, red-tiled roofs and trellised balconies. Every evening at the park, a little guy in a box madly flips switches to manipulate a **Music Fountain** choreographed to Hindi pop. *(2hr., show 6-8pm, Rs5.)* The art deco **Crown Theatre,** on Town Hall Rd. at the southwest corner of the park, screens Western films.

BEACH. Although it's not a hot-spot for sunbathers, the city's long, sandy **beach** lies just 2km from the city center, and is worth a visit. The view to the north includes a local mosque whose twin white minarets rise above the fishing boats gathered on the beach; to the south, food carts selling coconuts and various fresh and pickled fruits dominate.

MUSEUMS. The **Pazhassiraja Museum** is one of those all-purpose Indian museums that contains all the clutter that anyone ever thought of putting into a museum. Much of the museum is worth passing by, but a number of well displayed stone carvings downstairs might be worth a quick stop. *(East Hill, 5km from Calicut; rickshaw Rs25. Or take a 15min. bus ride for Rs2 from in front of the Hotel Malabar Mansion to West Hill. Get off at the stop opposite St. Michael's Church, take the first right, then left where the street ends, and right at that street's end. Head uphill on the left fork to the museum. Open Tu-Su 10am-5pm. Free.)* Around the back, the **Krishna Menon Museum** houses the personal belongings of the late Indian president (1896-1974), including his Seiko watch, monogrammed pen, and a couple metal-medallion engravings of Lenin. The **Art Gallery** upstairs, smelling pleasantly of dusty old wood, contains a collection of paintings by Raja Ravi Varma and Raja Raja Varma, in addition to some Tibetan and Japanese wood engravings and sketches. Check out the incredibly erotic "Siva Mohin" oil painting. *(Museums and gallery open Tu and Th-Su 10am-5pm, Wed. 1-5pm.)*

SHOPPING. The side-streets and alleyways of Calicut are bursting at the seams with commercial activity. A bit of bartering and haggling can provide plenty of entertainment, for a price. For giant quantities of spices, veggies, and fruits, visit the **market** around the old bus station on MM Ali Rd. east of GH Rd. The **Comtrust Store,** south of the park and just off Town Hall Rd. maintains a large showroom of the hand-loomed fabrics that made Calicut famous. *(Open M-Sa 10am-7pm.)*

MADHYA PRADESH

मध्य प्रदेश

True to its name, Madhya Pradesh (the "Middle State") stretches right across the center of India. Outside the fertile and heavily populated Narmada River Valley, the land is dominated by dense forests, scrubby hills, and ravines, which provide an unravaged homeland for the region's indigenous groups and a refuge for *dacoits* (bandits) and tigers. Also hidden and protected by the forests are the ruined cities of Mandu and Orchha, as well as the erotic temple carvings of Khajuraho.

During the 3rd century BC, the great Buddhist convert-king Ashoka founded Sanchi as a religious center. Mughal emperors ruled the region from the north until they lost control to the Marathas, who ruled until Independence. Today, 93% of the population is Hindu, and state politics are dominated by the BJP, but the landscape of Madhya Pradesh—from its ancient Buddhist pilgrimage sites to its timeless national parks—preserves vivid reminders of a rich and varied past. In November 2000, Madhya Pradesh was divided into two states, Madhya Pradesh in the north and **Chattisgarh** in the south. Our coverage includes no destinations in Chattisgarh, a region with few claims to fame except its natural resources.

HIGHLIGHTS OF MADHYA PRADESH

Madhya Pradesh has the largest tiger population of any Indian state. **Kanha National Park** (p. 367), which inspired the *Jungle Book,* is the best place to see them.

The middle-of-nowhere temple town of **Khajuraho** (p. 369), with its titillating erotic sculpture, is one of the world's great architectural marvels.

The 3rd century BC Buddhist *stupas* at **Sanchi** (p. 353), perched atop a lush green hill and pleasantly devoid of touts, are easily accessible and well worth any detour.

The ruins of the town of **Mandu** (p. 359) open a window onto the Muslim Malwa culture of the 14th century.

The fort in **Gwalior** (p. 382) is one of the most impressive in India.

BHOPAL भोपाल ☏ 0755

The capital of Madhya Pradesh, Bhopal (pop. 1.2 million) falls just short of high expectations. Its good range of hotels, great restaurants, two lakes, and several mosques are not sufficient to warrant a visit to Bhopal, save as a transit point to the nearby Buddhist retreat at Sanchi, or elsewhere. The program of civic improvements begun during the 19th century left the city with lakes and parks. However, the 20th century transformed Bhopal into an industrial metropolis that proved lethal when, in December 1984, thousands of people died in a toxic gas leak from a Union Carbide factory in northern Bhopal. Since then, the city has slowly been recovering. At times, Bhopal's lakeside sections resemble a beautiful seaside town; at others, the gutters overflow with raw sewage and Bhopal's poverty and lack of infrastructure become blatantly evident.

⌐ TRANSPORTATION

Flights: The **airport** is on Agra Rd. (☎2521277), 12km from the city center (taxis Rs100-150; rickshaws Rs80-100). **Indian Airlines** (☎2770480) is next door to the Gangotri Building in TT Nagar, past the Rang Mahal cinema 100m on the left. Open daily 10am-1pm and 2-5pm. To **Delhi** (2hr., 7:05pm, Rs4770) and **Mumbai** (2hr., 3pm, Rs5090) via **Indore** (30min., Rs2295). **MPSTDC,** also next door, deals with both IA and Jet Airways.

Trains: Railway station (☎131), down the street and off the bend in Hamidia Rd., 1km east of the bus station, exit through platform #5. Reservation office outside platform #1, on the far right as you face the station. Open M-Sa 8am-8pm, Su 8am-2pm. To: **Delhi** (8-12hr., 16-20 per day 12:40am-10:40pm, Rs221) via **Agra** (6-8hr., Rs174); **Gwalior** (4½-6hr., Rs138); **Hyderabad** (15-22hr., 2-4 per day 3:43am-11:35pm, Rs267); **Indore** (4-6hr., 4 per day 7:50am-9:40pm, Rs67) via **Ujjain** (3hr., Rs52); **Jabalpur** (7½hr., 1-2 per day 4 and/or 11pm, Rs81-126); **Jhansi** (3-4½hr., Rs112); and **Mumbai** (16hr., 6am and 4:50pm, Rs245).

Buses: Main Bus Stand (☎2540841), just off Hamidia Rd., west of the train station, 1km down on the right. Frequent departures for **Indore** (5hr., every 10min. 6am-6:30pm, Rs60) and other cities around the state, including **Sanchi** (1½hr., every 15-30min. 6am-9pm, Rs19).

Local Transportation: Auto-rickshaws charge Rs5.50 to start, and the metered rate is Rs3.75 per km. Insist that the driver use the meter, despite claims that it is broken. **Minibuses** will take you almost as far for much less. Minibus #9 goes from the railway station to TT Nagar; #7 and 11 go by Sultania Rd.; #2 goes from Hamidia Rd. to New Market and MP Nagar.

✈ 🛈 ORIENTATION AND PRACTICAL INFORMATION

The huge **Upper Lake** and smaller **Lower Lake** separate Old Bhopal in the northwest from the **New Town** in the southeast. **Hamidia Road** runs near the Taj-ul-Masjid (the city's largest mosque) on the western fringes of the old town, past the **bus stand** to the **railway station** in the east. If arriving by train, exit via platform #5 for Hamidia Rd. From the station area, with its many cheap hotels and restaurants, Hamidia Rd. turns right and runs south toward the new town and government center. The MPSTDC, Indian Airlines office, and the banks, are all in **TT Nagar. MPSTDC main office,** 6th fl., Gangotri Building, TT Nagar, New Town, offers tourist services and additional branches in the airport and railway station. (☎2774340. Open M-F and 1st and 4th Sa 10am-5pm.) In TT Nagar are the **State Bank of India,** Parcharad Building (☎2564118; open M-F 10:30am-2:30pm) and **IDBI Bank** (open M-F 10am-4pm and Sa 10am-2pm). The **police station** is on Sultania Rd. (☎2540880), and **Hamidia Hospital** is on Royal Market Rd. (☎2540222) and has a **24hr. pharmacy.** Look for fast connections at **Loveknot Photo State & Net Cafe,** at 1 Hamidia Rd. (☎2255712; Rs20 per hr.; open daily 7:30am-11pm). The **post office** is on Sultania Rd., opposite the Taj-ul-Masjid. (Open M-Sa 7am-6pm.) **Postal Code:** 462001.

Madhya Pradesh

Madhya Pradesh

RAJASTHAN

UTTAR PRADESH

BIHAR

JHARKHAND

CHHATTISGARH

ORISSA

MAHARASHTRA

GUJARAT

BUNDELKHAND

Kanpur
Varanasi
Allahabad
Son R.
Bandhavgarh National Park
Bilaspur
Mahanadi R.
Raipur
Rewa
Khajuraho
Panna
Satna
Murwara
Mandla
Kanha National Park
Kawardha
Chhatarpur
Orchha
Jhansi
Datia
Gwalior
Sind R.
Chanderi
Sagar
Jabalpur
Chhindwara
Nagpur
Kota
Shivpuri N.P.
Chambal R.
Udayapur
Udaigiri
Vidisha
Sanchi
Raisen
Bhojpur
Bhopal
Piparia
Pachmarhi
Betul
Chittaurgarh
Ujjain
Dewas
Indore
Mhow
Bhimbetka
Narmada R.
Omkareshwar
Khandwa
Burhanpur
Ratlam
Dhar
Mandu
Bagh
Maheshwar
Jalgaon
Ahmedabad
Baroda
Surat

60 miles
60 kilometers

▐ ACCOMMODATIONS

Hotels in Bhopal cater largely to business travelers. There are not many good budget places around, and every place in town levies taxes and service charges of up to 20%. This does mean, though, that "luxuries" like TVs, telephones, and attached bathrooms are pretty standard. **Hotel Sonali ❷,** on Radha Talkies Rd., has luxurious clean rooms with hot water showers, TVs, and 24hr. room service and check-out. (☎2740880, 2740990, or 2711176; fax 2710481. Singles Rs250-800; doubles Rs325-850.) **Hotel Meghdoot ❶** is left from the train station on Hamidia Rd. (☎2713407 or 2710131. Singles Rs125; doubles Rs170-400.) **Hotel Gulshan ❶,** around the corner from Hotel Sonali, has sparse but pleasant aqua rooms with basic amenities. (☎2740467. Singles Rs55-80; doubles Rs125.)

▐ FOOD

Restaurants in Bhopal offer a wide selection of surprisingly good fare. **Indian Coffee House ❶,** on Hamidia Rd., opposite Hotel Ranjit, and its sister franchises scattered around MP, is the friendliest restaurant in town with basic fare for Rs10-70 and superb coffee for Rs6-10. (Open daily 7am-10pm.) Equally pleasant is **Manohar Dairy and Restaurant ❶,** 6 Hamidia Rd., which offers good, cheap South Indian fare and lively service. South Indian snacks Rs10-40, fresh juices Rs12-20, pizza Rs30-40, a wide variety of desserts Rs12-45. (Open daily 6am-midnight.)

♫ ◎ ENTERTAINMENT AND SIGHTS

BHARAT BHAVAN. A cultural center that produces exhibitions of theater, music, poetry, and the fine arts, the Bharat Bhavan is one of India's finest museums. Architect Charles Correa crafted it into a charming public space with multi-layered courtyards overlooking the scenic Upper Lake. Check at the ticket office for scheduled performances. A library and cafe complete this cultural oasis. *(Lake Drive Rd., in New Town.* ☎ *2540353. Auto-rickshaw from Old Town Rs25-30. Open Nov. 1-Jan. 31 Tu-Su 1-7pm; Feb. 1-Oct. 31 Tu-Su 2-8pm. Rs10.)*

OLD TOWN. Bhopal's status as an independent, Muslim-ruled princely state until 1952 endowed the city with a strong Muslim character and a wealth of mosques. The old Muslim bazaar quarter, **Chowk,** wedged in the crook of a turn in Hamidia Rd., has the strongest Islamic flavor. The **Taj-ul-Masjid,** Bhopal's biggest mosque, is a spectacular illustration of Bhopal's Islamic tradition. The plans of the original builder, Nawab Shajehar Begum, were so grandiose that they have still not been completed. The 18-story minarets, the three huge domes over the prayer hall filled with students of the Qur'an, the vast courtyard, and the nearby river create a grand impression. The mosque can only be approached from Royal Market Rd. *(Open dawn-dusk. Free.)* The **Jama Masjid,** built by Kudsia Begum in 1837, has impressive gold-spiked minarets. The **Moti Masjid,** constructed in 1860 by Kudsia Begum's daughter, continues the Mughal tradition of small-scale, elegant, more "personal" mosques. Although less opulent than its big city counterparts, this mosque imitates many features (including the striped domes) of the Jama Masjid in Delhi. The mosques are illuminated by night; go up to the hill or on a balcony and enjoy the view.

TRIBAL HABITAT (MUSEUM OF MAN). The Tribal Habitat reconstructs the dwellings of various indigenous Indian tribes and attempts to provide a glimpse of actual tribal life. The open-air exhibition matches the natural surroundings of the tribal villages. *(Shamla Hill, close to Bharat Bhavan. 2km auto-rickshaw ride to exhibition area Rs15. Open Tu-Su 10am-6pm. Free.)*

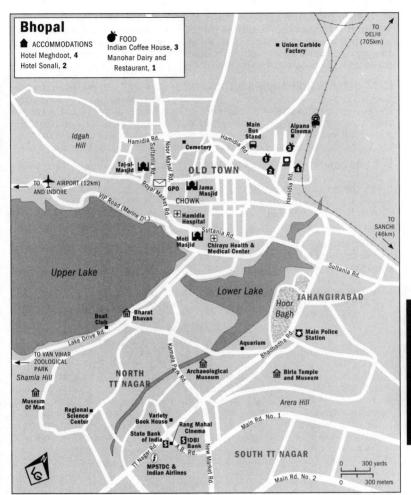

Bhopal

🏠 ACCOMMODATIONS
Hotel Meghdoot, **4**
Hotel Sonali, **2**

🍎 FOOD
Indian Coffee House, **3**
Manohar Dairy and
Restaurant, **1**

TO
DELHI
(705km)

■ Union Carbide
Factory

Idgah
Hill

Hamidia Rd.

■ Cemetery

Sultania Rd.

Noor Mahal Rd.

Main
Bus
Stand

Alpana
Cinema

Hamidia Rd.

Taj-ul-
Masjid

OLD TOWN

TO ✈ AIRPORT (12km)
AND INDORE

Royal Market Rd.

✉ GPO 🏠 Jama
Masjid

CHOWK

Hamidia Rd.

VIP Road (Marine Dr.)

✚ Hamidia
Hospital

Sultania Rd.

TO
SANCHI
(46km)

Moti
Masjid

✚ Chirayu Health &
Medical Center

Upper Lake

Sultania Rd.

Lower Lake

JAHANGIRABAD

Hoor
Bagh

Boat
Club

🏛 Bharat
Bhavan

Lake Drive Rd.

Kamala Park Rd.

🗡 Main Police
Station

Bhadbhada Rd.

TO VAN VIHAR
ZOOLOGICAL
PARK
Shamla Hill

Aquarium

**NORTH
TT NAGAR**

🏛 Archaeological
Museum

🏛 Birla Temple
and Museum

🏛
Museum
Of Man

Arera Hill

Regional ■
Science
Center

Variety
Book House

Rang Mahal
Cinema

Main Rd. No. 1

State Bank
of India

$ IDBI
Bank

New Market Rd.

TT Nagar Rd.

A.B. Rd.

SOUTH TT NAGAR

0   300 yards

ℹ️ MPSDC &
Indian Airlines

Main Rd. No. 2

0   300 meters

MADHYA PRADESH

OTHER MUSEUMS. The **Birla Museum** features a collection of 9th- and 10th-century sculptures from the Raisen, Sehore, Mandsaur, and Shahdol districts of MP. *(Arera Hill. Open Tu-Su 10am-5pm. Rs3.)* Next door, the **Birla Mandir** has yet another scenic view of the city, especially at night. *(Open in summer daily 6-11:30am and 4-9pm; in winter daily 6:30am-noon and 4-8:30pm. Free.)* The **State Musuem** has a small collection, with several noteworthy sculptures from this region, tribal art, and paintings from the Bagh Caves near Mandu. *(Banganga Rd. Open Tu-Su 10am-6pm. Rs30.)*

SANCHI सांची   ☎ 07482

In the 3rd century BC, the emperor Ashoka founded the Buddhist retreat at Sanchi as a haven for meditation. Sanchi re-entered the limelight when a British officer stumbled across its ruins in 1818. The large white *stupas*, with their exquisite sculptures, were named a UNESCO World Heritage site in 1989.

⌨ TRANSPORTATION. Frequent **buses** ply the roads between Bhopal's bus stand and Sanchi (1½hr., Rs19). Some take the long route via Raisen (2½hr.), so be sure to clarify the destination. Sanchi is on the main line from Bhopal to Delhi, but only two express **trains** from Bhopal stop at Sanchi (1hr., 8am and 2:40pm, Rs19). Other trains from Bhopal are extremely slow (2½-3hr.) and likely not worth taking.

◼◼ ◢ ORIENTATION AND PRACTICAL INFORMATION. The two main roads in Sanchi intersect. One leads southwest from the **railway station,** past the few budget hotels and the **police station,** and up a hill to the **main gate** of the ruins. The road to Bhopal crosses this street, continuing on to Vidisha, 10km to the northeast. The **market** and **bus stand** occupy the quadrant on the station side of the main road and the Bhopal side of the crossroads. There is a phone booth at the bus stand.

◢◻ ACCOMMODATIONS AND FOOD. Though many visitors see the sights in a couple of hours, accommodations are plentiful. The **Tourist Cafeteria ❷,** just before the museum, has bright, airy, spotless rooms. (☎62743. Singles Rs220; doubles Rs319.) The cafeteria serves the standard MPSTDC fare. (Snacks Rs12-25, entrees Rs20-45. Open daily 7am-10pm.) Near the railway station, the **Pathak** and **Rohit** restaurants serve basic Indian meals.

◧ SIGHTS. The main road from the railway station leads past a kiosk on the left that sells tickets for both the **archaeological museum** and the hilltop ruins. The museum holds a modest collection of statues unearthed at Sanchi. (Rs5. Closed F. No photography.) The useful *Sanchi* guide, published by the Archaeological Survey of India, is sometimes available here (Rs15). Past the museum, a road winds its way up the hill; if you're on foot, the steep staircase leading off to the right is the more direct route to the ruins. (Ruins Rs250. Video fee Rs25.)

The oldest structure at Sanchi, the **Great Stupa** was erected by Emperor Ashoka in the 3rd century BC. When the ruins were unearthed, archaeologists nearly destroyed the massive 16m *stupa* in their rush to find valuable artifacts before discovering that there was no treasure inside—the *stupa* was solid throughout.

In the 1st century BC, the Satavahanas tacked on Sanchi's richest addition: the four monumental gateways facing the cardinal directions. Archaeologists attribute the intricate sculpture to ivory carvers accustomed to making maximum use of minimum surface; the theory is borne out by a Pali inscription on the south gate.

The **north gateway,** less scarred by the ravages of time than its counterparts, is adorned on top by a partially preserved wheel of law. It shows the **Vessarkara Jataka** around both sides of the bottom rung. In the tale, the Buddha successively gives up a magic elephant, his horse and chariot, and his wife and children before being reinstated to his princedom.

While the upper registers of the **east gateway** repeat earlier scenes, the south pillar depicts the Buddha walking on water on the outside and facing a fearsome cobra on the inside. Below this scene is a depiction of villagers trying to make a sacrificial fire that won't light without the Buddha's permission. Hanging off the bottom right architrave is a *yakshi* (maiden).

The **south gate,** opposite the path to the ruins, was once the main entrance, as evidenced by the stump of a pillar erected by Ashoka to the right of it. A local *zamindar* (landlord) broke off the rest of the pillar to use in a sugarcane press. The middle architrave of the south gate shows Ashoka's army arriving at the last of the eight original *stupas* containing the Buddha's relics at Ramagrama, but Ashoka is prevented from carting off the loot (as he had at the other seven) by the army of snake people to the left. On the inside, the middle rung depicts the *Chhadanta Jataka;* above this scene are the trees and *stupas* of the *manushis.* The bottom rung shows the siege of Kushinagar (see p. 719), the archetypical story of Buddhist non-violence.

The **west gateway** is best recognized by the funny dwarves that support its architraves. The front face of the west gateway features (from top to bottom) more *manushis*, the Buddha's first sermon (note the wheel), and more scenes of the *Chhadanta Jataka*. Inside, the top two architraves show more wrangling over relics, and the bottom reveals the Buddha attaining enlightenment despite the distracting demons sent by Mara. On the southern pillar of this gate, the **Mahakapi Jataka** depicts the Buddha as a monkey turning himself into a bridge so that his brethren can escape to safety over a river.

There are four other *stupas* at Sanchi, all of them younger than the Great Stupa. **Stupa 3,** on the way to the Great Stupa, is marked by one gateway. **Stupa 2,** down the hill on the way back to the village, has no gateways but is decorated by interesting frescoes. Past the south gateway of the Great Stupa stand several *chaityas* (temples) whose style resembles that of ancient Greek temples. The largest of the remaining monasteries is **Monastery 51,** to the right of the Great Stupa and back toward the village. The **Great Bowl,** now broken, lies just past the monastery and once served as a depository for the monks' food and offerings.

INDORE इंदौर ☎0731

Indore (pop. 1.2 million) has not been endowed with any spectacular sights to attract visitors; nevertheless, it is a friendly, pleasant city of parks and broad avenues. As the commercial heart of Madhya Pradesh, Indore has solid infrastructure and the smog-choked air of modernity. Its markets are great for gift-shopping and are cluttered with everything from saris and silver to carpets. Well-connected via rail and road, Indore is an ideal base from which to visit the ancient cities of Mandu and Ujjain, as well as Maheshwar and Omkareshwar.

☐ TRANSPORTATION

Flights: The **airport** (☎2410452 and 2413747) is 8km west of the city center, along MG Rd. Auto-rickshaw Rs70-100. **Indian Airlines,** RS Bandari Marg (☎2431595 or 2431596). From Gandhi's statue, head away from the center, turn left, then right, and walk for 5min.; IA will be on the right. Flies daily to: **Delhi** (2hr., 11am, US$140) via **Bhopal** (30min., US$60); **Mumbai** (1hr., 5pm, US$95). **Jet Airways,** G-2 Vidyapati Bhawan, 17 Racecourse Rd. (☎2544592 or 2433211). Open M-Sa 9:30am-6pm, Su 9:30am-1pm. To: **Delhi** and **Mumbai** (1 hr., 2 per day, US$95-100). **Sahara Airlines,** G-6 Industry House, Agra-Bombay Rd. (☎2266399 or 2432637) also has a flight to **Mumbai.** Open daily 10am-6pm.

Trains: The **railway station** is on Station Rd. (☎131 or 2521685). The **reservation office** is on the street directly across from the main entrance, in a pink bldg. on the right. Open M-Sa 8am-8pm, Su 8am-2pm. To: **Ahmedabad** (express 10hr., 10:30pm, Rs250); **Bhopal** (6hr.; 4 per day Tu-F 6am-4:40pm, M and Sa-Su 6am-8:35pm; Rs155); **Kolkata** (36hr.; Tu, Th, Sa 8:45pm; Rs400); **Delhi** (21hr., 1 and 4pm, Rs300) via **Gwalior** and **Agra; Jaipur** (16hr., daily 9:50pm, Rs245); **Mumbai** (16hr., 3:50pm, Rs300); **Udaipur** (15hr., daily 5:55pm, Rs175); **Ujjain** (2hr., frequent 6am-8pm, Rs50).

Buses: Sarwate bus stand (☎2465688), at the intersection of Nasia Rd. and Kibe Compound Rd., 500m south of the train station. Turn right and go under the Patel overpass as you exit the railway station. To: **Aurangabad** (5am and 9pm, Rs197); **Bhopal** (4½hr., every 30min. 4:30am-12:30am, Rs86-130); **Mandu** (3½hr., frequent, Rs37); **Omkareshwar** (3½hr., frequent 6am-4pm, Rs34); **Ujjain** (2hr., every 15min. 6am-10pm, Rs27). **Gangwal bus stand,** about 3km west of the train station, serves **Mandu,** but you need to change buses in **Dhar** (4hr., frequent, Rs52). For a more comfortable ride to these and other destinations, including **Maheshwar,** try the

MADHYA PRADESH

private operators on the street opposite the train station, near the reservation office. However, these are far less frequent, leaving only when sufficiently full. Prices are about 2-3 times higher. For those with cash to spare and little time, a private taxi return trip to most of these destinations will run you Rs700-1000.

Local Transportation: English street signs are rare, and the wide, sidewalk-less roads are crammed with fast-moving traffic. Take advantage of the ubiquitous **auto-rickshaws** from Rs10 for short rides to Rs25 across town. Make sure that your driver uses his meter. Or jump aboard one of the **tempos** that ply the main thoroughfares (Rs3), though your driver will almost certainly not know English.

ORIENTATION AND PRACTICAL INFORMATION

The **train station** is in the center of Indore, and the railway lines bisect the city into eastern and western halves. To the east, workshops and business hotels are built on top of each other; to the west is the older part of town, containing most of the city's sights and endless bazaars. **Serafa Bazaar** is especially alluring, with its crumbling colonial buildings, mosques, and vendors selling jewelry and good luck charms. Two bridges link the two halves of the city. **Shastri Bridge** is 250m north of the railway station along **Station Road.** From Shastri Bridge, **Mahatma Gandhi (MG) Road** leads to the sights in the west and to the **Gandhi statue,** at the intersection with **RN Tagore Road** (known as "RNT Marg" by auto-drivers), in the east. A 500m walk south (right) from the railway station takes you under the Patel Bridge to **Sarwate Bus Stand.** A 5min. walk away from the railway lines from either the Patel Bridge or the bus stand takes you to the **Nehru statue** and to **Maharaja Yeshwantrao (MY) Hospital Road,** which leads southeast to the bank, GPO, and Central Museum. From the railway station, exit through platform #1 for the east side of the city and platform #4 for the west side.

Tourist Office: MPSTDC, RN Tagore Rd. (☎2528653). From MG Rd., turn right onto RNT Rd. at the Gandhi statue; it's in a park on the left. Open M-Sa 10am-5pm.

Currency Exchange: State Bank of India, Main Branch, Agra-Bombay Rd., on the left before the GPO and Central Museum. At least a 20min. walk from the train or bus station. Head east, past the Nehru statue, turn right at Indian Coffee House, then make another right. **IDBI Bank,** Agra-Bombay Rd. Follow directions to the State Bank of India, and take another left at the big intersection; it's on the left, 5min. down the road. AmEx **ATM** outside. Open M-F 10am-4pm, Sa 10am-2pm. ATMs also abound in the shopping complexes on MG Rd. and RNT Marg.

Police: (☎2464488 or 100 for emergencies), under the Patel overpass, between the railway station and Sarwate. Police Commissioner's Office (☎2513026).

Pharmacy: MY Hospital Pharmacy, MY Hospital Rd., between the Nehru statue and State Bank of India. Open 24hr. Or try one of the pharmacies across from the MY Hospital.

Hospital: Choithrom Hospital, Monik Barg Rd. (☎2362491).

Internet: There are many internet cafes on RNT Marg, most with fast connections. Be wary of those with private booths with webcams. **Cyber Dream,** 166 RN Tagore Rd., just past the Woodlands Restaurant. Rs30 per hr. Open daily 8:30am-11:30pm. **Valdilal Shop,** 7 MG Rd. (☎5068606), next to Ahinsa Towers, has modern facilities and cold drinks and ice cream. Rs20 per hr. Open daily 9am-midnight.

Post Office: GPO, Agra-Bombay Rd. (☎700244). Between the State Bank of India and the museum; turn right off MY Hospital Rd. Open M-Sa 8am-7:30pm, Su 10:30am-3:30pm. **Postal Code:** 452001.

ACCOMMODATIONS

Hotels in Indore fill up with businessmen, especially at the beginning of the month. The cheaper places, which are between the Sarwate bus stand and the Nehru statue, cater to middle-class Indians, and usually offer 24hr. check-out, TVs, phones, and *dhobi* service. Prices quoted do not include state tax of 10%.

Hotel Ashoka, 14 Nasia Rd. (☎465991 or 475496), opposite the Sarwate bus stand. The hallways may smell a bit funky, but even the most ordinary rooms on the top floor are very clean and modern. Rooms facing the interior courtyard are quite noisy. Singles Rs175-350; doubles Rs225-400. ❷

Hotel Royal Residency, 225 RN Tagore Rd. (☎705633; fax 405677). From the train or bus station, walk east to the Nehru statue, then turn right. This gorgeous, modern hotel is pure luxury, but its cheaper rooms are only standard. Check-out 9am. Singles Rs450-850; doubles Rs650-1050. MC/V. ❸

Hotel Neelam, 33/2 Patel Bridge Corner (☎466001 or 464616). From the Sarwate bus stand, take the alley that leads alongside the overpass; it's on the side street on the right. The higher up you climb the endless staircase, the brighter and airier the rooms get. Singles Rs175-350; doubles Rs250-400. ❷

FOOD

Indore is not a city of culinary delights, and most restaurants are in the better hotels near RN Tagore Rd. Fortunately, prices tend to be reasonable. There are bar-restaurants, fruit stands, and sweets-stalls to the left of the Sarwate bus stand.

Woodlands Restaurant, Hotel President, 163 RN Tagore Rd., near the Nehru statue. A respite from the frantic frenzy of outdoor Indore, Woodlands serves breakfast (Rs65-85), dinner (Rs70-100), and South Indian snacks (Rs30-50). Open daily 7am-11pm; meals served 7-11am, noon-3pm, and 7-11pm. ❷

Indian Coffee House, MG Rd., 250m past Gandhi Hall, on the left, inside a courtyard heading west toward Rajwada. As always, this stylish cafe serves the best coffee and cheap snacks. No item on the menu is more than Rs28. Superb outdoor tables in a small park at a 2nd location, opposite the MY Hospital (continue east past the Nehru statue). Both open daily 8am-10pm. ❶

SIGHTS

CENTRAL MUSEUM. Presenting religious sculptures, stone inscriptions, and Sanskrit copper plates from western MP among other things, the Central Museum has a collection that is both beautiful and unique. Unfortunately, poor presentation does little to illuminate cultural context. The pieces scattered outside in the grass make the art accessible to all. Ask one of the attendants for a tour. *(On the Agra-Bombay Rd. beyond the GPO. Open Tu-Su 10:30am-5:50pm. Rs30.)*

LAL BAGH PALACE. This British-style manor was built by the Holkar Maharajas between 1886 and 1921. Along with the usual stuffed wildcats, the house features an underground tunnel connecting the main house with the kitchens on the other side of the river, as well as imposing gates that are replicas of the ones at Buckingham Palace. Don't jump out of your *chappals* when a statue of a certainly-not-amused Queen Victoria pops up at the exit to see you off the premises. *(Between the train station and Gangwal Bus Stand. Open Tu-Su 10am-5pm. Rs2. Guidebooks Rs10.)*

OTHER SIGHTS. On the western side of town, off MG Rd., **Rajwada** pays homage to the faded splendor of the Holkars. This 18th-century palace was built in a style that blended Mughal, French, and Maratha influences. The mostly wooden structure did not prove very resistant to fires, so only the front facade survives today. Wander the streets of the lively **Khajuri Bazaar** on your way to the nearby **Kanch Mandir,** a Jain temple made entirely of mirrored tiles. The 1875 **Bada Ganapati,** otherwise uninteresting, houses the largest Ganesh statue in the world (8m). Finally, those interested in Raj-era architecture might want to visit **Gandhi Hall,** now a Town Hall, on MG Rd. just west of Shastri Bridge.

NEAR INDORE

▶ MAHESHWAR

Maheshwar is not connected directly with any major cities, but if you don't mind transferring, it's quite easy to reach. Frequent buses run to Dhamnod (30min., Rs5), from which there are connections to Mandu (2hr., Rs27) and Indore (3hr., Rs30). Four buses per day go to Omkareshwar (3hr., Rs30). For a much more comfortable and flexible ride, take a private taxi from Indore (round-trip Rs700-900).

Both the *Ramayana* and the *Mahabharata* mention **Mahishmati** (Maheshwar's previous incarnation), once a glorious city and the capital of King Arjuna Kartavirya's realm around 200 BC. The city fell into oblivion until the late 18th century, when the Holkar queen, Ahilyabai, made it her capital and built a fortified palace and two richly decorated temples along the Narmada River. The queen also established a center for producing fine, handloomed saris, and legend has it that she created the simple but distinctive geometric border design that makes Maheshwari saris famous throughout India today.

To reach the sights, clustered inside the **fort,** turn left out of the bus station and head straight across the main road. The right fork in the village road leads up to the fort. Past the main gate, a smaller gate leads into the palace grounds, where a two-room **museum** contains a jumble of broken statuary and Holkar dynasty paraphernalia. Through the gate to the left of the museum are steps down to the **sari workshop** and the temples and *ghats* below. The workshop at the top of the stairs, run by the Rehwa Society (established in 1978 to preserve Maheshwar's silk-cotton sari-weaving tradition), is set up for the benefit of tourists. In a dark, low, historic building lit by fluorescent tubes, workers, most of them women, weave material in a stunning array of colors and designs. The manager, who sits just inside the door, will call somebody up to show you around. Saris, *dupattas*, and other stunning woven items are for sale in the workshop's store (Rs250-2500). Prices are comparable to those in town, and while the proprietors do not bargain, you are ensured that your money is actually reaching those who made the crafts. Rehwa employs underprivileged women, many of them cast out by their families, and provides them with housing, decent pay, pension, family healthcare, childcare, and humane working hours. (Open W-M 10am-5pm. Free.) Past the sari workshop, at the bottom of the stairs, Maheshwar's **temples** are pressed into small courtyards that make them seem larger than they are. However, the sheer number and variety of these old temples makes Maheshwar a delight to explore. The relative lack of tourism leaves you free to walk along muddy *ghats* or perch next to shrines overlooking the greenery lining the pacific Rehwa river.

Aakashdeep Rest House ❶, at the base of the fort, has both clean and basic doubles, and also nicer, brand-new spotless rooms higher up, complete with balconies and big, soft beds. (✆07283 273326. Doubles Rs50-70; new rooms Rs200, with A/C Rs400.) For food, **VIP Cottage ❶,** on the main road 400m to the left of the bus stand, just over the bridge, has all the usual stuff (Rs15-150).

MADHYA PRADESH

▓ OMKARESHWAR (ONKARESHWAR)

Buses run directly from Omkareshwar to Indore (3hr., frequent 5am-4:15pm, Rs34). Four buses per day also make it to Maheshwar (3hr., last one 3:30pm, Rs30) on what long ago used to qualify as "roads." Buses run to Ujjain (5hr., 1 per day, Rs56).

For centuries, Omkareshwar, an island shaped like the holiest of all Hindu symbols, the "Om" (ॐ), has drawn pilgrims to its temples and *ghats*. With its endless night-and-day chants, repeated *Hare Om* greetings, and the buzz of flies, Omkareshwar is like a miniature Varanasi. Its temples rise up over jagged cliffs, while the *ghats* climb serenely from the banks of the Narmada and Kaveri rivers.

To reach the temples, follow the crowds through the village until you reach the footbridge that spans the deep gully dividing the island. Visit the public restrooms (Rs1-3) to the right of the bridge before the crossing; the trip around the island is long (at least 1½hr.) and toilets are almost nonexistent. Otherwise, descend to the *ghats* and take a ferry across (Rs5). Once across the river, follow the paved pathway to the left that runs along the riverside. The path leads pilgrims in a clockwise circle around the island. The route is scattered with innumerable temples and shrines of all sizes and shapes. The shrines are tended by caretakers who act rather like hawks, beckoning you to visit their particular shrine, and, of course, show your devotion in rupee form. The path leads to a rocky tip of the island, littered with stones in *linga* shapes, and uphill to the island's peak, populated heavily by large and outgoing monkeys, and finally winds down to the bridge again. The remarkably detailed five-story **Shri Omkar Mandhata,** home to one of only 12 *jyotirlingas* (naturally occurring phallic symbols that are a sign of Shiva) in India, is the reason why most people come to Omkareshwar. Compared to the *jyotirlinga* in Ujjain (see p. 362), this one seems embarrassingly small. The **Siddhnath Temple,** also worth visiting, is an early medieval brahmin temple.

The **police station** (☎344015; open daily 9am-5pm) and the **post office** (☎02780 71222; open M-Sa 9am-5pm) are near the bus station. There is no place in the village to change currency. From the bus station, a 3min. walk through the village takes you past the **Government Hospital** on the right (open daily 8am-noon and 5-6pm) and the **pharmacy** on the left (open daily 7:30am-9:30pm). **Yatrika Guest House ❷** is behind the bus station. (☎02780 71308. Singles Rs150; doubles Rs200.) For nicer rooms and more scenic views, try the **Hotel Aishwarya ❸.** Take the small side street directly across from the bus station, and follow the signs for 20min. (☎02780 71325 or 71326. Singles Rs275-325; doubles Rs375-475. 10% luxury tax.) For food, you're best sticking with one of the many nameless restaurants that line the main street, all serving *samosas* (Rs4), other fried fare, and decent *thalis* (Rs15-30).

MANDU माण्डव ☎02792

Mandu is the kind of agricultural idyll that India likes to promote in its tourist brochures. Goats munch on the grass surrounding the ruins, while women walk by with pots on their head, and children run over to say "hello." Stretched out on top of a narrow plateau in the Vindhya mountain range, the city was fortified as long ago as the 6th century. Mandu's golden age lasted from 1401 to 1526, when the Muslim rulers of the kingdom of Malwa called it their home, building walls, mosques, palaces, and pleasure domes in stone and marble across the length of the plateau. Five centuries later, their monuments still stand in a tranquil, underpopulated mountain region set against a backdrop of great natural beauty. The main tourist season is between October and March, but the monsoon season is perhaps the best time to visit, when the life-giving rains paint the surrounding countryside a lush green. Mandu is something of an earthly paradise; a cool and verdant landscape littered with ruins.

▐ TRANSPORTATION

Buses depart from the village square to: **Dhar** (1½hr., 14 per day 7am-6:15pm, Rs15); **Indore** (3hr., 5-6 per day 6am-4:45pm, Rs60); **Maheshwar** via **Dhamnod** (3hr., frequent, Rs32). Bus service is often less frequent during monsoon season. Inquire at Relax Point Restaurant for exact departure times, as the restaurant functions as an unofficial bus depot. The easiest and most pleasant way of getting around is on **bikes,** which you can rent from several villagers living on the main road or from **Ajay's Bicycle Shop,** also on the main road, just south of the square (Rs3 per hr., Rs30 per day), or inquire through your hotel. Alternatively, **Nitin Traders,** just south of the square opposite the Jain temple, will wheel out the one village **auto-rickshaw** (Rs100 per hr.) or call up private **taxis** to Indore. (Rs725, book 1½hr. before departure. Open daily 8am-8pm.)

▐▐ ORIENTATION AND PRACTICAL INFORMATION

The only way out of the village is from the north. The **main road** runs north/south, past the **village square** and **Jama Masjid,** ending at the **Rewa Kund** ruins 6km south of the village. **Jahaz Mahal Road** shoots out of the village square and leads to the **Royal Enclave** ruins. The sights around town are well-marked, and there are signs in English to direct visitors to the ruins. All the hotels and restaurants, as well as the **post office** (☎263222; open M-Sa 9am-5pm), **police station** (☎263223), and **pharmacy** (open daily 9am-7pm) are on the main road. There are several doctors' offices in Mandu, but the closest hospital is in Indore. There is no tourist office in Mandu, but the **MPSTDC** in Indore can help with hotel reservations (recommended in winter). Power outages are frequent, and phone lines are often down during the monsoon. **Postal Code:** 454010.

▐ ▐ ACCOMMODATIONS AND FOOD

All accommodations in Mandu are overpriced given the quality (or lack thereof) of lodging they provide. Despite this, it is worth staying here overnight. Ask the bus driver to drop you off at one of the hotels. **Hotel Maharaja ❷,** on Jahaz Mahal Rd., has small but clean rooms with attached baths and is the best deal in town. At first glance, the rooms may seem a bit too rustic, but they are quite comfortable and offer all the same amenities that the exorbitantly-priced hotels do. The friendly owner is also the mayor of Mandu and very eager to provide help should you encounter any problems during your stay. The Nepalese kitchen staff whips up Indian, Chinese, Continental, and, yes, Nepalese cuisine. (☎263288. Doubles Rs200; singles Rs150. Off-season Rs150/100.) The **Travelers' Lodge ❷,** 1km north of the square on the main road, has scenic views over the eastern ravine, but its dingy and slightly worn rooms have passed their prime. (☎263221. Singles Rs290; doubles Rs390.) The **MPSTDC Tourist Cottages ❸,** on the main road 2km south of the square, has better rooms in small cottages with lake views. (☎263235. Singles Rs350-750; doubles Rs450-850.) Both places charge 10% luxury tax but offer 25% discounts in May and June. Reservations can be made in any MPSTDC office (recommended in-season). MPSTDC has two comfortable but pricey hotels in Mandu. The MPSTDC Tourist Cottages both have **restaurants ❶,** with the standard menu of snacks (Rs5-40), continental dishes (Rs30-100), veg. (Rs20-45) and non-veg. (Rs30-100) options. (MPSTDC restaurants open daily 6-10am, noon-3pm, and 7-11pm; snacks available between meal times.) The **Rupmati Hotel ❷,** the best in town, has large rooms and magnificent terraces overlooking the ravine. (☎263270. Doubles Rs450-750; 10% luxury tax.) The **restaurant ❷** is more affordable than the rooms. The open-air pavilion, overlooking a landscaped lawn with swings and slides, serves veg. (Rs30-55) and non-veg. (Rs50-250) dishes. Beer Rs50-75. (Open daily 7am-11pm.) The **Relax Point Restaurant ❶**, in the main square, offers veg. *thalis* for Rs35 and an astounding array of packaged snacks, chocolates, cold drinks, and travelers' necessities. (Film, mosquito nets, toilet paper, etc. Open daily 8am-10:30pm.)

🔎 SIGHTS

Ruins are everywhere in Mandu, dominating the landscape, from the gateways you pass on the way into town to the mosque and tomb in the market square; from the crumbling houses along the sides of the main street to the palace at the tip of the plateau. The attractions are in three main areas: the **central group** in the village center, the **Royal Enclave** in the north, and the **Rewa Kund complex** in the south. The last group is 6km away from the village, and a bike is strongly recommended. All sights are open from sunrise to sunset and only some charge an entrance fee.

THE CENTRAL GROUP. In the middle of both the plateau and the village, the central group includes the beautiful **Jama Masjid,** one of India's largest mosques. Like the other monuments here, it typifies the austere architectural style imported from Afghanistan by Hoshang Shah. Reputedly modeled on the mosque in Damascus, and completed in 1454, the Jama Masjid is remarkable for both its sheer scale and the simplicity of its design. Hoshang Shah's son built a white marble **mausoleum** behind the Jama Masjid for his father. The structure inspired Shah Jahan to send his architects to study it before beginning the Taj Mahal. *(Mausoleum Rs100.)*

THE ROYAL ENCLAVE. Sultan Ghiyas Shah constructed the huge 15th-century **Jahaz Mahal** (or "ship palace"), inside the gateway, to house his huge harem. The long, narrow design and the two artificial lakes on either side are what give the building its name, especially apparent during the rainy season, when water comes cascading through the palace's complex system of pools and conduits. Behind the Jahaz Mahal stands the **Hindola Mahal,** an audience hall nicknamed the "Swinging Palace" due to its sloping buttresses, which look as if they're swinging out at an angle. Ghiyas Shah had a ramp built so that he could ride to the upper floor without the hassle of getting down from his elephant. Many other ruins, including **Dilwar Khan's Mosque,** the **Water Palace,** and **Gada Shah's Shop,** are also in this enclave. *(Jahaz Mahal Rd., next to Hoshang Shah's tomb, continues to the Royal Enclave. Rs100.)*

REWA KUND. The main road ends 6km from the sq., at the **Rewa Kund** complex, named after the tank that used to supply water to the nearby palaces. Baz Bahadur, the last independent ruler of Mandu, built his **palace,** the **Baz Bahadur,** in the 16th century to serve as a quiet retreat, with views of the surrounding greenery. But even this tranquil spot could not satisfy the stunning Rupmati, the sultan's favorite dancer. She was from the plains, and life up on the plateau made her homesick. According to legend, Rupmati demanded that Baz Bahadur build her a pavilion on the crest of a hill, from which she could see her former village in the Narmada Valley far below. No sooner had the dutiful sultan completed **Rupmati's Pavilion** than the jealous Akbar stormed Mandu to seize the renowned dancer. Baz Bahadur fled, Rupmati swallowed poison, and soon after, Akbar let his testosterone guide him to the next dancing girl (see **Orchha,** p. 377), leaving Mandu desolate. The views from the palace are not to be missed. *(Entrance to complex Rs100.)*

NIL KANTH TEMPLE. Originally a Mughal palace, complete with running water that once flowed over ribbed stones in front of candles, the temple today has been taken over by the Shaivites. From this spot on the valley slopes, just below the clifftop, people worship an incarnation of Shiva whose throat turned blue when he drank poison. Inscriptions on the walls date Akbar's time, and describe the futility of mavi's achievements: "Till when wilt thou boast that thy mansion has reached heaven? / They will laugh at our vainsome hearts. / Come take warning from the history of others / Before that they listen to our history." *(At the southern end of the village, a fork leads right, or west, from the main road to the Nil Kanth Temple, 3km away.)*

UJJAIN उज्जैन ☎ 0734

Ujjain's long and varied history stretches back to the 3rd century BC, when the city was the imperial seat of Ashoka, Buddhism's first patron. Later, Ujjain served as a major center of Indian astronomy. Long before the days of the prime meridian, Hindu stargazers made Ujjain into India's Greenwich. An 18th-century observatory on the southwestern side of town is still in use today. Ujjain is also among the holiest of holy Hindu cities; legend has it that when Hindu gods scrambled with demons for the nectar that grants immortality, one of the four drops of the nectar that fell to Earth landed smack dab in the middle of Ujjayini (Ujjain's ancient name, meaning "one who conquers with pride"). Ujjain is thus one of the four cities that hosts the **Kumbh Mela** festival every 12 years (the other four are Haridwar, Nasik, and Allahabad). The town attracts millions of people every year with the promise of a hard-earned space along the city *ghats* for a dip in the sacred river Shipra. While Ujjain's temples are not the grandest that India has to offer, its hectic religious atmosphere makes it a worthwhile day stop.

▐ TRANSPORTATION

Trains: The **railway station** is on Subhash Rd., 150m west of the bus station. A **reservation office** is on the left after exiting the main station building. Open M-Sa 8am-8pm, Su 8am-2pm. Use platform #1 to exit to town, platform #7 to the MPSTDC and Hotel Shipra. To: **Ahmedabad** (10hr., 9:05pm, Rs159); **Bhopal** (3-4hr., 6-8 per day 1am-10:15pm, Rs52); **Delhi** (17hr., 2:45 and 6:25pm, Rs280); **Gwalior** (10½hr., 2:45pm, Rs210); **Indore** (2-3hr., 14 per day 2am-8:40pm, Rs23); **Jaipur** (9hr., about 1 per day, Rs196); **Mumbai** (13hr., 5:35pm, Rs268).

Buses: Mahakal Bus Stand, on the corner to the right (northeast) as you leave the train station. To: **Bhopal** (5hr., 4 per day 6am-9:30pm, Rs78) and **Indore** (2hr., frequent 4:30am-9:30pm, Rs27). Buses to Indore are faster than trains. Other connections are through Indore.

Local Transportation: Things are spread out, and most **auto-rickshaw** drivers refuse to use meters. Bargain—the longest ride should cost no more than Rs30-35. **Tempos** #2 and 9 go to the Mahakaleshwar Mandir; #4 and 10 go to the Gopal Mandir.

✦ ▐ ORIENTATION AND PRACTICAL INFORMATION

Hemmed in by the **Shipra River** to the west and the **railroad tracks** to the south, Ujjain's **old city** charms visitors with many small shops and drives them crazy with frustratingly narrow lanes. There are no street signs, few landmarks, and countless little roads to nowhere. Most of the temples and *ghats* are within walking distance of one another, but other places require a rickshaw ride. The railway station, bus stand, GPO, and most hotels are all clustered around one intersection.

Tourist Office: MPSTDC has a booth in the railway station that provides great maps of the city. Open daily 8am-3pm. The staff at the reception desk of the **MPSTDC Hotel Shipra,** Vishva Vidhyalaya Rd. (☎2551495 or 2551496), will also provide information. Exit the railway station through platform #7. Go left and turn right on the wide avenue; the hotel is 200m down on the right. Open 24hr. Ask here for Raju Pawar, the only government-licensed guide in Ujjain (Rs300-600 for a tour of the city).

Currency Exchange: The closest place to exchange currency is in Indore.

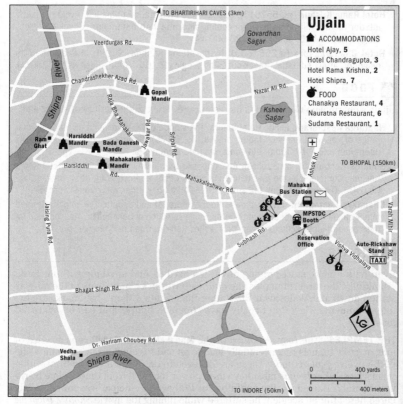

Ujjain

▲ **ACCOMMODATIONS**
Hotel Ajay, **5**
Hotel Chandragupta, **3**
Hotel Rama Krishna, **2**
Hotel Shipra, **7**

🍴 **FOOD**
Chanakya Restaurant, **4**
Nauratna Restaurant, **6**
Sudama Restaurant, **1**

MADHYA PRADESH

Police Superintendent: ☎ 2513300.

Hospital: Civil Hospital, Ashok Rd. From the train station, it's 200m beyond Mahakal bus stand and across the street. Also has a **24hr. pharmacy.** For private medical assistance, the MPSTDC recommends Dr. Rita Shinde or Dr. Bishi (☎ 2555067).

Post Office: GPO (☎ 2551023), behind the bus stand at the 2nd gate on the left. Open M-Sa 10am-10pm, Su 10am-2pm. **Postal Code:** 456001.

🏨 ACCOMMODATIONS

The only "luxurious" place to stay is MPTDC's Hotel Shipra (see below). All other budget hotels are pretty basic and grubby, with hot water in buckets and no showers. They cluster around the railway station. Prices listed do not include state taxes of 5% on rooms Rs60-149 and 10% on rooms Rs150 and above.

Hotel Shipra, Vishva Vidhyalaya Rd. (☎ 2551495 or 2551496; mptujjain@sify.com). Relatively expensive, but with spacious, airy rooms, sparkling showers with hot water, room service, and gorgeous balconies. Only the more expensive rooms have TVs. Singles Rs350-1790; doubles Rs390-1790. AmEx/MC/V. ❸

Hotel Ajay, 12 Dewas Gate, Mahakaleshwar Rd. (☎ 2550856 or 2551354), on the street opposite the bus station. The best choice among Ujjain's budget hotels. Sizable rooms are clean, and the staff is friendly. Singles Rs150-225; doubles Rs175-350. ❷

Hotel Rama Krishna (☎ 2557012), opposite the train station to the left. Avoid the stuffy interior rooms. All rooms have air-cooling and attached bathrooms. Check-out 24hr. Singles Rs150-500; doubles Rs225-600. ❷

Hotel Chandragupta (☎ 2561600), by the Rama Krishna. Slightly cheaper than its neighbor. Attached baths. Check-out 24hr. Singles Rs100-180; doubles Rs200-250. ❶

▐ FOOD

Ujjain's charm won't be found in its restaurants; stick to the variety of street eats.

Nauratna Restaurant, inside Hotel Shipra. The standard MP Tourism menu made up of a range of veg. and non-veg. Indian dishes (Rs15-175). Separate bar area. Open daily noon-3pm and 7-10:30pm, but can serve food anytime. ❷

Sudama Restaurant, on Subhash Rd., opposite the railway station, next to Hotel Rama Krishna. Contemplate the fascinating cut-mirror decor while chowing down on veg. fare (Rs6-45). Dinner after 7pm, but snacks (Rs6-32) all day. Open daily 9am-11pm. ❶

Chanakya Restaurant, on the ground floor of Hotel Chandragupta. The whole extended family can fit into one of the giant booths. Large selection of beer and spirits, and hard-to-miss pseudo-erotic sculpture. Veg.-only dishes Rs6-40. Open daily 8am-11pm. ❶

◉ SIGHTS

Even with a map, start praying now—it's hard to find anything without faith. Thankfully, the largest temples and *ghats* are within a 30min. walk of the railway station down Mahakaleshwar Rd. Rather than sights, Ujjain's landmarks are living monuments; they don't really have "opening hours" and can be accessed most days.

THE TEMPLES. The rosy *shikhara* of the **Mahakaleshwar Mandir** caps a series of long, narrow tunnels that eventually lead to an underground room containing one of the twelve *jyotirlingas*. These are believed to derive their power from within themselves; other *lingas* must have their power renewed from time to time by ritual. Amitabh Bachchan, the godfather of Bollywood cinema, was miraculously cured here after an accident he suffered while filming the movie *Sholay*. *(From the bus stand, Mahakaleshwar Rd. leads 1.5km directly to the temple.)*

As its name suggests, the **Bada Ganesh Mandir** enshrines a sculpture of Ganesh. (100m down the road that circles behind the Mahakaleshwar Mandir, to the right.) The **Harsiddhi Mandir,** the large temple complex behind high white walls, is the focal point of Devi worship. It marks the spot where Parvati's arm was severed when Shiva pulled her from her *sati* pyre. A famous image of the goddess Annapurna in the temple shrine. *(From the Mahakaleshwar Mandir, continue on the road past the Bada Ganesh Mandir into and over the marsh beyond; when you hit dry land, turn right.)*

Gopal Mandir (Ganesh Temple) sits behind a high, whitewashed, onion-domed fortification in the midst of a busy market square, where vendors display the season's most sought-after devotional paraphernalia. Inside, pilgrims lounge under the arched platforms that encircle the complex's perimeter, while in the sumptuous main hall, a figure of Ganesh sits obediently between figures of his parents, Shiva and Parvati. *(In the center of town, head north 300m on Spiral Rd.)*

THE VEDHA SHALA. The instruments of the Vedha Shala (Veda School) sit in a compound behind a gate with a sign reading "Shree Jiwagi Observatory." The mathematically inclined will wonder at the precision of gadgets like the parallel sundials on either end of a meter-high cylinder. Each side tells the time for exactly half the year. Located on top of a hill with a view of the river and fields beyond, the observatory would be a pleasant place to sit and admire the view, if it weren't for the truck traffic just outside the gate. *(On a road leading southwest from the back of the railway station, on top of the hill. Approximately Rs25 by rickshaw.)*

OTHER SIGHTS. Many holy sights are scattered throughout the city. If you are determined to see them all, consult the encyclopedic MPSTDC map-guide. The **Ram Ghat** is the largest, although not always busiest, of the long row of *ghats* that line both sides of the river. *(Take the road between the Harsiddhi Mandir back down the slope toward the river.)* Toward the northern end of the row, the **Bhartirihari Caves** are home to the hoop-earringed Kanpatha *yogis*. 3km north of town, worshippers still make offerings of sweets and alcohol at the Kal Bhairava Mandir.

JABALPUR जबलपुर ☎ 0761

The Madhya Pradesh tourism office heralds a series of scenic white cliffs as the main attraction to Jabalpur, a city of just over a million people. Besides the dazzling Marble Rocks, the city is rather anti-climactic, and mainly serves as a starting point for trips to Kanha and Bandhavgarh National Parks.

▐ TRANSPORTATION

Flights: To **Delhi** (3hr.; Tu, Th, Sa; US$200) via **Gwalior** (1½hr., US$135). Buy tickets at **3a Travels,** opposite the museum.

Trains: The **railway station** (☎2311132) is a Rs15 rickshaw ride to the east of Russel Chowk. Reservation office open M-Sa 8am-8pm, Su 8am-2pm. Window #2 serves tourists. To: **Bhopal** (7-8hr.; Tu, Th, Sa, Su 3:45am and 11pm; Rs136); **Kolkata** (23hr., 1:50 and 11:40pm, Rs329); **Delhi** (23hr., 3 and 3:55pm, Rs284-297); **Jalgaon** (11hr., 3-5 per day 5:40-11:30am, Rs245); **Patna** (16hr., 1-3 per day 4-6:15pm, Rs241); **Satna** for **Khajuraho** (3hr., 3-4 per day 4am and 1:50-4:35pm, Rs121); **Umaria** for **Bandhavgarh N.P.** (1hr., 5:50am, Rs121); **Varanasi** (10hr., 2-3 per day 9:40am-11:10pm, Rs187).

Buses: The chaotic **bus stand,** near the museum, has both public (MPSRTC) and private sections. To: **Bhopal** (9hr., every hr. 5am-9:30pm, Rs162); **Kanha National Park** (6hr., 7 and 11am, Rs68). For Khajuraho and Bandhavgarh you have to take a train to Satna and Umaria, respectively, and catch a bus from there.

Local Transportation: Tempos run from the museum to the Marble Rocks for Rs12.

▐ ▐ ORIENTATION AND PRACTICAL INFORMATION

Collectorate Road curves north from behind the **railway station,** past the hospital and Gothic High Court to the **clock tower,** which marks the beginning of the **bazaar area.** Russel Chowk, the center of town and home of the accommodations and bus stands, is 200m to the left through the bazaar. **Station Road** is south of the station.

Tourist Office: MPTDC (☎2322111), inside the railway station. Makes reservations for MPTDC facilities at Kanha and Bandhavgarh. In-season (Dec.-Mar.) bookings for park accommodations should be made at least 4 days in advance from any MPTDC office; full payment required. Open M-Sa 8am-8pm, Su 8am-4pm.

Currency Exchange: State Bank of India (☎2322259), opposite Hotel Rishi Regency, near the railway underpass. Open M-F 10:30am-4pm.

Police: Collectorate Rd., Civil Lines (☎2320352), in front of the clock tower.

Hospital: Medical College, Nagpur Rd. (☎2322117), 8 km south of the bus stand, has a **24hr. pharmacy.**

Internet: Honey's Cyber World, opposite Hotel Shivalaya on Russel Chowk. Rs20 per hr. Open daily 10am-10pm. Plus a slew of others near Russel Chowk.

Post Office: GPO, Residency Rd. From the station, turn left on Station Rd. and then right on the next main road. The GPO is 500m down on the left. Open M-Sa 10am-6pm. **Postal Code:** 482002.

ACCOMMODATIONS

Russell Chowk is the hotel epicenter. Accommodations become less upscale moving from Russell Chowk to Karamchand Chowk, but many will not take foreigners. 24hr. check-out and 15-20% tax are standard.

Lodge Shivalaya (☎2625188), opposite Jyoti Cinema on Russel Chowk. Clean rooms with attached bath and intermittently functional color TVs lead to enormous balconies overlooking the town center. Singles Rs110-132; doubles Rs176-220. ❶

Hotel Samdriyo Inn (☎5004137), Russell Chowk. Moderate to pricey rooms replete with all the extras, including TV, carpeting, attached baths, and overachieving service staff. Non-A/C singles Rs300-350; doubles Rs400-450. ❷

Hotel Natraj (☎310931), near Karamchand Chowk. Head north (away from Russel Chowk), cross Navdra Bridge, then take the right fork. Turn right after 100m; it's on the left. Best budget place, but usually full. Rooms with attached baths have TV, A/C, and hand-held showers. Singles Rs50-70; doubles Rs110-130. ❶

Hotel Kanishka (☎5004147), Russell Chowk. High ceilings somewhat compensate for the small size. Pleasant views. Functional rooms with attached baths. Singles Rs75-95; doubles RS150-190. ❶

Hotel Adarsh (☎2830502), in Bhedaghat, 40min. outside Jabalpur near the Marble Rocks. Comfortable, quiet doubles in a peaceful village setting. Doubles Rs250. ❷

FOOD

Indian Coffee House, Malaviya Marg, near Karamchand Chowk. Follow directions to Hotel Natraj (see above); the Coffee House is across the street. Vintage advertisements, wicker chairs, rock-solid tables plus the classic assortment of *dosas, uttappams* (Rs12-20) and superb coffee (Rs4.50). The chain has several equally good avatars around the city, including one opposite the bus station. Open daily 7am-10pm. ❶

Hotel Republic Bar, just over Navdra Bridge (from Russel Chowk); it's on the right. Rows of tall, straight-backed chairs and the no-nonsense Sikh owner behind the bar give the Republic a wild west feel. Butter chicken (Rs75) is their specialty. They also serve vegetarian dishes (from Rs15) and a full range of alcohol. Open daily 11am-11:30pm. ❶

SIGHTS

Jabalpur's star attractions are the **Marble Rocks,** where the Narmada River cuts through a spectacular white-cliffed gorge and then drops 100 ft. down a huge waterfall. Sightseeing rowboats (Rs15) leave from the village of **Bhedaghat,** 15km from Jabalpur. The waterfall and haphazard series of stairs, marble souvenir shops, and viewing platforms are 1.5km farther up the road. If local youth in swimsuits offer to dive into the rapids for Rs10-20, it's worth every rupee. (Tempos go to the Marble Rocks/Bhedaghat from in front of the museum for Rs100, Rs12 sharing.) On the way to the Rocks is the old grand fortress of **Madan Mahal,** testimony to Jabalpur's 12th-century status as capital of the Gond kingdom. A small **museum** on the road from Russell Chowk to the bus stand contains temple sculptures. (Open Tu-Su 10am-5pm. Free.)

PROJECT TIGER At the turn of the 20th century, there were more than 100,000 tigers in the wild; today, fewer than 6000 survive worldwide, and more than half of these are in India. Faced with this shocking drop in the tiger population, caused by rapid industrialization and persistent hunting, Indira Gandhi inaugurated a drastic initiative to save the tiger in 1973. **Project Tiger** set aside nine areas of tiger territory as national parks and hired a staff of armed guards to patrol the areas and protect the animals from poachers. Initially successful, the plan boosted the tiger population from just a few hundred to several thousand. Ten more national parks were eventually set aside. However, lately poaching has increased as the forces protecting the sanctuaries have become less formidable. Tiger products—many believed to have healing and aphrodisiacal properties—fetch high prices on domestic and international markets. The tiger remains an endangered species and some fear it could soon face extinction again. The best places in India to see tigers are at **Corbett** (see p. 666) and **Kanha National Parks** (see below).

◤ NATIONAL PARKS

If you visit a national park in Madhya Pradesh, keep your receipt—it will get you a 50% discount on visits to the state's other national parks for one year.

KANHA NATIONAL PARK

The park is most easily reached via Jabalpur, 160km to the northwest. Buses run from Jabalpur to Kisli, the main gate entrance, stopping first at Khatia Gate, near the Visitors Center, where most non-MPTDC accommodations and food can be found (6hr.; 7 and 11am, return buses at 8am and 12:30pm; Rs68). Kisli is 4km inside Khatia Gate. Mukki, another park gate, is 32 km southeast, and has only a handful of high-end resorts. Jeeps (Rs10 per km) are the necessary mode of transportation. The park is open Nov.-June sunrise to sunset. Entry fees Rs200 per person per day. Vehicles Rs100. Guides Rs90. When tigers are sighted, elephant rides are conducted for close-up viewing (20min., Rs300).

Beautiful Kanha and its animals have had an up-and-down history. The same Brits who cantered across the continent with their rifles, driving game to the brink of extinction, also set aside Kanha as a hunting preserve, saving it from the encroachment of the local population. Kanha became a wildlife reserve in 1933, and its nearly 2000 square kilometers of untainted jungle served as the setting for Rudyard Kipling's *Jungle Book*. With about 120 tigers in the park, sightings are frequent, and the tiger population only keeps increasing (though not too quickly, as the males like to nip competition in the bud by eating their sons). Once a tiger is spotted, it is held at bay by elephants until everyone gets a look. Besides the well-fed tigers, you can also see their friends (and food): leopards, deer, sambar, wild boar, bears, pythons, porcupines, and over 300 species of birds. Your chances of seeing a tiger here are better than anywhere in India.

Although some visitors catch one of the nightly man-eater films (7pm in English, at the Khatia Gate Visitor Center) or take the somewhat disorienting 1.5km **jungle walk** from Khatia Gate, most really come to see the law of the jungle at work. Jeep trips, the only way to go, run through Sher Jahan-land for around Rs400-600 plus sundry fees (Rs200 per trip), which can be split between a maximum of six passengers. Arrange your jeep beforehand, either directly with the battalion by Khatia Gate or through the manager of your hotel (usually an easier way to share). Bafati Khan (☎277272) is a superb guide; unlike many of the others, he knows more about the animals than just their names. Trips run in the morning (4-5hr., 6am) and afternoon (2-3hr., around 3pm). The morning trip, which makes a breakfast stop (fritters and *chai* Rs9) in Kanha village at the heart of the park, is usually a better time for sightings. If there are tigers about, your jeep can take you to an **elephant** (15-20min., Rs300) for closer, more silent viewing. Bring warm clothing and a blanket in winter.

More cost-effective accommodations have mushroomed around Khatia Gate, most of which double as restaurants and jeep stops. ▨**Van Vihar ❶**, 400m to the left when facing the gate, has simple doubles with bucket showers. The village atmosphere has made it a budget favorite. (Doubles Rs100-200.) Scattered around the woods to the right of the gate are the huts of the forest department **Jungle Camp ❷**, which has rooms with attached baths and an impersonal central dining hall. (Doubles Rs150.) Also to the right, but down the lane 200m, in front of the gate, is **Mogli Guest House ❸**. With hot water and air cooling or A/C, rooms are more expensive but include access to a swimming pool, and dammed pond with a *machan* (watchtower) where you can view deer coming to drink water. (☎277228. Reservations recommended. Doubles Rs400-1100.) There are two MPTDC-run accommodations. The **Baghira Log Huts ❸**, in the park, have posh doubles with private baths for Rs690-890. The **Tourist Hostel ❷**, in Kisli, offers dorms for an exorbitant Rs300 and also contains a depressing canteen with bland snacks. For information or reservations, contact one of the MPTDC offices in major Madhya Pradesh cities or in Mumbai, Delhi, and Kolkata; the head office is in Bhopal. (☎0755 2774340.) It's a good idea to book rooms in advance during high season. The MPTDC requires full payment in advance, though email reservations are supposedly more flexible. (mail@mptourism.com.) Tea stalls line the road to Khatia Gate (*thalis* Rs25-40). **Burman ❷**, close to the gate, is very popular and has phones. At Kisli, the two options are Baghira's restaurant (Rs50-120) and the hostel canteen.

BANDHAVGARH NATIONAL PARK

*From Jabalpur, take a train to **Umaria** (4½hr., 5:50am; or 3hr., Tu, Th, F, Su 10pm; sleeper Rs121). If you are coming from the north, catch the train to Umaria from **Katni**, 18km south of Satna. **Buses** sometimes run between Umaria and **Tala** Village, the sole gateway to Bandhavgarh; a better bet is the **shared jeeps** that depart from the market (1hr., every 30min. 6am-6pm, Rs20). The last two trains from Umaria to Jabalpur via Katni leave at 4:30 and 8:20pm. **Jeep safaris** start at sunrise and three hours before sunset for 3-4 hr. park tours (Rs400). Pay the relevant fees beforehand at the park office: Rs200 per person per day; vehicle fee Rs100; guide fee Rs90; camera fee Rs25. When tigers are sighted, **elephant rides** provide a closer look (25min., Rs300 per person).*

Often overshadowed by the nearby Kanha Park, Bandhavgarh is 170km northeast of Jabalpur and curiously reminiscent of a theme park. Rocky hills center around the ancient ruins of the 2000-year-old Bandhavgarh fort, which can be visited as an afternoon tour separate from the safaris (entry fees last all day, but vehicle and guide fees must be paid each time you enter the park). Three Sanskrit-scrawled **caves** below the fort can be unlocked for tourists—the rest house tigers. The park has 60 tigers, with at least half of those in the 67 sq. km tourist zone, creating one of the highest densities in India. Given its relatively easy accessibility from places like Varanasi and Khajuraho, the park has been attracting an increasing number of tiger-seekers. As a result, the small park can get quite crowded during peak season (Nov.-June) and in April 2003 two tourists were attacked by a tiger while their jeep was stuck in a traffic jam. There are accommodations near the park gate in Tala. Rooms at **Kumkum House ❷** are well insulated thanks to a double roof. (☎07627 265324. Singles Rs200; doubles Rs250.) **Tiger Lodge ❷** has a few clean, modest rooms (doubles Rs150) above **Nandu ❶**, the best *dhaba* in town (veg. *thalis* with *chipati* Rs30). **Maharaja's Royal Retreat ❹** is cheaper than some of the high-end resorts, but still landscaped and luxurious. (☎07627 265306. Doubles Rs700.)

KHAJURAHO खजुराहो ☎07686

This dusty hamlet (pop. 4680), isolated in northern Madhya Pradesh, plays host to one of India's major tourist attractions: the extraordinary temples of Khajuraho. These sites of worship, collectively designated a UNESCO World Heritage Site, are legacies of the Chandela dynasty, whose mighty capital rose and fell here a thousand years ago. The temples are (in)famous for the pulse-quickening, erotic sculptures adorning their walls; couples are shown prominently copulating in any and every position imaginable, with each explicit detail meticulously rendered in the sandstone facades. Surrounding the main temple area, the unavoidable souvenir stands are full of pocket paperback editions of the *Kama Sutra* translated into all of the world's major languages, and late-night conversation in the town's restaurants and cafes seems to focus on the advisability—indeed, even the possibility—of performing the feats of flexibility and ingenuity depicted here. But there is much more to Khajuraho's temples than a few exquisitely executed sex scenes. For all the attention they are given, the scenes represent only a small part of the cultural insight offered by these holy sites. From war to love, from joy to sorrow, the carvings cover the breadth of human experience.

▐ TRANSPORTATION

Khajuraho isn't really en route to anywhere, but it is most easily positioned between Varanasi and Agra. Buses are the only form of ground transportation to Khajuraho and connect regularly to the nearest railheads at Jhansi (175km away; convenient from Delhi or Mumbai) and Satna (117km; convenient from Varanasi or Allahabad). The last buses to Khajuraho leave Satna at 2:30pm, Jhansi 1:15pm, and Mahoba 5pm. Flying is a popular alternative if you can afford it. Flights stop during the low season, so check with the Indian Airlines for availability.

Flights: Khajuraho Civil Aerodrome, 6km south of town. Make reservations at least one day in advance at **Indian Airlines** (☎274035, airport office 274036), 2km south of town on Main Rd. Open daily 10am-1:15pm and 2-5pm. Daily flights to: **Agra** (45min., US$85); **Delhi** (1½hr., US$105); and **Varanasi** (45min., US$85).

Buses: The station, a 10min. walk south of Main Sq. on Link Rd. No. 2, posts English bus schedules and also hosts a computerized **train reservation office** from which you can reserve onward connections from Jhansi, Satna, or any other rail station. (Open M-Sa 8-11am and 2-5pm.) Buses go to: **Agra** (12hr., 9am, Rs190); **Bhopal** (12hr., 6 and 7pm, Rs200); **Gwalior** (6½hr.; 9, 11:15am, 4pm; Rs130); **Jabalpur** (12hr., 6am, Rs130); **Jhansi** (4-5hr., 7 per day 5:30am-4:15pm, Rs90); **Varanasi** via **Mahoba** (3hr., every 45min. 7:30am-4:30pm, Rs35) or **Satna** (4hr., 4 per day 9:30am-4pm, Rs50). There is one direct bus to **Varanasi** (13hr., 4pm, Rs175).

Local Transportation: Bicycles, the most practical mode of transport, can be rented at hotels or stands in the square for Rs15-30 per day. The few **auto-rickshaws** are over-priced. A **cycle-rickshaw** trip should cost Rs5-10. It is a 20-25min. walk from the Western to the Eastern Group.

▣▐ ORIENTATION AND PRACTICAL INFORMATION

Khajuraho is tiny, but unmarked roads make directions confusing. There is only one main road, which leads up from the airport in the south to the **Western Group** (the main temple complex) and the mess of hotels, restaurants, and postcard shops that comprise the "new village." **Jain Temple Road** leads east from here to the **Eastern Group** of temples (the second main group), scattered around the old village. The bus stand is on **Link Road Number Two,** south of Jain Temple Rd., a 10min. walk from the main group of temples and most accommodations.

MADHYA PRADESH

Tourist Office: Main Rd. (☎272348), opposite the Western Group. Distributes free copies of a hand-drawn Khajuraho map. Open M-F 9:30am-1:30pm and 2-6pm.

Currency Exchange: State Bank of India, Main Sq. (☎272373), opposite the Western Group, cashes traveler's checks and changes many currencies. Open M-F 10:30am-2:30pm and 3-4pm, Sa 10:30am-1pm.

Police: (☎274032), just beyond the bus stand on Link Rd. No. 2; 2nd booth more centrally located in Main Sq.

Hospital: Dr. R.K. Khare (☎274177, residence 272374). Recommended by local luxury hotels. His **clinic** is in the strip mall beside the bus station. Open M-Sa 10am-2pm and 6-9pm. There is a **24hr. pharmacy** (☎274453) to the right of Dr. Khare's clinic.

Post Office: Opposite the bus stand. Open M-Sa 9am-5pm. **Postal Code:** 471606.

ACCOMMODATIONS

The intense competition between guest houses in Khajuraho means you typically don't have to worry about finding a bed, even if you arrive late in the day in high-season. Most places are also good bargains. All incoming buses are met by hordes of rickshaw-*wallahs* and hotel agents; as usual, you'll be in a much better bargaining position if you hoof it instead of agreeing to go with one of them.

The cheapest guest houses in town are all centrally located near the Western Group, with a string of similar places lined up side-by-side along Jain Temple Rd. In low season (Apr.-June), prices typically plummet. All accommodations below offer hot water unless otherwise noted.

Hotel Jain, Jain Temple Rd. (☎272352; jainbanglesh@yahoomail.com), to the right of Main Sq. Cheap, clean rooms and friendly service. The owner's family home, rooftop restaurant, and 20 guest rooms are arranged around a central courtyard. Laundry service, bicycle rental available; Internet cafe attached. Dorms Rs40; singles Rs60-80, with bath Rs150-170; doubles with bath Rs100-250. Off-season 25% discount. ❶

Yogi Lodge (☎274158), down an alley on the left side of Main Sq. (with your back to the Western Group). Simple rooms in this popular guest house suffice for simple lodging. Most have hot water and air cooling. Singles Rs50-70; doubles Rs80-150. The owner, Yogi Sharma, also runs the quaint, smaller, and more secluded **Yogi Ashram Guest House,** 1.5km north of town on Main Rd. (on the left), where he gives free morning meditation lessons. Guests can use the communal kitchen and TV and enjoy fruit from the garden. Ask for an aura reading. Dorms and singles Rs50; doubles Rs100-150. ❶

Hotel Zen, Jain Temple Rd. (☎274228; oshozen@hotmail.com), the last in the chain of guest houses, all the way down on the right. A classy place offering well-furnished rooms with attached bath, marble floors, and a courtyard. Higher-end rooms have bathtub and A/C. Singles Rs200-450; doubles Rs250-650. Off-season 50% discount. ❷

Hotel Harmony, Jain Temple Rd. (☎274135), on the right from Main Sq. Air-cooled rooms with wood furnishings, TV, and attached bath. Courtyard garden. Doubles Rs250-350, with A/C Rs750; single occupants Rs100 less. Off-season 50% discount. ❶

Hotel Surya, Jain Temple Rd. (☎274145). On the right from Main Sq. Spacious, spotless rooms with bath, marble floors, and air-cooler; some with balconies. Singles Rs200-350; doubles Rs250–550. May 1-July 15 30-40% discount. ❷

Hotel Marble Palace, Jain Temple Rd. (☎274353), on the left, set back from the street, opposite Gole Market. Designed by a Japanese architect with marble floors and fixtures, sleek black beds, and maharaja-inspired arched doorways. The Marble Palace earns its name with class, though you'll pay for it. Sheets changed daily. All rooms have bathtubs. Singles Rs350; doubles Rs450, with A/C Rs650. Off-season 20% discount. ❸

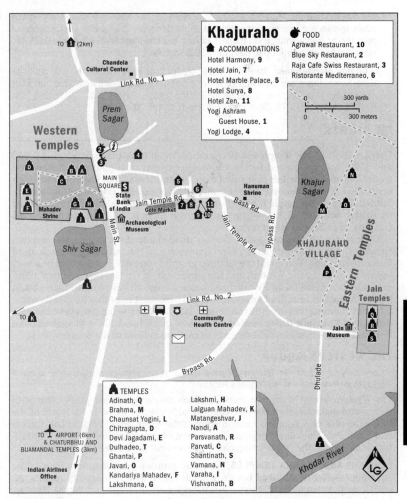

Khajuraho

🏠 ACCOMMODATIONS
Hotel Harmony, **9**
Hotel Jain, **7**
Hotel Marble Palace, **5**
Hotel Surya, **8**
Hotel Zen, **11**
Yogi Ashram
   Guest House, **1**
Yogi Lodge, **4**

🍴 FOOD
Agrawal Restaurant, **10**
Blue Sky Restaurant, **2**
Raja Cafe Swiss Restaurant, **3**
Ristorante Mediterraneo, **6**

0   300 yards
0   300 meters

Western Temples

Prem Sagar

Chandela Cultural Center

Link Rd. No. 1

TO 🏠 (2km)

MAIN SQUARE
State Bank of India
Jain Temple Rd.
Gole Market
Archaeological Museum

Main St.

Shiv Sagar

Hanuman Shrine

Bash Rd.

Bypass Rd.

Khajur Sagar

KHAJURAHO VILLAGE

Eastern Temples

Jain Temples

Jain Museum

Mahadev Shrine

Link Rd. No. 2

Community Health Centre

Dhulade

Bypass Rd.

TO ✈ AIRPORT (6km) & CHATURBHUJ AND BIJAMANDAL TEMPLES (3km)

Indian Airlines Office

Khodar River

TEMPLES
Adinath, **Q**
Brahma, **M**
Chaunsat Yogini, **L**
Chitragupta, **D**
Devi Jagadami, **E**
Dulhadeo, **T**
Ghantai, **P**
Javari, **O**
Kandariya Mahadev, **F**
Lakshmana, **G**

Lakshmi, **H**
Lalguan Mahadev, **K**
Matangeshvar, **J**
Nandi, **A**
Parsvanath, **R**
Parvati, **C**
Shantinath, **S**
Vamana, **N**
Varaha, **I**
Vishvanath, **B**

MADHYA PRADESH

🍴 FOOD

Raja Cafe Swiss Restaurant, Main Rd., directly opposite the Western Group. Run by two charming and gregarious Swiss sisters, the cafe dishes out full breakfasts (Rs80), Chinese and Indian food (Rs50-90), *au gratin* dishes (Rs80-150), *rosti* (Rs45) and spot-on Western desserts, like only an expat could make 'em. Tours and jungle stays can be arranged through the cafe as well. Open daily 8am-10pm. ❸

Agrawal Restaurant, next to Hotel Harmony. This modest joint serves up delicious *shudh shakahari*. South Indian dishes at friendly prices put the tourist restaurants in town to shame. Indian *thalis* and *paneer* Rs25-60. Open daily 8am-11pm. ❶

Blue Sky Restaurant, Main Rd. Just north of Main Sq. The restaurant's two-story terrace offers unparalleled views of the Western Group temples. Chef cooks a wide range of tasty Indian, continental, and Japanese dishes. Full breakfast Rs40-60; soups Rs25-40; main courses Rs30-60. Open daily 8am-10:30pm. ❷

Ristorante Mediterraneo, Jain Temple Rd., 200m from Main Rd., on the left, opposite Hotel Surya. This place serves up good (for India) pizza, pasta, and wine-sized bottles of chilled beer to a European crowd on the rooftop terrace. Pastas Rs50-130; pizzas from Rs130; crepes Rs40-75. Open daily 7:30am-10:30pm. ❷

🔾 SIGHTS

Construction of the temples at Khajuraho, which took place between AD 900 and 1100, was sponsored by the Chandela dynasty, a Rajput clan descended from Central Asian tribes that ruled over Central India from the 9th to the 13th centuries. When Chandela power waned, the temples were forgotten and lay hidden deep in the jungle for 700 years before the outside world—represented by British officer T.S. Burt—stumbled across them in 1838. Of the original 85 temples, only 25 still stand today.

Khajuraho's temples are conventionally divided into three groups; the Western Group contains the most famous and impressive of the temples, although all of them are stunning. You could see all three groups in one day, but it would be a very busy day. Splitting the Western and Eastern/Southern Groups between two mornings allows a more leisurely tour, and since almost all the temples face east, it brings the added benefit of enjoying the early morning light that highlights many intricate carvings that are difficult to see later on. For the biggest event in town, the annual **Khajuraho Dance Festival** (Feb. 14-20 in 2004 and 2005), the government brings in India's best classical dancers to perform in front of the temples.

THE WESTERN GROUP

Open daily sunrise-sunset. Tour groups roll in by 9 or 10am; show up by 8am at the latest. US$10, or Rs equivalent. Audio guide Rs50.

The Western Group of temples, most of which are contained in a grassy, fenced-in compound maintained by the Archaeological Survey of India, holds many of the best examples of Khajuraho's magnificent architecture, including the Lakshmana and Kandariya Mahadev Temples. The custom of *pradakshina* dictates that visitors walk around the whole group clockwise and circle each temple the same way.

LAKSHMI AND VARAHA TEMPLES. The first stop on your *pradakshina* is the least impressive: the **Lakshmi Temple,** a small shrine that 19th-century repairs left with a jagged cement roof. Next door, the open-air, 10th-century **Varaha Mandap,** built for Vishnu's avatar as a boar *(Varaha),* offers a more promising beginning. The huge, solid-sandstone boar is so well polished that it shines like glazed porcelain. It is covered with rows of tiny gods and goddesses that total over 764 figures, including the deities of the sacred rivers Ganga, Yamuna, and Saraswati.

LAKSHMANA TEMPLE. Dating from around AD 941, the magnificent Lakshmana Temple, opposite the Lakshmi and Varaha temples and dedicated to Vishnu, is one of the largest, oldest, and best-wrought in Khajuraho. Its plan features two pairs of transepts and reflects the classic, five-component design that characterizes Khajuraho's great temples: an **ardhamandapa** (entrance platform); a **mandapa** (hallway) directly behind the entrance; a **mahamandapa** (central hall) encircled by a small passageway and stone columns; a **garbagriha** (inner shrine), which houses a representation of the deity to which the temple is consecrated (for instance, a *linga* for Shiva or a monkey statue for Hanuman); and a **pradakshina** (closed passageway) around this sanctuary. The abbreviated, three-part Khajuraho temples lack the *mandapa* and *pradakshina* (for more on Hindu temple architecture see **Architecture,** p. 84). Secondary shrines are arranged at the four corners of the main Lakshmana platform; all five temples are oriented such that a devotee ascending the terrace steps faces each door simultaneously. The Lakshmana Temple's carvings are exceptionally intricate, from the *mandapa* ceiling inside to the two bands of sculptures (instead of the usual three) lining the outer walls and the panoramic friezes that wind around the base. These fantastic sculptures showcase an endless procession of elephants, horses, and soldiers marching together in riotous disorder. The hunting and battle scenes are interspersed with scenes of a different kind of conquest. The initial surprise at the candor of such couplings quickly fades into appreciation of graceful forms and the evocation of human passions on the cold, dispassionate medium of stone.

KANDARIYA MAHADEV TEMPLE. Straight ahead at the far end of the park, three temples stand together on the same platform. Built between AD 1025 and 1050 and dedicated to Shiva, the Kandariya Mahadev Temple, on the left, is the tallest temple in Khajuraho. It is considered the culmination of the Khajuraho school of architecture. The subordinate shrines that once graced the temple's four corners have long since disappeared, but the main shrine is extremely well preserved. An incredible wealth of sculptures adorns the walls, each exquisite specimen vying for the observer's attention. By one count, at least 226 statues line the interior, while 646 grace the exterior—872 in total, most nearly 3 ft. tall. A sex scene on the southern walls delights gaggles of gawkers, but the famous erotic scenes are just one part of a wide variety of superlative sculpture here. A recent chemical treatment to remove the black mold that mars some other temples has enhanced the intricacy of the Kandariya Temple's adornments.

MAHADEV SHRINE AND DEVI JAGADAMI TEMPLE. On the same platform, next to the Kandariya Temple, is the **Mahadev Shrine,** which houses one of the finest sculptures at Khajuraho, depicting a human figure grappling with a lion. It is thought that what remains here is merely the entrance portico of what was once a temple to Shiva. On the other side of the Mahadev Shrine is the **Devi Jagadami Temple.** Though smaller than the Lakshmana and Kandariya temples, it has some superb sculptures, most notably its directional guardians, who are stationed between boldly flirting women and delicate, sensual scenes. The image of Vishnu positioned over the doorway indicates that the temple was originally dedicated to him, though it now enshrines an image of Kali (Parvati painted black).

CHITRAGUPTA TEMPLE. Set apart from the other three temples along the back wall of the enclosure, this is Khajuraho's only temple to Surya (the sun god). Built circa AD 1000-1025, its plan is identical to Devi Jagadami's, though it is slightly more ornate and developed. Small processions run around the lower portion of the temple wall; higher up are many amorous couples. The damaged wall and roof were repaired with concrete. Most of the statues inside the temple have been decapitated, but the main image of Surya, driving his chariot across the sky, is missing only the arms.

PARVATI, VISHVANATH, AND NANDI TEMPLES. Continuing around the circuit, the next temple is the small and mostly reconstructed concrete **Parvati Temple,** overshadowed by the more spectacular **Vishvanath Temple** next to it, a large Shiva temple dating back to AD 1002 from an inscription inside. The stairs on the northern side are flanked by a pair of lions; the stairs on the southern side, by a pair of elephants. The bawdy sculptures on the Vishvanath Temple are some of the best and depict whole scenes in which the couples' attendants also get caught up in the action. There are also some fascinating sculptures of posing women (called *apsaras* if they are dancing and *surasundaris* if performing other daily tasks)—look for the one on the south side twisting her hair to dry, and the one on the ceiling inside, holding a tiny baby. Some of the figures are sculpted in astonishing detail down to their cuticles. The Vishvanath Temple originally had a shrine at each corner of its foundation as the Lakshmana Temple does, but only two remain. In front of the temple is the **Nandi Mandap,** an open square pavilion from which Shiva's bull, Nandi, gazes into the temple.

MATANGESHVAR TEMPLE. The three members of the Western Group that stray outside the fence are older and noticeably different from the others. Just over the fence from the Lakshmana Temple is the first, the Matangeshvar Temple. Built around AD 900, it is the only temple in this group that is still in use—more people come here to worship than to view the architecture. It is a relatively plain temple with only thin stripes of carving. Inside, a *linga* sits on top of a huge, stone platform. The temple's upper-level terrace has good views of the Lakshmana Temple.

CHAUSAT YOGINIS. Along the south side of Shiv Sagar Lake, a narrow, tree-lined path leads off to the right to the temple of Chausat Yoginis ("Sixty-Four Goddesses"). Built during the 9th century, Chausat Yoginis distinguishes itself as the oldest temple in Khajuraho and is made of crudely cut blocks of granite piled together like sandbags. Scarcely more than a large stone platform, the top is ringed by a gallery of empty shrines—only 35 of the original 64 remain.

LALGUAN MAHADEV TEMPLE. Five-hundred meters farther west from Chausat Yoginis lies this small, ruined Shiva temple. It is part granite, part sandstone and is similar in design to the Brahma Temple.

ARCHAEOLOGICAL MUSEUM. Across the street from the Western Group enclosure, the Archaeological Museum houses sculptures separated from their temples. A wonderful Ganesh dances in the entrance hall, while in the center of the Miscellaneous Gallery on the right, a king and queen—possibly the sculptor's Chandela patron—sit together making an offering. Also note the unfinished couple whose noses have been left stuck together, making them look like a pair of kissing Pinocchios. There are few pieces here to compare with the best sculpture still on the temples—the museum's main virtue is that it offers close-up views of sculptures otherwise hidden high up on the temple walls. *(Open M-Th and Sa-Su 10am-5pm. Rs250.)*

EASTERN AND SOUTHERN GROUPS

*To get to the Eastern Group from Main Sq., head down Jain Temple Rd. past Hotel Zen and bear left at the fork onto Basti Rd.; follow the sign to the old village. The temples are scattered throughout the village, with a few clustered in the Jain temple complex. The Southern Group is comprised of only three temples. Dulhadeo Temple is 600m down the paved road to your left as you walk out of the Jain temple complex. To get to the other two—Chaturbhuj and Bijamandal temples—cruise 3km south of town on Main Rd., take the first left after the bridge, and head down this paved road to the temples. The easiest way to tour these groups is by bike; see **Local Transportation,** p. 369, for pricing and information. Both groups open daily sunrise-sunset. Free.*

Located in and around Khajuraho village, the temples of the Eastern Group are not as stunning as those of the Western Group. But since they are visited by fewer people, they have an atmosphere of relative peace and seclusion that is often missing from the temples of the main group. The Southern Group's three temples are farther apart from one another than from either of the other two groups. By bike, you should be able to complete the tour leisurely in 3-5hr.

EASTERN GROUP. On the left heading to the old village, you'll pass a **Hanuman Shrine** containing one of the oldest sculptures in Khajuraho, a large *sindur*-smeared Hanuman (monkey god) image that dates from AD 922. Crossing Bypass

Rd. and entering Khajuraho village, the path veers to the left along the side of a seasonal pond called the **Khajur Sagar.** Not far along it on the left is the small **Brahma Temple,** misnamed by 19th-century art historians. A four-faced Shiva *linga* sits in the sanctuary, and Vishnu is carved on the lintel above the door. Continuing north and following the small path to the right brings you to the **Javari Temple,** which features a number of interesting pieces despite its small size and relatively simple design. The women dancing around the temple walls manage to look remarkably life-like and sprightly, though most of them had their heads knocked off centuries ago by Mughals. Continuing north on the main path leads to the **Vamana Temple.** As large as some of the temples in the Western Group, but simpler in design, it has slightly less impressive sculpture and decoration. Backtrack down the lakeside path and ask locals to point out the path to **Ghantai Temple,** or at least what remains of it—an entrance porch and tall pillars supporting a flat, ornate roof. The frieze illustrates the 16 dreams of Mahavira's mother.

Heading south and turning left on Jain Temple Rd. (follow the sign to the Jain temples) will bring you to the second subgroup of the Eastern Group, which consists of three Jain temples walled into a monastery complex on the far side of Khajuraho village. The old temples here are interspersed with newer ones. This mixture is embodied in the **Shantinath Temple,** the first temple as you enter the complex, which was built recently with heavy pillars and doorways taken from older temples. Inside the temple is a collection of photographs, posters of Jain pilgrimage sites, plenty of sculptures, and paintings of naked monks.

To the left of the Shantinath Temple is an enclosure housing the two adjacent remaining temples. The most impressive Eastern Group temple, the **Parsvanath Temple,** is notable for its simple design and the small shrine at the back. In addition to Jain *tirthankaras* (saints), the sculptures on the outside depict just about every major Hindu deity, suggesting that this was once a Hindu temple. Some of the most famous sculptures in Khajuraho are here, including one of a woman putting on ankle-bells and another of a woman applying her makeup. The **Adinath Temple,** whose porch has been reconstructed in concrete, features limber women climbing up the walls. Shiny black *tirthankara* images sit inside both temples.

Just outside the Jain temple complex, the small but worthwhile **Jain Museum** houses a gallery of Jain sculptures and architecture. *(Open daily 7am-6pm. Rs5.)*

SOUTHERN GROUP. The **Dulhadeo Temple** dates from around AD 1100, by which time standards had started to slip in Khajuraho—the sculpture here is generally held to be inferior to that of the other temples. There are still plenty of interesting little scenes, though, including numerous dragon-like mythical beasts and people going about their daily lives. At the southern end of the temple is a pair of dioramas showing first a man and then a woman unsuccessfully imitating some of the other sex-in-stone scenes so prevalent in Khajuraho. The *linga* inside the temple is overlaid with dozens of tiny replicas of itself, giving it a curiously scaly appearance. The *mahamandapa*, with its great rotunda ceiling, is carved in an elaborate star shape. By the time this temple was built, sculptors were getting so carried away with ornaments and jewelry on their human figures that the quality of the actual sculptures had begun to decline.

The trip to **Chaturbhuj Temple** is best made in the late afternoon, since Chaturbhuj is the only big temple in Khajuraho that faces west. The evening light shines warmly on its 2.7m *dakshinamurti* statue of three deities carved from one stone. This huge image is a combination of Shiva, Vishnu, and Krishna. The sculptures around the outside feature another interesting hybrid: on the southern side, an image of Ardhanarishvara (half-Shiva, half-Parvati) is split down the middle, illustrating the motif of male and female union that was so significant to those who produced the marvelous sculptures at Khajuraho. Chaturbhuj is well-worth the trip, despite the fact that it is the only temple at Khajuraho without any erotic sculptures.

From Chaturbhuj, you'll be able to catch a glimpse to the northeast of what looks like not too much more than a pile of rubble, but is actually the fascinating remains of **Bijamandal Temple.** To get there, follow the marked dirt path that forked left as you followed the paved path right to Chaturbhuj. This newest member of the Southern Group was just opened to visitors in 1999 and is still under excavation, but the lowest portions are clear and some tantalizing carvings (as well as the remains of a Shiva *linga*) poke out from the rock piles above. The temple is quite large, and will be a fantastic sight to behold once restoration is complete.

JHANSI झांसी   ☎ 0517

Travelers would be well advised to take a good, long look at the timetables before coming to Jhansi—this is not the kind of town you want to be stranded in. Jhansi (pop. 379,000), though technically in Uttar Pradesh, draws tourists because of its proximity to Orchha and its function as a railhead for Khajuraho, both in Madhya Pradesh. If schedules conspire to keep you here, you can while away the hours lamenting the recent price increases that have made two of the city's three time-killers, the Jhansi Fort and the Rani Mahal, quite expensive.

ᴱ TRANSPORTATION. Buses for Khajuraho leave from the railway station (4 per day 5:30-11am) and the bus stand (11:45am and 1:15pm, Rs75-85). Frequent Delhi-bound **trains** leave throughout the day, of which the fastest is the A/C *Shatabdi Exp. 2001*, which goes to **Delhi** (5hr., 5:55pm, Rs565) via **Agra** (2¼hr., Rs390) and **Gwalior** (1¼hr., Rs495). Frequent trains also run to **Bhopal** (express 4hr., 10:32am, Rs480) and **Jabalpur** (express 11½hr., 11:05pm, sleeper Rs166). **Tempos** for Orchha (Rs6) leave from the bus stand.

ᴴᴸ ORIENTATION AND PRACTICAL INFORMATION. Downtown Jhansi spans 5km from the **railway station** in the west to the **bus stand** in the east. Heading left out of the railway station and turning right at Chitra Crossing (1km from the station) brings you to **Shivpuri Road,** which leads toward the town's central crossing and the fort. As the town is quite spread out, you'll need auto-rickshaws to get around—they should take you anywhere local for Rs15. The **Madhya Pradesh Tourism** booth on platform #1 of the railway station provides transit info and maps of the city. (☎ 2442622. Open daily 10am-6pm.) The **State Bank of India,** in the center of town near Elite Crossing, changes only AmEx traveler's checks. (☎ 2443919. Open M-F 10am-4pm, Sa 10am-1pm.) The government **hospital** (☎ 2440572) is on Manik Chowk, the market at the base of the fort. The **police station** is on the Main Rd. (☎ 2440538). The **GPO,** Sadarj Marg, Civil Lines, is across the street from the Jhansi Hotel. (Open M-Sa 10am-6pm.) **Postal Code:** 284001.

ᴬᴰ ACCOMMODATIONS AND FOOD. Hotel Samrat ❷, Chitra Sq., Shivpuri Rd., 1km from the train station. All rooms come with attached bath, TVs, and phones. (☎ 2444943. Singles and doubles Rs250-800.) The **Prakash Regency Guest House ❷,** Sardari Lal Market, Civil Lines, just north of Elite Crossing (the center of town) on the right, offers pleasant mid-range lodgings, all with air-cooling and attached bath. The Prakash Regency also boasts—wonder-of-all-wonders for a budget hotel—a swimming pool. (☎ 2330133. Singles Rs275-375; doubles 350-450.) **Hotel Veerangana ❶,** 10min. past Hotel Samrat on Shivpuri Rd., is a UP Tourism-run place with clean dorms (men-only) and large, clean rooms. (☎ 2442402. Dorms Rs75; rooms Rs300-1100.) The **Hotel Sita Restaurant ❷,** Shivpuri Rd., serves first-rate food in a plush, climate-controlled environment. (Open daily 6:30-10:30am, noon-3pm, 7-11pm. Main courses from Rs45.)

⬛ **SIGHTS.** The **Jhansi Fort** is dedicated to Maharani Lakshmi Bai, a celebrated revolutionary who joined the anti-British sepoys in the Mutiny of 1857. As the British recaptured the region, Jhansi was one of the last rebel holdouts. The British policy of honoring a maharaja's or maharani's sovereignty and property rights was granted only to those with heirs. Lakshmi Bai had only an adopted child, so she was not protected under the laws. Infuriated, she fought valiantly against the British. Dressed as a man, her guns blazing, the maharani rode out into battle to meet her demise 180km from Jhansi. Today the fort serves primarily as an empty and decrepit home to bands of monkeys and bats, though the maze of archways, stairwells, turrets, and abandoned rooms can provide for some interesting exploration. However, for most, the view isn't worth the exorbitant admission fee. (Open daily sunrise-sunset. Rs250.) You can experience some of the fort for free just outside, along the southern wall as you approach the main entrance. Check out the bizarre life-sized model depicting a battle between heroic Indian freedom-fighters and their dastardly red-coat oppressors during the Mutiny of 1857. "Who cannot remain unimpressed by this life-like picturisation?" asks a nearby sign—a pertinent question, indeed.

The colorful **Rani Mahal** palace, down the other side of the hill from the fort and a few minutes to the left, was constructed in the late 18th century and today houses sculptures from the late Pratihar and Chandela periods. (Open daily 9:30am-5:30pm. Rs250. Same ticket covers fort and Rani Mahal.) The only reasonably priced way to kill time in Jhansi is the **U.P. Government Museum,** at the base of the road leading up to the fort, which houses more archaeological finds from the area, though to call the largely empty museum worthwhile might be a stretch. (Open July 1-Apr. 15 10:30am-4:30pm; Apr. 16-June 30 7:30am-12:30pm. Rs2.)

ORCHHA ओरछा ☎ 07680

On a loop in the Betwa River, 16km from Jhansi, the little town of Orchha sits in the shadows of an abandoned 17th-century city that once served as the capital of the Bundela kingdom. Raja Rudra Pratap Bundela founded the capital here in 1531, and Orchha continued to grow and prosper up through its golden age in the early 17th century. Throughout this period, the Bundelas managed to keep the neighboring Mughal Empire at bay. Raja Bir Singh Deo (r. 1605-27), the greatest Bundela king, befriended the emperor Jehangir and even welcomed him as a visitor in 1606. Under Bir Singh Deo, the Bundelas controlled the whole region of Bundelkhand, which still bears their name. Later rulers were less successful at appeasing the Mughals, and the kingdom's long, slow decline began as soon as the emperor Shah Jahan attacked Orchha. The city was abandoned in 1783, when the onslaught of Mughal and Maratha attacks became too much for the residents to withstand.

The Bundelas left a landscape filled with palaces and temples, and nothing but the forces of nature (and now tourists) have disturbed them in the two centuries since. Orchha, meaning "hidden," lives up to its name—when human rulers gave up the attempt to conceal the city from invaders, nature took up the challenge. The ruins are overgrown with trees and weeds, cracked walls are shrouded with vines, and empty palace courtyards echo the songs of squeaking bats.

⬛⬛ TRANSPORTATION AND PRACTICAL INFORMATION

Tempos (Rs6) and **auto-rickshaws** (Rs60) make the quick trip from Jhansi to Orchha. **Buses** between Jhansi and Khajuraho also stop just north of town; you can catch a *tempo* or walk the 1km to Orchha. The town itself is tiny, with only one **intersection.** If you're coming from Jhansi or Khajuraho, the road straight through the crossroads leads south to the *chhattris* and the Betwa River; to the left and east, a bridge crosses over to the palaces on Orchha Island; to the right and west are most of the accommodations in town, as well as the temples. Just north of the cross-roads on the righthand side is **Canara Bank,** which exchanges traveler's checks and US dollars. (Open M-F 10:30am-2:30pm, Sa 10:30am-12:30pm.) Just east of the crossroads is the **post office. Postal Code:** 472245.

 ## ACCOMMODATIONS AND FOOD

The best value in town is the new, brightly painted **Sharma Guest House ❶,** which offers clean rooms and a nice rooftop view. It's on the right as you head south from the crossroads. (Singles with bath Rs100; doubles with common bath Rs150.) Of the string of budget places lined up just west of the crossroads, the best is the **Shri Mahant Guest House ❷.** (☎52715. Doubles with attached bath Rs200-250.) The nearby **Hotel Mansarovar ❷** is much more basic. (☎52623. Doubles with bath Rs150.) The cheapest beds in town are buried inside the **Palki Mahal ❶,** the run-down palace to the right of Ram Raja Temple as you face it; the manager's office is opposite the entrance. (☎52633. Dorms Rs25; doubles with common bath Rs90.) The MPSTDC has converted an 18th-century palace in the middle of the ruins into the moderately priced **Sheesh Mahal Hotel ❸,** where only the most expensive suites are really palatial. The best rooms are decked out with rugs, marble baths, decorative hookahs, and unparalleled views of the entire complex of ruins. (mail@mptourism.com. Six ordinary rooms Rs590; 1 deluxe room Rs1990; and 1 royal suite Rs2990. Email for reservations at least 10-15 days in advance.)

Pintoo and Sintoo's Restaurant ❶, the 2nd shop from Sharma Guest House (when looking at Sharma), marked by Korean letters on lintel. Fresh, hot, and non-greasy basic Indian food, at rock-bottom prices. Unbeatable *thali* Rs15. Run by 2 brothers who are incredibly proud of their sweet *lassis* (Rs10). **Betwa Tarang Restaurant ❶,** near the bridge on the crossroads side, serves Indian food and the usual traveler fare (Rs20-50) on a rooftop with palace views. (Open daily 7:30am-10:30pm.) The **Orchha Resort ❶,** has a shiny, A/C, all-vegetarian restaurant that serves excellent meals for Rs85 and up. (Open daily 7am-9:30pm.)

⊙ SIGHTS

ORCHHA RUINS

All locations open daily 9am-5pm. Rs30 for a ticket that covers all the main sights, including the Lakshmi Narayan Temple and the chhattris. Photography Rs20. Walkman tour 2hr., Rs50, Rs500 deposit. Guides Rs100-200 for the three main palaces on the island, Rs200-500 for all sights. Guards at each site also serve as impromptu guides, showing you the best parts of the building and chasing off monkeys and dogs, for a tip of Rs10-20.

The ruins of Orchha are scattered along a bend in the Betwa, and they spill across from the main island to the present-day village and beyond. Nothing much has happened in Orchha over the past 200 years to clear them away, and nothing of consequence has been built here since the Bundelas shut up shop and left the place to the winds. The old buildings still dominate the landscape, and abandoned palaces and temples stand undisturbed amid the grasses and trees. Slumping towers and overgrown archways are everywhere, most of them unnamed and unmarked. MP Tourism offers a **walkman tour,** available at Sheesh Mahal Hotel, built into a wing of the Jehangir Mahal, that covers the three main palaces. This is well worth taking for the historical background, though you'll probably find your finger twitching over the fast-forward button from time to time as the breathless narrator launches into yet another dramatic "picture-the-scene" sequence. If any of the ruins are closed and locked as you make the tour, a complaint at the ticket office can often prompt someone to find the keys to the gate.

RAJ MAHAL. The Raj Mahal was the king's residence, with a room for his private audiences and several chambers for his harem. Constructed in the 16th century and one of the oldest buildings in Orchha, the palace lacks any notable ornamental features, though the walls and ceilings of many of the rooms are painted with intricate botanical patterns and murals depicting religious and mythical scenes. The king and queen's bedrooms hold the most ornate and well-preserved paintings of Ganesh and various epics; ask the guards to unlock these royal chambers. The top windows offer a good view of the town. Hours can be spent wandering the palace's myriad stairways and turrets—some have crumbled, leaving precipitous dead-ends. *(On the right as you approach the Sheesh Mahal Hotel.)*

RAI PRAVEEN MAHAL. Built and named for Raja Indramani's favorite dancing concubine, the smallest of the three main palaces was intended to be level with the treetops in the Anand Mandal Bagh gardens behind it. These can still be seen from the 2nd floor, and though neither the palace nor its gardens have exactly improved with age, it is still possible to imagine that this must once have been quite a nice place to kick back and relax after a long hard day spent wielding supreme executive power. *(Follow the road around to the left instead of heading up the stairs toward the hotel and the Raj Mahal.)*

JEHANGIR MAHAL. Built for Emperor Jehangir when he visited Orchha in 1606, the Jehangir Mahal palace surpasses anything else the Bundelas ever built in Orchha. Two elephants nod in welcome on both sides of the entrance, and inside, the Jehangir Mahal is filled with balconies, walkways, and railings. Traces of Islamic style can be seen in the stone screens, built for court ladies who wanted to see but not be seen, and decorated domes. The views from the 3rd floor balconies are some of Orchha's best: the Betwa river curls through the countryside and into the village, winding its way past the ruins. Throughout the palace are fine carvings of peacocks, parrots, snakes, and other animals. There is also a tiny **museum** on the ground floor, whose most interesting piece is a tremendous metal pot. *(Continue along the path to the right, past the camel stables, to the main entrance. Museum closed M.)*

TEMPLES
The three most important Bundela temples lie across the bridge from the ruins and to the right of the crossroads as you approach from Jhansi and Khajuraho.

RAM RAJA TEMPLE. The devout Raja Madhukar Shah had a dream in which Lord Rama appeared to him and ordered him to bring an image of the Lord to Orchha from Rama's holy hometown of Ayodhya. The king did as he was told, but arriving back in Orchha before his workmen had completed the temple designed to house the image, he decided to keep the holy image in his own palace until the temple could be completed. When the time came to relocate him, though, Lord Rama refused to budge. The palace had to be given up, and it became the Ram Raja Temple, where Rama has been worshipped in his role as a king ever since. Painted pink and yellow and overlooking a cobbled square, Ram Raja is now a popular temple. No firearms or leather goods are allowed inside. The evening worship is at 8pm, which brings hundreds of Ram worshippers, notorious for their enthusiasm, to shout and sing and pelt the shrine with flowers and sweets as police guards nervously try to control the chaotic crowd. *(Open daily 8am-12:30pm and 8-10:30pm.)*

CHHATURBHUJ TEMPLE. The massive but defunct Chhaturbhuj Temple is only marked by the remaining great arching assembly hall and several large spires. Spiral staircases at each corner of the cross-shaped floorplan lead to high lookout points that offer fantastic views of the palace complex across the river. The temple's ruined and eerie splendor is only enhanced by the dozen or so giant vultures who call the spires home. *(To the left of the Ram Raja Temple.)*

LAKSHMI NARAYAN TEMPLE. Isolated from the rest of Orchha and positioned at the crest of a hill, the Lakshmi Narayan temple's location seems fit for a fort, and it is built like one with four high walls, turrets at the corners, and two mighty stone lions standing guard at the entrance. Inside the temple are the best paintings to be found anywhere in Orchha, dating from the 17th to 19th centuries, including one fabulous post-Mutiny scene of British soldiers swarming around an Indian fort. Other scenes depict the Ramayana and Krishna stories and the marriage of Shiva. The breathtaking view from the top surveys all of Orchha, from the temples and palaces all the way down to the chhattris and beyond. *(Follow the westward path from behind Ram Raja Temple for 1km. Open daily 10am-4:30pm.)*

OTHER SIGHTS

On the island, turning left after passing through the **Royal Gate** and then walking through another archway brings you to the north end of the island, which is a good place to fight back the thornbushes and explore. The area is dotted with **old temples** that have been neglected and are now surrounded by small farms. People still dip into the ancient wells for their water here, and in some cases the temples have become makeshift tool sheds, kitchens, and cow barns. Though unfrequented by tourists, these temples are not to be missed. Their disrepair and the jungle's attempts to reclaim them only add to their charm. Ignore the small signs displaying each temple's name, and you'll feel as if you're the first foreign explorer to stumble upon these treasures. Some farmers and temple squatters double as unofficial guides and bushwhackers, fending off dogs, monkeys, angry bulls, and ornery brambles. They will also show you the safest and least smelly ascent to the upper levels of these old temples for around Rs50.

In town, to the right of the Palki Mahal palace, the **Phool Bagh Gardens** contain a formally laid out garden featuring a row of fountains and a small palace-pavilion. The Orchha kings retreated to a cool underground structure here to seek refuge from the summer heat.

Clustered along the peaceful, tree-lined banks of the Betwa river south of town is a series of 14 royal chhattris (cenotaphs). The Hindu Bundelas cremated their dead, but this did not stop them from borrowing the Mughal custom of mausoleum-building in order to commemorate the departed. Admission to the impressive complex is included in the same ticket that covers the rest of the sights in town. *(On foot, 10min. south of town and just past the Betwa Cottages and Orchha Resort.)*

GWALIOR ग्वालियर ☎ 0751

Currently boasting a population of almost one million, Gwalior has long been known for its massive fort, dubbed "the pearl amongst the fortresses of Hind" by Emperor Babur. Generations of conquerors have gazed down on the world from its mighty walls. During the Raj, the British granted the Maharaja of Gwalior one of only five 21-gun salutes ever bestowed upon Indian potentates in recognition of his loyalty during the Mutiny. This stands in stark contrast to the fate of Maharani Lakshmi Bai, who resisted the British from nearby Jhansi (see p. 376). The Scindia royal family is still the focus of Gwalior's civic pride—their palace, a 19th-century shrine to conspicuous consumption, offers a glimpse into a fairy-tale world of kitschy chaos and conforms to every preconceived notion of what a maharaja's house should look like.

▉ TRANSPORTATION

Flights: The **airport,** Bhind Rd. (☎2470272), is 10km northeast of the city. **Indian Airlines,** MLB Rd. (☎2326872, airport office 2368124). Open M-Sa 10am-1:15pm and 2-4:45pm. To: **Delhi** (45min.; M and F 1:15pm, Tu, Th, and Sa noon; US$75) and **Jabalpur** (1½hr.; Tu, Th, and Sa 8:25am; US$135).

Trains: Railway Station, MLB Rd., Morar (☎2341344). **Computerized reservation office** open M-Sa 8am-8pm, Su 8am-2pm. *Shatabdi Exp.* fares are for A/C chair-car; others are for sleeper class. To: **Agra** (2-3hr., frequent 4:15am-2:35am, Rs56); **Bhopal** (6-8hr., 15-20 per day 9:15am-3am, Rs140; *Shatabdi Exp. 2002*, 4½hr., 9:15am, Rs550); **Delhi** (5½-7hr., frequent 3:45am-2am, Rs123; *Shatabdi Exp. 2001*, 4hr., 7pm, Rs495); **Jhansi** (1½-2hr., frequent 3:45am-2am, Rs50); **Lucknow** (9hr., 11:15am and Tu 4:15am, Rs83); **Mumbai** (22hr., daily 10:25am, Rs310) via **Kanpur** (7hr.); **Mathura** (3hr., frequent 3:45am-1am, Rs82).

Buses: State bus stand (☎2340192), near the railway station, off MLB Rd. To: **Agra** (3hr., frequent 5am-9:30pm, Rs56-62); **Bhopal** (11hr., 7:30am, Rs180); **Delhi** (8hr., 18 per day 5am-9:30pm, Rs161); **Jhansi** (3hr., every 30min. 4am-10pm, Rs51); **Khajuraho** (8½hr., 7:25 and 8:30am, Rs133).

✱🛈 ORIENTATION AND PRACTICAL INFORMATION

Gwalior is quite spread out, wrapped in an irregular "U" shape around the **fort.** The city's sprawled shape combined with dusty, pedestrian-unfriendly roads makes it quite impossible to navigate without a *tempo* or auto-rickshaw. The **Old Town,** containing the **railway station** and the **state bus stand,** lies to the east of the fort. The **Morar** area, dominated by the gaudy **palace,** is to the southeast, and the **Lashkar** area (the heart of modern Gwalior and home to **Bada Chowk**) is in the southwest. **Maharani Lakshmi Bai (MLB) Road** runs across town from the northeast, near the station, to Lashkar. Tuesday is Gwalior's **business holiday.**

Tourist Office: MPSTDC (☎2540777), on Platform #1 of the railway station. Open M-Sa 9am-8pm. The main regional **tourist office,** Gandhi Rd. (☎2340370), is inside Hotel Tansen. Map guide Rs10. Open M-Sa 11am-5pm; if closed, ask at reception.

Currency Exchange: State Bank of India, Bada Chowk (☎2336291). Exchanges traveler's checks and foreign currency. Open M-F 10:30am-4pm, Sa 10:30am-1:30pm. SBI ATM directly across the street is supposed to be open 24hr., but is sometimes puzzlingly locked.

Police: Jayendra Ganj (emergency ☎100).

Hospital: Royal Hospital, Kampoo (☎2332711), near Roxy Cinema. A recommended private hospital, with doctors available 24hr. and a **24hr. pharmacy** as well. **Kasturba Medical Stores,** 6 Kasturba Market (☎2310953), is open 24hr.

Internet: Several places have sprung up along MLB Rd. and around town. Most charge Rs25-35 per hr. **Bhargava Computers,** opposite the Miss Hill School, Lakshmi Bai Colony (☎2428946). A short distance west of the Indian Airlines office, turn through the eastern gate to the colony; the store is 100m down on the left. Rs35 per hr.; after 5pm Rs25 per hr. Open daily 9:30am-9:30pm. A shop a few doors past Regal Hotel, MLB Rd., advertises "Internet" with a blue sign. Fast connection. Rs15 per hr. 10am-10pm.

Post Office: GPO, Bada Chowk. Open M-Sa 8am-8pm, Su 10am-6pm. **Postal Code:** 474001.

🏠 ACCOMMODATIONS

Accommodations in Gwalior are frustratingly expensive, and most hotels (including those listed below) will slap a **20% luxury tax/service charge** onto your bill to boot, but in most cases you get what you pay for (i.e. hot water bath and cable TV). Those really traveling on a shoestring can check out the budget hotels lining the market in front of the railway station, but in general, these are overpriced (from Rs135) for what you get (musty, very unappealing rooms).

Hotel Mayur, Padav (☎2325559). Turn right out of the railway station and go over the flyover; double back down the small road to the right, and look for the sign down an alley on the left. Clean, well-furnished, mid-range rooms with bath and cable TV. Dorms (men-only) Rs61; singles Rs270-360; doubles Rs330-420. ❷

Hotel Midway, MLB Rd. (☎2424392), 2km from the railway station. A complex with clean sheets and towels, satellite TVs, phones, and attached hot water baths. A Sikh *gurudwara* across the street provides chanting on megaphone from early morning to late evening. Singles Rs275-450; doubles Rs350-550. MC/V. 10% discount for *Let's Go* readers. ❷

Regal Hotel, Shinde Ki Chhawanii, MLB Rd. (☎2334469). Another decent place facing the main road, with slightly worn but fairly spacious rooms with TV and hot water bath. Paper-thin walls and water stains (in pricier rooms) detract slightly from the ambience. Breezy garden terrace upstairs and airless beer bar downstairs. Singles Rs250-475; doubles Rs275-500. ❷

Hotel Fort View, MLB Rd. (☎2423409). One of a string of places along the main road in the shadow of the fort. Decent rooms all come with attached hot water bath and TV. Check-out noon. Singles Rs300-500; doubles Rs350-550. Off season 10-15% discount (approx. Mar.-July). ❷

Hotel Surya, Jayendra Ganj, Lashkar (☎2331183). A bit removed from the tourist scene—you'll need a rickshaw to find it. Wood furniture, hot water, color TVs, and balconies. Singles Rs300-400; doubles Rs350-450 (non-A/C and A/C). ❷

Hotel Meghdoot, Padav (☎2326148), in the back of a commercial plaza next to the Indian Airlines office, just after the flyover from the railway station. Well-furnished rooms with wall-to-wall carpets. Good location for rail access. Dorms Rs100-150 (men and women separate); rooms Rs300-400. ❶

🍴 FOOD

Kwality Restaurant, Deendayal Market, MLB Rd. Chalk up another one for the dim, non-descript, A/C chain with a spelling problem. Standard range of North Indian veg. (Rs28-50), chicken (Rs40-160), and *biryani* (Rs20-40) dishes. Open daily 10am-11pm. ❶

Volga Restaurant, Tayendra Ganj, inside Hotel Surya. No Russian food at this chandeliered, A/C bastion of the *bourzhaozya,* but good Indian food and even a few Chinese dishes. Entrees Rs28-50. Open daily 9:30am-11pm. ❶

Feeder's 2000 Restaurant, Gwalior Rd., on the left, just north of the intersection with MLB Rd. It may look a little shady from the outside, but this underground lair serves up tasty Indian dishes (entrees Rs30-60) in a clean and tasteful environment. Open daily 9am-11:30pm. ❷

👁 SIGHTS

GWALIOR FORT

Open daily 8am-6pm. Admission to complex Rs0.20; additional joint ticket good for entry into Man Mandir Palace, Teli-ka Mandir, and Sas Bahu temples Rs250. English-language sound and light show (at Man Mandir Palace) daily 7:30pm; Rs100.

Gwalior's amazing fort, almost 3km long and at points 1km wide, dominates the city from 90m above, behind hulking 10m high walls. It has been the center of the region's power for all of recorded history. According to legend, King Suraj built the fort in the first century AD and named it after a holy hermit, Gwalipa, who cured Suraj's leprosy. Since then, the fort has been ruled by all of the region's succeeding dynasties: Rajputs, Delhi Sultans, Mughals, Mar-

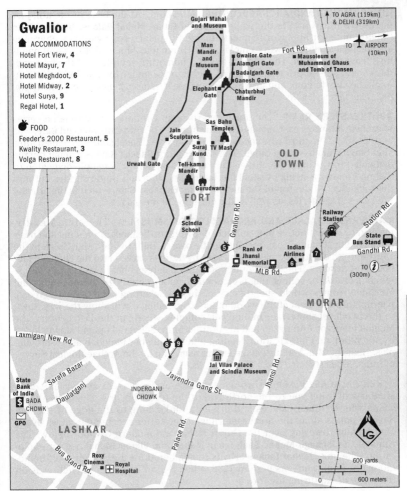

Gwalior

🏠 ACCOMMODATIONS
Hotel Fort View, **4**
Hotel Mayur, **7**
Hotel Meghdoot, **6**
Hotel Midway, **2**
Hotel Surya, **9**
Regal Hotel, **1**

🍎 FOOD
Feeder's 2000 Restaurant, **5**
Kwality Restaurant, **3**
Volga Restaurant, **8**

Gujari Mahal and Museum

Man Mandir and Museum

TO AGRA (119km) & DELHI (319km)

Fort Rd.

TO ✈ AIRPORT (10km)

Gwalior Gate
Alamgiri Gate
Badalgarh Gate
Ganesh Gate

Mausoleum of Muhammad Ghaus and Tomb of Tansen

Elephant Gate

Chaturbhuj Mandir

Sas Bahu Temples

Jain Sculptures

OLD TOWN

Suraj Kund

TV Mast

Urwahi Gate
Teli-kama Mandir

Gurudwara

FORT

Scindia School

Gwalior Rd.

Railway Station

Station Rd.

State Bus Stand

Gandhi Rd.

Rani of Jhansi Memorial

Indian Airlines

MLB Rd.

TO ℹ (300m)

MORAR

Laxmiganj New Rd.

Jai Vilas Palace and Scindia Museum

Jhansi Rd.

Sarafa Bazar

Daulatganj

INDERGANJ CHOWK

Jayendra Gang St.

State Bank of India

BADA CHOWK

GPO

LASHKAR

Palace Rd.

Bus Stand Rd.

Roxy Cinema

Royal Hospital

0   600 yards

0   600 meters

athas, and eventually the British. Since 1886, the fort has belonged to the Scindias, Gwalior's royal family. Through the ages, the fort has accumulated palaces and temples and more recently, a prestigious boys' school, a TV relay station, and two post offices.

There are two entrances to the fort: **Gwalior Gate** on the northeast side next to the Old Town, and **Urwahi Gate** on the southwest, which can be entered through a long gorge. Both have long, steep ramps that must be climbed on foot, although cars and taxis (but not auto-rickshaws) can enter through Urwahi Gate. The following sights are listed from northeast (Gwalior Gate) to southwest (Urwahi Gate); seeing them in this order is recommended as the view of Man Mandir's Palace above from Gwalior Gate yields a powerful first impression. (An auto-rickshaw ride from town should run about Rs20.)

GUJARI MAHAL AND ARCHAEOLOGICAL MUSEUM. At the base of the hill, just inside Gwalior Gate, is the well-preserved **Gujari Mahal Palace**, built by Man Singh Tomar for his favorite queen. Inside the palace courtyard is a charming **archaeological museum** with a melange of Hindu and Jain sculptures and paintings from the region. The curator keeps a miniature sculpture of the tree-goddess Gyraspur—a priceless piece of art history—under lock and key, but you might be able to coax him into letting you see it. *(Museum open Tu–Su 10am-5pm. Rs2; photography fee Rs2.)*

NORTHEASTERN RAMP. The northeastern ramp continues up through a series of arched gateways past Jain and Hindu shrines. The first gate, **Alamgiri Gate**, was built in 1660. The third (the second did not survive), **Badalgarh**, was named after Man Singh's uncle, Badal Singh. The 15th-century **Ganesh Gate** is a small temple dedicated to Gwalipa. The 9th-century **Chaturbhuj Mandir**, a temple dedicated to Vishnu, follows a string of small but interesting Jain and Hindu shrines cut into the rock face. At the top of the incline is the **Elephant Gate**, which is the 5th and final gate in the series, as well as the entrance to the palace.

MAN MANDIR PALACE AND ARCHAEOLOGICAL MUSEUM. The Man Mandir, marked by its distinctive blue-splotched towers, is the most interesting and best-preserved of Gwalior's palaces. Inside the palace, built by Raja Man Singh in the 15th century, are many small rooms split by lattices carved into the shape of animals and dancers. These elaborate, perforated screens bear witness to the system of *purdah*, or veiling, that is customary among certain groups of Hindus and Muslims. Women would spend much of their time sitting behind these screens, peering through them at the world outside. A flashlight will show the way down to the two-level subterranean dungeon complex where, in the 17th century, the Mughal emperor Aurangzeb had his brother Murad chained up and slowly killed by starvation and intoxication, feeding him nothing but boiled, mashed-up poppies. Near the Man Mandir Palace is a **museum**, run by the Archaeological Survey of India. *(Open M-Th and Sa-Su 10am-5pm. Rs2.)*

OTHER PALACES. Passing through the gate on your right as you exit Man Mandir will bring you to the north end of the fort. This area is a barren landscape where ruined palaces and dried-up tanks cling to the edge of the hill. Several points along the northeastern wall here offer spectacular views of the Man Mandir towering over the Gujari Mahal and modern Gwalior below. The ruins of the **Jehangir Mahal, Shah Jahan Mahal,** and **Vikram Mahal** beg for exploration. The huge **Jauhar Tank** nearby is remembered for the *jauhar* (self-immolation) of Rajput queens here in 1232, when Sultan Iltutmish of Delhi was on the verge of capturing the fort.

SAS BAHU TEMPLES. About halfway along the eastern edge of the hilltop are the Sas Bahu, or Mother-in-Law and Daughter-in-Law temples, built from the 9th to 11th centuries. The larger Mother-in-law (Sas) Mandir is dedicated to Vishnu, whom she worshipped, while the small Daughter-in-law (Bahu) Mandir is dedicated to Shiva. The temples themselves are shaped according to Jain aesthetics, but the statues and ornamentation are Hindu—a testament to the syncretism of the era. Aurangzeb defaced the thousands of figures and covered the whole surface of both temples with plaster, evidently enraged by the unapologetic idolatry of such depictions. The temples remained shrouded until Major J.B. Keith ordered their stripping and cleaning. The edge of the fort here offers a drab view of the city; the most interesting thing visible is the big, brown dome of Mohammed Ghaus' tomb. The west side of the fort has better views of the huge city and its craggy landscape.

TELI-KAMA MANDIR AND GURUDWARA. Toward the southern end of the fort, past the massive TV tower, stands the **Teli-ka Mandir** (Honeymoon Temple), a tall chunk of carved stone dating from the 9th century. It was once a Vishnu temple, but when the British occupied the fort in the 19th century, they turned it into a soda-water factory. There is nothing inside now but a fetid stink. The outside is pretty enough, though, with a Dravidian (southern Indian) roof and Indo-Aryan (northern Indian) decoration, a combination which is attributed to the marriage of a local prince to a Dravidian woman, for whose honeymoon the temple is named. Local legend has it that the amorous couples adorning the temple were teaching aids for a priest who resided over the newly married couple's sexual initiation.

Just east of the temple is the **Bandi Chhor Gurudwara,** a Sikh pilgrimage site that marks the spot where the 6th Sikh Guru, Hargobind, was imprisoned for two years by Emperor Jehangir. Ritual cleansing is required, and cloths are provided for you to cover your head before entering the *gurudwara.* Inside, men sit and chant Sikh scriptures above a sunken, silver chamber marking the guru's jail.

SOUTHWESTERN RAMP. Backtracking a bit north from the Teli-ka Mandir and passing through part of the grounds of the Scindia School brings you to the other main road connecting the fort with town. It snakes down through the long Urwahi Gorge, a natural rift in the hillside. Its walls are decorated with rows of **Jain sculptures** dating from between the 7th and 15th centuries. These figures of *tirthankaras* still stand impassively above the road, despite the best efforts of Mughal conqueror Babur, who damaged many of the statues by smashing their faces and genitals to pieces. Some faces have been repaired during recent restoration efforts. Unfortunately, a number of the faces are quite ugly and ill-fitted to the style of the bodies. One statue, an image of Adhinath, is 19m tall. More of these carvings are on the southeastern side of the fort, including one still used as a Jain shrine.

OUTSIDE THE FORT

JAI VILAS PALACE AND MUSEUM. Maharaja Jiyaji Rao Scindia commissioned a British architect to build this great white whale of a complex for him in an attempt to impress the Prince of Wales (later Edward VII) on his state visit here in 1875. Generations of Scindias have since filled it with the most outrageous *objets d'art* and kitsch imaginable. Today, part of it is open as the **Scindia Museum** (the rest is still the family's residence). Chairs, dressers, and tables from Versailles, a giant swing of cut glass and Italian rococo, a taxidermic trophy room of moth-eaten tigers poised to attack, rows of family portraits, and a dining table with tracks for a silver toy train that once wheeled around after-dinner brandy and cigars are only a few of the palace's notable features. From the gilded ceiling of Durbar Hall hang two enormous Belgian chandeliers, each weighing 3½ tons; below them is the largest handmade carpet in Asia. To test the strength of the hall's ceiling, 10 elephants were led up ramps onto the roof. *(Tell the rickshaw-wallah "Jai Vilas Museum"; a different entrance is used for the palace. Open daily M-Tu and Th-Su 9:30am-5pm. Rs175 for foreigners. Keep your ticket stub for entry to both wings.)*

MADHYA PRADESH

MAUSOLEUM OF MUHAMMAD GHAUS AND TOMB OF TANSEN. On a beautiful grassy expanse 10min. east of the fort's northeastern gate is the **Mausoleum of Sheik Muhammad Ghaus,** named for the Afghan prince and Muslim saint who helped the emperor Babur capture Gwalior Fort. The walls of this fine early Mughal monument are made up of a series of cut-stone screens carved into beautiful geometric patterns. The **Tomb of Tansen** is in the same graveyard; this 16th-century raga-singer was one of the greatest musicians in Indian history. Chewing the leaves of the tamarind tree near the tomb is supposed to make your voice as sweet as Tansen's. A classical music festival takes place here in November or December.

MAHARASHTRA

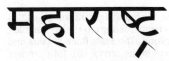

Maharashtra, the "Great Country," straddles the Indian Peninsula, from the tropical coast to the arid Deccan Plateau, from the fringes of the hot and hectic Ganga Plain to the balmier, palmier, more easy-going South, and from isolated villages to metropolitan Mumbai. From the sacred Godavari at Nasik and the giddy, red-robed, Birkenstock-clad acolytes of the Osho Commune to the businessmen and billboards of Mumbai, Maharashtra has more than enough to keep you happy. More than half of India's foreign trade and nearly 40% of its tax revenue flow from here, but two-thirds of Maharashtra's population still practices subsistence agriculture. Many people here are proud of the bold martial traditions of their state, and are quick to embrace the fierce regional independence of their forbears, the Marathas, hardy fighters bred in the rocky hinterland. This heritage is embodied in the warrior-king and folk-hero Shivaji (1627-80) and is currently exploited by the ruling Shiv Sena ("Shiva's Army") Party, a Hindu nationalist ally of the BJP.

HIGHLIGHTS OF MAHARASHTRA

The intricately carved **cave temples** at **Ajanta** (p. 429) and **Ellora** (p. 427), both UNESCO World Heritage Sites, are architectural wonders par excellence.

A hissing, buzzing helter-skelter of a city, **Mumbai** (below) will make your head spin, with its sights, sounds, nightlife, and inexhaustible energy.

MUMBAI (BOMBAY) मुंबई   ☎ 022

Mumbai unites all of India's languages, religions, ethnicities, castes, and classes into one heaving, seething sizzler of a metropolis. Rupee and dollar billionaires, film stars, models, and politicians flock to frolic at the city's hotels, discos, and restaurants. But Mumbai is by no means all glamor and glitz. The city is also home to more impoverished people than any other Indian city; the shantytown at Dharavi has become Asia's (and perhaps the world's) largest slum.

Mumbai sprang from modest roots. When the Portuguese acquired the islands in 1534, they called them Bom Bahia ("Good Port"); subsequently, Mumbai entered the hands of Charles II of England as a part of Catherine of Braganza's dowry. In 1687, Bombay became the capital of the East India Company's regional holdings.

After India's independence, disputes between the Marathi- and Gujarati-speaking populations ended in the partition of Bombay State into Maharashtra and Gujarat in 1960. Even during the conflict, the economy boomed, as it continues to do today. In 1995, politicians gave the city a new official name—Mumbai, from Mumbadevi, the local incarnation of the goddess Durga.

Today, the city makes the most movies in India, and India makes far more movies than any other place on earth—a fact that earned the local film industry its nickname, "Bollywood." The manic mix of London double-deckers and bullock carts, *sadhus* and stockbrokers, and the perpetual motion of it all is enough to floor first-time visitors. Mumbai defies stereotypes of an India filled with pot-bellied cows and ramshackle temples, though it has plenty of both. Instead, the city forces travelers to face an explosive fusion of development and despair.

✈ TRANSPORTATION

INTERNATIONAL FLIGHTS

Sahar International Airport, Vile Parle (☎28366700; Air India flight information 2836 6767), 20km north of downtown Mumbai. This chaotic, mosquito-ridden complex prepares arriving travelers for the continent beyond. The **State Bank of India** and **Government of India Tourist Office** operate counters in the arrival hall for currency exchange and info (24hr.). The easiest way to get downtown from the airport is by **pre-paid taxi** (1½hr.; Rs 300, Rs 370 for a car with A/C). Pay for a taxi at the counter in the arrival hall, then go outside to the line of taxis and find the one whose number matches the number on your receipt. The non-pre-paid drivers at the airport are not to be trusted, but from Mumbai to the airport, any metered cab will do. Allow 2hr. during rush hour (to the city 8-11am, from the city 5-8pm).

There is a Rs500 **departure tax,** which all travelers must pay before going through customs and leaving India (Rs250 if you're headed to another South Asian country). Many airlines do not include this tax in their ticket prices. Set aside enough cash for the tax before exchanging your last rupees.

INTERNATIONAL AIRLINES. Air India, Marine Dr., Nariman Pt. (☎22024142). Open M-Su 9:15am-5:15pm. **British Airways,** 202-B Vulcan Insurance Bldg., Veer Nariman Rd., Churchgate (☎22820888). Open M-Sa 9:30am-1pm and 2:45-5:30pm. **Cathay Pacific,** Taj Mahal Hotel, Apollo Bunder, Colaba (☎22029113). Open M-Sa 9:30am-5:30pm. **Delta,** Express Towers, Veer Nariman Pt., near Air India (☎28267000). Open M-Su 9am-5:30pm. **Lufthansa,** Express Towers, Nariman Point (☎22023430 or 22875264). Open M-F 9am-5:45pm, Sa 9am-1pm. **Royal Nepal,** 222 Maker Chamber SV, Nariman Point (☎22836197). Open M-Sa 10am-5:30pm.

DOMESTIC FLIGHTS

Santa Cruz Airport is 20km northeast of downtown, 3km from Sahar International Airport. The new Terminal 1A is for Indian Airlines, and 1B is for all private carriers; **free shuttle buses** connect the two (every 15min., 4am-midnight). Free shuttle buses also depart from both terminals to the international airport (every hr.). Take a metered auto-rickshaw (about Rs40) from the airport to the Andheri Railway Station, buy a ticket for any **city-bound train** (45min., 2nd class Rs5), and get off at Churchgate Station, or vice versa. Exit on the east side of Andheri Station to get a rickshaw to the airports. There are **no pre-paid taxis** from this airport, but the ones at the stand outside should follow the meter one-way (Rs200 to downtown; under Rs75 to Sahar International Airport).

DOMESTIC AIRLINES. There are three main carriers: **Indian Airlines,** Air India Building, Marine Dr., Nariman Point (24hr. inquiry ☎140 or 141; for reservations and confirmation ☎22876161). Open M-Sa 8:30am-7:30pm, Su 10am-1pm and 1:45-5:30pm; ticketing office at domestic airport open 24hr. **Jet Airways,** Amarchand Mansion, Madam Cama Rd. (☎22855788, reservations ☎28366111). Open M-Sa 10am-5:30pm. **Sahara India Airlines,** Maker Chamber V, Nariman Point (☎22835671 or 22835672). Open M-Sa 10am-6pm. The following are approximate flight schedules and rates. Contact each carrier for the best deals. Discounts for travelers under 26. To: **Ahmedabad** (1hr., 6-7 per day, US$75); **Aurangabad** (45min., 2 per day,

US$92); **Bangalore** (1½hr., 9-10 per day, US$168); **Bhopal** (2hr., 1 per day Su-F, US$130); **Bhubaneshwar** (3hr., 3 per week, US$250); **Kolkata** (2½hr., 5-6 per day, US$235); **Calicut** (1½hr., 3-4 per day, US$145); **Chennai** (2hr., 8-9 per day, US$160); **Cochin** (2hr., 4-5 per day, US$150); **Coimbatore** (2hr., 2 per day, US$180); **Delhi** (2hr., several, US$208); **Goa** (1hr., 4-5 per day, US$98); **Hyderabad** (1½hr., 6-7 per day, US$125); **Indore** (1hr., 2 per day, US$95); **Jaipur** (3½hr., 2 per day, US$160); **Mangalore** (1½hr., 2 per day, US$120); **Trivandrum** (2hr., 3-4 per day, US$200); **Udaipur** (2hr., 2 per day, US$130); **Varanasi** (5hr., 1 per day, US$235). Flights booked from abroad must be reconfirmed 72hr. before departure.

TRAINS

Western Railways connects Mumbai to Gujarat, Rajasthan, and Delhi. **Central Railways** serves Delhi and destinations to the east. Some long-haul trains also leave from **Dadar, Kurla,** 15km northeast of downtown, or **Bandra;** all are accessible by local train from Victoria Terminus. For train **schedules,** arm yourself with the indispensable *Trains at a Glance* (Rs25), available at railway station bookstalls.

CENTRAL RAILWAYS. Central Reservation Office, **Victoria Terminus (VT),** officially known as **Chhatrapati Shivaji Terminus** (inquiry ☎135 or 22695959, automated info ☎22656565), in the right wing of the complex. Go to the station at Churchgate for all west-bound trains (see **Western Railways,** below). Head for **Window 7,** the Foreign Tourist Guide (open M-Sa 9am-1pm and 1:30-4pm). They sell tickets for US$ or UK£, or for rupees with an encashment certificate. They release tourist quota seats on a first-come, first-served basis on the day *before* departure for trains leaving before 2pm, or on the day *of* departure for trains leaving after 2pm. The following trains, which leave from VT unless otherwise noted, are just a select few of the many available. To: **Agra** (22hr., 7:10pm, Rs326; 1-2 trains per day from Dadar Station 7:55am and 10:40pm); **Aurangabad** (7½hr., 6:10am and 9:20pm, Rs137); **Bangalore** (24hr., 1-2 per day 7:55am and 10:40pm, Rs310); **Bhopal** (14hr., 8am and 7pm, Rs244; 1-2 per day from Dadar Station 7:55am and 10:40pm); **Kolkata** (33hr., 3 per day 6am-9pm, Rs393); **Chennai** (24hr., 2 and 11:20pm, Rs314; daily from Dadar 7:50pm); **Ernakulam** (28hr., 1-2 per day 12:15 and 3:30pm, Rs207); **Hyderabad** (15-17½hr., 12:35 and 9:55pm, Rs151); **Margao** (11hr., 5:15am and 10:30pm, Rs225); **Pune** (4hr., 16 per day, Rs53); **Trivandrum** (44hr., 12:15 and 3:35pm, Rs256).

ON THE MENU

STIKKI CHIKKI

One thing that is bound to strike any visitor to Matheran, Lonavla, o Mahabaleshwar is the plethora o "*chikki*-marts" that line every street ir the tourist resort towns. There is a chikki store at every corner, and ven dors sell packaged *chikki* at bus sta tions, in hotels, and on the train *Chikki* is not just an industry in Maha rashtra, it is an institution.

A traditional sweet resembling crumbly peanut brittle, *chikki* is a Maharshtran specialty. Its two mair ingredients, ground nuts and suga cane (which is boiled down to jag gery), are staple agricultural products of the region. Historically, *chikki* pro duction was a trade handed dowr from father to son. Merchants would travel through the town, going door-to door to hawk their sweets. Some *chikki-wallahs* are now fourth- or fifth generation sweets-makers.

The *chikki* trade has strong agricul tural, economic, and historical ties to Maharashtra, but the sticky candy is also bound to the region's spiritua traditions. Each of Maharashtra's reli gious festivals is associated with a sweet to be produced, presented and consumed at that time. *Chikki* is associated with Makar Sankranti, the festival recording the passing o zodiac signs.

The *chikki*-marts of the hill-stations have a wide range of *chikki* flavors including pistachio, dried fruit, coco nut, chocolate, and the traditiona peanut. All stores are strictly "try before-you-buy," so join the rush to stock up on this delectable local spe cialty. Happy sampling!

WESTERN RAILWAYS. Western Railways, Churchgate Reservation Office, Maharishi Karve Rd., Churchgate (inquiry ☎131, booking info 22095959, arrivals from Delhi ☎132, from Gujarat 133). Across the street from Churchgate Station, in the same building as the Government of India Tourist Office. To get to the **Foreign Tourist Counter,** ignore the first reservation office and walk past the first floor tourist office; it's the next door on your left, upstairs. Tourist quota procedures are the same as at VT (see above), but here an agent is specially assigned to help you navigate the confusing process of ticket-buying. Open M-F 9:30am-1:30pm and 2-4:30pm, Sa 9:30am-2:30pm. The following trains leave from **Mumbai Central** (see **Local Trains,** p. 394) unless otherwise noted. To: **Ahmedabad** (7-8½hr., 5-7 per day 5:45am-9:50pm, Rs107; 4 per day from Bandra 3-8:50pm); **Delhi** (17-22hr., 5-6 per day 7:25am-10:40pm, Rs212; A/C 3-tier sleeper Rs1485; daily from Dadar station 10:40pm; daily from Bandra 10:25pm); **Jaipur** (18hr., 7:05pm, Rs184).

MUM'S THE WORD

Most tourists spin or stroll down Nataji Subhas Chandra Bose Rd. in Mumbai without even realizing it. They, like all the city's residents, know this street by its colonial name, Marine Drive. The new street names may be patriotic, but people continue to rebel against today's authorities by refusing to relinquish the street names of past oppressors. Nepean Sea Rd. is never Laxmibhai Jagmohandas Marg; even the bus conductors say Ridge Rd. for Bal Gangadhar Kher Marg. Shahid Bhagat Singh Marg elicits blank stares from taxi drivers—but everyone recognizes Colaba Causeway. On the rare occasions when Mumbai's citizens do accept the new names, the names are inevitably abbreviated beyond recognition: Sir Pherozeshah Mehta Rd. becomes PM Rd.; Doctor Dadabhoy Naoroji barely escapes as Dr. DN.

Mumbai's name game developed from small-scale civil disobedience against big-time politics. The Hindu nationalist Shiv Sena party, senior partners in the state's coalition government at the time, exerted their political control by renaming as many locations as possible, in accordance with Marathi names. In 1995, the Sena caused their biggest stir when they renamed the whole city Mumbai, derived from its "traditional" Marathi name, Mumbadevi. Residents and visitors alike can't seem to agree on which name to use, and most are interchangeable. Cheeky urbanites seem to have invented their own name for the city, laconically dubbing it "Slumbai."

BUSES

State Transport Terminal, JB Behran Marg (☎23074272 or 23076622), opposite Central Railway Station, next to the Maratha Mandir Cinema. **Maharashtra State Road Transport Corporation** runs quiet, comfortable, and expensive buses to the major tourist destinations in the state; services are cut back during monsoon. To **Aurangabad** (10hr., 2 per day, Rs204) and **Mahabaleshwar** (7hr., 2 per day, Rs150). For other destinations in Maharashtra, you have to book at the ASIAD office (☎24136835) in Dadar, or at an MTDC luxury service office, although trains are likely to be quicker and more convenient. **Goa State Transport** (Kadamba) runs a daily luxury bus to **Panjim** (15hr., 5pm, Rs280). **Gujarat State Transport** has at least 2 daily buses to **Ahmedabad** (12hr., 3 and 7pm, Rs168). **MTDC,** CDO Hutments, Madam Cama Rd. (☎22026713), runs buses Oct.-May, to **Mahabaleshwar** (7hr., 7am, Rs230). Services change frequently, so check for up-to-date route info.

Maharashtra

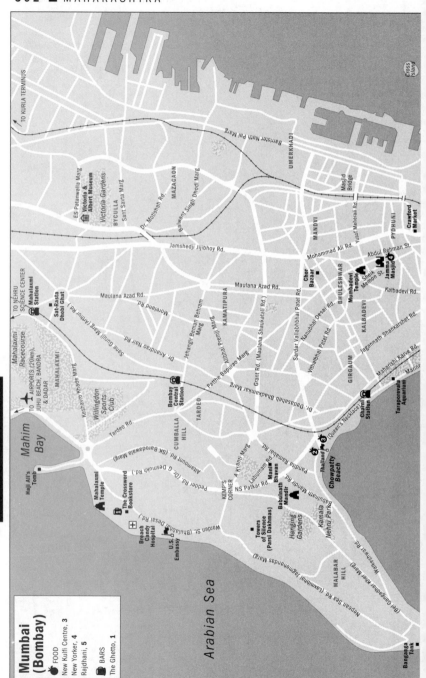

MAHARASHTRA

Mumbai (Bombay)

FOOD
New Kulfi Centre, **3**
New Yorker, **4**
Rajdhani, **5**

BARS
The Ghetto, **1**

Arabian Sea

Mahim Bay

TO KURLA TERMINUS

Cross Island

Barrister Nath Pai Marg

UMERKHADI

Maslid Bridge

MANDVI

PYDHUNI

Crawford Market

ES Patanwala Marg

Victoria & Albert Museum

Victoria Gardens

BYCULLA

Sant Savta Marg

MAZAGAON

Dr. Motiram Rd.

Bolivari Singh Dhodi Marg

Jamshedji Jijibhoy Rd.

Mohammad Ali Rd.

Yusuf Meherali Rd.

Abdul Rehman St.

Jamma Masjid

Sheik Memon St.

Chor Bazaar

BHULESHWAR

Mumbadevi Temple

KALBADEVI

Kalbadevi Rd.

TO NEHRU SCIENCE CENTER

Mahalaxmi Station

Sat-Rasta Dhobi Ghat

Maulana Azad Rd.

Maulana Azad Rd.

KAMATIPURA

Sardar Vallabhbhai Patel Rd.

Nanubhai Desai Rd.

Vithalbhai Patel Rd.

Jagannath Shankarshet Rd.

GIRGAUM

Maharishi Karve Rd.

Mahalaxmi Raceourse

Mahalaxmi Raceourse (20km), TO AIRPORTS (20km), JUHU BEACH, BANDRA & DADAR

MAHALAXMI

Keshavro Khade Marg

Willingdon Sports Club

Moreland Rd.

Dr. Anandrao Nair Rd.

Sane Guruji Marg (Arthur Rd.)

Jehangir Behram Behram Marg

Parthe Aitbha Premji Marg

Grant Rd. (Maulana Shaukatali Rd.)

Tardeo Rd.

Bombay Central Station

TARDEO

CUMBALLA HILL

Altamount Rd. (SK Barodawala Marg)

Dr. Dadasaheb Bhadkankar Marg

Chami Station

Taraporevala Aquarium

Queen's Necklace

Thallani

Pandita Ramabai Rd.

Chowpatty Beach

Babulnath Mandir

Babulnath Mandir Rd.

Kamala Nehru Park

Haji Ali's Tomb

Mahalaxmi Temple

The Crossword Bookstore

Breach Candy Hospital

U.S. Embassy

Warden St. (Bhulabhai Desai Rd.)

Peddar Rd. (Dr. G Desmukh Rd.)

KEMP'S CORNER

A Kranti Marg

Laburnam Rd.

NS Patkar Rd.

Mani Bhavan

Babulnath Bhavan

Towers of Silence (Parsi Dakhmas)

Hanging Gardens

MALABAR HILL

Nepean Sea Rd. (Laxmibai Jagmohandas Marg)

Bel Gangadhar Kher Marg

Walkeshwar Rd.

Banganga Tank

TO ELEPHANTA ISLAND

MALABAR POINT

Raj Bhavan

Ridge Rd.

Temple

Back Bay

Lines Station

(Netaj) Subhashchandra Bose Rd.)

Loksat Tilak Rd.

P D'Mello Rd

Victoria Terminus Station

GPO

Shahid Bhagat Singh Rd.

BALLARD ESTATE

FORT

Dr. Dadabhoy Naoroji Rd.

HORNIMAN CIRCLE

St. Thomas' Cathedral

Mahapalika Marg

Mahatma Gandhi Rd.

Shankar Marg

BALVANT PHADKE CHOWK

New Marine Lines

Govt. of India

Flora Fountain

Jehangir Art Gallery

Prince of Wales Museum

High Court

Rajabai Clock Tower

Regal Cinema

Bhaurao Patil Marg

Gateway of India

Maharshi Karve Marg

Veer Nariman Rd.

Churchgate Station

Jamshedji Tata Rd.

Bradbourne Stadium

MTDC

Madam Cama Rd.

Air India

Nathalal Parekh Marg

COLABA

Colaba Causeway (Shahid Bhagat Singh Rd.)

NCPA

NARIMAN POINT

KOLI VILLAGE

(Prakash Pethe Marg)

Cuffe Parade Rd.

CUFFE PARADE

World Trade Center

Afghan Church

SEE CENTRAL MUMBAI MAP

0   600 yards
0   600 meters

◧ LOCAL TRANSPORTATION

LOCAL BUSES

Trains are easier to deal with than buses, but if you're going to be in town for a while, it's worth the (Herculean) effort required to come to terms with the city's chaotic bus system. For a complete guide to stops and routes, pick up a city bus map (Rs20) from the bus terminal office on Colaba Causeway (open M-F 9am-5pm). Try to learn the Marathi numerals so that you can recognize the bus as it approaches (the Roman numeral and English destination are only written on the side—often visible too late to allow you to clamber on board before the bus roars off again). Red numbers indicate "limited" services, which supposedly stop less frequently and cost marginally less. No fare within the city should exceed Rs3, limited or otherwise.

BUS #	MARATHI	ROUTE AND DESTINATION
1 ltd.	१	Colaba-Regal-Flora-VT-Crawford Market-Mahim
3	३	Afghan Church-Colaba-Regal-Flora-VT-Jijanatra Velyan
6	६	Colaba-Regal-VT-Crawford-Byculla-Chesbus Colony
62	६२	Flora-Metro-Marine Lines-Mumbai Central-Dadar Station
61	६१	Mantulaya-Regal-Metro-Opera House-Mumbai Central-Dadar Station
81 ltd.	८१	VT-Kemp's Corner-Breach Candy and Haji Ali-Nehru Planetarium-Santa Cruz
91	९१	Mumbai Central-Dadar-Kurla
106	१०६	Afghan Church-Colaba-Regal-Chowpatty-Kamala Nehru Park
108	१०८	VT-Regal-Chowpatty-Kamala Nehru Park
125	१२५	Colaba-Crawford Market-Haji Ali-Worli Village
132	१३२	Regal-Churchgate-Breach Candy and Haji Ali
188 ltd.	१८८	Borivli (E)-Sanjay Gandhi NP-Kanheri Caves
231	२३१	Santa Cruz (W)-Juhu Beach
321 ltd.	३२१	Worti-Airport-Vile Parle (E)
343	३४३	Goregaon (E)-Film City

LOCAL TRAINS

Mumbai's commuter rail system runs along two lines. **Western Railways** runs one line from **Churchgate** through Mumbai Central, Mahalaxmi, Dadar, Bandra, Santa Cruz (for Juhu), Andheri (for the airports), and a dozen other stations before Borivli (Sanjay Gandhi NP) and beyond. The **Central Railways** line runs to and from **VT** (check the final destination; be sure you're on the right line) and tends to be of less use to the tourist. Most trains out of VT stop at Dadar, where you can cross the platform and change onto a Western train. One-way tickets (2nd class Rs3-10, 1st class Rs8-32) are sold at windows in each station. When boarding a train, check the illuminated display—the first letter code is the first letter of the final destination, the second code is the time, and the "F" or "S" indicates whether the train is (relatively) fast or (especially) slow. Fast trains skip the stations whose names are illuminated on the board below. That's right, the names that are lit up brightly are the **places it does not go.** There are special, less crowded cars exclusively for women on all trains.

TAXIS

Taxis rule in Mumbai, since auto-rickshaws aren't allowed in the downtown area and public transport is so crowded. Set the meter and go—this shouldn't be too much of a struggle unless it's very late or the weather's very bad. You pay roughly Rs16 per km—for the precise figure, consult the chart that the driver should carry. **Auto-rickshaws** only roam the suburbs; you pay about seven times the meter.

✈ ORIENTATION

The city of Mumbai reaches into the Arabian Sea like a cupped hand, the fingers and thumb forming a backward letter "c" off the western coast of India. For purposes of orientation, it is more important to familiarize yourself with the names of the city's different areas than specific street addresses, as most locals (and taxi drivers) navigate and give directions according to the names of neighborhoods and well-known landmarks. At the fingertip of **Colaba,** toward the southern end of the city, is the tourist ghetto. The area's main thoroughfare, **Colaba Causeway** (also known as SBS Marg), is where you'll find most of the budget accommodations and lost-looking backpackers. The Causeway ends in the north at a huge, circular intersection universally known as **Regal** because of the movie theater that presides over it. Directly west of Regal, jutting into the bay, are **Cuffe Parade,** an elite residential area, and **Nariman Point,** Mumbai's most prestigious corporate address, housing the offices of many international banks, airlines, and a few consulates. North of Regal, past the Prince of Wales Museum, stretches **Fort,** Mumbai's oldest neighborhood and its main financial district. Banks cluster near its most prominent landmark, **Flora Fountain (Hutatma Chowk).**

West of Fort and north of Nariman Point is the **Churchgate** neighborhood, where you'll find the Churchgate railway station and several trendy restaurants. **Marine Drive** (Nataji Subhash Rd.) runs along the western edge of the city, curving from Nariman Point in the south to Churchgate in the north, and farther still to **Chowpatty Beach.** North of Chowpatty are the upmarket **Malabar Hill** community and the northern suburbs.

Most travelers arriving by train will enter Mumbai at **Victoria Terminus (VT),** now officially called **Chhatrapati Shivaji Terminus (CST),** just north of the Fort. North of VT, **Crawford Market (Phule)** marks the beginning of the **bazaar district.**

☷ PRACTICAL INFORMATION

TOURIST AND FINANCIAL SERVICES

Tourist Office: Government of India Tourist Office, 123 Maharishi Karve Rd. (☎22033144), across the street from the Churchgate Station. Dispenses maps of Mumbai (free) and some useful info. Open M-F 8:30am-6pm, Sa 8:30am-2pm. Also at Sahar International Airport (☎28325331; open 24hr.) and at Santa Cruz Domestic Airport (☎26159200; open during flight arrival times). **Maharashtra Tourism Development Corporation (MTDC),** CDO Hutments, Madam Cama Rd. (☎22026713). From the Air India Bldg., walk away from Marine Dr. along Madam Cama Rd.; it's on the left, just past the giant Nehru statue. Open M-Sa 9:30am-6:30pm. Other offices at Santa Cruz Airport, Sahar International Airport, Churchgate Station, and the Gateway of India.

Consulates: Australia, Maker Towers E., 16th fl., Cuffe Parade (☎22181071). Open M-F 9am-5pm. **Canada,** 41/42 Maker Chambers VI, Nariman Point (☎22876027). Open M-Th 9am-5:30pm, F 9am-3pm. **Ireland,** Bombay Yacht Club, Apollo Bunder, Colaba (☎22024607). Open M-F 9am-5pm. **South Africa,** Gandhi Mansion, Altamount Rd. (☎23893725), near Kemp's Corner. Open M-F 9am-5pm. **Sri Lanka,** Jehangir Wadhwa,

1st fl., 34 Homi Modi St., Fort (☎22045861 or 22048303). Most visas obtainable upon arrival in Sri Lanka. Open for visas M-F 9:30-11:30am. **UK,** Maker Chambers IV, 1st and 2nd fl., J.B. Marg, 521 Nariman Point (☎22833602 or 22830517). Open M-F 8am-4pm. **US,** Lincoln House, 78 Bhulabhai Desai Rd., Breach Candy (☎23633611 or 23633617). Open M-F 8:30am-1pm and 2-3:45pm.

Currency Exchange: Hong Kong Bank, 52/60 MG Rd., Flora Fountain (☎22674921). Cash advances on MC and V. On-site **ATM** is connected to the Plus network. Open M-F 10am-6pm, Sa 10am-2pm. **Thomas Cook,** Dr. DN Rd., Fort (☎22048556). On the left, 2 blocks up from Flora, with the bright red sign. Cashes Thomas Cook traveler's checks for free; Rs30 per transaction for other brands. Open M-Sa 9:30am-6pm. **American Express,** Regal Cinema Bldg., Shivaji Marg (☎22048291), on Wellington Circle. Cashes AmEx traveler's checks for free; 1% fee on other brands. Open M-F 9:30am-6:30pm, Sa 9:30am-2:30pm.

LOCAL SERVICES

Luggage Storage: Cloak Room at VT, inside the station bldg., near platform 13. Rs10 per day, 31-day max. Similar facilities at all big stations. Bags must be locked. Don't lose the receipt. Limited space. Open 24hr. except 7:30-8am, 3-3:30pm, and 11:30pm-midnight.

Bookstore: ▓ Crossword Bookstore, Mahalaxmi Chambers, 1st fl., 22 Bhulabhai Desai Rd., Breach Candy (☎24924882). Look up for the yellow sign in the window. Open M-F 10am-8pm, Sa-Su 10am-9pm. Outdoor booksellers pack the sidewalk on VN Rd., between Flora and the Churchgate Station. **The Strand Book Stall,** Sir PM Rd., Fort (☎22661994). Just above Horniman Cir. Favorite of the Mumbai intelligentsia, the Strand's crowded collection is hand-picked. Search carefully for discounts. Open M-Sa 10am-7pm. **Nalanda,** Taj Mahal Hotel, 1st fl. (☎22022514). A fine selection of fiction, travel, and ethnographic literature. Open daily 8am-midnight.

Market: M Phule Market, north end of Dr. DN Rd. Universally known as **Crawford Market.** Anything from kitchen supplies and vegetables to puppies and European chocolates. See also **Shopping,** p. 405. Open M-Sa 6am-6pm.

EMERGENCY AND COMMUNICATIONS

Police: Police Commissioner's Office, Dr. DN Rd., Crawford Market (☎100), opposite the market building, behind an iron fence. You can report thefts at this head office; expect a bureaucratic nightmare, but miracles might happen. Open M-F 9am-4pm.

Pharmacy: New Marine Lines is lined with late-night chemists, such as **New Bombay Chemists,** Churchgate (☎22001173), opposite the cinema and next to the hospital. Open daily 8am-11pm. Also nearby is **Real Chemist,** 50/51 Kaka Arcade (☎22002497), which is open 24hr.

Hospital: Breach Candy Hospital, 60 Warden Rd., Breach Candy (☎23633651, 3671888, or 3672888), just past the American Consulate and the Breach Candy Swimming Club. Not near Colaba, but one of the most modern hospitals in Mumbai and accustomed to dealing with foreigners. Open 24hr. **Bombay Hospital,** 12 New Marine Lines (☎22067676). Modern, established, and centrally located. Open 24hr. **Ambulance** ☎102.

Internet: ▓ Diral Point, RM Nowroji Furdanji Rd., across from Waghela. Rs25 per hr., 20 computers. 8am-12:30am. **Meghdoot** (☎56311611) 288-270 SBS Rd., directly across from Welcome Hotel. Rs 25 per hr. 12 computers. 9am-midnight. **Waghela,** 23-B Nowroji Furdunji Rd., Colaba (☎22048718), around the corner from Leopold Cafe, off Colaba Causeway. Rs30 per hr. Open daily 8:30am-midnight. Both the American Cultural Council (Rs40 per hr.) and the British Council (Rs60 per hr.) also have Internet.

Post Office: GPO, W. Hirachand Marg (☎22620956). The huge stone building next door to VT, off Nagar Chowk. *Poste Restante* at counter #92. Open M-Sa 9am-8pm, Su 10am-5pm. **Postal Code:** 400001.

⚑ ACCOMMODATIONS

Most foreign tourists gravitate toward the peaceful, crumbling mansions of Colaba despite the area's proximity to Gateway of India touts and the (decidedly non-budget) Taj Mahal Hotel. Mumbai real estate being what it is, "budget" means something entirely different in this city from what it means elsewhere in India. Even bottom-of-the-barrel digs charge rates that would mortify any self-respecting budget traveler. Reservations are a good idea at any time, especially in season Nov.-Feb. Check-out is noon unless otherwise noted. Most hotels have a variety of rooms ranging from windowless cells to comfortable, airy digs.

COLABA

YWCA International Centre, 18 Madam Cama Rd. (☎22025053 or 22020598; fax 2202 0445; ywcaic@bom8.vsnl.net.in), a 4min. walk from Regal, on the left. Second fl. Open to men and women. Although it's more expensive than most budget hotels, you get your money's worth at the Y. Rates include all-you-can-eat buffet breakfast and dinner, TV lounge, daily room cleaning, telephones, and towels in spotless, spacious rooms with balconies. All have attached bath. Reserve 15 days in advance. Rs100 membership fee (good for 6 months). Dorms Rs625, singles Rs700, doubles Rs1300, triples and family rooms up to Rs3200. If reserved ahead: dorms Rs800, singles Rs900, doubles Rs1650. ❹

Salvation Army, 30 Mereweather Rd., Boman Behram Marg (☎22841824). Behind the Taj Mahal Hotel, under the arcade. Pistachio-green walls make it as drab and institutional as you'd expect, but if you're on a budget nothing beats it. Passable dorms and large, nondescript doubles. Breakfast included. No hot water. Lockers Rs50 per day. Max. 1-week stay. Check-in 10am. Check-out 9am. Dorms Rs135; doubles with or without bath Rs505-585 with 3 meals included. ❶

Hotel Sea Shore, 1-49 Kamal Mansion, 4th fl., Arthur Bunder Rd./Haji Niyaz Ahmed Azmi Marg (☎22874237 or 22874238). From Regal, follow the Causeway to Arthur Bunder, 9 blocks down on the left. The entrance to Kamal Mansion is on the right, down an alley before Arthur Bunder hits the ocean. The rooms range from claustrophobic cubicles to large, airy, ocean-view suites. Sparkling common bath. Singles Rs350; doubles with TV Rs450-500. ❸

Hotel Lawrence, 3rd fl., ITTS House, 33 Sri Sai Baba Marg, Rope Walk Ln. (☎22843618), first left off K. Dubash Marg when coming from B.G. Rd., just past the Sanuk Thai restaurant. Nine clean, airy rooms with shared bath and friendly, helpful staff. Breakfast included. Hot water upon request. Reserve 3 weeks in advance. Singles Rs400; doubles Rs500; triples Rs700. ❸

Hotel Prosser's, Curzon House, 2-4 Henry Rd., Apollo Bunder Rd. (☎22841715 or 22834937), located where Henry Rd. (the 6th left off the Causeway, south of Regal) meets the sea. High ceilings and spacious rooms. Common bath. 24hr. check-in. Noon check-out. Singles or doubles Rs400-600. Off-season Rs350/Rs550. ❸

India Guest House, 1/39 Kamal Mansion (2283 3769). Same directions as Sea Shore. Third floor. All rooms with common bath. Thin walls afford limited privacy. Singles Rs300; doubles with window Rs450, without window Rs400; triples Rs550. ❷

Hotel Carlton, Florence House, 12 Mereweather Rd., Boman Behram Marg (☎22020642 or 22020259), one block away from the Salvation Army, behind the Taj. The lively veranda, equipped with chairs and tables, allows residents to escape their cramped quarters for a glimpse of cathouse life across the street. Singles Rs350; doubles Rs550-600; triples with A/C and bath Rs1200; quads Rs900. ❸

Bentley's Hotel, 17 Oliver Rd. (☎22841474 or 22841733; bentleyshotel@hotmail.com). A peaceful refuge from Mumbai's bustle—vintage rooms with hardwood floors, white-washed balconies, and mosaic tiling. Individual baths, TVs, and breakfast included in price. 70 beds total. Singles Rs955, with A/C Rs1130; doubles Rs1220, with A/C Rs1420. ❺

BEYOND COLABA

Ship Hotel, Bharati Bhavari, 3rd floor, 219 P D'Mello Rd. Right next to Hotel Manama (see below). Newly renovated, with clean rooms and baths and very friendly staff. Meals at on-site canteen Rs25. TVs in every room. Check-out 9am. Dorms Rs125 (with built-in lockers!); singles Rs175; doubles Rs300. ❷

Hotel Oasis, 276 Shahid Bhagat Singh Rd. (☎22697886; fax 22626498). With your back to the GPO, head left on W. Hirachand Marg, then right onto SBS; it's on the right. Decent-sized rooms with phones and TVs. No advance booking for singles. Singles Rs490; doubles Rs640-980. ❸

Welcome Hotel, 257 Shahid Bhagat Singh Rd. (☎22612196 or 22617474; welcome_hotel@vsnl.com), near the Hotel Oasis. Glamorous and clean, with TVs and phones. Breakfast, morning, and evening tea included. Singles Rs590-850; doubles Rs850-1150; rooms with bath Rs900-2150. V/MC. ❸

Hotel Manama, P D'Mello Rd. (☎22613412; hotelmanama@vsnl.net), close to St. George Hospital. With your back to the GPO, head left on Hirachand Marg, then turn left on P D'Mello; it's on the right. Good-value, crowded, middle-class hotel. Doubles Rs624-832. ❹

🍴 FOOD

Eating in Mumbai can result in anything from gastronomical delight to gastrointestinal distress. The distinctive street food is a constant temptation, and the city's restaurants brim with the best international food in India, as well as every conceivable type of Indian cuisine, including a few (Parsi, Malvani) not to be found anywhere else. Not surprisingly, the Good Port of Mumbai is also renowned for its seafood. There is no better place to splurge on your meals. Serious eaters should refer to the *Mid-Day Good Food Guide* (Rs50). Some Mumbai specialties are **pao bhaji,** batter-fried balls of potato and chilies served on white bread, and **puri,** innocent-looking fried pastry shells, which come in two varieties—flat and disc-like or hollow and spherical—and can be filled with anything from green chutney, tamarind sauce, chili paste, fried vermicelli and puffed rice to potato, tomato, onion, green mango, and coriander.

COLABA

🍴 **Fort Central Vegetarian Restaurant,** Cawasji Patel Rd., Fort (☎22870080). From Flora, take VN Rd. away from Churchgate and turn left onto C. Patel. Spicy Punjabi food at its best. Great service. Open daily 8:30am-11:30pm. Delectable *masala dosa* Rs14, main dishes Rs24-50. ❷

🍴 **Trishna Restaurant,** 7 Sri Sai Baba Marg (☎22672176 or 22659644). Follow Dr. VB Gandhi Marg past Rhythm House, turn left at the first intersection and walk 2 blocks; it's on the right. Trishna started out as a food stall, and by word of mouth became Mumbai's trendiest seafood restaurant. Freakishly-sized shellfish at rock-bottom prices. Pomfret (enough for two) Rs300; crisp calamari Rs130. Reservations essential for dinner. Open M-Sa noon-4pm and 6pm-midnight, Su noon-4pm and 7pm-midnight. ❹

Picadilly Lebanese Food, Donald House, Colaba Causeway (☎22823217), next to Kamat and across from bus station. Stunning Lebanese cuisine at low prices. Falafel roll Rs40; homemade hummus Rs50. Also offers American fare including veggie burger Rs45. Open daily 8am-11pm. ❷

Olympia Restaurant and Coffee House, Rahim Mansion, opposite Leopold Cafe, Colaba Causeway. Time stands still in this 2-tiered, turn-of-the-century, Iranian-style cafe. Brain *masala* fry (Rs27) is their most famous dish, but no-brainers will also be satisfied. Mutton *biryani* Rs15. Open daily 11am-11pm. ❶

Sahakari Bhandar, to the right as you face the Regal Cinema. Don't let the garish, pseudo-western sign out front deter you from entering this fast and friendly snack joint. A convenient and dependable place for *bhel puri* (Rs14-16) and *pao bhaji* (Rs24). Don't miss the chickoo milkshake (Rs25). Great, cheap South Indian tiffin (*dosas* Rs15). Open M-Sa 8am-9pm. ❶

Majestic, Colaba Causeway, opposite Mondegar's, up a few stairs. Proves that there is such a thing as budget in Mumbai. Simple dishes (Rs18-50) and basic *thalis* (Rs25) served in a huge hall with low tables under whirring fans. Open daily 7am-11pm. ❶

Kamat Vegetarian Resaurant, Colaba Causeway (☎22874734), opposite Electric House. The self-proclaimed specialists in South Indian delicacies and North Indian dishes serve a wide variety of *dosas* (Rs20-48), great *thalis* Rs35, Kashmiri *dum aloo* (Rs55). Open daily 8:30am-9pm. ❷

Cafe Churchill, Colaba Causeway, between Walton and Garden Rd. This tiny, brightly colored cafe serves American snacks that taste better and cost less than those at the bigger tourist hangouts in the area. All-day breakfast skillets Rs40-60; sandwiches Rs40-60; brownies and cakes Rs25-50. Open daily 10am-11:30pm. ❷

Khyber Restaurant, 145 MG Rd. (☎22673227), where MG Rd. meets K. Dubash Marg. The finest Mughlai cuisine in all the city served amid lavish antiques and mirrors. Chicken *makhanwala* (Rs275) in thick, tangy tomato sauce; chicken *badami* (Rs275) is superb. Open daily 12:30-3:45pm and 7:30-11:45pm. Reservations a must. ❺

Sanuk Oriental, 30 K. Dubash Marg (☎22044233). Classy Thai food. Meat and veg. curries Rs180-280. *Pad thai* Rs120-220. Chinese lunch buffet Rs250. Open daily 12:30-3:30pm and 7:30-11:30pm. Reservations recommended. ❹

BEYOND COLABA

▨ **Cafe Universal,** 299 SBS Rd., (☎22613985, 22694893). The sibling offshoot of the ever-popular Leopold's Cafe. Lofty, sponge-painted walls, Art Deco ironwork and a versatile Chinese menu make this brand new cafe a hip spot for Szechuan Prawn (Rs70) or a Kingfisher beer (Rs70). Open 8am-midnight. ❸

ON THE MENU

SWEETS FOR THE SWEET

During your stay in India, salty *dal* fry, spicy mutton *masala*, savory *paneer*, and fiery chutneys may test the tolerance of your taste buds. If too much strong flavoring has your tongue exhausted, the antidote may not be to eat more bland foods, but rather to take a trip around the block to your nearest *mit hai* shop. *Mit hai* (literally "sweet") can refer to any of a dozen types of sweet bonbon. From tough rose *halwa* to fresh milk and coconut and pistachio rolls, India's *mit hai* will satisfy even the pickiest palate. Just the sight of the endless trays of multi-colored sweets—some pink, some sprinkled with multicolored nuts, some sheathed in silver—could be sufficient to send you into sugar shock. And while you might have spent hours haggling over a few paise with an understandably tight-fisted taxi driver, *mit hai* shopkeepers exhibit incredible generosity. Just glance at a variety and the next moment find a sample of the soft sweet in your palm. Don't be timid about accepting the gift, or about buying some more. After all, with so much Indian salt and spice assaulting your senses on a daily basis, don't you deserve it?

▨ **Chopsticks,** Manik Mahal, 90A VN Rd., Churchgate (☎22049284), near Marine Dr., across VN Rd. from Jazz and the Pizzeria. Join Mumbai's hoi polloi as you gorge on fresh-cooked aromatic Chinese cuisine. Four course lunch buffet Rs 225. Relaxing, A/C atmosphere and friendly Chinese chefs. Low-calorie and veg. options available. Starters Rs105-190, entrees Rs135-265. ➍

New Kulfi Centre, opposite Chowpatty, near the pedestrian overpass where SVP Rd. meets Marine Dr. Locals on the sidewalk wolf down creamy *kulfi* desserts in every possible flavor at this legendary street-side stall (Rs20-40). Ask for *mutka kulfi* (Rs40), served in small, earthen pots that you can take home. Open daily 10am-12:30am. ➊

Rajdhani, Sheikh Memon St. (☎23426919), opposite Mangaldas Market, near Crawford Market. From Crawford, look down the crowded lanes opposite Dr. DN Rd.; it's on the right of the lane with the white turret at the far end. Mumbai's richest Gujarati lunchtime *thalis* (Rs125). Open daily 11:30am-3:30pm and 7-11pm. ➍

Jimmy Boy Cafe, 11 Bank St., Fort (☎22700880), 1 block south of Horniman Cir., at Green Rd. Burgers and sandwiches (Rs40-75) are good, but even better are the sweet-and-sour spiced Parsi veg. or non-veg. meals served on a banana leaf (Rs80-100), the *saas-ni-machhi* (a spicy fish curry, Rs90), and the *kid gosht,* served in a bed of saffron rice (Rs80). Open M-Sa 11:30am-11:30pm. ➋

Samrat, Prem Court, J. Tata Rd., Churchgate. From Churchgate, it's on the left side of the road that leads to the right of Eros. Fancy, pure-veg. restaurant specializes in slightly sweet Gujarati *thalis* (Rs117-140). You can wash down the all-you-can-eat *chappatis, dal,* and vegetables with a bottle of beer (Rs95). Open daily noon-10:30pm. ➍

Indian Summer, 80 Veer Nariman Rd., Churchgate (☎22835445). You won't need to eat again for days after one of Indian Summer's upscale, sumptuous, all-you-can-eat Mughlai lunch buffets (Rs270 plus 20% tax). Epic seafood buffet M night (Rs300 plus tax), and a large *a la carte* menu, too. Chicken and lamb dishes Rs175, veg. Rs150-160. Live music Sa nights. Open daily noon-3:30pm and 7pm-midnight. ➎

New Yorker, 25 Chowpatty Seaface (☎23632923). America gets classy in this A/C eatery. Trendsetters down well-prepared plates of everything from pizza to sandwiches and enchiladas to Mexican falafel (Rs50-150). Open daily 11:30am-11:30pm. ➋

The Pizzeria, 143 Marine Dr., Churchgate (☎22856115), where VN Rd. meets Marine Dr. A cool bay breeze and eclectic pizza offerings. Margherita Rs130; Tandoori chicken sausage Rs165; Tangy *paneer* Rs225. Fresh dough made daily. Pasta dishes Rs165-185. Open daily noon-12:45am. ➎

⊙ SIGHTS

The Raj-era might have ended over half a century ago, but the mostly British-influenced areas of Mumbai continue to dominate the sightseeing scene.

COLABA

THE GATEWAY OF INDIA. The quintessential starting point from which to lose yourself in the endless metropolis is the Gateway of India. Built to commemorate the visit of King George V and Queen Mary in 1911, this Indianized triumphal arch stands guard over the harbor next to the Taj Mahal Hotel. With a cosmopolitan nonchalance typical of Mumbai, the gateway combines carved brackets derived from Gujarati temple architecture with Islamic motifs such as the minaret-like finials in a European building type. By day, the area is a sea of relentless touts. In the evening, however, the gateway is a favorite haunt of strolling couples, camera-happy tourists, peanut vendors, and snake charmers.

In the small park nearby stands an imposing equestrian statue of the great 17th-century Maratha leader **Shivaji Bhonsle.** The reputation of this historical king and legendary hero has been hijacked by the right-wing Maharashtrian party, Shiv Sena, which decks out the unwitting image in marigold garlands and saffron flags.

TAJ MAHAL HOTEL. While the modern tower of the Taj Mahal Hotel dwarfs Shivaji, the building's older wing is the real eyecatcher. Jamshedji Tata, one of India's first industrialists, built this Mumbai landmark in 1899 in retaliation against the Europeans-only policies of other Raj-era hotels. Like all the other Tata enterprises which dominate today's Indian economy, the Taj soared to success, monopolizing both the hotel industry and the city's early skyline.

AFGHAN CHURCH. Down at the southernmost end of the Causeway stands the 19th-century Afghan Church, built to commemorate the soldiers who died to keep the Khyber Pass British. This area also houses an old colonial cemetery and the now-defunct Colaba lighthouse.

KALA GHODA

PRINCE OF WALES MUSEUM. Opposite the Regal Cinema is the Prince of Wales Museum. The intervening gardens provide a buffer between the newly restored domed gallery and the relentless traffic outside. The most impressive exhibit is the collection of miniature paintings from the 16th to 18th centuries. These painstakingly detailed works showcase the various Rajasthani, Deccani, and Mughali schools of painting through scenes of palace life and Hindu mythology. Other areas of the museum feature cluttered displays of everything from Mughal miniatures to stuffed animals and fourth-rate oil paintings. Also of great interest are the collection of Ashokan sanskrit stone tablets in the ground floor's balcony and the second floor's history of Indian swords and weaponry. The first hall contains a trove of archaeological treasures dating back to the Indus Valley civilization, including well-preserved stone tools and burial urns from both Harappa and Mohenjo-Daro. Another highlight is the collection of metal deities. (☎ 22844484. Open Tu-Su 10:15am-6pm. Rs300, students with ISIC Rs6.) The spacious domed building across the street is the **National Gallery of Modern Art,** which hosts a fantastic array of rotating exhibits of Indian and international art. (MG Marg, corner with Madam Cama Rd. ☎ 22881969. Open Tu-Su 11am-6pm. Free.)

THE JEHANGIR ART GALLERY. The building next to the Prince of Wales Museum consists of several rooms, each hosting an exhibit by a different contemporary Indian artist. Even better, artists are on-site and happy to chat with you. New shows every week. A posterboard outside lists exhibits at other galleries around Mumbai. (☎ 22843989. Open daily 11am-7pm. Free.) Inside the museum, Cafe Samovar, opening onto a garden, provides a peaceful escape. Enjoy a light meal or munch on snacks there. (Open M-Sa 10:30am-7:30pm.)

NEAR MUMBAI UNIVERSITY. The buildings of Mumbai University and the **High Court** line the left side of MG Rd. from the Prince of Wales Museum to Flora Fountain. These Victorian-Gothic extravaganzas, centering on the 85m **Rajabai Clock Tower,** occupied the seafront until the Art Deco neighborhood opposite was built on reclaimed land in the 20s and 30s. Today, their finest facades face the Oval Maidan, one block to the west. The wide, grassy maidans, which now support enthusiastic cricket matches, used to separate the British residential communities in Fort from the Indian areas on the other side. (Open daily 11am-5pm.)

THE FORT AREA

Another group of sights stretches north from **Flora Fountain,** now renamed **Hutatma Chowk (Martyrs' Square)** in honor of the protesters who died agitating for a separate Marathi-speaking state in 1959-1960. Flora is lined by still more Raj-era Gothic buildings, now inhabited by foreign banks.

HORNIMAN CIRCLE. Horniman Circle is oddly anachronistic of the surrounding commercial hubbub. The elegant neoclassical colonnade faces the early-19th-century **Asiatic Society Library** (originally the Town Hall) across a small park complete with fountain. The neighboring **Mint and Customs House** also dates from the early 1800s. Mumbai's oldest English building is **St. Thomas's Cathedral,** at the southwest corner of the circle. Although begun by East India Company Governor Gerald Aungier in 1672, when Surat was still the capital of the Mumbai Presidency, St. Thomas's remained incomplete until 1718. The interior reveals a fascinating slice of colonial life with its endless marble memorials to long-gone English types. *(Open daily 6:30am-6pm.)*

NORTH FORT. At the northern edge of the Fort area stand the grand colonial edifices of the GPO (post office) and **Victoria Terminus (VT).** Opposite VT, the **Mumbai Municipal Corporation Building** comes as close to scraping the sky as any Victorian building could. The rotunda of the **Crawford Market** sends a lesser, yet equally improbable spire into the sky. Lockwood Kipling, Rudyard's father, designed the sculptures on the exterior during his tenure at the nearby art school. *(MJ Phule Market. A quick stroll up Dr. DN Rd. from VT, past the huge Times of India building and the Mumbai School of Art.)*

CHURCHGATE AND BACK BAY COAST

NEAR CHURCHGATE STATION. The red-and-white wedding cake of the **Eros Cinema** in the middle of this period-piece area exemplifies Mumbai's unparalleled wealth of interwar architecture. A functioning cinema, Eros shows Bollywood's latest hits. *(Advance booking open daily 9:30am-2pm and 4-7pm. Tickets Rs40-100. Buy tickets at least 3 days in advance.)* Some of the surrounding buildings, on the same sq. as Churchgate Station, have been restored to their original waxy, zig-zag glory, but most have suffered from the damp, salty air and landlords constrained by rent control. Visitors strolling down the side of the maidan from Churchgate will find it hard to believe that these dilapidated apartments fetch millions of dollars on the rare occasions when they come up for sale.

MARINE DRIVE. In the opposite direction from Churchgate, Marine Dr. runs along the rim of the Arabian Sea, stretching all the way from Nariman Point to Chowpatty Beach at the foot of Malabar Hill. Near the beach, the Drive is lined with backstock from the supply of massive, gray "tetrapods" that keep downtown Mumbai from the waves below. At sunset, people come to stroll, power-walk, and jog along the sea front, chatting, buying snacks, and treating their children to rides on toy cars and merry-go-rounds. Meanwhile, Chowpatty Beach comes alive with vendors, locals, and Kolis mending their nets. During the monsoons, tremendous waves crash down on the street, but its roasted-corn hawkers, buses, and cars seem unperturbed. At night, neon ads and a long string of streetlights transform the seaside strip into what is still popularly known as the **Queen's Necklace.**

KOLI VILLAGE. From the maidan, Maharishi Karve Rd. merges with Cuffe Parade Rd., where an abrupt gap in the land reclamation schemes has left a small bay between the towers of Nariman Point and the Cuffe Parade Extension. A fishing village, still populated by the original inhabitants of Mumbai, the Kolis, lines the shore here.

MALABAR HILL

Beyond the beach rises Malabar Hill, Mumbai's wealthiest residential district.

⊠ MANI BHAVAN. As the site of the first meeting of the Indian National Congress, Mumbai pays tribute to the Father of the Nation and one-time citizen of the city, Mahatma Gandhi. The Mahatma stayed at Mani Bhavan during his frequent visits to Mumbai. The building now houses a **museum** dedicated to the great man, with a huge research library on Indian history, Gandhi, and independence. Along with a film archive, the museum includes a small collection of old photos and a "look-and-see" diorama version of the great moments in Gandhi's life and the struggle for independence. *(19 Laburnum Rd. Walk up Babulnath Mandir Rd. and turn right at its end, then take the first left onto Pandita Ramabai Rd. Open daily 9:30am-6pm. Free.)*

BANGANGA TANK. The **Walkeshwar Temple** hides in one of the many old back streets that wind through Malabar, lined with bright flower stalls and renegade chickens. In local legend, the area harbored the banished hero of the *Ramayana*, Rama, and his brother Lakshmana, as they traveled south to free Rama's wife from captivity in Lanka. In order for Rama to perform his daily worship, Lakshmana had to bring a *linga* from far-off Varanasi. He was late one day, prompting Rama to make one from the only material he had, sand *(waluk)*, thus creating a *walukeshwar* ("sand god"). The temple's massive gray *shikhara* sits at the head of Banganga Tank, a huge rectangular pool of greenish water surrounded by jagged lines of rundown settlements and as full of legend as it is of bathers and *dhobis*. The thirsty Rama created the tank by shooting his arrow into the ground, and water began to gush forth to quench his thirst. What was once a celestial drinking fountain is now a glorified sink. Just behind the temple, the maze of *dhobi ghats* along the shore is crowded with row upon row of half-dressed washermen crouched low on the rocks and beating to smithereens the washables of everyone else in the city. The city has even more impressive *dhobi ghats* near the Mahalaxmi race course, but these are less accessible to most tourists.

THE GARDENS. The city's two most famous gardens are spread over the top of Malabar Hill. Sir Pherozeshah Mehta Garden, locally known as the **Hanging Garden,** is at the terminus of buses #106 and 108. Although its tree sculptures of various animals border on kitsch, the garden offers a welcome break from the bustling city. *(Open daily 5am-9pm. Free.)* The **Kamala Nehru Children's Park** across the street features a replica of the shoe that the old lady and all her children used to live in. *(Open daily 5am-8pm. Free.)* Old people, families, and young lovebirds come to the park to relax, walk among topiary and penguin-shaped trash cans, lounge on lawns and benches, and take in the views of the city. Crowning Malabar Hill are the seven massive **Parsi Towers of Silence,** where Zoroastrians set out their dead for vultures to eat. The whole complex is screened from sight by artful landscaping. The funerary customs of the Parsis nonetheless caused a stir a few years ago when the vultures threatened to contaminate the city's water supply by dropping leftover morsels in nearby reservoirs.

BABULNATH MANDIR. The entrance on Babulnath Mandir Rd. is an unassuming set of three small stone arches, seemingly held up by the throngs of flower sellers, holy men, and worshippers around their base. The gates open up to a world far removed from the jams of Marutis below, where a concert of blaring bells and chanting voices blankets the path up the stone-stepped hill, lined with the living quarters of worshippers. The temple itself is loudly alive during worship.

MAHALAXMI AREA

■ **TOMB OF HAJI ALI.** Just beyond Mahalaxmi, on an island in the middle of the Arabian Sea, the shrine of the Sufi saint Haji Ali battles the waves daily. The bright white building stands out against the blue or gray of the sea like a beacon to all camera owners. The narrow causeway to the island nearly disappears at high tide and during the monsoon storms, but at other times even non-Muslims can stride past the expectant rows of beggars as far as the outer chambers. On dry ground next to Haji Ali, the **Mahalaxmi Racecourse** cuts a green gash through the gray cityscape. *(Races run on weekends from Dec.-May.)*

MAHALAXMI TEMPLE. The Mahalaxmi Temple's patron goddess (like Mumbai itself) devotes herself to wealth and beauty, making this *mandir* the city's most popular. In addition to a depiction of Lakshmi riding a tiger, the temple contains images of Kali and Saraswati, two other major goddesses of the Hindu pantheon. *(North past the flyover-covered shopping hub of Kemp's Corner, near the sea on Warden Rd., also called Bhulabhai Desai Rd.)*

CENTRAL AND NORTHERN MUMBAI

West of Crawford stretches an endless string of bazaars: first **Zaveri (Silversmiths) Bazaar,** then **Bhuleshwar Market** near the Mumbadevi Temple, and finally **Chor (Thieves) Bazaar,** northward by Johar Chowk. Buy a small offering (Rs20) outside of Mumbaderi temple and stumble among the hordes to have your offering blessed and distributed. One block down Sheik Memon St., visit **Jamma Masjid** or just peer through the gates at the spotless edifice and rain-water cistern-cum-fish pond.

JUHU BEACH. Scruffy palm trees and litter make this a less-than-idyllic sunbathing spot, but that doesn't stop crowds of city-dwellers from flocking here as the sun sinks down into the Arabian Sea. In a carnivalesque atmosphere, you can bounce along in horse-drawn carriages, ride rickety ferris wheels, chow down at *chaat* stands, join in pick-up volleyball games, or simply stroll and wade along the water's edge. One of the best-known spots in the city, the Juhu area is also home to many a Bollywood star. The bungalow of the country's most famous actor, Amitabh Bachchan, is constantly surrounded by a small pack of curious crowds hoping to catch a glimpse of their hero. *(Take a local train from Churchgate to Santa Cruz station. (45min., Rs5.) Exit station on the west side, and take a rickshaw to Juhu Beach. Rs15.)*

BYCULLA. North from Johar Chowk along Sir JJ Rd., in the neighborhood of Byculla, the **Victoria and Albert Museum** (now Veermata Jijabhai) sees relatively few foreign tourists. The exhibits on Mumbai's history include the carved stone elephant that gave Elephanta Island its name. *(Open Th-Tu 9:30am-5pm. Rs2.)* For the real thing, head next door to Mumbai's spartan **zoo**. The adjacent **Botanical Gardens** are a more healthful setting for a stroll. *(Open Th-Tu 10:30am-4:30pm. Rs2.)* The architecture in Byculla, in contrast to the examples farther south, is dominated by congested housing complexes known as *chawls*, which flourished during the first half of the 20th century when Mumbai was enjoying its status as the country's premier spot for cotton manufacturing and textile production. The center of the city, where most of the factories were located, became the center of working class life. Today, 20% of Mumbai's population lives in this tenement-style housing, where 10 families might share one room, a kitchen, and a toilet.

SANJAY GANDHI NATIONAL PARK. The Sanjay Gandhi National Park features over 100 rock-cut caves, although only a few amount to much more than holes in the wall. Nonetheless, those planning to hit Ajanta, Ellora, or Karla and Bhaja can come here for a quick prep course, while others can treat this as a kind of consolation prize. Cave 3, a *chaitya* hall guarded by two huge standing Buddhas, is the most interesting place to explore. *(In the northern suburb of Borivili. Take the train to the Borivili stop. Open daily 9am-5:30pm. Rs2.)*

📷 ENTERTAINMENT

Check *This Fortnight* or the *Bombay Times* section of the *Times of India* for the weekly bulletin of the latest concerts and plays at the **Tata Theatre,** the **Nehru Centre,** and a host of smaller venues.

Nehru Centre, Dr. Annie Besant Rd., Worli (☎24920510), is in the same complex as the Nehru Planetarium, on the right just past the Mahalaxmi race course. Indian and Western classical music and theater. The **Planetarium** within has English shows Tu-Su at 3 and 6pm, Rs10.

National Centre for the Performing Arts, Marine Drive (☎22833737), at the very tip of Nariman Pt., just beyond the Oberoi. The compound houses a main theater, an experimental theater, and a third venue scheduled to open soon. More European and American offerings than at the Nehru, but good Indian music and theater, too.

Prithvi Theatre, Janki-Kutir, Juhu-Church Rd. (☎26149546). Along a lane that juts off the main road leading to the Juhu bus station. The theater hall here is a city legend and one of Mumbai's most popular, with performances in many languages. Tickets Rs100. Call for dates and times of English shows.

📷 SHOPPING

Like some enormous, quasi-tropical Mall of India, Mumbai can fulfill material needs and wanton consumer desire in every price range. A two-minute walk north from Flora Fountain leads to a part of MG Rd. known as **Fashion Street,** an endless chain of street stalls selling cheap and disorientingly similar merchandise. The hawkers of Western designer cast-offs can spot naive tourists a mile off, so bargain without shame. (Open daily roughly 10am-8pm.) For those who need a hiatus from haggling, **Cottage Industries Emporium,** Shivaji Marg, near Wellington Circle, offers a government fixed-price alternative. Though it's unabashedly geared toward tourists, and, compared to the chaos of the streets outside, rather sterile, you're guaranteed good quality and reasonably fair prices. The emporium is an almost-too-convenient, one-stop souvenir shop, proffering such wares as batik fabrics, silk Nehru jackets and scarves, and all things sandalwood. (Open M-Sa 10am-7pm. Accepts major credit cards and exchanges money.)

The **Khadi Bhavan Village Industries Emporium,** at the corner of Dr. DN Rd. and Sir P.M. Rd., Fort, offers hand-woven cotton cloth, *kurtas*, and traditional knick-knacks at reasonable prices. (☎22073280. Open M-Sa 10:30am-6:30pm.) The more upscale **Bombay Store** (formerly the Mumbai Swadeshi Store) is along Sir P.M. Rd. in Fort. The store's gleaming glass cases and polished hardwood shelves bear little resemblance to the *swadeshi* movement's spinning wheels and simple, home-made cloth. Like a department store specializing in "ethnic" merchandise, this is sterile, spoon-fed shopping, but the quality and selection is hard to grumble about. (☎22885048. Open M-Sa 10am-7:30pm, Su 10:30am-6:30pm. Major credit cards accepted.) Travelers with particularly fat wallets should head over to **Warden Road (Bhulabai Desai Road)** near Kemp's Corner. This line of stores is the place to go if you want to match, thread for thread, the clothing worn by Mumbai's hipsters.

MAHARASHTRA

MAHARASHTRA

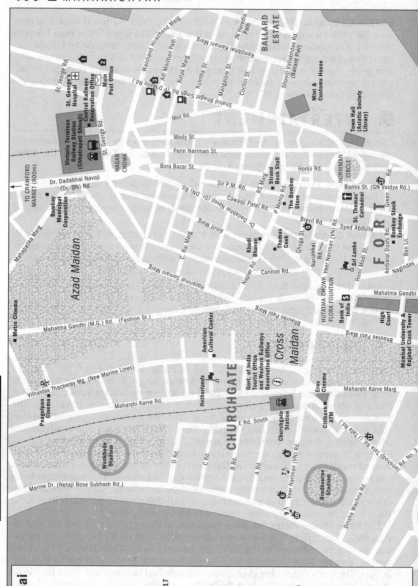

Central Mumbai (Bombay)

▲ ACCOMMODATIONS
Bentley's Hotel, **28**
Hotel Carlton, **22**
Hotel Lawrence, **16**
Hotel Manama, **2**
Hotel Oasis, **4**
Hotel Prosser's, **26**
Hotel Sea Shore, **30**
India Guest House, **31**
Salvation Army, **25**
Ship Hotel, **1**
Welcome Hotel, **3**
YWCA International Centre, **17**

☕ FOOD
Cafe Churchill, **27**
Chopsticks, **6**
Fort Central Vegetarian
    Restaurant, **5**
Indian Summer, **8**
Jimmy Boy Cafe, **12**
Kamat Vegetarian
    Restaurant, **23**
Khyber Restaurant, **14**
Majestic, **19**
Olympia Restaurant, **21**
Piccadilly Lebanese Food, **24**
The Pizzeria, **10**
Sahakari Bhandar, **18**
Samrat, **11**
Sanuk Oriental, **15**
Trishna Restaurant, **13**

♪ NIGHTLIFE
Leopold Cafe, **20**
Mocha, **7**
Not Just Jazz By the Bay, **9**
Voodoo, **29**

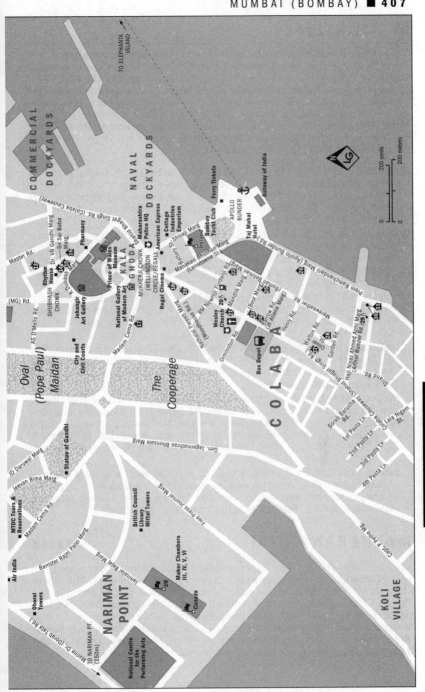

MAHARASHTRA

TO ELEPHANTA ISLAND

COMMERCIAL DOCKYARDS

NAVAL DOCKYARDS

Ferry Tickets

Gateway of India

APOLLO BUNDER

Bombay Yacht Club

Taj Mahal Hotel

N

200 yards
200 meters

Master Rd.

Prem Ramchandani Marg (Apollo Bunder Rd.)

Shahid Bhagat Singh Rd. (Colaba Causeway)

Rhythm House

SHUBHASH CHOWK

Sri Sai Baba

Dr. VB Gandhi Marg

Pharmacy

Maharashtra Police HQ

American Express

Cottage Industries Emporium

Chhatrapati Shivaji Marg

Prince of Wales Museum

KALA GHODA

MUKHERJI CHOWK (WELLINGTON CIRCLE/REGAL)

K Dubash Marg

Mahakavi Bhushan Marg (Lansdowne St.)

AS D'Mello Rd.

(MG) Rd.

Jehangir Art Gallery

National Gallery of Modern Art

Regal Cinema

Madam Cama Rd.

RM Nerowji Firdanji Rd.

Maharshi Karve Rd.

Oval (Pope Paul) Maidan

City and Civil Courts

Nathalal Parekh Marg (Woodhouse Rd.)

Wesley Church

Mandlik Marg

Barrow Rd.

JA Allana Marg

Bus Depot

Ormiston Rd.

Merewether Rd.

Henry Rd.

(Best Marg)

(Roman Behman Marg)

Walton Rd.

Garden Rd.

COLABA

The Cooperage

Gen. Jagannathrao Bhonsale Marg

Statue of Gandhi

JD Daruwal Marg

Jeevan Bima Marg

MTDC Tours & Reservations

Madam Cama Rd.

British Council Library Mittal Towers

Free Press Journal Marg

Jamnalal Bajaj Marg

Barrister Rajni Patel Marg

Air India

Oberoi Towers

NARIMAN POINT

Maker Chambers III, IV, V, VI

UK

Canada

Marine Dr. (Dorab Tata Rd.)

TO NARIMAN PT. (250m)

National Centre for the Performing Arts

Strand Rd.

Sorab Barucha (Shahid Bhagat Singh) Rd.

Colaba Causeway

1st Pasta Ln.

2nd Pasta Ln.

3rd Pasta Ln.

4th Pasta Ln.

Haji Niyat Ahmed Azmi Marg (Arthur Bunder Rd.)

Lala Nigam St.

KOLI VILLAGE

Capt. C Pyrne Mg.

❦ NIGHTLIFE

Unlike most cities in India, Mumbai knows how to party. International partiers pack the city's pubs and discos in search of the next "in" thing. Beware of the pervasive "couples only" policies on busy nights (although only single men are likely to be turned away), and the occasional refusal of dirty-looking T-shirted or sandal-clad travelers. Bars and clubs in Mumbai tend to close by 1-2am, causing a mass exodus to the 24hr. coffee shops at luxury hotels. If you're looking to splurge, try the **Taj Mahal Hotel,** Apollo Bunder (☎22023366), in Colaba; the **Ambassador Hotel,** VN Rd. (☎22041131) in Churchgate; the **President Hotel** in Cuffe Parade; or **The Oberoi,** Marine Drive (☎22025757), in Nariman Point.

❧ **The Ghetto,** 30 Bhulabhai Desai Rd., Breach Candy (☎24921556), located in an alley on the seaward side of the road, just before Mahalaxmi. Photos of the Edge and Jim Morrison, and loads of graffiti adorn the walls of this popular, yuppie-filled bar. Great atmosphere and music make this worth the Rs70 taxi ride from Colaba. Beer Rs100, spirits Rs70 and up. Open daily 7pm-1:30am.

❧ **Mocha,** 82 VN Rd., near Marine Dr., Nagin Mahal (☎56336070). Split into two venues, Mocha offers coffee, wraps (Rs250), and conversations on a breezy patio. The A/C bar inside serves wine (bottles Rs700-13,500) and tapas (Rs75-220). Urban sophisticates and artistes gather for sangria (pitcher Rs775) and puffs of sheesha on the many hookahs. Open daily 9:30am-2:30am.

❧ **Leopold Cafe,** Colaba Causeway, Colaba (☎22020131), 3 blocks down from Regal, on the left. The ultimate tourist hangout. The dimly lit A/C bar upstairs hosts the serious drinkers. Beer Rs130; pitchers Rs200. Open daily 1pm-1am. Downstairs open daily 8am-11pm.

Insomnia, in the Taj Mahal Hotel, Colaba (☎22023366). Test just how cool you are in the Taj's new brushed steel hipper-than-thou club, which attracts Mumbai's young heirs and hipsters in droves, despite the staggering Rs550 cover. Open daily 9pm-3am. F-Sa is especially crowded.

Not Just Jazz By the Bay, 143 Marine Dr. (☎22851876 or 22820957), right next to the Pizzeria, at the corner with Veer Narimar Rd. Caters to expats and the local elite, although it might as well be in London or New York. The "Jazz"'s great food, A/C, and live music every night compensate for the steep prices. Beer Rs130; spirits Rs150-300. Cover Rs150. Open daily 11am-2pm and 6pm-1:30am. Reservations necessary on F and Sa nights.

Voodoo, Arthur Bunder Rd., Colaba., 4 doors up on the left from the sea front. A dive for desperate straight men during the week, Voodoo transforms into Mumbai's only aboveground gay disco on Saturday nights. India's most famous gay rights activist, Ashok Rao Kavi, is a regular. Beer Rs65. Cover Rs180. Open daily 7pm-1:30am.

MATHERAN मथेरान ☎02148

Once an exclusive retreat for Raj-era *sahibs*, the hill station of Matheran (95km east of Mumbai) now swarms with Indian weekend vacationers. The village shuts down from mid-June to August, when the monsoon rains arrive in full. Frazzled Mumbaikers come here for the full-board resorts, and the cooler temperatures and relatively laid-back atmosphere can be a welcome relief for city-weary travelers. With numerous secluded paths winding through leafy forests and magnificent views over the surrounding plains, Matheran is a good spot for a few days of aimless wandering and general relaxation.

TRANSPORTATION. The access point for Matheran is the small town of **Neral,** which lies at the base of the hill. From Mumbai's VT Station, local trains to **Karjat** stop at Neral Junction (2hr., approximately every hr. 6am-1am, Rs19). Only a few of the Mumbai-Pune express trains stop at **Neral** (2hr., 6:40am and 8:45am, Rs35), leaving Neral for **Pune** (2½hr; 8:20 and 10:30am; Rs40). From Neral, Matheran is 21km up the hill. The best option is the **miniature train** (2hr; 9, 10:45am, 5pm, 12:10pm Sa and Su only, 7:30am in-season only; return 5:45am, 1, 4:10pm, 2:35pm Sa and Su only, 9:50am in-season only). The train is almost always full in peak season. Tickets for the train can be reserved up to 3 days in advance, but not on the day of departure, at Pune and Mumbai VT stations, as well as at Matheran for the return trip. During the monsoon, mini-train service is sporadic and may be cancelled entirely. If the train is full, a taxi will take you up the hill (Rs50 per person shared, Rs250 solo ride). Since motor vehicles are prohibited in Matheran, taxis cannot take you all the way into town. The taxi drop-off point is 3km north of town. To complete the trip, you're left with a gentle but sweaty 40min. hike (a porter will carry your bags for Rs40), a rocky but fun horse ride (Rs110), or a hand-pulled rickshaw (Rs150). Matheran levies an entry tax on all visitors (adults Rs25, children Rs5). Hold on to your ticket as you may be asked for it when you leave.

ORIENTATION AND PRACTICAL INFORMATION. Most of Matheran is strung out along the main road, **Mahatma Gandhi Marg (MG Marg),** which runs north-south. The miniature train pulls into the **Matheran Railway Station** at the north end of MG Marg, so most of the town is to the left (south) as you exit. The **Union Bank of India,** a 2min. walk south from the station on the right of MG Marg, will exchange travelers checks but not cash (☎230282. Open M-F 10am-2pm, Sa 10am-noon.) The **police station** is at the south end of town. Walk about 15min. south from the train station until MG Marg splits into 3. Take the right-hand road and the station is 100m down on the right. The **post office** is several buildings further down on the left side of MG Marg (Open M-Sa 9am-5pm). There is a separate **phone code** when calling from Mumbai: ☎952148.

ACCOMMODATIONS AND FOOD. Matheran is a resort town catering to wealthy Indian visitors. As a result, in-season (Sept.-May) prices are high. Almost all hotels are aimed at families; 2-4 person rooms are common, while single rates are rare. Prices for mid-week and longer stays are generally open to a bit of haggling, while in the off season prices plummet automatically. Basic hotels are clustered along MG Marg while larger resorts are set back from the chaos further uphill. Check-out times are distressingly early (7 or 8am is standard), and hotels will gleefully charge you for another half-day if you sleep in. North of the train station, on the opposite side of the tracks from MG Marg, the family-run **Hunjer House** ❹, offers one of the more pleasant budget options, with balconies on some of its basic but clean rooms and hot water in the mornings. Check-out 9am. (☎230536. Doubles Rs600. Off-season Rs250.) The **Hotel Prasanna** ❸, stands opposite the train station. It has simple but clean rooms with tidier-than-usual bathrooms. (☎230258. Doubles Rs400. Closed off-season.) Further into town on the right of MG Marg, the **Hotel Khan** ❸ is situated in an exotic palace-style building. Clean rooms with hot water 7:30-10am and attached restaurant. Make reservations in advance in-season. (☎230240. Doubles Rs400, off-season Rs200.) The cheapest room-and-board deal is the **Janata Happy Home** ❹, on Kasturba Rd. Heading south from the station, take the first right, and then turn left onto Kasturba. (☎230229; booking in Mumbai ☎022 6193899. Doubles Rs700-1000 including all meals. Off-season 30-50% less.)

There are several simple restaurants on MG Marg, south of the railway station. The board and lodging deals that resorts offer are a good choice in the heavily discounted off-season, when non-hotel meals are few and far between. The amiable **Kwality Restaurant** ❶ on MG Marg has *bhel puri* for Rs15 and *dosas* for Rs18-22. (Open daily 9am-9:30pm; closed June 25-Aug. 25.) Two doors down, the **Sakvill Restaurant** ❶ has vegetarian options for Rs20-40 as well as ices and fruit juices. Some hotels that serve non-guests are the **Hotel Prasanna** ❸ (open daily 8am-9:30pm) and the **Divadkar Hotel** ❸, just north of the train station, which has a large selection of Indian and Chinese dishes. (Beer Rs65. Open daily noon-2:30pm and 7-10:30pm.) Local specialties include *chikki*—a sweet, sticky, crunchy peanut brittle—and mango fudge, which tastes much better than it sounds (or looks, for that matter).

◙ **VIEWS.** The borders of the hill station are marked by numerous sheer cliff outcrops, many of which have been set up as viewpoints. The best views are at **Louisa Point** in the west and **Monkey Point** to the north, though **Porcipine (Sunset) Point** and **Alexander Point** are also justifiably popular. From Louisa Pt. you can see Neral and the coast in the distance. The views are most beautiful at sunrise and sunset when temperatures are also more bearable. All the viewpoints are about a half hour walk from town, though there are plenty of touts who would be happy to take you on horseback. Though there are some signposts, it is still easy to get hopelessly lost in the maze of trails that criss-cross the hilltop. Ask for directions whenever possible and bring the town map. Women are advised not to explore the more remote locales alone at night as the trails are isolated and poorly lit.

NASIK नाशिक ☎0253

Smaller than Mumbai or Pune but no less frantic, Nasik (NA-shik; pop. 1 million) is best known for the sacred Godavari River that runs through it. The city is believed to be the site where the demon Ravana abducted Rama's wife Sita, igniting one of the greatest match-ups in Hindu lore (see **The Ramayana**, p. 620). Today, Nasik's status as a religious haven seems threatened by the growth of industry. The jinglejangle of temple bells and the hypnotic humming of the meditative syllable *om* clash with the chug and spit of smokestacks and exhaust pipes. Nevertheless, every year thousands of devotees head to Nasik to walk along the same pathways their gods and goddesses once trod. Nasik plays host to the **Kumbh Mela** festival every 12 years (the next one here will occur in 2015). During the Mela, one of the most auspicious moments in the Hindu calendar, millions come here to take a purifying dip in the waters of the Godavari.

▐ TRANSPORTATION

Trains: Railway Station (☎561274 or 563625), Nasik Rd., 8km from the city center. As you leave the platforms, the booking office is on the left. To **Mumbai** (4-4½hr., 10 per day, Rs53-151) and **Nagpur** (12hr., 4 per day 12:20am-11:45pm, Rs225). For most other destinations around Maharashtra, it is easier to take a bus.

Buses: Central Bus Stand (CBS) Sharanpur Rd. (☎572854). To: **Ahmedabad** (12hr., 5 per day noon-1am, Rs90); **Aurangabad** (4½hr., every hr. 5:30am-2am, Rs97); **Mumbai** (5hr., every hr., Rs90); **Nagpur** (15hr., 10pm, Rs350); **Pune** (5hr., every hr., Rs110).

Local Transportation: Auto-rickshaws rule the road and are subject to meters. Fare is approximately Rs13 per unit on the meter.

➕ 🛈 ORIENTATION AND PRACTICAL INFORMATION

Nasik's spiritual life centers on the banks of the **Godavari River.** Its commercial heart is a couple of kilometers away, near the **Central Bus Stand (CBS),** at the intersection of **Sharanpur Road** and **Old Agra Road.** Going up Old Agra Rd. from the CBS will lead to **MG Road** (the first road on the right), Nasik's main street, which provides access to the Godavari River. Going down leads to **Trimbak Road** and the tourist office, post office, police station, and hospital. The **Nasik Road Railway Station** is 8km southeast of the CBS. Nearby is chaotic **Dwarka Circle** (bus to CBS Rs4; auto-rickshaw Rs40).

Tourist Office: MTDC T-1, Golf Club, Old Agra Rd. (☎570059). From the CBS, head down Old Agra Rd., past the State Bank. Turn right at the 2nd major intersection; the MTDC is 5min. down on the right. Open M-F and 1st and 3rd Sa 10am-5:45pm.

Currency Exchange: State Bank of India Old Agra Rd. (☎599935). Go right from the CBS; it's 200m after the intersection on the left. Open M-F 11am-5pm, Sa 11am-2pm.

Police: Police Commissioner's Office (☎570183 or 352122), off Sharanpur Rd.

Hospital: General Hospital Trimbak Rd. (☎576268). Same directions as to the MTDC (see above), but turn right at the 1st intersection.

Internet: Matrix Cyber Cafe, straight across from Hotel Basera, is faster than elsewhere. Rs30 per hr. Open daily 9am-midnight. **Citi Heart Cyber Cafe,** Chandakwadi, across from Pancharati. Fast connection, well-lit, and clean, with friendly staff. Rs25 per hr.

Post Office: GPO Trimbak Rd. (☎500141). Go down Old Agra Rd. towards MTDC from the CBS and turn left at the first major intersection. The GPO is on the right, beyond the next intersection. Open M-Sa 10am-6pm, Su 10am-1pm. **Postal Code:** 42001.

🏠 ACCOMMODATIONS

Budget hotels cluster near the CBS on Shivaji and Old Agra Rd., and along Dwarka Circle. Most have noon check-out.

Hotel Shilpa, 430 Ratan Bhuvan, MG Rd. (☎580271, 580272, or 572360; hotelshilpa@hotmail.com). From Old Agra Rd. toward the river, turn left at Hotel Shipa sign. It's on the right of the alley. Safe, friendly, and comfortable. Cable TV, balcony, and bath in each room. Singles Rs135-330; doubles Rs225-690; rooms for 3-6 people also available. MC/V. ❶

Raj Mahal Lodge, Sharanpur Rd. (☎580501; rajmahallodge@vsnl.com), opposite the CBS. Basic rooms, unbeatable location, and relatively cheap rates conspire to fill the Raj's rooms early, so act fast. 24hr. STD/ISD in the lobby, TVs and telephones in all rooms. Singles Rs190-500; doubles Rs260-600. ❷

Panchavati Guest House, 430 Chandakwadi (☎2578771), on MG Rd. Walking toward the river, turn left at the Shilpa mall sign. Panchavati is on the left, past the candy store. About as upscale as Nasik gets, the Panchavati offers sparkling marble-tiled rooms and multi-room suites. Singles Rs540-740; doubles Rs740-940; quads Rs800-1000. ❸

Hotel Basera, Shivaji Rd. 1st fl. (☎575616 or 575618). Cross the intersection from the CBS and head down the small alley on the left. Comfortable rooms all have TV and phone. Singles Rs230-400; doubles Rs350-500. Tax Rs9. ❷

Hotel Padma, Sharanpur Rd. (☎576837), opposite CBS. Simple, clean, cheap, and central. Singles Rs350-500; doubles Rs400-590. ❸

MAHARASHTRA

▌ FOOD

Shilpa Garden Restaurant, on Chandakwadi, around the corner from Hotel Shilpa. Charming outdoor dining complete with lanterns, bridges, and greenery. Offers hot, fresh, and cheap Indian and Chinese fare Rs25-90. ❶

Tandoor, 42 Meghdoot (☎2579744), opposite CBS Rd., in an alleyway next to Matrix Cybercafe. Offers tandoori specialities in a dark-walled brick interior with some sidewalk seating. "Chicken in the Basket" Rs36, non-veg. entrees Rs31-76, veg. entrees Rs21-51. Free home delivery. ❷

Samrat Restaurant, Old Agra Rd., in the Hotel Samrat, opposite the State Bank, serves up pure veg. Gujarati *thalis* (Rs70) that are popular with locals. The canteen-like ambience mixes well with the bus stand hullabaloo nearby. Open daily 8am-11:30pm. ❸

Suruchi Vegetarian Restaurant, around the corner from Hotel Basera, dishes out cheap Indian fare all day long to meet all your veg. needs. Open daily 6:30am-10:30pm. ❷

◉ SIGHTS

GODAVARI RIVER. The easiest way to get to the sacred Godavari River is to follow MG Rd. You don't have to walk far down the sloping pathways before you leave the thick traffic fumes behind and are surrounded by the clatter of candy, *kurta*, and cloth vendors. Just beyond the Old Quarter, shallow squares of murky water can be seen next to the **Santar Gardhi Mahara Bridge.** The first visible *ghat*, the square farthest upstream, is designated for ritual bathing and prayers. A white obelisk dedicated to Gandhi rises above it. The second *ghat* hosts hundreds of *dhobi-wallahs* scrubbing clothes, while the third washes filth off animals. Every 12 years, however, these *ghats* experience the onslaught of thousands of devotees who flood Nasik during the **Kumbh Mela.** Nasik's next Mela will take place during 2015, but it's not impossible to imagine the frenzied cacophony that ensues at festival time—one glance at the sprawling **market** directly behind the *ghats* will give you an idea. Rickety stalls sell row upon cluttered row of religious paraphernalia as well as fruits, vegetables, nuts, jewelry, carved statuettes, and bronze vessels.

OTHER SIGHTS. Among the market stalls around the *ghats* are several sites steeped in mythology. Nasik's religious focal point, several meters to the left of the **Ram Sita footbridge,** is the **Ram Kund,** a sacred *ghat.* Thousands of people immerse themselves here in order to purify themselves of sin. The waters here are also supposed to have the unusual power to dissolve bones; the remains of royalty and politicians (from members of the Nehru-Gandhi dynasty to Rama's father, King Dasharatha) rest here in the **Astivilaya Tirth** ("Bone Immersion Tank"). Up the hill from Ram Kund is **Kala Rama Mandir,** a temple at the site where, according to the *Ramayana*, Rama's brother Lakshman sliced off the nose (in Sanskrit, *nasika*—hence the town's name) of Ravana's monstrous sister, Shurparnakha. The *mandir* houses ebony images of the myth's protagonists. Sita's cave, or **Gumpha,** marks the site where Sita was abducted by the demon Ravana.

PUNE पुणे ☎020

As Mumbai has become increasingly congested and cosmopolitan, the steady stream of daily commuters between Mumbai and Pune (POO-nuh) has become more of a flood. Recent years have seen a mini-exodus to the cooler, more relaxed Pune, a 4hr. climb up the Deccan Plateau. Birthplace of the Maratha hero Shivaji, capital of his successors, and an almost purely Marathi-speaking city, Pune cer-

MAHARASHTRA

Pune

ACCOMMODATIONS
Green Hotel, 3
Hotel Alankar, 5
Hotel Toran, 11
National Hotel, 2
Samarat Hotel, 4

● FOOD
Coffee House, 12
The German Bakery, 10
Sagar, 1
Touché the Sizzler, 13
Vaishali, 7
Woodland Restaurant, 6

♪ NIGHTLIFE
10 Downing St., 8
Club Polaris, 9

MAHARASHTRA

tainly fulfills its claim as "cultural capital of Maharashtra" far more than its larger
and more cosmopolitan neighbor. Though much of the urban chaos (and accompanying pollution) that characterizes Mumbai also rules in Pune, the city has
plenty of greenery, fresh air, and pleasant strolling grounds. Particularly pleasant
is the Koregaon Park Road area, home to the famous ashram Osho Commune
International. The Birkenstock-clad crowd in their maroon robes (called *sannyasins*) come from all over the world to converge on Pune and undergo Osho's various meditation therapies. Every year the city plays host to the Pune festival, the
joint celebration of Ganesh and Marathi culture. The usually laid-back city bursts
with excitement for the ten days of the festival. At other times of the year, Pune
has a quiet atmosphere but with just enough of that big-city vibe, making it a great
place to rest for a few days on your way into or out from Mumbai.

▐ TRANSPORTATION

Flights: Airport, Pune-Nagar Rd. (☎6685591), 10km from the city. An ex-servicemen's
bus leaves every hr. from outside the GPO (Rs25). **Indian Airlines** (☎4260932), off
Garden Rd., parallel to Sassoon Rd., on Camp. To: **Bangalore** (1½hr., 2 per day,
US$155); **Delhi** (2hr., 2 per day, US$220); **Goa** (1hr., 1 per day, US$90); **Mumbai**
(35min., 2 per day, US$55). **Jet Airways** (☎6137181) flies to: **Bangalore** (1½hr., 1
per day, US$155); **Chennai** (3hr., 1 per day, US$185); **Delhi** (2hr., 2 per day,
US$220); **Mumbai** (35min., 2 per day, US$95). **Air Sahara** (☎6059003) flies to:
Delhi (2hr., 2 per day, US$220); **Kolkata** (4hr., 1 per day, US$290) via **Mumbai**
(35min., 1 per day, US$55).

Trains: Railway Station, MPL Rd. The booking office, the pink building to your left as you
face the station, deals with local tickets, reservations, and Mumbai trains. Reservations
office upstairs. To: **Bangalore** (24hr., 11:51am, Rs300); **Goa** (19hr., 5 and 10pm,
Rs250); **Hyderabad** (13hr., 1:45am and 4pm, Rs280); **Mumbai** (3hr., every hr. 6-
10am and 4-9pm, Rs80); **Neral** (2hr., 7:15am, Rs50).

Buses: Pune has three main state stations and many private carriers. The most convenient station for tourists is right next to the railway station. To: **Goa** (12hr.; 4 per day;
Rs250, sleeper Rs350); **Mahabaleshwar** (4hr., 10 per day 5:30am-6:30pm, Rs70-90);
Mumbai (3½hr., every hr. 5am-10pm, Rs180). Buses from **Shivajinagar Station** in Deccan head for: **Aurangabad** (6hr., 12 per day 5am-6pm, Rs150); **Lonavla** (1½hr., every
hr., Rs35); **Nasik** (5hr., every hr., Rs125). **Swargate Station** has buses to **Bangalore**
(20hr., 1pm, Rs500). Private bus companies around MPL Rd. and Sasoon Rd. offer
comfortable 'luxury' buses, some with A/C, and a few buses direct to Mumbai Airport.
It's worth shelling out a few extra rupees for a long journey. One reliable private carrier
is **Prasanna,** Connaught Rd. (☎6123137 or 6129721), just around the corner from
MPL Rd. Open daily 6am-11pm. Shared taxis leave regularly for Mumbai from in front of
the bus station and the train station (Rs315).

Local Transportation: The most convenient way to get around town is by **auto-rickshaw.**
Make sure the drivers use the meter. The fare is usually 5-6 times the meter reading—
ask the driver to see the chart. Instead, each rickshaw has a standard conversion chart
and the fare is usually 5-6 times the meter reading. **Local bus #4** goes to Deccan; **#5,
6,** and **31** go south toward Swargate bus station and the old town.

▐ ▐ ORIENTATION AND PRACTICAL INFORMATION

Although it's relatively quiet, Pune is still a huge city with a population of three
million. The city is divided into two vaguely defined sections: the **Camp** and the **Old
Town.** The railway station and one of the major bus stands rub shoulders in Camp,
between **Sassoon Road** (formerly part of Connaught Rd.) to the east and **MPL Road**

MAHARASHTRA

to the south. Camp's upscale shops and restaurants cluster around **MG Road**. A 10min. rickshaw ride west of here is the Old Town, where traditional *wadas* (mansions) surround the Swargate Bus Terminal, Raja Kelkar Museum, Phule Market, and the ruined Shaniwar Wada Palace. Farther west across the Mutha River is the middle-class neighborhood of **Deccan**, which stretches to Fergusson College Rd., home to Pune's students and a string of restaurants and cafes. The Koregaon Park suburb to the northeast of Camp, home to the **Osho Commune**, occupies its own distinctive physical (and psychological) space.

Street names can be confusing in Pune. The old Connaught Rd. is now called Sassoon Rd. north of its intersection with Byramji, and Sadhu Vaswani Rd. to the south, though it is essentially one street. Ambedkar and Moledina Rd. flow into each other in similar fashion. To make things worse, street signs are only in Hindi.

Tourist Office: MTDC (☎6126867), in the Central Bldg. Complex on Byramji Rd. Enter through the main gate and follow the road straight back. The MTDC is the first bldg. on the left after the road curves. Not worth the walk, unless you're really desperate. Open M-F 10am-5:30pm. The branch opposite the bus station (☎6125342) offers 15-point sightseeing tours of Pune (7½hr., 9am, Rs100). There is also a branch in the train station.

Currency Exchange: HDFC Bank, East Rd., in Camp, 10min. south of Moledina Rd., has a **24hr. ATM** for Cirrus/MC/Maestro. **American Express,** 9 Moledina Rd. (☎6055337), just past the intersection with Moledina. Open M-F 9:30am-2:30pm. **UAE Exchange** (☎4013493) is off Koregaon Park Rd., just behind the German Bakery. Open daily 9:30am-6pm.

Bookstore: Crossword Bookstore, Sohrab Mall, 1st fl. (☎6059602), across from Jehangir Hospital. Open daily 10:30am-9pm. **Manney's Bookstore,** 7 Moledina Rd., Clover Centre (☎6131683), in Camp. The best source for Pune maps. Open M-Sa 9:30am-1:30pm and 4-8pm. **Dragon Gallery,** 291 North Koregaon Park Rd., over the German Bakery, has a selection of second-hand guidebooks and a nice collection of postcards. Open M-Sa 9am-9:30pm, Su 9am-8pm.

Market: Dobrojee's, 1 Mahedena Rd., is a Western-style supermarket. Open M-Sa 9:30am-2pm and 3:30-9pm, Su 9:30am-1pm and 4:30-9pm.

Police: Bund Garden Station, Byramji Rd. (☎6122202), at the giant intersection next to the MTDC. Open 24hr.

Hospital: Jehangir Hospital and Medical Centre, 32 Sassoon Rd. (☎6122551 or 6050550). From MPL, turn left on Sassoon Rd. and cross the railroad tracks; it's immediately on the right. On-site **24hr. pharmacy**.

Internet: Cyber Cafe, Sadhu Yaswani Chowk. From MPL, turn right onto Sassoon Rd. It's on the block with many stores, immediately before the intersection. Rs30 per hr. Open M-W and F-Sa 8am-11pm, Th 8am-7pm, Su 8am-6pm. **Planet Internet Cafe,** Asok Jay Complex basement, the first right off MG Rd. going south. Not super-fast, but open 24hr. Rs20 per hr. **Yahoo Communications** is off North Koregaon Park Rd., just behind the German Bakery. Rs20 per hr. Open daily 9am-11pm.

Post Office: Sadhu Vaswani Rd. A domed, stone bldg. in the park on the right, 5min. south of the intersection of Sassoon and MPL Rd. *Poste Restante* at window #8. Open M-Sa 10am-6pm. **Postal Code: 411001.**

MAHARASHTRA

▶ ACCOMMODATIONS

Almost all of the budget hotels in Pune are within the **Wilson Garden** area across from the train and bus stations. Most of these 80-100-year-old buildings used to be opulent personal homes, though most are beginning to crumble. To get here, take the small lane to the left of the National Hotel and turn right at the corner.

More accommodations can be found near the Osho Ashram. The shady, tree-lined streets at the Koregaon Park area have more of a backpacker feel. There are plenty of rooms available in the **Raj Villas** area. (☎9822210666 or inquire at the German Bakery. Rs100-200 per night.)

National Hotel, 14 Sassoon Rd. (☎6125054 or 6127780), opposite the railway station. Stylish facade, large verandas and a well-tended garden characterize this 150-year-old palace-turned-hotel. Large, clean rooms with high ceilings and big windows, or smaller cottages with porch. Helpful and friendly staff will cook breakfast (Rs15-25) and serve tea or coffee (Rs5-10). Doubles have attached bath. Check-out noon. Hot water 7-11am. Singles (men only) Rs250; doubles Rs350-500. ❷

Green Hotel, 16 Wilson Garden (☎6125229). Stained glass and old wood furniture in reasonable rooms overlooking an interior courtyard. Check-out 5pm. Singles Rs200, with bath Rs300; doubles Rs300/350. ❷

Hotel Toran, Koregaon Park Terr. (☎6137171). Located in the laid-back area near the Osho Ashram, the Toran has large, clean rooms with private bath, or smaller ones with shared bath. Check-out noon. Singles Rs300, with bath Rs500; doubles Rs400/600. Off-season singles Rs150/250; doubles Rs300/400. ❷

Hotel Alankar, 14 Wilson Cir. (☎6120484). Simple rooms (some with balconies) along quiet corridors. All rooms with attached bath and hot water. 24hr. check-out. Singles Rs300; doubles Rs375; triples Rs425. ❷

Samarat Hotel, 17 Wilson Garden (☎6137964). Luxurious rooms with A/C, cable TV, room-service, and hot showers. Singles Rs900; doubles Rs1100-1300. MC/V. ❺

⬛ FOOD

Lieutenant Colonel Tarapore Marg, which crosses Sadhu Vaswani Rd. a block before Moledina Rd., becomes a huge open-air cafe in the afternoons and evenings. Countless food stalls tempt passersby in the balmy evening air. The area between the bus stand and the railway booking office is full of fruit carts and food stalls.

Sagar, Hotel Dreamland Bldg., MPL Rd, just before the intersection with Sassoon Rd. Look for the yellow Marathi sign. Popular and convenient place with good Indian, Chinese, and continental dishes in a large, comfortable interior. Entrees Rs40-70. Open daily 10am-11pm. ❷

Woodland Restaurant, inside Woodland Hotel, Byramji Rd., Camp. Go south along Sassoon Rd. and turn right at the first intersection. Mouth-wateringly good Chinese and Indian dishes, but with prices to match. A full meal will set you back about Rs100. Buffet breakfast Rs75. Open daily 7-10am, 11am-3pm, and 7-11pm. ❹

The German Bakery, North Koregaon Park Rd. From the Osho ashram, take a right at the gate, walk to the end of the road, turn left; it's on the right. Hippies, backpackers, and Osho *sannyasins* all enjoy a taste of home in this popular open-air chill-out spot. Coffee Rs20, pastries Rs25. Open daily 7am-midnight. ❶

Vaishali, Fergusson College Rd., Deccan, opposite Saraswat Bank. The tree-canopied backyard overflows during the day with the city's young and wealthy chatting over the ringing of mobile phones. At night, families flock here for the *bhel puri* and South Indian snacks (Rs15-30), ice cream, and shakes (Rs40-50). Open daily 7am-11pm. ❷

Touché the Sizzler, 7 Moledina Rd., Camp. The snappy, two-tier Tudor interior packs in Pune's yuppies for "sizzlers"—iron skillets filled with rice, vegetables, fries, and a choice of entree (veg. Rs100-120, non-veg. Rs150-200). Tandoori dishes also available (Rs70-200). Open daily 11:30am-3:30pm and 7-11pm. ❹

Coffee House, 2 Moledina Rd., Camp. Decent coffee and the standard array of Chinese and Indian dishes (Rs30-70), as well as fruit juices, ice cream, and milkshakes (Rs35). Tables are jammed with locals at peak times. Open daily for snacks 8am-11:30pm; meals 11am-3pm and 7-11:30pm. ❷

🔍 SIGHTS

OSHO COMMUNE INTERNATIONAL. Upwardly mobile meditators worldwide flock to Pune's famous ashram, a weird synthesis of health-club luxury and Eastern spirituality. Followers of the late, great, and intercontinentally controversial guru, Osho (also known as Bhagwan Shree Rajneesh), gather to practice his New Age meditation techniques in 40 acres of futuristic buildings and lush tropical grounds. The center's daily routine revolves around six daily meditations, but the classy facilities—including a swimming pool, library, bookstore, vegetarian canteen, jacuzzi, sauna, gym, and tennis courts—may ease the path to enlightenment. Meditations—which encourage you to "become an empty vessel" or engage in the cathartic explosion of "shouting wildly the mantra 'Hoo!'"—take place in the 3000-seat, pyramid-shaped (for efficient channeling of energy) Osho Auditorium. Visitors can become a true part of the Osho community at the Welcome Center to the right of the entrance way. Registration requires an HIV test (Rs1050), two passport photos, and Rs250 per day for the meditation program. All courses, food, and accommodations cost extra. Though the commune has its own guest house (singles Rs600; doubles Rs1800), most *sannyasins* rent rooms nearby for anywhere from two weeks to three months. *(17 Koregaon Park, in the northwest part of Camp. ☎ 4019999; www.osho.com. Visitors Center open daily 10am-noon and 2-3:30pm. 15min. silent guided tours approximately every 20min. Rs10.)*

SHANIWAR WADA. Amid the narrow, winding streets of Old Town sits the Shaniwar Palace, whose Delhi Gate is Pune's most celebrated landmark. The palace was built in 1732 as the chief residence of the Peshwa dynasty. By 1760, it was the bureaucratic center of the powerful Maratha empire and home to at least a thousand people. In 1828 the inner structures burned down in a fire that lasted 7 days and 7 nights. Only the foundation and the palace's outer walls and gates are left for tourists and picnickers to explore. *(Shivaji Rd. Open daily 8am-6pm. Rs100. Sound and light show W-M 8:30pm; Rs25.)*

RAJA KELKAR MUSEUM. The pack-rat passion of the late Dr. D.G. Kelkar, the museum's founder, has resulted in a vast collection of Indian life, religion, and art. Located in a sprawling house in the center of Old Town, the collection gradually unfolds over four floors and room after room of astonishing treasures. Everything is represented here, from the mundane (30 brass nutcrackers), to the divine (eight images of Ganesh carved on a bear), to the simply bizarre (elephant-shaped foot scrubbers and lion-headed noodle-makers). Objects are arranged roughly by theme, allowing a comparison across India's regions and history. Highlights include a painstakingly relocated and reconstructed 18th-century royal palace room from Madhya Pradesh, an 18th-century image of the goddess Mahishasarmardini slaying a demon, and a sandalwood and ivory *dhariat* showing a scene from the Bhawadgita. *(Baji Rao Rd. Open M-Sa 9:30am-6pm. Rs150.)*

TRIBAL AND CULTURAL MUSEUM. India has over 600 tribal communities, incorporating 67.7 million people—9% of the nation's population. This obscure gem of a museum celebrates those cultures and their craftwork with over 2000 artifacts, taken primarily from the 47 Maharashtrian groups. *(Koregaon Park Rd., just south of the railroad tracks. Open M-F 10am-5pm. Rs10.)*

MAHARASHTRA

HE HIDDEN DEAL

KAIVALYADHAMA YOGA INSITUTE

On the outskirts of Lonavla lies a retreat to refresh the body and purify the soul. The Kaivalyadhama Yoga Institute was founded in 1924 to pursue the scientific study of yoga and its healing properties. Its slightly ambitious mission includes "trying to develop a perfectly integrated personality, not only for the individual but for the whole of mankind."

While the Institute offers longer courses in yogic practice, philosophy, and religion, short-term visitors can stay at the attached Gupta Yogic Hospital to indulge in daily doses of yogic exercise, natural therapy, and medical consultation.

For stays of over eight days, participants can stay at the Centre (common bath singles US$10, with bath US$15; doubles US$16, with bath US$20). The price is inclusive of the Centre's daily routine, which begins at 5:30am with tea and gentle exercises and continues with lectures, assanas, natural health treatments and an evening *puja*.

Short-term visitors can also indulge in the "naturotherapy" offered at the hospital for a very modest fee. Services include mud bath (Rs10), immersion bath (Rs10), steam (Rs50), and full-body massage (Rs60). A week of outpatient yoga therapy is a steal at Rs150. More information is available at www.kdham.com. Visitors who wish to stay at the hospital must book in advance and send a Rs1000 deposit. Reception is open M-Sa noon-5pm.

PATALESHWAR TEMPLE CAVES. Almost overshadowed by the modern temple next door, the 8th-century Pataleshwar Caves exude a sedate spirituality. A circular stone gazebo (a Nandi *mandapam*) stands by the entrance to the small underground temple, where three rows of columns lead to the small rock-cut shrine. The peaceful and shady area makes for a marvelous escape from the bustle of modern Pune. (*On Jangali Maharaj Rd., near the intersection with Shivaji Rd. Free.*)

🎵 📷 ENTERTAINMENT AND NIGHTLIFE

One of the few disco-pubs around to cater to post-colonial partygoers is **10 Downing Street,** Boat Club Rd., off Bund Garden Rd., at the northern edge of town. Legions of students grind away on the strobe-lit upstairs dance floor, while a more mixed crowd throws back beers (Rs50) on the chill, ultraswank first floor Dance floor is couples and single women only. Live bands every Sa. (☎6128343. Open daily 7pm-12:30am.) Hip members of Pune's elite pack into the exclusive **Club Polaris** in the city's classiest hotel. (Taj Blue Diamond Hotel, 11 Koregaon Park Rd. Cover Rs300. W ladies free. Open daily 9:30pm-1:30am.) Huge crowds take in Bollywood flicks, afternoon and night, at Pune's theaters, including **Alankar Cinema,** Sassoon Rd. (☎6123333; Rs15-50), and **West End Cinema,** next to Touché the Sizzler on Moledina Rd., which also shows big Western releases. (☎4031447. Rs30-50.) **Bal Gandharva Theater,** Jangli Maharaj Rd. (☎5510844), has daily performances of traditional Marathi plays. (12:30pm, Rs80.) For listings and schedules, see the "Pune Plus" section of the *Times of India.* Celebrations of Maharashtra's most popular god, Ganapati, and Marathi culture, take place every September in the Pune Festival.

🔁 DAYTRIP FROM PUNE: SINHAGAD FORT

Take public **bus #50** *(40min., Rs13) or a* **taxi** *(Rs15) from Nehru Stadium. Ask around for one going in the right direction. From the bus drop-off, it's a 2-3hr. uphill* **hike** *to the fort—bring plenty of food and water—or a Rs25 per person* **jeep** *ride.*

Spread high atop the rugged green hills 24km southwest of Pune, Sinhagad Fort makes for a pleasant day's escape from the strain of city life. The fort is one of the most important historical sites in the area; its conquest by the great Maratha king, Shivaji, was crucial in reclaiming the area from the Mughals and in establishing the Maratha empire. The few ramparts and getaways that remain of the fort are spread out over the hillside, allowing visitors the unparalleled pleasure of wandering idly from one spectacular viewpoint to the next. The views over the entire city of Pune and the surrounding hills and river valleys are simply stunning, and highlight just how incredible a feat it was storming this near-impregnable hilltop fort. Plenty of locals make the weekend pilgrimage to their hero's mountaintop, wandering about the massive ruins, drinking the revered "sweet water," and snacking at the huts at the top of the fort area.

LONAVLA लोनावला   ☎ 02114

Founded in 1811 as a health resort, the town of Lonavla serves as a convenient stopover for travelers making their way between Mumbai and Pune. During the Raj Era, Bombay *sahibs* came here to relax and escape the searing temperatures of the coast in the forested hills that surround the station. Though little can be discerned of its sedate, colonial past in the hustle and bustle that is the modern Indian town, Lonavla retains its resort function. Families from Pune and Mumbai flock here for short getaways especially in season (April-June). The most compelling reasons to visit, however, are the Buddhist caves at nearby Karla and Bhaja, which date back to the first century BC.

⊡ TRANSPORTATION. Lonavla is on the main highway and railway line between Mumbai and Pune, so it is easily accessible by both bus and train. **Trains** are quickest and express trains leave for **Mumbai** (3hr., every hr., Rs44) and **Pune** (1½hr., every hr. except noon-2:30pm, Rs29). Local trains also leave regularly for Pune and Malavli. **Buses** head to: **Mumbai** (3hr., every hr., Rs60); **Pune** (1½hr., every hr., Rs35); and the **Karla** and **Bhaja** caves.

⊡ ORIENTATION AND PRACTICAL INFORMATION. The railway track divides Lonavla into two parts, North and South. Facing the same direction as Pune-bound trains, turning right (south) leads to the bazaar area and market stalls. Coming out the left (north) side of the station, the first on the left is **Shivaji Road.** The **post office** is 2min. down the road on the left. The road bends around to join the **Mumbai-Pune Highway** which runs parallel to the railway tracks. The **bus station** is at the intersection of these roads. **Balaji Computers** has speedy, reliable **Internet** access (☎275812; 8:30-10:30am, 12:30-11:30pm; Rs25 per hr., Rs15 per hr. from 5-9pm). Cross over the westernmost railway footbridge, then turn left and take the second right where you should be able to see a large red and white sign. Take the small stairway just before the sign to the 2nd floor. There is no place to exchange currency in Lonavla, so make sure you have enough cash before you arrive.

⌂⊡ ACCOMMODATIONS AND FOOD. Most of the tourists in Lonavla are families from Mumbai and Pune looking to splurge on resort-style, hill station living. Budget travelers have few accommodation options, especially in the high season (Apr.-June). By far the best budget choice in town is the family-run ▨**Hotel Ravishan ❸**. This hotel, run more like a homestay by the friendly owners, boasts large, airy doubles, clean bathrooms with showers, hot water, room service, and even home-cooked breakfasts. Space is limited (only 7 double rooms), so book ahead during the high season. Turn right onto the Mumbai-Pune Rd. from the bus station and take the first left. You should be able to see the sign from the road. (☎272267. Doubles Rs450.) About 100m to the left of the bus station on Shivaji Rd., the **Hotel Chandralok ❸**, with its clean baths and friendly staff, is another good choice if the Ravishan is full. (☎272294. Doubles Rs525-1190; small discounts for solo travelers.) If you're intent on saving your rupees then the **Hotel Mahalaxmi ❷** is the cheapest you'll find. Rooms come complete with dirty walls, concrete beds, squat toilets, and bucket showers, but not linen. Next door to the Hotel Chandralok. (Singles Rs150, doubles Rs250.) One of the nicest choices in Lonavla, the **Ardash Hotel ➒** comes with all modern conveniences including cable TV, telephone, room service, and showers. Even pricier rooms have a balcony and a sofa. Next to the bus station on Shivaji Rd. (☎272353. Doubles Rs900-1800. Reservations required in-season.)

The bazaar area south of the train station has cheap, simple restaurants and food stalls. Many of the hotels that are spread along the Mumbai-Pune Rd., particularly toward the western end, have attached restaurants. Particularly good is the **Hotel Chandralok ➌** which serves tasty, bottomless Gujarati *thalis.* Open daily 8am-10pm, Rs65. The **Udipi Restaurant ➊,** close to the bus station on the Mumbai-Pune Rd., is popular with locals and has both South and North Indian food for Rs20-40. Open daily 9am-11pm. For a splurge, the **Dynasty Restaurant ➍** is attached to the four-star Hotel Metropole and serves Indian and Chinese dishes in an elegant dining room. (Two buildings down from the Hotel Chandralok. Open daily 11am-3pm, 7-11pm; Rs90-150.)

◩ SIGHTS. Tourists come to Lonavla not for the town itself (which is eminently forgettable), but for the exquisite Buddhist caves chiseled into the high, basalt cliffs at nearby **Karla** and **Bhaja.** Buses to Karla leave about every half hour to an hour from Lonavla's bus station (30min, Rs8). From the bus stop, it is a steep 20min. walk up a stone staircase to the caves. There is really only one cave on view at Karla (smaller caves are open, but have no carvings) and this is the main *chaitya* (temple) hall. Carved in 80 BC by Hinayana Buddhists, the *chaitya* is the largest of its kind in India. Six large elephants flank the entrance to the cave and each of the 30 columns inside are topped by a double-elephant capital (all added later by Mahayana Buddhists). Many Hindus visit the modern Hindu shrine that obscures the entrance to the *chaitya.* The temple is packed with worshippers, particularly on a Sunday, when bands and dancers create a festive atmosphere. (Karla caves open daily 8am-6pm. Rs100.)

The Bhaga caves are about a 7km rickshaw ride south from the Karla steps (Rs60). Otherwise, local trains run between Lonavla and **Malavli** (Rs5). Follow the road over the highway and keep going for 20min. to get to the Bhaja stairs. A serene atmosphere prevails at these 18 calmer, less-frequented and better-preserved caves, which were carved in the second century BC. *Viharas* surround the main *chaitya* and include a celebrated relief of a war elephant tearing up trees in its path. Past the main area, there is a cave containing 14 identical *stupas* and a room with sculptured reliefs of the Buddha and Vishnu side-by-side. Farther still, down a narrow path, a lone *stupa* is tucked away behind a trickling waterfall. (Bhaja caves open 8am-6pm, Rs100.)

The area around Lonavla is dotted with forts dating back to the 16th and 17th centuries. This was the time when the **Mahratha** warrior Shivaji was battling over this land with the Mughal emperors in Bijapur. The closest fort to town is **Rajmachi.** Buses leave from the Shivaji Rd. Bus station (15min., every hr., Rs5).

About 5km south of town is Lonavla's most popular attraction during the monsoons, the **Bhushi Dam.** The dam has rock steps along part of its face, and at the peak of the rainy season, it overflows, allowing foamy water to spill down these stairs, where tourists and locals delight in the bubbles.

MAHABALESHWAR महाबलेश्वर ☎ 02168

Mahabaleshwar is Indian hill station life at its finest. Thirty viewpoints, several waterfalls, a lake, and numerous old temples make this the best of the Maharashtrian hill stations. Set amidst lush tropical scenery, the relaxed resort-town atmosphere and cool climate make Mahabaleshwar a rewarding escape from Pune or Mumbai. Though somewhat difficult to get to, Mahabaleshwar is well worth the effort. The town shuts down during the monsoons of mid-June-Sept.

▐ TRANSPORTATION. Buses run to: **Mumbai** (7hr., 5 per day 9:15am-9pm, Rs140-200); **Pune** (4hr., every hr. 6:30am-7:30pm, 70-90); **Satara,** for train connections (2hr., 11 per day 5:30am-3pm, Rs28). There are numerous private bus companies along Main St. These offer luxury coaches, occasionally with A/C, to **Mumbai** (Rs250), **Pune** (Rs150), **Goa** (12hr., Rs400, sleeper bus Rs550), **Ahmedabad** (13hr., Rs550), and **Bangalore** (24hr., Rs650.) **Taxis** loiter at the stand opposite the bus station; the universal local fare is Rs30.

▐▐ ▐ ORIENTATION AND PRACTICAL INFORMATION. All visitors to Mahabaleshwar are charged a Rs5 entry tax. The main part of the town is a few kilometers south of Old Mahabaleshwar. **Dr. Sabane Road (Main Street)** runs east-west. On this road is the town's bazaar, the heart of Mahabaleshwar. The **bus station** is at the far western end of Main St. **Masjid Road** runs parallel to Main St. to the north, and **Murray Peth Road** is parallel to the south. **Currency exchange** is available at the **Bank of Maharashtra,** up a small flight of stairs on the north side of Main St. near the Hotel Vaibhav. (Open M-F 10:30am-2:30pm, Sa 10:30am-12:30pm.) The **police station** is on the right, farther east on Main St. (☎260333 or 260420. Open 24hr.) **Morarji Gokuldas Rural Hospital** (☎260247) Shivaji Circle, is at the east end of Main St. up the flight of steps to the north. It has a **24hr. pharmacy.** You can also find **Internet** access available at the Hotel Sunny International, Masjid Rd., one block east of the bus station. (24hr., Rs15 per hr.) To get to the **GPO,** come out of the front of the bus station and turn left. Keep walking for 5min. and it will be on your right. (Open M-F 9am-4pm.) **Postal Code:** 412806.

▐ ▐ ACCOMMODATIONS AND FOOD. During the wet season, even the best hotels go for next to nothing; in season, however, rates can more than triple, and it takes an effort to find anything resembling budget accommodation. **Hotel Nells ❸,** Main St., offers the best cheap beds in town with spare but neat rooms with TVs. (☎260323. Doubles Rs400-600. 50% discount off-season.) The **Kalpana Excellency ❸** has clean, more upscale rooms with TVs surrounding a stone and marble courtyard. Make advance reservations in season. (☎260419. Doubles Rs1050, off-season Rs350-500.)

There are numerous restaurants in between the tourist stalls on Main St., which becomes the spot of choice after dark. Places serve fast food (pizza, burgers, chips) as well as Indian selections. The **Yogeshi Lunch Home ❶** on the north side of the street has complete "plates" for Rs25 on a balcony overlooking Main St. (Open daily 9am-11pm.) The popular **Rasoi Restaurant ❸** to the Kaplara Excellency (see above) has traditional Maharashtrian *thalis* (Rs70.) In addition, Mahabaleshwar is famous for its delicious ▐strawberries, which can be found in season all over town.

▐ SIGHTS. The hilltop town of Mahabaleshwar is surrounded by numerous steep drops which provide views of the surrounding countryside. The best view to be had is from **Arthur's Seat,** about 12km west of town. On a clear day in the dry season, you can see the ocean. **Bombay Port** to the south and **Kate's Port** in the north also provide good views over the surrounding countryside. Be warned that during the monsoon season, however, thick fogs make it hard to see anything more than the ground beneath your feet. There are boats for hire at nearby **Venna Lake** (Rowboats Rs160 per hr.; paddleboats Rs200 per hr.) though the atmosphere is spoiled by a nearby construction site.

The town of **Old Mahabaleshwar** has endless cobblestone streets, unfortunately filled with endless souvenir stalls open during the high season. Its quiet atmosphere (no cars allowed) as well as two historic temples make it worthwhile to explore. The **Panchaganga Mandir** contains five springs of five sacred Hindu rivers (Krisha, Koyna, Savitri, Veena and Gayatri). Inside the temple they merge into one flow which pours from the mouth of a stone bull into a pool. The brightly colored Mahabaleshwar Mandir encloses a natural rock *linga*.

Taxis run something of a cartel in the sightseeing business. In order to get to the sights, you'll have to take one of two non-negotiable tours for Rs280. One of these goes out to Arthur's Seat and Old Mahabaleshwar, while the other takes in Kate's Port and Bombay Port. The 17th-century Pratapgad Fort built under the rule of Shivaji also has good views. The fort is 24km from town and a taxi will cost Rs450.

AURANGABAD औरंगाबाद ☎ 0240

Cradled by the crags of the Deccan Plateau, Aurangabad (pop. 1,200,000) is a pleasant, mid-sized city with enough nearby sights to put its larger neighbors in its pocket. The city's proximity to the celebrated caves at Ellora and Ajanta, plus its remarkable tourist infrastructure, make it a must-see destination in Maharashtra. The boulevards are broad and clean, and run under 52 huge, 17th-century gates built by ultra-orthodox Aurangzeb, the last of the Mughal rulers. Right-wing Shiv Sena councilors recently renamed the city in honor of Sambhaji, Shivaji's son and Maratha Hindu hero. To most, the city is still named for Aurangzeb. The old square, the stone houses, the sizable Muslim population, and the silky *himroo* fabric (patterned after the paintings in Ajanta) give the city a distinctly Islamic air. These days, Aurangabad enjoys the economic boom typical of Maharashtra's hinterland. The brewing capital of India, Aurangabad is a mellow place to throw back a few locally made "Australian" lagers after a long day touring the nearby ruins.

☐ TRANSPORTATION

Flights: The **airport,** in Chikalthana, Jalna Rd., is 10km from the city center. Buses run to and from the city bus office at the railway station (Rs5), but are inconvenient as they don't run all the way to the terminal. A much better option are taxis (to town Rs50). **Indian Airlines,** Jalna Rd. (☎485421 or 483390), 150m west of Rama International Hotel. Open daily 10am-1pm and 1:30-5pm. **Jet Airways** (☎441770 or 441392), opposite Indian Airlines. Open daily 10am-1pm and 1:30-5pm. Under 40 25% discount. Both fly to **Mumbai** (45min., 1 per day, US$85). Indian Airlines also has service to **Delhi** (3½hr., 1 per day, US$185).

Trains: Railway Station, Station Rd. (☎331015, reservations and inquiry ☎131 and ☎132). Fares listed are 2nd class. Five days a week, the Sachkhand Express from **Nanded** to **Amritsar** arrives in Aurangabad at 12:30pm, and continues on to **Agra** (20hr., Rs393), **Bhopal** (12hr., Rs289), and **Delhi** (25hr., Rs425). Trains also run to **Mumbai** (8½hr.; Tapovan Express 2:40pm, Deogiri Express 9:20pm; Rs178).

Buses: Central Bus Stand, Dr. Ambedkar Rd. (☎331647), 2km north of the railway station, west along the continuation of Station Rd. Schedules and fares are for regular buses. The "semi-deluxe" buses cost about 30% more; full-on "deluxe" buses are 60% more. To: **Ahmedabad** (14hr., 9pm, Rs175); **Ajanta** (3hr., every hr., Rs47); **Daulatabad** (20min., frequent, Rs7); **Ellora** (45min., every 20 min., Rs15); **Hyderabad** (12hr., 3pm, Rs200); **Jalgaon** (4hr., 10 per day 6am-6pm, Rs50); **Mumbai** (10hr., 15 per day 8am-10pm, Rs170-250); **Pune** (6hr., every 30min. 5am-midnight, Rs101-120).

Local Transportation: Auto-rickshaws are convenient, but make sure that they use the meters. Cost-effective **tempos** function as mini-buses, scooting up and down major city routes. **Bicycles** are for rent just outside the railway station, on your left as you face the station. Rs3 per hr. or Rs20 per day.

MAHARASHTRA

TO AURANGABAD CAVES (4.5km)

Bibi-Ka-Maqbara

HIMAYATBAG

TO AJANTA (106km)

Delhi Gate

BEGAMPURA

JASINGPURA

KUTUBPURA

Ghati Rd.

KALA DARWAZA

Government Medical College Hospital

Panchakki

GPO

Juna Bazaar

Sarafa

TO DAULATABAD (14km), KHULDABAD (27km), ELLORA (29km), NASIK (190km), & PUNE (230km)

Begampura Rd.

Panchakki Rd.

Police Commissioner's Office

Dr. Ambedkar Marg

NIRALA BAZAAR

1

ICICI Bank

AURANGPURA

MILL CORNER

Aurangpura Rd.

Central Bus Stand

Siddarth Gardens

2

GULMANDI

3

Trade-wings

Kranti Chowk Police Station

State Bank of India

Jalna Rd.

TO AIRPORT (10km)

Dr. Rajendra Prasad Marg

KRANTI CHOWK

KARAN-PURA

4

Padampura Rd.

Kamal Nayan Bajaj Hospital

PADAMPURA

NARSINGPURA

Govt. of India

5

6

Station Rd. West

7

MTDC Holiday Resort

8

Station Rd. East

11

9

10

N

LG

Kham River

0   1 mile

0   1 kilometer

Aurangabad Railway Station

SHAHNOOR-WADI

MAHARASHTRA

Aurangabad

ACCOMMODATIONS
Hotel Devpriya, **2**
Hotel Natraj, **8**
Hotel Pushpak, **6**
Hotel Shree Maya, **5**
Tourist's Home, **7**
Youth Hostel, **4**

FOOD
Foodwala's Bhoj, **3**
The Kitchen, **9**
Lovely Juice Center, **11**
Pinky's, **10**
Smile Vegetarian Restaurant, **1**

☀ ⚡ ORIENTATION AND PRACTICAL INFORMATION

Tourist facilities are along **Station Road,** which has two branches: the western half runs north from the railway station to the bus stand; the eastern branch runs northeast past several hotels and restaurants to **Kranti Chowk,** a major business area. From Kranti Chowk, **Jalna Road** runs east to the airline offices and the airport. **Dr. Rajendra Prasad Marg** cuts back west to intersect Station Rd. North of this intersection, near the bus stand, Station Rd. becomes **Dr. Ambedkar Marg.** It ends at the north end of town near the Bibi-Ka-Maqbara and the Aurangabad Caves.

Tourist Office: Government of India Tourist Office, Krishna Vilas, Station Rd. (☎331217), on the right side of the main (western) branch of Station Rd., about 250m from the station. Open M-F 8:30am-6pm, Sa 8:30am-1:30pm. Also has counters at railway station and airport. The **Maharashtra Tourism Development Corporation (MTDC),** MTDC Holiday Resort, Station Rd. East (☎331513 or 331198), gives tours. Open M-F 10:30am-6pm.

Budget Travel: Classic Travel, MTDC Holiday Resort, Station Rd. E. (☎335598 or 337788), inside the lobby to the right. This friendly office provides tours. There is also a branch at the airport. Both open daily 7am-10:30pm. AmEx/MC/V. **Trade-wings,** Dr. Ambedkar Marg (☎3322677), opposite Hotel Printravel, provides basic travel services. Open daily 9am-7:30pm. AmEx/MC/V.

Currency Exchange: State Bank of India, Dr. Rajendra Prasad Marg, Kranti Chowk (☎351126 or 331872). Open M-F 10:30am-2pm, Sa 10:30am-noon. **ICICI Bank,** Tapadia Center, Nirala Bazaar, Samarth Nagar (☎342371). Open daily 8am-8pm.

Market: The Aurangpura area is one giant market, selling everything from chandeliers to pomegranates—a much better shopping spot than the tourist bazaars near the caves.

Police: Police Commissioner's Office, Mill Corner (☎334333, 321100, and 334675), north of the bus station.

Hospital: Government Medical College Hospital, Panchakki Rd. (☎331402 through 331410). 24hr. pharmacy. **Ambulance** (☎102 or 402415).

Internet: Many cyber cafes line Station Rd. East and West, but tend to cost more than elsewhere in India. **Bolbala.com** (☎5629270), down the alley from ICICI Bank, Nirala Bazaar. Rs20 per hr. Open 10:30am-11pm. **Cyber-dhaba,** Station Rd. W. (☎364520 or 330304), next to Trade-wings. Rs30 per hr. Open 7am-11pm.

Post Office: GPO, Juna Bazaar, Bazaar District (☎331420). Open M-Sa 10am-8pm. **Postal Code:** 431005.

⚐ ACCOMMODATIONS

Most of Aurangabad's budget hotels cluster around the railway station and the bus stand. Those around the railway station are nicer, but the budget hotel ghetto across from the bus will always have a cheap room ready. The Government of India Tourist Office also arranges homestays with local residents (Rs200-400).

■ **Hotel Shree Maya,** Bharuka Complex, Padampura Rd. (☎333093; shrimaya_agd@sancharnet.in). Walk north on Station Rd. from Government Tourist Office, take the first two right turns; it's 100m on right. Upscale and worth it. Attractive rooms with TVs, telephones, attached baths, and A/C. Great staff, room service, and Internet (Rs60 per hr). Check-out 24hr. Doubles Rs275-395. ❷

Youth Hostel (HI), Station Rd. W. (☎334892), 1km from the station, on the right just south of the intersection with Dr. Rajendra Prasad Marg. Well-run and spotless. Cheap, mosquito-netted dorms, warm-water baths, and cafeteria (breakfast Rs12, lunch and dinner Rs22). Check-in 7-11am and 4-8pm. Check-out 9am. Curfew 10pm. Unbeatable prices: dorms Rs40, non-members Rs60; doubles Rs160. ❶

Tourist's Home, Station Rd. W. (☎337212), a 5min. walk from the railway station. A sprawling complex of simple and clean rooms. Singles Rs100-150; doubles Rs150-200. ❶

Hotel Natraj, Station Rd. West (☎324260), just before the Tourist Home when walking from the railway station. This family-run house is cheap, clean, and well located. All with attached bath. Singles Rs125; doubles Rs180; triples Rs250; quints 350. ❶

Hotel Devpriya, Dr. Ambedkar Marg (☎332344 and 339032; fax 336129), just south of the Central Bus Stand. Despite the bus station cacophony, this giant place has plenty of color. The impressive hallway is its best feature, but the rooms are fine, too, and the staff is friendly. Attached baths and morning hot water. Same-day laundry service. Check-out 24hr. Singles Rs160-180; doubles Rs275-300; triples 360-400. ❷

Hotel Pushpak, (☎3244614), Bhaji Mandi, behind RTO. Walking towards Station Rd. East from Shree Maya, it's across from Hotel Indradep down an alley on the right. Shining, beautiful rooms with double beds, cable TV, and phone. Situated on a well-located but amazingly peaceful little street. Doubles Rs225-650. ❷

🍴 FOOD

🍴 **Smile Vegetarian Restaurant** (☎324841), Nirala Bazaar, opposite ICICI Bank. Smile resembles a sleek, modern, European bistro with its pale wood furniture and cheerful striped awning. It offers not only continental dishes but also Manchurian Szechuan, South Indian and Punjabi veg. dishes, tackling each cuisine adeptly. Clean, efficient kitchen and breezy patio seating add to a purely enjoyable eating experience. Entrees Rs24-38. Open daily 7am-11pm. ❶

Pinky's, Station Rd. E., next door to the The Kitchen. Choose from Mughlai, South Indian, and Chinese foods. Quick service and garrulous, open-hearted owner. A divine boneless chicken curry plate (Rs51). Entrees Rs25-100. ❶

The Kitchen, Station Rd. E., by the train station. The budget trinity of good, cheap, and clean converge in Kitchen's South Indian snacks, Western breakfasts, and Bengali dishes. Entrees Rs18-70. Open daily 6am-11pm. ❶

Lovely Juice Center, Station Rd. E., in the complex right across from the MTDC. Excellent shakes Rs15-30. Another location on corner of Station Rd. E. and Station Rd. W. Open daily 10am-11pm. ❶

Foodwala's Bhoj, Dr. Ambedkar Marg, in a big building 200m south of the bus stand, on the right, one floor up. A hideaway for Aurangabad's elite, with a small but classy central fountain. Tremendous *thalis* (Rs50) compensate for a limited menu. Punjabi dishes Rs20-30; *dosas* and *uttappams* Rs12-20. Open daily 11am-3pm and 7-11pm. ❷

👁 SIGHTS

If you're pressed for time or just want some comfort, try one of the MTDC or Classic Travels tours that cover both sights in Aurangabad and Ellora.

AURANGABAD CAVES. Aurangabad's cave temples are often eclipsed by the glamour that surrounds the caves at Ellora and Ajanta. Blissfully free of tour groups and touts, they remain a wonderful introduction to the breathtaking sculpture to be found all along Maharashtra's cave-trail. Split into western and eastern sections, these distinctive examples of Buddhist art and architecture were created

MAHARASHTRA

by two great dynasties during the 6th, 7th, and 8th centuries. The western caves, numbered 1 through 5, are off the dirt road at the top of a treacherous climb up winding stone steps. The third and most beautiful cave was once a *vihara* (residence hall) for the wandering Buddhist monks *(bikshus)* of the time, who gathered in monastic communities in caves like these around the state. Some fragments of the original paintings depict stories about the Buddha's previous incarnations. The fourth cave is a *chaitya* hall, used for congregation and prayer. The eastern caves at the end of the right fork, numbers 6 through 9, afford incredible views of the surrounding landscape, including a view of Bibi-Ka-Maqbara. The seventh cave greets visitors with lotus-framed *apsaras* (celestial dancing nymphs) at the entrance to the crypt. A shadowed Buddha sits inside the sanctuary, his feet surrounded by the frozen faces of the disciples. Outside the final cave is a giant (broken) sculpture of the Buddha after his death. Visit the caves early in the morning when few tourists are there. *(In the hills behind the Bibi-Ka-Maqbara, up the dirt road that leads past the tomb; 10min. by auto-rickshaw or a 1hr. walk. Open daily dawn-dusk. Rs100. Bring a flashlight.)*

BIBI-KA-MAQBARA. Constructed between 1650 and 1657, Prince Azam Shah's milk-white monument to his mother, Begum Rabi'a Durani, has been the object of scorn as an inferior Taj Mahal knock-off. The Bibi-Ka-Maqbara was important to the tradition of Mughal mausolea, but this rather small tomb could never have challenged the Taj, even if cash shortages had not forced ungainly corner-cutting, such as the abandonment of marble for plaster a meter up the wall. If you do hire a guide, decide on price prior to the tour. *(Open daily dawn-10pm. Rs100, or peek from the gates for free.)*

PANCHAKKI. The Mughal water mill at Panchakki is a good stopover on the return trip from the caves or Bibi-Ka-Maqbara. The mill was built in 1624 in honor of the Muslim saint Baba Shah Musafir to help feed the hundreds of orphans, paupers, and fakirs who were his devotees. In the Panchakki's heyday, the output was almost four tons of finely ground grain. Today, Panchakki has been reduced to a breeding ground for hawkers and crafts shops specializing in the city's unique *himroo* fabric. Nearby lies Musafir's tomb, though it's not much to look at. *(Panchakki Rd. Open daily 7am-8:30pm. Rs5.)*

▶ DAYTRIP FROM AURANGABAD

DAULATABAD दौलताबाद
Most buses from Aurangabad to Ellora stop at Daulatabad, Rs6. Open daily 6am-6pm. Closed Tu. Rs100.

Several important sights lie along the road between Aurangabad and Ellora. The most impressive is the **Daulatabad fortress,** on top of a hill 13km from Aurangabad. Originally erected in the 9th century, the fortress gained notoriety in the 14th century when Muhammad Tughlaq, the whimsical Sultan of Delhi, decided this was the spot for a capital. Rather than leave the development of a thriving city to chance, the not-so-savvy sultan marched the entire population of Delhi 1000km across India to people it. The small proportion of the deportees who did not die on the way greeted life in the Deccan with a resentment not conducive to prosperity. The Sultan abandoned his project after only eight years and marched the few survivors back home. Nevertheless, Daulatabad grew into an important city, and the fort itself is considered India's second most impenetrable, after the Amber Fort in Rajasthan. Today, the ruins of the fort are inhabited only by monkeys and lizards.

Behind the first gate, spiked to prevent elephant attacks, is a series of labyrinthine streets, designed to confuse the potential invader. A left turn after the first gate leads to a wall, but a right turn provides access to the ruined walled city. The pink **Chand Minar** victory tower, built in 1435, rises over a water tank. Across the water tank is the **Bharatmata Temple** (Mother India), a 10th-century Hindu structure that resisted several attempts to convert it into a mosque. A series of steps leads up the hill past ruined palaces to the blue-tiled **Chini Mahal,** where the last king of Golconda met his end. On top of the small tower next door, a re-creation of a cannon called Qila Shikan (Fort Breaker) points menacingly out at the horizon. From here, the defenses begin in earnest; you have to cross a moat to get into the sheer-walled citadel. Inside the fort's walls is a night-dark passage designed as an ambush path for intruders. A guide will save you from attack and lead you through it with a kerosene lamp, in anticipation, of course, of a little *baksheesh.* Endless stairs lead upward, reemerging into daylight and to a farther series of palaces lining the slope to the fort's summit. From the top, there are magnificent views of Aurangabad and the surrounding countryside. Bring a flashlight along on the journey, and don't forget to pack a bottle of water.

ELLORA इलोरा   ☎ 02437

The UNESCO-protected "caves" at Ellora and Ajanta make up Maharashtra's most celebrated tourist attractions. Though still referred to as caves, they are actually man-made architectural and sculptural wonders. A total of 34 caves were carved out of the volcanic basalt rock by several generations of artisans between AD 600 and 1000. Unlike the earlier, Buddhist-only structures at Ajanta, Ellora's Buddhist, Hindu, and Jain caves reflect the rise and fall of religions in India. Also in Ellora is the **Ghrashneshwar Temple,** one of the *jyotirlingas,* where Shiva is said to have burst from the earth. The same square also houses three ancient temple-like structures said to be the tombs of Shivaji's father and grandfathers—locals maintain that this village, not Pune, is Shivaji's birthplace. A mere 29km from Aurangabad, Ellora makes for an ideal daytrip from the city.

▐ TRANSPORTATION

The main road runs west from the bus stand by the entrance site, concealing one budget hotel amid stalls of trinkets and cold drinks. Frequent **buses** run to Ellora via Daulatabad (45min., 6am-6pm, Rs15). **Shared taxis** run from the stand opposite Aurangabad's Central Bus Station (Rs15). The jam-packed **jeeps** that cruise the Ellora-Aurangabad road cost about the same as the bus, and allow you to see both Ellora and Daulatabad in a day. MTDC's and Classic Travel's more expensive and comfortable **tours** do the same (see p. 396).

▐ ▐ ACCOMMODATIONS AND FOOD

The MTDC's **Kailas Hotel ❶** is clean and well-run. (☎244543 or 244468. Dorms Rs100; singles Rs500; doubles Rs350-1100.) Food options in Ellora involve sodas, *pakoras,* and a few minimalist restaurants. The **Kailas Hotel Restaurant ❷** serves *thalis* for Rs50. (Open daily 7am-9:30pm.) Ellora's best restaurant, **Hotel Milan ❶,** has veg. dishes for Rs15-50. (Open daily 8am-5pm and 8-11pm.)

▐ THE CAVES

Caves open daily except Tu sunrise to sunset. Cave 16 open daily except Tu 6am-6pm. Rs250 or US$5; video fee Rs25, exterior only. All other caves free.

Of Ellora's 34 caves, the oldest ones are Buddhist (built AD 600-800) and are numbered 1 through 12. The slightly more recent Hindu caves (AD 700-900) bear numbers 13-29, and include Ellora's greatest attraction, the **Kailasa Temple** (Cave 16). The youngest Jain caves (numbers 30-34; AD 800-1000) are a 10min. walk uphill or a short ride from the other caves.

M
A
H
A
R
A
S
H
T
R
A

BUDDHIST CAVES. With the exception of Cave 10, all Buddhist caves at Ellora are *viharas* (monasteries). They are quite simple in design and decoration and do not compare to the caves at Ajanta. **Cave 5** stands out among the first ten. The flat, low ridges in its floor are believed to have served as benches to make a community dining hall. The stern Vajrapani (the *bodhisattva* holding a thunderbolt) and the more forgiving Padmapani (in the form of a lotus-toting *bodhisattva*) presided over meals from the sides of the central shrine. **Cave 10,** the only *chaitya* (temple), is called Carpenter's Cave, after the ribbed ceiling designed to look like wood. The 3-floor **Cave 12,** with a courtyard and balconies, is the most recent and most ornate of the group, probably in order to compete with the elaborate Hindu caves. The top floor houses intricate and dynamic sculpture: *bodhisattvas* line the side walls, and the seven previous incarnations of the Buddha flank the main shrine. A different type of tree shades each Buddha, a symbolic technique developed at Sanchi (see p. 353) and other early Buddhist monuments. Traces of paint in the sanctum and chamber hint at the once colorful painting inside the caves.

HINDU CAVES. The densely sculptured temples share many repeating motifs, most often depicting the Hindu trinity: Brahma (creator), Vishnu (protector), and Shiva (destroyer, also known as Manesh). Shiva appears most often on Mount Kailasa playing dice with wife Parvati while a demon tries frantically, in vain, to dislodge him; at other times he dances "Nataraja," the dance of the gods. Vishnu crops up as Narasimha (the man-lion), Varaha (the boar), and, most commonly, as Narayan, asleep in the coils of a serpent floating on the cosmic sea. From his navel grows a lotus, out of which Brahma emerges to create the world. The image of the Seven Mothers, buxom goddesses with children, flanked by Kala and Kali (goddesses of death), also appears regularly. **Cave 14** was originally a Buddhist monastery, converted into a Hindu temple and dedicated to Shiva. **Cave 15** depicts Shiva emerging from a *linga*, among other things, while Brahma and Vishnu kneel before him—(yet another) testimony to Shiva-worship among Ellora's patrons.

Cave 16, the **Kailasa Temple,** is the highlight of Ellora and the climax of Hindu sculpting mastery. A replica of Shiva's home in the Himalayas, the Kailasa Temple, is the largest monolithic sculpture in the world, and was sculpted from the top down over the course of 150 years during the 8th and 9th centuries. The sheer scale of this structure defies belief, even before you consider the technical challenge of slicing it all out from one solid rock. Traces of white plaster (imitation of snow in the Himalayas) and paint bear witness to further decorative complexity. The central courtyard (80m deep) is surrounded by galleries and contains a massive shrine, flanked by a statue of an elephant on each side. Apart from countless other elephants, the temple contains images from Hindu mythology. Of these, the most impressive are the panels depicting scenes from the *Mahabharata* on the left of the temple, and from the *Ramayana* on the right sides. If you don't want to shell out the entrance fee for Cave 16 (though you should), you can climb up the stairs on the right of the cave for a view of the structure from above. The remaining 12 Hindu caves can be reached from the paved road to the left of the temple, but they pale in comparison to Kailasa.

Cave 29, with its view of a rainy-season waterfall, is Ellora's second-largest cave. Strangely enough, in comparison to more reverential depictions, you'll notice a dwarf baring his rear end under the auspice of Lord Shiva. The cave is also among the most structurally impressive, with three lion-guarded entrances protecting it.

JAIN CAVES. Ellora's most recent structures, the Jain Caves, date back to the 9th and 10th centuries, and reflect the temporary resurgence of Jainism in the region. Though some sections remain unfinished, others hold some of the most intricately detailed carvings anywhere in Ellora. Both **Cave 30** and **Cave 32** are smaller imitations of the Kailasa Temple. Cave 32 depicts the *tirthankara* (Jain saint) Gomatesvara so deep in meditation that he has not noticed the vines growing on his limbs or the animals surrounding him. This temple is dedicated to Indra, king of the gods, the pot-bellied god reposing under a banyan tree.

AJANTA अजन्ता   ☎ 02438

Ajanta is almost as remote today as it was in the first century BC, when it was a Buddhist retreat. Its architects chose a sheer cliff face above a horseshoe-shaped canyon along the Waghora River to render their contemplative spiritual visions in painting and sculpture. The 29 caves were carved out between the first century BC and the 6th century AD in two separate phases. Construction of the caves was halted when Hinduism became dominant in the 1st century AD. It wasn't until emperor Harisena of the Vakataka Dynasty, a Buddhist, came to power in the 5th century AD that excavation of Ajanta's caves resumed. After Harisena's death, the region descended into chaos and artists and monks abandoned the site. Only locals knew that these masterpieces even existed, until British army officer John Smith spied Cave 10 from the opposite ridge in 1819 while tiger hunting. Two thousand years might have chipped the paint, but Ajanta's colorful, meticulous wall paintings continue to tell stories of the Buddha's incarnations as *bodhisattva*—known as the *Jataka* tales—and other legends. The UNESCO-protected caves should make it onto every traveler's itinerary. It's best to visit the more ancient Ajanta prior to Ellora.

▐▀ TRANSPORTATION

Visitors have to suffer through a hot, jolting **bus** ride to get to Ajanta. Many buses stop at Ajanta between Aurangabad 108km south (3½hr., Rs65) and Jalgaon 58km north (1hr., Rs37), arriving at 5:30pm from Aurangabad and 6:30pm from Jalgaon. The best way to see the caves is to come from one town, leave your bags with the guards in the cloak room at the base of the caves (theoretically free), and to go to the next town the same evening. The MDTC organizes convenient tours from Aurangabad (Rs180; see p. 397).

▐▐ ACCOMMODATIONS AND FOOD

The MTDC runs the **Ajanta Travellers Lodge ❷** at the caves themselves. Their rooms are clean but spare, with balconies and common baths. (☎244226. Doubles Rs250-325.) A more luxurious but pricier option is the **Ajanta Holiday Resort ❹**, also run by the MTDC, in Fardapur, 1km from T-junction. (Doubles Rs750-900.) For a more budget option try the **New Ajanta Guest House ❶**, in Fardapur Village near the mosque. (4 basic rooms Rs100-200.) For reservations, call the regional MTDC manager in Aurangabad (☎2331198 or 2331513). A better but pricier option is the **Forest Rest House ❸**, 500m back down the road. It has two air-cooled doubles with hot water, a cook, mosquito nets, and a veranda. Book in advance with the Divisional Forest Officer, Osmanpura, Aurangabad. (☎2334203. Rs400 per person.)

FROM THE ROAD

IT'S LADIES' NIGHT!

The day started off innocently enough: I fell into a river and I rode the bus sitting on a burning hot gear-shift box with a villager's pants-less infant in my arms. I counted the hours until I could board the Seva-gram Express and sleep my way to a new day. When the night train finally arrived, I was enthusiastically tired and ready to go.

I found my way to the ladies' only coach. It was not the powder-room salon lounge I had anticipated. Women of all ages lay head-to-foot on wooden bunks and covered the floor underfoot. Yet as I stumbled with my unwieldy pack, they all jumped to help me. When they realized I was a foreigner, they gathered around and offered to share their *pakoras* and biscuits with me. Soon, they settled for sleep, chattering all the while. It was a slumber party, I decided, with 100 women on a train racing through India, perhaps, but a slumber party nonetheless. I turned on my walkman and a girl, Neha, asked to listen. She reacted indifferently at first, and then began swaying to Neil Young's tuneful twanging. It was a far cry from Indipop, but Neha grabbed my wrists to dance anyway.

When the train approached my stop, all the women roused themselves from their slumber to bid me farewell and give me their mailing addresses. I can't say that I will become close pen pals with any of them, but I definitely won't forget our night on the Sevagram Express.

-Min Lieskovsky, 2004

THE CAVES

Open Su and Th-Sa 9am-5:30pm. US$10 or equivalent; video fee Rs25, exterior-only guide Rs100. From the T-junction, take the shuttle bus (Rs10) to the entrance. The caves are up the steps behind the drink stands and over the rise.

The guided tours often rely on gimmicks but also illuminate some of the murals' convoluted story lines. As in Ellora, two types of caves are found here: *chaitya* halls (9, 10, 19, 26, and 29), where locals came to worship Buddha, and *viharas* (monasteries), where monks meditated away in their stone cells. Caves not described below are unfinished (3, 5, 8, 23-25, 28, 29); they are heaven for archaeologists, as they reveal the various stages of carving.

CAVE 1. This 5th-century cave was sponsored by Emperor Harisena himself and contains some of the most delicate paintings at Ajanta. The paintings are also among the best preserved, as the cave was never used for worship and was thus spared charring by smoke. With the exception of Persian blue, which was imported from present-day Iran, all colors used in the paintings are natural, local colors. All paintings show the use of perspective, a technique not discovered in Europe until the Renaissance. Just to the left of the rear shrine, a painting depicts the elegant Padmapani (the lotus-holding *bodhisattva*). Vajrapani stands guard to his right with his thunderbolt. The statue of Buddha (notice the lotus position, symbolizing meditation, and the teaching position of his hands) changes expressions (from meditative to serious to happy) when illuminated at different angles.

CAVE 2. Paintings on the left wall of this 6th-century cave show Buddha's mother's dream of a six-tusked elephant, foretelling his conception and miraculous birth. Farther on the same wall is the unfinished mural of a Thousand Buddhas. In the right-hand rear corner, a sculptural frieze of a classroom of 500 children depicts a student pulling the hair of the girl in front. Above to the right, the demon Hariti dances furiously. The ceiling at the back resembles a Persian rug, testifying to the influence of Persian culture at the time.

CAVE 4. Due to a ceiling collapse, the largest *vihara* at Ajanta is unfinished.

CAVE 6. The unusually high number of columns (16) in this cave is probably due to the presence of a second floor, a unique occurrence at Ajanta.

CAVE 9. This *chaitya* hall dates back to the first century BC. There are oblique references to the Enlightened One, including the pipal-tree-shaped window in the facade, signifying learning, and the huge *stupa* in the apse, symbolizing the relics of the Buddha.

CAVE 10. The oldest Hinayana *chaitya* at Ajanta, dating back to the 2nd century BC, was also the 1st one sighted by the British officers in 1819. Sadly, the majority of the cave was destroyed by vandals, including its "discoverer" John Smith, who inscribed his name on a rear column on the right.

CAVE 12. One of the oldest *viharas*, Cave 12 contains 12 cells, each with two rockbeds for Buddhist monks.

CAVE 16. Sponsored by the prime minister of Emperor Harisena, Varhadeva, this cave, known as the "Dying Princess," carries the inscription of his name on the left side-wall. The columns at the front are supported by *ganas* (Dwarf followers of Shiva), miserable Japanese sumo wrestlers, and shiny happy couples. The front left corner, the most celebrated fresco of all, shows a princess swooning in distress as her husband throws in the worldly towel. At the back sits the 5m tall Buddha in teaching position, the largest statue in Ajanta.

CAVE 17. This cave showcases the greatest number of surviving murals, mostly *Jataka*, and a number of tales of seductive beauties and bloodthirsty demons, depicted in remarkably accurate anatomical detail. The most significant *Jataka* tale, on the rear wall on the right, shows Buddha as an elephant who breaks off his own six tusks in order to avoid hunters. A Wheel of Life is on the left side wall.

CAVE 19. Believed to be the latest carved cave at Ajanta, this *chaitya* represents the culmination of Buddhist art in the region. Inside is a statue of Buddha with his palm pointing down, a so-called "giving" position.

CAVE 26. The most splendid example reclines along the left-hand wall of Cave 26: the Buddha on the verge of leaving this world, and entering *nirvana*. Below, a procession mourns his departure from earth; above, the heavens rejoice. Further back along the same wall sits Buddha in meditation so deep that he fails to notice the flirtatious Mara. The path in front of Cave 26 leads down the hill to a bridge. From here, a path to the right leads to views of a rainy-season waterfall that surges over the cliffs. Visitors can head left and then climb to a **viewpoint** to relive the astonishment of the Brits who stumbled across the caves back in 1819. The river's gorges were carved by its seven waterfalls. Backtracking down to the riverbank opposite the caves will bring you to the parking lot.

NAGPUR नागपुर ☎0712

Smack dab in the center of India, Nagpur is the hub of seemingly every major road and rail route. But it certainly doesn't *feel* as though an entire subcontinent revolves around this city of two million. The streets are filled with tattered tongas and auto-rickshaws rather than taxis and aggressive Tata two-tonners. The seat of the state legislature alternates between Nagpur and Mumbai, but Nagpur lacks the skyscrapers and concrete that characterize many other cities of its size. In fact, with all its parks and playgrounds, Nagpur is one of the greenest cit-

MAHARASHTRA

ies in India. Most visitors are corporate types attending conferences, and for tourists, there is little reason to come here unless you're heading for Sevagram or one of the national parks nearby.

⌨ TRANSPORTATION. The **airport** (☎260348 or 260433) is 9km from the city center; a taxi there should not cost more than Rs250. The **Indian Airlines office** is next to the Institute of Science, Civil Lines (☎2526069 or 2533962, airport ☎2532025. Open daily 10am-5pm.) **Flights** go to: **Bhopal** (45min., Tu and Sa 1:05pm, US$80); **Delhi** (1½hr., 10:30pm, US$135); **Hyderabad** (1hr.; M, W, F 8pm; US$135); **Kolkata** (1½hr.; Su, W, F 7:30am; US$150); **Mumbai** (1¼hr., 7:30am and 8:45pm, US$120). **Gujarat Airways,** c/o Handling Agents, Globe Travels (☎2560141), operates a flight to **Pune** (1hr., 3 per week, US$85). **Trains** go to: **Kolkata** (19-20hr., 5-7 per day 6:40am-8:15pm, Rs297); **Chennai** (15-21hr., 4-5 per day 6:05am-1:25pm, Rs290); **Delhi** (14-22hr., 7-10 per day 2:05am-11:05pm, Rs290); **Hyderabad** (2-4 per day 5:20am-6pm, Rs190); **Mumbai** (14-18hr., 5-7 per day, Rs244); **Sevagram** (1hr., 8 per day 4:20am-3:55pm, Rs29). The **local bus stand,** 2km south of the railway station, has buses to: **Indore** (16hr., 5:30am, Rs224); **Jabalpur** (6 per day 9:45am-11pm, Rs120); **Wardha** (2hr., 28 per day 7:15am-8:30pm, Rs33). It is not advisable to travel by bus to Madhya Pradesh, as the road is in a sorry state. **Tongas** and **rickshaws** Rs10-15 per km.

◼◼▣ ORIENTATION AND PRACTICAL INFORMATION. Nagpur's **railway station** is on **Central Avenue;** the tracks split the city into eastern and western halves. Central Ave. becomes **Kingsway Road** after the station. South of and parallel to Kingsway Rd. is **Palm Road.** Farther south is the tourist center, **Sitabuldi,** with shops and hotels. North and west of Sitabuldi is **Civil Lines. Wardha Road (NH 7)** runs parallel to the train tracks. The **State Bank of India,** Kingsway Rd., near the railway station, exchanges currency and cashes traveler's checks at the **foreign exchange office** in the center of the building on the left. (☎2521196, ext. 416. Open M-F 10:30am-2pm.) **Trade Wings,** Lokmat Bhavan 4th fl., also exchanges currency. (☎2538437. Open M-F 9:30am-5pm, Sa 9:30am-1pm.) **Mayo Hospital,** Central Ave. (☎2728621), near the railway station, has a 24hr. **pharmacy.** Send email home at **Liberty Internet Cafe,** Church bldg., 2nd fl., Sadar (☎2811296), opp. Liberty cinema. Rs30 per hr. The **GPO** is on Palm Rd. (Open M-Sa 8am-10pm, Su 9am-1pm.) **Postal Code:** 440001.

▣▣▣ ACCOMMODATIONS, FOOD, AND ENTERTAINMENT. The high traffic of business travelers in Nagpur has created an abundance of accommodations. A luxury tax of 14% is often added to basic room rates. The thickest tangle of disorientingly similar budget hotels is on Central Ave. and its arteries. **Hotel Blue Diamond ❶,** 113 Central Ave., Dosar Chowk, is a good bet if you think you can handle the huge psychedelic honeycomb. The cheap rooms share a common bath. (☎2727461; www.hotelbluediamondnagpur.com. Singles Rs130-140; doubles Rs180-550.) Taking your 3rd right turn after MG Rd. onto Amravati Rd., you'll find the best-kept lodging secret in all of Nagpur. Nestled in the lush grounds of the Mure Memorial Hospital, the Christian-run guest house **Die Arche (the Ark) ❷,** Sitabuldi, has spotless, sunny rooms with hot water and shared balconies. The staff is spectacularly friendly and conscientious. Book ahead. (☎2523220, ext. 22. Doubles Rs250.) Another cluster of cheapies is in **Sitabuldi,** in the heart of Nagpur's market district. Head east along MG Rd. away from Gandhi's statue and take the 3rd left. Modi No. 3 hosts a slew of mid-range hotels, including **Hotel Amrta ❸,** Sitabuldi. Recently upgraded, Amrta's rooms are comfortable and luxurious. (☎2543762. Checkout 24hr. Singles Rs450-1000; doubles Rs550-1100. AmEx/MC/V.)

Nanking ❸, Residency Rd., Sardar, next to the Bata shoe store, is the best-known, best-value Chinese place in town. (Chicken Rs65-100; seafood Rs75-150; veggies Rs35-90. Open Tu-Su noon-3pm and 6-10pm.) From the overpass by the Gandhi statue, take a right instead of going up MG Rd. toward **Haldiram ❶,** which offers a small menu of entrees, supplemented by an epic dessert menu. Entrees Rs18-40. **The Zodiac,** 24 Central Bazaar Rd., in the Hotel Centre Point, a popular spot among locals, is the most happening pub-discotheque in town. (☎2520910. Open for "jam sessions" W 2-6pm, Rs150 per couple; discotheque Sa 10pm-1am, Rs300 per couple. Open daily 7:30am-11:30pm.)

NEAR NAGPUR: SEVAGRAM

Trains from Nagpur to Mumbai and Chennai will stop at Sevagram (1hr., 8 per day 4:20am-3:55pm, Rs37) or at Wardha (1hr., 12 per day 11:50am-8:40pm, Rs29), 8km away. Frequent MSRTC buses also run from Nagpur to Sevagram and Wardha (2hr., 28 per day, Rs35). Shared auto-rickshaws travel between Wardha and Sevagram (Rs5). Buses also travel from Wardha to the ashram (15min., every 10min. 7:30am-8pm, Rs5). Ashram open daily sunrise-sunset.

Mahatma Gandhi founded an ashram in Sevagram (literally the "Village of Service") after he left his Sabarmati retreat in Ahmedabad (see p. 193) in 1936. From Sevagram, Gandhi directed the Independence movement with his policy of non-violence. The community continues to thrive and is a paragon of simple living and self-sufficiency. The town is also the site of the **Nai Talimi Sangh,** the university founded here by Gandhi. Far from the bustle of the rest of urban India, Sevagram is clean, serene, and contemplative. Even people with no prior introduction to Gandhi's works and philosophy will find themselves enchanted by the lifestyle and outlook he promoted, embodied by his ashram.

Sevagram Ashram has kept all of its original buildings and Gandhi's personal belongings intact, complete with explanatory English signposts. Erudite Ashramites will also gladly answer questions. (Open daily sunrise to sunset.) A shop near the entrance sells Gandhi's books and *khadi*, the hand-spun cloth that played an important role in the freedom movement, signifying *swaraj* (self-sufficiency) and a rejection of the reliance upon imported textiles. The *chakra* (wheel) that Gandhi used to spin the cloth now figures as the central motif on India's flag. Opposite the ashram, the **Gandhi Picture Exhibition** displays a photographic timeline of the Mahatma's life. (Open Sa-Th 10am-6pm. Free.) The neighboring town of Wardha, **Magan Nadi,** the home of Gandhi's nephew, has a history of *khadi* on display.

The Center of Science for Villagers, 4km away, devotes itself to explaining Gandhi's philosophy of village-based economics. The corresponding NGO is devoted to improving village life through the production of organic products, or through improved sanitation. Those with a great interest in such topics should contact the project's director, Dr. Soham Pandya; short- and long-term volunteer opportunities can be arranged. (Ecological Science & Technology Division, Centre of Science for villages P.B. No 21, Karla Wardha 442001; soham_csv@rediff-mail.com. Open daily 9am-1pm and 2-5pm. Free.) Adjoining the center is the **Leprosy Home,** Manohordham, Dattapur, Wardha, where patients engage in a variety of tasks, including agriculture, shoe-making, weaving, and spinning. Volunteer opportunities are available. (☎2248081, 2240639, or 2242714.)

The women who run **Vinobaji's Ashram** in Paunar, 3km away, are a living testament to the success of the self-sufficient community that Gandhi envisioned. A peer and respected friend of Gandhi, Vinoba Bhave was a social activist and reformer who advocated land reform and the eradication of caste hierarchy. **Vinobaji's Museum** has exhibits explaining Gandhi's and his efforts to get landlords to give land to the destitute. (Open daily 9am-noon and 2-5pm. Free.)

MAHARASHTRA

🏚**Sevagram Ashram ❷** hosts up to 60 guests in its spare but comfortable rooms. It is an incredible experience to take part in the ashram life established and practiced by Gandhi. (Rooms Rs30. Meals Rs40). If the ashram is full or if you are too busy to participate in its many daily activities, **Yatri Nivas ❶**, opposite the ashram, has rooms and meals for the same price. 🏚**Vinobaji's Ashram ❶** (☎ 07152 243518), in Paunar (3km away), prefers to house only women and requires advance notification by mail (Vinobaji's Ashram, Paunar, District Wardha, Maharashtra, 442111) or by telephone. For food, **Goras Bhandar Wardha ❶**, in the main square of Sevagram near the Central Bank (look for the cow on the sign), sells delicious bread and milk. Try the hot milk with cardamom for Rs5. (Open daily 10am-5pm.) **Food stalls** also line the main street, but their hours vary, so if you're looking for a square meal, you're better off going to Wardha.

NORTHEAST INDIA

The closest thing India has to a lost frontier, the northeast states have both rugged wilderness and governmental authority that is contested almost every day. At the heart of the region lies the Brahmaputra Valley, surrounded by mountainous borders with Bhutan, China, Myanmar, and Bangladesh. The Northeast is inhabited in part by *adivasis* (indigenous peoples) who have had little exposure to the industrialization that has overrun other parts of the Subcontinent. In 1963, these peoples' struggles for autonomy led to the splintering of what was then the single state of Assam into the "Seven Sisters": Arunachal Pradesh, Nagaland, Manipur, Mizoram, Tripura, Meghalaya, and a pared down Assam. For administrative purposes, the central government also includes Sikkim in Northeast India, a strategy to help bridge the gap between the region and the rest of the Subcontinent—and to drag its enormous tourist potential out from under the shadow of political instability.

The tradition of armed insurrection in Tripura, Mizoram, Nagaland, and Assam has only partially abated, and political violence is common in the Northeast. Most opposition comes from tribal groups demanding greater independence, an issue complicated by rival factions and accusations that the government plays favorites. Dissidents also generally claim that India plunders the region's rich natural resources, especially Assam's oil, and neglects its social problems and decaying infrastructure. Political instability, coupled with fears of a Chinese invasion (China still claims Arunachal Pradesh), kept the region closed to foreigners until 1995. Assam, Meghalaya, and Tripura are now open to tourism. The other states require **Restricted Area Permits,** which can be extremely tough to get (see p. 436). While Arunachal has some breathtaking Himalayan scenery, much of Manipur and Mizoram, and the eastern strip of Nagal remain underdeveloped and politically volatile. Unfortunately, recent crack-downs on illegal logging have shifted black market capital into drug trafficking and have left a small but growing number of youth with devastating addiction problems. The Northeast's difficult terrain has also inspired some insurgents to re-invent themselves as cross-border terrorists, operating from just within the borders of adjoining countries.

Visiting the parks and villages of Assam and Meghalaya doesn't involve jumping through hoops, and they offer ample natural beauty and cultural attraction. Tripura has a proud cultural legacy and is a good gateway into rarely-visited Bangladesh. The Northeast's lack of tourists—a traveler can go weeks without seeing another foreigner—can be a welcome escape from the bustle of India's major cities and a journey far off the beaten path in the remotest corner of India.

HIGHLIGHTS OF NORTHEAST INDIA

Assam's **Kaziranga National Park** (p. 444) teems with wildlife, including a large population of protected rhinos.

One of the wettest places on earth, **Meghalaya** (p. 448) welcomes visitors with hospitality, sublime scenery, and well-watered greenery.

ASSAM অসম

Stretching 800km through the Brahmaputra Valley, Assam is the largest of the seven northeast states. Despite appearances in both the *Mahabharata* and the *Puranas*, Assam doesn't appear in history textbooks until the 13th century, when a group of Thai Buddhists—the Ahom—conquered the area and established their capital in Sibsagar. The cultural victory, however, belonged to the Hindus, who quickly converted their conquerors. Even today, Assamese speakers perform *puja* alongside Indian pilgrims. In the 19th century, the Burmese took over Assam, but they soon deferred to the British, who built Asia's first oil refinery and took advantage of the hilly terrain and seasonal rains to establish plantations that today produce over half of India's tea.

Geographically as well as culturally, Assam is divided into three regions. In the north, the Brahmaputra Valley combines alluvial lands and islands, hilly tea estates and pristine jungle and wilderness. A decade of lackadaisical reform has finally curbed organized deforestation, but poll-sensitive officials continue to turn a blind eye on rampant cutting for local village use. The Cachar Hills, in the middle area, are inhabited by indigenous peoples and are the best alternative to a visit to the states of Nagaland, Manipur, and Mizoram. Close to the border with Bangladesh in the south, the Barak River Valley is home to a sizable Muslim population, the majority of whom speak a dialect of Bengali.

Though the state is known for its racial melange, the tide of public opinion has turned drastically against the increasing flood of Bangladeshi immigrants. At times tribal conflicts have escalated into violent confrontations, usually in more rural areas. In addition to these ethnic tensions, frustration over the region's poor economy and the sense that the central government is neglectful have led to the formation of the United Liberation Front of Assam (ULFA), whose tactics of bombing, kidnapping, and racketeering have fortunately slowed. The dream of autonomy has also motivated indigenous groups to take up arms. The recent agreement between the government and Bodo rebels is being railed as a milestone for peace, yet has triggered renewed opposition from other organizations fighting for tribal independence, as well as Indians with no tribal affiliation, who claim *their* rights are being compromised. However, the Northeast carries a "special category states" status, which guarantees them at least 10 percent of each union ministry's budget. Major changes should lie ahead.

WARNING. The Northeast states are politically volatile, so you should check the travel advisories issued by your government before visiting. Terrorist groups, tribal militias, and loosely affiliated bandits are all in effect here. Occasional attacks on trains and buses have persisted into 2003, and buses in the south sometimes travel in police-escorted caravans. Many incidents of political violence are murders or kidnappings of political adversaries and occur in the village areas outside of urban centers. Although tourists are rarely targeted, it is important to keep abreast of news and avoid all travel at night.

THE RAP ABOUT RAPS. Foreign tourists can visit the states of Assam, Meghalaya, and Tripura just like they can the rest of India but a special Restricted Area Permit (RAP) is required for entry into Arunachal Pradesh, Nagal, and Manipur or Mizoram. The exact reason why is as unclear as the process of gaining access. Some say it's because the area is a defensive buffer zone against an encroaching China, while others claim it is to protect the indigenous cultures and their traditional way of life. Some people who actually live there lament the center's policies of exclusion as an unfair excuse to ignore the region's development, and

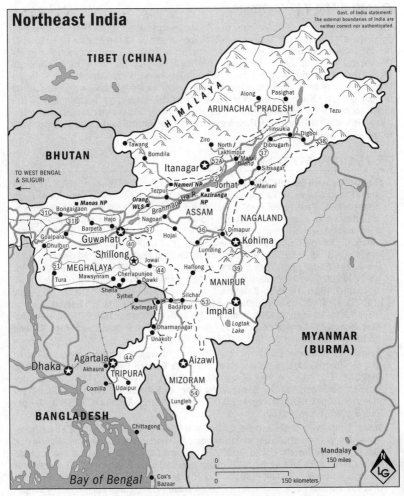

Northeast India

Govt. of India statement:
The external boundaries of India are
neither correct nor authenticated.

TIBET (CHINA)

HIMALAYA

ARUNACHAL PRADESH

Along • Pasighat

• Tezu

BHUTAN

Tawang •

Bomdila

Ziro • North /
Lakhimpur

Tinsukia • Digboi

Dibrugarh

38

37

Itanagar

52A

Majuli
Island

Sibsagar •

TO WEST BENGAL
& SILIGURI
←

Tezpur

Nameri NP

52

Jorhat •

• Mariani

Manas NP

Orang
WLS

Brahmaputra R.

Kaziranga
NP

31C Bongaigaon

31B

Hajo

Nagoan •

ASSAM

NAGALAND

Barpeta

Goalpara •
Dhulburi •

Guwahati

37

Hojai

36

Dimapur •

Kohima

Shillong

40

Jowai

Lumding •

51 MEGHALAYA

44

Haflong •

39

Tura

Mawsynram • Cherrapunjee

Dawki

MANIPUR

Shella

Sylhet •

Silchar •

53

Karimganj •

Badarpur •

Imphal

Dhaka

Agartala

Akhaura

44

TRIPURA

Comilla • Udaipur •

Dharmanagar •

Unakoti •

Logtak
Lake

MYANMAR
(BURMA)

Aizawl

MIZORAM

54

Lungleh •

BANGLADESH

Chittagong •

Mandalay •

150 miles

Bay of Bengal

• Cox's
Bazaar

0

0

150 kilometers

N

NORTHEAST INDIA

complain that a culture does not have to be frozen to be preserved. Officially, RAPs can be obtained in Delhi, but they are practically impossible to get. First go to the Ministry of Home Affairs in Khan Market (☎ 24633334 or 24612543. Open M-F 10am-noon). Here you will likely be directed to the Foreigners Registration Office, First Floor, Hansa Bhavan, Tilak Marg. They generally do not issue permits to solo travelers. As a tourist, your best bet is to apply as a group of at least four and with a governmental-approved travel agent or tour operator. The permit itself is free and allows for 5-15 days of travel, depending on the state. Alternatively, your chances of success increase if you are sponsored by a regional group such as an NGO. As a volunteer or aid worker, you can also be allowed to stay for longer periods. Though not unprecedented, sneaking across the border is never a good idea.

GUWAHATI ওৱাহাটি ☎ 0361

Though its name is derived from the Assamese phrase for the betel-nut market (*guwa hatt*), Guwahati is now much more—a gritty, sprawling metropolis that has surpassed the official seat of government at Dispur, and become effectively the capital of Assam. A crossroad of the Northeast, all the tribes, races, and cultures from the region's states pass through Guwahati's crowded bazaars. Just a few steps away from the bustle flows the majestic Brahmaputra, overlooked at its holiest point by Nilachal Hill. This is the site of the Kamakhya Temple, one of the most sacred of all Hindu *tirthas*. Despite its attractions, both sacred and mundane, Guwahati is little more than a gateway to the natural and cultural attractions to the south and east.

▐ TRANSPORTATION

Flights: Gopinath Bordelai Airport (☎2840279), is 24km from town in Borjhar. Taxis run from Paltan Bazaar (Rs300 or Rs70 per person to share). Buses go from Judge Field, next to Nehru Park, to VIP Point (every 30min., Rs3), 2km from the airport, where you can pick up an auto-rickshaw (Rs20). To get to Judge Field from the railway station, take a rickshaw (Rs5) or city bus. All three major airlines fly into Guwahati: **Indian Airlines, GS Rd.** (☎2264420), in Ganeshguri, a 10min. ride from Paltan Bazaar; **Jet Airways,** GNB Rd. (☎2662396), Guwahati Club; **Sahara Indian Airlines,** GS Rd. (☎2548676), Ulubari. Save some time by booking at **Network Travels** GS Rd. (☎2512700), in Paltan Bazaar. Open M-Sa 9am-5pm. To: **Agartala** (45min., daily 9:45am-2:45pm, US$55); **Bangkok** (2hr., Th 7:30pm, US$235); **Delhi** (2hr., daily 11:45am-3:40pm, US$220); **Dibrugarh** (35min., 12:45pm, US$65); **Imphal** (40min., daily 12:15-1:15pm, US$50); **Kolkata** (1hr., daily 11:40am-5:10pm, US$80). **Meghalaya Helicopter Service** (☎2840311) flies to the Air Force Helipad in **Upper Shillong** (30min., M-Sa 1-2 per day 9am-1:30pm, Rs725).

Trains: The main railway station in the Northeast, **Guwahati Junction,** is next to Paltan Bazaar. To book sleeper tickets, go to the **North Eastern Railways Reservation Bldg.** (☎2541799), 200m in front of the railway station. To: **Delhi** (36-41hr., 3-4 per day 8:15am-10:30pm, Rs442); **Dimapur,** for buses to **Kohima** and **Imphal** (5-6hr., 3 per day 2-10:30pm, Rs127); **Jorhat** (13hr., 7:30pm, Rs181); **Kolkata** (20-23½hr., 2-4 per day 5:30am-10pm, Rs370).

Buses: Both private buses and the Assam State Transport Corporation (ASTC) have buses of varying quality and service; whenever possible, check out the bus before you buy your ticket. **Network Travels,** GS Rd. (☎2522007), past MD Sah Rd., sends buses to: **Agartala** (24hr., 3:30 and 4pm, Rs330); **Dimapur** (10hr., 7-9:30pm, Rs220); **Itanagar** (10hr., 4 per day 7:30am-8:30pm, Rs200); **Jorhat** (7hr., 7 per day 6am-9:30pm, Rs140); **Kohima** (13hr., 6:30pm, Rs250); **Silchar** (12hr., 5 and 6pm, Rs215); **Siliguri** (14hr., 6pm, Rs250). For **Kasiranga** take a Jorhat bus to **Kohara** (4½hr., Rs110). All private buses leave from **Paltan Bazaar. Assam and Meghalaya State Transport** buses depart from the depot between the railway station and Paltan Bazaar. To: **Agartala** (24hr., 5 per day 4:30am-6:15pm, Rs335); **Jorhat** (7hr., 4 per day 8:30am-9:15pm, Rs140); **Shillong** (4hr., every hr. 6:30am-4pm, Rs60); **Silchar** (12hr., 6:30am and 5:45pm, Rs225); **Tezpur** (5hr., every hr. 7:30am-6:30pm, Rs78). **Sumos** are available at the same building (Rs 700 per day plus fuel, negotiable).

Local Transportation: Cycle-rickshaws and **auto-rickshaws** park on both sides of the railway station. City **buses** run on MG, AT, Shillong, and GS Rd. (Rs1-5 in the city). Buses go west along MG Rd. to Nilachal Hill and the Kamakhya Temple. **Ferries** run to Umananda (Rs10 per person), from Sukleshwar Ghat and the Deputy Commissioner's office. **River cruises** also leave from Sukleshwar Ghat (1hr., 5 and 5:30pm, Rs50).

NORHTEAST INDIA

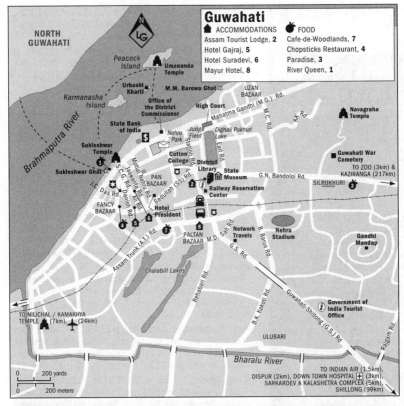

Guwahati

♠ ACCOMMODATIONS
Assam Tourist Lodge, **2**
Hotel Gajraj, **5**
Hotel Suradevi, **6**
Mayur Hotel, **8**

🍴 FOOD
Cafe-de-Woodlands, **7**
Chopsticks Restaurant, **4**
Paradise, **3**
River Queen, **1**

✴ 🛈 ORIENTATION AND PRACTICAL INFORMATION

The **Guwahati Junction Railway Station** is the heart of the town. South of it lies **Paltan Bazaar,** the departure point for buses. A 15min. bus ride along **Guwahati-Shillong (GS) Road** brings you to **Dispur,** where the government offices of Assam and other Northeastern states are located. Northwest of the station are the **Pan** and **Fancy Bazaars** (Rs5 rickshaw ride or a 10min. walk), the liveliest areas of town. **Mahatma Gandhi (MG) Road** runs behind Pan Bazaar along the river; government buses take this route to Kamakhya Temple (8km west) and Navagraha Temple (1km east).

Tourist Offices: Government of India Tourist Office, GS Rd. (☎2547407). On the left down a small lane to the G.L. Publication Complex, 400m after the Shree Hanuman Temple. From Paltan Bazaar, take a bus to Lachit Nagar. Open M-F 9:30am-5:30pm, Sa 9:30am-1pm. **Assam State Tourism Office,** Station Rd. (☎2544475), in front of the Tourist Lodge. Arranges package tours to Kaziranga (2 days, Rs2000) and North Cachar Hills (2 days, Rs2350), among others. Open M-Sa 10am-4:15pm.

Currency Exchange: State Bank of India, MG Rd. (☎2543576). International banking division is on the 3rd floor. Open for exchange M-F 10am-3pm, Sa 10am-1pm.

Police: In Pan Bazaar (☎2540106) and Paltan Bazaar (☎2540126). The **Superintendent of Police** (☎2540278) is near the District Court. Open M-Sa 10am-4:30pm.

NORTHEAST INDIA

THE LOCAL LEGEND

DIVINE DISMEMBERMENT

Shiva, an ascetic, fell in love with the beautiful, high-bred goddess Sati, and she was unfortunate enough to return his love. Her father, Daksha, disapproved. He snubbed Shiva, and at his grand sacrifice celebration, he invited every god but the vagabond groom. Furious, Sati flung herself weeping on the sacrificial pyre, where her tears boiled away and she burned alive. When Shiva learned of his wife's demise, he lifted her blackened body and sobbed so convulsively that the universe shook. To save the cosmos from being shaken into a pile of rubble, the god Vishnu stepped in and hacked at the charred corpse with his *chakra* (discus). With the corpse gone, Shiva was consoled, and the universe was saved. The spots on earth where bits of Sati's body landed became *shakti pithas*. These sacred sites, which number 4, 51, or 108, depending on who's counting, began as independent goddess shrines, but the myth of Sati's dismemberment provides a unifying thread. The most important *shakti pithas* are those from the most potent parts of Sati; Guwahati's Kamakhya Temple is the greatest of them all.

Hospital: Down Town Hospital, GS Rd. (☎2531003), Dispur, near Capitol Complex. Has fluent English speakers and a **24hr. pharmacy.**

Post Office: GPO, Meghdoot Bhawan (☎2541294), at AOB Rd. and MG Rd. near Pan Bazaar. Open M-F 10am-5pm, Sa 10am-3pm. **Postal Code:** 781001.

🏠 ACCOMMODATIONS

Paltan Bazaar has most of the transit hotels, if you can put up with the honks and growls of night buses. Pan Bazaar is quieter, cleaner, and more upscale, but you pay for these comforts.

🏨 **Mayur Hotel,** AT Rd. (☎2560824), opposite the ASTC bus station in Pan Bazaar. Floor-to-ceiling renovations in 2003 were so successful that now all taps dispense mineral water from a huge tank on the roof. Clean rooms have TVs and windows with city views. No liquor or meat allowed, but the restaurant serves good veg. dishes. Singles Rs132-176; doubles Rs209-276. ❶

Assam Tourist Lodge, Station Rd. (☎2544475), in front of the railway station. Spacious doubles have a balcony, a dressing room, and an attached bathroom with hot water. Popular bar. Singles Rs230; doubles Rs290. ❷

Hotel Suradevi, M. Nehru Rd. (☎2545050), 100m from SS Rd. Cheap and comfortable but windowless rooms make this the best value near Pan Bazaar. Dorms Rs70; singles Rs90-120; doubles Rs140-190. ❶

Hotel Gajraj, SS Rd. (☎2525071), between HB Rd. and Danish Rd. Rooms have squat toilets, TVs, and mosquito nets, but no linen. Singles Rs190; doubles Rs140-190. ❶

🍴 FOOD

Assamese cuisine features *khar* made from dried banana peels, *pitika* (potatoes pureed with vegetables) and fish, rice, and mustard. Most *dhabas* hover around the major intersections near the railway station, especially Paltan Bazaar.

🍽 **Paradise,** GN Bandoloi Rd., past Silpukuri pond. Excellent Assamese dishes in a soothing environment. The *thali* (Rs55) comes in 11 different varieties, including fried fish and chili chicken. Beer Rs65. Open daily 10am-3:30pm and 6-9:30pm. ❷

🍽 **Cafe-de-Woodlands,** AT Rd., opposite the Pan Bazaar bridge. A shot of southern-Indian comfort. The veg. *thali* special (Rs36-48) is incredible. Open daily 8:30am-9:30pm. ❷

Chopsticks Restaurant, SS Rd., in the Dynasty Hotel. Quality Chinese, Indian, and Continental food (Rs100-160) served amidst a forest of cast-iron lamp posts. Open daily 7am-11pm. AmEx/MC/V. ❸

River Queen, anchors at Sukleshwar Ghat. Although the food is not spectacular, the view from the boat of the late-afternoon Brahmaputra is. Prawn *masala* (Rs70). 1hr. river cruise leaves at 5pm (Rs50). Open daily 10am-8pm. ❸

SIGHTS

NILICHAL AND KAMAKHYA TEMPLE. Several crisscrossing paths lead up Blue Hill to 10 shrines dedicated to the various manifestations of the all-powerful mother-goddess, Shakti. By far the most important site is the Hindu Kamakhya Temple, built on the site where it is said that the goddess Sati's vulva fell when she was cut into pieces by Vishnu. The current temple, with its beehive-shaped spire, was built by King Naranarayana in 1665, after a brahmin priest who converted to Islam torched the original. Inside, the Mother-Goddess is worshipped in the form of a *yoni*, a crack in a rock, rather than as a sculpted image. The ancient stone bleachers that rise from the base of the temple provide seating to spectators eager to see sacrifices—goats tied to the posts at the main temple gate each morning are decapitated by the evening. The shrine inside the temple is open to non-Hindus; purchase a ticket from the window at the top of the stairs (Rs100, Rs500 to bypass the oft-long line) and bring a good deal of change for the host of guardian priests. Another shrine there is the peaceful **Bhubaneshwari Temple,** under a pipal tree at the top of Nilickal. From the Kamakhya bus stand, bear right and walk 20min. along the scenic route uphill. (*From Guwahati, ASTC bus #15 (Rs5) leaves Judge Field, opposite Nehru Park up the winding road to Kamakhya Temple—hop on anywhere along MG Rd. Other buses heading west on MG Rd. drop off at the bottom of the hill; catch a taxi or climb the path to the temple (30min.). The last bus leaves Kamakhya at 6pm.*)

BRAHMAPUTRA RIVER. The mighty Brahmaputra ("Son of Brahma") surges past the city's north edge. Though the river may look serene, during the rainy season it frequently overflows and washes away riverside settlements. Don't miss the beautiful virgin shoreline, as it may disappear with Delhi's plans for a US$3 million waterfront development. The run-down **Umananda Temple** to Shiva, on a small island in the middle of the river, has the best views. On the rocky outcrop nearby is the **Urbashi Kharti,** a British-built yardstick used to measure monsoon water levels; local legend says it's actually a beautiful woman transformed into a rock. Assam Tourism maintains two pleasant **riverfront parks,** one at Mathura Mohen Barowa Ghat, in Uzan Bazaar, and another at Sukleshwar Ghat, just east of the temple. Here the diminutive 1874 "Gateway of Guwahati" stands as the only piece of British brick architecture to survive the 1897 earthquake. (*Open daily 9am-7pm. Rs2.*) The Jolporee (5:30pm) and the River Queen (5pm) lead 1hr. **river cruises** from Sukleshwar Ghat. (*Rs50.*) Ferries run from Sukleshwar Ghat and the Deputy Commissioner's Office to Umananda. (*7am-4pm. Rs10 to share, or Rs100 for the boat.*)

NAVAGRAHA TEMPLE. Perched on a hill over the city, the Navagraha ("nine planets") Temple provides an ideal location for stargazing. An echo chamber holds nine *lingas* dedicated to the heavenly bodies identified by ancient Indians: the sun, the ascending and descending nodes of the moon, Mercury, Venus, Mars, Jupiter, and Saturn. A family of wild, territorial monkeys patrol the premises. (*On Citrachaila Hill in east Guwahati. Hire an auto-rickshaw from MC Rd., or take Navagrala Rd. past the War Memorial and through the gate at the end of the road. Open daily 10am-6pm.*)

NORTHEAST INDIA

OTHER SIGHTS. Assam State Museum, across from Dighali Pukhuri pond, has Assamese cultural artifacts, Japanese WWII weaponry, and an exhibit of photographs and documents from the Indian independence movement. The library next door is stocked with literature on regional cultures. *(Both open summer Tu-Sa 10am-5pm; winter 10am-4:15pm; closed 2nd and 4th Sa. Rs2.)* A cultural center, the **Sarkardev A Kalashetra Complex,** recently opened on the 6th mile of GS Rd. Named for an Assamese artisan who devoted his life to the promotion of regional culture, the center is a theme park of all things Assamese. The temple contains temples, an open-air amphitheater, a contemporary art gallery, and a beautifully landscaped "Heritage Park," which contains sculptures, paintings, and mosaics depicting scenes of rural Assamese life. *(Take a bus along GS Rd., or hire an auto-rickshaw from the Paltan Bazaar (Rs60). Open daily 10am-7:30pm. Rs5.)* The **Guwahati War Cemetery,** on a side street south of Navagraha Temple, is a quiet resting place for Guwahatis who perished in WWII.

TEZPUR ☎03712

Tezpur, the "town of blood," is a pleasant little place with a grim mythological past. According to legend, Hari (Krishna) and Hara (Shiva, in the form of Banasura) did battle here and drenched the town with their blood. Today, the red stains on the street are from *betel*-chewers. At **Da-Parbatia,** the stone foundation and gate are all that remain of one of the oldest temples in Assam. **Agnigargh,** 5km out of town, on a hill facing the river, contains the ruins of a rampart. However, the main reason to come to Tezpur is its location on the north bank of the Brahmaputra, close to Orang, Nameri, and Kaziranga National Parks. The city is also the gateway to the western part of Arunachal Pradesh, via the breathtaking Bomdila Road to **Tawang Gompa** (permits required; see **The Rap about RAPs,** p. 436).

Buses arrive at **Kekarapul,** the ASTC bus station, a 10min. walk from the town center. Buses run to: **Guwahati** (5hr., frequent 5am-3pm, Rs78); **Jorhat** (5hr., every hr. 6am-1:30pm, Rs55) via **Kohora** (2hr., Rs35); **Siliguri** (2:45 and 3:30pm, Rs267). The road opposite the bus station slopes downhill to Cole Lake, in Chitralekha Park, and the **public bus stand** (where you can catch cheaper, later, and less comfortable buses). As you exit the ASTC bus station, turn right on **Kabarkhana Road** to reach two blocks of travel companies. **Himalayan Holidays** (☎223580) runs Tata **Sumos** (4½hr.; 5:30, 11:30am, 12:30, 1:30pm; Rs160) and a bus (5hr., 5:30am, Rs130) to Bomdila. Another right turn connects to the **police station** (☎232800) and the **main road,** which runs parallel to Kabarkhana Rd. There are several **Internet** cafes on the main road. Walk one block past the police station and three blocks right to reach the **post office,** which exchanges dollars and pounds at outrageous rates. (☎220183. Open M-Sa 10am-4pm.) **Postal Code:** 784001.

Hotel Green View Lodge ❶, on the main road, 200m from the police station, has big, clean, quiet rooms. (☎230667. Singles Rs70-100; doubles Rs140-200.) **Basant Hotel ❷,** on the main road, 100m from the police station, is more expensive but has posh rooms with TVs and quality room service. (☎230831. Singles Rs165-195; doubles Rs220-350.) The **Tourist Lodge ❶,** Kabarkhana Rd., dispenses travel advice about local parks. (☎221026. Dorms Rs100; doubles Rs260.) **Flora Restaurant and Bar ❷,** Jonaki Cinema Rd., near the police station, is the local favorite for beer (Rs55) and food. Mood lighting is in effect at all hours of the day; bring a flashlight to see your food. (Open daily 10am-10pm.)

NATIONAL PARKS

Assam's national parks have now standardized rates. Adults Rs250 per day; camera fee Rs500; video fee Rs1000; vehicle fee Rs150.

NAMERI NATIONAL PARK

From Tezpur, take a bus from the private bus stand to Balipara (1hr., Rs7). Switch to a Bhalukpong Rd. bus, and get off at the Nameri elephant gate (45min., Rs8). From the road it is a 2.3km walk to the Forest Ranger Office and the ECO Camp, on the southern bank of the Bhoroli River. The camp is run by the Bhoroli Angling Association and sometimes fills up, so book in advance. Pay the Rs250 daily fee at the Forest Ranger Office (open daily 8am-5pm), and the ranger will arrange a ferry across the river.

Nameri comprises 220 sq. km of evergreen forest between the northern bank of the Jia Bhoroli River and the foothills of the Himalayas. Ideal elephant country, it is also known for orchids, a steadily increasing tiger population, and the endangered white winged wood duck. The best way to visit the park is on a 2hr. walk at sunrise or sunset, the only times you will see any wildlife. A guide, with rifle, will accompany you and point out birds, flowers, and footprints of fierce creatures. However, only 45 tigers live in the park, so it is unlikely that you will spot one. Friendly range officer **Mr. Sarma** arranges low-key rafting trips (3-4hr., Rs750). Catch-and-release angling is also popular, but you have to bring your own equipment and purchase a permit (Rs50) from the Divisional Forest Office in Dhulabari, Tezpur. (Open 10am-4pm.) The **ECO Camp ❶** next door to the Forest Ranger Office has luxury tents (Rs950, with attached bath Rs1050) and two dorms sharing a common bath (Rs120). Meals are served from 7am to 8pm (veg. plate Rs50).

ORANG WILDLIFE SANCTUARY

From Tezpur, take the Guwahati bus to Orang (1hr., Rs10). From here, another bus goes to Silbari, a 2km walk from the park. Alternatively, a car can be hired in Tezpur (Rs200). To stay in the park overnight you need permission from the Divisional Forest Officer in Mangaldoi located between Guwahati and Tezpur on most bus routes.

This "mini-Kaziranga" packs rhinos, elephants, rare birds (including the Bengal florican), and a few tigers into just 76 sq. km. Located at the edge of a village of Bangledeshi Muslims, 32km from Tezpur on the northern bank of the Brahmaputra, quiet Orang makes a great one-night getaway. Accommodations consist of two basic **forest bungalows ❶** (Rs60), the better of which is within the confines of the park. To stay overnight, contact **S.P. Vashishth,** Divisional Forest Officer in Mangaldoi, Barrang District (☎0914 230022, evenings 0914 230138; vashi_mld@epatra.com). Bring your own food; the ranger might help you cook.

MANAS NATIONAL PARK

*Expeditions into the park can be quite pricey, as they require both a 4-man guide and a security detail (Rs400-500 per day) and a sumo rental from Guwahata. To plan a visit, contact **Andjit Raban**, head of the **Tiger Project Office** at Baspeta Road, 42km from the park. (☎03666 261412 or 260288. Open 10:30am-4:30pm.) The park entry fee is Rs100 per person per day plus Rs150 for the vehicle.*

One of the most beautiful wildlife parks in all of Asia, Manas National Park is a UNESCO World Heritage Site and home to rhinos, elephants, and tigers. After serving as home to violent Bodo (National Democratic Front of Bodoland) rebels for many years, Manas reopened its doors to visitors in October 2002, several months in advance of the February 2003 Bodo Accord; however, it is still a good idea to check the latest news before entering the park. You can stay at the Assam State Tourism's Barpeta Road Lodge (☎03666 260749) or in the **Forest Department bungalows ❶** at Mathanguri, inside the park, for only Rs100.

▓ KAZIRANGA NATIONAL PARK

From Guwahati take a Jorhat bus to Kohora, the gate of the park (6hr., frequent 6am-9:30pm, Rs80). From Tezpur, take the Jorhat bus to Kohora (2hr., hourly 6am-8pm, Rs30). From Jorhat, take a Guwahati bus (3hr., frequent 6:15am-9pm, Rs40). The sanctuary is open from November to late April; during monsoon season, animals flee the flooded marshland for the muddy roads, making passage dangerous or impossible.

Kaziranga National Park, located in the heart of tea-country, 217km from Guwahati, is Assam's top tourist attraction and the most scenic park in the Northeast. Most visitors come here to see the Indian **one-horned rhinoceros**—Kaziranga is home to 65% of the world's population of this endangered species. Since 1966, the park's rhino population has tripled, despite the best efforts of horny horn hunters (the phallic snout is a much-coveted aphrodisiac). There is no doubt that the rhinos are the stars of the show, but Kaziranga's cast of supporting characters is also impressive. Your chances of seeing a tiger are close to nil (the park has only 86), but Asiatic wild buffalo (or *gaur*), equipped with mammoth horns, are all over the place. The park also houses four kinds of deer and packs of wild elephants. For bird-lovers, there are over 478 species, including fish eagles, gray-headed pelicans, and even the rare and much sought-after Bengal florican.

The 430 sq. km sanctuary is a broad floodplain of the Brahmaputra River. Grasslands and swamp give way to jungle, which rises up to deciduous forests and eventually to the evergreen slopes of the Karbi Anglong Hills. The park consists of four administrative zones, although rising annual floods and subsequent migrating wildlife cause so much havoc that several huge additions have been proposed. The **Forest Range Office** can say if there are any new sections to visit. (☎ 03776 2662428. Open M-Sa 7:30am-noon and 2:30-5:30pm.) The **Central Region,** or **Kaziranga Range,** starts at Kohora, the park's primary entrance and consists of wet grassland and forest filled with rhinos, elephants, buffalo and deer. The **Western Range,** at Baguri, 11km from Kohora, is pure grassland and has significant numbers of elephant and rhino; afternoons are the most likely time for sightings. The **Eastern Range,** at Azoratoli, 25km from Kohora, features a pelican colony and other major bird habitats. The barren **Burapahar Range,** at Ghorakati, is closed to the public.

There are two ways to visit the park—by jeep and by elephant. Jeeps cover an entire range in a matter of hours, but the best view of the animals is from the back of an elephant, as they are able to get much closer to the animals. Arrangements for either form of transport are made at the **Park Office** in Kohora (the sign outside says Interpretation Center; open daily 7:30-9:30am, 2-3:30pm, and 8-9pm). Jeep safaris depart from the office between 7:30 and 9:30am or 2 and 3pm. Each jeep holds eight people, so latch onto a larger group to save money. Punen Gogoi is an informed guide who speaks good English (☎ 03776 2662549). Elephant rides (1hr., 5:30 and 6:30am, Rs750) must be scheduled the night before. You will also need a jeep shuttle to the mounting point (Rs150), which is too far inside the park to walk. There are normally enough people around to split the cost for the short, popular central route (3hr., Rs680), but it is harder to find people for the western (4hr., Rs550) and eastern (6hr., Rs950) routes.

Buses arriving in the park drop visitors off on the side of National Highway 37, near a giant gate shaped like an elephant. Follow the sign to the tourist area, on the opposite side of the road, behind the **police station** (☎ 03776 2662426). After 10min., you will find the Kohora village, the **Park Office,** and the accommodations. Assam Tourism runs four lodges. To the left, **Bonani Lodge ❷** has spacious rooms and enormous bathrooms. (☎ 03776 2662423. Singles Rs220-350; doubles Rs280-410.) The reception at Bonani also deals with bookings for **Bonoshree ❷,** which has pleasant garden-view rooms (singles Rs210; doubles Rs260) and **Kunjaban ❶,** which has dorms (Rs50). To the right of the road is **Aranya ❹,** the park's attempt at a luxury hotel. (☎ 03776 2662429. Singles Rs540;

doubles Rs660.) The **Karbi-Anglong Forest Range Office,** along the way, books rooms. **Hotel Anindita ❶,** on the road into the park, is the tastiest dhaba around. (Veg. plate Rs20. Open daily 6:30am-8:30pm.) **Rhinorica Restaurant ❶,** by the police station, and the newer **Prashaanti Restaurant ❶,** across from the park office, serve virtually the same Indian and limited Contintental menu. (Open 8am-9pm.)

JORHAT   ☎ 0376

Mass exodus to a better life in Guwahati has left a languid Jorhat in its wake, although the city continues to be the commercial and academic center of eastern Assam. Wide streets and polite traffic make this city a good resting point en route to somewhere else. Buses stop here on their way to Sibsagar (seat of the Ahom empire for 500 years), the Gibbon Wildlife Sanctuary, and Majuli, a huge island and the site of several prominent *satras* (Vaishnava monasteries).

▐▄ TRANSPORTATION. Rowriah Airport (☎ 2340881) is 5km from Jorhat. **Jet Airways** flies to **Kolkata** (2¾hr., Th and Su 2:35pm, US$80) via **Guwahati** (50min., US$40). **Indian Air** also has flights to **Kolkata** (1¼hr., Tu and Sa 1:30pm, US$76). **Trains** run to **Guwahati,** but foreign tourists are not allowed to take them since the train passes through Nagaland for a fraction of its journey. The **ASTC bus station,** AT Rd. (☎ 2320307), sends buses to: **Gibbon Wildlife Sanctuary** via **Mariani** (45min., 3pm, Rs7); **Guwahati** via **Kohora** (7hr., every hr. 6:15am-1:30pm and 9pm, Rs140); **North Lakhimpur** (9hr., 6 and 6:30am, Rs125); **Sibsagar** (2hr., every 30min. 4:45am-5pm, Rs20). One block west, past JB College Rd., **private buses** line AT Rd., with schedules and fares similar to ASTC. **Network and Royal Tours** have the best luxury coaches. The **public bus stand,** at the intersection of AT Rd. and MG Rd., has local service to **Nimati Ghat,** where you can catch the ferry to **Majuli** (45min.; 7:45, 8:45, 9:45am, 1:30, 3pm; Rs8).

▟▐ ORIENTATION AND PRACTICAL INFORMATION. Jorhat is 80km east of Kaziranga, on the southern banks of the Brahmaputra. The town centers on a quadrant defined by **AT Road** and **KB Road,** running east-west, and **MG Road** and **Gar Ali Road,** running north-south. The **tourist office** (☎ 2321579) is on MG Rd., near the public bus stand. **Pelican Travels,** MG Rd., opposite the police station, books flights. (☎ 2321128. Open M-Sa 10am-5pm.) **State Bank of India,** on AT Rd., next to the Office of the Deputy Commissioner, between the ASTC bus station and the public bus stand, exchanges foreign currency. (☎ 2320098. Open M-F 10am-4pm.) You'll find the **police station** (☎ 2320022) next to the tourist office. The **post office** is near the bus stand. (☎ 2320045. Open M-Sa 10am-5pm.) **Postal Code:** 785001.

▐▐ ACCOMMODATIONS AND FOOD. Hotels crowd AT Rd., though most are noisy and dingy. The nicer options cluster on quiet Biman Baruah Rd., next to the ASTC bus station, but you pay for the convenience. **Hotel Dilip ❷** has compact rooms with attached bathrooms and color TV. (☎ 2321610. Singles Rs200; doubles Rs300.) **Arbees Guest House ❶,** in Restaurant La Belle, on AT Rd., 400m west of the ASTC bus station, has the most pleasant budget digs, thanks to a small, planted courtyard. (☎ 2320562. Singles Rs85; doubles Rs175.) The **Assam Tourist Lodge ❷,** in the same building as the Tourist Office, has spacious doubles with mosquito nets. (☎ 2321579. Singles Rs176; doubles Rs260.) The **Food Hut ❷,** near the police station on MG Rd., serves good Indian, especially Assamese, food. The duck and pigeon *thalis* (Rs50) provide a yummy change of pace. (Open daily 9:30am-9:30pm). The excellent, air-conditioned **Belle Amie's ❷,** on Gas Ali Rd., opposite the mosque, has an exhaustive Chinese and Indian menu—if you can get past the packed bakery and snack stand. (☎ 2323142. Open daily 11am-9:30pm.)

NEAR JORHAT ☎ 0376

 MAJULI

Buses leave Jorhat from the public bus stand for Nimati Ghat (45min.; 7:45, 8:15, 9:15 9:45am, 1:30, 3pm; Rs8), where ferries cross to Kamalabari Ghat (2hr.; 9, 10:30am, 2:30, 4pm; Rs10-15). From there, buses continue to Kamalabari, the largest town on the island (20min., Rs10), Garamur (40min., Rs15), and finally another ferry to North Lakhimpur. To get back, buses leave Garamur 2hr. before the ferry for Kamalabari, where they wait until 30min. before the ferry departs for Nimati Ghat (2-2½hr.; 7, 8, 9am, 2pm; Rs10-15). In the afternoon you may spot the endangered Gangetic dolphin.

Despite the top ranking that locals and Assam's tourist board like to claim, Majuli is actually only the world's sixth-largest inhabited island. Nevertheless, the vast landscape overflows with rich nature, indigenous culture, and, from June to August, the waters of the same Brahmaputra River that isolate it from the mainland. The peaceful remoteness of the island was perhaps what attracted Shankardeva, the 16th-century Vaishnava poet-saint, who established *satras* (Vaishnava monasteries) here. While the Shaivite *sadhus* who congregate along the Ganga worship Shiva, the song-and-dance-oriented Vaishnava cult considers Vishnu (Krishna) the supreme god. The roads between *satras* lead through fields filled with birds (such as the great stork), as well as backwoods villages, where a cup of *chai* with locals may be more fun than a *bhajan* singalong with the priests.

Foreign tourists are supposed to register at Kamalabari's **police station** (☎2573429), by the bridge. There is a **post office** in Kamalabari. (☎2573421. Open M-F 9:30am-4pm, Sa noon-4pm.) **Postal Code:** 785106. Limited lodging is available at Garamur's **Majuli Circuit House** (☎2320712; singles Rs40), but you must first visit the **Office of the Deputy Commissioner** in Jorhat. (☎2320496. Open M-F 10am-4:30pm.) However, staying at one of the *satras*, either in the guest house or directly with the monks, is a more enriching experience. The only alternatives to dining with monks or locals are a few mediocre *dhabas* along the main road.

While at its peak, Majuli was blessed with 65 *satras*. The river's constant war against the shoreline has brought that number down to 22, a handful of which are most worth visiting. To reach **Kamalabari Satra ❶,** where the monks are friendly and fond of dancing, take the dirt road by the bridge and walk 15min. along the river. Most Indian tourists check into the guest house here, which has common, Indian-style baths and tidy rooms off breezy hallways. (☎2573302. Rs60 per person.) **Auniati Satra ❶,** 5km outside Kamalabari, is the largest in Assam. Over 450 monks live (from the age of 6) in the broad, cleanly swept quads, and will eagerly offer travelers a spare bed and some of their staple *roti* and molasses. There is a museum-library stocked with ancient texts, decorative dishes and swords from the Ahom period. (Open daily 10am-5pm. Rs30.) The ritualized morning prayers (7-10am) may leave a more lasting impression. To reach Auniati, turn left at the main paved intersection in Kamalabari with the police station behind you. After 1km, pass the bamboo bridge and bear left when the road splits. The *satra* and guest house are across the big timber bridge ahead. (☎2573450. Rs75 per person.)

Garamur Satra ❶, 1km from the Circuit House, is the most famous of the island's *satras* due to the patronage of Sibsagar's Ahom kings. Today, only fallen stone pillars, a rusted canon, and a dozen original wooden effigies testify to this glorious past. Some monks are married and have families, so the community (one of the few non-celibate ones on the island) feels like a village. The guest house has flowers and a few rooms just outside the gate. (☎2574500. Rs50 per person.) The other large monastery, **Dakhimpat Satra,** is an 18km walk from Kamalabari, but the route rewards with beautiful scenic views. Passing vehicles will usually give you a ride.

NORHTEAST INDIA

■ GIBBON WILDLIFE SANCTUARY

From Jorhat, take a bus to Mariami (45min., Rs7) and then hire a rickshaw or walk 5km to the ranger's office, following signs for the Indo-US Primate Project. Entrance fee Rs250.

Twenty kilometers south of Jorhat, the Gibbon Wildlife Sanctuary is home to the largest number of primate species in India. Seven kinds of monkeys swing from the jungle branches here, making this the best spot to catch a glimpse of rare macaques and capped languors. The **Forest Department Bungalow ❷** has two doubles and staff that will cook for guests. To stay there, obtain a permit from the **Office of the Divisional Forest Officer** in Jorhat, at the end of the road between the post office and the Jorhat Government Boy's school, after it becomes an unpaved path. (☎ 2320008 or 2320456. Rs200-300 per person.) It's worth the hassle; wildlife is best observed at sunrise and sunset, and once you pay the entry fee you are free to wander throughout the forest as you please.

SILCHAR ☎ 03482

In the middle of the Barak River valley, Silchar, the biggest town in southern Assam, is a transit point for the lucky Manipur and Mizoram inner-line permit-holders, as well as for anyone bound for Tripura from Assam or Meghalaya. Silchar itself has nothing to distinguish it from any other small, rural, goats-on-the-sidewalk town of the Northeast. Travelers may want to take the 4hr. train ride north to the Cachar Hills, the best place to experience the indigenous groups of the northeastern hills. Foreigners need a permit before they can hop aboard one of the many Sumos that leave Silchar for Imphal and Aizawl, both restricted areas (see **The Rap about RAPs**, p. 436). The check-posts are heavily guarded.

▌ TRANSPORTATION. Given the inaccessibility of Nagaland to foreign visitors and the precarious condition of the Silchar-Imphal road, flying is the only practical way to get into Manipur. The **Indian Airlines** office is on Club Rd. by the police circle. (☎ 2245544. Open M-Sa 10am-4:30pm.) **Flights** connect Silchar to **Imphal** (30min., Tu and Sa 11:10am, US$35) and **Kolkata** (1hr., M-Sa 11:10am or 1:10pm, US$85). **Trains** go via **Haflong** to **Lumding,** where connections can be made to **Guwahati** (12½-14hr. to Lumding, 3-4hr. onward journey to Guwahati; 7:30am and 6:30pm; Rs185). Private **buses** leave from Club Rd. for: **Agartala** (14hr., 6:30am and 6:30pm, Rs180); **Aizwal** (9hr., 7pm, Rs165); **Guwahati** (13hr., 7am and 4-6pm, Rs215) via **Shillong** (10hr., Rs165); **Imphal** (12hr., 3:30am, Rs195). **Sumos** also leave from Club Rd. and are a much better option if you want to get to **Aizwal** (5-6hr., Rs200). Many bus companies operate around Club Rd. **Capital Travels** (☎ 2245761) has a branch near the railway station.

▌▌ ORIENTATION AND PRACTICAL INFORMATION. The Railway Station is an extension of Park Rd.; most buses arrive near Club Rd. **No currency exchange** is available in Silchar. The closest option is the State Bank of India in Karimganj, 45km away. The **Superintendent of Police** (☎ 2245873) lives on Park Rd., and he should be able to answer permit-related questions. **Postal Code:** 788001.

▌▌ ACCOMMODATIONS AND FOOD. Hotel Ellora ❶, near the police circle on Club Rd., is set back from traffic in a courtyard retreat. All rooms have fan, TV, and attached bath; deluxe rooms also have mosquito nets. (☎ 2247412. Dorms Rs50; singles Rs130-190; doubles Rs260.) **Assam Tourist Lodge ❶,** on Park Rd., a Rs5 rickshaw ride from Club Rd. or the train station, has large rooms with mosquito nets and a bathroom. (☎ 2232376. Dorms Rs50; singles Rs132; doubles Rs210.) **Bholanath Bakery ❶,** near the train station, sells fresh, crisp pastries and breads. (Open daily 7am-10pm.) **Restaurant Sreyashi ❷,** adjacent to Hotel Ellora, serves good Chinese and Indian food. Egg *masala* Rs40. (Open daily 10am-9:30pm.)

NORTHEAST INDIA

MEGHALAYA

Travelers who take the hilly roads through Meghalaya discover why the state is called the "Abode of Clouds." Cool mists shroud the slopes, bursting into violent rains that douse the valley and swell the Brahmaputra River. The rain makes Cherrapunjee and Mawsynram two of the wettest places on earth and supports a wealth of vegetation, from pine forests to steaming jungles. Three indigenous groups inhabit Meghalaya: the Garos (or Achiks) live in the Garo Hills to the west, and the Khasi and Jaintias inhabit the Khasi Hills to the east.

In the 19th century, Welsh and Italian missionaries and the officers of the British Raj arrived on the scene. The missionaries created stressed education, now demonstrated by Meghalaya's claim to have the second-highest literacy rate in India. In contrast, the British were more keen on using the hills as an escape from the torturous heat of the Brahmaputra plains. Having defeated (and beheaded) the local independence hero, U Tirot Sing Syiem, during the 1830s, they established a hill station in Cherrapunjee, only to be driven out by the rains. They decamped to Shillong, which they converted into the capital of Assam and furnished with such modern necessities as a golf course and tennis club. To this day the missionaries are remembered with fondness, while memories of the British are all but gone.

In 1972, Meghalaya gained independence from Assam and became India's 21st state. Despite the various outside influences, Meghalayans have managed to hold onto their unique traditional institutions, such as matrilineal descent and property inheritance. Offices, families, and bazaars are run primarily by women. Democratic values are supported by regional *syiem* (kings) who have long endorsed self-government through public discourse and referenda.

Opened to unrestricted tourism in 1995, Meghalaya, is only now beginning to attract foreign travelers. Most people come to enjoy the cool weather of Shillong and the Khasi Hills and to visit the wildlife sanctuaries of West Meghalaya. A small band of hard-core spelunkers return each year in January and February, when low water levels allow miles of the hills to be explored from the inside. Based on the volume of new caves mapped, the state was the world's fastest-growing caving region in 2002. The bumpy road that cuts west from Shillong to Dhulbari provides adventurous travelers the opportunity to explore the hill cultures in greater depth.

SHILLONG   ☎0364

From afar, the lovely hill station of Shillong looks much like any Scottish highland town, blessed with a cool climate and surrounded by green hills. But a visit to the Iewduh Market (Bara Bazaar), alive with the local cultures of Meghalaya, may convince you otherwise. The city, named for an incarnation of the Khasi creator god Shillong, is marked by its British past, visible in the churches, botanical gardens, and colonial cottages still dominating the old European town center. Although the city has as yet to attract the throngs of tourists seen in Darjeeling and Shimla, Shillong's solid infrastructure, unmatched in the Northeast, makes it an excellent spot for relaxation and a good base for walking expeditions in the hills.

⌐ TRANSPORTATION

Flights: The closest **airport** is in Guwahati. **Jais Travels,** MG Rd. (☎2222777), inside Rap's Mansion, opposite the Secretariat, is an official agent for **Indian Airlines, Jet Airways,** and **Air Sahara.** Also runs a Maruti **van** shuttle to Guwahati airport (3½hr., 7am, Rs200); reserve in advance. Open M-Sa 10am-5:30pm. The **Meghalaya Helicopter Service** (☎2223129), at MTC bus station, flies from the Air Force base helipad in Upper Shillong to Guwahati airport (30min., M-Sa 1-3 per day 9:40am-8:10pm, Rs725). Open M-F 9am-4:30pm.

NORHTEAST INDIA

Shillong

🏠 ACCOMMODATIONS
Earle Holiday Home, **2**
KJP Synod Guest House, **7**
🍴 Shillong Club, **6**

🍴 FOOD
Broadway Restaurant, **3**
Kim Poo Chinese Banquet, **4**
New World Chinese
Restaurant, **1**
Pizza (Fast Food), **5**

Trains: The **Shillong Out-Agency,** at the MTC bus station, books rail tickets for trains leaving from Guwahati station.

Buses: Government buses operate out of the **MTC bus station** in Police Bazaar. To **Guwahati** (4hr., every hr. 6:30am-4pm, Rs57); **Tura** and **Williamnagar Wildlife Preserve** (12hr., 4pm, Rs180). For **Aizwal** and **Imphal,** take a bus to **Silchar** (8hr., 7pm, Rs135), where connections are available. Frequent **private buses** depart from the Polo Ground for **Guwahati** and **Silchar** (7am-4pm); make reservations at any travel agency in Police Bazaar. **Network Travels** (☎2222747), at Police Bazaar point, runs a direct bus to **Argatala** (22hr., 7:30pm, Rs320). The **Khasi Hills Sumo Association** (☎2211712), MG Rd., near the State Bank of India, also services **Guwahati** (2½hr., every 30min. 10am-7pm, Rs90 to share). **Sumos** and **buses** for **in-state destinations** depart from Bara Bazaar and charge the best rates. Buses at the **private bus stand,** past the city bus stand in Bara Bazaar, head to: **Nongkhlaw** via **Nongstein, Mairang** and **Mawphlang; Ranikor** via **Mawkyrwat;** and **Jakrem** (you can also get off along the way and walk the 2km to **Mawsynram**).

Local Transportation: Shared taxis (Rs5 per head) barrel through the city streets without even coming to a complete stop to pick up passengers. Across the street from the Sumo Association, 100m closer to Police Bazaar, the **Khasi Hills Tourist Taxi Association**

(☎2223895) goes to **Guwahati airport** (3½hr., frequent 6am-6pm, Rs200 to share, Rs1000 for whole taxi), as well as the local sightseeing circuit To Umiam Lake Rs500, to Sohra/Cherrapunjee Rs1200, to Jowai Rs1200.

✳ 🛈 ORIENTATION AND PRACTICAL INFORMATION

Shillong is a hilly mess. Roads snake out from **Police Bazaar Point,** 100m uphill from the MTC bus station. **Guwahati-Shillong (GS) Road,** lined with budget hotels, bends westward and leads to **Bara Bazaar. MG Road (Kacheri Road)** winds southeast away from Police Bazaar and holds many government offices, the State Bank of India, the Post Office, the Shillong Club and, at its southern tip, the State Museum and Library. Apart from **Ward Lake,** most of the area's sights are outside of town.

Tourist Office: Government of India Tourist Office, GS Rd. (☎2225632), near Police Bazaar. Open M-F 9:30am-5:30pm, Sa 9:30am-2pm. **Meghalaya Tourist Information Counter** (☎2226220). On Jail Rd., opposite the MTC bus station. Open M-Sa 7:30am-5:30pm, Su 7:30-11am.

Currency Exchange: State Bank of India, MG Rd. (☎2224772). Accepts AmEx, MC, and Thomas Cook travelers checks. Open M-F 10am-4pm, Sa 10am-1pm.

Bookstore: Ka Ibadasuk Books Agency, on GS Rd., (☎2210027). Opposite Hotel Center Point. A remarkable range of titles, covering everything from orchids to Meghalaya's tribal sociology, crammed onto three walls. Open M-Sa 10am-6pm.

Market: The **Bara Bazaar** is an endless maze of market lanes selling everything from cow hooves to hand-woven shawls to electronic equipment. Every 8 days on the Khasi calendar, the streets become even more chaotic as vendors from outlying villages come to hawk their wares at the **Iewduh Market;** ask around for dates.

Internet Access: S.J. Pareek.com, next to New World Chinese Restaurant, in Police Bazaar. Reliable connections. Rs35 per hr. Open daily 10am-7pm.

Police: Superintendent of Police, MG Rd. (☎2224150), next to the Secretariat. Houses the **Foreigner Registration Office,** the best place for help and advice. Open M-F 10am-4pm.

Pharmacy: Economic Medical Hall (☎2224237). Open daily 8am-8pm, 24hr. for emergencies.

Hospital: Nazareth Hospital, Arbuthnot Rd. (☎2210188). The best care in town.

Post Office: GPO, MG Rd. (☎222302). Open M-Sa 10am-4pm. **Postal Code:** 793001.

⌂ ACCOMMODATIONS

Hotels between GS Rd. and Police Bazaar are uniformly cramped and dark. For space, light, and peace, you'll have to escape the jostling city center.

Earle Holiday Home, (☎2228614). From Police Bazaar take the steep incline between Jail Rd. and MG Rd. then turn left on the road to Ward Lake. The historic B. Baruah House has peaceful rooms backed by pine groves. Good canteen. Doubles Rs300. ❷

KJP Synod Guest House, MG Rd. (☎2228611), opposite the State Museum. Run by a tiny Khasi woman who will insist on being your surrogate mother. Breakfast, heater, and buckets of hot water are included. Hearty Khasi dinners available. Beds Rs75. ❶

Shillong Club, MG Rd. (☎2227497). The British spirit here is yet to be exorcised. Each room has a color TV, a fireplace, and a balcony overlooking Ward Lake. Guests are temporary members of the Club itself, with a reading room, billiard tables, and a bar (beer Rs40; open daily 1-9pm). Singles Rs509; doubles Rs600; triples Rs727. MC/V. ❸

FOOD

Cloned Chinese restaurants serve up decent food in Police Bazaar. The stalls along the Bara Bazaar offer traditional Khasi fare loaded with beef, pork, and fish.

Kim Poo Chinese Banquet, GS Rd., by the Monsoon Hotel. Authentic Chinese dishes complimented by a decorative fish tank. Great fried chicken dumplings (Rs70) and prawn rice noodles (Rs60). Open daily 9am-8pm. ❷

  Broadway Restaurant, GS Rd., in the Broadway Hotel. Delicate curry and tandoori flavors. Mutton curry Rs50; vegetable shish kebabs Rs50. Open daily 10am-9pm. ❷

  New World Chinese Restaurant, at the end of Police Bazaar. New World has come up with some very satisfying Szechuan, Thai, and Korean creations made with rice or noodles (Rs50-85). Choice people-watching spot. Open daily 10am-7pm. ❸

  Pizza (Fast Food), Jail Rd., Police Bazaar. Near the bus stand. American food with an Indian twist. The delicious special includes salad, cheese pizza, and an omelet (Rs90). Veggie burger Rs50. Open daily 9am-7:30pm. ❷

◉ SIGHTS

Shillong's wooden colonial houses are scattered over crooked hills and ridges; each hill has its own church and its own identity. Several sights on the outskirts of town make decent half-day excursions.

SHILLONG PEAK. Although hard to reach, Shillong Peak is the most spectacular sight near the city. Follow Howell Rd. up through Laban, where it turns into a stone path and enters a pine wood en route to **Shillong Observation Point** (1hr.). From here, follow the road right through the Northeastern Air Command military installation, past a heavily guarded gate, and through potato fields. **Bara Peak,** the highest point in Meghalaya, is off the road to the left, about 1km past the gate (1-2hr. from Shillong). To get back to town, follow the same road for another 3km through the woods until you hit the Shillong-Cherrapunjee road. Turn left and walk 600m to **Elephant Falls,** a series of cascades maintained as a business venture by local teenagers. *(Buses and jeeps can provide a lift down to Shillong (30min., 6am-7pm, Rs10). Open daily 8:30am-5pm. Rs2.)*

THE BUTTERFLY MUSEUM. During the 1930s, Shillong's Mr. S.K. Sircar began collecting brightly colored butterflies from the surrounding hills; by Independence, he had thousands, including such priceless items as 30cm poisonous stick bugs and the world's heaviest beetle. Although his daughter now maintains the museum in the family basement, the exhibition remains one of the city's rare treasures. *(From Police Bazaar, take GS Rd. past the Grand Hotel, then turn right onto Umsohsun Rd. At the fork, go left and follow the curving residential street for 500m. The museum is on the right, though the sign is difficult to see. (☎ 2223411.) Open M-F 10:30am-4pm, Sa 10:30am-1pm. Rs5.)*

▷ DAYTRIPS FROM SHILLONG

CHERRAPUNJEE
Buses for Cherrapunjee leave from the long queue in Shillong where Bara Bazaar Rd. approaches GS Rd. (2hr., 7am-5pm, Rs20). The nearby Sumos are quicker and more comfortable (1½hr., Rs330 or Rs30 per person). Transport arrives at Cherrapunjee Market, next to the Ramakrishna Mission. The last rides from Cherrapunjee to Shillong leaves around 4:30pm. Eight-hour guided tours depart from the MTDC office in Shillong daily at 8am, as long as at least 15 people sign up (Rs125).

NORTHEAST INDIA

Fifty-six kilometers south of Shillong, the town of Cherrapunjee is one of the wettest places on earth, with an average annual rainfall of 2063.3mm (almost 40 feet). During most of the year, countless waterfalls pour over the ridges, but during winter, water sources run dry and blue skies prevail. This lush landscape calls out to you to roam its hills and valleys. The road that runs up to the left of the Mission High School leads to **Nohkalikai Falls,** 4km away. Heading down from the bus stand takes you to **Nongsawlia,** the site where Welsh Calvinistic Methodists began their mission work in 1841. The **Circuit House ❶,** 500m farther down to the left off the main road, is meant primarily for government guests, but they do sometimes take tourists. Contact the Sub-Divisional Officer next door for reservations. (☎0927 235222 or 35326. Rs100 per mosquito-netted double.)

Five kilometers past the Circuit House, along the main road, is the village of **Mawsmai,** known for its cave and waterfalls. Souvenir hounds have broken off most of the stalactites, but the cave is still impressive. The short but dramatic limestone path leads to a lush, bright jungle on the other side. (Admission Rs10.) Ask about the second, unlighted cavern. The **Nohsngi Thiang (Seven Sisters) Falls** are a few meters off the main road that continues past Mawsmai village to **Shella** village. Beyond the Seven Sisters, 9km along the Mawsmai-Mawlong Rd., is **Thangkharang Park,** a popular picnic spot, and the **Kynrem Falls,** the tallest in Meghalaya.

JOWAI

Buses (2hr., Rs25) and Sumos (11½hr., Rs440 or Rs40 per person) leave for Jowai from opposite Anjalee Cinema Hall in Shillong.

Jowai, 64km from Shillong, holds the longest cave in India, the 21.6km **Krem Um Lawan.** For more information on tours or equipment rental, contact the **Meghalaya Adventurers Association** through the General Secretary, Brian (Kharpran) Daly (☎2224465 or 2548059). Generally, the group is more active during winter months when most caves are dry. Jowai is also the district headquarters of the **Jaintia Hills,** and the center of the Behdeinkhlam, a July festival to stomp out epidemics and pray for a healthy crop by dancing in a pool of muddy water.

The best accommodation in the area is undoubtedly the unique **Cherrapunjee Holiday Resort ❸,** in the Khasi village of Laitkynsewm, 20km outside Cherrapunjee. A taxi from Cherrapunjee market will cost Rs200. Run by a former banker turned environmentalist, this place is very relaxing and familial. Large rooms with comfortable furniture and hot showers feel like home—except they have amazing views of waterfalls (Mar.-Oct.) and the Bangladeshi floodplains. (Doubles Rs600-700. Call ahead to ask if jeep pick-up is available.) Nearby spring baths and plentiful options for trekking, caving, and angling provide ways to take in the scenery.

TRIPURA ☎0381

The tiny state of Tripura is a narrow finger of land poking into Bangladesh. At the southwestern corner of Northeast India, the state is distinct from its neighbors, both historically and ethnically. The Manikya, the traditional rulers of Tripura, submitted to Mughal authority but regained and retained control of the state during the Raj. It was a princely state until 1949, when it joined the Indian Union. Several ethnic groups continue to inhabit the state, but the majority of the population today is Bengali. Tripura has several beautiful forests and wildlife sanctuaries, but development is threatening these precious ecological preserves.

Agartala, Tripura's capital, has few attractions of its own, but it is a good hub from which to see outlying sights. **Buses** connect Agartala with **Silchar** (12hr., Rs180) and continue to **Shillong** (18hr., Rs320) and **Guwahati** (24hr., Rs360). Buses leave at 6am and 12pm from Sagar Travels on Laximinarayan Rd. near

NORHTEAST INDIA

the Palace. You can also **fly** out of the city to **Kolkata** (1hr.; M, W, Th, F, Su; US$55) and **Guwahati** (45min.; W, F, Su; US$50). The town is dominated by the **Ujjayanta Palace** at its center. This sprawling white structure was built in 1901 by Radhakishore Manikya and now houses the State Legislature. In the evening, the palace is lit by floodlights and features a "musical fountain," which is a regular fountain accompanied by a cassette player. (Open daily 5-7pm. Rs3.) At other times, the palace and its well-kept flower gardens are closed. Go to the back for the **Tripura Tourist Office**, Swet Mahal Palace Compound (☎225930 or 223893. Open M-F 10am-4pm, Sa 3-5pm.) The staff can direct you to the **currency exchange** bureau and the **Bangladesh visa office,** near Circuit House and the Palace (☎224807; open M-F 10am-5pm). The fee is US$5-50 and is processed within a day. Agartala seems to have more hotels than tourists. Among the cheapest and best is **Hotel Sausastra ❶**, on HGB Rd. (☎225573. Singles Rs58; doubles with attached bath Rs116.) The nearby **Hotel Ambar ❶**, has TV and telephone in every room. (☎223587. Singles Rs88; doubles Rs165.) **Hotel Moonlight ❶**, serves a set veg. lunch (Rs22) and hosts a lively crowd. A short rickshaw ride will take you to the Bangladeshi town of Akhaura. Frequent buses and 2 trains a day (2½hr., 12:20 and 6:30pm, taka130) leave for **Dhaka**. From Dhaka there are frequent buses to **Kolkata** (taka500).

The famed **Water Palace** at Neermahal is 53km south of Agartala. Built in 1930 as a summer resort for Bir Bikram Kishore Manikya, the palace is an exquisite example of Indo-Saracenic architecture. The red-and-white structure lies in the middle of a large lake. A **tourist lodge** and a few restaurants dot the shore, but the area is left blissfully deserted at night. Neermahal is 1km from Melaghar. Buses leave for **Melaghar** from Agartala's Battala bus stop on HGB Rd. (2hr., every 40min., Rs20). Temple aficionados might enjoy Matabari temple, near Udaipur. Buses, jeeps, and taxis leave the Battala stop for **Matabari** (1½hr., every 30min., Rs18).

OTHER NORTHEAST STATES. Manipur, Mizoram, Nagaland, and **Arunachal Pradesh** are unstable regions with little tourism. For those who wish to travel in these states, **permits must be obtained in Delhi.** These permits are obtainable from the **Ministry of Home Affairs** in Khan Market. (☎4693334 or 4612543. Open M-F 10am-noon). The officers, here, though, like to direct foreigners to the **Foreigners Registration Office,** 1st Fl., Hansa Bhavan, Tilak Marg. Your best bet for getting a permit, however, is to go through a tour operator, government-sponsored travel agent, or a regional NGO.

NORTHEAST INDIA

ORISSA ଓଡ଼ିଶା

Orissa's coastline stretches for almost 500km, and nearly all of the state's urban residents live within a stone's throw of the Mahanadi River Delta. Most of the rural population work in rice paddies; the rest can be found manning wooden fishing boats—a far cry from the maritime prowess of the Kalingas and other dynasties that once sent colonists as far away as Bali and Java. The thick forest cover of the Eastern Ghats has allowed the indigenous Adivasis to survive relatively undisturbed. Orissa's industry capitalizes on its rich ore reserves, making the state a center for the production of aluminum, steel and phosphatic fertilizers, the major hinterland goods for Paradeep, the country's deepest port.

Orissa has defended its independence for thousands of years as the kingdom of Kalinga. The Kalingas held out against the Mauryan Empire in the 3rd century BC, relenting only after a battle so bloody that it convinced Mauryan Emperor Ashoka to convert to Buddhism. Orissa withstood Muslim rule until 1568, long after surrounding regions had been conquered. The state's cultural autonomy has led to the development of distinctive art forms, including its glorious temple architecture and the *odissi* form of dance. Orissa's natural wonders include the wildlife sanctuaries of Nandankanan, the enormous lagoon at Chilka, the sun kissed beaches of Puri and Konark, and the rugged red earth dominated by the Mahanadi River.

In October 1999, the state of Orissa was ravaged by one of the worst cyclones ever to hit India. Over 10,000 people were killed. Orissans have been rebuilding their lives ever since, but the devastation was frightening, and the path to recovery has been a long and painful one.

HIGHLIGHTS OF ORISSA

On the coast of the Bay of Bengal, **Puri** (p. 464) juggles dual roles as religious center and beach-side resort.

Temple-packed **Bhubaneswar** (below) showcases the unique beauty of the region's varied and intricate Hindu architecture.

Konark (p. 461), the third point of Orissa's "Golden Triangle" of tourism, is the site of the spectacular **Sun Temple** and a wonderfully tranquil beach.

BHUBANESWAR ଭୁବନେଶ୍ବର ☎ 0674

Bhubaneswar has one of the finest collections of Hindu temples in India, and its mighty *lingaraj* spire forms the apex of Orissa's "Golden Triangle" of Bhubaneswar, Konark and Puri. The city also has a Buddhist Peace Pagoda and a Jain temple, demonstrating its other influences.

As the capital of the powerful maritime dynasties of the Kalingas who ruled the Bay of Bengal, Bhubaneswar was the center of trade and commerce in the area now known as Orissa. Members of the Hindu ruling classes erected the finest devotional structures, and under their patronage, temple architecture grew into an art form. Under Muslim and British rule, however, neglect and plunder reduced many of the monuments to rubble. When Bhubaneswar became the capital of the new Indian state of Orissa in 1950, it received a makeover; urban planners built monumental warrens along wide avenues. The preservation of the remaining temples became a religious and civic imperative. Today, the city exhibits both the outward characteristics of a modern state capital and the enduring spirit of the majestic kingdom that was classical Orissa.

TRANSPORTATION

Flights: Bhubaneswar Airport (☎2534472 or 2534084), southwest of the New Town. **Indian Airlines,** Gaputi Nagar (☎2530533 or 2530544), off Raj Path just before the intersection with Sachivalaya Marg. Open daily 10am-1:15pm and 2-4:45pm. To: **Kolkata** (1hr., daily, US$90); **Chennai** (2½hr.; M, W, F, Su; US$205) via **Visakhapatnam** (1hr., US$125); **Delhi** (2hr., 1 per day, US$220); **Hyderabad** (1½hr.; Tu, Th, Sa; US$165); **Mumbai** (2hr.; Tu, Th, Sa; US$255).

Trains: Bhubaneswar Railway Station, Station Sq. (reservations ☎2502042). To: **Kolkata** (8-13hr., 10-14 per day 4:20am-11pm, Rs154; *Janashatabdi Express,* 8hr., daily 5:45am, Rs484); **Chennai** (21-23hr., 2-4 per day 3:28am-10:53pm, Rs312); **Cuttack** (30min.-1hr., 12-14 per day 4:20am-10:15pm, Rs19); **Delhi** (31-42hr., 3-4 per day 8:15am-9:47pm, Rs374; *Rajdhani Express,* 25hr., W and Su 9:10am, Rs1725); **Hyderabad/Secunderabad** (21-24hr., 4 per day 7:25am-7:18pm, Rs286); **Puri** (2-3hr., 6-8 per day, Rs26).

Buses: Baramunda New Bus Station (☎2526977), on NH 5, 5km west of the city center. To: **Balasore** (4hr., every 10min. 4:30am-10pm, Rs70); **Berhampur** (4hr., every 10min. 5:30am-10pm, Rs50); **Cuttack** (1hr., every 10min., Rs7); **Kolkata** (13hr.; 4, 6, 6:30pm; Rs120); **Konark** (2hr., every 30min. 6am-5pm, Rs12); **Puri** (1½hr., every 15min., Rs18). Buses to nearby towns can also be caught at Kalpana Square.

Local Transportation: Minibuses cover all the major streets (Rs3-7). **Cycle- and auto-rickshaws** zip across town (Rs25-60). Although auto-rickshaws are unmetered, drivers will usually charge Rs10 per km.

ORIENTATION

Bhubaneswar consists of the well-planned commercial and residential **New Town** to the north and the chaotic temple-packed **Old Town** to the south. Large roads like the north-south **Jan Path** and the east-west **Raj Path** cut the New Town into squares called **nagars.** Each nagar, also called a **unit,** has a name and a number. Most shops and services cluster around **Station Square,** in front of the station, and **Rajmahal Square,** to the south. Puri Rd. (Lewis Rd.) and Vivekananda Marg run south from

ORISSA

Kalpana Square, an accommodations hub in the southeast, to the Old Town. There is no main road in the Old Town maze, but the **Bindu Sagar** tank is at its center and the tall **Lingaraj Temple** lies to the south.

🛈 PRACTICAL INFORMATION

Tourist Office: Government of Orissa Tourist Office, 5 Jayadev Nagar (☎2431299), from Kalinga Sq., head south down Lewis Rd.; it's just past the Panthanivas Tourist Bungalow, on the right. Open M-Sa 10am-5pm. Counters at the airport (☎2534006) and railway station (☎2530715) are open 24hr. Maps and basic information leaflets available. **OTDC** (☎2432282), behind the Panthanivas, arranges cheap tours of Bhubaneswar, Puri, Konark and Chilka Lake, and owns inexpensive Panthanivas accommodations all over the state. **Government of India Tourist Office,** B-21 BJB Nagar (☎2432203). From the railway station, take the last left before the fork that leads to Puri Rd.; it's on a side road 750m down on the right. Open M-F 9am-6pm, Sa 9am-1pm.

Currency Exchange: State Bank of India, Main Branch, Unit 1, Raj Path (☎2530894), near Raj Mahal Sq., opposite Capital Market. Open M-F 11am-3:30pm, Sa 10:30am-12:30pm. Bhubaneswar also has a convenient network of ATMs that accept MasterCard and Visa—the largest number belong to SBI and ICICI Bank and can be found near or at most petrol pumps.

Pharmacy: Kalinga Hospital Pharmacy (☎2300726), at Kalinga Hospital, Nalco Sq., Chandrashekharpur. Open 24hr. **Rabindra Medical Hall,** Raj Mahal Bldg., Rajmahal Sq., Bapuji Nagar (☎2531028), in the complex at the southeast corner of Raj Mahal Sq., on the side facing Raj Path. Open daily 8:30am-10:30pm. **Capital Hospital's pharmacy** is open 24hr., as is **Kar Clinic's.**

Hospital: Kalinga Hospital (☎2300726 and 2300997), see above. **Kar Clinic,** A/32 MLA Colony, Unit 4 (☎2516666 and 2518888). An excellent private hospital with pharmacy. **Capital Hospital,** Unit 6, Ganga Nagar (☎2400688 or 2401983). From Raj Mahal Sq., go south on Jan Path; after 1 block, turn right (west) on Udyan Marg and continue past Sachivalaya Marg; to the left is the 24hr. government hospital.

Internet: Hi-Tech Cyber Café, 137-6 Ashok Nagar (☎2539777). Head north up Jan Path from Raj Mahal Sq.; it's 100m on the right, upstairs. Internet (Rs15 per hr.) with A/C, ice cream, and cold drinks. Open daily 8am-11pm. There are hundreds of other cybercafes throughout the city, usually closest to STD/ISD/PCO phone booths; rates range from Rs15-60 per hr.

Post Office: GPO, PMG Sq. (☎2402132), from Station Sq., go northwest on MG Marg. It's at the intersection with Sachivalay Marg. Open daily 10am-6pm. **Postal Code:** 751001.

🛏 ACCOMMODATIONS

Lodging can be found throughout Buddha Nagar and Gautam Nagar, especially between Raj Mahal and Kalpana Sq. Those listed below have 24hr. check-out. More upscale hotels are located mainly in Nayapalli and Jaydev Vihar, to the west.

◪ **Hotel Padma,** 67 Buddha Nagar, Kalpana Sq. (☎2416626 or 2416628), on the left as you go up Cuttack Rd. A long, white ship of a hotel with friendly staff, spacious rooms, and rooftop garden. Singles Rs70-120; doubles with bath Rs200-250. ❶

OTDC Panthanivas, Lewis Rd. (☎2432314 or 2432515), near the Tourist Office. A large, clean hotel with friendly staff and a host of services. The tourist office is just below, so residents enjoy travel resources galore. The attached A/C restaurant serves good Indian food. Large well-lit doubles Rs450-750. ❸

ORISSA

Bhubaneswar

⌂ ACCOMMODATIONS
Bhubaneswar Hotel, **7**
Hotel Bhagat Niwas, **6**
Hotel Padma, **8**
Hotel Swagat, **5**
OTDC Panthanivas, **10**

🍴 FOOD
Hare Krishna Restaurant, **3**
Mayfair Lagoon Hotel/Food
Court, **2**
Pal Heights, **1**
Suruchi Food Plaza, **4**
Venus Inn, **9**

TO CUTTACK (35km),
NANDANKANAN ZOO (12km)
& KOLKATA

GOPA-
BANDHU
NAGAR
(9)

SATYA
NAGAR

Patel Marg

BHAUMA
NAGAR
(4)

Madhusudan
Marg

➕ Kar Clinic

INDUSTRIAL
AREA

Gopabandhu Marg

KHARAVELA
NAGAR
(3)

GPO
✉

KESHARI
NAGAR (5)

MG Marg

■ Secretariat

Cuttack Rd.

Vidyut Marg

TO 🍴 & 🍴 (1.5km)

Raj Path

ASHOK
NAGAR (2)

STATION
SQUARE

3

SURYA
NAGAR
(7)

Jan Path

Railway
Station

TO UDAIGIRI &
KHANDAGIRI CAVES (6km)

GANGA
NAGAR
(6)

Indian ■
Airlines

CAPITAL
MARKET

Railway St.

BUDDHA
NAGAR

Sachivalaya Marg

State Bank 💲
of India

RAJMAHAL
SQUARE

5

6

7

Daya West Canal

Ekamra Marg

Central
Hospital
✚

BAPUJI
NAGAR
(1)

8

KALPANA
SQUARE

Udyan Marg

GAUTAM
NAGAR

9

State
Museum

Govt. of India
Tourist Office
ⓘ

N
LG

Airport ✈

Ekamra Marg

Vivekananda Marg

ⓘ 10
Orissa
Tourist
Office

Lewis Rd.

Bhaskareswar

0   500 yards
0   500 meters

Barhabanda Sahi

Parsurameswar

Rajarani

Tankapani Rd.

Vaital

Mukteswar

Mahatab Rd.

Bindu
Sagar

Kedareswar

Puri Rd.

Lingaraj

TO DHAULI (8km),
PIPLI (7km)
& PURI (46km)

Brahmeswar

Bhubaneswar Hotel, Cuttack Rd. (☎2313245 or 2313246), just past Swagat. Not as fancy as it looks, this popular hotel has well-appointed rooms served by friendly bell-hops. Restaurant serves great breakfasts. Singles Rs150-300; doubles Rs200-400. ❷

Hotel Bhagat Niwas, 9 Buddha Nagar (☎2311345 or 2313708), in Kalpana Sq., behind Hotel Padma. A yellow maze of small rooms with TVs and attached bath. Staff does laundry. Singles Rs120-160; doubles Rs250-650. ❶

Hotel Swagat, Cuttack Rd. (☎2312686 or 2311934). Exit the east side of the railway station (not the main exit facing Station Sq.), turn right, and look for it on your right after 200m. Decent rooms, decent prices and room service that brings drinks until 10pm. Restaurant attached (open daily 8am-10pm). Singles Rs175; doubles Rs200-550. ❷

ORISSA

◘ FOOD

Bhubaneswar is the perfect place to sample traditional Orissan cuisine, served in small *ginas* on large *thalis*. The food is similar to South Indian food, but less spicy. Delicious veg. and non-veg. offerings can be found along Jan and Raj Paths. The larger city hotels are also home to number of popular restaurants.

▩ **Mayfair Food Court,** 8-B Jaydev Vihar, outside the slick Mayfair Lagoon Resort. A bright and friendly A/C restaurant with everything from pizzas (from Rs65) to South Indian *dosas* (from Rs40), as well as mineral water *pani puris* (Rs2) and freshly fried *jalebis* (Rs10) right outside on the porch. ❷

▩ **Venus Inn,** 217 Bapuji Nagar (☎2531738), from Raj Mahal Sq., take the 2nd right before the train tracks; it is 400m further, on the left. One of Bhubaneswar's oldest and best for veg. and South Indian food. Classy decor, A/C, and Hindi beats. Butter cheese *kofta* Rs30, *uttappams* Rs9-16, *dosas* Rs10-25. Open daily 6:30am-10pm. ❶

Pal Heights, J/7 Jaydev Vihar (☎2361156), close to the Mayfair Lagoon. Specializes in Indian, Chinese and Korean food, with top-notch quality. Pal is one of the city's newest metropolitan eating places, so call and reserve ahead. Munch on delicious Korean cabbage and ask for a huge, crisp, spiced complimentary *papad* while you browse the menu. Entrees Rs200-250. ❺

Suruchi Food Plaza, Eastern Market Bldg., Capital Market, off Raj Path. Dark and cool but full of hot, mouth-watering dishes, the plaza is highly recommended by locals; even the house *lassi*, a blend of yogurt, berries and nuts, is a culinary treat (Rs20). Indian and Chinese upstairs, South Indian below. Open daily 7:30am-11:30pm. ❶

Hare Krishna Restaurant, 1st fl., Lalchand Market, Jan Path (☎2534188), just north of Station Sq., on the right. Posh, shiny, low-lit establishment with a very serious atmosphere. The menu, though, is full of tasty interpretations of Braj country "delights." All veg. Entrees from Rs45. Open daily 11am-3pm and 7-10pm. ❷

◉ SIGHTS

It is said that there are more ancient temples in Orissa than in the rest of North India put together. Puri and Konark have more famous and monumental temples, but for sheer numbers, Bhubaneswar is the place to be. Carved between the 7th and 12th centuries AD, the sculptures tell the story of Hinduism's resurgence—the frequent depiction of a lion pouncing on an elephant represents Hinduism's triumph over Buddhism. Lakulisa, a 5th-century Shaivite saint who converted many Orissans, also appears on temple walls. Most of Bhubaneswar's temples are dedicated to Shiva, whose cult remains an important part of the lives of many of the region's inhabitants. The temples, in the middle of the Old Town around Bindu Sagar, can be explored in a few hours. Guides prowl the temples soliciting customers; ignore them. Certified guides can be hired from the state tourism office. Be wary of the men (universally called *pandas* in Orissa) with a "temple register" listing foreign contributions—it's a scam. The temples are open from dawn to dusk, with the exception of the Lingaraj temple.

LINGARAJ TEMPLE. The **Lingaraj** is one of Orissa's great temples, notable for the balanced placement of sculpture on its 45m spire. Completed around 1100 AD, it has a four-chambered temple structure: a sanctuary (under the spire), a porch, a dance hall, and an offering hall. Shiva is worshipped here in the form of Tribhubaneshwar (Lord of Three Worlds), hence the city's name. Devotional songs have been sung here since the temple was built. The compound contains ornate stonework as well—more than 50 smaller temples surround the main one. The second-largest temple in the compound, to the right in front of the main temple, is devoted to Shiva's consort, Parvati. The compound is closed to non-Hindus, but the British built a viewing platform next to the north wall. *(Open daily 6am-3pm and 6-9:30pm.)*

PARSURAMESWAR TEMPLE. The oldest and one of the best-preserved of Bhubaneswar's temples, the 7th-century **Parsurameswar Temple** exhibits many of the features characteristic of earlier Orissan temples, including a small, squat *shikhara* and an uncarved roof over the porch. The walls are resplendent with exquisite carvings, but it is most famous for its masterfully carved lattice windows, all in stone. Standing sentinel on the left side of the rear entrance, is a *linga* with 1000 other tiny *lingas* carved into it. *(From the New Town, turn down the road to the left just before the Bindu Sagar; the temple is on the left. No photography allowed.)*

MUKTESWAR TEMPLE. In contrast to its elder neighbor Parsurameswar, the **Mukteswar Temple** is a series of small monuments. The complex features a U-shaped archway at the entrance, an evolutionary link between the first and second phases of Orissan temples, and plenty of intricate sculpture. On the exterior, amongst thousands of other pictures in stone, monkeys are shown doing monkey things— riding crocodiles, picking lice, and falling into the clutches of crabs. Most of these animal storyboards are tales from the *Panchatantra*, an ancient set of fables written by Orissan scholar Vishnu Sharma. *(On the left, near Parsurameswar Temple.)*

KEDARESWAR TEMPLE. Opposite the Mukteswar Temple, the whitewashed **Kedareswar** is the most active temple in Bhubaneswar after the Lingaraj.

RAJARANI TEMPLE. Originally named for the *raja* (red) and *rani* (yellow) stones from which it was built, this now-defunct 11th-century temple is looked after by the Archaeological Survey of India. The **Rajarani Temple** is famous for its *shikhara*, built with miniature temple spires clustered around the main tower. Though common in other parts of India, this style is rare in Orissa. Even stranger, the temple lacks a presiding deity. For those who brave the high entrance fee, *nayikas* show women looking in the mirror, playing instruments, and, of course, engaging in amorous play. The large stone porch is sometimes used for dance recitals and cultural shows in winter. *(Up Puri Rd. behind the Mukteswar Temple; take a right on Tankapani Rd.; temple after 100m on the right, at the back of a rectangular park. US$5.)*

BHASKARESWAR AND BRAHMESWAR TEMPLES. The chunky **Bhaskareswar Temple** is no artistic triumph, but it does contain a 3m-high *linga* encased in what is thought to be an Ashokan column from the 3rd century BC. Wander down a lane to the right after the Bhaskareswar Temple to the 9th-century **Brahmeswar Temple**. The temple walls are carved in standard Orissan fashion and proportions, making it seem like a miniature version of the Lingaraj Temple. Indeed, it may well have been the model on which the grander temple was based. The temple has smaller Shiva shrines at the four corners of its compound. *(A short rickshaw ride down Tankapani Rd., 1km past the pretty sewage canal.)*

VAITAL TEMPLE. The **Vaital Temple**, sunk in the ground at a crossroads on the western side of the Bindu Sagar, has a unique style. Its oblong, barrel-shaped *shikhara* betrays a Buddhist influence, although local priests will insist that Vaital resembles a ship. Take a light with you inside to illuminate scenes of human sacrifice and gory tantric carvings, depicting the skull-clad goddess Chamunda with her attendant owl and jackal. Beside the Vaital Temple is the **Sisireswar Temple**, a near-duplicate of the nearby **Markandeswar Temple**. In both temples, images were carved directly into the walls, a technique that was later discontinued.

ORISSA

BINDU SAGAR. Central to the city's religious life is this Old Town landmark, Bindu Sagar, a large green tank at the foot of Vivekananda Marg. The waters of the **Bindu Sagar (Ocean Drop) Tank** are believed to contain droplets from all of India's holy pools and streams. Early-morning bathers come here to take advantage of the blessings the waters bestow. Every April during Orissa's Rath Yatra (Cart Festival), the Lingaraj's image of Lord Tribhubaneshwar comes to the tank for his own ritual washing.

MUSEUM. The **Orissa State Museum** contains a collection of palm leaf manuscripts and Orissan musical instruments, as well as ethnographic exhibits on Orissa's indigenous peoples. Study the assorted statues and stonework from various periods of Kalinga's history, from all over the state. *(Puri Rd., close to Kalpana Sq. Open Tu-Su 10am-1pm and 2-4pm. Rs5.)*

☒ DAYTRIPS FROM BHUBANESWAR

UDAIGIRI AND KHANDAGIRI CAVES

Auto-rickshaws from Bhubaneswar Rs70. Caves open daily 8am-6pm. US$5.

More vestiges of antiquity can be found at the **Udaigiri** and **Khandagiri Caves,** 6km west of Bhubaneswar. Cut into the hillside are 33 niches that functioned as retreats for Jain ascetics during the 1st and 2nd centuries BC. King Kharavela of the Kalinga Dynasty also took refuge here after the Kalinga War at Dhauli. A road now divides the Udaigiri caves (on the right) from the Khandagiri caves (on the left). An explanation of the carvings and paintings is in the "Inscription of Kharavela" at Udaigiri, near Cave 12.

The best sculptures are found in and around Cave 1 at Udaigiri, otherwise known as **Rani Gumpha** (Queen's Cave). Originally 10 stories high, the cave now has only 2 stories; the rest were wiped out by earthquakes. The central area of the first floor contains hiding places once used by the king and his ministers. Large holes in the ceiling served as communication channels, air tunnels, and water drains. Intricate carvings inside the caves depict the marriage of the gods. Cave 12 is carved as the gaping mouth of a tiger, and a triple-hooded snake decorates the facade of Cave 13. Cave 14, the **Hathi Gumpha** (Elephant Cave), has a ceiling inscription from the reign of King Kharavela of the Chedi Dynasty, the greatest of Kalinga kings and patron of the caves. Images from Jain legends, mythology, and iconography decorate **Rani Nur** and **Ganesh Gumpha** (Cave 10).

Though the caves of Khandagiri are not as well-carved, nor as well-maintained, they do house an old temple with 26 sadhus (hermits) and 26 goddesses carved in two rows. This temple is still an active religious center; the pundits (or *pandas*) are friendly, but beware of their fanatical pursuit of donations. An active **Jain temple** at the top of the hill offers fantastic views over Bhubaneswar. On a clear day, you can spot the Lingaraj Temple and Dhauli Hill (Dhauligiri). The best-preserved carvings at Khandagiri are in **Cave 3.** A few caves are fenced off because of risky ceilings or cave-ins, but you should be able to step into some of the ground-level caves at both Udaigiri and Khandagiri for a bit of 200 BC meditation charm. Just make sure your niche of choice is not already occupied by the caves' more regular visitors: hungry, all-too-common romancing Bhubaneswar teenagers. If you're interested in the caves' history, hire a certified guide (Rs100).

DHAULI

You can visit Dhauli as part of an ODTC guided bus tour. Auto-rickshaws cost Rs100 round-trip; buses (Rs4) drop you off 3km from the hill. Open daily 5am-8pm. Free.

Worry Free Travel is Just a Click Away

Trip Cancellation
International Medical Insurance
Emergency Evacuation
All Nationalities

Personalize your travel insurance needs
with our online Policy Picker®

USA / Canada: 1 800 234 1862
International: +1 703 299 6001

ww.Letsgo.WorldTravelCenter.com   Travel Insurance Experts

young fun & on the run

tell us you saw us in "Lets Go" for a **FREE** passport holder!

save some serious dough when you travel with contiki! our vacations for 18 to 35 year olds include accommodations, many meals, transportation and sightseeing **from $70/day**. so grab your passport and get movin'!

> **8 days london & paris getaway from $675***
  tower of london, big ben, notre dame, arc de triomphe

> **14 days european discovery from $1145***
  amsterdam, munich, venice, rome, florence, swiss alps, paris

> **14 days aussie beaches and reefs from $965***
  sydney, brisbane, cairns, port douglas, surfers paradise,
  great barrier reef and more!

  *prices subject to change, land only.

for more info on our trips...
see your travel agent
call 1-888-CONTIKI
visit www.contiki.com

CST # 1001728-20

contiki
VACATIONS for 18-35 year olds

> **europe** > **australia** > **new zealand** > **america** > **canada**

The hill of Dhauli (also known as Dhauligiri), 8km south of Bhubaneswar on the Puri road, is Orissa's greatest historical claim to fame. In a horrific battle here in 261 BC, the Mauryan emperor Ashoka (then "The Terrible") defeated his foes and claimed victory in the Great Kalinga War. But profoundly appalled by the bloodshed, he renounced violence forever, converted to Buddhism, and changed his surname to "The Righteous." A long-winded rock edict in Brahmi script at the foot of Dhauli Hill explains Ashoka's new theory of governance according to the principle of *dharma* (an English translation is posted near these inscriptions). In the rock above is one of India's earliest rock cuts—a simple head of an elephant commemorating the emperor's conversion. On the summit of Dhauli Hill, affording fantastic views of Bhubaneswar and the sandy River Durga, is the **Shanti Stupa** (Peace Pagoda), built in 1974 by the same team of Japanese Buddhists who created the almost identical *stupas* in Vaishali and Lumbini.

NANDANKAN ZOOLOGICAL PARK

Buses from Bhubaneswar cost Rs5 for the 1hr. trip; auto-rickshaws Rs120 each way. Open daily 7:30am-5pm. Rs40, vehicles Rs30.

This zoo and wildlife park, in a vast expanse of the Chandaka forest, has a huge collection of animals from all over the world, but the gardens are best known for their successful breeding of rare local species such as white tigers, gharials, and white peacocks. In fact, the extremely rare Bengal white tiger was first bred at **Nandankanan.** But fame turned to shame in July 2000, when several of those prized tigers died under mysterious circumstances. The park has both a section that houses animals in enclosures, as well as an attached preserve where animals roam free, coming back only to feed.

CHILKA LAKE

The best way to see Chilka Lake is to join an OTDC guided bus tour to Satapada or Barkul (Rs160-175, 8:30am-6pm). Unless you want to make least 3 train connections, your other bet is to hire a car for the day—ask at your hotel. OTDC charges Rs3-6 per km.

Nestled in the heart of coastal Orissa, **Chilka** is India's biggest inland lake. Spread over 1100 sq. km, and bordering 3 districts, it joins the Bay of Bengal at a narrow mouth, forming an enormous lagoon of brackish blue water. It is dotted with emerald green islands with colorful names like Honeymoon Island and Breakfast Island. The lake is home to a rich variety of marine life, and is also a winter sanctuary for thousands of migratory birds. The lake is also a source of wealth for hundreds of fishermen who set out in their boats daily to trawl for mackerel, prawn, and crabs. Of the many towns that border it, the most easily accessible are **Satapada,** a magnificent viewing point for dolphins, and **Barkul.** Both can be reached by separate OTDC bus tours. If you plan to stay over at Chilka's shores, stick with OTDC's **Barkul Panthanivas ❸** (☎06756 20488), which has a decent restaurant and organizes all manner of water activities. Doubles Rs450-800.

KONARK ଚକାଶାର୍କ   ☎06758

On this isolated stretch of Orissan coastline, life revolves completely around the glorious temple to the sun god Surya. Beginning at first light, tourists stream off buses to catch a glimpse of the temple, only rediscovered in the early 20th century. Even in its present dilapidated state, the chariot-shaped shrine still stands as one of India's greatest architectural and sculptural marvels. The adjacent "village" is a tiny collection of hotels, *dhabas*, and stores that sell basic supplies and camera film. It becomes quiet once the daytrippers leave, so if you're in the mood for exploring alone, you might want to stay

ORISSA

overnight. Unfortunately, accommodations are neither plentiful nor particularly good. The town is very popular for its annual **Odissi Dance Festival,** held around early December.

ORIENTATION AND PRACTICAL INFORMATION

Curiously, Konark's street plan resembles a setting sun on the horizon. The semi-circular arch is the main street, which contains the temple entrance and the town's few shops. The left horizon line is the road to Bhubaneswar; the right is the tree-lined Marine Rd. to Puri, which passes beautiful, deserted beaches along the way; the Sun Temple sits in the middle of the semi-circle. **Buses** depart from the intersection halfway between the Panthanivas and the temple entrance. To **Bhubaneswar** (3hr., every 30min. 5am-5:30pm, Rs20) and **Puri** (1hr., every 15min. 7am-8pm, Rs10). Labanya Lodge rents **bikes** (Rs25), and the **Orissa State Tourism Office,** inside the Yatri Nivas, can arrange for **taxis.** (☎236831. Open M-Sa 10am-5pm.) **Richa Cyber Dhaba** has Internet (Rs30 per hr.) and phones. (☎236745. Open 6am-11pm.) **Canara Bank,** just past Sun Temple Hotel, exchanges traveler's checks. (☎236825. Open M-F 10am-2pm, Sa 10am-noon.) **Police:** ☎235825. The **post office** is next to Geetanjali Restaurant. (Open M-Sa 9am-5pm.) **Postal Code:** 75211.

ACCOMMODATIONS AND FOOD

Orissa Tourism's **Panthanivas ❷,** next to the museum, is the best place to stay overnight in Konark. It has immaculate rooms, well-trimmed garden-courtyards, and a quiet atmosphere. The in-house **restaurant** and **snack bar ❷** are decent. (☎236820. Doubles Rs200-350.) The laid-back **Labanya Lodge ❶,** just out of town on the road to Puri, is a pink and teal palm-tree-filled bungalow popular with backpackers. (☎236824 or 236860. Singles Rs60; doubles with bath Rs75-150.) **Bijaya Lodge ❶,** on the junction with the road to Puri, has slightly cramped, dark rooms. (☎236478. Doubles with bath Rs100-200.) A decent meal can be found at the "ancient" **Sun Temple Hotel ❸,** just past the bank, on the right. (Entrees under Rs65. Open daily 7am-10pm.) **Sharma Mawadi Hotel ❷,** a little farther down towards the temple entrance, is a veg. eatery with slow-cooked but tasty *thalis* for Rs30-65. (Open daily 7am-10pm.) The pyramid-capped **Geetanjali Restaurant ❶,** next to the Panthanivas, has cheap North and South Indian breakfasts. (Open daily 6am-10pm.)

SIGHTS

THE SUN TEMPLE

The ticket booth is up to the left of the gated entrance. Another entrance to the grounds, the left after the Archaeological Museum, brings you to the outer wall of the complex, but you still have to walk around to the booth. Open daily dawn-dusk. Foreigners US$10.

Konark's **Sun Temple,** dedicated to the sun god Surya, is built in the form of a huge chariot, Surya's heavenly vehicle. With its intricate carvings, erotic imagery, and grand design, it is possibly the most impressive example of Orissan temple architecture anywhere. Originally sitting on the shoreline (it is now more than 3km from the sea, which recedes a little every year), the temple was used as a navigational aid by European sailors, who called it the "Black Pagoda" to distinguish it from Puri's similar but white **Jagannath Temple** (see p. 467). There has been a Surya temple in Konark as far back as the 9th century AD, but most of the existing structure dates from 400 years later, the time of Narasimha Deva I. Victim to centuries of pillagers and the weathering effects of nature, the crumbling temple is now preserved as an archaeological site and remains the central feature in the geographic—and economic—landscape of the area. Every year the ruins serve as backdrop to the **Konark Dance Festival** (Dec. 1-5), an open-air celebration featuring renowned *odissi* dances. Half the town, it seems, freelances as "guides" to the temple and its racy iconography, while the other half hawks trinkets from the street-side stalls surrounding the temple's entrance. Archaeologists are still debating if the sun temple at Konark, in Luxor, Egypt, is a relative of this one.

NATAMANDIRA AND JAGAMOHAN. Upon entering the walled compound, the first visible structure is the *natamandira* (dance or festival hall), a pillared platform decorated with carvings of *odissi* dance poses and flanked by two *gajasimhas*, the motif of a Hindu lion mounting a Buddhist elephant and trampling the desires of men. Beyond rises the staggering step-pyramid of the *jagamohan* (porch or assembly hall), the temple's most prominent feature at over 50m high. The porch's east-facing door was designed to catch the light of the rising sun and to reflect it into the sanctuary. To prevent the porch from collapsing, it was filled with concrete and sand in 1904, thus blocking the sanctuary's usual entrance.

PLATFORM AND PORCH. The *jagamohan* and the sanctuary are mounted on a heavily ornamented platform. Carved as a mythical chariot, the platform contains 24 giant wheels (representing the hours of the day and the fortnights of the year) and is driven by seven horses (symbolic of the days of the week) on the sides of the eastern staircases. (This chariot-wheel motif is regularly incorporated into the facades of contemporary Orissan buildings, having become the state's most enduring icon.) Images decorating the clock-like spokes of the wheels follow the progress of a typical day. Looking at the fourth wheel on the southern side, the first four spokes depict a woman bathing and performing housework, while the last four spokes—the nighttime hours—show her making love to her husband.

The carvings on the *jagamohan*, conceived to reflect the entirety of the world, are divided into three levels whose heights correspond to the age of their intended audience: G-rated animal parades line the platform's bottom edge, erotic images above entice the imaginations of young men and women, and slightly more pious, mature images fill the highest tier. Close inspection of the masterful friezes reveals a giraffe, priests, princes and dancers indulging in various kinds of amorous play.

SANCTUARY. Behind the porch, steps lead up to the exterior of the sanctuary and three beautiful images of Surya on the southern, western, and northern sides, show his increasing fatigue as he makes his daily run. Two modern staircases lead from the statues down to the remains of the sanctuary itself. Considering the breathtaking appearance of the sun temple as a whole, the sanctuary seems somewhat plain. A large amount of the adornment within, however, would have been in the form of murals, paintings, wooden carvings and silken banners, none of which have withstood the centuries that Nature had to ravage them. The Surya statue that once presided here no longer exists, and archaeologists can only speculate about its design. There is some archaeological evidence to support the legend that the idol, perhaps of magnetite, was suspended in the air between massive pieces of lodestone. According to the legend, the magnets were so powerful that they disrupted the compasses of seafaring ships that strayed close to shore, and angered some so much that in the 15th or 16th century, the statue was destroyed by disgruntled Portuguese sailors who had been tricked by the deity once too often. Perhaps you'll find it more likely that it rested on the chlorite pedestal that still exists. The frieze on the eastern side of the pedestal shows King Narasimha and his queen. The northern and southern faces portray their retinues.

MAYADEVI TEMPLE. Behind the sanctuary of the Sun Temple are the remains of a **Mayadevi Temple.** Now considered to be an earlier Surya temple, the small sanctuary and porch may have housed an image of one of Surya's wives once the main temple was built. More intricate sculpture decorates the exterior.

ORISSA

OTHER SIGHTS

NINE PLANETS SHRINE (NAVAGRAHA). A 6m-long, black marble monolith, exquisitely carved with the faces of the nine planets, used to rest above the eastern entrance to the *jagamohana*, truly a masterpiece. The British cut it in half in a botched attempt to plunder it one night and move it to a museum in England. Now the slab sits in a shed near the northeastern corner of the compound and is a center of local worship, as it used to be long before.

ARCHAEOLOGICAL MUSEUM. Sculptures from the temple were scattered about the site by successive waves of plunderers and collectors. Some of the finest fragments—cleaned, polished, and reconstructed—are now on display in the Archaeological Museum. (Other fragments from the temple's sculptures are kept in the Indian Museum in Kolkata and the Victoria and Albert Museum in London.) The museum also sells the Archaeological Survey's informative guide to the Sun Temple for Rs50. *(Just past the Panthanivas. Open Sa-Th 10am-5pm. Rs5.)*

🌊 BEACHES

Three kilometers down the road to Puri, the legendary Chandrabhaga (a waterhole where the original Surya image for the first Sun Temple was found) and a small fishing village give way to vacant expanses of white sand and endless sea. Beautiful and unspoiled, the beaches stretch for miles—however, sunning yourself on the marvelous beach and gaping at the scenery is all you can really do, as **the fast currents and uneven sea bed make it dangerous for swimmers.**

PURI ପୁରୀ   ☎ 06752

Despite the multitudes who have descended upon its shores throughout the ages, the small, quiet beach town of Puri still remains very much a pilgrim's paradise. As one of the four holy *dhams* of India, Puri and its skyline are dominated by the immense Jagannath temple, dedicated to the Lord of the Universe as his "place of eating." Under the temple's shadow, miles of white beach lure small armies of vacationers from landlocked cities all over India. Moreover, in the 1960s and 1970s, Puri's permissive attitudes (and plentiful supply of drugs) made it a popular stop along India's well-established hippie trail. Today, three distinct varieties of visitors haunt Puri, each claiming a section of town as their hangout and rarely intermingling. Hindu pilgrims tend to occupy the area near the Jagannath Temple (closed to non-Hindus) and the eight *dharamsalas* that line the Bada Danda (Grand Rd.); Indians on holiday or honeymoon populate the busy downtown boardwalk area called Swargadwar; and middle-aged men, bikini-clad women, youthful Japanese, and other international characters mellow out in the emptier, wallet-friendly eastern portion of Chakratirtha Rd. Besides the local deities, the city's most regular residents are probably the friendly, hardworking fishermen, still farming the seas in boats from a bygone era. Puri is best visited September-March, but some really good deals await in the low season, typically June-August, when most Indian tourists make the summer trip to warmer climates and prices fall.

🎫 TRANSPORTATION

Trains: Puri Railway Station (☎ 224995), Station Rd. and Hospital Rd. Express to: **Kolkata** (7-11hr., 7 and 9:40pm, Rs145) and **Delhi** (10-28hr., 3 per day 9:30am and 9pm, Rs380). There are regular trains to **Bhubaneswar** (2hr., 6-7 per day, Rs26), but the bus is more convenient, if not quite as comfortable.

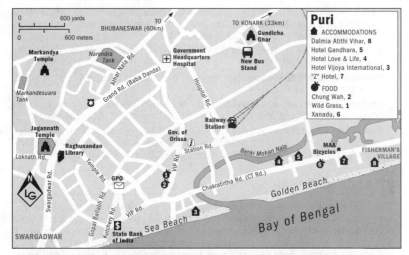

Buses: New Bus Stand (☎223786), at the east end of Bada Danda, next to the Guchinda temple. To: **Bhubaneswar** (2hr., every 10min. 5am-5pm, Rs25); **Kolkata** (16hr., 6am, Rs180); **Cuttack** (3½hr., every 30min. 5am-5pm, Rs25); **Konark** (1hr., every 15min. 7am-7pm, Rs20). Numerous private companies operate interstate buses. Tour agencies (including **Orissa Tourism**) and hotel desks make arrangements.

Local Transportation: Unrushed **cycle-** and **auto-rickshaws** pedal and hoot their way from one corner of Puri to another for less than Rs30—the going rate is Rs7 per km; expect to be charged more. **Local buses** (under Rs5) are often in poor condition. One useful route runs from the New Bus Stand to the Jagannath Temple, to the beach, and back (Rs5). **Maa Unique,** just past "Z" hotel on the inland side of CT Rd., rents bicycles (Rs15 per day), mopeds (Rs150 per day), and a variety of motorcycles (Rs150-250 per day). Deposit, payment, and license required. Open daily 7:30am-9pm.

ORIENTATION AND PRACTICAL INFORMATION

Puri's extra-wide main drag, **Bada Danda** or **Grand Road,** runs east-west through the northern (inland) part of town, with a number of old houses and shops with local handicrafts and appliqué work, then arches southwest near the **Jagannath Temple** to become **Swargadwar Road.** There are many hotels, restaurants and a large market at Swargadwar, mainly frequented by residents and Indian tourist families. The Bay of Bengal forms the town's southern border. Along the shore, **Chakratirtha (CT) Road** has a number of budget hotels and restaurants catering to more independent travelers, both foreign and Indian. As it heads west, CT Rd. intersects with **VIP Road** and eventually becomes **Marine Parade Road,** a seaside strip most popular with vacationing Indians.

Tourist Office: Government of Orissa Tourist Office, Station Rd. (☎222664). From the railway station, follow Station Rd. west for 200m. The office is on the right just before VIP Rd. Open M-Sa 10am-5pm. They run a helpful counter in the station as well (☎223637), but the Station Rd. office has more info on tours, accommodations, and hiring vehicles. Open daily 8am-8pm.

Currency Exchange: State Bank of India, VIP Rd. (☎223623). From the station, head west on Station Rd., turn left onto VIP Rd., then right at the Netaji Subhash Chandra Bose statue; it is 400m down on the left, just before Kutchery Rd. Open M-F 10am-2pm

ORISSA

and 2:30-3:30pm, Sa 10am-12:30pm. **Hotel Gandhara** changes traveler's checks for a fee. Open M-Sa 8am-8pm, Su 8am-2pm. In a pinch, five-star hotels normally change US dollars and traveler's checks at exorbitant rates.

Police: Town Police Station, Bada Danda (☎222039), near Jagannath Temple. **City Beach Police** (☎222025).

Hospital: Government Headquarters Hospital, Bada Danda (☎223742). Most hotels have doctors on call.

Internet: Nanako Tour and Travels, CT Rd. (☎229696). Internet Rs30 per hr. Open daily 8:30am-11:30pm. Many other CT Rd. establishments also have connections.

Post Office: GPO, Kutchery Rd. (☎222051). From CT Rd., go west past the Bose statue and turn right after the State Bank of India. Go north on Kutchery Rd.; the GPO is on the first street to the left. Open M-Sa 9am-6pm, Su 3-5:30pm. **Postal Code:** 752001.

ACCOMMODATIONS

There are literally hundreds of places to stay at in Puri. If you stroll along the seaside, you'll find you can stay at almost all beachfront properties at a price. Budget accommodations (including those listed below) are located along the length of CT Rd., becoming more concentrated at its eastern end. Most have early morning check-outs, no-guest policies, and loosely enforced curfews. Most hotels in Swargadwar and on Marine Parade Dr. are frequented by Indian tourists, so look among those for deals in the low season.

■ **"Z" Hotel** (☎222554), east of Hotel Gandhara, right at the center of CT Rd. This place is well known in its own right, so you won't have trouble finding it. Enormous and airy, "Z" (pronounced "Zed," of course) was once the home of the Maharaja of Serampore in Bengal. Hints of luxury are still found in the sea-view rooms and courtyard. Staff managed by a former chief minister of Orissa. Excellent cook and room service. Beach access. 6-bed dorms (women only) Rs60; singles Rs150; doubles Rs300-500. ❶

■ **Hotel Gandhara** (☎224117), 700m down CT Rd., just beyond Hotel Love & Life, opposite a path to the beach. The 19th-century bungalow in front contains a dorm and some budget rooms; the 5-story bldg. behind is pricier. Smart and well-run, with a travel agency, garden, and restaurant serving Japanese food for Rs100. Check-out 9am. Dorms Rs40-50; singles Rs110; doubles Rs150-750. AmEx/V. ❶

Hotel Vijoya International (☎223705), CT Rd., close to the Netaji statue end, next to the massive Hotel Mayfair. A very nice 4-star hotel with a lovely stretch of beach and a swimming pool. Efficient travel desk, good food and 24hr. room service make for a great stay. Standard non-A/C rooms Rs770, A/C rooms Rs1210-1870. MC/V. ❹

Dalmia Atithi Vihar, CT Rd. (☎225557), behind Hotel Pink House. An excellent sea-facing property with central A/C and a peaceful ambience. Older couples often frequent the place. Great strictly veg. **restaurant** ❶ with Rajasthani *thalis* (Rs60). Large ground floor rooms Rs900, airy 1st fl. rooms with great views Rs1100. ❹

Hotel Love & Life (☎224433; fax 226093), next to Hotel Gandhara. A long-time favorite with foreign budget travelers. Less romantic than the name suggests, but just as relaxed. Dorms Rs30; singles Rs80-125; doubles Rs100-250; cottages Rs200-250. ❶

FOOD

Food in Puri is cheap and tailor-made for foreign tourists, with an array of non-Indian options on CT Rd. Fish is as fresh as you'd expect it to be. Almost all hotels have a dining room or restaurant, which is not restricted to their own guests.

"Z" Hotel Restaurant. The kitchen staff does a superlative job of cooking up a spicy fish curry (Rs40). The *navaratan* (Rs30) and *aloo dum* (Rs15) are outstanding, and the beer (Rs70) always chilled. Bring insect repellent if you are sitting near the window. Open daily 7am-3pm and 6-10:30pm. ❶

Hotel Pink House Restaurant, next to the hotel. Open-air thatched hut with a Hindu Bob Marley mural, a superb stereo system, and a sea-breezin', wave-crashin' ocean just outside. International menu includes *thalis* (Rs24-40) and seafood. Open 7am-11pm. ❶

Xanadu, CT Rd., about 75m past Hotel Gandhara. This little shack-and-garden makes pretty much anything you could want. Polite service, mosquito coils, and many Madonna tunes included. Breakfast with baked beans Rs65. Open daily 7am-11pm. ❸

Chung Wah, VIP Rd. Head west on CT Rd. then right on VIP Rd., about 150m down on the left. Clean, cool, and the most authentic Chinese grub in Orissa. Veg. dishes Rs25-50, garlic fish Rs85. Open daily 11:30am-3pm and 6:30-10:30pm. ❷

Wild Grass, VIP Rd., around the corner from Chung Wah. Orissan sculpture and plenty of jungle all around—kind of hokey, but fun. Slightly pricey Chinese, Indian, and seafood (Rs50-120). Eat in your choice of tree-house or hut. Open daily 11:30am-11:30pm. ❷

◉ SIGHTS

JAGANNATH TEMPLE. Constructed in the early 12th century by the Ganga king Anantavaram Chodaganga, the Jagannath Temple is one of the most stunning examples of Kalinga-style temple architecture and one of the holiest sites in Orissa. With its central viman rising to a height of 65m, it is the main feature of Puri's skyline, the visible destination of many a pilgrim's journey, and a symbol of the power Jagannath, Lord of the Universe, continues to wield over the town below. Also observable from many miles out at sea, the white, sandstone temple is sometimes referred to as the "white pagoda," a name given by British sailors who used it as a navigational point.

Inside the tower, the mighty lord (an incarnation of Krishna), his brother Balabhadra, and his sister Subhadra reside in roughly-hewn, abstract, wooden bodies. Tiny arms extend from stumpy, legless abdomens; enormous eyes glare out from the disproportionately large faces. It is said that Lord Jagannath has no eyelids, so that he can continually look after the well-being of the world; his small arms stretch outward in a gesture of love. Temple priests cite ancient tales to explain the peculiarly shaped forms—the peeking eyes of a king's wife prevented the architect from finishing his work—while academics suggest that the deities have their origins in the traditions of Orissa's indigenous people. New evidence suggests that the peoples of the region had links with the ancient Sumerians, and the Jagannath Triad are descendants of Hittite and Assyrian religion. Some 6000 priests attend to the divine trinity, performing a set of daily activities that include bathing, feeding, dressing (five different changes), and brushing teeth. Every 12-19 years the pampered images are carved anew from specially chosen trees.

Patterned on the same architectural principles as the older Lingaraj Temple in Bhubaneswar, Jagannath's abode is strictly aligned from east to west and completely surrounded by a 20m high wall. There is an entrance at each compass point, but the eastern **simbhadwara** (lion gate), off Bada Danda, sees most of the temple's traffic. The *bhog mandap* (offering hall) and *nritya mandap* (dance hall) nearest to the entrance were 15th- and 16th-century additions to the original *jagamohana* (assembly hall). These halls and their white, pyramidal roofs lead up to the flag-and-wheel-crowned *deul* (inner sanctuary), the divine trio's resting-place. Protected by a second wall and raised on a platform, the centermost structures were originally surrounded by water and accessible

NO WORK, ALL PLAY

A TOUR OF THE UNIVERSE

Sweating, singing, shouting, and praying, exuberant crowds move *en masse* to enact an event of cosmic proportions. Though the **Rath Yatra** (Cart Festival) of Puri is celebrated two days after the new moon in the month of Ashadha (June-July), preparations begin a month beforehand. New *raths* (chariots) are built every year. On the full moon of the previous month, *Jyesththa* (May-June), the deities are bathed and retired from public view for 14 days of treatment and rest. They reappear, refreshed, invigorated, and ready to roll three days before the festival day kicks off. The grand day begins with the divine procession, or the **Pahandi Bije,** during which the gods are carried from the temple to their chariots in a rhythmical march called *pahandi,* accompanied by beating cymbals and drums and thousands of devotees chanting prayers. This is followed by the **Gajapati's** (the King of Puri) gesture of *chhera paharna,* ritually "sweeping" the chariots to symbolize humanity humbling itself in preparation for the mercy and goodwill of the gods.

As the mesmerizing chants and ecstatic shouts of "Jai Jaggannath" fill the air, some 4000 people pull the three chariots from the main gate of the temple east along Grand Avenue.

only by boat. Over the years, the moat was filled in to make the structure more stable and better protected from the cyclones that sweep in from the Bay of Bengal.

The massive temple compound hosts action-packed days of *darshan* and treats worshippers to devotionals and sacred dances at night. Over 20,000 people earn their livelihood in the complex: entire communities of artists and cooks work to produce the ritual materials, which include 56 different food offerings. Besides feeding the gods, the massive kitchen serves *mahaprasad* to 10,000 devotees every day (and up to 25,000 during festival time) in the adjacent **Ananda Bazaar.** The temple does not allow cameras, leather, or non-Hindus—even former Prime Minister Indira Gandhi was denied access because of her marriage to a Parsi.

To get a gander at the action beyond the temple walls, follow the monkeys and climb to the top of the **Raghunandan Library,** opposite the eastern gate. *(Open daily 7am-noon and 4-8pm.)* Other views may be obtained from the roofs of the buildings to the west of the compound; the landlord will request some *baksheesh* (Rs30-50).

🏖 BEACHES

Puri's beaches have a reputation for being the most beautiful in eastern India, although too-regular visits by foreigners, nationals, and toiletless locals mean that many are far from the image of a pristine paradise. Still, the sun, sand, and surf are inviting and all the entertainment many travelers need. At the main strip, **Sea Beach,** near the town center, Indian tourists wade in their customary fully-clothed style; farther east by CT Rd., **Golden Beach** has fewer coral-salesmen and oily massage-*wallahs* offering their services. Beyond the fishing village, you only have to share the white sands with a few pieces of driftwood. The lifeguards (locally called *nolias,* you'll spot them by their conical white hats) offer inner tubes, and it's usually a good idea to engage one's service to keep an eye on you even if you're a good swimmer (Rs50-100). Some of the local fishermen can be talked into providing a 3hr. tour (Rs150), though rough waters and tricky tides can make this a risky business. While the beaches are generally safe, **locals advise against going alone at night or bringing any valuables.**

👁 🎵 FESTIVALS AND ENTERTAINMENT

In a pilgrim city like Puri, festivals are common throughout the year, although locals don't always make them well-known. The granddaddy of them all is the **Rath Yatra Festival,** when Lord Jagannath, his brother Balabhadra, and his sister Subhadra are paraded through the city on large wooden chariots (see p. 468). Puri's **Beach Festival** showcases the best of Orissan folk dancing, music, and handicrafts. The Government of Orissa Tourist Office also arranges **dance and theatrical programs** (check their bulletin board for current information). You can always take an evening stroll along Marine Parade through the Swargadwar area and the **night market** of western Puri.

NEAR PURI

👁 LALITAGIRI, UDAYAGIRI, AND RATNAGIRI

Orissa's "Golden Triangle" of tourist points might be shaped by the Hindu shrines of Bhubaneswar, Konark, and Puri, but the state has a rich Buddhist heritage as well. Forming their own "mini golden triangle," Udayagiri, Lalitagiri, and Ratnagiri stand as remarkable ancient monuments to a religious culture steeped in art and learning. The site at **Lalitagiri,** dating from the 1st century AD, is the oldest in the region and also the most easily accessed. A large brick monastery, a ceremonial hall, and plenty of votive *stupas* lead up to a museum and, at the crest of the hill, a reconstructed *stupa*. **Ratnagiri,** the largest of Orissa's Buddhist sites, features two monasteries, a gorgeous green chlorite doorway, an impressive *stupa*, and several other shrines and sculptures over its extensive, fenced grounds. The Archaeological Survey of India **Museum** displays artifacts from the three sites, including two giant Buddha heads. (Open Sa-Th 10am-5pm. Rs2.) The remains of 7th-century **Udayagiri**—a square platform *stupa*, stone well, monasteries, and *bodhisvatta* sculptures— are the most unspoiled, having been only recently unearthed.

All three towns can be visited on a long daytrip from **Cuttack,** with lots of gorgeous natural scenery along the way. Buses from Puri to Cuttack leave daily every 30min. 5am-5pm (3½hr., Rs25). From the bus stand in Cuttack, take the 60km (1hr.) ride to **Chandikol** (Rs20). *Tempos* from the bus stop make the journey to Ratnagiri and stop at Udayagiri on the way back (Rs350 round-trip; add Rs100 for Lalitagiri). You can also climb aboard a *tempo* ferrying locals to villages near the sites; Balichandrapur and Patharajpur are the convenient turn-offs. It's possible to complete the entire circuit in this way for less than Rs40, but you will need very good karma to find tempos when you need them. Bring plenty of water—*dhabas* are ubiquitous in Chandikol, but bottled water is scarce. (All sites open daily dawn-dusk. Ratnagiri and Lalitagiri each have a US$5 foreigner entrance fee. Udayagiri is free.)

ORISSA

Find (Our Student Airfares are cheap, flexible & exclusive) great Student Airfares everywhere at StudentUniverse.com and **Get lost.**

 StudentUniverse.com

Student Airfares everywhere

PUNJAB AND HARYANA ਪੰਜਾਬ ਨ੍ਦ ਹਰਿਯਾਣਾ

When India gained its independence from the British in 1947, the Punjab (from the Persian *punj aab*, or five rivers) was divided up between India and Pakistan, but only two of the five rivers for which the region was named remained within India's new borders. Nineteen years later, the state was divided again, this time along linguistic lines, to form the states of Punjab and Haryana. These states share the neutral capital of Chandigarh, a fertile geography, and the pride of overcoming a violent history to become India's most prosperous region.

Punjab has long been considered the doorway to the Subcontinent. Both the Aryans (1500 BC) and the Mughals (AD 1562) invaded India via the Punjab, bringing with them a specter of violence that has continued to haunt the region well into the 20th century. During the massacres that followed Partition, more lives were lost in Punjab than anywhere else in India. But despite its battered past, Punjab has wielded great influence in India. The majority of Sikhs, and their holy city of Amritsar, are in Punjab (see **Sikhism**, p. 79); the perilous struggles of their homeland account for the religion's doctrine of military readiness. Any visit to Punjab results in considerable exposure to Sikh hospitality, from nights spent in one of the state's numerous *gurudwaras* to round-the-clock wanderings of Amristar's **Golden Temple,** the religion's welcoming holy site.

Other parts of the state are also marked by evidence of its dual identity as a long-suffering region and the bread basket of India. The capital, Chandigarh, was created following the country's victorious struggle for independence. Born of the optimism of India's newly independent government, the city is an example of meticulous Western planning. The Golden Temple is the embodiment of the coexistence of prosperity and turmoil in the region. Unfortunately, recent history yields the supporting evidence: in 1983-84, Sikh militants massacred Hindus and barricaded themselves within the temple; the Indian government responded by raiding the holy site. The militants were members of Punjab's *Shiromani Akali Dal* party, which demanded an independent Sikh nation, Khalistan ("Land of the Pure"). The siege of the temple led to desertions and mutinies within the Sikh army, and, eventually, to the murder of Indira Gandhi by her Sikh bodyguards. Thousands of Sikhs were killed in the Hindu rioting that followed the murder of the prime minister. Only recently has support for the Khalistan movement begun to wane in the region.

HIGHLIGHTS OF PUNJAB AND HARYANA

Amritsar's **Golden Temple** (p. 481), the most sacred site of the Sikh religion, astounds visitors with its dignified take on sparkling excess.

Weird and wonderful **Chandigarh's** (p. 472) pre-planned sectors and structures represent a French architect's dream of the future, set in pre-poured concrete.

CHANDIGARH चंडीगढ़ ਚੰਡੀਗੜ੍ਹ ☎ 0172

When Punjab (including present-day Haryana) was partitioned, its original capital, Lahore, lay across the border in Pakistan. A new capital was needed, and the Nehru government decided on the present site of Chandigarh. A team of Western architects, the most prominent being Le Corbusier, seized the opportunity to mobilize plans for a revolution in urban landscape. The result is a huge grid of broad, park-filled avenues and "sectors" that make up modern-day Chandigarh. Le Corbusier's dream of "sun, space, and silence" has largely been realized, at least by Indian standards. Chandigarh is much less crowded than most cities in the country, and, despite the abundance of concrete, the landscape's dominant color is green. The city also maintains a startling level of cleanliness—waste bins are found in strategic locations throughout the sectors, and their "Use Me" signs do not go unheeded. The city's residents take great pride in the city, which many of their fellow Indians believe to be the most beautiful in the country. Foreign tourists, most of whom do not come to India seeking reminders of home, may be disappointed by Chandigarh's orderliness—farm animals look out of place on the concrete plazas. Still, many come here to take a break and relax for a few days in somewhat familiar territory before entering the fray once again.

▐ TRANSPORTATION

Flights: Airport, 11km out of town (auto-rickshaw Rs120). **Indian Airlines** (☎ 703510) flies to: **Delhi** (40min., 10:30am, Rs3020) and **Goa** (5hr., 10:30am, Rs9440). Book well in advance for **Leh** (1hr., Th 9:30am, Rs3170). **Jet Airlines** (☎ 741465) offers daily flights to Delhi (1hr., 2:40pm, US$75).

Trains: The **railway station** is 8km southeast of town. Local bus #37 connects the station to the bus stand (20min., Rs8). Auto-rickshaws will go there for Rs20-30. **Train Reservation Inquiry** (☎ 653131), on the 3rd fl. of the bus stand. Open M-Sa 8am-8pm, Su 8am-2pm. To: **Amristar** (Rs160) and **Delhi** (Rs143) via **Ambala** (1hr., 5 per day 8am-1am, Rs121); **Shimla** via **Kalka** (30min., 5 per day 4am-10pm, Rs121).

Buses: As long as you're at the right station, you won't have to wait long for a bus in Chandigarh. The city is a bus transport hub, with five companies (Punjab Roadways, UP Roadways, Haryana Roadways, Himachal Pradesh Roadways, and Chandigarh Transport Undertaking) operating out of two terminals. The largest, **Interstate Bus Terminal 1,** is on the southwest edge of Sector 17, opposite the hotels in Sector 22. To: **Dehra Dun** (5½hr., 6 per day 7:30am-3:15pm, Rs100); **Delhi** (5½hr., every 30min. 7am-12:30am, Rs116; deluxe 3 per day, Rs 170); **Jaipur** (12hr., 6 per day 4am-2:50pm, Rs238); **Rishikesh** (6½hr., 1:40pm and 7pm, Rs116); **Shimla** (every 10min. 4:30am-7pm; Rs85). **ISBT 2** is in Sector 43. To: **Dharamsala** (8hr., 10 per day 5am-1am, Rs146); **Jammu** (8hr., 8 per day 5am-8pm, Rs147); **Manali** (12hr., 10 per day 3:30am-8pm, Rs263); **Dalhousie** and **Chamba** via **Pathankot** (8hr, Rs110).

Local Transportation: Cycle-rickshaws charge Rs15 for a 2-sector trip. **Auto-rickshaws** charge about double. Local **buses** leave from the main bus station, Sector 17. Bus #13 goes to the Rock Garden (15min., Rs8), bus #37 to the train station (20min., Rs8). CITCO (see below) rents **bicycles** (Rs100 full day with Rs500 deposit).

▐ ORIENTATION

No one could accuse Chandigarh of being illogical—the city was plotted on a massive grid—but it can be confusing, nonetheless, as all the roads look identical. The streets run northwest to southeast and northeast to southwest, dividing the town into 50 sectors. Each sector is a self-sufficient unit with its own market places and

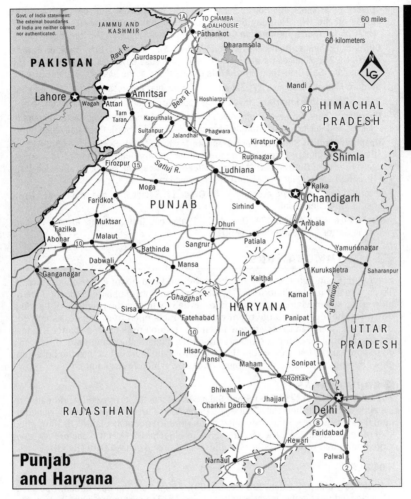

Govt. of India statement: The external boundaries of India are neither correct nor authenticated.

Punjab and Haryana

shopping centers. **Sector 1** is to the north, where the main government buildings, **Sukhna Lake** and the **Rock Garden,** are situated. The rest are numbered from west to east, then east to west, in rows proceeding to the south. **Sector 17** is the heart of the city. Most services, including the **bus station,** are located here. **Sector 22** has its share of cheap restaurants and hotels as well as several interesting temples.

🛈 PRACTICAL INFORMATION

Tourist Office: Chandigarh Industrial and Tourism Development Corporation (CITCO) (☎ 704614, railway station 658005) has an office upstairs from the bus stand (open M-Sa 9am-5pm) and at the railway station (open for arrivals). CITCO runs a "hop-on-hop-off" bus tour of the city, which makes stops at Sukhna Lake, the Rock Garden, and several other spots. The double-decker bus runs on the hour and stops at the tourist office on the ½hr. Half-day ticket Rs50. There are also **UP** (☎707649) and **HP** (☎708569) **Tourist Information Centres** at the bus stand. Open M-F 9am-5pm.

Currency Exchange: Banks cluster around "Bank Sq." in Sector 17B. **Bank of Baroda** (☎709692) exchanges traveler's checks and gives cash advances on MC/V. Open M-F 10am-2pm, Sa 10am-1pm. **24hr. ATMs** can be found at the post office and ISBT #1.

Market: Markets in sectors 17, 22, and 23 are popular with locals.

Police: Police Headquarters (☎742655), opposite Sector 9. Open M-Sa 10am-6pm.

Pharmacy: There are several pharmacies near the medical center in Sector 17 and in Sector 22-C, including **Anil and Co.,** Bayshop #42 (☎777565). Open daily 8am-9pm.

Hospital/Medical Services: Post Graduate Institute (PGI), Sector 12 (☎543823) is the best hospital in Chandigarh and one of the most reputable in India. 24hr. emergency services. **Government Medical College and Hospital,** Sector 32, Dakshin Marg (☎665253, emergency ext. 1200) has an ambulance service.

Internet: Cyber cafes are everywhere. Try **Cyber 17,** Sector 17C, near the theater. Rs35 per hr. Open 9am-9pm.

Post Office: GPO, Sector 17A. Open M-Sa 10am-5pm. **DHL** and other express couriers are in Sector 17. **Postal Code:** 160017.

▌ ACCOMMODATIONS

Staying in Chandigarh is easy on the wallet and can be an experience in itself. Treat yourself to simplicity in a ▌**gurudwara.** Stubborn persistence in the face of glowering, spear-wielding guards will eventually win you the privilege of bedding down for the night in a large room with floor mats open to everyone, usually for free. Unless you plan to stay in one in Amritsar, don't pass up this chance. No cigarettes, alcohol, or other intoxicants are allowed inside the compound. If this isn't quite your cup of tea, trot across the street from the bus station into the hotel jungle of Sector 22 or try the government *bhawan*, which fills up quickly.

▌ GURUDWARAS

The Sikh owners of ▌**Sri Guru Singh Sabha ❶,** Sector 19, are friendly and eager to instruct you about their faith, once you persuade them to let you stay. Large communal rooms are free, and there also clean double rooms available (Rs100). Max. stay of three days. Also, the *gurudwaras* in ▌**Sector 22 ❶** and ▌**Sector 9 ❶** have large communal rooms (free) or doubles with fan and shared bath (Rs50).

HOTELS

Hotel Satyadeep, Section 22B (☎703103), 250m from the bus station. Spacious, clean, and comfortable rooms with large balconies. The best budget hotel in town. ❷

Hotel Divyadeep, Section 22B (☎705191 or 721169). Under the same management as Hotel Satyadeep and offering similarly well-outfitted rooms. Doubles Rs250-650. ❷

Panchayat Bhawan, Sector 18 (☎780701), on the northeast side. Large rooms around a courtyard. Reservations recommended. Doubles with bath Rs400-900. ❸

Transit Lodge, ISBT #1 (☎712417). This recently-opened government hotel offers standard doubles with attached baths. Windows look out over the bustling scene below; unfortunately, they can't keep out all of the noise. A free *thali* at Tandoor restaurant included in all room prices. Dorms Rs100; doubles Rs350. ❶

Hotel Sunbeam (☎708100), Sector 22B, across from the bus station. Higher prices afford the expected upgrades—air-conditioning, sanitized toilets, and a higher marble-to-concrete ratio. Singles Rs1095; doubles Rs1495. ❺

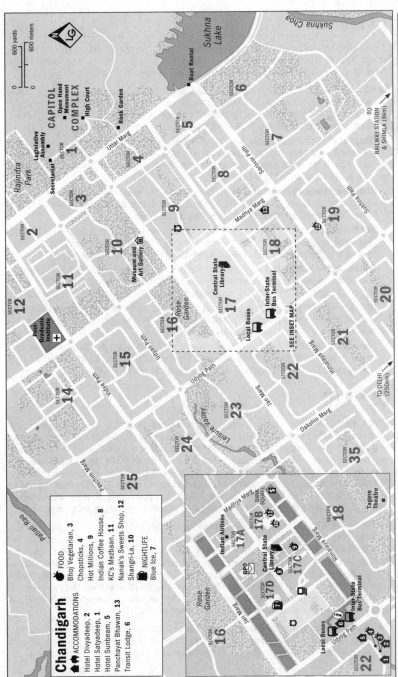

Chandigarh

🛏 ACCOMMODATIONS
Hotel Divyadeep, 2
Hotel Satyadeep, 1
Hotel Sunbeam, 5
Panchayat Bhawan, 13
Transit Lodge, 6

🍴 FOOD
Bhoj Vegetarian, 3
Chopsticks, 4
Hot Millions, 9
Indian Coffee House, 8
KC's Mezbaan, 11
Nanak's Sweets Shop, 12
Shangri-La, 10

NIGHTLIFE
Blue Ice, 7

0   600 yards
0   600 meters

CAPITOL COMPLEX
Open Hand Monument
High Court
Rock Garden

Legislative Assembly
Secretariat
Rajindra Park

Sukhna Lake
Boat Rental
Sukhna Choa

SECTOR 1
SECTOR 2
SECTOR 3
SECTOR 4
SECTOR 5
SECTOR 6
SECTOR 7
SECTOR 8
SECTOR 9
SECTOR 10
SECTOR 11
SECTOR 12
SECTOR 14
SECTOR 15
SECTOR 16
SECTOR 17
SECTOR 18
SECTOR 19
SECTOR 20
SECTOR 21
SECTOR 22
SECTOR 23
SECTOR 24
SECTOR 25
SECTOR 35

Uttar Marg
Madhya Marg
Udyan Path
Vidya Path
Sarovar Path
Sukhna Path
Himalaya Marg
Jan Marg
Dakshin Marg
Leisure Valley

Post Graduate Institute
Museum and Art Gallery
Rose Garden
Central State Library
Inter-State Bus Terminal
Local Buses

SEE INSET MAP

Patiali Rao
Passimm Marg

TO DELHI (250m)
TO RAILWAY STATION & SHIMLA (8km)

INSET MAP:
Rose Garden
SECTOR 16
Jan Marg
Madhya Marg
Indian Airlines
SECTOR 17A
SECTOR 17B
BANK SQUARE
Central State Library
SECTOR 17D
GPO
SECTOR 17C
Himalaya Marg
SECTOR 18
Inter-State Bus Terminal
Local Buses
Udyog Path
SECTOR 22
Tagore Theatre

FOOD

There's no shortage of restaurants in Chandigarh. Sector 17 offers pricey restaurants, American-style fast-food joints, and a scattering of cheap *dhabas*. *Thalis*, *samosas*, and local food can be found outside sectors 17 or 22.

KC's Mezbaan, Sector 17, on the north side, behind KC Cinema. Muslim-influenced culinary styles—from the *nawab* of Avadh's favorite *gushtaba* (Kashmiri meatballs in yogurt sauce, Rs140) to the *nizam* of Hyderabad's beloved *mury malai tikka* (Rs140). Flowers, fountains, and beer on tap (Rs30-35). Open daily 11am-11:30pm. ❹

Chopsticks, Sector 22B, down from Hotel Divyadeep. Stern waiters serve heaping plates of excellent Chinese under a sloping roof. Red lighting and a jungle of plants in the entryway add to the atmosphere. Vegetable dishes Rs85-95, chicken Rs140-160, steamed rice Rs60. Open daily 11am-11pm. ❸

Bhoj Vegetarian Restaurant, Sector 22B, directly below Hotel Divyadeep. Serves delicious enormous veg. *thalis* (Rs 70-72) and a full Indian dessert menu (Rs7-15) in a clean, comfortable environment. Open daily 11am-10pm. ❶

Hot Millions, Sector 17C, near the library. One of many fast food joints in Sector 17 offering pizza, burgers, and ice cream. A confusing self-service procedure adds a degree of excitement. Pizzas Rs75-121, burgers Rs44-63. Open daily 9am-10pm. ❷

Indian Coffee House, has 4 locations in Sector 17, all offering the same fare. Some of the best dressed waiters in town serve you your choice of 5 types of coffee (Rs7-15), 6 types of eggs (Rs7-26) and 7 types of *dosas* (Rs12-23). Open daily 9am-10pm. ❶

Nanak's Sweets Shop, Sector 19D, next to the 19D *gurudwara*. Brave palates will be rewarded with a chalky, dough-based taste-sensation. Strong whiskey-and-beer aperitifs. Chocolate, coconut, and pistachio *barfi* Rs80.❶

Shangri-La, SCO 96, Sector 17C. Nepali-run Chinese restaurant decorated with red paneling, dragon paintings, silk lanterns, and a picture of the Dalai Lama. Szechuan-style sliced lamb Rs100, jasmine tea Rs15. Open daily 11am-11pm. ❸

SIGHTS

ROCK GARDEN. Waterfalls, ferns, and numerous trees give this glorified trash heap more of a garden feel than you might expect. In 1985, road construction supervisor Nek Chand began turning Chandigarh's mountains of construction waste into an artistic wonderland. Four foot high doorways, armies of stone figures, and many household items went into the making of this masterpiece. Today, his still-expanding creation meanders over 40 surreal acres. *(Sector 1, near the Capitol Complex. Open daily Apr.-Sept. 9am-1pm and 3-7pm; Oct.-Mar. 9am-6pm. Rs10. Appointments with Nek Chand, the garden's creator, occasionally available; inquire at the ticket window.)*

CAPITOL COMPLEX. Le Corbusier's plan for the city mimicked the anatomy of the human form. He built the city's Capitol Complex in Sector 1 as the "head" to the city's "body" (the parks are the "lungs"). The slab concrete, exposed brick, and *bris-soleil* (lowered sun-screens) style distinguishes the Capitol Complex from other Indian municipal buildings. The **High Court** and **Open Hand Monument** are much more accessible than the **Legislative Assembly** and **Secretariat;** only avid architectural enthusiasts should consider braving the hour long bureaucratic snarl that will yield them permission to wander the latter two buildings.

PARKS. Sukhna Lake, in the north, is a reservoir-turned-tourist-trap with a cafeteria, pub, mini-amusement park, and paddleboats. Come at sunset, hop in one of the **swan boats,** and float to the mangrove **alcoves** across the lake. *(2-seater Rs40 per*

30min., 4-seater Rs80 per 30min.) Le Corbusier used the term **Leisure Valley** for the long parkland which stretches through the heart of Chandigarh. The highlight of this public park is the **Zakir Rose Garden,** off Jan Marg in Sector 16, which is the largest rose garden in Asia and features 4000 species of roses. They are in bloom Jan.-Mar.; in February, the garden hosts the giant Rose Festival.

🎭 🎵 NIGHTLIFE AND ENTERTAINMENT

Chandigarh has a well-developed beer-drinking culture, and 25 pubs to prove it. The latest hot spot is **Blue Ice ❷,** Sector 17D. Everything from Punjabi pop to P. Diddy blasts over the sound system as you down imported brews (Rs150) with local hipsters. The blue and silver decor may require some eyeblinking adjustment time. Beer Rs60-150. A 200m crawl will take you to **Gymkhana ❷,** Sector 17D, another popular bar. With soft music and dim lighting, it's a bit more understated than its neighbor, and conversations are less of a vocal-chord-stretching ordeal. Beer Rs65-85; liquor Rs50-120. For an even more hushed experience in one of Chadigarh's classiest pubs, try the basement of **KC's Mezbaan,** which has Thunderbolt on tap. All of these bars offer snacks to soak up the booze, but if you'd prefer to have a dry night and a little more culture, head to the **Tagore Theatre,** Sector 18 (☎774278), which stages Shakespeare in Punjabi and dancing exhibitions.

AMRITSAR ਅਮ੍ਰਿਤਸਰ ☎0183

Modern-day Amritsar stretches far beyond the narrow winding streets between the 20 gates of the old city, but it continues to be defined by the awe-inspiring monument at its heart. The Golden Temple casts a long shadow over the largest city in Punjab, giving it the distinction of being the focal point of the Sikh faith. Guru Ram Das started construction of the temple in AD 1579, but the city, which is named for the sacred tank or "pool of immortal nectar" that surrounds the temple, did not begin to form until the Sikh holy book, the Guru Granth Sahib, was enshrined here by the fifth Guru, Arjun. Centuries of Mughal invasions kicked-off a cycle of destruction and reconstruction, and the calamities continued into the 1980s. Today, however, an atmosphere of peace and serenity envelops the Golden Temple, which seems to stand oblivious to its own turbulent history. Most tourists limit their tour of Amristar to the city's precious centerpiece, but there is still plenty to see beyond the walls of the complex, including some extremely well-stocked bazaars and nearby **Wagah,** the only open border crossing between India and Pakistan.

🚍 TRANSPORTATION

Flights: Raja Sanhsi Airport, 12km northwest of town. To **Delhi** (2hr., Tu and Sa 4:35am, Rs4065). Book at the **Indian Airlines** office, Court Rd. (☎2213392), halfway between Albert Rd. and Mall Rd. Open M-Sa 10am-5pm.

Trains: The **computer reservation** complex (☎2562811) is in the south end of the railway station. Open M-Sa 8am-1:30pm and 2-8pm, Su 8am-2pm. To: **Agra** (15hr.; 5:30, 8:15am, 4:10pm; Rs270); **Delhi** (5½-8hr.; 7 per day 5:15am-9:30pm; Rs124-270, express Rs565); **Haridwar** (12hr., 8:55pm, Rs150); **Jaipur** (19hr., W and Su 2:20pm, Rs310); **Lucknow** (18hr., 5 per day 5:45-9:15pm, Rs322); **Mumbai** (33hr., 8:45am and 9:30pm, Rs530); **Patna** (34hr., 5:45 and 6:30pm, Rs380).

Buses: Inquiry Office (☎2551734). Departure times change frequently. To: **Attari** (1hr., every 30min. 6am-8pm, Rs12); **Dalhousie** (6hr., 9:10am, Rs110); **Dehra Dun** (7hr., 7am, Rs188); **Delhi** (9hr., frequent 5:45am-9pm, Rs205); **Dharamsala** (7hr., 6am,

Rs113); **Jammu** (7hr., every 30min. 5am-4:30pm, Rs82); **Shimla** (11hr., 6am, Rs190). You may also reach **Shimla** via **Chandigarh** (5hr., every 30min. 4:20am-8:30pm, Rs105) or **Pathankot** (3hr., 4:30am-8pm, Rs46).

Local Transportation: Bicycle rental at **Raja Cycles,** across the street from the bus stand. Full-day Rs20 with Rs1000 deposit. Open M-Sa 5am-9pm. **Cycle-rickshaws** will run anywhere in town for Rs10-20. In the "new sections," **auto-rickshaws** can speed things up, but they move at a snail's pace through the old parts of the city.

✦ ORIENTATION

Amritsar's railway tracks divide the city into northern and southern sections. The older, livelier section of the city is to the south of the railway beyond the gates. **Bhandari Bridge** is the major vehicle conduit connecting north and south. North of the bridge is **Ram Bagh** park and the modern parts of the city. The old town is farther south, enclosed by **Circular Road,** which runs where the wall once stood. The Golden Temple is at the center of the circle. Most tourists limit their tour of the city to the temple compound and the area immediately north of it, but the maze of alleys and bazaars to the south and west also capture the feel of old Amritsar. The **bus stand** is northeast of the center, on the road from Delhi to the **railway station.**

🔃 PRACTICAL INFORMATION

Tourist Office: Punjab Government Tourist Office (☎2402452), in the Palace Hotel, opposite the railway station. Open M-Sa 9am-5pm. There is also a helpful **Information Center** at the Golden Temple (☎2553954). Open daily 7am-8pm.

Currency Exchange: State Bank of India (☎2531400), across from the Town Hall, exchanges currency and traveler's checks. Open M-F 10am-2pm, Sa 10am-noon. The railway area also has several offices that change **Pakistani rupees.** There are a number of licensed money changers in the Golden Temple area. **Satija Trading Co.** (☎2293517), located behind the Hargobind Niwas Gurudwara on Gail Sangal Wali Rd., is an official Western Union branch office. Open 24hr.

Market: The **bazaar** immediately in front of the main entrance to the Golden Temple carries a wide selection of merchandise, from Rajasthani shoes to Sikh daggers and swords. The steel bracelets (kara), worn by all Sikhs to symbolize strength of will and determination, are sold here. Each narrow lane south and west of the shrine specializes in a particular product or craft. Locals go to the Hall Bazaar area between Town Hall and Gandhi Gate for a wider, cheaper range of pretty much everything.

Police: (☎2211864 or 2220043). The main station is in the town hall building.

Pharmacy: Chemists cluster on Cooper Rd., around the corner from Crystal Restaurant, several blocks northeast of the railway station. One of these, **Sham Medicine** (☎2228905) is particularly well-stocked. Open daily 8:30am-10pm.

Hospital: Kakkar Hospital, Green Ave. (☎2210964). Near the intersection of Mall and Albert Rd. The most reputable in town; enough people know the name to point the way. **24hr. emergency room** on Mahna Singh Rd., in the Golden Temple area.

Internet: Cyber City (☎5097459), off Lawrence Rd., near the intersection of Queens and Lawrence Rd. Rs20 per hr. Open daily 7am-midnight. **Cyber Net** (☎2549537) is closer to the Golden Temple, but more expensive. Rs40 per hr. Open daily 10am-10pm.

Post Office: Court Rd. (☎2566032), northwest of the railway station. Open M-Sa 9am-5pm. The **Golden Temple Post Office** is open M-Sa 9am-5pm. **Postal Code:** 143001.

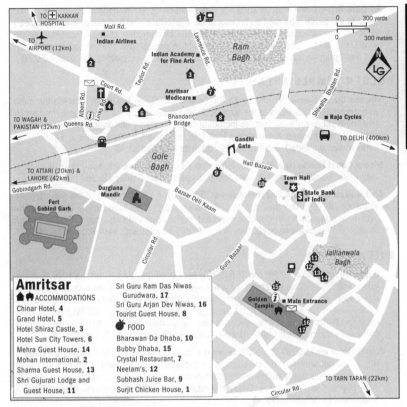

Amritsar

♠♦ ACCOMMODATIONS

Chinar Hotel, **4**
Grand Hotel, **5**
Hotel Shiraz Castle, **3**
Hotel Sun City Towers, **6**
Mehra Guest House, **14**
Mohan International, **2**
Sharma Guest House, **13**
Shri Gujurati Lodge and
   Guest House, **11**

Sri Guru Ram Das Niwas
   Gurudwara, **17**
Sri Guru Arjan Dev Niwas, **16**
Tourist Guest House, **8**

♥ FOOD

Bharawan Da Dhaba, **10**
Bubby Dhaba, **15**
Crystal Restaurant, **7**
Neelam's, **12**
Subhash Juice Bar, **9**
Surjit Chicken House, **1**

⚑ ACCOMMODATIONS

Amritsar's hotels are in three parts of the city: by the bus stand, near the railway station, and around the Golden Temple. The cheapest places are near the bus stand, but many of these are neither clean nor safe—over the years the area has become a red-light district. A number of hotels near the railway station are decent, especially if you're anxious to keep the heart of the city at a safe distance. Hotels near the temple are more scarce, but this is the most vibrant part of the city. The best place to stay is in the temple compound itself.

INSIDE THE GOLDEN TEMPLE

🕮 **Sri Guru Ram Das Niwas Gurudwara,** on the east side of the temple compound past the community kitchen. Foreign guests sleep on beds or floor mats within the packed confines of an open-ceiling bunker. No reservations accepted; get there in the afternoon and place some of your belongings (nothing valuable!) on a bed to increase your chances of getting it for the night. No smoking or drinking allowed. Prayers broadcast periodically through the courtyard. Foreign compound is guarded 24hr. In-house closets provided. Donations at the charity box are appreciated. Max. stay 3 days. ❶

Sri Guru Arjan Dev Niwas (☎ 255953; sgpc@vsnl.com), 100m north of Pram Das Niwas. If the free digs are a bit too free for your taste, the temple also maintains nearly 500 clean doubles with attached bath. All booking is done by computer at Arjan Dev Niwas or via email. You will be randomly assigned to any of five *gurudwaras*. The quality of rooms vary, but don't plan on having a say in the matter. No smoking or drinking. Doubles Rs50. ❶

GOLDEN TEMPLE AREA

Sharma Guest House, Mahna Singh Rd. (☎ 5551757), on the street between the main and the eastern entrances to the temple. Great location, familial atmosphere, and excellent room service. Clean doubles including some sparkling new rooms with seat toilets, cable TV, and phones. A few rooms look into Jallianwala Bagh. Check-out 24hr. Reservations recommended. Singles Rs150; doubles Rs200-500. ❷

Mehra Guest House (☎ 2291940), a few doors down from Sharma. Rooms are air-cooled, clean, and boast comfortable beds and fresh paint jobs. Doubles Rs250-500. ❷

Shri Gujrati Lodge and Guest House (☎ 2557870), a block in front of the main temple entrance, next to the passage to Jallianwala Bagh. The 8-bed dorm overlooks the memorial park; cramped doubles with seat toilets open onto Amritsar's chaotic central market. No reservations accepted. Dorms Rs80; doubles with bath Rs165-300. ❶

RAILWAY AREA

Tourist Guest House, GT Rd. (☎ 2553830), near Bhandari Bridge, on the road from the bus stand to the railway station. 50 years ago, a British colonel turned his mansion into this guest house; since then, tourists have flocked here for a taste of the Raj lifestyle. Rooms vary widely—some rooms have high ceilings, air cooling, and TVs; others have common baths. Bring your earplugs; trains signal their arrival in Amritsar just as they pull even with the guest house. Dorms Rs85; doubles with bath Rs100-250. ❶

Grand Hotel (☎ 2562977), as you leave the railway station, just to the right on Queens Rd. Small but well-kept rooms surround a pleasant courtyard with a garden and lawn chairs. Attached baths with seat toilets, running hot water, and color TV. Room service 7am-10pm. Check-out noon. Excellent restaurant and bar downstairs. Singles Rs395-900; doubles Rs500-1000. ❸

Hotel Shiraz Castle (☎ 220886), off Queen's Rd., a 10min. walk from the station. Large rooms with color TVs, seat toilets, and hot water, the best deal in a row of similarly flavored hotels. Room service 7am-11pm. Check-out noon. Singles Rs350-550; doubles Rs425-1075. ❸

Mohan International, Albert Rd. (☎ 2227801). One of several four-star hotels on this strip just off of Court Rd. Doorman, oh-so-plush carpets, and wall-size windows overlooking the hazy city outside. Singles Rs1500; doubles Rs2500. ❺

Hotel Sun City Towers, Queen's Rd. (☎ 2224636). All rooms air-conditioned, clean, and comfortable, with sparkling baths, but otherwise unexciting. Be sure to bargain. Singles Rs800-1000, doubles Rs1050-1250. ❺

Chinar Hotel, Links Rd. (☎ 2564655). A half-block up from the railway station. Moderately clean, with huge front-side rooms. Rooms come with TV and air coolers. Check-out noon. Singles Rs300-500; doubles Rs400-600. ❷

 FOOD

You should try to eat at least one meal in the Golden Temple itself—the *dal* might leave you yearning for more.

Crystal Restaurant, at the corner of Queens Rd. and Lawrence Rd. Taste the chicken curry (Rs140) and you'll probably be a convert. A wide range of Italian dishes (Rs100-140) and "Global Hits International" (Rs120-140). If the prices are too high for you liking, they run a take-out counter outside, where they also sell soft ice cream in such exotic flavors as "Green Apple" and "Blue Hawaii" (Rs15). Open 11am-11pm. ❹

Neelam's, a few doors down from the entrance to Jallianwala Bagh. A/C and cushy booths make it the most comfortable *dhaba* in the temple area. Big and tasty portions. *Malai kofta* Rs40; excellent *masala dosa* Rs25. Open daily 9am-11pm. ❷

Subhash Juice Bar, 1 block southwest of Gandhi Gate. Recently renovated with the bright coats of paint to match the colorful juice and shake offerings. Now making a foray into the fast-food business as well, with a full menu of pizzas, burgers, and the like. Mango shake with *pista badam* Rs15. Open daily 7am-11pm. ❶

Bharawan Da Dhaba, opposite the Town Hall and next door to Punjab National Bank. Well-known, well-stocked, well-lit cafeteria with superb *thalis* (Rs35-50). Great *paneer* dishes Rs40. Speedy service and foreigner-friendly. Sibling store **Brothers,** does its best to grease it up Western fast food-style next door. Pizzas Rs50-65, burgers Rs30-35. Both open daily 8:30am-11pm. ❷

Surjit Chicken House, right below Cyber City, off Lawrence Rd. The best grilled chicken in town (Rs65) according to locals. Open daily 11am-11pm. ❷

Bubby Dhaba, directly in front of the main temple entrance, provides a standard menu. Relax in the A/C room in the back, and watch all the action in front of the Golden Temple or stay up front to chat with the cooks. Open daily 6:30am-11pm. ❷

● SIGHTS

THE GOLDEN TEMPLE

Golden Temple Information Centre (☎ 2553954) is on the northeast side of the complex. No tobacco, alcohol, or stimulants of any kind are allowed, and visitors must deposit cigarettes 200 yards away from the temple's entrance. Shoes, socks, and umbrellas must be left at free depositories at each of the main entrances or at the Tourist Information Centre. Visitors must rinse their feet in the tanks in front of the entrances. Photography is allowed inside the temple complex, but not inside the temple itself. Head-coverings are required at all times inside the temple. They are available for free at the Information Centre and for sale (Rs10) outside the temple, but any scarf, hat, or towel will do. Information Centre open daily 7am-8pm. Complex open daily 24hr. Free.

No matter what you choose to call it—the Golden Temple, Hari Mandir, or Darbar Sahib (as it's known in Punjabi)—Amritsar's main monument is inspiringly beautiful, hauntingly serene, and oblivious to the grind and grime of the city beyond its walls. Its current state of tranquility is especially impressive given the tumultuous history of the Sikhs and of the site itself. Since its initial construction nearly 400 years ago, the temple has been plagued by almost incessant attacks. Its holiness is undiminished and all Sikhs try to make a pilgrimage here at least once in their lifetime. The temple sparkles throughout the day, but the best time to visit is at night, when lanterns impart an ethereal glow to the place of worship.

Although Guru Nanak, the founder of Sikhism, once lived near the site of the modern tank, it was **Guru Ram Das** who ignited the growth of a religious center here when he began work on the pool in 1574. That project was completed under Guru Arjun 15 years later, when the area was named Amritsar. Guru Arjun built the **Hari Mandir** at the center of the tank and placed the Guru Granth Sahib, the Sikh holy book, inside it. A series of destructive Mughal invasions followed the completion of the temple in 1601, and the temple alternated between Mughal and Sikh control for 150 years. In 1762 Ahmad Shah Abdali captured it, and, taking no chances, blew it to smithereens. Five years later, under the leadership of Punjab ruler Maharaja Ranjit Singh, the Sikhs regained control of the site. The one-eyed maharaja rebuilt the complex, decorated parts of it with marble and copper, and coated the newly built Hari Mandir in gold leaf. The British assumed a less-than-reverent management of the temple during the 19th century, and it wasn't until the 1920s that the practice of Sikhism was restored within the temple's walls.

Unfortunately, violence has also marred the temple's recent history. The 1980s saw the rise of a vocal Sikh militant group that called for the creation of an independent Sikh nation. Tensions came to a head in 1983, when the movement's leader, Sant Bhindranwale, sequestered himself in the Golden Temple and incited acts of violence against Hindus. With over 350 Hindus killed by the summer of 1984, Indira Gandhi ordered the national army to storm the temple, a plan dubbed **Operation Bluestar.** What was intended as a commando raid became a three-day siege. When the smoke had cleared, more the 750 people were dead, including Bhindranwale and 83 soldiers. Consequently, Indira Gandhi was assassinated by an angry Sikh shortly after the standoff. Tour guides and brochures tend to be hush-hush about this latter-day violence, emphasizing instead historically distant bloodbaths and the site's current state of peace.

PARIKRAMA. The main entrance to the Golden Temple is on the north side of the complex, beneath the **clock tower.** It is flanked by the main shoe depository and the **Tourist Information Centre,** which provides informative brochures about the temple and the Sikh religion and conducts tours in English every hour. The clock tower leads to the Parikrama, the 12m-wide marble promenade that encircles the tank. The four entrances to the temple complex symbolize an openness to friendly visitors from all sides. Guru Arjun once exclaimed, "My faith is for people of all castes and all creeds from whichever direction they come and to whichever direction they bow." Traffic generally moves clockwise around the Parikrama. Here, the **68 Holy Places** represent the 68 holiest Hindu sites in India—just to walk along this northern edge, Guru Arjun declared, is to attain the holiness a Hindu takes a lifetime to acquire. Some of the holy sites have been converted into the **Central Sikh Museum,** or Gallery of Martyrs, housed in the northern part of the temple complex; the entrance is to the left of the main gate. Lining the walls are portraits of renowned Sikhs, including Baba Deep Singh and Sevapanthi Bhai Mansha Singh, who swam across the tank through gunfire to keep the temple lit. The display of heavy-duty arms includes everything from spears to blunderbusses. Graphic images of Sikh martyrs are not for the faint of heart. *(Open daily 8am-6pm. Free.)*

On the eastern side of the tank (to the left as you pass through the main entrance) is a small tree said to have been the site of the miraculous healing of a cripple; today the healthy, wealthy, crippled, and destitute alike seek the benefits of the tank's curative powers at the adjoining **bathing ghats.** Just next to the *ghats* is one of four booths where priests read from the Guru Granth Sahib. Ongoing readings are meant to ensure the survival of Sikh beliefs. Each priest recites for three hours; a complete reading takes 50 hours. Looming overhead are the **Ramgarhia Minars,** two brick towers that were damaged when tanks rumbled through this entrance in 1984. The entryway below leads to the Guru-ka-Langar, the communal kitchen, and the *gurudwaras.* On the south side of the tank, opposite the main entrance is a shrine to **Baba Deep Singh,** whose struggles made him a Sikh hero. When the Mughal Ahmad Shah Abdali blew up the Golden Temple in 1761 and filled the sacred tank with trash, Baba Deep Singh began a defense of the desecrated temple. On his way, however, his head was cut off by a Muslim soldier. Disembodied and with head in hand, the Sikh leader trudged on, eventually crossing the temple's gates and plopping his head in the water before dying. The west end of the tank has several notable structures. The first window is where devotees collect *prasad*, the sweet lumps of cornmeal used as an offering inside the Hari Mandir. Moving clockwise, opposite the entrance to the Hari Mandir, is the **Akal Takhat,** the second-holiest place in the temple. Guru Hargobind, the sixth Sikh guru, built the Akal Takhat in 1609 as a decision-making center. Many weapons, fine pieces of jewelry, and other Sikh artifacts are stored here. The two towering flagstaffs next to the Akal Takhat represent the religious and political facets of Sikhism; the two are joined by the **double swords of Hargobind,** demonstrating how intertwined these aspects of Sikhism are. Illuminated at the very top, the poles are intended as beacons for pilgrims heading into Amritsar. Near the flagstaffs is the shrine to the last and most militant guru, Gobind Singh. The last noteworthy spot along the Parikrama, other than the Hari Mandir itself, is the 450-year old **jujube** tree under which the Baba Buddhaja, the temple's first priest, used to spend his time. The tree is thought to bring fertility to anyone who touches it.

HARI MANDIR. Seemingly afloat in the middle of the tank, the Hari Mandir is the holiest part of the entire complex, and conspicuously so. Its architecture fuses Hindu and Muslim styles, particularly evident in the synthesis of the Hindu temple's rectangular form with the domes and minarets of the Muslim mosque. The three stories of the Hari Mandir, capped by an inverted lotus dome, are made of marble, copper, and about 100kg of pure gold leaf. Inside the temple on the ground floor, the chief priest and his musicians recite *gurbani* (hymns) from the Guru Granth Sahib. People sit around the center and toss flowers and money toward the jewel-studded canopy, where the silk-enshrouded Guru Granth Sahib lies.

The **Guru Granth Sahib** (considered by the Sikhs to be a living teacher, not just a book) is brought to the temple from the Akal Takhat each day and returned at night. The morning ceremony takes place at around 3:30am, the procession at 10pm. Arrive about an hour early to observe the ceremony from the second floor of the Hari Mandir. Hymns echo through the building before the book is revealed and the priest takes over the prayers; he chants, folds the book in gold leaf and more silk, and finally places it on the golden palanquin. Head downstairs at this point, and you might end up in the line of devotees pushing each other for the privilege of bearing the holy burden. Finally, a blaring serpentine horn and communal drum signal a final prayer that puts the book to bed, near the flagstaff. The entire ceremony lasts about an hour and a half.

GATAKA: THE ART OF WAR
The Sikhs' success in withstanding centuries of oppression is partly due to their skill as warriors. Through countless battles, they developed a martial art known as *gataka*. Today, young would-be warriors practice *gataka* on the roof of the Guru-ka-Langar (daily 8:30-11pm). They enjoy having visitors watch as they wield their *neja* (spears), swords, bamboo sticks, and other ancient weapons and practice *talwar baji* (fencing), or as it's more bluntly known, *kirpan* (the art of stabbing). The most impressive weapon is the *chakkar*, a wooden ring with stone spheres dangling from it by 4-ft. strings. The warrior stands in the middle and spins the ring so that the whirling balls form a barrier around him. He then tosses it up into the air (still spinning) for someone to catch. Watching the spectacle is exciting, but participating is even better and the warriors will often let you give it a go. To really indulge in *gataka*, they recommend heading out to Raia, 50km outside of Amritsar, where you can visit Baba Bakala, the training center for the most hard-core students.

Step outside to the left (north) side onto the *pradakhina*, the marble path leading around the temple. On this side is a stairwell leading to the second floor, where flowers, animals, and hymns ornament the walls. From here, you can catch a good look at the procession and Adi Granth below. A small *shish mahal* (hall of mirrors) fills the east side of this floor. Once occupied by the gurus, the halls now reverberate with the voices of priests engaged in the *akhand path*, the ongoing reading of the holy book. The Har-ki-Pari (Steps of God), on the ground floor of the temple's east (back) side, allows visitors easy access to the most sacred section of the tank's waters.

AROUND THE COMPLEX. No visit to the Golden Temple would be complete without a meal at the Guru-ka-Langar, the enormous community kitchen characteristic of all Sikh temples. Sikh founder Guru Nanak instituted the practice of *pangat* (dining together) to reinforce the idea of equality; today, the custom continues in the dining hall, where basic meals are dished out daily to rows of thousands who sit together, regardless of wealth or caste. As one row eats, the next gathers, in an ongoing cycle. The meal consists of all-you-can-eat *dal* and *chappatis;* simply hold out cupped hands as the *chappati* chappie walks by, and he'll toss you more. Don't let the man wielding the bucket of *dal* splash too much of the stuff on your plate; out of respect, you should leave it clean and avoid waste. Afterwards, leave a donation in one of the charity boxes—these meals are largely funded by such contributions.

Just south of the Hargobind *gurudwara* is the nine-story **Tower of Baba Atal Rai,** named after the son of Guru Hargobind. According to legend, he performed a miracle at age nine, which annoyed his father to no end. In shame, the young *baba* came here and died. On the first floor are some detailed miniatures depicting episodes from Guru Nanak's life and a *nagarah* (drum). The other floors are empty, but you can climb to the top for unsurpassed views of Amritsar, the Golden Temple, and the tank of Kamalsar to the south.

OTHER SIGHTS

JALLIANWALA BAGH. About two blocks north of the temple's main entrance is Jallianwala Bagh, the site of one of the most horrific moments in the history of colonial India. On April 13, 1919, peaceful crowds filled Jallianwala Bagh to protest a law allowing the British to imprison Indians without trial. British Brigadier-General Reginald E.H. Dyer was brought in to quell the disturbance. Dyer stood behind 150 troops in front of the main alley, the only entrance and exit to the compound and ordered his men to open fire without warning on the 10,000 men, women, and children who had gathered here. In all, about 400 people died and 1500 were wounded. The massacre sparked a rallying cry for Indian insurgence. The Bengali poet Rabindranath Tagore, who had been knighted after winning the Nobel Prize for Literature in 1913, returned his knighthood after the massacre. Dyer was reprimanded and relieved of his duties but never charged with crime. In 1997, Queen Elizabeth II visited Jallianwala Bagh. Although no official apology was made during her controversial visit, the British monarch expressed regret for the massacre and laid a wreath at the memorial to the victims. Today, Jallianwala Bagh is a calm garden, frequented by students and picnickers. The stone well is a monument to the drowned Indians who jumped to their deaths in an attempt to flee the attack. The Martyr's Gallery features portraits of some of those involved in the massacre. *(Open daily in summer 9am-5pm, in winter 10am-1pm and 3-7pm.)*

RAM BAGH. Northeast of the railway station is Ram Bagh, the park between The Mall and Queens Rd. At the south edge of the park, the impressive Darshani Deorhi Gate is all that is left of the solid ramparts and moat that once surrounded the area. At the northwest corner stands a menacing statue of Maharaja Ranjit Singh, the Sikh leader who was responsible for the early 19th-century restoration of the Golden Temple. Ram Bagh served as his summer residence between 1818 and 1837, and the central building now houses the Ranjit Singh Museum, which contains oil paintings, weapons, manuscripts, and miniatures from the maharaja's era. The tourist office's pamphlet, *Amritsar: Spiritual Centre of Punjab*, is a good guide to the museum. *(Museum open Tu-Su 10am-4:45pm. Rs5.)*

DURGIANA MANDIR. The high profile of the Golden Temple overshadows the tiny Hindu shrines tucked into the alleyways all around it, as well as the impressive Durgiana Mandir. This temple, set back from the busy street four blocks northwest of the Golden Temple, honors the goddess Durga.

 DAYTRIP FROM AMRITSAR: TARN TARAN ਟਰਨ ਟਜ਼ਨ

Once the Hari Mandir has whetted your appetite for shiny, golden Sikh temples, head 22km south to the town of Tarn Taran. Buses leave every 30min. from the main bus stand (1hr., Rs12). From the Tarn Taran bus stand, it's a 15min. walk along the main road and through the narrow alley of the bazaar up to the local *gurudwara*. Its founder, Guru Arjun Dev, built the temple in 1768 to commemorate Guru Ram Das, who slept side-by-side with a leper to show his compassion. Though local doctors can't provide any evidence for the common belief that the water here cures leprosy, they do attest to its curative effects on several minor skin conditions. The architectural style here resembles that of the Golden Temple complex; the *parikrama* encircling the still waters is actually larger than its counterpart in Amristar. The *gurudwara* provides decent rooms (free) in the large yellow building just outsides the west entrance.

 BORDER WITH PAKISTAN: WAGAH

> **⚠ WARNING.** As of August 2003, foreign governments have been advising against travel to Pakistan. While violence has decreased, acts of terrorism against Westerners still occur. If you do decide to go, try to blend in, maintain a low profile, and **make sure you have a Pakistani visa and that your Indian visa allows multiple entries.** For more information, see **Surrounding Countries,** p. 11, **Border Crossings,** p. 41, and **This Year's News,** p. 71.

The *only* border crossing between India and Pakistan is at **Wagah,** 32km from Amritsar. **Buses** go to **Attari** (1hr., every 15min. 7am-6pm, Rs12), 2km away; from there, it's a Rs15 rickshaw ride to the border. There are several better options, including taking a bus or van directly from the Golden Temple (Rs80 round-trip; 4pm departure) or hiring an auto-rickshaw in front of the train station (Rs100-150 round-trip). The border is open daily from 10am-4pm. If you only wish to visit, wait until after 4pm, or better still, arrive even later for the flag-lowering ceremony (see **Border Ballet,** below). The ceremony's start time varies by season—it begins at 6:45pm in the middle of summer, and around 6pm in winter. Arrive at least 30min. ahead (1hr. ahead on Sunday) to get a good seat. If you are crossing over, pass through customs on the left and walk the remaining 200m to the actual line. The **train** from Amritsar to **Lahore** was suspended effective January 1, 2002. The direct **bus** service between Delhi and Lahore was also suspended, but has resumed as of July 11, 2003. The last bus to **Amritsar** leaves Attari at 6pm. If you are here for the flag ceremony, you will have to take an auto-rickshaw back (Rs70).

BORDER BALLET A few people go to Wagah to *cross* the border, but a huge crowd always shows up to *watch* the border. A half-hour before sunset, an elaborate nightly ritual accompanies the closing of the border and the lowering of the flags. Three to six thousand visitors clamor around the spiked gate on either side and jostle for the best views. The ceremony unfolds more on less on schedule. As one officer barks an order and another follows with furious stomping and wild high-stepping, the audiences on both sides break into raucous applause and scream out patriotic chants. The scene is more like a cricket match than a solemn ritual. The military police shove the roaring throngs back behind an imaginary line, only for the masses to retake their turf the moment the officers push on. After some more machismo-packed face-offs and lengthy siren-like yells, the respective flags are lowered, the lights go bright, the bugles blare, and the visitors mob the gate for a glimpse of the faces on the other side—or for a chance to toe one of the world's most famous white lines.

At Wagah, **Punjab Tourism,** just behind the check-point, supplies the standard outdated brochures and maps (open M-Sa 10am-4pm). Next door, the **State Bank of India** changes traveler's checks but not Pakistani rupees (open 11am-4pm). The money-changers do change Pakistani rupees. There is a **post office** for last minute send-offs. There is no lodging in Wagah, but there are plenty of tea stalls at which to socialize before the big show.

RAJASTHAN

राजस्थान

The northwestern desert state of Rajasthan is India's "Land of Kings," ruled for more than a millennium by the legendary Rajput warrior clans. Life in Rajasthan is the stuff that tourist-brochure dreams are made of: camels and elephants mosey alongside cars and traffic, turbaned men twirl their foot-long moustaches, and women in brightly colored saris balance water jugs on their heads. Few people leave Rajasthan without some fantastic pictures and a new set of tales to tell.

But Rajasthan is not all desert sunsets and romantic palaces. Behind the enchanting facade lies a haunting history of bloodshed. In the 6th and 7th centuries, the Rajputs emerged as the rulers of the area now known as Rajasthan. Much of the history of Rajasthan is comprised of struggles between the contending feudal states of the warrior Rajput clans, and a series of conflicts as the Mughals extended their power across northern India. Most of the Rajput royal houses, too individually weak to resist the burgeoning Mughal empire, kowtowed to its mighty rulers. The threat from the Mughals receded after the death of the last great Mughal emperor, Aurangzeb, in 1707, but then the Rajputs had to contend with the Marathas. When the British came, the Rajput royal houses leapt at the chance to exchange their support of the Raj for British protection. After Independence in 1947, the single state of Rajasthan was pieced together from the various Rajput kingdoms, and Jaipur emerged as the capital.

Today, its picture-perfect exterior belies a state ridden with poverty, India's lowest literacy rate, and immense caste and gender inequalities. A decade-long drought has further squeezed villagers onto the economic and social margins. And while the tourist boom has brought money and a much-needed infrastructure to Rajasthan, it has also resulted in a fiercely competitive clamor for dollars, pounds, and yen. Nearly everyone who approaches you in the tourist center is working some angle, making genuine cultural exchange almost impossible. However, with a little effort travelers can look past Pushkar's pushy *pandas*, Udaipur's touts, and Jaipur's rickshaw mafia to catch a glimpse of Rajput's former storybook splendor. The colored *bandhani* cloth of Jaipur's marketplaces, the camel rides at sunset over the dunes of the Thar Desert, the serene waters of exotic Lake Pichhola in Udaipur—these are but a few of the wonders to be experienced in Rajasthan.

HIGHLIGHTS OF RAJASTHAN

Jaipur is Rajasthan's most popular destination. Its **City Palace** (p. 497), teeming bazaars (p. 497), and **Amber Fort** (p. 498) are worth all the hype.

The **Lake Palace** of **Udaipur** (p. 518) has long been the ultimate romantic draw for honeymooners and secret agents alike—one glimpse of the sunrise city and you'll see why.

Jaisalmer's illuminated fort (p. 540) satiates most tourists' cravings for a taste of life in the middle ages—the restful journey into the desert on the hump of a camel.

Peaceful **Pushkar** (p. 510) is a quiet oasis, soothing weary pilgrims and travelers 361 days a year. The four-day **Pushkar Camel Fair** (p. 513) is another story entirely.

RAJASTHAN

Rajasthan

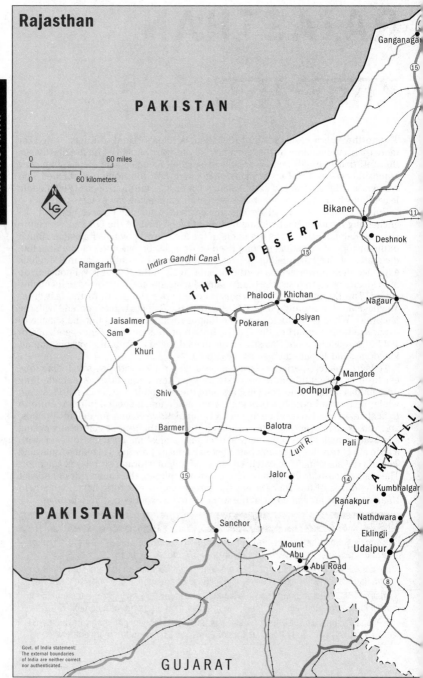

PAKISTAN

0 _____ 60 miles
0 _____ 60 kilometers

PAKISTAN

THAR DESERT

Ganganagar

Bikaner

Deshnok

Indira Gandhi Canal

Ramgarh

Phalodi   Khichan

Nagaur

Jaisalmer
Sam

Pokaran

Osiyan

Khuri

Mandore

Jodhpur

Shiv

Balotra

Barmer

Luni R.

Pali

ARAVALLI

Jalor

Kumbhalgar

Ranakpur

Nathdwara

Sanchor

Eklingji

Udaipur

Mount
Abu

Abu Road

Govt. of India statement:
The external boundaries
of India are neither correct
nor authenticated.

GUJARAT

RAJASTHAN

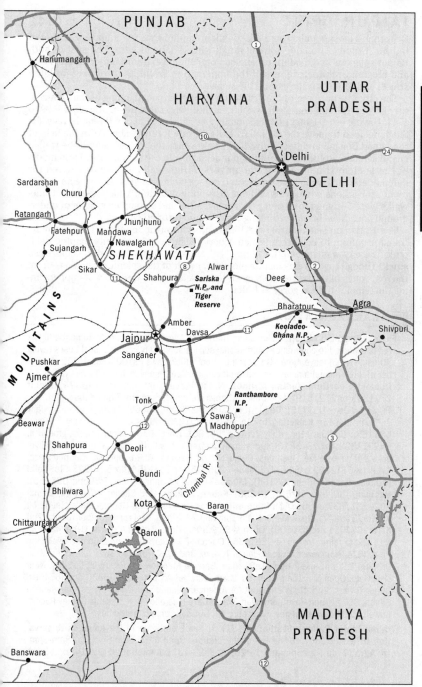

JAIPUR जयपुर ☎ 0141

Rajasthan's most popular tourist destination, Jaipur forms the southwest corner of India's "Golden Triangle," joining ranks with Delhi and Agra. The seat of both Rajput splendor and modern urban squalor, Jaipur's extraordinary bazaars, forts, and elegant architecture, assail the imagination while its throbbing polluted streets and ruthless touts assault the senses.

The city was born out of the vision and prudent urban planning of the 18th-century Rajput leader Maharaja Sawai Jai Singh II, who ruled the region from 1699 to 1744. Having established political stability in his territories by the mid-1720s, Jai Singh decided to move the capital from its hillside fort in Amber. With the help of renowned Bengali architect Vidyadhar Chakravarti, the maharaja built the walled city of Jaipur, carefully laying out Jaipur according to the mathematical grid model of the ancient Hindu map of the universe. High walls were constructed for defense, and the entrances to stores and homes were placed on side streets so that royal processions could pass without disrupting daily life. Wide streets and sidewalks were designed to permit pedestrian traffic, and a complex system of underground aqueducts brought drinking water to the fortified city.

The British presence during the 19th century brought about a drastic cosmetic transformation; to celebrate Prince Albert's visit in 1856, the city painted itself pink. The city was dubbed the "Pink City," and both the name and the colorwash stuck. Though the city has lost its pink hue, much of the splendor remains—from the rosy tones of the bazaars at sunset, to the sea of monkeys and worshippers lining the temple-studded gorge at Galta.

⎅ TRANSPORTATION

Flights: Sanganer Airport, 15km south of the city, currently serves only **domestic** flights but is expected to commence international service soon. Very crowded local buses (every 30min., Rs4-5) leave Ajmeri Gate for the airport. Rickshaws Rs100, taxis Rs200. A number of international airlines also have offices in Jaipur, many in Jaipur Towers on MI Rd. **Domestic carriers: Indian Airlines,** Nehru Place, Tonk Rd. (☎2743324, airport 2721333 or 2721519). Open daily 10am-1pm and 2-5pm. To: **Ahmedabad** (1hr.; Tu, Th, Sa 6:10pm; US$115); **Delhi** (40min., daily 8:30pm, US$65); **Jodhpur** (40min., daily 7:20am, US$85); **Kolkata** (2hr.; Tu, Th, Sa; US$230); **Mumbai** (3½hr., daily 7:10am, US$165); **Udaipur** (1hr., daily 7:10am, US$80). **Travel Care,** Jaipur Towers, ground fl. (☎2371832; fax 2373810), has a computerized link with IA, and can book and deliver tickets at no extra fee. Open daily 9am-9pm. **Jet Airways,** MI Rd., opposite Ganpati Plaza, 1st fl. (☎5112222 or 5112223, airport 2551352 or 2551354; fax 5112227). To: **Delhi** (40min., daily 9:45am, US$65); **Mumbai** (3hr., 7:25am; 1½hr., 7:30pm; US$165); **Udaipur** (1hr., daily 7:25am; US$80). **Sahara Airlines,** 203 Shalimar Complex, Church Rd. (☎377637 or 365741). **International carriers: Air India,** Ganpati Plaza, 1st fl., MI Rd. (☎2368047). Open M-F 9:30am-1pm and 2-5:30pm. **Air France,** Jaipur Towers, 2nd fl. (☎2377051 or 2370509). Open M-Sa 9:30am-6pm. **British Airways,** Usha Plaza, MI Rd., next to Jaipur Towers (☎2361065). Open M-F 9:30am-1pm and 2-6pm, Sa 9:30am-2pm. **KLM/Northwest Airlines,** Jaipur Towers, 2nd fl., MI Rd. (☎2367772). Open M-Sa 9:30am-1:30pm and 2-6pm. **Lufthansa,** Saraogi Mansion, MI Rd. (☎2561360). Near New Gate. Open M-F 10am-6pm, Sa 10am-2pm. **Jet Air Ltd.** (☎2375430 or 2367409), Jaipur Towers, 2nd. fl., is an agent for American Airlines, Austrian Airlines, Bangladesh Biman, Gulf Air, and Royal Jordanian. **Travel Care** (see above), represents Cathay Pacific, Kuwait Air, Malaysia Airlines, Singapore Air, Swissair, United, and others.

Trains: Jaipur Railway Station (☎131). To book early, go to the **Advance Reservation Office** (☎135), to the left of the station. Open M-Sa 8am-8pm, Su 8am-2pm. To: **Agra** (7½hr., 1:25pm and 11:20pm, Rs83-133); **Ahmedabad** (9½-14hr., 3-5 per day, Rs218); **Ajmer** for **Pushkar** (2-3hr., 5-7 per day, Rs43-68); **Bikaner** (10hr., 9pm, Rs148); **Delhi** (5-8hr., 8-11 per day, Rs127); **Jodhpur** (6hr., 4-5 per day, Rs127); **Mumbai** (18½hr., 2:05pm, Rs329); **Udaipur** (12hr., 10pm, Rs162); **Varanasi** (20hr., 1:25pm, Rs295).

Buses: Sindhi Camp Central Bus Stand, Station Rd. Platforms serving different destinations have different inquiry and ticket counters. All deluxe buses depart from platform 3, in the back. **Platform 1** to **Ahmedabad** (15hr.; 5:30, 10pm; Rs271); **Sariska** (counter #8, 2½hr., every 30min. 5am-10pm, Rs53). **Platform 2** (☎2206055) to **Sawai Madhopur** (5hr., 5:15pm, Rs74). **Platform 3,** for deluxe buses (☎2205621), to: **Abu Road** (11½hr., 8pm, Rs249); **Agra** (5hr., 14 per day 6am-11pm, Rs128); **Ajmer** for **Pushkar** (2½hr., 15 per day 4am-midnight, Rs66); **Chittaurgarh** (7hr., 5 per day 10am-midnight, Rs141); **Delhi** (5½hr.; every 30-60min. 5:30am-1:30am; Rs203, A/C Rs353); **Jaisalmer** (13hr., 9:45pm, Rs252); **Jodhpur** (7hr., 7 per day 4am-11:30pm, Rs141-163); **Udaipur** (9hr., 8 per day 10am-1am, Rs201). **Platform 4** to: **Bikaner** (7hr., 9 per day 5am-10pm, Rs123); **Jhunjhunu** (4hr., every 30-60min. 3:45am-11pm, Rs87) via **Nawalgarh** (3hr., Rs60). **Private buses** depart from the same stand. Private bus companies line Station Rd. and Motilal Atal Rd., off MI Rd.; most hotels make reservations.

Local Transportation: Unmetered **auto-rickshaws** are the quickest way to get around. Prepaid rickshaws leave from the train station and the RTDC Tourist Hotel. **Cycle-rickshaws** are cheaper (bus or train station to Bani Park Rs10; GPO to Ajmeri Gate Rs10). **Local buses** leave from the Central Bus Stand, all sights, and most major intersections every 5-15min. **Taxi stands** are opposite the RTDC Tourist Hotel and outside Sanganeri Gate. **Cars** can be rented (with driver) from **RTDC Tours and Travels,** RTDC Tourist Hotel (☎2375466; open daily 7am-8pm) or **Sita World Travels,** Jaipur Towers, 2nd fl. (☎5102020). Roughly Rs5 per km for A/C, plus an additional Rs100 per night for the driver's lodgings. **Bicycle rental** is available at many of the hotels and guest houses. Jaipur Inn rents at Rs50 per day.

ORIENTATION

Jaipur's wide, straight roads make getting around easy. The walled **Pink City,** which contains most of Jaipur's tourist attractions, is in the northeast; the **new city** sprawls south and west. From **Jaipur Railway Station,** on the western edge of town, **Station Road** leads past the **Central Bus Stand** on its way to **Chand Pol,** the western gate into the Pink City. The Pink City's main thoroughfare changes names four times—**Chandpol, Tripolia, Ramganj,** and **Surajpol Bazaars**—before exiting the walled city under **Suraj Pol,** the eastern gate. The **City Palace complex** is just north of Tripolia Bazaar. **Johari Bazaar** is the principal shopping street in the old city. **Mirza Ismail (MI) Rd.,** the new city's main thoroughfare, is lined with shops, restaurants, and tourist services. Just south of New Gate and beyond the Ram Niwas Gardens, **Jawaharlal Nehru Marg** runs south past several hospitals and the Birla Mandir.

PRACTICAL INFORMATION

TOURIST AND FINANCIAL SERVICES

Tourist Office: Indian Tourism, in Hotel Khasa Kothi (☎1363 or 2372200; indtourjpr@raj.nic.in). South of the MI Rd. and Station Rd. intersection. Open M-F 9am-6pm, Sa 9am-1:30pm. Other offices include the **Rajasthan Department of Tourism Office** (☎5110598), in the RTDC Tourist Hotel bldg. (through the "TRC Information Counter" door. Open daily 8am-8pm), the conveniently located and 24hr. **RTDC Tourist Information Bureau** (☎2200778), on platform 1 of the railway station, and at the **Central Bus Station** (Open daily 8am-8pm). Next door to the RTDC Tourist Hotel Office is the sister

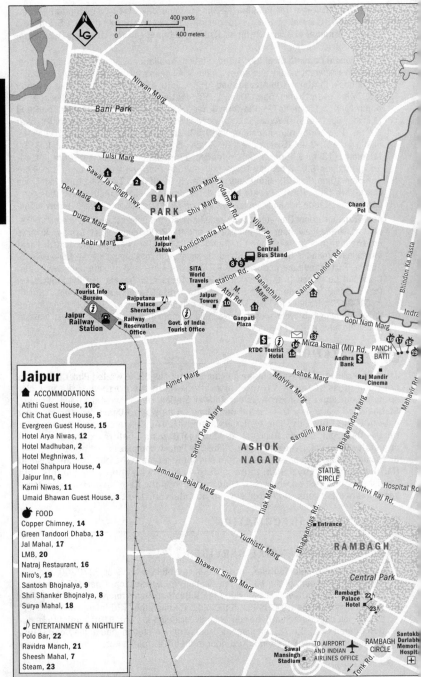

Jaipur

🏠 ACCOMMODATIONS
Atithi Guest House, **10**
Chit Chat Guest House, **5**
Evergreen Guest House, **15**
Hotel Arya Niwas, **12**
Hotel Madhuban, **2**
Hotel Meghniwas, **1**
Hotel Shahpura House, **4**
Jaipur Inn, **6**
Karni Niwas, **11**
Umaid Bhawan Guest House, **3**

🍎 FOOD
Copper Chimney, **14**
Green Tandoori Dhaba, **13**
Jal Mahal, **17**
LMB, **20**
Natraj Restaurant, **16**
Niro's, **19**
Santosh Bhojnalya, **9**
Shri Shanker Bhojnalya, **8**
Surya Mahal, **18**

♪ ENTERTAINMENT & NIGHTLIFE
Polo Bar, **22**
Ravidra Manch, **21**
Sheesh Mahal, **7**
Steam, **23**

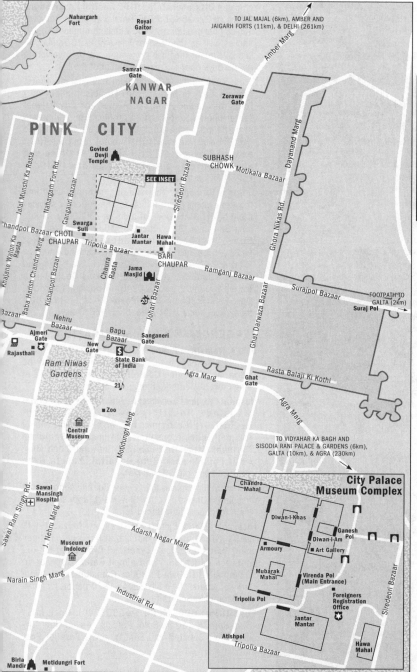

Nahargarh
Fort

Royal
Gaitor

TO JAL MAJAL (6km), AMBER AND
JAIGARH FORTS (11km), & DELHI (261km)

Amber Marg

Samrat
Gate

KANWAR
NAGAR

Zorawar
Gate

PINK   CITY

Dayanand Marg

Govind
Devji
Temple

SUBHASH
CHOWK   Motikala Bazaar

Sireodeori Bazaar

SEE INSET

Jalal Munshi Ka Rasta

Nahargarh Fort Rd.

Gangauri Bazaar

Swarga
Suli

Chandpol Bazaar   CHOTI
CHAUPAR

Tripolia Bazaar

Jantar
Mantar

Hawa
Mahal

BARI
CHAUPAR

Ghora Nikas Rd.

Khajane Walon Ka
Rasta

Baba Harish Chandra Marg

Kishanpol Bazaar

Chaura
Rasta

Jama
Masjid

Johari Bazaar

Ramganj Bazaar

Ghat Darwaza Bazaar

Surajpol Bazaar

FOOTPATH TO
GALTA (2km)

Suraj Pol

Bazaar

Nehru
Bazaar

Ajmeri
Gate

Rajasthali

New
Gate

Bapu
Bazaar

Sanganeri
Gate

State Bank
of India

20

Ram Niwas
Gardens

21

Agra Marg

Ghat
Gate

Rasta Balaji Ki Kothi

Agra Marg

Zoo

Motidungri Marg

Central
Museum

TO VIDYAHAR KA BAGH AND
SISODIA RANI PALACE & GARDENS (6km),
GALTA (10km), & AGRA (230km)

Sawai Ram Singh Rd.

Sawai
Mansingh
Hospital

J. Nehru Marg

Adarsh Nagar Marg

Museum of
Indology

Narain Singh Marg

Industrial Rd.

Birla
Mandir   Motidungri Fort

**City Palace
Museum Complex**

Chandra-
Mahal

Diwan-I-Khas

Ganesh
Pol

Diwan-i-Am

Armoury

Art Gallery

Mubarak
Mahal

Virenda Pol
(Main Entrance)

Tripolia Pol

Foreigners
Registration
Office

Jantar
Mantar

Sireodeori Bazaar

Atishpol

Tripolia Bazaar

Hawa
Mahal

IN RECENT NEWS

WATER RUNS DRY

The ferry boat-*wallahs* used to do brisk business ferrying tourists on Fateh Sagar Lake in Udaipur. Today, tourists can walk across the cracked and crevassed lake-bottom to what was once the island of Nehru Park. Extremely low water levels in Rajasthan's lakes are an all too common sight in a region parched by a decade-long drought.

Farther west in the expanding reaches of the Thar Desert, the effects of the absent monsoons are much harsher. The village economies in this arid region revolve around camel and goat herding. Skeletal camels and goats range farther across the scrubland to nibble at what scarce thorny brush remains. Trucks and tractors from Punjab and Gujarat haul in bursting loads of fodder in enormous canvas sacks, but the grain is too expensive for those who need it most. As a result of the fodder shortage, many herders have been selling or abandoning their animals. Before the drought, a healthy young camel would have fetched Rs15,000 (roughly US$300) at the Pushkar camel fair. Today, they go for as little as Rs500 (US$10).

The state government has taken a variety of steps to alleviate the economic suffering in the desert areas. The Governor recently declared 40,000 villages drought-affected and eligible for state aid. However, only the prodigal monsoon can quench the growing thirst in the region. Until then, Rajasthanis will continue to adapt to scarcities that characterize desert survival.

office for **Uttaranchal.** The **RTDC Central Reservations Office** (☎2202586), RTDC Hotel Swagatam Campus, makes bookings for 46 RTDC hotels throughout Rajasthan as well as the Pushkar Fair and RTDC Tourist Village. Payment for Pushkar tents must be received in full 60 days prior to commencement of the fair.

Tours: RTDC runs half- and full-day bilingual **city tours.** (Usually daily in high-season, 10 person minimum.) Tours may include stops at Amber, the City Palace, Jantar Mantar, and the Central Museum, Nahargarh and Jaigarh Forts. Book the day before by phone (☎2375466) or at any RTDC hotel. Both the RTDC and the Government of India Tourist Office can arrange government-approved **guides** (half-day Rs280 for up to 4 people).

Currency Exchange: The following exchange cash and traveler's checks, in addition to offering other services listed below. **State Bank of India** (☎2565001), MI Rd., near Sanganeri Gate. Open M-F 10am-2pm and 2:30-5pm, Sa 10am-2pm. **Andhra Bank,** MI Rd. (☎2374529), near Panch Batti. Gives cash advances on MC and V (1% commission). Open M-F 10am-2pm and 2:30-3:30pm, Sa 10am-noon. **Thomas Cook,** Jaipur Towers, ground fl. (☎2360940). Moneygram services. Open M-Sa 9:30am-6pm. **Citibank,** on MI Rd. near Ganpati Plaza., has a 24hr. **ATM** (Cirrus/MC/Plus/V).

EMERGENCY AND COMMUNICATIONS

Police: Rajasthan Police Headquarters (☎2606111 or 2606122). Inside the City Palace complex, behind the Hawa Mahal. **Police Control Room** (☎2565555), in King Edward Memorial Bldg., near Ajmeri Gate.

Hospital/Medical Services: Ambulance (☎102). **Sawai Mansingh Hospital,** Sawai Ram Singh Rd. (☎2560291). Government-run, large, and efficient. Of the many private hospitals, the best are **Santokba Durlabhji Memorial Hospital,** Bhawani Singh Marg (☎2566251), and **Soni Hospital,** Kahota Bagh (☎2571123), off J. Nehru Marg.

Pharmacy: Pharmacies line Station Rd. and surround the hospitals. One is also on Shiv Marg, opposite Jaipur Inn. Most open daily 8am-10pm.

Internet: Elpha Cybercafe, Ganpati Plaza, 1st fl. (☎5108777), has 8 computers at Rs30 per hr. Open daily 9:30am-9:30pm. **Cyberland Cybercafe,** MI Rd., between Panch Batti and Ajmeri Gate. Rs30 per hr. Open daily 11:30am-11:30pm. **Communicator,** Jaipur Towers, ground fl. (☎5103204). Rs30 per hr. Open M-Sa 9am-9pm, Su 11am-4pm.

Post Office: GPO, MI Rd. (☎2368740). Open M-Sa 8am-8pm, Su 10am-6pm. Parcels heavier than 2kg must be inspected and sent from the **Foreign Post**

Office around back (bring a box). Open M-Sa 10am-5pm. Branches near the Government of India Tourist Office and at the Central Bus Stand. Open M-Sa 9am-5pm. **Postal Code:** 302001.

ACCOMMODATIONS

The budget hotel scene in Jaipur is frustratingly competitive. On arrival, you will be mobbed by rickshaw drivers prodding you to a particular hotel and telling you the one you want is either full, "finished," or that it had a terrible fire the previous night. If you've arrived by train you can bypass the hassle by going to the pink prepaid rickshaw kiosk in front of the station (up to 2km Rs14, 4km Rs22, 6km Rs31. Additional luggage and nighttime charges). Otherwise you can hoof it to your hotel or at least a few blocks to find slightly less ruthless local transportation. Hotels around MI Rd., near the bus and railway stations, offer easy access to the services of the new city but are noisier. Those in the residential area of Bani Park provide a more peaceful environment. Few hotels are within the Pink City itself. Hotels offer discounts of 25-40% off-season (Apr.-Aug.). Homestays can be arranged through the tourist office at the railway station (Rs100-1500 per night).

ON AND AROUND MI ROAD

▨ **Atithi Guest House,** 1 Park House Scheme, MI Rd. (☎2378679; atithijaipur@hotmail.com). Near All India Radio. Sparklingly-clean, airy rooms with marble floors, attached baths, and phones, run by the friendly Shuka family. Garden and plant-filled rooftop terrace provides a safe getaway from the noise. Great veg. cooking and attentive staff. Internet Rs55 per hr. Reservations recommended. Singles Rs450-500; doubles Rs500-550, with A/C Rs750-800. ❸

▨ **Hotel Arya Niwas,** Sansar Chandra Rd. (☎2372456 or 2371773; www.aryaniwas.com). A popular, well-run hotel in a light and airy bldg. brimming with potted plants. Spotless rooms are simple but modern and pleasant with clean attached baths. All rooms with coolers, most with TVs. Lawn seating area surrounded by meticulous flower garden. Singles Rs350-450, with A/C Rs550; doubles Rs450-600, with A/C Rs700-800. ❸

Evergreen Guest House (☎2363446 or 2362415; evergreen34@hotmail.com). Off MI Rd. A huge, staggeringly popular guest house, set around a lush green courtyard. Centrally located and a good place to meet other travelers, but rooms (all with attached bath) are rather bare and service can be brusque. Internet Rs1 per min. Singles Rs150-250; doubles Rs175-350, with A/C Rs500. ❷

Karni Niwas, Motilal Atal Rd. (☎2365433 or 2216947; karniniwas@hotmail.com), behind Hotel Neelam. Run by four brothers, Niwas has 13 clean, comfortable rooms, most with private terraces, in a residential area. Free pickup at train or bus station. Singles Rs300-500, with A/C Rs750; doubles Rs350-600/Rs850. ❷

BANI PARK AND ENVIRONS

Jaipur Inn, B-17 Shiv Marg (☎2201121; jaipurin@sancharnet.om). Started in 1976 as campsite for overlanders, the Bhagava family has added 16 rooms, a dorm, and a beautiful rooftop restaurant. Nightly buffets (which guests occasionally cook), a ping pong table, and free Internet for guests contribute to the home-away-from-home feel. Free pickup from train and bus station, phone ahead or from station. Dorms Rs100; singles Rs150-400; doubles Rs250-700. Camping Rs50 per night. ❶

Umaid Bhawan Guest House, D-1/2-A Via Bank Rd., Bani Park (☎2316184; www.umaidbhawan.com). Behind Collectorate. Elegantly furnished rooms with spotless baths and TVs, most with balconies. A classy place run by an extremely helpful family. Great value. Phone or email ahead for free pick-up from the bus or train station. Pool,

R A J A S T H A N

Internet, restaurant. Non-A/C budget rooms go for Rs450-550, but the more expensive rooms are better value. Rooms with A/C Rs650-750; beautiful suites Rs900-1050. ❹

Hotel Shahpura House, Devi Marg, Bani Park (☎2202293; www.shahpurahouse.com). Former residence of the King Shahpura seems out of place in this residential area. King still owns the 20-room hotel decorated with heirlooms from his estate. Beautiful common spaces, well-appointed rooms. Deluxe A/C single Rs1100, suite Rs1800; deluxe A/C double Rs1400; suite Rs2200. ❺

Hotel Meghniwas, C-9 Jai Singh Hwy. (☎2202034; email@meghniwas.com). Twenty-seven tastefully furnished and decorated rooms all with attached hot water baths, cable TV, and minibar. Guests can play croquet on the manicured front lawn or lounge around the pool in the rear garden. Attached Restaurant. 10% off tariff if you book by Internet. Standard single Rs1000, deluxe Rs1600, suite Rs1800; standard double Rs1200, deluxe Rs1800, suite Rs2000. ❺

Hotel Madhuban, D-237 Behari Marg (☎2200033; madhuban@usa.net). Antique styled furniture fills sharp, clean rooms, all with attached hot water bath. Small garden, pool, and restaurant fill out the property located in a quiet section of Bani Park. Free station pickup. Singles Rs550-1000; doubles Rs1000-1800. ❸

Chit Chat Guest House, D-160 Kabir Marg, Bani Park (☎2201899). An intimate place with six simple rooms set far away from the noise. Excellent value. Huge restaurant serves good food in a relaxing setting. Adjoining cybercafe Rs30 per hr. Rooms Rs80, with attached bath Rs100-150. ❶

🍴 FOOD

For cheap eats, the *bhojnalyas* (diners) on Station Rd. are local favorites, while the more expensive restaurants are on MI Rd. For those with a sweet tooth, the *mishri, mawas,* and *ghevars* of Jaipur are the best in the state; **Lassiwala,** on MI Rd., also whips up a delicious sweet *lassi* (Rs10). If you're desperate for international fast food, **Pizza Hut** is on Ganpati Plaza, and **McDonald's** is on Panch Batti.

Santosh Bhojnalya and **Shri Shanker Bhojnalya,** Station Rd., west of the bus stand. Join the locals at these unpretentious joints for lip-smacking all-you-can-eat *thalis* at great prices. Two of the most popular *bhojnalyas* in town. *Thalis* (Rs30) and *tandoori.* Open daily 9am-11pm. ❶

Niro's, MI Rd., near Panch Batti. A Jaipur institution, very popular with both locals and tourists. All your old Indian, Chinese and Continental favorites are here, and yours for only Rs75-175. Open daily 10am-11pm. AmEx/DC/MC/V. ❸

Copper Chimney, MI Rd. (☎2372275). Opposite the GPO. Huge portions of yummy Indian food (Rs65-175), and free home delivery. Open daily 11:30am-3:30pm and 6-11:30pm. DC/MC/V. ❸

Surya Mahal, MI Rd. Next to Niro's. Popular among businessmen, families, teens, and tourists alike. Specializes in South Indian, Chinese, and pizza. *Dosas* Rs38-70, veg. dishes Rs46-87. Open daily 8am-11pm. Its affiliated bakery, **Bake Hut,** around the back, is full of Westerners with pastries in hand. Open daily 9am-10:30pm. ❷

Natraj Restaurant, M.I. Rd., on the strip with the other eateries. "A vegetarian's paradise" has an extensive, mostly Indian menu. Dig into your *thali* (Rs75-160) at a table in the cave room upstairs. Entrees Rs35-160. Open daily 9am-11pm. AmEx/MC/V. ❷

LMB, Johari Bazaar in the old city. Incredible veg. food in a quirky A/C environment. Try not to fill up first at the attached sweet shop. Indian entrees Rs50-120. Open daily 8am-11:30pm. ❷

Green Tandoori Dhaba, off MI Rd., down the street opposite Hotel Shaan. Next to Old Green Tandoori Dhaba. Prices are cheaper if you can manage to order off the Hindi menu. Full *tandoori* chicken Rs90, chicken curry or chicken *muglas* Rs45-55. Open daily 11am-11pm. ❸

Jal Mahal, MI Rd., next to Surya Mahal. Perfect for dessert after a meal at any of the MI restaurants. Tasty ice cream cones, floats, shakes, and sundaes go for Rs18-55. ❶

◎ SIGHTS

THE PINK CITY
The avenues of the Pink City are broad and meticulously planned. At the heart of the Pink City lies the **City Palace Complex,** which contains the City Palace Museum, the Hawa Mahal, and the Jantar Mantar observatory. The main entrance to the complex is 200m north of the Hawa Mahal off **Siredeori Bazaar.** The **bazaars** surrounding the complex are as interesting as the palace itself and provide lots of shopping opportunities (see **Shopping,** p. 478).

RAJASTHAN

CHILLIN'—MAHARAJA-STYLE The current maharaja of Jaipur, Sawai Bhawani Singh, is a man of refinement and verve. Paying him a visit is about the coolest thing you can do in Jaipur. An old military man, the maharaja is an avid polo player who enjoys driving fancy cars and talks with excitement about computers and ham radio. The maharaja typically grants **private audiences** to visitors on weekdays. To make an appointment, ask at the main entrance of the City Palace for the ADC (Aide de Camp) Office. There you can speak with the PPS (Principal Private Secretary), who organizes the maharaja's schedule. It's best to give the PPS a couple of days' advance notice. Be persistent in confirming the date and time of the appointment. Throughout the process, modest, respectful clothing and behavior are expected.

CITY PALACE AND MUSEUM. Built between 1729 and 1732 by Jai Singh II, founder of Jaipur, the City Palace encompasses nearly 15% of the Pink City's total area. Early maharajas filled the palace with scientific and artistic treasures. Others cultivated a lively palace harem, which reputedly held over 1000 women. In recent decades, the palace has taken on a new public role in the life of the city. It opened to tourists in the 1950s, and scenes from over 400 films—including *North by Northwest* and the Errol Flynn version of Rudyard Kipling's *Kim*—have been shot within its walls. As the home of the current maharaja, Sawai Bhawani Singh, much of the palace is off-limits, but what you can see is delightful.

There are two entrances to the **museum** once you've entered the City Palace complex; the main one is via **Virendra Pol,** near the Jantar Mantar. From the center of the first courtyard, Jaleb Chowk, head left through the south gateway and follow the road to Virenda Pol. The building directly ahead as you enter through Virendra Pol is the **Mubarak Mahal,** carved out of white marble. The ground fl. is occupied by the offices of the palace's director, a museum complex, and a library that is accessible only with permission. The 2nd fl. of the bldg. houses a **Textile Museum,** with collections of cloth and costumes, including the big robes of the notorious "Fat Maharaja," Sawai Madho Singh I, who reportedly weighed over 250kg. Behind the Mubarak Mahal to the right, in the northwest corner of the same courtyard, is the **Arms and Weapons Museum.** Apart from some amusing greetings on the walls, spelled out in English using various instruments of death, the armory is more memorable for the exquisite mirror-work and gold-leaf paintings on the ceilings.

Adjacent to the armory is the elaborate **Rajendra Gate,** whose massive brass doors, flanked by two marble elephants, lead to a second courtyard. At the center is the **Diwan-i-Khas,** or Hall of Private Audience, which contains two huge silver urns. With the Guinness-certified distinction as the largest pieces of silver in the world, these urns were used to store a reserve of holy Ganga water for Maharaja Madho Singh, who refused to drink, bathe in, or use any other water.

Through the door on the right (on the eastern side of the courtyard) is the **Diwan-i-Am** (Hall of Public Audience), which houses the **Art Gallery,** whose hodge-podge of objects includes an extensive collection of manuscripts, miniature paintings, carpets, and a 16th-century edition of Aristotle. As you exit the Art Gallery, **Peacock Gate,** on the opposite side of the courtyard leads into a third courtyard. On an adjacent wall of the courtyard is the **Chandra Mahal,** the maharaja's residence. Parts of the first floor are infrequently open to the public. *(☎ 2608055. Open daily 9:30am-5pm. Entrance fee Rs150; camera fee Rs50; video fee Rs150. No photography in the galleries. Government-authorized guides for 1-4 people Rs150.)*

HAWA MAHAL (PALACE OF WINDS). Jaipur's most recognizable landmark, the Hawa Mahal's five-story pink sandstone edifice was built in 1799 as a comfortable retreat for Maharaja Sawai Pratap Singh. Designed to catch the breeze, the Hawa Mahal was named for the many brass wind vanes that adorned it until the 1960s. Underground tunnels connected the palace to the harem. A small **government museum** displays some sculptures on the ground floor. Shopkeepers opposite the edifice will direct shutterbugs up a flight of stairs for the best vantage point (no *baksheesh*). *(To reach the entrance from the front of the facade, head south down Siredeon Bazaar, turn right on Tripolia Bazaar, and take your 1st right. ☎ 2618862. Open daily 9am-4:30pm. Museum closed on Friday. Entrance fee Rs5; camera fee Rs30; video fee Rs70.)*

JANTAR MANTAR. The largest stone observatory in the world, Jantar Mantar ("instrument of calculation") is one of the Maharaja Jai Singh's most conspicuous additions to Jaipur. Before building it in 1728-34, Jai Singh sent emissaries abroad in search of cutting-edge technical manuals, including a copy of La Hire's "Tables." After it was built, Jai Singh found that the Jantar Mantar produced readings 20 sec. more accurate than La Hire's. The observatory features 16 instruments, including a 30m sundial—impressive, but incomprehensible without a guide or a solid knowledge of astronomy. *(South of the City Palace. ☎ 2660494. Open daily 9am-4:30pm. Rs10, free M; camera fee Rs50; video fee Rs100. Guides negotiable, around Rs100-150 for 2.)*

GOVIND DEVJI TEMPLE. Surrounded by sprawling gardens, Govind Devji Temple contains an image of Lord Krishna as Govind Devji, the patron deity of the royal family, and his mate, Radha. *(North of the City Palace, off Siredeori Bazaar. Darshan times change every two months but are always clearly posted outside the temple. The following may have been changed, so be sure to get updated hours before visiting: 5-5:15, 7:45-8:45, 10-10:30, 11:30-11:45am, 5:45-6, 6:30-7:30, 8:30-8:45pm. Free.)*

SWARGA SULI. This towering minaret lies southwest of the City Palace and is the highest structure within the walls of the Pink City. The maharaja would sometimes bring criminals to the top of the tower and throw them to their deaths below.

NORTH OF THE PINK CITY

The sights north of the Pink City can be approached via turnoffs from the same road and, thus, are most conveniently visited in the same trip. A round-trip rickshaw to all of the following sights should cost Rs250. The cheapest way to see the forts without too much hassle to see them all is to bus to Amber Fort (Rs5), hike from Amber to Jaigarh Fort (20min.), hire a rickshaw to Nahargarh Fort from Amber (Rs100), and walk from Naharagh 2km down the footpath to the Old City and over to Royal Gaitor.

AMBER FORT. Standing guard over the Pink City, the three Garland Forts dominate the northern horizon. Foremost among these is the Amber, the ancient capital of Jaipur State. Built in 1592 by Raja Man Singh, Amber synthesizes both Hindu and Islamic architectural styles. While Jaigarh Fort was built primarily for defensive purposes, Amber was intended mainly as a residential fort, and its elaborate palace complex features decorative artwork and many other comforts.

Buses and rickshaws will drop you off at the base of the mountain; you can either walk the 15min. up to the fort or hop on an elephant (Rs400 round-trip for up to 4 people) or jeep (Rs100 round-trip per person). From the main courtyard, a flight of stairs leads to **Diwan-i-Am** (Hall of Public Audience). To the right is the mosaic-tiled **Ganesh Pol**, the main gate into the palace. Just inside are the maharaja's former apartments, with a maze of corridors, balconies, terraces, and rooms built for the maharaja, his 12 wives, and the 350 women of his harem. Parts are in poor repair, but some, like the famous **Jai Mandir** (Hall of Victory), are in better condition. To the left as you pass through Ganesh Pol into the Jai Singh I garden courtyard, the halls exhibit blinding mirror-work and beautifully preserved coloring. Other attractions include the **Sheesh Mahal,** the original private chambers of the maharaja, just behind the Jai Mandir and the **Sukh Mahal** (Pleasure Palace), opposite the courtyard from the Jai Mandir. The wall opposite Ganesh Pol separates the garden from the palace proper. While not as well preserved as the halls and rooms off the garden, the palace corridors make for a great wander. Down from the main courtyard, on the right of the ticket booth, is the **Shri Sila Devi Temple** whose majestic silver doors lead to a shrine for the goddess of strength. The government-approved **guides** are extremely well-informed. They make the palace come alive with their stories. *(11km north of Jaipur. Amber-bound buses leave regularly from the Central Bus Stand and from the front of the Hawa Mahal; Rs5. Open daily 9am-4:30pm. Entrance fee Rs50; camera fee Rs75; video fee Rs150. Guides Rs100 for 2 people.)*

JAIGARH FORT. Stocky Jaigarh, the second in the Garland trio, is perched on an even higher hill with a breathtaking view of Amber Fort. It once served as the royal treasury, and some people still think there's some royal treasure hidden somewhere on the grounds; even the Indian government ransacked it in 1976 in the hopes of finding it. Inside is a moderately interesting **museum,** and an **armory,** with the usual instruments of death. The highlight of the fort is the gigantic **Jaivana,** the largest wheeled cannon in the world. This 50 ton behemoth has a 22 mi. range and requires 100kg of powder per shot. Serving as the ultimate deterrent, Jaivana was never tested on the field of battle, and has only been fired once. If you're curious about the current maharaja's whereabouts, look to the flagpole on the adjacent tower. Two flags flying means he is town, a solitary banner indicates he's abroad. *(The fort can be reached by a 20min. climb, by jeep (Rs200-250), or by rickshaw. Open daily 9am-4:30pm. Rs20, free with City Palace ticket stub; camera fee Rs20; video fee Rs100.)*

JAL MAHAL (WATER PALACE). About 6km north of Jaipur along the road to Amber is the Jal Mahal, which appears to float on a lake and resembles the Lake Palace in Udaipur. Unfortunately, you can't go inside.

NAHARGARH FORT. Also known as the Tiger Fort, Nahargarh Fort provides visitors with amazing views of Jaipur from the palace roof. Inside, the painted floral patterns brighten the walls of its many chambers, which are strung together in a maze-like floorplan. Because of Nahargarh's isolated locale, be wary of bringing valuables or traveling here alone. *(Accessible via a winding 15km road from Jaipur or a steep 2km hike from the northwest corner of the old city. Open daily 9:30am-5:30pm. Entrance fee Rs15; camera fee Rs30; video fee Rs70. Guides available; negotiate price ahead of time.)*

ROYAL GAITOR. Just north of the old city, are the memorials to the maharajas of Jaipur. The older ones are toward the back of the complex, including the beautifully carved cenotaph of Jai Singh. On the hill to the left, you can see Nahargarh Fort; to the right, steps lead 20min. uphill to a **Ganesh temple.** *(North of Samrat Gate. Open daily 9am-4:30pm. Free; camera fee Rs10; video fee Rs20.)*

SOUTH OF THE PINK CITY

BIRLA MANDIR. Officially called the Lakshmi Narayan Mandir, this blindingly-white and industrially-sponsored temple is rapidly becoming one of Jaipur's most beloved buildings. Built by the wealthy Birla family, the temple was styled with the family's multi-denominational approach to religion in mind: the three domes have each been styled according to a different type of religious architecture. The theme of pluralism is further evident in the artwork of the *parikrama*—done by a Muslim—and the pillars flanking the temple, which include carvings of Hindu deities as well as depictions of Moses, Jesus, Zarathustra, and Socrates. Underneath the temple the Birla family museum exhibits some of the family silver, jewelry, furniture, and clothing. Near the entrance to Birla Mandir are a variety of small temples. On the hill overlooking the Birla Mandir are the remains of **Motidungri Fort,** owned by the maharaja. The fort complex contains a **Shiva temple** that is open to the public only on Shivaratri, during the first week of March. *(At the intersection of Jawaharlal Nehru Marg and Bhawani Sing Marg. Open daily Nov.-Feb. 6:30am-noon and 3-8:30pm; Mar.-Oct. 6am-noon and 3-9pm. Museum free.)*

CENTRAL MUSEUM AND RAM NIWAS GARDENS. Ram Niwas Gardens shelters Jaipur's Central Museum, often called **Albert Hall.** The building itself, a mixture of pillars, arches, and courtyards adorned with murals, is more interesting than the museum. The halls contain exhibits on traditional Rajasthani dance, musical instruments, and decorative arts. *(In the Ram Niwas Gardens, south of the old city. Open Sa-Th 10am-4:30pm. Rs30, M free. Photography prohibited inside.)*

CENTRAL PARK. Solitude and fresh air in the center of Jaipur is not just another desert mirage. Developed in 2001, the largest park in the city extends from Statue Circle to Rambagh Palace. It encompasses a golf course, running path, and plenty of green space for primary schoolchildren to play *kolda chamarka* (duck, duck, goose) and tourists to stretch out and take a few deep breaths. In the mornings and evenings check out the musical fountain near the entrance. *(Entrance south of Statue Circle off Bhagwander Rd. Solo visitors should be careful at night.)*

MUSEUM OF INDOLOGY. The eccentric, privately-funded Museum of Indology features the encyclopedic treasure troves of Vyakul (recently deceased poet, painter, and pack-rat)—ancient manuscripts, curio pieces, and some real treasures. In one room, the marriage contract of the last Mughal emperor competes with a grain of rice with a full-color map of India drawn on it. *(About 500m south of the Central Museum, just off J. Nehru Marg. Open daily 8am-6pm. Admission with guide Rs40.)*

EAST OF THE PINK CITY

GALTA (MONKEY TEMPLE). This series of beautifully frescoed temples and pavilions lines a rocky valley 3km east of Jaipur. The temples are grouped around a sacred pool in which worshippers bathe and swim while monkeys scamper and splash nearby. The best time to visit is before noon, when the tide of worshippers is at its fullest. The most direct route to Galta is a steep 2.5km foot path that begins just outside Suraj Pol and takes about 30min.; this route takes you past the **Surya Mandir,** with exquisite views, before leading you down into the gorge. The lazier route is a 10km drive via Agra Marg (auto-rickshaw Rs150 round-trip).

SISODIA RANI KA BAGH & PALACE AND VIDHYADHAR KA BAGH. The **Sisodia Rani Palace and Gardens,** 8km east of Jaipur on Agra Marg, was built by Jai Singh in 1710 for his princess. The delicately painted palace and pavilions are washed in a pale yellow—the original color of the Pink City. Nearby, the **Vidhyadhar Gardens** provide a pocket of green wedged between two sheer rock faces. If you're driving to Galta, both make a pleasant stop right on the way. *(Both open daily 8am-6pm. Rs5.)*

🎭 🎵 ENTERTAINMENT AND NIGHTLIFE

THE ARTS. Most regularly scheduled performances take place only during the high season. Many of the high-end hotels put on a dance, music, or puppet show every night. Try the Rajputana Palace Sheraton, the Man Singh Palace, or the Rambagh Palace. **Ravindra Manch** (☎2619061), in Ram Niwas Gardens, offers occasional evening performances of Rajasthani dance, music, and plays. The Modern Art Gallery upstairs is free. (☎2618531. Open M-Sa 10am-5pm.) **Jawahar Kala Kendra,** Jawaharlal Nehru Marg (☎2706501), run by the Department of Art and Culture, shows regular in-season Rajasthani plays and performance.

FESTIVALS. The **Gangaur Fair** celebrates the union of Shiva ("Gan") and Parvati ("Gauri") on Mar. 23-24, 2004. Along with performances and parades, the **Elephant Festival** brings elephant polo and a man versus beast tug-of-war (Mar. 6, 2004). The **Teej Fair** (Festival of Swings) celebrates the monsoon (Aug. 19-20, 2004).

CINEMA. Jaipur's 16 cinemas are packed with people at every Hindi film showing. The world-renowned **Raj Mandir Cinema,** just south of Panch Batti, is an experience in itself. The showings are *always* sold out, so arrive *at least* 1hr. ahead to get tickets and look for the tourist/student queue. (☎2374694. Screenings daily noon, 3, 6:15, 9:30pm. Advance booking for next-day shows 10am-6pm. Tickets Rs20-80.)

CHOWKI DHANI. A traditional Rajasthani village is re-created surprisingly well at Chowki Dhani, 20km south of the city. The admission fee includes a traditional (spicy and very heavy) Rajasthani dinner, served on leaf plates in a large mud hut, after which you can roam freely about the "village" to watch performances of traditional palmistry, snake charming, *mehendi* hand-art, puppet shows, acrobatics, and a (man-powered!) ferris wheel. Just like Disneyland, but not at all. (Dinner Rs50. *Baksheesh* expected at some performances. Open M-Sa 6-11pm and Su 11am-11pm. Auto-rickshaw 45min. one-way; Rs250 round-trip.)

BARS. Only hotels can legally serve anything stronger than beer. For classy, A/C boozing, try the **Polo Bar** or **Steam,** both in Rambagh Palace, off Bhawani Singh Rd. (Polo Bar open daily 11am-midnight; cocktails Rs225-275. Steam open W-M 7pm-late; beer Rs125.) The latter is the only bar hitched to a 1915 Bagnall UK steam engine. Another classy option is the **Sheesh Mahal,** in the Rajputana Palace Sheraton near the railway station (open daily 11am to 11pm; cocktails Rs200). For laid-back budget sloshing, pick up a few brews from reception at Jaipur Inn and relax on their rooftop. Open late.

🛍 SHOPPING

Jaipur is the shopping capital of Rajasthan—you'll find a huge assortment of handicrafts, pottery, silk, textiles, jewelry, and perfumes. Shopping here can be draining because you have to haggle incessantly, but the effort is worth it. Rajasthan is known for its colorful, unbeatable selection of tie-dyed fabrics called *bandhani*. The jewelry and gem work of Jaipur are world-famous and remarkably inexpensive, but be on the lookout for scams. The fixed-price emporium **Rajasthali,** opposite Ajmeri Gate, carries a variety of goods from throughout Rajasthan. (Open M-

Sa 11am-7:30pm.) In front is the **Rajasthan Handloom House,** the government emporium for textiles. More high-quality crafts can be found at the award-winning showroom in the **City Palace museum,** but beware of the insanely inflated prices. The **bazaars** of the palace complex also offer great shopping. The Johari Bazaar and two lanes off it—Gopal ka Rasta and Haldiyon ka Rasta—are the prime spots for **jewelry;** Nehru Bazaar and Bapu Bazaar specialize in **textiles, perfumes,** and **shoes.** Tripolia Bazaar and Chaura Rasta sell a variety of items and **trinkets.** Watch master **carpet-makers** at work in Siredeori Bazaar, find exquisite **marble sculpture** on Khajane Walon Ka Rasta, which crosses busy Chandpol Bazaar and behold **shoemakers** at work on Ramganj Bazaar. (Most stores open M-Sa 10am-8pm.)

BHARATPUR भरतपुर ☎ 05644

A convenient stop on the tourist route between Agra (56km) and Jaipur (172km), Bharatpur's spectacular Keoladeo Ghana National Park is one of the best bird sanctuaries in the world. During the winter, the beautifully maintained park draws millions of migrating birds. Founded by Badan Singh in 1733 as a princely state, Bharatpur soon became known as home of the fierce armies of Suraj Mal. The Mughals recognized Bharatpur as autonomous and the area successfully resisted two attacks by the British before it was finally captured by Lord Combermere in 1826. It became part of Rajasthan after Independence.

E TRANSPORTATION. The **train station** is several kilometers north of town. To: **Delhi** (3½-5hr., 5 per day 6:15am-2:43am, Rs68-141) via **Mathura** (1hr.); **Mumbai** (19-22hr.; 10:15am, 6:20, 7:45pm; Rs215-397). No trains run from Bharatpur to Jaipur; you must change trains in Mathura. The **bus station,** on the western edge of town, sends buses to: **Agra** (1½hr., every 30min. 7am-8:30pm, Rs30) via **Fatehpur Sikri** (30min., Rs12); **Alwar** (3½hr., every 45min. 6am-7:15pm, Rs41); **Bikaner** (12hr., 1pm, Rs197); **Delhi** (5hr., every hr. 5:30am-8:30pm, Rs92); **Jaipur** (4hr., every 30min. 5:30am-9pm, Rs62-75); **Udaipur** (14hr., 7:45am and 7:45pm, Rs251). **Rickshaws** cost Rs15-20 to the hotel area. **Tempos** (Rs4) run between the train and bus terminals. You can rent **bicycles** at several hotels near the sanctuary (Rs20-30 per day).

■ ☑ ORIENTATION AND PRACTICAL INFORMATION. The bird sanctuary and the hotels are a few kilometers south of the town center, along the road to Agra and Fatehpur Sikri. If you arrive by train or by bus from Jaipur, you'll need to take a rickshaw to get there (Rs15-20); if coming by bus from Agra or Fatehpur Sikri, hop off the bus early (look for guest house signs) and head down the main drag. The town center sprawls around the ruins of an ancient fort and is best avoided unless you need practical services. The **RTDC Tourist Reception Centre,** in the middle of the strip opposite government-run Hotel Saras (a local landmark), sells a small brochure with map for Rs10. (☎ 222542. Open M-Sa 10am-5pm.) The **State Bank,** near B. Narayan Gate, a 15min. walk northwest of Birdland, changes currency and traveler's checks. (☎ 222441. Open M-Sa 10am-2pm.) There is also the **police** (☎ 223116), and the **Arora Hospital,** Krishna Nagar (☎ 224667), which has a **24hr. pharmacy. Post Office,** near Gandhi Park. (Open M-Sa 6:30am-6pm.) **Postal Code:** 321001.

Г ☐ ACCOMMODATIONS AND FOOD. All the hotels below are out of town, along a main strip leading to the park entrance. Most establishments rent bicycles, binoculars, and field guides. Prices listed are for the winter; from April to August rates drop by as much as 50%. Reserve ahead during high season (Nov.-Feb.).

    ⊠Jungle Lodge ❷, at the end of the strip, has spotless rooms and a peaceful garden overflowing with all things related to birding. (☎ 225622. Doubles with attached bath Rs150-350.) Next door, the **New Spoonbill ❷** has four amazing,

just-completed rooms with terraces and attached baths. (Doubles Rs200-400.)
The original **Hotel Spoonbill ❶**, behind Hotel Saras, is less well-manicured but
equally welcoming. (☎223571. Dorms Rs50; doubles with attached bath Rs100-
400.) **Falcon Guesthouse ❷**, on the other side of Jungle Lodge, has nice rooms,
TVs, an Internet connection (Rs60 per hr.), and second-story balconies.
(☎223815. Doubles with attached bath Rs150-400.) Between the park entrance
and Hotel Saras is backpacker favorite **Hotel Pelican ❶**, a good value with a
decent restaurant to boot. (☎224221. Dorms Rs50-70; doubles with attached
bath Rs200-250.) A second colony of family-run guest houses has started up on
nearby Rajendra Nagar, parallel to the highway across from the park entrance.
■**Kiran Guest House ❶**, also serves up painstakingly prepared meals. (☎223845.
Doubles with common bath Rs60-80.) Serious nature-lovers might want to consider the **Forest Rest House ❹**, inside the park, to the right of the second guard
check-post. Better than the spacious rooms are the views and immediate access
to the birds. Contact Deputy Chief Warden B. Praveen or Mr. Satish of the Forest Office for booking inquiries. (☎222777. Open M-Sa 10am-5pm. Doubles
Rs600. Includes 3 meals for 2 people.)

The restaurants attached to guest houses in Bharatpur feature monotonous,
mediocre food at inflated prices, but it's so far to the town center that few travelers put up a fight. If you've got a bike, a good compromise is **Jeet Restaurant ❶**,
5min. down the road to Bharatpur from Hotel Saras (the sign is in Hindi). This
favorite serves up rich Punjabi food (Rs15 per plate)—after a burning *masala
channa*, the ice-cold Kingfisher might just be the best bird you've seen all day.

⬛ SIGHTS. Foreigners flock to Bharatpur to go cuckoo over the hordes of birds
at Keoladeo Ghana National Park. If you're in town and sick of binoculars, you
could check out the 18th-century **Lohagarh** (Iron Fort), on an artificial island surrounded by a wide moat in the center of town. Built by Maharaja Suraj Mal, the
fort has acquired a reputation for its resistance to attack; British weapons are said
to have bounced off the walls. Inside are two towers, **Jawahar Burg** and **Fateh Burg**,
built by Suraj to commemorate his victories over the Mughals and the British, as
well as the decaying remains of three former palaces. One of them contains a
museum with three large galleries of Jain sculpture and fort artifacts. *(Open M-Th and
Sa-Su 10am-4:30pm. Rs3.)*

⬛ KEOLADEO GHANA NATIONAL PARK. Internationally renowned for its bird-
watching opportunities, Keoladeo Ghana National Park started out as a 29 sq. km,
anything-goes play zone for the maharaja of Bharatpur and his buddies to indulge
their passion for hunting in the late 19th century. The protected deer-shooting site
was flooded at the turn of the century to create an artificial duck-shooting reserve.
A sandstone plaque near Keoladeo Temple chronicles the astonishingly large bags
of ducks and geese felled by royalty from around the world (4276 in one long,
record-breaking day in 1938). Since then, the area has been declared a national
park and a UNESCO World Heritage Natural Site.

The park has plenty to offer, even if your interest in birds doesn't normally go
much beyond backyard bird feeders. Known as the finest wetland reserve in northern India, Keoladeo is home to such waterfowl as storks, cormorants, egrets, herons, and spoonbills. These locals nest during the monsoon season (starting mid-
Aug.), populating the park with eager, young chirpers by early winter. Starting in
September, the park also hosts species that migrate south for the winter from as
far as Siberia and Tibet. At its peak bird population from November to January, the
park houses around 375 species, 130 of which are year-round residents. Addition-
ally, the dry-land sections of the park (about two-thirds of the total area) house
large numbers of spotted deer, sambar, and invasive cattle.

As motor vehicles are allowed only 1.7km inside Keoladeo's sole entrance, and the park is too expansive to be traversed on foot, you'll need to hire transportation. Going solo on a rented **bike** (Rs20-30 per day, available at the entrance gate and local hotels) allows you to explore at your own pace; this is especially recommended if you intend to venture beyond the central marsh area (where the birds are located) and check out the dry-land scenery. However, be forewarned that many paths in the park are extremely rocky. If you're planning to visit just the main bird area, you can hire a **tonga** (horse cart; Rs100 per hr.) or an authorized **cycle-rickshaw** (look for the yellow ID tag and number; Rs50 per hr.). Either way, a **guide** will eagerly accompany you for Rs70 per hr. One of the more qualified of the many self-titled "naturalists" milling around the gate is Goverdhan Singh (☎ 221284). The best way to see the birds is on an early-morning boat trip, which allows you to float up to hundreds of nesting herons, egrets, cranes, storks, and spoonbills. You can hire a **boat** for up to four people in season *(1hr., Rs30 per person).*

Just past the ticket counter, a small **Orientation Center** features nests, eggs, and stuffed specimens, as well as a color map of the park. A stall at the second checkpost, 1.7km past the entrance gate, sells bird-books and postcards. *(Open daily 8:15am-5:30pm.)* At the rear of the building, across the road, a small **canteen** sells beverages. No food is available within the park, so plan to bring your own. Most guest houses happily pack lunches for birdwatchers. *(Park Office ☎ 222777. Park open daily sunrise-sunset. Rs200 per entry; video fee Rs200.)*

SHEKHAWATI

The muralled *havelis* of Shekhawati sets this region apart from the rest. Located 150km northwest of Jaipur, the many painted mansions built by the merchant class present beautifully-painted facades and intricate architecture. Along with the forts, palaces and cenotaphs spotted throughout the region, these outdoor displays of art will dazzle any visitor. The slower pace of rural life also provides a welcome respite from the urban pace of Jaipur and Delhi.

Rajput princes descended from Rao Shekha, the stalwart 15th-century ruler from whom Shekhawati derives its name, resisted Jaipur control in the 17th and early 18th centuries and established the region's independence. An important stopping point on the Delhi-Persia trade route, rich merchants built their *havelis* here. The merchants patronized the artists that created the beautiful artwork.

Descendants of these merchants still live in many of the *havelis*. Others are administered by caretakers. Most are open for visiting during daylight hours, some require a (technically illegal) Rs10-20 entrance fee for upkeep. Be sure to ask which rooms of the *haveli* are open before poking around any private quarters. A knowledgeable guide, usually available at any hotel, will enhance any visit.

The region is accessible by bus or train from Jaipur, Delhi, or Bikaner. Jeep and car tours are the most hassle-free way to travel within the region. It's best to arrange tours from Nawalgarh (see below) or Mandawa (see p. 506) as the drivers and guides are more knowledgeable than their Jaipur or Delhi counterparts.

NAWALGARH नठळगट ☎ 1594

Nawalgarh's concentration of well-preserved *havelis* and its central location within the region make it a nice base for exploration. Founded in 1737, the town was centered around its fort, now houses the Bank of Baroda and bazaar and bounded by its four gates. Today many of the *havelis* lie just outside these gates, while the bazaar spills out from the fort in the old city.

✈ 🎫 ORIENTATION AND PRACTICAL INFORMATION

Nawalgarh is in the heart of the Shekhawati Region, 145km northwest of Jaipur, 275km from Delhi, and 225km from Bikaner. The town is on the Sikar-Delhi line and the **train station** (☎222025) is 2km west of the town center. Station Rd. runs from the station, intersects with the state highway after 1km, and continues into town. The main bus stand is on the state highway 1km west of the town center. Buses to: **Bikaner** (5½hr., 2pm, Rs84); **Delhi** (7hr., every hr. 7am-7pm, Rs100); **Jaipur** (3½hr., every 15min., Rs50); via **Sikar** (40min., Rs10). Buses to Bikaner leave hourly from Sikar. Auto-rickshaws from the bus or train station will cross the street or cross town for the same fixed Rs30 fare. Shared rickshaws run from the station to the Old City when they fill up (Rs4; passengers must get off at the point nearest their destination on the main roads). Thasil Rd. runs from the bus stand parallel to Station Rd. to Nansa Gate, the southern portal into the Old City. Local buses to **Parasurampura** leave from a stand 1km south of Nansa Gate. (45min., every hr. 7am-7pm, Rs8.) Local buses leave from the bus stand just north of **Barwari Gate,** the northern gate into the Old City, to: **Dundlod** (15min., every 10min. 6am-late, Rs4) and **Fatehpur** (2½hr., every hr. 7am-7pm, Rs20). A **regional map** and **town maps** of Nawalgarh, Mandawa, Fatehpur, Dundlod, and Parasurampura are available at **Rajesh Jangid's Tourist Pension** near the **Maur Hospital.** There is no currency exchange in Nawalgarh. In case of a medical **emergency,** call ☎222006; **police** (☎222046). The **GPO** is on the east side of town, take the first right after passing through the eastern gate into the Old City. (☎32009. Open M-Sa 10am-5pm).

🏠 🍴 ACCOMMODATIONS AND FOOD

Nawalgarh has a variety of accommodation options. The oldest guest house in town, **Rajesh Jangid's Tourist Pension ❷,** near the Maur Hospital, is also the best value. The Jangid family maintains 7 clean, simple rooms all with attached hot water bath. They also have loads of information on places of interest in Shekhawati. Internet Rs60 per hr. Call ahead for bus or train pick-up. (☎224060; touristpension@yahoo.com. Singles Rs180-280; doubles Rs200-300.) The Jangid family's other property, the **Apani Dhani ❹,** 500km north of the bus stand off the state highway, emphasizes 🌱**sustainable tourism.** Solar panels provide the electricity for the 8 well-appointed, clay brick huts, all with spotless attached hot water baths. (☎222129; rcjangid@yahoo.com. Singles Rs600; doubles Rs725.) On the other side of town, 1½km east of the Old City, the **Roop Niwas Palace ❺** hints at luxury. Overpriced rooms are large but not well-kept. (☎4220078. Singles Rs1500-1700; doubles Rs1700-1900.) Near the Roop Niwas Palace the **Shekhawati Guest House ❷** (☎224658; gss2@satyam.net.in; singles Rs300, doubles Rs400) and **D.S. Bungalow ❷** (☎222703; singles Rs250, doubles Rs450) sit side-by-side. Both offer basic rooms with attached hot water bath.

Outside of the hotels, Nawalgarh has few restaurants. **Apani Dhani ❸** offers a fully organic menu using ingredients from their vegetable farm. Notify the kitchen in advance. **Rajesh Jangid's Tourist Pension ❹** serves tasty veg. *thalis* (Rs120) and **Shekhawati Guest House ❹** has veg. *thali* (Rs150) and non-veg. *thali* (Rs200).

📷 SIGHTS

Nawalgarh has some of the nicest *havelis* in the region. A 3hr. walking tour covers all the major points of interest. A guide will greatly enhance your tour and can be arranged at any of the hotels. Krishan at the Apani Dhani is a reliable bet (Rs200). Walking east up Thali Rd., the second left after passing Gandhi Park on your right leads to **Murarka Haveli.** Though only open during the winter wedding season the dome over the door shelters a Krishna mythology sequence. The **Aath Haveli** complex is across from Murarka, a bit farther down the road on the right. The second *haveli* on the left is the most interesting; it serves as a graphic timeline of style and content. The oldest paintings, completed in the early 19th century, are on the right. The middle section was done in the late 19th century, while the left side depict a modern train engine and automobile finished in the early 20th century. With the 2nd *haveli* on your left, a left on the next road will wind toward the **Khedwal Bhawan Haveli** with its beautiful courtyard. The paddle-shaped objects hanging over the interior doorway are wedding *tharons*—tokens of remembrance for the daughters of the house who have married and moved out (as is the custom). To the north of Podar Gate the **Bhagton Ki Haveli** opens all of its doors to visitors (Rs10). The family courtyard (the second one) has family portraits in good condition. On the 2nd fl. portraits of the former owner and his wife flank the wall of the terrace overlooking the public courtyard. Also visible from the terrace is a Neem tree, with your back to the front door it's on the right. Artists would feed these leaves to the cows and use the bovine urine to make their yellow color. On the east side of town the **Polar Museum** houses a collection of bright costumes, traditional instruments, and well-preserved paintings on its walls. (Open daily 9am-sunset. Rs50.) South of Nansa Gate off Ram Devra Rd. the **Ganga Mai Temple** has a painting of the Ramayana on the ceiling right in front of the shrine.

Jeep tours of the region can be arranged at the hotels. Rajesh Jangid's Tourist Pension runs tours from Parasurampura to Ramgarh and points in between (up to 4 people Rs1000-1500). They also arrange treks to the nearby Aravalli Mountains. The Roop Niwas Palace runs horse treks through the desert as far as Pushkar. (www.royalridingholidays.com.)

MANDAWA मड़ाठा   ☎ 05192

Founded in the mid 18th century, Mandawa is 30km north of Nawalgarh and 22km east of Fatehpur. The Forr, current home of the Castle Mandawa, the nicest hotel in the region, dominates the main bazaar and marks the center of town. Mandawa's *havelis* have seen better days but a few worthwhile depictions remain.

■ ⚑ ORIENTATION AND PRACTICAL INFORMATION

Mandawa is a small, compact town, easily seen on foot. The center of town is the **main bazaar.** The bus stand forms the terminus of the bazaar, with the road to Fatehpur continuing west just to the north of the stand. The T-intersection with the southbound Nawalgarh road marks the eastern end of the bazaar. The bazaar road continues east toward Jhunjhunu. Buses depart from the bus stand but can be flagged down anywhere. Buy tickets on board. Buses to: **Bikaner** via **Fatehpur** (3hr., 6 per day, Rs80); **Delhi** via **Jhunjhunu** (4½hr., 10 per day, Rs112); and **Jaipur** via **Nawalgarh** (3½hr., 10 per day, Rs72). Local buses run frequently to **Fatehpur** (40min., Rs10), **Jhunjhunu** (40min, Rs10), and **Nawalgarh** (1hr., Rs15), where rail connections can be made to the larger cities. There is **no tourist office.** The **State Bank of Bikaner** and **Jaipur,** across the bazaar just to the west of the entrance to the **Castle Mandawa** exchanges currency. (☎223073. Open M-Sa 10am-2pm.) **Pharmacies** can be found on the Main Bazaar. (Most open daily 8am-9pm.) The only **Internet** access in town is at **Hotel Shekhawati** (Rs50 per hr.). The **GPO** is just off the Main Bazaar neat the T-intersection with the road to Nawalgarh.

☗ ⬛ ACCOMMODATIONS AND FOOD

Mandawa has the highest concentration of mid-range and luxury lodgings in all of Shekhawati. The **Castle Mandawa ❺** serves dual purposes as the most luxurious hotel in the region and one of its more popular sights. Palatial deluxe rooms are the best value if you want to splurge. Ordinary rooms vary so ask to see a couple before choosing. (☎0140 371194; reservation@castlemandawa.com. Singles Rs1850; doubles Rs2400; deluxe singles Rs2995; deluxe doubles Rs3995; royal suite Rs5995.) The same owner has another hotel 1km south of town off Nawalgarh Rd., the **Desert Resort ❺**, where guests can stay in nicely furnished mud huts. (Contact Castle Mandawa. Single Rs1800; doubles Rs2350; deluxe cottages Rs2500-3500; royal suite Rs5995.) The beautiful **Hotel Mandawa Haveli ❺**, next to Sonthaliya Gate, off the main bazaar, is the oldest frescoed *haveli* in Mandawa. Wonderfully-preserved rooms, some with private courtyard, all have attached hot water baths. (☎223088; hotel mandawahaveli@yahoo.com. Doubles Rs1100-1750.) The best budget option in town is the **Hotel Shekhawati ❶**, southeast of the T-intersection; follow the signs off the road to Nawalgarh. Colorful rooms all include attached hot water bath and a painting by an Italian artist named Filomena. (☎223036; hotelshekhawati@sity.com. Air-cooled rooms Rs100-400; A/C rooms Rs500.) Like Nawalgarh the only restaurants that cater to tourists are in the hotels. Hotel Shekhawati offers cheap meals (lunch buffet Rs130, dinner buffet Rs160).

☗ SIGHTS

Though Mandawa's *havelis* aren't as well-preserved as the ones in Nawalgarh, they are more conveniently clustered together and easier to see all at once. A 1.5km walking loop starting at the bus stand and finishing back at the main bazaar, with tours of the Castle Mandawa and Hotel Mandawa Haveli (both free), covers all the town's highlights. A guide can make the tour much more enjoyable. Vicky at the Hotel Shekhawati and Surendra at the Castle Mandawa are both informative and reliable. (Rs150-200 per 2hr. walking tour.)

The tour starts at the **Goenka Haveli** across from the bus stand. Ramnath Goenka, the owner of the now-defunct India Express newspaper, owned a number of *havelis* in town. A second Goenka *haveli* is on the right side of Fatehpur road as it heads out of town. A right at the next alley leads to the **Murmuria Haveli,** the first building on the left. The paintings of the *haveli* reveal the influence of Italian traders in the 19th century, many of whom did business with the Murmuria family. Continuing back on Fatehpur Rd., the road that is the next left leads past the **Harlalka water well** on the right and the **Harlalka cenotaphs** (*chattri*) a bit farther west. On the south side of the well, camels attached by rope to the well bucket would walk along the long ramp, hauling up bucketloads of water. Past the well back on the road the **Saraf Haveli** sits above a propane gas tank distributor. The paintings in the first courtyard have been repainted, but still give a good idea of what many of the *havelis* looked like a century ago. Across from the Saraf is the **Gulabria Ladia Haveli,** which has some of the best preserved paintings in town on its outer walls. A right turn after walking between **Saraf** and **Gulabria Ladia** leads to the **Chowkhani Double Haveli** with its large double courtyard. A camel, elephant, and horse race is depicted up on the left wall of the left *haveli*. (Admission Rs10. The only *haveli* in town that charges.) Following the warren of roads and alleyways north will lead back to the main bazaar. Many of the hotels offer jeep tours of the Shekhawati Region arranged by request. Camel safaris can also be arranged (Rs300 per 2hr.).

RURAL ETIQUETTE Shekhwati is a rural region that sees only a trickle of the tourists that flood Rajasthan. In this conservative area it is especially important to understand the effect tourists can have on the local culture and economy (even the solitary backpacker) and to practice responsible tourism.

-Do not embrace, kiss, or hold hands with your partner in public.

-Avoid wearing tank tops, shorts, revealing or transparent clothing.

-Protect the authenticity of spontaneous contact. Do not distribute anything (candy, pens, money, shampoo, samples, etc.) to children or teenagers. If the children can receive by begging for a few hours what their father earns after a day of labor, they can be reluctant to continue their schooling.

-Use the traditional Indian greeting of "Namaste" with hands pressed in a prayer gesture when meeting strangers. Local teenagers get their kicks by making physical contact with female strangers, a practice which is frowned upon by local custom until marriage.

-Refrain from photographing people as much as possible. If you must, try to do so after establishing some sort of extended contact with the person.

-Try to participate in the local economy as often as possible by purchasing directly from local vendors.

Adhering to these guidelines will help slow the transformation of the local culture while still allowing for genuine cultural exchange, the goal of responsible tourism.

AJMER अजमेर ☎ 0145

The busy town of Ajmer (pop. 490,138), 132km west of Jaipur in the middle of the Aravalli Mountains, is significant to Muslims as the final resting place of Khwaja Muin-ud-din Chishti. This Sufi saint's tomb is considered the holiest Islamic shrine in India, second only to Mecca in the hearts of Indian Muslims. Hundreds of thousands of Muslims and Hindus make a pilgrimage to Ajmer during the annual Urs Ajmer Sharif, a six-day festival that starts with the new moon in the seventh month of the Islamic calendar. The rest of the year, most travelers chug straight through to the nearby backpacker mecca of Pushkar, and with good reason—Ajmer has a relatively poor selection of hotels and restaurants. The town's few worthwhile sights are easily visited on a half-day excursion from Pushkar.

▐▘ TRANSPORTATION. Ajmer is on the major Delhi-Ahmedabad broad-gauge line. The railway reservation office is on the second floor above the main entrance to the station. (Inquiries ☎ 131, reservations 2431965. Open M-Sa 8am-8pm, Su 8am-2pm.) To: **Ahmedabad** (10hr., 2-5 per day, Rs182) via **Abu Road** (5hr., Rs127); **Delhi** (7-10hr., 3-6 per day, Rs167); **Jaipur** (2-3hr., 5-8 per day, Rs68). Meter-gauge trains also head to **Udaipur** (9-10hr., 1:37 and 7:50am, Rs124) via **Chittaurgarh** (5hr., Rs84). Buses run from the **main bus stand** (☎ 2429398) to: **Abu Road** (9hr., 6 per day 5:45am-midnight, Rs147); **Ahmedabad** (14hr., 4 per day 5:45am-midnight, Rs218); **Bikaner** (7½hr., 11 per day 5am-1am, Rs115); **Chittaurgarh** (5hr., every hr. 6am-1am, Rs77); **Jaipur** (3hr., every 20min. 7:30am-10:30pm, Rs55); **Jodhpur** (5hr., every hr. 5am-2am, Rs87); **Udaipur** (7hr., every hr. 5:30am-1am, Rs119). **Private bus** companies lining Kutchery Rd. send deluxe buses to most destinations. Buses to **Pushkar** leave regularly from both the main bus stand and the Station-Kutchery Rd. intersection (100m to the right as you exit the train station). For Rs10-25, cycle- and auto-**rickshaws** will get you anywhere. Crowded **tempos** charge Rs3-5.

ORIENTATION AND PRACTICAL INFORMATION. Ajmer is a small town, only about 3km long. Heading right (north) out of the train station along **Station Road** leads to the **Pushkar Bus Stand** and the town's main intersection, where Station Rd. meets **Kutchery Road.** A left on Kutchery leads to the bazaar of the Old City; a right leads to the **Main Bus Stand,** 1.5km northeast. The main **tourist office** is nearby, inside the Hotel Khadim. (☎2627426. Open M-Sa 8am-6pm.) A small branch is also at the train station. Both distribute useful maps. The **Bank of Baroda,** Prithviraj Marg, opposite the GPO, changes traveler's checks and issues AmEx/MC/V cash advances. (☎2422575. Open M-F 10am-3pm, Sa 10am-12:30pm.) **24hr. ATMs** can be found on Jaipur Rd., near the Hotel Embassy. The **police** (☎2431251) are opposite the railway station. Dr. Yadava's **Pratap Memorial Hospital,** Kutchery Rd. (☎2426406), the best private hospital, has a 24hr. **pharmacy** in front. Back toward the station intersection, **Satguru Internet,** Kutchery Rd., is open for surfing. (☎2623749. Rs30 per hr. Open daily 9am-9pm.) The **GPO** is near the Station-Kutchery Rd. intersection. (☎2427603. Open M-Sa 10am-5pm.) **Postal Code:** 305001.

ACCOMMODATIONS AND FOOD. Ajmer has a disappointing selection of hotels and independent restaurants, but if you haven't booked something ahead in Pushkar for the Mela, they may provide a cheaper alternative. Numerous dirt-cheap, no-frills hotels catering to Muslim pilgrims lie opposite the railway station and are scattered throughout the bazaar area. The most appealing budget option is **Nagpal Tourist Hotel** ❷, Station Rd., 50m to the left as you exit the train station, where the cheapest rooms have TVs and attached baths. (☎2627427. Check-out 24hr. Singles Rs175-800; doubles Rs300-1000.) The best of the cheapies is **Bhola Hotel** ❷, Prithviraj Marg, near Agra Gate, which has well-decorated rooms with tiled bathrooms and a tiny terrace. (☎2432844. Singles Rs150; doubles Rs200.) For top value, try the historic, family-run **Haveli Heritage Inn** ❸, Kutchery Rd., 200m from the station intersection. Nehru and Gandhi stayed here when the *haveli* was the Ajmer headquarters of the British National Congress. (☎2621607. Doubles Rs450-650; triples Rs800.) Formerly on the north shore of the rapidly evaporating Ana Sagar Lake, **Mansingh Palace** ❺, Vaishali Nagar, 2km from Agra Gate, offers Western-style hotel amenities at Western-style prices. (☎2425956; http://fhrain-dia.com/hotel/Amjer/Mansingh. Singles Rs2000; doubles Rs3000; suites Rs4500.) The **Bhola Hotel** ❶ has an excellent and inexpensive restaurant that serves up veg. dishes for Rs30-60. (Open daily 9am-11pm.) The **Honeydew Restaurant** ❶, Station Rd., to the left of Nagpal Tourist Hotel, serves Indian and Chinese dishes and ice cream galore in a clean, calm environment with two pool tables. (Entrees Rs30-170. Pool Rs40 per hr. Open daily 9am-11pm.) Nearby, in an alley, to the left of the clock tower opposite the station, **Jai Hind Restaurant** ❶, also serves very good veg. food. (Entrees Rs24-47. Open daily 8am-11pm.)

SIGHTS. Thousands of people flock to Ajmer during the Urs Ajmer Sharif to see **Dargah,** the tomb of the Sufi saint **Khwaja Muin-ud-din Chishti,** who died here in 1236. On the west side of town, in the old city, the tomb looms high above the surrounding bazaars. The elaborate marble complex constitutes one of the most important destinations for Muslim pilgrims in South Asia; Emperor Akbar himself used to pay regular homage to Dargah and even walked here twice all the way from Agra. Originally a simple brick cenotaph completed by Humayun, Dargah has been expanded and improved upon as subsequent rulers have paid tribute. A tall, elaborate gateway, added by the Nizam of Hyderabad, leads to the first courtyard, where two massive cauldrons called *degs* are filled with rice that is sold to devotees as *tabarukh*, a sanctified food. Akbar's mosque is to the right, and Shah Jahan's grand mosque is farther inside. The actual tomb of the saint is in the central domed marble mosque, encircled by silver railings and overflowing with flower offerings and legions of devotees. Just outside the tomb, *qawwali* singers perform the same hypnotic tunes that have been sung here for the past 700 years. You will inevitably be approached by **"guides"** when you enter Dargah, but they are not necessary; be firm. Similarly, decline any offers to sign a **"visitor's book,"** which only serves as a slippery slope to demands for large donations. A **head scarf** is required to enter certain parts of the complex; pick one up from the bazaar that leads up to the tomb. Be sure to keep a close eye on your personal belongings when you enter. Respectful behavior and a small donation are expected.

On the same road, about 500m past Dargah, is the **Adhai-Din-ka-Jhonpra** (Mosque of Two-and-a-Half Days), named for the remarkably short time it took Muhammad of Ghur to add the massive arched screen that converted the former Sanskrit college into a mosque in 1193. The breathtaking screen consists of seven arches carved with Persian calligraphy. The pillared hall behind it is also a beautiful architectural specimen. The striking, red **Nasiyan Temple,** in the bazaars near Agra Gate, houses a museum where the Jain conception of the universe is illustrated using a two-floor golden model. A local Jain family used over 1000kg of gold to construct the exhibit in 1865, and the project—with its kaleidoscope of mirrors, colored glass, and gilded figures—took 20 artisans 40 years to complete. (Open daily 8:30am-5:30pm. Rs5.) Not too far away, through the gate 100m to the left as you face Bhola, is **Akbar's Palace** (Daulat Khona), an uninspiring structure built by the emperor in 1570. Inside, a small **government museum** exhibits ancient tablets, sculptures, and weaponry. (Open M-Th and Sa-Su 10am-4:30pm. Rs3; M free.) The **Daulat Bagh** gardens on the northwest side of town, by the banks of **Ana Sagar Lake,** contain marble pavilions built by Shah Jahan in 1637. (Paddleboats Rs40 per 30min.)

PUSHKAR पुश्कर ☎ 0145

Tiny Pushkar (pop. 13,000) is a major pilgrimage center. Devout Hindus are expected to dip in the waters here at least once in their lifetime, and for many, this is the final stop on a tour of India's sacred sites. A staggering number of devotees converge upon Pushkar during the full moon of the Hindu lunar month of Kartika (Oct.-Nov.), which coincides with the world-famous Pushkar *oont mela* (camel fair). During the fair, the largest of its kind in the world, the tiny town is transformed into a swarming beehive of activity—don't miss it.

Given its sacred atmosphere, picturesque surroundings, and *mela*-induced fame, Pushkar was powerless to escape its fate as a backpacker mecca. The main street—a jumble of Internet cafes, shops, and rooftop restaurants—feels more like a traveler's fantasyland than India. Venture out of the bazaar to the other side of the lake or up into the surrounding hills and you'll discover the magic that drew people to Pushkar in the first place.

▅ TRANSPORTATION

Ajmer, 11km south of Pushkar, is the most common gateway to Pushkar.

Buses: Ajmer Bus Stand, Ajmer Rd. To: **Ajmer's Pushkar Bus Stand** (30min., every 15min. 6am-8:30pm, Rs5). **Marwar Bus Stand** serves: **Bikaner** (6½hr., 10 per day 5:30am-11pm, Rs107); **Jodhpur** (5hr., 9am, Rs83). All other destinations can be reached via the **Main Bus Stand** (☎ 2429398) in Ajmer. **Private bus** companies line Sadar Bazaar and the area around Marwar Bus Stand. Most private buses depart from Ajmer, though free transport from Pushkar to Ajmer's Main Bus Stand is typically included. **Ekta Travels** (see below) has daily buses to major cities in Rajasthan.

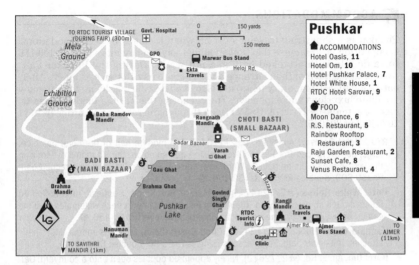

Pushkar

▲ ACCOMMODATIONS
Hotel Oasis, 11
Hotel Om, 10
Hotel Pushkar Palace, 7
Hotel White House, 1
RTDC Hotel Sarovar, 9

🍴 FOOD
Moon Dance, 6
R.S. Restaurant, 5
Rainbow Rooftop
   Restaurant, 3
Raju Garden Restaurant, 2
Sunset Cafe, 8
Venus Restaurant, 4

RAJASTHAN

❈ 🛈 ORIENTATION AND PRACTICAL INFORMATION

Pushkar is a small, tourist-friendly town, so it's hard to get lost. Most travelers arrive at **Ajmer Bus Stand,** Ajmer Rd., in the southeast part of town. As it winds into town, Ajmer Rd. becomes **Sadar Bazaar,** the main thoroughfare, which follows the northern shore of **Pushkar Lake** and ends on the west side of town, near the **Brahma Mandir.** Roughly speaking, the eastern half of the town is referred to as **Choti Basti (Small Bazaar),** and the western half is known as **Badi Basti (Main Bazaar).** A right turn on any one of the twisting side streets off Sadar Bazaar leads to the road that marks the northern boundary of the town, which contains **Marwar Bus Stand.**

Tourist Office: RTDC Tourist Information, near RTDC Hotel Sarovar. Friendly government tourist agents distribute maps (Rs2), brochures, and info on trains, buses, accommodations, and *mela*. Open daily 9am-5pm.

Currency Exchange: State Bank of Bikaner and Jaipur (☎2772006), Sadar Bazaar. Changes only traveler's checks. Open M-F 10am-2pm, Sa 10am-noon. Money-changers along Sadar Bazaar change cash at decent rates, but count your rupees carefully.

Police: Main Police Station (☎2772046), on the northern side of town. Tourist-friendly and English-speaking. Open 24hr.

Pharmacy: Pharmacies can be found in the northern part of town near the hospital and in Sadar Bazaar. Most open daily 8am-8pm.

Hospital/Medical Services: Dr. Sanjay Gupta (☎2772672), between Hotels Om and Sarovar, runs an excellent clinic that provides medical assistance to travelers. Open daily 10am-8pm; on call after-hours. **Government Community Hospital** (☎2772029), near Marwar Bus Stand. English-speaking staff. Open 24hr. for emergencies.

Internet: All over town. Most places charge Rs1 per min., Rs50 per hr. **Cyber Space,** Sadar Bazaar, blows away the competition with 20 computers.

Post Office: GPO (☎2720022), on the north side of town. There is a branch on the eastern side of Sadar Bazaar. Open M-Sa 9am-5pm. **Postal Code:** 305022.

ACCOMMODATIONS

Pushkar is a shoestring traveler's dream when it comes to accommodations. Competition is so intense that you shouldn't have to pay more than Rs100-150 for a double with attached bath and hot water. During the Pushkar Fair, reserve at least a month in advance and expect to pay 10 times as much. Alternative lodgings (temporary tents) are also available during the *mela*, but many are quite luxurious and expensive. The cheapest, the RTDC's **Tourist Village ❷**, has dorm tents. (☎2772074. US$5.) Book through the reservation office (☎0141 202586; fax 201045.)

RTDC Hotel Sarovar, Ajmer Rd. (☎2772040). The modern half of the hotel has nice, large, but overpriced (for Pushkar) rooms. The real gems are the six rooms overlooking the lake in the adjoining palace. Worth every rupee. Singles Rs150, with attached bath Rs350-800; doubles Rs250/Rs450-900. ❷

Hotel White House (☎2772147), near Marwar Bus Stand. Spotless, marble-floored rooms around an airy courtyard. The rooftop restaurant features fresh vegetables from the garden below. Free welcome mango tea. Internet. Doubles Rs150-450. ❷

Kanhaia Guest House (☎2772416), Choti Basti. Clean, spacious rooms. Most have attached hot-water bath. Yoga lessons. Singles Rs60-80; doubles 80-250. ❶

Hotel Om, Ajmer Rd. (☎2772672). Nicely appointed doubles open onto a courtyard. Garden restaurant and spartan rooftop terrace. Singles Rs50-150; doubles Rs150-250. ❶

Hotel Oasis (☎2772100), near Ajmer bus station. All rooms have hot water bath and balcony. Some with satellite TV and A/C. Swimming pool. Doubles Rs200-650. ❷

Hotel Pushkar Palace (☎2772001), southeast corner of Pushkar Lake. A Heritage Hotel with posh decor, minibar, satellite TV, and great views of the lake. The nicest hotel in Pushkar. Singles Rs1900-4000; doubles Rs2200-5000. Add 10% tax. ❺

FOOD

Pushkar is a holy town so you won't find meat, eggs, or alcohol on any menus. Also, imposters are everywhere—don't be fooled by restaurants bearing remarkably similar names to more popular places.

Rainbow Rooftop Restaurant, near Brahma Mandir. Well-prepared Indian and Western cuisine from a menu almost as stunning as the lakeside view. Falafel Rs30-100, homemade pasta Rs45-75, chocolate truffles Rs15. Open daily 8am-10:30pm. ❶

Venus Restaurant, Sadar Bazaar, Choti Basti. A popular multi-cuisine restaurant with particularly tasty Indian dishes (Rs15-40) and fresh juice (Rs12). A prime people-watching spot. Absurdly cheap prices. Open daily 7am-11pm. ❶

Moon Dance, across from Rangji Mandir. Appealing garden setting, some mats and low tables for lounging. Mexican (Rs40-60), Chinese (Rs30-60), Italian (Rs60-80), and Indian entrees (Rs20-65). Pool table Rs80 per hr. Open daily 8am-11:30pm. ❶

Sunset Cafe, near Hotel Pushkar Palace, on the lake. Major backpacker hangout. *The place to be at sunset*, though the view is superb at any time. Standard Indian dishes and an extensive Italian menu (Rs50-110). Open daily 8am-11:30pm. ❷

R.S. Restaurant, opposite Brahma Mandir. Quite possibly the only restaurant on tourist-dominated Sadar Bazaar where you will see Indians eating. All-you-can-eat *thali* Rs40, spaghetti Rs50, fresh juices Rs15-25. Open daily 7am-11:30pm. ❶

Raju Garden Restaurant, Sadar Bazaar, Badi Basti. International cuisine, "all cooked with love by Raju." Lakeside view. Indian dishes Rs25-60. Open daily 8am-11:30pm. ❶

👁 SIGHTS

PUSHKAR LAKE. Legend has it that at the beginning of time, Lord Brahma dropped a *pushkara*, or lotus flower, into the desert. A holy lake sprang up where the flower fell and became a place where pilgrims could be cleaned of all their sins. This lake is still the central attraction in Pushkar. Fifty-two broad *ghats* (one for each of Rajasthan's maharajas) line its shores. The most important are: **Gau Ghat,** where an assortment of politicians, ministers, and VIPs have paid their respects; **Brahma Ghat,** which Brahma himself is said to have used; and the central **Varah Ghat,** where Vishnu once appeared in the form of a boar. Signs in hotels instruct visitors to remove their shoes and to refrain from smoking and taking photographs. All around town local priests accost pilgrims and tourists, offering a small orange flower. This flower is an invitation to perform the Pushkar *puja*, a ceremony of scripture-reading and flower-scattering. Ask beforehand about the number of donations in the ceremony; some priests have been known to add donations (for the charities of Pushkar and now one for my family and let us not forget Shiva...) at the end. Do not feel pressured into donating the exorbitant amounts that the priests insist are "standard." An honest brahmin will be happy with any donation as long as it comes "from the heart." After the *puja*, your patronage is officially recognized with a red wristband—the "Pushkar Passport"—theoretically allowing you to visit *ghat*s and stroll around town without priestly harassment.

TEMPLES. Most of Pushkar's 540 temples were rebuilt after 17th-century pillaging raids by the Mughal emperor Aurangzeb. Several are open only to Hindus. The most popular is the **Brahma Mandir,** the only temple in India dedicated to Brahma, the Hindu creator-god. Note the status of the *hans* (goose; Brahma's vehicle of choice) over the entrance. Other temples of interest include the **Rangji Mandir,** with its white stone facade, the **Hanuman Mandir,** a colorful tower depicting Hanuman's exploits, the turquoise-green **Baba Ramdev Mandir,** and the 800-year-old **Rangnath Mandir.** Two major temples crown hills on the northern and southern sides of Pushkar, commanding superb views of the valley. Named for two of Brahma's wives, **Savithri Mandir,** to the south, and **Gayatri Mandir,** to the north, are both rewarding 1½hr. hikes from the town center.

CAMELS. Camel safaris into the desert are becoming increasingly popular in Pushkar, along with camel treks across the desert to Jaisalmer, Jodhpur, or Bikaner. Most hotels and travel agents can make arrangements; expect to pay around Rs350-450 per day for a good camel safari. If you don't have enough time for a safari, but want to get close to a dromedary, try a camel ride—a loop around the city costs Rs50 per hr.

📷 FESTIVALS

The annual Pushkar *mela* (Camel Fair; Nov. 18-26, 2004; Nov. 8-15, 2005) crowds 200,000 people from all over the world bathe in the lake's holy waters to seek redemption for their sins. Beyond the lake, the dry desert teems with more than 50,000 camels that race, parade, primp, participate in auctions, and carry tourists on desert safaris. Stalls selling handicrafts from all over India fill the streets, and street performers jump and juggle on every corner. Contributing to the mayhem of the festival are carnival rides set up next to the camel campgrounds. The first half of the *mela* sees the majority of camel trading, while the second half is more of a religious jamboree that attracts legions of devotees.

CHITTAURGARH चित्तौड़गढ़   ☎ 01472

Rajasthan boasts many impressive forts, but none can rival the rich history or air of tragic nostalgia surrounding Chittaurgarh. "Chittaur" epitomizes the community's concept of Rajput valor, particularly the traditional insistence upon death-before-dishonor. Three times the fort had fallen under siege, and all three times the residents of Chittaurgarh responded according to the legendary Rajput code of honor: the men slapped on their saffron robes of martyrdom and rode out of the fort, despite the overwhelming odds; and the women, unwilling to live with military defeat, immolated themselves in a huge funeral pyre. The stories have been told and retold with much gusto, and by now the estimates of total Rajput lives lost to *jauhar* has grown to 30,000 women and 40,000 warriors. The fort today, Asia's largest, is a 5km stretch of awe-inspiring views, the last vestiges of the city's past glory. The only invaders these days are tourists pursuing their photographic plunder. Chittaurgarh's fort is well worth the day-long detour to get here.

▐ TRANSPORTATION

As Chittaurgarh's rail lines are still undergoing conversion from meter- to broad-gauge, most destinations remain most easily reached by bus.

Trains: Railway Station, Station Rd. (inquiries ☎240131). Reservation office open daily 8am-8pm. To: **Ahmedabad** (15hr., 2pm, Rs157); **Jaipur** (8hr., 5:50am and 9:50pm, Rs133) via **Ajmer** (4½hr., Rs88); **Udaipur** (4hr., 6:40am and 2pm, Rs42).

Buses: Roadways Bus Stand (☎241177). To: **Abu Road** (8hr., 7am and midnight, Rs150); **Ahmedabad** (9hr., 8am, Rs153); **Bundi** (6hr.; 8:30, 10:30, 11:15am, 6pm; Rs60); **Jaipur** (8hr., every hr. 5am-10pm, Rs131-151) via **Ajmer** (5hr., Rs80-90); **Jodhpur** (8hr., 10:30am and 6pm, Rs133); **Kota** (7hr.; 7:30, 8:30, 10:30am, 1:30, 6pm; Rs89); **Udaipur** (2½hr., every hr. 6am-7:45pm, Rs47). **Private buses** on Station Rd. go to most places.

Local Transportation: Shared **auto-rickshaws** are the most common mode of transport (within town Rs3-5, to the fort Rs15-20). **Bicycles** can be rented (Rs2 per hr.) from shops near the railway station.

◄∗ ▐ ORIENTATION AND PRACTICAL INFORMATION

Chittaurgarh is too spread out to get around on foot. The **railway station** is on the southwest side of town. **Station Road** heads north through Pratap Circle. The next right leads across the tracks to **Ajmer Road** on its way to **Collectorate Circle.** From here, **City Road** heads east, passing the **Roadways Bus Stand** before crossing the **Gambheri River** and proceeding toward the Fort. To reach the Fort's entrance take a right off of City Rd. onto Fort Rd. just after Aspara Cinema. The main commercial area and the **new city** spreads between City Rd. and Fort Rd. Fort Rd. zigzags steeply up to the **Fort,** which sprawls 5km across the plateau. One main road loops inside the Fort and leads to Chittaurgarh's major sights.

Tourist Office: Tourist Reception Centre, Station Rd. (☎241089). Free maps. Open M-Sa 10am-1:30pm and 2-5pm. **Tours:** Of the nine licensed guides in Chittaurgarh, **Mr. Sudhir Sukhwal** (☎243245) stands out as one of the best—he speaks excellent English and makes the fort's history come alive (half-day Rs230). Find him, or one of his relatives, at the fort entrance.

Currency Exchange: Due to problems with phony traveler's checks, no banks in Chittaurgarh will exchange money. **Raj Tours** and **Travels** (☎245376), off Udaipur Rd., opposite Hotel Panna, offers private exchange services for a fee.

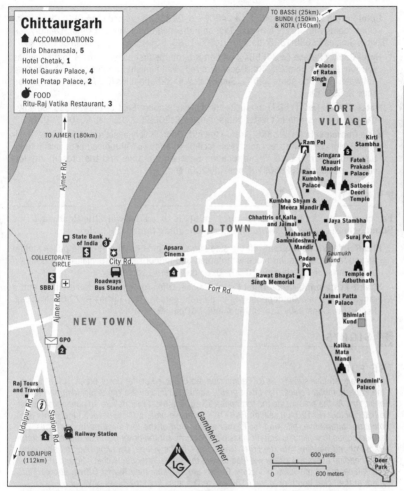

Chittaurgarh

🏠 ACCOMMODATIONS
Birla Dharamsala, **5**
Hotel Chetak, **1**
Hotel Gaurav Palace, **4**
Hotel Pratap Palace, **2**

🍎 FOOD
Ritu-Raj Vatika Restaurant, **3**

TO AJMER (180km)

TO BASSI (25km),
BUNDI (150km),
& KOTA (160km)

Palace
of Ratan
Singh

FORT
VILLAGE

Kirti
Stambha

Ram Pol

Sringara
Chauri
Mandir

Fateh
Prakash
Palace

Rana
Kumbha
Palace

Satbees
Deori
Temple

Kumbha Shyam &
Meera Mandir

Chhattris of Kalla
and Jaimal

Jaya Stambha

Mahasati &
Sammideshwar
Mandir

Suraj Pol

OLD TOWN

State Bank
of India

Apsara
Cinema

Gaumukh
Kund

Padan
Pol

Temple of
Adbuthnath

COLLECTORATE
CIRCLE

City Rd.

SBBJ

Roadways
Bus Stand

Fort Rd.

Rawat Bhagat
Singh Memorial

Jaimal Patta
Palace

Bhimlat
Kund

NEW TOWN

GPO

Kalika
Mata
Mandi

Raj Tours
and Travels

Padmini's
Palace

Railway Station

TO UDAIPUR
(112km)

Gambheri River

0   600 yards
0   600 meters

Deer
Park

RAJASTHAN

Police: Main Police Station (☎241060), opposite the bus stand. Open 24hr.

Hospital: General Hospital, Ajmer Rd. (☎241102). English-speaking consultations daily
in winter 9am-1pm; in summer 8am-noon. **Pharmacy** and emergency open 24hr.

Post Office: GPO, Station Rd. (☎241159), near the railroad crossing. Open M-Sa
7:30am-6:30pm. **Postal Code:** 312001.

🏠 ACCOMMODATIONS

Budget hotels in Chittaurgarh tend to be basic and not very well maintained, and
the acceptable ones are overpriced. However, huge discounts (30-60%) are often
negotiable at Chittaurgarh's nicer hotels, so try your hand at bargaining before
resigning yourself to one of its more unsavory options (which, if you're desperate,
are clustered around the train and bus stations).

RAJASTHAN

Hotel Pratap Palace, Ajmer Rd. (☎240099 or 243563), opposite the GPO. Clean, spacious rooms with wicker furniture, TVs, and attached baths with hot water. Laundry service. Singles Rs630-1325; doubles Rs660-1380. 50% discounts even in season. ❹

Hotel Gaurav Palace (☎246904), off Fort Rd., on the first big side street to the right as you move away from City Rd. Decently sized, well-furnished rooms, all with attached hot-water bath and some with TV. Singles Rs200-325; doubles Rs270-425; honeymoon suite Rs550. ❷

Hotel Chetak (☎241589), opposite the railway station. Best of the railroad lodgings, has clean rooms with hot water baths. Singles Rs200-600; doubles Rs300-700. ❷

Birla Dharamsala (☎245386), inside the fort. Offers 8 very basic rooms (catering to pilgrims) with common toilet (no shower facilities), and two VIP rooms upstairs with furniture and attached bath. Prime location between the ruins and the present-day fort village. Basic rooms Rs50; VIP rooms Rs200. ❶

FOOD

For cheap eats in Chittaurgarh, your best bet is to head toward the Roadways Bus Stand, where roadside *bhojnalyas* serve steaming *thalis* (Rs25-30).

Ritu-Raj Vatika Restaurant, off the side street that runs to the left of the police station as you face it. A popular place with garden and indoor seating specializing in *tandoori* and South Indian dishes (Rs20-50). Open daily 8am-11pm. ❶

Shakti Restaurant, inside Hotel Pratap Palace. Offers quiet, comfortable dining and a range of cuisines. Outdoor seating in the rear garden. Veg. dishes Rs20-65. Non-veg. Rs40-100. Open daily 7am-3:30pm and 7-10pm. ❶

SIGHTS

THE FORT

*Open daily sunrise-sunset. Rs100 admission fee collected at the ticket booth 100m before the Rana Kumbha Palace. The ticket grants admission into all the sights including the Tower of Victory. As the area inside the fort spans 13 sq. km, most visitors hire an auto-rickshaw for a half-day tour (Rs120, off-season Rs100). If you have time, walking between the sights is a pleasant alternative, allowing for further exploration of the fort's ramparts and walls. An added bonus to walking is that it's possible to circumvent the ticket booth by turning left from Ram Pol and heading into the Fort Village. Once in the village, doubling back on any other road heading out of the village will lead toward the sights. Attendants check tickets at Padminis Palace and at the Tower of Victory. Guides are available (see **Tourist Office**, above). Find them at the ticket booth or at the RTDC cafeteria across from the Tower of Victory.*

Jutting out abruptly from the plateau below, the Chittaurgarh Fort is one of the most historically significant in all of Rajasthan. Believed to have been constructed by the Pandava brother Bhima, of *Mahabharata* fame, the fort contains 113 temples, in various stages of decay, as well as 84 tanks, 20 of which still contain water.

ASCENT AND ENTRANCE. Padan Pol is the first gate *(pol)* in a series of seven that punctuate the steep, 1km climb to the top. Near the second *pol* are the chhattris (cenotaphs) of the heroic martyrs Kalla and Jaimal, who died in the third sacking of Chittaurgarh in 1568. The seventh and final gate, Ram Pol, was originally the back entrance to the fort but is now the main one.

SRINGARA CHAURI MANDIR. Often the first stop on a counterclockwise tour of the fort's sights, this 15th-century Jain temple shows Hindu influences in its elaborate decoration. It also shows Muslim influence at its top—after the Mughals conquered Chittaurgarh, they knocked off the Hindu *shikhara* (spire) and replaced it with a dome to make the temple look more like a mosque. The thick stone wall that now stops just short of the temple is also of interest, for it was part of a conspiratorial plot against Prince Udai Singh. Banvir Singh, the royal cousin, tried to seize power and have the prince killed. The prince's nurse, Pannadhai, discovered Banvir's dastardly scheme and sacrificed her own son, switching him with the prince, whom she whisked away to safety. When he learned that the prince was still alive, Banvir partitioned the fort, hoping that this would allow him to share power with the young prince. He conveniently constructed the wall so that his section of the fort included the treasury and the tax-paying residential area.

RANA KUMBHA PALACE. The impressive remains of the 8th-century Rana Kumbha Palace are believed to be where Chittaurgarh's first *jauhar* (self-immolation) took place in 1303, in an underground tunnel leading to Gaumukh Kund. All that remained after the siege of the city were stables (including a stable said to house Genda Hathi, a sword-wielding military elephant) and a Shiva temple. In the back on the right is the nurse's palace, where Pannadhai's son was slain in the place of the young prince. Also nearby are the elegant **Meera Mandir,** which honors the Jodhpuri mystic poet Mirabai, the towering **Kumbha Shyam Mandir,** built in 1448, and the notable **Jatashankar Mahadev.**

FATEH PRAKASH PALACE AND SATBEES DEORI TEMPLE. The incongruous **Fateh Prakash Palace** (built within the last century) today houses an unexciting **museum** of archaeological finds from Chittaurgarh and surrounding areas. *(Rs3. Open M-Th, Sa-Su 10am-4:30pm.)* Just south lies the elaborate 11th-century Jain **Satbees Deori Temple,** consisting of three main shrines and 24 subsidiary ones (one for each *tirthankara*).

JAYA STAMBHA. The subject of every Chittaurgarh brochure and postcard, the Jaya Stambha (Tower of Victory) is an imposing gray limestone tower whose 37m high exterior walls tell the story of the city's gory past. The tower's construction began in 1458 to commemorate a victory over the Muslim rulers of Malwa and Gujarat and took 10 years to complete. The view from the top is breathtaking. *(Open daily 7:30am-7pm. Climbing free with ticket.)* The 11th-century **Sammidheshwar Mandir** is down the hill from the Jaya Stambha. Nearby is **Mahasti,** a series of cenotaphs (memorials) marking the supposed spot of the second *jauhar* in 1537, committed by Queen Karnawati and 16,000 Rajput women. The **Gaumukh Kund** (Cow's Mouth Tank), farther south, features a carved cow who fills the tank with water.

PADMINI'S PALACE. According to legend, it was here that Ala-Ud-Din Khilji caught a glimpse of the beautiful Padmini (seated on the pavilion steps below) in a palace mirror, prompting him to set his sights on her (and his army on Chittaurgarh). After the siege proved successful, Padmini and 13,000 Rajput women committed *jauhar* rather than face the humiliation of capture. Visitors can simulate Khilji's gaze in the rear domed compartment facing the smaller water palace. The mirror on the opposite wall reflects the same steps where Padmini once primped. The palace also houses a lush garden. The **Kalika Mata Mandir,** directly opposite, was dedicated during the 8th century to the sun god Surya but now pays tribute to Kali. Still the most active temple in the Mewar region, it comes alive on Sundays when devotees from all over the countryside flock to pay their respects.

BHIMLAT KUND. The road loops south past the often-empty **Deer Park** to the quiet Bhimlat Kund. This legendary tank was created by the Pandava brother Bhima to satiate his mother's thirst. The giant Bhima, who was said to have the strength of 1000 elephants, stomped his foot down in this spot, and the lake was formed by the imprint it left. Much later, this was also the supposed site of the third *jauhar* in 1567, in which 'only' a few hundred Rajput women threw themselves upon that well-used Chittaurgarh pyre. The road then turns north again past **Suraj Pol,** the eastern gate of the fort, originally the main entrance.

KIRTI STAMBHA (TOWER OF FAME). Built by the *Digamber* (nudist) Jain sect, the 12th-century, 23m Tower of Fame is covered with images of the Jain pantheon, particularly that of Adinath, the first *tirthankara*, to whom the tower is dedicated. Like the Tower of Victory, it's also scalable (provided you can locate the attendant to unlock the door and negotiate the narrow entrance and staircase).

UDAIPUR उदयपुर ☎0294

Udaipur, City of Sunrise, is one of Rajasthan's biggest tourist draws. Its cobblestoned old city hugs the shore of green Lake Pichhola, whose serene waters harbor two exotic island palaces. On shore, its whitewashed *havelis*, lush gardens, and massive City Palace complex inspire hours of awe and contemplation. Although this longtime capital of the Mewar kingdom hasn't altogether managed to fend off the chaos and pollution of industry, the old city has nevertheless somehow managed to retain its romantic flavor. A city of monumental architectural and aesthetic importance, Udaipur should certainly take up several days in tourists' itineraries.

Maharaja Udai Singh II moved the Mewari capital to Udaipur after the final siege of Chittaurgarh in 1568. Upon his death four years later, he was succeeded by his son, Pratap, who remains the most revered of the Mewari Rulers for his legendary heroism during the repeated Mughal attacks that followed. As the city thrived, the Udaipuri school of miniature painting developed and many of the city's majestic palaces were built. In 1736, the city was crippled by the mighty Marathas, but it bounced back again with British aid, somehow managing to remain firmly independent. Since then, the city's arts have continued to flourish, James Bond films notwithstanding (yes, Roger Moore's *Octopussy* was filmed here).

▐▀ TRANSPORTATION

Flights: Dabok Airport (☎2655453), 25km east of Udaipur (taxi Rs150-200). **Indian Airlines,** Delhi Pol (☎410999). Open daily 10am-1:15pm and 2-5pm. To: **Delhi** (3hr., 6:10pm, US$115); **Jaipur** (2hr., US$95); and **Jodhpur** (40min., US$75); **Mumbai** (1hr., 9:30am, US$135). **Jet Airways,** Blue Circle Business Centre (☎2561105), near the GPO. To: **Delhi** (2½hr., 8:10am, US$115) via **Jaipur** (1hr., US$95); **Mumbai** (1½hr., 8:50am and 7:25pm, US$135). **Gangaur Tour 'n' Travels,** 28 Gangaur Ghat (☎2411476), is the only authorized IA and Jet agent in the Jagdish Temple Area. Open daily 8am-9:30pm.

Trains: Udaipur City Station (inquiries ☎131, reservations 2483979). Several km southeast of the old city; **don't get off at Udaipur Station,** which is much farther north. Advanced computerized reservation open daily 8am-8pm. To: **Ahmedabad** (9hr., 7:45pm, Rs124); **Delhi** (19-23hr., 8:20am and 6:15pm, Rs241) via **Chittaurgarh** (4hr., Rs38) and **Ajmer** (8-12hr., Rs124); **Jaipur** (11hr., 6:15pm, Rs164).

Buses: Main Bus Stand (☎2484191). To: **Ahmedabad** (6hr., every 30min. 5am-10pm, Rs108; deluxe 5½hr., 10am and 10pm, Rs120); **Bikaner** (15hr., 4:30pm, Rs225); **Chittaurgarh** (3hr., every 30min. 6am-10pm, Rs47; deluxe 2½hr.; 8:15, 10:15am, 12:30, 3:45pm; Rs55); **Delhi** (15hr.; 1:30, 4, 6:15pm; Rs275; deluxe 3:45pm, Rs410); **Jaipur** (9hr., every hr. 5am-11:30pm, Rs175; deluxe 9hr., 9 per day 8:15am-11pm, Rs200) via **Ajmer** (7hr., Rs115-145); **Jodhpur** (7hr.; 7, 9am, 3, 6, 8pm; Rs111; deluxe 7hr.; 5am, 3, 10, 10:30pm; Rs128) via **Ranakpur** (3hr., Rs37); **Mt. Abu** (5hr., 10 per day 5am-8pm, Rs68; deluxe 8:15am and 2:30pm, Rs75). Many companies offer **private buses** to major cities (see **Budget Travel,** below).

Local Transportation: The old city is navigable on foot, but to get anywhere else you'll need wheels. **Vijay Cycles,** BC, next to Raj Palace Hotel, rents bikes for Rs20 per day. Scooters Rs200-300 per day. Open daily 9:30am-8pm. **Heera Cycle Store,** Gangaur

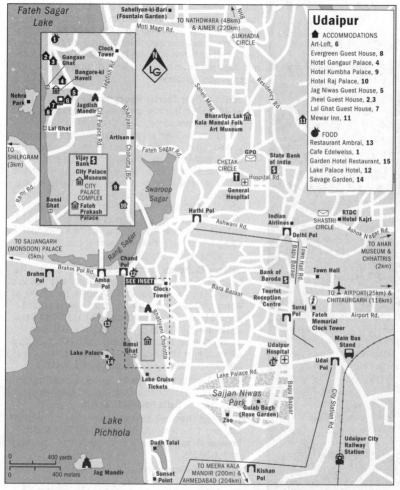

Udaipur

🏠 ACCOMMODATIONS
Art-Loft, 6
Evergreen Guest House, 8
Hotel Gangaur Palace, 4
Hotel Kumbha Palace, 9
Hotel Raj Palace, 10
Jag Niwas Guest House, 5
Jheel Guest House, 2,3
Lal Ghat Guest House, 7
Mewar Inn, 11

🍴 FOOD
Restaurant Ambrai, 13
Cafe Edelweiss, 1
Garden Hotel Restaurant, 15
Lake Palace Hotel, 12
Savage Garden, 14

Marg, inside Badi Haveli. Bikes Rs25 per day; scooters Rs150-200 per day; motorcycles Rs300 per day. Open daily 7:30am-9pm. **Auto-rickshaw** fares from Jagdish Mandir to the bus station Rs15; to Bansi Ghat or Chetak Circle Rs20. Full-day sightseeing Rs150-200. **Taxis** can be hired through travel agents for daytrips around Udaipur.

■ ORIENTATION AND PRACTICAL INFORMATION

Udaipur rests in the shadows of the Aravalli mountains, 113km southwest of Chittaurgarh. The **Old City** curves along the northeastern bank of **Lake Pichhola**; the **New City** expands to the north, east, and south. Most budget travelers base themselves in the area of the Old City around **Jagdish Mandir** and **Bhatiyani Chohotta (BC)**, a stone's throw from Udaipur's two most famous monuments, the **City Palace** and

THE LOCAL LEGEND

ONE HELLUVA HORSE

The cow might be a more common object of worship for Hindus, but the Rajputs of Rajasthan have a special place in their hearts for a certain white stallion named Chetak. Indeed, his name lives on in Udaipur's main circle and is emblazoned across the carriages of Rajasthan's main express trains.

Chetak, whose statues are a common sight in Udaipur, was the loyal battle companion of Rana Pratap. At the famous bloodbath of Haldighati in 1532, Chetak's leg was cut by an enemy elephant wielding a broadsword in its trunk; Pratap was also wounded. Though hobbled, Chetak carried his master from the battlefield through a narrow passage, leaping a 3m crevice before coming to rest under a tree 6km away. Having saved his master's life, poor Chetak breathed his last. Many tours of the Udaipur area stop at Haldighati to pay respects at Chetak's tomb and hear the tale of the horse's valiant death.

Lake Palace. The **train** and **bus stations** are on the east side of town, far beyond walking distance from the main accommodations area. The four main entrances to the old city—**Udai Pol, Suraj Pol, Delhi Pol,** and the **Hathi Pol**—serve as major landmarks. **Chetak Circle,** beyond Hathi Pol, is home to the **GPO. Bapu Bazaar** and **Bara Bazaar,** which intersect at Suraj Pol, are two major shopping streets.

Tourist Office: Tourist Reception Centre, Suraj Pol (☎2411535). Has free maps and arranges home stays (see **Accommodations,** below). Open M-Sa 10am-5pm, closed 2nd Sa. There are also small branches at the **train station** (open M-Sa 8-11am and 4-7pm, closed 2nd Sa) and **airport** (open when flights arrive and depart). More convenient and more helpful is the bi-monthly *Out and About,* available at the West Zone Cultural Center in Bangore-ki-Haveli and throughout the Jagdish Mandir area (Rs10). **RTDC Hotel Kajri,** Shastri Circle (☎2410501) offers half-day sightseeing tours of the city for Rs74, excluding admission fees. City tours run from 8am-1pm. A do-it-yourself, all day **rickshaw tour** will cost about Rs200 (excluding the Monsoon Palace).

Currency Exchange: State Bank of India, Hospital Rd. (☎2528857). Exchanges foreign currency and traveler's checks. Open M-F 10am-4pm, Sa 10am-1pm. **Bank of Baroda,** Bapu Bazaar, north of Suraj Pol (☎2420671; open M-F 10am-3pm, Sa 10am-noon) and **Vijaya Bank,** inside the City Palace complex (☎2411381; open M-F 10am-3pm, Sa 10am-12:30pm). Both offer credit card advances for a 1% commission. Numerous licensed money changers populate the area around Jagdish Mandir.

Police: Tourist police (☎2412693, superintendent 2413949). A major police station is at every gate. The biggest are at **Delhi Pol** and **Udai Pol.**

Pharmacy: There are several pharmacies on Hospital Rd. and Udai Pol. Most open daily 7am-9:30pm. **Udaipur Hospital** has a well-stocked 24hr. pharmacy (☎5101011).

Hospital: Maharana Bhopal General Hospital, Hospital Rd. (☎528811 to 528817). Government-run. **Udaipur Hospital** Gulab Bagh Rd. (☎5101011), near Udai Pol. Has excellent facilities. Both hospitals are English-speaking and open 24hr.

Internet: The usual rate in the Jagdish Mandir area is Rs40 per hr. The biggest bank of computers is at **One Stop Shop,** 35 Lal Ghat (☎2419810). Open daily 8am-11:30pm.

Post Office: GPO (☎2528622), off Chetak Circle. Parcels sent M-F 10am-4pm, Sa 10am-1pm. Open M-Sa 10am-6pm, Su 10am-3pm. *Poste Restante* mail is held at the **City Post Office,** Shastri Circle (☎2413905). Open M-Sa 10am-7pm. **Postal Code** (both offices): 313001.

ACCOMMODATIONS

The hotels in the Jagdish Mandir area on the beautiful east bank of Lake Pichola offer some of the best valued rooms in the city. To avoid touts, it's easiest to ask your rickshaw driver to drop you off at Jagdish Mandir and then walk to your hotel of choice. On the other side of Chandpol a cluster of mid-range and luxury hotels features rooms with clearer views of the City Palace in addition to the Lake Palace. The next best collection of budget hotels is along **Lake Palace Road** and **BC**. Hotels in the **new city** are cheap and noisy. There are over 70 **guest houses** in Udaipur, but only 10 to 20 offer genuine homestay experiences (Rs100-500 per night, depending on amenities and location); contact the tourist office for more information. Bargain hard in the off-season (Mar.-Sept.), especially for mid-range rooms. Most hotels listed below have laundry, travel agencies, attached restaurants, and hot water.

Hotel Gangaur Palace, Gangaur Ghat (☎2422303 or 2523427). In the 250-year-old Ashoka *haveli*. Soft mattresses and spotless bathrooms in spacious rooms around a central courtyard. Helpful staff, excellent attached restaurant (see **Food**). Rooms with common bath Rs80, with attached bath Rs150-250, with lake view Rs350. ❶

Art-Loft, Lal Ghat. (☎2420304 or 2420163). Breezy rooms with marble floors and attached baths, most with lake views. Run by a chef and artist family, this intimate six-room guest house offers art and cooking lessons (2hr. lessons Rs250-350) and serves excellent food. Room prices nearly halved in off-season. Doubles Rs450-600. ❸

Pushkar Palace, 93 BC (☎2417685). Five huge, well-kept rooms above courtyards and a family home in this intimate converted *haveli*. The most expensive rooms are a fantastic value. Breakfast only. Rooms Rs80; with attached bath Rs100-150. ❶

Hotel Raj Palace, 103 BC (☎2410364 or 2527092; fax 2410395). Beautiful rooms all have stained-glass windows, marble floors, and cushioned window seats. The deluxe rooms have bathtubs and A/C. Good service. It's a little pricey, but a better value than others in this price range. Singles Rs250-1000; doubles Rs300-1250. ❷

Hotel Kumbha Palace, 104 BC (☎2422702). Distinctive rooms have colorful stained-glass windows, Jaisalmeri desert decorations, as well as attached baths and air coolers. Lovely garden area borders the walls of the City Palace. Run by an Indian-Dutch couple. Singles Rs80, with attached bath Rs150-250; doubles with bath Rs150-200. ❶

Jag Niwas Guest House, 21 Gangaur Ghat Marg (☎2416022). No longer owned by the Maharaja, but still has style. Spacious rooms with attached baths and air-cooling. Good restaurant upstairs; chef lets guests watch him prepare the meals. Singles Rs100-350; doubles Rs150-400. ❶

Lal Ghat Guest House, 22 Lal Ghat. Popular with budget travelers. Dorms Rs50; rooms Rs75-150, with attached bath Rs200-350. If the self-serve kitchen doesn't suit you, head next door to the lake-view restaurant at **Evergreen Guest House,** which also has simple rooms. Singles Rs100, with attached bath Rs150; doubles Rs150-250. ❶

Jheel Guest House, 56/52 Gangaur Ghat (☎2421352). Rooms spread across two buildings across the street from each other. The newer bldg. on the lake has rooms with marble floors and attached baths (Rs200-500; deluxe with balcony Rs600); those across the street are more basic (Rs150, with attached bath Rs200-250). ❷

Mewar Inn, 42 Residency Rd. (☎2522090; fax 2525002), a 15min. walk north of Delhi Gate. If the Jagdish Mandir area proves too much of a hassle, seek out this quiet, laid-back hotel well north of the Old City. The gigantic diamond deluxe room is an outstanding value. Some english spoken. Discounts for youth hostel card holders. Singles Rs39; doubles Rs52-112. ❶

FOOD

Udaipur has a good range of restaurants to choose from, many of which are graced with nightly screenings of *Octopussy*.

■ **Lake Palace Hotel** (☎2528800), floating in the middle of Lake Pichhola. The ultimate Udaipur dining experience: unbelievably delectable food, amazing views, and unparalleled ambiance. It's the ultimate splurge. Reserve ahead, wear your least-grubby outfit, and bring your own water—the food's worth paying for, but the water (Rs50) is not. Buffet Rs625 for lunch, Rs750 for dinner; includes boat transport from Bansi Ghat. Lunch 12:30-2:30pm. Dinner 7:30-10:30pm. Folk dance performance nightly 7pm (free). ❺

■ **Restaurant Ambrai,** Panch Devri Marg, in Amet Haveli, beyond Chand Pol. Clinches the romantic dining cliche. Recommended for dinner, when palaces are lit and music is played. Veg. dishes Rs45-65, non-veg. Rs75-110. Open daily 7am-11pm. ❸

Savage Garden, near Chand Pol. Breaks the mold with its indigo walls, small but thoughtful menu (meals Rs75-135), and tasty food. All vegetables washed with purified water. All open daily 9am-10pm. The kitchen also bakes the tasty pastries served at **Cafe Edelweiss,** 36 Gadiya Devra, Chandpol Rd., and **Coffee.com,** Lal Ghat. Open daily 8am-8pm. ❸

Garden Hotel Restaurant, opposite main gate to Sajjan Niwas Park. This circular restaurant next to a vintage car museum serves Gujarati *thalis* (Rs50 includes sweets). Here you can literally eat like a maharaja since the chef's first *thali* is sent to the City Palace for the big man himself. Open daily lunch 11am-3pm, dinner 7-10pm. ❷

Natural City View Restaurant, inside Hotel Gangaur Palace. When you've had your fill of Udaipuri romance and are ready to re-embrace banana pancakes and free movies, head to this 3-tier rooftop restaurant. Most popular at dinner time, when unobstructed views of the sunset are followed by two movies (both 7pm), one of which is *Octopussy*. Veg. dishes Rs30-50, tasty baked goods Rs20-55. Open daily 7:30am-11pm. ❷

SIGHTS

LAKE PICHHOLA

Lake Pichhola is not as stunning nowadays as it usually is; a string of weak monsoons over the last few years has left it pretty dry. However, the lake seems remarkably full when compared to the mud flats that once were Fatah Sagar Lake. Rumor has it that Mother Nature has received a helping hand from the government in keeping Udaipur's centerpiece adequately watered.

JAG NIWAS (LAKE PALACE). The Lake Palace occupies the entirety of Jag Niwas island, giving the impression that the former summer residence of the royal family is floating in the middle of the lake. Converted into a luxury hotel in the 1960s, the palace still houses stunning garden courtyards and an exquisite interior, but it's hard to get a look at them if you're not a guest. The best way to get onto the palace grounds is to treat yourself to a meal at the hotel's restaurant (see **Food,** p. 522). It's worth every penny.

JAG MANDIR ISLAND AND LAKE CRUISES. The slightly smaller Jag Mandir island, just south of the Lake Palace, is home to **Jag Mandir,** the palace that sheltered the Mughal Emperor-to-be Shah Jahan in 1623-24 as he led a revolt against his father, Jehangir. Several centuries later, Jag Mandir also served as a refuge for British women and children during the Mutiny of 1857. The palace today isn't in as good condition as some of its counterparts in Udaipur, but a few rooms are open for exploration, and there's a very nice garden in back. Some beautiful stone carvings, including a mighty row of huge elephants encircling the island, also make the trip worthwhile. The only way to see Jag Mandir up close is to take a boat cruise from Bansi Ghat (the City Palace jetty); the ½hr. cruise gets you only a glimpse of the elephants, while the hour long cruise earns you a 25min. stopover. *(Boats depart every hr. 10am-5pm. ½hr. cruise Rs100, 1hr. cruise Rs175.)*

CITY PALACE COMPLEX

The jewel of Udaipur is its grand palace complex, the largest in Rajasthan, begun in 1559 by Udai Singh, the proud Mewar migrant who founded the city. An architectural amalgam reflecting the efforts of more than 20 kings, today the City Palace is part museum, part luxury hotel, and part royal residence (the 76th Maharaja of Mewar, who lacks political power but still plays a role in civil life, lives here).

CITY PALACE MUSEUM. The two sections of the City Palace of interest to visitors are the **Mardana Mahal** (men's quarters) and **Zenana Mahal** (women's quarters), which have been reincarnated as the City Museum. Before entering the palace, note the two large stone indentations—they were once elephant beds. Inside, **Ganesh Deoti Gate** marks the point past which commoners were not allowed and at which the museum begins. The museum is a maze of rooms and courtyards interconnected by narrow passages. Colored glass mosaics, detailed miniature paintings, and beautiful mirror-work can be seen throughout. The most notable areas of the palace include: **Mor Chowk,** home of the famous inlaid glass peacocks whose visage stares out from many a Rajasthan tourist poster. **Chitram Ki Bung,** a small room bathed in miniature paintings (dedicated to Krishna Kumari, a 16-year-old princess who committed suicide to prevent a war between vying suitors from Jaipur and Jodhpur); and the **Bari Mahal,** which encloses a beautiful garden courtyard. The Zenana Mahal (women's quarters) next door, is now a gallery of Mewar School miniature paintings surrounding a courtyard (today used for social functions). *(The museum is accessible via the main entrance to the City Palace, just down City Palace Rd. from Jagdish Mandir. Open daily 9:30am-4:30pm. Entrance fee Rs50; camera fee Rs100; video fee Rs300. Tours for up to 5 people Rs70 per hr.)*

ELSEWHERE IN UDAIPUR

JAGDISH MANDIR. Built by Maharaja Jagat Singh, this 17th-century temple in the center of the old city is dedicated to Vishnu's avatar Jagannath, whose black marble image resides in the sanctum. The outer structure is a pyramid-like *shikhara* decorated with elephants, *apsaras,* and figures from Mewari mythology. A bronze Garuda, Vishnu's mount, guards the entrance. The cornerstone at the left base of the stairs supposedly brings good luck to those who rub it seven times. The central dome teems with mythological figures and houses a huge silver bed meant for the gods. *(Open daily 5am-2pm and 4-10:30pm; Oct.-Feb. 5:30am-2pm and 4-10pm. Free.)*

SHILPIGRAM. Another link in the government-sponsored chain of "rural arts and crafts complexes," Shilpigram seeks to educate foreign and Indian tourists about the rural and indigenous communities of Rajasthan, Gujarat, Maharashtra, and Goa with life-size models of their traditional homes, complete with imported traditional families. At any given time, four or five "habitats" feature cultural performances (puppetry, singing, dancing, etc.) and offer live demonstrations of their crafts (e.g. pottery). Tips and purchases help to sustain the "village." The complex has an undeniably artificial feel—it strikes some as little more than a human zoo—but even those who feel uncomfortable patronizing the village should find the uninhabited model homes interesting. The complex is at its liveliest during the annual **Shilpigram Festival** (Dec. 22-31). *(Off Rani Rd., west of Fateh Sagar Lake 5km from the Jaddish area. Open daily 11am-7pm. Entrance fee Rs10; camera fee Rs10.)*

BHARATIYA LOK KALA MANDAL FOLK ART MUSEUM. This museum exhibits a variety of items ranging from colorfully painted masks to clay figure dioramas of local festivals. The museum's highlight is its collection of traditional Rajasthani **puppets** called *kathpurli*. Don't miss the free and excellent 10min. **puppet show,** repeated every 20min. *(Saheli Marg, just past Chetak Circle. Museum open daily 9am-6pm. Entrance fee Rs25; camera fee Rs10. Longer puppet-and-traditional-dance shows performed nightly; see* **Entertainment,** *below.)*

CHHATTRIS AND AHAR MUSEUM. More than 200 *chhattris* (cenotaphs) of Mewari maharajas and their families are in a plot northeast of the city. These were overgrown and inaccessible to the public until a recent project unearthed them. Most are simple in design and haphazardly arranged (that of Sangram Singh is a notable exception), but their isolation from the city makes them a great addition to Udaipur's sights. *(Open 24hr. Free.)* The nearby **Ahar Museum** exhibits 4000-year-old relics from the civilization of the same name, unearthed from an excavation behind the museum. *(Shared rickshaws departing from Shastri Circle pass both sights Rs3. Open M-Th and Sa-Su 10am-4:30pm. Rs3.)*

SAHELIYON-KI-BARI. The 18th-century Saheliyon-ki-Bari (Garden of the Maids of Honor), built by Maharaja Sangram Singh for his wife and her friends and servants, lies 2km to the north of town. These days the garden, with its palm trees and lotus pool, is more of a tourist site than a refuge. Note that the fountains and irrigation system are both powered by water pressure from the lake, so the garden is most spectacular during and after the monsoon. *(Open daily 8am-8pm. Rs5.)*

FATEH SAGAR LAKE. Lake Pichhola's less celebrated sister lies not too far west of Saheliyon-ki-Bari. As of spring 2003, the lake was nearly completely dried up; a good monsoon should revitalize it. On an "island" in the middle of the lake, **Nehru Park** is spread over fountain-sprinkled grounds, with domed cupolas and swaying palm trees. When there's water, small boats leave from the east side of the lake every 20min. in season but you can walk out to the park when the lake is dry. *(Open daily in winter 8am-6pm; in summer 8am-7pm. Rs10 includes admission and shuttle boat.)* The once-booming Fateh Sagar paddleboat industry is another victim of Mother Nature's capricious cycles. Should the rains return, so too will the watercraft (Rs100 per hr.) A few minutes from the jetty is **Moti Magri** (Pearl Hill), whose gardens and statue memorialize the legendary Mewar hero Maharaja Pratap Singh.

🎵 📷 ENTERTAINMENT AND FESTIVALS

Traditional **Rajasthani folk dances** and music performances, involving a blend of local trance dances and circus-like balancing stunts, take place at **Meera Kala Mandir,** near the Pars Theater in Sector 11, a Rs25-30 rickshaw ride from the old city. (☎583176. Shows held M-Sa 7-8pm. Tickets Rs60.) Book right in the heart of the tourist ghetto. The government-run **West Zone Cultural Center** hosts cultural performances; these aren't as professional, but feel perhaps more authentic. (In Bangore-ki Haveli, Gangaur Ghat. Daily 7pm. Rs60.) **Bharatiya Lok Kala Folk Art Museum** offers a nightly show that consists of half-folk-dancing, half-puppetry. See **Elsewhere in Udaipur,** above. Shows daily noon and 6pm, Rs50). The **Mewar Festival** (Mar. 23-24 2004; Apr. 11-12, 2005), dedicated to Parvati, celebrates the arrival of spring with music, fireworks, and a colorful procession down to the lake.

🛍 SHOPPING

Clothing, jewelry, textile, and handicraft shops are crowded into the areas around Jagdish Mandir, Lake Palace Rd., and Bara and Bapu Bazaars. They sell wares from all over Rajasthan at inflated but negotiable prices. *Never* accept an invitation into a shop by a rickshaw-*wallah* or tout. That is, unless you're feeling generous enough to pay their 30% commission. The shopping areas are easily navigable on foot, so you should have no problem on your own. **Miniature painting** is an Udaipuri specialty, and in many shops you can watch skilled artists work without any obligation to buy. It's best to shop in stores that are run by the artist himself. Prices depend on the intricacy and level of detail rather than the size of the painting. Beware of artists approaching you on the street claiming to have shown their work in the most famous galleries in (insert your country here). Pretending that they need to practice their English for an upcoming exhibition is another ruse used by the artists to get you in their shops. Also note that miniatures done on "camel bone" and "coconut wood" are most likely done on ivory and formica respectively. Honest dealers don't employ these tactics or make such claims. Two dealers who sell high-quality paintings at reasonable prices are: **Artisan,** 40 BC; and **Ashok Art,** inside Hotel Gangaur Palace. Artists at Ashoka give miniature painting lessons and will even touch up first attempts gone slightly awry (2hr. lesson Rs150). Tailors are also particularly abundant and cheap in Udaipur.

🗝 DAYTRIPS FROM UDAIPUR

Nagda, Eklingji, and Nathdwara are easily visited together in a half-day excursion from Udaipur. Most convenient is to rent a **motorbike** or hire a **car** and driver through a travel agency (about Rs500). **Rickshaws** can take you to Nagda and Eklingji (Rs250 round-trip) but are not permitted as far as Nathdwara. Frequent **local buses** go between Udaipur and Nathdwara via Eklingji (2.5km from Nagda). **RTDC Hotel Kajri,** Shastri Circle, offers a rushed tour to Eklingji and Nathdwara (☎ 2410501; daily 2-7pm depending on demand; Rs105). You can visit the Jain temple at **Ranakpur** as a (long) daytrip from Udaipur.

EKLINGJI AND NAGDA

> *Buses* run to Eklingji from Udaipur (45min., frequent 4am-9:30pm, Rs13). Eklingi temple open daily 4:15-6:15am, 10:30am-1:30pm. Nagda temples open daily 5am-6pm.

The village of **Eklingji,** 22km north of Udaipur, is home to a magnificent Shiva temple. The marble temple encloses a four-faced, solid, black image of Shiva and is adorned with silver doors, lamps, parcels, and a solid silver bull. According to legend, this marks the spot where a hermit (depicted above the entrance) bestowed a blessing upon the feudal lord Bappa Rawal (the first Mewar suzerain, rendered in statue form opposite the entrance) to found a great dynasty. The original temple was erected in AD 734, but the 107 other temples in the complex, added over the next 750 years by Bappa Rawal's royal descendants, proves the hermit's prophecy. Two kilometers down a path that turns left off the main road just before Eklingji is **Nagda,** legendary birthplace of Bappa Rawal and the first capital of the Mewar kingdom (preceding the capital at Chittaurgarh). Today Nagda remains the home of the **Sas Bahu** (Mother and Daughter-in-Law) Temples, which were rendered inactive by Mughal attack. Even though the central icons were destroyed, these 10th-century temples have retained their beautiful carvings.

NATHDWARA

> *Buses* run to Nathdwara from Udaipur (1½hr., every 15min. 4am-9:30pm, Rs19-23). Temple hours are highly variable but are approximately 6-6:30am, 7:15-7:45am, 9:15-9:30am, 11:30am-12:15pm, 3:30-3:45pm, 4-4:15pm, 5-5:15pm, 6:30-6:45pm. Free.

Forty-eight kilometers north of Udaipur is the Vaishnava pilgrimage site of **Nathdwara,** built entirely around its incredible **Sri Nathji Mandir,** a temple dedicated to Krishna's *avatar* as the baby Sri Nathji. Legend has it that during the

17th century, a chariot carrying Krishna's image from Mathura to Udaipur became trapped inexplicably in the mud; the bearers interpreted the situation as a divine signal and built a temple on the spot. The image of Sri Nathji, with blazing diamond-studded eyes and Mughal dress, is found on decorative items in households all over India. The stalls outside the temple have commercialized the image, and Krishna paraphernalia abounds. Although the temple's architecture is a visual feast, the evening ceremonies (5pm, following the ritual feeding, bathing, and putting-to-bed of the image) are far more interesting. For each *darshan* (viewing window), a different backdrop is displayed behind the statue in order to depict various scenes from Krishna's life.

RANAKPUR रनकपुर ☎02934

Eighty kilometers northwest of Udaipur stand Ranakpur's superb Jain temples, which comprise a complex that rivals Dilwara on Mt. Abu. The main white-marble **Chaumukha Temple,** built in 1439, is dedicated to Adinath, the first *tirthankara* (Jain teacher). Inside, there are 29 halls, 80 domes, and 1444 pillars (no two of them alike), all intricately carved and sculpted. The temple's most intricate carvings surround a four-faced image of Adinath in the innermost sanctum. In addition to this Adinath temple, the complex contains three other shrines: the smaller but equally superb **Parsavath Temple,** straight ahead to the left as you enter the complex, and the less notable **Neminath Temple** and Hindu **Sun Temple** farther back to the right. (Open to non-Jain tourists daily 11:30am-5pm; to Jains and Indians 7am-8pm. Menstruating women are not supposed to enter. Camera fee Rs40.)

Ranakpur is a good stopover on the long bus journey between Udaipur (2½-3hr.) and Jodhpur (4½hr.). Make sure the driver knows you want to get off at Ranakpur. Buses stop by the *chai* stand on the main road en route to: **Abu Road** (5hr., 5:30am, Rs85); **Jodhpur** (4½hr.; 8am, noon, 2, 5:30, 11pm; Rs80); **Udaipur** (3hr., every hr. 7am-7pm, Rs35; deluxe 2½hr.; 10am, 4, 7pm; Rs37). As there's nothing to see in "town" besides the temples, you could conceivably move on to your next destination the same night or even do a daytrip to Ranakpur from Udaipur, but Ranakpur is a pleasant enough place to stay. The **RTDC Hotel Shilpi ❷,** 150m up the road (toward Jodhpur) from the bus stand and temples, has spacious, pleasant rooms with bath and serves reasonably priced meals. (☎285074. Singles Rs200-600; doubles Rs300-700.) The **dharamsala ❶,** inside the temple complex offers very basic lodgings and plentiful meals. (☎285019. Meals Rs20. Rooms Rs60.)

MOUNT ABU माऊंट आबू ☎02974

Situated on a plateau near the Gujarati border, Mt. Abu (pop. 16,000; elev. 1220m) is unique among Rajasthan's tourist destinations. Besides being Rajasthan's only hill station, it's far more popular with Indian tourists than with foreigners. Some come to worship at the breathtaking Dilwara temples, to take a dip in the holy waters of Nakki Lake, or to honor Vashishta, the sage who gave rise to the five Rajput clans. Families come here to seek refuge from the heat at lower altitudes, and honeymooners come to frolic among the ice-cream shops and endless parade of pony rides. With so many worldly delights, the few foreign visitors to the city are unlikely to leave disappointed—the Dilwara temples are nothing less than spectacular, there are virtually no touts or high-pressure sales tactics, and the cool temperatures and abundant greenery make the town a fantastic place to relax for a few days before heading back into the thick of things.

RAJASTHAN

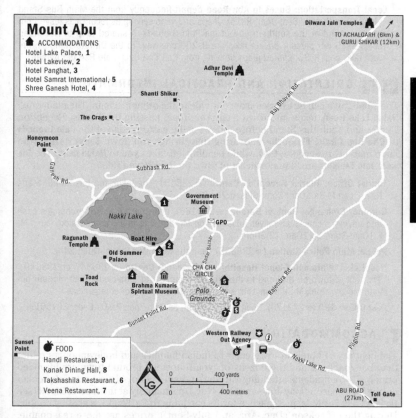

Mount Abu

🏠 ACCOMMODATIONS
Hotel Lake Palace, **1**
Hotel Lakeview, **2**
Hotel Panghat, **3**
Hotel Samrat International, **5**
Shree Ganesh Hotel, **4**

🍴 FOOD
Handi Restaurant, **9**
Kanak Dining Hall, **8**
Takshashila Restaurant, **6**
Veena Restaurant, **7**

▆ TRANSPORTATION

A Rs10 tourist tax is levied on all visitors at the end of the long climb up the mountain, so keep some small change handy.

Trains: Abu Road Railway Station (☎222222), 27km from town; it's on the main broadgauge line between Delhi and Mumbai via Ahmedabad. **Western Railway Out Agency,** Nakki Lake Rd. (☎38697), next to the bus stand, handles reservations to Delhi and Mumbai. Open M-Sa 9am-1pm and 2-3pm, Su 9am-noon. To: **Ahmedabad** (4½hr., 6 per day 11:30am-5:20am, Rs83); **Jodhpur** (6hr., 3pm and 1am, Rs85-130); **Jaipur** (8hr., 3-5 per day 10:20am-9pm, Rs180) via **Ajmer** (5hr., Rs145).

Buses: Main Bus Stand (☎235434). To: **Ahmedabad** (7½hr., 5 per day 6am-9pm, Rs95); **Jaipur** (12hr., 11:30am, Rs180; deluxe 6:30pm, Rs220); **Jaisalmer** (11hr., 6am, Rs187); **Jodhpur** (7hr., 6:45am, Rs130); **Udaipur** (6½hr., 3 per day 8am-7pm, Rs81; deluxe 8am, Rs95). **Private bus companies** line Nakki Lake Rd. **Shobha Travels** (☎238302) is next door to Hotel Samrat. Open daily 7am-10:30pm. Bus transportation arranged in Mt. Abu departs from Mt. Abu proper, but arrangements made in other cities for service to Mt. Abu may only come as far as Abu Rd., 1hr. away. Check in advance.

Local Transportation: Buses to **Abu Road** depart frequently from the Main Bus Stand (1hr., every 30min. 6am-9pm, Rs15). Jeeps and vans serving as local **taxis** leave from the taxi stand at the southern end of the Polo Grounds. A shared **jeep** to Abu Road costs Rs15 per person; private taxis are Rs200 one-way. To the Dilwara Temples, private taxis cost Rs30; shared jeeps, leaving from Cha Cha Circle, are Rs4 per person.

ORIENTATION AND PRACTICAL INFORMATION

The small town can be crossed from one side to the other in 25min. The main drag, **Nakki Lake Road,** leads into town from Abu Road, passing the Tourist Reception Center and Main Bus Stand before following the eastern edge of the **Polo Grounds** to **Cha Cha Circle.** From there, bearing right brings you down **Sadar Bazaar** (the main market) toward the **GPO,** while heading left takes you to **Nakki Lake.** The **Dilwara Jain Temples** are 3km northeast of town on Raj Bhavan Rd.

Tourist Office: Tourist Reception Centre (☎235151), opposite the bus stand. Maps Rs2. Open M-Sa 10am-5pm. Closed 2nd Sa.

Currency Exchange: Bank of Baroda (☎235166), near the taxi stand, exchanges cash and traveler's checks and gives advances on MC and V for a 1% commission. Open M-F 10am-3pm, Sa 10am-12:30pm.

Police: Main Police Station (☎238333), near the Main Bus Stand. Open 24hr.

Hospital: J. Watumull Global Hospital and Research Centre (☎238347 or 238349), 1km out of town on the road to the Dilwara Temples. An ultra-clean, ultra-modern private facility. Open M-Sa 9am-1pm and 3-5pm. Open 24hr. for emergencies.

Post Office: GPO (☎243170). Open M-F 9am-3pm, Sa 9am-2pm. **Postal Code:** 307501.

ACCOMMODATIONS

The majority of hotels in town cater to Indian families and honeymooners rather than backpackers, and the dozens of "youth hostels" around town are intended principally for students attending Mt. Abu's private schools. Room rates skyrocket during high season (May-June and Oct.-Nov.), particularly at the time of **Diwali** (see **Holidays and Festivals,** p. 89), when tariffs can jump to Rs1000 for a shabby double. During the off-season (Dec.-Apr. and July-Sept.), prices are more reasonable. Buses will drop you off within walking distance of most of the hotels in town. Unless otherwise noted, all hotels listed have a 9am check-out.

Shree Ganesh Hotel (☎243591 or 237292; lalit_ganesh@yahoo.co.in), on the road to the Old Summer Palace. The rooms are comfy, but what sets this place apart is the hospitality and range of facilities. The only hotel in Mt. Abu that caters primarily to foreigners, Shree Ganesh keeps a foreign-tourist quota until 10pm and offers free pickup and drop-off at the station. Internet Rs1 per min. Jeep tours to Achalgarh and the Dilwara temples (Rs60 per person). Free yoga lessons twice daily. Singles Rs150-175; doubles Rs200-250. Off-season Rs50 discount. ❷

Hotel Panghat, Nakki Lake (☎238886). Unexciting but adequate rooms, all with attached baths and TVs. Good values considering their lakeside location, though the carnival vibes from the streets below might test your patience after a while. Rooms Rs350-450. Off-season Rs125-150. ❸

Hotel Lakeview, Nakki Lake (☎238659). Another lakeside hotel with good views. Geared toward honeymooners and hippies—some rooms bedecked in reams of red velvet, others upholstered with tie-dye. Deluxe rooms have lakeside swings for two. All rooms with attached baths. Hot water 7-11am. Rooftop restaurant. Rooms Rs300-700. Off-season Rs200-400. ❷

Hotel Samrat International, Nakki Lake Rd. (☎235173 or 235153). Beautiful, clean, modern room, all with TV, sitting areas, and attached baths. Hot water 7-10am. A great choice if it's in your price range. Good restaurant too (see below). Rooms Rs500-820. Off-season 50% discount. ❹

Hotel Lake Palace, Nakki Lake (☎237154), on the quieter eastern shore. Spacious clean, bright rooms all with TV and hot water, some with private balconies. Lots of space for lounging on the rooftop and in large side garden. Room service, rail and bus station pickup. Room prices fixed Rs400-800. ❸

☕ FOOD

Thanks to the abundance of Gujarati tourists in Mt. Abu, you'll find Gujarati food as often as you will the typical Rajasthani, Punjabi, and Chinese items.

Kanak Dining Hall, near the Main Bus Stand. Come at lunchtime to see stainless steel fly. Gujarati *thalis* Rs45. Smiling, speedy service. Deliciously sweet. Open daily 11am-3pm and 7-10:30pm. ❷

Veena Restaurant, Nakki Lake Rd., opposite the Bank of Baroda, known as "where the taste and quality meets." Fast food joint specializing in South Indian food. Twist your hips to Hindi pop as you munch on a tasty *dosa* (Rs20-45) or a veg. meal (Rs20-60). Open daily 7am-midnight. ❶

Handi Restaurant, in the Hilltone Hotel, south of the Main Bus Stand. Superb food (Rs60-150) served in an upscale environment. Indoor or garden seating. Attached bar. Open daily 7am-11pm. ❸

Takshashila Restaurant, in Hotel Samrat. Tasty veg. food in a central location. Indian, Kashmiri, and Chinese options Rs40-75. Open daily 8am-3pm and 7-11pm. ❷

☕ SIGHTS

Many travel agencies offer half- and full-day tours of Mt. Abu and its environs, but these tend to be very rushed (e.g. less than 1hr. at the Dilwara complex) and cater to Indian tourists (most are in Hindi), so it's more advisable to wander by yourself.

DILWARA JAIN TEMPLE COMPLEX

The temples are 3km northeast of town, along Raj Bhavan Rd. Jeeps from Cha Cha Cir. head to the temples every 15min. for Rs4; chartering a taxi costs Rs30-40. The walk between town and Dilwara is most pleasant on the way back, when it's downhill. The complex is open to non-Jains noon-6pm; Jains can visit sunrise-sunset. Photography and leather items prohibited; don't bring anything you wouldn't feel comfortable leaving at the mandatory storage area. Menstruating women are not supposed to enter.

The Jain temple complex at Dilwara is one of the architectural highlights of India. The temples are famed for the incredible intricacy and detail of their white-marble carvings. Even more impressive though, is the amazing variation of figures and ornamentation; from the pillars to ceiling reliefs, no two designs are identical.

The first temple, straight ahead from the entrance past the guidebook stand, is the small, modest **Temple of Mahaveer Swami,** built in 1582 and dedicated to the 24th *tirthankara.* Next up on the right is the **Hasti Shala** (elephant cell), which contains three rows of huge, beautifully carved pachyderms.

Opposite the Hasti Shala sits the original and most famous temple at Dilwara, the **Vimal Vasahi,** built during the 11th century by Vimal Shah, Chief Minister to the Solanki King of Gujarat. The "dancing dome" just inside the entrance features statues of the 16 *Vidhyadevus* (goddesses of education), and magnificent carvings line the pillars supporting the dome and the main sanctuary just behind it. Surrounding the sanctum itself is a circumambulatory corridor with 57 cells, each of which contains a *tirthankara* statue and is embellished by a unique beam. The best artwork is carved into the ceiling panels in front of the cells. The statue of Adinath at the center of the temple is modeled on a 3500-year-old granite statue housed in the temple. The dome and walls of the sanctuary were left undecorated to avoid distracting meditators.

The next temple, the **Luna Vasahi,** known as the Tejpal Temple, was built two centuries after the Vimal. Its marble carvings are more intricate and delicate. Workers carved the tiered lotus dome from a single block of marble. The Tejpal is dedicated to Neminath, the 22nd *tirthankara*, and the 52 cells along the corridor contain images of the *tirthankaras*. The last two temples are the **Pittalhar** (c. 1315-1433) and **Parshwanath** (c. 1458).

⛰ HIKING AND OUTDOOR ACTIVITIES

NAKKI LAKE. Visiting Nakki Lake, where most of Mt. Abu's activity is focused, is like attending a carnival—popcorn sellers, photo stalls, and brightly decorated **ponies** (rides Rs100 per hr.) crowd the streets, and mobs constantly clamor for **paddle-boats** and **rowboats** available at the dock (Rs50 per 30min.). The festive atmosphere tends to obscure the religious significance of the lake, thought to contain holy waters because it was dug out by the *nakh* (nails) of a god. Taking a scenic walk along the left bank, from which you can see **Toad Rock,** leads past the small **Ragunath Temple** to a quiet side of the lake lined with huge estates and stately homes.

VIEWPOINTS AND HIKES. Sunset Point lies 500m west of the Polo Grounds along Sunset Pt. Rd. (a short but very nice nature trail runs parallel to the main road). Though it offers a beautiful view of the setting sun, the crowd of tourists has made it a much better people-watching spot. A similar fate has befallen **Honeymoon Point,** off the road leading northwest behind Nakki Lake. The view from here is also superb, and the name draws newlyweds by the dozen. From here you can see the **crags** or hike up a little farther to the **Shanti Shikhar** for dazzling panoramic views. A left off the northeast road to Dilwara leads to the base of a 30min., heart-pumping trek up 360 steps to the mountain-top **Adhar Devi Temple.** Dedicated to the patron goddess of Mt. Abu, the "temple" is a natural cleft in the rock that can only be entered by crawling on all fours. It commands a spectacular view of the valleys below. Numerous other hiking possibilities exist for those looking to take advantage of Mt. Abu's fantastic scenery, uniquely green for Rajasthan. For suggested hikes, see the sign near Sunset Point. Friendly ◪**Lalit** at the Shree Ganesh Hotel leads hikes through less-trampled places; non-guests might be able to tag along after eating at the restaurant or utilizing the hotel's travel services.

> ❗ **WARNING.** A number of tourists have been mugged while hiking alone on the trails around Mt. Abu. Do not hike alone. Better still, go with a local guide who knows how to handle would-be thieves (as well as the occasional bear).

JODHPUR जोधपुर ☎ 0291

Once the capital of the state of Marwar ("Land of Death"), founded by the warrior clans of Rathore, Jodhpur (pop. 1 million) borders the Thar Desert and is the second-largest city in Rajasthan. Despite its size and activity, Jodhpur has yet to emerge as a tourist destination in its own right, though it's a pleasant enough place to spend a few days before continuing on to more exotic destinations like Jaisalmer and Udaipur. The city's highlights include its formidable and lavishly decorated fort, a bustling bazaar, and a sea of color-washed homes that have earned Jodhpur the nickname, "The Blue City." These sights can be seen in a day, after which many travelers tack on a daytrip to the nearby desert villages of the Bishnoi.

▛ TRANSPORTATION

Flights: Jodhpur Airport, Airport Rd. (flight info ☎ 142), 6km from the city center. 25min. from town by auto-rickshaw (Rs50) or taxi (Rs100). **Indian Airlines,** Airport Rd., (☎ 2510757 or 2510758, airport office 2512617). Open daily 10am-1:15pm and 2-4:30pm. To: **Delhi** (2hr., 7:20pm, US$80) via **Jaipur** (40min., US$60); **Mumbai** (2½hr., 8:20am, US$111) via **Udaipur** (40min., US$48).

Trains: Jodhpur Railway Station, Railway Station Rd. (☎ 131 or 132). Most trains also stop at **Raika Bagh Railway Station,** on the east side of town. Reserve at the **Advance Reservation Office,** Station Rd. (☎ 2636407), next to the GPO. Open M-Sa 8am-8pm, Su 8am-2pm. To: **Ahmedabad** (10hr.; 6:45am, 3:15, 6:15pm; Rs183) via **Abu Road** (5hr., Rs72); **Bikaner** (5hr., 10:15am and 8:35pm, Rs116); **Delhi** (11-12hr., 7:30 and 9:30pm, Rs218); **Jaipur** (4-7hr.; 5:45, 7am, 5:15, 7:30, 10pm; Rs122); **Jaisalmer** (6½hr., 6:10am and 11:15pm, Rs122).

Buses: Main Bus Station (☎ 2544686 or 2544989), near Raika Bagh Railway Station. To: **Ahmedabad** (11hr., 6 per day 6:30am-7:30pm, Rs185; deluxe 9pm, Rs208); **Ajmer** (4½hr., every 30min. 5:15am-midnight, Rs84); **Bikaner** (6hr., 12 per day 5:30am-7:45pm, Rs102); **Delhi** (14hr.; 9, 10am, 3:30, 9:30pm; Rs260; deluxe 4pm, Rs371); **Jaipur** (7½hr., 11 per day 5:15am-midnight, Rs139; deluxe 11am, noon, 4, 10, 10:30, 11pm, midnight; Rs162); **Jaisalmer** (5hr., 12 per day 5am-5:30pm, Rs80); **Mount Abu** (7hr., 11:45am, Rs127); **Udaipur** (8hr., 10 per day 5:30am-10:30pm, Rs111; deluxe 7hr.; 5:30, 11:45am, 3, 10:30pm; Rs111) via **Ranakpur** (4hr., Rs79). There are dozens of **private bus companies;** most are along High Court Rd., near the main railway station.

Local Transportation: Local **buses** (Rs2-7) and **tempos** (Rs1-5) are the cheapest options, provided you can figure out their routes. **Auto-rickshaws,** the best way to maneuver through the streets of the old city, congregate around the major sights and stations (Rs10-30 to most destinations). **Prem Cycle Store,** opposite the railway station, rents bikes (Rs3 per hr., Rs15 per day). **Taxis,** available in front of the tourist office (Rs3 per km, Rs60 minimum), are good for longer hauls.

◪ ▞ ORIENTATION AND PRACTICAL INFORMATION

Much of modern Jodhpur lies beyond the old city walls. **Jodhpur Railway Station** is in the southwestern part of town, along **Station Road.** Nearby are the two most important gates to the old city and Jodhpur's modern commercial centers—**Jalori Gate,** at the end of the road running perpendicular to the station, and **Sojati Gate,** to the right as you exit the station, along Station Rd. **High Court Road** continues east from Sojati Gate past the **Umaid Gardens** and the **Tourist Reception Center** to **Raika Bagh Railway Station** and the **bus stand.** The city's main artery, **Nai Sarak,** leads north from the old city walls to **Sardar Bazaar** (the main market area), which is punctuated by the **Clock Tower.** Looming over the tangled web of old-city streets are **Meherangarh Fort** and the memorial **Jaswant Thada.** The old city is almost impossible to navigate—take a rickshaw or be prepared to ask for lots of directions.

Tourist Office: Tourist Reception Centre, High Court Rd. (☎ 2545083), in RTDC Hotel Ghoomar. Free maps. Open daily 8am-8pm. Daily tours visit the fort, the Umaid Bhawan Palace and Garden, Jaswant Thada, and Mandore Gardens (9am-1pm or 2-6pm, 6-person minimum, Rs85 without entrance fees). For info on **village safaris,** see p. 535).

Currency Exchange: Bank of Baroda, Sojati Gate (☎2439746), under Hotel Arun. Changes currency and traveler's checks, MC/V cash advances on MC and V have a 1% commission. Open M-F 10am-3pm, Sa 10am-2pm.

Markets: High Court Road, Nai Sarak, and **Sardar Bazaar** are the main shopping areas. There are fresh fruit and vegetable stalls in Sardar Bazaar and along **Station Road.** Most stores open daily 10am-9pm.

Police: Ratanada Rd. (☎2633700). **Police Control Room** (☎2547180), at the intersection of Nai Sarak and High Court Rd., is also helpful in an emergency.

Pharmacy: Most pharmacies are near the hospitals, around Sojati and Jalori Gates, and along Nai Sarak are open M-Sa 8am-10pm.

Hospital: Mahatma Gandhi Hospital, Mahatma Gandhi Hospital Rd. (☎2636437), between Sojati and Jalori Gates. Also accessible from Station Rd. **Goyal Hospital,** Residency Rd. (☎432144). Near the Medical College. One of the best private hospitals. Both open 24hr.

Internet: Govind Hotel and a few small STD places along the Nai Sarak offer Internet services (Rs1 per min.). Most open 8am-11pm.

Post Office: GPO, Station Rd. (☎2636695), near Sojati Gate. Open M-Sa 8am-8pm. **Postal Code:** 342001.

ACCOMMODATIONS

Budget hotels line Station Rd. and High Court Rd. Accommodations on the other side of the railroad tracks are more peaceful but necessitate heavy reliance on auto-rickshaws to see the rest of town (about Rs20 to Sojati Gate/Nai Sarak). Several smaller guest houses are sprinkled around the clock tower (tout city) and throughout the old city—these can be charming, though hard to find and lacking modern amenities. The tourist office also arranges homestays.

Govind Hotel (☎2622758; govindhotel2000@yahoo.com), opposite the GPO, a 5min. walk from railway station. Modern, well-kept rooms, most with hot-water bath and TV. Govind's central location, its helpful owner Jagdish, and its good rooftop veg. restaurant (with fantastic views of the fort) make it a popular budget choice. Narrow but clean 6-bed dorm Rs60; singles Rs200-300; doubles Rs250-350, with A/C Rs550-600. ❷

Durag Niwas Guest House, 1st Old Public Park (☎2510692; maharaja_m2k_4u@hotmail.com). Family-run guest house with spotless, beautifully decorated rooms. Manager well-attuned to backpackers' needs. Fantastic value. Free informal cooking classes. Ask about their unique village safari. Rooms with attached hot-water bath Rs150-500. ❷

Cosy Guest House, Novechokiya Rd., Bhram Puri, Chuna Ki Choki (☎2612066). Deep in the old city, a 5min. walk from the fort's back gate. Look carefully for the signs. Formerly known as Joshi's Blue House, this intimate lodge has cramped but quaint rooms in the oldest part of the city. Rooftop restaurant with wonderful views serves home-cooked food. Dorms Rs60; small doubles Rs150, with hot-water bath and TV Rs250. ❶

Haveli Guest House, Makrana Mohalla (☎2614615; havelighj@sify.com). 5min. on foot from the clock tower in the old city. Another popular refuge for travelers, housed in a beautiful 250-year-old *haveli*. Rooms are smallish but bright and clean. All have attached hot-water bath. Amazing views from the rooftop veg. restaurant. Pricey but worth it. Older 1st fl. rooms Rs200; rooms with A/C, tub, and a view Rs800. ❷

FOOD

Local specialties include *mawa* sweets, available at shops at the intersection of Nai Sarak and High Court Rd., *chakki-ka-sagh*, wheat sponge cooked in rich gravy, and the *makhania lassi*, a thick, sweet *lassi* flavored with saffron.

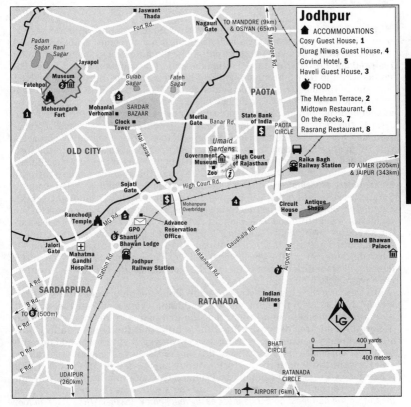

Jodhpur

🏠 ACCOMMODATIONS

Cosy Guest House, **1**
Durag Niwas Guest House, **4**
Govind Hotel, **5**
Haveli Guest House, **3**

🍴 FOOD

The Mehran Terrace, **2**
Midtown Restaurant, **6**
On the Rocks, **7**
Rasrang Restaurant, **8**

🍽 **The Mehran Terrace,** on top of Meherangarh Fort. Enter via the elevator to the left after you pass through the main gate. Candlelit dinners in the rooftop veranda or out on the terrace overlooking the twinkling city, 120 ft. above the rest of the fort. Set menu served on a silver *thali*. An unsurpassed dining experience. Veg. Rs200, non-veg. Rs250. No alcohol. Nightly Indian folk music. Open daily 7:30-10pm. ❺

🍽 **On the Rocks,** Airport Rd., next to Ajit Bhawan Hotel. Excellent Indian, Chinese, and continental food served in a relaxing outdoor courtyard. Popular with locals and tourists alike. Veg. dishes Rs45-80, non-veg. Rs80-210. Sa-Su live Indian classical music. Open daily 12:30-3pm and 7:30pm-midnight. ❸

Rasrang Restaurant, B Rd. in the heart of Sardarpura. Sign is in Hindi. Look for the silver counter that wraps around the corner across from Krishna Temple. Popular outdoor fast food spot. Worth the trip off the beaten track. Fantastic milkshakes Rs10-25. South Indian snacks Rs20-25. Open daily 9:30am-11:30pm. ❶

Midtown Restaurant, Station Rd., in Shanti Bhawan Lodge, opposite the railway station. A great introduction to Rajasthani cuisine, this veg. restaurant has a range of local specialties (Rs35-70). Sample everything with a *Rajasthani Maharaja Thali* (Rs80). Open daily 7am-11pm. ❷

👁 SIGHTS

MEHERANGARH FORT. Rising magnificently above Jodhpur, Meherangarh is one of the best-preserved forts in Rajasthan. It may be quite small compared with some of its sprawling counterparts, but the interior has been beautifully restored and now houses a fascinating collection of artifacts. The addition of a fantastic audio tour more than justifies the admission fee hike and makes the fort one of the most worthwhile sights in all of Rajasthan. The fort was originally built in AD 1459, by Rao Jodha, but has been expanded over the years by subsequent maharajas. Seven *pols* (gates) mark the various entrances. The **Jayapol**, the main entrance, commemorates the military achievements of Maharaja Man Singh. The impressive **Fatehpol** (Victory Gate), created by Maharaja Ajit Singh after his return from exile, marks the original entrance into the fort. The **Lohapol** (Iron Gate) features 15 handprints that honor the *sati* sacrifice of Maharaja Man Singh's widows in 1843. The centerpiece of the modern fort, the **Meherangarh Museum**, sits in a red sandstone palace beyond the final gigantic **Surajpol**. Filling its halls are extravagant silver *howdahs* (elephant seats), exquisite wood and ivory artifacts, a weapons room, the royal dumbbells of the maharaja, a beautiful 250-year-old tent canopy (a prized acquisition seized during a raid on the Mughals in Delhi), 150 types of cannons, fancy baby cradles, musical instruments, miniature paintings, and a 300-piece turban collection. Of particular interest are the **Phool Mahal** (Flower Palace), an elaborate, mirrored dance hall embellished with gold, and the **Moti Mahal** (Pearl Palace), a conference room with a glass and gold ceiling.

After exiting the museum, you can stroll along the ramparts to the southern end of the fort, which commands a breathtaking view out over the wash of blue, old-city homes. Some claim that the distinctive color was intended to denote brahmin residences, while others hold that the copper sulfate was added primarily because of its protective powers against termites and mosquitoes. The **Chamunda Temple** is also at this end of the fort. The guards will allow you to walk the length of the fort without paying the entrance fee if you request to see only the Chamunda Temple. This method, however, will not allow you to see the museum or listen to the audio tour. (*The main entrance to the fort, in the northeast corner, is most easily reached by rickshaw; (Rs40), or on foot from the clock tower through the old city (15min.). Most people exit the same way; Fatehpol gate, an alternate exit, leads to the southwest. Open daily 9am-5pm. Rs250 includes camera use, audio tour, and museum admission; video fee Rs100.*)

UMAID BHAWAN PALACE. This majestic marble and sandstone palace dominates the eastern part of the city. Built just before Independence, the palace is impressive, but lacks some of the charm of Rajasthan's older palaces. The current maharaja, Gaj Singh II, and a luxury hotel occupy most of the palace, but six rooms have been converted into a **museum** and are open to the public. The eccentric collection includes antique clocks, opulent furniture, Chinese vases, stuffed animals, and miscellaneous relics—all property of the maharaja. (*Open daily 8:30am-5:30pm. Entrance fee Rs50. Cameras strictly prohibited.*)

JASWANT THADA. This impressive white-marble memorial to the beloved Maharaja Jaswant Singh II was erected by his wife in 1899. Adjoining the memorial are four smaller cenotaphs of rulers who followed; those who came before him are memorialized at Mandore. The view is spectacular. (*10min. downhill from the main fort entrance. Open daily 9am-1pm and 2-5pm. Entrance fee Rs20; camera fee Rs25; video fee Rs50.*)

ENTERTAINMENT

The **Ajit Bhawan** hotel organizes performances of Rajasthani folk singing and dancing to accompany the delicious buffet dinner (in-season nightly 7:30pm, Rs350; off-season times vary, check with reception). For those with a less cultural form of entertainment in mind, **On the Rocks** and **Gossip** have well-stocked bars, though nothing stays open after midnight. The annual **Marwar Festival** (Oct. 26-27, 2004; Oct. 16-17, 2005) showcases local history, dance, art, and most of all, food.

SHOPPING

The **Sojati Gate** and **Nai Sarak** areas, especially **Sardar Bazaar** by the Clock Tower, are crammed full of shops peddling everything imaginable. Aromatic **spices** are very popular purchases among visitors. There are numerous spice shops around the clock tower, but everybody's favorite is **Mohanlal Verhomal,** stall 209B at the *sabzi* (vegetable) market. Beware of imitators. Mohan Gehani, the owner, might charge a little more than some of his competitors, but he's very knowledgeable, and he offers reliable mail-order service.

Another major Jodhpur specialty is **antiques.** The area leading to Umaid Bhawan Palace is filled with huge treasure troves of Rajasthani paraphernalia (both genuine and "instant" antiques). Most, however, are not for popular tourist consumption—items run on the large and expensive side (e.g. elaborately painted wooden furniture) and are geared toward Western art and antique dealers and overseas exporters. Still, the collections are fun to peruse, and most of them also offer modest selections of smaller (and more affordable) items in wood, brass, marble, iron, clay, *papier mâché*, and textiles—all handmade in Rajasthan. Two good places to start are **Lalji Handicrafts** (☎2510887; open daily 9am-7:30pm) and **Ajay Art Emporium** (☎2510269; open daily 9am-8pm), both on Umaid Bhawan Palace Rd.

DAYTRIPS FROM JODHPUR

Almost as strong a draw to Jodhpur as the fort and bazaars are the popular daytrips. During a half- or full-day trip, it's possible to visit the desert villages of the Bishnoi people; in another day it's possible to see the exquisitely sculpted Jain temples at Osiyan.

BISHNOI VILLAGES

The only practical way to see these villages is with an organized tour, since they're spread out far from each other and a translator-guide is necessary for any meaningful communication. Many hotels in Jodhpur offer village safaris (5hr. visit to four villages Rs350-450 per person), as does the tourist office (Rs1100 per vehicle, seats up to 8). Take care when selecting an operator, as a poor choice can be the difference between a fulfilling cultural experience and a tacky shopping expedition. The tourist office, Hotel Govind, Durga Niwas Guest House, and Cosy Guest House run reputable operations.

The Bishnoi people, established as a group in the 15th century, are well-known for their devotion to environmental protection. They regard all fauna as sacred (they're pure vegetarians), as well as some flora (in 1730, 363 Bishnois sacrificed their life to save the Khejri tree), and live their lives according to 29 conservative principles (*"bishnoi"* means "29"). Bishnoi villages are scattered throughout northwest India, including the area southeast of Jodhpur (along the road to Pali), and "village safaris" from Jodhpur are a popular way for tourists to view a bit of rural Rajasthani life. In traditional desert homes, typically cow dung complexes or thatched huts, visitors can learn about herbal medicines, taste desert cuisine, and watch local craftspeople spinning, making pottery, and weaving carpets.

OSIYAN

*65km north of Jodhpur. **Buses** run to Osiyan from Jodhpur (1½-2hr., every 30min. 5:30am-9pm, Rs23). Alternatively, rent a **jeep** from the tourist office (1hr., Rs700). Mahavira Jain Temple Rs5; camera fee Rs40.*

The desert town of Osiyan houses Rajasthan's largest group of early Jain and Hindu temples. From the 8th to the 12th centuries, this was a prosperous trading town, and its primarily Jain merchants poured their wealth into beautifully sculpted, fairly well-preserved temples. You can visit them on a daytrip from Jodhpur or, if you don't have the time to go to Jaisalmer or Bikaner, you can stay longer and organize a camel trek from here.

Right near the bus stand is the oldest group of temples, consisting of the red 8th- and 9th-century **Vishnu** and **Harihara** temples. Follow the main road from Jodhpur to Phalodi, then continue straight toward the town center as the road bends right. In the middle of town is the massive and very busy **Sachiya Mata** temple, perched atop a large staircase. Women and men line up separately and are admitted in alternating waves, but no matter what your sex, be prepared to push and shove when it comes time for you to enter the main temple. The principal worshipping area dates from the 12th century, though the mirrorwork in the main hall is modern. The central idol is Sachiya, the ninth (and last) incarnation of Durga. As you promenade down the exit ramp from the temple, continue straight ahead down the path directly opposite the exit to reach the third group of temples. The **Mahavira Jain Temple,** built in the 8th century and renovated in the 10th, is arguably the most impressive at Osiyan, as it's much more peaceful and spacious than Sadhiya Mata. The dome of the *mandapa*, lined with beautiful *apsara* sculptures, is supported by 20 intricately-carved pillars. Inside, the sanctum features a colorful, restored frieze and a stunning gold-coated icon of Mahavira, the last of the Jain *tirthankaras*. A few minutes' walk beyond the Mahavira temple are two more temples to Surya. Visit the temples in the afternoon when they are less crowded.

For those who want to stay in Osiyan, English-speaking priest Bhanu Sharma runs a small **guest house ❷** opposite the Mahavira temples. (☎02922 or 274296. Rs150.) Mr. Sharma also organizes short camel rides and trips to Bishnoi villages.

JAISALMER जैसलमेर   ☎02992

Providing perhaps the most dramatic approach to any city in Rajasthan, the golden Jaisalmer Fort rises above the desert welcoming weary travelers numbed by the endless sea of scrub. The "Golden City" of Jaisalmer (pop. 40,000), in the heart of the Thar Desert, 285km west of Jodhpur and 100km from the Pakistani border, is named for the color diffused through its sandstone skyline by the setting sun. The labyrinthine streets of the old city are filled with scores of breathtakingly carved *havelis* (royal mansions); and then of course there's the heart and soul of the Jaisalmer tourist industry: the camel safari.

After a dark medieval period characterized by Mughal sieges and dramatic *jauhars*, the city enjoyed a "golden age" (16-18th centuries) during which art and architecture flourished. Under the British, sea trade eclipsed the desert routes, and in 1947 Partition cut them off altogether, diminishing Jaisalmer's wealth and importance. With rising Indo-Pakistani tensions of the 1960s, Jaisalmer once again became a military outpost. Today, the heavy army presence provides a source of income rivaled only by the booming tourism industry.

⌐ TRANSPORTATION

Flights: Jaisalmer Airport, Sam Rd. (☎250048 or 252960), 5km from the city center, is accessible by auto-rickshaw (15min., Rs30-40). After a two-year hiatus, domestic service is supposed to return to Jaisalmer in 2003-2004. **Crown Tours Limited,** Sam Rd. (☎251912), near Hanuman Circle opposite the Collectorate, is the only agent in town for **Indian Airlines.** Open daily 9:30am-8:30pm. Flights in Oct.-Mar. to: **Delhi** (3½hr.; Tu, Th, Sa; US$165); **Jaipur** (2hr., US$135); **Udaipur** (55min., US$110).

Trains: Jaisalmer Railway Station (☎252354, inquiry 251301), a Rs15 rickshaw ride from Gopa Chowk. Connected by meter-gauge line to **Jodhpur** (6-7hr.; 7am, 3, 11:15pm; Rs44-152). Connecting reservations can be made at the **computerized reservation counter** (open M-Sa 8am-1:45pm and 2-8pm, Su 8am-2pm).

Buses: The Main Bus Stand (☎251541) is near the railway station. Most government buses originate at a **second bus stand** near Hotel Neeraj, south of Hanuman Circle. **Private buses** arranged through hotels or agencies on Hanuman Circle leave from Hanuman or the station near Hotel Neeraj. To: **Bikaner** (7½hr., 4 per day 6:30am-8:30pm, Rs117); **Jaipur** (12hr., 5pm, Rs201) via **Ajmer** (8hr., Rs202); **Jodhpur** (5½hr., every hr. 5:30am-6pm, Rs80; deluxe 5hr., 5pm Rs92); **Mt. Abu** (12hr., 5:30am, Rs176).

Local Transportation: It takes 15-20min. to cross the city on foot. Unmetered **auto-rickshaws** are everywhere, except in the fort during peak tourist hours (Oct.-Mar. 8am-noon and 4-7pm), when they are not permitted to enter. A ride from the train or bus station to Gopa Chowk should cost Rs15. **Bicycles** are available for rental at Gandhi Chowk (Rs30 per day). Agencies at Hanuman Circle and many hotels rent **jeeps** (Rs3.50 per km) and **cars** (Rs4-5 per km) if you are looking to venture beyond the city.

★ ⁊ ORIENTATION AND PRACTICAL INFORMATION

Hanuman Circle, littered with jeeps, buses, and taxis, is just outside **Amar Sagar Pol,** the main entrance to the old city. Just inside Amar Sagar Pol is **Gandhi Chowk,** the main commercial square, which hosts money exchanges, shops, and tour operators. Narrow, shop-lined **Bhatia Market** (the main commercial artery) connects Gandhi Chowk to **Gopa Chowk,** at the base of the **Fort** (the entrance to the fort here is also known as **Fort First Gate**). Heading north leads into the tangled web of Jaisalmer's old-city streets, with their exquisitely carved golden *havelis.* **Gadi Sagar Road** leads from Gopa Chowk to **Lake Gadi Sagar** and Jaisalmer's culture museums. Walk 10min. outside Gadi Sagar Pol to reach the **railway** and **bus stations.**

Tourist Office: Tourist Reception Centre (☎252406). Exit Gadi Sagar Pol and turn right at the first intersection. Provides unbiased information on hotels and safaris and free maps. Open Sept.-Mar. M-Sa 8am-8pm; Apr.-Aug. M-Sa 10am-5pm. Many private travel agents off Gopa Chowk book safaris, train, and bus tickets. **Joshi Cyber Cafe** (☎250455) and **Hotel Fort View** (☎250740) operate reputable travel counters with competitive rates on bus and train tickets and safaris.

Currency Exchange: State Bank of Bikaner and Jaipur, Ring Rd. (☎252329), near Neeraj bus stand, just inside the old city. Exchanges British and American currency and traveler's checks. Open M-F 10am-2pm, Sa 10am-noon. **Bank of Baroda** (☎252402), just inside Amar Sagar Pol, grants MC/V cash advances for 1% commission plus Rs100. Open M-F 10am-2pm, Sa 10-11am.

English-Language Bookstore: Bhatia News Agency, Court Rd. (☎252671), just east of Gandhi Chowk, buys used books. Decent selection of fiction. Open daily 9am-9pm.

Pharmacy: Government Pharmacy, outside the Government Hospital. Open 24hr.

Hospital: Sri Jawahar Government Hospital, Sam Rd. (☎252343). Open daily 8am-noon and 5:30-7pm.

Police: Main Police Office (☎252233), south of Hanuman Circle.

Internet: Scattered shops throughout the fort and Bhatia Market offer internet access for Rs20-50 per hr. **Joshi Cyber Cafe,** Gopa Chowk, is the biggest and most convenient. Rs20 per hour. Open daily 6am-midnight. **Sumit Cyber Cafe,** Gandhi Chowk. Rs30 per hr. Rs10 discount for repeat customers. Open daily 8am-midnight.

Post Office: GPO (☎252407 or 251377), south of the police station, 5min. from Amar Sagar Pol. Offices around the city. Open M-Sa 9am-5pm. **Postal Code:** 345001.

ACCOMMODATIONS

Ordinarily, the amazing depth of budget accommodations in Jaisalmer (the competition is stiffer than Mr. Desert's moustache, see p. 540) would spell backpacker heaven. However, camel safaris are much more lucrative than budget rooms, and hotels (and the touts they employ) will offer incredible room rates (Rs10), provided you go on their camel safari. The tourist office, recognizing these headaches, has set up a **Tourist Protection Force** to keep the touts at bay. To bypass the touts, some hotels send vehicles to pick up travelers free of charge.

Budget hotels in town, mostly on the two parallel streets off Gandhi Chowk, tend to be basic and cheap. The slightly pricier hotels in the fort have more charm and most offer great views of the desert. A large number of hotels in Jaisalmer have an ungenerous 9am check-out. During high season (Oct.-Mar.), the pressure to validate the hotel space you take up by going on safari is at its most intense; things relax a bit between seasons (July-Sept. and Apr.). Huge discounts are available in May and June. During the **Desert Festival** (Feb. 4-6, 2004; Feb. 21-23, 2005), expect rates to at least double.

🏨 **Hotel Renuka,** Chainpura St. (☎252757; hotelrenuka@rediffmail.com). Family atmosphere and clean, basic rooms. Rooftop restaurant with spectacular views. Look for their jeep at the station. Hot water 8am-noon and 6-9pm. Singles Rs60-80, with attached bath Rs100-150; doubles Rs80-100 with attached bath Rs150-200. **Hotel Ratan Palace** (☎253615), down the street, is run by the same family and boasts spacious, upscale rooms that are good value. Rooms with attached bath Rs150-350. ❶

🏨 **Hotel Paradise** (☎252674; hotelparadisejsm@yahoo.com), in the fort. This beautiful *haveli* is built around a pleasant garden. Bright, tasteful, clean rooms make for a very popular choice. Great rooftop views. Breakfast only. Hot water 7am-noon, 5-10pm, and on request. Call for free pickup. Rooftop budget digs Rs50; singles Rs70-100, with attached bath Rs250-500; doubles Rs150-250, with attached Rs400-850. ❶

Hotel Suraj (☎251623; hotelsurajjaisalmer@hotmail.com), next to the Jain Temples. Five huge, unique rooms in a 500-year-old *haveli*. Many still have the traditional pillars. Great rooftop views. Hot water "nearly" 24hr. Beware of copycat hotels with similar names— many may be lurking nearby. Doubles Rs350-650. ❸

Deepak Rest House (☎252665 or 252070; vyasdinesh@yahoo.com), behind the Jain temples. A backpacker institution with 25 clean, colorful rooms (most with attached hot bath), a chill rooftop restaurant, and a sitting area set into the fort wall. Dorms Rs25; singles Rs50, with attached bath Rs75; doubles Rs80-120, with bath Rs150-350. ❶

FOOD

The main reason to eat in Jaisalmer is the rooftop view, but the desert cuisine found here is unique. Be sure to experience *ker sangri* (a mix of capers and beans that looks like a bundle of gravied twigs), *gatta dal* (flour dumplings), and *kadhai pakoras* (a yogurt-based appetizer).

Jaisalmer

ACCOMMODATIONS
Deepak Rest House, **8**
Hotel Paradise, **10**
Hotel Ratan Palace, **2**
Hotel Renuka, **1**
Hotel Suraj, **9**

FOOD
Man Bhavan, **5**
Midtown Restaurant, **6**
Monica Restaurant, **7**
Natraj Restaurant, **4**
Trio Restaurant, **3**

RAJASTHAN

TO BADA BAGH (7km).
Rambagh Rd.
TO AIRPORT (3km),
AMAR SAGAR (5km), &
SAM SAND DUNES (42km)

Government Museum

Crown Tours
Sam Rd.
Collectorate

Government Hospital
HANUMAN CIRCLE
Rajasthali Government Emporium
GPO

Mainpura St.
Chainpura St.
Amar Sagar Pol
Thar Safari
GANDHI CHOWK
Royal Safari
Bhatia News

Narayan Niwas Palace
Cinema
Nathmalji-ki-Haveli
BHATIA MARKET

Malka Pol

Kishanghat Pol

Salam Singh-ki-Haveli
Patwon-ki-Haveli

GOPA CHOWK
SEE FORT INSET
FORT
Ring Rd.

Gadi Sagar Pol
Gadi Sagar Rd.
Desert Cultural Centre Museum
Jaisalmer Folklore Museum
Tilon-ki-Pol
Lake Gadi Sagar

Station Rd.
Hotel Neeraj
Bus Stand

Jaisalmer Railway Station
TO BIKANER (328km) & JODHPUR (285km)
Barmer Rd.
TO BARMER (153km)
Main Bus Stand

Jaisalmer Fort

Hotel Fort View
Sahara Travels
GOPA CHOWK
Fort First Gate
Laxminath Temple
Parmar Jewelers
Palace
DASAHARA CHOWK
Emporium
Jain Temples
Ring Rd.

O WORK, ALL PLAY

WELCOME TO MR. DESERT COUNTRY

Moustaches twisted to follicular perfection, camels dripping with shells, mirrors, and buttons, and turban-tying pros await those willing to brave the onslaught of tourists at the annual Desert Festival of Jaisalmer (Feb. 4-6, 2004; Feb. 21-23, 2005). The event kicks off with a procession of ships of the desert" and local bands followed by an odd assortment of competitions: tug-of-war, turban tying, a battle of the moustaches, camel racing, camel decoration, and, the high point of the festival, the "crowning of Mr. Desert." This prestigious and lucrative title is bestowed upon he man who best epitomizes Rajasthan—the one who exudes masculinity in his traditional dress, bushy beard, and gravity-defying moustache. Mr. Shri Laxmi Narain Bissa captured the crown for four consecutive years before being forcibly removed from the competition and bestowed with the lifelong title "Mr. Desert Emeritus." His face can now be seen staring out of haveli windows on posters promoting Rajasthan and gracing advertisements for Jaisalmer-brand cigarettes, a stint that has earned him the title "The Indian Marlboro Man."

Monica Restaurant, Gopa Chowk. A *betel*-spit to the left from the fort gate. Tasty Indian and Chinese food; a great place to try Rajasthani specialties (*thalis* Rs80). Nightly live music by local musicians. Entrees Rs35-100. Open daily 7am-11pm. ❸

Trio Restaurant, Amar Sagar Pol. (☎252733). Considered by many to be the best restaurant in Jaisalmer, Trio features great views, well-prepared specialties (Royal Safari soup Rs60), and traditional Rajasthani music from 6:30pm. A tad pricey (veg. dishes Rs40-85, non-veg. Rs60-145) but worth it. Open daily 7:30am-11:30pm. ❷

Midtown Restaurant, Gopa Chowk. Standard traveler's cafe, with the usual Indian (Rs40-50) and Chinese dishes (Rs30-50), as well as pizza and some Western desserts. Good breakfast place. Rajasthani *thalis* Rs50. Open daily 7am-11pm. ❷

Natraj Restaurant, near Salam Singh-ki-Haveli. Well-prepared Indian and Mughlai dishes (Rs40-110) and a rooftop view of the *haveli.* A/C. Open daily 8am-11pm. ❷

Man Bhavan, to the right (as you face Fort First Gate) around the base of the fort from Gopa Chawla. Serves delicious South Indian, Bengali, Gujarati, and Rajasthani food for under R60. Popular with the locals and tourists alike. Open daily 7am-11pm. ❷

SIGHTS

JAISALMER FORT

Founded in 1156 by Maharaja Jaisal, a king of the Bhati clan of Rajputs, and surrounded by 99 circular bastions, Jaisalmer's fort is the second oldest in Rajasthan (after Chittaurgarh). Like Chittaurgarh, the fort is exceptional in that it continues to be a "living" fort with current inhabitants. From Gopa Chowk, enter the fort through **Akhaipol** (a.k.a. **Fort First Gate**). A paved ramp winds its way to the last gate, **Hawapol,** which opens onto the **Main Chowk.**

RAJ MAHAL (FORT PALACE MUSEUM). The Royal Palace, which dominates the fort's Main Chowk, consists of five smaller palaces built by various Maharawals. Some tile and mirror-work as well as some wall paintings and stained glass remain intact, but the main attraction is the fine architecture of the building itself. The view from the top of the fort and old city is fantastic. *(Winter open daily 9am-6pm; summer open 8am-6pm. Entrance fee Rs50; camera fee Rs50; video fee Rs100.)*

JAIN TEMPLES. A string of eight Jain temples exhibit extraordinary workmanship along the southern fort wall. Six of the temples are closed to non-

Jains. *(The first two temples on the right-hand side as you approach from the Main Chowk are open to tourists; follow the alley past Hotel Paradise. Open daily 7am-noon. Entrance fee Rs10; camera fee Rs50; video fee Rs100. No leather or menstruating women permitted inside.)*

OTHER TEMPLES. The fort also contains many Hindu temples inside, the most famous of which is the **Laxminath Temple.** Built in 1495, the temple is simpler than its Jain counterparts, but boasts a heavily decorated, white marble central icon.

HAVELIS

A walk through the old city will bring you past numerous beautiful open-air mansions, or *havelis* (Persian for "air-house"), but three are particularly impressive and open to the public.

PATWON-KI-HAVELI. The most celebrated of Jaisalmer's *havelis* is actually a complex containing five different homes (constructed 1800-1860), one for each of the five prosperous merchant Patwa brothers. Today their common golden facade soars four dramatic stories, each fitted with stone balconies topped by arched stone umbrellas and exquisite latticed windows. Counting from the main gate, the first, second, and fifth *havelis* are open to the public. *(Entrance to first haveli on the right. Open daily 9am-7pm. Entrance fee Rs20; camera fee Rs10. Entrances to the 2nd and 5th havelis are on the left. Both open daily 10am-5pm. Entrance fee Rs2.)*

SALAM SINGH-KI-HAVELI. This *haveli*, with peacock buttresses adorning its exterior, was built around 1800 by the notorious prime minister Salam Singh Mohta. Considered a tyrant for his crippling taxes, he tried to add two additional levels to his own *haveli* to make it taller than the maharaja's. The maharaja, however, had the offending appendages torn down and its audacious builder assassinated. Moti Mahal, on the top floor, is an elaborately decorated ballroom with a beautiful carved balcony. *(Open daily 8am-6pm. Entrance fee Rs25.)*

NATHMALJI-KI-HAVELI. Once a Prime Minister's home, this *haveli* has only one room open to the public at present, but it features some very nice paintings. The two artisan brothers who built the *haveli*, Lalu and Hathi, split it right down the middle. *(Open daily 9am-8pm. Donation requested.)*

OTHER SIGHTS

LAKE GADI SAGAR. Constructed in 1367, Lake Gadi Sagar was once Jaisalmer's only source of water. Today, the reservoir is frequented by bathers, *dhobi-wallahs*, and visitors who come to view the nearby museums. The other attraction is the **Tilon-ki-Pol,** a yellow sandstone gateway with grand arched windows. This gateway once held beautifully carved rooms where the royal family stayed during the monsoon. Built by the king's chief courtesan, the gate was a source of great controversy for the town's citizens, who refused to allow women to walk beneath the "tainted" creation. As a compromise, a smaller entrance to the lake was built to the right. The lake is now decorated with royal stone *chhattris*.

MUSEUMS. Both museums between Gadi Sagar Pol and the lake promote local desert culture through collections of traditional instruments, clothing, and artifacts. The **Folklore Museum** is near the lake, and the **Desert Cultural Centre Museum** is next to the tourist office. Both host nightly puppet shows. Besides the usual ancient fossils, coins, and sculptures, the **Government Museum,** 1km southwest of Hanuman Chowk, exhibits Jaisalmeri textiles and puppets. *(Folklore Museum open daily Aug.-Mar. 8am-6:30pm; Apr.-July 4:30-7:30pm; Rs10. Desert Museum open daily 10am-5pm; free with stub from Folklore Museum. Puppet shows Rs50. Government Museum open M-Th and Sa-Su 10am-4:30pm. Rs3; M free.)*

RAJASTHAN

RAJASTHAN

CAMEL SAFARIS

By far the best and most popular way to get a taste of desert life is to go on a camel safari. By day you'll cross paths with women picking berries and boys tending herds of goats; by night you'll sleep under some of the starriest skies you've ever seen. As for the mode of transportation, the strange smells and noises that come from both ends are sure to provide hours of entertainment.

Though longer cross-desert safaris (e.g. to Bikaner) are possible, the most popular safari routes are two-to-four-day loops around Jaisalmer. Due to Jaisalmer's proximity to the Pakistan border, the government has laid down heavy restrictions on safari routes. Most safaris are concentrated in a small, easily accessible area to the north and west of town and tend to take in a pretty standard set of well-trampled sights (Lodurva, Amar Sagar, Bada Bagh, Sam Dand dunes, etc.), though the reputable agencies have started to branch out from this track. Between sunrise and sunset you can expect anywhere from 3-6hr. of camel riding, punctuated by meals, sightseeing stops, and at least one extended break. The following agencies have good reviews.

> **WARNING.** Choosing your safari operator carefully can make the difference between an amazing experience and a completely miserable one. When selecting a safari, beware of scams and hidden charges, such as charging Rs50 for a bottle of water. A realistic minimum for a safari is Rs400 per day, but simply agreeing to pay isn't equivalent to clinching a satisfactory safari experience. Reputation is *key*. Ask how often the agency sends out safaris and then peruse the comment book to see how frequently clients rave about their trip. Ten glowing reviews over the past two months is a lot better than ten over the past two years. The most reliable safaris are those booked through independent agencies, whose sole concern is building good reputations for their safaris. Before booking, be sure to ask plenty of questions. Among the things you might like to know are whether camel carts are included in the price quote, where the safari starts, what kind of food will be served, and what supplies will be provided.

Sahara Travels (☎252609; sahara_travels@yahoo.com), near Fort First Gate, is quite popular and run by Mr. Desert himself (see p. 540); he can easily form groups. Basic safaris Rs450 per day.

Thar Safari (☎254296; tharsafari@yahoo.com), off Gandhi Chowk. Offers a range of safaris. More expensive tours include tent, guide, meals, camel cart, and jeep support (Rs550-950). Mineral water Rs10.

Hotel Paradise, offers well-reviewed budget safaris from Rs400 per day.

Hotel Renuka, is also well-reviewed. Safaris include jeep transport to the starting point and fantastic campsites. Water included. 1½ days Rs750, each additional day Rs150.

Royal Safari (☎252538; rsafari@sancharnet.in), in Nachana *haveli,* off Gandhi Chowk. Rs1550 per day.

ENTERTAINMENT

For the wildest time in Jaisalmer, come to the annual **Desert Festival** (Feb. 4-6, 2004; Feb. 21-23, 2005; see **No Work, All Play,** p. 540). Prices double (at least) and tourists mob the place, but you'll still be able to enjoy traditional music and dance, camel races, camel polo, camel dances, puppeteers, **moustache contests,** and more. RTDC sets up a tourist tent-village for accommodations.

Other diversions include **swimming** in Lake Gadi Sagar or at Narayan Niwas Palace's indoor pool (near Patwon-ki-Haveli, Rs100). Film fans can indulge at Hindi **cinemas,** including **Ramesh Talkies** (☎252242; Rs7-25), near Patwon-ki-Haveli.

SHOPPING

Jaisalmer is a haven for **handicrafts,** including embroidery, patchwork, leather goods, and mirror-work, stone carving, silver, and pottery. Bargain hard, and don't even think about shopping during the Desert Festival. **Gandhi Chowk** and the main road connecting it to Gadi Sagar Pol are the primary commercial areas. The **Rajasthani Government Emporium,** just outside Amar Sagar Pol, sells a vast selection of Rajasthani handicrafts in brass, silver, wood, and textiles, as well as carpets and paintings, all at fixed prices. (☎252461. Open daily 9:30am-8pm.) **Parmar Jewelers Emporium** has a good selection of silver and semi-precious jewelry. (☎251373. Open daily 9:30am-8pm.)

DAYTRIPS FROM JAISALMER

The sights below are most easily visited on camel safaris (often you'll visit some or all of them by jeep before commencing the actual camel-riding portion of the safari). Of all the places below, only Khuri is accessible by public bus, so you'll need a jeep to visit them if you don't go on safari. Access to the area 45km west of Jaisalmer is restricted because of border disputes, and special permission (forget it) is required from the District Magistrate Office, near the police station.

BADA BAGH, AMAR SAGAR, AND MOOL SAGAR

Gardens open daily 8am-8pm. Admission Rs10. Temple fee Rs10; camera fee Rs50; video fee Rs100. Menstruating women are not allowed to enter. Garden Palace entrance fee Rs5.

About 7km north of Jaisalmer is **Bada Bagh,** where 500-year-old sandstone cenotaphs stand next to the 300-year-old mango trees of the royal garden and in the midst of towering year-old windmill turbines. To the far left is the most recent tomb, constructed in 1991 for the grandfather of the current maharaja. The gardens, which used to supply food to all of Jaisalmer, are a popular picnic spot in wet season (if there is a wet season). Another well-known spot for tea and tiffin is **Amar Sagar,** 5km northwest of Jaisalmer, where a beautifully carved Jain temple, constructed under the orders of Maharaja Amar Singh, guards a lake and fertile gardens. The green oasis of **Mool Sagar Garden Palace,** 7km southwest of Jaisalmer, was once the maharaja's picnic place.

SAM SAND DUNES

The tourist office runs sunset jeep tours to Sam for Rs125 per person.

The Sam Sand Dunes are 42km west of Jaisalmer, and they're far from undiscovered. The scene here at sunset is nothing less than a circus, with legions of Indian and foreign tourists and an almost comical number of camels and camel drivers chasing after them. This is not the place to come for solitude, but it is nevertheless a stunning place to be at sunrise or sunset, and if you're in the market for a camel ride, you couldn't pick a better locale (Rs10-20 for a sunset stroll). Those who want to stay the night but aren't satisfied sleeping under the stars can stay at the clean but pricey **RTDC Sam Dhani ❸,** right next to the dunes. (Rooms with attached bath Rs500. Book through the tourist office.) Nearby **Hotel Lala ❶** provides a mattress and blanket in a hut, along with breakfast and dinner, for Rs100.

KHICHAN

Khichan is difficult to reach by public transport. However, if you are travelling between Jodhpur and Jaisalmer by car, it's a sight that should not be missed.

Khichan, a slight detour off the dusty road from Jodhpur to Jaisalmer (about midway near Phalodi) is unremarkable as a town but quite remarkable as the site where thousands of **demoiselle cranes** *(Anthropoides virgo)* feed upon grain spread by villagers each morning and evening from September to March.

BIKANER बीकानेर
☎ 0151

Bikaner, the fourth-largest city in Rajasthan (pop. 420,000), has been trying to draw tourists, but its remote location and formidable competition from desert neighbors has proven to be a major hindrance. Those who make the trek out here are rewarded with Jain temples, an amazing fort, *havelis*, and lots of camels. Bikaner, much lower-key than Jaisalmer, is a good place to arrange a camel safari. It's also near the moderately terrifying but indisputably fascinating "Rat Temple" at Deshnok.

Founded in 1488 by Rao Bika, a Rathore prince descended from the founder of Jodhpur, Bikaner was originally a stop on the Silk Route, as well as an important center for camel breeding. In the 16th century, its maharaja, Rei Singh, became one of the most successful generals in Emperor Akbar's all-but-invincible army. By the 18th century, Bikaner was a power to be reckoned with, a deadly enemy of Jodhpur, and the home of the legendary Bikaner Camel Corps. Since Independence, the city has been almost exclusively concerned with its own economic advancement, leading to increased industrialization. Only recently has Bikaner looked to tourism as an avenue for economic development. The city's **Camel Festival** (Jan. 6-7, 2004), a celebration of food, music, and all things camel, is yet another attraction designed to draw visitors.

▐▘ TRANSPORTATION

Trains: Bikaner Railway Station (☎ 131 or 132, computerized inquiry 1330), a Rs20-30 auto-rickshaw ride from anywhere in the city. The computerized **Advance Reservation Office** (☎ 2523132) is next to the railway station. Open M-Sa 8am-8pm, Su 8am-2pm. To: **Delhi** (10½-12hr.; 8:40am, 5:55 and 7:45pm; Rs203); **Jaipur** (5-10½hr.; 5am, 2:15, 8:30pm; Rs177); **Jodhpur** (5hr.; 1:30, 9:35am, 12:35pm; Rs148).

Buses: Central Bus Stand (☎ 2523800), 3 km north of the city, near Lalgarh Palace. To: **Ahmedabad** (14hr., 7:20am and 1:30pm, Rs282); **Ajmer** (7hr., every hr. 5:15am-11:30pm, Rs112); **Delhi** (12hr., 6 per day 5:15am-6pm, Rs196); **Jaipur** (7hr.; every hr. 5am-10pm; Rs130; deluxe 7:45am) via **Fatehpur** (4hr., Rs59); **Jaisalmer** (7hr.; 5am, noon, 9pm; Rs117); **Jhunjhunu** (5hr., 4 per day 6:30am-7pm, Rs90) **Jodhpur** (6½hr., every hr. 4:45am-12:30am, Rs103); **Udaipur** (12hr., 6:30pm, Rs226). **Private buses** can be arranged behind the fort and through hotels, excursion agents, and the bus agencies around Goga Gate, south of Kote Gate.

Local Transportation: Unmetered **auto-rickshaws** take you anywhere in the city for Rs15-30. **Bicycles** can be rented from stores opposite the police station on Station Rd. (Rs3 per hr., Rs15 per day. Open daily 8:30am-10pm). **Jeeps** can be rented near the railway station and opposite the fort's front entrance for Rs3-5 per km.

▜ ▟ ORIENTATION AND PRACTICAL INFORMATION

Station Road, the main budget hotel strip, runs parallel to the tracks in front of the **railway station.** To the right of the station, it intersects the main commercial thoroughfare, **KEM Road,** and then continues to **Junagarh Fort.** A left turn on KEM Rd. leads to **Kote Gate,** the main entrance to the **old city.** A left on Station Rd. from the station leads past the **Clock Tower** through two intersections; take a left at the second intersection to reach **Ambedkar Circle.** The city is spread out and best traversed by rickshaw.

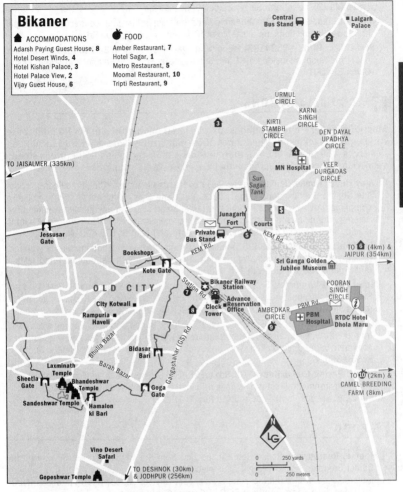

Bikaner

🏠 ACCOMMODATIONS
Adarsh Paying Guest House, 8
Hotel Desert Winds, 4
Hotel Kishan Palace, 3
Hotel Palace View, 2
Vijay Guest House, 6

🍎 FOOD
Amber Restaurant, 7
Hotel Sagar, 1
Metro Restaurant, 5
Moomal Restaurant, 10
Tripti Restaurant, 9

Tourist Office: Tourist Reception Centre (☎ 2544125), on the RTDC Hotel Dhola Maru campus, near Pooran Singh Circle. Officers can steer tourists toward particular safaris. Maps Rs10-20. Open M-Sa 10am-5pm. For helpful information on Bikaner, check out www.realbikaner.com.

Currency Exchange: Bank of Baroda (☎ 2545053), opposite the railway station. Changes traveler's checks only. Open M-F 10am-3pm, Sa 10am-12:30pm. **State Bank of Bikaner and Jaipur** (☎ 2544034), near the fort entrance. Changes cash and traveler's checks. Open M-Sa 10am-2pm.

Police: District office (☎ 2200840), next to the railway station. Open 24hr.

Pharmacy: Hospitals (see below) both operate 24hr. pharmacies. Other pharmacies line Hospital Rd.

Hospital: PBM Hospital, PBM Rd. (☎2525312). Large and government-run. **MN Hospital** (☎2544122), near Karni Singh Stadium. Privately run.

Internet: Shops at Kirti Stambh Circle have the "fastest" Internet connections. Rs25 per hr. Slower connections are available at STD shops along Station Rd.

Post Office: GPO (☎2524185), behind Junagarh Fort. Open M-Sa 10am-6pm. Branches near PBM Hospital, inside Kote Gate, and near State Bank of Bikaner and Jaipur. **Postal Code:** 334001.

ACCOMMODATIONS

Most of Bikaner's budget options are clustered on Station and GS Rd., but these can be pretty lackluster. The tourist office can arrange **homestays** with local families (Rs80-750 per night). A lethargic tourist industry keeps hotel prices steady year-round, except during the annual Camel Festival, when prices skyrocket.

Vijay Guest House, Jaipura Rd. (☎2231244; camelman_vijay@rediffmail.com), opposite Sophia School. Consummate hosts Vijay and Daisy offer outstanding service, a complimentary rum cocktail hour, and large, clean suites. Many guests overstay their itinerary. Complimentary use of motorbike, scooter, or bicycle. Also runs camel safaris (see p. 548). Double rooms with attached hot-water bath Rs100-400. ❶

Hotel Palace View (☎2543625; opnain_jpl@sancharnet.in), just off the palace grounds. Clean, well-decorated rooms with sitting areas and spotless bathrooms. Good restaurant. Rooms Rs300-550, with A/C Rs600-800. ❷

Hotel Desert Winds (☎2542202), opposite Karni Singh Stadium, next to MN Hospital. Small, 7-room guest house run by the former Deputy Director of RTDC. Large, bright rooms all with attached bath. Doubles Rs250-350, with A/C Rs450-550. ❷

Hotel Kishan Palace, 8B Gajner Rd. (☎2527762). Budget rooms of varying sizes away from the Station Rd. bustle. Better than any of the Station Rd. hotels. All with attached hot-water baths. Free pickup. Very basic rooms Rs80-200, with fresh linens and A/C Rs350-650. ❶

Adarsh Paying Guest House, GS Rd. (☎2548716). Tiny place with basic rooms in a family environment. Most rooms have attached baths (hot water by the bucket). Checkout 24hr. Singles Rs80-130; doubles Rs100-180. ❶

FOOD

Moomal Restaurant, Panch Sebi Circle, 2km from the city center, on the way to the Camel Breeding Farm. A large, air-cooled veg. restaurant serves everybody's favorite Indian dishes: well worth the 20min. walk. Fast service. Entrees Rs40-70, *dosas* Rs20-40. Open daily 11am-3pm and 6:30-10:30pm. ❷

Hotel Sagar, near Lalgarh Palace. Opposite the bus station. Quiet restaurant in a mid-priced hotel. A tad expensive, but the food and service make up for it. Veg. dishes Rs40-75. Open daily 6am-11pm. ❷

Tripti Restaurant, Hospital Rd., Ambedkar Circle. A popular local haunt with a bizarre thatched-hut-meets-blacklight decor. Entrees Rs30-60, South Indian snacks Rs20-48. Open daily 10am-10pm. ❷

Amber Restaurant, Station Rd. Very conveniently located. Decent food is popular with tourists. *Dosas* Rs20-38, veg. dishes Rs35-58. Open daily 6am-10pm. ❷

Metro Restaurant, at the front of the fort near Sadul Singh Circle. Tri-level, air-cooled restaurant. Veg. dishes Rs30-70, non-veg. Rs40-150. Open daily 8am-10:30pm. ❷

👁 SIGHTS

OLD CITY. A stroll through the old city is an essential component of any visit to Bikaner. The wealth brought in by camel caravans is reflected in over 200 towering *havelis;* those of the **Ramapuria Estate,** on Jail Rd., near Kotwali police station, are of particular interest. The only portion of the complex that is open to the public is the Hotel Bhanwar Niwas. You may be able to sneak a peek by feigning interest in a room, but you'll have to admire the rest of the estate from outside.

JUNAGARH FORT. Rajasthan certainly has no shortage of forts, but Bikaner truly has one of the most magnificent. Along with Meherangarh at Jodhpur, **Junagarh** is one of Rajasthan's two forts to have undergone significant restoration. Built in 1589 by Rai Singh, it is one of the few in the country that has never been conquered, despite the fact that it doesn't command a hilltop position. The fort is a solid structure whose 986m long wall is capped with 37 bastions and surrounded by a 9m-wide moat. Near the second fort gate, **Daulat Pol,** are 24 handprints, left behind by the women who performed *sati* here after their husbands perished in an attempt to hold off a siege. The fort's main entrance, the **Suraj Pol** (Sun Gate), is a large iron-spiked door flanked by two stone elephants.

The fort is an intricate complex of 37 palaces, courtyards, pavilions, and temples. The **Karan Mahal,** built after an important victory over the Mughal army of Emperor Aurangzeb, features gold-leaf paintings and the silver throne of Lord Karan Singh. The breathtaking **Anup Mahal,** decorated by the same artist, boasts Italian tiles, inlaid mirrors, and more intricate gold-leaf paintings. Upstairs in the **Gaj Mandir** is the **Sheesh Mahal** (Mirror Palace), the Maharaja's glittering bedroom. **Hanuman Temple** is filled with an array of swords, saws, spears, and nails, which are danced upon every January by fakirs from neighboring villages. The **Phool Mahal** (Flower Palace) was constructed under Gaj Singh a hundred years later. The **Chandra Mahal** (Moon Palace) is a beautifully painted *puja* room adorned with representations of Hindu gods and goddesses. These last two rooms are under restoration but can be accessed with a donation to one of the tour guides. The **Ganga Singh Hall,** the last portion of the fort, houses a **museum** with a collection of weapons and various relics including a World War I biplane. *(Open daily 10am-5pm. Rs50; camera fee Rs30; video fee Rs100. Guides may barrage you as you approach the entrance but are by no means necessary, a guided tour is included in the price of admission.)*

Also in the fort complex is the **Prachina Museum,** which displays, among other things, portraits of the Bikaneri royal family and a beautiful array of traditional embroidered dresses. *(Open daily 9am-6pm. Rs25.)*

LALGARH PALACE. This red sandstone palace was designed in 1902 for Maharaja Ganga Singh, in commemoration of his late father, Lal Singh. The royal family of Bikaner still lives in part of the palace, two luxury hotels take up some more space, and the **Sri Sadul Museum** occupies the rest. The museum is essentially a shrine to the House of Bikaner's three greatest and most beloved rulers, Maharaja Ganga Singh (r.1887-1943), his son Maharaja Sadul Singh (r.1943-1950), and his grandson Maharaja Karini Singh (r.1950-88). Its corridors and halls are filled with everything from a picture of Ganga Singh signing the Treaty of Versailles to his grandson's personal effects, including an electric toothbrush and a rifle from the 1960 Olympics. *(3km north of the city, near the Central Bus Stand. Palace tours at Laxmi Niwas Hotel daily 8am-7pm. Free. Museum open M-Sa 10am-5pm. Rs20.)*

JAIN TEMPLES. In the southern end of the old city, past a spice market, stand two extraordinary 16th-century Jain temples. The first, the stunning **Bhandeshwar Temple,** is decorated with gilded-floral motifs painted by Persian artists from Emperor

HE LOCAL LEGEND

TURBAN LEGENDS

Once upon a time, no one wore turbans in India. This changed forever when the turbanned Mughals poured into northern India in 1526, an invasion that sent shockwaves through the world of South Asian fashion. Originally worn as a sign of respect when one appeared before a Mughal official, turbans soon became a symbol of the Sikh religion and an indicator of status among high-caste Hindus. In Rajasthan today, turban colors and styles vary according to region. In Bikaner, Brahmins wear a yellow turban except when mourning, when they cut their hair off and switch to white. Bikaner Rajputs, a *kshariya* caste, wear brightly colored, striped, or *bandhani* (tie-dyed) turbans wrapped around one ear with a long tail in the back. Jats and Bishnois, the farming castes, wear enormous white turbans called *safas*. *Vaishya* castes wear small turbans known as *pagoris*. Untouchables and *shudras* are not allowed to wrap their heads at all. Turbans can be deeply symbolic; exchanging turbans signifies deep friendship; placing one's turban at another's feet is a request for mercy; and having one's turban forcibly removed in public (as is often done with debtors and criminals) brings great shame. In earlier times, the value of a turban was sometimes literal as well as symbolic; earlier moneylenders often made loans only after mortgaging the borrower's turban!

Akbar's court. Fifty years, 500 laborers, and 40,000kg of ghee went into its construction. The ghee was used in place of water to make the temple's cement foundation. Each of the temple's three floors houses different tirthankara idols, a total of 12; the other 12 (the Jain religion features 24 prophets in total) are housed in the neighboring **Sandeshwar Temple.** This smaller temple isn't nearly as amazing as the main one, but has some nice carvings and painted pillars. Next to the Jain complex is the Hindu **Laxminath Temple,** a carved stone temple with superb views of the desert and city. (*Bhandeshwar and Sandeshwar temples open daily 7am-1pm and 4-8pm. Free; camera fee Rs20; video fee Rs30. Laxminath Temple open daily 6am-1pm and 5:30-10:30pm. Free. No socks, shorts, umbrellas, watches, cameras, or leather goods.*)

☈ SAFARIS

Although the industry here cannot compare with the one in Jaisalmer, camel safaris have grown increasingly popular in Bikaner. Three-day loops around Deshnok are most popular; also common are longer safaris to Phalodi (6 days) and Jaisalmer (13-14 days). This latter, one-way trip typically involves a camel cart, which accommodates heavy luggage and weary bums. The best valued safaris are run by **The Camel Man** Vijay Singh Rathore, whose safaris include tasty meals, mineral water, tents, mattresses, a camel cart, and jeep transport. Most also include an English-speaking guide and a musical performance. Vijay organizes trips out of his guest house. (☎231244; www.camelman.com. Safaris Rs600-900.) The lower-end safaris (including those operated by the agencies below) do not include any jeep transport or mineral water. A few hotels organize safaris, but book directly through independent agencies to avoid commission headaches. Friendly Vinod Bhojak runs **Vino Desert Safari** and organizes safaris for Rs450-650 per day. Vinod operates out of his guest house, near Gopeshwar Temple, a 15min. walk south of the old city. (☎270445; www.vinodesertsafari.com. Open daily 8am-5pm.)

☞ SHOPPING

Bikaner is a good place to shop for **handicrafts.** The main commercial areas are **KEM Road** and the **old city.** Cloth and textile stores are clustered just inside Kote Gate on the left. The government-approved **Abhivyakti,** recently relocated to outside the camel breeding farm (see below), sells handicrafts from villages around the city. (Open M-Sa 3-5pm.)

DAYTRIPS FROM BIKANER

DEVIKUND SAGAR
8km west of Bikaner.

This area contains the marble and red sandstone *chhattris* (cenotaphs) of Bikaner rulers and their wives and mistresses, whose handprints commemorate their self-sacrifice. The women's spirits are worshipped at a *sati* temple. It all surrounds a tranquil lake inhabited by pigeons and peacocks.

CAMEL RESEARCH AND BREEDING FARM
10km south of the city. ☎ 230070. Round-trip auto-rickshaw Rs80, including 45min. wait. Open M-Sa 3-5pm. Free; camera fee Rs10. Government-authorized guides Rs50 per person.

The largest camel research and breeding farm in Asia, with an average population of 280 camels, produces 50% of India's bred camels. In the afternoon, visitors are allowed to watch the camels' mass procession back to the farm. The trip is most worthwhile during breeding season (Dec.-Mar.), when there are lots of baby camels. A walk around the grounds includes a tour of the stud quarters, where overeager male camels fidget and froth at the mouth in anticipation. In season they bear the responsibility of inseminating up to six or seven female camels per day.

KARNI MATA TEMPLE (RAT TEMPLE)
In Deshnok, 30km from Bikaner. The temple is accessible by taxi (Rs200 round-trip), and by bus from Bikaner (45min., every 30min. 4:45am-12:30am, Rs11-13). Open daily 4am-10pm. Camera fee Rs20; video fee Rs50.

According to local legend, the patron deity of Bikaner, Karni Mata, was asked to resurrect her favorite nephew. She summoned Yama, the god of death, who told her that the boy had been reborn as a rat and that all her male descendants would be born as rats in her temple at Deshnok. As a result thousands of holy rats run rampant at the feet of worshippers, who bask in their footsteps. The temple's magnificent solid silver gate was donated by Maharaja Ganga Singh. The best time to visit is during the Navratri festival in March, when the temple swarms with people (and rats).

SIKKIM

सिक्किम

Shambhala, Tazik, Shangri-La—whatever you want to call it, most people agree that Sikkim is heaven. Its natural beauty is unparalleled. The tropical valleys support rice, mustard, papaya, wheat, and millet farming, while vertical ridges hide small villages and monasteries. Bordered by Nepal, Tibet, and Bhutan, the state's cultural bounty is just as appealing; the native Lepchas peacefully coexist with Tibetan Bonpos and Bhutanis. Sikkim is so peaceful, in fact, that it once appeared in the *Guinness Book of World Records* for going 10 years without a single criminal case. Perhaps the most charming aspect of the state, however, is its seclusion. Because foreigners are only allowed to visit for a limited period of time, the state has thus far escaped the crushing tourist influx of neighboring Nepal.

Hindu Nepalis currently represent 75% of the population, although Sikkim, which is home to over 250 monasteries, is historically a Buddhist kingdom with close ties to Tibet. The earliest known inhabitants of Sikkim were the Naong, Chang, and Mon tribes. The Lepchas arrived from the north sometime around the 8th century. A second wave of immigration 500 years later brought the Bhutia people from Tibet, who set themselves up as rulers and appointed the first *chogyal* (king) of Sikkim in 1641. The British protectorate, begun in 1861, brought Hindu Nepalis to Sikkim to work on tea plantations, and they soon outnumbered the Lepchas and Tibetans. This ethnic diversity has resulted in a friendly confluence of cultures. People from the flatlands to the south are "Indian," while those who grew up in the mountains identify themselves by their ancestry: Nepalese, Bhutanese, Tibetan, or Lepcha.

When India became independent in 1947, Sikkim was made a semi-independent Indian protectorate. Strife between the traditional monarchy and mainly Nepalese middle class caused the *chogyal* to ask the Indian government to intervene. The result was a 1975 referendum, in which 97% of Sikkim's electorate voted to become India's 22nd province. Many Sikkimese, however, resent Indian dominion. Some even accuse the Indian government of staging the internal conflict as an excuse to bring in the troops and take over. There is still a *chogyal* of Sikkim, but he has retired to a monastery and holds no official power. Sikkim has only recently opened its borders to tourists, and it still remains largely undiscovered. The government has carefully fostered an eco-friendly tourism industry that also respects and preserves Sikkimese cultural traditions; a visit to Sikkim is refreshingly hassle-free and tranquil. The best times to visit are from late March to May, when the flowers are in bloom, and October to November, when clear views are guaranteed. **Visitors to Sikkim must obtain permits first** (see **Sikkim Permits**, p. 552).

HIGHLIGHTS OF SIKKIM

Peaceful **Pelling** (p. 559) is a good place to relax and soak up the views, or to begin the scenic, four-day **Local Trek** (p. 561) for some breathtaking views.

Headquarters of the *karma-pa* sect of Tibetan Buddhism, the hilltop village of **Rumtek** (p. 557) is an ideal spot to sit back, relax, and watch the vegetables grow.

Sikkim

TIBET (CHINA)

Kanchenjunga
8586m

Lachen

Yumthang

Lachung

Kabru
7338m

NEPAL

Chungthang

SIKKIM

Mangan

0 ———— 10 miles

0 ———— 10 kilometers

Phensang

Khechopari
Lake

Yuksam

Phodong

Nathu La

Rathong River

Tashiding

Rumtek

Tsomgo
Lake

Pelling

Geyzing

Kewzing

Gangtok

Legship

Singtam

Namchi

Rangpo

BHUTAN

Jorethang

Melli

Govt. of India statement:
The external boundaries
of India are neither correct
nor authenticated.

WEST BENGAL

Kalimpong

GANGTOK ग्याङटोक   ☎ 03592

Carved out of the hillside, Sikkim's capital is dwarfed by its spectacular surroundings. Though by Sikkimese standards Gangtok is a big, noisy city, it still manages to maintain the relaxed and friendly atmosphere that is characteristic of the entire state. In addition to being a good base for trips to neighboring attractions like Rumtek Monastery and Tsomgo Lake, Gangtok also has monasteries, vista points, and other sights of its own to offer. The tourist industry dominates the town's infrastructure so thoroughly that you can't throw a stone without hitting an agency. As such, this is the best place to shop around for both organized treks and store-bought goods and supplies, to extend Sikkim permits, and to send off a batch of emails. You'll also be able to find plenty of information about other destinations in Sikkim from the tourist office, travel agencies, and other travelers.

▐ TRANSPORTATION

Flights: The nearest airport is **Bagdogra,** near Siliguri. **Josse and Josse,** MG Rd. (☎224682; jossegtk@hotmail.com), next to Raj Enterprise, are authorized agents for Jet Airways, Indian Airlines, Sahara Air, and Necon Air. Open daily M-Sa 8:30am-8pm, Su 8:30am-2pm. The proprietor of the **Green Hotel,** MG Rd. (☎225057), is a sub-agent for Indian Airlines and Jet Airways.

Trains: The **railway reservations window,** at the south end of the SNT Bus Terminal, can make reservations for any train in India. Open M-Sa 8am-2pm, Su 8am-11am.

Buses: Sikkim Nation Transport (SNT) Bus Terminal (☎222016), down from the National Hwy., at the north end of town. Book tickets early (the previous day for morning departure) at the far left window. Open daily 5:30am-4pm. The crowded **buses** are the cheapest and slowest mode of transport. To: **Geyzing** (6hr., 7am, Rs70); **Jorethang** (4hr., 7am, Rs55); **Kalimpong** (4hr., 7:15am, Rs55); **Namchi** (4hr., 7:15am and 2pm, Rs55); **Rumtek** (1½hr., 4pm, Rs17); **Siliguri** (4½hr., 7 per day 6am-12:15pm, Rs70-90). **Shared jeeps,** also called "private buses" by locals, are available at the private bus stand, on the National Highway just south and downhill from the tourist office. Shared jeeps make more frequent trips than buses and are faster and more expensive. To: **Darjeeling** (4hr., every hr. 6am-2pm, Rs100); **Kakarbhitta** at the Nepal border (4½hr.; 6, 7, and 8am; Rs130); **Kalimpong** (3hr., every hr. 7am-3pm, Rs70); **Pelling** (5hr., 7 and 8am, Rs130); **Rumtek** (1hr., frequent 7am-4pm, Rs25), **Siliguri** (3½hr., every ½hr. 6am-5pm, Rs100).

Local Transportation: Mini-van taxis run up and down the National Highway and side along the north end of MG Rd., near the tourist office. Negotiate first; it shouldn't cost more than Rs25 to traverse the city. **Shared taxis** run from Gangtok to Deorali, 2km down the road, for Rs7.

SIKKIM PERMITS. The Sikkim permit process can seem endlessly bureaucratic, but in fact, it's pretty simple. Most people only need the basic permit, called an ILP (Inner Line Permit), which is free and can be obtained instantly from the Sikkim Tourist Office in New Delhi, Kolkata, or Siliguri. Bring a passport photo. You can get a similar permit in Darjeeling with more hassle but without a passport photo.

The easiest option way to get a Sikkim permit is to apply for one along with your Indian visa. The permit is then stamped onto the visa and begins when you arrive in Sikkim. An equally painless alternative for those heading to Gangtok is to get a permit at the border post at Rangpo. Passport photo required. Regardless of where you obtain the permit, it's valid for 15 days and allows for travel in the southern half of Sikkim: Gangtok, Mangan, Geyzing, Namchi, Soveng, Ravangla, Pakyong, Rongli, Singhik, Yuksam, and Tashiding, as well as other towns inside this boundary. Permit Extensions are available from the Foreigner Registration Office in Gangtok and the District Administrative Office in Tikjuk, near Pelling. You are allowed up to two extensions (a total stay of 45 days). Apply for an extension a few days before your permit runs out. After your permit expires, you'll have to wait three months until you can enter Sikkim again.

Permits, as well as passports and visas, are checked at the Sikkim border. Beyond a basic area permit, all special permits *must* be handled through a tourist agency. There are two kinds of special permits: a PAP (Protected Area Permit) and a Trekking Permit. Special permits are only available in Gangtok and require a minimum of four people. The PAP covers destinations like Tsomgo Lake (one-day) and Yumthang (five-day). **Sikkim permits are only issued for tourism,** so if you're in Sikkim for another reason (religious pilgrimage, studying the flowers), it's best to just lump it all under "tourism" when applying for a permit.

⚫✶⚡ ORIENTATION AND PRACTICAL INFORMATION

The **National Highway** cuts northeast, diagonally up the hill, with roads branching off horizontally above and below. The **SNT Bus Terminal** is 100m off the highway at the northern end of town. **Mahatma Gandhi (MG) Road,** which serves as the center of town, branches south off the highway, 50m downhill from the intersection that leads to the SNT Bus Terminal. The large, hard-to-miss **tourist center** sits at the intersection of MG Rd. and the highway. A road which leads up from the tourist office passes the giant **Lal Market** to join **Tibet Road,** which is where most of the backpacker-friendly hotels are located. If you're coming to town by jeep, you'll arrive at the **private bus stand,** on the National Highway just south of and downhill from the tourist center. MG Rd. continues further south to a four-way intersection: the road on the left is the downhill end of Tibet Rd., the road on the right leads down to a **local jeep stand,** and MG Marg continues straight ahead to become **Naya Bazaar,** with a particularly dense concentration of shops.

Tourist Office: National Tourist Centre (☎223425 or 221634), at the corner of MG Rd. and the highway. In addition to providing helpful information and brochures, the office also organizes 20min. helicopter tours of Kanchenjunga (4-person flight Rs25,000). Open M-Sa 10am-4pm, Office open in season daily 9am-7pm; off-season open M-Sa 10am-4pm, closed Su and every second Sa.

Sikkim Permit: Getting a Sikkim Permit extension is a fairly painless process at the **Foreigner's Registration Office.** To get there follow, Tibet Rd. downhill toward its southern intersection with MG Marg, but before reaching the end bear left up the set of steps climbing to Kazi Rd.; turn right on Kazi and follow it until you see a path leading down and around to the office, which is marked with a yellow sign. Open 10am-4pm M-Sa, 10am-noon Su and every second Sa.

Tours: Tour companies provide comprehensive trek services, including permits, guides, and equipment. Tours cost around US$25 per day. One professional operation is **Modern Tours and Treks,** MG Rd. (☎227319; moderntreks@hotmail.com), in the same bldg. as the Gangtok Lodge, opposite the tourist office. Run by the proprietors of the Modern Central Hotel, the tours are mid-range in price and well-equipped. Open daily 7am-8pm. **River rafting** in the Teesta River is popular; tour agencies, including several along MG Rd., organize trips. **Brothers Tours and Travels** (☎224220; www.brothertours.com), along the west side of Lal Bazaar, among the vegetable stands, specializes in rafting and trips on the Teesta and Rangit Rivers from Sept.-May. Four person minimum. Daytrips Rs550 per person; Rs750 with food and transport. 2-day trips Rs1850; equipment, food, and transport included.

Currency Exchange: State Bank of India, MG Rd. (☎222824), opposite the tourist office. Changes AmEx and Thomas Cook traveler's checks and cash on the 3rd fl. (Rs100 commission). Open M-F 10am-2pm and 2:30-4pm, Sa 10am-1pm.

Police: (☎222033; emergency 100), on the National Hwy. across from the tourist office.

Pharmacy: There are a number of pharmacies along MG Rd. and Naya Bazaar. Locals often go to **Chiranjilal Lalchand Pharmacy,** MG Rd. (☎229680), opposite the Green Hotel. Open daily 8:30am-8:30pm.

Hospital: Sir Thutab Namgyal Memorial (STNM) Hospital, National Hwy. (☎222059), 50m north of the tourist office. Enter via the footbridge overpass.

Internet: Though often crowded, the cheapest place for Internet in Gangtok is the unassuming **Dot Com,** Tibet Rd., 20m uphill from the Modern Central Lodge. Rs30 per hr. Open daily 8:30am-8pm. More upscale and with slightly more reliable connections is **Somani Cyber-Cafe,** MG Marg (☎223813), 100m south of the intersection with Tibet Rd. Rs40 per hr. Open daily 8:30am-8pm.

Post Office: (☎225668), halfway down the road leading to the SNT Terminal from the National Hwy. Open M-F 9am-3pm, Sa 9am-2pm. **Postal Code:** 737101.

SIKKIM

▛ ACCOMMODATIONS

Many of Gangtok's hotels cater to wealthier Indian tourists, and the few budget places are usually crowded. Always ask for a discount—many managers take pity on travelers. Consider staying near the **Rumtek Monastery** (see p. 557), 24km away. During peak season (Sept.-Dec. and Mar.-May), prices rise and hotels fill up.

▨ **Kewzing Home,** Helipad Bye Pass Rd. (☎223702 or 223735; www.discoversikkim.com/kewzing.htm). From the bottom of the hill past the SNT Bus Terminal, take the upper fork in the direction of the big sign to "Holiday Hill." Kewzing is a 4-story yellow bldg. with prayer flags 150m down the road, past the small bridge. The 4 rooms have attached baths, hot water, and TVs. Guests are invited to eat with the family and relax in the living room with mug of millet *chang*. ❷

Modern Central Lodge, Tibet Rd. (☎224670; www.modernhospitality.com). Go up the road that climbs up from MG Rd. opposite the tourist office. At its end, turn left on Tibet Rd. and walk 100m up. Very popular with backpackers, and for good reason. The front rooms have nice views of the valley, there's a TV room upstairs, and the restaurant serves tasty meals. Dorms Rs40-50; singles Rs150; doubles Rs180, with toilet Rs200, with toilet and hot shower Rs250. Bargain, particularly off-season. ❶

Gangtok Lodge, MC Marg (☎226562), near State Bank of India. A sightly more upscale offering than Modern Central Lodge under the same management. Centrally located, with comfortable rooms, all with attached bath. Rs300, with satellite TV Rs350. ❷

Green Hotel, MG Marg (☎224439 or 225057). In the dead center of town, Green is a convenient and popular spot with tourists. Has STD, fax, travel agency, money changer, restaurant, and TV. Rooms range in quality but all have attached baths with hot shower. Singles Rs150-250; doubles Rs250-450. Off-season: up to 50% discount. MC/V. ❷

Travel Lodge, Tibet Rd. (☎223858), 50m south of the Modern Central. Big, spotless, lime-green rooms all have attached baths, carpets, and TVs; some with balconies. Breakfast, lunch, tea, and dinner Rs350 per day. Doubles Rs380, with balcony Rs480; triples Rs680; quads Rs780. 10% service charge. Off-season 30% discount. ❸

Hotel Mig-Tin, Tibet Rd. (☎224101), 200m south of the Modern Central. Clean and roomy doubles have attached baths with seat toilets and hot water. The upstairs rooms have terrific views of Gangtok and the hills beyond. Dorms Rs100; singles Rs400; doubles Rs500. Off-season: rooms Rs200-300. ❶

▛ FOOD

Food can be expensive in Gangtok. Bulk foods for hiking are available along **Naya Bazaar,** which has the best selection in Sikkim. Fresh fruits and vegetables can be purchased at the giant party that is Lal Bazaar.

▨ **Roll House,** from MG Marg, go 10m down the narrow side street across from the Thali Restaurant, under the sign for the Sarda Emporium. In addition to the fastest and cheapest *momos* and chow mein you're likely to find anywhere, this hole-in-the-wall lunch counter also offers its own unique "rolls:" vegetables, egg, or cheese rolled up inside a fried *chappati*. There's no place to sit, but you won't be waiting long. Plate of 8 *momos* Rs10, chow mein Rs10, rolls Rs10-30. Open daily 7am-7pm. ❶

Snow Lion Restaurant, Paljor Stadium Road (☎222523), on the road to the SNT Bus Station, inside Hotel Tibet. A good place if you're looking for a place to take your sweetheart or just craving creme caramel. Though pricey, it has a vast menu of well-prepared Chinese, Tibetan, and Indian dishes and the elegant dining area features the intricate wood carvings and colorful painting usually reserved for monasteries. Most entrees Rs65-85; whole mandarin fish Rs435; creme caramel Rs40. 5% service charge. ❸

Hungry Jack Restaurant, National Hwy. (☎228138), south of the lower taxi and private bus stand, beyond the gas pumps. Elegant, spacious, western-style restaurant and bar. The portions are as generous as the name suggests. North Indian entrees Rs20-50, sandwiches Rs25-50. 10% tax. Open daily 8am-8:30pm. ❶

Crispy Cuisine, MG Rd., 10m south of the Tibet Rd. intersection. A pleasant place overlooking a busy corner of MG Marg. Serves Indian and Tibetan, and a particularly strong and varied selection of Chinese dishes (Rs30-65). Open daily 8am-7pm. ❷

Parivar Restaurant, MG Rd. (☎227409), in the basement of the Yama bldg., 100m south of the tourist office. This all-veg. restaurant is popular with Indians. It serves standard favorites at reasonable prices. *Paneer kofta* Rs32. Open daily 8am-9pm. ❷

Blue Sheep Restaurant, MG Marg, next door to the tourist office. Actually two restaurants in one. The fast-food joint downstairs, while neither fast nor especially cheap, is a convenient place to grab a familiar bite, while the posh restaurant upstairs has a classier atmosphere and an extensive menu. Fast food: chow mein Rs30-40, fish and chips Rs35. Open 8:30am-7pm. ❷

Durga and **Laxmi Sweets,** MG Rd., across and a bit south from the Green Hotel. A popular pair of adjacent snack shops. Pastries Rs5-10. Open daily 7am-8pm. ❶

ⓒ SIGHTS

Many of the sights can be visited on foot or by taxi, and many tour agencies also operate whirlwind tours (Rs300-600). Contact the Tourist Department (see p. 553) for more information. Also, look for the helpful *Gangtok in a Nutshell* (Rs30), a map guide available in some stationery stores around the city.

SIKKIM INSTITUTE OF TIBETOLOGY AND DO DRUL CHORTEN. The nearby town of Deorali is home to a hilltop complex containing the enormous **Do Drul Chorten,** the **Sikkim Institute of Tibetology,** and a flower garden that has orchids and giant ferns. The Institute, founded by the Dalai Lama in 1957, contains one of the largest collections of documents in the world. The upper-floor library houses roughly 30,000 volumes of Tibetan documents (mostly wooden boards called xylographs). Of greater interest to non-scholars is the ground-floor collection of *thankas*, but there are also some macabre ritual items, such as *kanglings* (wind instruments made from human thighbones) and a *kapala* (bowl made from a human skull). Further up the hill, the impressive Do Drul Chorten, surrounded by 108 prayer wheels, is one of the

ON THE MENU

CHANG-TASTIC

Cheaper, somewhat tastier, and alleged to be more potent than beer, Sikkimese millet chang is a regional delicacy, traditionally served in a bamboo or stainless steel jug called a *tomba*. The drink is prepared by pouring hot water on the fermented millet and then letting it settle for two or three minutes, after which time the juicy mixture can be sucked up through a special filtered straw.

In order to make chang, locals have to stock up on some millet (*mincha* in Bhutia, *kodo* in Nepali) and *pho* (yeast). The millet is then washed and soaked, after which it must be carefully sorted through to remove any stray sand and pebbles. Millet is like rice in that it is allowed to cool for a couple of hours, followed by grinding the pho and mixing it into the millet. To exacerbate the difficulty of making the delicacy, the millet mixture is then wrapped in cloth and left to sit for two nights, only to be followed by a one- or two-week fermenting session.

IN RECENT NEWS

ENVIRONMENTAL CONSERVATION: KEEPING SIKKIM GREEN

With the central government preoccupied by pervasive poverty, disputed borders, and inter-ethnic conflict, it is little wonder that India's environmental health is often overlooked. Token cleanup efforts such as the "Keep India Green" postering campaign in India's urban centers have proven unsuccessful as the mounds of refuse keep growing. In Sikkim, however, environmental action is no joke. In 1999, the state's Chief Minister Pawan Kumar Chamling was honored by environmentalists as India's most green-friendly state head when he instituted a complete ban on the use of plastic bags. In recognizing Chamling, the Centre for Science and Environment expressed hope that the rest of India might soon follow suit.

Forty-three percent of Sikkim is covered by forests, many of which are protected lands. For more information about environmental conservation in India or to subscribe to their newsletter, visit the Centre for Science and the Environment's website, www.cseindia.org.

most important *stupas* in Sikkim. Below the institute is a flower garden, with a number of benches. *(Deorali is 2km south of Gangtok on the National Hwy. Institute ☎ 222525. Open M-Sa 10am-4pm. Rs5. Chorten and Garden free.)*

ENCHEY MONASTERY. The Enchey Monastery is on the landing spot of Lama Druptob Karpo, who is said to have flown over from Maenam Hill over 200 years ago. The building itself dates from 1909 and has beautiful views of Kanchenjunga, and Gangtok. The main hall is small but richly decorated, with a large statue of Sakyamuni Buddha. *(Next to the TV Tower, a 30min. walk from downtown Gangtok. Head uphill to Ridge Rd., and walk north past the White Hall. At the rotary, follow the sign pointing to Raj Bhawan; when you see the Raj Bhawan arch take a right towards the Siniokhu Lodge and follow the winding road to the monastery. Open to the public M-Sa 6am-4pm.)*

TSUGLA KHANG. The murals of the **Tsugla Khang**, or Royal Chapel, enclose collections of scriptures. Generally, the monastery and chapel are not open to tourists, but you may be able to peek through an open window at the elaborate murals and carvings inside. *(Inside the royal palace complex at the south end of Ridge Rd., overlooking Bhanu Path and the government offices of Tashiling.)*

GANESH TOK AND THE HIMALAYAN ZOOLOGICAL PARK. A 30min. walk from Enchey monastery, **Ganesh Tok** ("Tok" means ridge) provides great views of the city and surrounding valleys. At the viewpoint itself there is a small shrine and a paved platform with benches. Just across the road is the sprawling **Himalayan Zoological Park.** An "immersion exhibit," the animals are housed in relatively large pockets of forest spread across the ridge. While you'll be lucky to see many animals, the walks along the wooded paths are enjoyable in themselves. *(With your back to the entrance to Enchey monastery, turn right road downhill towards the sharp bend. From here, take the rougher path leading up the hill. Continue uphill until the jeep road. From here the viewpoint is a short walk to the left. Zoo open daily 8am-4pm. Admission Rs10.)*

FLOWER EXHIBITION CENTRE. The best time to visit this indoor garden is in March, during the annual flower show, when orchids and other blooming beauties vie for top honors. The flowers remain on display until June and are brought out again Oct.-Dec. With a pool full of carp and plenty of benches, it's a quiet place to spend a few moments relaxing or reading. *(On Ridge Rd., just south of the White Hall. Open daily 8am-5pm. Entrance fee Rs5; camera fee Rs5.)*

SHOPPING

The government-run **Directorate of Handicrafts and Handloom** serves as a "factory" for handicrafts and furniture. Follow the National Hwy. 20min. north of the tourist office. (Showroom open M-Sa 10am-4pm.) The best local market for everything from prayer flags to potatoes is **Lal Market,** in the huge complex between MG Marg and Tibet Rd., uphill from the tourist office.

⚡ DAYTRIPS FROM GANGTOK

RUMTEK

The SNT bus (1½hr., 4pm, Rs20) is the cheapest option, although you can take a shared jeep (45min., Rs25) or a taxi (round-trip Rs400, including 1hr. wait; Rs250 one-way).

Rumtek is a tranquil village only 24km away, on the opposite side of the valley from Gangtok. The centerpiece of the town is the **Rumtek Monastery,** the headquarters of the Karma-pa (Black Hat) sect of the Kagyu-pa order of Tibetan Buddhism. Forced to flee Tibet, after the Chinese invasion, the sect's leader, the 16th Gyalwa Karmapa, chose Rumtek to be the site of his new headquarters. Built in the 1960s, the monastery is modeled on the main Kagyu-pa monastery in Tsorpu, Tibet. The main hall of the monastery houses a large statue of Sakyamuni Buddha, flanked on either side by his disciples Shariputra and Mangalputra. Ensconced in the back walls are hundreds of small Buddha statues representing all the Buddhas that will come to the world. In front of the statues are the thrones of the Karmapa, his regents, and other Rinpoches. At the center of the monastery courtyard stands a pillar on which the history of the monastery is inscribed in Tibetan. The building directly behind the main monastery houses the **Golden Stupa,** protected by a glass window and surrounded by elaborate *thankas*. The *stupa* contains the remains of the 16th Gyalwa Karmapa, who died in 1981.

Behind the monastery is the **Karmae Shri Nalanda Institute for Higher Buddhist Studies,** opened in 1981 and affiliated with the Sanskrit University of Varanasi. There is a small **Buddha Shrine** in the courtyard, and you might be allowed into the shrine room on the 4th fl. Step outside and you can grab a cup of tea (Rs5) and challenge the monks to a game of carom.

Following the path up and past the monastery to the left will lead you on a wood hike that affords views of the monastery complex and surrounding countryside.

The Rumtek Monastery is also the site of a number of important Buddhist **pujas** and **chaam** mask dances. The best times to visit are around *Losar* (in February) and on the 10th day of the fifth month of the Tibetan calendar (sometime in July). Check with the tourist office in Gangtok for events. A 20min. walk along the main road past the police check-post is the smaller but still impressive **Old Monastery,** where the 16th Gyalwa Karmapa practiced for a short time before the construction of the Rumtek monastery was completed. Restored in 1983, the Old Monastery's intricate woodcarvings and wall paintings shine in spite of its name.

Accommodations around Rumtek are cheaper and more peaceful than those in Gangtok, but they are also less convenient for those with business in the capital. The best value in town is the **Hotel 93 ❶,** tucked away (without any sign) behind the Kunga Delek, just south of the courtyard in front of the monastery. Pristine attached baths, hardwood floors, hot water showers, and majestic views grace every room. It is mainly intended for visiting monks and is almost always full during festivals. (☎252250. Doubles Rs100.) Up the hill past the check-point for the monastery is the larger and more upscale **Sun-gay Guest House ❷,** with big, sunny rooms with balconies, attached baths with hot showers, and a lively staff who serves up great food. (☎252221. Doubles Rs150.) Another good budget option is the **Sangay Hotel ❶**, further up the hill towards the monastery, run by a friendly family. (☎252238. Singles Rs60; doubles Rs100.)

▨ TSOMGO LAKE

A 1hr. jeep ride east of Gangtok (round-trip US$10; 4 person minimum). Book with any local travel agent.

Cradled at the top of some of Eastern Sikkim's highest peaks, the sacred **Tsomgo Lake** (3700m), also known as Tsonga Lake or Changu Lake, has something to offer year-round. The lake is frozen December-January, ringed with snow until April, and surrounded by wildflowers in the warmer seasons. The **jeep tour** is well worth the price. For the energetic, a short, steep hike up to the ridge overlooking the lake gives a spectacular, 360° panorama which includes the lake, the Kanchenjunga range, and the mountains of Tibet and Bhutan (4000m, 1hr. ascent, 20min. descent). Garishly decorated ▨**yaks** can trot you about the lake for Rs20-100. Tsomgo Lake also has a snack bar (*momos* and chow mein Rs20 at any of the cafeterias). Sunglasses are necessary protection from the blinding light in snowier months. A special permit is required for Tsomgo (see **Sikkim Permits,** p. 552), but your tour company should take care of it.

WESTERN SIKKIM

Most travelers to Sikkim make the small villages and vertical ridges of the west the focus of their visit, and for good reason: blessed with attractions like the Pemayangtse Monastery and Khechopalri Lake, Sikkim's natural beauty, rich cultural heritage, and serene atmosphere are deeply felt in Western Sikkim. The easiest way to enter Western Sikkim is by bus from Gangtok or Darjeeling. Transportation to the region will usually stop in Geyzing or Pelling, transit points for treks or rides to the rest of Western Sikkim. Most towns are a 5-6hr. walk apart. The trip is only slightly shorter if you travel over the roads by bus or jeep.

GEYZING गेजिङ ☎03595

Geyzing (also known as Gayzing or Gyalshing) is the district headquarters of Western Sikkim and it is the departure or termination point for many of the local buses and jeeps. It also has a number of facilities (e.g. a hospital) unavailable elsewhere. The town has no tourist appeal (aside, perhaps, from its **Sunday markets**), and new arrivals would do better to head up the hill to Pelling for a bed. Geyzing's **SNT Bus Terminal** (ticket office open daily 6:30am-4pm) is 100m downhill along the main road from the central sq., at the bend in the road. **Buses** run to: **Gangtok** (5hr., 7:30am, Rs70); via **Legship** (30min., Rs10); **Khechopalri** (3hr., 2pm, Rs30); **Siliguri** (5hr., 7:30am, Rs95) via **Jorethang** (1hr., Rs30); **Yuksam** (3hr., 2pm, Rs35) via **Tashiding** (2hr., Rs20). **Jeeps** leave from the lot uphill from the SNT Terminal; the ticket offices (open daily 6:30am-4pm) are above the lot. Most depart when full for: **Gangtok** (4hr., 7am-1pm, Rs105); **Jorethang** (1hr., 7am-4pm, Rs50); **Kakarbhitta** (5hr., 6:30am, Rs140); **Kalimpong** (3hr., 7am and 12:30pm, Rs90); **Khechopalri Lake** (2hr., 11am-1pm, Rs50); **Siliguri** (4hr., 7am and 12:30pm, Rs100); **Tashiding** (1½hr., 1pm, Rs50); **Yuksam** (3hr., 11:30am-1pm, Rs60).

Currency exchange is not available anywhere in Western Sikkim. The **police** (☎250833) in Geyzing are 25m up the steepest hill leading uphill from Kanchanjanga Hotel. Geyzing's **hospital** (☎250823), 100m up the road that curves left past Kanchanjanga Hotel, is pretty dismal. **Gupta Medical Store** (☎250289), 30m north of the main sq. along the same road, has a doctor on call 24hr. (Open daily 6am-9pm.) The **post office** is 10m off the main square. (Open M-Sa 9am-5pm.) **Postal Code:** 737111.

Accommodations in Geyzing are limited. Unless you're catching an early bus or jeep, there's no reason to stay the night. Most hotels are in the central sq. area. Your best bet is **Hotel No Name ❶**, with bright clean rooms and concrete floors. Attached bath doubles have seat toilets and cold showers. (☎250722. Singles Rs50; doubles Rs100, with attached bath Rs150.) The hotel restaurant is also one of Geyzing's nicer eating establishments (veg. chow mein Rs25, *thukpa* Rs20). A slightly less appealing alternative is the **Kanchanjanga Hotel ❶** 20m up the main road from the central sq. The big rooms are clean but bare, and all have common bath. ,(☎250789. Doubles Rs120.)

A BON-AFIDE RELIGION

Among its many wonders, Sikkim is home to Bon, one of the oldest and least understood religions in Asia, which predates Buddhism by hundreds, if not thousands, of years. Followers of Bon (known as Bonpo) adhere to the teachings of their own enlightened one, **Tonpa Shenrab.** Bon was one of Tibet's earliest organized belief systems, but the arrival of Buddhism in the 8th century did not bode well for its future. Bonpos were forced to convert or were driven from the country. Time, however, has mended the wound, and today the two religions are so remarkably similar that Bon is often considered the "Fifth Sect" of Mahayana Buddhism. Many of the rituals are similar to, if not the same as, their Buddhist counterparts; both sides claim that they invented them. However, there is one obvious difference in the direction of ritual motion: Bonpos do everything counter-clockwise, opposite from the Buddhists.

Over the years, the number of Bonpos has dwindled, and the number of contemporary adherents outside of Tibet is small. Sikkim, though, harbors a sizable population, and is home to one of the three Bon monasteries in India. The **Yungdrung Kundrakling Bon Monastery,** just outside the town of Kewzing, has a small community of monks and struggles to preserve its traditions. While the monastery is small and its facilities modest, the monks leap at the chance to show visitors around. They'll even let you sit in on their morning and evening rituals (daily 6am and 6pm), which last about 30min. At the monastery, ask for **Kalsang Nyima,** the resident painter, who speaks English.

Kewzing sits on the front road between Gangtok and Legship. From Gangtok, any Kewzing-, Legship-, Geyzing-, Pelling-, or Jorethang-bound bus or jeep will pass by the monastery, about 5km before town. While in Gangtok, you can meet with the monastery's head Lama, **Yungdrung Lama,** at his photo store opposite the tourist office, on MG Rd.

PELLING पेल्लिंग   ☎03595

An 8km drive uphill from Geyzing, Pelling is the jumping-off point for tours in Western Sikkim. Paths to Yuksam, Tashiding, and Khechopalri Lake all start from here, and the town's many comfortable accommodations can provide detailed information for trekkers. On clear days Pelling is blessed with spectacular views of Kanchenjunga and friends, and the nearby monasteries, waterfalls, archaeological ruins and Lepcha villages inspire many travelers to spend an extra day or two before continuing further north.

■ 🔁 **ORIENTATION AND PRACTICAL INFORMATION.** Upper Pelling is on the top of a ridge. Everything you'll need is there; you won't have to descend the ridge unless you're setting out for Khechopalri Lake. The best point of orientation is the town's single crossroads at the top of the ridge: roads follow the ridge east (toward Pemayangtse and Geyzing) and west (toward Sanga Choeling Monastery), and descend the ridge to the north (toward Middle Pelling) and south (toward smaller villages). Most **buses** leave from Geyzing, but a bus to **Siliguri** (5½hr., 7am, Rs105) via **Geyzing** departs daily from the SNT office in Middle Pelling. In addition to the frequent **jeeps** to **Geyzing** (30min., 6am-6pm, Rs10), there is also direct service to **Gangtok** (5hr., 6am and noon, Rs120), and **Kalimpong** (4hr., 6am, Rs100). Jeeps depart from or pass through Pelling's main intersection. For **police** or **medical** assistance, you'll have to head to Geyzing. Phones are available at **Hotel Window Park,** next to Hotel Garuda. As of March 2003, there were no **Internet** facilities in Pelling itself, but a few hotels were planning to offer Internet pending an imminent upgrade of Pelling's telephone exchange. Hotel Kabur's **Cyberzone** was ready and waiting to start. (Rs50 per hr. Open daily 7am-10pm.) You can also head to the government-run **Community Information Centre,** with a fast satellite link. (Rs20 per hr. Open M-Sa 9am-5pm, Su 10am-noon.) The Centre, along with the office for **Sikkim Permit extensions,** is in the District Administrative Office at Tikjuk, a 45min. walk from Pelling on the road to Geyzing, past the Rabdentse ruins. (Permit extensions available M-Sa 10am-4pm.) Pelling's **post office** is next door to the Sikkim Tourist Centre. (Open M-F 9am-4pm, Sa 9am-2pm.) **Postal Code:** 737113.

⌐⌐⌐ ACCOMMODATIONS AND FOOD. Upper Pelling has a range of good accommodations to suit every budget. Most can also provide up-to-date trekking and transportation information. The most popular choice among backpackers is **Hotel Garuda ❶,** Pelling's oldest, just below the town's central intersection. Staff members give out a helpful area map, and have a detailed trekking logbook and book exchange. The attached restaurant serves Sikkimese, Chinese, and continental food (dishes Rs20-40). You can store your gear here and grab a packed lunch before you go gallivanting about. (☎258319. Dorms Rs50; doubles with common bath Rs90-120, with attached bath Rs200-350.) Another great bargain is **Hotel Kabur ❶,** 50m uphill from the main intersection on the road toward Geyzing. Great views and attached baths in every room, and good advice for trekkers. (☎258504. Dorms Rs40; singles Rs50; doubles Rs100-150.) Pelling's most luxurious place to stay is the **Hotel Phamrong ❷,** also at the main intersection. Rooms feature wooden furniture, satin-covered blankets, and marble baths with hot showers. All are excellent, but the more expensive rooms have better views. Phamrong's restaurant is unquestionably the best in town, offering a set menu of Sikkimese specialties (Rs150; give 24hr. advance notice) in addition to a broad array of Chinese and Indian standards (dishes Rs30-80). (☎2582218; mailphamrong@yahoo.com. Singles Rs500-850; doubles Rs600-1050; suite Rs1500. 10% service charge.) If these prices seem steep, try the **Ladakh Guest House ❶,** 20m from the main intersection on the road toward Sanga Choeling Monastery. Rooms are basic but clean; common baths are outside. The attached restaurant is a great place to grab *momos* (Rs15) or chow mein (Rs25). (Dorms Rs50; doubles Rs100. Bucket showers Rs10.) For a change from hotel fare, **Anjela Havmor Fast Food ❶,** just off the main intersection, has all-veg. South Indian fast food and outdoor seating. (*Dosas* Rs15-30; *momos* Rs15; open daily 7am-8pm.)

VOLUNTEER OPPORTUNITIES. Up the hill from Pelling, toward Pemayangtse Monastery on the main road, is the **Denjong Padma Choeling Academy,** a school for disadvantaged Sikkimese children, many of whom are orphans. The school seeks English-speaking volunteers to teach everything from math to art, as well as help with various tasks from carpentry to computers. The school provides food and housing for its volunteers, as well as optional instruction in classical Tibetan and Nyingma Buddhism. Volunteers can extend their stays in Sikkim beyond 45 days. To find out more, drop by the school, or contact the school's director (the *lama* at the Pemayangtse Monastery), Yapo S. Yongda. (*DPC Academy, Yongda Hill, Drakchong Dzong 737113, West Sikkim, India. ☎ 250760; www.satya.com/sikkim.)*

NEAR PELLING

PEMAYANGTSE पमयाइको

The monastery is a 30min. walk from Pelling along the road to Geyzing. A sign will direct you uphill toward the monastery. Open to the public daily 7am-4pm.

Founded in 1705 by Lhatsun Chenpo, one of the three "Great Lamas" of Yuksam, the **Pemayangtse Monastery** (Monastery of the Sublime Perfect Lotus), is the third-oldest monastery in Sikkim. Currently the key *Nyingma-pa* (Red Hat) monastery, it is also one of the most artistically stunning in the region. Intricate wall paintings incorporate everything from wrathful deities to serene and detached *bodhisatt-vas*. An enormous pair of terrifying Dorje Taras guard the main room, while an enlightened Guru Padma Sambhava looks on from the top of a lotus. The monastery's centerpiece, though, is the ◪**Sang Thog Palri**, a detailed, 7m high wooden rendering of the Maha Guru's paradise. The Sang Thog Palri is encased in glass and occupies the monastery's top room. Given plenty of advance notice (at least six months), the monastery's head **lama**, Yapo S. Yongda, can arrange to host students who wish to study Buddhist philosophy, meditation, and classical Tibetan at the monastery. Contact Mr. Yongda for more details (☎ 250141).

RABDENTSE PALACE RUINS
Slightly beyond the turnoff for Pemayangtse along the road toward Geyzing, a sign points the way toward the palace. Follow the path into a meadow, and then a cobblestone path for 10min.; signs mark the way.

The second king of Sikkim, Tenzung Namgyal, moved the capital from Yuksam to this spot in 1670, and it served as the seat of royal power until 1814. On the right as you climb through the ruins are the remains of the stable and military headquarters; on the left is the site of the main throne. The view from here takes in the holiest areas of Western Sikkim, including Yuksam and Tashiding. At the top of the hill, on the right, you can see the remains of a public temple.

SANGA CHOELING MONASTERY
The monastery is about a 45min. hike from town, in the opposite direction from Pemayangtse. The road soon reaches a football field; bear left around the small hill and take the lower road when it splits in two. This path leads all the way to the monastery. The same trail continues past Sanga Choeling—it's easy to miss; watch for the faded wooden sign. The forested ridge behind it is a popular destination for day hikes.

Though it can't boast artwork as flashy as its newer neighbor at Pemayangtse, the Sanga Choeling Monastery's serene hilltop location sets it apart. Ancient pine forests surround the monastery complex, and the (literally) breathtaking climb is worth the trip. Three large statues watch over the main prayer room--and the wall paintings, many erotic, remain vivid despite their age—the Buddha on the left, Dorje Sempa in the middle, and Guru Padma Sambhava on the right. In front of the entrance to the main building, a flat rock covers a small hole. Local legend has it that this hole leads all the way to a cave near Legship, and that this cave is the source of the eerie wind that emanates from the hole. Whatever its actual source, the gusts are real: drop a few blades of grass in and watch them blow back out.

◪ TREKKING IN WESTERN SIKKIM

The best way to take in the lakes, monasteries, jungles, and villages of Western Sikkim is by foot. Though the most popular sites are connected by road, the most enjoyable (and most challenging) routes are the unmarked "shortcuts." It's easy to get lost since these trails have many branches, but there are plenty of farmers around who will help you find your way. Keep in mind that while finding dinner and a place to sleep is rarely a problem, lunch or bottled water is generally unavailable along the trail. Many hotels will provide a packed lunch for Rs20-30.

THE LOCAL TREK
The Local Trek is very popular, and with good reason. More of a walk than a trek, it is relatively easy, does not require much advance planning, and takes you to some of the most impressive sights and scenery of Western Sikkim. The trek is a four-day loop, which starts and ends in

Pelling, passing through villages along the way. Food and accommodations are available on the route, and the towns are connected by jeep service. The route described is the longest and proceeds in the more popular (and more auspicious) clockwise direction.

DAY 1 (4½-6½HR.): PELLING TO KHECHOPALRI LAKE. From the tourist office in Pelling, the road bends sharply and heads down the ridge past the Alpine Restaurant. Follow this road into lower Pelling until you see the sign for Mondol Lodge. In front of this sign, a concrete path descends to the right and heads down to the river. The concrete disappears, and the path begins to fork regularly. Almost all of the forks will take you where you want to go, but when in doubt, favor the more downhill option. The descent to the Rimbi river takes 45min. to 1½hr. At the river, there's a rickety bamboo bridge, and then the trail climbs quickly to the road. Follow the road east for about 20min., until a clearly-marked road splits off toward Khechopalri, 10km away. Numerous shortcuts traverse the initial switchbacks, and locals point them out. The road eventually levels, winds up the valley, crosses a stream, and then spins back out and around the next ridge before reaching the lake. Snacks and bottled water are available at some of the roadside villages.

Khechopalri Lake is considered the holiest lake in Sikkim, and legend says that if even a single leaf falls on its surface, a bird will pluck it up. Local tradition says that it can grant wishes, so wish wisely! **Swimming is not allowed.** The main shrine is on the eastern side of the lake; a small platform extends from it to the lake's edge. A "trail" of sorts continues on and circles the lake, but it's hard to follow in some places. Also accessible from the lake (but in opposite directions from each other) are the **Chubuk** and **Dupuk caves,** where local monks meditate and perform religious ceremonies, and the **"footprint rock,"** a legendary rock that a monk stepped on. Ask at the trekkers' hut for directions. A small monastery above the lake commands excellent views.

The best accommodation at the lake is the privatized **trekkers' hut ❶,** on the road 200m before the lake. The serene ambience and friendly staff are complemented by huge communal dinners for Rs30. (☎258562. Double rooms Rs50 per bed.) The **pilgrims' hut ❶,** by the entrance to the lake, has a grander exterior, but a drabber interior (dorms Rs50). A **jeep** runs from Geyzing to Khechopalri Lake at noon (Rs50), and an SNT **bus** makes the trip at 3pm (Rs20).

DAY 2 (3-5HR.): KHECHOPALRI LAKE TO YUKSAM. From the lake, a short-cut trail descends off the main road just opposite the trail leading up to the monastery. The trail drops past a few houses and some rows of white prayer flags, and after 45min. to 1hr., crosses a stream. From there, you can follow the downhill road or take the much steeper path over the ridge. Either way, you will have to join the path that crosses the crystal-clear Rathong River on a suspension bridge. The steep shortcut to Yuksam climbs up from the road just a few hundred meters past the bridge. The trail zig-zags through fields all the way up to an unused stretch of road 1hr. away. Follow the road to the right all the way to **Yuksam.** The road snakes around to the left and passes a school before arriving at the town 5min. later.

Yuksam itself is relatively developed, for it is the starting point for the popular treks to **Dzongri** and **Goch La.** Yuksam (Lepcha for "three *lamas*") became the first capital of Sikkim in 1641 when three *lamas*, Lhatsun Chenpo, Rigdzin Chenpo, and Nadak Sempa Chenpo, met here to consecrate the first king of Sikkim, Phontsog Namgyal. The spot of the ceremony, a white stone throne, is still intact, and is known as the **Norbugang Chorten.** This dignified monument rests in a wooded glade 10min. down the road past Hotel Tashi Gang. The capital has long since moved, but Yuksam still has some basic services. There is a **police outpost** on the main road, 150m north of the Wild Orchid Hotel, and a **hospital** another 100m north on the road that curves to the right. Yuksam's ultra-modern **Community Information**

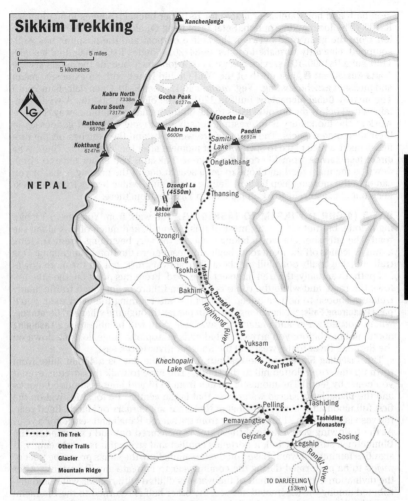

Sikkim Trekking

0   5 miles
0   5 kilometers

Kanchenjunga

Kabru North
7338m

Gocha Peak
6127m

Kabru South
7317m

Goeche La

Rathong
6679m

Kabru Dome
6600m

Pandim
6691m

Kokthang
6147m

Samiti
Lake

NEPAL

Onglakthang

Dzongri La
(4550m)

Thansing

Kabur
4810m

Dzongri

Pethang

Tsokha

Bakhim

Yuksam to Dzongri & Gocha La

Rathong River

Yuksam

Khechopalri
Lake

The Local Trek

Pelling

Tashiding

Pemayangtse

Tashiding
Monastery

Geyzing

Sosing

Legship

Rangit River

TO DARJEELING
(13km)

•••••• The Trek
- - - - Other Trails
    Glacier
    Mountain Ridge

SIKKIM

Centre, established by the Government of India as part of a larger project to bring remote areas in Sikkim and the Northeast States online, has blazingly fast satellite-fed **internet,** and probably qualifies as a sight in its own right. The centre is on the road to the Norbugang Chorten; look for the satellite dish. (☎241270; sik_yoksum@hub.nic.in. Open daily 10:30am-4:30pm. Internet Rs50 per hr.) **STD/ ISD** is available at the Information Centre and at the Hotel Tashi Gang.

The best bargain accommodation in town is the **Hotel Yangrigang ❶,** at the bend in the main road, just south of the bazaar. The rooms are clean, the lobby has comfy couches, and the restaurant dishes out veg. chow mein for Rs25. (☎241217. Dorms Rs50; doubles with bath Rs150. Bucket shower Rs10. Off-season: Rs40/ 100.) Though not quite the seductive paradise its name suggests, **Wild Orchid Hotel ❶,** just south of the main bazaar, is another reliable option. All rooms have a common bath and hot water is available for Rs10 per bucket. (Singles Rs50; doubles Rs100.) The local luxury option, **Hotel Tashi Gang ❹**, along the road that diverges left from the main road between the police outpost and the hospital, has well-equipped, elegantly furnished rooms. (☎241202. Singles Rs650-900; doubles 900-1150; suite Rs1500. 10% service charge.) For a good meal outside the hotels, try the **Gupta Restaurant ❶**, just north of the Wild Orchid Hotel, with an extensive menu and pleasant gazebo seating. (Veg. *momos* Rs12, beer Rs40. Open daily 6am-7pm.) The nearby **Dubdi Monastery**, built in 1701, is the oldest in Sikkim. A well-maintained trail below the hospital leads to the hilltop monastery 45min. away. The artwork at the monastery is interesting, mostly portraying gods and goddesses in their fearsome aspects. The grounds are well-kept and the benches on the premises make a nice place to spend a quiet moment after the long climb. There is **no direct jeep service** from Khechopalri Lake to Yuksam. You either have to climb down to the main road and hope to get a seat in one of the passing jeeps, or you can take the morning jeep back to Pelling or Geyzing, which leaves from the trekker's hut at 6:30am (Rs40). Catch a jeep to Yuksam from there.

DAY 3 (4-6HR.): YUKSAM TO TASHIDING. The walk from Yuksam to Tashiding is long, but not strenuous; most of it is downhill, and much of it is along the road. The only shortcut worth taking comes at the very beginning. From Yuksam, a trail descends off the main road, beginning just before the Hotel Yangrigang. This trail cuts diagonally downhill for about 2km; at every fork, opt for the more downhill path. Eventually, the trail intersects the road. From this point on, the hike follows the road, and while the route is lovely and there is not much traffic, many trekkers choose to hop on a jeep for this leg. after joining the main road, you'll pass **Phamrong Falls;** farther along, the path passes through the village of **Gerethang,** where bottled water and snacks are available. You will be able to see **Tashiding** about an hour before you arrive. Tashiding is on top of a ridge, looking down on the Rathong River to the west and the Rangeet River to the east.

The **Tashiding Monastery,** the real attraction of the day, is a 45min. hike from town up the *stupa*-dotted hill to the south. (You have to walk this stretch, even if you come by jeep.) The monastery dates from 1716 and houses about 50 monks and the **Bhumchu,** a sacred water vase that is the center of a local festival on the first full moon after Losar, the Tibetan New Year in February or March. Each year, the vase is filled with 21 jugs of water from the sacred Rangit and sealed for a year. At the following year's festival the water is measured out and examined. If the Bhumchu is still nearly full, it portends conflict and strife; if it is nearly empty, it signifies famine and want. Based on their examination, the lamas prescribe a set of *pujas* to be performed during the coming year to mitigate any ill portents. After the divination is complete, half of the water is diluted with regular water and distributed among the assembled masses; the other half is returned to the Bhumchu and mixed anew with water from the Rangit for next year's festival. The **Thong Wa Rang To Chorten,** considered the holiest *chorten* in Sikkim, is also on the premises. Simply beholding its glory is said to wash away all sin.

If you are looking for a place to stay in Tashiding, keep your eyes peeled for the **Hotel Blue Bird ❶**, just north up the hill from the main intersection. Rooms are simple, and all share a common bath. There's a comfortable sitting area upstairs, and free buckets of hot water are provided. (☎243248. Dorm Rs30; singles Rs40; doubles Rs80.) The restaurant serves cheap meals (veg. rice Rs25, chicken rice Rs30).

Jeep service for this part of the trek runs mostly in the early morning (1hr., departure before 6:30am, Rs30); it is possible to visit Tashiding early and then continue on to either Legship or Pelling in the evening.

DAY 4 (5-7HR. OR 3-5HR.): TASHIDING TO PELLING OR LEGSHIP. You have two options from Tashiding: one is to take the shortcut trail directly down to the river and up the other side to Pelling; the other is to follow the road down to Legship, where buses and jeeps run up to Pelling, Gangtok, Jorethang, and Siliguri.

Heading straight to Pelling requires more energy. The shortcut trail departs directly from the town of Tashiding (ask at the Hotel Blue Bird) and after 1½-2½hr. reaches a suspension bridge. Across the river, the trail begins to ascend; at the few forks in the trail, veer toward the more uphill path. This eventually leads to **Naku Chumbong Village** (2½-3hr.), where a number of paths converge. Take the most uphill trail, which will take you to Pelling in 1-1½hr.

The other option is to follow the descending path to Legship, a better choice for those headed to other parts of Sikkim or West Bengal, since most buses and jeeps pass through Legship. Navigation is easy, just follow the road, but keep in mind that there is no food or water available on the way. The road crosses the Rangeet River (1½-2½hr.), winds downstream, and crosses again at Legship (1½-2½hr.). It's a long walk, but the path is mostly downhill. **Jeeps** run from Tashiding to Legship before 8am (45min., Rs20). Trucks on the route often stop for trekkers (Rs10).

In Legship, **buses** run to **Gangtok** (4hr., 8:30am, Rs65) and **Siliguri** (4hr.; 6:30, 8:30, 9am; Rs65). **Jeeps** head to: **Geyzing** (45min., frequent 7:30am-5pm, Rs20); **Jorethang** (1hr., frequent 7:30am-5pm, Rs25), for connections to Gangtok; **Siliguri** (4hr., frequent 8:30am-4pm, Rs70). The only real accommodation in town is the **Hotel Trishna ❶,** up the street from the bus terminal, at the main intersection. Their rooms are clean, and they'll wake you up for early buses and jeeps. (☎250887. Free buckets of hot water for common bath. Doubles Rs100 per person.) Ask the hotel for directions to the **hot springs,** a half-hour walk from town.

OTHER TREKS

For serious trekkers, the more challenging (and more costly) **Dzongri Trek** (5-6 days) leaves from Yuksam and ascends well above 4000m. It must be booked ahead of time in Gangtok, and the cost of US$20-25 per person per day will cover food, tents, a guide, and porters. The trek goes from **Yuksam** (1780m) to **Dzongri** (4024m) over a period of two or three days. The **Goeche La Trek** (8-10 days) continues for three more days to the Goeche La pass (4940m) before returning to the "lowlands." The newly-opened **Singalelah Trek** (10-15 days) also ends up at Dzongri, but follows a circuitous, less traveled, more spectacular route along the Sikkim-Nepal border. The trek crosses into Nepal at several points, but no visa is necessary. The best months for these treks are Mar.-May and Sept.-Nov. In March the routes are less crowded, but don't go too early or you may be forced to turn back due to poor snow conditions. April is popular for its blossoming rhododendrons, but the trails tend to be packed with Indian tourists on their annual school vacations. Although these treks are guided and relatively safe, read up on Acute Mountain Sickness (AMS) before you go (see p. 35).

TAMIL NADU
தமிழ் நாடு

The southernmost state in mainland India and the heartland of Dravidian culture, Tamil Nadu is defined in its morning life, when intricate rice *kollamo* are drawn on the streets in front of homes, piles of fragrant jasmine garlands await to adorn braids and buses, and coffee is hypnotically poured from stainless steel cups to bowls and back again. Here tourism is often, although not exclusively, synonymous with pilgrimage, and travelers can expect high standards of hospitality. Few worry about falling victim to overzealous trinket-dealers or undercooked chow mein. Bright bougainvillea greet you more frequently than touts as you travel across Tamil Nadu's green rice paddies and red-tiled earth on the coast to foggy hill stations and bustling cites.

The state is a stronghold of Hindu practice and one of the most conservative and traditional parts of the country. Some of the finest temples in India are in Tamil Nadu: vividly colored towers and gateways that soar over huge temple-city complexes and shrines that buzz with worshippers. But here too, India exhibits its religious diversity. Don't be surprised to wake at 5am to a *muezzin's* call to prayer or to find yourself daytripping to a site of the Virgin Mary's appearance.

Centuries ago, Tamil Nadu was ruled by three rival dynasties: the Cholas, the Pandyas, and the Cheras. By the 4th century AD, the Pallava kingdom had risen to power and ruled until the 9th century, when it was toppled by the Cholas, who eventually came to rule the whole of South India. Under the British, Tamil Nadu was part of the Chennai Presidency, which included parts of present-day Andhra Pradesh, Kerala, and Karnataka. It has nurtured South India's oldest literary tradition in its mother tongue, Tamil, since the 1st century, as well as India's most popular classical dance form, *bharatretyam*. Today, the state remains proudly separatist and refuses to welcome Hindu into its schools, making English the more common *lingua franca*.

HIGHLIGHTS OF TAMIL NADU

The sweeping grounds and serene *gopurams* of the **Brihadishwara Temple** (p. 605) in tiny **Tanjore** (p. 603) are a masterpiece of Chola-era architecture and recognized by UNESCO as a World Heritage Site.

Hanuman leapt across **Rameswaram** (p. 617) to Sri Lanka to save Sita from the evil clutches of Ravana. Today, you can leap across its pristine beaches on your way to the **Ramanathaswamy Temple** (p. 618).

A unique cultural mix distinguishes **Pondicherry** (p. 590), the former capital of French India, now home to the famously surreal **Aurobindo Ashram** (p. 594).

Kodaikanal (p. 624), in the Western Ghats, has all the standard hill station amusements, set against some of India's finest film-grade scenery.

CHENNAI (MADRAS) சென்னை ☎044

Dubbed the "Gateway to the South" by its champions, Chennai is India's fourth largest city and the first stop in Tamil Nadu for most travelers. If you're arriving from a big city elsewhere in India, you may be pleasantly surprised by the relative calm that manages to survive here, underneath the traffic fumes and mad wheeling thrum present in all

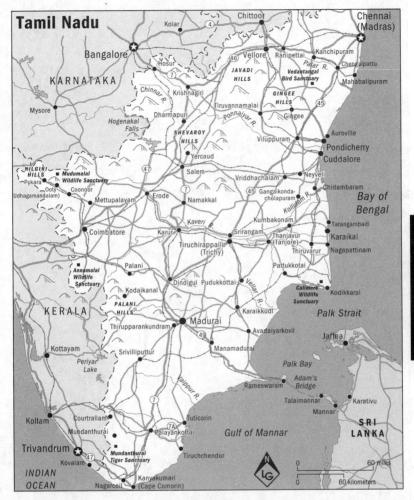

Tamil Nadu

Chennai (Madras)
Kolar
Chittoor
Bangalore
KARNATAKA
Hosur
Vellore
Ranipettai
Kanchipuram
Palar R.
JAVADI HILLS
Chengalpattu
Vedantangal Bird Sanctuary
Mahabalipuram
Chinnar R.
Krishnagiri
Tiruvannamalai
GINGEE HILLS
Dharmapuri
Ponnaiyar R.
Gingee
Mysore
Hogenakal Falls
SHEVAROY HILLS
Viluppuram
Auroville
Yercaud
Pondicherry
Cuddalore
NILGIRI HILLS
Mudumalai Wildlife Sanctuary
Salem
Vriddhachalam
Neyveli
Pykara
Ooty (Udhagamandalam)
Coonoor
Mettupalayam
Erode
Namakkal
Gangaikonda-cholapuram
Chidambaram
Kollidam R.
Bay of Bengal
Coimbatore
Karur
Srirangam
Kumbakonam
Tarangambadi
Kaveri R.
Thanjavur (Tanjore)
Karaikal
Tiruchirappalli (Trichy)
Thiruvarur
Nagapattinam
Annamalai Wildlife Sanctuary
Palani
Pattukkotai
KERALA
Kodaikanal
Dindigul
Pudukkottai
Vellar R.
Calimere Wildlife Sanctuary
Kodikkarai
PALANI HILLS
Karaikkudi
Palk Strait
Thirupparankundram
Madurai
Avadaiyarkovil
Jaffna
Kottayam
Srivilliputtur
Manamadurai
Palk Bay
Periyar Lake
Vaippur R.
Adam's Bridge
Rameswaram
Talaimannar
Karativu
Mannar
SRI LANKA
Kollam
Courtrallam
Tuticorin
Mundanthurai
Palayankottai
Gulf of Mannar
Trivandrum
Kovalam
Mundanthurai Tiger Sanctuary
Tiruchchendur
INDIAN OCEAN
Nagercoil
Kanyakumari (Cape Comorin)

0   60 miles
0   60 kilometers

TAMIL NADU

subcontinental cities. In Madras, as it was known before being swept up in India's wave of politically motivated name changes, the burning heat and bustle is offset by tree-lined streets and long, lazy stretches of sand along the Bay of Bengal.

Chennai's climb from humble fishing village to horn-honking metropolis began in 1639, when East India Company worker Francis Day founded a trading outpost. French forces stormed, seized, and sacked the city in 1746, but Madras it continued to develop as a thriving economic center. By the late 19th century, its factories were spinning out thousands of bales of cotton clothing for export throughout the Empire. Today, Chennai is the capital of the state and a bastion of South Indian culture, and its dance and music festivals attract bigger crowds than the few sights sprinkled within the city limits. Nonetheless, Chennai has never been much of a tourist destination, and most travelers get out of town as soon as they can.

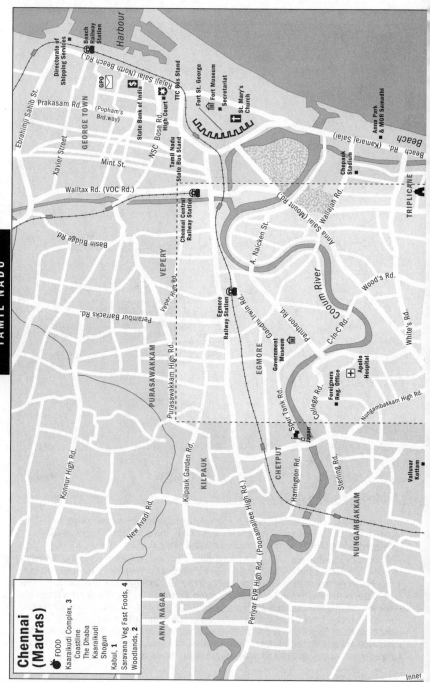

Chennai (Madras)

FOOD

Kaaraikudi Complex, **3**
Coastline
The Dhaba
Kaaraikudi
Shogun
Kabul, **1**
Saravana Veg Fast Foods, **4**
Woodlands, **2**

TAMIL NADU

Harbour

Directorate of Shipping Services
Beach Railway Station

Rajaji Salai (North Beach Rd.)

Ebrahimji Sahib St.

Prakasam Rd.

GPO

(Popham's Brd.way)

GEORGE TOWN

State Bank of India

Xavier Street

Mint St.

NSC Bose Rd.
High Court

Tamil Nadu State Bus Stand

TTC Bus Stand

Fort St. George
Fort Museum

Secretariat

St. Mary's Church

Anna Park & MGR Samadhi

Beach Rd. (Kamaraj Salai)

TRIPLICANE

Walltax Rd. (VOC Rd.)

Basin Bridge Rd.

VEPERY

Chennai Central Railway Station

Chepauk Stadium

Wallajah Rd.

A. Naicken St.

Anna Salai (Mount Rd.)

Perambur Barracks Rd.

PURASAWAKKAM

Veper High Rd.

Purasawakkam High Rd.

Egmore Railway Station

Gandhi Irwin Rd.

Pantheon Rd.

EGMORE

Government Museum

Coourm River

Wood's Rd.

C-in-C Rd.

White's Rd.

Foreigners Reg. Office

Apollo Hospital

Nungambakkam High Rd.

Konnur High Rd.

KILPAUK

Kilpauk Garden Rd.

New Avadi Rd.

Spur Tank Rd.

CHETPUT

College Rd.

Japan

Harrington Rd.

Sterling Rd.

Volluvar Kottam

Periyar EVR High Rd. (Poonamallee High Rd.)

ANNA NAGAR

NUNGAMBAKKAM

Inner

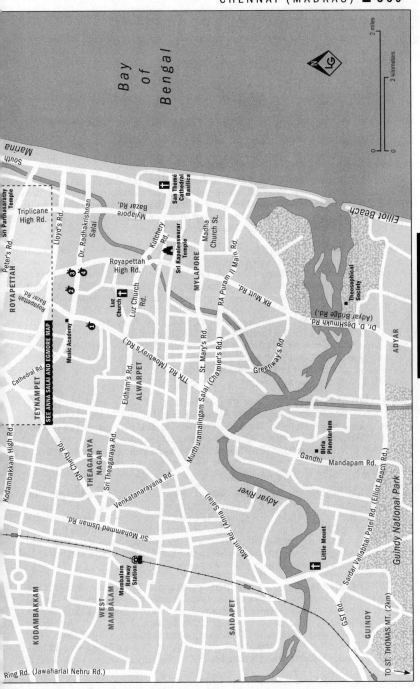

TAMIL NADU

Bay
of
Bengal

South Marina

Sri Parthasarathy Temple
Triplicane High Rd.
Peter's Rd.
Lloyd's Rd.
Dr. Radhakrishnan Salai
ROYAPETTAH
Royapettah Bazar Rd.
Royapettah High Rd.
Cathedral Rd.
Music Academy
TEYNAMPET
SEE ANNA SALAI AND EGMORE MAP
Luz Church
Luz Church Rd.
Kutchery Rd.
Mylapore Bazar Rd.
San Thomé Cathedral Basilica
Sri Kapaleeswarar Temple
MYLAPORE
Madha Church St.
Elliot Beach
Eldham's Rd.
TTK Rd. (Mowbray's Rd.)
ALWARPET
St. Mary's Rd.
RA Puram II Main Rd.
RK Mutt Rd.
Greenway's Rd.
Dr. D. Deshmukh Rd. (Adyar Bridge Rd.)
Theosophical Society
ADYAR
Murthuramalingam Salai (Chamier's Rd.)
Kodambakkam High Rd.
GN Chetty Rd.
THEAGARAYA NAGAR
Sri Theagaraya Rd.
Venkatanarayana Rd.
Sir Mohammed Usman Rd.
KODAMBAKKAM
WEST MAMBALAM
Mambalam Railway Station
Mount Rd. (Anna Salai)
Adyar River
Birla Planetarium
Gandhi Mandapam Rd.
Little Mount
SAIDAPET
GUINDY
Guindy National Park
Sardar Vallabhai Patel Rd. (Elliot Beach Rd.)
GST Rd.
TO ST. THOMAS MT. (2km)
Ring Rd. (Jawaharlal Nehru Rd.)

0   2 miles
0   2 kilometers

◪ INTERCITY TRANSPORTATION

FLIGHTS

Chennai Meenambakkam is not as heavily used as the airports in Delhi and Mumbai, making Chennai a relatively peaceful port of entry and exit. The city center is 16km north of the airport, and there are a number of ways of getting there. **Local buses** (#52, 52A, 52B, 52D, 52E, 52G, 60E, 60G; Rs15) are too crowded to be useful unless you are carrying all your luggage in your pockets. The **minibus service** running between the airport and the major hotels (Rs100) is a tedious and time-consuming way of making it into the city. Tickets are sold at a counter in the international terminal. The **pre-paid taxi booth** inside the international terminal will fix you up with a taxi downtown for about Rs250; regular taxis are likely to cost substantially more. **Auto-rickshaws** are not allowed inside the airport compound, so you will have to hike to the main road before you can start haggling over a fare, which should be Rs150-200. Another option is the urban **train** system; it runs from Tirusulam Station (a short walk from the terminals) to Egmore Station, the site of a number of cheap hotels (Rs5; last train at around midnight).

INTERNATIONAL AIRLINES. Most airline offices are open M-F 9:30am-5:30pm and Sa 9:30am-1:30pm. A reliable travel agent is **Mecotronics,** near the cinemas. **American Airlines,** 43-44 Thaper House, Montieth Rd. (☎28592564). **Air France** White's Rd. (☎28554894). **Air India,** 19 Marshalls Rd. (☎28554488 or 28554477). **British Airways,** Alsa Mall Khaleeli Centre, Montieth Rd. (☎28554680). **Delta Airlines,** 47 White's Rd., Royapettah (☎28525655 or 28525755), open M-F 9:30am-5:30pm, Sa 9:30am-1:30pm. **Gulf Air,** 52 Montieth Rd. (☎28554417 or 28553101). **Lufthansa** 167 Anna Salai (☎28523272). **Sri Lankan Airlines,** 76 Cathedral Rd. (☎28261535), opposite Chola Hotel. **Swiss Air,** 191 Anna Salai (☎28522541). **Thai Airways, United Airlines, SAS, Air New Zealand,** and **Varig Airlines** (☎28226150 or 28226149) share an office at the Malavikas Centre, 144 Kodambakkam Rd. Sri Lankan Airlines and Air India both fly to **Colombo, Sri Lanka** (1½hr., 4-5 per day, US$90).

DOMESTIC AIRLINES. Jet Airways, Thaper House, 43-44 Montieth Rd. (☎8414141), open M-Sa 8:30am-8:30pm. **Indian Airlines,** 19 Marshalls Rd. (☎8555200). Daily flights to: **Bangalore** (7-8 per day, US$70); **Cochin** (1-3 per day, US$125); **Coimbatore** (2-3 per day, US$95); **Delhi** (6-7 per day, US$265); **Hyderabad** (3-4 per day, US$110); **Kolkata** (2-3 per day, US$225); **Mumbai** (7-9 per day, US$165); **Trivandrum** (2 per day, US$110).

TRAINS

Chennai has two main train stations: **Egmore,** for travel within Tamil Nadu, and **Chennai Central,** for trains to other parts of the country. Both are in the north of town near Periyar EVR Rd. (Poonamallee High Rd.). For **arrival and departure information,** call ☎1361 and dial the train number after the beep. Southern Railways maintains an extremely useful and up-to-date website of schedules and route maps that finally relegates *Trains At A Glance* to the status of an ancient abacus. Ride the rails at www.srailway.com or www.southernrailway.org.

CHENNAI CENTRAL. Long-distance trains arrive at and depart from Chennai Central, in Georgetown, near the Buckingham Canal, not far from the hotels of Gandhi Irwin Rd. The reservation counter is upstairs in the administrative building, the 10-story concrete structure to the left of the huge red station. The helpful "Foreigners Assistance Cell" is upstairs on the first floor. (General inquiries ☎132. Open M-Sa 8am-8pm, Su 8am-2pm.) To: **Ahmedabad** (35hr., 9:30am, Rs485); **Bangalore** (7hr., 6-7 per day 6am-11pm, Rs118-505); **Coimbatore** (8½hr., 7-8 per day 6am-9:45pm, Rs143-

235); **Delhi** (35hr., 4 and 10pm, Rs537); **Ernakulam/
Cochin** (13½hr., 3-4 per day 11am-8pm, Rs299); **Hydera-
bad** (14½hr., 4 and 6:30pm, Rs319); **Kanyakumari** (16hr.,
5:15pm, Rs284); **Kolkata** (33hr., 9am and 10:30pm,
Rs469); **Madurai** via **Kodaikanal** (10hr., 5-6 per day 7am-
9:30pm, Rs223); **Mangalore** (19hr., 11am and 7:15pm,
Rs318); **Mumbai** (30hr.; 6:50, 11:45am, 9:30pm; Rs389);
Mysore (12hr., 10:45pm, Rs215; express 7hr., Th-Tu
6am, Rs680); **Tirupati** (3hr.; 6:25am, 1:50, 4:15pm;
Rs64); **Trivandrum** (17hr.; daily 7:30pm, Su-F 4:40am;
Rs235); **Varanasi** (39hr., Th and Su 5:30pm, Rs513).

EGMORE RAILWAY STATION. Most trains to desti-
nations within Tamil Nadu depart from the Egmore
Railway Station, though many trains now run from
Tambaram, 1hr. away (see below). Egmore Station is
north of Gandhi Irwin Rd. The reservation counter is
to your left as you enter. The tourist cell at Chennai
Central deals with bookings for trains out of both sta-
tions. (☎ 132. Open M-Sa 8am-8pm, Su 8am-2pm.) To:
Chidambaram (5½hr., 4 per day 8:45am-9pm, Rs70);
Kodaikanal (8hr., 4 per day 5:15am-9:30pm, Rs110);
Madurai (8hr., 6 per day 7am-9:30pm, Rs118); **Trichy**
(7hr., 9 per day 7am-10:30pm, Rs87-97).

TAMBARAM. Some trains within Tamil Nadu now run
from Tambaram, 1hr. from Chennai. Suburban trains
run between Tambaram and Egmore (every 15min.
4am-midnight, Rs8). Destinations served from Tambaram include: **Chidambaram** (6hr., 4 per day 8:45am-
10:35pm, Rs64); **Kanyakumari** (15hr., 5:45pm, Rs289);
Kumbakonam (8hr., 8:45am and 10:45pm, Rs93);
Rameswaram (17hr., 1 and 9pm, Rs268); **Tanjore** (8hr., 9
and 11pm, Rs169); **Trichy** (5hr., 10 per day 7:35am-11pm,
Rs83-102); **Trivandrum** (16hr., 8pm, Rs299).

BUSES

Buses to most parts of Tamil Nadu leave from **Chennai Mofussil Bus Terminus (CMBT),** 15km southwest of
the city, to: **Bangalore** (8hr., every 30min. 5:30am-
1:30am, Rs150); **Chidambaram** (5hr., every hr. 5am-
11pm, Rs82); **Coimbatore** (12hr., every 30min.
5:30am-10:15pm, Rs204); **Kanchipuram** (2½hr., every
hr. 5am-9pm, Rs25); **Kanyakumari** (15hr., every hr.
5am-9:15pm, Rs275); **Kodaikanal** (13hr., 5:40pm,
Rs208); **Kumbakonam** (7hr., every 30min. 5am-11pm,
Rs112); **Madurai** (10hr., every hr. 5:30am-11pm,
Rs181); **Mahabalipuram** (2hr., every hr. 5am-9pm,
Rs35); **Mysore** (10hr., 5 and 8pm, Rs180); **Ooty** (13hr.,
5 and 7:30pm, Rs251); **Pondicherry** (4hr., every 10min.
4am-11pm, Rs70); **Rameswaram** (14hr., 5:45pm,
Rs223); **Tanjore** (8hr., every hr. 5am-11pm, Rs125);
Tirupati (4hr., every 30min. 4am-midnight, Rs70);
Trichy (7hr., every 30min., Rs123).

IN RECENT NEWS

SEX, LIES AND VIDEOTAPE

While many of India's politicians
involuntarily participate in the entertainment industry, Tamil Nadu's current Chief Minister, Jayalalitha
Jayaram, can actually claim to have
been a star of the silver screen. In
1990, the former actress and dancer
and now leader of the regional
AIADMK party came to power in the
first installment of an up-and-down
political saga that ran throughout the
rest of the decade. JJ, or "Amma," as
she is affectionately called by her
groupies, quickly became embroiled
in corruption charges that forced her
to make a hasty exit in 1995. However, JJ made a sensational comeback in early 2001, when she
managed to have herself re-elected,
despite the charges against her.
Doubts about the legitimacy (and
even the legality) of JJ's re-election
were, however, not about to cramp
her style, and one of her first acts
after moving back into the Chief Minister's residence was to have several
of her biggest rivals rounded up and
arrested on charges of—you guessed
it—corruption.

As if her political career weren't
melodramatic enough, JJ's personal
life has also been substantial tabloid
material, including past romances
with playboy-politician M.G. Ramachandran, who founded AIADMK
and rumoured shadowy lesbian lovers. In any event, JJ's biggest fan is
herself. The city of Chennai and
much of the state, is peppered with
huge cutout images of Amma, sometimes 10-15 times larger than life.

BOATS

There are weekly sailings from Chennai to Port Blair in the **Andaman Islands** (2½ days, once a week, Rs1330-4320 depending on class). To purchase tickets, you will need two passport photos (get them done at one of the shops on Anna Salai), a photocopy of your passport and Indian visa, and a "proof of residence form" issued by the hotel where you are staying. Contact the Deputy Director of Shipping Services, Andaman & Nicobar Administration, NSC Bose Rd. (☎25226873. Open daily 8am-4:30pm.) Don't forget the special permit needed for travel to this restricted area, for which you will need two more ID photos and yet another photocopy of your passport and visa (see p. 574).

■ ORIENTATION

Chennai is a massive, sprawling city, extending more than 15km along the western shores of the **Bay of Bengal.** The city can be divided into three distinct sections. Northernmost is **Georgetown,** an area of long, straight streets running south to **Fort Saint George** and the **Central Railway Station.** Georgetown's major east-west artery is **NSC Bose Road,** which runs across town, parallel to **Prakasam Road (Broadway),** to the shoreline, where it meets **Rajaji (North Beach) Road,** which leads south to Marina Beach. **Parry's Corner,** at the intersection of NSC Bose and Rajaji Rd., is the wheeling, dealing market area. The city's **local bus stand** is here. **Chennai Central railway station** is in the southwest corner of this neighborhood. The brand new **Chennai Mofussil Bus Terminus (CMBT),** the intercity bus station, is 13km southwest of the city. The southernmost part of town is 10km south of Georgetown and stretches from **Mylapore** in the north to the residential areas south of the **Adyar River.** To the west are the **Guindy National Park** and **Saint Thomas Mount.** Royapettah contains some nice upscale hotels and restaurants. **T. Nagar** and **Dr. Radhakrishnan Salai,** in the south of the city, are great areas for stores and restaurants.

Between Georgetown and Mylapore is the real center of the city, including **Egmore** and **Anna Salai (Mount Road),** the longest and busiest street in Chennai. Many of the city's tourist services are along Anna Salai, which runs northeast to southwest. North of Anna Salai is the congested Egmore area, full of cheap hotels. Egmore's northern boundary is **Egmore Railway Station,** just off hotel-rich **Gandhi Irwin Road. Pantheon Road** runs parallel to and south of Gandhi Irwin Rd. **Periyar EVR Road (Poonamallee High Road)** is to the north. Perpendicular to both are **Commander-in-Chief (C-in-C) Road** and, farther southwest, **Nungambakkam High (NH) Road,** two busy streets where many of Chennai's businesses are. **Triplicane** is a mix of hotels, residences, and businesses near the coast and just south of Anna Salai.

☰ LOCAL TRANSPORTATION

AUTO-RICKSHAWS

The streets of Chennai are infested with swarms of auto-rickshaws, probably the easiest (though not cheapest) way of getting around. It is important to agree on a price before getting in, though the first price you're offered will almost always be about double the going rate. Rs20-30 is a typical fare between two downtown destinations. Most rickshaw-*wallahs* will meet you at your hotel in the morning or will take you around town for the day—simply discuss your plans beforehand and agree on a lump sum in advance (Rs80-200). If you have serious trouble with a driver, threaten to take down his number (on the back of the vehicle or on a black pin worn on his shirt) and report him to the police.

TAXIS

Taxis are much less common and about twice as expensive as auto-rickshaws. Most have meters, but again, it's often best to fix a price beforehand. Expect to pay at least Rs100 from the railway stations to Anna Salai or to Triplicane.

LOCAL BUSES

The very thought of getting onto an Indian city bus is enough to make some people ill. However, Chennai's bus system is efficient and reliable when compared with others. Also, it is (marginally) less crowded than those in Kolkata, Delhi, and Mumbai. Most public buses are green and have their destination displayed at the front and on the side. There is a bus stand every few blocks throughout the city. Rush hour (7:30-10:30am and 5:30-7pm) is for masochistic crowd-lovers only.

Buses are boarded from behind. The conductor will soon amble along and extract payment (usually Rs2-3). Many buses are unofficially segregated by sex—women on one side, men on the other. Regular bus service runs 5am-10pm. Night buses are less frequent and run only along select routes.

BUS #	ROUTE
22, 27, 27B, 29A	Egmore-Triplicane
23C	Egmore-Anna Salai-Adyar Depot
9, 10, 17, 17E	Egmore-Central via Broadway
9, 10	Parry's Corner-Central-Egmore-T. Nagar
9A, 17D	Parry's Corner-Central-Egmore
18A, A18, 52B	Broadway-Anna Salai-Airport-Mylapore
21G	High Court-Adyar-Guindy National Park-Airport-Tambaram
21	Parry's Corner-Central-Mylapore
17A, 17G, 25B, 25E	Anna Salai-Nungambakkam-Vadapallani
25B, 27, 40	Anna Salai-Triplicane-Egmore via Marina Beach
23A, 23B, 23C, PP23C	Adyar Bus Depot-Anna Salai-Egmore
25, 25A	Anna Salai-Triplicane-Vadapallani
40, 40A	Triplicane-Egmore

MOPEDS

You need an international license to rent a moped (Rs150 per day). For your own wheels, check out **U-Rent Services Ltd.,** 36 II Main Rd., in the Gandhi Nagar district, south of the Adyar River. (☎24910838. Open daily 8:30am-8pm.)

SUBURBAN TRAINS

Two suburban train lines run along the eastern and western extremities of Chennai. These trains—cheap, frequent, and only packed during morning and evening rush hours—are the best means of reaching places south of the city center. From **Beach Railway Station,** near the Head Post Office in Georgetown in the north of the city, trains run south to Egmore, Park (close to Chennai Central), Nungambakkam, Mambalam (for T. Nagar), Guindy, St. Thomas Mt., and then on to the airport and Tambaram. The eastern line runs south from Beach Railway Station to Triplicane, Luz, and Gandhi Nagar. Trains run every 10-15min. between 4am and midnight, and fares for most journeys are Rs8 or less.

◪ PRACTICAL INFORMATION

For up-to-date information, tourists should pick up a copy of **Hallo! Madras,** a monthly listings pamphlet detailing everything from practical information to sights and shopping. Copies are available from the tourist information center and from bookshops around town.

TOURIST AND FINANCIAL SERVICES

Tourist Office: Government of India Tourist Office, 154 Anna Salai (☎28460285 or 28461489; indtour@vsnl.com), at the corner of Clubhouse Rd. The best place to start collecting informational pamphlets on Chennai, Tamil Nadu, and the country beyond. Open M-F 9am-6pm, Sa 9am-1pm. There are also smaller **information counters** in the domestic and international airports, and at Egmore and Central railway stations. Open daily 6am-9:30pm. **Tamil Tourism Development Corporation (TTDC) Office** (☎5353351), near Chennai Central RW Station, books TTDC tours. Open daily 24hr. Many **regional tourist agencies** (including those for Kerala, Rajasthan, Uttar Pradesh, and Himachal Pradesh) share an office at 28 C-in-C Rd. (☎8279862). Open M-Sa 10am-5pm, closed 2nd Sa.

Consulates: Australia, 115 Mahatma Gandhi Rd. (☎8276036). **France,** 202 Prestige Point Bldg., 16 Haddows Rd. (☎8266561). **Germany,** 49 Ethiraj Salai (☎28210810). **Netherlands,** Catholic Center, 64 Armenian St. (☎24473309). **Sri Lanka,** 196 TTK Rd., Alwarpet (☎24987696), open M-F 9am-5:15pm. **UK,** 24 Anderson Rd. (24 hr. ☎28257422). **US,** 220 Anna Salai, at Cathedral Rd. (☎28112000), open M-F 1:30-4:30pm. 24hr. emergency.

Immigration Office: Foreigners Registration Office, Sastri Bhavan Annex, 26 Haddows Rd. (☎28275424), off NH Rd. Applications dropped off in the morning are usually available later the same day. Bring 2 passport photos and copies of your passport and visa. Issues special permits for restricted areas such as the Andaman Islands. Open M-F 9:30am-6pm.

Currency Exchange: Dozens of banks and money changers all over town exchange most major currencies and traveler's checks. The **State Bank of India** is open M-F 10am-4pm, Sa 10am-1pm, individual transactions in back building on Anna Salai. Many of the other big national and international banks are on Anna Salai. **Citibank,** 766 Anna Salai (☎8522151), 500m past the tourist office, on the left as you head south, has 24hr. ATM machines that take international cards. Open M-F 10am-4:30pm, Sa 10am-1:30pm. **Thomas Cook,** El Dorado Bldg., 112 NH Rd. (☎28274941), and Ceebros Centre, 45 Montieth Rd. Open M-F 9am-6:30pm, Sa 9am-6pm. **American Express** (☎28523638), in Anna Salai, ground fl. of Spencer Plaza Mall. Open M-F 9:30am-6:30pm, Sa 9:30am-2:30pm.

LOCAL SERVICES

Bookstores: Landmark, Apex Plaza, 3 NH Rd., is a huge store with a wide selection. Open M-Sa 9am-9pm, Su 10:30am-9pm. **Higginbothams,** 814 Anna Salai. Open M-Sa 9am-8pm. **Giggles,** attached to the Taj Connemara hotel on Binny Rd., just off Anna Salai. The cramped, narrow premises are covered in towering piles of serious reading. In the back sits the most knowledgeable bookseller in all of Chennai. Shipping available. Open M-Sa 11am-8pm.

Cultural Centers: Alliance Française, 40 College Rd., Nungambakkam (☎8279803). Open M-Sa 9am-1pm and 3:30-6:30pm.

Markets: You can find everything from carnations to computers at **Parry's Corner,** NSC Bose Rd., in Georgetown, northeast of the city center. The nearby **Burma Bazaar** hawks imported goods. **Spencer Plaza Mall** on Anna Salai is a huge, modern, A/C shopping mall, with several good bookstores and ice cream parlors. Open daily 9:30am-9:30pm.

EMERGENCY AND COMMUNICATIONS

Police: Stations are all over town. Those closest to major tourist enclaves include: **Anna Salai** (☎28521720), **Egmore** (☎8250952), **Triplicane** (☎25365610).

Hospital and Pharmacy: Apollo Hospital, 21 Greams Ln. (☎1066 emergency). The best hospital in Chennai. Hospital and attached pharmacy both open 24hr.

Internet: You will have no difficulty getting on line in Chennai; Internet facilities are everywhere. Particularly convenient for travelers are: **BPM Exports,** Shop No. 119, 1st fl., Spencer Plaza, Anna Salai. Rs30 per hr. Open daily 9:30am-9:30pm. **Iway,** on the left at the end of Kennet Lane as you walk toward Egmore railway station. Rs40 per hr. Open daily 6:30am-11pm. **Gee Gee Internet Centre,** just before Broadlands on Vallabha Agraharem St., Triplicane. Rs20 per hr. Open daily 24hr.

Post Office: The **GPO** is north of Parry's Corner in Georgetown, on N. Beach Rd. Open M-Sa 8am-8:30pm, Su 10am-5pm. **Postal Code:** 600001. More convenient is the **Head Post Office** on Anna Salai. Open M-Sa 10am-8pm. **Postal Code:** 600002. There is also a branch office in Egmore, on Kennet Ln. Open M-Sa 10am-4pm. **Postal Code:** 600008.

◗ ACCOMMODATIONS

Hotels in Chennai cater to virtually every budget. Budget hotels are concentrated in Triplicane and around Gandhi Irwin Rd. and Kennet Ln. in Egmore. There are posher places along Anna Salai and in Royapettah. Reservations are wise, especially during peak times (Oct.-Apr.). Check-out is 24hr., unless otherwise noted.

YWCA International Guest House, 1086 EVR Periyar Salai (☎25324234). Removed from the noisy streets by a tree-filled courtyard, the YWCA has beautiful lilac-scented rooms and bathrooms with seat toilets. Comfy wicker chairs and large TVs in common areas. Attached restaurant. Breakfast included. Very popular with middle-class family groups. Reservations recommended. Singles Rs550-860; doubles Rs710-1000. ❹

Hotel Dasaprakash, 100 EVR Periyar Salai (☎28255111), north of Egmore Station. This creaky old place has huge rooms with sitting areas and plenty of wooden furniture. A good mid-range option with atmosphere and decrepit charm. Attached restaurant and ice cream parlor. Singles Rs300-600; doubles Rs600-1070. ❷

Broadlands, 16 Vallabha Agraharem, Triplicane (☎28545573), opposite Star Theaters. This labyrinthine villa has been around for nearly 50 years. Lots of crumbling walls, plenty of old-world atmosphere, and Bangladesh-bound busloads of bearded backpackers. Singles Rs160; doubles Rs200-350. ❷

Taj Connemara, Binny Rd. (☎28520123), near Anna Salai. A circular driveway, white columns, and carpeted floors greet you on your way to business class rooms with TV. Singles Rs4250-12,000; doubles Rs4750-12,000. ❺

Ramada Raj Park, 180 TTK Rd., Alwartet (☎24987777). Glitter, lights, and costumed bellboys make this place worth the price. Doubles Rs2800. ❺

Dayal-De Lodge, 486 Pantheon Rd. (☎28193208), west of the intersection with Kennet Ln. A driveway leads to this villa removed from the hectic rush of the main road. High-ceilinged rooms and attached seat toilets. Singles Rs185; doubles Rs300. ❷

Hotel Pandian, 9 Kennet Ln. (☎28191010; hotelpandian@vsnl.com). The luxuries offered here—satellite TV, complimentary towels and soap, round-the-clock moneychangers, and room service—all help you to deal with those jet-lagged, culture-shocked, first-night blues. Singles Rs450-800; doubles Rs700-1200. ❸

Hotel Regal, 15 Kennet Ln. (☎28191122). Slightly run-down, standard-issue budget hotel. Rooms come complete with satellite TV and attached (squat) bathrooms. Attached restaurant. Singles Rs180-380; doubles Rs230-460. ❷

◖ FOOD

EGMORE

There are plenty of cheap places to eat in and around the budget hotels close to Egmore railway station, many of them all-but-identical "meal" joints serving up banana leaf *thalis* and other simple South Indian snacks.

TAMIL NADU

◙ **Vasanta Bhavan,** at the corner of Gandhi Irwin Rd. and Kennet Ln. The South Indian restaurant that follows you wherever you go. Excellent selection of food and extremely cheap prices ensure constant crowds. "Meals" Rs24-45. Open daily 6am-11:30pm. ❶

Raj, 9 Kennet Ln., attached to Hotel Pandian. Good mid-range hotel restaurant with icebox A/C and sound system. Tandoori and Chinese dishes as well as all the usual stuff. Most main courses Rs30-75. Open daily 6:30am-11pm. ❷

Ceylon Restaurant, 15 Kennet Ln., in front of Hotel Mass. Popular, mostly non-veg. cross between whirring *thali* joint and A/C hotel restaurant. Mutton dishes Rs26-40, chicken Rs25-50, chicken *biryani* Rs35. Open daily 7am-11pm. ❶

ANNA SALAI AND TRIPLICANE

◙ **The Fruit Shop,** 11 Greams Rd., next door to the Galloping Gooseberry. Barrel-loads of fruit are on display all over this small, A/C haven, ready to be pulped into mineral water juice cocktails. Dozens of different fresh fruit juices (Rs20-75), shakes, and smoothies (Rs20-70). Open daily 10am-midnight. ❶

◙ **Anna Lakshmi,** 804 Anna Salai. Business-class elegant restaurant with plush red carpet, rich wooden carvings, and branches around South India and Southeast Asia. Mix of North and South Indian set multi-course meals, starting at Rs350 per head. Open Tu-Su noon-3pm and 7:30-10pm. MC/V. ❺

Southern Chinese Restaurant, 683 Anna Salai, on your right as you head south, just before the Thousand Lights mosque. Small and romantic, with red lanterns, painted dragons, and delicious, authentic Chinese meals. Szechuan chicken Rs65, egg-drop soup Rs25, pork dishes Rs55-65. Open daily 11:30am-3pm and 6-10:30pm. ❷

The Galloping Gooseberry, 11 Greams Rd., north of Anna Salai. Chennai's only "authentic Italian American eatery" comes as a welcome change of pace. Immaculately clean with plenty of natural light and genuine American light rock muzak. Club sandwich Rs75, pasta Rs75-95, American fried chicken Rs75. Open daily 11am-11pm. ❸

Cakes 'n' Bakes, 32 NH Rd., 1km from the southernmost end of Anna Salai. Small, popular, A/C bakery sells ice creams and plays English language radio. Cakes Rs10-20, chili chicken roll Rs35. Open daily 10am-10:30pm. ❶

Hotel Maharaja, Triplicane High Rd., at the Wallajah end. Quality breakfast *idlis* (Rs6), lunchtime "meals" (Rs30-50), and dinner time *dosas* (special *masala dosa* Rs13) for the backpackers camped out in Triplicane. Open daily 7am-11pm. ❶

MYLAPORE, ALWARPET, AND T. NAGAR

It's well worth making a short dinnertime trek out to some of the restaurants that dot the Mylapore/Alwarpet area of town; many of them have a menu and an ambience that even the more upscale competition on Anna Salai can't match.

◙ **Kabul,** 35 TKK Rd. This place gets rave reviews from locals, with good reason: waiters move at the drop of a napkin, serving kebabs (Rs125-135) so soft you can cut them with a straw. Open daily noon-3pm and 7pm-midnight. Major credit cards accepted. ❹

Saravana Veg Fast Foods, 57 Dr. Radhakrishnan Salai. The champion of the South Indian restaurant world. Superb food at unbeatable prices, served in a clean, open-air environment. *Masala dosa* Rs17, fresh fruit juices Rs18-28. Open daily 6am-11pm. ❶

Coastline, Kaaraikudi, The Dhaba, and **Shogun,** at the Kaaraikudi Complex, 84 Dr. Radhakrishna Salai. Four different restaurants in one complex: seafood, kebabs, Far Eastern, and South Indian food. Open daily 11am-4pm and 7-11:30pm. ❶

Woodlands, 72/75 Dr. Radhakrishnan Salai, attached to the New Woodlands Hotel. Good-value hotel restaurant; efficient, prompt service in cool surroundings. South Indian *thali* Rs45, *idli* Rs10, *dosas* Rs18.50. Open daily 6:30am-10pm. ❶

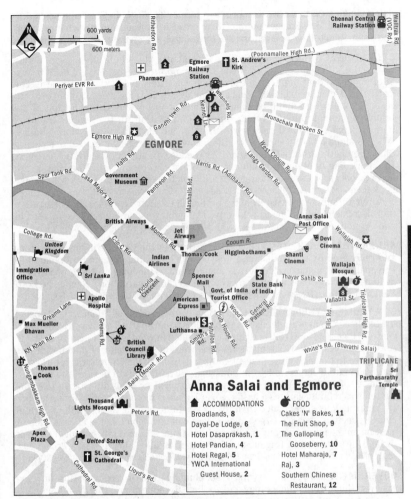

Anna Salai and Egmore

ACCOMMODATIONS
Broadlands, 8
Dayal-De Lodge, 6
Hotel Dasaprakash, 1
Hotel Pandian, 4
Hotel Regal, 5
YWCA International
Guest House, 2

FOOD
Cakes 'N' Bakes, 11
The Fruit Shop, 9
The Galloping
Gooseberry, 10
Hotel Maharaja, 7
Raj, 3
Southern Chinese
Restaurant, 12

TAMIL NADU

◉ SIGHTS

For a city of six million, Chennai is not big on sightseeing. However, the city is a proud center of Carnatic culture, and the performances of traditional music and dance at one of its many *sabhas* are well worth a visit. (Free admission.)

MARINA BEACH. The 12km of the Marina Beach, one of the world's largest city beaches, are spectacular at dusk, when the setting sun casts an iridescent glow as peddlers hawk roasted peanuts and balloons. Palm readers lure customers, telling fortunes with the aid of seashells and tarot parrots. Few people swim here, in part because of the dangerously strong tides, in part because of the social current—wearing a swimsuit in public is frowned upon. Near the beach are **Anna Park** and the antenna-like **MGR Samadhi,** memorials to former Tamil Nadu Chief Ministers C.N. Annadurai and M.G. Ramachandran. There are also several decrepit swimming pools and a slimy aquarium. Deserted areas of the beach are often unsafe, especially at night.

SRI KAPALEESWARAR TEMPLE. The Vijayanagar kings built the present structure in the 16th century and the majestic 37m *gopuram* (gateway) at its entrance after a much older temple on the shoreline was destroyed by the Portuguese. The great saint Ugnanasambandar sang a hymn here to Lord Kapaleeswarar in order to resurrect a girl who had died of a snake bite; a shrine and statue in front of the temple commemorate the event. Another explanation for the temple's name is derived from a mythical meeting of Brahma and Shiva on top of Mount Kailas. When Brahma failed to show Shiva the respect and courtesy due to him, an angry Shiva plucked off one of his *kapalams* (heads). In an act of regretful penance, Brahma came to Mylapore and installed Shiva's *linga* himself. Non-Hindus are allowed only as far as the outer courtyard, which houses a shrine to Parvati in peacock form. *(Mylapore, off Kutchery Rd. Open daily 5:30am-noon and 4-9:30pm.)*

About a 10min. walk west from the Sri Kapaleeswarar Temple is the Portuguese-built **Luz Church,** the oldest in the city. The whitewashed church has an altar in good condition and still retains a good deal of old-world atmosphere.

SRI PARTHASARATHY TEMPLE. Originally built by the Pallavas in the 8th century and renovated by the Cholas and Vijayanagar kings, this temple is dedicated to Krishna. Its distinguishing feature is that it contains the images of four of Vishnu's avatars: Varaha (boar incarnation), Narasimha (lion incarnation), Rama, and Lord Venkatakrishna. *(Triplicane, west of South Beach Rd. Open daily 6am-noon and 4-8pm.)*

SAN THOME CATHEDRAL BASILICA. Built over the tomb of Thomas the Apostle, the basilica is an important pilgrimage site. It is believed that Thomas arrived in Kerala from Palestine in AD 52, and that he was killed in what is now Chennai in AD 72. About 1000 years later, Thomas's remains were carried inland, and a church was built close to the site of the present cathedral. In 1606, the church was refurbished and made into a cathedral by the Portuguese, who carted off most of the relics to Rome. All that is left here of Thomas now is a small piece of his little toe. In 1896, the church was rebuilt again, as a basilica. San Thome is more interesting for its historical and religious significance than for its aesthetic appeal, although the peaceful church sanctuary bears a large stained glass window depicting the apostle's life. A **museum** on the premises contains the cathedral's most prized relics: a small piece of the apostle's bone and a fragment of the spear that killed him. *(Eastern Mylapore, 6km south of Egmore. Open daily 6am-6pm. Museum open M-Sa 9:30am-12:30pm and 2-5:30pm.)*

GOVERNMENT MUSEUM. A string of six buildings, the Government Museum covers everything from archaeology and zoology to modern art. The main highlights are the excellent collection of stone sculpture in the main building, and the free-standing **bronze gallery,** whose unparalleled collection of Chola bronzes includes a complete set of characters from the *Ramayana* and a succession of excellent dancing Shivas. West of the bronze gallery is the less-than-thrilling **Children's Museum** with its large plastic dinosaurs. Next door is the **National Art Gallery,** housed in a splendid Indo-Saracenic edifice, built in 1906, that is more impressive than most of the stuff inside. *(Pantheon Rd., south of Egmore Station. Open Sa-Th 9:30am-4:30pm. Rs3. Camera fee Rs200. Free tours at 10am, noon, 2, 4pm.)*

FORT ST. GEORGE. Foremost among the city's traditional attractions, the huge Fort St. George was the first fort built by the British in India and a major enclave of colonial power for more than 300 years. This is where the modern city, not Chennai, began, when East India Company official Francis Day won permission from a local ruler to begin work on fortifications here in 1639. Work on the first buildings was completed (appropriately enough) on St. George's Day, 1640, and the fort continued to be the center of local administration until Independence and beyond. Many of the original buildings were damaged or destroyed during mid-18th-century French attacks, though several remain. These days, the fort complex is home to Tamil Nadu's state government, which has closed much of it to tourists.

Amid the everyday workings of the Tamil Nadu Legislative Assembly and Council, the ghost of the fort's colonial past lingers in the **Fort Museum,** which displays an impressive assortment of items from colonial times, including uniforms, weapons, coins, lithographs, and a collection of manuscripts written by Robert Clive. *(Open Sa-Th 10am-5pm. Rs100.)*

South of the museum, the fascinating **St. Mary's Church,** consecrated in 1679, is the oldest Anglican church east of the Suez. The walls are covered with plaques dedicated to the immortal memory of various long-forgotten Englishmen and their wives. The church was built with a bomb-proof ceiling to withstand the frequent attacks on the fort. *(Open daily 9:30am-5pm. Services Su 9am, closed 9:30am-1pm.)*

Not far from Fort St. George rise the minarets of the **High Court** and the **Law College,** constructed in an Indo-Saracenic style in the mid-19th century and still in use.

LITTLE MOUNT AND ST. THOMAS MOUNT. Just south of the Adyar River is **Little Mount,** a complex of mildly interesting caves where St. Thomas led the life of an ascetic, occasionally offering sermons from his rocky pulpit. According to local lore, the impressions in the caves are St. Thomas's handprints. Little Mount has two churches, both of which attract plenty of pilgrims. The older church was built over the caves in 1551 by the Portuguese. The newer one, Sacred to Our Lady of Health, was consecrated in 1971. *(Little Mount is approx. 8km south of the city center. Autorickshaws from downtown Rs40-50.)* About 5km southwest of Little Mount, 134 steep steps lead up to **Saint Thomas Mount (Great Mount),** where St. Thomas is said to have been killed after fleeing his home at Little Mount. The Portuguese church at the top was put up in 1523 on the site of a church built by Armenian traders nearly 1000 years earlier. The altar is supposed to stand on the very spot where St. Thomas died, and legend holds that the paintings over the altar were done by St. Luke. The "bleeding cross" that hangs above the altar was discovered while digging the foundations for a new church here in 1547. It is believed to have been shaped by the hands of the saint himself, and legend has it that the cross was seen to sweat blood on several occasions during the 16th century. The cool, stone church is a very mellow and atmospheric place, and there are fantastic views of the city and the airport from the hilltop. To get there, take a suburban train south from Egmore to St. Thomas Mt. station (Rs5). It is a 20min. walk or short auto-rickshaw ride from the station to the bottom of the steps leading up to the church. Those with an interest in Chennai's present-day Christian community can visit the largest church in India—the 15,000 member congregation of New Life Assembly of God. *(Near Little Mount. English services Su 8am and 4pm.)*

OTHER SIGHTS. Guindy National Park is a peaceful, though increasingly scruffy, place where herds of deer, antelope, and mongoose are supposed to run wild, but your chances of seeing anything more exciting than an occasional monkey are slim indeed. Before you can enter the National Park, you will need to get official permission from the wildlife warden, who can normally be found drinking tea with his cronies inside the Children's Park within the same grounds, in front of the entrance to the National Park itself. *(Open W-M 9am-5pm. Rs5.)* Also on the premises is an uninspiring **Snake Park.** *(Open W-M 8:30am-5:30pm. Rs3; camera fee Rs10.)* Eastern Adyar harbors the headquarters of the **Theosophical Society,** a spiritual movement founded by a pair of Americans in 1875. The mansion is surrounded by elaborate gardens, containing "The Great Banyan Tree," one of the largest in the world. *(☎ 2491 7198. Open M-Sa 8:30-10am and 2-4pm.)*

🎦 ENTERTAINMENT

Chennai is home to India's second-largest film industry; taking in a Tamil talkie is a fun way to spend a couple of hours. You don't need to know much Tamil to figure out the plot, and you'll probably leave the theater having learned *something*. A cinema is on nearly every corner and many screen English-language movies. Two of the best movie theaters are on Anna Salai, opposite the Head Post Office. **Devi** (☎ 28555660) has showings at 1, 4, 7, and 10pm, mostly in Tamil, but occasionally in Hindi or English. (Tickets Rs10-60, advance booking office open 9am-12:30pm and 3-5pm. Advance bookings recommended.) **Shanti** (☎ 28549086), next door, has only Tamil films at 3, 6:30, and 9:45pm. (Tickets Rs10-40, no advance booking.) Women should be careful—dark cinemas are popular hangouts for dirty old men. *The Hindu* has listings of screenings and cultural events.

Performances are often given at the city's various music and dance academies *(sabhas)*. The **Carnatic Music and Dance Festival** takes place every year from early December to mid-January. **The Music Academy** (☎ 28112231), 115 E. Mowbray's Rd., often gives away free tickets for shows.

🛍 SHOPPING

Before you bust your wallet, take a moment to reflect on your itinerary. Many crafts and silks can be had for considerably less in smaller towns, where you can purchase handicrafts directly from the people who make them. Dozens of makeshift shops line the streets in **Luz** (directly south of city center in **Alwarpet**) and **Ranganathan Street** in **T. Nagar**, which is a bazaar of the South Indian variety: "cut-piece junctions" jockey for space with bangle and *bindi* sellers. Also in T. Nagar is **Usman Road,** home to a million silk houses and gold jewelry stores. It becomes riotous during wedding season. The best places to shop are at the new **Nalli** and **Kumaran** stores, across the street from each other. **Radha Silk House (RASI),** 1 Sannadhi St., Mylapore, next to the Kapaleeswarar Temple, is a favorite for silk fabrics and saris of all styles and colors. The basement has a decent selection of gift items, wooden carved boxes, brassware, and paintings. (☎ 24941906. Open daily 9am-9pm. MC/V.) Also of interest are more glitzy shopping plazas, such as **Alsa Mall,** 149 Montieth Rd., Egmore, where you can buy beautiful *salwaar kameez*, and **Spencer Plaza** on Anna Salai, where local social climbers go on Saturday afternoons to see and be seen.

🍸 NIGHTLIFE

Tamil Nadu only recently repealed its prohibition laws, and there is still a stigma attached to alcohol consumption. Most bars have heavily tinted windows and doors, as if to obscure the shameful goings-on inside. The situation is slightly better in Chennai than in most other places in Tamil Nadu, and nearly every three-to-five-star hotel has its own permit room. Most permit rooms are stocked with whatever liquor the owners can get their hands on. In a few of them, there is almost enough light for you to see what you're drinking. The bars in the **Pandian** and **New Victoria** hotels, both on Kennet Ln., are both reasonably pleasant by local standards. Around the corner in the Hotel Chandra Towers, **Bon Sante** has a good selection of the day's papers, which you can just about read by the flickering half-light of the (relatively restrained) TV in the corner. A good place for a pre-dinner drink if you're eating at one of the restaurants on Dr. Radhakrishnan Salai is the bar in the **Hotel Savera,** next to the New Woodlands Hotel. It's well-lit, with comfortable bamboo chairs and well-behaved TVs, and your beer comes with a tasty selection of munchies and snacks. Most bars are open daily 11am-11pm.

If you're looking for more serious kinds of nightlife, you've come to the wrong place. For glitzy discos and other forms of stroboscopy, the five-star hotels are the venues to look into, though many of these places seem to come and go with the seasons. The **G2 (Gatsby's)** disco, in the Park Sheraton at the bottom of TTK (Mowbray's) Rd., is one of the few places open for late-night dancing.

KANCHIPURAM காஞ்சீபுரம் ☎ 04112

A small, dusty, and bustling city surrounded by open plains and dominated by the towering *gopurams* of its ancient temples, Kanchipuram is a major center of pilgrimage and one of Hinduism's seven most sacred cities. The city's name comes from the words *Ka* (another name for Brahma, the creator) and *anchi* ("worship")—Brahma worshipped Vishnu and the goddess Kamakshi here. Some magnificent temples were built in the city between the 4th and 8th centuries, when Kanchi was the capital of the Pallava kings. Kanchi was also the seat of the guru Shankara (AD 780-820) and has been a center of philosophy and learning ever since. Today, Kanchipuram is well-known for its *sari*-producing silk emporiums, found along the city's major thoroughfares. With temples and shopping, Kanchipuram has something to offer to everyone, and—unless you're a serious pilgrim looking to stay longer—the city makes a great daytrip from Chennai.

⊫ TRANSPORTATION

Trains: Railway station, Railway Station Rd. (☎ 223149). At the northern end of Railway Station Rd. and northeast of the Vaikunta Perumal Temple. From the bus stand, go north on E. Raja Veethi, and follow the signs. This is not a busy place; there are only five passenger trains a day, which run to: **Arakkonam** (40min.; 8:53am, 6:44 and 8:57pm; Rs8); **Chennai Beach** (2¼hr.; 5:35, 7:15, and 10am; Rs20); and **Chengalpattu** (40min., 6:36am and 6:06pm, Rs9).

Buses: The chaotic **bus stand** is at the intersection of Kamarajar and Nellukkara St., hidden behind storefronts. To: **Chennai** (#76B, 2½hr., every 30min., Rs20); **Chengalpattu** (#212B, 1½hr., frequent 4:15am-10pm, Rs8.50); **Mahabalipuram** (#212A, 2hr., 10 per day 4:15am-8:30pm, Rs25); **Vellore** (#156, 2½hr., every 30min. 5am-10:30pm, Rs15.25). Frequent buses to **Pondicherry** depart from Chengalpattu.

Local Transportation: Auto-rickshaws can be flagged down on Kamarajar St. or Gandhi Rd. or picked up next to the bus stand. A ride from the bus stand to the outskirts of town should cost no more than Rs25, so be sure to bargain the price before getting in.

✳ ⁊ ORIENTATION AND PRACTICAL INFORMATION

The **bus stand** has one main entrance on **Kamarajar Street,** which runs north-south through the center of town, where many shops and eating places are located. The bus stand also empties out onto **Nellukkara Street,** which runs perpendicular to Kamarajar St. at its northern end. Much of the food and accommodations in Kanchipuram can be found here, with temples spreading out to the north. **Gandhi Road** runs parallel to Nellukkara St., about 500m down from the bus stand, turning into **T. Nambi Koil Street.** Most of Kanchi's famous silk emporiums are along these roads.

Tourist Office: There is no official tourist office, but you can get basic info and see a map at the TTDC-sponsored **Hotel Tamil Nadu,** Railway Station Rd. (☎ 222553 or 222554).

Currency Exchange: None of the banks in Kanchipuram deals with foreign exchange. In an emergency, try one of the big hotels, such as the Baboo Soorya (see below).

Market: Rajaji Market, at the intersection of Railway and Gandhi Rd. Sells all the fruit, vegetables, and mutton you could want. Open daily 8am-8pm.

Police: Taluk Police Station, Kamarajar St. (☎222181).

Pharmacy: Tamil Nadu Medicals, 75 Nellukkara St. (☎222285). West of the intersection with Kamarajar St. Open daily 8am-11pm.

Hospital: Manohar General Hospital, Railway Rd. (☎222102). A private facility.

Post Office: GPO, Railway Station Rd. Open M-F 10am-4pm, Sa 10am-1pm. **Postal Code:** 631501.

▛ ACCOMMODATIONS

Most of Kanchi's budget hotels are along the busy, noisy streets around and south of the bus station. For longer than a one-night stay—and if fresh air and clean bathrooms are a priority—this is a good place to upgrade your accommodations.

Hotel Baboo Soorya, 85 E. Raja Veethi (☎222555; fax 222556). near the Varkunta Perumal Temple, a 5min. walk from the bus stand. If you want glitz and polish, you've come to the right place. One of the best hotels in town, and you get what you pay for: immaculate rooms, an airy atrium, seat toilets, and the morning paper. All rooms have Star TV. Attached restaurant (Kanchi Woodlands, see below). Singles Rs300, with A/C Rs450; doubles Rs375, with A/C Rs525; 4-bed suites with A/C Rs900. Add 20% tax. AmEx/MC/V. ❷

Hotel Jaybala International, 504 Gandhi Rd. (☎224348). Marble-floored, mid-range hotel under the same management as the neighboring restaurant Hotel Saravana Bhavan (see below) and a successful silk emporium. For customers in A/C rooms they provide satellite TV and soap. Solitary rupee-pinching backpackers may find the non-A/C singles (no attached bath) stuffy, cell-like, and sparse. When windows look out onto hallways, check to make sure they are locked. Singles without A/C Rs125; doubles with A/C Rs340. Rs25 deposit, returned at check-out. AmEx/MC/V. ❶

Sri Rama Lodge, 20 Nellukkara St. (☎222435). Take a right out of the bus station onto Kamarajar Rd., and a left onto Mellukkara St. Just 10m on the left. Simple and clean rooms with attached (squat) bath, TV, and colorfully-printed bedspreads. Some windows look out onto airshaft. Cafe of the same name attached. Non-A/C singles Rs95; doubles Rs170, with A/C Rs420. ❶

Hotel Tamil Nadu (☎223553 or 222554; fax 222552), a two-minute walk from the station on Railway Station Rd. It might just be worth putting up with the inflated prices for the peaceful of this little-used government hotel; one of the few hotels where you won't be disturbed by the noise of buzzing buses all through the night. The secluded location may make it difficult to find at night, especially if you're coming from the bus station. Spacious doubles with attached (seat) bath and wide bay windows. Doubles Rs350, with A/C Rs490. Quads Rs490, 6-bed dorm Rs550. ❸

Rajam Lodge, 9 Kamarajar St. (☎222519). Take a left out of the bus stand; the lodge is 15m down on the left. Fun tile tesselations on the floor, but no A/C and some fluorescent lights that struggle to turn on. Squat toilets. Singles Rs80, doubles Rs130. ❶

▐ FOOD

Ananda Bhavan, on Nellukkara St., near the junction with Kamarajar St. Snacks and "pure *ghee* sweets" displayed in immaculate glass cases and doled out by the kilo. Kick back at the intimate round cafe tables and enjoy the cashew *halwa* (Rs200 per kg), the Bombay mix (Rs130 per kg), and the A/C. Open daily 8am-10pm. ❷

Kanchipuram

🏠 ACCOMMODATIONS
Hotel Baboo Soorya, **2**
Hotel Jaybala International, **8**
Hotel Tamil Nadu, **1**
Rajam Lodge, **7**
Sri Rama Lodge, **6**

🍎 FOOD
Ananda Bhavan, **5**
Kanchi Woodlands, **3**
Hotel Saravana Bhavan, **9**
Hotel Sakthy Ganapathy, **4**

TAMIL NADU

Hotel Saravana Bhavan, 504 Gandhi Rd., next to Hotel Jaybala International. A bustling, lively spot with about a dozen tables and A/C that is somewhat stymied by the large, open doors. *Ghee masala dosa* Rs42, "quick lunch" Rs30. Also has a self-service counter with clean marble counters and floors. Hearty mini-*tiffin* Rs30. Full service 10am-4pm, 7-10pm. Self-service available noon-10pm. ❷

Hotel Sakthy Ganapathy, E. Raja Veethi St., about 2min. north from the bus stand. Typical South Indian "meals" joint serving all your old favorites. An always-crowded cross between a Salvation Army soup kitchen and a summer camp cafeteria. *Rava dosa* Rs16. Lunch meal Rs20. Open daily 5:30am-9:30pm. ❶

Kanchi Woodlands, inside Hotel Baboo Soorya. Igloo-like restaurant with white ceilings, white walls, white floors, A/C and no windows. Helpful waitstaff, diverse menu, which includes North and South Indian, Chinese, and American fare. South Indian *thali* Rs30. American breakfast Rs60. Open daily 7am-11pm. ❷

☉ SIGHTS

The temples here are spread out along the northern side of town. Auto-rickshaw *wallahs* will ask for Rs150-200 for a tow, including "waiting charges"—try to bargain down. Below, the temples are arranged in clockwise order with the must-see temples first.

SRI KAILASANATHA TEMPLE. Don't let this temple's remote location down a bumpy path prevent you from visiting. The trip is worth it: of Kanchi's temples, Sri Kailasanatha is the cleanest, most peaceful, and in the best condition. Built by Rajasimba Pallava in the first quarter of the 8th century, this temple is the oldest building in Kanchi. Its relatively modest size and soft amber sandstone are both characteristic of Pallava temples; the famous shore temple at Mahabalipuram was built by the same team at about the same time. The interior of the wall surrounding the shrine is marked by a row of 58 small meditation chambers. In some, traces of the temple's frescoes can still be seen. On the rear wall of the sanctum are carvings of Shiva performing the Urdhwa Tandava dance of destruction. The inner sanctum houses a *linga* to which it is believed Vishnu prayed for help in defeating the demon Tripurantaka. The temple is often relatively empty since most visitors opt for either the Kamakshi Amman or Sri Ekambaranathar temples in the center of town. (*1½km out of town. Follow Nellukkara St. westward until it becomes Putteri St. Sri Kailasanatha is on the right past a small lake. Open daily 8:30am-noon and 4-6pm. To make the most of your visit, arrive before sunset.*)

SRI EKAMBARANATHAR TEMPLE. As the biggest temple in Kanchi, the magnificent white *gopuram* of the Sri Ekambaranathar Temple dominates the skyline across the northern part of town. Inside, its dark, mysterious *linga*-lined and columned hallways evoke a sense of timelessness. The focal point of the temple is nearly timeless itself: a huge, supposedly 3500 year old mango tree stands in the center of the inner sanctum. It is from this tree that the temple derives its name—the root "Eka" means "mango tree." Each of its four branches—they represent the four books of the Vedas—are said to produce a different type of leaf, as well as fruit of a different taste. Locals believe that eating the fruit cures women of infertility, and many women hang brightly colored ribbons and offerings from the branches.

The origins of the temple are recorded in the *sthalapurana*, which recounts Parvati's mischief when she jokingly covered the eyes of her soon-to-be husband Shiva and upset the process of creation and destruction. Shiva was so angry that he ordered Parvati down to earth, where she came to a mango tree on the banks of the river Kampa in Kanchi and fashioned a *linga* of sand. To test her devotion, Shiva placed numerous obstacles before her, all of which Parvati overcame. Finally, Shiva let the Ganga flow from his hair, hoping to inundate Kanchi and wash the *linga* away. But Parvati's devotion was so great that she held tight, protecting the *linga* through the torrent. Duly impressed, Shiva took her back and they were wed under the temple's mango tree. The *linga* is housed in the inner sanctum of the temple.

Although non-Hindus are generally not allowed into the inner sanctum, they can feed puffed rice to the fish in the temple's *ghat*-enclosed pool. Colorful works are displayed during the temple's festivals in April and July. Shiva and Parvati's wedding anniversary is celebrated during the full moon in March. (*Taking Puthupalayam St. leads north directly to the temple. Open daily 6am-12:30pm and 4-8:30pm. Puja 6 and 7am, noon, 4, 5, and 9pm.*)

KAMAKSHI AMMAN TEMPLE. Painted elephants will greet you inside Kamakshi Amman and bless your head with their trunks if you offer a few paise donation. *Gopurams* cast in soft shades of yellow, green, and pink and capped with tiny wooden spires adorn this temple, dedicated to Kamakshi, an incarnation of the goddess Devi and the town's resident deity. The temple is one of India's sacred *shakti pithas*, sites devoted to the worship of the female element in creation (*shakti*). The inner sanctum (inaccessible to non-Hindus) is a squarish chamber with inscriptions on all sides. Outside, a golden tower gleams in the sunlight. The sacred tank in the back is also steeped in legend—Vishnu supposedly sent two servants-turned-demons to bathe here in order to cleanse them of their evil ways. There is also an art gallery under a tent in front which houses depictions of various figures from Hindu mythology. *(From W. Raja St., turn right onto Amman Koli St. Photography not permitted. Open daily 6am-12:30pm and 4-8:30pm.)*

VAIKUNTA PERUMAL TEMPLE. This temple, dedicated to Vishnu, is one of the oldest in Kanchipuram as evidenced by its won gray stone sculptures. Ancient texts proclaim that those who worship devotedly on the holiday of *Maha Shivaratri* will have sons who will be followers of Vishnu. The courtyard surrounding the inner sanctum is lined with granite pillars and carvings depicting the Pallava kings, battle scenes, and musicians. The back left corner has a panel showing Xuanzang, the Chinese Buddhist pilgrim who traveled all over India during the 7th century.

The central spire contains three images of Vishnu, one on top of the other. On the ground floor he is seen sitting; on the second floor, reclining on the serpent *ananta;* on the top, standing in an ascetic pose. A small walkway around the *vimana* is filled with well-preserved panels of Vishnu and Lakshmi. *(From E. Raja St., turn right; the temple is several hundred meters ahead. Open daily 8am-noon and 4-7:30pm.)*

⌐ SHOPPING

Each Kanchi sari is woven by hand and takes between 15 days and one month to complete. Kanchi silks start around Rs1000 and skyrocket into the tens of thousands for elaborate wedding saris. Expect to pay at least Rs3000 for a good quality sari with a fair amount of *zari* (pure gold thread) and an intricately woven *pallu* (the part that drapes over the shoulder). Store owners should give you at least a Rs1200 "discount" off the first price named. Most owners will gladly take you to the back of the stores to show you silk yarn and demonstrate the process of adding *zari* designs onto saris. Turn right onto the road perpendicular to Sannadhi St. (outside Varadaraja Perumal Temple), and take a left at **Ammangar Street,** which is full of silk weavers who are eager to demonstrate their craft. Weavers' cooperatives cluster near temple entrances, where you'll probably be accosted by salesmen wielding business cards.

MAHABALIPURAM (MAMALLAPURAM)
மஹாபலிபுரம்
☎ 04114

Until about 20 years ago, Mahabalipuram was a quiet little fishing village on the Bay of Bengal. And then came the tourists, drawn here by the prospect of sun, sand, sea, and the unique collection of stone sculptures left behind from Mahabalipuram's glory days over 1000 years ago, when it was the major sea port of the Pallava dynasty. Although the incessant push of the tourist trade can be overwhelming (there is even a Tourist Dance Festival devoted to all the foreign visitors from late December to late January every year, when the tourist madness really hits its peak), it's worth striking out for the fresh fish, beach breezes, and serene temples that make Mahabalipuram a mecca for backpackers traveling in Tamil Nadu.

⌐ TRANSPORTATION

Buses: The **bus stand** is on E. Raja St. To: **Chennai** (2hr., every 20min. 4:30am-9pm, Rs17-23); **Chengalpattu** (1hr, every hr. 5:20am-9pm, Rs9); **Kanchipuram** (2hr., every 2hr. 5:20am-9pm, Rs19); **Kovalam** (40min., every hr. 5:30am-8pm, Rs7); **Pondicherry** (2hr., frequent, Rs30); **Tirupati** (5hr., 3 per day 5am-3pm, Rs50-60).

Local Transportation: Auto-rickshaws and **tourist taxis** wait outside the bus stand, but you won't need them unless you stay at one of the beach resorts outside town. Several places rent **bikes,** including Moonraker's, on Othavadai St. (Rs25 per day).

> **WARNING.** Swimming in the Bay of Bengal can be very dangerous, and many people drown every year. Ask at the tourist office and at your hotel about the feasibility of swimming. Even if you are an experienced swimmer, don't underestimate the force of the undertow.

✦❷ ORIENTATION AND PRACTICAL INFORMATION

Finding your way around Mahabalipuram is a cinch. From the **inter-city bus stand,** it's a 5min. walk north (left) along **East Raja Street** to the intersection of **TKM Road.** As E. Raja St. crosses TKM Rd., it becomes **Kovalam Road,** which leads out of town to the Tiger Cave and beach resorts. Off E. Raja St. before TKM Rd., is **Othavadai Street,** which takes a sharp right turn before the fishing beach and has most of the town's restaurants and hotels on it.

Tourist Office: TTDC, Kovalam St. (☎242232). Open M-Sa 10am-5:45pm.

Currency Exchange: LKP Forex at the intersection of E. Raja and Othavadai St. Changes cash, traveler's checks. **Indian Overseas Bank,** TKM Rd. Walk north on E. Raja St., and turn left onto TKM Rd. Changes cash and AmEx and Thomas Cook traveler's checks. Open M-F 10am-2pm, Sa 10am-noon.

Police: Police Station, Kovalam St. (☎242221), next to the tourist office. Open 24hr.

Hospital: Suradeep Hospital, Thirukula St. (☎2442390 or 2442448), next to Baskin Robbins, has a **24hr. pharmacy.** If you're seriously ill, your best bet is to go to Chennai.

Internet: VAT Telecom Center, 144 E. Raja St. (☎242711), just north of Othavadai St. Open 6am-10pm, Rs50 per hr.

Post Office: On a small lane off E. Raja St., near the tourist office. Open M-Sa 8am-4pm. **Postal Code:** 603104.

⌐ ACCOMMODATIONS

You won't struggle to find a place to stay in Mahabalipuram. Dozens of cheap hotels have sprung up to cater to high-season tourists. Most of the cheapest places are on or near E. Raja, Othavadai, and Thirukula St. The posher resorts are north and south of town.

Seashore Guest House (☎242074 or 242047). Clean, colorful bedspreads and an ocean view set over a relaxed beach side restaurant. Doubles Rs300-500. ❶

Surya Camping Site (Resort), Thirukula St. (☎242292), just off Othavadai. Not a camping site at all. Newly built, lovely cottages with a lagoon or garden-view. Doubles Rs350-750. Add 20% tax. ❶

ACCOMMODATIONS
Hotel Sea Breeze, **6**
Mamalla Bhavan Annexe, **4**
Seashore Guest House, **3**
Sterling, **10**
Surya Camping Site (Resort), **5**

Mahabalipuram (Mamallapuram)

TO TIGER CAVE (3km) &
COLLEGE OF SCULPTURE (1km)

Indian Bank
TKM Rd.

Trimurti Cave

Othavadai St.
LKP

Mandapam

Krishna's Butterball
Ratha

Ganesha Ratha
Ratha

Mandapam

Dhamaraja Lion Throne
Varaha Mandapam

Koneri Tank

Arjuna's Penance

Krishna Mandapam

Rayala Gopuram

Ramanuja Mandapam

Mandapam

Shiva Temple
New Lighthouse

Mandapam

Mandapam

Adivartha Temple

TO THE 5 RATHAS (250m)

Shore Temple Rd.

Tank

Shore Temple

Bay of Bengal

Fishing Beach (no swimming)

Swimming Beach

0   100 yards
0   100 meters

Unpaved Trails
Paved Trails

FOOD
Golden Palate Restaurant, **6**
La Vie En Rose, **9**
Mamalla Bhavan, **8**
Moonrakers, **2**
New Papillon Restaurant, **7**
Santana Beach
 Restaurant, **1**

TAMIL NADU

Sterling (☎243914, 243915), up the guarded driveway off Shore Temple Rd. Classical music, seashell encrusted columns, and a huge vaulted pavilion will greet you. Room rate includes impeccable service, A/C, yoga and meditation, and an evening cultural program. Doubles Rs2200. Add Rs275 tax. V/MC. ❺

Lakshmi Lodge, 5 Othavadai St. (☎242463), down the road to the right after Moonrakers Restaurant. Sea-side lodge full of foreigners. Bright, well-kept rooms, many overlooking the sea. Most bathrooms have seat toilets. Staff will arrange practically anything for guests, including bikes, massage, and astrology readings. Attached rooftop restaurant. Check-out noon. Singles Rs100-200; doubles Rs100-350. ❶

Hotel Sea Breeze (☎243035; fax 243065), at the end of Othavadai St. after it turns right. Marble floors, wooden furniture, balconies. Non-guests use the pool for Rs100. Breakfast included. Singles Rs300; doubles Rs490-975. Add 10% luxury tax. ❷

Mamalla Bhavan Annexe, 104 E. Raja St. (☎242060). The swankiest and most luxurious budget spot in town. Spacious rooms have marble-tiled floors with double beds and cable TVs. Attached restaurant. Doubles Rs400-700. ❷

▶ FOOD

Mahabalipuram is full of restaurants offering backpackers' favorites like *muesli*, banana pancakes, and seafood, but you'll have a difficult time finding straightforward Indian food. Beer is available, though it's not on most menus—you'll have to ask for it. Many places close down off-season; most of the restaurants listed below should be open throughout the year.

■ **Moonrakers,** Othavadai St. European breakfasts are popular (*muesli* and yogurt Rs40), but the mellow vibes keep travelers here throughout the day. The most-visited backpacker hangout in town. Fish and chips Rs100, calamari Rs100, honey crepes Rs25. Ask to see the fish for freshness. Open daily 7am-1am. ❷

Santana Beach Resort, at the end of Othavadai St. A simple little place on the beach, with tables set in the sand overlooking the sea. Fish Rs75-150, calamari Rs100. Open 7am-10:30pm. ❷

New Papillon Restaurant, Shore Temple Rd. Opposite the turnoff for Sterling. Quaint pastel-painted place with clean tablecloths and a selection of Western music. Grilled snapper Rs70, jumbo prawns Rs100, fresh fruit juices Rs25. Open daily 8am-10pm. ❶

La Vie En Rose, E. Raja St., near the bus stand, 150m down on the left-hand side. Small and quiet upstairs balcony, away from the heat and hassles of the street. Despite the French name, the menu here is pretty much the same one you will see in every other restaurant in town. Grilled fish Rs70, beer Rs70. Open daily 7am-10:30pm. ❶

Golden Palate Restaurant, 104 E. Raja St., inside Mamalla Bhavan Annexe. Good, classy A/C joint with professional service and a good range of North and South Indian food. *Tandoori gobi* Rs55, *malai kofta* Rs45, South Indian *thali* Rs55. Open daily 6am-9:30pm. ❶

Mamalla Bhavan, off E. Raja St., opposite the bus stand. The most popular "meals hotel" around. If you can't take the tourists anymore, come here for your daily dose of *dosas*. Special "meals" Rs27. Open daily 6am-9:30pm. ❶

◉ SIGHTS

Mahabalipuram has an incredible collection of well-preserved sculpture in a peaceful enclosed park-like area west of E. Raja St., thankfully removed from the madness of touts and tourists. Scholars agree that most of these masterpieces were sculpted under the patronage of the 7th-century Pallava leader Narasimhavarman I, who went by the fearsome name Mamalla, which means "Great Wrestler"—hence the town's (official) name. The sights are all in the southern part of town, within easy walking distance of most of the hotels.

SHORE TEMPLE. Dedicated to Shiva and Vishnu, Mahabalipuram's famous shore temple was constructed during the 8th century and was probably the first South Indian temple built entirely of stone. The Pallavas' maritime exploits helped spread their culture far and wide, and echoes of the Shore Temple's lion carvings and stocky spires can be seen in much South Asian temple architecture from the period. Inside the temple are a flower-strewn image of Vishnu reclining on the serpent Sesa and a broken, fluted-granite Shiva *linga*. Outside the temple, carved panels depict scenes from the lives of its Pallava creators. There has been speculation that the Shore Temple once served as a lighthouse, which would explain its oddly elongated *vimana*. It is now protected and maintained by the Archaeological Society of India. *(On Shore Temple Rd., jutting into the Bay of Bengal, 1km right of the bus stand. Open daily 6am-5:30pm. US$5 or equivalent in Rs includes admission to the five Rathas.)*

ARJUNA'S PENANCE AND KRISHNA MANDAPAM. One of the largest bas-relief sculptures in the world, Arjuna's Penance is the most impressive sight in town. Particularly engaging are the elegant, humorous depictions of animals and birds which include whimsical renderings of an elephant family and an ascetic, meditating cat surrounded by dancing rats. The spectacle itself is easy enough to admire, but scholars are still scratching their heads trying to figure out what it's all supposed to mean. According to one widely accepted theory, Arjuna's Penance depicts a story from the *Mahabharata*—the scrawny man standing on one leg is the penitent archer Arjuna, who is gazing through a prism and imploring Shiva to give him the *pashupatashastra*, a powerful magic arrow. Other historians believe that the images represent Rama's ancestor, Bhagiratha, begging the gods to give the River Ganga to the people of the world. The gods have agreed to comply with Bhagiratha's request, and the whole of creation has turned out to watch the miracle of Ganga gushing down from the Himalayas. *(In town, just behind the bus stand on W. Raja St.)* **Krishna Mandapam,** a large mid-7th-century bas-relief, shows Krishna holding up Mount Govardhana to protect his relatives and their cows from the floods brought on by the god Indra. Other panels illustrate scenes from Krishna's life, including his flirtatious play *(lila)* with the milkmaids *(gopis)*. *(Just meters away from Arjuna's Penance, to the left as you face the monument.)*

RATHAS. This collection of worn yet stunning monoliths known as the **Pancha Pandava Rathas,** was carved during the reign of Narasimhavarman I, and they are thought to be scale models of temples known to the Dravidian builders of the 7th century. The five temples were clearly influenced by Buddhist temple architecture and are named for the five Pandava brothers, the heroes of the *Mahabharata.* The largest, the **Dharmaraja Ratha,** is adorned with various carvings of demi-gods and Narasimhavarman. The complex also includes life-size animals carved out of stone. *(About 1.5km south of town along E. Raja St. US$5 or the equivalent in Rs, includes admission to the Shore Temple.)*

MANDAPAMS AND SURROUNDING MONUMENTS. The hilly area behind the bus stand and Arjuna's Penance is strewn with massive boulders and 10 small **mandapams** (cave temples), which depict tales from Hindu mythology. Finding your way from one *mandapam* to the next is not difficult; a well-marked path links most of the main monuments. Just around the corner to the right from Arjuna's Penance is the **Ganesha Ratha,** containing an image of the elephant-headed son of Shiva and Parvati. North of the *ratha* and off to the left is **Krishna's Butterball,** a massive boulder balanced on the side of a hill. The name comes from popular stories of Krishna's youth, which recount an incident when the baby Krishna was caught stealing *ghee* from an urn. North of the Butterball and next to a Pallavan water tank is the **Trimurti Cave,** which contains shrines to Shiva, Vishnu, and Brahma; all are depicted with their right hands in the *abhya* or blessing pose. The **Kotikal Mandapam,** dating from the turn of the 7th century, is down the hill to the left. A small cell in the back is guarded by stone carvings of female attendants.

Heading south back toward Arjuna's Penance, you'll first pass the 7th-century **Varaha Mandapam.** Its four panels represent the goddess Varaha raising the earth from the ocean. Most impressive is the one on the left, which depicts Vishnu in the form of a boar with the goddess Bhumidevi (Earth) seated in his lap. Another panel depicts the goddess of wealth, Lakshmi, accompanied by elephants.

Up the steep hill directly west of the Krishna Mandapam is the decaying **Rayala Gopuram.** This uncompleted structure bears slender vertical panels that portray the 10 incarnations of Vishnu. From the Krishna Mandapam, it's a short walk south to the **Ramanuja Mandapam,** built in the mid-7th-century and almost completely ruined by vandals who chiseled away at many of the temple's elaborate panels. From here, you can see the 100-year-old **New Lighthouse.** Next to the lighthouse is a Shiva temple at an especially high elevation which was used as a lighthouse until the turn of the last century.

TIGER CAVE. The so-called Tiger Cave is actually the remains of an 8th-century Pallava temple sacred to the mighty goddess Durga. A large rock-hewn monument survives and is decorated with a dozen or so carvings of snarling tigers, Durga's constant companions. Several meters away, down a small flights of steps, is a small, wind-worn Shiva temple. *(About 3km north of Mahabalipuram on the beach just off the main road to Chennai.)*

GOVERNMENT COLLEGE OF SCULPTURE AND ARCHITECTURE. Hundreds of artists-in-training learn their craft at this lively seaside complex. Contact the tourist office or college directly to make an appointment for a look around. *(☎ 242261. About 3km north of Central Mahabalipuram along Kovalam Rd.)*

CROCODILE BANK. The crocodile bank in Vodanammali, a small town about 15km north of Mahabalipuram on the main road to Chennai, was set up about 30 years ago in an attempt to breed endangered species of alligators and crocodiles in captivity. The project has been a big success, and the park now contains thousands of crocodiles, including many very rare breeds. Next door is the government-run **Snake Venom Extraction** facility. *(☎ 246332. 15km north of Mahabalipuram. Open daily Tu-Su 8am-5:30pm. Rs20.)*

PONDICHERRY பா டிக்செழ்   ☎ 0413

Although once the capital of French India, Pondicherry ain't Paris. It is, however, home to a comfortable Indian middle-class, a magnet for European tourists and devotees, and a trendy vacation spot for fashionable North Indian families. In other words, Pondicherry is a relaxing, chic, and relatively pricey city.

Pondy is split geographically and culturally by a narrow canal. To the west is plain old Pondy, your basic, bustling, medium-sized South Indian city. To the east of the canal is *Pondichérie*, where bougainvillea bursts over whitewashed walls, the streets are well-kept, restaurants serve French food, and the architecture is European. Most of the city's elaborate buildings were constructed during the French occupation, begun in 1673 by François Martin, who hoped to gain a commercial advantage for his country over the Dutch and English. For the next two centuries, the French ruled their South Asian colonial enclaves from here. In 1954, they handed over their scattered territories to the Indian government. With Pondicherry as their capital, these became a semi-autonomous Union Territory.

Today, the overwhelming influence on the city is the Sri Aurobindo Ashram, established in 1926. Sri Aurobindo Ghose, a Bengali poet, philosopher and former freedom fighter, popularized his spiritual teachings here with the help of French artist Mirra Alfassa (later known as "the Mother.") The fruits of their efforts are readily apparent today: the ashram owns huge chunks of real estate in Pondy, and followers from around the world still live in the Mother's experimental utopian community at **Auroville,** 12km north of the city.

▐▀ TRANSPORTATION

Trains: The **railway station** (☎ 2336684) is on South Blvd. Reservations Counter open M-Sa 8am-2pm. Call for schedules to **Villupuram** on the Chennai-Rameswaram line, which is undergoing repairs as of July 2003.

Buses: The massive bus station is on Lal Bahadur Shastri Salai. There are several reservation and inquiry counters. Timetables are posted in English. **Bangalore** (8hr., 5 per day 7:30am-midnight, Rs110); **Chennai** (3hr., every 15min., Rs55); **Chidambaram** (2hr., frequent, Rs20) via **Cuddalore** (Rs7); **Coimbatore** (9hr., 3 per day 8:30-10:30pm, Rs150); **Kanchipuram** (frequent, Rs30) via **Tindivanam; Mahabalipuram** (2hr., every 30min., Rs40); **Trichy** (5hr., 10pm, Rs70); **Trivandrum** (16hr., 5pm, Rs261); **Vellore** (8hr., 5am and 4:30pm, Rs100).

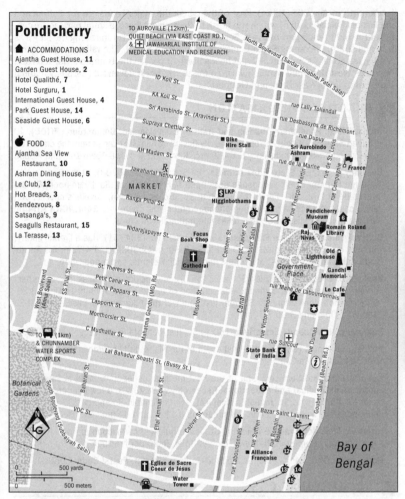

Pondicherry

🏠 ACCOMMODATIONS
Ajantha Guest House, **11**
Garden Guest House, **2**
Hotel Qualithé, **7**
Hotel Surguru, **1**
International Guest House, **4**
Park Guest House, **14**
Seaside Guest House, **6**

🍴 FOOD
Ajantha Sea View
   Restaurant, **10**
Ashram Dining House, **5**
Le Club, **12**
Hot Breads, **3**
Rendezvous, **8**
Satsanga's, **9**
Seagulls Restaurant, **15**
La Terasse, **13**

TO AUROVILLE (12km),
QUIET BEACH (VIA EAST COAST RD.),
& ✚ JAWAHARLAL INSTITUTE OF
MEDICAL EDUCATION AND RESEARCH

North Boulevard (Sardar Valliabhai Patel Salai)

ID Koil St.
KA Koil St.
Sri Aurobindo St. (Aravindar St.)
Supraya Chettiar St.
C Koil St.
AH Madam St.
Jawaharlal Nehru (JN) St.
MARKET
Ranga Pillai St.
Vellaja St.
Nidarajapayer St.

rue Lally Tollendal
rue Desbassyns de Richemont
rue Dupuy
Sri Aurobindo
Ashram
rue de la Marine
■ Bike
Hire Stall
Pondicherry
Museum
Romain Roland
Library
Raj
Nivas
Old
Lighthouse
Government
Place
Gandhi
Memorial
Le Café
rue Mahé de Labourdonnais

St. Theresa St.
Petit Canal St.
Sinna Pappara St.
Lapporth St.
Monthorsier St.
C Mudhaliar St.
Lal Bahadur Shastri St. (Bussy St.)

West Boulevard (Anna Salai)
SS Pilai St.
Baharati St.
VOC St.
South Boulevard (Stobbayah Salai)

TO 🚌 (1km)
& CHUNNAMBER
WATER SPORTS
COMPLEX

Botanical
Gardens

Mahatma Gandhi (MG) Rd.
Mission St.
Ellai Amman Covil St.
Cazwar St.
Canal

Focus
Book Shop
Canteen St.
Capt. Xavier St.
Ambur Salai
🛒 LKP
Higginbothams
Cathedral

rue François Martin
rue de St. Louis
rue Compagnie
France

rue Victor Simonel
rue Surcouf
State Bank
of India 💲
rue Labourdonnais
rue Suffren
rue Romain Roland
rue Bazar Saint Laurent
Alliance
Française

Goubert Salai (Beach Rd.)
rue Dumas

Eglise de Sacre
Coeur de Jésus
Water
Tower ■

Bay of
Bengal

0 ⊢ 500 yards
0 ⊢ 500 meters

TAMIL NADU

Local Transportation: Auto-rickshaws are everywhere, as usual. Pay no more than Rs25 for a trip between the bus stands and the French side of town. **Bicycles** are available to Park Guest House guests for Rs20 per day, or from the cycle stalls 2-3 blocks north of JN St. on Mission St. (Open daily 7:30am-9pm. Rs3 per hr. or Rs25 per day.)

🧭 ORIENTATION

Pondy is a well-planned city, bordered on the east by the **Bay of Bengal** and divided into eastern and western sections by a covered canal that is more easily identifiable by smell than by sight. Streets are laid out in a simple grid. The three major east-west commercial thoroughfares in north to south order, are **Jawaharlal Nehru (JN)**, **Ranga Pil-lai**, and **Lal Bahadur Shastri** (Bussy Street). Lal Bahadur Shastri leads past the **bus stand**. West of the canal, the major north-south avenue is **Mahatma Gandhi (MG) Road**, which leads north to **Auroville** (12km). East of the canal, the major roads are **rue Suffren** and **rue Romain Roland**, both of which run north to **Government Place**, a small park at the center of the old French part of town. **Goubert Salai** (Beach Road) runs along the shore as it heads south, becoming **South Boulevard** (Subbaiyah Salai). The **railway station** is off Subbaiyah Salai. As Subbaiyah Salai heads north, it passes the Botanical Gardens and becomes **West Boulevard** (Anna Salai). To the north, **North Boulevard** (Sardar Vallabhai Patel Salai) links West Blvd. and Goubert Salai.

⚡ PRACTICAL INFORMATION

Tourist Office: Pondicherry Tourism and Transport Development Corporation (PTTDC), 40 Goubert Salai (☎2339497). **Tours** of the city (including Auroville) depart from the office (full-day Rs70, 9am-5:30pm; half-day Rs60, 2pm-5:30pm). Open daily 8:45am-1pm and 2-5pm.

Currency Exchange: State Bank of India, rue Surcouf (☎2336208). At the intersection with rue Suffren. Foreign exchange desk open M-F 10am-2pm, Sa 10am-noon. On the west side of town, **LKP Forex,** 185 Mission St., exchanges cash, traveler's checks, and gives cash advances against international credit cards. There is a **24hr. ICICI ATM** on the north end of Mission St. that takes international ATM cards.

Cultural Centers: Alliance Française, 38 rue Suffren (☎2334351). Has a French library, cultural events and art displays. Open M-Sa 8:30am-12:30pm and 4-7pm. **Sri Aurobindo Ashram** (see p. 594) also offers films, special events, and a bookshop.

Bookstore: Focus, 204 Mission St. (☎2345513), is considered by locals to be the best bookshop in town. Also carries a wide selection of music. Open 9:30am-1:30pm, 3:30-9pm. **French Bookshop,** rue Suffren, just south of the Alliance Française. Open M-Sa 9am-12:30pm and 3:30-7:30pm.

Pharmacy: New Ananda Emporium, 160 JN St., just west of the intersection with MG Rd.

Police: rue Dumas (☎2337243), just south of rue Mahe de Labourdonnais; turn left off Goubert Salai at Le Cafe.

Hospital/Medical Services: One of the best medical colleges in India is **Jawaharlal Institute of Medical and Educational Research** (☎2372380), a few km north of town; take NH 45 straight. **St. Joseph's Hospital,** 16 rue Romain Roland (☎2339513), has an emergency ward open 24hr. Consultations 8-11am and 4-6pm.

Internet: Sree Netcorner, 54 Mission St., is the quickest connection in town. Rs30 per hr. Open daily 9am-8pm. **Netsurf,** Goubert Salai. Rs20 per hr. Open daily 9am-9pm.

Post Office: GPO, Ranga Pillai St. Open M-Sa 8am-5:30pm. **Postal Code:** 605001.

🏠 ACCOMMODATIONS

Apart from a few luxury hotels catering to the business crowd and jet-set North Indians on holiday, accommodations in Pondy fall into two basic categories: standard Indian lodges and ashram guest houses. The ashram guest houses offer some great deals and include the option of extremely cheap meals at the ashram dining hall as long as you don't mind a few rules (no drinking, no smoking, and no fun after lights-out) and photos of Sri Aurobindo and the Mother over every doorway. All ashram guest houses close their gates at 10:30pm. They were originally set up to accommodate devotees, so unrepentant materialists in search of nothing more than a good time may feel slightly out of place.

▨ **Seaside Guest House** (☎2336494), at the northern end of Goubert Salai. Brand new ashram guest house with gleaming white tile floors, attentive service, buffet meals, and relaxing balconies. Pictures of Sri Aurobindo and the mother available upon request.

Check-out noon. Doubles Rs350, with ocean view Rs450. MC/V. ❸

■ **Park Guest House,** Goubert Salai (☎2344412). The best setting in all of Pondicherry—right at the Southern end of Goubert Salai, with balconies looking out over manicured lawns to the Bay of Bengal beyond. Cleaned daily, rooms have couch, desk, comfy bed, mosquito net, and bureau. Attached baths with seat toilet, towels, soap, showers. Bike rental Rs20 per day. Attached restaurant. Check-out noon. Doubles Rs300-600. ❷

Hotel Qualithé, rue Mahe de Labourdonnais (☎2334325), a crumbling building with old-world charm overlooking Government Plaza. Has large rooms with attached bath (seat toilets). No drinking restrictions here; the popular open-air bar downstairs is open till 11pm. Check-out noon. Singles Rs200; doubles Rs400; quads Rs500. ❷

Hotel Surguru, 104 SV Patel Salai (☎2339022), in the northern end of town. Classy mid-range hotel with the town's best veg. restaurant. Doubles Rs410-780. ❸

Garden Guest House, 6 Akkasamy Madam St. (☎2220797). Extremely cheap and clean ashram guest house in a leafy neighborhood in the north end of town. Rooms with attached bath (squat toilets) Rs40. ❶

International Guest House, 47 Gingy St. (☎2336699). One of the largest ashram-run guest houses, but often full. Spacious and sparkling clean, white rooms overseen by ashram devotees. Minimum 2-day stay. Singles Rs100; doubles Rs150-450. ❶

Ajantha Guest House, 22 Goubert Salai (☎2338898), south of the tourist office. Stuffy rooms could use some light, but the location (right on the ocean) tries to compensate. Attached baths with seat toilets. Check-out 24hr. Doubles Rs300. ❷

🍴 FOOD

Eating out in Pondicherry comes as a welcome change of pace. Pondy's colonial legacy includes a handful of glitzy European restaurants serving French food and cheapish beer and cocktails. You can find better-than-average North and South Indian food at inflated prices on both sides of the canal.

■ **Satsanga's,** rue Labourdonnais. Quite the lovers' nest at night, with its high arches, potted jungle plants, and candlelight. Perfectly-cooked pasta (Rs85-105) and pizza (Rs95-120) as well as a wide range of meat and fish dishes (Rs120) make this *the* place to eat in Pondicherry. Open Tu-Su 8am-noon and 3-7pm. ❸

THE BIG SPLURGE

LA VIE 'CHERIE

The influence of French colonial culture lives on in the white-trimmed **Hotel de l'Orient,** a colonial-era *manoir* just a few blocks from the oceanfront in Pondicherry. With period furniture, wide teak shutters, and Indian fineries adorning each of the hotel's fourteen suites, l'Orient provides travelers with a luxurious escape from Indian reality. Sleep soundly on a walnut four-poster bed, and pamper your feet on the plush Savonnerie rugs, woven on the looms of Jaipur.

L'Orient's genteel staff will meet you at the airport in Chennai, arrange day excursions around Pondicherry, to outlying Mahabalipuram, or to the stunning temple sites at Chidambaran or Gangaikondacholapuram. The hotel's central garden court restaurant is an elegant brunch spot. If you feel like you've been missing out on the chance to indulge, the hotel invites you to experience life in "a graceful era when leisure was no idle man's sin." Whether you'll be agitating for independence from this kind of colonial rule remains to be seen.

Hotel de l'Orient, 17 Rue Romain Rolland (☎2343067; orient1804@satyam.net.in). Doubles Rs1750-3500, extra bed Rs300.

Seagulls Restaurant, 19 rue Dumas, at the southernmost end of the street, overlooking Park Guest House. Surrounded by palm trees and just steps from the Bay of Bengal, the open-air dining area is the perfect spot for a quiet evening beer (Rs42). The food's not bad either. *Paneer masala* Rs45, chicken *korma* Rs60. Open daily 11am-10:30pm. ❷

Rendezvous, 30 rue Suffren, on the corner with Bussy St., east of the canal. Rooftop dining, tuxedoed waiters, and elegantly folded napkins. Pasta with sauce Rs60-100, rich mousse Rs25. Open M and W-Su 8-10:30am, 11:30am-3pm, 6-10:30pm. MC/V. ❸

Le Club, 33 rue Dumas. This is a great place to come for dinner, especially if you're not paying. Open-terraced French restaurant with excellent food and graceful service in English or French. Three restaurants in one: **Bistro Cafe,** 7am-6pm; **Le Club,** 6-10pm; and **Indochine,** Southeast Asian, Vietnamese and Chinese fare, 7-10pm. AmEx/V. ❸

La Terasse, 5 South Blvd., a short jaunt west from the southern end of Goubert Salai. Relax in a small courtyard under a bamboo-slatted roof as the scent of the wood-fire oven wafts into the dining area. Thin-crust pizza Rs60-125, fresh fruit juices Rs20, Indian veg./non-veg. dishes Rs40-60. Open M-Tu and Th-Su 8:30am-10pm. ❷

Hot Breads, Gingy St., next to Higginbothams. Air-conditioned cafe-patisserie selling fresh-baked bread (Rs11 per loaf), scones (Rs10), and croissants (Rs10) as well as a range of snacks and meals (sandwiches Rs25-35, pizza Rs35-65). The closest thing you'll find to a French cafe in Pondicherry. Open daily 7am-9pm. ❷

Surguru Restaurant, in the hotel of the same name. Local families pack the place every night for the best veg. food in town. Kanchipuram *idli* (Rs12), tandoori *idli* (Rs15).

Ashram Dining House, on Ranga Pillai St. Just east of the post office. Guests at the ashram guest houses can buy Rs20 vouchers in advance that entitle them to three meals. Piles of *basmati* rice and fresh fruits will be heaped upon your metal platter. Serving daily 6:40-7:45am, 11:15am-12:30pm; dinner 5:45-7pm or as posted. ❶

Ajantha Sea View Restaurant, 22 Goubert Salai, upstairs from the hotel of the same name. Good views out over Goubert Salai to the sea; very popular place to sit with a drink in the evenings. Good range of seafood, chicken, and mutton dishes (Rs60), as well as the veg. standards (Rs35) and beer (Rs40). Open daily 10am-11pm. ❷

 SIGHTS

SRI AUROBINDO ASHRAM

Rue de la Marine. Children under 3 not permitted. Photography allowed only with prior permission. Open daily 8am-noon and 2-6pm. Free.

The "integral yoga" of Bengali mystic **Sri Aurobindo Ghose** was an attempt to reconcile the principles of yoga with the findings of modern science. The eventual aim was the summoning of a "supramental consciousness" that would enable Aurobindo and his disciples to evolve to a "level beyond the human." Whether he succeeded or not depends on your point of view. Born in Kolkata in 1872 and educated in England, Aurobindo returned to India to head an Indian nationalist newspaper; in 1908, his opposition to British rule led to his imprisonment. From inside his prison cell, he underwent a series of profound spiritual experiences, and in 1910 he gave up politics and headed for French-ruled Pondicherry. Here, Sri Aurobindo met **Mirra Alfassa,** an artist and ascetic who had come from France to India to further her spiritual development. Later known as "the Mother," she eventually became Aurobindo's constant companion.

The ashram was founded in 1926, as Sri Aurobindo writes, "not for the renunciation of the world but as a center and field of practice for the evolution of another kind and form of life which would in the final end be moved by a higher spiritual consciousness." To this end, the ashram includes businesses, educational centers, farms, and all kinds of other money-spinning ventures among its many facilities.

It was largely the charisma and energy of the Mother that brought these projects to life, as she supervised growth of the ashram during Aurobindo's later life and after his death in 1950. When the Mother died in 1973, the ashram faced tumultuous internal struggles over the future direction of the ashram; tensions were especially high with regard to the fate of Auroville, the ashram's experimental community (see **Auroville**, p. 596). These days, the ashram houses the flower-strewn **samadhis** (mausolea) of Sri Aurobindo and the Mother. At any time of the day, devotees mill around the perimeter of the *samadhis*, bowing their heads in silent prayer and prostrating themselves on the grass, following the teachings of Sri Aurobindo. Maps and brochures are available at any ashram shop, guest house, or from the Bureau Central, on the western side of the canal, around the corner from Telecom Complex. **Autocare,** 3 blocks north, just over the canal, conducts tours of ashram industries and of the Matrimandir (see **Auroville**, p. 596) in Auroville (Rs42).

OTHER SIGHTS

Aside from the ashram, most of Pondicherry's attractions are clustered around **Goubert Salai (Beach Road),** the promenade where locals go to see and be seen in the evening hours. During the day, the street is peaceful and deserted, disturbed only by tourists and the occasional ice cream vendor. Early mornings are when locals come for a jog or stroll. On weekend nights, Indian tourists, local families, and young people descend on the area for a wholesome, rollicking good time (and a little ravenous drinking). The 1.5km-long rocky beach is pretty to look at but not safe for swimming. Along the beach is a 4m-high statue of Mahatma Gandhi, surrounded by eight elaborately sculpted monoliths, as well as some elegant French architecture, including a monument built in memory of Indians who died fighting on the French side during WWI. Near the beach, the French side of town is a scenic walk full of pristine villas and crumbling old colonial relics that give this part of Pondicherry an atmosphere quite different from anywhere else in India.

Just west of Goubert Salai is the **Government Place,** a grassy quadrangle framing a solemn, neo-classical monument dating from the time of Napoleon III. On the northern edge of the park is the elegant, French-built **Raj Nivas,** now the plush residence of Pondicherry's Lieutenant Governor. Next door is the **Pondicherry Museum,** which displays dusty 19th-century French furniture, a small collection of Chola bronze sculpture, and an assortment of pottery and other objects dug up at the nearby site of Arikamedu. (Museum open Tu-Su 10am-5pm. Rs2.)

Follow Goubert Salai to South Blvd. to reach the **Botanical Gardens.** Planted in 1826, the gardens contain species from around the world. (Open daily 9am-5:30pm.) On your way to the gardens, have a look at the **Eglise du Sacré Coeur de Jésus,** where the altar is flanked by stained-glass panels depicting the life of Christ.

🎵 ENTERTAINMENT

By Tamil Nadu's conservative standards, alcohol flows quite freely in Pondicherry; bars are quite common on the French side. One of the best places for an evening beer is the open-air seafront terrace at the **Seagulls Restaurant** (see p. 594).

Chunnamber Water Sports Complex (☎2066816), 10km out of town on the backwaters of the Bay of Bengal, offers boat rentals (kayak, paddle, sail, water scooter

TAMIL NADU

Rs10-75). It is also possible to go deep-sea fishing or take a dolphin-watching **sea cruise.** Contact the tourist office (☎ 2339497) for more information.

🎇 DAYTRIPS FROM PONDICHERRY

AUROVILLE ஆரோவிடு

*For a brief visit to Auroville, **tours** are sponsored by the tourist office in Pondicherry (Rs60-70) or by Autocare (2pm, Rs50). Another option is to get a **auto-rickshaw** in Pondy (Rs150-200 plus waiting charges) or go solo down East Coast Rd. by **bike.** Look for the "To Auroville" sign about 6km out of Pondy; this leads you left off the main road onto a smaller dirt track that runs (uphill!) for 8km or so to the Information Center.*

The utopian New Age community of Auroville, about 12km north of Pondicherry, was an attempt to realize the Mother's dream of creating a place where seekers from all over the world could come together to live a progressive life in the service of Divine Truth. Auroville was designed to be a peaceful international city of the future, arranged in the shape of a galaxy around the huge golden golf-ball shaped **Matrimandir** (Mother Temple) at its center.

At the community's inauguration in 1968, children from 124 countries gathered to place handfuls of their native soil in a large urn. Today, there are around 1500 people living here, more than two-thirds of them foreigners, including some of the original settlers. The town covers an area of over 50 hectares. Aurovilleans are pushing to buy up the last bits of land necessary to fulfill the Mother's vision. they are competing with developers who seek to capitalize on the relative wealth that Auroville's international community brings.

Citizens are grouped into small rural settlements around the urn and the Matrimandir. A geodesic dome housing a huge crystalline meditation chamber, the solar-powered Matrimandir symbolizes the goals of the Mother by integrating science and meditation within a peaceful, industrious international community.

For now, the real center of the community is the **Solar Kitchen,** where many residents gather for lunch or an afternoon cappuccino and email in the rooftop cafe. Residents live in small settlements named after development goals such as Utility, Certitude, and Revelation. Entrepreneurial and research institutions include a Building Research Center dedicated to new, low-cost housing technologies, and Aurelec, the town's computer company. There are also innovative agricultural and environmental projects, schools, and a village development program.

🔲 **VISITING AUROVILLE.** Understandably, residents are unappreciative of tourists who lack sincere interest in their way of life and come to gawk at them as a relic of the 1960s. As part of a **tour** group, you'll avoid the hassles of transportation and the bureaucracy of getting to see the Matrimandir, though you may feel rather herded. The tour goes first to the Visitors' Information Center, which sells brochures and displays photos and exhibits detailing Auroville's mission and development, including a model of the proposed town. A 20min. video about the community is shown regularly between 10am and 3:30pm every day except Su. Just across from the exhibits is a boutique, selling all things New Age. (Open M-Sa 9am-1pm and 2-5:30pm.) A small **cafe ❶,** opposite the Information Center, sells drinks and snacks (chocolate cake Rs15) throughout the day and serves dinner at 6:30pm every day except Su. (Open M-Sa 8:30am-9:30pm, Su 8:30am-6pm.) The Matrimandir is open for viewing from 4-5pm, and for meditation from 5-6pm. Passes must be obtained from the Information Center (free, last pass issued at 4pm). A strict code of silence is enforced as visitors are ushered down a gravel path and up a ramp past construction work to glance inside the otherworldly meditation chamber, which houses a large crystal ball surrounded by a ring of slender white columns. The crystal is illuminated by sunlight reflected from a mirror on top of the dome; when the sky is overcast, solar-powered lamps provide the necessary light. Stepping into the Matrimandir is a bit like entering another dimension—don't be surprised if even this quick peek leaves you dazed; buy a separate ticket for a meditation session and spend an hour regrounding yourself. The gardens next to the Matrimandir are open daily 8:30am-3pm.

To go solo, you can take a **auto-rickshaw** or even a **bike.** One advantage of visiting the community on your own is that you'll have a better chance of actually meeting Auroville settlers, though it is a good idea to proceed to the Visitors' Center first to gain a bit of background on the community and obtain a map and newspaper. It is also possible to eat lunch at the Solar Kitchen (12:15pm) if invited by a resident, or sometimes by contacting Guest Services above the kitchen at around 9:30am.

⊓ STAYING ON. If you are intrigued by Auroville, you might consider a longer stay in one of the **guest houses ❷** for Rs150-750 per day. Many of the accommodations include bath, laundry, and meals. The Visitors' Information Center will provide a list and make arrangements. For more information, contact the **Visitors' Information Center** in Auroville directly. (☎ 2622709. Open daily M-Sa 9am-1pm and 1:30-5:30pm, Su 9am-1pm and 2-4 pm.) **Youth Camp ❶,** in the residential area of Fraternity, is a fun, clean place to stay (Rs120 per person per night). Not restricted to kids, excellent breakfast and dinner are served, and the place is run by the ultra-laid-back Samrat Das, former Aurobindo ashramite turned Aurovillean. To plan in advance, contact **Auroville Guest Service,** Solar Kitchen building, Auroville 605101. (☎ 2622357; avguests@auroville.org.in.)

CHIDAMBARAM தடபரடி   ☎ 04144

Chappals in hand, locals casually cut through the grounds of the grandiose temple complex at Chidambaram, another one of the remarkable architectural initiatives of the Cholas, who made Chidambaram their capital in AD 907. This is the "only place in the universe" where dance is allowed inside a temple's sanctum sectorum, and with good reason. It was here that Shiva descended from the divine firmament as Nataraja ("King of Dance") and performed the *ananda tandavam* ("Cosmic Dance"). The forested clearing where Nataraja danced became sacred ground; the town that grew around it was dubbed "Chit Ambaram," the "Hall of Wisdom."

Every February, prominent dancers from throughout the country converge in Chidambaram to present dance-offerings to Nataraja in the **Natyanjali Festival.** During the **"car festivals"** in mid-December and mid-June, thousands come to watch ritual chariots glide through the four streets bearing their names. The Tamil New Year (April 14th every year) is also a time of huge celebration. The town itself, despite being home to a prominent university, is small and quiet, and worth a daytrip from Pondicherry or Tanjore.

⊏ TRANSPORTATION

Trains: The sleepy railway station is little more than a rural outpost. Most travelers stick to the buses, which are normally quicker. The reservation counter is open M-Sa 8am-8pm, Su 8am-2pm. To: **Chennai** (7hr., 11:50am, Rs54); **Rameswaram** (12hr., 6:30pm, Rs101); **Trichy** (6hr., 2:30 and 3am, Rs56) via **Tanjore.**

Buses: The **bus stand,** just off the eastern end of S. Car St., services all parts of Tamil Nadu. To: **Chennai** (5½hr., 20 per day 4:30am-midnight, Rs66-76); **Kumbakonam** via **Tanjore** (2½hr., every 20min., Rs22); **Madurai** (8hr., 5 per day 4am-5:30pm); **Pondicherry** (2hr., frequent, Rs20); **Trichy** (5½hr., 12 per day, Rs51).

✦ 🔁 ORIENTATION AND PRACTICAL INFORMATION

Chidambaram is small and easy to navigate. **North, South, East,** and **West Car Street** form a rectangular border around the temple. To reach them from the bus stand, turn right out of the bus stand and then take your first right onto Venugopal, a.k.a **VGP Street.** After 500m, VGP St. turns into S. Car St. To get to the **Tourist Office** from the bus stand, take a left and then another left about 200m later onto **Pillaiyar Koil Street.** Cross over the **Khan Sahib Canal** before making your first right onto **Railway Feeder Road.** The railway station is at the end of this street, with the tourist office just before it on the right.

Tourist Office: TTDC (☎238739), at the beginning of Railway Feeder Rd., next to Hotel Tamil Nadu, on the way to the railway station. Open M-F 10am-5:45pm.

Currency Exchange: The nearest place to change money is in Pondicherry.

Police Station: Chidambaram Police Station, W. Car St. (☎222201). Open 24hr.

Pharmacy: There are many in town, and most are open until 10 or 11pm. Try **Srinivasa Medicals** on S. Car St. near Star Lodge. Open daily 9am-10:30pm.

Hospital: Raja Muthandi Medical College and Hospital (☎238147), 3km southeast of the bus stand. To get there take an auto-rickshaw.

Internet: Pick Up Internet Browsing Centre, 100m up W. Car St., on the right as you head north. One floor up inside the Saba Lodge bldg. Rs30 per hr. Open 24hr.

Post Office: A tall, cream-colored bldg. covered by a patchwork of orange squares at the western end of N. Car St. Open M-F 10am-4pm, Sa 10am-1pm. **Postal Code:** 608001.

🏠 ACCOMMODATIONS

The accommodations listed have 24hr. check-out.

Hotel Akshaya, 17-18 E. Car St. (☎220192), on the left hand side heading north, toward the end of the street. Good value hotel, offering nice rooms with attached bath (seat toilet). Rooftop terrace offers a spectacular aerial view of the temple. Excellent attached restaurant (see below). Singles Rs200-500; doubles Rs250-600. MC/V. ❷

Hotel Saradharam, 19 VGP St. (☎221336), opposite the bus stand. Where the car loads of middle-class Indian families stay and the local Rotary Club meets. Sparkling rooms, attached restaurant (see below). Doubles Rs325-1000. MC/V. ❸

Star Lodge (☎222743). At the eastern end of S. Car St. near the intersection with E. Car St. Small, basic rooms with attached bath (squat toilet) and windows onto a sunlit hallway. A budget option for a quick night in town. Singles Rs60. ❶

🍴 FOOD

Hotel Saradharam, opposite the bus stand. Three different restaurants, each with its own flavor. **Pallavi ❶,** in front, serves the best veg. food in town and is always crowded. South Indian "special" dishes Rs 15-30. Open 6am-10:30pm. **Annu Pallavi ❶,** in back, cooks up spicy, non-veg. dishes. Open daily 11am-11pm. **The Pizza Shop ❶,** serves pizza and burgers (Rs30) and has Internet access (Rs40 per hr.). Open 11am-11pm.

Aswini Restaurant, 17-18 E. Car St., in the Hotel Akshaya. Menu features all the standard items, served in a cool, quiet A/C dining room. Veg. curry Rs20, *aloo gobi* Rs22. Open daily 7-10am, 11am-3pm, and 6-10pm. Non-veg. meals noon-3pm, 6-10pm. Veg. meals 7-10am, 1:30-10pm. ❶

◎ SIGHTS: SABHANAYAKA NATARAJA TEMPLE

Open daily 6am-noon and 4-10pm. Puja at 7, 9, 11am, noon, 6, 8, 10pm.

One of the few temples where Shiva and Vishnu are enshrined together, the Sabhanayaka Nataraja Temple draws crowds of thousands daily. It was here that the dance duel took place between Kali and Shiva, the Lord of the Dance (Nataraja). The temple is also one of the five Shiva temples in South India dedicated to the five Vedic elements; Chidambaram is dedicated to the "Ether of Consciousness." The other four are at Kanchipuram or Thiruvarur (earth), Kalagasi (air), Thivumalai (fire), and Srirangam (water).

Covering more than 54 hectares, the temple dominates central Chidambaram. Scholars believe that work on the temple began during the 10th century, but local tradition holds that there has been a temple on this site for thousands of years. The present Nataraja Temple, according to legend, was built in the 6th century when the Kashmiri monarch Simhavarman II (r. AD 550-575) made a pilgrimage to Chidambaram, hoping that bathing in the tank of the ancient Nataraja Temple would cure his leprosy. When he recovered soon after his bath, the king—thereafter known as Hiranyavarman, or the "golden-bodied one"—gave orders for the temple to be enlarged. In addition, Hiranyavarman decreed that the holy entourage of 3000 brahmin priests *(Dikshitars)* who had accompanied him from Kashmir should remain behind at Chidambaram to serve the temple. Lepers still come to the temple for its holy healing powers, and descendants of the *Dikshitars* still live in Chidambaram. You'll recognize them by the knot of hair on top of their heads.

THE OUTERMOST EDGE. Most visitors enter through the eastern or western *gopuram* (gateway), where **guides** immediately accost any foreign-looking person. Also beware of English-speaking individuals trying to usher you to a priest who will anoint you with *kumkum* for a "voluntary" donation. To avoid most of the general hassle, use the northernmost gate instead.

The temple's four massive, pyramidal *gopuram* are painted every 50 years in a rainbow of pastel tones, and each has a distinctive character. The eastern *gopuram* is supposed to invoke a feeling of love, with the worshipper approaching the Nataraja as he would approach his beloved. From the south, the soul approaches as a child, and from the west, as a friend. One enters the northern *gopuram* in a position of subservience. The 42m-high northern *gopuram*, erected in the 14th century, bears an inscription claiming that it was built by a 16th-century Vijayanagar king. Its interior is embellished with carvings of the 108 dance poses associated with *bharatnatyam*. The southern *gopuram*, put up in the 12th century, contains a set of impressive carvings of the goddess Lakshmi. Each of the four *gopurams* still has its original granite base, although the brick towers have been replaced numerous times, often falling victim to the winter monsoon. Across the front of each base are carvings of Shiva and Parvati.

On the eastern side of the temple is a depiction of Ganesh taken from a story in which Lord Shiva held a contest between his two sons, Ganesh and Kartikkeya. The deal was that a delicious mango would be given to the son who could go around the universe first. Kartikkeya leapt onto his peacock and set off, confident of victory. The short, plump Ganesh had only a little mouse for a mount. He thought for a while and then rode around his parents, Shiva and Parvati. When Shiva asked his son what he was up to, Ganesh replied: "Going around the supreme Lord Shiva and Goddess Parvati who create and contain the universe is equivalent to going around the universe." Shiva smiled in satisfaction and presented the mango to his slow-footed but quick-witted son.

TAMIL NADU

The **Shivaganga Tank** is to the left as you come in through the northern gate. This is where King Simhavarman bathed, emerging with golden-hued skin. Opposite the tank is the **Shivakumarasundari Temple,** dedicated to Shiva's consort Parvati. On the other side of the tank, in the northeast corner of the temple grounds, stands the 103m-long **Raja Sabha,** the temple's "1000-pillared corridor" where the victory processions of the Pandavas, Cholas, and other local powers were held. The corridor has only 999 pillars; Shiva's leg serves as the 1000th.

THE INNER CHAMBERS. The inner chambers are accessible from the north and south. On the eastern side of the enclosure, the **Devasabha,** or "Hall of the Gods," is where images of deities are stored when they are not being used; this is also where temple meetings were held. In the southwest corner of the second enclosure, the **Nritya Sabha** (Dance Hall) marks the spot where Shiva and Kali had their famous dance duel. The hall is adorned with 56 pillars representing various dance poses.

Inside the innermost shrine, accessible from the southern side of the second enclosure, it is possible to get a glimpse of the gold-roofed Chit Sabha and Kanaka Sabha, the holiest points in the entire complex. The atmosphere here is often highly charged, particularly during evening *puja,* when crowds pray to the raucous accompaniment of horns, drums, and temple bells. Five silver-plated stone steps lead to the Chit Sabha; they represent the five Sanskrit letters that spell out the famous Hindu Panchakshara mantra, "Nama Shivaya." The Chit Sabha contains images of Nataraja and Parvati. To the right, behind a string of leaves, are the Chidambara Rahasyam ("Secret of Chidambaram") and the Akasa Linga, representing the elusive and invisible element *akasa* (ether). In the passageway to the sanctum is a hallway that leads to the Govindaraja Temple, dedicated to Vishnu.

KUMBAKONAM கும்பகோணம் ☎ 0435

Millions flock to Kumbakonam every twelve years, when the waters of the nine sacred rivers are supposed to flow into the Mahamakham Tank. The next gathering is set for early 2004. The rest of the time, Kumbakonam is a quiet and relaxing place to spend a few days. In addition to the five major temples within the town itself, Kumbakonam is also a good base for daytrips out to the Chola-era sites at Darasuram and Gangaikondacholapuram.

▐ TRANSPORTATION

Trains: The **railway reservations counter** (☎2430052) is open M-Sa 8am–8pm, Su 8am-2pm. To: **Chennai** (9½hr., 10:45am-8pm, Rs101) and **Villupuram** (4hr., 10:15am and 8pm, Rs27-45). As of August 2003, service to **Rameswaram, Tanjore** and **Trichy** remains suspended for repairs.

Buses: The bus stand is at the eastern end of the city, not far from the railway station, a 1km walk out of town from Mahamakham Tank along Kamaraj Rd. and then right, through the market. To: **Bangalore** (11hr., 6:30pm, Rs132); **Chennai** (6hr., every hr. 8am-11:45pm, Rs71-94); **Chidambaram** (frequent, Rs29); **Karaikal** (2hr., every 30min., Rs13); **Tanjore** (1½hr., every 30min., Rs10); **Tirupati** (10hr., 9pm, Rs114); **Trichy** (2½hr., every 20min., Rs23).

▐⁕▐ ORIENTATION AND PRACTICAL INFORMATION

Kumbakonam is relatively easy to navigate, though locals are helpful if you're lost. To get from the train station to the center of town, turn right out of the station and take your first left on **Kamaraj Road;** it's 1km ahead. From the bus stand, exit right, go through the market, turn right at the T-junction and then left onto Kamaraj Rd., which runs into **Head Post Office (HPO) Road** near the large **Mahamakham Tank.** Turn right on HPO Rd., head past Hotel Raya's and take the 2nd left onto **Ayikulam Road.** A few hundred meters down, a street on the right takes you to **TSR Big Street,** marked by VPR Hotel Siva and many jewelry shops. It runs parallel and to the north of the Ayikulam Rd. These two streets flank the **Potramai Tank** at the back of the **Sarangapani Temple.**

Currency Exchange: City Union Bank Ltd., 140 TSR Big St. (☎2432322). **State Bank of India,** also on TSR Big St. Both open M-Sa 10am-3:30pm, Su 10am-noon.

Police: West Police Station, Ayikulam Rd. (☎2421450), opposite the Sarangapani Temple, near the Athityaa Hotel.

Hospital: ST Hospital, HPO Rd. (☎2430839), between Ayikulam Rd. and Hotel Raya's. Attached **24hr. pharmacy.**

Internet: Vendan Internet, 35 HPO Rd. (☎2402191), by the Mahamakham Tank near Hotel Raya's. Rs25 per hr. Open daily 7am-11pm.

Post Office: The **Head Post Office,** HPO Rd., next to Hotel Raya's. Open M-Sa 10am-6pm. **Postal Code:** 612001.

ACCOMMODATIONS

The following have 24hr. check-out policies. Prices do not include tax.

Hotel ARK, 21 TSR Big St. (☎2421152), opposite City Union Bank Ltd. Rooms have color TVs, sofas, and seat or squat toilets. Doubles Rs400-600. ❸

Hotel Chela, 9 Ayikulam Rd., (☎2430336). Sparkling foyer and polished rooms near the train and bus stations and the Mahamakham Tank. Doubles Rs425-600. ❸

VPR Lodge, 102/3 TSR Big St. (☎2421949), at the end of the road. Spare but clean rooms with attached seat toilets in an airy building. The octogenarian owner houses a clan of wild monkeys on the second floor. Singles Rs90; doubles Rs120. ❶

FOOD

Arul, near the Sarangapani Temple, opposite Pandiyar Hotel. Whirring floor fans and dim lighting create a relaxed setting for excellent *thalis* (Rs25-30, 10am-4pm only). Open daily 6am-10pm. ❶

Sathars, inside Hotel Raya's, on HPO Rd. Excellent restaurant serves a wide range of chicken, mutton, and seafood dishes. Entrees Rs30-60. Open daily 11am-11:30pm. ❷

Pandiyar Hotel, opposite the main entrance to the Sarangapani Temple. Banana leaf *thali* (Rs15) is constructed one heaping spoonful at a time. Open daily 9am-7pm. ❶

Arogya, in the Hotel Athityaa, near the Sarangapani Temple. Standard mid-range hotel restaurant popular for its never-ending "meals" (Rs20). Open daily 11am-11pm. ❶

SIGHTS

There's a temple around every corner in Kumbakonam. While they may at first look similar, each has a distinct and fascinating history and religious significance.

MAHAMAKHAM TANK. Hindus believe the tank to be the place where the sacred nectar from Brahma's *kumbh* was collected after its original container was shattered by an arrow from Shiva. A multi-functional pond where people go to swim, do laundry, or worship, the tank is especially pleasant in the evening, when you can rent paddle-boats (Rs5 per person per 30min.). Every 12 years, the tank's tranquility is disrupted by a huge festival that invites pilgrims to Kumbakonam to bathe in the waters here. When Jupiter passes Leo, the waters of the Ganga and 8 other sacred Indian rivers—the Yamuna, Kaveri, Godavari, Narmada, Krishna, Saraswati, Sarayu, and Tungabhadra—are believed to flow into the tank. The last festival, in 1992, brought well over one million devotees to Kumbakonam. When controversial political leader and current Chief Minister of Tamil Nadu, Jayalalitha Jayaram, went to take her purifying dip, a stampede ensued that killed 60 pilgrims. *(At HPO Rd. and Kamarajar Rd. Open 24hr. Next festival scheduled for 2004.)*

SARANGAPANI TEMPLE. Along with Srirangam near Trichy (see p. 609) and Tirupati in Andhra Pradesh (see p. 116), Sarangapani is one of the three most sacred Vishnu shrines in India. On the left of the main sanctum is a golden shrine to Lakshmi, the goddess of prosperity, which depicts her seated on a thousand-petal lotus, worshipping Vishnu. Legend holds that she was discovered in this position in the temple's tank. Later, Vishnu came to Kumbakonam to marry her. Around the inner sanctum are fine carvings of Vishnu's 10 avatars. Within the sanctum is a huge reclining Vishnu, ornamented with silver and watched over by his two wives, Lakshmi and Saraswati. *(From the corner of Ayikulam Rd. and HPO Rd. With Hotel Raya's and the Mahamakham Tank to your left, walk 200m west, then turn right. The temple will be on your left. Open daily 7am-noon and 4:30-9pm. Puja 9, 10am, noon, 6, 8, 9pm.)*

NAGESHWARA TEMPLE. Built during the 10th century, the Nageshwara Temple, dedicated to Shiva, is thought to be the oldest temple in Kumbakonam. The sculpted figures adorning the *gopurams* are some of the best examples of early Chola workmanship. Many of the temple's finest sculptures are within the sanctum itself surrounded by niches containing carvings of Shiva and Parvati. Sunlight passes through the opening in the *gopuram* three times a year and illuminates the shrine's image. It is believed that Surya (the sun god) worships Shiva at these times. *(From the Mahamakham Tank at your back, walk 200m down HPO Rd. and take your first left. The temple is at the end of the road. Open daily 6am-noon and 4:30-8pm. Puja on the hour.)*

KUMBESHWARA TEMPLE. Facing east, this temple is the largest and most important Shiva temple in Kumbakonam. The *linga* enshrined here is believed to have been shaped by Shiva himself. According to legend, Brahma anticipated the Great Deluge, "Mahapralaya," and entreated Shiva to save creation from destruction. Shiva instructed him to place a pot, or *kumbh*, containing sacred nectar and the seed of creation on top of Mount Meru in the Himalayas. The Great Deluge carried the sacred *kumbh* south to Kumbakonam, where Lord Shiva, in the guise of a hunter, shattered the pot with an arrow and spilled the nectar. He then gathered the broken shards and shaped the *linga* that now stands inside the temple. Nectar from the broken pot trickled to five other places within a 16km radius of Kumbakonam, as well as to the Mahamakham Tank. Traditionally, pilgrims visit these shrines before coming to Kumbeshwara. *(At the western end of Ayikulam Rd., across from the Potramai Tank. Open daily 7am-1pm and 4-9pm. Puja 7, 8:30am, noon, 5, 7, 8:30pm.)*

▶ DAYTRIPS FROM KUMBAKONAM

GANGAIKONDACHOLAPURAM
Buses every hr. from Kumbakonam (1hr., Rs10). Open daily 6am-noon, 4-8pm.

An exquisitely maintained UNESCO World Heritage Site, the beautifully restored temple complex at Gangaikondacholapuram is perhaps second only to the Brihadeshwara Temple in Tanjore in demonstrating the Chola-era architectural style. Gangaikondacholapuram, which means "the city of the Chola who conquered the Ganga," was built by King Rajendra I (r. 1012-1044), son of Raja Raja, after he brought the lands north of the Ganga under the control of a

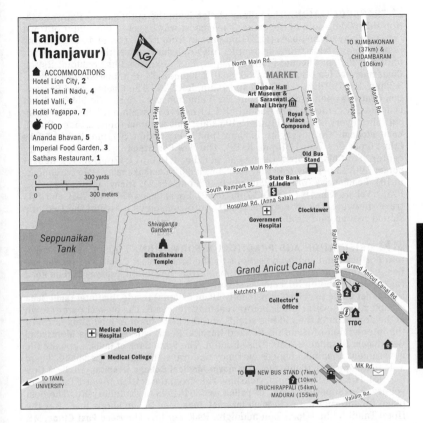

Tanjore (Thanjavur)

🏠 ACCOMMODATIONS
Hotel Lion City, **2**
Hotel Tamil Nadu, **4**
Hotel Valli, **6**
Hotel Yagappa, **7**

🍎 FOOD
Ananda Bhavan, **5**
Imperial Food Garden, **3**
Sathars Restaurant, **1**

southern dynasty for the first time. To commemorate his victory, the king had water from the Ganga transported to the temple's tank. The temple is dedicated to Shiva—a large Nandi guards the entrance—and among the most impressive carvings is a frieze that depicts Shiva and Parvati crowning King Rajendra. Worship still goes on inside the temple's candle-lit interior. The upper stories, which served as a fortress, are accessible to visitors—and bats!

TANJORE (THANJAVUR) தத்சா/ஸி ☎ 04362

Not many foreign tourists make it here, but they're missing out. Tanjore is well worth the 2hr. bus ride from Trichy or Kumbakonam to see the Chola's greatest monument: the noble Brihadishwara Temple, which is deservedly recognized by UNESCO as a World Heritage Site. Tanjore's other best-kept secret is its impressive collection of Chola-era bronze statues, beautifully housed in an old 16th century Nayak Palace. For more than 400 years, until the end of the 13th century, Tanjore was the most important city in the Chola empire, which at its height encompassed most of southern India and stretched as far south as Java. Today Tanjore is a small but prosperous commercial city of 250,000.

E TRANSPORTATION. The **railway station** is on the aptly-named Railway Station Rd., 600m south of the canal. The easiest way to get to the center of town is to take any of the buses (Rs2) that pass in front of the station to the Old Bus Stand, a 5min. walk from the temple. Auto-rickshaws cover the same route for under Rs20. To: **Chennai** (11hr., 8:20pm, Rs89; express 9hr., 8:30pm, Rs97); **Chidambaram** (6hr.; 3 per day 6:30, 8:20, 8:30pm; Rs24-45); **Rameswaram** (5½hr., 8:20pm, Rs45); **Trichy** (2hr., 6:20 and 10am, Rs12-26). The **Computerised Reservation Centre** is open M-Sa, 8am-8pm, Su 10am-2pm and 3-5pm. The **Old Bus Stand** is in the city center, where Gandhiji Rd. turns into East Main Rd. It serves **Chennai** (8hr., every 30min. 8-11pm, Rs105-130); **Chidambaram** (4hr., 2:15am, Rs30); **Kumbakonam** (1hr.; every hr. 5:30am-1pm, every 30min. 8-11pm; Rs13); **Trichy** (1hr., 6 per day 7am-11:15pm, Rs18). The **New Bus Stand** is 7km from the city center. To: **Chidambaram** (3½hr., 25 per day 1:10am-11:47pm, Rs36); **Kanchi puram** (8hr., 2 per day 6:43 and 10:08am, Rs90); **Kumbakonam** (1½hr., frequent, Rs16); **Pondicherry** (5hr.; 3:40am, 6:20, 9:20pm; Rs56); **Trichy** (1¼hr., frequent, Rs15); **Vellore** (8hr., 6:17am and 7pm, Rs90). Local buses #74, 74A, 74B, and 74D travel between the two stands (Rs2). Auto-rickshaws between the two bus stands cost around Rs40.

■ ⁊ ORIENTATION AND PRACTICAL INFORMATION. Tanjore is divided into northern and southern sections by the **Grand Anicut Canal**. The **railway station** is in the southernmost part of town. From the station, **Railway Station Road** (also called Gandhiji Rd.) curves slightly as it heads north, passing a branch of the **tourist office** (☎230984, open daily 10am-5:45pm) inside the **Hotel Tamil Nadu** complex, and several hotels before reaching the canal. The busiest part of town is the area around the old bus stands and the **clock tower** immediately north of the intersection of Gandhiji Rd. and **Hospital Road,** where the **Raja Merusudad Government Hospital** (☎231023) is situated. The **State Bank of India,** opposite the government hospital, changes currency and traveler's checks. (☎230698. Open M-F 10am-4pm, Sa 10am-1pm.) **Thanjavur Medical College Hospital,** Medical College Rd. (☎240851), a 15min. rickshaw ride from the station toward Tamil University. The superintendent of **police** (☎230451) is on Kutchery Rd. The best place for Internet is the **Netclub Internet Zone,** one of the shops just after the Hotel Tamil Nadu. (Open 9am-midnight, Rs30 per hr.) The **Head Post Office,** MK Rd., is off Railway Station Rd. in the southern part of town. (☎231022. Open M-F 10am-6pm, Sa 10am-3pm, Su noon-6pm.) **Postal Code:** 613001.

⻖ ☪ ACCOMMODATIONS AND FOOD. Places south of the canal tend to be quieter than those overlooking the bus stand. All hotels have a 24hr. check-out policy. Perhaps the best of the lot is **Hotel Tamil Nadu ❷**, a large, white complex on Railway Station Rd,. about 100m before the canal from the railways station. Comfortable rooms with attached bath built around a mini-jungle courtyard are big enough to settle down in. Attached bar and restaurant. (☎231421. Doubles Rs285-600.) **Hotel Valli ❷**, 2948 MK Rd., is on a well-shaded side-street, a 5min. walk east from the railway station. Rooms have attached baths with squat and seat toilets; the hotel has an attached restaurant. (☎231580. Singles Rs185; doubles Rs252-304.) Overlooking the canal is the fancy **Hotel Lion City ❸**, at 130 Gandhiji Rd. Marble, marble everywhere, and they even take credit cards. (☎275650, 275926, or 275927. Singles Rs350-495; doubles Rs495-700). Attached **Imperial Food Garden ❶** has *tandoori*, chinese, veg. and non-veg. cuisines. (Open 12pm-10pm.) **Hotel Yagappa ❷**, 1 Trichy Rd., south of the station, has clean rooms with attached squat toilets and bucket bath. Sheets and hot water are available. (☎276552. Singles Rs175-250; doubles Rs626-700.)

There are plenty of vegetarian restaurants around the bus stand. **Ananda Bhavan ❶**, Railway Station Rd., up the street on your left as you walk away from the station into town, serves simple banana leaf meals for Rs15. Its location makes it a key stop for locals going to work, so expect morning crowds. (Open daily 6:30-10:30am, 11:00am-10:30pm.) **Sathars Restaurant ❷**, 167 Gandhiji Rd., is just north of the canal on your right as you walk away from the railway station. Excellent non-veg. meals in a dark, fan-flapped setting just off the main road. Chicken dishes Rs30-60, mutton *rogan josh* Rs26-105, brain fry Rs30. (Open daily 6am-11:30pm.)

◨ SIGHTS. The ◪**Brihadishwara Temple,** the pride of Tanjore, is recognized by the United Nations as a World Heritage Site. One of the most stunning monuments in southern India, its sweeping lawns and castle-like walls make the temple seem like a movie set. But no, the temple is still functional: an elephant will bless you at the front gate and you may find a man quietly meditating in the lotus position inside. Awe-inspiring by day, the temple acquires an added aura of magic at sunset as couples stroll and families picnic in its park-like atmosphere. When night falls, artfully-placed lights bring the sculptures into sharp relief.

The temple complex is guarded by a giant sculpture of Nandi (Shiva's bull). This massive sculpture weighs over 25 tons, making it one of the largest in India. Over 1000 smaller Nandis and 252 *linga*s also keep careful watch from the walls. The temple stands as an impressive reminder of the city's glory under the reign of the Chola King Raja Raja I (r. 985-1014). Legend has it that he built the temple to save his own life. Unable to find a cure for his leprosy, Raja Raja turned to his religious tutor for guidance, who advised him to build a temple to Shiva using a *linga* from the Narmada River. Raja Raja rushed to the river and pulled a *linga* from the water; as he pulled, the *linga* grew and grew, and Raja Raja had no choice but to build a massive temple to enclose it. By the time the temple was completed in 1010, the Cholas had brought virtually the whole of southern India under their control. The temple now stands as a symbol of its builder's power.

Above the *linga* rises the *vimana*, a stepped superstructure representing Mt. Meru, the cosmic mountain at the center of the Hindu universe. In an inversion of traditional South Indian architectural order, the *vimana* soars over the *gopurams*, or entry gates. The set of exquisite carvings on the frontal face, depicting Shiva, Parvati, and other gods on top of Mt. Meru, has earned the temple the local nickname "Himalaya of the South." The monolithic *stupa* that caps the *vimana* was raised via a ramp more than 6km long. Also within the temple's courtyard walls are a 16th-century temple to Krishna, famed for its intricate miniature carvings, and another to Ganesh and Parvati.

A pathway to the left as you leave the temple leads 100m down a small lane to the **Shivaganga Gardens,** where couples and families throw picnic leftovers at caged monkeys and peacocks. (Take the #2 bus from the railway station to the temple. Open daily roughly 6am-noon and 4-9pm. Shivaganga Gardens, Rs2.)

The large **Royal Palace** was built as a residence by the Nayaks in the 16th century and was subsequently refurbished by the Marathas. These days, the palace has been colonized by a number of incongruous outfits, including a secondary school, an agricultural office, and a martial arts academy. The only real reason to come here is the excellent collection of Chola bronzes and stone sculptures in the **Durbar Hall Art Museum.** (Once inside the palace, follow signs for the art gallery. Open daily 9am-1pm and 3-6pm. Rs10, Rs30 camera fee.) The **Saraswati Mahal Library,** also in the palace, houses thousands of palm-leafed manuscripts. With 33,433 holdings, the collection is one of the world's finest. Most of the collection is closed to the public, but a small selection of weird and wonderful pieces is on display in a room by the entrance. (Open Th-Tu 10am-1pm and 1:30-5:30pm. Free.)

TAMIL NADU

TIRUCHIRAPPALLI (TRICHY) ருசிராபபழின்

☎ 0431

For a growing industrial center of over a million people, Tiruchirappalli (commonly referred to as Trichy or Tiruchi) is a relatively sane and manageable city. Its biggest attraction is the temple town of Srirangam, 5km north of the city center. The city has been occupied for over 2000 years and controlled at various times by the Cholas, Pandyas, Pallavas, and Nayaks, whose prosperous reign brought about the creation of the imposing Rock Fort, still the city's dominant landmark. Since the late 19th century, when the railways brought industry to South India, Trichy has been ruled by manufacturing—today, the city produces staggering quantities of *bindis* and costume jewelry. Trichy is also a convenient bus, rail, and air transportation hub to destinations farther south, and is only one of a handful of Indian cities with Sri Lankan Air flights to Colombo.

◧ TRANSPORTATION

Flights: The **airport** (☎ 2341063, 2341601 or 2340020) is 8km south of the city. Take an auto-rickshaw (Rs75) or taxi (Rs125). **Indian Airlines,** Dindigul Rd. (☎ 2480233 or 2481433), about 1.5km southwest of the intersection with Junction Rd. To: **Chennai** (M, W, F, Su; US$90); **Calicut** (Tu and Sa, 2:30pm; US$105); and **Trivandrum** (Tu, Th, Sa, Su; 4:15pm; US$105); **Sri Lankan Airlines,** Williams Rd. Hotel Femina Complex (☎ 2460844 or 2462381). Open M-Sa 9am-5:30pm. Flights to **Colombo, Sri Lanka** (1hr.; M-W, F, Su; one-way Rs6730).

Trains: The **Trichy Junction Railway Station** in the south of town, off the intersection of Junction and Madurai Rd. The **Reservations Building** (☎ 132) is the small white structure to your left as you approach the main station complex. Open M-Sa 8am-8pm, Su 8am-2pm. To: **Chidambaram** (6hr., 5 and 6:30pm, Rs56); **Tambaram** for **Chennai** (12hr., 2 per day 5 and 6:30pm, Rs99); **Madurai** (3hr., 7 per day 12:30pm-3am, Rs28-51); **Rameswaram** (7hr., 3 per day 6:40am-9:30pm, Rs40-67); **Tanjore** (1½hr., 14 per day 4:55am-1am, Rs12-26); **Tirupati** (10hr., Th and Su 12:20pm, Rs104).

Buses: The **State Bus Stand** at the intersection of Rockins and Royal Rd. To: **Bangalore** (8½hr., 3 per day 8:30am-10pm, Rs147); **Chennai** (7hr., 2 per day 6:15am and 11pm; Rs91-104); **Coimbatore** (6½hr., every 20min., Rs70); **Dindigul** (3hr., every 30min., Rs35); **Kodaikanal** (6hr., 6:40am and 11am, Rs70); **Madurai** (3¼hr., every 30min., Rs35); **Tanjore** (1hr., frequent, Rs15).

Local Transportation: Trichy's **local bus** system is probably the most efficient in all of Tamil Nadu. A fleet of shiny silver buses, most equipped with deafening sound systems, shuttles passengers around the city. The **#1 bus** is every tourist's best friend; it passes the railway station, the State Bank of India, and the Head Post Office on its way to the Rock Fort (Rs2) and the Srirangam Temple (Rs3.50). Buses depart every few min. from the State Bus Stand. Trichy also has hordes of hardly-used **rickshaws,** which congregate in the bus stand/tourist office area. They aren't really necessary, unless you need to get to the airport (Rs70-75).

◪ ▮ ORIENTATION AND PRACTICAL INFORMATION

Trichy is split into two segments by the **Woyakondan Channel,** with the **Kaveri River** forming its northern border. The northernmost portion (nearest to the Kaveri River) is Trichy's industrial area, full of textile shops and dominated by the majestic **Rock Fort** and the town's **railway station.** To the south of the channel is the busy **Trichy Junction**

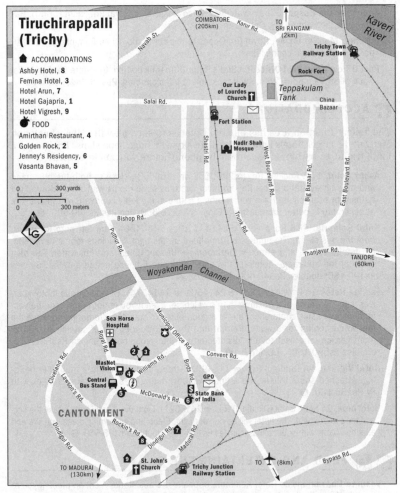

Tiruchirappalli (Trichy)

🏠 ACCOMMODATIONS
Ashby Hotel, **8**
Femina Hotel, **3**
Hotel Arun, **7**
Hotel Gajapria, **1**
Hotel Vigresh, **9**
🍴 FOOD
Amirthan Restaurant, **4**
Golden Rock, **2**
Jenney's Residency, **6**
Vasanta Bhavan, **5**

TAMIL NADU

area, where you'll find the city's main **railway station.** The streets around the railway station are full of hotels and banks. This area also contains the **bus stands,** the tourist office, and the HPO. **Srirangam** is north of the Kaveri River.

Tourist Office: Government of Tamil Nadu Tourist Office (☎ 2460136), on the corner of McDonald's Rd. and Williams Rd, across from the central bus stand. Open M-F 10am-5:45pm. Information counters also at the airport and railway junction.

Currency Exchange: State Bank of India. Turn left at the end of McDonald's Rd., after Jenney's Residency; it's on the left. Exchanges cash and AmEx (US$ only) and Thomas Cook traveler's checks (US$ and UK£ only). Open M-F 10am-4pm, Sa 10am-noon.

Swimming Pools: Jenney's Residency (see below). Rs100. Open daily 6am-7pm.

Police: Cantonment station on Municipal Office Rd. Open 24hr.

Pharmacy and Hospital: The private **Sea Horse Hospital,** 6 Royal Rd. (☎2415660). Has a well-stocked pharmacy. Open 24hr.

Internet: MasNet Vision, Royal Rd. Opposite the bus stand. Open 8am-midnight. Rs10 per hr. for lethargic connections.

Post Office: Head Post Office, on Bird's Rd., 500m walk up from the State Bank of India. Open M-Sa 9am-6pm. 24hr. speedpost in the adjacent bldg. **Postal Code:** 620001.

ACCOMMODATIONS

The Trichy Junction area has plenty of places to stay, all with 24hr. check-out. Many of the larger hotels light up the night sky with huge neon signs. Trichy sees a lot of traffic, so try to reserve a room by phone before you pull into town.

Ashby Hotel, 17-A Rockins Rd. (☎2460652 or 2460653), close to both the bus stand and the railway station. This Raj-era place features large rooms with TVs and attached baths with seat toilets. Have your morning coffee in the leafy courtyard restaurant. The attached bar is better than average. Singles Rs215-650; doubles Rs300-800. ❷

Hotel Gajapria, 5&6 Royal Rd. (☎2414411; fax 2466456). Turn left onto Royal Rd. from the bus stand. The hotel is 500m ahead on the right. Spacious rooms have modern furniture, TVs, and attached bathrooms with seat toilets and hot water. The best value of the mid-range hotels in the area. Attached Chinese restaurant/bar. Singles Rs190-450; doubles Rs340-600. DC/MC/V. ❷

Femina Hotel, 14-C Williams Rd. (☎2414501 or 2414274). The cavernous lobby sparkles with the polish of a businessman's welcome. Even if you're not in town for the vacuum cleaner sales conference, this is a good place to stay if you're hoping to leave the real world behind for a while. Retreat into the A/C wonderland of satellite TV, 24hr. room service, and seat toilets "disinfected for your protection." Singles Rs350-1150; doubles Rs550-1600. DC/MC/V. ❸

Hotel Vigresh, I-A Dindigul Rd. (☎2414991) Great, clean rooms in a triangular building. Attached squat toilets and a tinted-window dining area downstairs. Singles with TV Rs135-180. ❶

Hotel Arun, 24 State Bank (Dinidigul) Rd. (☎2415021). From the railway station take the second road to the right. The hotel will be on your right. Clean and welcoming place with TVs and attached baths with squat toilets. Singles Rs175-199; doubles Rs195-550. ❷

FOOD AND ENTERTAINMENT

Vasanta Bhavan, inside Hotel Abhirami, opposite the bus stand. A cheap place if you're craving South Indian food. Lunchtime "meals" Rs20, *dosa* Rs12, *uttappam* Rs12, served by armies of blue-uniformed men and boys. Open daily 6am-11pm. ❶

Jenney's Residency, 3/14 McDonald's Rd. Operated by the Park Sheraton chain, Trichy's top 5-star hotel has 2 excellent restaurants, both serving the same multi-cuisine menu. Chandeliers, tablecloths, and marble floors make for a swanky setting at **Suvya ❸,** open daily 7am-11pm. The popular **Peaks of Kunlun ❸** is open for dinner only, 7-11pm. Fish Manchurian Rs90, sliced lamb in garlic sauce Rs80, chili pork Rs70, and fish and chips Rs120. Jenney's also has the most original watering hole in town, the **Wild West Bar ❷,** an old-fashioned saloon complete with swinging doors and a well-watered cowboy clutching an economy-size bottle of liquor. Open daily 11am-11pm.

Amirthan Restaurant, Ramyas Hotel on Williams Rd., near the tourist office. Small and tidy well-lit A/C place, ideal for a quick lunch. *Masala utthappam* Rs18, "meals" Rs25-40, chili *gobi* fry Rs35, black coffee Rs6. Open daily 11am-11pm. ❶

Golden Rock, inside the Femina Hotel. Small, A/C cafe serving all the standard Indian and Chinese items around the clock. *Navaratan korma* Rs50, *palak paneer* Rs40, veg. noodles Rs55, Chennai meals Rs50. Open 24hr. ❷

👁 SIGHTS

ROCK FORT. One old lump of rock, this citadel was erected long ago by the Pallavas and later by the Nayaks. Today, most people who reach the summit are Hindu pilgrims visiting the temples at the top or camera-happy tourists on the hunt for good views. At the bottom of the 400 rock-cut steps leading to the top is a small shrine to Ganesh; remove your shoes before starting your climb. From the top of the fort you should be able to make out the meandering Kaveri river and the *gopurams* of the Sri Ranganathaswamy and Jambukeshwara temples in nearby Srirangam. The main Shiva temple is off-limits to non-Hindus, but not the smaller Vinayaka (Ganesh) shrine at the top, where a viewing platform affords superb 360° views of the surrounding countryside. *(Take bus #1, Rs2, and get off at the Lady of Lourdes Church; turn right, walk through the arch, and continue along the bazaar road until you come to a temple entrance on the left. Steps from here lead up to the fort. Open daily 6am-8pm. Rs1; camera fee Rs10.)*

OTHER SIGHTS. Between 7 and 11am, the banks of the **Kaveri River** are the site of a series of ceremonies and rituals. Here pilgrims bathe for good fortune, priests pray for childbirth, and mourners scatter ashes. The lack of rainfall onto the parched riverbed remarkably hasn't put a damper on things; there's still quite a religious scene going on. *(Take the #1 bus and ask to be let off at Amma Mandapam, Rs4.)* **Our Lady of Lourdes Church,** a Catholic church modeled after the Basilica in Lourdes, is worth a stop on your way to the Rock Fort. Back in town on Dindigul Rd., near the bus stand, **St. John's Church** (1816) is a colonial-era Anglican Church, complete with louvered doors and the usual array of florid plaques to the fallen victims of cholera, malaria, enemy bullets, and other ailments. Open daily 6am-6pm.

NEAR TRICHY

SRIRANGAM ஸ்ரீரங்கம்

Five kilometers north of central Trichy, on a peninsula formed by the Kaveri River and its tributary, is **Srirangam,** home of the **Sri Ranganathaswamy Temple.** The sheer size of the temple, dedicated to Vishnu in his role as "Director of the Universe," makes it unique—over the centuries, the seven concentric walls have come to absorb an entire town. The walk through the first three walls passes through a pleasant market shaded by a high, thatched ceiling. You don't need to remove your shoes until you reach the fourth wall, beyond which are the elaborate sculptures that make this temple a rewarding masterpiece even for non-Hindus denied access to the sanctum itself. The fantastical *yalis* (face of lion, body of horse, legs of tiger, trunk of elephant, tail of cow) that greet you are a Nayak invention perhaps representing Hinduism's victory over Buddhism, symbolized by the elephant crouched under the *yali.* A little further along is access to the roof, with its fantastic views and large statue of Garuda, Vishnu's vehicle. On the eastern side of the fourth enclosure is the "1000-pillared hall," containing 936 carved columns depicting horsemen atop rearing steeds. The 16th-century Vijayanagar horse pillars portray the battle between the forces of good (horses) and evil (tigers). Behind them are the 10 avatars of Vishnu.

Unusually, the entrance to the temple complex faces south rather than east; the reason, like so many things in India, is the stuff of which legends are made. Vibishana, the good brother of the demon Ravana (see **Ramayana,** p. 620), was awarded a

TAMIL NADU

statue of Vishnu in recognition of his valor in war, with the stipulation that the *murti* should never be allowed to touch the ground. When Vibishana stopped by the Kaveri River to bathe, he gave the statue to a clumsy young boy who dropped it. Infuriated, Vibishana chased the boy to the sight of the Rock Fort and struck him, at which point the boy was transformed into a statue of Ganesh. The fallen Vishnu image was affixed to the place where it had fallen and bade Vibishana to rule Sri Lanka with the words, "I will watch over you to the South."

The **Amma Mandapam,** by the banks of the Kaveri, is on the way to the **Sri Ranganathaswamy Temple.** Pilgrims come here to purify themselves before offering further *puja* at the temple. Many of the ceremonies take place on the 10th day after birth or death; you may also see a plantain ceremony aimed at preventing second marriages, or small bags that have been tied to trees in hopes of pregnancy. This site has been sacred since ancient times, and the older gods and goddesses of the earth are remembered in the worship of snake sculptures placed under a spreading tree. *(Take the #1 bus from Trichy Bus Stand, Rs4, or take the #1 bus from Sri Ranganathaswamy Temple, Rs2. Get off at Amma Mandapam.)*

The **Vaikunta Ekadasi Festival** (Dec.-Jan.) draws thousands of pilgrims to go swimming at the site; during the festival, a procession enters through a doorway called the "Gateway of Heaven" to ensure everlasting afterlife.

MADURAI மதுரை ☎ 0452

According to legend, Shiva once stood over Madurai to dry his matted hair. The nectar that fell from his holy locks soaked the city and gave it its name, derived from the Tamil word *madhuram* (sweetness). The sugary buzz is still going strong in modern Madurai, a turbulent temple city that energizes the thousands who visit here every day. Most of these are pilgrims in search of a little auspicious action from mother Meenakshi, giving this otherwise fast-paced city a neighborly, small town feel.

Madurai has thrived as a cultural center since it was founded as the capital of the Pandya kingdom that ruled much of South India in the 4th century BC. The powerful Vijayanagar Kingdom reigned from here throughout the 15th and early 16th centuries, when the city's famous Meenakshi Amman Temple was built. From 1559 onward, Madurai was ruled by the Nayak dynasty, which built the city's other main attractions, the Teppakkulam and the Nayak Palace. The Nayaks lost power in 1736, when the East India Company bought and de-fortified the city, tearing down its walls and filling in the moat that once stood where the Veli streets run today.

Madurai has survived to become an important commercial hub. For all its vibrant clamor, Madurai still moves to the rhythm of the temple's activities, and the towering *gopurams* of the Meenakshi temple can be seen from almost everywhere in the city. Huge crowds descend on Madurai during the city's many **festivals,** the most important being the **Chittrai Festival** (April-May). This celebrates the marriage of Meenakshi (Parvati) to Lord Sundareswarar (Shiva).

▐ TRANSPORTATION

Flights: The **airport** (☎ 2671333) is 13km south of the city center. A taxi into town costs around Rs200. City buses also run infrequently between the airport and the city center. **Indian Airlines,** 7A W. Veli St. (☎ 2341234, airport 2690333), opposite the railway station. Open M-Sa 10am-5pm. To: **Chennai** (daily, US$100) and **Mumbai** (daily, US$200).

TAMIL NADU

Madurai

▲ ACCOMMODATIONS
Hotel Grands Central, **5**
Hotel Keerthi, **4**
Hotel Rathna Residency, **2**
Hotel Tamil Nadu, **12**
New College House, **7**
T.M. Lodge, **6**
YMCA, **11**

◆ FOOD
Hotel Mahal, **9**
New Arya Bhavan, **10**
Priya, **3**
Ruby Restaurant, **8**
Surya, **1**

Vaigai River

TO KODAIKANAL

TO MATTU THAVANI BUS STAND, LAKSHMI SUNDHARAM HALL & GANDHI MUSEUM

TO ANNA BUS STAND & HOSPITALS

TO VANDIYUR MARIAMMAN TEPPAKULAM

Victor Bridge

Kalpalam Rd.

Workshop Rd.

Tamil Sangam Rd.

N. Masi St.

Munichalai Rd.

E. Veli St.

E. Market St.

E. Masi St.

Palace Rd.

Tirumalai Nayak Palace

E. Avani Moola St.

E. Chittrai

N. Chittrai

Meenakshi Treasures

Madurai Gallery

Meenakshi Amman Temple

S. Chittrai

Parameswari Stores

W. Chittrai

S. Masi St.

Old Kosavar Pilayam Rd.

W. Veli St.

TO ARAPALAYAM BUS STAND

N. Veli St.

GPO

MADURAI MAIN MARKET

Town Hall Rd.

Khadi Gramodyog Bhavan

Nethaji (Dindigul) Rd.

W. Vadampokki St.

State Bank of India

Indian Airlines

Malligai Book Centre

Madurai Junction Railway Station

Periyar Bus Stand

W. Perumal Maistry St.

W. Veli St.

Kudal Alagar Perumal Temple

S. Veli St.

TO (15km)

TTDC

TO TUTICORIN, KANYAKUMARI & THIRUPPARANKUNDRAM (8km)

TO BODINAYAKKANUR

150 yards
150 meters

Trains: Madurai Junction Railway Station, W. Veli St. (☎ 132 or 2340135). Reservations open M-Sa 8am-8pm, Su 8am-2pm. To: **Bangalore** (10½hr.; daily 7:40pm; Rs124, with reservations Rs245); **Chennai** (10hr.; 8 per day 6:40am-11pm; Rs118, with reservations Rs215) via **Trichy** (Rs50); **Coimbatore** (5hr., 6:40am and 11pm, Rs66-360); **Kanyakumari** (6hr., daily 2:20am, Rs70-166); **Rameswaram** (4½hr., 5 per day 4:30-5:40am, Rs27-50); **Tirupati** (12hr., Th and Su 9:30am, Rs135-245). Change at **Trichy** for **Chidambaram, Tirupati,** and **Tanjore** (9am direct train).

Buses: There are 2 interstate bus stands. You can get in between the two by bus (Rs2-3) or auto-rickshaw (Rs40). **Mattu Thavani Bus Stand** has service to: **Bangalore** (10hr., 8 per day 6am-1am, Rs180); **Chennai** (10hr., every 30min. 4:30am-12:30am, Rs171-176); **Rameswaram** (3½hr., 1:30am and 2:30pm, Rs67); **Pondicherry** (8hr., 8:45, Rs125); **Tanjore** (3½hr., 2 per day 12:30pm and 1am, Rs65); **Trichy** (3hr., every 30min., Rs36-41); **Trivandrum** (7½hr., 9:30pm, Rs125); **Cochin** and **Kanyakumari. Arapalayam Bus Stand** serves the north. To: **Coimbatore** (every 20min., Rs66); **Kodaikanal** (5hr., 5 per day 3:15am-5:50pm, Rs37); **Munnar** (4hr., 8am, Rs50).

Local Transportation: Local buses leave from the **Periyar Bus Stand** on W. Veli St., a 2min. walk right out of the railway station. **Anna Bus Stand,** another local bus stand, is across the river. Auto- and cycle-**rickshaws** are everywhere; the main stand is right outside the railway station. A pre-paid rickshaw booth opens when trains arrive.

✦⌕ ORIENTATION AND PRACTICAL INFORMATION

Madurai stretches north and south of the often dry **Vaigai River.** The city is bordered on the south and west by railway tracks and is dominated by the **Meenakshi Temple.** The **Periyar Bus Stand** and **Madurai Junction Railway Station** are off **West Veli Street,** 1km west of the temple. To reach the city center and the budget hotels from the railway station, turn right onto W. Veli St., and then left again on Town Hall Rd., which leads east toward the temple; from Periyar Bus Stand, follow the wider **Nethaji (Dindigul) Road,** marked by the Hotel Empee. Streets are arranged concentrically around the temple, forming an irregular grid. Closest to the temple are North, East, South, and West **Chittrai Street.** Farther from the temple are North, East, South, and West **Avani Moola Street.** North, East, South, and West **Masi Street** are encircled by North, East, South, and West **Veli Street.** To cross the Vaigai River, head 1km northeast of the temple and across **Victor Bridge.**

Tourist Office: Tamil Nadu Tourism Development Corporation (TTDC), W. Veli St. (☎2334757), next to the Hotel Tamil Nadu. Turn right out of the railway station and walk straight down W. Veli St.; it's on the left. Open M-F 10am-5:45pm; Sa 10am-1pm. There are also offices at the airport and railway station. Open daily 6am-9pm.

Currency Exchange: State Bank of India, 6 W. Veli St. Sangam Towers (☎2342127), north of the railway station and across the street. Changes a wide range of currencies and traveler's checks. Open M-F 10am-4:30pm, Sa 10am-1:30pm.

Bookstore: Malligai Book Centre, 11 W. Veli St., opposite the railway station. Open M-Sa 10am-2pm and 4-9pm. There are also many book stalls on W. Veli St. around the railway station.

Police: Police Control Room (emergency ☎100). The B-7 station, on W. Veli St. (☎2336665), just past the tourist office, is the closest to the hotel area.

Pharmacy & Hospital: There are plenty of pharmacies along Town Hall Rd. and around the budget hotel area, most of them open 8am-10pm. The private **Jawahar Hospital,** 14 Main Rd., KK Nagar (☎2650021), on the northern bank of Vaigai, and the **Apollo Hospital,** Lake View Rd. (☎2650892), also in KK Nagar, both have a 24hr. **pharmacy.**

Internet: Global Soft, in the New College House complex at the corner of the Town Hall Rd. and W. Perumal Maistry St. Rs25 per hr. Open daily 6am-11:30pm.

Post Office: Head Post Office, on N. Veli St. Open M-Sa 9:30am-2:30pm, and 4-7pm, Su 9am-5pm. **Postal Code:** 625001.

ACCOMMODATIONS

Nearly all of Madurai's hotels are within walking distance of the Meenakshi Temple and the city's transportation hubs. Many budget places are on West Perumal Maistry St., parallel to W. Veli St., a 1min. walk from the railway station. Standards tend to be higher in Madurai than in most other places—probably due to the high volume of pilgrims passing through town. Most have 24hr. check-out.

New College House, 2 Town Hall Rd. (☎2342971). Huge, labyrinthine place with over 100 large, clean rooms with TVs and attached baths with seat toilets. Your best bet during peak season. A self-contained mini-village with barber shop, restaurant, and textile emporium offers relief from the congestion of the area. Singles Rs185. ❷

Hotel Rathra Residency, 109 W. Perumal Maistry St. (☎2348400). A fancy place with spacious, luxurious rooms catering to a business crowd. All the major newspapers are yours for the reading in the cushy foyer. Singles Rs375-800; doubles Rs425-900. AmEx/MC/V. ❸

YMCA International Home and Service Centre, Nethaji Rd. (☎2346649 or 2340861; www.ymcamadurai.org), near the corner of W. Masi St. It's fun to stay at the YMCA. Clean rooms along airy balconies; friendly staff. Ask about their local service projects. Singles Rs250-450; doubles Rs350-550. ❷

T.M. Lodge, W. Perumal Maisty St. (☎2341651). A touch above most other places in this price range. Rooms come with TV and attached bath with squat toilets, towels, soap, and hot water. Singles Rs199; doubles Rs320-480. MC/V. ❷

Hotel Grands Central, 47 W. Perumal Maistry St. (☎2343940). Good-sized rooms with clean sheets and TVs. Attached bath with seat toilet and hot water. Singles Rs195; doubles Rs495. ❷

Hotel Keerthi 40 W. Perumal Maistry St. (☎2341501; fax 2341510), 2 blocks north of Town Hall Rd. Polite staff and white-washed rooms with spotless sheets, ample lighting (but few windows), TVs, and phones. Clean attached baths with hot water. A/C rooms have seat toilets. Singles Rs175; doubles Rs253-345. ❷

Hotel Tamil Nadu, W. Veli St. (☎2337471), turn right out of the station and walk straight for 5min.; it's on the left. Clean rooms off a balcony. Singles Rs100; doubles Rs125-300. ❶

FOOD

The best restaurants in Madurai are in and around the hotels on W. Perumal Maistry St. and Town Hall Rd. Many of the hotels have rooftop dining, which usually means quiet surroundings, cool breezes, and great temple views.

Surya, 110 W. Perumal Maistry St., on the roof of Hotel Supreme. Relax with a few beers (Rs80) in a pleasant open-air setting on the 10th fl. *Dosas* Rs25, *Malai kofta* Rs40, veg. sizzler Rs90. Rooftop restaurant open daily 6am-midnight. A/C restaurant on ground fl. open daily 6am-11pm. AmEx/MC/V. If you're in the mood for surreal basement noise, try the **Apollo 96 Bar** downstairs. Once upon a time, this is what people thought the world would look like in AD 2001. Open daily 11am-11pm. ❶

Ruby Restaurant, W. Perumal Maistry St., next to Ruby Lodge. A peaceful courtyard lined by marble topped tables and pea plants. An entire section of the menu is devoted to mushrooms. Ginger mushroom Rs40, peas *masala* Rs30, *chappati* Rs10. ❶

New Arya Bhavan, 268 W. Masi St., at Nethaji Rd., on a corner on your left as you head from N. Perumal Maistry toward the temple. A calm oasis with wooden booths on a busy street, this local favorite serves up delicious *masala dosas* (Rs12), *uttappam* (Rs11), and all the rest. A/C banquet booths available upstairs for heat-hassled tourists in need of a quick cool-down. Attached sweet shop. Open daily 6:30am-10:30pm. ❶

Hotel Mahal, 21 Town Hall Rd., on the left as you head toward the temple. Long narrow room filled with whirling fans and lined with dining booths. The menu here is the most varied in town: *madura* chicken Rs45, roast leg of lamb Rs80, beer Rs70. Popular with foreign tourists. Open daily 11am-midnight. ❷

Priya, 102 W. Perumal Maistry St., in Hotel Prem Nivas. Typical dimly lit mid-range hotel restaurant, with good Indian food, A/C, and foreigner-friendly luxury items like corn flakes (Rs20). *Aloo gobi* Rs25, veg. sandwich Rs20. Open daily 7am-10pm. ❶

 SIGHTS

MEENAKSHI AMMAN TEMPLE

The temple complex is accessible via any of the 4 gopurams. Open daily 5am-12:30pm and 4-9:30pm. General entrance free; a few interior sanctums have entrance fees of Rs10-15. Camera fee Rs30.

The Meenakshi Amman Temple is a carnival of color—a spectacular, larger-than-life structure that attracts more than 10,000 people every day. Visitors are dazzled by the 65,000 sq. meters of the complex, its 30 million sculptures, and its twelve *gopurams*, the tallest of which is nearly 50m high. It's not all bells and whistles, though—the temple's candy-striped **ghats**, colorfully-painted ceilings, and hibiscus-lined Golden Lotus Tank make it a calm retreat from the hustle and bustle of the city. Dedicated to Shiva (Sundareswarar), as well as to his consort Parvati (Meenakshi), the temple was originally a humble shrine built by the Pandyas, but was later embellished and expanded upon by the Vijayanagar kings. The complex grew further when the Nayaks came to power in the 16th century and began work on the temple's famous towering *gopurams*. The temple was opened to Untouchables after Gandhi's visit here in 1946.

Legend has it that Pandya King Malayadwaja was childless and desperate for a male heir, so the king appealed to the gods for help and set about performing a series of *yagnas*, or fire sacrifices. Much to the king's surprise, a three-year-old girl emerged from the flames to stand before him one day—a beautiful girl with fish-like eyes ("Meenakshi" means fish-eyed), three breasts, and a whole lot of divine attitude. The king was a trifle troubled by his daughter's unconventional appearance, but a voice from above assured him that her third breast would disappear once she found the man who would one day become her husband. Meenakshi eventually grew up to become a beautiful princess, and eventually set out to conquer the world. One after another the gods fell before her, powerless in the face of her beauty and power, until only Shiva was left. When she confronted Shiva, Meenakshi's heart turned to *ghee*. Her third breast disappeared, and her wild ways were soon a thing of the past. Meenakshi and Sundareswar (Shiva) were married in Madurai and ruled the Pandya kingdom together. The **Meenakshi Kalyanam** festival commemorating the wedding takes place for 10 days in April or May and reportedly draws over 100,000 people.

POTRAMARAI KULAM. The corridors around the Potramarai Kulam (Golden Lotus Tank) are often crowded by devotees relaxing in the shade or taking in the spectacular view of the temple's southern *gopuram*. When the tank isn't closed for construction, it is frequented by pilgrims seeking a purifying bath in its light green waters, following the tradition of Indra, who is said to have bathed here. In ancient times, the Tamil Sangam (Academy of Poets) met in the area around the tank. Locals claim that the Sangam judged the merit of literary works by tossing submissions into the tank. If a work sank, the aspiring writer's hopes went along with it. Only works that floated were deemed worthy of the Sangam's attention.

KILIKOOTU MANDAPAM. The northwest corner of the tank leads directly to the Meenakshi Shrine, closed to non-Hindus; the corridor surrounding the shrine, however, is open to all. Called the Kilikootu Mandapam, or Parrot Cage Corridor, the space was once used to keep green parrots, lucky birds who were trained to repeat Meenakshi's name in offerings to the goddess. Now all that is left of the corridor is two large cages full of squawking green parrots outside a small shrine. (*In the corner south of the Meenakshi shrine and west of the Golden Lotus Tank.*)

ASHTA SHAKTI AND MEENAKSHI NAYAKKAR MANDAPAMS. In the southeastern corner is the brightly painted Ashta Shakti Mandapam (Eight Shakti Corridor), where hawkers peddle postcards, curios, and *puja* offerings. The passage was named for the eight avatars of the goddess Shakti carved on its pillars. Other sculptures and paintings depict the miracles *(tiruvilayadal)* of Shiva. The Meenakshi Nayakkar Mandapam has two rows of pillars carved with images of the *yali*, a mythological beast with the body of a lion and the head of an elephant, commonly used as a symbol of Nayak power.

OONJAL MANDAPAM. The golden images of Meenakshi and Sundareswar are carried into the neighboring 16th-century Oonjal Mandapam (Swing Corridor), placed on a swing, and sung to every Friday at 5:30pm. The shrine has a three-story *gopuram* guarded by two stern *dwarapalakas* (watchmen) and is supported by golden, rectangular columns that bear lotus markings. Along the perimeter of the chamber, granite panels of the divine couple overlook the crowds.

KAMBATHADI MANDAPAM. North of the Oonjal Mandapam is the **Sundareswar Shrine,** with its eight-foot image of Ganesh (Mukkuruni Vinayakar). The idol was discovered in the 17th century when King Tirumalai Nayak began digging the Mariamman Teppakulam in the southeastern corner of the city. To the right, in the northeast corner of the enclosure, is the Kambathadi Mandapam, adorned with elegant pillars, each of which bears a sculpture of Meenakshi or Shiva. Sculptures of Shiva and Kali trying to out-dance one another are pelted with balls of *ghee* by devotees. On the left are two sculptures of Shiva killing the demon child. A golden flagstaff with 32 sections symbolizes the human backbone and is surrounded by various gods, including Durga and Siddhar. The inner chamber contains the image of Sundareswar and an image of Nataraja, unique for having his right foot raised.

AYIRAKKAL MANDAPAM. East of the Kambathadi Mandapam is a lively market, where vendors sell postcards and religious trinkets. These stands surround the Ayirakkal Mandapam (Thousand Pillar Hall), which contains 985 carved pillars (no word on the other 15). It has been converted into a quiet **museum** with a substantial collection of sculptures. (*Open daily 7am-7:30pm. Rs2; camera fee Rs10.*)

TAMIL NADU

OTHER SIGHTS

GANDHI MUSEUM. The Mahatma visited Madurai several times, but this museum--one of only five (the others are in Pune, Mumbai, Delhi, and Kolkata)--does more than merely chronicle his stops. One section presents a fiery version of the events leading up to Independence; the other focuses on samples of Gandhi's correspondence and houses relics such as the loincloth he was wearing when he was killed. The museum is housed in a lovely, white, palace-like building with extensive, well-maintained, and peaceful gardens and grounds. The complex also houses a non-circulating library and research facilities, outdoor amphitheater, peace garden, and children's "science park." *(Take bus #3 from Mattu Tharani bus stand or from Periyar to Anna bus stand. Auto-rickshaw Rs20. Open 10am-1pm and 2-5:30pm. Free. Camera fee Rs10; video fee Rs50.)*

TIRUMALAI NAYAK PALACE. All that remains of Tirumalai's grand 17th-century palace is the cavernous **Swargavilasam** (Celestial Pavilion), a expansive courtyard lined with pillars and arcades. Nayak rulers held their public audiences under the domed ceiling of the pavilion. A passage at the back of the audience chamber leads to the former dance hall, large parts of which have been fully restored. This is the most impressive part of the palace—carvings of gargoyle-like dragons and elephants line the rich crimson and cream walls, and give a hint of the palace's former grandeur. The palace houses a small collection of stone carvings and early terracottas. *(1.5km southeast of the Meenakshi Temple. Open daily 9am-1pm and 2-5pm. Rs1. Sound and light show daily, 6:45pm in English, Rs10; 8:15pm in Tamil, Rs5.)*

VANDIYUR MARIAMMAN TEPPAKULAM. This square water tank has a tree-surrounded **shrine** in the center. The tank was built in 1646 by Tirumalai Nayak, who retired with his harem to the central shrine. These days the tank is usually dry, and the only activity in the area is boys playing cricket. Every year, a colorful float festival (Jan.-Feb.) commemorates the birth of its builder. *(Kamarajar Rd., 5km southeast of the railway station. Bus #4 or 4A from Periyar Bus Stand.)*

THIRUPPARANKUNDRAM. Though not as awe-inspiring as Meenakshi Amman, Thirupparankundram is an impressive cave-temple dedicated to Lord Subramanya guarded by sculptures of prancing horses. It is in a sleepy little village which sees few foreign tourists. The **inner sanctum** is carved right out of the rock in the side of a mountain and is accessible to non-Hindus. *(8km south of town from Periyar Bus Stand. Bus #5 or 48, 15min., Rs2.50. Open 5am-1pm and 4-9:30pm.)*

🎵 📷 ENTERTAINMENT AND SHOPPING

There are five **cinemas** near the Periyar Bus Stand. *The Hindu* has the latest listings for English-language films. Check with the tourist office for **cultural programs** such as classical dancing and music in Lakshmi Sundaram Hall, Tallakulam. Madurai is full of **textile shops** and sari showrooms. Tailors keen to make you an exact copy of whatever you're wearing for a nominal cost will accost you wherever you go. As always, beware of auto-rickshaw drivers who steer you toward a particular handicraft store—they're just after the commission. Even if you don't plan on buying anything, you may find yourself slurping down yet another free 7-Up as a smooth-talking salesman tries to talk you into buying that Rs500 parakeet-embroidered pillowcase you never knew you wanted. **Parameswari Stores,** 21 South Chittrai St., just outside the southern *gopuram* of the Meenakshi Temple, is well-known for its silk-cotton blends. (☎2347988. Open daily 9am-10pm.) **Khadi Gramodyog Bharan,** 26 Town Hall Rd., is a good place to buy gifts and wooden carvings. (Open M-Sa 9am-9pm, Su closed.) For the full Kashmiri-carpet experience, try the large multi-story **Madurai Gallery,** 19 N. Chittrai St. (☎2627051 or 2624064. Open daily 8:30am-9pm.) **Meenakshi Treasures,** worldwide shipping services, N. Chittrai St., has a beautiful, expensive jewelry collection upstairs, as well as an extensive range of silks, sandalwood, and silverware. (☎2630240. Open daily 9am-8:30pm.)

RAMESWARAM இராமேசுவரம் ☎04573

Situated on a remote island off the country's southeastern coast, the tiny town of Rameswaram is surrounded by pristine, nearly unpopulated beaches and aquamarine ocean. The town is also dominated by one huge monument, the Ramanathaswamy Temple, which draws thousands of Hindu pilgrims from all over India. The town is the setting of some of the most important scenes in the *Ramayana* (see **The Ramayana,** p. 620). It was from this venerated spot that Rama, the epic's hero, launched an attack on Ravana's fortress on the island of Lanka. According to a later myth, Rama made a *linga* of sand here after defeating Ravana, to honor Shiva and expiate the sin of murder. Rameswaram is also significant as the southern holy *dham* (abode), one of India's four sacred places marking the cardinal directions. (The others are Dwarka in the west, Badrinath in the north, and Puri in the east.) A number of major festivals take place in Rameswaram, including **Thai Amavasai** (Jan.), **Masi Sivarathiri** (Feb.-Mar.), and **Adiammavasai** (July-Aug.). For the rest of the year, Rameswaram is a quiet, slow-paced little town that sees relatively few foreign tourists, and is home to the Sub-continent's most relaxed bus drivers. It is a gorgeous place to kick back and watch the waves for a few days.

▐ TRANSPORTATION

Trains: Rameswaram Station (☎221226), 1km southwest of the temple. To: **Tambaram** for **Chennai** (12hr., 12:05 and 3:10pm, Rs145); **Coimbatore** (12hr., 7pm, Rs99); **Madurai** (5hr., 2:30pm, Rs20-51); **Palghat** (12hr., 7:30am and 4:10pm, Rs55); **Trichy** (7hr., 1 and 9:30pm, Rs73).

Buses: The **bus stand** is on Bazaar Rd., 2km west of the temple. Frequent buses run between the temple and the bus stand around the clock (10min., Rs2). Express buses to: **Chennai** (12hr., 5pm, Rs223); **Kanyakumari** (9hr., 7:30am and 8pm, Rs110); **Salem** (10hr., 7:15am and 7:45pm, Rs143); **Madurai** (every 10-15min., 12:15am-10:45pm); **Tanjore** (7hr., 4 per day 6:55am-4:05pm, Rs75); **Trichy** (7hr., 20 per day, Rs72); **Tiruppatur** (11 per day, 4:15am-6:05pm); **Thiruchundur** (7hr., 16 per day 5am-6:30pm, Rs60); **Rajapalayam** (7hr., 5 per day 4:45am-3:25pm, Rs76); **Aruppukottai** (6hr., 8 per day 5:05am-5:45pm, Rs40).

Local Transportation: Unmetered **cycle-** and **auto-rickshaws** go all over town; an auto-rickshaw from the railway station to the temple should cost Rs20. **Horsedrawn covered carts** are also available (railway station to temple, Rs15). Silver-and-red **local buses** shuttle between the bus stand and E. Car St. **Bikes** can be hired (Rs3 per hr.) from a stall around the corner from Hotel Maharaja's, on West Car St.

◢◼ ? ORIENTATION AND PRACTICAL INFORMATION

Getting around Rameswaram involves wandering the four **Car Streets**—North, East, South, and West—surrounding the **Ramanathaswamy Temple.** Most of the hotels and restaurants are on these four streets and on **Sannadhi Street,** which runs east from the middle of E. Car St. to the Bay of Bengal. To reach the temple from the railway station, walk out of the main entrance and follow the road for about 300m as it

TAMIL NADU

curves slightly, then turn left (north) when you hit the principal north-south thoroughfare. Walk north for 500m until you reach **Middle Street,** which leads east (right) to the middle of W. Car St. and the western entrance to the temple.

Tourist Office: (☎221371 or 221373), located at the bus stand. Open M-F 9am-5:40pm. The **Tourist Information Centre,** open daily 6-11am and 1-4pm, is inside the railway station and has brochures and maps of Rameswaram. The Temple Information Centre, on the east side of the temple, is often unmanned.

Police station: (☎221246), in a red brick bldg. at the junction of E. and N. Car St. Open 24hr. Also a small coastal station on the beach near Dhanushkodi.

Pharmacy: Sekar Medicals, on the corner of Middle and Bazaar St., 200m up the road from Hotel Maharaja's. Open daily 7:30am-10:30pm.

Hospital: There is a **government hospital** (☎222036), near the railway station, but you might find more helpful and better medical resources in Madurai. Open 24hr. The small **Lakshmi Hospital** (☎222116) is just a one-doctor clinic but is open 8am-10pm daily. On Bazaar St. across from govt. hospital, small attached pharmacy.

Post Office: (☎221230), on Middle St., 500m down on the left-hand side as you head away from the temple toward the bus stand. Open M-Sa 9am-3:30pm. **Postal Code:** 623526

🏠 ACCOMMODATIONS

Except for the TTDC Rest House, most hotels are in the immediate vicinity of the Ramanathaswamy Temple. Accommodations are basic, catering to pilgrims looking for a cheap place to crash for the night. Rameswaram's tap water can be salty, and showers are extremely rare, so test the plumbing before checking in. Reserve ahead during the pilgrimage season (July-Aug.), and in April-May, when schools are out and families flock to the area.

Hotel Maharaja's, 32 Middle St. (☎221271 or 221721). Pleasant rooms with cable TV and a view of the temple's *gopurams*. Attached squat toilets are the cleanest around; hot water available. Check-out 24hr. Singles Rs180; doubles Rs266-495. ❷

Hotel Tamil Nadu (☎221277 or 221064). On the beachfront, just past the holy bathing spot. More expensive, but further from the temple noise. The rooms here are clean and blessed with more air, light, and life than those in most TTDC-run hotels. All rooms have attached baths with seat toilets and hot water showers. Good attached restaurant and bar with a view of the sea. Doubles Rs425-650. ❸

Hotel Guru, 12 E. Car St. (☎221134 or 221531), at the northern end of the street. Rooms have attached bath and squat toilets. Singles Rs100; doubles Rs175-650. ❶

🍴 FOOD

For the most part, dining options in the town are restricted to all-but-identical "meals" joints serving up the familiar *idlis*, *dosas*, and *sambar* rice.

Vasanta Bhavan, at the southern end of E. Car St. Quality food at unbeatable prices. "Meals" Rs15. Open daily 6am-10:30pm. ❶

Ganesh Mess, near Hotel Maharaja's and the western gate. Another popular "meals" place serving all your South Indian favorites. Onion *uttappam* Rs10, special *dosa* Rs10, "meals" Rs17. Open daily 7am-3:30pm and 7-10pm. ❶

👁 SIGHTS

THE RAMANATHASWAMY TEMPLE. The most enjoyable of Tamil Nadu's temples, especially on a hot day, the Ramanathaswamy Temple is the pilgrim's equivalent of a water park. The Bay of Bengal and the 22 tanks of the

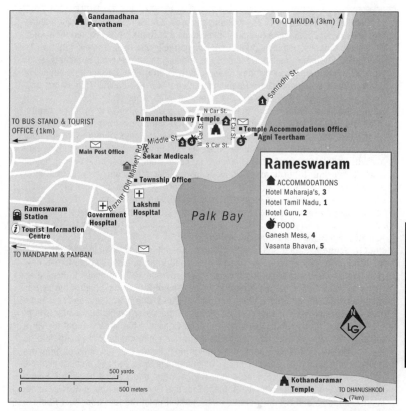

TO OLAIKUDA (3km)

Gandamadhana
Parvatham

TO BUS STAND & TOURIST
OFFICE (1km)

N Car St.

Ramanathaswamy Temple

Middle St.

Main Post Office

Sekar Medicals

W Car St.

S Car St.

E Car St.

Temple Accommodations Office
Agni Teertham

Township Office

Palk Bay

Bazaar (Old Market) Rd.

Lakshmi
Hospital

Rameswaram
Station

Government
Hospital

Tourist Information
Centre

TO MANDAPAM & PAMBAN

Rameswaram

🏠 ACCOMMODATIONS
Hotel Maharaja's, 3
Hotel Tamil Nadu, 1
Hotel Guru, 2
🍴 FOOD
Ganesh Mess, 4
Vasanta Bhavan, 5

0   500 yards
0   500 meters

Kothandaramar
Temple

TO DHANUSHKODI
(7km)

TAMIL NADU

Ramanathaswamy Temple form part of one of the most sacred pilgrimages a
Hindu can make; its spiritual power is akin to jumping in the waters of the
Ganga at Varanasi (see p. 721). Before taking *darshan* at the temple's resident
deities, pilgrims first bathe in the sea at **Agni Teertham** ("Holy Fire Water") and
then proceed to the wet temple where they are led from holy tank to holy tank.
To expedite the process, temple employees are on hand to dump buckets of
salty water on devotees. The best time to visit is at dawn, when water-splash-
ing is at its peak and thousands of dripping-wet pilgrims scurry from one wet
washing place to the next. If you're so inclined, a squad of guides and friendly
touts will compete to help get your hair wet as well. Taking part in the ritual
without their help may be tricky, as certain parts of the temple complex are
off-limits to non-Hindus.

The inner sanctum houses two *lingas*, one of which was fashioned out of sand
by Rama himself. According to a later version of the *Ramayana*, Rama returned
to Rameswaram after he had killed Ravana in Lanka, only to discover that Ravana
had been a brahmin and that his murder was therefore a grave sin. Rama sent
Hanuman to bring back a *linga* with which Rama could worship Shiva and expiate
his guilt, but the monkey was slow in returning, and Rama had to make do with a
linga of sand, fashioned by his devoted wife, Sita. When Hanuman finally returned
and tried to replace the makeshift *linga*, so great was Sita's devotion that it would
not budge; the new *linga* was installed to the left of it.

THE RAMAYANA Arguably the most culturally influential work of literature in India, the *Ramayana* (literally, "the romance of Rama") has inspired thousands
of dances, paintings, shadow puppet shows, inter-religious riots, and even its own TV
mini-series. The epic's main characters, Rama and Sita, are revered as archetypes of
those who unwaveringly follow their *dharma* (duty or fate). The Sanskrit poet Valmiki is
thought to have composed the *Ramayana* around 400 BC, basing it on events that
took place between 1000 and 700 BC. Here's our take two:

Act I, Scene 1: Rama is born to King Dasaratha's wife Kausalya in Ayodhya, capital
of Kosala. Dasaratha's other wives, Kaikeyi and Sumithra, bear him Bharata and the
twins Lakshman and Shatrugna, respectively. **Scene 2:** Rama journeys with his guru
Viswamitra to the kingdom of Mithila, where he falls in love at first sight with King Janaka's beautiful daughter, Sita. But winning her hand is not an easy task. Fearing he will
lose his daughter to an unworthy man, Janaka declares that only he who is able to
break Shiva's divine bow can have her hand in marriage. **Scene 3:** Rama successfully
breaks the bow, and the two kingdoms delight in the wedding of Rama and Sita. **Scene
4:** The aging Dasaratha names Rama as his successor, but his wife Kaikeyi refuses to
accept Rama as king, forcing Dasaratha to banish Rama to the forest for 14 years.
Kaikeyi's son Bharata is crowned king instead.

Act II, Scene 1: Rama, Sita, and Rama's faithful brother Lakshman leave Ayodhya for
the forest. The sorrowful Dasaratha soon dies, and Bharata rushes to the forest, begging Rama to return to claim the throne. Unwilling to break his promise to his father,
Rama stays in the forest for the next 14 years. **Scene 2:** Ravana, chief of the *asuras*
(demons), abducts Sita to his island kingdom of Lanka. **Scene 3:** Rama and Lakshman
journey in search of Sita, encountering, en route, the clever monkey Hanuman, son of
the wind god. Rama sends Hanuman to Lanka to assess the situation and deliver a
token to his beloved wife. Hanuman sets fire to the entire capital of Lanka before he
leaves. **Scene 4:** With the help of a Lankan spy, Rama and his army of monkeys
advance on Lanka. The valiant monkeys build a bridge to Lanka, and a celestial battle
ensues. Rama emerges victorious, vanquishing Ravana and winning back Sita. **Scene
5:** 14 years are up, and Rama, Lakshman, Sita, and Hanuman return to Kosala. Rama
is crowned king, and Ayodhya erupts in celebration upon the revelation that Rama is
an avatar of Vishnu. **Scene 6:** Sita's fidelity during Rama's absence is questioned.
Subordinating his trust in Sita to his princely duty, Rama subjects her to an ordeal of
fire, from which she emerges unscathed and vindicated. However, mortified by Rama's
lack of faith, she prefers to be swallowed by the Earth than to be his queen. **The end.**

Construction of the temple, famous for its sculpted pillars and long wet corridors, began in the 12th century under the Chola empire; the last major alter-
ations to the temple were made in the mid-18th century by the Raja of
Ramnathapuram, Muthuramalinga Sethupathi. The eastern *gopuram* was
completed during the 20th century. *(Wet temple open daily 4am-8pm. Rs7 for entrance
to bath; Rs10 for water-pouring guide. Inner sanctum closed noon-4pm. Watch out for bats.)*

OTHER SIGHTS. The Gandamadhana Paravtham, a simple, white-washed temple
on top of the highest hill in town, houses an imprint of Lord Rama's feet and commands splendid views of the sandy island terrain. *(3km north of the Ramanathaswamy
Temple. Head away from Ramanathaswamy Temple along Middle St., and turn right at the first
crossroads. Follow the road straight uphill to the temple.)* The southeastern end of the
island forms a great finger of sand pointing toward Sri Lanka. The railway line to
Dhanushkodi was destroyed by a cyclone that roared through in 1964, but it is accessible today by bus. *(Take bus #3 from E. Car St. to the end of the road; 15min., buses every*

30min., 5am-8:30pm, Rs4; from there it's 6km of sand, seashells, and surf to the village itself.) The **Kothandaramar Temple,** 2km along the road to Dhanushkodi, dedicated to Rama, is said to mark the site where Ravana's brother, Vibhishana, was crowned king of Lanka after Ravana's death. Painted scenes from the *Ramayana* line the walls of the interior. *(Accessible by the #3 bus to Dhanushkodi. Open daily 6am-5pm.)* Touts and tour guides near the temple and holy bathing spot will compete to take you out **snorkeling** over the beautiful coral reefs that lie a few kilometers offshore. Prices vary enormously according to supply and demand; bargain hard, and aim to pay around Rs200-300 for an afternoon's float. For a genuinely friendly guide, it is worth seeking out **A. "Vijay" Kulanthaisamy** (☎ 223393), a young spear fisherman who lives in the village of Olaikuda, a few kilometers north along the coast.

KANYAKUMARI க�
ற் யாகுமாஸ் ☎ 04652

Kanyakumari (Cape Comorin), the southernmost tip of the Indian Subcontinent, is particularly auspicious for Hindus because it is the meeting place of three major bodies of water—the Arabian Ocean, the Bay of Bengal, and the Indian Ocean. Hindu pilgrims come by the thousands to the sacred point to watch the sun set into one ocean and rise out of another. Just as South India's beach resorts provide sun, sand, and tropical fruits in one easy-to-swallow package for Western tourists, so Kanyakumari provides an equally irresistible dose of patriotism, spirituality, and tacky shell art for Indian tourists. Monuments to Gandhi and Swami Vivekandanda compete for visitors with the Kumari Amman Temple, dedicated to Devi Kanya, a virginal incarnation of Parvati. Although tour buses parked along the seafront disgorge seemingly endless masses of pilgrims into the waiting arms of beach vendors hawking cheap souvenirs, the natural beauty and power somehow manage to rise above it all. When the sun begins descending and the hyperactive pilgrims slow their pace to munch on deep-fried peppers and bananas at lit-up street stalls, any prior carnivalesque grimness dissolves into the seas.

▆ TRANSPORTATION

Trains: Railway station, on Main Rd., a 15min. walk from the sea. Reservations open daily 4am-8pm. To: **Bangalore** (20hr., 6:40am, Rs300); **Chennai** (17hr., 4:10pm, Rs289); **Ernakulam** (10hr., 4:40 and 6:40am, Rs140); via **Trivandrum** (2½hr., Rs62).

Buses: The **bus stand** posts schedules in English. All buses also stop on Main Rd.; save yourself the walk and get off opposite the Government Hospital. **Tamil Nadu State Express Transport** (☎ 246019) runs buses to: **Chennai** (16hr., 5 per day 9:30am-8:30pm, Rs280); **Coimbatore** (11hr., 5:30 and 6:30pm, Rs180); **Kodaikanal** (10hr., 8:45pm, Rs130); **Madurai** (6hr., every hr. 9:30am-8:45pm, Rs104); **Ooty** (14hr., 5:30 and 6:30pm, Rs236). Buses also go to **Nagercoil** (30min., every 5min., Rs6-8), where there are frequent connections to many other cities. **KRSTC** buses leave from platform #4 of the bus station and go to: **Ernakulam** (8hr., 7 and 9am, Rs130); **Kovalam** (3hr., 4 per day 6:20am-4:30pm, Rs40); **Trivandrum** (2½hr., 12 per day 5:45am-9pm, Rs32). The Kovalam schedule is particularly variable; it may be easiest to go to Trivandrum and take a local bus from there.

▆▆ ORIENTATION AND PRACTICAL INFORMATION

Buses from Trivandrum and Madurai head south down **Main Road** past the **railway station,** stopping just north of **South Car Street,** where most people descend. Buses then turn west onto **Bus Stand Road,** past the **lighthouse,** to the **bus stand.** Main Rd. continues south past the junction to the **tourist office** (on the left) and peters out at the seafront by the **Gandhi Memorial.** Running east from Main Rd. Junction, Bus Stand Rd. crosses **Sannadhi Street** before ending at the **ferry service station.** Sannadhi St. heads south through the stalls to the **Kumari Amman Temple,** at the very tip of the Subcontinent.

Tourist Office: Main Rd. (☎246276). On the right, in a circular building north of the Gandhi Memorial. Open M-F 10am-5:45pm.

Currency Exchange: Canara Bank, Main Rd. (☎246249), a 5min. walk north of Main Rd. Junction, on the left. Changes AmEx and Thomas Cook traveler's checks. Gives cash advances on AmEx/MC/V. Allow at least 1hr. Open M-F 10am-2pm, Sa 10am-noon.

Police: Main Rd. (☎246224), just off Main Rd. Junction.

Pharmacy: Sastha Pharmacy (☎246455), on Main Rd., halfway between the railway station and the tourist office, just beyond Hotel Sangam. Open daily 8:30am-9:30pm.

Hospital: Dr. Arumugam's clinic, E. Car St. (☎246349). Between Hotels Manickham and Maadhini.

Internet: Sri Uttira, Main Rd. on the left about 50-100m shy of the Gandhi memorial. Rs40 per hr. Open daily 10am-9pm.

Post Office: GPO, Main Rd., just south of Canara Bank. Open M-Sa 8am-noon and 1:30-4:30pm. **Postal Code:** 629702.

ACCOMMODATIONS

Every second building in Kanyakumari provides lodging of some kind. Prices begin to soar in August and peak between October and February. There is no such thing as tranquility here—families wake up noisily at 5:30am to catch the sunrise. All hotels listed have attached restaurants.

Hotel Maadhini, E. Car St. (☎246787), on the shore, 200m north of the temple. Carpeted rooms with bright lighting and large disinfected baths with soap, towels, and hot water. Lime green walls and balcony views of the fishing villages (in some rooms) make a stab at elegance. Check-out 24hr. Doubles Rs300-450; triples Rs550. ❷

Manickam Tourist House, N. Car St. (☎246387), near Hotel Maadhini. Decent amenities in green rooms, spacious attached baths, and small balconies with views of the sea. Facilities are a little tired, but cheap. Clean rooms with attached bathrooms and balconies. Check-out 24hr. Singles Rs250; doubles Rs300-400. ❷

Hotel SeaView, E. Car St. (☎247841). Heading toward the sea, take a left down the hill about 100m past Hotel Sangam; it's straight ahead. Modernist monstrosity, glass gone amok, call it what you will: this is simply a beautiful hotel. Pristine, palatial rooms with TV and sliding plate-glass windows offer stunning panoramic views encompassing the Bay of Bengal and the Indian Ocean. Almost every convenience; you name it, they've got it. Doubles (w/o view) Rs600, deluxe (with view) Rs820. ❹

Hotel Sangam, Main Rd., (☎246351), opposite the GPO. Less-than-tranquil location. Rooms with great natural light have sea views and spotless baths with seat toilets and towels. Rooftop views of the sunrise. Room service. Singles and doubles Rs300-900. ❷

Hotel Ramshath, S. Car St. (☎247759). Follow directions to Hotel SeaView, but look left at the bottom of the incline. Bare lodging with some rooms overlooking the ocean. Rooms Rs200-250. ❷

🍴 FOOD

Since people come to attend to spiritual affairs and buy souvenirs, it's perhaps not surprising that material matters, like food, lean toward simple and uninspiring. The stalls, which set up at night at the junction of Main and Bus Station Rd., will slap down a banana leaf in front of you and serve excellent fast meals (chicken or fish fry with a veg. curry and *parathas*) for less than Rs25.

Hotel Saravana has two very popular branches: one on Sannadhi St., 50m in front of the temple, and another around the corner toward Main Rd. Junction. South Indian breakfasts (excellent *masala dosa* Rs20), and Gujarati, Rajasthani, Punjabi, and South Indian veg. *thalis* (Rs27-40; served 11am-3pm). Both open daily 6:30am-10:30pm. ❷

Hotel Triveni, Main Rd., opposite Hotel Sangam. Wide variety of veg. dishes, including a deliciously crisp onion *utthappam* (Rs16), served under portraits of the kitchen's creations. Fresh juice Rs7-22, meals Rs25-37. Open daily 6:30am-11pm. ❶

Archana Restaurant, East Car St., attached to Hotel Maadhini. This tourist-laden dig has spacious garden surroundings sunken from the street and an extensive menu comprising both Indian and Continental. Open daily 7am-10:15pm. ❷

Hotel SeaView Restaurant, East Car Street, in the hotel. The virtues of the hotel create a slightly forced ambience in the restaurant (dependably cheesy hotel still-lifes of flower vases on the wall), but the food is excellent. South Indian *thalis* Rs45, North Indian *thalis* Rs55. Open daily 11am-11pm. ❷

👁 SIGHTS

KUMARI AMMAN TEMPLE. The seaside Kumari Amman Temple, with its unmistakable red-and-white vertical temple stripes, is at the very tip of India. Dedicated to Kanya Devi, an incarnation of Parvati, the temple celebrates the penance she did in the hope of winning Shiva's hand in marriage. Shiva consented and set off for the midnight wedding ceremony. The other gods, wanting Kanya Devi to retain her divine *shakti* by remaining a virgin, hatched a plot to spoil the wedding. The sage Narada, assuming the form of a rooster, crowed for dawn long before sunrise to make Shiva think he was late for the ceremony. Shiva fell for the trick and went home, leaving poor, heartbroken Kanya Devi an eternal virgin. Foreigners should expect an entrance fee and will find it difficult to shake guides claiming "temple-worker" credentials. Visitors must remove their shoes, and men must go shirtless. *(Open daily 4:30am-noon and 4-8:15pm. Rs10. Camera fee Rs2.)*

GANDHI MANDAPAM. This unusual rendition of Orissan-style architecture, this time in bright pink, overlooks the southernmost tip of India. A black marble box marks the spot where the ashes of Mahatma Gandhi were stored before being scattered seaward, and photographs of "the great soul" line the walls. The *mandapam* rises 23m (79 ft.), one foot for each year of Gandhi's life. It was designed so that it is hit by rays of sunlight at noon every year on October 2, his birthday. *(At the seaward end of Main Rd. Open daily 7am-7pm.)*

VIVEKANANDA MEMORIAL. Accessible only by ferry, the two rocks marking the Vivekananda Memorial sit in the Bay of Bengal east of Kanyakumari. The Hindu reformer Swami Vivekananda swam here and meditated on top of the rocks for several days in 1892 before heading to Chicago for the 1893 World Religions Conference. The Memorial temple commemorates the event, and a meditation chamber below the temple, decorated with a shiny green "Om" in the darkness, allows you an attempt at empathy with the Swami. Arrows mark a path around the island, which also houses a temple built around one of the **goddess Parvati's footprints.** The notice board at the ferry terminal on the mainland gives information on sunrise times. If you have sensitive feet, wear socks or come in the morning: large stretches of stone exposed to the sun tend to get piping hot. Expect a wait for the ferry to get back. *(Ferries daily 7:45am-4pm. Rs10. Memorial entrance fee Rs10.)*

WANDERING MONK EXHIBITION. Infinitely more tranquil, if a little less picturesque than the other monuments, this small museum is devoted to the life of Swami Vivekananda. Panels chronicle his life, his wanderings, and his goals. For those with little prior knowledge of the Swami, it is well worth a wander, but a serious perusal of all the information could take half the day. *(At the junction of Bus Stand and Main Rd. Open daily 8am-noon and 4-8pm. Rs2.)*

FISHING VILLAGE. The village on the east coast north of the hotel district has many charms—bright yellow and lavender houses, small church-shrines, and a thriving catamaran fishing business. The elegant and imposing **Holy Land of Ransom Church,** with its impressive facade, towers over the southern edge of the village. The area can be a bit intimidating after dark, however, as one can easily get turned around and disoriented in the back-alleys.

THIRUVALLUVAR STATUE. Impossible to miss, this impressive stone statue rises from a rocky island next to the Vivekananda Rock Memorial and commemorates the Tamil poet who lived over 2000 years ago. His *Thirukkural* consists of 1330 couplets on ethical and moral themes. Accordingly, the statue stands 133 ft. high. *(First stop for the Vivekananda ferry; ferries daily 7:45am-4pm.)*

◗ FESTIVALS

Kanyakumari's **Pongal Festival** (Jan. 14-16, 2004) marks the end of the rice harvest with the ritual cooking and offering of South India's beloved sweet (sticky rice in earthen pots) to the goddess. The tourist office runs trips to nearby villages to watch the festivities, where most of the merriment is concentrated. The tourist office also organizes the **Cape Festival** at the end of December, a celebration of Tamil culture, especially *bharatnatyam* dance. Finally, **World Tourism Day** (Sept. 27) is a party of free cultural shows, free food, and free garlands for foreigners.

◗ DAYTRIP FROM KANYAKUMARI

SUCHINDRAM TEMPLE. The beautifully carved Suchindram Temple, 13km from Kanyakumari, is dedicated to the holy trinity of Hinduism—Shiva, Vishnu, and Brahma—and contains large numbers of sculptural odds and ends, including India's only depiction of a female Ganesh. Also of note are several hollow pillars, each sounding a different musical note when hit, a huge Hanuman statue, and a stone pillar (hidden among hundreds) depicting a man with a massive erection. *(Suchindram can be visited by taking bus #303 from Kanyakumari. Rs4.50 to Suchindram, Rs12 to Padmanabhapuram. Open daily 4:30am-noon and 4:30-8:45pm.)*

KODAIKANAL கொடை · கானடு ☎04542

Hours away from the nearest major city and surrounded by towering cliffs and protected forests, Kodaikanal is one of the most popular (and most beautiful) hill stations in southern India. The heady scent of eucalyptus mingles with the fresh breezes that blow across Kodai's mountainside, covered in blue-gums and *kurinji* blossoms. During the hottest months of the year (Apr.-June), the town swarms with tourists, who descend *en masse* to stroll along the gentle slopes and breathe in the crisp country air—a trend that's been popular ever since the Brits set up shop here in the 1840s to escape the sweltering, malaria-infested plains. Today, the constant influx of tourists has taken its toll on the town, scarring it with a jumble of tour buses and cheap hotels, and littering some of Kodai's natural wonders with garbage. But Kodai's setting remains one of the most stunning of any hill station. The high season often coincides with a thick persistent "Scotch mist" cloud cover that can obstruct Kodai's famous views; the winter months (Jan.-Feb.) are supposed to be clearer. Temperatures are 10-20°C cooler than in Chennai, and nights are often nippy enough for warm shawls and fireplaces. Peak season here is Apr.-June.

⊏ TRANSPORTATION

Trains: Kodaikanal Road Station (☎ 454338226), just off Anna Salai, near the bus stand, is a 2¾hr. bus ride from town. From Kodaikanal Rd. to **Chennai** (4 per day 12:30-1pm, Rs203). The train reservation center is open M-Sa 8am-noon and 2:30-5pm, Su 8am-noon.

Buses: The **bus stand** is a paved lot just off Anna Salai, on Wood Will Rd. A reservation and inquiry booth is open daily 9am-1pm and 2-4pm. To: **Bangalore** (12hr., 5:30 and 6pm, Rs275); **Chennai** (10hr., 6:40pm, Rs225); **Coimbatore** (5½hr., 4:30 and 8:30pm, Rs165); **Dindigul** (3 hr., 8 per day 8am-6:20pm, Rs27); **Kanyakumari** (10hr., 8:45am, Rs165); **Madurai** (4hr., 11 per day 7am-4:30pm, Rs37); **Palani** (3hr., 11 per day 6:30am-7:15pm., Rs20); **Trichy** (5½hr., 1:30 and 5:30pm, Rs65); **Kodai Road Station** (2¾hr., 3 per day 11:40am-4:20pm, Rs27). A number of **private bus** operators on Anna Salai offer minibus service to Bangalore, Chennai, Coimbatore, Madurai, and Ooty (Rs100-700).

Local Transportation: The best way to get around town is on foot or by bike. **Bikes** are available for hire from stalls along the lakeside for Rs10 per hr. **Taxis** are also available outside the bus stand to help you deal with Kodai's hilly roads (minimum charge Rs60). A taxi tour of Kodai's environs should cost Rs350, off-season Rs300 (8 sites), and Rs550, off-season Rs500 (12 sites).

⚡ 🔼 ORIENTATION AND PRACTICAL INFORMATION

Buses pull into a lot on the corner of **Anna Salai** and **Wood Will Road,** by the Hotel Astoria. Going uphill on Wood Will Rd. (toward the bus reservation booth) leads to **Coaker's Walk,** the Youth Hostel, and then on to **Pillar Rocks** and other scenic spots and viewpoints. Downhill from the bus stand on Anna Salai are most of the budget hotels and the post office. Along Anna Salai in the other direction is a large rotary intersection with **PT Road,** home to many of the town's restaurants. From here, the lake is down the hill to the left.

Tourist Office: (☎ 241675), on the northern side of Anna Salai, a 2min. walk downhill from the bus stand; on the left. Open M-F 10am-5:45pm. For more information on hikes around Kodaikanal, visit the **District Forestry Office** (☎ 240287) to get a brochure and an application for the (free) trekking permit. Turn left off Anna Salai after the police station and follow the road downhill for about 5min. Open M-Sa 10am-5:30pm.

Budget Travel: For bus, train, and airline bookings, try the **Almond Travel Agency** (☎ 243376 or 243508. Open daily 9am-9pm) or **Kurinji Tours and Travels** (☎ 240008 or 244006), near Hilltop Towers Hotel, Club Rd. Open daily 9am-9pm.

Currency Exchange: Indian Bank, Anna Salai, on the left as you head toward the lake from the bus stand, changes cash and traveler's checks in most major currencies. Open M-F 10am-2pm, 2:30pm-3:30pm, Sa 10am-12:30pm.

TAMIL NADU

Internet: Alpha Net, above Valliapa Medicals on PT Rd. in the Heritage Complex. Rs50 per hr. Open daily 9am-10pm.

Supermarket: Spencer's, downhill from Hilltop towers on Club Rd., heading toward the lake, is a well-stocked supermarket selling donuts, CDs, and apple-scented shampoo. Open daily 9am-7:30pm.

Hospital: Van Allen (☎241254). A reputable private hospital near Coaker's Walk. Doctor on call M-Sa 8:30am-5pm. Intensive Care, in rear, open daily 24hr. for emergencies.

Pharmacy: Valliappa Medicals, on PT Rd., next to the Royal Tibet restaurant. Open daily 10am-9pm.

Police: (☎240262). On Anna Salai, on the left, past Snooze Inn as you head downhill.

Post Office: on Anna Salai, opposite Snooze Inn. Open M-Sa 9am-4:30pm. **Postal Code:** 624101.

▐ ACCOMMODATIONS

Every other building in Kodai seems to have rooms for rent. Most of the cheapest places are along Anna Salai. As you move away from the town center, quality and prices increase exponentially. The high season runs from April to mid-June.

Greenland's Youth Hostel, St. Mary's Rd. (☎240899 or 241099). From the bus stand, go uphill on Wood Will Rd. and past Coaker's Walk on St. Mary's Rd. for 10min. In a secluded spot near a cliff, the grassy terraces command stunning views of the plains and ridges in the distance. Private rooms have attached toilets and fireplaces. Hot water available 7-9am. Friendly room service also builds you fires (firewood Rs50 per bundle). Laundry service Rs8 per piece. Check-out 10am. Dorms Rs55; singles Rs200-300; doubles Rs275-390. ❷

Villa Retreat, St. Mary's Rd. (☎240940 or 243940; www.villaretreat.com). At the start of Coaker's Walk, uphill from the bus stand. The views here rival those from the Youth Hostel. Tastefully furnished rooms and cottages with hot water, phone, and TV. Check-out 9am. Doubles Rs590-790; cottages 990-1690. ❹

Hotel Astoria (☎240524; astoria1@vsnl.com). Just next to the bus stand at the intersection of Wood Will Rd. and Anna Salai. Classy mid-range hotel popular with the imported suitcase crowd. Bay windows, large beds, seat toilets, satellite TV, and hot water. Check-out high-season 9am, off-season 24hr. Doubles Rs700, off-season Rs350. ❹

Hotel Strawberry Park, 7/200 Anna Salai (☎242340 or 242341; straw-berry@eth.net). No strawberries to be found, but digital TVs instead. Deluxes have bathtubs and balconies. High-season check-out 10am. Doubles Rs460-960. ❸

Snooze Inn, Anna Salai (☎240837; fax 660657). Downhill from the bus stand, on the left. Spacious but slightly stuffy rooms (with or without faded tatty carpet) with clean sheets, towels, and the Bible. Attached bathrooms with seat toilets and hot water. 24hr. check-out. Doubles Rs295-450, off-season Rs250-425. ❷

International Tourist Lodge, Anna Salai (☎240542). On the right as you head downhill from the bus stand. One of the better rock-bottom places. Simple rooms with attached (squat) bath. 24hr. check-out. Doubles Rs300, off-season Rs150. ❷

▐ FOOD

In addition to the North and South Indian standard cuisines, Kodaikanal's colder climate and tourist economy support surprisingly good homemade chocolates and local, fresh honey. Sweet teeth welcome here.

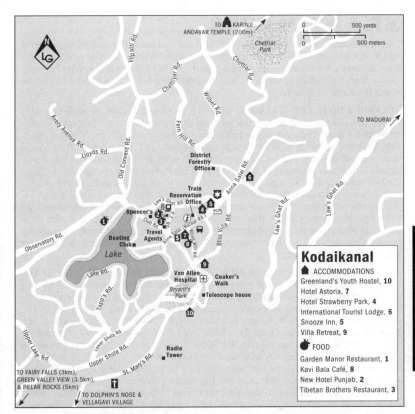

Kodaikanal

🏠 ACCOMMODATIONS
Greenland's Youth Hostel, **10**
Hotel Astoria, **7**
Hotel Strawberry Park, **4**
International Tourist Lodge, **6**
Snooze Inn, **5**
Villa Retreat, **9**

🍎 FOOD
Garden Manor Restaurant, **1**
Kavi Bala Café, **8**
New Hotel Punjab, **2**
Tibetan Brothers Restaurant, **3**

Garden Manor Restaurant, on Lake Rd. near Convent Rd. Away from the town, beautiful garden setting overlooking the lake and excellent food—from chicken sizzlers (Rs80) to Kerala-style fish curries (Rs50). Indian and Chinese entrees Rs45-60. Beer Rs90. Open daily 7am-10:30pm. ❷

Hotel Astoria. (See above.) Join the crowds and sit back to enjoy some quality people-watching as you demolish yet another mountain range of rice and *sambar*. Surrounded by mahogany carvings and attentive service. *Bindi* (okra) fry Rs35, tomato onion *utthapam* Rs23. Open daily 7am-9:30pm. ❶

Tibetan Brothers Restaurant, PT Rd., 2nd flr., on the left. A greasy spoon with pop tunes in the background and cheerful orange trimmed windows. Crisp vegetable *momos* (Rs30), Tibetan bread (Rs10), and lemon tea (Rs25) are perfect for a cool day in Kodai. Open daily noon-4pm and 5:30-10pm. ❶

New Hotel Punjab, PT Rd. Dark interiored, North Indian non-veg. restaurant with an extensive menu. Mutton *keema* Rs80, *tandoori* chicken Rs50. Open daily 11am-10:30pm. ❷

Kavi Bala Café, opposite the bus stand. Good veg.-only dishes served in this dim, classy hotel restaurant. South Indian *thali* Rs45, *malai kofta* Rs35. Open daily 6:30am-10pm. ❷

👁 🏞 SIGHTS AND SCENERY

The mountains around Kodai are breathtaking and lend themselves to peaceful hikes. In contrast, the town itself provides a weird wonderland of artificial out-door adventure—sights, including a man-made lake and garden park, mostly frequented by Indian tourists and some school groups. Head out of town to make the most of your trip.

DOLPHIN'S NOSE AND VELLAGAVI VILLAGE. A pleasant stroll through a hillside village and shimmering eucalyptus leads to the breathtaking promontory known as **Dolphin's Nose.** Because you actually have to hike there and can't take a maxi-cab, Dolphin's nose gets fewer visitors, less trash, and more heart-lifting views than any other place around Kodai. Go in the early morning to avoid the dense clouds. The views continue as the rocky path winds downhill, eventually reaching the terraced farms of Vellagavi, a small village you can almost make out from Dol-phin's Nose. *(From Coaker's Walk, follow the signs past the Youth Hostel to La Salette shrine; walk past the radio tower and the thermometer factory, and then continue down the cobbled road to the right of the Salette Church. When the road dips, take the small dirt path to the left. Cross the bridge when you come to it and stay left, following the winding path downhill. Make another left at the sign for Voyce, down the steep, root-rutted path. 90min. down to Dolphin's Nose. For Vellagavi, allow 4hr. each way.)*

PILLAR ROCKS, GREEN VALLEY VIEW, AND BERIJAM LAKE. For some of the best views around, follow the crowds out to **Pillar Rocks,** a popular viewpoint about 8km from town, overlooking soaring cliffs and miles of green-carpeted val-leys. Unfortunately, the experience is marred by vast quantities of litter left by the crowds, but the road is well-signed from Coaker's Walk and Greenland's Youth Hostel and makes a nice, if long, 7km walk from town. *(From town, walk 7km up Upper Shola Rd. past Fairy Falls and the Golf Club. Garden park open daily 8am-8pm.)* Expect to share the road with a convoy of noisy tour buses on their way out to **Green Valley View** and Pillar Rocks. Three kilometers farther on up the road is another lookout spot—**Moir's Point.** From here, the road splits to continue downhill to town via Observatory Rd. (9km), or to **Berijam Lake** (15km). *(Permission from the District Forest Officer in Kodai is required for travel to the lake by car or to Silent Valley or Cap Play View. Get a permit at least 1 day in advance. ☎ 240287. Open M-F 10am-6pm. Free.)*

COAKER'S WALK. Kodai's most famous scenic promenade is Coaker's Walk, a 10min. stroll along a paved precipice that traces an arc from Taj Villa to Green-land's Youth Hostel. On clear mornings, the views of the surrounding hills and plains are amazing—you can see as far as Madurai. A small **telescope house** near the far end gives you a closer look at the surrounding countryside. *(Open daily 6:30am-7pm. Rs2; camera fee Rs5; telescope house Rs1.)*

THE LAKE AND ENVIRONS. Tourist activity centers around the man-made lake; which can get a bit mucky around the edges. The 6km path around the lake makes for a pleasant bike or horseback ride. **Bike rentals** and **horseback riding** are between the boat club and Bryant Park on Lake Rd. *(Bike rental Rs10 per hr.; horses Rs80 for 3km, Rs160 for 6km.)* Hire those cute little paddleboats from the **Boathouse** (2 seat paddleboat Rs20 per ½hr. with Rs20 deposit; four-seat paddleboat Rs40 per ½hr. with Rs40 deposit. Open 9am-5:30pm.) Just south of the lake is **Bryant's Park,** with a **botanical gar-den** dating from 1902. *(Open daily 8:30am-6pm. Rs5; camera fee Rs25, video fee Rs500.)*

CHETTIAR PARK. The secluded Chettiar Park is the center of attention every 12 years, when the chronically shy *kurinji* plant springs into bloom. The next sched-uled blossoms are not due until 2006, though there are a few plants whose biologi-cal clocks are off-kilter. The gardens here attract few daytrippers, making them a peaceful place to visit. *(Walk straight down Anna Salai, and then continue down along the leftmost of the 2 roads at the bottom. Walk uphill past the Zion School, and then take the steep steps to the right as the road curves left and winds its way slowly uphill. The park is at the very top of the steps.)* Just past Chettiar Park is the **Kurinji Andavar Temple** dedicated to Murugan, with a viewing platform. *(3km northeast of the bus stand.)*

COIMBATORE ☎ 0422

If you want to get somewhere, go to Coimbatore first. As a stop along several major criss-crossing continental train routes, Coimbatore's four bus stands and railway station overflow with travelers, most going to or from Ooty, Kerala, or Karnataka. Most travelers stop here just long enough to check email and grab a few hours of sleep before taking off for their next destination and leaving most of this pulsating industrial city unexplored.

Coimbatore's **airport** is 11km outside of the city, towards Salem Rd. Indian Airlines (☎ 2399833) flies to: **Chennai** (Tu, Th, Sa; Rs3965); **Mumbai** (daily 2:10pm, Rs6850); and **Cochin** (M, W, F; Rs1980). **Jet Airways** (☎ 2575275 or 2212034) flies to: **Bangalore** (8:30pm, Rs2720); **Chennai** (Rs3925); and **Mumbai** (2:40pm, Rs6985).

Coimbatore Junction Railway Station is on Bank Rd., in the southern part of the city. (Reservations office upstairs ☎ 131. Open M-Sa 8am-8pm, Su 8am-2pm). To: **Bangalore** (7hr., 5 per day, Rs158); **Chennai** (8hr., 5 per day 6:25am-11:10pm, Rs186); **Cochin** (5hr., 12:40am, Rs109); **Delhi** (20hr., 2-3 per day 3:15-8:20pm, Rs492); **Kanya-kumari** (15hr., 12:40am and 4:50am, Rs196); **Madurai** (6hr., 4 per day 7:40am-10:10pm, Rs115); **Mettupalayam** for the "toy train" to **Ooty** (1hr., 5:55pm, Rs104); **Mumbai** (34hr., 2 per day 5:15am and 5:50pm, Rs363).

Three of the city's four **bus stands** are at the northern end of Dr. Nanjappa Rd., 1½km from the railway station. The **Town Bus Stand** (known as **Gandhipuram**), marked by the pedestrian overpass on Dr. Nanjappa Rd., provides efficient local service, including buses to the railway station (take #3, 56, or 84 or just ask the bus attendant; many buses go to the railway station). If you're coming into town by bus, you'll probably disembark at either the **SETC Bus Station** or the **State (Central) Bus Stand** which flank Gandhipuram. The SETC has reservations desks for Tamil Nadu (open daily 6am-10pm) and Kerala (open 24hr.) state buses. Note that "State Bus" does not indicate destination, but ownership. For instance, Kerala State Buses is owned by Kerala, but run to destinations in other states as well. SETC buses go to **Bangalore** (9hr., 2 per day 9:15 and 10pm, Rs160) and **Ooty** (3hr., every ½hr. 3:15-8am and 1:45pm, Rs28) among other places. The State (Central) Bus Stand services **Mysore** (5hr., 3 per day 6:45am-11:25pm, Rs80) and **Ooty** (3hr., every 10min., Rs21), as well as a host of other cities in South India. Private "travels" services abound around SETC and will provide A/C and some semi-sleeper buses to almost anywhere for a higher (but always negotiable) fee. If you can't get train reservations for a long ride, these are a good option.

A fourth stand, **Ukkadam,** 3km south of the other three, services mostly smaller towns to the south and is surrounded by a dense, bustling commercial district. Buses to: **Kodaikanal** (6hr., 10am, Rs50); **Madurai** (6hr., 5 per day 6am-4pm, Rs61); **Udumalpet** for buses to **Munnar,** Kerala (1½hr., several per day, Rs20); **Palani** (3hr., every 10 min., Rs30). From Gandhipuram, **local buses** run to Ukkadam. A PP bus runs from Ukkadam to the railway station.

The north-south thoroughfare of **State Bank Road** heads north from the railway station. Walk left out of the railway station on State Bank Rd. to get to the **State Bank of India,** which changes most currencies and traveler's checks. (☎ 2303251. Open M-F 10am-4pm, Sa 10am-1pm.) Across the street is **Medpus Medicals,** a 24hr. pharmacy (☎ 2301317, RHR bldg., opposite State Bank of India.) At the end of State Bank Rd., on **District Trasting Road**, are the enormous, fenced-in grounds of the

Commissioner of Police (☎ 100). Turn right onto District Trasting Rd., and then right at the rotary and **KG Hospital** (☎ 2212121, if busy try any of the numbers between 2212121 and 2212128) will be at the corner of Art College Rd. **Internet** access is at **Netsea** in Raj Rajeswara Tower, opposite Gandhipuram bus stand. (Rs20 per hr. Open daily 8:30am-11:30pm.) The **Head Post Office** is off Goods Shed Rd. From State Bank Rd., walk straight through the railway station and turn right; it's on the left after 600m. (Open M-Sa 10am-6pm, Su 9am-4pm.) **Postal Code:** 641001.

You won't need to wander far from Coimbatore's bus stands or railway station to find a host of polished budget lodging options. If you need to catch an early train, the best thing to do is try to get your hands on one of the nine **railway retiring rooms ❸**, upstairs in the station building, opposite the computerized reservation centre. However, these are often full, and advance bookings are not possible. (Rooms Rs350-400.) A small path across the street from the railway station entrance leads to Geetha Hall Rd., a lively and safe area with several good budget options, including **Aiba Regency ❷**, 28A Geetha Hall Rd., which has clean rooms, seat toilets, and a classy A/C lift. (☎ 2303737. Singles Rs190-450; doubles Rs350-550.) For cheap food, head to **Sree Annapoorna ❶**, at the State Bus Stand on Dr. Nanjappa Rd., where you will find many travelers slurping *sambar* by the bucketful. (Meals Rs20. Open daily 6:30am-10:30pm.) **Gaythri Bhavan ❷**, opposite the Hotel Blue Star on Nehru St., is a palm-treed, waterfalling, wooden-bridged fantasy restaurant. Back in the railway station neighborhood, chow down at **Royal Hindu Restaurant ❶**, 27 State Bank Rd., across from the bank in the RHR Bldg.

OOTY (UDAGAMANDALAM) உௌᵗᴵᴶ ☎ 0423

Shrouded in mist and movie mystique, the verdant hill station of Ooty is South India's most popular hill station and a favorite backdrop for Indian filmmakers. Established in 1821 by John Sullivan, an enterprising collector with the East India Company, Ooty quickly earned a reputation as a high-class getaway. No longer the exclusive retreat of the gin-and-tonic-at-sundown crowd, Ooty is often overrun by tourists: exhaust fumes sully the crisp mountain air, sewage clogs the once-pristine lake, and the booming hotel and package-tour industries noisily exploit Ooty's quiet charm. It's not difficult, however, to escape the crowds. The mighty Mt. Doddabetta, which, at 2638m, is about as close as you can get to heaven in South India, is just a stone's throw away. The tribal villages of the Nilgiris are an easy day's hike and a quick getaway from the hordes of holiday-makers.

Just a few kilometers off the beaten path you'll find yourself face-to-face with what made Ooty special in the first place: the laid-back locals, the acres of tea plantations and the verdant, hilly scenery. Ooty can be crowded most of the year, but particularly so during the season (Apr.-mid-June and Sept.-Oct.) when prices soar. Monsoon season runs from July to August. Ooty's cold, relatively dry winter stretches from November to March.

▰▰ ▱ ORIENTATION AND PRACTICAL INFORMATION

With its streets skirting the valley and snaking up the surrounding mountainsides, getting around Ooty can be tricky. Not to worry—the town itself is fairly small, and locals are used to directing tourists. The **bus stand** and **railway station** are next door to each other at the south-west. They sit between **Ooty Lake** to the west and the **race course** to the east. **Lower Bazaar Road** runs northeast from the bus stand, becoming the town's busiest road, **Commercial Road,** after 1km. Commercial Rd. runs on to **Charing Cross,** the center of Ooty. Northwest, up the hill behind Charing Cross, **Garden Road** continues northeast to the **Botanical Gardens** and **Ettines Road** loops back toward the race course.

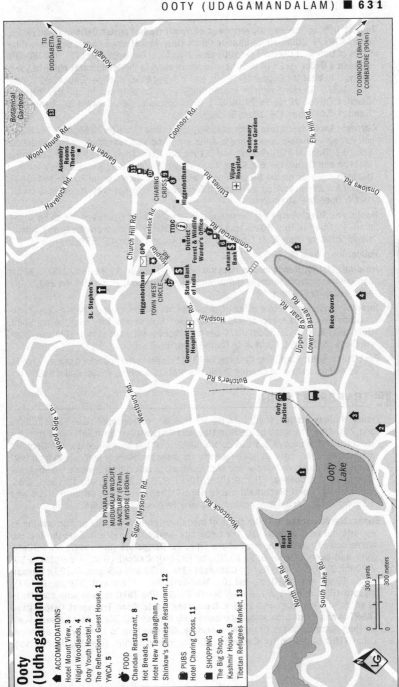

TAMIL NADU

Ooty (Udhagamandalam)

♠ ACCOMMODATIONS
Hotel Mount View, **3**
Nilgiri Woodlands, **4**
Ooty Youth Hostel, **2**
The Reflections Guest House, **1**
YWCA, **5**

♦ FOOD
Chandan Restaurant, **8**
Hot Breads, **10**
Hotel New Tamilaagham, **7**
Shinkow's Chinese Restaurant, **12**

♣ PUBS
Hotel Charing Cross, **11**

🛍 SHOPPING
The Big Shop, **6**
Kashmir House, **9**
Tibetan Refugees Market, **13**

632 ■ TAMIL NADU

Tourist Office: The new **Government of Tamil Nadu Tourist Office,** Wenlock Rd. (☎ 2443977), 200m above Charing Cross. Open M-F 10am-5:45pm. Organizes daily tours of Ooty and Coonoor (Rs100) as well as local film-spots (Rs175). The **Wildlife Warden's Office** (☎ 24444098) can organize stays in the **Mudumalai Wildlife Sanctuary,** a habitat for elephants, tigers, and many species of birds. Dorms Rs25; doubles Rs310. Trekking permits for the Nilgiris can be obtained in one day from the **District Forest Office** (☎ 2444083). Both offices are on Steward Hill behind the Tourist Office. Open M-F 10am-5:45pm.

Currency Exchange: State Bank of India, Town West Circle (☎ 2444099). The pleasant foreign exchange desk changes AmEx and Thomas Cook traveler's checks in US$ and UK£. Open M-F 10am-2pm and 3-4pm, Sa 10am-1pm. The attached **ATM** takes Maestro and Cirrus. The **Big Shop,** Commercial Rd. (☎ 2444136) changes cash and travelers cheques on the second floor. **Canara Bank,** Commercial Rd. (☎ 2444087), to your left as you look up the steps to Town West Circle. Gives cash advances on MC and V. Open M-F 10am-2pm.

Bookstore: Higginbothams, Commercial Rd. (☎ 2443736), between the co-op supermarkets. Open Th-Tu 9:30am-1pm and 3:30-7:30pm. Another branch is on Commissioner Rd. near Town West Cir. Open M-Sa 9:30am-1pm and 2-5:30pm.

Police: Town West Cir. (☎ 2443973).

Hospital: District Headquarters Hospital, Jail Hill, Hospital Rd. (☎ 2442212). A better and cleaner establishment is the private **Vijaya Hospital,** Ettines Rd. (☎ 2442248), behind Alankar Theatres.

Internet: There are a whole string of small Internet shacks around Charing Cross. Connections tend to be reasonably fast. **Globalnet,** Commercial Rd., near the Big Shop. Open daily 8:30am-10:30pm. Rs30 per hr. **Cyber Planet,** Garden Rd., 50m from Charing Cross on the right. Open daily 10am-1pm. Rs40 per hr.

Post Office: GPO, Town West Circle (☎ 2443791), behind the collector's office. Open M-Sa 9am-5pm. Another at Charing Cross, south of Coonoor Rd. **Postal Code:** 643001.

⌐ TRANSPORTATION

Trains: Railway Station, North Lake Rd. Reservations counter open daily 8am-12:30pm and 2:30-4pm. The small gauge Blue Mountain Railway (the "toy train") takes you on a spectacular ride through tea and potato plantations and past waterfalls; like Ooty, it's often crowded, so make advance reservations in-season. Railway buffs are in for a treat as the route between Coonoor and Mettupalayam is pulled by a genuine, no-nonsense steam train. To: **Coonoor** (1hr.; 9:15am, 12:15, 3, 6pm, return 7:45, 10:45am, 1:35, 4:30pm; Rs7) and **Mettupalayam** (3½hr.; 9:15am and 3pm, return 8:10am and 1:15pm; Rs12). For full train connections, take the bus to **Coimbatore.**

Buses: The **bus stand** is 100m south of the railway station. Regular and private buses operate out of one dusty lot. The departure bays are labeled in English, and the buses actually use them, most of the time. To: **Bangalore** (8hr., every hr. 7:30am-2pm and every 30min. 8:30-10:30pm, Rs140); **Calicut** (6hr.; 4 per day 6:30, 7:30am, 2:15, 3:15pm; Rs70); **Chennai** (12hr., 4:30 and 6:30pm, Rs223); **Hassan** (8hr., 10am and 11:30pm, Rs110); **Madikeri** (9hr., 11am and 5:30pm, Rs107); **Mysore** (6hr., every 1-2hr. 8am-5:30pm, Rs62). The **TSTC** reservations counter is open daily 10am-1pm and 2-9pm. **Karnataka State Road Transport Corporation (KSRTC)** has a reservations counter open daily 6:30am-10:30pm. Make reservations for long-distance buses (Bangalore, Mysore, Chennai) up to two days in advance. Local **TTRC** buses go to: **Coonoor** (30min., every 10min. 6am-10:30pm, Rs5);

Doddabetta Junction (20min., every 30min. 6:30am-4:30pm, Rs4); **Mettupalayam** (every 15min. 5:30am-8:30pm, Rs14); **Mudumalai** (3hr., every 30min. 6am-8:45pm, Rs31); **Pykara** (30min., every 30min. 6:30am-4pm, Rs6).

Local Transportation: Unmetered **auto-rickshaws** charge at least Rs15 for a ride from the railway station to Charing Cross.

ACCOMMODATIONS

Ooty is a resort town with many hotels. Prices skyrocket in-season, however, making hostel dorms the only real budget option. Hotels in town tend to be grungier and marginally cheaper, while rooms in the lake area are quiet and pleasant.

The Reflections Guest House, North Lake Rd. (☎2443834; reflectionsin@yahoo.com), 500m west of the bus stand. The proprietress, Mrs. Dique, is legendary in backpacker circles for her home-cooked meals and maternal disposition. Wildflowers, lake view, and a cozy sitting room. Clean but simple rooms with evening hot water. Will arrange day-treks to the Toda tribal villages (Rs300). Call ahead in-season. Doubles Rs400, quad Rs450. Off-season Rs280/300. ❸

Ooty Youth Hostel, 42 South Lake Rd., Fern Hill (☎2447506; www.ootyhostel.org). Crowded but fairly pleasant 8-bed dorms with clean attached bath. Organizes sight-seeing tours (Rs100) and has attached restaurant. Dorms Rs80, YHI members Rs60; doubles Rs250-350. Off-season, everybody gets the member's rate. ❶

YWCA, Ettines Rd. (☎2442218), 500m from the racetrack. Homey cottages with wicker chairs and seat toilets. Sunlit sitting room in the main bldg. with TV and piano. Bare 30-bed dormitory lacks the same charm. A great deal in the off-season when prices are nearly cut in half. Attached restaurant. Dorms Rs110; cottages Rs400-900. Off-season Rs99/125-700. ❶

Nilgiri Woodlands, Ettines Rd. (☎2442551 or 2442451), up a forking garden path. This elegant 100 year-old bungalow has spacious suites, wood floors, antique furniture and bathtubs with hot water. Smaller, cheaper rooms are in the former stable block. Reserve ahead in-season. Rooms Rs500-1300. Off-season Rs400-1100. AmEx/MC/V. ❸

Hotel Mount View, Ettines Rd. (☎2443307). House-turned-hotel with spacious rooms and pine-wood floors. The cheapest rooms are nothing special. Seat toilet, hot water 5:30pm-10am. Doubles Rs600-1400. Off-season Rs300-700. 15% luxury tax. ❹

THE LOCAL LEGEND

WHISTLE BLAST FROM THE PAST

The Nilgiris Mountain Railway, commonly known as the Blue Mountain Railway, is Asia's longest and steepest meter-gauge railway. Over the course of forty-five kilometers, it traverses some of the most treacherous and spectacular terrain ever covered by rail.

The railway to Coonoor was begun in 1891, and the relatively simple extension to Ooty was added in 1908. The toughest section of track runs from Mettupalayam on the plains to the tea-growing region of Coonoor. The train claws its way up extremely steep ground through the use of a rack-and-pinion system. Each engine has a cog which fits into a grooved rail running down the center of the track. Invented by Swiss engineer Riggenback, the system was designed to help negotiate the pesky Alps. The train has to fight for every inch of ground it covers; maximum speed on the rack section is just thirteen kilometers per hour. And going down can be almost as bad as going up—each carriage has its own brakeman who operates a hand-powered brake on signals transmitted from the engine by whistle blasts.

While the rail was originally designed to carry supplies to an ammunitions factory in Coonoor, it now serves a much sunnier purpose. Indeed, aboard the Blue Mountain Railway, today's passengers have the opportunity not only to marvel at a classic feat of engineering, but also at the stunning Indian countryside it traverses.

▐ FOOD

Apart from the very cheapest snack joints, eating in Ooty tends to be expensive. Restaurants attached to guest houses are usually good options. Shops up and down Commercial Rd. sell **homemade chocolate** in a dizzying variety of flavors.

Chandan Restaurant, Commercial Rd. In Hotel Nahar, 100m from Charing Cross. Carefully spiced but pricey vegetarian selections (Rs60-80) are served in heated *kadhais*. Popular with Indian families. Open daily noon-3:30pm and 7-10:30pm. ❸

Hotel New Tamilaagham, Commercial Rd., near the Big Shop. Cleanest and tastiest of the *dosa* dives, its clientele come for Rs5 *idli*, Rs10 *puri-sabzi* sets, and an eye-popping Rs20 chili mushroom. Plus, there's ice cream. Open daily 8am-10pm. ❶

Shinkow's Chinese Restaurant, 38-42 Commissioners Rd., opposite the State Bank of India, Town West Cir. Serving mouth-watering but overpriced stir-fry to locals and tourists since 1954. Varied menu includes sliced beef with broccoli (Rs50-70) and cashew chicken (Rs80-100). Open daily 12:30-3:45pm and 6:30-9:45pm. ❸

Hot Breads, Charing Cross, at the intersection with Garden Rd. Warm, fresh baked breads, pizzas (Rs38-48), and foot-long sandwiches (Rs60). Open daily 10am-9pm. ❷

♫ ▐ ENTERTAINMENT AND SHOPPING

If occupied at all, **bars** in Ooty usually have just a few sorry-looking men mumbling to each other in a darkened corner. A slightly more cheerful watering hole is the bar at **Hotel Charing Cross.** (☎ 2444624. Beer Rs40-75. Open daily 10:30am-10:30pm.) Close to the Botanical Gardens in the **Assembly Rooms Theatre,** which shows not-too-dated American flicks. (Daily shows at 6pm. Rs15-20.) The **Race Course,** near the bus stand, is a 1¼ mi. loop where jodhpured jockeys run their horses to the delight of riotous but low-betting crowds. Races Apr.-June.

Shopping in Ooty revolves around locally made body oils and textiles. **Kashmir House,** Charing Cross, has some better quality goods without the pressurized sales pitch. (Open daily 9:30am-9pm.) **The Big Shop,** halfway between Charing Cross and the Lower Bazaar on Commercial Rd., sells kitschy knick-knacks on the first floor, but has nicer silver jewelry and handicrafts upstairs. (☎ 2444136. Open daily 9:30am-8:30pm. Traveler's checks, AmEx/MC/V.) A **Tibetan Refugees' Market,** along Garden Rd., near the Botanical Gardens, has stands selling mohair sweaters and colorful wool blankets. (Open daily 8:30am-5:30pm.)

◎ SIGHTS

BOTANICAL GARDENS. Ooty's Botanical Gardens were originally established in 1847 and spruced up again in 1995. A century and a half after they were opened, they are as green as ever. With more than 2000 species on display, the gardens have come a long way from their original purpose of producing "English vegetables at reasonable costs." Some of the more bizarre highlights include a map of India done entirely in shrubbery and a rather phallic twig, said to be a fossilized tree trunk. *(Open daily 8am-6:30pm. Rs10; camera fee Rs30, video fee Rs500.)*

CENTENARY ROSE GARDEN. Four terraces on a hill overlooking the town show-case India's largest collection of roses. Over 2200 varieties, with names as diverse as "Taj Mahal," "American Dream," and "Margaret Thatcher," are interspersed with benches and literary quotations. Flowering Apr.-Sept., reaching a colorful climax in May. *(Open daily 9am-6:30pm. Rs10; camera fee Rs30.)*

LAKE. Just west of the railway station and bus stand is Ooty's lily-filled, sewage-stopped **lake,** constructed in the 1820s by good old John Sullivan. A pretty dismal "fun park" has shops and cafes as well as a variety of dubious attractions including **boat rental** (Rs60-100 for 30min.) and **miniature train** (Rs10). **Horse rentals** near the lake are Rs150 per hr. *(1km down North Lake Rd. Admission Rs3; camera fee Rs10.)*

NEAR OOTY

⚡ COONOOR

*Trains creak along narrow-gauge tracks to **Mettupalayam** (2hr., 4pm, Rs8) and **Ooty** (1hr., 4 per day 7:45am-4:30pm, Rs7). **Buses** go to: **Coimbatore** (2hr., every 15min. 6:30am-8pm, Rs16) via **Mettupalayam** (1hr., Rs9); **Dolphin's Nose** and **Lamb's Rock** (30min., every 2hr. 7:30am-6:30pm, Rs4); **Ooty** (45min., every 10min. 5:30am-10:30pm, Rs5). Getting around the sights can be tricky, so it's probably easier to hire a taxi (Rs250-400) or to join one of the daily tours from Ooty (Rs100-150). **Auto-rickshaws** run between Lower and Upper Coonoor (Rs20-25); the **local buses** along Mount Rd. follow the same route for less (Rs2).*

Deep in the tea-growing region of the Nilgiris, Coonoor is quieter and less fre-quented than its larger neighbor Ooty, only 18km away. Though there are places to stay, most make it an easy daytrip from Ooty—coming in on the Blue Mountain Railway, then whizzing around the tea plantations and viewpoints that surround the town. The town is separated into two parts: the railway station and bus stand are in the town center of Lower Coonoor, down in the valley; most of the attrac-tions, as well as the quiet and calm, are in Upper Coonoor, around **Bedford Circle.** The **railway station** and **bus stand** are on the Ooty-Mettupalayam Rd., near **Mount Road,** which winds 2km up to **Upper Coonoor.** The **police station** (☎ 2206100), **Sagayamatha Hospital** (☎ 2206979), and **post office** (open M-F 9am-2pm, Sa 9am-noon) are all on Balaclava Hill.

Conoor's main attractions are its stunning viewpoints from where, if the world is not shrouded in mist, you can gaze out over the Coimbatore plains. **Lamb's Rock,** 12km from Lower Coonoor is one of the most popular. It's a short walk up the hill behind the road. Four kilometers farther is **Dolphin's Nose,** a rock formation with views of a gaping, waterfall-filled gorge. For all those who thought that all tea came in tea-bags, a visit to the ⚑**Highfield Tea Estate** should be an informative expe-rience. Wander the fields, tour the factory, and enjoy the free samples of tea in the very fields it was grown. (Open daily 8am-5pm, Rs5.) From Sim's Park (see below), the estate is 2km up Kotagiri Rd., but it is accessible from the park via a shortcut along the park's eastern edge; take a sharp left as you exit the east gate. In Janu-ary, there's a week-long Tea and Tourism Festival.

Coonoor's response to Ooty's Botanical Gardens is **Sim's Park,** high on **Gray's Hill** on the road to Kotagiri, 3km from the Coonoor bus stand. Set in a small ravine, the park displays varieties of flowers and plants not found in Ooty. (Open daily 8am-6:30pm. Rs10, children Rs2, camera fee Rs25.) The **YWCA "Wyoming" Guest House ❷,** off Upasi Rd., between Church of the Sacred Heart and Nankem Hospital, a delightful place to stay and a good reason to turn Coonoor into more than a day-

TAMIL NADU

trip. Spacious rooms in the 150-year-old house overlook tea and flower gardens from a bluff above the bazaar. Home-cooked meals Rs40-60. (☎2234426. Singles Rs220, doubles Rs440.) From the bus stand, go straight across the railway tracks past the Gandhi statue, 200m up the road, and take the steps up the steep slope to the left. The **Quality Restaurant ❷,** Mount Rd., near Bedford Circle, has a big North and South Indian buffet lunch (Rs50). Open daily 8am-10:30pm.

UTTARANCHAL

उत्तरांचल

Uttaranchal, whose name means "Northern Mountains," embodies the holy and the hilly in one mountainous package. Comprising the regions of Garhwal and Kumaon, with its 7000m peaks, frenetic hill stations, ashrams, and sacred rivers, the state encompasses enough to enthrall, enlighten, and amuse any visitor.

In the early 19th century, Garhwal and Kumaon were overrun by the Nepali commander Amar Singh Thapa. He was ousted in 1816 by the Brits, who set up regimental headquarters and made Garhwal and Kumaon part of the United Provinces. After Indian independence, the mountainous area then called Uttarakhand was united with the plains to form Uttar Pradesh. In November 2000, after ten years of struggle, the hilly northern regions of Uttar Pradesh won the right to form a new state: Uttaranchal. While Uttar Pradesh and today's Uttaranchal (UA) remain bound by the Ganga and Yamuna Rivers, UA remains distinct from its flat southern neighbor. The state's Himalayan setting affords a cool, comfortable climate as well as majestic mountain vistas from almost every village.

Nevertheless, Uttaranchal's most significant distinguishing characteristic is its culture. Long before the 9th century, when Indian saint Shankara established Hinduism in Garhwal, the region already had religious ties. Parts of the *Mahabharata* and *Ramayana* had already occurred here, enshrouding the hills of Uttarakhand with religious mystique. Today, people flock to UA from all over the globe to take part in or merely observe the religious rituals enacted here, as well as to absorb the small town charm that pervades the state.

HIGHLIGHTS OF UTTARANCHAL

Ashram towns such as **Rishikesh** (p. 653) and **Haridwar** (p. 648), pilgrimage centers like **Gangotri** (p. 662) and **Yamnotri** (p. 660), and national reserves such as **Corbett National Park** (p. 666) and the **Valley of Flowers** (p. 665) beckon lovers of the natural and the supernatural alike to Uttaranchal's hills.

DEHRA DUN देहरादून   ☎ 0135

Dehra Dun is not exactly a tourist town. As Uttaranchal's thriving capital city, it has most of the advantages, and many of the drawbacks, of big-city life in India. But there is another, more gentle side to Dehra Dun found outside the downtown area, a result of its proximity to quieter mountain villages. Bus drivers and rickshaw-*wallahs* jockey for room on the congested roadways here just as they do everywhere else on the Subcontinent, but at least they do it with a smile. Most travelers stop in Dehra Dun for a day or two en route to the northern hills or to the hill station of Mussoorie, whose lights are visible from the city at night. There is plenty to do here—temples, parks, and springs—but in the end, there's too much "city" and not enough "town" to keep visitors here for more than a couple of days.

Uttaranchal

HIMACHAL PRADESH

TIBET (CHINA)

Yamnotri

Barkot

Gangotri

Kedarnath

Hemkund

Uttarkashi

Badrinath

GARHWAL

Joshimath

Mussoorie

Tehri

Gwaldam

Nanda Devi
▲ 7817m
Nanda Devi
Sanctuary
■—*Pindari Glacier*

Dehra Dun

Rajaji
National
Park

Rishikesh

Haridwar

Baijnath

Song

Munsiyari

Saharanpur

Kosi River

Kausani

Bageshwar

KUMAON

Ranikhet

Pithoragarh

Muzaffarnagar

Corbett
National
Park

Ramnagar

Almora

NEPAL

Nainital

Bhowali

Kathgodam

UTTAR
PRADESH

Haldwani

Meerut

Mahendranagar

Moradabad

Rampur

Pilibhit

Hapur

Govt. of India statement: The external boundaries of India are neither correct nor authenticated.

▛ TRANSPORTATION

Trains: As a terminus of the **Northern Railway,** Dehra Dun sends trains all over India. The inquiry office is in the main terminal, but for day-of tickets the booking office is toward Gandhi Rd. The computerized reservation complex is across the parking lot. Open M-Sa 9am-8pm, Su 8am-2pm. To: **Delhi** (7hr., 4 per day 5:10am-9:15pm, Rs300-400); **Haridwar** (1½hr., 8 per day 6am-9:15pm, Rs150); **Lucknow** (12hr., 2-3 per day 7:30-8:30pm, Rs250.)

Buses: Several companies operate from the **Delhi Bus Stand,** next to Hotel Drona. **UP Roadways** (☎ 2653797) runs buses to: **Delhi** (6hr., every 30min. 5am-10:15pm, regular Rs120, deluxe Rs203); **Haldwani** (9hr.; 7, 8am, 7, 8, 9pm; Rs138); **Haridwar** (2hr., every 30min. 5am-7pm, Rs28); **Rishikesh** (1½hr., 14 per day 5am-7pm, Rs20). **Himachal Bus Lines** (☎ 2623435) sends buses to **Shimla** (10hr.; 6, 8, 10am; Rs163) and **Amritsar** (14hr.; 7:30am, Rs175). **Punjab Roadways** (☎ 2624410) goes to **Amritsar** (14hr., 5:30am, Rs175). UP Roadways also leaves from the **Mussoorie Bus Stand.** To: **Almora** (12hr.; 5am, 2, 4pm; Rs250); **Mussoorie** (1½hr., every 30min. 6am-8pm, Rs23); **Nainital** (11hr.; regular 7, 8:30am, 5pm, Rs165; deluxe 8pm, Rs210); **Uttarkashi** (9hr; 6, 8:30am; Rs127). **Highway Motors,** 69 Gandhi Rd. (☎ 2623644), next to the railway station, serves **Hanuman Chatti** (8hr., 8am, Rs100). Daily deluxe buses run by Hotel Satkar, 30 Patel Rd., to **Delhi** (6hr.; 11am, 10pm; Rs300). **Shared taxis,** opposite the bus stands, run as far as **Mussoorie** (Rs80 per person).

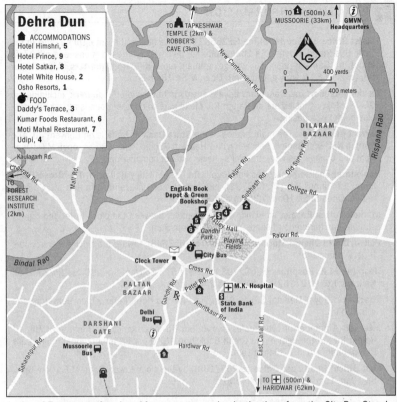

Dehra Dun

▲ ACCOMMODATIONS
Hotel Himshri, **5**
Hotel Prince, **9**
Hotel Satkar, **8**
Hotel White House, **2**
Osho Resorts, **1**

◆ FOOD
Daddy's Terrace, **3**
Kumar Foods Restaurant, **6**
Moti Mahal Restaurant, **7**
Udipi, **4**

TO ▲ TAPKESHWAR TEMPLE (2km) & ROBBER'S CAVE (3km)

TO ▲ (500m) & MUSSOORIE (33km) ⓘ GMVN Headquarters

New Cantonment Rd.

DILARAM BAZAAR

Kaulagarh Rd.

Chakrata Rd.

Mall Rd.

TO FOREST RESEARCH INSTITUTE (2km)

Rajpur Rd.

Subhash Rd.

Old Survey Rd.

College Rd.

Rispana Rao

English Book Depot & Green Bookshop

3 **4**
5 **2**
6
Astley Hall
Gandhi Park

Playing Fields

Raipur Rd.

7
✉
Clock Tower ■ 🚌 **City Bus**

Bindal Rao

Cross Rd.

PALTAN BAZAAR

Gandhi Rd.

Patel Rd.

R̴

8
☧ **M.K. Hospital**

$ State Bank of India

Amritkaur Rd.

DARSHANI GATE

Delhi Bus 🚌

ⓘ

Hardiwar Rd.

East Canal Rd.

Mussoorie Bus 🚌

Sahaanpur Rd.

9

🚗

TO ☧ (500m) & HARIDWAR (62km)

0 ___ 400 yards
0 ___ 400 meters

Local Transportation: Local **buses** go to nearby destinations from the City Bus Stand, by the parade ground. **Tempos,** known locally as *vikrams*, are common, clean, and cheap. They run along ten fixed routes (with the route number painted clearly on the rear of the vehicle) and cost Rs3-5 per ride. **Auto-rickshaws** are more expensive but will take you exactly where you want to go.

✹ ORIENTATION

Dehra Dun can be broken down into three main areas: the **railway station** area, the **Paltan Bazaar** clock tower area, and the **Astley Hall** area. The railway station is the farthest to the southwest; the **Mussoorie Bus Stand** is between the train station and the Bazaar, and the **Delhi Bus Stand** is a 5min. walk north along **Gandhi Road,** an unmistakable collection of vehicles. Following Gandhi Rd. away from the train station leads to the second main focus of the city, the area around the tall **clock tower.** The **city bus stand** and Gandhi Park are farther away from the station. The bus stand is toward the parade ground, while Gandhi Park is on Rajpur Rd., where many shops and high-end hotels are located. This strip is referred to as Astley Hall or **Dilaram Bazaar** farther north. The web of streets between the clock tower and the train station is known as Paltan Bazaar; the part of the bazaar nearest the railway station is **Darshani Gate.** Most streets are unlabeled, but store signs often have the street name in English.

UTTARANCHAL

PRACTICAL INFORMATION

Tourist Office: UA Tourist Office (☎2653217), attached to the Hotel Drona, next to the Delhi Bus Stand. Open M-Sa 10am-5pm. For trekking trips, reservations, and other info about the Garhwal region, try the government-run **GMVN Headquarters,** 74/1 Rajpur Rd. (☎2746817; www.gmvnl.com). Open M-Sa 10am-5pm.

Trekking Agency: There are many private agents in town who arrange treks, including the GMVN. Most agencies are on Rajpur Rd. Make sure to compare prices at several agencies before purchasing.

Currency Exchange: The main branch of the **State Bank of India** is on Convent Rd. and **Punjab National Bank** is between Astley Hall and Gandhi Park. Both are open M-F 10am-4pm and change cash and traveler's checks without commission.

Bookstore: English bookstores line Rajpur Rd. in the Astley Hall area. **The Green Bookshop,** 17 Rajpur Rd. (☎2653382), has tourist maps of Dehra Dun and the Garhwal region. Open M-Sa 10am-1:30pm and 3-8pm.

Market: Paltan Bazaar, stretching over a kilometer between the clock tower and railway station, has hundreds of shops. Open daily 9am-9pm.

Police: Dhara Chowki Station, Rajpur Rd. (☎2653648), toward the clock tower from the Hotel Ambassador.

Hospital: M.K. Hospital (☎2652798 or 2657667), Convent Rd. at Cross Rd. **CMI,** 54 Haridwar Rd. (☎2720238), both with 24hr. service.

Pharmacy: Goyal Medical Store, 4 New Rd., next to Hotel Relax. Open 9am-2pm and 4-8:30pm.

Internet: A number of cyber cafes line Rajpur Rd. near Astley Hall. Internet Cafe, 17 Rajpur Rd., to the right of the Green Bookshop. Rs40 per hr. International phone calls Rs6 per min. Open 7:30am-11pm.

Post Office: Head Post Office (☎2657168), by the clock tower. Open M-F 10am-6pm, Sa 10am-1pm. **Postal Code:** 248001.

ACCOMMODATIONS

Hotels around the bus stands and the clock tower tend to be either bland high-end boxes or dingy budget dives, though tolerable if you're only staying a night. Nicer (and sometimes cheaper) hotels line Rajpur Rd., by Astley Hall and beyond.

Hotel Satkar, 30 Patel Rd. (☎2652561). Its central location in a surprisingly quiet neighborhood keeps the walking to a minimum, but still makes relaxation possible. Despite being a bit sparse, the rooms have attached bath with seat toilet, TV, and A/C. Very helpful staff. Check-out noon. Singles Rs250; doubles Rs400. ❷

Hotel White House, Subhash Rd. (☎2652765). Near enough to Astley Hall for great shopping and good eats, but far enough from downtown to avoid most of the grime and congestion. Huge but dark rooms with shower in a sterile building surrounded by gardens. Singles Rs240; doubles Rs345-380. AmEx. ❷

Hotel Prince, 1 Haridwar Rd. (☎2627070), two blocks south of the Delhi Bus Stand and two blocks east of the Mussoorie Bus Stand. Good for early morning buses and trains. Rooms face the inner courtyard and are therefore insulated from the noise and dirt of local auto shops. Great top-floor views and basic rooms with fans, desks, and hot water (but no showers). Pricier rooms are bigger and have A/C, TV, and shower. Checkout noon. Singles Rs250-750; doubles Rs300-900. ❷

Hotel Himshri, 17 Rajpur Rd. (☎2653880), in the same strip mall as Green Bookshop. Located in the heart of the clock tower and Astley Hall area, its rooms are comfortable. Those looking for something a little more upscale but still inexpensive will be pleased with the attached baths, A/C, and TV. Singles Rs400-750; doubles Rs500-900. ❸

Osho Resorts, 111 Rajpur Rd. (☎2749522), 1km beyond the GMVN Tourist Office. Rooms with TVs, hot water, and super-guru Osho himself (see p. 417). Read Osho books, watch Osho TV, or seek enlightenment in the lush meditation center. All rooms have a shower. Yoga and massage also available. The attached restaurant, **Heaven's Gate,** serves excellent food. Singles Rs490-1190; doubles Rs590-1290. ❸

◖ FOOD

Restaurants near Astley Hall and on Rajpur Rd. are a bit more up-market than the ones in the grime of the bus stand. The Paltan Bazaar area has good bakers and sweets vendors, plus a row of fruit stands near the clock tower. The **Venus Restaurant** (62 Gandhi Rd., opposite Hotel Grand, open 6am-6pm) and **Ahuja Restaurant** (80m from Venus away from the train station) restaurants are open throughout the day, especially during breakfast when most other places are closed. Street stands selling *thalis* and other set menus (Rs15-125) are generally safe for foreigners with stronger stomachs, but stands between the clock tower and Hotel Ambassador are cleaner and more reputable. As a general rule of thumb, the more Indian customers you see, the better a restaurant's food is likely to be.

Udipi, 16A Subhash Rd. (☎2657666). Huge, multi-cuisine selection which is attentively served. The upscale atmosphere is perfect for a break from fast-food or lunch counters, but with prices comparable to each. *Thalis* Rs55-70. Filling chicken and sweet corn soup Rs40. Open 8:30am-10:30pm. AmEx. ❷

Kumar Foods Restaurant, 15B Rajpur Rd., just after Hotel Ambassador. Located away from the clock tower, between the post office and Motel Himshri. Delicious renditions of Indian specialties—the *rogan josh* (Rs65) and chicken *tikka masala* (Rs130) are superb. Great service in a quiet and classy atmosphere. Open daily 11am-4pm and 7-10:30pm; closed last Tu of the month. ❸

Moti Mahal Restaurant, on Rajpur Rd., opposite the Hotel Ambassador, has a quiet atmosphere that makes it a pleasant place to escape the heat. Quality non-veg. food from a large menu. Tandoori chicken Rs60-100, mutton *shahi korma* Rs60, *dal makhani* Rs40. Open daily 9am-10:30pm. ❸

Daddy's Terrace, Rajpur Rd., just past Astley Hall, away from the clock tower. This western-style burger joint with quick service is a good place to grab lunch. A varied menu includes pizza (Rs 40-60), fries (Rs22), and theme burgers, including the "Daddy's Twin Burger" (Rs50). Open daily 9:30am-8pm. ❷

◗ SIGHTS

Most of the sights lie outside the city. Buses and *tempos* will take you where you want to go from the city bus stand; taxis and auto-rickshaws charge Rs150-250 for trips to any of the sights and Rs400-500 for a full day. If you really want to take your time, pick a destination and make it a full day's excursion. The GMVN's day-long bus tour, **Doon Darshan,** covers the FRI, Tapkeshwar Temple, Malsi Deer Park, and Sahastra Dhara (Rs100). The bus stops for 45-90min. at each place (daily at 10:30am, returns at 5pm). Contact **Drona Travel,** 45 Gandhi Rd., by the Hotel Drona. (☎2653309. Open daily 9am-5pm.)

FOREST RESEARCH INSTITUTE (FRI). Established under British auspices in 1906, the FRI works toward a better understanding of the uses and abuses of forestry, botany, and biodiversity conservation. Even if you're not into forestry, there's still quite a bit to do here: six museums covering 7 acres focus on different aspects of forest life, from the chemicals in the leaves to the bugs in the bark, as well as the social culture of forests in India. The green lawn of the institute's Botanical Gardens, behind the main buliding, is a wonderful picnic spot. There is a canteen for afternoon tea or snacks (cold drinks Rs10) and a visitor's center cataloguing the various furniture uses of wood. The peace and quiet of the Institute make this is *the* place to escape the big-city sound and atmosphere of Dehra Dun. *(Visitors' gate 5km west of town on Chakrata Rd. Take the Pream Nagar bus or #7 route auto-rickshaw. Museums 2km straight through the gate. Open M-F 9:30am-5pm. Museums open M-F 9:30am-5:30pm. Gate Rs2. Botanical Gardens Rs10. Guide Rs50 for up to 6 people.)*

TAPKESHWAR TEMPLE. Built over 100 years ago into the cliffs and caves beside a stream where water bubbles up through the rocks, this Shiva temple is the most important temple in the area. There are several shrines around the temple's entrance, and the stream also serves as a popular swimming hole. The temple also hosts the **Shivaratri celebration** during the last week of March and the first week of April. *(6km northwest of town. Take the Garhi Cantonment bus from the city bus stand. Follow Tapkeshwar Rd., take the first right, and after the bend to the left, take the right fork. The temple is at the end of the road. Open daily 5:30am-9pm.)*

ROBBER'S CAVE. A 200m-long, 15m-high gorge, the so-called Robber's Cave or **Guchu Pani**, is a popular picnic spot. So popular, in fact, that commercialism is slowly eroding its peaceful atmosphere. The natural beauty remains mostly untouched, but be sure to wear sandals if you choose to bathe in the water. Some of the rocks in the stream can be sharp. *(8km north of town. Take a bus from the city bus stand to Supply, Rs3. Auto-rickshaws Rs30 one-way, Rs60 round-trip. From Supply, walk right at the fork and turn left at the end of the paved road (Anarwala); follow the broken cement road to the Robber's Cave.)*

MUSSOORIE मसूरी ☎0135

The mountain hill station of Mussoorie, a convenient access point to the forest treks nearby, certainly isn't for everyone. Travelers looking to shun commercialism in favor of spirituality should stay in nearby Haridwar or Rishikesh to avoid Mussoorie's high prices and overcrowding. Those hoping for mountain tranquility would be better off making a pilgrimage (see **Garhwal Pilgrimages,** p. 658).

A favorite destination of heat-fleeing tourists from Delhi (it's the closest hill station to the capital), the town was settled in 1827 by an Englishman, Captain Young. British officials developed Mussoorie into a Victorian home-away-from-home, complete with an exclusive club, several libraries, and an Anglican Church. The central promenade, the Mall, was made for afternoon strolls and chit-chat in full view of the snow-peaked Himalayas and the Doon Valley.

Where once the British rulers ascended 11km carried by porters, Indian throngs now cruise up the scenic drive from the plains. Peak season is between May and July, when prices are high, hotels are full, and the Mall is packed. Mid-season extends from July to October (the foggy monsoon months) and from March to May. The off season, November through March, brings snow and solitude.

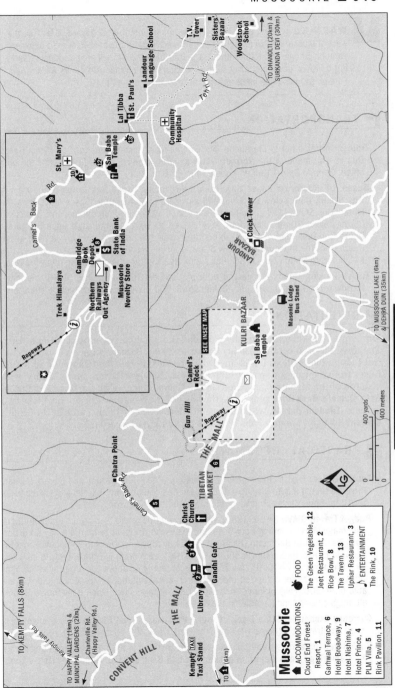

UTTARANCHAL

TO DHANOLTI (20km) & SURKANDA DEVI (30km)

Sisters' Bazaar
Woodstock School
T.V. Tower
Landour Language School
St. Paul's
Lal Tibba
Tehri Rd.
Community Hospital
St. Mary's
Sai Baba Temple
Camel's Back Rd.
10 11
9
8
Cambridge Book Depot
State Bank of India
Northern Railways Out Agency
Mussoorie Novelty Store
Trek Himalaya
Ropeway
Clock Tower
7
LANDOUR BAZAAR
Masonic Lodge Bus Stand
TO MUSSOORIE LAKE (6km) & DEHRA DUN (35km)
KULRI BAZAAR
Sai Baba Temple
SEE INSET MAP
Camel's Rock
Gun Hill
Ropeway
THE MALL
6
Chatra Point
Camel's Back Rd.
Christ Church
5
TIBETAN MARKET
3 4
Gandhi Gate
Library
THE MALL
Kempty TAXI Taxi Stand
CONVENT HILL
TO (6km)
TO HAPPY VALLEY (1km) & MUNICIPAL GARDENS (2km)
Charleville Rd. (Happy Falls Rd.)
Kempty Falls Rd.
TO KEMPTY FALLS (8km)

400 yards
400 meters
0
0

Mussoorie

▲ ACCOMMODATIONS
Cloud End Forest Resort, 1
Garhwal Terrace, 6
Hotel Broadway, 9
Hotel Nishima, 7
Hotel Prince, 4
PLM Villa, 5
Rink Pavilion, 11

🍴 FOOD
The Green Vegetable, 12
Jeet Restaurant, 2
Rice Bowl, 8
The Tavern, 13
Uphar Restaurant, 3

♪ ENTERTAINMENT
The Rink, 10

> **WARNING.** There is an Indian Army encampment at **Chakrata,** 82km north-west of Mussoorie. No foreigners are allowed north of the east-west road between Yamuna Bridge and Kalsi without a permit from the army. Foreign tourists heading by road for Shimla or eastern Himachal Pradesh must do so via Herbertpur. Foreign tourists have been arrested for traveling north of Kalsi.

◗ TRANSPORTATION

Trains: No trains run to Mussoorie, but computerized reservations for trains from Dehra Dun can be made at the **Northern Railways Out Agency,** on the Mall, below the post office. Open M-Sa 8-11am and noon-3pm, Su 8am-2pm.

Buses: UP Roadways buses leave from the **Masonic Lodge Bus Stand** or the **Library Bus Stand,** both below the Mall, and service only **Dehra Dun.** Buses leave from the Library Bus Stand (1½hr., every hr. 7am-6pm, Rs23), and from the Masonic Bus stand (1½hr., every 30min. 7am-6pm, Rs23). Several signs around town advertise direct Dehra Dun-Delhi deluxe service, but state buses and taxis are the only ways to get to Dehra Dun. The **Mussoorie Novelty Store,** opposite Northern Railways Out Agency, runs A/C buses to **Delhi** (7hr., 11am and 10pm, Rs275) from the clock tower in Dehra Dun.

Taxis: Booking stands are next to both bus stands. To: **Dehra Dun** (Rs400 per car), **Haridwar** (Rs900 per car), and **Rishikesh** (Rs900 per car). Taxis cannot be shared.

◗ ORIENTATION

Mussoorie is 15km long, stretching around the mountain overlooking Dehra Dun. The town has two centers, **Library Bazaar** and **Kulri Bazaar,** connected by a 20min. walk along **the Mall,** which is lined with murals, hotels, and shops of all kinds. Buses from the valley stop near both bazaars. The plaza in front of the library, with a statue of the Mahatma, is called **Gandhi Chowk;** the gate by the library is **Gandhi Gate.** Camel's Back Road runs along the back of the mountain and connects the two bazaars. **Landour Bazaar,** with its large clock tower, is a 10min. walk east of Kulri. **Convent Hill** is on Kempty Falls Rd., past the library, away from Kalri.

◗ PRACTICAL INFORMATION

Tourist Office: Next to the ropeway, halfway between Kulri Bazaar and Library Bazaar. Provides tourist maps. May 15-July 15 open daily 10am-5pm; July 16-May 14 open M-Sa 10am-5pm. Closed 2nd Sa of the month in the off season.

Budget Travel: GMVN (☎2631281), at the Library Bus Stand. Runs tours to the northern pilgrimage sites departing from Delhi and Rishikesh. Trips range from a 6-day excursion from Rishikesh to Badrinath (Rs3000) to 10-day trips from Delhi to Yamnotri, Gangotri, Kedarnath, and Badrinath (Rs5000). Open daily 8am-6pm. For travel into the hills, try **Trek Himalaya** (☎2630491; fax 2631302), on the Mall, above the ropeway office. Provides assistance for organized trips and drop-in consultations. Mussoorie guides available for Rs500. Fully planned excursions US$45 per person. Open daily 9am-8:30pm, although closing time is earlier in the off season.

Currency Exchange: State Bank of India, Kulri Bazaar (☎2632533). Exchanges currency and traveler's checks (Rs5 commission). Open M-F 10am-4pm, Sa 10am-1pm.

Bookstore: There are several bookstores along the Mall in Kulri. For books in English try the **Cambridge Book Depot,** opposite the State Bank of India. Open daily 9am-11pm.

Market: Tibetan Market, above and below the Mall, halfway between the Library Bazaar and the Gun Hill Ropeway. **Library Bazaar** and **Kulri Bazaar** have many curios, woolens, and tourist trifles. Bazaars generally open 9am-9pm. The smaller **Sisters' Bazaar** is on the road above Tehri Rd., near the TV tower. Metal workers, tailors, and dry-goods stores can be found in **Landour. Rubal Stores** and **Ram Chandir and Bros.**, next to the clock tower, sell food and are both open daily 9am-10pm.

Police: (☎2632005). Above the Mall, opposite Hakman's Grand Hotel. Open 24hr.

Hospital: Community Hospital (☎2632541), in Landour, 1.5km east of the clock tower above Tehri Rd., provides 24hr. emergency care. For private care, try Dr. Garg's **clinic** (☎2633232, cell 2632822), next to the post office. Open daily 10am-2pm and 5-8pm.

Internet: Cyber Corner, Gandhi Chowk. Rs50 per hr. Open daily 9am-11pm. In Landour, **Omi's** charges Rs40 per hr. Open daily 9:30am-9pm. In Mussoorie, all Internet is dial-up and sevice is extremely slow. Slip into an empty cafe for faster service.

Post Office: (☎2632206). Opposite the State Bank of India. Open M-F 9am-5pm, Sa 9am-2pm. **Postal Code:** 248179.

ACCOMMODATIONS

Most low-end hotels are near **Kulri Bazaar.** Places in Landour are quieter, but there are fewer options. It's a good idea to book ahead of time in peak season (May-June), when rates are higher. Expect discounts mid-season (Mar.-May and July-Oct.) and much lower prices Nov.-Mar. Rates vary, so try your hand at a little haggling. Unless otherwise noted, check-out is 10am and doubles are the same price even if used as a single.

KULRI AND LANDOUR

Hotel Broadway, Camel's Back Rd. (☎2632243), next to The Rink. This converted English guest house retains its peaceful charm away from the noise of the nearby Mall. Rooms with balconies have breathtaking valley views; some with showers, some with TV. May-July singles Rs300; doubles Rs350-600. Off-season 60% discount. ❷

Hotel Nishima, Landour Bazaar (☎2630298), a 5min. walk past the clock tower. Rest easy on thick mattresses behind heavy metal doors in the quieter part of town. TV in the lobby, food available, and seat toilets for the lucky few. May-July doubles Rs250-550, Aug.-Apr. Rs125-250. ❷

Rink Pavilion, Camel's Back Rd. (☎2630291, Delhi office ☎5734598), in the same building as The Rink. Newly built and finished in varnished wood, the high end rooms here have TVs, full baths with shower, and walls of windows overlooking the valley. For added entertainment, open the door and watch those struggling on The Rink's skating floor. Super deluxe room Rs2500. ❺

Garhwal Terrace (☎2632682), on the Mall, between Kulri Bazaar and Library Bazaar. This GMVN-run hotel has dormitories opening up to a lovely veranda with valley views. Pricey doubles are worth it if location is important. Reserve in advance during peak season. Dorms Rs150; rooms Rs1300-1600. July 16-Apr. 15: Rs100/800. ❶

LIBRARY AREA

▨ **Hotel Prince** (☎2632674), off the Mall, up the alley 30m toward Kulri from the library. Once a British hotel, this magnificent site is high above the Mall in a century-old summer getaway. Regal halls, huge rooms, and high ceilings are enhanced by the attention of a family staff. One of the few hotels that offer both mountain and valley views. May 15-July 15 doubles Rs500-1500. Off-season 50% discount. ❸

ON THE MENU

STRANGE BREW

Though an Englishman founded Mussoorie, it took an unruly Scot to set the tone for the revelry that has outlasted the Brits in the hill station. In the 1880s, a fellow named Mackinnon discovered limestone springs near present-day Gandhi Chowk. Mackinnon thought that the waters here might be good for brewing, and he built a brewery on the land, which soon began producing Garhwal's first beer.

From the beginning, Mussoorie was a fun-loving town, and the beer-brewing led to a level of bacchanalian debauchery that wrinkled more than a few official brows. Local lore has it that one English lass, well versed in the appreciation of the Scotch-Indian brew, stood on a chair on Mall Rd. and sold kisses for Rs5. That spelled trouble for Mackinnon.

Since an outright ban on Mackinnon's operation would have been illegal, the authorities shrewdly crippled him by refusing him the right to import barley on the government road. Shut down but not broken in spirit, Mackinnon would not be snubbed—especially by the English. In a daring scheme, he built his own road, 20km long, fitting it with carts to transport his barley. He even set up a watchtower and tollbooth and ran it as a private highway.

Aside from barley, much of the heavy European furniture in Mussoorie was brought up on "Mr.

PLM Villa (☎2631090), off Camel's Back Rd., up the 2nd ramp. Small garden-front home popular with Indian families. Furniture-stuffed rooms have spectacular views and complete silence. Doubles Rs300. Off-season 50% discount. ❷

OUTSIDE MUSSOORIE

Cloud End Forest Resort (☎2632242; www.cloud-end.com), away from Kulri past the library; accessible only by an 8km jeep ride. Set within 400 acres of forest on a ridge overlooking the town, this building dates back to 1838 and is one of Mussoorie's oldest. The period ambience has been scrupulously preserved in the old photographs, plush armchairs, and dark wooden beds of the resort, but the beautiful walks to the George Everest House (30min.) and several temples (8km) are the highlights of a visit. Restaurant serving unusually flavorful food and tea and snacks beside a bonfire at night. Reserve a day ahead for jeep pickup from the library or taxi pickup from Dehra Dun. Dorm bunks Rs400; doubles Rs1200-1800. Camping Rs900 for a 2-person tent, Rs200 if you have your own tent. Off-season 75% discount. AmEx/MC/V. ❸

☕ FOOD

Roasted and boiled *masala* corn (Rs5-15) is sold along the Mall, and sweets are scooped up at **Krishna's and New Delhi Sweet Shop** in Kulri. Restaurants that serve balanced meals can often be hard to find. The fast food can be so fast that your stomach may thank you for avoiding it.

▨ **The Green Vegetable,** Kulri Bazaar. Delicious veg. food at reasonable prices, though a long stream of customers can render it impossible to find or keep a table. For breakfast, try the "Green Special *Paratha*," stuffed with peas, *paneer*, cashews, and raisins (Rs20). *Raita* Rs20-40, Chinese food Rs40-70, and an extensive dessert menu. Open daily 8am-5pm and 7:30-11:30pm. Off-season open 8am-4pm and 7:30-10:30pm. ❷

Uphar Restaurant, on the Mall, in Library Bazaar. This lively ice cream parlor and restaurant has veg. fare on the cheap. Breakfast daily 8am-noon, including *dosas* (Rs25-55). Ice cream Rs30. Open daily 8am-10:30pm. ❶

The Tavern, In Kulri Bazaar, across from the Four Seasons Restaurant. Only Indian and Chinese cuisine on the menu. Upscale atmosphere with cloth napkins and prices to match, but the food is worth it. Seafood Rs300, *tandoori* chicken Rs180, and sweet and sour chicken Rs90. Open daily 11am-9pm. ❹

Jeet Restaurant, Gandhi Chowk. Between the library and Jeet Hotel. Watch the chaos outside while grabbing a quick bite to eat. Veg. fare Rs30-55, chicken curry Rs45, *samosas* Rs30. Open daily 8am-11pm. ❷

Rice Bowl, Kulri Bazaar, in Rialto Gate. Cubicles with street view. Chinese and Tibetan food. *Thukpa,* a Tibetan soup, Rs28-40, garlic chicken Rs60, mutton *momos* Rs30. Open daily 10:30am-11:30pm. ❷

👁 SIGHTS

GUN HILL. Directly over the town hovers this extinct volcano named after the pre-independence ritual in which guns were fired from the top at midday—the townspeople used to set their watches by it. You can walk for 20min. up the path, which starts at the main police station. However, the most scenic way to go is via Mussoorie's **ropeway**—come early or at lunchtime to avoid the long lines. *(Open daily 8am-10pm; last car up at 8pm. Off-season open 10am-7pm. Rs40 round-trip.)*

LAL TIBBA. On the far side of the mountain with the TV Tower is Lal Tibba, a glorious **lookout point** for the distant Himalayas. Take the path from the right side of the Community Hospital and turn right at the next highest road. Follow the road, taking the left switchback, to Chardukhan. At St. Paul's Church, turn left and continue past the food stands. The walk takes 45min.-1hr., but taxis are also available. The 30min. walk from Lal Tibba to the TV Tower and Sisters' Bazaar affords an even more serene retreat.

CAMEL'S BACK ROAD. This road, which connects the Library Bazaar and Kulri Bazaar by winding around the mountain on the side opposite the Mall (3km total) has excellent silent views of the Himalayas. Points of interest include the **cemetery** (if the main gate is closed, try the side gate), studded with interesting British tombstones, **Camel's Back Rock** (guess at its shape; Rs10 for a peek through a telescope), and a slightly dilapidated **Chatra (Umbrella) Point,** where you can buy *chai* and snacks. The entire walk, from one bazaar to the other, takes 45min. On a clear day, the sunset view from the road is spectacular.

MUNICIPAL GARDENS. Although the same commercialism reigns here as everywhere else, there are several opportunities to get away from the crowds. Bring food or buy from one of the stands and have a picnic on the well-manicured lawns. The back corners are the most intimate. Work off lunch by biking to the **bassistand,** the local name

Buckles' Bullock-Cart Train," as the venture was called. And so, Mussoorie had its beer.

To thank his consumers, Mackinnon threw a massive bash, where he cracked a huge wooden cask of new brew. The rollicking horde polished off most of the barrel, noting repeatedly that it tasted better than any beer in brewing history. But a scream of horror suddenly broke up the festivities, and the party collapsed into pandemonium—in the dregs of the cask lay a rotting human body. Apparently, an impatient imbiber had slipped into the cellar, packed down a few too many, and fallen in with the hops. The brew was through.

Mackinnon's ruined brewery looms on the Lynndale Estate 3km west of Mussoorie, but his bullock-cart road now forms 20km of the present road to Rajpur.

for old Mackinnon brewery, 2km away down the path that runs from the far end of the boat pond. *(3km past the library away from Kulri on Charleville Rd. Rs90 for round-trip rickshaw with 1hr. wait.)*

ENTERTAINMENT

Most Indian visitors walk the Mall until late at night (midnight), watching their fellow Delhi-*wallahs* go by. The younger generations can be found at **The Rink,** in Kulri, India's largest indoor roller-skating rink. The wooden floor and its building date back 125 years to when British couples experimented with what was then all the rage back home. (Open daily 8:30am-8pm. Admission including rental Rs65.)

NEAR MUSSOORIE

KEMPTY FALLS. Located in a valley 15km from Mussoorie, Kempty Falls are the highest falls in the region. Visitors can either stay at the top and watch the water rush under the bus-filed roadway or descend the steps to the crash basin for a refreshing dip. Sadly, this popular "retreat" is slowly degenerating from an idyllic spot overlooking pristine, rushing falls and peaceful pools into a glitzy hotspot indistinguishable from the rest of town. GMVN runs a 3hr. bus trip to Kempty Falls. (Times vary; check at the GMVN office at the Library Bus Stand. Rs50.) Taxis leave from the Kempty Taxi Stand, a 10min. walk up Kempty Rd. from the library (Rs350 per 5-person taxi round-trip.)

HIKING. Most hiking in or around Mussoorie starts outside of town and provides little in terms of lodging. The exceptions are those hikes that start at **Cloud End** (see **Accommodations,** p. 646), which are fairly untouched. From here, a 30min. walk through apple orchards brings you to the **George Everest House,** the home of the First Surveyor General of India. Directions are available at reception for more hikes, or simply wander the 400 acre farm. Famous British-Indian author Ruskin Bond lives near the Masonic Lodge Bus Stand and always welcomes friendly visitors. On the other end of Mussoorie, 25km past Landour, in **Dhanolti,** are orchards and dense deodar forests. Past Dhanolti is **Surkanda Devi** (35km from Mussoorie). This temple, at the top of the highest mountain in the area (3300m), provides great views. It's a strenuous 2km walk to the temple from the road head.

HARIDWAR हरिद्वार ☏ 0133

Steeped in legend, cloaked in forests, and bordered by the Ganga as it emerges from the mountains to carve its winding way across India, Haridwar (Gateway to the Gods) is one of Hinduism's sacred sites. The city's spiritual pre-eminence is rooted in the belief that the Ganga flows here in its purest form at the Har-ki-Pairi (Footstep of God), the main *ghat* to the Ganga. Today, tens of thousands of Hindus bathe in, drink from, and pray to the Ganga. At sundown, *arati* is performed at Har-ki-Pairi where pilgrims float leaf bowls filled with flowers and lit candles down the Ganga to the sound of *bhajans*. A major pilgrimage destination, Haridwar hosts the Kumbh Mela every 12 years when millions of people rush the Har-ki-Pairi *ghat* at a precisely calculated moment. During the other 11 years the city is filled with Indians, pilgrims, and foreigners, all focused on the Ganga.

UTTARANCHAL

Haridwar

▲ ACCOMMODATIONS
Hotel Alaknanda, **2**
Hotel Madras, **5**
Hotel Mahaalakshmi, **8**
Hotel Samrat, **4**
Rahi Motel, **1**
Shiv Vishram Grah Lodge, **9**

🍴 RESTAURANTS
Big Ben Restaurant, **3**
Chotiwala Restaurant, **6**
New Mysore Kwality
    Restaurant, **7**

Map labels:
Mansa Devi Temple
TO BHARAT MATA MANDIR (1km), RISHIKESH (27km) & DEHRA DUN (54km)
Broken Bridge
Ganga Mandir
Har-ki-Pairi Ghat
VIP Ghat
MOTI BAZAAR
Pant Dweep Island
Gau Ghat
Rajaji National Park
Ropeway
Upper Rd.
Kusha Ghat
Vishnu Ghat
Shatabdi Bridge
GPO
Govt. Hospital
GMVN & UP Tourism
Clock Tower
State Bank of India
Railway Station
TO DELHI (214km)
Laltare Bypass Rd.
Sadhubela Rd.
Ganga River
Nil Dhara
Lalta Rao Bridge
Railway Rd.
UA Tourism
TO CHILLA
Chilla Wildlife Park
TO PARESHWAR MAHADEV & DAKSHA MAHADEV TEMPLES (1km)
TO CHANDI DEVI TEMPLE (1km)

Vertical tab: UTTARANCHAL

▣ TRANSPORTATION

Trains: Northern Railway Station, opposite the bus stand on Railway Rd. The inquiries office is in the building on the right. The reservation counter is in the building on the left. Reservations can be made daily 8am-8pm. To: **Dehra Dun** (2hr., 16 per day 4:12am-7:20pm, Rs50); **Delhi** (7-8hr., 5 per day 5am-10:40pm, Rs71); **Rishikesh** (1hr., 3 per day 5am-5pm, Rs70); **Varanasi** (20hr., 8:15pm, Rs309).

Buses: The **bus stand** is opposite the train station, at the end of Railway Rd. away from Har-ki-Pairi. **UP Roadways** (☎ 223770) runs buses to: **Agra** (11hr., every hr. 4:30am-9pm, Rs150); **Dehra Dun** (1½hr., every 30min. 6am-7:30pm, Rs28); **Delhi** (5hr., every 30min. 4am-11pm, Rs100); **Lucknow** (14hr., 3:30pm, Rs231); **Rishikesh** (45min., every 30min., Rs15); **Shimla** (12hr., 4 per day 10:30am-10:30pm, Rs200).

Local Transportation: Auto-rickshaws and *tempos* are not allowed in the northern half of town (past the post office), so **cycle-rickshaws** are best for transport to Har-ki-Pairi and the surrounding area. They'll go anywhere in the city for Rs10, though most of the river-side bazaar lanes are too narrow for them. *Tempos,* which congregate around the train station, post office, and Har-ki-pairi, are the best option for temples outside the city.

ORIENTATION AND PRACTICAL INFORMATION

Haridwar runs along the banks of the Ganga, which flows from northeast to south-west or from the **Har-ki-Pairi** to the train station. The **bus stand** and **railway station** face each other at the southern most end of **Railway Road**, the town's main thor-oughfare. The post office is halfway between the train station and the Har-ki-Pairi. Just south of the post office is a barricade that prohibits four-wheeled traffic from continuing up Railway Rd. North of this barricade, Railway Rd. becomes **Upper Road;** the Har-ki-Pairi is at the northeast end of Upper Rd. The main bazaar, **Moti Bazaar,** runs parallel to and between the river and Upper Rd.

Tourist Office: GMVN, Railway Rd. (☎224240), and **UP Tourism** (☎227370) are at the Railway Rd. end of Lalita Rao Bridge. Tourist maps, package tours, and trekking infor-mation are available. Both open M-Sa 10am-5pm. GMVN operates an info desk inside the train station, open daily 5:30am-4pm. **UA Tourism,** in Rahi Motel, is opposite the railway station. Open M-Sa 10am-5pm.

Budget Travel: Ashwani Travels, Railway Rd. (☎224581), opposite the train station in Hotel Sachin. Offers package tours for pilgrimages. Open daily 7am-8pm. **Shivalik Travels,** Upper Rd. (☎226855), opposite Gorakh Nath Ashram. Open daily 7am-3pm and 5-10pm.

Currency Exchange: State Bank of India, towards the river from Hotel Madras on Sadhubela Rd. Changes US dollars. Rs50 for encashment receipt. Open M-F 10am-2pm and 3-4pm, Sa 10am-1pm.

Market: Moti Bazaar, on the narrow streets just south of Har-ki-Pairi. Features a wide selection of brass, wooden goods, food stalls, and items needed for spiritual worship.

Police: Main Station, Upper Rd. (☎226200 or 225200), next to the post office.

Pharmacy: Milap Medical Hall, Railway Rd. (☎227193), opposite the hospital. Open M-Sa 8am-10pm. **Dr. B.C. Hasaram & Sons,** Upper Rd. opposite the police station. Spe-cializes in Ayurvedic medicines. Open daily 8am-9pm.

Hospital: Government Hospital, Railway Rd. between Lalita Rao Bridge and the post office. Two buildings, separate for women and men, with clinic open daily 8am-2pm. Also offers 24hr. emergency care.

Internet: Balkrishan Dinesh Kumar's self-titled phone booth, Railway Rd. (☎227615), just south of the hospital. Internet access for Rs1 per min.

Post Office: Railway Rd. (☎227025), north of Lalita Rao Bridge. Open M-F 10am-5pm, Sa 10am-2pm. **Postal Code:** 249401.

ACCOMMODATIONS

Though the *dharamsalas* may look inviting, most are not open to foreigners. However, the famous **Shantikunj** (☎2260260; shail@de12.vsnl.net.in) is open to for-eigners looking to ascend to higher spiritual states. For those familiar with Shan-tikunj practices, the ashram offers courses of varying lengths in meditation, music, medicine, and chanting. Reservations are required for both specific seminars and regular visits. Single or two-day stays are also possible (payment by donation).

Except for a few diamonds in the rough, most hotels in Haridwar are old and run-down. The prices listed below are for high (pilgrimage) season.

Hotel Mahaalakshmi, Upper Rd. (☎227238), next to the path to Mansa Nevi. Well-kept, marble-tiled rooms come with seat toilets, TVs, and hot water. Reservations highly recommended during pilgrimage season. Singles Rs450-800; doubles Rs650-950. ❸

Hotel Samrat, off Railway Rd. (☎227380), 2 blocks toward Lalita Rao Bridge, from the train station. Turn right after the Kailash Hotel. Although the rooms are no-frills, they are well-kept and priced accordingly in a town of inflated rates. Location also can't be beat—a quiet side-street near the train station. Doubles from Rs250. ❷

Shiv Vishram Grah Lodge, Upper Rd. (☎227618). This large complex in the Moti Bazaar has rooms facing the quiet inner courtyard. Air-cooled doubles with attached bath. Filled with Indian families during pilgrimage season. Doubles Rs400. ❸

Hotel Madras (☎226356), off Railway Rd., 2 blocks north of the railway station. Turn right after the Kailash Hotel. On the left after Hotel Samrat. The oldest hotel in town has bare-bones rooms with common bath. Singles Rs100; doubles Rs120. ❶

Hotel Alaknanda (☎226379). Cross Lalita Rao Bridge, turn right onto the walkway along the river, and walk 1km. Though pricey and far from most of the sights, it's the best place for peace and quiet, with a little lawn, flower garden, and a strip of riverbank on the holy Ganga. All rooms have air-cooling, attached bath with shower, and TV. Check-out noon. Laundry available. Dorms Rs100; air-cooled rooms Rs600-800, A/C rooms Rs1300-1600. Off-season 20% discount. ❶

Rahi Motel, Railway Rd. (☎426430), 1 block from the bus stand away from Lalira Rao Bridge. Good location for late arrivals. Huge rooms with seat toilets, hot showers, and air cooling. Singles Rs500-1000; doubles Rs660-1440. ❸

☐ FOOD

Purity of diet follows purity of spirit in Haridwar, so alcohol and meat are not available. Most major restaurants are on Railway Rd., midway between the bus stand and Har-ki-Pairi. Street vendors in Moti Bazaar near Har-ki-Pairi offer sugar-filled *jalebis* that look like clogged arteries even *before* you eat them. Sit-down restaurants can be hard to find, but be sure the place is relatively clean: the Ganga can cleanse your soul, but not your digestive tract.

Big Ben Restaurant, 2 blocks toward the Har-ki-Pairi from the train station inside Hotel Ganga Azure. The promise of A/C dining will lure you in while the Indian and continental fare will keep you here. *Thalis* Rs55, Big Ben Special Dinner Rs95, and set breakfast Rs65. Open daily 8am-10:30pm. ❸

Chotiwala Restaurant, Railway Rd., opposite the GMVN office. One of the nicest sit-down places in town. North and South Indian food served in a relatively quiet A/C environment. *Thalis* Rs55-70. Open daily 8am-8pm. ❸

New Mysore Kwality Restaurant, on Railway Rd. between police station and Hotel Mahaalakshmi. Unassuming atmosphere, cool air, and great prices. *Thalis* Rs35, *dosas* Rs14-28, and *utthapam* Rs16-28. Open daily 7am-10:30pm, in winter 7am-9pm. ❶

☉ SIGHTS

HAR-KI-PAIRI GHAT. The most important spot in Haridwar is the holy *ghat* of Har-ki-Pairi, site of Vishnu's footprint and the place where the sacred Ganga flows out into the plains. Many pilgrims fill a bottle or two to take home for use in religious ceremonies. The *ghat* itself is a huge set of stadium-like stairs facing a man-made island, connected to land by several pedestrian bridges. The small channel allows for safer bathing conditions. The **Ganga Mandir,** a small temple on a man-made island in the channel, marks the spot where the drop of sacred nectar fell during the mythical match-up between the demon *asuras* and the good-guy gods that is now celebrated during the Kumbh Mela. Many people bathe at the *ghat* at sunrise, though you'll see people here throughout the day; there are chains to keep bathers from getting swept off to Varanasi by the strong under-tow. The area is constantly crowded with pilgrims, beggars, lepers, *sadhus*, and several uniformed men who wander the area asking for donations for various "trusts." Many of these individuals pocket their earnings—donate via the charity boxes around the area or at the office of Ganga Sabha, above the temple at the *ghat*. Every evening at sundown, the sublime and spectacular **aarti** ceremony takes place. Thousands gather to pay tribute to the gods with *diyas* (cupped leaves filled with flower petals and a lit candle) that are set free to float down the river. Arrive early (around 6:45pm) in high season. Recently, overly enthusi-astic worshippers have started jumping into the Ganga from the bridges span-ning the channel and some have gotten hurt. The police cordon off the bridges an hour before sunset, making the best viewpoints either upstream or on the island near the clocktower. Check your shoes if you want to go down to the tem-ples, but avoid the 8pm shoe-return stampede.

MANSA DEVI AND CHANDI DEVI TEMPLE. Haridwar is dotted with temples, but the two most important and beautiful can only be reached by ropeway or trek. Just above the city, on top of Bilwa Parvat, is the **Mansa Devi Temple,** ded-icated to the goddess by the same name who can make the wishes of faithful and holy people come true. Mansa is believed to have bathed at Har-ki-Pairi every morning. The temple houses two intricately carved statues of the god-dess—one with five arms and three mouths, the other with eight arms. To get to the shrine, stand in line for a ropeway trolley to whisk you up and over a garden to the hilltop, where views, vendors, and the temple await. You can avoid the long wait in line by making the 30min. hike uphill yourself. The **Chandi Devi Temple** is across the river a few kilometers from town, but the rope-way operator below Mansa Devi offers a package deal including a bus to the base of Chandi Devi's ropeway. The temple itself is smaller than Mansa Devi, but the breathtaking views of the Himalayas, Haridwar, and the Ganga make it well worth the trip. *(Mansa Devi ropeway trolley open daily Apr.-Nov. 8:30am-6:30pm; Nov.-Mar. 8am-6pm; Rs30 round-trip. Chandi Devi ropeway trolley open daily 8:30am-5:30pm; Rs60 roundtrip. Package tour Rs120; includes A/C bus between both ropeways, as well as ropeway fares.)*

BHARAT MATA MANDIR AND ENVIRONS. North of Haridwar, just off the road to Rishikesh, is a group of unusual temples that appear more gaudy and over-done than opulent and justly grand. Nevertheless, visiting even a few of them can help make plain just how many different kinds of Hindu temples there really are. *Tempos* from just upstream of the Har-ki-Pairi are the best way to get to the first stop (Rs5-15). After that, however, they are all within easy walking distance of each other. One kilometer from Har-ki-Pairi, on the left just under the train bridge, is the **Bhimgoda Tank,** where Bhima, one of the strongest of the five Pan-davas, took a bath. Most of the year it is a murky brown pool surrounded by cement stairs, but it is still used for some festivals. A little farther toward Rish-ikesh on the right is the **Jai Ram Ashram,** a large pink and yellow complex. Its bone-white sculptures, depicting the battles between gods and demons, are a departure from the colorful deities that characterize most Hindu temples.

To get to the next temple continue toward Rishikesh until you cross a low bridge. Turn right just before the large green building and follow the road around until it becomes Swami Shukhdevanand Marg. The **Pawan Dham,** with its pristine white facade, is 1km ahead on the left. Its many shrines are made entirely of mirrors and stained glass. Shiva and Arjuna ride on mirror-covered horses while Krishna eyes his 100 lovers. The road then proceeds first to **Bhuma Nikotan,** recognizable by the huge globe above its entrance, and then to **Maa Vaishnodevi,** 200m past Bhuma Nikotan on the left, with an entrance guarded by a towering monkey statue. Both attempt to simulate the experience of visiting a cave in Kashmir, complete with fake rocks, large animals, and running water, but Bhuma Nikotan has the added bonus of automation. At the end of the tour pay Rs2 to enter a room filled with jerky robotic scenes of Hinduism's formative movements.

From here, you will be able to see the **Bharat Mata Mandir,** an eight-story shrine to Mother India and her leaders. The *mandir* resembles a modern apartment building capped by colorful temple domes. The top story houses the Hindu gods while the floor below hosts the goddesses, including Ganga and Saraswati, goddess of knowledge. The lower floors honor the saints of India's various religions (from Guru Nanak of the Sikhs to the Buddha and Swami Vivekenanda), saintly sisters (including Gandhi's devotees Annie Besant and Sister Nivedita), and freedom fighters. The fifth floor has paintings highlighting characteristic features of India's states, and the ground floor has a giant relief model of the country. Around the bend in the road, the farthest from Haridwar, is **Saptrishi Ashram** with its seven temples. It's believed that when Ganga arrived, the seven sages were involved in deep *tapasya* (austerities). To please all seven, she divided herself at this spot into seven streams and flowed on to their feet. The seven streams of the Ganga were distinctly visible as recently as 10 years ago.

RISHIKESH ऋषिकेश ☎ 0135

Most travelers come to Rishikesh to find something—a cure to some deep-rooted ailment, a spiritual leader, or, more often, themselves. There is a spirituality here that can only be matched in the northern *yatras*, but Rishikesh also offers the comforts of a large city. Because most people come to Rishikesh to find peace, they create it as wellc, giving the areas outside the city proper, especially Swargashram, a calmer atmosphere than most other cities in Garhwal. Compared to Haridwar, *aarti* ceremonies on the Ganga are smaller and more foreigner-friendly. Every year, thousands turn up for the **International Yoga Week** (Feb. 2-7, 2004) on the banks of the Ganga. Even the Beatles sought a new path here in 1968 under the guidance of the Maharishi Mahesh Yogi (see **Instant Karma,** p. 658). There are fewer temples in Rishikesh than in Haridwar, but more Westerners, more foreigner-accepting ashrams, and more opportunities for relaxation. Summer is the off season for yoga. Winter sees fewer Indian tourists. No matter the time of your visit, Rishikesh is a good place to rest before heading north to the *yatras* and trekking.

▐ TRANSPORTATION

Trains: Railway Station, at the end of Railway Rd. (sometimes Station Rd.) Reservations office open M-F 8am-8pm. Most connections to major destinations start in Haridwar. To **Haridwar** (1½hr., 3 per day 7:35am-6:35pm, Rs43) and **Delhi** (10hr., 7am, Rs81).

Buses: Rishikesh has two bus stands. Smog-belching buses heading for the plains leave from the **UP Roadways Main Bus Stand** (☎ 2430066), at the corner of Hiralal Rd. and Adarash Nagar. To: **Agra** (12hr., 5:30pm, Rs180); **Chandigarh** (7hr., 4 per day 4:30am-9:30pm, Rs130); **Dehra Dun** (1hr., every 30min. 5am-7:30pm, Rs20); **Delhi** (6½hr., every 30min. 5am-10:30pm, Rs150); **Haridwar** (every 30min. 4am-10:30pm, Rs15). For buses to the northern pilgrimage sites, go to the **Yatra Bus Stand** (☎ 2430008), on Dehra Dun Rd. A rickshaw from the UP stand to the Yatra Bus Stand costs Rs20. Tickets for Yamnotri, Gangotri, Kedarnath, and Badrinath can be purchased 1 day in advance. To: **Badrinath** (12-13hr.; 3:30, 4, 5am; Rs180); **Chamoli** (7hr.,

3:30-11:30am, Rs120); **Gangotri** (12hr., 5am, Rs155); **Hanuman Chatti** (11hr., 5am, Rs132); **Kedarnath** (8hr., 4 and 5am, Rs127); **Tehri** (3½hr., every 30min. 3:30am-4pm, Rs46); **Uttarkashi** (7hr., 7 per day 3:30am-1pm, Rs90). Uttarkashi serves as a launch point for Yamnotri and Gangotri. **Shared taxis** to **Uttarkashi** (5hr., Rs1200 per cab, up to 5 seats) leave from Haridwar and Dehra Dun Rd.

Local Transportation: Getting to Ramjhula and Lakshmanjhula from Rishikesh is best done via one of the **tempos** that run along Lakshmanjhula Rd. (Rs5-10). Both bridges must be traversed on foot—there is no public transportation on the bank opposite Rishikesh. *Tempos* also leave from anywhere on Haridwar Rd. to Haridwar (Rs30).

ORIENTATION

Rishikesh is divided into three parts by the **Ganga** and the **Chandrabhaga Rivers.** Opposite Rishikesh, across the dry bed of the Chandrabhaga River, is **Ramjhula,** and farther away from Rishikesh is **Lakshmanjhula.** Both straddle the Ganga and their halves are connected by footbridges. The eastern part of Ramjhula is known as **Swargashram** and the western part is called **Muni-ki-Reti** (named for the nearby hill where Lord Hanuman brought herbs to cure Lord Rama's illness). Ramjhula is where most accommodations and ashrams can be found. It's a 5km hike into Rishikesh if you're staying in Lakshmanjhula, but the distance from the noise and clutter of the station makes the walk well worth it.

The tiny business center of Rishikesh is on the land mass between the Chandrabhaga and the Ganga Rivers. The river banks are lined with temples and *ghats*. A grid of streets covers the rest of the land, where the train station, bus stands, and most shops and services are located. **Dehradun Road** runs along the Chandrabhaga, intersecting with Haridwar Rd. at the end closest to the Ganga. **Kailash Gate,** 1km toward Rishikesh from the Ramjhula taxi stand, is a major landmark.

PRACTICAL INFORMATION

Tourist Office: GMVN Trekking and Mountaineering/Yatra Office (☎2430799), 1 block toward Rishikesh from Kailash Gate. Offers info on treks and rents equipment at great prices. Open daily 10am-5pm. Off-season closed Su. **UA Tourism,** Railway Rd. (☎2430209), 3 blocks toward the train station from the State Bank of India, up the outdoor flight of stairs by the white statue. Open M-Sa 10am-5pm, closed 2nd Sa.

Currency Exchange: State Bank of India (☎2430780). Changes currency with no commission at its main office, on the north side of Railway Rd., a 5min. walk from Lakshmanjhula Rd. Open M-F 10am-2pm and 2:30-4pm, Sa 10am-1pm. **Bank of Baroda,** 74 Dehradun Rd., does credit card advances. Open M-F 10am-4pm, Sa 10am-12:30pm.

Market: Main Bazaar, in Rishikesh, towards the river from the post office. Each street has an unofficial specialization such as metalsmiths, sari emporiums, or *dhabas*. Yoga books, Ayurvedic herbs, and henna adornment can be had in Swargashram.

Police: Main Rishikesh Office, Dehradun Rd., next to the hospital (☎2430100). 24hr.

Pharmacy: Kailash Medical Hall, opposite the Government General Hospital. 24hr.

Hospital: Government General Hospital, Dehradun Rd. (☎2430402), next to the police station. Clean, well-staffed, and open 24hr.

Internet: Blue Hill Travel (☎2433836), in Swargashram. Rs20 per hr. Open daily 8am-10pm.

Post Office: Main office (☎2430340), near the entrance to the Main Bazaar, next to the Hotel Basera. **Ramjhula branch,** Swargashram. **Lakshmanjhula branch,** a 5min. walk south from the bridge. All open M-Sa 9am-5pm. **Postal Code:** 249201.

ACCOMMODATIONS

Seekers of the inner light may want to stay in an ashram around Muni-ki-reti. The less spiritually-inclined will find their best options in Swargashram on the bank of the Ganga opposite Rishikesh. Only those needing an early getaway should stay in the loud and congested center of Rishikesh near the railway station and bus stand.

HOTELS AND GUEST HOUSES

Most hotels in Rishikesh can arrange massages, yoga, and music lessons upon request if they don't offer them already. Check-out time is noon unless otherwise noted.

▨ **High Bank Peasant's Cottage** (☎2431167). From Muni-ki-reti, head toward Lakshman-jhula. Take Bypass Rd., which branches left; 50m later, turn right at the sign. Large, clean rooms with attached baths, valley views, and homey feel. It is the perfect place for a quiet retreat from the otherwise chaotic tourist scene. Doubles Rs300-500. ❷

▨ **Brijwasi Palace** (☎2435181 or 2435918), behind Gita Bhavan, in Swargashram. A friendly staff, yoga classes, (Rs50), and massages (Rs250 per hr.) to go along with clean rooms and bathrooms. Although the rooms are sparse and mostly cement, it helps to keep the oppressive heat under control without need of A/C. Singles Rs120, with TV Rs250; doubles Rs150/Rs300. ❶

▨ **Green Hotel** (☎2431242), one block from the Brijwasi Palace. Follow the numerous signs from Ramjhula Bridge. Immaculate rooms, seat toilets, hot showers, and a great Italian restaurant. Attached STD booth. Singles Rs100-200; doubles Rs150-300. ❶

Yoga Niketan Guest House, Muni-ki-reti (☎2434778), before the Ramjula taxi stand. Clean and spacious rooms boast high-powered fans, white tile floors, seat toilets, and shower. All rooms with balconies overlooking well-groomed garden and steps leading down to the Ganga. Convenient location near the Ramjhula bridge ensures easy access to Rishikesh proper and Swargashram, although it is not as quiet as accommodation across the river. Free yoga and meditation classes at the nearby Yoga Niketan Ashram. Singles Rs400; doubles Rs600; prices include meals. ❸

Bhandari Swiss Cottage (☎2432939), just opposite High Bank. Peasant Cottage. Recent construction projects have created double rooms with attached baths and amazing valley views. Balconies for contemplating the long hike back to town. Lots of services, including internet (Rs30 per hr.), phone, and German bakery. Foreign exchange available. Doubles Rs150-400. ❷

ASHRAMS AND YOGA

No matter which yoga position you manage to twist yourself into, an ashram is never far from sight in Rishikesh. Most Westerners head to Swangashram for ashram stays, which often include yoga and meditation classes as well as meals. Staying in an ashram is not like bunking up in a hotel—the meditative atmosphere comes with a series of strict rules that generally include: no meat, no eggs, no smelly food, no alcohol, no tobacco, no drugs, and no noise. Most demand daily bathing (always a good plan), request that menstruating women stay out of the ashram centers, and have strict curfews. Though some are set up for pilgrims and Hindu worshippers and do not allow foreigners, most ashrams in the Ramjhula and Swargashram area, are very welcoming.

Ved Niketan (☎2430279), at the end of Swargashram farthest from the bridge. This large, yellow and orange complex claims a large chunk of the Ganga's bank. The main guru, now in his 90s, still lives here, but others do the teaching of the day-long yoga and meditation syllabus. There is no required length of stay. Yoga is Rs100 per day. Rooms with attached bath: Singles Rs70, doubles Rs120. Food for Rs20 per meal. Six month intensive course available. STD/ISD facilities. Sometimes there are specific seminars underway so calls ahead are appreciated.

Yoga Niketan (☎2430227), in the hills above Lakshmanjhula Rd. With wide views of the Ganga. This ashram is a world unto itself. 15-night min. stay includes 3 meals, 2 yoga classes, and 2 meditation classes per day. Visible security force ensures compliance with the rules at this yoga boot camp. Rooms with squat toilets, no showers. Guests are expected to help with weekly cleaning and attend all classes. Curfew 9:30pm. Office open 8:30am-noon and 2-5pm. Rs250 per day per person.

Omkarananda Ganga Sadan, Muni-ki-reti (☎2431473 or 2430763), next to Ramjhula Taxi Stand, not to be mistaken for the Omkarananda Ashrani opposite the GMVN office, which takes no foreigners. One of the swankiest ashrams in town—dazzling white rooms and bathrooms (all attached, some with Western toilets). Try for a river view. Staff's attitude is as sterile as the outside of the building. Yoga instruction Rs600 per week with 1 lecture course each evening. Indian music, dance, and Hindi lessons also available. 3-night min. stay. Breakfast (Rs25), lunch and dinner (Rs40 each). Rooms Rs200-250.

Yoga Study Centre (☎2433837), at the end of Haridwar Rd., away from Muni-ki-reti, on the river side of the road. Well-known place to learn *iyengar yoga*, though without accommodations it lacks the community feeling of the ashrams. Beginning yoga classes Jan., Mar., May, June, and Dec. M-Sa 6:30-8am. General class July-Nov. 2hr. per morning. Pay on a donation basis.

◎ FOOD

Restaurants in Rishikesh don't serve meat, eggs, or booze. However, years of vegetarianism has made the dishes particularly clean and delicious.

⬛ Little Italy Restaurant, inside Green Hotel in Swargashram. The Italian-trained chefs turn pasta (Rs75-85) and pizza (Rs60-90) very true to the real thing. The *gnocchi* with creamy tomato sauce (Rs70) is a filling break from *thalis* while the Nutella chocolate pancake (Rs35) is the western version of *nirvana*. Also has extensive Indian and Middle Eastern menu. Open daily 8am-10pm. ❸

Amrita, on the western bank of the Ganga in Muni-ki-reti, beneath the rickshaw stand. From Omkarananda Ganga Sadan take the stairs down to the public *ghat* and turn left; it's at the end of the building. Fresh is the name of the game at this little-known place, from the fruit to the entrees. Eat the spaghetti with a delicious, spicy marinara sauce (Rs70) outside, along the Ganga, or grab a book from the in-house bookcase to enjoy with a banana pancake (Rs30). ❸

Madras Cafe, in the Ramjhula rickshaw stand area. Indian food, whole-foods style, with lots of sprouts and whole wheat. Himalayan Health *Pullao,* with sprouts, curd, and Ayurvedic herbs Rs50, hot lemon-ginger-honey tea Rs15, and fresh bread baked daily. Open daily 6:30am-10:30pm. ❷

Chotiwala and Chotiwala Restaurant, in Swargashram near the bridge; The 2 parts, side by side, were divided by 2 brothers. Both serve similar, standard Indian food. *Paneer* butter *masala* (Rs55). Open daily 7am-10pm. ❷

Ganga View Restaurant, opposite Bombay Kshetra in Lakshmanjhula. This is where the foreign tourists staying in Lakshmanjhula come together to enjoy good conversation and the Ganga view. Serves imaginative and tasty breakfast fare, like Nutella and banana toast (Rs15). Open daily 7:30am-8:30pm. ❶

Ganga Darshan, next to Ganga View, closer to the bridge. Very similar to the Ganga View except the focus here is on lunch and dinner. Not worth a special trip from outside Lakshmanjhula unless dirt cheap prices are essential. *Dosas* Rs12-20; *thalis* Rs35. Open daily 6:30am-8:30pm. ❶

◎ ♫ SIGHTS AND ENTERTAINMENT

Triveni Ghat, on the opposite end of the Main Bazaar from Haridwar Rd., is believed to be the place where the Yamuna, Ganga, and Saraswati rivers meet, and therefore it is the most sacred spot in Rishikesh. The **arati** ceremony takes place here, and at the *ghat* next to the clock tower in Swargashram, every evening at sundown. This is also a popular site at which to make river offerings at dawn, when the pilgrims make it a sea of saffron. An ancient **Lakshman Temple** stands on the west bank between the Lakshmanjula taxi stand and the bridge. **Boats** head across the Ganga at Ramjhula, below Sivananda Ashram (Rs5 one way, Rs8 round trip). Another way to go with the flow is to **raft the rapids** along the Ganga. Companies in the Kailash Gate area, such as **Step Himalayan Adventures** (☎2432581), run daily 3-4hr. rafting trips (Rs100-300). Multiday trips also available (2-6 days, Rs300-600 per person per day). Another good option are the professionals at Garhwal Himalayan Explorations. (☎2433478; www.thegarhwalhimalayas.com.) Fixed departure rafting trips can include stays at their river camp, Ganga Nature Camp, 11km from Rishikesh.

Not content with mere meditation and vegetation, many visitors also take **music lessons. Sivananda Ramesh Music School** (☎2437581; take a left at the sign on the far side of the bridge on Lakshmanjhula Rd., just after Tehri Rd.) will

INSTANT KARMA When the Beatles came to Rishikesh to study Transcendental Meditation in February 1968, it was the culmination of several years of Western pop's infatuation with the Mysterious East. George Harrison-inspired sitar licks had been turning up in an increasing number of places for several years, and the Beatles had already attended lectures by the Maharishi Mahesh Yogi during 1967. They recorded tracks for "The Inner Light," one of their most India-inspired songs, just before heading out for the Himalayan foothills.

In Rishikesh, George, John, Paul, and Ringo embraced the typical ashram experience —they eased off on the drugs, meditated, and mostly just hung out with other Westerners (including Mia and Prudence Farrow, the Beach Boys' Mike Love, and 60s pop anomaly, Donovan). They also wrote songs. Most of the "White Album," and much of what later became *Abbey Road* was written during the group's stay in Rishikesh. The most famous of these is "Dear Prudence," an entreaty to the latter Farrow to come out and join in the meditative fun: "The sun is up, the sky is blue / It's beautiful and so are you / Dear Prudence, won't you come out to play?"

Eventually though, the blue skies clouded, and the Beatles became disillusioned with the Maharishi and his vegetarian diet. Less than a month after they left Rishikesh, John Lennon and Paul McCartney announced they'd ended their relationship with the guru. Some of the bitterness they felt comes through in the thinly veiled lyrics of a John Lennon song that appears on the second disc of the White Album: "Sexy Sadie, what have you done? You made a fool of everyone...."

teach you to make the voice soar, the tabla ring, or the sitar gently weep. Rs100 per lesson. 1-month course Rs3000; 2 weeks Rs1500. If your back has seen better days than the long ones spent on Indian buses, then settle in for a **massage** at the well-advertised **Baba Health and Massage Centre** in Rishikesh, 100m down the first right after the Chandrabhaga River. You can enjoy an Ayurvedic, Swedish, Thai, or relaxation full-body massage (they even massage your ears) in a dark, cool room. (☎ 2433339. Open daily 7am-10pm. Rs250 per session except Thai Rs350.) They also teach massage, either a basic, 1-week course (Rs3000) or 12-week Ayurvedic course (Rs5500). Lodging is an extra Rs50 per day.

🔌 DAYTRIP FROM RISHIKESH

NEEL KANTH MAHADEV. The trip to the temple at Neel Kanth Mahadev makes another good day-hike. The place is so popular with pilgrims bearing milk, *ghee*, and Ganga water that the *linga* has been eroded so that it is now just a few inches tall. The jungle trail along the way, inhabited by wild elephants, is what really makes the hike worthwhile. Go early (5am) since it's a 4-5hr. climb with no stops, and the temple is more likely to be peaceful early in the day. Jeeps leave for the trailhead from the Chotiwala Hotel near the taxi stand between Lakshmanjhula and Ramjhula on the opposite side of the river from Rishikesh (12km; round-trip Rs80). Regular jeeps return to Rishikesh.

GARHWAL PILGRIMAGES AND TREKS

Gurus, *sadhus*, and *sants* have been coming to meditate among the snow-capped mountains of Garhwal and Kumaon for centuries. Until the 1960s, just getting here was enough to test a person's faith. The northern pilgrimage sites could only be reached by foot from the plains, but new roads have made them more accessible. Since that time, a steady stream of package-tour pilgrims has made the peaceful isolation of the sites a distant memory. However, for true believers, the pilgrimage experience is suffused with a holiness that even diesel, mud, and commercialization cannot spoil.

The temples and many of the towns at the pilgrimage sites are open from May to November, though it is dangerous to go during the monsoons, as frequent landslides and heavy rains often render the roads impassable. Rattling, non-A/C local buses and overcrowded shared jeeps are the only things that make the journey up the narrow roads from Rishikesh or Uttarkashi. Between pilgrimage sites and towns off the established bus routes, you might find buses or shared jeeps going your way, if you're lucky. If not, you will have to either book a package tour or hire a taxi from one of the major cities. Most *dharamsalas* do not welcome foreigners, although this is slowly changing—you'd be well-advised to book a guest house room during high season (May-June) at least a month in advance.

UTTARKASHI उत्तरकाशी   ☎ 01374

This busy town, on the banks of the Bhagirathi River, is the administrative center of the Uttarkashi District, as well as the last place to stock up on supplies before heading out for a trek. Despite its recent commercial development, Uttarkashi has retained its small town feel, making it as much a destination as a pit stop. Temples line the river and trekking paths cover the hills.

TRANSPORTATION. Uttarkashi is also a major transportation hub for the pilgrimage sites to the north. **Buses** head to: **Barkot** (for Yamnotri: 3hr., every hr. 5:30am-3pm, Rs50); **Gangotri** (4hr., every hr. 5am-3pm, Rs60) via **Bhatwari** (for treks to Sahasratal and Kedarnath, 1hr., Rs15); **Gaurikund** (9hr., 4:30am, Rs145); and **Rishikesh** (6hr., every hr. 5am-1pm, Rs90). Morning **taxis** to Rishikesh wait at the bus stand (Rs1200 per car).

ORIENTATION AND PRACTICAL INFORMATION. Most visitors arrive at the **bus stand**, on the left bank of the river, smack in the middle of the shops and services. The road splits at the end of the **Main Bazaar** and to the left is **Gangotri Road.** The right bank of the river is mostly residential. The **GMVN tourist office,** where Gangotri Rd. meets the Main Bazaar, provides little help for trekking. Instead, try **Mountain Support Trekking** (☎ 222419), about 10min. past the bus stand along Gangotri Rd., opposite the Alpine Public School. The office supplies area guides for Rs400 per day or organizes trekking trips of all lengths for Rs1400-1600 per day per person. The Main Bazaar, extending to the right of the bus stand, primarily has electronics stores, tailors, and fruit stands. There is **no currency exchange** available, so be sure to plan ahead in Rishikesh or another city. The **police roost** is on Gangotri Rd., 15min. from the bus station, on the right. The 24hr. emergency **District Hospital** (☎ 222467) is off Gangotri Rd. Take the first right fork, 300m past the bus stand, and follow the road around; turn left at the chowk. The **Penguin Cyber Space,** 3min. into the Main Bazaar from the bus stand, offers Internet for Rs40 per hr. Open daily 9:30am-9pm. Uttarkashi's **Post Office** is immediately next to the river; turn right at the end of the bazaar and it is at the end of the road on the right. Open M-F 10am-5pm, Sa 10am-2pm. **Postal Code: 249193.**

ACCOMMODATIONS. For visitors who aren't just passing through Uttarkashi, the **Monal Guest House ❷,** 2km outside of town, is the most relaxing retreat. The rooms in this converted house open up onto terraces overlooking the river below, and the kitchen can be rented for extended stays (Rs300-500). The

THE BIG SPLURGE

MEET THE MOUNTAIN

Trekking in the Himalayas can be difficult. If you're serious about tackling the big peaks, you can hone your skills at the **Nehru Institute of Mountaineering (NIM)** in Uttarkashi.

The forest-covered hills above the Bhagirathi River is the ideal setting for perfecting the skills to scale the world's highest peaks. Courses are offered in Basic Mountaineering (28 days), Advanced Mountaineering (28 days), and Adventure Courses (15 days). Trainees are taught by mountaineering experts, including military officers and forestry professionals. The late Tenzing Norgay, who summited Everest with Sir Hillary in 1953, was associated with the school. Campus amenities include housing, a gym, and an extensive mountaineering library. The Himalayan peaks loom over the training ground, beckoning students.

A course in mountaineering would not be complete without practice outdoors, and there is ample opportunity for this in northern Garhwal. Practice trips not only introduce first-timers to the sport, but to the gorgeous Indian mountain-scape, as well.

Nehru Institute of Mountaineering (☎ 01374 222123, 224663; www.nimindia.com). Mountaineering courses for foreigners US$500, adventure courses US$250. Contact Principal Lieutenant Colonel A. Abbey.

owner is a trained guide who can provide information on undisturbed trekking routes. (☎ 222270. Doubles Rs250-450; triples Rs400-550; call for free pick-up from town.) The **Hotel Shivananda** ❸, at the bus stand, is clean, quiet, and convenient for late arrivals or early departures. (Doubles with attached bath May-June Rs400-600; all other months Rs200-400.) Next to Hotel Shivananda, **Bhandari Hotel** ❶ offers more room variety and a lobby restaurant. (Dorms Rs40 per bed; singles Rs75-125; doubles Rs250-400.) **GMVN** ❶, past the hospital, near the river, has 6-bed dorms and clean rooms with hot water. (☎ 222271. May-June dorms Rs110, doubles Rs275-950; July-Oct. Rs100/Rs200-700; Nov.-Apr. Rs60/Rs140-480. Book one month in advance for May, June, and Sept.)

YAMNOTRI यमनोत्री

The source of the Yamuna River and the first stop on the Garhwal pilgrimage circuit, Yamnotri attracts around 1500 pilgrims per day during the tourist season. Yamnotri, whether or not it qualifies as a town, consists of the two temples devoted to the goddess Yamuna and the river bearing her name, the hot springs, and the *dhabas* lining the trail up to the temples. The original structure was built by Rani Gularia of Jaipur during the 19th century but was soon worn down by heavy snowfall. The elements continue to erode away at the temple that took the place of the original, making it essential to rebuild the structure every few years. The temple's architecture is not special—just a slapdash construction with dressed-up concrete walls and a corrugated metal roof. It is open from May to Nov., after which the image is carried to Kharsoli, a village opposite Janki Chatti.

⬛ TRANSPORTATION. Yamnotri is accessible only by a 14km **trek** from the town of **Hanuman Chatti** (2134m) or by a **shared jeep** ride on unkept roads to Janki Chatti (2575m), 8km past Hanuman Chatti, and then a 6km trek. To reach Hanuman Chatti, either take a bus directly from Rishikesh (209km) or take a bus from Uttarkashi to Barkot (84km, Rs50). From Barkot, shared jeep taxis go to Hanuman Chatti (Rs25 per seat) and Janki Chatti (Rs45 per seat). They leave only when full (10 people), so be prepared to wait.

⬛ PRACTICAL INFORMATION. There are **police** posts in Janki Chatti and Hanuman Chatti, as well as a seasonal one in Yamnotri. A small **pharmacy** sells the basics in Hanuman Chatti, while there are **clinics** in both Hanuman Chatti's and Janki Chatti's main markets. Janki Chatti's clinic is only open

May-Oct. The only **public phone** close to Yamnotri is in Janki Chatti's Hotel Arvina Annex. A year-round **post office** is in Hanuman Chatti's main market. **Postal Code:** 249141.

⌂ ACCOMMODATIONS. here are GMVN lodges at Barkot ❷ (☎013752 24236; May-June doubles Rs350-550, July-Oct. Rs280-450, Nov.-Apr. Rs180-300); Hanuman Chatti ❶ (May-June dorms Rs130, rooms Rs700; July-Nov. and Apr. Rs100/Rs560); and Janki Chatti ❷ (May-June dorms Rs150, rooms Rs380-700; July-Nov. and Apr. Rs120/Rs325-525. Closed rest of year). Reservations can be made through the Rishikesh GMVN office. During the pilgrimage season, many of these accommodations are fully booked for package tours operated by GMVN. At this time, Barkot is most likely to have open rooms, following a night there with early morning transport to Hanuman Chatti. There are also private lodges in Janki Chatti (Rs50-350 per room), but quality varies drastically from no electricity or water to attached bath with bucket showers.

⊠ TREK FROM HANUMAN CHATTI TO YAMNOTRI. As the road from Barkot comes into Hanuman Chatti, it splits—the right fork is the trail and road to Yamnotri via Janki Chatti. For the first several kilometers it moves up the right side of the Yamuna Valley on a ridge above the river. The slope is gentle until the road quickly switchbacks, turning right with the river. A slight decline leads to the outpost of **Phool Chatti** and a small bridge to the left side of the valley. **Janki Chatti** is 2km further up the valley where the road ends at the shared jeep taxi stand on the town's doorstep. If you are trekking from Hanuman Chatti to Janki Chatti (8km, 3½ hr.), leave early as there is no shade or cool drink stands.

At the taxi stand, the trail to Yamnotri turns into a paved sidewalk through Janki Chatti, where food and drinks are readily available. Although its pavement ends on the other side of town, the trail gets steeper and rockier for a kilometer. Just after it levels off, a teahouse forces the trail to fork around it—both forks will keep you on track. For the last 3km, the still rocky trail gets steeper, crossing a small footbridge, and starts to switchback in order to gain the height of the temple. Shady spots are few and far between.

The final approach is slightly downhill, delivering trekkers to the temples and their surrounding *dhabas* nestled at the base of small rapids (6km, 2hr.). The temples are on the far side, uphill from the hot springs, and stand next to each other. On the right is the **Yamuna Mouth Temple,** spouting hot water and

THE HIDDEN DEAL

WARM WATER WELCOME

For those who live high in the Himalayas, hot running water is not to be taken for granted. While residents of northern Garhwal may be accustomed to bathing under chilly conditions, cold bucket showers can rattle both the teeth and nerves of visitors. Fortunately, the goddess Yamuna has an alternative for those apprehensive about shivery showers and it's free to those who worship at her temple: the Yamnotri hot springs.

Located just below the twin temples at Yamnotri, the same hot water that springs forth and is worshipped at Yamuna Mouth Temple is collected and channeled to a waiting cement pool. Here, all visitors to Yamnotri are welcome to dive, soak, or float their way clean as the steam curls into the cold mountain air. Changing rooms are provided for both sexes and all that is asked of the bather is that he or she wear appropriate attire-boxers or shorts for men and opaque pants and shirts for women. Arrive early to beat the 10am crowd who makes the journey on horseback.

So if your muscles ache from pounding the trekking pavement and cold bucket showers have made you gasp on one too many mornings, go warm both body and spirit at the Yamnotri hot springs. The only hard part will be maintaining that squeaky-clean feeling for the 14km trek back to Hanuman Chatti.

steam into the air even as offerings are placed before it. On the left is the temple to Yamuna herself, the daughter of the sun. Visitors to the temple bring rice and potatoes wrapped in muslin to be boiled in the natural hot springs and then left at the feet of the statue. Both the river and the hot springs are just below the temples and are open for bathing. Even if you didn't bring rice or potatoes, the *pujari* are more than happy to perform the *puja*. Do not heed to their insistence that a minimum Rs500 donation is required; Rs10-20 is enough.

🔌 **RETURNING FROM YAMNOTRI.** The return trip to Janki Chatti is roughly the same length (1½hr.) because of the trail's rockiness. Janki Chatti to Hanuman Chatti (2hr.) is faster, but should not be done in the afternoon heat. To get back to Uttarkashi and the rest of Garhwal, first take a shared jeep taxi to Barkot (Rs25). From there, buses run frequently to Dharasu Band (Rs35) where buses to Uttarkashi (Rs20) are available.

GANGOTRI गंगोत्री ☎ 013772

After Bhatwari, the road from Uttarkashi narrows and the surrounding mountains become more severe, until the shimmering slopes of **Mt. Sudarshan** (6500m) finally come into view, towering above the small town of Gangotri. At an altitude of 3140m, Gangotri (sometimes called Bhagirathi), 98km northeast of Uttarkashi, is a major center for *sadhus* from all over India. It is here that the goddess Ganga made her descent from heaven. Shiva sat on a *linga*, visible during times of low water below the Gaurikund waterfall, and cushioned her fall with his hair. It was also here that Raja Bhagiratha worshipped Shiva at the sacred stone **Bhagiratha Shilla.** The present **temple,** near Bhagiratha's stone, was built by the Gorkha commander Amar Singh Thapa in the early 18th century as a replacement for an older structure. The temple is open only from May to Nov. because of heavy winter snowfall. Steps lead down to the *ghat*, where pilgrims and other visitors bathe. The sheer beauty of Gangotri's surrounding hills is enough to draw many visitors. However, there are also treks in the area, including one to Gaumukh, the melting glacier from which the Ganga flows.

🚍 **TRANSPORTATION.** To get to Gangotri, take a **bus** or a **shared taxi** from Uttarkashi (see p. 659). From the Gangotri bus stand, **buses** run to: Gaunikund for Kedarnath (18hr., 8am, Rs205); Hanuman Chatti (12hr., 9am, Rs110); Haridwar (11½hr., 5 and 7am, Rs165); Rishikesh (11hr., 5 and 6am, Rs150); and Uttarkashi (5hr., every hr. 5am-3pm, Rs60).

🔲🔢 **ORIENTATION AND PRACTICAL INFORMATION.** Gangotri is located at the juncture of the **Bhagirathi** (called the Ganga further south) and the **Kedar Ganga** rivers, which come from the Gaumukh and the Kedar Tal respectively. The town is situated on the banks of both rivers, as well as the spit of land between them, connected by no less than three bridges. From the bus stand, the **Main Bazaar** extends up the valley to the **Ganga Maa temple.** A bridge from the **bus stand** arches over the Bhagirathi (the name of the river after the two merge) to the bank where most ashrams and accommodations are found. Restaurants are in the bazaar.

Tourist Information: Most young men in the town would list guide as their profession. Since there is no official tourist office, get several opinions before acting and try to get references when hiring a guide. The only, and therefore best, map of Gangotri is hand-painted on the outside wall of the **GMVN reception office** near the Gaurikund.

Markets: The **Main Bazaar** runs between the bus stand and the Ganga Maa temple. Little else is sold beside the makings of temple offerings and woolen outer layers for the unprepared.

Police: Building is just below the bus stand.

Hospital: Across the Bhagirathi from the Ganga Maa *ghat*. Treatment Rs2. Open daily May-Oct. 8am-2pm.

Post Office: Toward the bus stand from the hospital. Open May-Oct. M-Sa 6-10am and 4-6pm. **Postal Code:** 249135.

🛏 🍴 ACCOMMODATIONS AND FOOD. The **GMVN Guest House ❶,** across the bridge from the bus stand, is extremely clean and friendly, with one of the better restaurants in town. Hot water Rs10 per bucket. (May-June dorms Rs140; rooms Rs380-880; July-Nov. and Apr. Rs100/Rs290-650.) Most ashrams in Gangotri do not accept foreigners, but the **Yoga Nilutan,** toward the Ganga Maa temple from GMVN, does. There is the choice between single rooms or double cottages (May-June Rs200 per person; rest of year Rs100 per person; prices include food). The yoga hall is also available for use, and classes are occasionally offered. For simpler living, try the **Krishna Ashram** on the spit of land between the two rivers. Unadorned rooms and a meditative atmosphere provide relaxation and excellent views of the *ghat*. Payment by donation. If ashram food is too simple, the **Ganga Putra Restaurant ❶,** at the fork in the Main Bazaar, has plentiful biscuits and *thali* options.

📷 🥾 SIGHTS AND TREKS. Dedicated to the goddess Ganga, the Ganga Maa Temple at Gangotri is the place where she touched earth for the first time. In addition, legend says that the Pandavas performed the "Deva Yagna" here to atone the deaths of their kinsmen in the battle of *Mahabharata*. Most pilgrims actually pay more attention to the *ghat* located just below the temple, as it provides a spiritual place to bathe, wash clothes, and perform a ritual *puja*. The daily temple timings are: Mangalaarti 6am, Hawan 8am, Raj Bhog 9am, closed 2-3pm, Aarti 7:45pm, Raj Bhog 8:30pm, closed 9pm. Even those not familiar with the Hindu ceremonies can appreciate the temple's breathtaking setting and Himalayan backdrop. If bathing in and drinking from the Ganga aren't enough, the 17km (one-way) trek to Gaumukh (Cow's Mouth) will bring you to spot where the Bhagirathi emerges from the Gangotri glacier. Here the sacred Ganga is at its purest. It is also at its coldest, but that does not deter pilgrims from swimming in the waters. Although the trek is easy, it cannot be done round-trip in one day. There is a hotel 14km from Gangotri where most trekkers spend the night. The next day's trek is to Gaumukh

ON THE MENU

COMA TOAST

Hashish and tobacco, smoked through a chillum, are a big part of the daily intake of most sadhus, but the really hip holy men try something else.

A krait (an extremely poisonous snake) is rolled up between two unbaked rotis with its tail sticking out, and then shoved into the fire. When the *rotis* are fully baked, the sadhu removes the deadly sandwich from the fire and pulls at the snake's tail, ripping off the skin and bones. Then, preparing himself, he puts a jug of water by his side, takes two to three bites of the snake, and immediately goes into a coma.

Every 8-10hr. the sadhu wakes up to drink some water and take another bite, sending himself back into a poisoned stupor. The whole process lasts three to four days.

Warning: this requires 30 years of practice—don't try this at home, or anywhere else!

and then a return to Gangotri. A further destination is Tapovan, 6km past Gaumukh. A large field filled with wild flowers, it gives magnificent view of Shivling peak. The trail to Gaumukh starts to the right of the booking office at the bus stand. The other river that runs through Gangotri springs to life at the Kedar Tal (lake), 18km from Gangotri. Pictures and views of this impressively calm lake are graced with the Thalaysagar peak. The trek is very difficult but well worth the effort. Hire a guide from Gangotri (Rs200-300 per day depending on who supplies the tent and sleeping bags) and carry plenty of supplies since there are only awe-inspiring views available along the way. The trail to Kedar Tal starts as a paved one, 20m toward Ganga Maa from the GMVN.

KEDARNATH केदारनाथ ☎01364

One of the chosen abodes of Shiva, Kedarnath is home to one of the 12 *jyotirlingas* in India. The **temple** here was constructed thousands of years ago when the Pandavas came to serve their penance to Shiva. Viewing the Pandavas as sinners for having killed their own kin in battle, Shiva disguised himself as a bull to escape their notice. When the Pandavas discovered the ruse, Shiva turned to stone and tried to escape into the ground. But as his front half vanished, Bhima, one of the Pandavas, managed to catch Shiva's rocky rear end. Pleased with the Pandavas' diligence, Shiva appeared in his true form and forgave them. The back half of that stone form is now worshipped at Kedarnath. Shiva's front half broke off and re-emerged in Nepal, where it is venerated at the **Pashupati Temple** (see p. 826). Other parts of Shiva turned up at Tungnath (arm), Rudrandath (face), Madhyamaheshwar (navel), and Kapleshwar (locks); together, they form the **Panch Kedar** (Five Fields) pilgrimage circuit.

Kedarnath remains open from May until late October and serves as the starting point for many beautiful treks. **Buses** take pilgrims as far as Gaurikund, 216km from Rishikesh (around Rs100). From there, it's a steep 14km, 4-6hr. trek. **Horses** are also available for hire. Standard hotel rates are Rs200-300 for a single and Rs400-600 for a double in season. **GMVN ❷** has two guest houses in Kedarnath, one on your left as you approach the town (☎27210) and a second across the river and below the hillside (☎27228. Apr. 16-June: dorms Rs150, rooms Rs350-800. July- Nov. 15: Rs100/250-600. Closed rest of the year.) Many ashrams will not accept foreigners, but the **Bharat Seva Ashram** and the **Temple Committee** will.

BADRINATH बद्रिनाथ ☎01381

The temple town of Badrinath (3133m) is the northernmost compass-point (*dham*) of India's sacred geography. Once the abode of Lord Vishnu, Badrinath is the most famous of Garhwal's Hindu pilgrimage sites, attracting the faithful during its summer season, May-Nov. Badrinath sits alongside the Alaknanda River, 305km from Rishikesh, not far from the Tibetan border, and it serves as one of the Ganga's twelve water channels. Its accessibility by road attracts growing numbers of pilgrims and tourists every year, who forego the austerity of a walking pilgrimage (once required) in favor of a harrowing bus ride. Badrinath can be reached by **bus** from Rishikesh via Srinagar, Rudraprayag, and Joshimath (12hr., 5 per day 3:30-6am, Rs170). Buses also come here directly from Kedarnath (Rs40).

The colorful Badrinath **temple** has a long main entrance gate (the Singh Dwara) that worshippers must pass through for *darshan* of the meter-high Badrivishal image inside. Probably a Buddhist temple in ancient times, the current temple is an unusual mixture of Buddhist and Hindu styles. Before visiting the temple, worshippers bathe in the **Tapt Kund** hot spring, often in preparation for a dip into the icy waters of the Alaknanda. Very basic accommodations are available at numerous *dharamsalas,* the **Garhwal Hotel,** or the **GVMN hotel ❶** (☎ 22338. May-June dorms Rs50, rooms Rs300-1000; July-Aug. Rs150-550; Sept.-Oct. Rs50/Rs225-750. Reserve 1 month in advance Apr.-July.)

JOSHIMATH जोशीमथ   ☎ 01389

A stopping point for those on their way to Auli, the Valley of Flowers, Hemkund Saheb, and other local treks, Joshimath's tourist industry has blossomed in recent years. It is now possible to find cheaper, cleaner places to eat and sleep here than elsewhere in the region. Nestled into a mountain overlooking a roaring river and snow-capped peaks, Joshimath itself is an attractive destination for those seeking peace and quiet in the hills.

From Rishikesh, Joshimath is accessible via Badrinath-bound **buses** (11hr., 5 per day 3:30-6am, Rs152). From Almora, take a bus to Karnaprayag (7hr., 8am, Rs90) and then a jeep to Chamoli (Rs20) and a jeep from Chamoli to Joshimath (Rs35).

Transport drops you off near a fork in the road; the **upper (right) fork** leads to **Upper Bazaar,** which has most of the town's good hotels, restaurants, and supply shops. Buy as much food, water, and other essential goods as you can in Joshimath, because further along you will have to pay up to 2-3 times the maximum retail price for these items. For trekking and camping gear and guides, try **Eskimo Adventures,** in the middle of Upper Bazaar, across from Hotel Sriram.

Hotels in Joshimath generally charge Rs300-500 for clean rooms with good views. **Hotel Mount Elephant ❶,** in Upper Bazaar, has a tidy six-bed dorm and private rooms. (☎ 222742. Dorms Rs100; doubles start at Rs250.) **GMVN ❶** operates two Rest Houses in Upper Bazaar (☎ 222118 and 222226. May-June dorms Rs130, rooms Rs300-700. July-Oct. Rs100/Rs275-530. Nov.-Apr. Rs70/Rs150-350.) For food, **Maharaja Restaurant ❶** in Upper Bazaar has great, cheap chow mein (Rs20). The restaurant in **Hotel Sriram ❷** offers the only pizza in town (Rs50).

AULI औली   ☎ 01389

Skiing? In India? What next? Home to 20km of seasonal (Jan.-Mar.) ski slopes, Auli has been the winter sports capital of UP since the 1970s, when the government decided that ski resorts were more fun than military training camps. **Equipment** can be rented (half-day Rs200, full-day Rs250) at the GMVN. The spectacular scenery (including views of Nanda Devi, which at 7820m is the second-highest peak in India) keeps Auli open in the summer for **cable car rides** up from Joshimath (4km, Rs300 round-trip). Alternatively, you can take a jeep up the muddy 14km road (40 min., Rs300-350 per car round-trip). There is a **GMVN lodge ❶** in Auli. (☎ 223208. Nov.-June dorms Rs80, rooms Rs840-1200. July-Oct. Rs60/760-950.) Rooms are also available at Joshimath (see above), where you can take the ski lift to Auli.

VALLEY OF FLOWERS फूलों की घाटी

One of the most awe-inspiring sights in all of India, this alpine valley hidden high in the Himalayas has been attracting pilgrims and nature lovers since its "discovery" in 1937 by Frank Smith. Ten kilometers long, two kilometers wide, and enclosed by snow-capped peaks, the valley is cut in two by the Pushpawati River. Snow covers the valley floor from November to late May, when the area is inaccessible to visitors. In late May, the snow begins to melt, and the first flowers start to bloom in early June. The valley is usually opened to visitors in mid-June. Peak bloom is in late July and August, but it's worth it to come in late June or early July, when there are far fewer tourists, and you might even have the valley to yourself. There are over 500 species of flowers in the valley; many of them, such as the Himalayan blue poppy, are extremely rare. When the valley was first explored in the late 1930s, the plant species count was 5000. The serious ecological decline of the area has prompted the government to declare it a National Park; camping and cooking are prohibited except in Ghangharia. Be aware that the trail leading into the Valley of Flowers is narrow, muddy, and requires crossing streams and steep patches of ice. **Do not attempt this trek during or immediately after rainfall.** From Joshimath, take a shared jeep (Rs20) to Govind Ghat, 14km away. Leaving early in the morning, around 5 or 6am, will help you to manage the 14km uphill trek from Govind Ghat to Ghangharia. The walk takes about 5-7hr., but you can also ride a horse up (3hr., Rs300).

In Ghangharia, finding a place to stay can be a frustrating experience as some of the hotels in town are dirty, overcrowded, and overpriced. If you stay at a private hotel, you can expect to pay Rs600 for a cramped cell with boards for mattresses. Power can be sporadic and running water may be hard to find. Hot water is free at GMVN, but costs Rs10-15 elsewhere. Rooms at the **GMVN Tourist Rest House ❶** are, again, overpriced (Rs700-950), but dorms (Rs140) are reasonable. Reserve at least a week in advance through **GMVN Yatra Pilgrimage Tours and Accommodations Office** in Kailash Gate, Rishikesh (☎ 2431793).

Ghangharia's tourism oligopoly is even more blatant when it comes to food. The **restaurants ❷** in town have almost identical menus (even the same typos!) with a price disparity of Rs5 here and there. All serve up similar, bland Punjabi dishes (Rs35-55). It's even difficult to make your own meals, because scarcely available foodstuffs (such as bread, jam, and biscuits) cost 2-3 times what they do in Joshimath. The tough living in Ghangharia is sure to make you take your time on the trek to avoid returning to town too soon.

After spending the night in Ghangharia, set off the next morning on the Valley of Flowers trail (it branches off to the left after you pass the stream) and pay the hefty admission fee at the gate (Rs350 for foreigners, Rs30 for Indian citizens). After a 1½hr. climb, you will emerge into the splendor of the valley. Have a picnic, walk around, or just sit and stare at the 360 degrees of idyllic beauty, before returning to Ghangharia for the night.

HEMKUND SAHEB
From miles around, Sikhs of all ages, from 8 years to 80, make the pilgrimage to Hemkund Saheb, the temple that sits atop a 4500m mountain 5km from Ghangharia. On the Valley of Flowers trek, you'll be sharing paths and hotels with the thousands of Sikhs who make the 4hr. pilgrimage between June and August of each year to witness waterfalls, mountain views, and a beautiful (but freezing cold!) mountaintop lake in which the Sikhs bathe. The trip up and down from Ghangharia is doable in a day, but for those who weather the climb, there is also a 1000-bed *gurudwara* at the top where you can eat or snooze for free (donation suggested). Foreigners are allowed.

CORBETT NATIONAL PARK कोरबट ☎ 05947

Corbett was India's first national park, founded in 1936 and named for James Corbett (1875-1955), a British gentleman renowned for his ability to kill tigers and other large animals with a shotgun. Corbett gave up killing tigers for kicks during the 1920s but was still called upon to shoot tigers and leopards from time to time when they threatened human lives. He became famous for his photographs of tigers and for the books he wrote, including *The Man-Eaters of Kumaon.*

In 1973, the Indian government, with support from the World Wildlife Fund, launched "Project Tiger" in an effort to save the country's dwindling population of tigers. The 1288 sq. km Corbett Tiger Reserve, comprised of the national park and the adjoining Sonandi Wildlife Sanctuary and Reserve Forest, was the first target area of this ambitious project. The 2001 census recorded 138 tigers in the reserve. Sightings of the big cats are frequent, but even if you don't get that lucky, Corbett's other wildlife will make sure you don't leave entirely disappointed. The endangered gharial crocodile, herds of wild elephant, leopards, deer, over 500 species of birds, and monkeys coexist peacefully in the same habitat. The park's landscape, particularly around Dhikala, is as much a treasure as its wildlife. By not feeding the animals, disposing of cigarettes and other refuse in designated trash receptacles, and keeping noise to a minimum you are helping to preserve the park's delicate ecosystem. Since attacks by tigers are not unheard of, never walk outside of the camp perimeter, and be careful at night.

TRANSPORTATION

The main hub for visiting Corbett is **Ramnagar,** accessible from Delhi by both bus (7hr., numerous 6am-9pm, Rs120) and train (#*5013A*, 6hr., 10:45pm). The **train station** is about 2km from the park office; just follow the road straight, bearing left through the bazaar. To **Delhi** (6hr., 9pm, Rs135); **Varanasi** (19hr., 9pm, Rs297). The government **bus stand,** near the park office, spills out onto the street, as queues of private buses. To **Delhi** (7hr., many 9am-8pm, Rs120); **Nainital** (3hr., 6am-1:30pm, Rs35). If your next stop is **Ranikhet,** get off the bus at Dhangarhi Gate and wait by the side of the road for buses headed north (4hr., last bus 2pm, Rs47). Private buses also run from below the bazaar to Nainital and **Moradabad** (4hr., 6am-8pm, Rs38), where there are many more road and rail connections. You can also hire **jeeps** from in front of the Park Office for Rs4.50-6.50 per km.

ORIENTATION AND PRACTICAL INFORMATION

Corbett has five **zones** accessible to tourists. These zones are exclusive of each other, which means that you have to exit the park and pay another hefty fee to enter another zone. **Dhikala** is the most scenic and the most popular, offering a range of accommodations, two restaurants, film screening facilities, and a library. **Bijrani** has the most tiger sightings, a smaller tourist complex than Dhikala in more desolate surroundings, and sees the most traffic from jeeps on daytrips. The other three zones feature greater solitude but fewer services (there are no restaurants and no electricity). **Jhirna** is an exceptionally beautiful area of the park on the edge of the restricted core zone; **Lohachavr** is the best place for birding; those looking for a more rugged experience and close encounters with wild elephants should head to **Halduparao.** Jhirna is accessible to visitors year-round, but the rest of the park closes during the monsoon (mid-June to mid-Nov.). The wildlife viewing is better during the summer (Mar.-June) than the winter (Nov.-Mar.), because the heat keeps animals predictably close to the shade and water.

The park has 8 entrance gates, but most visitors pass through one of the major portals. Here, you have to cough up the park entry fees (Rs200 for your vehicle and driver, plus an individual entry fee that depends on the gate), and a guide fee (Rs100). If you are going on a jeep safari, **Amdanada Gate,** 2km north of Ramnagar, is the entrance for Bijrani. (Entry fees of either Rs200 for 4hr. or Rs400 for 3 days. Open 6am-6pm; in winter 6:30am-5pm. Last entry 30min. before gate closing.) **Dhangarhi Gate,** 16km north of Ramnagar, is the entrance to Dhikala. (Entry fee Rs450 for 4 days. Open 6am-6pm; in winter 6:30am-5pm. Last entry 1½hr. before closing.) Before leaving Dhikala, all visitors must obtain a free **clearance certificate,** which should be turned in at Dhangarhi upon leaving.

Visitors must stop at the **Park Office,** opposite the Ramnagar bus stand, to secure a permit and to reserve and pay for accommodation within the park. (☎251489. Open daily 8am-noon and 1-4:30pm.) Prospective passengers for the two conducted bus trips can also sign up here: a safari and transport to and from Bijrani (4hr., 8am, Rs1200). There are kiosks outside the gates that sell snacks and water, but Ramnagar is your last chance to stock up on more essential items like toilet paper before trekking off into the great unknown. There is no currency exchange.

🏠 🍴 ACCOMMODATIONS AND FOOD

RAMNAGAR

Most of the cheaper accommodation in Ramnagar is in the vicinity of Russell Chowk. More expensive cottage and tent resorts are outside town, between Amdanada and Dhangar. Do not be fooled by the government **Tourist Rest House ❶,** next to the park office; even ignoring the noisy gas and bus stations next door, the rooms are way overpriced (☎251225. Dorms Rs60; doubles Rs400-800). The main road and bazaar have clean rooms with attached baths, a couple come with A/C at the same price and the meals are good (☎251277. Doubles Rs150). **Hotel Rameswaram ❶,** in the middle of Tesil Chowk, has modest rooms with high ceilings and attached baths (☎252664. Doubles Rs150). **Tiger Camp ❺,** 10km along the Ramnagar-Dhangari road, has luxury tents and cottages in a nice garden (☎284101. Tents Rs900-1000; cottages Rs2300-2750 including excellent meals). The few restaurants with standard Indo-Sino-Continental fare fall on the block past the bus station from the rest house. **Govind Restaurant ❷** serves excellent food behind its sweets shop facade. The friendly owner can show you his captivating notebooks on the park, penned by diners. (Banana pancakes Rs35; *lassis* Rs20. Open daily 8am-10pm.) Food is expensive inside the park, so stock up before you get here.

IN THE PARK

Lodging inside the park, which must be reserved through the Park Office in Ramnagar, is exorbitantly expensive. Although it affords the most immersive experience, the high cost—on top of already hefty entry fees—discourages some foreign tourists. If you decide to ante up, call ahead: there is often no same-day vacancy, since reservations with full payment by bank draft need to be made up to 1 month in advance. Visitors wishing to extend their stay may be told to wait until evening to see whether space is available, so it is possible you'll get stuck inside the park without accommodation, in which case you will have to hire a jeep out before the curfew. The only tourist complexes with (overpriced) canteens are at Dhikala, Gairal, and Bijrani. Dhikala has log-hut **dorms, tourist "hutments"** (3 beds), and **cabins** (2 or 3 beds) ❷. The log hut, just one step away from the great outdoors, has austere bunks, stacked three-high and 12 to a room, and lockers but no locks or bedding. Squat toilets and showers are in a separate building. Tourist hutments and cabins have linen and attached bathrooms. Bijrani has a dismal 12-bedded dormitory and a concrete-pretending-to-be-adobe forest rest house with 2 single and 4 double rooms. Gairal has hutments and doubles. (Check-out 11am. Log hut dorm bunks Rs200; tourist hutment Rs1200; cabin Rs1200-2000.) The other **Forest Rest Houses ❶** dotted around the tiger reserve tend to have nothing much to offer except for good old-fashioned peace and quiet. Old British **hunting lodges ❹** come complete with fireplaces, carpets, and attached bathrooms. Cooking utensils and firewood are provided, but other essentials must be brought from Ramnagar. (Lodges Rs600/1200/2000.) There is also a Rs100 "housekeeping fee."

◪ THE PARK

There *are* ways to get down and dirty in Corbett without breaking any rules. If you are in **Dhikala,** the best option is an **elephant ride.** For Rs100, four passengers per beast (not counting children) get bumped, shrugged, and shouldered across the prairie and through the jungle. This is the best way to try to see a tiger or to come close to wild elephants and other animals (not to mention what seems to delight tourists most: the acres of 3m-high cannabis plants). Besides the 6 elephants at Dhikala, rides are also available at **Gairal, Bijrani, Sarapduli, and Jhirna.** Sign up for a ride at the station office at least a day in advance during the high season. Tours depart at sunrise and sunset, approximately 6am and 4pm in the summer and 7am and 3pm in the winter. (2hr.; Rs250, Rs200 for students.) Sightings are equally likely at either time, but the weather is cooler in the morning. If you do spot a tiger, your guide will expect a "sighting" tip (Rs50-100).

Bijrani is the only place you can go on an elephant ride without staying in the park; however, there is always the risk that after paying your entry fees you may reach the rest house only to find that guests have taken all the spots (they have first priority). Then you might as well go on a **jeep safari,** the preferred choice of visitors who do not intend to stay inside the park. Up to eight can share the jeep with the mandatory guide. This mode of transport covers more ground than the elephants, but is also loud enough to startle much of the wildlife. Jeeps can be hired from Dhangari and the park office in Ramnagar (it is occasionally possible to get stuck in Dhikala waiting for a jeep). Prices are highly negotiable so bargaining between several drivers will always pay off. *(The best times for jeep tours are 5-11am and 4-7pm. Rs400-700, plus Rs100 for a guide.)*

NAINITAL नैनीताल ☎ 05942

Splashed on the shores of an eye-shaped lake, Nainital offers something that most hill stations don't—more views of itself than of the distant Himalayan peaks. Most tourists are happy to relax in cafes and rowboats and let their gazes rest on the tower, the town's shimmering centerpiece. Originally conceived as a summer getaway by the British, Nainital is now beloved by the beleaguered masses of UP, who flock here during May and June to quell blazing temperatures on the plains. You may be better off avoiding Nainital during these times, as prices, noise levels, and crowd sizes rise astronomically. At other times, the spot is no less picturesque, even during the monsoon when the surrounding hills hem in low-flying clouds, forming a misty canopy over the town.

▮ TRANSPORTATION

Trains: The nearest station is in **Kathgodam,** 34km away. The **rail office,** next to the UP Roadways bus station, books tickets to **Delhi** (8½hr., 8:35pm). Book well in advance during high season. Arrangements can also be made with local travel agents, who can also provide a bus ticket to Kathgodam.

Buses: Buses arrive to and depart from the lakefront in **Tallital.** Schedules change frequently. To: **Almora** (3hr., 7am, Rs42); **Bhowali** (1hr., every 30min. 6am-6:30pm, Rs6); **Dehra Dun** (11hr.; 5:30, 6, 7am; Rs170; deluxe 6 and 8pm, Rs215); **Delhi** (9hr., 5 per day 5:30am-7pm, Rs152); **Kathgodam and Haldwani** (1½hr., every 30min. 5am-6:30pm, Rs25); **Ramnagar** (4½hr., 7am, Rs55); **Ranikhet** (3hr., 8am, Rs42). Many travel agencies on the Mall sell tickets for deluxe tourist buses to Dehra Dun (Rs350) and Delhi (Rs200, with A/C Rs325). The major regional transportation center with buses almost every hour to most mountain cities is **Bhowali.** Buses leave every 30min. from Haldwani to **Nainital** (6am-7pm). After 7pm, there are jeeps and taxis (Rs40 per person).

Local Transportation: Cycle-rickshaws charge Rs5 to drive the length of the Mall. Queues form at the ticket booths in Mallital and Tallital; prepayment required. Local **jeeps** and **taxi-vans** are available to go to other places at all times. During high-season, the Mall closes to motor vehicles and cycle-rickshaws from 6-9pm.

◼ ⁊ ORIENTATION AND PRACTICAL INFORMATION

Nainital is split into two major parts—**Tallital** on the southern end of the lake and **Mallital** on the northern end. These are connected by **the Mall,** which runs along the east side of the lake. Buses arrive at Tallital, at the southern tip of the lake. From here, it's a 15min. walk along the lake to Mallital. The main market, **Bara Bazaar,** is in Mallital. Most hotels and restaurants are on the Mall. **The Flats,** a common area used for football and field hockey, lies along the lake north of Mallital.

Tourist Office: The **KMVN Tourist Information Centre** (☎235656), in Tallital, next to the cycle-rickshaw booth, provides information about the town and region, and arranges day tours by taxi and bus to nearby towns and lakes, including one to Bhimtal, Nauku-chiatal, Sat Tal, and Hanumangarh (half-day, Rs90). Open daily 8am-9pm.

Currency Exchange: State Bank of India (☎235645), in Mallital, just beyond the Flats, cashes AmEx traveler's checks. Open M-F 10am-2pm, Sa 10am-noon.

Trekking Agencies: Many travel agents along the Mall advertise small-scale and local trekking packages. For more advanced trekking, **Snout Adventures and Rescue Unit** (☎231749; snoutadventure@rediffmail.com), can take you off the beaten path. They usually work with groups, but will accommodate individuals. Be prepared to pay through the nose—all-inclusive packages start at Rs1000 per person per day.

Market: Bara Bazaar, in Mallital, is a good place to stock up on locally-made Kumaoni candles and woolen goods. The **Tibetan Market,** in the western part of the bazaar, sells brand-name clothes (fake) and junk (real). Open M-Sa 9am-9pm.

Police: Mallital Station (☎235424), across from the rickshaw stand. **Tallital Station** (☎236470), next to the post office.

Pharmacy: Indra Pharmacy (☎235139), by the bus stand in Tallital, is well-stocked. Open M-Sa 7am-10pm, Su 7am-2pm. Mallital branch (☎235686), in Bara Bazaar. Open M-Sa 9am-9:30pm, Su 3-9:30pm.

Hospital/Medical Services: B. D. Pandey Hospital (☎235012), Mallital, just up from the State Bank of India. Open daily 8am-2pm. **Dr. D.P. Gangola** (☎235039), a physician at **Indra Pharmacy,** keeps hours in the Mallital (M-Sa 8am-8pm) and Tallital (M-Sa 10am-2pm) branches.

Internet: Connections are consistently slow and spotty. **Cyberia,** on the Mall near the Mallital rickshaw stand, is no exception, but you can surf the web (Rs35 per hr.) with butterscotch ice cream in hand (Rs10 per scoop). Open daily 8am-11pm.

Post Office: GPO, on the north side of Mallital, a few blocks up from the Mall's extension. **Postal Code:** 263001. In Tallital, facing the bus stop, or on the Mall near Mallital, next to the Grand Hotel. **Postal Code:** 263002.

⌐ ACCOMMODATIONS

During Nainital's high season (May-June and October), Indian tourists flood the town and hotel prices skyrocket. Accommodation is at least twice as expensive here as in other parts of Kumaon during this time, making a stay by the lake very costly. Listed prices are peak-season rates, except where noted; outside of May-June and Oct., expect a 25-75% drop. Most establishments along the Mall are quiet with beautiful views of the lake, though there are quieter and better views further uphill. Most have 10am check-out.

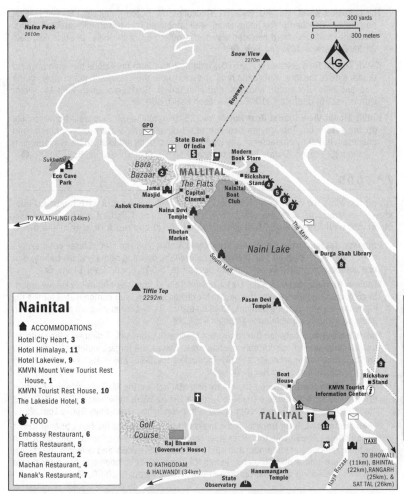

Nainital

🏠 ACCOMMODATIONS

Hotel City Heart, **3**
Hotel Himalaya, **11**
Hotel Lakeview, **9**
KMVN Mount View Tourist Rest House, **1**
KMVN Tourist Rest House, **10**
The Lakeside Hotel, **8**

🍴 FOOD

Embassy Restaurant, **6**
Flattis Restaurant, **5**
Green Restaurant, **2**
Machan Restaurant, **4**
Nanak's Restaurant, **7**

Hotel Lakeview (☎236489 or 235632; hotellakeview@rediffmail.com), Tallital, behind Hotel Mansarovar. Clean, spacious rooms with decorative photographs and paintings of the local scenery and wildlife. Balconies have superb views of the lake. Mr. and Mrs. Shah treat all their guests like family. Room service, laundry, TV and golf lessons on request. Doubles Rs550-900; suites Rs1800. ❹

Hotel City Heart (☎235228), near Mallital, on the Mall opposite the Nainital Boat Club. Spectacular views of the lake from every room, as well as a courteous and well-informed staff. Rooms are spacious and spotless, but are overshadowed by their shiny-tiled baths. Room service, clean bedding, and a rooftop restaurant with views of the entire lake. Doubles Rs800-1500. Off-season 50% discount. ❺

Hotel Himalaya (☎235258), Tallital, just up the hill from the bus station. Low-end place offers small, tidy rooms with squat toilets for the lower prices. Doubles Rs350-1000. ❸

The Lakeside Hotel, Mall Rd. (☎235220;alkahotel@vsnl.com), halfway between Mallital and Tallital. Polished place offers clean, well-appointed rooms with fully-outfitted baths. Pleasant verandas afford elevated views of a quiet part of the lake. Doubles Rs1300-2100. Off-season 40% discount. ❺

KMVN Tourist Rest House (☎235570), Tallital, 200m from the Tallital bus stand toward the far side of the lake. Above the road and away from the noise, with grand views of the lake and hills. Hot water, showers, and seat toilets. Restaurant open 7am-10:30pm. Dorms Rs100; doubles Rs1000. Off-season Rs80/600. ❶

KMVN Mount View Tourist Rest House (☎235400), Mallital, a 2km walk from the Mall up the extension. This government-run rest house is moderately-priced, clean, and uncontaminated by character of any kind. Only dorm beds are likely to be available during the high season. Dorms Rs100; doubles Rs675-1000. Off-season Rs375-800. ❶

FOOD

Along the Mall are countless clean and well-priced restaurants with beautiful lake views—restaurants at either end of town in Mallital and Tallital are generally less clean and well-frequented. Most restaurants have cheap outdoor seating—a must.

Embassy Restaurant, between the library and Mallital, on the Mall. Classy yet inexpensive restaurant is packed with hip young *dilliwallahs* downing *rajma* (kidney beans) and rice combo platters (Rs42) and cheap pizzas (Rs45-54). Open 10am-11pm. ❷

Machan Restaurant, Mall Rd., 100m toward Tallital from the Mallital rickshaw stand. Slightly upscale place serves the best meat dishes in town, and compensates for slightly higher prices with heaping portions. Chicken dishes Rs75-175; mushroom and spinach in garlic sauce Rs60; Szechuan vegetables Rs50. ❷

Flattis Restaurant, between the library and Mallital, on the Mall. A dimly-lit place with an unusually large and comfortable seating area. Serves the largest variety of Indian and Western food in the area. Pizza Rs60-75, sizzlers Rs80-95, *dosas* Rs30-40, *thalis*, and a homesick Tuscan salad Rs30. ❸

Nanak's Restaurant, between the library and Mallital, on the Mall. A wannabe Western fast-food place with burgers (Rs30-50), pizza (Rs70-125), milkshakes (Rs30-40), and mango sundaes (Rs90) in a room aglow with neon lights. Open daily 9am-11pm. ❸

Green Restaurant, Bara Bazaar, in the heart of Mallital; look for the large banner. Don't let the name deceive you–this diner-style eatery doesn't limit itself to just one color with veritable rainbows of streamers and lights decorating the walls and ceilings. The festive surroundings and a diverse menu (Indian/Chinese/Western/non-veg.) compensate for the cramped eating quarters. Chicken *masala* Rs65; pizzas Rs50-60. ❷

SIGHTS AND SCENERY

VIEWPOINTS. Any number of nearby hilltops and mountainside perches offer views of the city. If the clouds cooperate, you can sometimes see Himalayan peaks as far away as the Tibetan border. The best way to take in the views is to rent a **horse** from one of Mallital's stables (at the mouth of Mallital before Bara Bazaar) and clip-clop up to the top. Expect the ride—which runs up steep, loose-stone trails against the honking chaos of the oncoming traffic—to be difficult. *(Round-trip Rs150, with the guide jogging alongside your milk-white steed. Expect to pay more if you want to stop and enjoy the view for more than 1hr.)* But the easiest way to get a view of Nainital is to forsake horse and foot altogether and take the **ropeway** to **Snow View** (2270m). It leaves from a clearly marked building 30m up from the Mall in Mallital. Enjoy the 3min. in the gondola—it may be one of the smoothest rides you'll have in India.

The low-effort nature of this little excursion makes it extremely popular during high-season; book one to two days in advance, or try your luck in the morning at opening time (8am). The last cable car leaves Mallital at 6pm. The last car returns from Snow View at 7pm. *(Round-trip Rs65, with a 1hr. stop at the top. KMVN has a cottage at the top. Doubles Rs500-600.)*

Another popular viewpoint is **Naina Peak** (2610m), formerly known as Cheena Peak. Naina Peak is 6km away, roughly 1hr. by horse (Rs150) or 3hr. by foot. At the top is a snack shop and several places to sit and muse over the view. If the weather permits, you can get a fantastic view of Naina Lake and the city, not to mention the peaks of Garhwal, including Nanda Devi (7817m). You can either start from Mallital or take a taxi to Tonneleay on Kilbury Rd., and walk from there. **Land's End,** behind **Tiffin Top** (immediately west of the lake), affords views over the valley to the west.

NAINI LAKE. The town's pride and joy is the lake itself. If you want to get out into the middle of Parvati's emerald eye, **boats** are available for hire. *(Paddleboats Rs40-60 per hr.; boatman-guided rides Rs40-60; you will be overcharged if you don't bargain.)* You can rent **yachts** from the Nainital Boat Club (Rs80 per hr.). Another option is walking the perimeter. A **stroll along the Mall** becomes more peaceful from 6-9pm, when the road closes to traffic and an earsplitting chorus of bicycle bells and car horns no longer provides the dominant melody.

OTHER SIGHTS. The road heading west from Tallital leads to the colonial-era **Raj Bhawan** (Governor's House), an impressive castle-like mansion surrounded by an expansive lawn, from which you can view the UP Plains. The government of Uttaranchal now occupies part of the building, but most of it is open to visitors. *(Open 11am-1pm and 3-5pm, when KMVN guides conduct tours. Rs50. No pictures allowed.)* The **Raj Bhawan Golf Course** offers tight fairways and blind holes. It's also a perfect spot to catch sight of some local wildlife—everything from leopards to Himalayan blue whistling thrushes make their homes in the course's environs. *(Entry permit Rs50. Greens fees. Foreigners Rs1000, Indians Rs150-200. Caddy Rs150. Full set of clubs Rs100.)* Three kilometers along the road to Kathgodam is a small temple, **Hanumangarh,** home to a 6ft. bright-orange statue of Hanuman. Just beyond the temple is an state astronomical observatory. *(Open daily 7-9pm, slide show 2-4pm. Admission Rs15.)* In 1880, a landslide killed 151 people and wiped out public space. Today, the **Flats** are a a favorite hang-out of snake-charmers and musicians and are often busy with football and hockey games. In October, the **Autumn Festival** features sports competitions by day and music and dancing by night.

ENTERTAINMENT

With its cotton candy sellers and excited family crowds, Nainital may at times feel more like a carnival than a hill station; entertainment options follow the same pattern. Video game arcades and billiard halls line the Mall, and two cinemas (**Ashok** and **Capital**) play Bollywood flicks in the Flats area (Rs15-30). After scooching your way through some tight crevices at the **Eco Cave Park,** an underground attraction near Sukhatal, you can take in a sound and light show at its musical fountain. (Open daily 9am-7pm. Admission Rs10, light show Rs20.) There is also a roller rink, near the ropeway building in Mallital (Rs50 per 30min, Rs80 per hr.). The icing on the cake is the recently-opened **Himalaya MiniGolf,** next to the Himalaya Hotel in Tallital. The nine-hole course may be the first such attraction in North India; the carpet greens were imported from America. (Open 7am-10pm. Rs65.)

UTTARANCHAL

⚡ DAYTRIPS FROM NAINITAL

If you're looking for lakeside solitude, there are a number of places not far from the rickshaws of Nainital that offer lovely views and peace and quiet.

SAT TAL. Hidden deep in pine and oak forests 26km from Nainital are the lakes of Sat Tal. As the name suggests, there were once seven, but three have succumbed to evaporation. Perhaps sensing that the others face the same fate, developers have left most of the area untouched, making it a peaceful place to spend the day and enjoy natural surroundings. If you'd like a quiet night, as well, the **Sat Tal Christian Ashram** offers tranquility on a forested ridge between two of the lakes. Founded in the 1920s by Stanley Jones, an American missionary interested in Hindu thought and meditation, the complex is well-maintained by its welcoming staff *(Room Rs50. Food Rs100 per day. Notify the management prior to your arrival. Write to: The Manager, Sat Tal Christian Ashram, P.O. Mehrogaham, Nainital, UA 263001.)* Rent boats (Rs100 per hr.) and buy snacks from stalls along the lakefront, near the **KMVN Resthouse ❶.** Most tour agencies bus to Sat Tal and the surrounding lakes (Rs100).

BHIMTAL. A smaller and cleaner version of Nainital, Bhimtal, 22km away, has a good reputation as a being a center for waterskiing, sailing, and boating. The lake is a popular tourist destination, and these days there's more concrete here than pine and blue-sky beauty. Bhimtal is also home to two environmental groups: Himalayan Man and Nature Institute (HIMANI) and the Action Group for Environment and Humanity, both situated at the Tallital end. One kilometer along the road to **Naukuchiyatal** is a Kumaoni Folk Art Exhibition. (Open M-Sa 11am-6pm.) Tour buses don't stop here; you'll have to take a taxi. As usual, government accommodations are the cheapest. The **KMVN tourist bungalow ❶,** on the opposite side of the lake from Bhimtal, is about as quiet and cheap as Bhimtal lakeside hotels get. (☎247005. Dorms Rs60; tidy doubles Rs300-400.) One of the prettiest lakes, Naukuchiyatal, 4km from Bhimtal, offers plenty of solitude and lots of opportunities to fish and spot migrating birds. The lake is said to have nine corners *(nau kuchiya)*, and good luck is supposed come to those who see all nine at once. The **KMVN tourist bungalow ❶** at Naukuchiyatal has a comfortable lounge and a beautiful garden in front. (☎247138. Dorms Rs70; doubles Rs300-400.)

RANIKHET रानीखेत ☎ 05966

Ranikhet's citizens are proud of their hillside haven, one of the most peaceful in Kumaon. The same notion may not spring to mind as you sidestep yet another soldier marching through Sadar Bazaar, the town's main strip, but despite the town's large military presence, dating back to the arrival of British troops in 1869, Ranikhet is a rather calm place. Resting in the shadow of Nainital, Ranikhet receives fewer visitors than its hectic neighbor to the south, and consequently remains a more relaxed setting. Look away from the crowded town center to find the peace—to the Himalayan peaks, including Nanda Devi, rising silently on the horizon, or to the surrounding forests, where only the barks of deer break the stillness.

⌐ TRANSPORTATION

Buses: UP Roadways (☎220645) runs buses to: **Dehra Dun** (12hr., 8:30am and 3pm, Rs202); **Delhi** (12½hr.; 4, 4:30, 5pm; Rs190); **Kathgodam/Haldwani** (4hr., every 30min. 7am-5pm, Rs60); **Ramnagar** (5hr., 8:30am, Rs67). **KMOU** (☎220609) has buses to: **Almora** (2hr., 5 per day 5:30am-2:30pm, Rs35); **Kathgodam/Haldwani** (4hr.; 8:30am, noon, 2:30pm; Rs60); **Kausani** (3hr., 4 per day 5:30am-noon, Rs42); **Nainital** (3hr., 11:30am, Rs38); **Ramnagar** (4½hr., 8 per day 6:30am-2:30pm, Rs60).

Trains: Northern Railways Out Agency, above the UP Roadways Bus Stand, books tickets for the Kathgodam-Delhi train. The price includes a one-way bus ticket from Ranikhet to Kathgodam. Reserve at least 3 days in advance. Open M-Sa 10am-2pm.

Shared Jeeps: Jeeps service local sites and more distant destinations. From above the Alka Hotel to: **Chaubatia** (Rs10) and **the Mall** (Rs10). Uphill from UP roadways to: **Almora** (Rs40); **Doonagiri** (Rs50); **Dwarahat** (Rs40); **Kausani** (Rs50). From the KMOU stand to: **Bhowali** (Rs50); **Hare Khan Temple** (Rs5); and **Nainital** (Rs60).

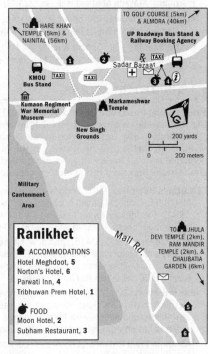

Ranikhet

▲ ACCOMMODATIONS
Hotel Meghdoot, **5**
Norton's Hotel, **6**
Parwati Inn, **4**
Tribhuwan Prem Hotel, **1**

🍴 FOOD
Moon Hotel, **2**
Subham Restaurant, **3**

UTTARANCHAL

✳ 🛈 ORIENTATION AND PRACTICAL INFORMATION

The town center, **Sadar Bazaar,** contains most services and many of the hotels and restaurants. **Buses** arrive at either end of the bazaar; **UP Roadways** stops at the downhill end, while **KMOU** buses arrive and depart on the west end. the Mall area, 4km above the bazaar, is a tranquil setting for some of the better hotels. To get to the Mall, keep to your left along the road next to the **Alka Hotel** (up the mountains and away from the chaos). It's a bit of a hike—take a shared taxi (Rs5) if you're carrying a heavy pack. There is a mural-sized map of Ranikhet opposite the **Rajdeep Hotel** listing area attractions. Monday is Ranikhet's **business holiday.**

Tourist Office: (☎220227). Downhill from the bazaar, up the stairs near the UP Roadways bus stand. Open May-June and Sept.-Oct., M-Su 8am-8pm. Off-season open 10am-5pm.

Currency Exchange: The nearest currency exchange is in Nainital or Almora. Try the kind staff at Hotel Moon if you are in a pinch.

Markets: Stores in **Sadar Bazaar** sell has stores selling traditional Kumaoni silver and gold jewelry, as well as Kumaoni woolens and shawls. Also, try the showroom across from the Nan Singh Stadium for the locally produced garments.

Pharmacy: Mayank Medical Hall (☎222432), by UP Roadways. Open Tu-Su 8am-8pm.

Medical Assistance: The **clinic** of Dr. O.P.C. Srivastava (☎20101) is on the bazaar, uphill from the Mayank pharmacy. Open daily 9am-5pm.

Post Office: The main branch is along the Mall, 2km from town center. Another branch is near the Mayank pharmacy. Open M-F 9am-5pm, Sa 9am-noon. **Postal Code: 263648.**

📱 ACCOMMODATIONS

Hotels along the bazaar tend to be noisy and a bit unkempt, but still expensive during the high-season months (April-June and Sept.-Oct.). Do a little walking and find better quality for the price at one of the hotels on either end of the bazaar. Walk even farther to the hotels on the Mall and find much nicer rooms in a secluded setting. In-season rates are quoted, so expect a 40-60% discount off-season. Always bargain a little before accepting a room.

🏨 **Norton's Hotel** (☎220673; nortonsranikhet@yahoo.com), uphill from Kumaar Lodge on Mall Rd. Colorful old British bungalow with much of its original furniture (dating back to 1880). The friendly owner refuses to subdivide the spacious sitting room or raise the rock bottom prices. Doubles Rs300-600. Off-season Rs50 discount. ❷

Hotel Meghdoot (☎220475), just downhill from Norton's on Mall Rd. A quiet, airy bungalow, with spacious rooms and huge bathrooms (seat and squat toilets). Balcony offers unobstructed views of the valley. Cable TV and restaurant. One standard double room Rs500; all others Rs750-1100. ❸

Parwati Inn (☎220325), above UP Roadways bus stop; look for large signs. The most elevated hotel in Ranikhet, it has clean, well-lit rooms, large baths with showers and seat toilets, and super views from its lounge. Deluxe rooms have balconies. Room service and hot water. Singles Rs350-450; doubles Rs500-800. ❸

Tribhuwan Prem Hotel (☎220524), on the west end of the bazaar, just before the KMOU bus stand. A 3-building behemoth, isolated from most hotels but still close to the main road's racket. Squat toilets and bucket showers. Panoramic valley views from balconies. Deluxe rooms are larger, carpeted, and have TVs. Doubles Rs350-650. ❸

🍴 FOOD

Moon Hotel, Sadar Bazaar, opposite Hotel Rajdeep. Don't let the spacious cafeteria-style seating fool you—this restaurant serves up well-crafted meat dishes at hefty prices. The "Moon Chicken Baghdad" (Rs260) is one shining example. The food is spicier than the standard regional fare. Open daily 7am-11pm. ❺

Subham Restaurant, in the Parwati Inn. The dimly lit interior isn't especially inviting, but an attentive staff and good, plain food make this a dependable restaurant. Chinese (Rs35-60), Indian (Rs25-60), and continental dishes (Rs40-80). Open daily 7am-10pm. ❷

👁 🎵 SIGHTS AND ENTERTAINMENT

CHAUBATIA GARDEN. The most popular attraction in the area, the hillside Chaubatia Garden features terraced fruit and flower gardens, which are in full bloom June-Aug. It is also a "Fruit Research Centre"; sneaky travelers sometimes do research of their own as they follow the trails through the forests. Apricots, apples, pears, and peaches grow here and are sold at reasonable rates at the shop at the entrance, along with fresh-squeezed apple, strawberry, lychee, and baransh juice (cup Rs10, bottle Rs15). In high season, Indian vacationers fill the garden. *(11km from Ranikhet. Seven buses head to Chaubatia from the UP Roadways stand (40min., 8am-6pm, Rs5). Shared taxi Rs10. Garden open daily 24hr. Shop open M-Su 9am-5pm.)*

FESTIVALS. The **Autumn Festival** in late Sept. is Ranikhet's largest, with sports tournaments featuring hockey, cricket, and tennis, as well as a potpourri of cultural exhibits from around Kumaon. For 10 days in June, you can stop in at the **Nar Singh Stadium** (also called the Nar Singh Ground) for the evening **Summer Festival,** a country fair featuring games, magic shows, song and dance performances, kiddie rides, a motorcycle show, and plenty of fried food.

OTHER SIGHTS. Closer to Ranikhet, 7km from the town center along the Mall, is the Hindu temple of **Jhula Devi,** another name for Durga, depicted here sitting on a swing *(jhula)*. It dates back to the 14th century, and it has been visited frequently—the thousands of bells hanging around it signify the many requests that have been fulfilled after a prayer has been made at the temple. A bit further uphill is the **Ram Mandir** temple. One-hundred meters closer to Sadar Bazaar is the impressive, albeit new (1994), **Mankameshwar Temple,** next to the Nan Singh Grounds. Five kilometers down the road leading west past the KMOU stand is the **Har Khar Temple.** *(Shared taxi Rs5.)*

KAUSANI कौसानी ☎ 05962

Shortly after his two-week stay here in 1929, Mohandas Gandhi mused, "Why would Indians go to Switzerland when they have Kausani?" Indeed, the range of snow-clad Himalayan peaks that rises on Kausani's doorstep makes European mountains look more like glorified ski jumps, but local brochures still call the area "the Switzerland of India." Perhaps the title is fitting for the little town, which consists of one main road, a few restaurants, and a few more hotels. Here, you can temporarily forget about the crush of humanity that makes India the 2nd most populous nation on earth. With so much extra breathing room, it's a good place to take in fresh air and world-class views outside of the summer season (May-Sept.).

⊏ TRANSPORTATION. Buses and **jeeps** leave frequently from the town center for Bageshwar, Almora, Gwaldam, Ranikhet, Bhowali, Kathgodam, and Haldwani. Inquire at the tourist office about departure times and prices.

▦ ⁊ ORIENTATION AND PRACTICAL INFORMATION. The center of town is marked by the three-way intersection. Stairs lead uphill from the intersection to a pedestrian walkway which is home to a number of shops, restaurants, and hotels. The **tourist office** is 50m downhill from the bus stop, on the main road. (Open M-Sa 10am-5pm.) The nearest **currency exchange** is in Almora, though the folks at **Krishna Mountview Hotel** have been known to help a foreigner in need carrying US dollars. The **Sunil Medical Store** is on the pedestrian walkway up the mountain. (Open daily 8am-8pm.) The **post office** is next to the tourist office. (Open M-Sa 9am-5pm.) **Postal Code:** 263639.

⊓ ⊡ ACCOMMODATIONS AND FOOD. A number of pricey resort hotels in Kausani advertise magnificent views of the Himalayas, but these behemoths don't have a monopoly on the region's nature beauty. The bright and cozy rooms at the **Hotel Uttarakhand ❷** have unobstructed mountain views, and are far enough away from the town center to offer a modicum of peace and quiet. Follow the stairs above the bus stand. (☎245012. Doubles Rs200-300. Off-season Rs100-150.) Many of Kausani's nicer hotels are along one strip of road 1.5km above the town center. **Amar Holiday Home ❷** offers the best quality for the price, with modest-sized rooms, hot water, and a homey atmosphere. The rooms on the peaceful balcony were recently remodeled. (☎245015. Doubles Rs300-650. Off-season Rs200-350.) Travelers tired of bucket showers may want to splurge for a room at the **Sun 'n' Snow Inn ❺,** one of Kausani's more exclusive hotels, just uphill from Amar. The "executive" option (Rs1425) includes panoramic views from a wall-size window, a cushioned window seat and sitting area, and a sparkling new bathtub. (☎245010. Check-out 10am. Doubles Rs950-1425.)

Good cheap eats are a bit harder to find than cheap beds. There are a few other options if you opt to leave your hotel for a bite to eat. Attached to Hotel Uttarakhand, the **Ice Rock Restaurant ❷** is one of the best in town, with accommodating cooks who will whip up anything from creamy tomato soup (Rs25) to *dum aloo* (Rs35) on request. (Open daily 7am-11pm.) The **Hill Queen Restaurant ❷** (not to be mistaken for name-usurper Old Hill Queen Restaurant), offers cheap Punjabi food (Rs35-50) and some of the best views in town from a large balcony. They've been known to have **Internet,** but the connection is hit or miss. (Rs50 per hr.)

◧ ♫ SIGHTS. The main sights in Kausani are the sunrise and sunset; these are also the best times to see the distant mountains, which are enveloped in clouds during the summer and monsoon season (May-Aug.).

If the skies haven't cleared and your feet start itching, consider abandoning the view and taking the pleasant walk to the nearby town of **Baijnath.** The 7km trail begins just below the Uttarakhand Hotel and passes through pine forests on its way down the hillside to the village, the site of a group of 18 ancient temples. The complex features an intricately carved black granite statue of Parvati in the main temple. The temple also features a large brass *linga* where *aarti* is held daily at 8am and 7pm. The temples are situated on the banks of the Conti River, which is home to a number of enormous fish. You can also take a bus or shared jeep to Baijnath (Rs8, 30min.), but the trail is a much more enjoyable route. Hiring a jeep back is always an option. Another way to explore the countryside is by **mountain bike. Yogi's Uttarakhand Cycle Tours** (☎245012), next to the Hotel Uttarakhand, rents bikes and organizes tours for Rs350 per day. The German expat owner usually opens his business from Sept.-Nov.

ALMORA अल्मोड़ा ☎5962

Legend has it that Almora was once the city of the gods. To proclaim their divine presence here, the gods left behind an abundant source of pure water, delivered to this mile-high city from over 120 underground wells. The mystical setting has drawn peace-seekers from the likes of Gandhi and Nehru (who used to meet here to talk) to Swami Vivekananda and Timothy Leary. Now, most of the soul-searching crowd heads to the nearby hills (see **Kasar Devi,** p. 681), where honking horns and screeching brakes do not impose on the peace and quiet. There are other rewards for those who stay in town. The most central hill station in Uttaranchal, Almora was created as the seat of the Chanda dynasty 400 years ago, and a stroll through the old bazaar evokes those bygone days. The buildings may be falling down, but colorful facades still persist and the cobblestone streets still echo with the sounds of centuries past. The mountains remain oblivious to the passing decades and dynasties and show themselves, mighty and lasting, on clear days. Most hotel rooms in town afford some sort of view as long as you book at the right time—the post-monsoon months of Sept.-Nov are best for mountain gazing. During May and June, Almora attracts many visitors hoping to escape the heat of the plains, but the weather is dry, and dust and smoke cloud the air and hide the view.

☞ TRANSPORTATION

Almora's **buses** stop on the Mall at the center of town. **KMOU,** in the green and white building next to the bus parking lot, sends buses to: **Kausani** and **Bageshwar** (2½hr., 6 per day 6:30am-4pm, Rs46/56); **Kathgodam** and **Haldwani** (3½hr., 5 per day 6:30am-noon, Rs40); **Ranikhet** (2½hr., 4 per day 8am-3pm, Rs32). **UP Roadways,** down the steps and across from Bank of India, services: **Bhowali** (2½hr., 10 per day 6am-5pm, Rs43); **Dehra Dun** (12hr., 6am and 4pm, Rs215); **Delhi** (11hr.; 3:30pm, 4:30pm, and 5pm; Rs200); **Kausani** (2½hr., 7am, Rs35); **Ranikhet** (2hr., 7am and 12:30pm, Rs26). The **Dharananla Bus Stand,** on the road that runs along the other side of the ridge from the Mall Rd., serves **Pithoragarh** (5hr., 4 per day, 7am-2pm, Rs70). There is no direct bus service to Nainital. To get there, take the bus to Bhowali and a **shared jeep** from there (½hr., Rs10). In Almora, shared jeeps leave frequently from the main bus area for most destinations listed above. They typically cost Rs5-10 more than a bus, but are faster and can be more comfortable, depending on how many passengers the driver manages to cram inside.

⬛🔢 ORIENTATION AND PRACTICAL INFORMATION

Most hotels and services are found along **the Mall,** the major thoroughfare for traffic, which slopes downward to the northeast. The crowded area where buses and taxis stop, at the midway point of the Mall, passes for a town center. Much of the town's activity, however, occurs along the **Main Bazaar (Javhari Bazaar),** the major pedestrian street that runs parallel to the Mall on the ridge above it. Many ramps and stairways connect the two streets. Sunday is Almora's **business holiday.**

Tourist Office: The **UA Tourist Office** (☎230180), 100m off the uphill end of the Mall on the road that splits off across from the post offices towards Hotel Savoy. Carries information about Almora and Kumaon but keeps inconsistent hours. Try M-Sa 10am-5pm. A better bet for information is one of the local **trekking companies,** including **Discover Himalaya** (☎231470) on the end of the Mall opposite the post office, and **High Adventure** (☎231441), 50m downhill. See **Trekking in Kumaon** (p. 682) for more information on planning a trek.

Currency Exchange: There is no place to exchange cash in Almora. State Bank of India (☎30048), on the Mall, near the bus stop, changes only AmEx traveler's checks. Open M-F 10am-2pm, Sa 10am-1pm. As of August 2003, the buzz around town was that an SBI **ATM** was nearly ready for operation.

Police: (☎23023), upstairs off the same ramp as the Tourist Office.

Pharmacy: The best-stocked pharmacy in town is the **Prakash Medical Store,** 100m up the road that ascends the hill across from Hotel Shikhar. Open daily 7am-10pm.

Hospital: Civil Hospital (☎230025, emergency 230064), up a short flight of stairs from the bazaar. Open daily 8am-3pm. 24hr emergency service. **Base Hospital** (☎230012), 3km from town, is cleaner and less crowded. Open daily 8am-3pm.

Internet: The **STD booth** to the left of Discover Himalaya charges Rs65 per hr. Open M-Sa 9am-10pm. **Hotel Shikhar,** on the far end of the Mall from the post office, has reliable connections for Rs60 per hr.

Post Office: (☎230019), on the uphill end of the Mall, 600m southwest of the bus stand. Open M-Sa 10am-6pm. **Postal Code:** 263601.

⌂ ACCOMMODATIONS

Almora has a limited range of hotels with a number of cheap and dingy establishments, though there are a few exceptions to the rule. Most are along the Mall. Many travelers bypass the town's noisy bustle for more relaxed accommodations in the surrounding hills (see **Daytrips from Almora,** p. 681). Besides quiet, these places usually afford better views and fresher air. The off season is July-August and November-March.

Hotel Shikhar (☎230238), at the lower end of the Mall. Throughout town, large billboards proclaim Shikhar's "three-star" presence. Though the rating system is unclear, the hotel offers excellent facilities at low prices. The rooms are spacious and well-lit, with attached bath, private balconies, and comfortable beds. Room service available. Doubles Rs250-1000. ❷

Kailas Hotel (☎230624), up the stairs next to Discover Himalaya. Kailas attracts an international backpacking crowd in search of character and comfort. The rooms could be cleaner, and the shared outdoor baths are a pain, but the pleasant garden, occasional home-cooked meals and incomparably charming 85-year-old owner, Mr. Shah, makes this the most welcoming hotel in Almora. Doubles Rs120-180. ❶

Hotel Savoy (☎230329), at the end of the ramp that veers upward opposite the post office. Those who crave quiet will find it here, several hundred meters from the incessant honking of the Mall Rd. Large rooms with TVs and attached baths. The higher price yields a room with a balcony and better views of the valley, more windows, and an extra sitting room. Doubles Rs300-800. Off-season 25% discount. ❷

KMVN Holiday House (☎222250), uphill from the bus stop on the Mall Rd. Set apart from the rest of the town, this pleasant and clean government hotel has a well-manicured garden and a valley view. Dorms have bucket showers. Dorms Rs100. Doubles Rs450-650. Off-season dorms Rs70, doubles Rs300-400. ❶

🍴 FOOD

Glory Restaurant, opposite Hotel Shikhar on the ascending road. Low ceilings, red lanterns, and New Age Indian music on the stereo lend this restaurant an unusual amount of character. Try the Glory Special *Dosa* (Rs35) for a great breakfast treat. Open daily 8am-10:30pm. ❶

Swagat Restaurant, 50m uphill from Hotel Shikhar on the Mall Rd., down the steps. An airy place with a grand view. Try the excellent special veg. *thali* (Rs40), or the veg. *korma* (Rs45). Open daily 8am-10pm. ❷

Sunrise Restaurant, uphill on the Mall Rd., past the post office in Hotel Surmool. Mix it up with creamy and heavy Punjabi and Chinese food as you contemplate the bronze rock sculpture. *Shahi paneer* Rs35, chow mein Rs30. ❷

Soni Restaurant, next to the Police assistance booth on the Mall Rd. Small and impersonal, but unique in its wide variety of meat dishes, including tandoori chicken (Rs90). Open 8am-10pm. ❸

Sangam Restaurant, near the town center inside Hotel Himsagar. Has decent food at cheap prices. Great views and all-veg. food. *Dal makhani* Rs30, spicy chow mein Rs35. Open daily 7am-10pm. ❷

👁 SIGHTS

Across the street from the bus stop is the small, government-run **G.B. Pant Museum,** which features tools and other artifacts from the Katyuri and Chanda dynasties. (Open M-Sa 10:30am-4:30pm. Free.) **The Nanda Devi Temple,** on the Main Bazaar, pays homage to the goddess of newlywed brides and draws religious and architectural enthusiasts alike. The **Nanda Devi Fair** is held here during the last week of August or the first week of September. A walk along the road that ascends the hill across from Hotel Shikhar offers stunning views and a peaceful atmosphere, as long as no crazed shared taxi drivers are bearing down on you. The walk is punctuated by the **Anandima** and **Patal Devi** temples, which both offer terrific views of the sunset. Another popular spot to watch the sunset is **Sunset Point** at the Brighton End Corner, a 2km walk uphill on the Mall Rd. past the post office.

MARKETS. Even if you don't enjoy the bustling Indian markets, stroll through the cobblestone streets of **Jauhari Bazaar** above the Mall to catch a glimpse of the intricately carved **Chanda-era wooden architecture.** Also, drop by the **jewelers** past the Raja stores to buy or look at traditional Kumaoni jewelry. Almora is the center of production of *tamtas*, silver-plated copper pots, which line the lower region of the bazaar. **Anokhe Lal** sells these pots, though they are pretty heavy to carry around.

🎒 DAYTRIPS FROM ALMORA

KASAR DEVI. Scattered along a ridge 8km from Almora, this hamlet draws backpackers who prefer clean air and quiet to the bustle of the nearby town. Many are long term visitors, and hang around the nearby teas stands with the well-adjusted airs of guests who have stayed for far too long. The scene centers around the **Mohon Cafe**, which offers tasty cappuccino (Rs15) and a variety of desserts, as well as a patio with a view. Ask around there to see where people are staying. **Akash Deep Guesthouse**, just down the road, is a good bet, with adequate rooms and shared baths (Rs60). *(The hamlet is 8km from Almora, reachable by a long hike upward on the road that ascends the hill opposite Hotel Shikhar. One-way shared taxi Rs10 per person.)* The main attraction on the village is the **Kasar Devi Temple,** spectacularly positioned at the top of Kashyap Hill. The temple is known as a center of spiritual energy— Swami Vivekananda came here to meditate—and inspiration is in large supply. Views from a giant, sloping, mountaintop rock afford sweeping panoramas of the whole area and are marred only slightly by the television antenna that shares the point. *(Two trails ascend the hill from the main road through Kasar Devi. Walk towards the television antenna until you see one.)*

TRANQUILITY RETREAT. Wedged between two hills and far from everything but its own splendor and jaw-dropping views, the Tranquility Retreat is a tiny getaway paradise for the short- or long-term visitor. Now in its seventh year, Tranquility has grown to five rooms and five cottages (complete with kitchens), with an organic garden and beehive. French expatriates busily tend the garden, bake bread (7 loaves per day) and steaming scones served with homemade honey. They cook up a vegetarian storm—French and continental mainstays with the occasional Indian touch—while exuding a warmth and compassion that keeps their contented guests from leaving the nest. There are two paths to Tranquility Retreat from the Kasar Devi road. If you are walking toward Kasar Devi, look for a blue sign high in a tree on the right 10min. after the Research Institute for Yoga Therapy. When walking away from Kasar Devi, there will be a sign on your left 15min. down the mountain from the Kasar Devi Temple. Write or call for reservations. *(Tranquility Guest House c/o Kishan Joshi, Sariya Pari Estate, Almora, Uttaranchal, 263601, India. ☎ 280318. Food is available 7am-10pm for casual visitors as well as guests. Doubles Rs100.)*

CHITAI TEMPLE. This temple is one of the most unique and important in the area. The King Golu Dev used to sit here as the bearer of justice. Today, locals come here to seek retribution if they feel they have been wronged. Plaintiffs paste or hang letters in the temple, describing disputes or hardships in the hopes that divine intervention can deliver the justice that the court system could not. Thousands of bells have also been hung in thanks after justice was done. *(8km towards Jageshwar. Shared taxi Rs10.)*

JAGESHWAR AREA. The temple complex of Jageshwar is 38km from Almora in a valley surrounded by deodar trees. Made up of 124 temples, the complex contains one of the 12 *jyotirlingas* of Shiva. The main temple features two statues of Deep Chand and Pawan Chand, two kings who were patrons of the complex. Photography is not allowed in the main temple. Two kilometers before Jageshwar is **Dandeshwar**, a smaller temple complex. The historical spot of **Lakhudiyar**, 15km toward Jageshwar, features ancient rock paintings, some of the first examples of art in Kumaon. *(Shared jeeps leave infrequently from Jageshwar. Rs40; Lakhudiyar Rs20.)*

TREKKING IN KUMAON

🔳 PINDARI GLACIER TREK

The trek to **Pindari Glacier** is a good introduction to the Indian Himalayas, an easy week-long trip that follows a Raj-era stone trail through high altitude pastures, terraced hillsides, colorful villages, and numerous waterfalls. While the journey is beautiful, the biggest rewards come at the end of the trail. By the time you've reached the saddle of rough-hewn rock at Zero Point, the familiar green hills will have yielded to their geological superiors: 6000m peaks and a giant wall of ice will hem you in on three sides, making for a truly breathtaking sight.

The trail is well-suited to the casual walker, so it draws everyone from primary school children to elderly Bengalis, especially during the summer months (May-June). But if you're hesitant about embarking on a trek which is as much a social activity as it is an athletic one, there are several escape routes, including trails to **Kafni** and **Sunderdhunga Glacier**, which are less peopled and more challenging.

The Pindari trailhead is in **Song,** a small village with a row of shops offering snacks and bottled water, but not much else. Trekkers must pass through a gauntlet of potential porters and guides. Do not be swayed by their eager offerings—a guide is not necessary for the easy, well-marked trail ahead; neither is a porter if you're traveling with a light enough load. The trail begins as a narrow cement path that leads up the hill behind the shops. It soon crosses a dusty jeep road, which makes a less direct ascent to **Upper Loharket;** stick to the trail for shade and more picturesque surroundings. Painstakingly constructed during British rule, the cobbled path to Khati has fallen into some disrepair. After climbing through terraced fields and fragrant gardens, the trail crosses a bridge in Loharket, a moderately-sized village with a PWD rest house and several guest houses. The trail continues up the rocky hill on the other side, criss-crossing the jeep road before revealing Upper Loharket (Kalidhar), where a KMVN guest house awaits. This is a more secluded spot to spend the night if you've made a late start, and views of the terraced hillsides of the Danpur Valley provide a preview of the scenery to come.

The Indian flag marks the spot where locals want to build a Gandhi memorial; the government wants to build a restaurant in the same spot.

UPPER LOHARKET TO DHAKURI. The trail scrambles up the hillside for another hot and dusty kilometer after Upper Loharket. The jeep road, which is still under construction, can make things confusing here—follow the red arrows for the shortest route into the oak forests above. At 3km, a tea house waits on the crest of a hill, offering *chai*, snacks, and a view of the route you took to get there.

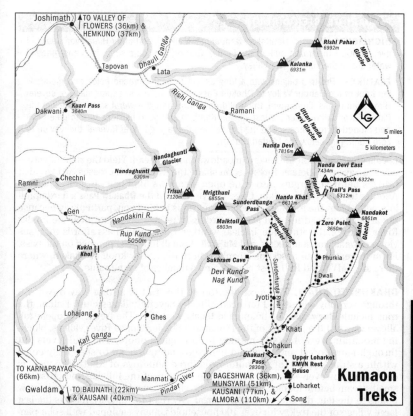

Joshimath ● TO VALLEY OF FLOWERS (36km) & HEMKUND (37km)

Dhauli Ganga

Tapovan ● Lata

Rishi Pahar 6992m

Milam Glacier

Kalanka 6931m

Rishi Ganga

Dakwani ● Kuari Pass 3640m

Ramani ●

Uttari Nanda Devi Glacier

Nanda Devi 7816m

Nanda Devi East 7434m

N LG

0 — 5 miles
0 — 5 kilometers

Ramni ● ● Chechni

Nandaghunti Glacier

Nandaghunti 6309m

Trisul 7120m

Mrigthuni 6855m

Sunderdhunga Pass

Nanda Khat 6611m

Pindari Glacier

Changuch 6322m

Trail's Pass 5312m

● Gen

Nandakini R.

Maiktoli 6803m

Sunderdhunga Glacier

Zero Point 3650m

Nandakot 6861m

Kafni Glacier

Rup Kund 5050m

Kukin Khol

Kathlia ●

Sukhram Cave ■

Devi Kund
Nag Kund

Sunderhunga River

Phurkia ●

Dwali ●

Jyoti ●

● Lohajang

● Ghes

Khati ●

Dhakuri ●

Debal ●

Kali Ganga

Dhakuri Pass 2830m

Upper Loharket KMVN Rest House

TO KARNAPRAYAG (66km)

Gwaldam ● | TO BAIJNATH (22km) & KAUSANI (40km)

Manmati ●

Pindar River

TO BAGESHWAR (36km), MUNSYARI (51km), KAUSANI (77km), & ALMORA (110km)

● Loharket

● Song

Kumaon Treks

UTTARANCHAL

PINDARI GLACIER CIRCUIT

TRANSPORTATION: Direct jeeps are the easiest way to get to the trailhead at Song, but can be expensive (Rs1000-Rs1200). Otherwise, take a bus from **Almora** to **Bageshwar** (2½hr., 6 per day, Rs56), a shared jeep from there to **Bharari** (1hr., Rs15), and another shared jeep from **Bharari** to **Song** (½hr., Rs10).

SERVICES: Food and lodging are available in numerous villages along the way, so it's possible to pack light and forgo the porter. **KMVN** (Kumaon Mandal Vikas Nigam) rest houses cost more than **PWD** (Public Works Department) and private guest houses, but provide more amenities.

VILLAGE	ALTITUDE	TIME
Song	1400m	start
Loharket	1600m	30min.
Upper Loharket (Khalidhar)	1750m	30min.
Dhakuri Pass	2830m	4hr.
Dhakuri	2620m	15min.
Khati	2210m	2hr.
Dwali	2580m	3½hr.
Kafni (sidetrip from Dwali)	3810m	6hr. (return)
Phurkia	3260m	1½hr.
Zero Point	3650m	2½hr.

PINDARI GLACIER CIRCUIT

HIGHLIGHTS: Views of Nandakot, Nandakhat, Maiktoli, and other Himalayan peaks of over 6000m. The frozen bulk of the Pindari Glacier, the sharp-shorn hills and graceful waterfalls of the Pindar River Valley.

FEATURES: The trail begins with a long ascent through terraced fields and meadow-land out of the Danpur Valley to Dhakuri Pass, which affords sweeping views of several Himalayan peaks. From there, the trail drops down through several small villages in the Pindar River Valley. After the last village, Khati, the terraced hillsides turn to green oak and rhododendron forests, and the trail follows the raging Pindar River all the way up to Zero Point, just below the Pindari Glacier.

Locals graze cattle on the several meadows that lie ahead. Yield the right of way—cows always win. Denser forests soon shade the trail, which crosses two wooden bridges before emerging into wide open meadows 5km from Upper Loharket. Another tea house sits at 6km. Once you've reached the **Dhakuri Pass** a hard uphill kilometer later, the toughest ascent of the trip is behind you, particularly because the area is hotter, drier, and less rewarding in terms of scenery, than the Pindar River Valley on the other side. In clear weather, the Dhakuri Pass affords gorgeous views of **Nandakot, Nandakhat, and Maiktoli**. A small temple is perched on the pass. From there, the trail descends steeply 1km to the grassy knoll of **Dhakuri**, where there are KMVN and PWD rest houses, and a number of restaurants.

DHAKURI TO KHATI. The next section of the trail is a long way downhill, through scrubby woods and terraced hillside. Several villages cluster along the trail, include **Bagwanpur**, at 1.5km, and **Umala**, at 3.5km. The frequently open trail allows views of the junction of the Pindar and Sunderdhunga River valleys, blocking mountain views but still making for a magical photo. The trail levels out through more forest and farmland before rounding a bend to seemingly come within a stone's throw of the rainbow-colored buildings of Khati. The view is deceiving, however—the trail follows the contour of the hillside and crosses a small stream before looping around into the village. Just below town, a red arrow points to the left, the trail to **Sunderdhunga**; stay right for Pindari. **Khati** is the last large village of the trek, with over 100 households, many equipped with solar panels and satellite television. Accommodations and food are plentiful here, but make the 1km climb past the village to the KMVN rest house for a more secluded stay.

KHATI TO DWALI. After the rest houses, the trail turns to dirt, first veering uphill to avoid a large landslide area, and then beginning a long descent through oak forest towards the **Pindar** riverbed. The trail is shady here, but Nandakot, rising majestically at the head of the valley, is still visible at points. At 5km, the trail emerges in a massive landslide area, and continues next to the Pindar for the next 1km before reaching tea houses at **Maliadhor**. A shaky wooden bridge with no railings allows for the first crossing of the Pindar here. When the monsoon hits, the bridge is impassable. Across the river, the trail climbs a steep hillside before leveling off. The valley tightens into a gorge, and the river, which can be seen from the trail, achieves an impressive flow. The trail drops down to the riverbed, and several waterfalls splash off the hills across the way, making for a graceful contrast with the raging river below. After traversing a steep hillside and crossing three rickety wooden bridges, the trail passes over the Pindar for the second time, this time over a well-made bridge (complete with handrails). Across the way is Dwali, where the usual establishments (KMVN and PWD rest houses; restaurants) await. Dwali lies on the part of land between the **Kafni** and Pindar rivers, and presides over the junction of the two valleys. It's quite the spot, with hills closing in on all sides, marred slightly by the landslide area to the river's left. Facing upstream, the Kafni is on the right and the Pindar is on the left. The trail to Kafni heads uphill to the right of the KMVN rest house, while the trail to Pindari continues behind the tea house at the bottom of the hill.

DWALI TO PHURKIA. From Dwali, the trail passes through rhododendron and birch forests and over several streams. Before the monsoon, five to six of the tributaries are blanketed by ice and snow. The crossings are manageable, but be careful not to slip in rainy weather. In clear weather, **Nanda Devi East** peeks up over Nandakhat, at the head of the valley. There are many waterfalls on the opposite side of the river, which cut their way down into the pools below. **Phurkia,** 5km from **Swali,** is a good place to spend the night and acclimate before making the final assault on the glacier. The last rest houses and restaurants are found here.

PHURKIA TO ZERO POINT (PINDARI GLACIER). To ensure views from **Zero Point** before the clouds roll in, set out early in the morning. The trail to Zero Point is open the whole way, passing by fields of wildflowers and blooming rhododendrons, and crossing several more snowy streams. Sheep dot the hills along the way, and several shepherds' encampments can be seen. A *sadhu*, or holy man, Swami Dharmanand, keeps an ashram 1km below Zero Point. Stop here for some morning tea or maybe a meal, and chat with the lively *baba*, who has lived here for 14 years and is happy to share his knowledge. Swami Dharmanand also welcomes guests seeking rest in the new "cave" behind the house, but bring your own sleeping bag. Donations are accepted. From here, the trail ascends 1km to Zero Point, crossing the river once. A landslide has washed away much of the land around Zero Point, so stay to the right. The views from Zero Point are quite spectacular, a wonderful reward for the journey, as snowy peaks close in on three sides—Nandakhat to the left, Nandakot to the right, and **Changuch** in the center.

ZERO POINT TO SONG. The return to Song follows the same route and takes two to three days. On the way back, the toughest ascent leads up to Dhakuri Pass from Umala. From there, it's smooth sailing (downhill). Just watch your knees.

SIDETRIP TO KAFNI. If you're feeling fit and have an extra day, consider making the daytrip to **Kafni Glacier.** The trail begins in Dwali and ascends 12km to the glacier. There are no tea houses or rest houses along the way, so Kafni is a one-shot deal (same-day return), unless you have a tent. This makes it more difficult than the climb to Pindari. **Be careful: landslides have washed out the trail in many places, and a fair amount of scrambling is required.** You will be rewarded for your efforts, however—Kafni is considered even more beautiful than Pindari, with a better view of monstrous Nandakhot and a view of Nanda Devi East.

Because the trip to Song can take quite a long time (6-7hr.), plan on a mid-afternoon start. This will give you enough time to reach Upper Loharket, a short 4km uphill, but the next stopping-off point, Dhakuri, may be too far (12km). From Upper Loharket, the trip to Khati involves a long preliminary uphill followed by a lengthy descent after Dhakuri, and is a good day's journey of 16km. On the third day, make the 16km ascent to Phurkia, leaving terraced fields and villages behind for more secluded surroundings. Zero Point can be reached the next day. Many trekkers choose to return to Dwali (19km, 12km downhill) the same day, then make the trip to Dhakuri the fifth day (19km) and trek out on the sixth. However, there's no rush—enjoy the mountain views and travel at the pace that suits you.

◙ OTHER TREKS

The Pindari/Kafni trek is the most popular route in the region by far, but there are many other possibilities. More difficult routes require you to carry a tent, cooking gear, and a 3-4 day supply of food, as villages and rest houses can be scarce, especially after the first two days of hiking. Hiring a guide can be a good idea on these routes, as the trails are more difficult to follow than the trail to Pindari. A knowledgeable guide will point the way to the best routes and rewarding sidetrips along the way, and can be a help on snow and ice at higher altitudes. Finding such a guide can be difficult, however. **Discover Himalaya** and **High Adventure Trekking** offer guides for about Rs500 per day, but despite certifications and professed experience, the level of quality (or fitness) is not a certainty. The agencies also arrange all-inclusive packages for Rs800-1100 per person per day. Be wary of these, as commissions are charged, and the trip becomes much more costly than it would have been if you had taken the steps of making the arrangement yourself. Your best bet may be to rent equipment at one of these stores and pay for some trip advice, then hire a porter. Porters often end up being more helpful than guides, and will cost you much less money. Just make sure you shop around for one who seems fit, experienced, and can speak decent English.

The 6-day trek to **Sunderdhunga Glacier** (96km) begins on the same trail as the Pindari trek, but branches off just before Khati, after two days. The trail crosses the Pindar River, and then the Sunderdhunga River before ascending to **Jyoti**, the last village. **A tent and food supplies are needed after this point.** The trail continues up the Sunderdhunga Valley past a campsite at **Kathlia** before the glacier and Maiktoli (6803m) come into full view. Many call this view more beautiful than Pindari, and you'll be much less likely to enjoy it in the company of dozens of Indian schoolchildren. The trip also allows for several other options—ascents of nearly 5000m and a sidetrip to an area of caves. Hire a guide who knows the rates and is willing to take you there if you hope to do this.

Another less-traveled and more strenuous option is the 8-12 day trek to **Milam Glacier** (155km). The trail begins in **Munsiyari**, 220km from Almora. Again, the trek requires a tent and food supplies after the second day. Though the trail comes close to the border with Tibet, no special permit is required. Highlights of the trek include views of the Milam Glacier and many Himalayan peaks over 6000m, including Nanda Devi East, Nandakot, Nandakhat, Rishi Pahar, and Hardeol. Many sidetrips and routes make it a good idea to hire a guide who knows the area.

UTTAR PRADESH
उत्तर प्रदेश

Uttar Pradesh, the "Northern State," is the true heartland of India, a vast expanse of fertile plains that served as the cradle of Indian civilization from the time of the Aryan chieftains to the reign of the great Mughal emperors. "UP," as the state has been known ever since the British carved it out as the United Provinces, gave India the *Ramayana*, the Hindi language, and eight of its 13 prime ministers. The state's fascinating history, diverse and sophisticated cuisine, distinctive holy sites, and incredible Mughal-era monuments attract a large tourist crowd, which the country's most populous state (pop. 140 million) absorbs with ease.

Unfortunately, the state has also been the focus of bitter communal and inter-caste violence. In 1992, its BJP government encouraged the destruction of the Babri Masjid in Ayodhya, leading to thousands of deaths in communal riots across India. In the spring of 2000, a bicycle bomb went off in Ayodhya, injuring more than a dozen people. The disputed site still makes UP a flashpoint for Hindu-Muslim tensions, though tourists need take no more precaution than an informed perusal of the recent newspapers before traveling here. Radical affirmative action politics for Dalits (former Untouchables) also have a strong base in UP. Few people visit India without visiting UP, yet no single image could ever wholly represent the state—neither the sacred city of Varanasi, nor the Taj Mahal in the Mughal capital of Agra, nor the old Muslim city of Lucknow. There is no quintessential UP, but this fact more than any other is what makes UP so quintessentially Indian.

HIGHLIGHTS OF UTTAR PRADESH

Agra (p. 687) is home to several of India's most famous and beautiful monuments, including a gem of a royal **fort** (p. 697), the abandoned Mughal capital of **Fatehpur Sikri** (p. 700), and a little ditty in marble known as the **Taj Mahal** (p. 696).

The sacred *ghats* of **Varanasi** (p. 721), Hinduism's holiest city, invite millions of pilgrims to wash away their mortality in the waters of the Ganga.

AGRA आगरा   ☎ 0562

Over the last decade, the average tourist's stay in Agra has declined from one and a half days to barely 12 hours. Everyone seems to be mumbling the same thing: Agra is a dump. It is not difficult to see why visitors who arrive expecting some kind of mystical Shangri-La—"the immortal city of undying love," according to the official literature—might leave feeling more than just a little bit disappointed. The monuments are every bit as magnificent as they are hyped up to be; the problem is that most of the tourist literature omits any mention of the parts of the city around and between its UNESCO-sanctioned sites. The main budget hotel center, Taj Ganj, is a powerful lesson in what happens when too many over-aggressive rickshaw-*wallahs* and rug vendors try to chase too many grungy backpackers down too few overcrowded streets. There *are* parts of Agra where visitors are treated to more than just urban grime and indigestion, but they are few and far between. The city's Rasputinesque offi-

Uttar Pradesh

BIHAR

Sunauli
Nautanwa
Kasia
Kushinagar
Ghazipur
Sasaram
Gorakhpur
Ghaghara R.
Sarnath
Mughal Sarai
Basti
Varanasi
Chunar
Balrampur
Ayodhya
Faizabad
Jaunpur
Mirzapur
Chandraprabha Wildlife Sanctuary
Gonda
Sultanpur
Bela
Bahraich
Allahabad
MADHYA PRADESH
Fatehpur
Rae Bareli
Rewa
Ganga R.
LUCKNOW
Kanpur
Banda
Chitrakut
Kalinjar
Satna
Farrukhabad
Kannauj
Khajuraho
Murwara
Orai
Etawah
BUNDELKHAND
Firozabad
Orchha
Patna Bird Sanctuary
Yamuna R.
Jhansi
Gwalior
Sagar
Mathura
Agra
Fatehpur Sikri
RAJASTHAN

UTTAR PRADESH

Govt. of India statement: The external boundaries of India are neither correct nor authenticated.

cials route the motorcades of visiting dignitaries through the Cantonment area, where there are wide, clean streets, upscale establishments and a string of shady parks. Luckily, Agra's biggest draw, the incomparably grand Taj Mahal, is still no less than breathtaking to behold.

Agra's monuments were built under the Mughals, who swept in from Central Asia early in the 16th century. At the Battle of Panipat in 1526, the Mughal warrior Babur crushed the ruling Lodi dynasty creating a great South Asian empire, which included Agra, the Lodi capital. For the next 150 years, the site of the Mughal capital shifted between Delhi and Agra, leaving each city rich with a host of beautiful landmarks. With the slow decline of Mughal power in North India, Agra fell on hard times. Under the British, Kolkata (and later Delhi) became the capital, and Allahabad rose to surpass Agra as the local political powerhouse.

Lately, Agra has gained notoriety for its political pocketbooks, which are rumored to be absorbing much of the money earmarked for the city's development. The latest scandal involved semi-secret plans to build a shopping mall behind the Taj Mahal. After an international outcry and angry threats from UNESCO officials, construction was stopped. There *are* signs of progress, however—ticket prices are expected to come down, and larger percentages of the foreign money flowing into the city's economy will (supposedly) be going back into the city. Hopefully, in a few years, some of those underemployed rickshaw-*wallahs* and touts will be put to work, returning Agra's streets to a state of grandeur that complements that of the Taj.

For now, it may require great reserves of patience and magnanimity to rise above the temptation to scream back at the persistent crowd that follows your every step. But despite its irritations, Agra is well worth the effort. The monuments remain serene and beautiful, and memories of the Taj at dawn will stay with you long after you have forgiven and forgotten the rickshaw driver who refused to take you anywhere but his uncle's diamond warehouse.

 WARNING. Agra, like all major tourist hubs in India, has a number of swindlers who'd love to take a bite out of your wallet. Rickshaw charges are often excessive. On the other hand, if the price they agree to (or offer) seems suspiciously low, prepare for a few sidetrips; the commissions incentive means drivers will often try to take you to the hotel or restaurant of their choice. More often, they'll point you to a marble shop or jewelry store. These aren't necessarily dangerous or undesirable situations, as some stores do offer high-quality or at least interesting hand-made goods, but be careful—know where you are on the map, take a good look at the store before you enter, and be aware of your situation. The driver will try to extend the tour for as long as possible—from the start be firm, be insistent, and be prepared to walk away. Never let yourself be browbeaten into anything (don't reward them for hassling you). Always keep change on hand. If the driver isn't happy with the tour (you didn't buy anything) he'll try to whine his way out of giving you the correct change, thereby inflating the initial agreed-upon price. Also beware of crafty salesmen who persuade tourists with "parties," tea, and sweet-talk to buy rugs and jewels to resell back home. Numerous schemes (credit card fraud, false identities, and even rape) can result from this, so don't get lured in. (See also **Touts, Middlemen, and Scams,** p. 15.)

TRANSPORTATION

Flights: Agra's **Kheria Airport** is 9km southwest of the city (inquiry ☎2302274). To **Delhi** (40min.; M, W, F 6:15pm; Rs2315) and **Varanasi** (2hr.; M, W, F 1:35pm; Rs4425) via **Khajuraho** (40min., Rs3250). **Indian Airlines** office (☎2360190), in the Hotel Clarks-Shiraz complex. Open daily 10am-1:15pm and 2-5pm.

UTTAR PRADESH

Agra

■ ACCOMMODATIONS
Agra Hotel, **1**
Hotel Akbar Inn, **8**
Hotel Clarks-Shiraz, **9**
Hotel Rantandeep, **11**
Hotel Safari, **14**
Hotel Sakura, **4**
Mughal Sheraton, **13**
Pawan Hotel, **5**
Tourists Rest House, **2**

◆ FOOD
D. Priya Restaurant, **12**
Dasprakash Veg.
  Restaurant, **3**
Lakshmi Villas, **7**
Only Restaurant, **10**
The Park Restaurant, **6**

UTTAR PRADESH

Buses: Most leave from **Idgah Bus Terminal** (☎2366588), northeast of Agra Cant. Railway Station. To: **Bikaner** (14hr., 11:30am, Rs232); **Delhi** (4hr., every 30min. 5am-11:30pm, Rs100); **Fatehpur Sikri** (1hr., every hr. 6am-6:30pm, Rs18); **Gwalior** (3hr., every hr. 4am-11pm, Rs56); **Jaipur** (6hr., every 30min. 5:30am-midnight, Rs104) via **Bharatpur** (1½hr., Rs30); **Jhansi** (5hr., 6 per day 5am-10pm, Rs100); **Khajuraho** (14hr., 5am and 9pm, Rs190); **Mathura** (1½hr., every hr. 4am-midnight, Rs28).

Local Transportation: Despite hassles, **rickshaws** are still the most convenient way to get around. Pay no more than Rs15-20 for a cycle-rickshaw or Rs25-30 for an auto-rickshaw going between the railway or bus stations and Taj Ganj or Agra Fort. Bicycles are another good option, especially for those who are all hassled out, as rickshaw drivers won't bother people who have their own set of wheels. Braving the traffic might be just another headache, however, and the quality of the bicycles is usually somewhat poor. **Raja Bicycle Store,** at the tonga stand, 100m south of Cyberlink, rents cycles (Rs10 per hr., Rs40 per day). Open daily 7am-8:30pm. Many hotels and travel agencies will also rent you a **car and driver** from one of the places around the tourist centers. **Tourist Rest House** gives an all-day tour that includes the Taj, Agra Fort, and Fatehpur Sikri (Rs1600 with monument and guide fees included).

🔋 PRACTICAL INFORMATION

Tourist Office: Government of India Tourist Office, 191 The Mall (☎2226378 or 2226368), opposite the post office. The most reliable and informative of Agra's tourist offices. Open M-F 9am-5:30pm, Sa 9am-4:30pm. The **UP Tourism Office,** 64 Taj Rd. (☎2226341), near Clarks-Shiraz, offers maps and tour packages. Open M-Sa 10am-5pm. They also have an office at Agra Cant. Railway Station (☎2368598), opposite the inquiry booth. Open daily 8am-8pm.

Currency Exchange: State Bank of India (☎2330449), next to Hotel Ganga Ratan, just off Fatehabad Rd. Exchanges currency and traveler's checks. Open M-F 10:30am-4pm, Sa 10:30am-1pm. **Andhra Bank,** Sadar Bazaar (☎2225036), in the black glass above the modern book depot. Exchanges currency and traveler's checks and gives credit card advances. Open M-F 10am-4pm, Sa 10am-12:30pm. **LKP Forex,** Fatehabad Rd. (☎2330481), in the tourist complex area just left of Pizza Hut. Exchanges traveler's checks and major currencies for a 1% commission. Open M-Sa 10am-7pm. Outside these hours, black-market opportunists in Taj Ganj will be more than happy to take your dollars from you—although *Let's Go* doesn't recommend doing business with them. Many of the larger luxury hotels will also change money for a fee.

ATM: There are two **UTI Bank** ATMs, one near the East Gate in Taj Ganj, the other on Sadar Bazaar. The ATM on Sadar Bazaar is open 24hr., and has a guard at all times.

Market: Taj Ganj is a high-pressure, hassle-a-minute hustler's hang-out where you are constantly urged to buy everything from toilet paper to mini marble and plastic Taj Mahals. **Old Agra** is one big bazaar for buying belts, shoes, car parts, and plastic buckets. **Kinari Bazaar,** extending northwest from the fort, is especially well-stocked. Shop around, and always, always bargain hard (even if a sign claims fixed prices).

Police: City control room (☎2361120; Taj Ganj branch ☎2331015), west of the hub, across from Shahjahan Hotel.

Pharmacy: Pharmacies dot the major tourist areas and also cluster around Hospital Rd. and Sarojini Naidu Hospital. Some near the hospital are open 24hr.

Hospital: Sarojini Naidu (S.N.) Hospital, Hospital Rd. (☎2361318), west of Old Agra, near Bageshwarnath Temple and Kali Masjid. **Shanti Manglik,** Fatehabad Rd. (☎2330038). Provides 24hr. emergency assistance and local ambulance service.

Internet: Cyber Space, Gopi Chand Shivare Rd. (☎2225532), on the first fl. of the shopping arcade north of Zorba the Buddha. A/C with fast ISDN connections. Rs30 per hr. Open daily 8:30am-midnight. **Cyberlink,** Thana Chowk (☎2230104), Taj Ganj. Just west of the hub at the first major crossing. Cyberlink has more computers than its rivals and is run by English-speaking staff. Rs40 per hr. Open daily 8am-9pm.

Post Office: GPO, The Mall (☎2353674). Opposite the tourist office. Massive but notoriously inefficient. Open M-Sa 10am-6pm. **Postal Code:** 282001.

🔳 ORIENTATION

Agra is a large and spread-out city, most of which sprawls west from the banks of the **Yamuna River,** along which are both the Fort and the Taj Mahal, separated by 1.5km, and the **Shah Jahan Park. Yamuna Kinara Road** runs along the river's western banks from the Taj Mahal to **Belan Ganj,** a bustling neighborhood 1km north of **Agra Fort Railway Station,** where trains from eastern Rajasthan pull in. Tourist facilities cluster south of the Taj Mahal and Agra Fort. Bargain-basement backpacker dives crowd the streets of **Taj Ganj,** an unremitting ugly and irritating rabbit-warren of hotels, restaurants, and souvenir shops that strangles the Taj Mahal from the southern side. **Mahatma Gandhi (MG) Road, Gwalior**

Road, and **General Cariappa Road** are major thoroughfares that cross both **The Mall** and **Taj Road.** From the upscale but none-too-beautiful **Sadar Bazaar,** which is squeezed between MG and Gwalior Rd., it's 2km due west to **Agra Cant Railway Station;** 2km northwest along **Fatehpur Sikri Road** is the **Idgah Bus Stand.**

ACCOMMODATIONS

Agra's hotels split themselves between two areas—Taj Ganj and everywhere else. Prices vary by season; in December, the rates listed below may inflate by as much as 200%. Most check-out times are 10am.

TAJ GANJ

The area immediately south of the Taj Mahal testifies to the benefits of competition. Rooms here are surprisingly cheap—there's no need to pay more than Rs150 for a decent double except for during peak times. This is where most budget travelers stay, and many cheap restaurants have sprung up to keep them watered and fed. The area also swarms with touts, con-men, and remarkably persistent rickshaw-*wallahs*, who collect commissions from most of the nearby hotels. The majority of the hotels have rooftop views of the Taj—often little more than a blurred glimpse of a marble minaret through the brown haze and electrical wires. The best way to orient yourself is to start with the central hub, the area in front of Joney's Place.

Hotel Kamal (☎2330126; hotelkamal@hotmail.com), on the left as you walk east from the hub. A roof with a view, and a good one at that. Rooms are clean and bright but somewhat cramped. Staff members offer good advice about how to navigate the wilds of Taj Ganj. Singles Rs120-150; doubles Rs140-450. ❶

Shahjahan Hotel (☎2331159). One of the oldest of the Taj Ganj budget places and still one of the more popular. The cushion-equipped rooftop chill-out area has good views of the Taj and a sunset swing. The manager is very eager to please. Singles Rs80-150; doubles Rs150-250. ❶

Hotel Sidhartha (☎2230901), 100m south of Western Gate. Clean, wallpapered rooms with sheets changed daily. Singles with bath Rs100-150; doubles Rs150-250. ❶

Hotel Sheela (☎2331194 or 2333074), East Gate. Just far enough from the noise of the hub without being more than a couple of minutes' walk away from the you-know-what. Rooms are standard for the area but somewhat pricey. This is understandable when you consider the amount of work it must take to keep the courtyard's gorgeous gardens so green on those 45-degree summer days. Strictly a no-commission, no-scams, no-rugs-or-knick-knacks zone. Singles Rs150-250; doubles Rs200-400. ❷

Shanti Lodge (☎2330900), 50m on the left as you walk east from the hub. The tallest hotel in Taj Ganj, Shanti has a rooftop restaurant with a view of the Taj. Bright rooms with armchairs at varying levels of upkeep. Singles Rs100-150; doubles Rs200-250. ❶

CANTONMENT AREA

The scam-a-second intensity ebbs a bit a few kilometers from Taj Ganj, especially if you're staying within the fortress-like walls of one of the area's five-star hotels. If you decide to splurge a bit and stay in one of Agra's nicer arrangements, **make sure to bargain,** despite the glossy tariff card and well-heeled surroundings (five-star receptionists aren't above calculating prices that will "fit your budget"). There are also several good budget options, including the best one in town (below), though most mid-range options are sorely lacking. Most of these establishments are within a 10min. rickshaw ride of the world's most talked-about tomb.

UTTAR PRADESH

CITY CENTER

▨ Tourists Rest House, Kachahari Rd. (☎2363961; dontworrychickencurry@hotmail.com), near Meher Cinema off Gwalior Rd., northeast of the GPO. Agra's best budget deal by far—spotlessly clean rooms (with soap, toilet paper, and clean towels) around a green garden courtyard. 24hr. STD/ISD, email facilities, and a multi-lingual manager. Singles Rs95-250; doubles Rs120-350. ❶

Agra Hotel, Field Marshal Cariappa Rd. (☎2363331; fax 2265830), 500m from the fort. Agra's oldest hotel still in operation (since 1926), it's beginning to show its age. However, the friendly management and mellow atmosphere make it a good deal. Attached restaurant. Singles Rs200-500; doubles Rs250-650. ❷

Hotel Safari, Minto Rd. (☎2333029), opposite Hotel Swagat and near the All India Radio station. Middle-of-the-road rooms with sitting areas and bathtubs. A pleasant rooftop patio and bicycles for those who want to cruise to the Taj (2km). Doubles Rs250-350. ❷

Pawan Hotel, 3 Taj Rd., Sadar Bazaar (☎2225506, pawotel@sancharnet.in). The only hotel in the main Sadar strip, this sprawling and slightly run-down hotel is well-placed for restaurants, bars, and auto-rickshaw tours of the world. All rooms have air-cooling. Singles Rs200-350, with A/C Rs500; doubles Rs250-500, with A/C Rs600-900. ❷

Hotel Sakura, 49 Old Idgah Colony (☎2369743), 100m from the bus station. A fairly uninspiring place with rooms that run the gamut from luxurious to drab. The bathrooms are all very clean, however, and the hotel provides towels, soap, and toilet paper. Air-cooled singles with attached bath Rs150-350; doubles Rs200-400. ❷

Hotel Clarks-Shiraz, 54 Taj Rd. (☎2226121; www.hotelclarksshiraz.com). A swimming pool, plush carpets, chilly rooms, and restaurants out the wazoo at slightly more digestible prices than its Mughal competitor. Rooms Rs3000. ❺

Hotel Rantandeep, Fatehabad Rd. (☎2331074). The rooms are somewhat dim but comfortable, with tile floors, televisions, and clean baths. Singles Rs400, with A/C Rs600; doubles Rs700-900. ❸

Mughal Sheraton, Fatehabad Rd. (☎2331701; mughal@welcomgroup.com). A full-blown five-star resort hotel, with everything from mini-golf to an in-house astrologer. Singles US$130-600; doubles US$140-600. ❺

Hotel Akbar Inn, 21 The Mall (☎2268036), halfway between Taj Ganj and the railway station. A lot of long walks and rickshaw rides are required from this secluded spot. The cheapest rooms are small and stuffy. Singles Rs60-150; doubles Rs150-250. ❶

◪ FOOD

Most of Agra's foreigner-friendly restaurants are clustered around Taj Ganj, Sadar Bazaar, and other tourist centers south of the old heart of town. Most travelers tend to stick to places close to (or inside) their hotels, but there are some excellent restaurants in Agra. None are in Taj Ganj, and the good food comes at a price.

TAJ GANJ AREA

The restaurants near the Taj Mahal are notorious for poor hygiene; most who stay more than a few days get the "Agra aches," akin to "Delhi belly." Several years ago, a truly ghastly scam came to light—allegedly restaurants were deliberately poisoning guests and then pocketing a percentage of the charges levied by the dodgy doctor who helped the victim "recover." In some cases, the "victim" was in on it, and false insurance claims were filed. Those hotels and restaurants have since been blacklisted by the Agra police, though (in the true fashion of the city) the list is no longer available. Many continue to operate under different names, but there have been no new reports. For the most part, you are unlikely to develop anything more than a mild case of underfed boredom—unless, of course, your waiter morphs into a tout at the end of a dirt-cheap meal and whisks you off to a dazzling showroom.

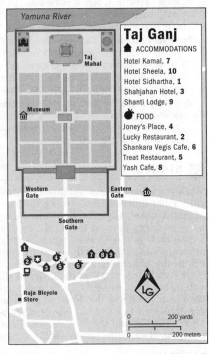

Taj Ganj

♠ ACCOMMODATIONS
Hotel Kamal, **7**
Hotel Sheela, **10**
Hotel Sidhartha, **1**
Shahjahan Hotel, **3**
Shanti Lodge, **9**

🍴 FOOD
Joney's Place, **4**
Lucky Restaurant, **2**
Shankara Vegis Cafe, **6**
Treat Restaurant, **5**
Yash Cafe, **8**

Joney's Place, at the main hub of Taj Ganj. The original Taj Ganj Diner, Joney's Place has not grown much since its humble, one-table beginnings, but the place is as friendly and reliable as ever. Renowned 🗺 banana *lassis* Rs15. Breakfasts (Rs20) are also good, as is the *malai kofta.* ❶

Shankara Vegis Cafe, Chowk Haghzi, just east of the hub. The most popular of the rooftop gathering points. Games like Connect 4, tunes from Bob Dylan to Bob Marley, and decent views of the local all-marble dome go with the filling *thalis* (Rs50) and other treats (beer Rs55-70). Open daily 7am-11pm. Happy Hour daily 6-7pm and 9-10pm. ❷

Yash Cafe, 75m east of the hub, next to Shanti Lodge. Red bricks, green paint, and Christmas lights make for a festive—if not just plain strange—atmosphere on this balcony restaurant. Standard menu of Western and Indian favorites. Pizza (Rs50-80) and *koftas* (Rs25-40). Open daily 7am-11pm. ❷

Treat Restaurant, at the Taj Ganj hub, south side, opposite Joney's Place. Tiny, wooden-benched place with four colors of light bulbs. Prompt service, dirt cheap. Serves *thalis* (Rs25-45), mini-breakfasts (Rs15), and the usual stuff. Open daily 6am-10:30pm. ❶

Lucky Restaurant, west of the hub, near Cyberlink. A silver television and air-cooler blast away while you plow through basic Indian fare (Rs25-50). Open daily 6am-10:30pm. ❶

CANTONMENT AREA

Here you'll find better, safer restaurants with slightly elevated prices. The cloth napkins and superior cuisine are well worth the monetary difference.

🗺 **Dasprakash Veg. Restaurant,** 1 Gwalior Rd., in the Meher Cinema complex. Part of the Dasprakash family of high-quality international restaurants, Dasprakash serves up excellent South Indian veg. meals and desserts. Filling *thalis* (Rs100-150) make for a great sampler of South Indian cuisine. Open daily 10am-11pm. ❹

Lakshmi Villas, Taj Rd., just east of The Park Restaurant and the main strip of Sadar Bazaar. Good South Indian veg. without fuss. Service is speedy for the 23 different *dosas* (Rs28-55) and a variety of milkshakes (Rs35-40). Open daily 7am-11pm. ❷

UTTAR PRADESH

D. Priya Restaurant, behind Hotel Ratan Deep, off Fatehabad Rd. Large dining hall with kitschy posters of Bollywood stars. Tasty Indian fare (from Rs60) including a Shah Jahan *thali* (Rs280) that could feed a royal tiger for a week. Open daily 7am-11pm. ❸

The Park Restaurant, Sadar Bazaar, just to the left of the main Sadar Bazaar strip. Airy, A/C dining room with tables set far apart on the marble floor. Listen to hits from 1980s flicks while deciding between Chinese and continental standards and excellent Indian food (the slightly overbearing waiters will be happy to help). *Dum aloo kashmiri* Rs90, szechuan vegetables Rs70. Open daily 9am-11pm. ❸

Only Restaurant, The Mall, on the roundabout near Clarks-Shiraz. Serves up pricey non-veg. under a shiny bamboo roof. Rajasthani dance in the garden patio outside on some nights. Try the *murg kadaiwala* (chicken with cinnamon, onion, tomato, and curry). Open daily 7am-11pm. ❸

◉ SIGHTS

While Agra contains several interesting monuments from the heyday of Mughal rule, most tourists come to see the marble jewel in India's crown, the Taj Mahal. Capitalizing on one of the most famous buildings in the world, the money-hungry folks at the Agra Development Authority and similar-minded bureaucrats at the Archaeological Survey of India increased admission prices several years ago. Recently, pressure from the local business community paid off, as the ASI cut their fees in half. As of press time, ADA was due to reduce their fees before 2004, at the order of the Supreme Court. Ticket prices will still be high (around Rs500), but even the most frugal backpacker will have a hard time justifying the decision to settle for hazy rooftop views of the city's big draw now that the bill has dropped below the going rate for a meal back home. The Taj and the Fort do not allow re-entry, so make the most of your one visit. Most sights charge Rs25 for cameras.

TAJ MAHAL

Open Sa-Th 6am-7:30pm. Rs750 for foreigners (ASI Rs250, ADA Rs500).

Despite all the hype and hoopla, the sheer beauty of the place is so overwhelming that no amount of overexposure can diminish it. Especially at dawn and dusk, even the most jaded of globe-trotters often find themselves smiling in wonder as they behold the Taj. Emblazoned across the signs of a million-and-one restaurants, T-shirts, and biscuit tins the world over, this marble prima donna, unofficially crowned by her ardent fans as "the most beautiful building in the world," remains India's ultimate must-see.

The tale of the Taj is a sad, sweet love story. When he became Mughal emperor in 1628, Shah Jahan brought to the throne a great many virtues, among them intellect, political acumen, and a passion for fine architecture. Three years after becoming emperor, he received news that broke his heart: after 18 years of marriage, his favorite wife, Arjumand Banu Begum, had died giving birth to their 14th child. In his grief, Shah Jahan decided that his beloved should be buried in a tomb of timeless beauty, a "tear [that] would hang on the cheek of time," in the words of Bengali poet Rabindranath Tagore.

Work on the Taj began in 1632, one year after the death of Arjumand Banu Begum. Marble was quarried in Makrana, Rajasthan, and precious stones were brought to Agra from Yemen, Russia, China, and Central Asia. Architects were sent over from Persia, and French and Italian master craftsmen had a hand in decorating the building. In all, nearly 20,000 people worked non-stop on the construction of the Taj. By the time the tomb was completed in 1653, a great many things had changed—the Mughal capital had been moved from Agra to Delhi, the deceased Arjumand Banu Begum had become popularly known as "Mumtaz Mahal" ("Elect of the Palace"), and one of Shah Jahan's sons, Aurangzeb, had come to power. In 1658, Aurangzeb staged a coup, violently surmounting the opposition of his three brothers and imprisoning his father in Agra Fort. Shah Jahan lived out his days under house arrest, staring out across the Yamuna River at the Taj Mahal. When the deposed emperor died in the winter of 1666, his body was buried next to his wife's.

The path to the Taj from the original entry arch (now the exit) is one of the most well-designed architectural approaches in the world. The tomb building and the four principal minarets rest on a large pedestal of white marble. Up close, the Taj is hardly white at all: delicately inlaid precious stones create meandering floral patterns framed by elegant Arabic script (it is said that the entire Qur'an is written on the walls of the Taj). While much of the tomb's interior is off-limits, visitors can enter the dimly-lit, domed chamber that contains the cenotaphs of Shah Jahan and Mumtaz Mahal; the latter is inscribed with the 99 names of Allah. The tombs themselves lie directly below in a room not accessible to the public. The **mosque** is to the west and the **Jawab** ("Answer"), its architectural mirror, is to the east. A popular local myth has it that Shah Jahan planned to construct a second Taj of black marble, to the north, on the other side of the Yamuna River. A small **museum** on the west side of the gardens showcases paintings of Shah Jahan and Mumtaz Mahal and some other curios, but few take the time to visit it. *(Open Sa-Th 10am-5pm. Rs2.)*

If you prefer a serene, private audience, show up at dawn—you'll have the place practically to yourself, save a few like-minded backpacker types who will be happy to take your picture. At other times, the monument is crawling with tourists and security guards, but it's worth it to stay for a while and see the Taj at different times during the day—changing light patterns affect the appearance of the Taj. Depending on the time of year and on Agra's air quality, sunsets are often the most beautiful.

AGRA FORT
To the west of Yamuna Kinara Rd., 1.5km up river from the Taj Mahal. Open daily sunrise-sunset. Rs300 for foreigners, with a Taj Mahal ticket Rs250. Light and sound shows daily 7:30pm; Rs75.

There aren't nearly as many restaurants named after Agra's fort, but it's a close second to the Taj on most visitors' checklist itineraries. Don't expect to be swept off your feet for a second time in one day, however—the fort's bulky sandstone walls and marble places aren't nearly as captivating as the tomb down the river. Still, the fort is a sight to behold. Construction began under Emperor Akbar in 1565. Its fortifications were gradually strengthened over the years—the 2.5km of bulky, red sandstone walls that enclose it were not completed until the time of Emperor Aurangzeb. Of the three outer gates that lead through the walls and into the fort, only the **Amar Singh Gate,** decorated with colorful glazed tiles, is accessible to the public. The gate is named for the Rajasthani maharaja who killed the royal treasurer before the emperor's eyes and then jumped from the walls here in 1644 to escape the guards.

Due north of the Amar Singh Gate and straight through the second gate is the breezy **Diwan-i-Am** (Hall of Public Audience), a low structure that is open on three sides. It served as Shah Jahan's court while Agra was the Mughal capital. At the height of Agra's Mughal fame, the Diwan-i-Am was filled with nobles, courtiers, and regal accoutrements. Shah Jahan's throne sat on the platform at the east side of the hall. The low marble platform in front of the throne was reserved for his chief minister. The tomb at the center of the courtyard is that of a British officer who was killed here during the Mutiny of 1857.

Agra Fort

The **royal chambers** are between the eastern end of Diwan-i-Am and Agra Fort's ramparts; here the emperor's many needs were attended in private. He also slept and prayed here from time to time. From Diwan-i-Am, the first chamber is the expansive **Macchi Bhavan** (Fish Palace), which gets its name from the stock that was dumped into its water channels so that the emperor could amuse himself with rod and reel. Unfortunately, the chamber is missing blocks of mosaic work, and huge chunks of the royal bath have been pillaged over the centuries. In the northwest corner of the Macchi Bhavan (left as you face the river) is the **Nagina Masjid** (Gem Mosque), built by Shah Jahan for the women of his harem.

Southeast of the Macchi Bhavan is the fabulous **Diwan-i-Khas** (Hall of Private Audience), completed in 1637, where the emperor would receive visitors. The **terrace** just east of Diwan-i-Khas offers classic views over the Yamuna to the Taj Mahal. Just south of the terrace is the two-story **Musamman Burj** (Octagonal Tower), which features delicate inlay work. Legend has it that Shah Jahan spent his final hours here, as a prisoner, gazing wistfully at his Taj Mahal, which was reflected in mirrors positioned at every angle in his cell. The emperor, meanwhile, is said to have enjoyed watching as men, tigers, and elephants were pitted against one another in the cramped area between the inner and outer walls.

Heading south from the tower, it's a hop, skip, and a jump to the **Sheesh Mahal** (Palace of Mirrors), where the women of the court bathed. South of the Sheesh Mahal is an enclosure that includes the **Anguri Bagh** (Vine Garden). On the east side of the garden are three buildings. The **Khas Mahal** (Private Palace) is at the center, flanked by the **Golden Pavilions.** Rendered in cool marble, the Khas Mahal is supposedly where the emperor slept. The pavilions were women's bedrooms, with walls discreetly packed with jewelry. Note the pavilions' roofs, which were built to resemble roofs of Bengali thatched huts. The **Jehangir Mahal,** the large sandstone palace to the south, (back out through the second gate) was designed for the Hindu queen Jodh Bai. In front of the palace is a large tub, thought to have been where Queen Nur Jahan took her baths. The **Moti Masjid,** to the north, is closed to visitors (as is much of the rest of the fort).

OTHER SIGHTS

ITIMAD-UD-DAULAH. The so-called "Baby Taj," the Itimad-ud-Daulah, is a small, all-marble tomb that is always less crowded than its rival down the river, though the exquisite example of pre-Taj craftsmanship would certainly receive much more attention in any other city. The tomb was built between 1622 and 1628 for Ghiyas Beg, a Persian diplomat who served as Emperor Jehangir's chief minister and was dubbed Itimad-ud-Daulah (Pillar of Government) for his exemplary service. Set in an intimate garden, the demolished tomb was designed by Ghiyas Beg himself but built by his daughter Nur Jahan, whom Jehangir married in 1611. The dazzling, semi-precious stone inlay work on white marble is perhaps the most beautiful in Agra. Several of Nur Jahan's relatives were subsequently buried in the central tomb. *(Cross the second bridge over the Yamuna and head north 300m; the tomb is on the left. Open daily sunrise to sunset. Foreigner entrance fee Rs10.)*

SIKANDRA. A town just outside Agra (though it appears to be a mere extension of the city's sprawl), Sikandra is famous as the home of **Akbar's Tomb.** Mughal emperor from 1556 to 1605, Akbar was a great patron of the arts and a respectful admirer of Hinduism. The most impressive structure at the complex is the **Buland Darwaza** (Gateway of Magnificence), embellished with geometric patterns and Qur'anic inscriptions. The central mausoleum is sparsely adorned with colonnaded alcoves and marble domes. A narrow passageway leads down to the remarkably simple crypt itself, with its flickering candlelight and smoking sticks of incense. The dome is a wonder of acoustics, and echoes reverberate for 10 seconds or more. Ask one of the guides to show you how to have secret conversations with your friends through the solid plaster walls on the outside. Mornings and evening are less crowded, while the rest of the time the joint jumps with the usual mix of hawkers, hustlers, and picnickers. The grassy area between the northern wall of the mausoleum and the wall that encloses the entire complex is an interesting place—monkeys, deer, peacocks, and amorous couples enhance the architectural grandeur of the tomb. Feeding the animals can be dangerous and is not recommended. People have been mauled by monkeys here. Sikandra is accessible by **auto-rickshaw** (Rs100 round-trip from Agra) or by one of the **buses** bound for Mathura, which board at the station and along Mathura Rd. *(Open daily dawn-dusk. Rs110.)*

DAYAL BAGH. Some say this temple, which has been under construction since 1915, will rival the Taj for grandeur once completed, supposedly in another 80 years. It is being built by members of the Radh Surami sect, founded by Swami Shiv Dayal in 1861. Currently, the unfinished facade rises two stories off a slab of marble. The sculpted depictions of various fruits and flowers, inlay work, and dozens of carvings of the initials "RS"—no two the same—are remarkable, but the true draw is the opportunity to see the painstaking process unfold as workers hunch over marble slabs in the yard out front. *(Ratan Muri Marg. Reachable by an Rs60 auto-rickshaw ride. Open dawn-dusk. Free.)*

JAMA MASJID. The Jama Masjid (Friday Mosque), Agra's main mosque, is 100m west of Agra Fort Railway Station. Built in 1648 by Shah Jahan, its sandstone walls are spliced with ornamental marble in a zig-zag pattern. The mosque complex was damaged during the Mutiny of 1857, when British forces deemed its main gate a threat to the strategically important Red Fort; the gate was promptly leveled along with some of the front cloisters of the mosque. For a while during the uprising, the Jama Masjid was, in a sense, held hostage—the mosque was planted with explosives, and the British authorities loudly proclaimed that if the Mutiny gained a large enough following in Agra, the Jama Masjid would suffer the consequences. The building remained standing, though it is in bad shape today.

CHINI-KA-RAUZA AND RAM BAGH. Six hundred meters north of Itimad-ud-Daulah is the **Chini-ka-Rauza** (China Tomb), the decayed burial chamber of Shah Jahan's chief minister, Afzal Khan. Glazed tiles once covered the entire structure—the few that remain are severely dulled and weathered. *(Open daily sunrise-sunset. Free.)* Two hundred meters farther north and past the bridge intersection is **Ram Bagh,** a three-tiered garden said to have been designed by Babur. Once an amorous playground with water wheels and baths, today the grounds are an unimpressive tangle of weeds and stone. Only a few locals and some peacocks find the ruins a worthwhile respite. *(Open daily sunrise-sunset. Foreigner entrance fee Rs100.)*

FATEHPUR SIKRI फ़तेहपुर सीकरी ☎ 05613

Fatehpur Sikri is split between two distinct parts—a silent hilltop city of abandoned palaces and crumbling store facades, and an unremarkable tangle of a village below. Most tourists, unimpressed by the familiar mud-splashed streets and ubiquitous awnings, opt to spend a few hours taking in the sights before heading back to Agra for the night. Emperor Akbar, who ruled the Mughal Empire from 1556 to 1605, followed a similar route, though his stay was much longer. He arrived in the village a desperate man—he could not produce a male heir, and had left Agra to wander North India in search of help. In Sikri, he came across a Sufi mystic named Shaykh Salim Chishti, who consoled the ruler and promised him no fewer than three sons. When, a year later, the first foretold son arrived, Akbar repaid the saint by naming his son Salim (the future emperor Jehangir) and moving the entire court close to the saint's village of Sikri. Palaces, mosques, and battlements were hastily constructed, and Fatehpur Sikri served as the Mughal center for 15 years before shifting back to Agra. The reasons for the move are unclear—some say water shortages forced them away, while others claim the death of Shaykh Salim prompted the shift. The decision left a pristine ghost-palace and abandoned city behind. Fatehpur Sikri casts a haunting spell on visitors, especially at dawn and dusk, as sunlight and shadows whirl across the barren sandstone buildings.

⏺ ⓘ TRANSPORTATION AND PRACTICAL INFORMATION

Vehicles drive into Fatehpur Sikri from an access to the east of the palace complex. The deserted city is on a hilltop overlooking the modern village of Sikri to the south. From the bus or train stations, it's a 5min. walk up the hill to the ruins. **Buses** head to **Agra** (1hr., every 30min. 6am-8pm, Rs18) and **Bharatpur** (every hr. 9am-5pm, Rs12). **Trains** run daily to **Agra** (9:30am and 4pm, Rs8). No trains run to Jaipur. For **currency exchange,** head back to Agra or ask at one of the hotels.

Fatehpur Sikri

🏠 ACCOMMODATIONS
Gulistan Tourist Complex, 4
Hotel Ajay Palace, 2
Hotel Goverdhan Tourist Complex, 3
Maurya Rest House, 1

UTTAR PRADESH

🏠 🍴 ACCOMMODATIONS AND FOOD

Everything in Fatehpur Sikri is within walking distance of the palace. In peak season (Oct.-Mar.), hotels can fill up. Most travelers opt to stay in Agra and make a daytrip to see the palace (there isn't much else to see). A good budget option in town is the family-run **Hotel Ajay Palace ❶,** just to the left as you come out of the bus station, which offers four very clean rooms. (☎282950. Doubles Rs150.) Down the road that heads toward Agra, on the right-hand side just before the turn-off for the railway station, the **Hotel Goverdhan Tourist Complex ❶** has spacious rooms and a friendly manager; amenities include towels, air coolers, and some TVs. (☎882643. Dorms Rs50; doubles Rs100-250. Also offers Internet access Rs50 per hr.) The rooms at UP Tourism's **Gulistan Tourist Complex ❸** are overpriced, but the quiet, shady garden courtyard provides a safe haven from bothersome guides. (☎282490. Singles Rs525-700; doubles Rs575-900.) **Maurya Rest House ❶** (☎282348), just down the steps from the Jama Masjid, offers slightly cramped rooms and gorgeous views of the palace above and village below. (Singles Rs60-90; doubles Rs150.) For food, the ☒**Hotel Ajay Palace Restaurant ❷** is your best bet. Homemade cheese and mineral-water ice put this place in a different league from roadside joints (*thali* Rs60, including mineral water). The restaurant at the **Gulistan Tourist Complex ❺** has large lunch and dinner buffets (Rs260).

👁 SIGHTS

All sights open daily dawn-dusk. Entrance fee Rs260.

Before entering the sights at Fatephur-Sikri, tourists must pass through gauntlets of eager guides; even once inside, prospective guides continue to pester tourists who have chosen to wander the palaces alone. Many of these "guides" falsely claim to be licensed; others insist they are students whose "duty" it is to show you around, only afterward whining for *baksheesh* or leading you into their handicraft shops. Ask to see proper ID. Often they're of the laminated napkin variety, in which case you should stay away. Official guides should charge around Rs40-50 for a tour of the monuments, but it may not even be worth this much—guides are rarely informative and the sandstone signposts can usually tell you more than a live tour guide will.

Coming from the east (the side closest to Agra), you'll pass the **Naubat Khana** (Drum House), which was used to signal the emperor's arrival, and the ticket office for the palace complex. A path leads around into the **Diwan-i-Am**, the court where, from a throne set in a large sandstone pavilion, the emperor would hear the pleas and petitions of common men, as well as review the animals of rival stables. Straight through the doorway on the path that leads from the ticket office is the to the west toward the throne is the main palace courtyard. To the right is the **Diwan-i-Khas** (Hall of Private Audience), where Akbar is thought to have met with VIPs and relatives. The hall is a massive chamber supported in the middle by one ornate column shaped like a budding flower. Behind it is a meticulously carved gazebo, probably the sitting chamber of either the treasurer or royal astrologer. If you walk toward the far side of the courtyard, the **royal banquet hall** should be straight ahead. Finely carved columns and walls decorate the **Turkish Sultana's Palace,** to the left. The large tank with the two narrow footbridges across it is **Anup Talao,** the choice venue of legendary Mughal crooner Miyan Tansen. **Diwan Khana-i-Khas,** the emperor's chambers, sits just behind it. The emperor made appearances in the southern window, known as Jharokha Darshan. The five-story **Panch Mahal** tower dominates the courtyard from its western edge. Steps lead up past 176 intricately carved stone columns to the fifth floor, where Akbar sat on hot summer nights and enjoyed the breeze. Unfortunately, tourists are not allowed to do the same—access is restricted to the base. From here, exit the courtyard to the west. As you enter the next courtyard, **Miriam's Palace** is on your left. This was once home to Akbar's Christian wife, with faded wall paintings left over from the palace's glory days.

Proceed south and cut right to the entrance of **Jodh Bai's Palace,** one of Fatehpur Sikri's largest buildings. In the courtyard, symmetrical patterns and sandstone flowers carved into the walls surround a central fountain. This complex was probably used for the emperor's harem. Note the azure glazed tiles on the roof along the second story. Nearby **Birbal's Palace** was the residence of either the minister's daughters or one of Akbar's queens. Leaving the palace complex and heading down past the Karen Saria, a path leads to the **Hiran Minor,** a 22m tower with protruding tusk-shaped stones. The minaret was built as the memorial tomb for Akbar's favorite elephant, Iran. The 360° view from the top makes the dark and difficult climb worthwhile.

At the far western end of the complex, near the village, the base of the **Buland Darwaza** sits 13m above street level, and its gate stands 40m above that, making it the tallest doorway in Asia. The gate was added to the complex in 1595, following Akbar's triumph in Gujarat, and its style was copied in other Victory Gates around the country. As you pass through the gate, take off your shoes. The head of the

Jama Masjid is off to the left, facing Mecca. In the middle is the pure white **mausoleum** of Shaykh Salim Chishti, the sage who prophesied the birth of Akbar's sons. The core of the tomb is made from mother-of-pearl. Visitors hoping for Shaykh Salim to intercede on *their* behalf hang threads from the marble latticework on the walls inside. Incense sticks burn inside the tomb, and musicians sometimes sit and play outside. Next to the mausoleum is a series of royal cenotaphs. The tiny white one holds the remains of the royal pigeon. To the right of the mausoleum is the tomb of Islam Khan, Governor of Bengal during Jehangir's reign. The **Badshahi Darwaza** leads out of the courtyard.

MATHURA AND VRINDABAN मथुरा AND वृन्दावन ☎ 0565

The ancient, cultured city of Mathura, once known as the "Athens of India," is best known today as the temple-loaded birthplace of Krishna. Countless pilgrims come here every year for **Krishna Jayanti**, the celebration of Krishna's birth, to pay homage to the blue-skinned hero of Hindu lore. Even outside the main festival season, Mathura hums with holiness. Thousands of pilgrims and priests crowd the city, mingling saffron and incense with the dirt and grime of the streets. Despite their contributions, however, Mathura's landscape is not distinguished by a divine appearance—muddy drainage ditches sit stagnant on every street corner, trees are few and far between, and dust hangs heavy in the air. Tourists with no connection to Krishna may come away more annoyed than enchanted.

The nearby pilgrimage town of Vrindaban is a more pleasant place to visit, with quiet, leafy streets and plenty of empty winding alleys that make for great hassle-free exploring. It is also the main religious center of the area, where Krishna performed the deeds that made him famous: lifting up Mt. Govardhan, playing his flute, and cavorting with all the *gopis* (milkmaids) he could find. Ever since the Bengali teacher Chaitanya discovered the site's importance, Vrindaban has been a huge draw for pilgrims, whose ashrams are maintained by wealthy devotees and ISKCON, the International Society for Krishna Consciousness (Hare Krishnas). Devotees most prominently show their love for Krishna during **Holi,** the Festival of Colors, when they satiate his playful spirit by throwing colored powder and water at each other. Watch out for mischievous monkeys: they grab for food and have been known to snatch eyeglasses from peoples' faces.

▐ TRANSPORTATION

Trains: Mathura Junction Station is a chaotic, non-English-speaking place 1.5km south of the State Bank of India. To: **Agra** (45min.-1½hr., 20 per day, Rs28); **Delhi** (3-5hr., 20 per day, Rs47-57); **Gwalior** (3-4hr., 9-11 per day 7:40am-11:30pm, Rs60); **Jhansi** (4-6hr., 8 per day 7:40am-11:44pm, Rs165).

Buses: From the **new bus stand,** buses head every hr. or so (most frequent 6am-10:30pm) to: **Agra** (1½hr., Rs28); **Bharatpur** (1hr., Rs20); **Delhi** (3hr., Rs71); **Jaipur** (6hr., every hr. 6:30am-10:30pm, Rs95). From the **old bus stand,** UP Roadways buses head to **Haridwar** (8hr., 10pm, Rs154) and **Varanasi** (16hr., 6:30pm, Rs250).

Local Transportation: Stretch **tempos** cruise from the New Bus Stand to Vrindaban (Rs5) and around town, as do **cycle-** and **auto-rickshaws** (Rs100 to Vrindaban). **Horse-drawn wagons** also cruise the streets and cost about the same as cycle-rickshaws.

UTTAR PRADESH

■ 🄻 ORIENTATION AND PRACTICAL INFORMATION

At the heart of Mathura is the bazaar, which stretches north from Holi Gate in the eastern part of town near the Yamuna River. The old bus stand is 500m south of Holi Gate, and the more frequently used new bus stand is on Chowki Bag Bahadur Road, about 500m northwest of the State Bank of India and 2km southwest of Holi Gate. The town's most important landmark is the temple Shri Krishna Janmasthan (Janmabhoomi), built on the site of Krishna's birth, 2km northwest of the new bus stand. Vrindaban is 15km north of Mathura on the banks of the Yamuna.

In Vrindaban, tempos drop off on the main road from Mathura, near several unremarkable and under-frequented ISD/STD booths. Temples lie to the north (straight ahead) and northwest. The easiest way to tour the sights is to hire a cycle-rickshaw by the hour. (Rs25 per hr.) If you'd rather go temple-hopping on your own, start walking, but don't expect to make your way through the winding lines of Vrindaban without asking for directions a few times.

Tourist Office: UP Tourism (☎2405351), 200m southwest of the State Bank, on the road to the train station. Open M-Sa 10am-5pm.

Currency Exchange: State Bank of India (☎24075770), Junction Rd. crossing. Exchanges US and UK currency and traveler's checks. Open M-F 10am-2pm. Sa 10am-noon. SBI runs an extension branch at the ISKCON temple in Vrindaban.

Market: The **bazaar,** selling everything from chutneys to drums, extends just south and a long way north of Holi Gate. There is a **fruit market** next to the Jama Masjid.

Hospital: District Hospital (☎2403006 or 2500986), just north of the old bus stand. **Methodist Hospital,** Jaising Pura, Vrindaban Rd. (☎2406032 or 2404806).

Internet: City Net (☎2401625), 100m south of Holi Gate. Rs25 per hr. Open 7:30am-10pm.

Post Office: The GPO (☎2405863) is 2km south of the old bus stand in the Civil Lines area. Open M-Sa 10am-4:30pm. There are more convenient branches in Vikas Bazaar, between the old bus stand and Holi Gate, and at the Shri Krishna Janmasthan complex. **Postal Code:** 281001.

🄻 ACCOMMODATIONS

In Mathura, hotels tend to be found in three areas: around Shri Krishna, Janmasthan, near Holi Gate, and along Chowki Bag Bahadur Rd. The bazaar near Holi Gate is the liveliest and noisiest part of town, though the temple area is fairly loud as well; stay on CBB Rd. if you want a modicum of peace and quiet. Mathura has a few **ashrams,** including the **Keshvjee Gaudig,** opposite the district hospital (Rs30 per room). In Vrindaban, the only lodging options are ashrams, and the restaurant scene is not well developed.

International Rest House (☎2423714), at the eastern end of the Shri Krishna complex. Cheap, simple rooms for pilgrims, as well as a garden where they can kick back. Attached restaurant open 11am-3pm and 6:30-10:30pm for a "pious lunch and dinner." Singles Rs50; doubles Rs150. ❶

Hotel Surya International, Chowki Bag Bahadur (☎2409344), across from the new bus station. The management offers one standard type of room—air-cooled and spacious with a large window and comfortable bed. Singles Rs300; doubles Rs400. ❷

Gaurav Guest House (☎2406192). From the government museum traffic circle, head 100m south down the road with the cupola at its end. Look for the unmarked blue and white hotel down an alley on the left. Uninspiring but clean rooms far from the temple ruckus. Singles Rs150-300; doubles Rs250-350. ❷

Hotel Brijwasi Royal, Station Rd. (☎2401224; hotelbr@datainfo-sys.com), at the State Bank intersection. A/C, full baths, high "hygienic" standards, and other perks for a price. The staff is generally friendly. Singles Rs900-1250; doubles Rs1050-1950. ❺

Gajan Gardens, Chowki Bag Bahadur Rd. (☎2461646), 200m northwest of the bus station. With a large green lawn and tent setup, this place caters to wedding parties, but the super clean, recently finished rooms are still an option for the budget traveler who craves a degree of comfort. Most rooms have A/C. Singles Rs500-800; doubles Rs500-800. ❸

🍴 FOOD

The restaurant scene in Mathura is a bit lacking, and could stand a good culinary kick in the behind. Most restaurants that serve up food that a foreign stomach could digest are found in hotels.

Brij-Bhoj Restaurant, inside Hotel Mansarovar Palace, 100m east of the State Bank of India. The food takes longer than usual to emerge from the kitchen, but after the first bite it's clear that the delay was due to careful preparation and not lackadaisical service. Fine breakfasts Rs75-100, *paneer khoya* Rs55. Open daily 7am-midnight. ❸

Brij Raj Cafe, opposite the Shri Krishna complex, next to Hotel Brij Raj. Good *thalis* (Rs20), hard benches, no kowtowing to the foreign tourist. Open daily 9am-11pm. ❶

Cyber Cafe, just south of Holi Gate. No computers here, but an intimate cellar with hanging lamps and clay plates sets the mood for almost-romantic pizza (Rs50-80) and Chinese (Rs30-50) dinners. South Indian dishes Rs20-50. Open daily 10:30am-10pm. ❷

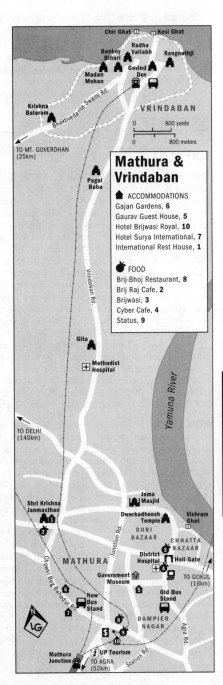

Mathura & Vrindaban

🏠 ACCOMMODATIONS
Gajan Gardens, **6**
Gaurav Guest House, **5**
Hotel Brijwasi Royal, **10**
Hotel Surya International, **7**
International Rest House, **1**

🍎 FOOD
Brij-Bhoj Restaurant, **8**
Brij Raj Cafe, **2**
Brijwasi, **3**
Cyber Cafe, **4**
Status, **9**

UTTAR PRADESH

Brijwasi, just north of Holi Gate. No real eats, but oodles of sweets. The shop is famous around the Mathura and always crowded, despite having four other branches in different parts of town. *Pera* Rs90 per kg. Open daily 7am-10pm. ❷

Status, inside Hotel Brijwasi Royal. The classy food you'd expect from a restaurant with a name like this. Indian and Chinese staples come in hefty proportions. The menu's promises of continental food, however, are most likely false. Indian dishes Rs50-92, Chinese Rs55-75. Open daily 6:30-11am, noon-3pm, and 7pm-11pm. ❸

SIGHTS

MATHURA

SHRI KRISHNA JANMASTHAN TEMPLE. Most of the sights in Mathura revolve around Krishna, whose birth here has given this otherwise unremarkable town its status as one of the holiest places in India. The most important site for pilgrims is the constantly buzzing Shri Krishna Janmasthan temple complex, which marks the spot of Krishna's appearance—the original temple, Kesava Deo, was destroyed by Aurangzeb and replaced with a mosque. The similar histories of the temples here and at the birthplace of Rama in Ayodhya (see p. 715) have made the authorities particularly cautious—visitors must check all belongings (bags, cameras, etc.) at the cloakroom off to the left, pass through a metal detector, and undergo a zealous frisking. Scattered around the towering temple and among the souvenir shops are several small temples and shrines. The most important of these, at the back right side of the complex, is a small, dimly lit room believed to mark the exact site of Krishna's birth. The room is designed to represent the prison cell where the joyous god was born while the nefarious King Kamsa held his parents captive. Barbed wire and uniformed guards with guns stand around the complex between the temple and the mosque, which can only be entered through a separate, much less conspicuous gate 100m down the road. Out the main gate and up the road is **Potara Kund,** where baby Krishna's diapers were washed. *(A straight, 1.5km walk west from Holi Gate. Open daily 5am-noon and 5-9pm. Kesana Deo closed noon-4pm. No bags allowed.)*

OTHER SIGHTS. The **Government Museum** houses a large collection of ancient Indian sculpture. Its pieces shed light on Mathura's religious and cultural significance—for nearly 1200 years it was the artistic center for early Indian and visiting Hellenistic cultures. The museum contains several excellent examples of the mottled red sandstone sculpture for which the area is famous. *(600m west of the old bus stand. Open daily 10:30am-4:30pm. Rs25.)* Mathura's other attractions are on the east side of town. As you head north from the Holi Gate, the **Dwarkadheesh Temple** is 500m up on the left. Built in 1814 by local merchants, this temple is the main point of worship for local Hindus. The building's glossy, colorful exterior only hints at the finery within; sparkling shrines, trickling fountains, and a trail of embedded coins brighten the interior. *(Open daily 6:30-10:30am and 4-7pm.)* Just 100m south of Dori Bazaar, the street forks off to the right toward the river and the sacred **Vishram Ghat,** where Krishna came to rest after slaying the menacing King Kamsa, and where many priests, guides, and beggars now congregate. From the *ghats,* **boats** take visitors on an overpriced, hour-long tour of the city's shore (Rs100), with a prime view of the dilapidated **Sati Bur,** built in 1570 and dedicated to the *sati* of Behari Mal. Sunset boat trips offer a unique view of the nightly *arati* ceremony, when priests bring fire to the sacred water amid the sound of gongs. The **Jama Masjid,** Mathura's main mosque, was built by Abo-in Nabir Khan in 1661. The mosque

UTTAR PRADESH

is unusually colorful, its teal and white facade brightening up the already striking bazaar and fruit market. *(A 1km walk northwest on the main road from Holi Gate through the bazaar.)*

VRINDABAN

KRISHNA BALARAM TEMPLE. None of the holy places in Vrindaban draws more foreigners than the Krishna Balram Temple, the dazzling marble house of worship built by **ISKCON**, the International Society for Krishna Consciousness. The founder of the society, Srila Prabhupada, lived and worked here before embarking at the age of 69 on a world tour to spread "Krishna Consciousness." As you enter, the shrine to the left with a curved marble staircase houses a golden, life-sized replica of the *swami* sitting eternally peaceful over the site of his burial. An international congregation of Hare Krishnas mingles here and around the two other shrines, many of them eager to chat with newcomers. The temple echoes throughout the day with the sounds of chants, drums, and clicking beads, though the pervasive atmosphere of serenity somehow manages to rise above all the commotion. *(Temple open daily in summer 4:30am-8:45pm, and in winter 3:30am-8:15pm. Periodic breaks for meals.)* The Hare Krishnas serve a free meal of *dal* and rice mush in front of the temple at 10am and 5pm. There is also a **guest house ❷** (☎ 2540021; ramamani@sancharnet.in), offering 44 clean doubles with attached baths (Rs200-500). The temple is likely to be full during August, September, and March. An attached **restaurant ❸** offers clean, sit-down dining, decent *thalis* (Rs80), and some Western fare. *(Open daily 8-10am, noon-3pm, and 6:30-9:30pm.)* Outside the guest house, a **museum** dedicated to Prabhupada displays the *swami's* rooms, including books, clothes, Vaseline, and other bits of holy paraphernalia that he used while still contained within his mortal body. *(Museum open daily 9:30am-1pm and 4:30-8:30pm. Free.)*

OTHER SIGHTS. In many of the town's temples, the original idols were removed to Jaipur when Aurangzeb attacked in 1670. Since the temples were pillaged by Muslims, some are no longer considered fit for worship. Those that still invite worshippers are often brimming with pilgrims and closed to non-Hindus, making temple-touring a challenging undertaking. Still, there's a lot to see. Most of the following temples close for three to four hours during the early to mid-afternoon. The large, thick-walled **Govind Dev Temple** is one of the oldest in Vrindaban. It lacks the characteristic *gopuram* of most temples, and the top four stories were destroyed by Aurangzeb and never replaced. These days, monkeys have conquered the place and locals may usher you away if rulers have been grumpy of late. One hundred meters northeast of the Govind Dev is the **Rangnathji Temple,** India's longest at over 200m. Seth Govind Das combined Rajput and South Indian designs when he built the temple in 1851. The 15m **Dhwaja Stambha,** the central column, is said to be plated in gold. Non-Hindus are not permitted inside, but can catch a glimpse through the back (eastern) entrance. Northwest of the temple stop near the river in Bankey Bihari (literally "crooked Krishna") one of the most visited temples in town. An electronic neon sign rounds out a full set of decoration within. Nearby, the **Madan Mohan Temple** has a small shrine in the base of its 19m sandstone tower, which is colored by a good amount of vegetation. Launch off from **Chir Ghat** for a **boat ride** on the Yamuna River (Rs80-100). Evening cruises are especially picturesque, as the sun sets behind the glowing skyline of Vrindaban accompanied by the mellow *bhajans* echoing through its tangled streets.

LUCKNOW लखनऊ ☎ 0522

Despite its status as the capital of Uttar Pradesh and its distinguished history, Lucknow (population 2 million), appears to be experiencing an identity crisis. Ten-story cement office buildings stand amid crumbling *nawab*-era ruins, and teenagers in faded jeans walk side by side with *kurta*-clad gentlemen. Spend enough time in one neighborhood and you're bound to swear that *this* is Lucknow—narrow, winding streets jammed with juice vendors and cycle-rickshaws, gutters overflowing with trash, sidewalks packed with close-quartered vegetable markets and tiny fabric shops. A few blocks over, you'll find a completely different scene—shady parks, freshly swept sidewalks, and tree-lined avenues with traffic that is, inexplicably, moving on the correct sides of the median strip. This appears to be Lucknow's newest face, though it is hardly its dominant one.

In the not-too-distant past, Lucknow was a leading center of culture and academia. The distinction dates back to 1775, when the city became the capital of Avadh. A series of ambitious building projects soon thrust Lucknow forward to challenge Delhi and Kolkata for the title of India's most sparkling city. When the British formally annexed Avadh in 1856, they sent the last *nawab*, Wajid Ali Shah, into exile in Kolkata. The Indian Mutiny and siege of the Lucknow Residency followed a year later in 1857.

Since Partition, when many of the city's Muslims fled to Pakistan, Lucknow has faded from prominence as a major cultural center, and its potential for greatness has been diminished by repeated political corruption scandals. Still, many traditions live on. Local products such as *chikan* embroidery and *attar* perfume (see **Insider's City**, p. 712) endure, and it is still common to see signs written in Urdu rather than Hindi. The Muslim religious presence also survives; the most important event in Lucknow's religious calendar continues to be the Shi'a Muslim commemoration of **Muharram**—a mourning for the martyrdom of Imam Husain (grandson of the Prophet) and his 72 companions. During the celebration, marchers wail laments as they carry replicas of Husain's tomb to the fire-walking ceremonies that take place in the *imambaras*.

▐ TRANSPORTATION

Flights: Amousi Airport (☎ 2435401 or 2436327), 11km from Charbagh. **Indian Airlines** (☎ 2220927), in the Clark's Avadh Hotel. Open daily 6am-8pm; ticketing 10:30am-4:30pm. Flies to: **Kolkata** (3½hr.; Su, Tu, Th, Sa 5:20pm; Rs6265); **Delhi** (1hr., 1-3 per day, Rs3075-3950); **Mumbai** (3½hr., 5:20pm, Rs8995); **Patna** (1hr.; Su, Tu, Th, Sa 5:20pm; Rs4065); **Varanasi** (40min., 11:10am, Rs2870).

Trains: Charbagh Railway Station, Charbagh, 3km from Hazratganj. To get to the station, flag down an auto-rickshaws making the run from Hazratganj. The shared ride costs Rs5 from MG Marg; a private cycle-rickshaw will run Rs10-15. To: **Agra** (6hr., 11:15pm, Rs163); **Allahabad** (4-8½hr., 6 per day 6am-10:25pm, Rs123); **Delhi** (6½-9hr.; at least 12 per day 5:30am-1:30am; Rs215. express Rs695); **Faizabad** (3-4hr., 7-8 per day 4:54am-12:30am, Rs121); **Gorakhpur** (5-7hr., 11-15 per day, Rs148); **Varanasi** (5-13hr., 7-8 per day 3:20am-11:15pm, Rs157).

Buses: The **Charbagh bus stand** is on Station Rd. From the railway station, walk to the main road. Take a left; the station is 300m down on the right. To: **Agra** (10hr., 7 per day 4:30-10:30pm, Rs157); **Allahabad** (5hr., every hr. 4:30am-10:30pm, Rs104); **Ayodhya** (4hr., every 30min. 5am-midnight, Rs73); **Delhi** (12hr., 7 per day 3:30-10:30pm, Rs246); **Faizabad** (3½hr., every 30min. 5am-midnight, Rs71); **Gorakhpur** (8hr., every 30min. 5am-midnight, Rs127); **Varanasi** (5 per day 6am-10pm, Rs135). The **Kaiserbagh bus stand,** northwest of Hazratganj, near the high court, is the main departure point for buses to **Delhi** (12hr., every hr., Rs243).

Local Transportation: Shared **auto-rickshaws** and **tempos** run from Charbagh to Hazratganj and as far as Husainabad. They usually cost about Rs5. City **buses** also ply the routes for Rs2-3. **Cycle-rickshaws** are everywhere and are often most convenient.

Lucknow

⌂ ACCOMMODATIONS
Carlton Hotel, **2**
Hotel New Ram Krishna, **6**
Hotel Paradise, **12**
Hotel Vishwanath, **13**
Pal Hotel, **11**

🍴 FOOD
Falaknuma Restaurant, **1**
Mahabeer Restaurant, **7**
Moti Mahal, **10**
Mu Man's Royal Cafe, **9**
Shanghai Surprise, **4**
Tunday's Kababi, **8**

🍺 PUBS
Simbha Bar, **3**
Tashna Bar, **5**

UTTAR PRADESH

✴ 🛈 ORIENTATION AND PRACTICAL INFORMATION

Lucknow occupies the south bank of the **Gomti River** and extends far inland. In the center of the city is **Mahatma Gandhi (MG) Marg,** along which are several bookstores, the police station, and most of the city's restaurants and shops. The downtown area known as **Hazratganj** centers on this strip. To the northwest is **Husainabad,** the oldest part of the city, where many of the monuments are located. The main bus and railway stations are in the area of **Charbagh** to the southwest of Hazratganj. The areas of Hazratganj, Husainabad, and Charbagh form a sort of triangle around **Kaiserbagh** and **Aminabad,** an old bazaar area.

> **Tourist Office: UP Regional Tourist Office,** 10 Station Rd. (☎2638105). From the intersection of Station Rd. and Vidhan Sabha Marg, head down Station Rd. 100m toward the railway station; the unmarked office is hiding at the end of the alley before the stationery store. Open M-Sa 10am-5pm. The **Tourist Reception Centre,** inside the railway station, is almost useless for foreigners. Open daily 24hr. **UP Tours** (☎2612659), in Hotel Gomti, runs daily tours of the city on non-A/C buses (8am-1:15pm, Rs100). The tour has a minimum of 5 people.

Currency Exchange: State Bank of India, MG Marg (☎2229805), down an alley across from Lalbagh. Open M-F 10:30am-4pm, Sa 10:30am-1pm. There are several **24hr. ATMs** nearby on MG Marg that accept international (Cirrus, Plus, etc.) cards.

Bookstore: There are many indistinct book hawkers on MG Marg. For something different, try **Ram Advani Booksellers** (☎2223511), on the corner of Lalbagh and MG Marg. Specializes in academic works on India and the Lucknow/UP area, though it's still versatile enough to keep the new Harry Potter in stock. The friendly proprietor will be happy to share his knowledge of Lucknow and recommend some good light reading.

Market: The main bazaars are at **Aminabad, Hazratganj,** and **Chowk.** Most shops are open from 10am-8pm, but hours often vary.

Police: Hazratganj Police Station, MG Marg (☎2229999). Turn left onto Hazratganj from Vidhan Sabha Marg. The police station is on the right side, next to the Kashmir Government Arts Emporium.

Pharmacy: Atul Pharma Medicals, 39/54 Ram Tirath Marg (☎2286941). Take the right-hand fork of Ram Tirath Marg after Hotel Naresh. Open daily 8am-10pm.

Hospital: Nishat, 3JC Base Rd. (☎2229674), Kaiserbagh. A small, private hospital with many doctors on call. Go to **Balarampur Hospital,** Golaganj (☎2224048) for emergency services. Both open 24hr.

Internet: Cyberfast Internet Cafe, Fast Business Centre, 1st floor (☎2210592). From MG Rd., turn down Lalbagh; FBS is the first major bldg. on the right. Rs35 per hr. Open 9:30am-midnight. **Sahu Talk Point** (☎2287109), across from Atul Pharma Medicals on Ran Tirata Marg, offers less reliable connections. Rs20 per hr. Open 6am-midnight.

Post Office: GPO, Vidhan Sabha Marg (☎2222887). Take a right from MG Rd. onto Vidhan Sabha. The GPO is the large yellow colonial bldg. with the clock tower. Open M-Sa 8am-6pm. **Postal Code:** 226001.

◤ ACCOMMODATIONS

Most of Lucknow's budget hotels are in Hazratganj and Charbagh, near the bus station. Plusher options can be found in the streets off MG Marg. Rock-bottom budget deals aren't the greatest—but there are plenty of good mid-range choices.

Hotel Vishwanath, Subhash Marg (☎2450879; markanday_202@hotmail.com). Standard rooms are a steal, with televisions, air-coolers, small sitting areas, and no dirt in sight. Good location for quick getaways. Singles Rs350-1300, doubles Rs450-2100. ❸

Hotel Paradise (☎2450793; hotelparadiselko@rediffmail.com). Take the first major left off Subhash Marg walking away from Station Rd; it's on the left. Brand-spanking new as of July 2003, and the proud owners plan to keep it looking that way. Bright paint on the walls, polished woodwork, sparkling bathrooms, air-cooled and A/C rooms available. Singles Rs400-600; doubles Rs450-700. ❸

Hotel New Ram Krishna, 17/2 Ashok Marg (☎2286380). A 5min. walk up past the main intersection with MG Rd., on the left. Popular, freshly painted place that is trying very hard to replace the original next door. All rooms with attached bath and wall-to-wall carpeting. Check-out 24hr. Singles Rs200; doubles Rs250-650. ❷

Pal Hotel, Ram Tirath Marg (☎2229476), 50m down on the right. In the heart of Narhi Bazaar, a no-frills, few-thrills hotel with reasonably clean, matrix-walled rooms and common or attached bath. Check-out 24hr. Singles Rs110-195; doubles Rs135-225. ❶

Carlton Hotel, Rana Pratap Marg (☎2222439). Turn left from Ashok Marg onto Rana Pratap Marg. The Carlton is 400m down on the left. Despite the facilities, this old palace maintains an air of forgotten luxury with huge furnished rooms, bathtubs, filtered water, and extensive porches. Bar, restaurant, and stuffed tiger downstairs. Free breakfast in the verdant courtyard gardens. Singles Rs500-1050; doubles Rs700-1350. ❸

🍴 FOOD

Lucknow owes its reputation for rich and refined cuisine to the *nawabs*. For the famous Avadhi kebabs, you will either have to hit one of the big hotel restaurants or sift through the small kiosks in the old city. Lucknow is also well known for its mangoes—the fruit market on Ram Tirth Marg is open every day.

Mu Man's Royal Cafe, Hazratganj, in front of Capoor's Hotel. A long, dark, and hushed hall serves up tastefully presented meals from Rs55. Excellent *pakoras* (Rs30) and pizzas (Rs55-75). Milkshakes with ice cream Rs30. Open daily 11am-11pm. ❷

Shanghai Surprise, Sapru Marg, near the intersection with Shah Najaf Marg, next to Hotel Ganti. High-end Chinese and Thai food. Eat "a drunken seaman's sizzling clay pot" (Rs150)—in layman's terms, a grilled fish fillet—while taking in Far Eastern decor. Thai dishes from Rs80; seafood Rs150-225. Open daily noon-3:30pm and 7pm-11pm. ❹

Falaknuma Restaurant, Clarks Avadh Hotel, 9th fl., on the MG Rd. traffic circle, after the cricket stadium. Carefully prepared food at high-class prices, and a dining room with unparalleled views of the city. Menu includes Lucknow classics and a full range of lamb and chicken kebabs (Rs160-285). A good place to play Avadh *nawab* for an evening, if you can afford it (mineral water Rs40). *Ghazal* singing starts every night except Tu at 8pm. Lunch 1-3pm, dinner 7-11:30pm. ❺

Moti Mahal, 75 Hazratganj, opposite the police station. Look for the trademark golden arches. The A/C restaurant upstairs is popular with the family set, and serves up Chinese and South Indian specialties from Rs50. **Mini-Mahal,** downstairs, serves breakfast, fast food, and cakes. Open daily 8am-11pm. ❷

Mahabeer Restaurant, at the intersection of Sapru Marg and Ashok Marg. Quiet, classy, family-run restaurant serves sumptuous veg. food and tasty sweets. The staff is very attentive. Great mini-meals Rs35-40, *thalis* Rs50-60. Open daily 10am-10:30pm. ❷

👁 SIGHTS

Most of what remains of old Lucknow's glittering mosques and flamboyant palaces is concentrated around the older **Husainabad** area to the northwest of the city, a 20min. rickshaw ride from the din of Hazratganj.

THE HIDDEN DEAL

TUNDAY'S KABABI

Six men sit on a platform above the narrow street, skillfully attending to the cooking tasks they'll repeat hundreds of times over the course of the day. One flattens the dough for the *paratha*, then fries up the bread; the next works with his hand in a large bucket of orange sauce, submerging whole uncooked chickens before handing them to his partner to roast. The fourth hunches over a large blue bucket of ground beef, right hand rolling small patties at lightning speed before popping them on the hot griddle in front of him. This is the scene in front of Tunday's Kababi, the second branch of Lucknow's oldest and most renowned *kabab* house. The menu card at Tunday's is as stripped-down as the décor, right down to the single digit prices that match up to five of the eleven items. Rs14 buys a full meal. The *parathas* are soft, feathery, and red hot on arrival, and the beef *kabab* has been browned to tender perfection. While Tunday's Kababi holds a prominent place in the hearts of the city's residents, it does not occupy a conspicuous spot on the main drag of Hazratganj. The first branch, which offers only beef *kabab*, is tucked away in the mazelike streets of Chowk. The second is just north of Aminatad's market. Take an Rs10 rickshaw to the neighborhood and start wandering. Ask around and you're bound to find a fan happy to point you—and your appetite—in the right direction.

(Old Najirabad Rd. Open daily 11am-10pm.)

THE INSIDER'S CITY

SNIFFING THE SUBCONTINENTAL SUBLIME

Mention India and odor in the same sentence, and you're likely to get a less-than-positive reaction. Indeed, for many a traveler, India is The Land of the Wrinkled Nose. In Lucknow, though, olfactory observation is more likely to run along the lines of *eau de toilette* than *eau de* toilet: this is a center for production of *attar*, India's finest class of perfumes. For centuries, *attar* has remained the scent of choice in both the secular and religious domains of Indian culture. The *attar* oil is extracted from pre-dawn flower buds and left in a large container of water. As the sun rises, the buds secrete an oily film which is then carefully preserved. There is an *attar* for every season and time of day: for summer, rose and Indian jasmine; for winter, musk. The undisputed raja of Lucknow's perfume biz is the **Azam Ali-Alam Ali Industry**, renowned for authentic attars since Mughal days. Their products are sold all over India and have been worn by the likes of Empress Nur Jahan and Princess Diana.

The best places to shop for *attar* in Lucknow are the shops in and around Chowk. Rs30-6000.

HUSAINABAD AREA

THE RESIDENCY. If the British Raj still governed India, the ruins of Lucknow's Residency would be one of its proudest monuments. One of the lengthiest struggles of the great uprising (the Indian "Mutiny" or "Revolt," depending on who's talking) took place when rebelling *sepoys* (Indians enlisted in the East India Company's army) besieged Lucknow's British residents from June to November of 1857 (see also **Sepoy Mutiny and Aftermath**, p. 67). The against-the-odds defense of the Residency was to leave a lasting impression on the colonial psyche. Once they had taken back the city, the British left the ruins as a monument to the stiff-lipped stubbornness and resilience of the thousands trapped and killed inside. The area surrounding the battered remains of the Residency has been converted into a shady green park near the center of the city. Many residents of Lucknow take leisurely walks there, especially during the early morning hours. Strangely enough, many are also extremely eager to give foreign visitors a tour.

The siege began when news reached Lucknow of *sepoy* rebellions throughout the region. The Residency, a mansion for the East India Company's agent in Avadh, was turned into a fortress for the 3000 local British and Raj supporters seeking refuge there. After five months, the British finally succeeded in breaking the siege, and the remaining survivors—less than a third of the original population—were evacuated to Allahabad. Meanwhile, the battle to take back the rest of the city raged on, and Lucknow was not completely back under British control until March of the following year.

As you enter the complex through Ballie Gate, there are several buildings on the right and left that were used during the siege as hospitals and armories. The Residency building itself, with only one pock-marked tower still standing, sits at the top of the hill amid palm trees and wide lawns. A museum and model **gallery** on its southern end houses a miniature version of the complex, along with several old weapons, prints, and a copy of the florid, jingoistic poem that Tennyson knocked off to commemorate the event. Below is the basement where many British women and children hid. Not far from the main building, the ruins of a small church and a cemetery hold the graves of the British "martyrs," including that of the unfortunate Sir Henry Lawrence, who, according to his epitaph, "tried to do his duty." *(Off MG Rd., northwest of Hazratganj. Open daily sunrise-sunset. Rs100.)*

BARA IMAMBARA. Marking the resting place of Asaf-ud-Daula and his wives, the Bara Imambara was constructed in 1784 as part of a food-for-work program instituted in the wake of a great famine. An *imambara* is a replica of the tomb of an *imam*, a martyred descendant of the Prophet Mohammed, revered by Shi'a Muslims. Dedicated to Husain Ibn Ali, grandson of the Prophet, the Bara Imambara is the center of April's Muharram festival, which mourns his death. Chandeliers hang from the 15m high ceiling of the great hall, which, without a single pillar of support, still stands as one of the largest vaulted spaces in the world. A staircase to the left side of the main building leads up to the roof and into the **Bhulbhalaiya,** a multi-level labyrinth designed for the entertainment of the *nawab*'s harem. A guide is not necessary, but proceed cautiously as dark, narrow passages turn suddenly and drop off into the great hall and its courtyard, 50 ft. below.

To the side of the Bara Imambara is the beautiful **Asafi Mosque,** built by Asaf-ud-Daula; it is closed to non-Muslims. Opposite the Asafi mosque is the **bauli,** once a spiraling series of water-cooled state apartments, now home to a green pool of algae and chattering bats. Straddling Husainabad Trust Rd. outside the *imambara* is the **Rumi Darwaza,** another work of Asaf-ud-Daula. This 20m-high gate, intended as a copy of the Sublime Port in Istanbul, is covered by a spine of trumpets. *(Open daily 7am-7pm. Rs10, includes entry to the bauli, the Rumi Darwaza, and the Picture Gallery.)*

OTHER SIGHTS IN THE HUSAINABAD AREA. Two kilometers further down off Husainabad Trust Rd. is the **Chota Imambara** (literally, "little *imambara*"), was commissioned in 1837 by Nawab Mohammed Ali Shah. Two Taj-shaped buildings in the courtyard mark the tombs of the *nawab*'s daughter and her husband. Ali Shah himself is buried below the main *imambara* structure. Inside are the *nawab*'s silver-plated pulpit, religious regalia used during Muharram, and dozens of dusty mirrors and chandeliers. *(Open daily 7am-7pm. Free.)* Farther up, past the sights of Hudainabad Trust Rd. on the left, is the **Jama Masjid,** Lucknow's largest mosque, and another conspicuous reminder of Ali Shah's legacy. The mosque is closed to non-Muslims. The **Picture Gallery,** inside a summer house built by the *nawabs*, displays forlorn-looking busts of Dante and Aristotle. *(Next to the clock tower. Open daily 8am-6pm. Entrance fee included in Bara Imambara ticket.)*

HAZJATGANJ AREA

SHAH NAJAF IMAMBARA. North of the Hazratganj area and west of the Botanical Gardens is the Shah Najaf Imambara. The monument holds the tomb of Nawab Ghazi-ud-din Haidar (r. 1814-27) and served as a rebel base in 1857. The treasures found inside include dusty chandeliers, grandfather clocks that no longer tell time, and doll house-sized replicas of mosques. Shi'a Muslims come here to express their devotion to Shah-i Najaf, the first Shi'a *imam*, and to the spiritual successor of the Prophet, Ali Ibn Abi Talib. On the fifth day of Muharram, fire-walking takes place in the *imambara*'s complex. *(Open daily 7am-7pm. Free. Tours Rs20.)*

LA MARTINIÈRE. The Martinière school is one of Lucknow's most distinctive and intriguing architectural survivals. Frenchman Claude Martin, money-lender and architectural advisor to the *nawab* as well as military man and colonial entrepreneur *par excellence*, designed this building as his own mausoleum after deciding to live out his final days in India. Martin built and owned dozens of houses throughout India, but his final creation, built in the late 1700s, is the only one to have survived intact, thanks to its conversion into a school in 1840. Described by one observer as a product of "the heterogeneous fancies of a diseased brain," La Martinière is an eclectic mishmash of architectural styles and flavors. Startled-looking lions cling to colonnades, while a chorus of sprightly figures strikes dignified poses on the rooftop. A large turbaned pillar completes the ensemble. Report to the principal's office first if you come during school hours. *(Off Kalidas Marg, southeast of Hazratganj. Rickshaws cost Rs15 and take about 15min. From May-June, it's best to arrive before 1pm, as office hours are shortened.)*

SIKANDAR BAGH. Once the site of Nawab Wajid Ali Shah's pleasure garden, this is where the final battle for the relief of the Residency took place, on November 16, 1857. Not much is left of the 137 sq. m compound, though the palm trees are impressively large. Across the street, the **National Botanical Research Institute** maintains lush gardens and nurseries, especially popular with early-morning, sneaker-clad walkers. *(At the intersection of Ashok Marg and Rana Pratap Marg. Gardens open daily 5-8am and 2-4:30pm. Free.)*

VOLUNTEER OPPORTUNITY

There are many English language schools in Lucknow, several of which accept volunteer teachers. La Martinière Boys College tends to accept (male and female) volunteer teachers most frequently. Stints last up to nine months. Write Mr. E. de Souza, the Principal, La Martinière College (Polo Grounds), Lucknow, 281001, UP, India, for more information. La Martinière Girls College accepts only female volunteers, and does so less frequently. To inquire, write Mrs. F. Abraham, the Lady Principal, La Martinière Girls' College, Moti Mahal Marg, Lucknow, UP, India.

♫ 📷 ENTERTAINMENT AND SHOPPING

Lucknow's legacy of self-indulgent rulers seems not to have trickled down to the commoners; the city's nightlife does not sparkle. A few **pool halls** hide on the upper floors of Hazratganj buildings, and budget **bars** are found along Station Rd. Pricier drinks are available in the **Falaknuma Restaurant** (see above). The only proper bar in Hazratganj is the pine-paneled **Tashna Bar,** Sapru Marg, in the Hotel Gomti. Full of chain-smoking, hard-drinking local businessmen crowded around a petite TV, this small, dark, air-conditioned place serves booze and basic munchies. (Beer Rs80; liquor from Rs50. Open daily 11am-10:30pm.) A little farther from the city center, the **Simbha Bar** at the Carlton Hotel has about the same stuff on tap, but the bar area is more informal, with couches, lounge chairs, and psychedelic paintings of animals on the walls. (Open daily 10am-10:30pm.) **Novelty Cinema,** on Lalbagh, opposite Aahar's Restaurant, regularly shows Hollywood movies (usually dubbed) as well as a regular slate of Bollywood hits in a large air-conditioned theater with comfortable seats (Rs15-45; Hollywood shows daily 10:30am). Lucknow is also home to the **Bhatkhande Music College,** one of two major schools of kathakali dance in India. Performances take place in several auditoriums in town, including **Uma Nath Bali Auditorium** in Kaiserbagh and **Gandhi Bhavan Auditorium.** Check at the tourist office for information; ticket prices are minimal. **Aminabad,** west of Hazratganj, is one of Lucknow's old bazaar areas and the best place to shop for crafts. Items of clothing with *chikan* embroidery cost Rs20-5000 per piece.

FAIZABAD फैज़ाबाद ☎ 05278

Before the *nawab* moved to Lucknow in 1775, Faizabad was the capital of Avadh. Today this mid-sized city is something of a pit stop—pilgrims and tourists spend the night here before heading to Ayodhya for the day, usually only stopping long enough between hotel and tempo to sample the local mango shakes. Several monuments from the city's heyday remain, including the mausolea of Nawab Shuja-ud-Daula and his wife Bahu Begum, the city's great patroness. Of course, Faizabad is only as unremarkable as an Indian city could possibly be—the bazaars are still bustling, the traffic is still outrageous, and cheap treats lie around every street corner. Show your curious foreign face on a trip through some of the town's back streets and you're bound to come away with a few stories.

TRANSPORTATION. Rickshaw rides from the bus and train stations to the Chowk area average 10min. (Rs10). **Buses** head to: **Allahabad** (every 45min. 5:30am-12:30am, Rs70); **Delhi** (16hr., 2-3 per day 1:30-5:30pm, Rs301); **Gorakhpur** (4hr., every 45min. 5:30am-12:30am, Rs61); **Lucknow** (every 45min. 5:30am-12:30am, Rs56); **Varanasi** (6hr., 2-3 per day 5am-2pm, Rs90). Bus departures can be erratic and unpredictable. **Tempos** to Ayodhya leave regularly from the Gurdi Bazaar, Chowk (Rs4), and the bus station (Rs6). **Trains** run to: **Delhi** (12½-14hr., 1 per day, Rs258); **Lucknow** (2½-4hr., 5-7 per day 6:20am-6:55pm, Rs44); **Varanasi** (4-5½hr., 3-5 per day 11:30am-9:20pm, Rs59).

⚡ 🔢 ORIENTATION AND PRACTICAL INFORMATION. There are two main areas in Faizabad: the **Civil Lines** region, where the bus and train stations are located, and **Chowk**, a much busier section 2km to the east. The bus station is on **Civil Lines Road,** which becomes **Rekavganj** 400m after the intersection with **Station Road.** The railway station is off Station Rd. Rekavganj leads to Chowk, where large sandstone gates mark the intersection with **Fatehganj.** The **Moti Bagh** area is to the right. The **Regional Tourist Office** is in an alley off Station Rd. 100m before **Krishna Palace,** on the right after the Shane Avadh Hotel. The alley is just before Krishna Palace, on the right. (☎223214. Open M-Sa 10am-5pm.) The **State Bank of India,** off of Station Rd., exchanges AmEx traveler's checks. Coming from Civil Lines, take the first right after Krishna Palace. **Cyber Zone,** at the intersection of Civil Lines and Station Rd., provides internet access (Rs25 per hr.; open daily 9:30am-9:30pm). The bank is on the left. (☎220430. Open M-F 10am-2pm, Sa 10am-noon.) Faizabad's **post office** is on Station Rd. (☎222301. Open M-Sa 10am-6pm.)

🔢 🔢 ACCOMMODATIONS AND FOOD. Budget lodgings are found in both areas of town. The Civil Lines area is quieter and more convenient than Chowk; most travelers choose to stay here, close to the bus and train stations, as well as the road to Ayodhya. All of the hotels listed below have restaurants; other than these, simple roadside *dhabas* are the only other places to eat. The **Tirupati Hotel ❷,** Civil Lines Rd., near the bus station, is probably the best option here—the spacious, well-furnished rooms come with soap, towels, and attached bath (☎223231). The **Shane Avadh Hotel ❷,** next door to Tirupati, offers similar digs, though the beds are a bit harder. (☎223586. Singles Rs175-590; doubles Rs200-690.) The attached **Mezbar Restaurant ❶,** serves the usual trifecta—Chinese, Indian, and Continental—in a dim, air-conditioned dining room (open daily 7am-10:30pm). If you'd prefer a more comfortable stay in Faizabad, **Hotel Krishna Palace ❸,** on Station Rd. toward the railway station, offers clean, carpeted rooms with large color TVs and sweet-scented bathrooms—even at the low end of the price scale. (☎221367. Singles Rs400-1100; doubles Rs500-1300.) Its **Caveri Restaurant ❷** serves the usual cuisine at slightly elevated prices. (Open daily 8am-11pm.) For livelier surroundings, the best option in Chowk is **Abha Hotel ❷,** in an alley off Fatehganj in the Moti Bagh area (a 15min. rickshaw ride from the railway station). All rooms have baths and TVs. (Singles Rs150-250; doubles Rs200-300.)

AYODHYA अयोध्या ☎ 05238

Ayodhya is one of India's holiest places, a village where the temples seem to outnumber the houses, and at least one slow-moving *sadhu* is always in sight. According to legend, the city was founded by the Hindu law-giver Manu, and it was also the birthplace of Lord Rama, hero of the *Ramayana* epic and the seventh incarnation of Vishnu. Many of Ayodhya's most important sites are devoted to him and his faithful servant Hanuman, the monkey god. For the past ten years, pious worship and a massive police presence have been forced into an improbable coex-

UTTAR PRADESH

istence. Ayodhya catapulted into the limelight in 1992, when Hindu-Muslim unrest broke out over the controversial Babri Masjid (see **Sights,** below). Thousands were killed in the nationwide riots that followed, and Ayodhya has since remained a flash point for community violence. Foreigners are unlikely to encounter any difficulties, but should check the news before visiting, especially during the unpredictable **Ramanavami** festival celebrating Rama's birth.

A major pilgrimage destination for thousands of Hindus, Ayodhya today sees few foreign visitors—a stay here makes a welcome break from the stresses and strains of some of India's more popular tourist destinations. Off the main road, every street and alley is home to at least one temple, and usually a peaceful air of religious serenity pervades the air.

🚆 **TRANSPORTATION.** Frequent, sporadic **trains** depart from the **Railway Station,** 400m south of NH 28 and the Sri Ram Hospital. To: **Faizabad** and points west (30min., 10:40am, Rs18); **Varanasi** (4hr., 11:35am, Rs57). It is much easier to catch trains from Faizabad. **Buses** between Faizabad and **Gorakhpur** (3½hr., every hr., Rs64) stop briefly; catch them at the new **bus stand** near the bridge on NH 28. **Tempos** and **taxis** run the most convenient service to Faizabad (Rs4-6).

🔦🔢 **ORIENTATION AND PRACTICAL INFORMATION. National Highway (NH) 28** cuts through Ayodhya on its way from Faizabad to Gorakhpur. The **railway station,** tourist bungalow, and most of the major sights (including Hanuman Gardhi and Kanak Bhavan) are on either side of the highway, within walking distance of the bus station and *tempo* stop. Ayodhya is not a big city; it's not much more than a 20min. walk from one side of town to the other along the main highway. The best way to see Ayodhya is to escape as quickly as possible from the clamor of the built-up strip and walk north through the winding, climbing, temple-packed streets on your way to the *ghats,* or head in the opposite direction, into the more spaced-out but no-less-temple-filled south. There is a **tourist office** stand opposite the railway station, but it is only open during festivals. The reception desk at Hotel Sakhet, 100m from the railway station, functions as a tourist office and keeps more consistent hours. To get there, turn right from the bus station, walk down NH 28 toward Faizabad, and take a left onto the first road. At the train station, turn left; the hotel is 100m down on the left. (Open daily 10am-5pm.) For **currency exchange,** head to Faizabad. **Sri Ram Hospital** (☎ 232840) is 150m west of the bus stand (to the right, if you're facing away from it). The **post office** is at Shrinagar Hat, on NH 28 as you head towards Gorakhpur. (☎ 232025. Open M-Sa 10am-6pm.)

🔦🔲 **ACCOMMODATIONS AND FOOD.** Ayodhya offers only a limited range of accommodations. For the most part, ashrams, occasionally with single rooms (and attached bath and fan), are the most popular and sensible choice for the thousands of pilgrims who descend upon Ayodhya each year. Directly opposite the bus station, the **Birla Dharamsala** ❶ is located in a peaceful garden compound next to the quaint and serene temple. (☎ 232252. Singles with bath Rs100; doubles Rs150.) Those who wish to stay in hotels usually spend the night in Faizabad, though there are several decent options in Ayodhya. **Hotel Sakhet** ❶ (the UP tourist bungalow), 100m to the left of the train station, offers institutional comfort, with uninspiring but clean rooms in a very quiet locale. (☎ 232435. Dorms Rs60; singles with bath Rs225; doubles Rs250-500.) The equally dull **restaurant** ❷ has a small menu and a vegetarian *thali* for Rs45, but only serves food to guests. (Open daily 7am-10pm.) Say "restaurant" to any rickshaw driver in town and you'll probably end up at **Shyam Restaurant** ❶, in the **Ram Hotel** ❷, just down the street off NH 28 opposite Hanuman Fort. It's the best (and perhaps the only) sit-down, A/C place in town, and serves all-veg., including tasty *dosas* (Rs10-25). The attached hotel boasts high-ceilinged rooms with air-coolers and glossy walls. (☎ 234241. Doubles Rs300.)

◙ **SIGHTS.** With sacred sites practically around every corner, Ayodhya is a temple-lover's paradise. *Sadhus* and pilgrims are everywhere, and fluorescent stalls selling sparkling bangles and cone-shaped piles of red and saffron *tilak* powder line the streets between temples. Many of the most important religious sites are within a 5-15min. walk of the bus and train stations, but Ayodhya is not the kind of place that comes with a convenient checklist of must-see attractions—the whole town is really one huge temple complex, alive with a continuous stream of holy hustle and bustle. The best way to drink in the atmosphere is to do as the *sadhus* do and let your unhurried footsteps lead you from one shrine to the next.

The **Ram Janam Bhumi** (known as **Babri Masjid** to Muslims) is the contested holy site that led to Hindu-Muslim clashes in 1992 and brought international attention to Ayodhya. The trouble began over the location of a mosque, built during the 16th century by the Mughal Emperor Babur on a site that many Hindus hold to be the birthplace of Rama, hero-king of the *Ramayana* and incarnation of Vishnu. The mosque became a symbol for the resentment and prejudice many Hindus felt (and still feel) toward Indian Muslims. Hindu Nationalists, such as the Vishwa Hindu Parishad (VHP) used the Babri Masjid as a rallying cry, and the mosque was eventually closed due to the controversy. On December 6, 1992, religious fervor turned to violence when 200,000 VHP-led militant Hindus (most of them from outside Ayodhya) descended on the town, smashing through police barricades to destroy the Babri Masjid and erect a makeshift temple in its place. Today, pilgrims, archaeology enthusiasts, and students of contemporary Indian politics huddle through a maze of cage-like fences surrounded by armed soldiers for a glimpse of the shrine, a glittering altar in a small military tent, and the mosque rubble below. Expect a thorough frisking and even a police escort. **Bring your passport.** No cameras or bags are allowed. (From the bus stand, take the first major left off NH 28 into the north half of town; keep heading up and to the left. Open daily 7-11am and 2-6pm.)

The **Hanuman Garhi,** in the white fort above the bus station, is one of Ayodhya's most important temples. It is abuzz with worshipers all day and into the night. Supposedly marking the spot where Hanuman sat guard in a cave overlooking Rama's birthplace, the main tile-covered shrine is at the top of a flight of over 75 steps. Leave your shoes at the bottom and look out for monkey droppings. The **Jain Temple** complex on Hanuman Rd. houses a 10m-high marble statue of Lord Kishabhadev. To get there from the bus station, walk away from Faizabad on NH 28 and take the 2nd right. The temple is on the right 50m past the first major intersection. (Open daily 5am-8pm. Inquire at the complex office for a free tour.) Other temples include the Kanak Bhawan (open daily 8am-noon and 4:30-9pm), off the main road farther up and east from the Hanuman Garhi, and the **Nageshwar Nath** temple, by the canal and river **ghats** over on the east side of town.

GORAKHPUR गोरखपुर   ☎ 0551

As the major transportation hub between India and Nepal, Gorakhpur is more often traveled through than to, and few people arrive here without definite plans to move on again as soon as possible. Buses leave regularly for the border, and the main railway station sends trains to major cities in India, so getting out is easy enough—a good thing, as Gorakhpur offers little to the visitor. Founded around AD 1400 and named for the Hindu saint Gorakhnath, Gorakhpur still hosts the temple of the patron saint of the Natha Yogis, 4km from the railway station on Nepal Rd. Gorakhpur became an army town under the Mughals and again under the British, who used it as a base for recruiting Gorkha soldiers from Nepal; it is still a major military center today. Insect repellent is a must if you're going to be overnighting here; hungry mosquitoes seem to penetrate even the most carefully netted hotel room windows.

⊏ TRANSPORTATION

Trains: Railway Station, Station Rd. To: **Allahabad** (11hr., 5am and 10:30pm, Rs172); **Kolkata** (18-23hr., 1-2 per day, Rs320); **Delhi** (13-18hr., 5:10pm, Rs317); **Jhansi** (12hr., 1 per day, Rs250); **Lucknow** (4-6½hr., 9-14 per day 4am-12:45am, Rs140); **Varanasi** (6hr., 4 per day 5am-10:30pm, Rs134).

Buses: Gorakhpur Bus Station, 300m down the road from the railway station. To: **Faizabad** (4hr., every hr. 5am-9pm, Rs65); **Kushinagar** (1hr., every 30-60min. 5am-8pm, Rs22); **Lucknow** (8hr., every 30-60min. 5am-9pm, Rs117); **Sunauli** (2hr., every hr. 5am-10pm, Rs43). Buses to **Varanasi** (6hr., every 30-60min. 5:30am-10pm, Rs90) and other points south depart from **Kacheri Bus Stand,** 1.5km south of the railway station. Regular buses (every 30-60min. 6am-8pm) also run from the intersection before the railway station to the border with **Nepal;** make sure you are getting on a government bus. From the border, you will have to change buses and buy a new ticket. There are many **private buses** to the border operating from the same area, but they tend to charge up to twice as much for tickets through to **Kathmandu** or **Pokhara.** The so-called "direct" service offered on these buses is, in fact, no faster than the government bus route. Either way, you will have to spend several hours at the border arranging your visa and switching buses in Nepal. For more information, see **Sunauli,** p. 875.

✴❼ ORIENTATION AND PRACTICAL INFORMATION

Most of Gorakhpur lies south of its **railway station.** Inside the station is a small tourist information booth (sporadically open 10am-5pm). Budget hotels and restaurants are on **Station Road,** directly opposite the station. The downtown area, **Golghar,** also contains some cheap places to eat and spend the night. It centers on **Jalkal Chawan Road,** which intersects with Station Rd. just west of the railway station. The road south from the railway station's entrance leads to the **main bus stand,** 300m away, before becoming Park Rd; this marks the beginning of the **Civil Lines** region. The **State Bank of India,** on Bank Rd. downtown, cashes AmEx traveler's checks and exchanges US and UK currency. (☎2338497. Open M-F 10am-2pm, Sa 10am-noon.) The **GPO** is located near the southern end of Bank Rd., by the district hospital. (☎2333018. Open M-Sa 10am-6pm.) **Postal Code:** 273001.

⌂ ACCOMMODATIONS

Several decent budget hotels are located directly opposite the railway station, beyond the swarm of young men competing to serve you breakfast or put you on a bus bound for Nepal. In the center of the city and at the western end of Station Rd. (Rs10-15 rickshaw ride from the station) are a couple of mid-range options, which are a bit quieter, but also a bit less convenient. Most places have 24hr. check-out, single-Hindi-channel black-and-white TVs, and great views of the station chaos; for a quieter night try to get a room in the back.

Hotel Elora, Station Rd. (☎2200647). Opposite the railway station. Simple, clean rooms with attached bath and eager room service. Those at the back are away from most of the Station Rd. noise. Singles Rs125-350; doubles Rs150-450. ❶

Hotel Siddhartha, Station Rd. (☎2209139), past Hotel Elora. The rooms are pretty standard for the area, but the enthusiastic manager brightens things up. Currency exchange available. Singles Rs125; doubles Rs175. ❶

Hotel Marina (☎2337630), Golghar, on an alley off Jalkal Bhawan Rd., behind Hotel President in the center of town. Slightly more upscale than most, its large, clean, carpeted rooms with attached baths are decorated with seashell curtains and pastel color schemes. Singles Rs225; doubles Rs275-650. ❷

Hotel President, Jalkal Bhawan Rd. (☎2337654). Gorakhpur's answer to high-end accommodation is no great shakes, though the rooms are a bit more clean and comfortable, the A/C is chillier, and the colorful murals in each room brighten things up. A/C doubles Rs550-3000. ❸

■ FOOD

Plenty of small, open-air restaurants serve snacks and simple meals along the strip opposite the railway station. For anything more elaborate, sanitary, or comfortable, you'll have to make the trek into town.

Bobi's Restaurant, Jalkal Bhawan Rd., across from Hotel President. A proper and popular place with a nicely finished interior. The Indian dishes are excellent and filling, but you'll be missing out if you don't save room for dessert from the confectioner's shop out front. Open daily noon-10:30pm; full meals served noon-3pm and 7-10:30pm. ❷

Queen's Restaurant, in Hotel President. Veg. and non-veg. standards (Rs30-160) served up under orange ceiling lights and powerful fans. Open daily 8am-11pm. ❸

King's Bar, across the alley from Queen's Restaurant. The perfect place to drown your sorrows if you've just missed the bus to Nepal. Beer Rs70-90, spirits Rs25-65. ❷

Vardan Restaurant, Station Rd., between Hotel Standard and Hotel Elora. Small, with occasional blasts of A/C, this is probably the best of the many places dotted around the station area. Food ranges from omelettes to *tandoori* dishes (Rs22-75) and spring rolls (Rs35-40). "Wine not allowed." Open daily 8am-11pm. ❷

KUSHINAGAR कुशीनगर ☎05563

"All things must pass. Decay is inherent in all things." Buddha uttered this final message before taking his last breath here in Kushinagar, where he was cremated and went on to attain the ultimate happily-never-after of *parinirvana*. Having been the site of such an auspicious end, the town flourished for several hundred years before the 12th-century decline of Buddhism in India spelled Kushinagar's own devolution as a major religious destination. Its temples and monasteries soon fell into forgotten ruin. 700 years later, a group of archaeologists working under the auspices of the East India Company unearthed a series of *stupas* and images that provided enough evidence to ascertain Kushinagar's holy heritage.

Today, the town has returned to prominence as a major religious center. The transition has been eased by foreign influence and investment, and it's evident to the casual observer: the paved streets are flat, smooth, and (mostly) free of trash, as are the carefully-tended lawns and gardens of the many temples that line the way. The money is still rolling in—a group of Americans and Europeans is financing the construction of a 500 ft. statue of Buddha in the coming years. Very much a beggar-free, truck-free, cow-free zone, Kushinagar is a small village remarkable for its pervasive air of peace and prosperity, small enough to be visited on a daytrip from Gorakhpur, but worth an overnight stay.

■ TRANSPORTATION. Small buses go regularly between Kushinagar and **Gorakhpur** (1¼hr., every 30min. 6:30am-8pm, Rs24). The **bus station** is in the town of **Kasia,** 3km from Kushinagar. Ask to be let off at Buddha Dwar gate; otherwise, you will have to get another bus back to the gate from Kasia station (Rs6). **Tempos** also make frequent runs between Gorakhpur and Kushinagar for a slightly higher fare than buses. Either form of transport can be caught from the post office on NH 28.

■■ ▧ **ORIENTATION AND PRACTICAL INFORMATION.** Fifty-one kilometers east of Gorakhpur, Kushinagar is on **National Highway (NH) 28.** All the places of worship, tourist attractions, and accommodations are on Kushinagar's L-shaped main road, **Buddh Marg,** which can be entered through the **Buddha Dwar gate** at the highway. The **Regional Tourist Office** is 200m down Buddh Marg, on the right, across from the Myanmar Temple and next to the Shree Birla Buddhist temple. (Open M-Sa 10am-5pm.) Internet access is available at **Shukla Communication Center,** at the crook of the L, for Rs60 per hr. The **post office,** next to the **police station,** is a small, white building opposite the Buddha Dwar on NH 28. (Open M-Sa 10am-4pm.) **Postal Code:** 274403.

▧▧ **ACCOMMODATIONS AND FOOD.** The main tourist season in Kushinagar runs from October to March; many hotels and restaurants close down completely in the off season. Those listed below are open throughout the year. The **Linh-Son Chinese Rest House ❷,** at the Chinese Temple on Buddh Marg, next to the Myanmar Temple, maintains two stories of spotlessly clean, 3-bed rooms with attached bath. (☎271019. Rs250-350.) The monks of the **Myanmar Buddhist Temple and Guesthouse ❶,** next door, offer simple dorms to pilgrims and visitors on a donation basis. (☎271035. At least Rs50.) **Hotel Pathik Niwas ❸,** Buddha Marg, 200m past the tourist office on the right, offers a wider range of accommodations. A white-walled complex built around manicured gardens and lined with paintings depicting the life of the Buddha, this UP government hotel's rooms and bathrooms are clean (toilet seats "sanitized for your protection"), and sheets and towels are changed daily. (☎272038. Singles Rs400; doubles Rs500; A/C deluxe rooms Rs900-975; small, kitchen-equipped "American huts" Rs700-800.) The **restaurant ❷** does everything from cheeseburgers (Rs30) to *malai kofta* (Rs40), as well as the obligatory chow mein menu. (Open 6am-10pm.) The **Yama Kwality Cafe ❶,** in front of the Myanmar Temple, is the only other restaurant open all year. Run by a friendly Bengali-Nepalese family, the cafe dishes out excellent *thukpas* (Rs25-40), fried rice (Rs20-40), and tourist information (free) and maintains a good selection of newspapers and magazines.

▧ **SIGHTS.** Kushinagar's main attractions are the ancient *stupas* and images rediscovered here during the last century. These range along the main Buddh Marg stretch. Dotted between the historical remains are several modern temples and an expansive green **Meditation Park.** Set on beautiful green lawns next to the Myanmar Temple is Kushinagar's holiest site, the **Buddha Mahaparinirvana Temple,** said to mark the spot where the Buddha was liberated from the cycle of rebirth and attained the ideal state of *parinirvana.* Extensive traces remain of the original temple, and a 6m reclining Buddha survives inside the main temple building. Behind the image is a large, modern *stupa,* built to protect the age-weathered original beneath it. The original *stupa* is believed to contain a portion of the Buddha's cremated remains. Left out of the temple grounds and farther down Buddh Marg just as the road shifts left, the small **Matha Kunwar Temple** stands on the site of the Buddha's last sermon and contains a small, golden statue of the Buddha. Another 500m down Buddh Marg on the left is the **Government Buddha Museum.** The impressive building is a bit large for the collection of Hindu, Jain, and Buddhist art objects within. Still, it's worth a look—some statues date back to 80 BC. (Open Tu-Sa 10:30am-4:30pm, Rs4.) One kilometer further down the road, past the Japanese and Korean temples and the impressive Thai *wat,* is the remains of the **Ramambhar**

Stupa, built on the site of the Buddha's cremation. Pay no attention to the Indian tourists: climbing on the *stupa* will do your karma no good. (*Stupas* open daily sunrise-sunset. Free.) For a more comprehensive tour of the area, the owner of Yana Kwality Cafe leads day-long nature hikes to various villages and holy sites. (Rs100; includes tea or coffee, refreshments, and lunch.)

VARANASI (BENARAS) वाराणसी ☎ 0542

For Hindus, Varanasi (also known as Benaras) is the holiest place on earth and the chosen residence of Lord Shiva, said to abide in every nook and cranny of the city. Those who die in Varanasi are guaranteed *moksha,* or liberation from the cycle of death and rebirth, no matter what they may have done in their life-times. This otherworldly confidence in the city's spirituality has made Vara-nasi the chosen residence of over 1.6 million people. In addition, countless thousands of pilgrims come here every day to bathe in the sacred waters of the Ganga and to pay their respects at the temples that stretch all along the river-side *ghats,* numerous sets of stone steps that lead down to the river.

The modern city takes its name from the two rivers that bind it, the Varuna to the north, and the Assi to the south. The Old City is a maze of tortuous lanes congested with animals and people. Small boys make small fortunes guiding for-eigners to the Golden Temple through little-used alleys. The city's denizens and most of its visitors are extremely religious. For many Hindus, a visit to Kashi (the ancient name of the city, meaning "The Luminous One") is roughly analogous to the Muslim pilgrimage to Mecca. Around the city, dead bodies are a common sight, delivered to the funeral pyre accompanied by the traditional chant, *"Ram Naam Satya Hai"* (The Name of Lord Ram is The Truth).

In the early days of Aryan settlement in India, Varanasi gained fame as a North Indian trading post and as a center of spiritual life. Teachers and ascetics came to mingle with the local deities in the ponds and rivers of Anandavana and in the For-est of Bliss, which grew here before the city developed. The Buddha came to Sar-nath, on the outskirts of Kashi, to preach his first sermon. Varanasi's Hindu priests were active in developing their religion through the millennia. The city itself soon became an object of worship: a holy place inhabited by holy beings and bounded by a holy river. Due to five centuries (AD 1200-1700) of levelings at the hands of Muslims, no building in Varanasi is more than 300 years old. However, the city was never totally wiped out—Varanasi today stands as one of the world's oldest con-tinuously inhabited cities.

 WARNING. Rickshaw-*wallahs* in Varanasi often collect commission from hotel owners for delivering guests. Beware of anyone who offers you a "ride any-where" for "Rs5 only"; you will have very little control over your destination. Be firm about where you want to go, and don't believe your rickshaw-*wallah* when he tells you that the hotel you asked for is "full" or "closed." If you have any con-cerns or doubts upon arrival, call a hotel yourself from the train station, or ask the staff at the tourist office to do so for you.

▐ TRANSPORTATION

Flights: Babatpur Airport, 24km northwest of Varanasi Junction Railway Station. The **Indian Airlines** booking office (☎ 2343746 or 2345959), Cantonment. Just off the Mall. To: **Agra** (1hr.; M, W, F 4pm; US$115); **Delhi** (1½hr., 4pm, US$185); **Kathmandu** (1hr.; Tu, Th, Sa 11:40am; US$71); **Mumbai** (4hr., 4pm, US$255).

UTTAR PRADESH

Trains: Varanasi Junction Railway Station. Rs20 by cycle-rickshaw or Rs35 by auto-rickshaw from Godaulia Crossing. To: **Allahabad** (2-3hr., 7-11 per day 4am-11:30pm, Rs50); **Delhi** (12-15hr., 5 per day 2:10-11pm, Rs248); **Gorakhpur** (5-8hr., 4 per day 12:15am-4:30pm, Rs92); **Lucknow** (4½-7½hr., 6-7 per day 5:10am-6:35pm, Rs120); **Mumbai** (26hr., 11:30am, Rs340); Patna (4-6½hr., 4-6 per day 2:05am-9:10pm, Rs97); **Satna** (5½-9hr., 5-9 per day 4am-11:10pm, Rs100). Satna is a 4hr. bus ride to **Khajuraho.**

Buses: Cantonment Bus Station, 300m to the left on Station Rd. as you exit the train station. To: **Agra** (16-18hr., 5pm, Rs247); **Allahabad** (3hr., every 30min. 4am-11pm, Rs54); **Delhi** (18hr., 7pm, Rs309); **Gaya** (7hr., 6:30am, Rs91); **Gorakhpur** (6hr., every hr. 5am-7pm, Rs80); **Lucknow** (8hr., 8 per day 5-10:30am, Rs135); **Sonauli** (10hr., 10 per day 6:30am-6:30pm, Rs134).

Local Transportation: Auto-rickshaws from the Cantonment to Sarnath should cost Rs50. All other destinations in the city should cost less than Rs50. **Cycle-rickshaws** can traverse the winding lanes and alleys (gullies or galis) of the Old City. Drivers here make careers out of over-charging visitors. **Tempos** run from Lanka Crossing to Ramnagar Fort (Rs20-30). **City buses** connect Varanasi Station and Sarnath (Rs10).

■ ORIENTATION

Varanasi's city limits are marked by the **Varuna River** to the north and the **Assi River** to the south. **Panch Koshi Road,** which circles greater Varanasi's 16km radius, marks the boundary of the sacred zone of Kashi. The **Old City** is stacked and squeezed up along the western banks of the Ganga at the point where the river begins to flow straight north. The old residence of the Maharaja at Ramnagar Fort lies on the east bank. Steep steps from the river *ghats* lead into a labyrinth of narrow street and alleys lined with temples, shrines, budget hotels, and restaurants. Finding your way through this tangle may seem impossible at times, though many of the main backpacker hang-outs are well marked, and the *ghats* are clearly labeled in English. Be wary of accepting offers of help in finding your way as lost-looking foreigners are easy targets for touts. Copycat hotels also abound—as soon as one place becomes popular, half the hotels around it change their names to something confusingly similar.

Sticking to the river is the best way to navigate Varanasi, as most points of interest are along the waterfront. **Dasashwamedh Ghat,** the city's main *ghat*, is easily reached via **Dasashwamedh Road** from **Godaulia Crossing,** a central traffic circle. The surrounding area near the **Kashi Vishwanath Temple (Golden Temple),** known as **Godaulia,** contains many of the budget hotels and is connected to the northern parts of Varanasi by **Chowk Road,** one of the few roads near the *ghats* wide enough for cars. Trains from the east cross the **Malaviya Bridge,** just beyond Raj Ghat. The railway and bus stations are inland in the northern part of the city. This is where things become more open and less chaotic, around the luxury hotel and tourist services of the leafy **Cantonment,** as well as on the campus of Benaras Hindu University, at the city's southern tip, near **Lanka Crossing.**

■ PRACTICAL INFORMATION

Tourist Office: The **UP Regional Tourist Office** (☎2346370) is located within the main railway station and can be quite helpful. Open daily 6am-8pm. The **Tourist Bungalow** (☎2343413), Parade Kothi, Cantonment. A short walk south of the railway station. Open M-Sa 10am-5pm. The **Government of India Tourist Office,** 15B, The Mall (☎2501784), Cantonment. Next to the Tourist Bungalow. Open M-F 9am-5:30pm, and Sa 9am-2pm.

The Mall
State Bank of India
Govt. of India Tourist Office
Indian Airlines
THE CANTONMENT
Varanasi Junction Railway Station
U.P. Tourist Office
Station Rd.
ENGLISHIA LINE
CHETGANJ
Fatman Rd.
Bharat Mata Temple
SIGRA
Aurangabad Rd.
Annie Besant Rd.
SIGRA CROSSING
SIDDH GIRI BAGH
GODAULIA/ DASASHWAMEDH
Luxa Rd.
Shri Ramakrishna Marg
BHELUPURA
NAGWA
Pilgrims Book House
Durga Temple
Tulsi Manas Mandir
Sankat Mochan Temple
University Rd.
Panch Koshi Rd.
Malviya Bhawan Museum
Sir Sunderlal Hospital
New Vishwanath Temple
Bharat Kala Bhawan School of Performing Arts
BENARES HINDU UNIVERSITY

TO BABATPUR AIRPORT (24km)
Varuna River
TO SARNATH (8km)
Sarnath Rd.
City Railway Station
Grand Trunk Rd.
JAITPURA
Raj Bazar Rd.
National Highway 2
ADAMPURA
KOTWALI
Bare Ganesh Temple
Kala Bhaironath Temple
Clock Tower
Kashi Railway Station
Raj Ghat
Malaviya Bridge
RAJGHAT
Adi Keshava
Chowk Rd.
Kabir Chaura Rd.
Chetgang Rd.
Bindu Madhava Temple
Dharhara Mosque
Panchganga Ghat
CHOWK
SEE CENTRAL VARANASI MAP
Vishwanath Temple
Manikarnika Ghat
Gai Ghat
Trilochan Ghat
TO MUGHAL SARAI (19km) AND PATNA (240km)
Dasashwamedh Ghat
Pandey Ghat
Sonarpur Rd.
Bengal Tola
Chowki Ghat
Kedar Ghat
Harishchandra Ghat
Hanuman Ghat
Shivala Ghat
Chet Singh Ghat
Panchkot Ghat
Jain Ghat
Bachhraj Ghat
Tulsi Ghat
Assi Ghat
Durga Kund
Lolarka Kund
Hanuman Temple
RAMNAGAR
Ganga River
Heritage Hospital
LANKA CROSSING
Ramnagar Rd.
Pontoon Bridge (Nov.-June)
Ramnagar Fort
Grand Trunk Rd.
Vidyapith Dr.
TO ALLAHABAD (128km)

0   800 yards
0   800 meters
N
LG
Ramnagar Rd.
National Highway 7

Varanasi
▲ ACCOMMODATIONS
Ganges View Hotel , 7
Hotel Arya, 4
Hotel Temple on Ganges, 8
🍎 FOOD
Bread of Life Bakery, 5
Malika Restaurant, 2
Mandarin Restaurant, 1
Pizzeria Vatika, 6
Yelchico Bar & Restaurant, 3

UTTAR PRADESH

Currency Exchange: State Bank of India (☎2343445), The Mall, Cantonment, down the street to the right of the Best Western (or Kashika) Hotel. Open M-F 10am-2pm, Sa 10am-noon. **Bank of Baroda** (☎2401471), Godaulia. On the left, just before Vishwanath Gali, as you head down Dasashwamedh Rd. towards the *ghat*. Gives advances on MC/V. Open M-F 11am-3pm, Sa 11am-1pm.

Market: Fruit vendors cluster around **Dasashwamedh Ghat**. Pilgrim supplies and souvenirs can be found along **Vishwanath Gali,** and saris in **Thatheri Bazaar** and **Kunj Gali.**

Police: Dasashwamedh Police Station (☎2321283).

Hospital: Heritage Hospital (☎2367977 or 2366726), Lanka Crossing, has a **24hr. pharmacy.** From Godaulia Crossing, take an auto-rickshaw (Rs25) toward Benaras Hindu University. The entrance is through the market complex. You can usually see an English-speaking doctor right away. **Sir Sunderial Hospital** at B.H.U. (☎2310290 or 2310292) is also reputable.

Internet: Zee Services (☎2451800), 100m up Dasashwamedh Rd. from the south end of the *ghat,* on the left, is one of many Internet options in the area. Rs20 per hr. Open daily 6:30am-10:30pm. **Tiwari Travels,** Assi Ghat (☎2366727), to the left of Harmony, has good connections. Rs40 per hour. Open daily 8am-9pm.

Post Office: Head Post Office (☎2332090). 400m east of the intersection of Chowk and Kabir Chaura Rd., on the right. Open M-Sa 10am-6pm. **Postal Code:** 221001.

ACCOMMODATIONS

Dozens of budget hotels are packed into the winding maze of the Old City around Godaulia Crossing. Mid-range hotels can be found throughout Varanasi, especially along Vidyapith Rd., on top of the *ghats,* and on the main streets in Godaulia. Luxury hotels and some pricier budget places in the Cantonment area north of the railway station seem a world away from the traditional life of the city, but are close to local transportation and the train station.

■ **Hotel Plaza Inn,** 116H Parade Kothi (☎2205504; www.hotelplazainn.com), Cantonment, opposite the station and bus stop. One of the city's most comfortable and classy budget hotels. The Plaza is a smart hotel with large, centrally air-conditioned rooms, cable TV, direct-dial phones, 24hr. room service, and an efficient travel desk. Check-out noon. Singles Rs500-850; doubles Rs700-1050. ❶

■ **Hotel Temple on Ganges,** Assi Ghat (☎2368640 or 2368703; hotel_temple@hotmail.com). A 20min. walk (or boat ride) down from Dasashwamedh, just off the *ghat* road. Spotless place offering massage, Internet, and free yoga lessons. The hotel restaurant serves veg. goodies to guests anywhere in the hotel. Nice rooftop terrace. All rooms have attached bath and hot water. Singles Rs150-350; doubles Rs350-650. ❶

Shivam Hotel, S-21/115 Parade Kothi (☎2201055), Cantonment, next door to Hotel Plaza Inn. Clean and airy rooms with attached bathrooms and friendly staff. The attached Mandarin Restaurant is a popular place for Chinese food. Singles Rs350-400; doubles Rs425-650. ❶

Golden Lodge, D 8/35 Kalika Gali (☎2393832 or 2328567). Head up Vishwanatha Gali and look for signs 150m on the right. Clean, simple, slightly shabby-looking budget hotel offers "homely and comfortably staying." A/C and satellite TV. Attached Fagin's Restaurant serves Indian, Western, and Israeli favorites. Check-out 10:30am. Singles Rs60-80; doubles Rs100-250. ❶

Vishnu Rest House, Pandey Ghat (☎2450206 or 2450744). From Dasashwamedh Ghat walk south 200m until you see "Pandey" written above the *ghats.* At low tide it's a rather steep climb up to the hotel. The most popular backpacker hang-out in town, this riverfront property fills up quickly. Breezy, colorful rooms with tie-dyed sheets. Terrace restaurant offers superb views of the Ganga (open 7am-10pm). Bring your own locks. 12-bed dorms Rs45; singles Rs70-80; doubles with bath Rs150-250. ❶

Shanti Guest House (☎2392568 or 2400956), near Manikarnika Ghat. Huge hotel that could pass for a small international city. Rooftop restaurant serves as Party Central for the Old City and has some of the best views in town. Freshly painted rooms of all shapes and sizes, currency exchange, motorcycle rentals, and boat rides. Singles Rs60-150; doubles Rs75-600. ❶

Ganges View Hotel, Assi Ghat (☎2313218). Next to the Harmony Book Shop. Family-run guest house with exquisitely-decorated rooms, glass chandeliers, and velvet curtains in the main dining room. Elegant furniture and art in all the rooms. Hosts free lectures and concerts during the regular season. Doubles Rs650-1200. ❸

Central Varanasi

♠ ACCOMMODATIONS
Golden Lodge, **2**
Shanti Guest House, **1**
Vishnu Rest House, **8**

Benya Park

CHOWK

0   150 yards
0   150 meters

Chowk Rd.

■ Thatheri Bazaar

Ganga Mahal Ghat

Gyana Vapi Mosque

Annapurna Temple

Vishwanath (Golden) Temple

Scindhia Ghat
Manikarnika Ghat

Nepali Temple

Lalita Ghat

Chetganj Rd.

Luxa Rd.

GODAULIA CROSSING

Bank of Baroda

Dasashwamedh Ghat Rd.

Mir Ghat

DASASHWAMEDH

Universal Book Co.

Ganga River

GODAULIA

Mandanpura Rd.

Man Mandir Ghat

Dasashwamedh Ghat

Shitala Temple

FOOD
Keshari Restaurant, **3**
New Monga Restaurant, **5**
Yelchico Bar & Restaurant, **4**
♪ ENTERTAINMENT
International Music Centre, **6**
Triveni Music Centre, **7**

Pandey Ghat

UTTAR PRADESH

Hotel Arya, B 8/47 Sonar Pura (☎2276426), 1km south of Godaulia Crossing, on the main road to Assi Ghat, near Harishchandra *ghat*. Convenient location and resourceful manager make (almost) everything easily accessible. Bike rentals, railway station pick-up, and rooftop restaurant. Spacious rooms with attached bath, some with TVs and balconies. Singles Rs150-200; doubles Rs250-350. ❶

🍴 FOOD

Dining options in Varanasi range from the local, pilgrim-friendly, vegetarian eateries to those trying to satisfy the Western palate with interpretations of Italian, Mexican, Israeli, and Chinese dishes; only a few of these are worth seeking out.

▨ **Keshari Restaurant,** off Dasashwamedh Rd. Near Godaulia crossing, down an alley opposite the La-Ra India Hotel, on the right. Rows and rows of booths for hungry shoppers. Good *thalis* (Rs40-120) and countless other veg. dishes (Rs30-100). Open daily 9:30am-10:30pm. ❶

▨ **Mandarin Restaurant and Bar,** in the Shivam Hotel, next to the Hotel Relax, near the railway station. This clean, calm restaurant serves a wider, tastier selection of Chinese dishes than most other places. Spicy Szechuan and Manchurian-style cooking. Veg. Manchurian Rs60, garlic chicken Rs80. Open daily 7am-11pm. ❶

Pizzeria Vatika Café, Assi Ghat (☎ 2315189), up to the right of the steps, in a garden of potted plants. A slice of the Mediterranean on the banks of the Ganges. Mellow out over wood-oven pizza (Rs50-70), pasta (ravioli Rs55), and the distant sound of temple bells. Ask the manager, Mr. A. Singh, for a Varanasi resident's take on the city's celebrity status. Open daily 8am-10pm. ❶

Bread of Life Bakery and Western Restaurant, B3/322, Shivala (☎ 2275012), on the main road between Assi Ghat and Godaulia. The vision of an American interior designer and his German wife, this bistro is far removed from Varanasi's *dhabas*. Western favorites from tuna fish sandwiches (Rs60) to *moussaka* (Rs80). Open daily 8am-9pm. ❶

Malika Restaurant, in Hotel Padmini, 400m down Sigra Mahmoor Ganj Rd. from Sigra Crossing. Look for the flags. All aboard this miniature train for Western breakfasts (Rs90-100) and a good range of Indian/Mughlai dishes. Delicious chicken/mutton *jhal frezi* Rs80. Open daily 7:30am-10:30pm. ❶

Shanti Guest House Rooftop Restaurant, near Manikarnika Ghat. With fantastic views of the Ganga and Manikarnika Ghat and a pool table, this high-in-the-sky patio is the top backpacker hangout in town. The food is unremarkable, but no one seems to notice. Guest house gate closes at midnight, but knock loudly to enter. Meal Rs100. ❶

New Monga Restaurant, Dasashwamedh Ghat Rd., just after Godaulia Crossing, on the right. Low-hanging wicker lamps, white tablecloths, bow-tie service, and underground seclusion make for an almost romantic setting. Thumping Hindi pop keeps things lively. Veg. *thalis* Rs50-90. Open daily 10am-10pm. ❶

Yelchico Bar and Restaurant, 2 branches in Varanasi. The first is near Godaulia Crossing. As you approach from the river, it's just past Mandanpura Rd., down a flight of stairs on the left. The only place in the Old City where you can get a glass of beer (Rs80). Open daily noon-10pm. The 2nd branch, at Sigra Crossing, is more of a civilized bar than a restaurant, though it serves meals. Open daily 11am-10:30pm. ❶

🄖 SIGHTS

THE GHATS OF THE GANGA

A little religious imagination and some knowledge of what is going on at the city's countless sacred sites can help, but to experience the life and vibrancy of Varanasi—its crowded temples and teeming *ghats*—all you really need are your five senses and an open mind ready to be bent gently out of shape.

The holy Ganga draws millions of pilgrims to Varanasi, and the series of **ghats** (steps) that line the river are at the heart of city life. Abuzz with crowds of people from before dawn until long after nightfall, the *ghats* are where the pounding pulse of the ancient city beats fastest. Thousands come at dawn to make offerings to the heavenly water, but the *ghats* are far from reserved for purely sacred activities. People stroll, meditate, play cricket, and play music along the banks. Dive-bombing teenagers crash into the river from the steps, while others bathe and wash their clothes in the waters. The Ganga draws all sorts of life and death as well. **Cremations** are viewed as auspicious events (a reversal of traditional beliefs). They take place right on the *ghats* rather than out of town on inauspicious soil, as they do everywhere else. Very rarely, the bodies of those who can't afford cremation, as well as those of holy men, pregnant women, and children under 12, are dumped straight into the river and can sometimes be seen floating in the water. Water buffalo also bathe in the river, and sewers dump directly into the Ganga.

The steps themselves are huge and sometimes number more than 100 from top to bottom, though some are hidden when the water is high. The name of each *ghat* is painted on the retaining walls in large letters in both Devanagari and Roman script. Memorizing the location of some of the major *ghats* will make finding your way around a lot easier. A **boat ride** along the river is one of the highlights of any Varanasi itinerary. The best time to do this is at dawn, when the *ghats* are their most crowded and the whole city shines like gold in the early-morning light. (A small boat seating four people should cost no more than Rs150 for an hour's trip from Dasashwamedh.) The *ghats* are presented here from south to north.

ASSI GHAT. The southern end of Varanasi's riverfront begins with Assi Ghat, a broad clay bank at the meeting point of the Ganga and Assi rivers. Assi Ghat is one of the busiest and most important of all the bathing *ghats*. Its muddy banks are alive throughout the day with pilgrims crowding to pay their respects to the large Shiva *linga* that stands in the shade of a pipal tree just a few feet from the water's edge. Shops, drink-stalls, and restaurants make this a popular destination for non-religious travelers too. If you are seeing the *ghats* by boat, consider starting your ride here, and getting dropped off closer to the city center. Assi Ghat is surrounded by temples, several of them among the most popular in the whole city.

TULSI GHAT. Tulsi Ghat, named for the famed 16th century Hindi poet, Tulsi Das, who wrote his famed *Ramcharitmanas* at the house sitting at the top of the steps, is the next significant *ghat* after Assi. Back from the water above Tulsi Ghat is one of Varanasi's most ancient sacred spots, the Lolarka Kund. Sunk deep into the ground, this tank was at one time the site where early Hindus worshiped Surya, the sun god. Today, it is a major pilgrimage spot during the annual festival of Lolarka Shashthi (Aug. or Sept.), when thousands of couples come here to pray for children.

HARISHCHANDRA GHAT. Varanasi's second most important cremation ground is distinguished by the spires of black smoke that rise throughout the day from the funeral pyres. It also houses an electric crematorium. The constant stream of mourners and attendants makes Harishchandra one of the busiest *ghats*. Though widely believed to be the oldest cremation site in Varanasi, it has not been accorded quite the same level of religious importance as Manikarnika farther north. Photography is strictly prohibited.

KEDAR GHAT AND CHOWKI GHAT. The *ghat* with the red, white, and green stripes is **Kedar Ghat.** Kedar means "field," and this is the field in which liberation is said to grow. The Kedar Temple, one of Varanasi's oldest and most important Shiva temples, is so holy that just resolving to come here is enough to liberate a person from the accumulated sins of two whole lifetimes. The stone mound that marks Shiva's presence here is thought to be the oldest *linga* in the city. **Chowki Ghat** has a fierce collection of *nagas*, early aquatic snake-gods at the top of its steps, around a central tree. Its name comes from the old British *chowki* (outpost) that used to exist here long ago. From here to Dasashwamedh Ghat, a long stretch of *ghats* used for laundry is marked by a collage of colorful saris and lungis stretched out to dry. If you look up above at the walls on **Raja Ghat,** along the way, you can see just how high the monsoon-filled Ganga flooded in 1967 and 1978.

DASASHWAMEDH GHAT. The most crowded *ghat* in Varanasi, Dasashwamedh is often referred to as the **"Main Ghat."** Every morning, busloads of pilgrims make their way past the fruit stalls and flower sellers that line the wide road leading to the steps. Dasashwamedh is said to be the spot where Brahma performed 10 royal horse-sacrifices *(ashwamedhas)* with the mythical King Divodasa. Bathing here is supposed to bestow on pilgrims all the benefits of ten horse sacrifices. On the *ghat* is **Brahmeshwar,** the *linga* that Brahma established here after performing his sacrifices. Just south of Dasashwamedh Ghat, Shitala, the goddess of small-pox and other diseases, is worshiped in the **Shitala Temple.** Adorned with colorful paint, tinsel, and flags, this small box of a temple is more popular than any of the *lingas* of Dasashwamedh.

MAN MANDIR GHAT TO LALITA GHAT. Man Mandir Ghat is topped by one of the observatories built in the 18th century by Maharaja Jai Singh of Jaipur. Climb up on the right side of the building to see a collection of astronomical scales made of stone. Above **Mir Ghat** and **Lalita Ghat** are several important temples. The colorful **Vishalakshi Temple** belongs to a "Wide-Eyed" local goddess, but it is also a Shakti *pitha*—the eye of the goddess Sati (or by some accounts her earring) is said to have landed here when she was chopped apart in the heavens. Nearby, a well, the **Dharma Kup,** marks the site where Yama, the god of death, paid homage to Shiva. At the top of Lalita Ghat, a **Nepali Temple** contains ornate woodcarvings (Rs10).

MANIKARNIKA GHAT. An axis of holiness runs between the **Vishwanath Temple** and the next *ghat*, Manikarnika Ghat. Manikarnika is the most sacred of all the *ghats* and the final stop on the popular *panchathirthi* pilgrimage, which leads devotees along the length of the city's riverside banks. Bathing here and worshipping at Vishwanath is a daily routine for many Benarsis and an essential part of any pilgrimage. Manikarnika Ghat takes its name from **Manikarnika Kund,** the small white tank just past the cremation grounds, which Lord Vishnu himself is said to have dug out at the beginning of time and filled with his sweat while trying to locate Parvati's bejeweled earrings *(manikarnika)*. Vishnu's footprints are nearby, under a circular shelter.

The area just south of Manikarnika has become the city's **primary cremation ground.** Boats full of wood are moored here, and the pyres burn day and night, consuming the corpses of those lucky enough to have been liberated here. Bodies are carried on stretchers down the winding streets to the riverside, where they are dipped in the Ganga before being burned for about three hours on fires lit from an eternal flame on the *ghat*. When the burning is complete, the eldest son of the deceased throws a pot of Ganga water onto the fire, and the ashes are sprinkled in the river. Above the *ghat* are hospices where the dying come to wait their turn. Visitors can watch the cremations from boats or buildings above the *ghat*, but you are likely to offend and upset mourners and workers if you linger too long or too conspicuously on the *ghat*. **Photography is strictly prohibited.**

SANKATA GHAT AND NORTHERN SIGHTS. Next is **Sankata Ghat,** above which is the blue and yellow temple of **Sankata Devi,** a powerful mother-goddess. The important bathing site is **Panchganga Ghat.** Five rivers are said to converge here: the Ganga, Yamuna, and Saraswati (said to run underground), which flow from Allahabad, and the Dhutapapa and Kirana, which have dried up. Vishnu chose this place as the greatest spot in Kashi, and his **Bindu Madhava** temple sits above the *ghat*. During the month of Karthik (Oct.-Nov.) the temple and the *ghat* are lit by lamps at night. For the rest of the year the most prominent feature of Panchganga Ghat is the **Dharhara Mosque,** built over the ruins of an earlier Bindu Madhava temple by Emperor Aurangzeb. The mosque is closed to visitors due to threats from Hindu zealots. A statue of a cow at **Gai Ghat** watches over an array of Shiva *lingas*. Nearby is **Trilochan Ghat,** with the popular temple of the "Three-Eyed" Shiva. **Varanasi Devi,** the patron-goddess of Varanasi, also inhabits the temple.

Despite being in the oldest part of the city, the *ghats* farther north are more spaced apart and less crowded than those in the southern part of the city. The next *ghat* of visible importance is **Raj Ghat,** the last before the Malaviya Bridge. This is the crossing-point where, since ancient times, traders have ferried across the Ganga. The temple of **Adi Keshava (Original Vishnu)** sits on a high bank to the north of the bridge and marks the northern city limits. Vishnu washed his feet here, and the image inside the temple was shaped by Vishnu himself. Other than the Ganga and some pasture land, however, there is not much to see here nowadays.

THE BANKS AND BEYOND

THE VISHWANATH TEMPLE (GOLDEN TEMPLE). Up Dasashwamedh Rd. from the river and right through a temple-like archway, signs lead to the temple of Shiva as Vishwanath (Lord of All). Nicknamed the "Golden" Temple, it contains the Vishweshwar *linga*, the first one on earth and one of India's 12 *jyotirlingas*, which are said to have shot up from the ground as shafts of light. All of Varanasi is measured in circles around Vishwanath, the city's center and its most important pilgrimage site. The temple is closed to non-Hindus, but shopkeepers across the road happily charge visitors for the view from their rooftops (Rs10). The temple's shining spire, encrusted with over 280kg of gold, soars up into the city, and bells chime at the many smaller temples that lead to it. There has been a Shiva temple on this site since ancient times, but the present building dates back only to 1777. Earlier temples here were repeatedly destroyed by waves of Muslim invasions. The last of these took place in 1669, when the temple was torn down by Aurangzeb. The Jnana Vapi Mosque was constructed on top of the half-demolished ruins of an earlier Vishwanath Temple and still stands today, surrounded by soldiers and a cordon of barbed wire. Hindu extremists have made repeated threats to destroy the mosque and reclaim the old holy site.

GYANA VAPI MOSQUE. Under a pavilion, in between the temple and the mosque, is the Gyana Vapi itself, a "Well of Wisdom" said to have been in existence since the very beginning of the world. The waters that sprang up here when Shiva dug up the earth with his trident were the first pure waters anywhere on earth.

ANNAPURNA TEMPLE. The most important goddess temple in Varanasi is dedicated to Shakti, the divine embodiment of power or energy and Shiva's consort, in the form of Annapurna. Armed with spoons and saucepans, Annapurna is a provider of food. A **Mountain of Food Festival** occurs here in late October or early November, Annakut, and only then is the sacred golden idol revealed to worshippers. *(Opposite Vishwanath, just down the lane. Closed to non-Hindus.)*

KALA BHAIRONATH. Once an angry and sinful form of Shiva, Kala Bhaironath (also known as Kal Bhairava) chopped off the fifth head of the god Brahma after he failed to recognize Shiva, embodied in a shimmering *linga* of light, as supreme among all the gods. As punishment, the rotting head stuck to his hand, and for years, Bhairava had to wander remorsefully around the whole of India, using the skull as a begging bowl for his food. It was not until he got to Varanasi that the head miraculously dropped from his hands, and Shiva appointed him the Lord Protector of the sacred city. He keeps an eye on Varanasi's residents, devours their sins as they are washed away by the Ganga's holy waters, and metes out instant retribution for the accumulated misdeeds of those who die here. The temple is often crowded with supplicant sinners offering incense, garlands, and all things saffron to the image of this holy police chief. Not too far away, on the other side of the Chowk-Kabir Chaura Rd. crossing, is the temple of **Bare Ganesh**, the central Ganesh shrine in Varanasi. *(Just south of the HPO on Kabir Chaura Rd.; head up Chowk Rd. from Godaulia and turn right towards the post office. Open daily 5am-noon and 2-10pm.)*

DURGA TEMPLE AND KUND. The impressive red tower of this temple stretches up into the sky above its adjacent tank. It is believed that the goddess Durga rested here after saving the world from an otherwise unassailable demon, Mahisasura, and she continues to be regarded as the protectress of Southern Kashi. The walls inside the temple, constructed in the 18th century, are inscribed with Tulsi Das's verses and adorned with paintings, the most notable of which depicts the love of Bharat, Rama's step-brother, who worshipped Rama's wooden sandals for the 14 years of Rama's exile. The shrine is also known as the "monkey temple." *(Straight west off Assi Ghat, a 5min. walk from the river. Open 5am-11pm.)*

UTTAR PRADESH

TULSI MANAS MANDIR. Built of white marble and flanked by palm trees, this modern Vishnu temple was erected in 1964 in honor of Tulsi Das, the premier poet of the Hindi language who translated the Sanskrit epic, the *Ramayana*, into Hindi in the 16th century. The complete epic is inscribed on the inside walls in the poet's Hindi script, and painted depictions of scenes from the story line the temple walls. Toward the back of the temple, a collection of brightly painted mechanical figures acts out the timeless tale to the delight of parents and children passing through. A mechanical mock-up of the great poet himself sits, book in hand, by the temple door. *(Just south of the Durga Temple. Open daily 5am-noon and 4-8:30pm. Rs1.)*

SANKAT MOCHAN TEMPLE. The Sankat Mochan Temple, in a patch of trees southwest of Assi Ghat, is dedicated to Hanuman. Orange *sindur* smears attest the devotion of pilgrims. Each spring the temple is home to a popular music fair. *(Open daily 4:30am-10:30pm.)*

BENARAS HINDU UNIVERSITY (BHU). Founded in 1916 by the reformer Madan Mohan Malaviya, the university was intended to merge modern ideas with traditional Hindu learning. The campus has two places suited to shorter visits. The **Sri Vishwanath Temple,** the largest temple in the city, has a large, white spire modeled on the one knocked down by Aurangzeb in 1669. *(Open daily 4am-noon and 1-9pm.)* **Bharat Kala Bhawan,** the BHU museum, has an extensive collection of miniature paintings, artifacts, and sculptures. The second floor contains the sculptures and paintings of Alice Boner, a renowned Indophile who claimed to understand India "on its own terms." There is plenty here from Varanasi as well, from 19th-century etchings of the *ghats* to a statue of Krishna lifting Mt. Govardhana. The most stunning artifacts, a collection of coins, ornate jewelry, and emperor's jade dagger hilts, are kept in a safe room in the **Nidhi Gallery.** *(Lanka Crossing, at the south end of town. Museum open M-Sa 11am-4:30pm. Rs40.)*

RAMNAGAR FORT. The Ganga's eastern shore has one point of interest, Ramnagar Fort, the castle of Varanasi's maharaja. The fort also contains a **royal museum.** While most exhibits are rather dilapidated, the royal family's sedan chairs, swords, and an extravagant astronomical clock are all on display. *(Open daily 9am-5:30pm; Rs7.)* Ramnagar is probably not worth the trip unless it's for the boat ride across the river and fabulous views of Varanasi, or the **Ram Lila,** the festive Ramayana pageant, held in September and October. *(In the village of Ramnagar opposite BHU at the south end of the city. Ferries at the end of Rawnagar Rd. cross the river for Rs2.)*

BHARAT MATA TEMPLE. A spirit of urbane and modernized Hinduism can be seen in the Bharat Mata Temple, on the city's western outskirts, south of the Cantonment. Mahatma Gandhi inaugurated this temple, which has a marble, swimming-pool-sized relief map of Mother India as its presiding "deity." If you can get one of the temple's "residents" to unlock them, the upper balconies provide the best views. *(A 15min. walk down Vidyapith Rd. from the railway station. Open daily 7am-6pm.)*

🎵 MUSIC

Varanasi is a center for Indian classical music (see p. 87), and many westerners come here to study the sitar or tabla. The best resource is the School of Performing Arts at **Benaras Hindu University** (☎2307641). Though the school itself only offers degree courses in Hindi and English, the faculty unofficially give **private music lessons.** These tend to be costly, so ask for recommendations of other reputable teachers. A good but touristy place to learn sitar or tabla is the **Triveni Music Centre** (☎2452266), on Keval Gali in Godaulia, near the Vishnu Rest House. Instructor Nandu and his brother give lessons (Rs50-100 per hr.) and performances (M, Th, and Su 8-10pm, Rs40). They also sell instruments at inflated prices. The well-established **International Music Centre,** south of Dasashwamedh Rd., also offers private sitar and tabla lessons (Rs100-150 per hr.), as well as evening concerts.

If you're interested in **purchasing musical instruments** in Varanasi, there are many sitar and tabla stores in the Old City. The faculty at BHU recommends the shop of **Mr. Nitai Chandra Nath,** a sage of string instruments and a true artisan. From Godaulia Crossing, facing Dasashwamedh, turn right onto Madandura Rd., and turn down the third lane on your left (25m after Universal Book Co.); the Jangambali (Bengali Tola) Post Office will be on your left, and the unmarked sitar store is several doors down. If you cannot find the shop, ask in the street for **Nitai Babu,** and someone will show you the way. (Sitars Rs4000-7000.) **Imtiyaz Ali,** Siddh Giri Bagh, is a tabla shop recommended by Mr. Nath. Hop in a cycle-rickshaw and ask for the Maulavi Bagh Masjid in Siddh Giri Bagh; the store is to the right of the mosque. (Brass tablas Rs2000; copper tablas Rs2500.)

SHOPPING

Varanasi is famous for its silk, and the touts will never let you forget it. There are several shops in Varanasi with fixed prices and government-enforced quality control. Two of the oldest and most reputable stores are on Vishwanath Gali in the Old City: **Mohan Silk Stores,** 5/54 Vishwanath Gali (☎2392354), and **Bhagwan Stores,** D10/32 Vishwanath Gali, both on the right-hand side shortly after the main gate leading off from Dasashwamedh Rd. toward the Golden Temple. Two other silk shops are in Sindhu Nagar, near the intersection of Aurangabad and Vidyapith Rds.: **M/S Bhagwanlila Exports,** 41 Sindhu Nagar Colony, Sigra, (☎2222533), and **Mahalakshmi Saree House,** 10 Chandrika Nager, Sigra (☎2221319). Also recommended is "The King of Banares Sarees," **Chowdhary Brothers,** Thatheri Bazaar, (☎2320469), a short walk up Chowk from the police station, on the right. **Mehrotra Silk Factory,** SC21/72 Englishia Line (☎2345289), Cantonment, with its seemingly infinite selection of silks, may be the best of these shops. The store carries shawls (US$8-9), tapestries (US$10-20), and raw fabric (US$5 per m). To get there, walk up Vidyapith Rd., with the railway station in sight, make a right onto Station Rd., and then look for signs about 100m on the left. It's a good idea to visit these shops to get a sense of the prices of top-thread silk before bargaining in the Chowk or Old City. (Shops open daily 10am-8pm.) When buying silk, also remember to insist on buying both a horizontal and vertical thread. Real silk, when burned, has the odor of burning hair, and when you mention quality, most sellers will insist they show you this test. Many fabrics in the market are woven with silk in one direction and a synthetic fiber in the other. When the fake thread is burned, it will smell like paper or plastic.

DAYTRIP FROM VARANASI

SARNATH

Auto-rickshaws putter wherever the money takes them (Rs50 to Varanasi). Buses go to the railway station (frequent 7am-7:30pm, 40min., Rs5). Tempos go to many different points in Varanasi, including the railway station (Rs10). To get to the temples, cross the intersection at the bus stand; the gate to the modern temple's park is 200m down Dharmapal Rd., on the right. Open daily 4-11:30am and 1:30-8pm. Entrance to stupa and ruins park US$5. Archaeological museum open Sa-Th 10am-5pm. Rs2. Chowkahndi Stupa is open dawn-dusk. Free.

In the wooded suburbs north of Varanasi lies **Sarnath,** a quiet and well-maintained site of ruins marking the location of Gautama Buddha's first sermon, the famous "Sermon in the Deer Park." After the Buddha attained enlightenment in Bodh Gaya, he walked the 200km to Sarnath, with lotuses blooming where his feet touched the ground. Gathering his former companions here, among the deer and peacocks, he revealed the Noble Eightfold Path. In later years, he occasionally returned to this quiet grove to meditate. In the 3rd century BC, when the region was under the rule of the Mauryas, *stupas* were built to commemorate the Buddha's visits. This construction continued until the 4th century AD, when the Hindu Guptas rose to power and Buddhist influence began to wane. Sarnath's prestige as a center of Buddhism came to an abrupt end during the 12th century when it was demolished by the Muslim Sultan of Delhi, Qutb-ud-din Aibak.

Sarnath makes for a pleasant stroll. Even in the time-tired state they are in today, the monuments here provide impressive evidence of the rich Buddhist culture that once flourished here and the importance that Buddhist philosophy once held throughout much of northern India. There has been little modern development in Sarnath since its monuments were excavated and explored during the 19th century by spade-*wallah* supreme, General Sir Alexander Cunningham. With a bit of selective squinting, it is still possible to imagine Sarnath as it might have been when the Buddha walked through its woods more than 2000 years ago.

Sarnath is contained within a triangle of road. From the south, Sarnath Rd. comes from Varanasi and splits in two by the Rangoli Garden Restaurant. The branch heading northwest is **Ashoka Road** and runs past the Archaeological Museum. The branch going northeast goes past the UP Tourist Bungalow. Connecting these two roads after they diverge is the main road, **Dharmapal Road,** which runs east-west and contains almost all of the sights. The **bus stand** is at the intersection of Dharmapal Rd. and the road that passes the UP Tourist Bungalow. The **post office** (open M-Sa 8am-4pm) is near the bus stand and opposite the **UP Tourist Bungalow.** There's a small information counter in the bungalow, which gives out maps of the sites. (Open M-Sa 10am-5pm.)

Most of Sarnath's points of interest are recently excavated piles of rubble: this is a place with more atmosphere and history than sights to write home about. However, the first stop on the way to the archaeological enclosure is intact and relatively new. The sandstone spires of the modern Buddhist temple, **Mulgandha Kuti Vihar,** rise above the main gate. Its peaceful interior was decorated by the Japanese artist, Kosetsu Nosi, with grandiose murals inspired by the *Buddhacarita* (The Acts of the Buddha). Nearby stands a pipal tree that is supposed to be a relative of the tree under which the Buddha attained enlightenment. Behind the Mulgandha Kuti Vihar's grounds, a manicured garden leads to a small zoo and the **Deer Park.**

In the next enclosure over from the modern temple, the **Dhamekh Stupa,** the only ancient structure left intact by Qutb-ud-din's armies, looms 39m above the trees. It commemorates the spot where the Buddha delivered his first sermon. First constructed by the Mauryas in 200 BC, it was rebuilt several times, the last sometime during the 5th or 6th century, in the twilight of Buddhist dominance in North India. It remains unfinished. The bottom is made of decorated stone, with eight niches that once held images of the Buddha. Next to the Dhamekh Stupa lie the remains of the **Dharmarajika Stupa,** an impressive shrine in its day, although today only the foundations remain. The *stupa* was built by the Mauryan emperor Ashoka in the 3rd century BC to house the relics of the Buddha. Ashoka is thought to have come here to meditate in what was once a major monastic center. The structure was reduced to rubble in the 18th century by locals and British hunting for treasure.

Next to the *stupa* are the remains of the **Main Shrine,** built by Ashoka to mark a favorite meditation spot of the Buddha. At the end of the ruined structure, down a shallow well, is the bottom portion of **Ashoka's pillar.** The column is engraved with

Buddhist edicts in Brahmi script that warn Buddhist monks and nuns against creating rifts among the followers of the Buddha (the advice wasn't taken). The capital from Ashoka's pillar is one of the great masterpieces of early Indian art and is preserved at the **Archaeological Museum,** opposite the main entrance to the Dharmarajika Stupa compound and at the intersection of Dharmapal and Ashoka Rd. The museum's collection is well-maintained and includes a number of excellent pieces, including a teaching Buddha from the Gupta period and two giant, umbrella-toting *bodhisattva* statues.

Beyond the main strip of Dharmapal Rd. shrines, 600m south of the Archaeological Museum on Ashoka Rd., rises the curious melange of Buddhist-Mughal architecture that is the **Chowkhandi Stupa.** The rectangular Gupta-period foundation commemorating the site where the Buddha met his five disciples is topped by a crowning tower in the octagonal Mughal style. It was rebuilt later to mark the site where Emperor Humayun once spent the night. Also worth visiting is Sarnath's collection of temples dotting the town. Each displays a unique style of architecture and can make a busier urban India seem years away.

ALLAHABAD इलाहाबाद ☎0532

The holy city of Allahabad stands at the sacred *sangam*, or confluence, of the Ganga and the Yamuna rivers. Into these two rivers flows a third, the mystical underground Saraswati, river of wisdom. Lord Brahma called this spot *Tirth Raj* ("King of Pilgrimage Sites"), and all devout Hindus try to bathe in the waters at least once in their lives. Known for thousands of years as *Prayag* (Confluence), the city was renamed "Ilahabad" in Mughal times after Emperor Akbar's religious philosophy of *Din-e-Ilahi*. The name morphed into "Allahabad" under the British.

The Brits declared Allahabad the capital of the United Provinces in 1901. The Indian Independence movement was strongly rooted here, thanks to the work of the Nehrus, the Allahabad family that forged a political dynasty after Independence. The Indian National Congress met here routinely, at the Nehru home in Anand Bhawan. A relatively tourist-free city, Allahabad is well worth a couple of days. It becomes the focus of national attention every 12 years when it hosts the **Maha Kumbh Mela,** the most important of all Hindu festivals in which millions of pilgrims converge at the Triveni Sangam. In recent times, Hindu fundamentalists have demanded that Allahabad's name be changed back to **Prayagraj.** Since Hindus and Muslims have coexisted peacefully in the city for hundreds of years, however, the movement has received little popular support.

▐ TRANSPORTATION

Trains: Allahabad Junction Railway Station, Leader Rd. To: **Agra** (11½hr., 4:35am, Rs179); **Delhi** (7hr., 28 per day 1am-10:55pm, Rs245; *Rajdhani Exp. 2301* and *2309* 7hr.; Tu, W, Sa, Su 2:45am; Rs975); **Gorakhpur** (9-11hr, 9:15pm, Rs151); **Gwalior** (11-15hr., 1-3 per day 6:35am-6:30pm, Rs169); **Kanpur** (32 per day, 4:40am-1:20am, Rs107); **Khajuraho** (7hr., 11 per day 6:20am-3:35am, Rs124); and **Lucknow** (3-5hr., 4 per day 6:20am-10:30pm, Rs109).

Buses: Civil Lines Bus Stand, MG Rd., next to the Hotel Ilawart. To: **Ayodhya** (5hr., every hr. 6am-10pm, Rs72); **Gorakhpur** (8hr., frequent 6-10am, Rs124); **Lucknow** (6hr., frequent 4am-8pm, Rs86); **Varanasi** (3hr., every hr. 4am-5pm, Rs72). The **Leader Road Bus Stand,** opposite the main Allahabad Junction Railway Station, sends buses to **Agra** (13hr.; 11am, 3 and 7pm; Rs205) and **Delhi** (20hr., 6pm and midnight, Rs268). **Zero Road Bus Stand** is north of Chowk.

Local Transportation: Cycle-rickshaws from the Allahabad Junction Railway Station to the Civil Lines area are Rs20-30. Within Civil Lines, no ride should be more than Rs15. From Civil Lines to the Sangam costs Rs40-50. **Tempos** and auto-rickshaws wait at the bus or railway stations. To reach the Sangam, take a *tempo* to Daraganj Railway Station (Rs30) and walk south from the tracks.

■ ? ORIENTATION AND PRACTICAL INFORMATION

North of the railway tracks is the tree-shaded, British-built **Civil Lines** area, with all of its roads laid out in a grid; south is the congested and gritty **Chowk** area. The **Yamuna River** flows south of Allahabad until it reaches the sacred confluence point at the southeastern extremity of the city. The Ganga flows down along the eastern edge of the city. In Civil Lines, **Mahatma Gandhi (MG) Road,** with its hotels, restaurants, and ice cream stands; it is lined with tall and distinctive statues that make good landmarks. The hub of Civil Lines is around the crossroads of MG Rd. and **Sardar Patel (SP) Road,** where the Tourist Office is located. **Kamla Nehru Road** turns up from MG Rd. toward Allahabad University. **Leader Road** runs along the tracks on the Chowk side. The **Grand Trunk Road** (NH 2) streaks through the heart of Chowk. **Triveni Road** leads from the Grand Trunk Rd. to the Triveni **Sangam.**

Tourist Office: UP Tourism, MG Rd. (☎2601873), in the Hotel Ilawart complex. Just around the corner from the Civil Lines Bus Stand. Extremely helpful staff has maps and a list of government-approved guest houses. Open M-Sa 10am-5pm.

Currency Exchange: State Bank of India, 4 Kacheri Rd. (☎2608653), near District Court. Changes major currencies, AmEx and Thomas Cook traveler's checks. Open M-F 10am-2pm, Sa 10am-noon.

Bookstore: M/S A.H. Wheeler Book Shop, MG Rd. (☎2624106), to the right of the Palace Theatre, on the left side of the road. Facing away from the Tourist Bungalow, walk 500m to the left. One of the best bookstores in UP. Open M-Sa 10am-7pm.

Market: A large fruit market is at **Khuldabad Mandi Bazaar** near the clock tower, at the intersection of Dr. Katiu and Grand Trunk Rd. Open daily 7am-9pm. The main **Chowk Market** is famous for its spices and fried goods. Open M-Sa 7am-9pm.

Police: Control Room (☎2652000). **Civil Lines** (☎2622592), on the main road that leads from All Saints' Cathedral to Allahabad Junction Railway Station.

Hospital: Nazareth Hospital, 13/A Kamla Nehru Rd. (☎2600430), from the intersection of MG and Kamla Nehru Rd., it's 1km to the northeast, on the left, marked by a red cross and a Hindi sign. The best private hospital in town, with a fully stocked **pharmacy.**

Internet: Cyber-cafes line MG Rd. in the Civil Lines area, some charging as little as Rs10 per hr. Also try **Modi Internet,** SP Rd., 1 block north of Bridges restaurant. Rs25 per hr.

Post Office: GPO, Sarojini Naidu Rd. (☎2624374). From the Civil Lines, head west on MG Rd. until you reach All Saints' Cathedral. Turn right and walk for 1 block. Also has an attached "volleyball complex." Open M-Sa 10am-5pm. **Postal Code: 211001.**

▛ ACCOMMODATIONS

There are a number of expensive hotels in the Civil Lines area, mostly along MG Rd. and SP Rd. This area is also home to decent budget accommodations. The real cheapies, however, are near the bus stand, around Leader Rd.

Hotel Ilawart, 35 MG Rd. (☎2601440; fax 2611374), next to the Civil Lines Bus Stand. Formerly named the Tourist Bungalow, UP Tourism's newly-renovated hotel is clean and convenient. Great location, with the tourist office downstairs. Restaurant open daily 6am-11pm. Bar serves beer (Rs80) daily noon-11pm. Check-out noon. Dorms Rs100; singles Rs450-1000; doubles Rs500-1200; suites Rs800. ❶

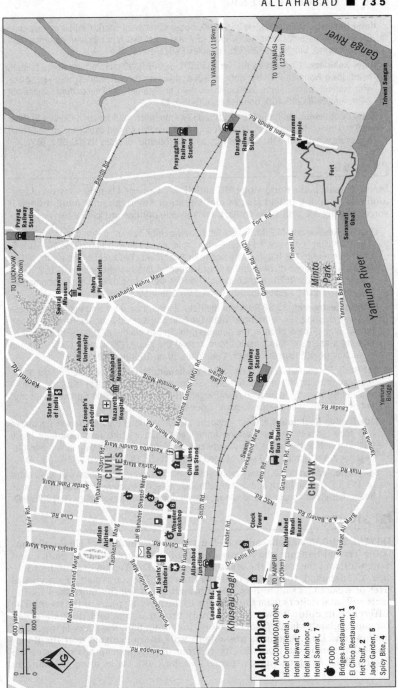

UTTAR PRADESH

TO VARANASI (119km)

TO VARANASI (125km)

Ganga River

Triveni Sangam

Benti Bandh Rd.

Daraganj Railway Station

Hanuman Temple

Fort

Prayagghat Railway Station

Bandh Rd.

Fort Rd.

Saraswati Ghat

Prayag Railway Station

TO LUCKNOW (200km)

Swaraj Bhawan Museum

Anand Bhawan

Nehru Planetarium

Jawaharlal Nehru Marg

Triveni Rd.

Minto Park

Kachari Rd.

Allahabad University

Allahabad Museum

Grand Trunk Rd. (NH2)

City Railway Station

Yamuna Bank Rd.

Yamuna River

State Bank of India $

St. Joseph's Cathedral

Nazreth Hospital

Kamla Nehru Rd.

Mahatma Gandhi (MG) Rd.

Pannalal Marg

Lala Sitaram Rd.

Lauder Rd.

Yamuna Bridge

Yamuna Rd.

Muir Rd.

Clive Rd.

Sardar Patel Marg

Telpahadur Sapru Rd.

CIVIL LINES

Patrika Marg

Kasturba Gandhi Marg

Civil Lines Bus Stand

7

4

Swami Vivekanand Marg

Zero Rd. Bus Station

Grand Trunk Rd. (NH2)

NSC Rd.

Zero Rd.

CHOWK

A.P. Baneji Rd.

Tilak Rd.

Maharshi Dayanand Marg

Sarojini Naidu Marg

Indian Airlines

Tashkent Marg

Lal Bahadur Shastri Marg

Smith Rd.

2

3

Wheeler Bookshop

6

5

Colvin Rd.

Clock Tower

Khuldabad Mandi Bazaar

9

Shaukat Ali Marg

Purshotamdas Tandon Marg

GPO

Nawab Yusuf Rd.

All Saints' Cathedral

Allahabad Junction

Leader Rd.

Dr. Katju Rd.

8

TO KANPUR (200km)

Leader Rd. Bus Stand

Khusrau Bagh

Chatappa Rd.

600 yards

600 meters

N

Allahabad

▲ ACCOMMODATIONS
Hotel Continental, 9
Hotel Ilawart, 6
Hotel Kohinoor, 8
Hotel Samrat, 7

🍴 FOOD
Bridges Restaurant, 1
El Chico Restaurant, 3
Hot Stuff, 2
Jade Garden, 5
Spicy Bite, 4

Hotel Samrat, 49A MG Rd. (☎2561200; hotelsamrat@vsnl.com), Civil Lines, opposite El Chico restaurant. Conveniently located 3-star hotel that is a peaceful distance from the bus stand. Singles Rs725-825; doubles Rs875-1075. ❹

Hotel Kohinoor, 10 Noorulla Rd. (☎2655501 or 2656323). From the railway station, head down Noorulla Rd.; the hotel is 300m down on the left. Classy, well-kept place with tasteful rooms, some overlooking a lawn and garden. A/C restaurant. Check-out 24hr. Singles Rs250-400; doubles Rs300-450. ❷

Hotel Continental, Dr. Katiu Rd. (☎2652058). From Allahabad Junction Railway Station, walk to Leader Rd., turn right, then left onto Dr. Katiu Rd. A good choice for an early train departure. Check-out 24hr. Singles with bath Rs250-500; doubles Rs300-600. ❷

◖ FOOD

Dining outside is the norm along MG and SP Rd. Crowded benches surround fast-food stalls serving Indian snacks and imitation American junk food, though if you're craving A/C and tablecloths, more upscale options are available.

El Chico Restaurant, MG Rd. Take a left from the Hotel Ilawart; it's on the right after the 4-way crossing, opposite the Hotel Samrat. A family-run establishment, for 40 years, El Chico pioneered the multicuisine scene in Allahabad. Their menu has a fine mix of Indian and Chinese dishes, and you can expect a fine meal for about Rs150. Good Indian (*dum aloo* Rs70) and continental dishes as well as delicious mushrooms and baby corn in garlic sauce (Rs100). Open daily 10am-10:30pm. ❸

Bridges Restaurant, 22 SP Rd. From the Hotel Ilawart, take a left and then a right at the four-way crossing; it's in the Hotel Vilas. Dimly lit and as cold as a Siberian funeral parlor (which can be a boon in the summer), this place claims to "bridge" the world by offering a choice of fine cuisines from around the globe. Chow mein (Rs50-75) and omelettes (Rs40) lead the charge. Open daily 10am-10:30pm. ❷

Hot Stuff, Sardar Patel Marg. From the Hotel Ilawart, take a left and then a right at the four-way crossing; it's on the left after 300m. Allahabad's coolest fast-food joint. If you've just been dying for a "Boyish Burger" (Rs30) or a "Hot Stuff Special Foot-Long" hot dog (Rs50), then search no more. Open daily 10am-10pm. ❷

Jade Garden Restaurant, MG Rd, opposite the former Hotel Harsh. Sparsely decorated and accented with dark red window frames and paintings, this restaurant feels like a ballroom with a lowered ceiling. A wide selection of veg. and non-veg. Indian and Chinese food. Veg. spring roll Rs45, *channa masala* Rs35. Open daily 10am-11pm. ❶

Spicy Bite, left out of the Hotel Ilawart and across the street. One of several good stalls on MG Rd. for late lunch and dinner, although it seems to be serving customers at all hours. A lively atmosphere, and cheap, tasty Indian and Chinese dishes (Rs10-65). ❶

◉ SIGHTS

TRIVENI SANGAM. Allahabad's chief attraction for millions of Hindu pilgrims is the Triveni Sangam, the meeting point of the rivers Ganga, Yamuna, and Saraswati, and the site of the **Maha Kumbh Mela.** The Yamuna skirts the south side of Allahabad; the Ganga flows to the east. The Saraswati, the mythical river of wisdom, is said to flow underground. For a fee (no more than Rs100) **boats** will take visitors from the fort side to the meeting place of the rivers. The difference in color between the muddy brown Ganga and the pale green Yamuna is plainly visible from the shore. In the summer, the water is warm and shallow, and it is sometimes possible to walk to the Sangam over the flood-plains that spread out from the city. Millions of pilgrims camp here during the Kumbh Mela. At other times, especially at dusk, the banks along the Sangam offer good views of the fort, with the city in the background. Alongside the road approaching the Sangam is the **fort** built by Emperor Akbar in 1583. The Indian Army still finds the confluence strategically important, so the fort houses soldiers, and visitors are not allowed to enter.

HANUMAN TEMPLE. In the shadow of the fort's outer wall facing the Sangam is the Hanuman Temple, dedicated to the monkey god. The temple itself is only a shed with many red and gold flags out front, but it's extremely popular nonetheless (and not to be confused with the relatively new Shankar Viman Mandapammulti, the multi-storied affair grinning out over the trees). A stream of chanting worshippers snakes around the tiny temple, showering flowers on the image of the god that lies smeared with vermilion below ground level. The floodwaters are said to flow over Hanuman's feet each year before they recede. *(Open daily 4am-10pm.)*

ANAND BHAWAN. Once the mansion of the **Nehru family,** Anand Bhawan is now a museum devoted to their legacy. Independence leader Motilal Nehru, his son, Prime Minister Jawaharlal Nehru, and Jawaharlal's daughter and Prime Minister, Indira Gandhi, all lived and worked here, hosting meetings of the Independence movement. The Mahatma even had a room and working area in Anand Bhawan. The surprisingly modest Nehru showcase exhibits the family's passion for books—their bookshelves are stacked with everything from Roman Law to Tagore, and all the volumes can be peered at through glass panels. There are even handwritten letters from Jawahar to a baby Indira, and nothing brings history to life like seeing the pajamas of India's first Prime Minister hanging in his bedroom. One of the most interesting, historically significant, and well-presented museums in UP, the Anand Bhawan is definitely worth a visit. *(At the northeast corner of the city, close to Allahabad University. Open Tu-Su 9:30am-5pm. Rs5.)* Next door is the **Swaraj Bhawan Museum,** the home of patriarch Motilal Nehru. This mansion has an excellent sound and light show in Hindi, which gives you a tour of the house while leading you through the events of the Independence movement. Apart from the show, however, there's not much else here. *(Open Tu-Su 9:30am-5pm. Show Rs5.)*

ALL SAINTS' CATHEDRAL. The boldest reminder of the British in Allahabad is All Saints' Cathedral, with its soaring Victorian gothic spires and stained glass windows. It was designed by Sir William Emerson, the architect who designed the Victoria

NO WORK, ALL PLAY

THE KUMBH MELA

The Maha (Great) Kumbh Mela at Allahabad in 2001 set the record for the world's largest human gathering. An estimated 20 million people came to the city to be present at Hinduism's greatest festival, which marks the holiest time to bathe in the Sangam. Every 12 years, at one precisely calculated moment, all the pilgrims splash into the water in a ritual act believed to undo lifetimes of sin. Columns of charging *sadhus*, often naked and smeared with ash, are among the most zealous bathers.

The story behind the Kumbh Mela concerns a *kumbh* (pot) that is said to have contained an immortality-bestowing nectar. The demons battled the gods for this pot in a struggle that lasted 12 days, during which time four drops of the divine nectar were spilled. One landed at Haridwar, one at Nasik, one at Ujjain, and one at Allahabad.

The mythical 12-day fight translates into 12 human years, the length of the festival's rotation between cities. Every three years a Kumbh Mela is held in one of the four cities in January or February. The Maha Kumbh Mela, held at Allahabad every 12th year, is the greatest of all. Smaller *melas*, known as Magh Melas, are held in Allahabad in off-years during the month of Magh (Jan.-Feb.). In the sixth year, midway between Maha Kumbh Melas, an Ardha ("Half") Kumbh Mela is held. In 2004, the Kumbh Mela will take place in Nasik.

Memorial in Kolkata. There are now more weeds on the lawn and more bats in the belfry than during the British era. *(In Civil Lines, at the intersection of Mahatma Gandhi Rd. and Sarojini Naidu Marg.)*

KHUSRAU BAGH. If All Saints' is the most Raj-reminiscent relic in Allahabad, then Khusrau Bagh is the most impressive reminder of Mughal rule. These gardens hold the speckled tombs of Khusrau (a son of Emperor Jehangir) and his mother. Following Mughal royal family tradition, Khusrau plotted against his father and was subsequently murdered in 1615 by his brother, the future emperor Shah Jahan. The gardens, shaded by fruit trees and lined with paths, are a popular place for people to come and relax. In the evenings, the place comes alive with games of cricket. *(In the Chowk area down Leader Rd., past the bus station.)*

OTHER SIGHTS. Beyond the fort, on the bank of the Yamuna, is **Saraswati Ghat,** where boats dock and evening ceremony lamps are floated down to the confluence. Follow Yamuna Bank Rd. away from the fort to reach **Minto Park** on the right, where Lord Canning proclaimed in 1858 that India would be ruled by the Queen of England. Independent India has reclaimed the historic site by renaming the park for **Madan Mohan Malaviya** (an Independence figure and critic of the caste system) and erecting a part-Mauryan, part-Italian monument. *(To reach the other side of the fort, take either a boat ride or detour through the fenced-off military installation behind the fort.)* The **Allahabad Museum,** Kamla Nehru Marg, has a large sculpture collection, including many terracotta figures from Kausambi, the ancient city and Buddhist center 60km from Allahabad. There is also a room with photographs and a few Nehru mementos. *(Open Tu-Su 10:15am-4:30pm. Rs150 for foreigners.)*

WEST BENGAL

পশ্চিম বঙ্গ

West Bengal is India's most densely populated state, with nearly 800 people to every one of its 90,000 sq. km. With this crush of humanity comes a history and culture that has dominated India for hundreds of years and which continues to thrive today. In the 19th century, Bengal was at the center of literary and religious revival and a hotbed of national activism—the Bengali Renaissance produced some of India's finest writers, thinkers, and social reformers, including Rabindranath Tagore, India's first Nobel laureate for literature, and Swami Vivekananda, who attempted to infuse Hinduism with Western ideas of material progress.

The French, Dutch, and British discovered the bounty of Bengal throughout the 17th century, setting up trading posts along the coast. The British headquartered the East India Company and soon gathered the ire of the local Muslim Nawab. The province came to prominence as the foundation of the British Indian Empire after the Battle of Plassey in 1757, when Robert Clive defeated Nawab Siraj-ud-Daulah and his French allies to claim Bengal for Britain. In 1905, the infamous Partition of Bengal divided the state along religious lines: East Bengal (later East Pakistan, then Bangladesh in 1971) and Assam held a strong Muslim population; West Bengal, with Bihar and Orissa, was largely Hindu. The tragic, bloody partition paved the way for the bigger, bloodier tragedies that accompanied Partition in 1947. Today, Bengal revels in its enlightened non-communal Marxist traditions—the Communist Party of India has ruled since the 1960s.

Nature has endowed the state bountifully with tall snow-clad peaks perched above emerald green tea estates and lush paddy fields. From the bustling metropolis of Kolkata, to the coconut palm fringed mud villages of the Sunderbans, to the golden beaches of Digha, West Bengal has it all.

HIGHLIGHTS OF WEST BENGAL

Kolkata's temples, monuments, museums, and parks (p. 752) are rivaled only by the unchecked exuberance of the city's denizens.

Darjeeling (p. 766), "the land of thunderbolts," perched on the roof of Bengal at an altitude of 2134m, seduces heat-weary travelers with superb views.

The Sunderbans (p. 764), the extensive mangrove islands and winding waterways of southern Bengal, are home to birds, crocodiles, and the eminent tiger.

KOLKATA (CALCUTTA) কোলকাতা

☎ 033

Bursting at the seams with nearly 13 million people, even to its own residents, Kolkata often seems like a human cyclone. You don't just walk down the street—you step into it, jump over it, and try to scoot your way around the worst parts of

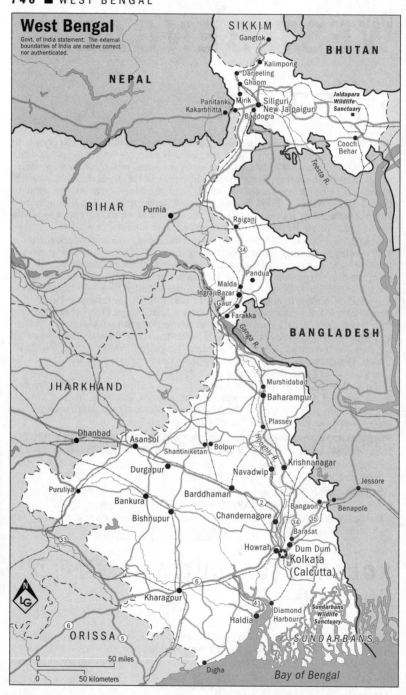

WEST BENGAL

it. Wherever you go, you can't avoid breathing in layers of black soot. Street vendors hawking everything from *biryani* to "Galvin Gline" wristwatches rule the sidewalks, while errant taxi drivers rule the streets—and everywhere there is the mad rush of people. But glance under this veil and you will see that this is a vibrant city full of history, of rich traditions, colonial and otherwise; a city perpetually bustling like a living thing, full of sights and sounds from all over India, and yet fiercely individual; a city that is the hub of consumerism in Eastern India with malls and bazaars galore; a city where cricket balls fly on acres of green by a holy river; a city that lights up like a festival every night. That's Kolkata.

The city's name derives from the word "Kalikshetra" (Ground of Goddess Kali), and the worship of Kali is an essential part of the city's character. The Durga Puja in October is the highlight of the year for many. Despite the scores of Indian temples scattered along the River Hooghly, Kolkata still bears the indelible imprint of the Raj. In 1690, East India Company agent Job Charnock bought the land that is now Kolkata, helping to build it into a prosperous trading post and industrial base. When Kolkata became the capital of the Raj in 1773, Bengalis got their first taste of a British education under the first governor-general, Warren Hastings (r. 1774-1785). The new literati proved too proud to submit to a foreign power, however, and the 19th century witnessed the elite-led Bengali Renaissance. Ram Mohan Roy (1774-1833) started the Brahmo Samaj movement, which pushed for social and religious reform within Hinduism. Upper-class salons hosted a revolution in the arts, culminating in the work of Nobel Prize-winning poet Rabindranath Tagore. Kolkata also became a center for anti-colonial politics; when the British moved to partition Bengal in 1905, their efforts were met with bombs and boycotts. The state has been ruled by an atheist non-partisan Communist government since the 1960s, one that most Kolkatans now accept as *de rigueur*.

✈ INTERCITY TRANSPORTATION

FLIGHTS

Officially known as the Netaji Subhas Chandra Bose International Airport, **Dum Dum Airport** (☎ 25118787 or 25119846) is 2km northeast of the city, in the suburb of Dum Dum. The **pre-paid taxi stand** in the domestic terminal is the most convenient way to catch a ride into downtown Kolkata, via the Eastern Metropolitan Bypass (30-40min., Rs175-200). City buses #46, 303, and 510 (Rs5) and the less direct E3 (Rs7-10) all run between the Esplanade and the airport. There is also a **minibus** (Rs20) that goes from BBD Bagh (Dalhousie Square) to the airport. Look for the route name on the bus. The airport has a reasonably well-stocked **duty free store** with liquor, tobacco, and lots of reasonably-priced Indian handicrafts, a **foreign currency exchange counter**, a **post office**, and **governmental tourist offices**. The **train ticket counter** serves Delhi, Mumbai, and Chennai only. The Airport Manager (☎ 25119846) in the domestic terminal can arrange beds in the waiting room for tired travelers with a layover of 24 hours or less. A valid ticket/boarding pass and photo ID is required.

INTERNATIONAL AIRLINES. All carriers have offices at the airport, as well as downtown. **AeroFlot,** 1st fl. Lords Building, 7/1 Lord Sinha Rd. (☎ 22829831). Open M-F 10am-5pm, Sa 10am-1pm. **Air France,** Chitrakoot Building, 230A AJC Bose Rd. (☎ 22408646). Open M-Sa 9am-5:30pm. **Air India,** 50 Chowringhee Rd. (☎ 22822356, 22822359, 22821187, or airport 25119864). Open daily 10am-5pm. **Air Nippon** and **Continental** Camac Tower, 3C Camac St. (☎ 22174913 or 22294464). **Alitalia,** Ground fl., Landmark Building, 228 AJC Bose Rd. (☎ 22471777 or 22871089). Open M-F 9:30am-6pm, Sa 9:30am-2pm. **American Airlines,** 230A AJC

Kolkata (Calcutta)

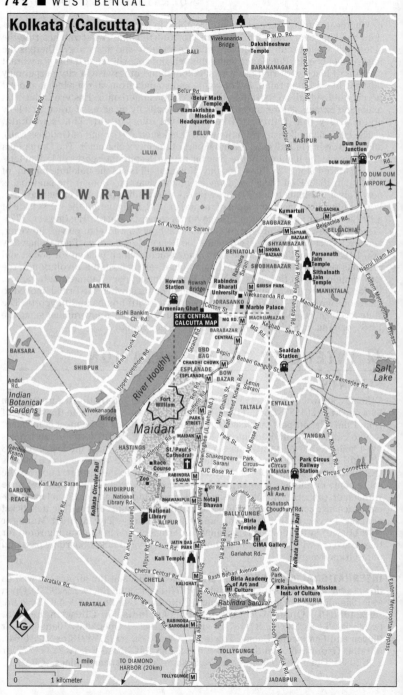

SEE CENTRAL CALCUTTA MAP

WEST BENGAL

As you leave the airport, you will likely encounter a number of taxi drivers who will solicit you for a trip to the city and offer accommodations at a specific hotel to which they are affiliated. Despite these offers, it's usually a good idea to get a taxi from the **pre-paid taxi stand** so that you can get a fixed destination and price. Should your driver claim that the accommodations you request are inaccessible or not as good as some other place he knows, insist on going to the hotel you want. Drivers are often paid commission by rival hotels and may therefore try a number of schemes to dissuade you from venturing to your intended lodgings. If you arrive late at night, you may want to consider staying overnight at the airport and getting a ride the next morning.

Bose Rd. (☎22801335). Open M-Sa 9am-5pm. **Austrian Airlines,** Vasundhara Building, 2/7 Sarat Bose Rd. (☎24745091). Open M-Sa 9am-1pm and 1:30-5:30pm. **Bangladesh Biman,** 33C Chowringhee Rd. (☎22292844 or 22497309). Open M-F 9:30am-4:30pm, Sa 9:30am-12:30pm. **British Airways,** 41 Chowringhee Rd. (☎22883452 or airport 25118424). Open M-F 9am-1pm and 2-4pm. **Cathay Pacific,** 1 Middleton St. (☎22403211). Open M-F 9:30am-1pm and 2-5:30pm, Sa 9:30am-1:30pm. **Delta, SAS, South African, Virgin Atlantic, Air New Zealand,** and **United Airlines,** Landmark Building, 228 AJC Bose Rd. (☎22405182). Open M-F 9:30am-1pm and 2-5:30pm, Sa 9:30am-1pm. **KLM** and **Northwest,** Jeevan Deep Building, 1 Middleton St. (☎22830151/0152/0153). Open M-F 9:30am-6pm, Sa 9:30am-1:30pm.

DOMESTIC AIRLINES. Indian Airlines is the country's primary domestic carrier, along with its subsidiary Alliance Air, but newer private carriers like Jet and Air Sahara have succeeded in opening up smaller Indian cities to air travel, and so prices are always competitive. **Indian Airlines** and **Alliance Air,** 39 Chittaranjan Ave. (☎22110730 or airport 25119637). Open M-F 7am-8:30pm. **Jet Airways,** Stephen Court, 18D Park St. (☎22292227 or airport 25119894). Open daily 9am-7pm. **Air Sahara**, Sahara India Sadan, 2A Shakespeare Sarani. (☎22828969 or airport 25119545). Open M-Sa 10:30am-5pm.

Indian Airlines flies to most of the following destinations, unless otherwise indicated. To: **Agartala** (1½hr., daily, Rs1900); **Ahmedabad** (2½hr.; M, Tu, Th, F; Rs8400); **Allahabad** (Sahara only; 1½hr.; M, W, F; Rs4700); **Bangalore** (2½hr., daily, Rs9000); **Bhubaneshwar** (1hr., daily, Rs3000); **Chennai** (2hr., daily, Rs7750); **Delhi** (2hr., daily, Rs6875); **Gorakhpur** (Sahara only; 2hr.; Tu, Th, Sa, Su; Rs3500); **Guwahati** (1hr., daily, Rs2700); **Hyderabad** (2hr., daily, Rs7200); **Jaipur** (2½hr.; M, Tu, Th, F; Rs8000); **Lucknow** (Sahara only, 2½hr., daily, Rs5000); **Mumbai** (2½hr., daily, Rs6850); **Nagpur** (1½hr.; M, W, F; Rs5800); **Patna** (1hr., daily, Rs3200); **Port Blair** (2hr., daily, Rs6700); **Shillong** (1hr.; M, W, F; Rs2500); **Tezpur** (1hr., Tu and Sa, Rs2800); **Vishakhapatnam** (1½hr.; Tu, Th, and Sa; Rs4700). International service to: **Bangkok,** Thailand (2½hr., daily, Rs13,400); **Dhaka,** Bangladesh (1½hr.; M, Tu, Th; Rs5300); **Kathmandu,** Nepal (1½hr.; W, F, Su; Rs6500).

TRAINS

Kolkata has two major inter-city railway stations: **Sealdah Station,** in northeast Kolkata going away from Park Street on AJC Bose Rd., for trains going primarily to the north, and the much larger **Howrah Station,** across the River Hooghly from Kolkata, for trains going all over India. Although any public bus stopping at Sealdah or Howrah will usually pull right up to the entrance of the station, a taxi may be a better bet if you have heavy luggage to carry. Taxis will likely drop you off at the car parking area next to the inquiry booth. Taxi from the city center to: Howrah Station Rs100-120, Sealdah Station Rs100. At Howrah, there is a **pre-paid taxi stand** at the station (Rs120-150 to downtown Kolkata) and a **West Bengal Tourist Information**

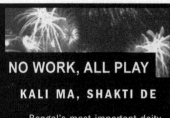

NO WORK, ALL PLAY

KALI MA, SHAKTI DE

Bengal's most important deity is the Mother Goddess, Kali. The Goddess embodies Shakti, or Power, in all her incarnations (Parvati, Durga, Chandi, Sati and many more) and is the consort of the Lord Shiva, the Destroyer of the Universe.

Every October, the whole state's affairs come to a screeching halt to celebrate the coming of Durga, Kali's maternal incarnation. Durga Puja is the most important festival for Bengalis, and it's a spectacle not to be missed by any visitor to the area. Preparations start with the onset of the monsoon. The crowds of family artisans in northern Kolkata's Kumartuli ("Potter's Lane") shape structures of bamboo and straw that are then covered with fresh monsoon clay and molded into idols of the deity and her family. Over three months they are shaped, dried, painted beautifully, and dressed in heavenly finery. By September, most of the million or so idols that will find their way to community halls, tents, and homes all over the city for the festival are nearing completion. It is an auspicious time.

As the five-day festival, as dictated by the lunar calendar, approaches, Kolkata moves into festive mode. Most stores have a month-long 20-50% off sale in celebration, for this is also the time when new acquisitions can be blessed. People all over the city put together *pandals* (large cov-

Counter (☎26602518; open daily 7am-8pm). Tickets can be purchased at the main **Railway Booking Office**, 6 Fairlie Place (☎22203496), near BBD Bagh. The **Foreign Tourist Office** is on the first floor. Foreign currency or rupees with encashment certificate accepted. (Open daily 9am-1pm and 1:30-4pm.) An excellent source for all Indian Railways status enquiries, ticket prices and schedules is their website, where you can even reserve tickets online, accessible at www.indianrailways.com or www.indianrail.gov.in.

From **Howrah Station** to: **Bhubaneswar** (6-9hr., 12 per day 8:25am-3:50am, Rs174); **Chennai** (28-34hr., 6 per day 1:15-10:20pm and 3:50am, Rs436); **Delhi** (23hr., 5-6 per day 9:10am-8:15pm, Rs377; express 18hr., 5pm, Rs1450); **Mumbai** (32-36hr., 5 per day 10:40am-8pm, Rs430); **Patna** (8-10hr., 9 per day 9:15am-11pm, Rs202; express 7hr., 1:45pm, 3-tier A/C Rs915); **Puri** (11hr., 6:05 and 9:45pm, Rs194); **Varanasi** (8-17hr., 5 per day 9:15am-11pm, Rs271). **Sealdah Station** to: **New Jalpaiguri** (13hr., 6 per day 6:25am-9:15pm, Rs206).

BUSES

Private buses go to Siliguri (12hr.), a departure point for Darjeeling. West Bengal Tourism runs the most direct bus, which leaves Kolkata at 6pm, reaching **Siliguri** (6am, Rs205) and **Jalpaiguri** (6:15am, Rs210). Buses also run to **Digha** (5hr., 7am, Rs150) and **Jaigon** (19hr., 6pm, Rs250). Tickets must be purchased in advance at the booth at the Esplanade; to get there, take a left from Chowringhee Rd. onto SN Banerjee Rd. The booth is on the right just before the tram tracks. Other private bus company booths are to the left (follow the tracks). Alternatively, you can call the Tourism Office (☎22485917 or 22488271) in advance and collect your ticket there for a little extra.

BOATS

Two to three ships sail each month to **Port Blair** in the Andaman and Nicobar Islands; the exact schedule depends on the weather and varies from year to year. Tickets and a tentative schedule for a six month period are available from the **Shipping Corporation Office** 13 Strand Rd., two blocks south of the Fairlie Place Railway Booking Office. (☎22462354. Open M-F 10am-1pm.) Arrivals and departures are announced about a week in advance. Ticket sales begin seven days before the scheduled departure, often selling out in the first couple of days. Bring three passport photos and acceptable photo ID, usually your passport will be required to purchase tickets. (3-4 days; ordinary bunk Rs1500, deluxe 2nd class Rs2500, 1st class Rs3500.) Boat conditions vary greatly, but less so in deluxe and first class.

✹ ORIENTATION

Expansive as it is, Kolkata's layout is relatively straightforward. The **River Hooghly** cuts through town, separating Kolkata proper from **Howrah;** these two areas are linked by one of the world's most heavily-used bridges, the **Rabindra Setu** (also called the **Howrah Bridge**), and farther south, by the new suspension **Vivekananda Setu.** Howrah's centerpiece is the frenetic **Howrah Station,** easily visible and accessed from Kolkata by the Howrah Bridge. The main road in Howrah is the **Grand Trunk Road,** which runs parallel to the river and connects the Botanical Gardens in the south with the Belur Math up north.

Across the river from Howrah along the river's eastern bank is the **Maidan,** a grassy field broken up by streets and dotted with monuments. The central city hugs the Maidan and **Strand Road** cuts between the Maidan and the river. At the Maidan's northeastern corner is **the Esplanade,** the central bus and train terminus. A couple of blocks north is **BBD Bagh** (formerly **Dalhousie Square**), around which are the tourist office, GPO, railway and shipping companies, and several banks. To the east of BBD Bagh is **Old Court House Road. Netaji Subhas Road,** north of the GPO, and **Chittaranjan Avenue** to the east, are the major roads leading to North Kolkata.

Running along the east side of the maidan is the majestic **Chowringhee Road** (now **Jawaharlal Nehru Road**). Several major streets make their way east from the Chowringhee. These include **Park Street** and **Shakespeare Sarani** (formerly **Theatre Road;** *Sarani* means "street"), with fancier restaurants, hotels, banks, and shopping malls. **Sudder Street** is two blocks north of Park St., walking in the direction of the grand Indian Museum, and is home to a majority of foreign budget travelers. At the eastern end of Sudder St. is the north-south **Mirza Ghalib Street** (formerly **Free School Street**), with a range of eating and shopping facilities, as it forms the main access route to **New Market** from Park St. Parallel to this even farther east is **Acharya Jagadish Chandra (AJC) Bose Road** (formerly the **Lower Circular Road**), which circles the lower east of the city center today, an area which marked Kolkata's city limits 150 years ago. To the south it curves back westward and leads to St. Paul's Cathedral and the Victoria Memorial, both at the Maidan's southeast corner.

East of it all is **Park Circus** at the end of Park St., leading to the city's Chinatown at **Tangra** and then the clean and efficient **Eastern Metropolitan Bypass** which runs alongside the entire city, connecting the airport and the north to the areas of **Gariahat** and

ered tents), street shows, exhibitions, and *melas* (fairs) as the excitement mounts and the anticipation rises and there are bright lights in the streets. Finally, the five-day festival begins when Durga returns to earth with her children to visit her parents, Himalaya and Menake.

The myth also harkens back to the time when the evil demon king Mahisasura had taken over the earth, and terrorized all mortals, when even the gods were powerless against him. They channeled all their powers into creating a new incarnation of Shakti—one with ten arms and the power of Good—Goddess Durga. As she revisits the earth every year, she reminds everyone of the power of Good over Evil, and this is why all her idols depict her slaying Mahisasura. The next few days are spent rejoicing and worshipping her stay.

On the fifth day, as Durga gets ready to bid farewell, the whole city heads to the river in large processions, each with their own idol, to send her off. At dusk, people launch their clay idols of Durga onto the water, adorned with candles and garlands of flowers, and watch as she makes her way to the sea, with her return to earth assured the next year.

Ballygunge in southern Kolkata as well as the city center via the Park Circus Connector. This is the route taxi drivers should take to bring you into town. East of the Bypass is **Salt Lake City** (also called **Bidhannagar**), a major residential and commercial suburb which was planned in the 1970s and has developed along less unruly lines than the rest of the city.

In the south, Chowringhee Rd. becomes **Ashutosh Mukherjee Road,** which continues into southern Kolkata. To the west is the upscale area of **Alipur,** which also contains the zoo and the National Library; south of Alipur is **Kalighat,** home to the Kalighat Temple.

▐▔ LOCAL TRANSPORTATION

Kolkata's busiest streets in the city center can best be negotiated, as the popular local saying goes, on "the #11 bus" (your own two legs). For greater distances, you'll be spoiled in your choice for a mode of transportation. This is one of the only cities in the world where you can not only hop into a taxi or on a bus, but also duck into an electric tram, slip inside a noiseless subway train on the Metro or even clamber onto a rickshaw (auto-, cycle- or hand-pulled). Traffic rules, while frequently bent with great finesse by Kolkatans, are strict and enforced with hefty fines by the Kolkata Police (check them out in their white uniforms and red bikes). Most thoroughfares which are too narrow to allow traffic both ways go one way in the morning and the other in the afternoon and evening.

BUSES

Buses in Kolkata are cheap and, as in any city with a burgeoning population, always crowded. Most buses charge Rs3-5 for average inner-city distances. You will see three major kinds of public buses plying on Kolkata streets: 1) the government-run **state transport buses** which are generally red, orange-and-white or orange-and-green, and which stick to their schedules (available at larger city post offices and West Bengal Tourism bureaus) and stop only at bus stops and shelters; 2) the slightly rickety silver colored buses inexplicably called **"privates";** and 3) the small **yellow-and-crimson minibuses** which have their routes emblazoned in large blue letters on their sides. While all of these buses will stop at actual bus stops, you can get on the non state-run buses just about anywhere—you'll see seasoned locals just put their hands out and the driver will slow down. If the bus is moving too fast for them to feel comfortable running alongside and jumping aboard, shouting *"aaste!"* ("Slow!") usually does the trick. You should identify a major destination close to yours in order to most easily find a bus on that route, and if your bus is crowded, start moving towards an exit a short while before your destination so you don't make your fellow passengers wait too long at a stop.

TRAMS AND THE SUBWAY

Trams leave from the central Esplanade to major destinations throughout south Kolkata and to Sealdah and north Kolkata and the Howrah Bridge (Rs3-12). There are also long north-south routes that will take you through the oldest sections of Kolkata on cobbled streets that were made for tram traffic right down to Ballygunge. They are slow and sometimes hard to get on at busy intersections. A list of routes is available at larger city post offices, West Bengal Tourism bureaus, and at the Calcutta Tramways website, www.calcuttatramways.com. India's first **subway** (metro) extends in a virtually straight line from Tollygunge, up Chowringhee Rd. (via the Maidan, Park St. and the Esplanade), to Dum Dum Station. From this station, a taxi or auto-rickshaw to the airport takes 15-30min. (Rs40). The Metro is relatively uncrowded and the fastest, most reliable mode of transportation available. Be sure to buy a ticket at the counter before boarding (Rs5-15). If you are in the city for a longer period of time and are staying downtown, much of your travel might be on the Metro, so it could be cheaper to get a weekly (Rs100) or a monthly pass (Rs220). (Open M-Sa 7am-9:20pm, Su 2:35-9:20pm. Trains every 10min.)

TAXIS AND RICKSHAWS

Taxis are the most convenient way to cover long distances in Kolkata. All taxis in the city are now required to have tamper-proof electronic meters for the fare, and you should avoid any taxi still using one of the large, easily-tampered-with chic-in-London-circa-1920 mechanical meters. The electronic meter begins at Rs10, and the fare is 1.4 times the meter reading. If you're worried about being taken around in circles to up the fare, negotiating on a price beforehand might be a good idea. However, new rules following the introduction of the new meters may not allow your driver to cooperate, in which case asking a friendly local how long your trip should take and how much you should expect to pay might be avoidable. Howrah to downtown Kolkata costs Rs100-120, rides around the city center are Rs14-30. The prepaid taxi counters at the airport have long lines, but they are worth the wait (Rs175-200). The city's fleet of **hand-pulled rickshaws,** the last in the world, is quickly dwindling. They are cheap, but you can usually walk faster than they can pull. **Cycle-rickshaws** are quicker, but like the hand-pulled and the three-wheeled **auto-rickshaws,** they are banned from major streets in most of Kolkata and Howrah.

◪ PRACTICAL INFORMATION

TOURIST AND FINANCIAL SERVICES

An excellent all-in-one resource for travelers in Kolkata is the fortnightly *CityInfo Kolkata* (Rs30), a compendium of important phone numbers and addresses published by Explocity Publications (☎22872194, www.explocity.com). Apart from their comprehensive website, copies are available at many hotels, restaurants and bookstores in the city, as well as at major post offices and at the tourist bureaus mentioned below. A similar publication, although less frequently published and not as readily available, is *Cal Calling* (Rs25). Listings in the metro sections of local dailies such as *The Telegraph (Metro)* and *The Times Of India (Cal Times)* are also great resources for important happenings and events in the city, especially weekend editions that devote entire sections to art and entertainment.

Tourist Office: Government of India Tourist Office, 4 Shakespeare Sarani, (☎22821475 or 22825813), provides maps and brochures, and up-to-date travel information from Kolkata to the rest of India. You will need to contact this office for information on traveling to Bangladesh, and the staff can direct you to the right place in case you have visa or travel permission queries. The office also provides a list of guest houses, host families and *dharamsalas* for other accommodation options. Open M-F 9am-6pm, Sa 9am-5pm. **West Bengal Tourism Center,** 3/2 BBD Bagh East. (☎22485917 or 22488271), provides city tours (daily 7:30am-5pm, Rs150), information and tours for all of West Bengal, and passes for nature reserves and wildlife sanctuaries in northern Bengal and the Sunderbans. You need to obtain permission here to visit the Marble Palace. Open M-F 10am-5pm, and over the weekend only for city tour information. **Tourist Information Counters** at the **airport** (☎25116026) and **Howrah Station** (☎26602518) are open daily 7am-8pm.

Consulates: Bangladesh, 9 Circus Ave. (☎22475208). Open M-F 9am-5pm. **Canada,** Duncan House, 31 Netaji Subhas Ch. Bose Rd. (☎22250163). Open M-F 10am-4pm. **France** and **Germany,** 1 Hastings Park Rd. (☎24791141). Open M-Th 8am-4pm, F 8am-1pm. **Israel,** Viswakarma Building, 86C Topsia Rd. S. (☎22800028). Open M-F 10am-5pm. **Nepal,** 1 National Library Ave. (☎24791224). Open M-F 10am-4pm. **Sri Lanka,**

WEST BENGAL

Nicco House, 2 Hare St. (☎22485102). Open M-F 9:30am-5:30pm. **South Africa,** 225D AJC Bose Rd. (☎22470253). Open M-F 10am-5pm. **UK,** 1 Ho Chi Minh Sarani. (☎22885172 or emergency 22886536). Open M-F 9am-noon and 1-4pm. **USA,** 5/1 Ho Chi Minh Sarani. (☎22823611). Open M-F 8am-5pm.

Immigration Office: Foreigner Regional Registration Office, 237 AJC Bose Rd. (☎22837034). **All foreign citizens planning to stay in India for more than six months must register here.** The office provides emergency passport/visa assistance as well as visa extensions for tourist and work visas. Open M-F 11am-5:30pm, and over the weekend only for emergencies.

Currency Exchange: 24hr. ATMs are all over Kolkata, and all major banks have attached ATMs unless otherwise noted. All branches mentioned offer currency exchange services for a fee. **ABN-AMRO Bank,** 5th. fl. ITC Building, 4 Russell St. (☎22260853). Open M-F 10am-5pm. **American Express,** 21 Old Court House St. (☎22101389 or 22486283). Open M-F 9:30am-5:30pm, Sa 9:30am-2pm. Travel services also available. **Bank of America,** Ruby House, 8 India Exchange Pl. (☎22422042). Open M-F 10am-5pm. No ATM; but useful for transferring money from the USA. **Citibank,** 43 Chowringhee Rd. (☎22492484). Open M-F 10am-2pm, Sa 10am-noon. **HSBC,** 31 BBD Bagh. (☎22201833 or 22102347). Open M-Sa 10am-5pm. **ICICI Bank,** 1/1 Ashutosh Choudhary Ave. (☎22807681). Open M-Sa 10am-5pm. Major branch at the corner of Park St. and Camac St. **Standard Chartered Bank,** 19 Netaji Subhas Chandra Bose Rd. (next to the Reserve Bank of India). (24hr. help line. ☎22428888.) Major branches with ATMs at the corner of Camac St. and Shakespeare Sarani, corner of Park St. and Chowringhee Rd. (opp. Asiatic Society) and at 41 Chowringhee Rd. **State Bank of India,** 1 Strand Rd. (☎22489331). Open M-F 10am-5pm, Sa 10am-2pm. Major branches with ATMs at Jeevan Deep Building (Middleton St.) and at the corner of Middleton St. and the Chowringhee. 24hr. foreign exchange counter at Dum Dum Airport, international terminal. **Thomas Cook,** Chitrakoot Building, 2nd fl., 230A AJC Bose Rd. (☎22474560; fax 22475854.) Open M-Sa 10am-5pm. Travel services also available.

BOOKSTORES

Landmark, Emami Shopper's City, 3 Lord Sinha Rd. (☎22822617). Open everyday 9am-9pm. Has the largest range of books in the city; a paradise for music, toys or gifts. All major credit cards accepted. **Oxford Bookstore Gallery,** 17 Park St. (☎22297662), below The Park Hotel. Open M-Sa 10am-8:30pm. One of the city's oldest bookstores, it is on three levels of richly polished wood with a space for its popular author readings and also houses a coffee and *chai* bar. Look for lithograph prints from old Calcutta. All major credit cards accepted. **Rupa & Co.,** 15 Bankim Chatterjee St. (☎22416597), is a major Indian publisher of foreign books at comparatively affordable prices. You can also try **Family Book Shop,** 1A Park St., next to the Asiatic Society (☎22293846). **College Street** is lined with colleges and book stalls that sell everything from hefty modern medical esoterica to peeling secondhand paperbacks.

CULTURAL CENTERS

Academy of Fine Arts, 2 Cathedral Rd. (☎22234302). Regularly exhibits paintings by prominent national artists. Frequent art and photography exhibitions from all over the world. **Alliance Française,** 3 West Range (☎22815538). French language classes, a small library, the center also sponsors French drama workshops and cultural studies. The British Council (see above) promotes English theater in the city and sponsors annual drama and cultural festivals. **Rabindra Sadan,** corner of Cathedral and AJC Bose Rd. This state-run cultural center hosts Bengali plays, dance performances and Indian classical music. The adjacent **Nandan** center hosts various exhibitions and has two movie theaters that have a number of annual theme film festivals. **Swabhumi Heritage Park,** across the Eastern Metropolitan Bypass from the Hyatt Regency, just past Salt Lake Sta-

River Hooghly

Armenian Church of Our Lady of Nazareth

Mahatma Gandhi Rd.

MG ROAD

(Harrison Rd.)

Biplabi Rash Bihari St.
Netaji Subhas Rd.

Armenian St.
Rabindra Sarani
Ezra St.

Nakhoda Mosque

Kolutola St.

CALCUTTA UNIVERSITY

BARABAZAR

Fairlie Pl.

Railway Booking Office

Lyons' Range

Bentinck St.

Tiretta Bazar St.

CENTRAL

Ashutosh Museum

College St.

Surya Sen St.

GPO

Writers' Building

Police Headquarters

Strand Rd.

Hare St.

BBD Bagh

Lal Bazaar

Chittaranjan Ave.

Sashi Bhusan Dey St.

St. John's Church

BBD Bagh W.

BBD Bagh E.

West Bengal

TIRETTA

BAITAKKHANA

High Court

Waterloo St.

Weston St.

Ganesh Ch. Avenue

Bepin Behari Ganguli St.

American Express

Vidhan Sabha

Raj Bhavan

Auckland Rd.

Old Court House Rd.

Indian Airlines

CHANDNI CHOWK

Eden Gardens

Esplanade Row

Curzon Park

Chittaranjan Ave.

BOW BAZAR

Ranji Stadium

Garden Rd.

ESPLANADE

Esplanade

Lenin Sarani

Ochterlony Monument (Shahid Minar)

Oberoi Grand Hotel

Lighthouse Theatre

Surendra Nath Banerjee Rd.

Red Rd.

Metro Theatre

New Empire Theatre

New Market

Mirza Galib St. (Free School St.)

Rafi Ahmed Kidwai Rd.

SEE INSET

Fort William

Dufferin Rd.

Lindsay St.

Sudder St.

Alimuddin St.

PARK STREET

Kyd St. (Dr. M. Ishaque Rd.)

TO MISSIONARIES OF CHARITY (500m)

ATM

Park Hotel

Ripon St.

MAIDAN

Jawaharlal Nehru Rd.

Russell St.

Royd St.

Casurina Ave.

British Airways

Middleton Row

Park Street

Acharya Jagadish Chandra Bose Rd.

MAIDAN

ATM

KLM & Cathay Pacific

Middleton St.

Camac St.

Wood St.

Chowringhee

Ho Chi Minh

Little Russel St.

United Kingdom

Short St.

Loudon St.

Queen's Way

Birla Planetarium

United States

Shakespeare Sarani

Govt. of India

Park Street Cemetery

Victoria Memorial

Air India

Hungerford St.

(Theatre Rd.)

Lord Sinha Rd.

Lindsay St.

Globe Theatre

St. Paul's Cathedral

St. Joseph's Home for the Aged

Cathedral Rd.

Academy of Fine Arts

Rabindra Sadan & Nandan Complex

AJC Bose Rd.

(Lower Circular Rd.)

Rawdon St.

Sudder St.

Indian Museum

Hartford Ln.

RABINDRA SADAN

Foreigners' Reg. Office

Hotel Hindustan

Chowringhee Ln.

Elgin Rd.

0   200 yards

0   200 meters

Kyd St. (Dr. M. Ishaque Rd.)

Biman

Central Kolkata (Calcutta)

ACCOMMODATIONS

Gujral Guest Hosue, **13**
Hotel Plaza, **12**
Middleton Inn, **7**
Shilton Hotel, **14**
Sikkim House, **8**

FOOD

Aaheli, **2**
Aminia, **11**
Anand Vegetarian Restaurant, **1**
Bar B-Q, **6**
Flury's Tearoom and Confectionary, **5**
Haldiram Bhujiawala, **9**

ENTERTAINMENT

Anticlock, **10**
Someplace Else, **3**
Tantra, **4**

WEST BENGAL

dium (☎23215486). This large complex is tastefully modelled on the style of a 19th century Bengali mansion, with handicrafts and art sold around an open courtyard with a stage and seating gallery that hosts dance, music, and dramatic performances.

EMERGENCY AND COMMUNICATIONS

Emergency: Police ☎ 100, **Fire** ☎ 101, **Medical** ☎ 102.

Police: Headquarters, **Lalbazar** (☎22145000 through 22145010).

Pharmacy: Dey's Medical Stores 6/2B Nellie Sengupta Sarani (☎22499810), opposite New Market's main entrance. Open M-F 9am-9pm, Sa 9am-5pm. **Frank Ross** 55 Gariahat Rd. (☎24755595). Open daily 8.30am-8pm. **Lindsay Blue Print** 21 Chowringhee Rd. (☎22492405). Open daily 8:30am-10:30pm.

Hospital: Belle Vue Clinic 9 Loudon St. (☎22472321), on the right two blocks down Loudon from Park St. **Woodland Hospital** 8/5 Alipur Rd. (☎24567079). Both have state-of-the-art facilities and 24hr. emergency rooms.

Internet: Three companies have established an extensive chain of broadband surfing centers all over the city. Call their downtown locations given below to ask for the franchise closest to you. Rates range from Rs15-30 per hr. **Satyami Way** (☎22493244), 59B Park St. **Dishnet DSL** (☎22171788), Gr. fl. Park Plaza, 71 Park St. **Junction96** (☎24743831), 2/1A Gariahat Rd.

Post Office: GPO (☎22201451). BBD Bagh. Open M-Sa 7am-8:30pm. **Major Branch Post Offices:** Airport, Russell St., Park St., New Market, Mirza Ghalib St., Ballygunge, Park Circus, Salt Lake City. **Postal Code** 700 001.

⌐ ACCOMMODATIONS

Kolkata offers travelers a wide range of places to spend the night. If its a dirt-cheap backpacker's hostel you want, then Sudder St. and Mirza Ghalib St. are the places to go (Rs500 and below per day). The rock-bottom prices will only give you shabby, spartan housing in the rather cramped, squalid—but centrally-located—part of town that is popular with backpackers. The Park St.-Middleton St.-Chowringhee Rd. area as well as Ballygunge and Gariahat in south Kolkata offer pricier digs—you'll be surprised how the quality improves with every Rs100.

Ramakrishna Mission Institute of Culture, Gol Park (☎24641303; rmic@vsnl.com), the circle at the end of Gariahat Rd. and Southern Ave. The fastidiously clean lodging for the Kolkata headquarters of the Ramakrishna Mission is built around a wonderful garden, an oasis of peace in hurly-burly Kolkata. Spacious, comfortable rooms in a great location. Apply at least two weeks in advance in writing (fax or email). All meals included. Gate closes 10pm, inform the gate if you'll be out later. Singles Rs380-500, with A/C Rs600; doubles Rs600, with A/C Rs850. ❸

Sikkim House, 4/1 Middleton St. (☎22815328), just into Middleton from the Chowringhee, after the Jeevan Deep building, on the right. The Sikkim state guest house in Kolkata. Large, clean A/C rooms, all doubles, with TVs and phones. Centrally located, close to the Maidan Metro station. Reserve at least a week ahead. Rooms Rs550-900. ❸

Hotel Galaxy, 3 Stuart Ln. (☎22464565), opposite the Astoria Hotel, closer to the Mirza Ghalib St. side of Sudder St. Though slightly more expensive than other budget places in the area, Galaxy is a steal. The staff is friendly and will deliver food ordered from local places for free, though you still have to pay for the food. Open, airy rooms have color TVs, carpets, and wooden furniture. Non-A/C doubles with bath Rs500-700. ❸

WEST BENGAL

Shilton Hotel, 5A Sudder St. (☎22521512 or 22451527; shiltoncal@hotmail.com), set back from the bustle on Sudder St. by a large courtyard; look for signs. Huge airy rooms have clean shared baths, large windows, cable TV, and phones. Singles Rs225, with attached bath Rs265; doubles Rs350; triples Rs400; quads Rs675. ❷

Middleton Inn, 10 Middleton St. (☎2216449; mi_inn@yahoo.com), on the left opposite Sikkim House. A luxurious executive hotel with the living comforts of a five-star, including marble floors, mini-refrigerators, cable TV, individual phones, 24hr. room service, travel desk and a doctor on call. A central location at an unbeatable price, compared to the city's full blown five-star hotels. Singles Rs1500-1800, Doubles Rs1800-2000. ❺

Hotel Homelyraj, 10/2 Manoharpukur Rd. (☎24754344; rajrest@cal2.vsnl.net.in), near the Kalighat temple. A bright and modern hotel in southern Kolkata has clean, well-appointed rooms with cable TV and attached bathrooms. There is provision for safe deposit with the office, and the hotel is close to the Kalighat Metro station. Singles Rs525, with A/C Rs775-875; Doubles Rs700, with A/C Rs875-975. ❸

Gujral Guest House, Lindsay St. (☎22440392). Circle around the right side of Lindsay Hotel and turn left onto an alley behind it; look for the painted signs. Comfortable, well furnished rooms await on the 3rd fl.; deluxe doubles have cable TV. Common TV room. Bed tea and breakfast included. Singles with shared bathroom Rs300; doubles with attached bathroom Rs400-1000. ❷

Hotel Plaza, 10 Sudder St. (☎22492435), closer to the Chowringhee end of the street. Cheerful staff, neat medium-sized rooms with carpets and attached bathrooms. Bed tea and breakfast included. All rooms are doubles, Rs400-525, with A/C Rs770-900. ❸

Astoria Hotel, 6/2/3 Sudder St. (☎22451514; astoria@hotmail.com), toward the Mirza Ghalib St. end of Sudder St. An excellent hotel; rooms are spacious, carpeted, and furnished well. All have A/C, TV, direct-dial phones, and attached bathrooms. Room service. Reserve a week ahead. Singles Rs650; doubles Rs985-1200. ❹

⌑ FOOD

Food is one of Kolkata's great pastimes. Here you can enjoy Bengali cuisine at its best, dominated by its seafood and sweets—don't miss the excellent coconut *golda-chingri* (tiger prawns), mustard *hilsa* (an excellent saltwater fish similar to the North American shad), mutton curry, and the *rossogolla* (a round, syrupy Bengali sweet). British influences are everywhere at foodstalls sell delicacies called rolls, chops, and cutlets, but which look nothing like their Western counterparts. The thriving Muslim population brought with it Mughlai cuisine many years ago, with kebabs, *kathi* rolls (rolls stuffed with skewered kebabs) and *biryani* (saffron-flavored fried rice cooked with meat and spices).

⧈ Shiraz Golden Restaurant, 56 Park St. (☎22477702), at Mullick Bazaar crossing. This place makes Kolkata's best and most famous *biryani,* take your pick of extremely filling chicken or mutton (Rs41), or go with the whole hog and order specials of each (Rs63) which come with extra portions of meat and Kashmiri saffron. *Chaap* curry, kebabs, and other *tandoori* dishes Rs20-80. Delivery available. ❷

Aaheli, The Peerless Inn, 12 Chowringhee Rd. (☎22280301). Waiters don traditional *dhotis* and *kurtas* while serving excellent Bengali *thalis* (Rs220-250). If you like seafood, go for the famed *Chingri Machcher Malai Curry* (large prawns in a coconut curry) (Rs200) with plain white rice (Rs40). Open daily noon-2:45pm and 7:30-11:30pm. ❺

Haldiram Bhujiawala, AJC Bose Rd., at the corner of Chowringhee Rd., next to the Aeroflot office. This veg. eat-and-run sweet-and-snack chain, popular with Kolkata's middle class primarily serves non-Bengali food. S*amosas, chanachur* (a sweet-and-sour fried mix), *dhokla* (spongy Gujarati cakes made out of *dal* and served with a sweet sauce), *jalebis,* and all things fried Rs10-60. ❶

WEST BENGAL

Suruchi, Elliot Rd., just after Mullick Bazaar. Delicious *bhepe ilish* (mustard coated *hilsa* fish) with white rice, or mutton curry with a large quantity of *luchis* (lightly fried flat bread). Go for their large seafood variety; no meal combination for one person will be over Rs80. Open for lunch only. Part of the proceeds fund the social service center for women that runs the establishment; check out their handicrafts at the back. ❸

Tung Fong, Mirza Ghalib St. (☎22174969), just inside from Park St. and on the left. One of the city's newer Chinese restaurants, this joint has a lovely ambience with its solid wood furniture and papered walls. Specializes in Szechuan cooking. Chili chicken Rs60; meal for one Rs150-250. Open daily noon-10:30pm. ❹

Anand Vegetarian Restaurant, 19 Chittaranjan Ave., between the IA office and Chowringhee Rd. A haven for vegetarians in the midst of meat-and-fish-crazy Kolkata. Great South and North Indian food on 2 fl. behind tinted glass. Most dishes Rs30-65. ❷

Flury's Tearoom and Confectionery, 18 Park St., the large white building on the corner of Middleton Row alongside Music World. English breakfast every morning. Stroll over to the confectionery section while you wait for your tea to pack some delectable cakes and pastries for home (Rs9-20 per piece). Open daily 7am-7pm. ❶

Aminia, New Market, near Eliot Cinema. Serves Nizam's-type staples, including kebabs and rolls, but Aminia's delicate rose-water flavored *biryani* is finger lickin' good (Rs36-42). Another legendary meal is the innocuously-named Aminia Special (pieces of mutton and chicken along with an egg in a rich spicy tomato gravy), with rice and rounded off with *firni* (a thick sweet Muslim rice pudding) for about Rs50. ❷

Bar B-Q, 43 Park St. (☎22299916). This elegant, spacious restaurant with extensive Chinese and Indian menus rewards with an escape from the grime. Their Szechuan and Manchurian dishes are spot on but don't order your food spicy unless you've got coolant in your belly. Szechuan chili chicken Rs125. Excellent bar upstairs. Reserve ahead on weekends. Open daily noon-3pm and 7-10.30pm. ❹

Grain Of Salt, 5th fl., Pantaloons/Westside Bldg., 22 Camac St. (☎22811313). One of the city's large multicuisine restaurants, this is a pricey establishment that covers 25,000 sq. ft. and features delectable buffets on select nights. They are noted for their Continental, Thai, and Indian food, all served in great style, and you can even watch your food being cooked. The adjoining bar is well-stocked but expensive, with stylish futuristic furniture and rock salt decor. A full spread with drinks about Rs300-400. ❺

🧭 SIGHTS

The best way to experience Kolkata and to see the sights is by **walking.** If it's not too hot, equip yourself with a copy of Prosenjit Dasgupta's *Ten Walks in Kolkata* (available at most city bookstores, Rs200) and a good map and take to the streets for a few hours every day. An interesting, if slow experience is West Bengal Tourism's Heritage tram ride (☎22485917 or 22488271) that starts early in the morning—see Kolkata's oldest parts the way you would have during the British Raj. If you're in a hurry, but want to see *everything*, hop on West Bengal Tourism's **full day tour** (7am-5pm, Rs150). They'll rush you around the city in 10 hours.

MAIDAN, PARK STREET, AND NEW MARKET AREA

VICTORIA MEMORIAL

Museum open Tu-Su 10am-4:30pm; Nov.-Feb. 10am-3:30pm. Foreigner entry Rs150-200; Indian citizens Rs10. Photography not permitted. Sound and light show Tu-Su 8:15pm. Rs10. Gardens open dawn-dusk.

The southern end of the Maidan is dominated by the famous Victoria Memorial, the most impressive reminder of Kolkata's past as capital of the British Raj. The British spent 15 years and 7.5 million 1920 Rupees (many, many millions today) putting together this strange cross between Buckingham Palace and the Taj Mahal, designed to stand in loving memory of the self-proclaimed "Empress of India." Untouched by the pollution and chaos of the rest of Kolkata, this silently overpowering monument to British imperialism since 1921 seems quite out of place amid the vibrant grime of the City of Joy. Four minarets surround a central dome of white marble, lugged from the same quarries of Makrana, Rajasthan that furnished the building blocks of the Taj Mahal. But unlike the living sensuality of Agra's great white monument, the "VM" is shaped by the angles and spheres of the Italian Renaissance, with a 16-foot tall bronze winged statue of Victory atop its majestic dome. A statue of an aging Queen Victoria stands guard at the entrance to the complex, and a much younger Victoria sits inside the building, now a **museum** chock-full of British war memorabilia and state portraits which form a rich, if uncomfortable legacy for the Indian people. A huge canvas (6m by 3m) of Edward VII entering Jaipur in 1876 is the largest painting in Asia. The most impressive exhibit is undoubtedly the **Calcutta Gallery,** a timeline that chronicles the city's history and features examples of artwork, literature, and craftsmanship by leading Bengali figures. Be sure to check out the heart rending letter written by Rabindranath Tagore in which he declines his knighthood to protest the Jallianwalla Bagh Massacre. In the early mornings the immaculate gardens are a joggers' haven, in the evenings a lovers' paradise. It's traditional to sample the fried goods and take a trip around VM in one of horse-drawn *tongas*. The entire monument is illuminated at night; don't miss the fabulous sound and light show, an audio-visual history of Kolkata.

ST. PAUL'S CATHEDRAL

At the south end of Chowringhee Rd., on Cathedral Rd., opposite the Victoria Memorial. Open M-Sa 9am-noon and 3-6pm; services Su 7:30, 8:30, 11am, and 6pm.

The Gothic spire of St. Paul's attracts Christians and non-Christians alike to Midnight Mass on Christmas Eve, one of the city's best known services. The cathedral was consecrated as the first Episcopal church in the Orient in 1847, designed the British Major General William Forbes and built by workmen from the city and from Yorkminister. The long nave is patterned on Norwich Cathedral. Old paintings of the Cathedral (at the Indian Museum down Chowringhee) show a large spire, which was destroyed twice by earthquakes in 1897 and 1934. In its place a new spire was erected, modeled on the Bell Harry Tower of Canterbury Cathedral, England. There are some splendid stained glass windows; especially grand is the one overlooking the west portico and the Maidan.

BIRLA PLANETARIUM AND ACADEMY OF FINE ARTS

North of St. Paul's. Permanent collection open Tu-Sa noon-6:45pm; Rs10. Local artists' exhibition open M-Sa 3-8pm; free.

For celestial viewing, head to the **Birla Planetarium,** a *stupa*-esque edifice (modeled on the real Sanchi *stupa*) just south of St. Paul's Cathedral. It's the largest of its kind in Asia. *(English show 1:30pm. Rs20.)* The **Academy of Fine Arts** is part of Kolkata's ongoing cultural buzz, holding exhibitions of local artists' work. Established in 1933, the permanent collections here feature contemporary Indian art, medieval textiles, miniatures, 19th century prints of Bengal and many works by Rabindranath Tagore and the Bengal School of painters.

INDIAN MUSEUM

At the corner of Sudder St. and Chowringhee Rd. Open Mar.-Nov. Tu-Sa 10am-5pm; Dec.-Feb. Tu-Sa 10am-4:30pm. Entry Rs50.

Housed in a classic Corinthian palace built in 1814, the nation's largest and oldest museum contains a remarkable collection of artifacts, pottery, paintings, and sculpture from around India and the world. Galleries opening out onto cloisters of Ionic columns crowded with the most marvelous exhibits (albeit dusty, faded, and in need of restoration) surround a central quadrangle in six sections: Art, Archaeology, Anthropology, Geology, Zoology, and Botany. Stone Age artifacts and pottery from the Indus Valley Civilization and late medieval sculpture coexist with a 50,000-piece chronological coin collection. The Bharhut Gallery houses the reconstructed magnificently carved remains of the Buddhist *stupa* at Bharhut, and the centerpiece of the Egyptian Gallery is a 4000-year-old mummy. An enormous dinosaur skeleton of uncertain provenance, giant prehistoric coconuts, a perfectly preserved goat with four ears and eight legs, and bangles from the belly of an ancient crocodile form other interesting exhibits you won't see anywhere else.

SOUTH PARK STREET CEMETERY

Southeast end of Park St., just before AJC Bose Rd. and on the right. Open daily 7am-4pm. Free.

The final resting place of British colonials since 1767, the cemetery is one of the city's most serene spots. Among the most notable of the many huge gravestones here is that of a Major General Sir Charles Stuart of the East India Company. You'll also see the romantic poem "Rose Aylmer" by 19th century British poet Walter Savage Landor adorning the epitaph on a slight spiral obelisk which marks the mortal remains of the poet's lost love, Rose Witworth Aylmer herself. Not many of these people were particularly famous, and yet walking among their remains, seeing their names, their birthplaces, their accomplishments, and the dates on the worn stones has a curious way of transporting you to a time that no longer exists. Ask for the guidebook (Rs30) at the gate, where you can also make a small donation to the upkeep of the sight.

THE MAIDAN AREA

The Maidan is a mix of unkempt nature and splendid gardens—the "lungs" of Kolkata—three sq. km of parkland dotted with trees and criss-crossed with roads and footpaths. It was a dense forest infested with tigers and wildlife until Bengal's first British administrator, Lieutenant Governor Sir Robert Clive (who defeated the Nawab of Bengal at Plassey in 1757 and ensured that a trading post became an Empire), cleared out this vast field to give his soldiers a clear shot from the new **Fort William,** and the old cannons dotting the Maidan echo its military past. Unfortunately, Fort William itself forms the Indian Army's Eastern Headquarters and remains closed to the public. During the Raj, the Maidan was the posh palace-to-be where the good ol' boys of the East India Company sat back and watched cricket. These days the Maidan belongs to the masses. Here schoolchildren and college-students converge to skip classes and play cricket or hold hands. In addition, the Maidan also hosts festivals, parades, fairs and *melas* year-round. The whopper of them all is Asia's largest **Book Fair** held yearly Jan-Feb. At the northwest corner of the Maidan, near the river, are the **Eden Gardens** *(free),* a pleasant respite from the crowds and congestion just outside its walls. These were laid in 1835 by Governor General Lord Auckland, and named for his sisters, Ladies Emily and Fanny Eden. A picturesque Burmese pagoda brought in parts from Myanmar and reconstructed at the artificial lake in the center of the Gardens in 1856 sits in the shadow of the enormous **Eden Gardens Cricket Stadium,** where ▓cricket is played before crowds that regularly top 150,000. The stadium has hosted World Cup matches and is notorious for the rowdy nationalistic fervor of the fans—Kolkatans take their cricket seriously. Near the northern edge of the Maidan is the **Shahid Minar** (Martyrs' Tower), built by the British in 1828 as the **Ochterlony Monument**. Originally built as a tribute to David Ochterlony, who led royal forces in the victorious Nepal Campaign of 1814-16, the obelisk—renamed in 1968—is now a symbol of India's freedom struggle.

BBD BAGH (DALHOUSIE SQUARE) AREA

Most of Kolkata's historic buildings are near its commercial center, north of the Maidan. The area's hub used to be Tank Square (named for the artificial tank that was a water source for the city), later called **Dalhousie Square** to honor Lord Dalhousie, then Lt. Gov. of Bengal. It was renamed **BBD Bagh** in free India in honor of Benoy, Badal, and Dinesh, three freedom fighters hanged by the British for lobbing a bomb at Dalhousie during protests following the 1905 partition of Bengal. The **Lal Dighi** ("Red Tank"), sits in the center. Up Netaji Subhas Rd. to the left of the **Writers' Building** is Kolkata's financial district. On **Lyons Range**, Kolkata's very own Wall Street, *bakda-wallahs* sell stocks in the street. To the south of the Writers' Building, down Netaji Subhas Rd. past it is the **General Post Office (GPO)**, whose white Corinthian pillars stand on the site of the original Fort William, which was destroyed by the Nawab of Bengal Siraj-ud-Daulah in 1756 soon after the infamous incident of the "Black Hole of Calcutta." The Black Hole was actually the tiny (just 24 sq. m) guardroom of the Old Fort, in which the Nawab imprisoned many Britishers after his attack, and as a result of intention or freakish negligence, many of them died that horrible night. The very next year Sir Robert Clive threw open two centuries of British involvement in India by defeating the Nawab at Plassey and creating out of the East India Co. trading post, the foundation of the British Indian Empire. Today just a plaque marks out the site of the Fort and the Black Hole. To the east of the Writer's Building is **Lalbazar,** home to Kolkata Police HQ and music stores that sell everything from guitars to *ghungroos*.

ST. JOHN'S CHURCH

Government Place West. Open M-F 9am-noon and 4-6pm. Services M-F 9am, Su 8am.

Built in 1787, St. John's Church is the first Anglican Cathedral in the region. Amidst its lush green grounds lies the octagonal mausoleum of Kolkata's founder, Job Charnock. Within the church is the famous painting of *The Last Supper* by John Zoffany, some marvelous stained glass windows and memorial tablets naming distinguished Kolkata citizens of yore. Several relics of historical interest, including some belongings of Warren Hastings, the first Governor-General of India are kept in the vestry and can be examined with permission at the premises.

RAJ BHAVAN AND THE KOLKATA HIGH COURT

Diagonally opposite St. John's.

Formerly home to British governors-general and viceroys, the vast grounds of Raj Bhavan (Government House) are now part of the official residence of the Governor of West Bengal. It was completed in 1805, a replica of Keddleston Hall, Lord Curzon's ancestral home in Derbyshire. The interior is suitably palatial, with rare antiques and glittering chandeliers (as well as India's first elevator, introduced by Lord Curzon—it still works!), but it's not open to the public, so unless you are royalty or know someone high up on the governmental ladder, you'll have to be content with enjoying the outside. Nearby, on the other side of Government Place West, are the State Legislature and the cheerful, tricolor Gothic-style Kolkata High Court, built in 1782 (an impressive replica of the Town Hall of Ypres, Belgium), where you can observe robed and wigged lawyers going about their business.

NORTH KOLKATA

One of the oldest and most fascinating parts of the city, North Kolkata was home to the educated Bengali elite of Kolkata—the Tagores, Chakrabortis, Mullicks, and Debs—during the colonial period. Tourists can visit many of the area's sprawling bungalows (some of which house stunning antiques, artwork, and statuary, like the Mullick family's **Marble Palace**) with permission from the owners. **Chitpur Road** (now officially **Rabindra Sarani**) is a narrow, crowded street lined with all kinds of shops—metal-workers, shoe-menders, wig-makers, and tailors. Just off the street is the red sandstone **Nakhoda Mosque.** The shops around the mosque sell cheap, if unhygenic Mughlai food, *attar* (flower oil based perfumes) and *surma* (a thick yet cooling eyeliner)—all traditionally Muslim goods, which indicates the Islamic majority of the population in the area. There are also shops selling *sherwanis* (long warm Muslim tunics) and Lucknowi *pajamas* (loose cotton trousers) to go with them. At the corner of Chitpur Rd. and Muktaram Babu St. is the **Jorasanko Thakurbari,** Rabindranath Tagore's ancestral home, the current location of **Rabindra Bharati University.** At the end of Chitpur Rd. about two blocks north, is the area of **Kumartuli (Potter's Lane),** a colony of craftsmen who create beautiful terracotta pottery and statues all year long, especially images of Hindu gods and goddesses, which are then exquisitely painted in time for various *puja*s and festivals.

MARBLE PALACE (MULLICK BARI)

Muktaram Babu St., off Chittaranjan Ave. Open Tu-W and F-Su 10am-4pm. Free, though permission from the WB Tourism Office is required. (☎ 22485917 or 22488271.)

Built in 1835 as a mansion for the *zamindar* (a title conferred by the British on local landed nobles who collected revenue) Raja Rajendra Mullick, the Marble Palace features almost 130 different types of marble from all over the world in all kinds of colors, covering floors, wall panels, stairways, and tables. The Mullick family still lives in parts of the house. Highlights include the intricate ceilings and the solid gold clock on the first floor. The artwork includes original masterpieces by Reynolds and Rubens. The mansion's Grecian columns, its Italianate courtyard and its ornamental pool flanked by a Hindu temple, Roman naiadas and Egyptian sphinxes (to say nothing of equally enigmatic pelicans who fish in the pool to the right as you enter) are frozen, as if suspended in time. Overgrown with weed and moss, but nonetheless splendid in decay, the Mullick's museum home is a riveting metaphor of all Kolkata. If you're lucky, you might even get to meet a family member who will spend a few minutes showing you around.

PARASNATH JAIN TEMPLE

Open daily 6am-noon and 3-7pm. Entry free.

Built by a prominent city jeweler in 1867, this shimmering palace is dedicated to Sheethalnathji, the 10th of the 24 Jain *tirthankaras*. It is built in the form of four Burmese pagoda-like shrines set in geometrical gardens and ponds. The impressive interior is decorated with colored Venetian glass and a host of mirrors inlaid with sparkling and intricate designs. A number of handpainted panels depict scenes from Jain mythology. The main deity is made of white marble, and like most temple idols in India, regularly bathed and decorated with fresh flowers and jewels. In one corner is an "ethereal lamp" that has been burning constantly since the temple was founded.

DAKSHINESHWAR KALI TEMPLE

10km from the city center, far north on the Kolkata side of the River Hooghly. Take Bus #32 from the Esplanade (Rs7) or a taxi. Open daily 6am-9pm. Free.

This temple is one of the most important Hindu pilgrim centers in India. It was built in 1847 by a rich Kali-worshipping Muslim widow, Rani Rashmoni. The main 12-spired Kali Temple houses a magnificent silver lotus with a thousand petals on which is placed the idol of Goddess Kali standing on the prostrate body of Lord Shiva, and is surrounded by twelve little temples dedicated to Shiva and containing Shiva *lingas*. The temple gardens are serene and ideal for meditating—especially under the *Panchavati*, a congregation of five ancient trees. It was here that the Hindu spiritual leader and seer Sri Ramakrishna Paramhansa had his vision of the Mother Goddess and the unity of all religions. One day, a brash, young agnostic walked into the compound, asking for proof of God's existence. Promising revelation, Ramakrishna led him into an adjacent chamber, where the young man was shown God—in his heart. Later, he came to be known as Swami Vivekananda, a spiritual leader who traveled around the world spreading the message of spiritual unity. Vivekananda founded the **Ramakrishna Mission** in memory of his *guru*, and the Mission continues to spread the message of social and religious unity today from its headquarters at Belur Math, across the river from Dakshineshwar.

HOWRAH

BELUR MATH

Taxis from downtown Rs80-120. Ferry ride across the Hooghly from Dakshineshwar Rs30. Open Apr.-Nov. Tu-Su 7-11am and 4-7pm; Oct.-Mar. 7-11am and 4-6pm.

This site serves as the center of the Ramakrishna Mission movement founded in 1899 by Ramakrishna's disciple Swami Vivekananda who established the shrine by placing the ashes of Sri Ramakrishna at this spot (see **Dakshineshwar Temple,** above). The soaring temple dominates the grounds, but the most peaceful spot on the compound is at the end of the grounds, in the small cottage where Vivekananda spent his last days. His bedroom has been preserved, and an attached museum contains some of his belongings. The unique architecture of the main shrine reflects the message of religious unity—each one of the temples' four facades is designed to represent a different place of worship—church, temple, mosque, and *gurudwara*. Belur Math is the Ramakrishna Mission headquarters.

BOTANICAL GARDENS

Ferries from Armenian Ghat, Babu Ghat, or Chandpal Ghat Rs10-20. Open dawn-dusk. Free.

This is one of Kolkata's most relaxing spots—if you go during the week, you'll have few companions other than storks, cranes, insects, and an amazing range of plants from every continent. It is the oldest botanical garden of its kind in the country and sprawls over 273 acres, housing 35,000 varieties of fruits and flowers and 15,000 medicinal plants in addition. The 250-year-old **Great Banyan Tree** is the largest in the world, with roots stretching out nearly a mile from the treetop. A series of cyclones killed the main trunk decades ago, but its standing roots still survive and flourish under the expansive canopy. The Gardens also have a well-equipped library containing a store of books on botany and related subjects.

SOUTH KOLKATA

KALI TEMPLE AT KALIGHAT

Open daily 6am-10pm. Free. Entry may be restricted to Hindus only.

The famous shrine at Kalighat is dedicated to the Mother Goddess Kali (also known as the Goddess Parvati or Durga, in different incarnations, but in all forms she is the consort of Lord Shiva), the patron goddess of Kolkata. The temple was built in 1809 with a 30m high double-canopy peculiar to medieval Bengali temple

WEST BENGAL

architecture. Legend has it that when Lord Shiva, disturbed by the death of his consort Kali (who had sacrificed herself in her incarnation as Sati), danced the cosmic dance of destruction, Lord Vishnu, the preserver of the Universe, intervened and sliced Sati's body into 51 pieces and the toe of the goddess fell on this very spot, Kalighat. The idol here depicts the angry incarnation of Kali, also known as Shakti, Goddess of Power. Inside, you can gaze into her wise and terrifying red eyes, reproduced on dashboards and posters all over Bengal. Westerners may not be allowed inside. Non-Hindus may also not be allowed to view ritual sacrifices of goats during **Durga Puja** and **Kali Puja** in October.

NETAJI BHAVAN

Elgin Rd., near Chowringhee. Open Tu-Sa noon-4pm. Rs10.

For many, the peaceful tactics of Gandhi are no way to bring about real progress. Their hero is Subhas Chandra Bose, erstwhile leader of the Indian National Army, who sought to wrest control of the country from the British by force when Britain was destabilized by war in the early 1940s. Netaji Bhavan was the home of Bose, who collaborated with the Japanese and led troops against the British during WWII. It features a museum with Bose's belongings and a history of his achievements. Every January 23rd, his birthday is celebrated here.

ZOOLOGICAL GARDENS

Alipur Rd., opposite the Taj Bengal Hotel. Taxi from Park St. Rs40-50. Open F-W 9am-5pm. Zoo Rs150; camera fee Rs250. Aquarium Rs20.

Established in 1876, Kolkata's zoo sprawls over 41 acres and contains India's foremost collection of predatory felines; the centerpiece is the large island home of the zoo's tigers. It has an entire family of white tigers, and cross-bred lions and tigers (strange beasts called tigons and litigons). Sightings are rare during the hot season, but don't fret—the lions and tigers are also on display in cages, where they laze in the open more frequently. The lake in the middle (home to a 100-year-old Giant Tortoise) is visited by hordes of migratory birds during the winter. A reptile house and an aquarium add to the attractions. Avoid weekends, when the zoo is absolutely swarming with visitors.

ENTERTAINMENT

The **Kolkata Information Centre,** in the same complex as the Nandan center, provides information on theater, film, and other cultural events. (☎22481451. Open M-F 1-8pm.) Check newspapers for listings and go early for tickets.

PERFORMING AND FINE ARTS. Kolkata supports a thriving performing arts scene. Bengali music, dance, and drama are staged throughout the city. The Drama Theater at the back of the **Academy of Fine Arts** has daily performances. (☎22234302. Performances, plus daily 6:30pm and Sa 10am and 3pm. Rs20-40.) On the corner of Cathedral and AJC Bose Rd. is **Rabindra Sadan** (☎22239936 or 22239917), an important concert hall dedicated to Tagore and Bengali dance and music. **CIMA (Center for International Modern Art),** Sunny Towers, 43 Ashutosh Chowdhary Ave., regularly exhibits contemporary and traditional art from India and abroad.

CINEMAS. Although Kolkata is home to India's artsiest film industry, its cinemas, such as the **Globe Theater** on the corner of Madge and Lindsay St., and **Metro Cinema** two blocks further north, tend to show the usual Indian and American fare, the latest Bollywood and Hollywood releases. The gigantic **New Empire** and **Light House** movie theaters, side-by-side just northwest of New Market, both favor recent hits, be they Hindi, Bengali, or English. **Nandan Theater,** alongside Rabindra Sadan has both English and Bengali films.

NIGHTCLUBS. Most nightclubs are full of grooving Kolkatans, even till early in the morning. **Tantra,** Park Hotel, Park St., plays new-age and techno—anything goes. They say the best dressed people in town find their way here every night. (Cover Rs350. Women enter free. Open 8pm-4am.) **Anticlock,** Hotel Hindustan, Kolkata's first disco, is still popular when Tantra gets too full, but this is still the college-student yuppie crowd. (Cover Rs350. Open 9pm-2am.) **Someplace Else,** Park Hotel, Park St., is a ritzy place to grab a drink and listen to some of Kolkata's best live bands play, including legends like Hip Pocket, KrossWindz, and Cognac. The cool, slightly grizzled folk share barstools with the uninitiated here. West Bengal law prohibits alcohol sales after 10:30pm, so be sure to drink early. (Beer Rs130. Cover Rs150-350 depending on the night. Open Th-Sa 7pm-2am. Bands typically play until midnight.) **London Pub,** The Golden Park, 13 Ho Chi Minh Sarani, is a classy pub with good music. (Open 9pm-2:30am. Happy hour 5-8pm.) **12 Down Inn Street,** The Peerless Inn, 12 Chowringhee Rd., is a discotheque that blasts Indipop and the latest Bollywood remixes. (Free entry many nights.) **Trinca's Bar and Restaurant,** at the Park Hotel, has live music and food every night from 5:30pm-midnight.

📑 SHOPPING

Kolkata has perennially been a shopper's paradise. From old-fashioned raucous bazaars where you'll have to haggle over every price you're offered, to slick state-of-the-art shopping malls that are mini-cities themselves, you'll find everything here. Almost all businesses open by 10am and start closing their doors by 8pm.

New Market (or the SS Hogg Market), north of Lindsay St., is definitely one of Kolkata's great misnomers, being its oldest existing indoor market (1874). It is a huge enclosed bazaar that sells everything, almost literally. Fruits, vegetables, all kinds of food, jewelry, clothes, books, music, shoes, appliances, bric-a-brac, and pets. It's especially famous for its confections, the Chinese leather stores, and the cheap porcelain and glassware stores that line the front (Lindsay St.) side. The market's Gothic tower clock is wound every alternate Su; just watch for the ladder. The newer wing (the aptly named **New New Market**) is mainly for clothes, as is the **Treasure Island** complex, also attached. **Shreeram Arcade** is north of this complex, opposite the New Empire movie theater and is a more modern mall. Closes at 2:30pm Sa and closed Su.

AC Market, 1 Shakespeare Sarani. It was Kolkata's first air-conditioned market, and the name has stuck. A haven for really cheap gadgets at one end of the spectrum, including imported phones, TVs, cameras, stereos, and video games, and everything a diva could possibly need at the other: clothes, Indian and Western alike, accessories, cosmetics and jewelry are all on sale. Closed M.

Fancy Market, Khidirpur Rd., close to the docks. To satisfy your urge to acquire contraband, this is the place in Kolkata to buy imported (um, smuggled) goods sold without duties, and, alas, without branded boxes or guarantees either. Incidentally, the origins of its name stem not from the English "fancy," but from the Bengali *phansi* (or "hanging"), a quaint remembrance of the area's past as a regular gallows. Haggling is an essential skill here. Closed Su.

Gariahat Market, The area is South Kolkata's most popular bazaar. Especially look out for cheap Indian clothes and saris from all over India. Haggling is a must. Open until 1pm Su; open later other days.

Strand Rd. Flower Market, just before Howrah bridge, on the left. Start bargaining by stating you will pay exactly half of the vendor's quote for a garland or a bunch of flowers. Open M-Sa 8-11am. Closed Su.

VOLUNTEER OPPORTUNITIES

Even after her death, Mother Teresa's organization continues to care for the destitute and dying. Now headed by Sister Nirmala Das, the **Missionaries of Charity** have bases around the city. Their **Mother House**, 54 AJC Bose Rd., has an excellent orientation program for foreigners interested in volunteering. While the Sisters always welcome those willing to help, they do expect a certain degree of dedication, commitment, and fortitude. Sister Nirmala registers all volunteers and is available before 9am and in the afternoon around 3pm. No prior arrangements have to be made, and you can volunteer for as long as you want, at the homes for destitutes **Prem Dan** (Park Circus) or **Nirmal Hriday** (Kalighat) or to work with children at **Shishu Bhawan**. On AJC Bose Rd., **St. Joseph's Home for the Aged,** across from Hotel Hindustan, is run by the **Little Sisters of the Poor.** They welcome volunteers at all times of the year to visit with their wards. Contact the Mother Superior about a week before you can start work. The **Ramakrishna Mission** does charity work and is engaged in a number of social work programs in which it welcomes volunteers. Contact them at their Belur Math or Golpark, Kolkata headquarters (see above) for details on which projects you might be able to help with and in what way. A number of the city's schools and colleges are run by missionaries (like **St. Xavier's College/School,** Park St., **Loreto House,** Middleton Row and **Don Bosco School,** Park Circus) and are involved with volunteer efforts.

SILIGURI AND NEW JALPAIGURI

শিলিগুড়ি নব জলপাইগুড়ি ☎ 0353

Since Siliguri and New Jalpaiguri function as the main transit point to Nepal, Sikkim, and the Northeast, most travelers can't avoid stopping here at some point. Linked by urban sprawl, these joined-at-the-armpit cities have managed to capture all the congestion, noise, and filth of urban India with none of the beautiful scenery or fresh air that their location might seem to promise. Because of their low elevation (114m), the climate of Siliguri and New Jalpaiguri has much more in common with Kolkata's scorching heat than with the cooler temperatures of nearby Darjeeling (80km north). This self-proclaimed "gateway to the Indian Himalayas" offers hardly a hint of the natural splendor that awaits just up the road

⊏ TRANSPORTATION

Flights: Bagdogra Airport lies 16km west of Siliguri. Take the Hill Cart Rd. bus from NJP Station or the Tenzing Norgay Bus Terminal (Rs3). From Bagdogra hop on a rickshaw to the airport (Rs10). The trip takes 1hr. **Jeeps** also run to the airport from Hill Cart Rd. in front of the bus terminal (30min., Rs30). **Indian Airlines** (☎ 2511495), 400m north of the bus station, on the second floor of the Hotel Mainak complex on the east side of the road. Open M-Sa 10am-1pm and 2-4:30pm. AmEx/MC/V. Flights to: **Kolkata** (1hr.; Tu, F, and Su 3:55pm; US $90); **Delhi** via Patna (2½hr.; Tu, Th, and Sa at 1:05pm; US$195) and via Guwahati (4hr., M and F 2pm, US$195); **Guwahati** (50min.; M and F 2pm; Tu, Th, and Sa 10:25am; US$60); and **Patna** (45min.; Tu, Th, and Sa 1:05pm; US $90). **Jet Airways,** Hill Cart Rd. (☎ 2435876 or 2538001; fax 2435890), 200m south of the bridge on the west side of the street (look for the sign in the window of their 2nd fl. office), has flights to: **Kolkata** (1hr., daily 1:30pm, US$90); **Delhi** direct (2 hr.; M, W, and F 2:15pm; US $195); via Guwahati (3½hr.; Tu, Th, Sa, and Su 12:35pm; US$195); and **Guwahati** (50min.; Tu, Th, Sa, and Su 12:35pm; US$60). 25% discount for passengers under 30. Open M-Sa 9am-6:30pm, Su 9am-5pm.

Trains: All trains stop at **New Jalpaiguri Station,** Hill Cart Rd., before continuing on to the Northeastern states. Reservations can be made at the **Central Rail Booking Office** (☎2423333), near the Hospital Rd. and Hill Cart Rd. police traffic booth, a little more than 1km south of the bridge. The office is marked by the large sign for the **Computerized Reservation Office,** a few steps down the road. Open M-Sa 8am-8pm, Su 8am-2pm. Trains leave New Jalpaiguri Station for: **Kolkata** (10-12hr.; 8:05am, 4, 6:15 and 8:05pm; Rs245); **Delhi** (24hr.; 5am, 12:15, 5:30. and 11pm; Rs405); **Mumbai** (32hr.; M and Th 2am, Tu 11pm; Rs481). All trains to Delhi stop in **Patna** (Rs205). There are frequent trains to the Northeast states; all stop in **Guwahati** (Rs180). The **toy train to Darjeeling** leaves from New Jalpaiguri Station (10 hr.; 9am; 2nd class Rs22, 1st class Rs192, plus Rs15 "reservation fee"), but you can save some time (and rickshaw fare) by taking the train from the **Siliguri Junction Station,** 100m west of Hill Cart Rd., just behind the Tenzing Norgay Bus Terminus (the train stops in Siliguri at 9:25am).

Buses: Private and government buses leave from the Tenzing Norgay Bus Terminus, about 250m north of the bridge. Government buses are cheaper, but you may prefer the extra comfort of private buses, especially for longer journeys. Government buses go to: **Kolkata** (12hr., 6:45 and 8pm, Rs203); **Darjeeling** (3½hr., 6:30am, Rs43); **Gangtok** (4hr., 6am, Rs75); **Guwahati** (12hr., 5pm, Rs202). Tickets for **private buses** are available at the counters farther away from Hill Cart Rd.; buses go to: **Kolkata** (12hr., 7:30pm, Rs250); **Darjeeling** (3½hr., every half hour 5:30am-5pm, Rs53); **Gangtok** (4hr., every hr. 6:30am-3:30pm, Rs75); **Guwahati** (12hr.; day buses 9 and 10:30am, night buses every hour 4-7pm; Rs275); **Kalimpong** (3hr., every half hour 6am-4pm, Rs48); . **Jeeps** gather in the lot opposite the bus terminal, and run from 6am-6pm when they have sufficient passengers. They are the fastest but most expensive option. Prices given here are per person based on a full car. To: **Darjeeling** (3hr., Rs62); **Gangtok** (3½hr., Rs100); **Kakarbhitta, Nepal** (1hr., Rs35); **Kalimpong** (2½hr., Rs40). The **Sikkim Nation Transportation (SNT) Centre** on the east side of Hill Cart Rd., just north of the tourist office, has buses to: **Gangtok** (4hr.; 5 per day 7am-1:30pm; Rs70, deluxe Rs90); **Pelling** (6hr.; 11:30am; Rs84, deluxe Rs105; other buses available in high season, Mar.-May and Oct.-Dec.); **Geyzing** (high season only, 5½hr., 12:30pm, Rs78). Deluxe buses are newer and have more spacious seating. Buses for **Kathmandu** leave from Kakarbhitta, Nepal. You can go to the border town of **Panitanki** by jeep (1hr., Rs40) or by bus. Buses to Panitanki leave from Tenzing Norgay Bus Terminus, or alternatively, you can flag down one of the buses cruising Hill Cart Rd.—listen for a conductor yelling "Nepal! Nepal!" (1½hr., Rs10). Once in Panitanki, you can make the 10min. walk across the bridge or take a cycle rickshaw (Rs10). If you take a rickshaw, make sure to establish in advance whether you will be paying in Nepali or Indian rupees. Touts may claim they can put you on a bus going direct to Kathmandu. They can't. Don't believe them. You'll have to cross over to Kakarbhitta (see p. 890) on the Nepali side and buy a ticket there. If you are **coming from the Nepal border** via the bus from Panitanki, take note: the bus follows Hill Cart Rd. from **north to south** and may not stop at the bus terminal unless you specifically request it. If it doesn't stop at the terminal, it will continue south across the bridge before turning around on Hospital Rd.

✈ 🛈 ORIENTATION AND PRACTICAL INFORMATION

Everything you want to find in Siliguri is either on or near **Hill Cart Road (Tenzing Norgay Road),** with its blaring horns, kamikaze rickshaw drivers, and carbon monoxide fumes of truly Indian proportions. The most useful landmark is the **Mahananda River Bridge,** 250m south of the **Tenzing Norgay Bus Terminus.** Buses, jeeps, and budget accommodations are north of the bridge, while most shops and services are crowded together along Hill Cart Rd. south of the bridge. Just over 1km south of the bridge, **Hospital Road** splits off from Hill Cart Rd. towards the east; the road leads to the post office and is the last stop for many buses coming from the Nepal

HE LOCAL STORY

RABINDRANATH TAGORE

The Bengali poet Rabindranath
Tagore (1861-1941) was the youngest son in the large family of the
prominent zamindar and Brahmo
Samaj leader Debendranath Tagore.
Dropping out of school at an early
age, Rabindranath taught himself
English and Sanskrit. Before long, he
broke new ground creating English
forms previously unknown in Bengali.

He traveled around Bengal looking after his family's estates; many of
his poems and stories concern the
lives of villagers in Bengal, and his
songs draw from the melodies of
Bengali folk music. Tagore also translated many of his verses into rhythmic English prose, catching the
attention of Western readers.

In 1913 he received the Nobel
Prize for Gitanjali (Song Offerings), a
collection of poems showing a hope
to become one with God. Tagore was
knighted by the British in 1915 but
renounced his title after the Jallian-
wallah Bagh massacre in Amritsar.

In his later years, Tagore experimented with novels, plays, and elaborate songs; toward the end of his
life he took up painting as well. Gandhi and other political leaders considered Tagore an inspiration, visiting
him frequently at Shantiniketan, the
school he founded in 1901.

Verses by Tagore are now the
national anthems of India and Bang-
adesh. His plays are widely produced, and his songs are a genre of
their own. Bengalis are fiercely fond
of their poet-patriot; try quizzing anyone on the street on "Rabi Babu"
and get a couplet in response.

border. Siliguri's twin city of **New Jalpaiguri,** 6km to
the south, is home to the **New Jalpaiguri Railway Station** and little else. It's 30min. by auto-rickshaw
between train station and bus terminus (Rs60).

Tourist Office: West Bengal Tourism Centre
(☎2511974; fax 2511979). In the orange bldg.,
100m south of the bus terminal on the east side of
the road. Makes advance bookings for Jaldapara
Wildlife Sanctuary. Open M-F 10:30am-5:30pm.
There are also information counters at the NJP Railway Station (☎2561118) and at Bagdogra Airport
(☎2551794). **Sikkim Permit: The Sikkim Tourist
Office** (☎2512646), inside the **Sikkim Nationalized
Transport** building, 50m south of the bus station on
the east side of the road, issues **Sikkim permits** for a
passport photo. Open M-F 10am-4pm.

Passport Photo: Studio Ellora, Hill Cart Rd.
(☎2432028), 160m south of the bridge, a few steps
south of the State Bank. Five instant digital photos
Rs60. Necessary for Sikkim permit and Nepal visa.
Open M-Sa 8am-8pm.

Currency Exchange: State Bank of India, Hill Cart Rd.
(☎2431362), 150m south of the bridge on the east
side of the road; currency exchange is on the 3rd
floor. Changes cash and Thomas Cook and AmEx traveler's checks. Rs100 fee per transaction. Open M-F
10am-3pm, Sa 10am-noon. Many banks and hotels
on Hill Cart Rd. change money.

Luggage Storage: Tenzing Norgay Bus Terminus, on
the right as you enter (Rs5 per item per 12 hr.) or **NJP
Station,** on track 4.

Police: (☎2510046), on Hill Cart Rd., opposite the bus
station and 50m north.

Pharmacy: Medical booths dot the city. Look around or
ask a local. Most close by 10pm.

Hospital: North Bengal Clinic (☎2510441 or
2518667; ambulance ☎983 2063138; www.north-
bengalclinic.com). Head 300m north from the bus
terminal and turn right at Dipti's Bakery, just past
Hotel Simla. Follow that road for 200m and take a
right at the sign reading "C.T. Scan North Bengal
Clinic." The clinic is the gray bldg. 50m ahead. A private hospital with state-of-the-art facilities and a
highly trained staff.

Internet: There are a number of Internet cafes on Hill
Cart Rd. south of the bridge. **CyberSpace**
(☎2432211), one floor above the Jet Airways office
is air-conditioned and provides fast ISDN connections
for only Rs25-30 per hr. Open daily 9am-9pm.

Post Office: **Head Post Office,** Hospital Rd. (☎2538850; express office ☎2421950). Turn left (east) at the 3rd police traffic booth south of the bridge on Hill Cart Rd., and follow the road for 200m. Main office open daily 10am-3pm; express office open M-Sa 7am-7pm. **Postal Code:** 734401.

▐▌▐▌ ACCOMMODATIONS AND FOOD

"Come as a guest, go as a friend," proclaims the warm, family-like **Siliguri Lodge ❶** 200m north of the bridge on the east side of Hill Cart Rd. and opposite the bus station. This peaceful, alcohol-free establishment has a garden, complete with mini-gazebo, a TV in the lobby, and a choice of squat or Western-style toilets. (☎2533290. Check-out noon. Singles Rs100; doubles Rs150-225; quads Rs200-350.) Seventy-five meters north on the same side of the street is the more up-market **Hotel Mount View ❷** offering a variety of rooms at a variety of prices, though all have private bath and TV. The basic rooms are institutional, but large and comfortable; higher end rooms have color TVs, hot water, carpeting, and in-room phones. Reservations are recommended. (☎2425919 or 2531958. Check-out noon. Singles Rs200-350; doubles Rs250-425; triples Rs300-450; quad Rs375. MC/V.)

There are a few decent restaurants on Hill Cart Rd., south of the bridge. The **New Ranjit Restaurant ❷** in the Ranjit Hotel, less than 1km south of the bridge, on the west side of Hill Cart Rd., is popular for its all-veg. menu and smoke-free atmosphere (entrees Rs24-66; open daily 6am-10:30pm). The slightly cheaper **Anand Restaurant ❶** about 50m south of the bridge on the east side of the road, serves a solid variety of North Indian cuisine for Rs15-45. (Open daily 8am-10pm.) If you're staying north of the river, you can save yourself a hike across the bridge by eating at the **Hotel Mount View Restaurant ❷** which serves all your familiar favorites at reasonable prices (veg. entrees Rs15-50; non-veg. Rs45-75).

▐▌▐▌ JALDAPARA WILDLIFE SANCTUARY

Jaldapara is truly a site fit for kings—or so the kings of Bhutan and Coochbehar (now part of West Bengal) believed some 100 years ago, when each jealously coveted the land as a royal rhinoceros-hunting ground. The British arrived to "settle the dispute" in true imperial fashion by claiming the entire Dooras ("gateway") region as their own, and over time, they gradually converted thousands of acres of lush jungle into vast tea plantations. This ecological upheaval left only a few large pockets of dense forest; the well-preserved Jaldapara Wildlife Sanctuary, officially designated a national park in 1985, is one of them. Though at 216 sq. km it's one of India's smaller wildlife sanctuaries, Jaldapara is one of a handful of parks left in India with a sizable population of rhinos. It also contains over 100 species of birds and is home to monkeys, deer, buffalo, boar, and elephants.

Jaldapara is just about the only reason not to flee straight into the hills from Siliguri, and its well-run services ensure a comfortable wildlife-viewing experience. Best of all, the park is still relatively undiscovered by the tourists who flock to India's other wildlife sanctuaries. (In season Oct.-Apr.; closed June 15-Sept. 15. Entrance fee Rs100; vehicle entry fee Rs50; camera fee Rs20.)

There are two lodges in the area. Both are excellent, though prices are very high. Rooms should be booked in advance through the tourist office in Siliguri. At the edge of Madarihat, the **Jaldapara Tourist Lodge ❷** has large, comfy rooms and a huge yard. All meals are included. The staff is friendly and attentive. (☎03563 262230. Check-out noon. Dorms Rs300; two-person cottages Rs650; doubles Rs1050.) The alternative is the **Hollong Forest Lodge ❺**, within the confines of the park. Spot the wildlife or the sunrise from your balcony overlooking a prim, colonial-era garden. (☎ 03563 262228. Doubles Rs1175, includes meals.)

Visitors can cruise the park by taking an **elephant ride** (Rs120). These powerful pachyderms pack four riders and lumber through dense forests and open plains, giving you a 90min. tour of Jaldapara's various flora and fauna. Your long-trunked guides will likely be accompanied by several little ones who are just along for the ride. Tours leave at dawn from the Hollong Forest Lodge. If you're staying in the Tourist Lodge, they'll drive you up to Hollong for a fee (Rs150 plus vehicle entry fee). **Elephant rides are not guaranteed.** If an elephant is sick or called off on other duty, or if there has been some activity among the wild elephants in the sanctuary, you might find yourself disappointed. There are also many more beds than there are seats on the elephants, so book ahead.

Another option is to go on a **jeep safari**, where, after a slow drive through the park, you'll stop at a look-out tower which provides a good vantage point for spotting wildlife. Jeep safaris leave from both the Jaldapara Tourist Lodge and Hollong Lodge at 6:30am and 3pm and last approximately 90min. Prices vary depending on the occupancy of the vehicle, ranging from Rs150 for a full (4 or more person) car to Rs515 for a lone visitor. Fifty meters down the road from the Jaldapara Tourist Lodge, a number of leopards pace back and forth in cages. As the sign outside this **Rescue Center** points out, this is not a zoo. It is a sanctuary for leopards who have been disturbed from their natural habitat and will soon be returned to the wild.

Jaldapara is about 125km east of Siliguri, which provides the only major access point to the park. **Madarihat,** the town near the park's entrance, is accessible by **buses** running to and from Siliguri (4hr., every hr. 5:30am-5:30pm, Rs53). If direct buses to Madarihat are not available, frequent buses going to **Alipurduara, Hashimara, Joygoin,** or **Phuntsholling** can drop you there. Buses returning from Madarihat to Siliguri run roughly from 6am-6pm. When you arrive in Madarihat, you can walk (about 10min.) or take a rickshaw (Rs15) to the Jaldapara Tourist Lodge, which is in the wooded area just off the main road. If you are staying at the Hollong Lodge, you'll have to take a taxi (roughly Rs150, plus vehicle entry fee).

ANIMAL HOUSE Tourists aren't the only ones starved for nightlife in early-to-bed, early-to-rise Northeast India. The natives are apparently getting restless as well. In fact, in recent years drunken gallivanting and late-night carousing have been on the rise among local populations...of elephants. Last call at many of the popular pachyderm watering-holes comes in late November when Jaldapara's streams fall victim to the winter dry season. Rather than resort to a winter on the wagon, wild elephants have been hitting the human hot spots (usually people's huts) in search of *hariya*, a locally micro-brewed rice wine; if you hear gunshots while staying at the Jaldapara Tourist Lodge, it's most likely villagers trying to ward off the thirsty beasts. But the hedonism does not stop there. With their booze-fed libidos primed, the wild male elephants cruise for chicks at the makeshift brothel which hosts domesticated female touring elephants. After having their way, the tuskers stagger back to the jungle—presumably to sleep the bender off.

SUNDARBANS NATIONAL PARK   ☎ 03219

The 70-odd islands at the river-delta border between West Bengal and Bangladesh comprise the Indian portion of the Sundarbans, a 4000 sq. km wildlife sanctuary of mangrove islands and winding waterways. The park's most famous attraction—the tiger—shuns human contact, especially the thundering motorboats full of chattering

Indian tourists who frequent the park on weekends. You are more likely to see the other famous resident, the estuarine crocodile, surfacing for air or wallowing in shaded mudbanks. You should also spot plenty of their prey, including spotted deer, turtles, monkeys, and unlucky villagers. The soothing sounds of birds, along with the rich green mangroves, are enough to make you feel you've been one of the few tourists to discover the long, rickety ride to paradise.

TRANSPORTATION

The complex journey to the Sundarbans is possibly as interesting as the park itself. Going on your own can be a bit bewildering, but that is half the fun. Sajnekhali, the gateway town, is roughly 120km southeast of Kolkata. First, go to the **West Bengal Tourism office** in the southeast corner of Dalhousie Sq., Kolkata, and secure a **permit.** (Open M-F 10am-4pm.) Permits are free and processing takes only one hour. Once you have the precious paperwork, you can board the bus to **Sonakhali.** The bus leaves from the bus stop (the green tin awning opposite the row of orange cargo trucks) at **Babu Ghat,** near the Eden Gardens (3½hr., 7am, Rs30); it's best to come 30min. early to be safe. At Sonakhali, follow the red brick path to **Dok Ghat.** Here you should be able to find a **bhut-bhut** (the local name for power boats) headed to **Gosaba** (1½hr., Rs8). If not, jump on a ferry across the channel to **Basabti** (Rs1). On this shore, **tempos** run to **Mojit Bati** (30min., Rs10), across the river from Gosaba. A second ferry will take you over (10min., Rs1). At Gosaba's van stand, through the bazaar and to the right, **cycle rickshaws** run to **Pakhirala** (40min., Rs20). The park is at **Sajnekhali,** 10min. away by **ferry** (Rs3). The entire journey takes 6hr. and costs around Rs75. In peak season, boats to Gosaba are also available from **Canning,** accessible by rail from Kolkata's Sealdah-station (1½hr., 17 per day, Rs14). The Dalhousie Sq. tourism office can provide more information about the park and **group tours** for less adventurous travelers. The Rs2500 price tag includes food, accommodation, and three days of group sightseeing, minus time to get from Kolkata and back. The **last bus** leaves Sonakhali for Kolkata at 2pm. The shops and pharmacies in Gosaba Bazaar are the best place to stock up on food and ointment for those tiger bites.

ACCOMMODATIONS AND FOOD

In Sajnekhali, the only accommodation is the **Tourist Lodge ❷,** which needs to be booked in advance through any West Bengal Tourism Office (Rs650). Although prices include relatively tasty meals, the

THE LOCAL LEGEND

BIG CATS OF BENGAL

Catching a glimpse of the Bengal Tiger, a majestic beast with a deep reddish tan, black stripes, and white-furred belly, is a rare event. Most of the tigers in West Bengal are found in the swampy mangrove forests of the Sundarbans, though they have occasionally been known to stray. In 1974, a tiger made it all the way to a village 80km outside Kolkata, where it killed a local woman. Only about 4% of tigers are "man-eaters," but all will attack if disturbed. Forest guards wear fiberglass head- and neck-protectors—these are the parts most vulnerable to attack. Honey-gatherers wear masks on the back of their heads since tigers tend to attack only when people are looking away. Researchers are trying to train tigers to stay away from humans by positioning electrified dummies in the forest—a 300V shock is administered if the tiger attacks. The experiment has been successful so far, but some people refuse to enter the Sundarbans without being escorted by *fakirs,* religious men who have the power to ward off tiger attacks.

dormitory (Rs220) seems more like a large, cluttered closet next to the generators. The tree-level doubles are nowhere near as lofty as the tariff (Rs650). Across the great divide in Pakhirala, the **Krishnakunj Hotel ❷** has a calming garden, breezy rooms with attached baths, and flawless concrete (Rs300-400). **Hotel Aram ❷** is considerably less luxurious. (Doubles Rs200.) Aluminum-sided **Madhuban Hotel ❶** offers the very bare essentials. (Doubles with common bath Rs100.) If everything is full, turn back and return to Gosaba, where you'll find **Kamal Kamini Hotel ❶**, in the bazaar. The hotel has simple rooms with fans and mosquito nets (Rs60-70). **Anapuran Hindu Hotel ❶** has rock-bottom singles (Rs70) and doubles (Rs100) that share a miserable common toilet. The semi-luxurious **Surya Tapa Lodge ❷** has rooms with showers. The upstairs rooms are quieter and more comfortable. (☎52509. Rs300.) The bazaar in Gosaba offers a number of decent Bengali eateries and sweet shops. Pakhirala has one pay telephone, a few tea stalls, and a store, but no restaurant. The hotels cook Bengali meals at high prices.

▨ WATCHING FOR TIGERS

To enter the park, you need to obtain clearance from the Park Office in Sajnekhali, next to the watchtower and nature observation center. (Open daily 8am-5pm.) To get clearance, you must have a permit (from Kolkata) and pay the daily fees (Rs10 per person, Rs25 per camera). The only way to see the park is by taking a boat tour. Boats depart 7-8am from in front of the office. Both the boat rental fee (half day Rs550-600, full day Rs850) and the mandatory guide fee (Rs200) can be split between passengers. The biggest boats seat 35, but they have the loudest engines and can't get into the smaller estuaries. Most groups consist of weekenders from Kolkata who are more interested in spending time away from smog and beggary than in waking up early in the prime tiger-spotting hours. Booking in advance with travelers serious about wildlife will pay off. The quietest times to visit are week-days in February and March. Usually the boat trips go to one of the three watch-towers, where you can disembark and spy on wildlife. The Netidhopani tour takes you as close to the core area as tourists are allowed. (8hr.)

KILLER KITTIES Catching a glimpse of the tiger, a majestic beast with a deep reddish tan, black stripes, and white-furred belly, is a rare event. Most of the tigers in West Bengal are found in the swampy mangrove forests of the Sundarbans, though they have occasionally been known to stray. In 1974, a tiger made it all the way to a village 80km outside Kolkata, where it killed a local woman. Only about 4% of tigers are "man-eaters," but all will attack if disturbed. Forest guards wear fiberglass head- and neck-protectors—these are the parts most vulnerable to attack. Honey-gatherers wear masks on the back of their heads since tigers tend to attack only when people are looking away. Researchers are trying to train tigers to stay away from humans by positioning electrified dummies in the forest—a 300V shock is administered if the tiger attacks. The experiment has been successful so far, but some people refuse to enter the Sundarbans without being escorted by *fakirs*, religious men who have the power to ward off tiger attacks.

DARJEELING দার্জিলিং ঢার্জলিন্ড ☎0354

Darjeeling has been a spoke in the wheel of the tourist industry since the 19th century, and it has grown very good at it over the years. The city of 350,000 manages to be both laid-back and cosmopolitan, with tasteful and well-priced hotels and restaurants, a lively city center, and significant amounts of greenery. Tottering on the brink of a knife-edged ridge, the city looks out over the Himalayan foothills and all the way up to Kanchenjunga, the third-highest mountain in the world. On the other side, the ridge drops away to the tropical valley floor thousands of meters below. When the British chanced upon this wooded ridge in 1828, they were so enraptured with the cool climate and majestic mountain views that they convinced the king of Sikkim to let them use the area as a health resort. Darjeeling's popularity as a getaway for heat-stricken colonials grew, and by 1861, Sikkim was forced to cede this great playground of colonial India to the British.

Today, Darjeeling is famous not only for its spectacular scenery, but also for its role as the starting point for the earliest Everest expeditions and as a center for tea production. The region's Gorkha inhabitants, most of them brought by the British from Nepal as laborers, never abandoned their language, dress, or blend of Hindu and Buddhist beliefs. Despite major differences in language, lifestyle, and livelihood from the plains below, Darjeeling and the other hill stations remained tagged to West Bengal after Indian independence; the Gorkha National Liberation Front's struggle for a separate state culminated in the 1958 formation of the Darjeeling Gorkha Hill Council (DGHC), a semi-autonomous body that now governs the area. Tensions persist: the DGHC still occasionally holds *bandhs* (strikes) during which the entire town closes for a day, and Darjeelingites often confide to foreigners their resentment of the Bengalis and other "Indians" who sweep over the town during peak tourist season.

▐ TRANSPORTATION

Trains: The **Computerized Reservation Centre** (☎2252555), at the **railway station,** issues tickets for any Indian Railways train. Open daily 8am-2pm. The station services the **Toy Train,** which traverses the route between Siliguri and Darjeeling to **Siliguri** (7hr.; 9:15am; 1st class Rs217, 2nd class Rs38). It also makes a daily trip to **Kurseong,** roughly the mid-point (3hr., 3pm; 2nd class only, Rs12) and an overpriced daily "joy ride" to **Ghoom** and back (2hr.; 10am and 12:50pm; first class only, Rs220; 10min. stopover in Ghoom; minimum of six passengers).

Buses and Jeeps: Most buses (including private ones) and jeeps heading out of Darjeeling leave from the main bus stand at the Chowk Bazaar on Hill Cart Rd. Other jeeps leave from the intersection of Laden La Rd. and Hill Cart Rd. and from the area around the clocktower. **Buses** to: **Gangtok** (Mar.-May and Sep.-Nov. only, 4½hr., 7:30am, Rs90), **Kalimpong** (4½hr.; 7:45am, 12:45, 1:30pm; Rs45), **Rimbik** (4hr., 7am and 1pm, Rs57) via **Manebhanjang** (1½hr., Rs28) and **Siliguri** (3½hr., frequent 6am-4:30pm, Rs50). **Jeeps** to: **Gangtok** (4hr., every ½hr. 6:30am-2:30pm, Rs 120), **Jorethang** (2hr., every ½hr. 8:30am-3pm, Rs80), where service is available to points in Sikkim; **Pelling** (5hr., 1pm, Rs140), **Manebhanjang** (1hr., every hr. 7am-2pm, Rs35), **Siliguri** (3hr., frequent 6am-4:30pm, Rs65), and **Ghoom** (10min., frequent 6am-5:30pm, Rs10), available only from the jeep stand near the train station.

 WARNING. Don't ride in cars bearing black license plates with white numbers; **they are not authorized to carry passengers** and may be detained by the police.

▐ ORIENTATION

Darjeeling is draped like a blanket on a clothesline over either side of a narrow, north-south ridge, and its steep, tangled streets, alleys, and stairways will strain both your legs and your sense of direction. Fortunately, locals are ready to offer assistance with directions. It helps to think of the town as a series of nearly paral-

WEST BENGAL

DISORIENT EXPRESS Ninety kilometers in nine hours? Sounds like a fast-paced trek, but the "toy train" uses every minute to lug some 80 passengers up more than 2000m of vertical ascent. Recently declared a UNESCO World Heritage Site, the train is a feat of 19th-century engineering brilliance. Built between 1879 and 1881, the rail line was the first of its kind, employing a number of revolutionary techniques to make its steep climb into the Indian Himalayas. Most notable are the famous "Z" turns, where the train goes into reverse for a short stretch, zig-zagging its way up the slope. The completion of the rail line cut travel time to Darjeeling from 5-6 days to less than 12hr., thus making Darjeeling accessible as a hill station and summer retreat. At 7408 ft., the station at Ghoom is second only to Cuzco in the Andes as the highest train station on earth.

This little engine that can (most of the time) hauls three cars and manages the climb (and descent) by traversing the main auto road at least 100 times. Service is sporadic, due to seasonal weather variations and constant mechanical problems. However, if the train is running, the breathtaking views make the experience one that should not be missed. The two time-saving alternatives are to ride the train to Kurseong, roughly the mid-point, and then catch a bus (2hr., Rs25) or a jeep (1½hr., Rs35) the rest of the way; you can also experience the train for the 1hr. ride between Darjeeling and Ghoom (although this may be the most boring part of the trip). And don't worry if part of the train slips from its 60cm tracks (this has been known to happen); locals will emerge from the woods bearing poles to lever the carriage back on course.

lel streets that zig-zag their way up the slope, occasionally connected by small stairways. The railway and bus stations are along **Hill Cart Road,** downhill on the west side of the ridge. This is the smelly, exhaust-filled part of town. Don't be discouraged—the rest of Darjeeling is quite nice. It's quite a climb from Hill Cart Rd. to **Chowrasta,** the town's central plaza near the top of the ridge. The Chowrasta intersection has a statue at the north end and a fountain and tourist office at the south. To the right of the fountain descends **Nehru Road** (also called **The Mall**), one of the town's main avenues filled with shops and restaurants. **Laden La Road** runs right below, connecting Nehru Rd. and Hill Cart Rd. At the intersection of Nehru and Laden La Rd. sits the **clocktower.** The road to the left of the fountain in Chowrasta (past the ponies) leads to the TV tower area, home to many budget hotels.

⚡ PRACTICAL INFORMATION

Tourist Office: West Bengal Tourist Office, Chowrasta (☎2254102), on the south side, just above the Indian Airlines office; enter to the right, up the ramp. Friendly, English-speaking staff provides a map of Darjeeling (Rs3), helpful transportation info, and free luggage storage for trekkers. Open M-F 10am-4:30pm. The **Darjeeling Gorkha Hill Council Tourist Office** (☎2255351) is in the wood and glass building 50m north of Chowrasta on Mall Rd. W. In addition to providing an array of useful maps and brochures, the office arranges jeeps to Tiger Hill (Rs65 per person), 1-day rafting expeditions on the Rangit and Teesta rivers (Rs350-650 per person), and rental of trekking equipment through the affiliated **Office of Adventure Sports** (see **Trekking Around Darjeeling** p. 775). Open daily high-season (mid-Mar.-end of May, mid-Sept.-end of Nov.) 9am-6pm; off-season open M-Sa 10am-4:30pm, Su 10am-1pm.

Sikkim Permit: The process of securing a Sikkim permit (valid for 15 days), is a three-step bureaucratic adventure that usually takes one to two hours. (It's much easier at the office in **Siliguri**–see p. 760.) The formalities are reasonably straightforward, but there's a fair amount of walking involved. You need your passport at every step. First go to the

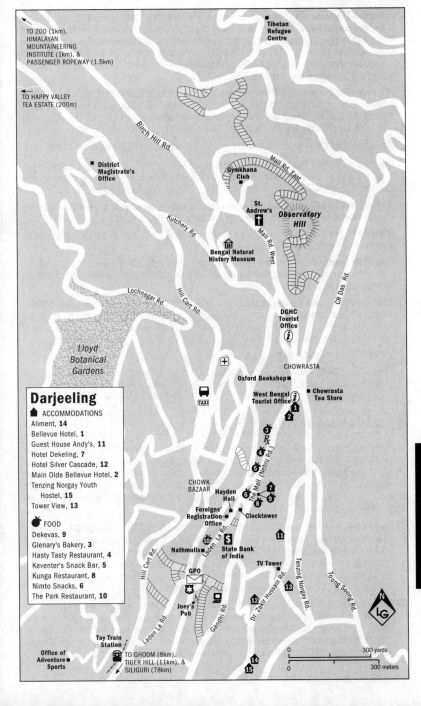

TO ZOO (1km),
HIMALAYAN
MOUNTAINEERING
INSTITUTE (1km), &
PASSENGER ROPEWAY (1.5km)

TO HAPPY VALLEY
TEA ESTATE (200m)

Tibetan
Refugee
Centre

Birch Hill Rd.

Mall Rd. East

District
Magistrate's
Office

Gymkhana
Club

St.
Andrew's

*Observatory
Hill*

Kutchery Rd.

Mall Rd. West

Bengal Natural
History Museum

CR Das Rd.

Lochnagar Rd.

Hill Cart Rd.

DGHC
Tourist
Office

*Lloyd
Botanical
Gardens*

CHOWRASTA

Oxford Bookshop ■

TAXI

West Bengal
Tourist Office

■ Chowrasta
Tea Store

1
2

3

Rx

4

5

CHOWK
BAZAAR

Hayden
Hall

The Mall (Nehru Rd.)

6
7
8
9

Foreigns'
Registration
Office

Clocktower

11

Hill Cart Rd.

Nathmulls ■

10

State Bank
of India

TV Tower

Tenzing Norgay Rd.

Toong Soong Rd.

GPO

13

Dr. Zakir Hussain Rd.

Laden La Rd.

Joey's
Pub

Gandhi Rd.

12

14
15

Toy Train
Station

Office of
Adventure ■
Sports

TO GHOOM (8km),
TIGER HILL (11km), &
SILIGURI (78km)

0   300 yards

0   300 meters

N

Darjeeling

ACCOMMODATIONS
Aliment, **14**
Bellevue Hotel, **1**
Guest House Andy's, **11**
Hotel Dekeling, **7**
Hotel Silver Cascade, **12**
Main Olde Bellevue Hotel, **2**
Tenzing Norgay Youth
    Hostel, **15**
Tower View, **13**

FOOD
Dekevas, **9**
Glenary's Bakery, **3**
Hasty Tasty Restaurant, **4**
Keventer's Snack Bar, **5**
Kunga Restaurant, **8**
Nimto Snacks, **6**
The Park Restaurant, **10**

District Magistrate's Office, 10min. down Hill Cart Rd., north of the bus stands; look for the "Sikkim Pass" sign. The office is on the 2nd floor of the building to the rear. Open M-F 11am-1pm and 2:30-4pm. With the stamped form, go to the **Foreigners' Registration Office,** Laden La Rd. (☎2254203), next door to Hayden Hall, for an official endorsement. Open daily 10am-5pm. Then, return to the District Magistrate's Office for the final signature. The permit is free.

Currency Exchange: State Bank of India, Laden La Rd. (☎2253589), just downhill from the clocktower, changes US dollars and British pounds in cash; AmEx traveler's checks in US dollars or Euros; and Thomas Cook traveler's checks in US dollars, Euros, or Pounds. Rs100 commission per transaction. Open M-F 10am-3pm, Sa 10am-12:30pm.

Luggage Storage: Free at the tourist office, most hotels, and trekking companies.

Bookstore: Oxford Bookshop, Chowrasta (☎2254325), has an extensive selection on the history, culture, and religion of the Subcontinent, with a good array of fiction and classics. Open M-F 9:30am-7pm, Sa 9:30am-2:30pm, Su in season. AmEx/MC/V.

Police: (☎2254422). Police assistance booths are all over town; there's one in Chowrasta, one at the intersection of Nehru and Laden La Rd., and one opposite the GPO.

Pharmacy: Frank Ross Pharmacy, Nehru Rd. (☎2254029), next to the cafe of the same name. Open daily 1am-7:30pm.

Hospital: Sardar Hospital (☎2254218), the yellow bldg. above the north end of the main bus stand. Many pharmacies along Nehru Rd. also have private doctors who do consultations.

Internet: Compuset Centre, Gandhi Rd. (☎2256901), on the right side, about 200m south of the clocktower, has plenty of computers and a well-chosen soundtrack. Rs30 per hr. Open daily 9am-7:30pm. **Glenary's Bakery** offers Internet in a posh cafe atmosphere, but at twice the price (Rs60 per hour).

Telephones: Most **STD/ISD** booths are open 8am-8:30pm.

Post Office: GPO, Laden La Rd. (☎2252076), down the road past the state bank, just after the sharp bend. Open daily 9am-5pm. There is also a **FedEx** branch at the Chowrasta. **Photo Studio,** Chowrasta (☎2255373). Open M-Sa 9am-6pm.

⚑ ACCOMMODATIONS

Darjeeling is home to a wide array of high-quality, inexpensive hotels; there's no need to settle for the wrong place or price. Off-season (mid-June to Aug. and Dec.-Feb.), there's plenty of space, and discounts of up to 50% are sometimes available; in season (Sept.-Nov. and Mar.-May), you may have to hunt a bit for a room. Budget accommodations are clustered along Dr. Zakir Hussain Rd., especially at the top of the hill near the TV Tower.

■ **Tower View,** 8/1 Dr. Zakir Hussain Rd. (☎2254452; fax 254330), just off Dr. Z's Rd. by the TV Tower. The friendly owner, a former Gorkha soldier, welcomes foreigners and shares his regional knowledge and the tourist log, which has good trekking tips. Rooms look out over Kanchenjunga, facing the sunrise. Backpacker-filled restaurant serves good meals. Laundry service and Internet (Rs30 per hr.). Dorms Rs50; singles Rs80-100; doubles Rs100-150. Off-season: Rs40-120. ❶

■ **Aliment,** 40 Dr. Zakir Hussain Rd. (☎2255068). From Chowrasta, take the road to the left of the fountain and bear right when it splits into three. After the TV tower (on the right), take a right up the hill and follow Dr. Z's around to the left. The owner's tips and the detailed tourist log are helpful in planning treks. All rooms have private bath. Dorms Rs50; singles Rs70; doubles with bucket shower Rs150, with hot shower Rs200. ❶

Guest House Andy's, 102 Dr. Zakir Hussain Rd. (☎2253125; http://users.big-pond.net.au/cfunk/gha/), close to Chowrasta, 150m past the *puri* stalls. Run by an engaging and friendly Gurung woman, Andy's has a relaxed, family feel. Large, spotless rooms with seat toilets. Fantastic view from the roof. The more expensive rooms have hot shower. Doubles Rs200-300. Off-season: Rs150-250. ❷

Hotel Dekeling, 51 Gandhi Rd. (☎2254159 or 2253298; www.dekeling.com), above the Nehru-Laden La intersection. If you want to splurge, this is the best place to do it. Primped and carpeted, with a palatial lounge area, Dekeling will make you feel a lot richer than you probably are. Cozy beds, attached bathrooms with hot showers, and TV sets in most rooms. Run by a friendly Tibetan couple, Dekeling retains a family atmosphere despite the luxury. In addition to regular off-season discounts, the hotel can sometimes give discounts of up to 50%, so be sure to ask. Doubles Rs600-1100. ❹

Bellevue Hotel, Chowrasta (☎2254075; www.darjeeling_bellevuehotel.com), on the south side of the plaza. Although pricey, the ski-lodge atmosphere, all wood interiors, private baths, and fantastic views make it worth the extra rupees. For real decadence, snatch up the top-floor corner room, complete with panoramic views, a wood burning stove, and a bathtub (Rs1200). Doubles Rs500-1000; Rs100 less for single occupancy. Off-season: Rs350-880. ❸

Main Olde Bellevue Hotel, 1 & 5/1 Nehru Rd. (☎2254178 and 2253977; www.dar-jeelinghotels.com), just a few steps down Nehru Rd. from Chowrasta. This grand hotel has 2 separate bldgs.: the new wing is comfortable, though uninspiring rooms, while the 19th-century "olde" wing, has slightly worn but beautifully furnished Raj-era suites. Phone ahead and they will send someone to pick you up. New wing doubles Rs500-1200; old wing Rs700-1000. Off-season discounts of 40-50%. ❸

Hotel Silver Cascade, 9 9/1 Cooch Behar Rd. (☎2250256), near the TV Tower, on the road leading to Aliment and the Youth Hostel. Unabashed luxury seekers can take refuge in Silver Cascade's palatial rooms, all with marble bathrooms, satin bedspreads, balconies, heaters, and TVs. The official prices are high, but the management routinely offers incredible discounts (sometimes over 50%), especially during the off season. Singles Rs1000; doubles Rs1400; suite Rs1800. ❺

Tenzing Norgay Youth Hostel, 16 Dr. Zakir Hussain Rd. (☎2256794), 30m up the hill from the Aliment. Named after Everest's 1st conqueror. The expansive balcony circling the bldg. compensates for sterile, institutional dorm rooms. In the off season call ahead to make sure the hostel is open. Dorms Rs40; doubles Rs120; quads Rs200. ❶

🍴 FOOD

Darjeeling is crammed with restaurants; **Aliment** and **Tower View** are the best of the hotel variety. **Vegetable stands** and **snack stalls** serving tasty food line Dr. Zakir Hussain Rd. just as it leaves Chowrasta, although you'll have to suffer the hungry stares and smelly deposits of the adjacent horses.

☒ The Park Restaurant, Laden La Rd., opposite the State Bank of India. With its soundtrack of synth soft-pop and ivy-draped faux Ionian columns, The Park maintains its reputation as the best restaurant in town. In addition to a new menu of Thai specialities (Rs45-135), the Park also serves the best Indian food you'll find in this part of Bengal. Indian dishes Rs30-90. Open daily 11am-3pm and 6-9pm. ❸

☒ Hasty Tasty Restaurant, 13 Nehru Rd. Line cooks prepare all-veg. fast food. The extensive menu covers a range of Indian, Chinese, Continental, and American fare. Quick and friendly service. Entrees Rs20-50, ice cream Rs14-20. Open daily 8:30am-8:30pm. ❷

☒ Nimto Snacks, at the intersection of Nehru and Laden La Rd., opposite the police booth. A tiny eatery carved out of the wall, with an intimate, relaxed atmosphere. The all-veg. snacks and sweets are cheap and tasty. Excellent Tibetan *momos* (4 pieces with hot soup Rs6) and chow mein (Rs20). Open daily 10am-7:30pm. ❶

Glenary's Bakery, Nehru Rd., 100m uphill from the Hasty Tasty. This is the central branch of a chain that spans North Bengal. The self-proclaimed master baker lives up to his own billing. Donuts, scones, macaroons, and rolls Rs10-40. American burger and pizza fare Rs20-90. Open daily 7:30am-8:30pm. ❷

Dekevas, Gandhi Rd., below the Hotel Dekeling. Colorfully decorated and elegant, Dekevas serves a comprehensive menu of Tibetan dishes in rather ambient surroundings. ❷

Kunga Restaurant, Gandhi Rd., above the Nehru-Laden La intersection, next door to Dekevas. Excellent Tibetan fare at competitive prices; quite popular with locals. *Thukpa* Rs30-40, *momos* (plate of 10) Rs30-60. Open daily 8am-8pm. ❷

Keventer's Snack Bar, 1 Nehru Rd., at the corner before the intersection with Laden La Rd. Those in search of a taste of Raj-era Darjeeling should head to "Kev's," famous for its hearty English breakfasts (Rs25-60). Rooftop deck makes for a fantastic brunch spot. Open daily 7:30am-8pm. ❷

◐ SIGHTS

TIGER HILL. Darjeeling's most popular sight lies 11km out of town. A favorite with Indian tourists, early risers flock in droves to catch the sunrise from Tiger Hill, which offers the area's best views of **Kanchenjunga** (8586m), the world's 3rd-highest mountain. An observation tower on top of the 2590m rise offers views stretching from the flood plains of the Ganga delta to the snowcaps of the Himalayas, each peak lighting up in turn as the sunlight inches west. Everest is sometimes visible. The only drawback is the noisy crowd, but a little more seclusion is available on the upper floors of the observation tower for Rs20-40. The spring haze and summer monsoon clouds may obscure the view. On the way back, jeeps queue up as a local priest anoints the steering wheel of every vehicle with *sindur*. *(The DGHC Tourist office and most hotels and agencies organize morning excursions. Alternatively, catch a jeep from the hordes idling at the Nehru-Laden La intersection. Jeeps leave for Tiger Hill 4-5am, Rs60 round-trip. General admission to the Tiger Hill area Rs5. If you tire of sardine tourism, consider taking the comfortable 3hr. walk back via Ghoom; see **Trekking Around Darjeeling** for details.)*

HIMALAYAN MOUNTAINEERING INSTITUTE (HMI). Darjeeling has long been connected to mountaineering: when Nepal was a closed country, the earliest Everest trips took off from here. Founded by Nehru a few years after Edmund Hillary and Tenzing Norgay's historic ascent of Everest, the Institute still carries out its mission of promoting the sport of mountaineering in India by commemorating the achievements of the past and training the climbers of the future. The main appeal for tourists are the **Everest Museum** and the **Mountaineering Museum**, both choc-a-bloc with everything from butterflies to ice picks to relief models of the Himalayas. In a glassed-in gazebo around the corner, a telescope stands aimed at Kanchenjunga. It was a gift from Adolf Hitler to one of Nepal's Rana prime ministers (closed to visitors). Above the HMI is the cenotaph of **Tenzing Norgay,** the famous Sherpa climber who made the first ascent of Everest with Sir Edmund Hillary in 1953. Tenzing was the long-time director of the HMI, and his ashes now rest here. The Institute offers 28-day climbing courses, which are open to foreigners; see **study opportunities** (p. 774) for details. *(20min. walk from Chowrasta on Mall Rd. W, which becomes Birch Hill Rd., just beyond the zoo; see below. Museums open F-W 8:30am-4pm. Rs5.)*

HAPPY VALLEY TEA ESTATE. As the closest tea estate to Darjeeling, Happy Valley is the best place to witness the metamorphosis of tea leaves from flora to flavor. Except in the off season (Dec. 15-Mar. 15), pickers work through the shrubs on the hills around you, and a factory worker will guide you through the plantation's antique drying, sifting, and sorting equipment. If you arrive out of season, you'll still be able to get a tour, but the factory will be empty and lifeless. *(Walk along Hill Court Rd. 200m past the District Magistrate's Office, turn left at the sign, and walk down a winding road to the tea estate below. Open daily 8am-4pm. Free, but tip the guides.)*

ZOOLOGICAL PARK. Darjeeling has more to offer than just mountains. The Padmaja Naidu Himalayan Zoological Park, better known as the Darjeeling Zoo, gives its animals larger and leafier spaces than most Indian zoos, and houses an astonishing array of mostly high-altitude species, including snow leopards, Siberian tigers and red pandas. Fifteen minutes further down the road, the **Breeding Center** is attempting to produce a sustainable population of snow leopards and red pandas from a program that began with only a pair of each species. The center offers visitors the opportunity to see these animals, particularly the snow leopards, at closer quarters than at the zoo itself. *(Adjacent to the HMI. Both open F-W 8:30am-4pm. Zoo entrance Rs5; breeding Center entrance Rs10.)*

OBSERVATORY HILL. A fine spot from which to take in Darjeeling's magnificent views, Observatory Hill is more importantly the site of a temple to Mahakala, a fearsome manifestation of Shiva, that is sacred to both Hindus and Buddhists. It is also believed to be the resting place of Indra's thunderbolt-casting scepter, or *dorje (Dorje-ling,* "land of the thunderbolt"). Protected by a grove of stately pines, woven together by thousands of prayer flags, and tirelessly guarded by an army of fearless monkeys that would make Hanuman proud, the hill is a world apart from commercial Chowrasta only minutes below. Don't miss the cave below and to the left, complete with carvings of Vishnu, Ganesh, and company. *(Stairs to Observatory Hill begin 50m north of Chowrasta on Mall Rd. E.)*

RANGEET VALLEY PASSENGER ROPEWAY. Clockwise around the ridge from the HMI is the starting point for the Rangeet Valley Passenger Ropeway. The cable car no longer makes the full trip to Singla Bazaar in the north, but it does go for a scenic 30min. dip over the tea shrubs. The cars won't operate until full (at least 8 people), so service can be erratic. *(Cars run daily 10am-4:30pm. Round-trip Rs66.)*

GHOOM MONASTERY. Founded in 1850, Yiga Choling Gompa, or Ghoom Monastery, is the region's oldest and most famous monastery. The Ghoom Monastery's large shrine contains a 5m golden statue of the Maitreya Buddha (the future Buddha). The murals inside have been recently refurbished by painter **Dawa Bhutia** and appear beautifully reborn. Don't confuse this with the new and not terribly interesting Samten Choling Ghoom Monastery below the road to Ghoom. *(In Ghoom, 8km from Darjeeling. Jeeps run here from the taxi stand near the train station between 6am and 5:30pm for Rs10; alternatively, it makes a convenient stop on a walk back from Tiger Hill. In Ghoom, walk 50m from the Ghoom Railway Station on the road back toward Darjeeling, turn left at the sign, and follow the road for about 1km to the monastery.)*

OTHER SIGHTS. The **Bengal Natural History Museum** has an extensive collection of stuffed, dried, and bottled creatures in varying states of preservation and decay. *(From Chowrasta, the road at the far left, past the Hotel Sunflower; bear left at the bottom of the road and you'll begin to see signs. Open F-W 10am-4pm. Rs5.)* Below the bus stand are the expansive and well-maintained **Lloyd Botanical Gardens,** specializing in alpine foliage. As Darjeeling's largest green space, the gardens make a pleasant reading or picnicking spot. *(Open daily 7am-5pm. Free.)*

SHOPPING

Darjeeling's main product is its excellent **tea,** available in shops and stalls all over town. The most reputable (though pricey) shops are **Nathmulls,** on Nehru Rd., opposite the State Bank of India, and the **Chowrasta Tea Store,** in Chowrasta. Prices range from Rs150-5000 per kg. Cheaper tea, along with everything else imaginable, is sold at the **Chowk Bazaar,** the market surrounding the main bus station. **Hayden Hall,** Laden La Rd. (☎2253228), across from the clocktower, is a women's cooperative that sells locally handmade blankets, rugs, bags, and sweaters. Proceeds go to needy women in Darjeeling. (Open M-Sa 9am-5pm.) A larger collection of handmade goods is available at the **Tibetan Refugee Self-Help Centre,** a 30min. walk beyond and below Observatory Hill. From Chowrasta, take CR Das Rd. (which starts near the police booth and runs below Mall Rd. E) north and west around the ridge. Follow the right fork, and descend along the zig-zagging main road until you reach the center. Established by Tibetans who fled here in 1959, the center has a shop selling carpets, sweaters, and woodcarvings. The workshops are on the premises and open to the public for viewing. (Open M-Sa 9am-5pm.)

Tibetan thangka paintings are available in the curio shops all over town, but if you're looking for something really special, contact master painter **Dawa G. Bhutia,** who was also responsible for the beautifully restored murals at Ghoom monastery. Though he works only on commission and a single *thangka* may take several weeks to finish and cost upwards of Rs10,000, his natural, stone-based colors and years of experience yield unrivalled results. (☎98320 16825; dawa_g@yahoo.com; or inquire with the manager of the Bellevue Hotel.)

NIGHTLIFE

Darjeeling is mostly dead after 8pm. One notable exception is ⚑**Joey's Pub** (☎2252748), 10m down the small street across from the post office. Joey, a Darjeelingite who spent two years in London in the 70s, has succeeded in recreating the British pub scene—Darjeeling style. The relaxed, informal, and coal-heated atmosphere, along with the steady stream of old-school rock-and-roll, invariably make for a pleasant evening. (Beer Rs70; hard drinks Rs35-125; in-season, mid-Mar.-May and Sept.-Nov., open 11am-10pm; off-season open 5-10pm.) The other option for an evening out is **The Buzz** (☎2254315), which is praised by locals (despite the fact that few actually seem to go themselves). The soft-pop soundtrack and chain restaurant ambience may give solace to homesick Americans. (Beer Rs80, whiskey Rs50-250. Open 2-10pm.)

STUDY OPPORTUNITIES

Founded in 1988 with the blessing of the Dalai Lama, Darjeeling's **Manjushree Institute** has already established itself as one of the world's foremost centers for the study of the Tibetan language, particularly modern spoken Tibetan. The Institute offers two classes every year, Beginner (modern Tibetan) and Advanced (classical Tibetan). Both classes meet for four hours each day and are divided into three three-month trimesters, the first starting in mid-March and the last ending in mid-Dec. Students are required to commit to a minimum of three months of study. Tuition rates for 2004: three months US$210, six months US$320, nine months US$430, registration US$30; for more information, contact the Institute or speak with Mr. Tshering Norbu Dekevas, the owner of Hotel Dekeling and the Institute's co-founder. (Manjushree Institute of Tibetan Culture, 8 Burdwan Rd., Darjeeling, West Bengal, India; ☎2254159 or 2256714; fax 2252807 or 2253298; www.kreisels.com/manjushree/.) The **Himalayan Mountaineering Institute** offers regular 28-

day mountaineering courses that are also open to foreigners. The HMI's Basic Mountaineering course is offered six times per year in Mar.-May and Sept.-Nov. Conducted on the Rathong Glacier in Sikkimand, the course covers first aid, altitude sickness, glacier travel and rescue, and other vital skills. Theoretically, foreigners are required to apply three months in advance but in practice this rule is rarely followed. Tuition for the Basic Mountaineering course is US$500. For more information, contact the institute. (☎ 2254083 or 2254087; hmi@dte.vsnl.net.in.)

◙ TREKKING AROUND DARJEELING

The hills around Darjeeling offer excellent trekking: permits are not required, a network of huts and lodges make guides and porters unnecessary, and the uncrowded trails lead through a spectacularly diverse landscape. Treks consist of 5-7hr. hikes between villages, where small lodges (usually Rs40-50 per person) and food are available. On some stretches of the trail, provisions are unavailable and snacks should be packed along with warm clothes and rain gear. Lodges usually provide blankets, but it's still a good idea to bring a sleeping bag—especially if you're planning to trek between Dec. and early Mar., when the temperature can drop below freezing indoors. Trekkers must also bring their **passports,** which are required at Moneybhanjang, Rimbik, and sometimes at the Tumling check-post. The routes are a mix of trails and rough jeepable roads. For the most recent information consult the DGHC's useful "Himalayan Treks" pamphlet and the tourist logs at the Bellevue, Tower View, and Aliment hotels. If you're short on trekking gear, you can rent sleeping bags, packs, down coats, tents, and boots from the DGHC's **Office of Adventure Sports** or **Trek-Mate,** a local trekking agency. The Office of Adventure Sports is a bit further from the center of town, but charges substantially less. Sleeping bag Rs5-10 per day, jacket Rs7-10 per day. To get to the office, walk 50m along the road into town from the railway station. If you look down the ridge to your left you will see a building below with the words "Lowis Jubilee Complex" painted on the roof; a narrow road branches off from the train tracks and zigzags down the hill to the complex, where the Office of Adventure Sports is marked with a small sign. (Open M-Sa 10am-4pm, Su 10am-1pm.) **Trek-Mate** is two floors down inside the Hasty Tasty and Keventer's Snacks. Rates are higher, but boots are also available. Sleeping bags Rs20 per day, jackets Rs20 per day, boots Rs30 per day. (☎ 2274092. Open daily 10am-5pm.) Some hotels, such as the Tower View, also rent out gear, but usually only to their own guests. There are currently no stores in Darjeeling offering trekking gear for sale.

TIGER HILL TREK

Though it scarcely qualifies as a trek (despite the DGHC's billing it as such) the walk back from Tiger Hill is still a great way to spend the morning after watching the sunrise, and to get a better sense of the area around Darjeeling. The steep path leading down from Tiger Hill itself is easy to follow and returns to the main road after a little over an hr. Fortunately, there's no need to take the main road all the way back to Darjeeling. After following the main road for a few minutes you will come to a three-way intersection by the police post at Jhorebunglow. From here, follow the uphill road in the direction of the yellow sign labeled "Kata Pahar." Before heading back to Darjeeling, though, it's worthwhile to walk 10min. further up the main road to Ghoom for a look at the Ghoom monastery. The flat, untrafficked road from Jhorebunglow follows the side of the wooded ridge toward Darjeeling, eventually becoming Tenzing Norgay Rd. and leading directly into Chowrasta. The only sight worthy of note is the Aloo Bhari Gompa, a small Nyingmapa monastery in the town of Aloo Bhan. Also called "Mag Dog," which means "warding off the war," the monastery was built between 1941 and 1919, in the shadow of World War I, and was dedicated to the cause of world peace. The original monastery suffered substantial earthquake damage and the monastery that stands today is largely the result of reconstruction efforts of the 1930s. The monastery isn't always open, but a lama usually arrives at 8am to perform *pujas* and will let you have a look around then.

SANDAKPHU OR PHALUT TREK

Treks in the Darjeeling area all cluster around the Singalila Range, the ridge separating West Bengal and Nepal. The main route is roughly in the shape of an upside down horseshoe, with Manebhanjang and Rimbik at the two ends and Phalut at the apex. From either end one can make a short excursion and return via the same path, or continue part of the way up, cut across, and return along the other leg of the horseshoe. Most people choose to start from Manebhanjang rather than Rimbik, because you'll spend a lot more time walking with your back to the mountains, and the steep path from Rimbik to Sandkphu or Gorkey to Phalut is a lot more brutal going up than down.

KALIMPONG কালিম্পং कालिम्पोङ্ ☎ 03552

According to a little-known story, in the years of the Raj a goldsmith of Kalimpong, Karbir Sunwar, was moved by feelings of goodwill to send a silver **tong-ba** to Queen Victoria as a token of his humble regards. Apparently the Queen took his gift kindly: after a lapse of six months the goldsmith received word from across the ocean that as a sign of her majesty's appreciation he would be gifted the whole of Kalimpong or 1,000 rupees, whichever was more to his liking. After his initial shock and subsequent deliberation, Mr. Sunwar decided to take the cash. Had he chosen otherwise, he would have inherited what is today one of the West Bengal hills' most fertile and sleepily scenic districts. Nowadays Kalimpong's chief claims to fame are its colorful flower nurseries and its numerous reputable schools, and aside from a few historic monasteries it has little in the way of sights that one can easily point to. But for visitors it offers a chance to spend a few quiet days among green hills and colorful flowers, and to get a feel for life in West Bengal hills outside of the bustle and hype of Darjeeling. Kalimpong remains a center of the Gorkha Independence Movement, any *bandh* that shuts down Darjeeling also renders Kalimpong inaccessible.

⊏ TRANSPORTATION

Buses and Jeeps: Buses and jeeps depart from the **motor stand,** with booking offices along the perimeter. **Buses** to: **Darjeeling** (3hr.; 7, 7:30am, and 12:30pm; Rs45); **Gangtok** (3hr.; 7:30, 8am, 1, 1:30pm; Rs45); **Panitanki,** on the Nepal border (3½hr.; 5:35, 5:50, 6:15am, 1:45pm; Rs60); **Siliguri** (2½hr., frequent 6:20am-5pm, Rs45). **SNT** runs 2 daily buses to **Gangtok** (3½hr., 8:30am and 1pm, Rs55). Open daily 7am-2pm. **Jeeps** run to: **Darjeeling** (2½hr., frequent 6am-4pm, Rs65); **Gangtok** (2½hr., 7 per day 7:30am-3pm, Rs70); **Geyzing** (5hr., 7:30am, Rs90); **Kakarbhitta** (3½hr., 12:30pm, Rs70); **Pelling** (5½hr., 1:15pm, Rs120).

◼✦ ORIENTATION

The **motor stand** sits in a large square in the center of town. On the east of the motor stand is Hotel Cosy Nook; on the west are the Himalaya Lodge and Sikkim Nationalized Transport (SNT) office. Just south of the motor stand is the old **football field,** also known as the **Mela Grounds. Ongen Road** runs north-south and crosses the square at the west end. Parallel to and just west of Ongen Rd. is **Main**

Road, the town's major thoroughfare and primary axis. The 200m central stretch of Main Rd. is capped at both ends by traffic intersections; the bus stand lies just east of the north intersection. Main Rd. continues north and becomes **Rishi Road.**

▟ PRACTICAL INFORMATION

Tourist Information: DGHC Tourist Reception Centre, 30m north of Main Rd.'s north intersection. Organizes sight-seeing tours of the area (Rs40 per vehicle of 4) and rafting expeditions on the Rengeet and Teesta rivers (Rs350-650). Also sells photocopies of a well-drawn map of Kalimpong (Rs5). Open daily from 9:30am-5:30pm.

Budget Travel: Shangri-La Services, Rishi Rd. (☎259403), 50m north of Main Rd.'s north intersection. An authorized agent for Jet Airways, Blue Dart Express, Sita World Travels, and **FedEx,** Shangri-La also organizes rafting on the Tista River (1-day trip Rs1200-1500 per person; multi-day $45 per person) and treks in Sikkim ($45 per person per day for a group of 4). Open daily 8am-6pm.

Currency Exchange: Because of a counterfeiting scam that happened a few years ago, none of Kalimpong's banks change currency. The only legal place to change money is the **Soni Emporium** (☎255030), 100m north of the tourist office, just off Rishi Rd. to the right. Soni exchanges traveler's checks and cash at reasonable rates, and he will then invite you into his back room and persuade you to spend your newly acquired rupees on his collection of Indian and Tibetan art. Open daily 8am-8pm.

Bookstore: Kashi Nath and Sons, opposite the tourist office. Stocks a good selection of everything from Hardy to the Hardy Boys. Open daily 7:30am-7:30pm.

Police: (☎100 or 55268). On the corner at the south intersection of Main Rd.

Pharmacy: Shree Tibet Stores, Main Rd. (☎255459), near the north intersection. Open daily 8:30am-8:30pm. Doctor available 9:30am-1pm and 2-6:30pm.

Hospital: Sadar Hospital (☎255245), northeast of town. Heading north from Main Rd.'s north intersection, take a left just after the tourism office, then a left at the next fork.

Internet: Odyssey Internet Cafe, Main Rd. (☎258964), on the 2nd fl. of the supermarket on Main Rd., has 8 terminals. Rs40 per hr. Open daily 9am-7pm.

Post Office: GPO, Main Rd. East (☎255990), 30m south along the road to the left of the police station. Open M-F 9:30am-3pm, Sa 9:30am-1pm. **Postal Code:** 734301.

▛ ACCOMMODATIONS

Most of Kalimpong's budget hotels are clustered around the noisy motor stand, but you'll better appreciate Kalimpong's mellow atmosphere if you stay at one of the quieter places further afield.

▨ **Deki Lodge,** Tripai Rd. (☎255095 or 255621; www.geocities.com/dekilodge). From Main Rd.'s north intersection, head north on Rishi Rd. for about 600m; Tripai Rd. branches left, and Deki is visible from here. Deki's peaceful location, perpetually smiling staff, and relaxed, backpacker atmosphere set it apart from the rest. A wide range of rooms, hot showers, and a small family of friendly cats and dogs. Singles Rs80-300; doubles Rs200-350; deluxe 2-person suites Rs500-900. ●

▨ **Cloud 9,** Rinkingpong Rd. (☎259554; cloud9kpg@yahoo.com). Follow the main road 300m south of the post office, and take the left, upper road at the fork. Follow the road for 400m, continuing after Hotel Chimal for another 400m. Cloud 9 is a little pricier, but very much worth it. 5 rooms (and common room with TV), all pristine, well-furnished, carpeted, and with attached seat toilet and hot shower. The downstairs restaurant serves the best food in Kalimpong. On Saturday evenings, the owner brings together some musically- inclined friends for an informal jam session of mostly

THE BIG SPLURGE

THE ORCHID RETREAT

Kalimpong's main attractions are its flower nurseries and its relaxing atmosphere, and there is no better place to enjoy either than the The Orchid Retreat, a set of six cottages tucked inside the garden of the Ganesh Mani Pradham Orchid nursery. The cottages themselves are faced with wood and bamboo that preserve the natural equilibrium of the garden, while inside they are well-appointed with carpets, wooden furniture, and immaculate green marble bathrooms. The Orchid Retreat is an ideal place to sit back, relax, and contemplate the flowers and mountains over a glass of fruit juice, but if you're feeling active you can try your hand in the nursery's garden or even in the rice paddies of a nearby village. Meals of fresh organic produce are eaten in the nursery's elegant main house with the warm and welcoming Pradham family, who take time to chat, share recipes and gardening tips, and can also arrange tours to any of the local sights.

(Single-occupancy cottages Rs1000; double-occupancy cotages Rs1500; meals Rs100-150. ☎274517 or 274275; fax 274489; www.theorchidretreat.com.)

classic rock. Guests are welcomed to join in. Doubles Rs600-800; single occupancy Rs475-675; 20% off-season discount. ❸

Shangri-La Guest House, Tripai Rd. (☎255109). Up above Dr. Graham's homes along the road to Deolo Hill, this aptly-named hotel is worth the 45min. walk from town. Beautiful and secluded, with kitchen facilities, private baths in each room, and a surrounding garden that provides fresh produce for meals. Check with Shangri-La Services (see **Budget Travel,** above) in town for info on availability and directions before walking up. 4 doubles Rs350 each. ❸

Lodge Himalshree, motor stand (☎255070), 20m to the right of the SNT office. Run by a family who disapproves of "hanky-panky," i.e. loud noise and alcohol. Hot water buckets Rs7. Doors lock at 9pm. "Dorms" (2 beds in the lobby) Rs70; doubles Rs150; triples with bath Rs250; quad without bath Rs200. ❶

Lodge Cosy Nook, (☎255541), on the east side of the motor stand. The betel-chewing owner offers advice on seeing the sights. Rooms are plain, but surprisingly clean and roomy, and all have attached bath (bucket hot water Rs5). Singles Rs150; doubles Rs200; triples Rs300; quads Rs400. ❶

◘ FOOD

Kalimpong has a scant selection of good restaurants, but some Chinese eateries have popped up around the motor stand. Main Rd. is lined with veggie snack stalls.

▩ **Kalsang Restaurant,** by the football field, 20m from Market Sq. Follow the road leading southeast away from the jeep stands, and descend the steps just past the football field into a Tibetan family's home. Cheap, delicious Tibetan food. *Momos* Rs10, veg. *gyathuk* Rs15. Open daily 6am-7pm. ❶

▩ **Glenary's,** Main Rd. and Rishi Rd. The master baker rears his doughy head in Kalimpong on Main Rd., 20m north of Kalash. The same great pastries as in Darjeeling—swiss rolls (Rs8), black forest cake (Rs15), donuts (Rs10). Open daily 8am-7pm. ❶

Fresh Bite, Rishi Rd., opposite the tourism office. Speedy service and classic rock distinguish this popular lunch spot. Sandwich and burger fare Rs15-60, North Indian dishes Rs18-50, sumptuous sundaes and floats Rs40-60. Open daily 10am-7pm. ❷

Evergreen Restaurant, Main Rd., across from Kalash on the lower level. A humble restaurant with a well-earned reputation for the best vegetable momos in town. Particularly popular with the after-school crowd. Plate of 8 *momos* with soup Rs12; *thukpa* Rs10. ❶

Kalash Vegetarian Snacketeria, Main Rd., opposite the State Bank of India. The best selection of veg. snacks in town. North and South Indian as well as continental favorites. Great *dosas* Rs18-35, curries Rs20-40, *momos* Rs15. Open daily 8am-7:30pm. ❶

Mandarin Restaurant, at the motor stand, has above-average ambience and wide selection of authentic Chinese dishes that go well beyond the usual chow mein and chop suey. The mostly non-vegetarian entrees range from Rs20-80; their specialty Mandarin fish must be ordered in advance. (Open 10am-8pm). ❷

👁 🎵 SIGHTS AND ENTERTAINMENT

One of Kalimpong's main attractions—the town's bountiful bouquet of orchids, amaryllises, roses, gladioli, and dahlias—is most impressive from March to June, but there's sure to be something blooming whenever you arrive. Several nurseries are scattered around the outskirts of town. **Ganesh Mani Pradhan Nursery,** 4km north of town on Rishi Rd., specializes in orchids and has a beautifully well-kept garden. Call before you visit to make sure someone will be available to let you in and show you around. The nursery also has a number of cottages that make for a unique night's stay. (☎274517; www.ganesh-villa.com; Open daily 9am-5pm.) The **Tharpa Choling Monastery,** a Geluk (Yellow Hat) monastery, was founded in 1892 and is still in the process of renovation; visitors are likely to see wood carvers and artisans at work. The monastery retains evidence of its Chinese influences, particularly in the long white temple uphill from the main building. Above the main compound where Chinese script adorns the entry pillars, a distinctly Chinese statue (Ling Kesar) stands, and all the tools and texts necessary for Mo divination are present (see **Local Legend,** p. 779). (Walk 15min. up Tripai Rd. from Deki Lodge. Directly across from the bright pink house, just before another road joins from above, there's a small path leading off to the right which then curves left to a small white archway.)

Kalimpong is well-known for its English-language schools. The oldest and most distinguished of these is **Dr. Graham's Homes,** which was built in 1900 when a Scottish minister set up a home for six orphaned students. The school eventually acquired the whole hilltop, and is almost entirely funded by alumni. It now has over 1200 students and is the model for many other schools devoted to poor and handicapped children. (20min. beyond the Tharpa Chaling Monastery on the same road.) If you con-

THE LOCAL LEGEND

ONE MO MONASTERY

Kalimpong's Tharpa Choling Monastery, of the Geluk-pa (Yellow Hat) sect, exhibits a particularly strong blend of Chinese and Tibetan influences. Most striking, perhaps, is the practice of Mo, a form of fortune-telling closely related to the I-Ching. Visitors are welcome to watch and join in. The first step is the casting of the Sho, a large seed split into two parts. While kneeling and thinking of a particular question or problem, the supplicant casts the seed onto the ground. If both sides land face up or face down, he or she isn't ready to continue; each person can take as many as three throws to get one side face up and the other face down. Next, the supplicant is given the Tonje, a large bamboo cup filled with 100 numbered bamboo sticks. The Tonje must then be shaken back and forth until one of the 100 sticks pops out. The number of this stick is then taken to the enormous Chinese (and corresponding Nepali) text, where the often-enigmatic fortune is read. Like the I-Ching, these fortunes are heavy on symbol and light on specifics. So if you can't decide what to do with your life, or maybe just where to go to dinner, Mo knows.

tinue farther on this road, it leads up to the top of **Deolo Hill,** the highest point in the area. The views are peerless—from the top you can see Kanchenjunga, Darjeeling, Sikkim, Kalimpong, the confluence of the Teesta and Rangit rivers, and the border with Bhutan. The DGHC has built a number of free gazebos that are perfect for a picnic lunch. A 200m footpath leads to a more secluded side of the hill. (Admission to the complex Rs5.)

Closer to town sits the **Bhutanese Monastery,** or Thongsa Gompa. Established in 1630, the monastery is the oldest and the closest thing to Bhutanese culture you're likely to see without a US$200 per day visa. The monks and students are primarily Bhutanese, but the temple draws many local worshipers, particularly on Sundays. (Follow Rishi Rd. 100m past the turn-off for Tripai Rd. and Deki Lodge, where another road on the right will join it from below. Backtrack 20m down that road, take the first turn on your left, and head down this road for 100m until it ends at the monastery gate. Open to the public daily 5am-7pm.) Kalimpong's other major monastery, the **Zong Dog Palri Fo-Brang Gompa,** sits at the opposite end of the ridge, 5km south of the town center. A Nyingmapa monastery founded in the mid-1970s, Zong Dog is notable for its unusual artwork and good views afforded by its hilltop location. Close to the ceiling of the main chamber, a number of miniature caves are sculpted out from the wall; each contains an image of one of Guru Rinpoche Padma Sambhava's 25 disciples. The room on the 2nd fl. houses an elaborate model of Guru Rinpoche's heavenly palace, the Zang Dog Palri, and a rare **3-D mandala,** which bears a striking resemblance to a *stupa*. (From Cloud 9, follow the road uphill for 30min., past the Morgan Tourist Lodge, until you reach a traffic rotary; follow Jammel Mahmood Rd. for another 10min. to the monastery.)

NEPAL स्नाल
LIFE AND TIMES

LAND, FAUNA AND FLORA

The legends are true: Nepal has the most dramatic mountains in the world. The massive Himalayan range was thrust up 50 million years ago when India collided with the rest of Asia. Today, Nepal is nearly 75% mountain, and it contains eight of the world's 10 highest peaks.

At the northernmost reach of the Indo-Gangetic Plain, the relatively flat **Terai** is fertile, low-lying (200m), hot, and humid. This whole area was once covered in dense malarial forest that supported only wild animals and hungry mosquitoes, but recent years have seen vast deforestation, and today it is the hub of Nepal's growing population. Jutting 1500m out from the Terai, the forested **Chure Hills** run parallel to the 3000m Mahabharat Range farther north. Between the Chure and the Mahabharat Hills are the broad basins of the **Inner Terai,** cut by the deep, north-south river gorges of Nepal's three biggest rivers—the Karnali, the Narayani, and the Kosi. At altitudes of 500 to 2000m, the **Pahar** region, north of the Mahabharat, is marked by flat, fertile valleys, including the Kathmandu, Banepa, and Pokhara Valleys. This region has been inhabited and cultivated longer than anywhere else in Nepal. Over 40% of the population lives there today.

The **Himalayas** are inhabited only in pockets. Human settlements are sparse after 4000m. Nepal's plant life thins out as altitudes increase, with the dense timber forests yielding to alpine pastures of spruce, birch, and rhododendron. Beyond 4900m, nothing but mountains grow. Ten mountains in Nepal are higher than 8000m, including **Mount Everest** or *Chomolungma* (8848m), the highest point on earth. North of the peaks is the high desert plateau of the **Trans-Himalaya.**

The Terai is inhabited by tigers, leopards, *gaur* (wild ox), elephants, and deer. Many can be seen in the **Royal Chitwan National Park** (see p. 880), a UNESCO World Heritage Site. The Rapti Valley is one of the last refuges of the endangered Indian rhinoceros. The Himalayas are also home to the mythical yeti *(Homo nivosus abominabilis)*, of four-toed footprint fame.

HISTORY

Nepal has a history and a culture as unique and diverse as its geography. Proximity to India has led to Indian influence in the Terai. The central hills and mountain valleys, including Kathmandu, have tended toward independence but not isolation. Deep in the mountains, life has gone on without much outside influence at all.

EARLY NEPAL (20,000 BC-AD 1200). Nepal's early history is shrouded in myth. Stone Age settlers arrived around 20,000 BC, and written references to the region appear in the first millennium BC. The **Kiratis,** a Mongol people who migrated into Nepal during the 8th century BC, were the first known rulers of the

PRIME MINISTER CHAND RESIGNS

Democracy in Nepal, still a relatively new institution, suffered a major setback on May 30, 2003 when Lokendra Bahadur Chand resigned from his position as prime minister. Chand was a senior leader of the National Democratic Party (NDP) who had served previous terms in 1983, 1990, and 1997. In the week leading up to his resignation, political news coverage focused on the stress created by ongoing Maoist peace talks within the government. Nevertheless, for many, the resignation marked a sudden, shocking failure in the efforts toward effective multi-party government.

With Maoist rebels threatening lives in the hills of Nepal, successful peace talks are crucial to rebuilding a safe and tranquil country. Unfortunately, despite all desire to meet this end, politicians have been unable to agree on a means toward it. Disputes caused by dissention within Nepal's multi-party government system have further impeded the peace process. The main political groups opposing Chand are the Communist Party of Nepal (Unified Marxist-Leninist) and the Communist Party of Nepal (Marxist). The differences between the CPN(UML) and the CPN(M) might seem nominal to the layperson, but they have been sufficient to derail efforts to find a common vision for Nepal's future.

Kathmandu Valley. Small kingdoms developed in the Terai region around 500 BC in response to the powerful Aryan kingdoms to the south. **Siddhartha Gautama,** the Buddha, was born into one of these early tribal confederations, the Sakya clan, during the 6th century BC. Three centuries later, the emperor **Ashoka** converted to Buddhism, leading to this religion's rise throughout Nepal.

During the 4th and 5th centuries AD, the **Licchavis** arrived from the Indian plains and overthrew the Kirati kings. They brought Hinduism and the caste system to Nepal and set to work viciously oppressing the Buddhist masses. Under the Licchavis, the Kathmandu Valley enjoyed economic and artistic growth, which continued despite the wars and poor administration of the reign of the **Thakuri dynasty,** which rose to power in the 9th century.

The first of the Thakuris were led by King Amsuvarman in AD 602, but conflict again set foot into the region during Nepal's Dark Ages. This period exposed the country to the rule of the **Thakuris of Nuwakot** (AD 1043), and a second Rajput dynasty in AD 1082. Despite the ongoing turmoil, trade flourished in the region, and trade-route settlement expanded into the Himalayas.

MALLA KINGDOMS (AD 1200-1742). A new dynasty, the **Mallas,** emerged in the Kathmandu Valley in 1200. After somewhat shaky beginnings, it ushered in a golden era in Kathmandu Valley culture and ruled for over 500 years. In 1482 after the death of Yaksha Malla, the greatest of the Mallas, the kingdom he had ruled from Bhaktapur was split among his three children. Kathmandu, Patan, and Bhaktapur developed into rival city-states. Despite constant feuding over trade with Tibet, all three kingdoms reached new heights in art and culture—the great wood-screened temples and the many cobbled **Durbar Squares** of the valley date from this time.

THE SHAH DYNASTY (1742-1816). Gorkha, 50km west of Kathmandu, was ruled by the **Shahs.** These rulers were the most ambitious of the many immigrant Rajput clans that had arrived between the 14th and 16th centuries, driven out of India by Muslim invaders. In 1742 King **Prithvi Narayan Shah** ascended to the throne of Gorkha, and within two years he set out to conquer Nepal's richest region, the Kathmandu Valley. After 25 years of war and attrition, the three cities of Kathmandu, Patan, and Bhaktapur surrendered. The nation declared its independence that year, 1768, and Shah successfully laid the foundation for modern Nepal. Shah's Gorkha army proceeded to conquer the eastern Terai and hills. Prithvi Narayan closed the doors of his new nation to the outside world, a policy that kept Nepal isolated until the 1950s. Prithvi Narayan's kingdom deteriorated soon after his death in 1775, as the monarchy passed from one infant Shah to another and nobles battled to act as regent.

Eventually the shrewd chief minister **Bhim Sen Thapa** took control and united Nepal by launching a war against the west, annexing the Garhwal and Kumaon sections of Uttaranchal, as well as Himachal Pradesh, regions that are now a part of modern India. However, with these new land acquisitions came additional problems. From 1788 to 1792 Nepal fought with Tibet and China, and in 1814 its expansion into the Terai provoked the hostility of the East India Company.

The **Anglo-Nepalese War** was not the easy victory the British expected. In spite of superior numbers and weaponry, the British were repeatedly defeated by the Nepalese soldiers, who held their hilltop forts and charged at the redcoats with *khukuri* knives. It was two years before the British broke through and won in 1816. A treaty signed in Segauli (1816) ending the war forced the defeated to accept a British Resident at Kathmandu. It also stripped Nepal of Himachal Pradesh, Garhwal, Kumaon, and much of the Terai, establishing the eastern and western borders of the country, where they remain today. The prospect of another insurrection encouraged the British to adopt a more sensitive stance toward Nepal. As a result, Nepal has survived as one of the few countries in Asia that has never been colonized.

STAGNATION AND COUP D'ETAT (1816-46). Prime Minister Bhim Sen Thapa kept the country stable by strengthening the army. However, chaos ensued when he fell from power in 1837, and several palace factions struggled to replace him. On September 14, 1846, a powerful minister was murdered, and the queen assembled the entire royal court in an attempt to discover the culprit. The personal guards of **General Jung Bahadur,** cabinet minister for the army, surrounded the court and opened fire, killing 32 of Kathmandu's most powerful nobles in the Kot Massacre. Over the next few hours, Jung Bahadur and the queen came to a secret agreement, and the general was appointed prime minister.

RANA RULES (1846-1951). Jung Bahadur took the title of **Rana,** and under this name his family maintained an iron grip for 105 years, amid countless family feuds and outrageous nepotism. Jung Bahadur eventually stripped the king, Rajendra, of his power. After a visit to London in 1850, Jung Bahadur kicked off a series of reforms designed to drag Nepal into the modern world. He bureaucratized the government: he did away with patronage and started to keep track of who was spending what and why. He

According to the May 2003 country report of The Economist Intelligence Unit, the three-way power struggle between the monarchy, rebel Maoists, and the multi-party aggregate will most likely continue in the upcoming years. Ceasefires are perennially declared, but the unsteady government system does not seem equipped to deal with a truce. The 1990s constitution, a valuable product of democratic progress, remains suspended in Nepal's current political situation. The country no longer maintains an elected parliament and the last remaining members completed their terms in July of 2003. Meanwhile, the king has postponed elections indefinitely. A decisive moment for Nepal's political structure does not seem to be on the horizon, but daily newsworthy drama continues.

instituted registration of land tenure so that landlords could no longer arbitrarily evict tenants from their land. In 1856, Jung Bahadur gave himself the title of Maharaja and made the position of prime minister hereditary. As a result, central power was transferred to the prime minister, and kings gradually became mere figureheads.

The Indian **Mutiny of 1857** provided an opportunity for Nepal to flex its muscles and win British support. Jung Bahadur sent 10,000 men to aid the British. In return, the British gave back the Terai lands they had taken in 1816. The British gave Nepal "guidance" on its foreign policy, but Nepal remained independent, scoffing at British demands for more trading rights and keeping strict tabs on Gorkha recruitment. The Rana prime ministers, however, proved to be more interested in advancing their family fortunes than in helping their country. When Jung Bahadur Rana died in 1877, his successors turned out to be equally wicked and a whole lot less competent.

Indian Independence in 1947 gave Nepal a new neighbor to deal with. Indian Prime Minister Jawaharlal Nehru disapproved of the Rana regime. In 1947 the **Nepali Congress** was formed, in the tradition of the Congress that had led India to freedom. Several renegade members of the Rana family who favored democratization fled to India and joined the growing anti-Rana resistance. Throughout the 104 years of Rana rule, the Shah kings remained in the background more as symbolic leaders than as reigning monarchs. The turning point arrived in 1950 when **King Tribhuvan,** a palace figurehead since 1911, also fled to India. By this time, he had captured popular support. The king, the prime minister, and Congress leaders met in Delhi, where Nehru engineered the **Delhi Compromise of 1951,** effectively bringing the Rana regime to an end.

NEPAL AFTER THE RANAS (1951-1990). After the Ranas' defeat, Nepal's foreign policies underwent dramatic changes. The Delhi Compromise was replaced in 1959 by a new constitution that called for a democratically elected assembly. The Nepali Congress won a large majority in the elections, and its leader, **B.P. Koirala,** became prime minister. But the state of affairs was fragile. King Tribhuvan had died in 1955, and his son **Mahendra** was less enthusiastic about political reforms, claiming that Nepal wasn't yet developed enough to handle them. He dismissed the Congress government almost as soon as it took power, and threw its leaders in jail. In 1962, a new constitution replaced the national assembly with a system of *panchayats* (village councils) to elect members to district councils, which, in turn, elected a National Panchayat. Political parties were banned, and the new system, supposedly a "special" kind of democracy uniquely suited to Nepalese traditions, effectively marked a return to absolute monarchy.

King Birendra, who came to power in 1972 (for astrological reasons he wasn't crowned until 1975), supported the *panchayat* system. Early in his career Birendra declared Nepal a "Zone of Peace" (a declaration of neutrality that angered India) and tightened visa restrictions for foreigners. The *panchayat* system continued to provoke dissent, however, and resistance came to a head in 1979 with riots in Kathmandu and Patan. In response, Birendra called for a national referendum to decide between the *panchayat* system and multiparty democracy. The *panchayats* won by a narrow margin, and the monarchy hung on another decade, kept in place by censorship and police brutality.

DEMOCRATIC NEPAL (1990-PRESENT). Inspired by revolutions in Eastern Europe and provoked by an economic blockade imposed by India, the outlawed opposition parties banded together in 1990, and pro-democracy demonstrations filled the streets of Kathmandu. When the king realized that mass arrests would not quell the uprising, he gave in and lifted the ban on political parties. The major parties formed an interim government and wrote a new constitution. In 1991, parliamentary democracy came into effect, with Birendra as constitutional monarch.

Elections gave a majority to the Nepali Congress, which had led the democracy movement. The **Communist Party of Nepal** became the main opposition. The new prime minister was **G.P. Koirala,** brother of the late B.P. Koirala. Rising inflation gave rise to general discontent (again), and an agreement with India over the Mahakali Dam project on Nepal's western frontier brought accusations of selling out to India. Unimaginative and stubborn, Koirala alienated many in his own party and was forced to resign in 1994.

The elections that followed brought the Communists to power in a minority government. Prime Minister **Man Mohan Adhikari** launched a series of populist schemes, including the "build-your-own-village" program, which gave large cash grants to local governments. Adhikari then resigned, hoping to gain a parliamentary majority for his government through another election. The king approved Adhikari's call for elections, but the Supreme Court ruled against the maneuver. No elections were held, and the Congress party took power by allying itself with the right-wing **National Democratic Party (NDP).** New Congress Prime Minister **Sher Bahadur Deuba's** efforts to bolster ties with the NDP were waylaid by intra-party dissent, and a March 1997 no-confidence motion brought the government down. A breakaway NDP faction led by **Lokendra Bahadur Chand** formed a coalition government with the CPN-UML, pushing Nepal into a new era of instability. In 1998, guerrillas from the **Communist Party of Nepal (Maoists)** turned violent and killed several NGO workers, alleging that they had mishandled funds.

TODAY

THIS YEAR'S NEWS

Tourism slumped and Maoist activity increased in the aftermath of the **royal massacre** of June 2001, when a drunken Crown Prince Dipendra killed his father King Birenda and eight other members of the royal family before turning his gun on himself. The current king is **Gayendra Bir Bikram Shah Dev.**

The Maoist insurgency continued to gain momentum, and a national **state of emergency** was declared in November 2001 in response to a series of violent attacks on government facilities and personnel. The country was thrown into even greater turmoil just days before the state of emergency was due to end in late May 2002, when Prime Minister Sher Bahadur Deuba was expelled from his own party after he threatened to dissolve parliament.

At the end of January 2003, another cease-fire was called as a prelude to peace talks. Since then, the cease-fire has held, and government leaders have been talking with the Maoist insurgents. However, activists protest against the establishment of what is seen as an undemocratically elected government. Nationwide strikes *(bandh)* called by Maoist leader Baburam Bhattarai have repeatedly affected transport and communications across major tourist areas, and although foreigners are not normally the primary targets of violence, there have been several instances of armed attacks on foreign tourists or tourist facilities. Businesses and NGOs with American affiliations have been targeted on several occasions, and there has been an increase in anti-Western rhetoric in recent months. These public demonstrations should be avoided. **Consult your government's travel warnings for more information before traveling to Nepal.**

GOVERNMENT AND POLITICS

Nepal became a constitutional monarchy with a parliamentary system of government on November 9, 1990. The power of the sovereign, a position held first by **King Birendra Bir Bikram Shah** (killed by his son the crown prince in June 2001), is limited, and real power is in the hands of the prime minister (currently **Sher Bahadur Deuba**), chosen by the 205-member House of Representatives. Members are elected by universal suffrage for a term of five years. An upper house, the 60-seat National Assembly, is made up of both appointed and elected members.

The main political parties in Nepal are the moderate Nepali Congress (NC), the Communist Party of Nepal—the Maoists, and the right-wing National Democratic Party (NDP). Other minor parties include the National People's Front, the Nepal Goodwill Party, the Workers and Peasants Party and the United People's Front. The Maoists, led by **Baburam Bhattarai,** have been engaged since 1996 in a violent struggle to overthrow the government and impose Communist rule. As of January 2003, a cease-fire between the government and the insurgents has indicated steps toward peace.

ECONOMICS

Nine of 10 Nepalis depend on subsistence farming. Nepal is one of the poorest countries in the world, where annual per capita income is equal to approximately US$240. An isolated agrarian society until the 1950s, Nepal entered the modern era with little infrastructure, lacking schools, hospitals, roads, telecommunications, electric power, industry and civil service. Nepalis use hillsides for terrace farming, but landslides and erosion wipe out crops regularly. In the more fertile Terai, where farming is more lucrative, high population growth makes even subsistence farming difficult. Many people's hopes for the future hinge on the hydroelectric potential of Nepal's raging rivers, with hydroelectricity plants popping up on the Kosi, Trisuli, Gandaki, Kulekhani and Marsyangdi rivers. However, development of this resource stands at odds with the bankable tourist appeal of pristine valleys for rafting and hiking. Meanwhile, roads are expensive to build and maintain, and the Indian border is the only easily negotiable channel of trade. Heavy industry is concentrated in the Terai, and most manufactured goods and machinery have to be imported from India.

Nepal's biggest source of foreign exchange is the export of carpets and textiles. International relations also comprise foreign aid from India, the Republic of China, the United Kingdom, the United States, Japan, Germany and the Scandinavian countries. International aid also comes from the World Bank, Asian Development Bank and the UN Development Program. In May of 2000, Nepal began accession negotiations to the WTO, though its status remains that of an observer country.

PEOPLE

DEMOGRAPHICS

Nepal has nearly 26 million people, representing 60 ethnic, linguistic, and caste groups. The country's cultural variety is largely the result of its rugged and often impassable terrain, which has kept areas isolated from each other. The cultures of Nepal have ancient roots in the land, but the country itself is young. Until two hundred years ago, a "Nepali" was somebody from the Kathmandu Valley, and it is still normal for people to identify themselves by their native region: *pahari, madeshi,* or *bhotia* (hills, plains, or northern-border dwellers), rather than Nepal.

Nepal is a nation of villages, and 90% of the population live in small market towns and rural settlements. Settlement is thickest in the fertile Terai, Nepal's bread-basket and a booming industrial region. Up in the highlands and the Trans-Himalayan valleys, almost no land is under cultivation, and these areas remain populated only by a few nomads.

Most Nepalis are Indo-Aryan Hindus, though Buddhism is also strong. The **Newari,** the earliest known arrivals in Nepal and the original settlers of the Kathmandu Valley, practice a blend of Buddhism and Hinduism. Only 4% of the total population today, the Newari have produced some of Nepal's most celebrated art. **Rais, Limbus,** and **Sunwars** live in the eastern hills, and the Terai is populated by **Tharus, Yadavas, Safars, Rajvanshis,** and **Dhimlas,** who speak dialects of Hindi (such as Bhojpuri and Maithili). The **Gurungs** and **Magars** of west central Nepal, are also thought to be among Nepal's earliest inhabitants. Today, 45% of the population claims Tibeto-Burmese descent. The Tibeto-Burmese settled mostly in the higher altitudes of the north, where Buddhist culture predominates. Among the most recent immigrants from Tibet are the **Tamangs,** the largest of Tibeto-Burmese ethnic groups, and the **Sherpas.** Other ethnic groups include the Brahmans, Chetris, Newars and Tharus.

LANGUAGE

The official language is **Nepali,** (also called Gorkhali). The mother tongue of half the population, Nepali is spoken by 90% of the population and understood by nearly everyone. As a descendent of Sanskrit, like the languages of North India, it uses the Devanagari script. (For basic Nepali, see the **Phrasebook,** p. 936.)

The **Newari** language is Tibetan in origin, although it uses the Devanagari script and takes half of its vocabulary from Sanskrit. Recent large-scale migrations from Tibet have brought **Tibeto-Burmese** languages and Tibetan Buddhist culture to Nepal. Tibetan refugees continue to seek asylum in Nepal, and the use of Tibetan, with its Sanskrit-based script, is not uncommon. In addition to Nepali, twelve other languages plus approximately 30 major dialects are spoken in Nepal. English is also widely spoken, though "*namaste*," a Sanskrit term meaning "I salute the God in you," makes an excellent greeting no matter what your native language happens to be.

RELIGION

Nepal is the cultural crossroads between India and Tibet. About 86% Hindu and 8% Buddhist (with small Muslim, Christian, and Jain minorities), Nepal is a unique mix-and-match of religious fusion. Although Nepal is the only country in the world with Hinduism as state religion, most Nepalis follow some combination of Hinduism and Buddhism, with plenty of local traditions thrown in. In general, northern regions near Tibet tend to be Buddhist, and areas closer to India are Hindu. Areas between (including the Kathmandu Valley) have the most complex blend of the two.

HINDUISM

Hinduism arrived in the Kathmandu Valley with the conquering Licchavi dynasty in the 4th and 5th centuries AD. It has long been Nepal's religion of status—**brahmins** (the priestly caste) and **chhetris** (the Nepalese warrior caste) have traditionally been at the top of the social hierarchy. Various legal reforms long ago tried to force lower-class Buddhists into an occupational caste system; this practice still survives, though few Buddhists accept the caste system.

Shiva is the most popular Hindu god; he is a fitting lord for this mountainous land, since he began his career as a Himalayan wanderer. He commonly appears as **Bhairava** or "Bhairab," a ghoulish figure who chases away demons, though he is also the compassionate **Mahadev,** worshipped out of love and devotion. In his form as **Pashupatinath,** the benevolent Lord of Animals, Shiva is Nepal's patron deity, and Nepal is often referred to as Pashupatinath Bhumi (Land of Pashupatinath). The temple of Pashupatinath near Kathmandu is the most important Hindu site in Nepal (see p. 826).

Vishnu, the cosmic "preserver," is also popular. In Nepal he is often called "Narayan," a name that comes from his role in the Hindu creation myth—he sleeps on the cosmic ocean while the creator god, **Brahma,** sprouts from his navel. Nepal's grandest festival, **Dasain,** is held in honor of the goddess **Durga.** Nepal also holds a special place for **Annapurna,** goddess of abundance and distributor of food.

Each goddess is an individual in her own right, but the goddesses are also the consorts of male deities, embodying the female aspect *(shakti)* of each god. In the Nepalese religious tantras, this *shakti* is considered the most powerful and active force in the cosmos. (For a general introduction to **Hinduism,** see p. 75.)

BUDDHISM

Buddha was born during the 6th century BC in Lumbini, in modern Nepal. Although he left Lumbini as a young man and did most of his traveling and teaching in India, his doctrines are popular in the land of his birth.

Most Nepali Buddhists follow the **Mahayana** (Great Vehicle) school, which differs from the older **Theravada** (Way of the Elders) school. Mahayana Buddhism, with its doctrine of salvation for all, developed in India during the first century AD and predominated in Tibet, China, Japan, and other parts of East Asia. The more orthodox Theravada school persisted in Sri Lanka and Southeast Asia. Hinduism beat out Buddhism in India, but an Indian-influenced Mahayana Buddhism survived in Nepal.

Mahayana Buddhism developed after a disagreement over monastic law *(vinaya)* in Buddhist communities. The Mahayana doctrines put less emphasis on the individual quest for nirvana, stressing instead the need for compassion for all beings. In the Mahayana tradition, the Buddha was not just a wise teacher and holy man—he was a cosmic being with magical powers and countless incarnations. The concept of a *bodhisattva,* who vows to put off his own enlightenment for the sake of saving all sentient beings, is very important in the Mahayana tradition, and a number of *bodhisattvas* are worshiped alongside the Buddha. (For a general introduction to **Buddhism,** see p. 80.)

TIBETAN BUDDHISM

In Tibet, a unique form of Buddhism developed when the Mahayana and Vajrayana (Thunderbolt Vehicle) traditions blended with the indigenous religion, **Bon** (see p. 559). Although Buddhism was originally brought to Tibet via Nepal, Tibetan traditions exerted a greater influence on the religion as it is practiced in Nepal than vice-versa. As a result of the Chinese occupation of Tibet, many Tibetan Buddhists have immigrated to Nepal, bringing prayer wheels and prayer flags blowing the mantra *Om Mani Padme Hum* ("Hail to the jewel in the lotus") all across Nepal's mountains and hills. Tibetan Buddhism divides the Buddha's nature into five "aspects," reflected in each of the five elements (earth, water, air, fire, and space). It is also noted for its monastic tradition—before the Chinese takeover, 25% of all Tibetans belonged to a religious order. Of the 6000 Tibetan monasteries in existence at the time of the occupation, only five remain. **Tibetan monasteries** are headed by teachers called lamas, addressed by the title *rimpoche* (precious one). Lamas are believed to have cultivated wisdom over many lifetimes, transmitting their knowledge to each reincarnation. The reincarnated lama is identified by astrologers who consult the Tibetan oracle and have the young candidates identify the former lama's possessions.

TANTRA

Tantra holds that polar opposites are merely two manifestations of the same consciousness, and that transcending these opposites leads to knowledge of the true nature of the mind. Consumption of meat, fish, and alcohol are off-limits. Tantric rituals also involve the harnessing and release of different energies in the body through sexual intercourse.

Tantra has much in common with the Hindu traditions of *shakti* and yoga. Between the 7th and the 9th centuries, tantra became popular throughout India as a part of both Hinduism and Buddhism, and its influence can still be seen today in Tibetan Buddhism, though it died out in India long ago. Some aspects of Tibetan Buddhism belong to the **Vajrayana** (Thunderbolt Vehicle) school, separate from both Mahayana and Theravada traditions. Vajrayana inherited much of its symbology from tantra—the major symbols of Vajrayana are the *vajra* or *dorje* (thunderbolt) and the *ghanti* (bell), which represent male compassion and female wisdom, respectively. The conscious release of bodily energy, achieved by meditation on goddess figures, is also prominent. These figures are often depicted in erotic poses, symbolizing reconciliation of dual energies.

INDIGENOUS TRADITIONS

CLIMB (ALMOST) EVERY MOUNTAIN

Mountaineers sometimes climb within meters of a summit, then forgo the pleasure of those last few steps out of deference to the mountains' resident gods and sacred powers. Hindus believe mythical Mt. Meru to be the center of the universe and the axis of all power. Mt. Kailash in Tibet is Shiva's stomping ground, and the Gauri-Shankar and Annapurna mountains in Nepal are both named after gods. Most of the Himalayan peaks, including those with more mundane names—such as Macchapuchare, which means "fish tail," and Kanchenjunga, which means "five treasures"—are considered sacred. In fact, the Himalayan range itself is said to be the father of Shiva's consort, Parvati.

Most people worship indigenous gods too, regardless of any other religion they might follow. Common in the Kathmandu Valley is the worship of the **Kumari,** a young girl recognized as an incarnation of the Hindu goddess Durga. The living goddess spends her entire childhood secluded in a palace, until she reaches puberty and reverts to the status of a mortal (see **The Living Goddess: Kumari,** p. 819). The Newaris also worship **Macchendranath,** a god born of a fish and identified both with Lokesvara, Shiva's form as "Lord of the World," and with the *bodhisattva* of Compassion, Avalokitesvara. Macchendranath's towering chariot makes his festivals distinctive highlights of the religious calendar. The Newari craftsmen of the Kathmandu Valley have also turned **Bhima** (or Bhimsen), the hero of the *Mahabharata* epic, into their patron deity. Also prominent in the valley is **Manjushri,** the valley's creator god, associated with Saraswati, the Hindu goddess of learning.

Outside the Kathmandu Valley, different ethnic groups preserve many of their local beliefs despite the widespread acceptance of Buddhism and Hinduism. The local gods are worshipped in return for good harvests and healthy children, and animal sacrifices to the gods are common. Shamans lead many religions and mediate between the human and supernatural worlds.

CULTURE

FOOD AND DRINK

Dal bhat tarkari (lentils, rice, and curried vegetables) is the staple dish for most Nepalis. Indeed, *bhat*, the word for cooked rice, is often used as a synonym for *khana* (food). Food in Nepal differs little from Indian food, except for a few Tibetan dishes on Nepalese menus. Ravioli-like **momo** and **thukpa,** a noodle soup, are popular. Newari food is largely buffalo meat. **Choyala** is buffalo fried with spices and vegetables.

The most popular breads are **chappati,** identical to the ones you see in India. Most Nepalis don't really eat breakfast, though it is commonly served in tourist restaurants and hotels. Vegetarians will probably have a better time with the food than meat-eaters.

Milk, or **dudh,** is an important staple and is often served hot, making it safe to drink if you know it has been boiled. **Chiya** (tea) is served hot with milk and lots of sugar. Yogurt *(dahi)* forms the base for **lassis** and the Newari delicacy **juju,** made from yogurt, cardamom, and cinnamon. Most sweets, including **barfi** and **peda,** are milk-based.

Nepalis drink beer and **chang,** a homemade Himalayan brew. **Raksi** is a stronger *chang* that tastes and feels like tequila. **Tong-ba** is a Tibetan brew made from fermented millet and sipped through a straw.

THE ARTS

Nepali arts draw from a synthesis of regional styles. Absorbing Indian and Tibetan aesthetics, the Newari artisans of the Kathmandu Valley developed a distinct style, mostly in woodwork that has since disappeared, but many of the valley's masterpieces remain in their original settings. Nepalese art has been inspired by religion, funded by kings, and executed by anonymous craftsmen.

Thanks to the boom in tourism, just about anything made in Nepal can be bought in Kathmandu, but many handicrafts are cheaper and available in a better and wider selection in their place of origin. For woodcarving and pottery, head to Bhaktapur; for papier-mâché masks and puppets, go to Thimi; for metalwork, Patan; and for Tibetan crafts like *thankas*, the best place to go is Boudha.

ARCHITECTURE

The oldest remaining structures in the Kathmandu Valley are **stupas,** sacred mounds of earth layered with centuries of plaster. They are large hemispherical domes, usually marking Buddhist holy places or sacred relics. Nepalese *stupas*, such as the amazing **Boudhanath Stupa** (see p. 841) in the Kathmandu Valley, display distinctive symbols on the square, golden spire at their top. These **chakus** are painted with the Buddha's eyes surveying the four cardinal directions and the number one (?) to represent universal unity. *Stupas* are often accompanied by **chaityas,** small stone shrines holding written mantras or scripture.

The greatest architectural achievements of the Kathmandu Valley are wood-and-brick **pagodas,** many of which resemble elaborate *chakus*, from which they perhaps evolved. Nepal is the birthplace of the pagoda—a 13th-century architect named Arniko exported the pagoda form to Kublai Khan's Mongolia, where it later spread to the rest of Asia. Most of Nepal's pagodas are Hindu temples built around central sanctums that house their deities. The sanctum is brick, with intricately carved wooden doors, window frames, and pillars. The pillars and struts on the outside support the tiered, sloping, clay-tiled roof. Despite appearances, the upper portions of the temple are not separate stories; they are left empty because of a belief that there should be nothing above the deity except the roof and the heavens. The whole structure sits on a terraced stone base resembling a step pyramid.

The Newaris also planned and built **bahals,** blocks of rooms surrounding a rectangular courtyard. These compact community units were used either as monasteries or as blocks of houses. *Bahals* are designed to be perfectly symmetrical, and the main doors and windows usually appear along the group's central axis.

Despite their xenophobic foreign policy, the Rana prime ministers, who reigned from 1846 to 1951, embraced European neoclassical architecture for the buildings they put up as part of their various modernization drives, and some parts of Kathmandu's Durbar Square would not look out of place in London's Trafalgar Square.

SCULPTURE

Early work in the Kathmandu Valley was influenced by North Indian styles of stone sculpture. Newari artisans of the Licchavi period made devotional images of Vishnu and the Buddha that strongly resembled the work of the Mathura school. Written accounts indicate that wooden sculpture also flourished at this time, though none has survived.

Stone sculpture in Nepal reached its heights between the 7th and 9th centuries and virtually disappeared after the 10th. Metal became the medium of choice for medieval Nepalese sculpture, again as a result of Indian influence. During the 17th and 18th centuries, the dominant influence was Tibetan. Newari artisans made bronze images of tantric aspects of the Buddha, which were exported to Tibetan monasteries—many "Tibetan" bronze sculptures were actually made in Nepal. Nepalese artists of the Malla period also created fantastic wood sculptures as architectural ornaments. Temple roof struts and window grilles were made of wood ornately carved with plant and animal forms.

Over the last two centuries, the crafts of bronze-casting and wood-carving have declined because of a lack of patronage. Foreign-funded restoration projects have recently given sculptors some business, and the demand created by tourism has encouraged the mass production of consumer-oriented crafts.

PAINTING

The earliest paintings to have survived in the Kathmandu Valley were painted on palm leaf manuscripts. A few examples have survived from as far back as the 10th century, but most are badly decayed. More common in Nepal today are Tibetan *thankas* (intricate scroll-paintings of deities) and *mandalas* (circles symbolizing the universe in Hindu and Buddhist art). During the medieval period, a distinctive Newari style of *thanka* developed, called a *paubha*. These were painted on coarser cloth and without the landscape background typical of traditional Tibetan *thankas*. Later paintings in Nepal were heavily influenced by the detailed miniatures of the Indian Mughal and Rajasthani styles.

MUSIC

Music in Nepal is a part of everyday life. The **gaine,** a caste of musician-storytellers, once wandered the hills, accompanying themselves on the *sarangi* (a four-stringed fiddle). Music of a traditional *panchai baja* (five-instrument) ensemble is often played for weddings, processions, and rituals. The women of most Indo-Nepalese castes are usually excluded from music-making, though they are allowed to sing in public during rice-planting and at the *teej*, an annual women's festival.

Several traditional styles of hill music still exist. Most popular is the *maadal*-based (double-sided drum held horizontally) *jhyaure* music of the Western Hills. The **Jyapu** farming caste developed an upbeat rhythmical style that uses numerous percussion instruments, including the *dhime* (a large two-sided drum), and woodwinds to accompany nasal singing. The *selo* style, developed by the Tamangs but shared by others, keeps rhythm with the *damphu* (a flat one-sided drum).

Music is vital to Hindu and Buddhist ritual. In traditional Newari communities, most young men complete a musical apprenticeship that enables them to participate in festival processions. Newari Buddhist priests chant ancient tantric verses as part of meditation exercises, and on sacred occasions ritual dancing accompanies these hymns. The music of the Sherpas derives much of its character from the ancient rituals of Tibetan Buddhism.

The continued presence and influence of Indian classical music in Nepal is a relic of the days when it was all the rage at the court of the Malla kings. The Rana prime ministers were such fervent patrons of Indian classical musicians that they banned Nepalese folk performers from their courts altogether.

DANCE

Nepalese dance, in both folk and classical styles, is usually based on dramatic retellings of sacred Buddhist and Hindu stories. The Newaris of the Kathmandu Valley are the chief exponents of **classical dance.** Newari performers enter a trance and become vessels possessed by the spirit of the deity. They gyrate and gesture and generally put on quite a show, dressed in elaborate costumes and ornately painted papier-mâché masks. On the tenth day of the Dasain festival (in Sept. or Oct.), the *nawa* dancers of Bhaktapur perform the vigorous dance-drama of the goddess Durga's victory over the buffalo demon.

Tibetan Buddhism also uses music and dance in festivals, ceremonies, and sacred rites. Performances often involve intricate hand gestures, ritual objects, and a number of unusual and symbolic musical instruments. **Cham** is a dance-drama specific to Tibetans and Bhotiyas, in which monks don masks and costumes to enact various Buddhist tales.

HOLIDAYS AND FESTIVALS

Hindu, Buddhist, and Jain festivals correspond to the lunar calendar, so the dates vary from year to year with respect to the Gregorian calendar. Secular holidays in Nepal follow the official Vikram Sambat calendar, the official calendar of Nepal, in which the year starts in mid-April of the Gregorian calendar. The dates given here are for 2004; the dates given are approximate.

DATE	HOLIDAYS AND FESTIVALS
January 1	**New Year's Day.** This traditional Nepali festival culminates in drunken revelry at midnight. Held annually.
January 11	**Prithvi Narayan Shah's Birthday** honors the late king who united Nepal.
February 2	**Lhosar,** the Tibetan New Year, is a three-day festival celebrated by Tibetans and Sherpas who flock to Boudhanath Stupa in Nepal and in Dharamsala in India.
March/April	**Macchendranath Rath Yatra,** a popular festival, during which a massive chariot holding Lokesvara, a patron deity of Kathmandu, is pulled through the streets of Nepal by hundreds of worshippers.
April 14	**New Year's Day** of the Vikram Sambat Year 2060, celebrated throughout Nepal.
April 11	**Ramanavami** celebrates Rama's birth, with readings of the *Ramayana* in Hindu temples all over India and Nepal.
May 16	**Buddha Jayanti** honors the Buddha's birthday and his attainment of *nirvana.*
July 7	**Birthday of King Gyanendra** is a national holiday commemorating the birth of Nepal's current ruler.
August 12	**Janai Purnima (Raksha Bandhan)** celebrates the Hindu sea god Varuna; the holiday is associated with brother and sisters.
September 9	**Indra Jatra,** when Kathmandu celebrates the capture of the King of Gods, Indra, in the Kathmandu Valley; processions and the annual blessing of the King of Nepal by the Living Goddess Kumari.
October 2-9	**Dussehra** (also known in some parts as **Navaratri**), a 9-10-day festival, celebrates the vanquishing of demons and honors Durga, the demon-slaying goddess. Known as **Dasain** in Nepal and **Durga Puja** in West Bengal.
October 25-27	**Tihar,** the Festival of Lights, an important holiday in Nepal.

ADDITIONAL RESOURCES

GENERAL

Nepal, by Jon Burbank (1994). A reference that touches upon the landscape, geography, history, culture, people, government, economy and religion of Nepal.

Culture Shock! Nepal, by Jon Burbank (1992). A guide to Nepali customs and etiquette aimed at those planning to live and work in Nepal.

Plants and People of Nepal, by Narayan P. Manandhar and Sanjay Manandhar (2002). A detailed examination of the ecology, landscape, and ethnicities of Nepal.

TREKKING

Life and Death on Mt. Everest: Sherpas and Himalayan Mountaineering, by Sherry B. Ortner (2001). An exploration of the world of the Sherpas and their mountaineering culture.

Into Thin Air: A Personal Account of the Mount Everest Disaster, by Jon Krakauer (1998). Intimate first-hand account of the May 1996 Everest expeditions, in which 12 died.

Trekking in the Nepal Himalaya, by Stan Armington (2001). The most comprehensive trekking guidebook available. It includes maps, day-by-day descriptions, and altitude charts for the most popular treks.

Trekking in Nepal, by Stephen Bezrucha (1997). Detailed route descriptions and a comprehensive section on planning and health concerns. Especially rich in historical, cultural, and biological commentary on Nepal's trekking routes.

HISTORY AND POLITICS

Massacre at the Palace: The Doomed Royal Dynasty of Nepal, by Jonathan Gregson (2002). One account of the murder of the royal family in 2001.

Nepal in the Nineties: Versions of the Past, Visions of the Future, edited by Michael Hutt. A collection of essays recounting the country's transition to democracy in 1990.

Politics in Nepal 1980-1990, by Rishikesh Shaha (1990). Once banned by the government, these essays look at recent political history.

Nepal: Profile of a Himalayan Kingdom, by Leo E. Rose and John T. Scholz (1980). Covers history, politics, culture, and economics.

RELIGION

Short Description of Gods, Goddesses, and Ritual Objects of Buddhism and Hinduism in Nepal. Published by the Handicraft Association of Nepal, this short but comprehensive book includes illustrations and is a valuable (and portable) reference. Available in Kathmandu bookstores.

LITERATURE

Arresting God in Kathmandu, by Samrat Upadhyay (2001). Written by one of the first Nepali authors writing in English to be published in the West, this is an anthology of short stories reflecting notions and traditions toward love and matrimony in modern Nepal.

Himalayan Voices: An Introduction to Modern Nepali Literature, by Michael Hutt (1991). The best English anthology of Nepali poetry and prose.

Nepali Visions, Nepali Dreams: The Poetry of Laxmiprasad Devkota, by Laxmi Prasad Devkota, photographs by David Rubin (1980). A good introduction to Nepal's most prominent modern poet.

WHAT'S SO SPECIAL ABOUT THE HIMALAYAS?

Trekking enthusiasts flock to the Himalayas, where Qomolangma (Mt. Everest or Sagarmatha), the tallest peak in the world, is located. (2003 marked the 50th anniversary of the first successful summiting of Qomolangma.) What makes the Himalayas so special? Why did the highest peak in the world develop here?

Population density along the foothills of the Himalayas is among the highest in the world. Every year, the monsoon moistens sediments that have been newly brought down from the high mountains, creating fertile ground for agriculture. However, people in Nepal and northern India are also living on the edge (figuratively). Massive landslides and flooding accompany the monsoon every year, while destructive earthquakes strike often, killing many thousands at a time. All these elements of nature are direct consequences of the active rising of the Himalayas, which began with the collision between the Indian and Asian continents about 50 million years ago.

This immense but slow process becomes evident if we begin our journey in South India. Here, one finds pervasive, parallel striations marking this plain of massive granite, and strewn boulders as large as the huts that huddle beside them. These are the footprints of an immense ice sheet that once covered much of southern India when this continent was near the South Pole. Farther north on the Deccan plateau, the red soil comes from weathered basalt that erupted over northwestern India when the continent passed by the Kerguelen islands in the southern Indian ocean about 65 million years ago. When India reached the Northern Hemisphere, its northern edge collided with Asia and the Himalayas were born.

As we continue the journey northward, the great influence of the Himalayas first appears on flood plains of the Brahmaputra and the Ganges rivers where the weight of the high mountains caused the northern Indian continent to bend down, making a natural trough to receive sediments carried by rivers rushing down from the Himalayas. Heading upstream toward the foothills, fine grain sill and sand gives way to gravel and boulders. During the monsoon season (June through August), flooding is nearly constant. Clean up and reconstruction can last well into October. It is common to see huge boulders (as large as some houses), which unlike the ones borne by ancient glacier ice at Hyderabad, were carried down by landslides and flood waters.

With abundant moisture, the northern edge of the Indian subcontinent has dense vegetation (and insects). Farm fields cover not only the lowlands but also many hill slopes in the form of terraces.

Nevertheless, some wooded areas, either old or secondary growth, still remain. For instance, the sal tree, a dense, strong hardwood, is common near the vast Chitwan National Park in southern Nepal. The sight and aroma of a blooming sal forest in April make a memorable spectacle. Meanwhile, because people must make do with what they have, locals also inefficiently use the sal trees for fuel.

Currently, the rate of shortening across the Himalayas is about 30 millimeters (just over an inch) a year. Our fingernails grow at about the same rate so the motion may appear to be insignificant. Geologically, however, this is a tremendous speed—1,500 kilometers (about 1,000 miles) in 50 million years! Moreover, the entire front of the Himalayas, over a length of 2,000 kilometers, moves at this rate. So this seemingly innocuous geologic process becomes evident even to a casual observer, and consequences of the process affect a vast, populous region.

What accounts for severe erosion in the Himalayas? The first factor is heavy rain that causes fast-running water in rivers. The towering mountains impede the trade wind, which is packed with moisture from the Indian Ocean, forcing most of the precipitation as monsoon rain along the southern slopes of the Himalayas. (On the flip side, vast, arid regions extend in the hinterland, including much of northern Tibet, the Taklimakan desert of western China and the Gobi desert of Mongolia.)

The second factor is cold temperature due to high elevation. During the hot summer months, people who have the means escape the heat of the Indian subcontinent by fleeing to resort towns at moderate elevations, such as Darjeeling and Dehra Dun. Because with every mile in elevation, air temperature drops by about 17 degrees Fahrenheit, so even in the summer, the snow line is just three miles above sea-level in the Himalayas. Regions above the snow line are the domain of glaciers. Glacial ice, being a solid, has an even greater power of erosion than running (liquid) water in rivers. All high peaks in the Himalayas, including the Qomolangma and others fabled by Tibetans and Hindus alike, are survivors of glacier erosion, attaining their stature at the expense of deep valleys beside them.

In short, the Himalayas are special because the interplay among earthquakes, mountain building, erosion, monsoon, and possibly global change of climate is strong, directly affecting a significant fraction of the world's population. There are few other places on our planet where the link between nature and humanity is as vividly evident, and in such a magnificent setting.

Wang-Ping Chen is a seismologist with a Ph.D. from the Massachusetts Institute of Technology in Cambridge, MA. He is a professor of geophysics at the University of Illinois.

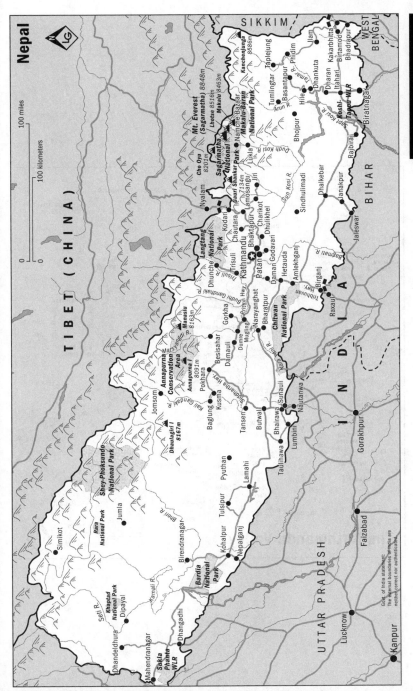

Nepal

NEPAL

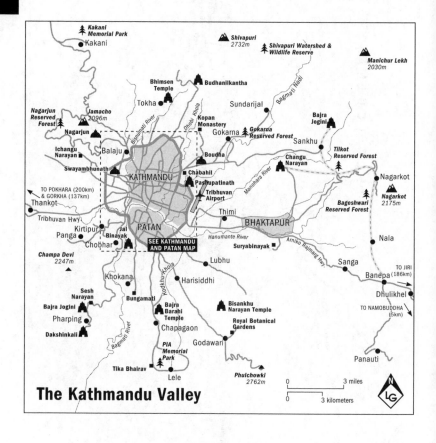

Kakani
Kakani Memorial Park

Shivapuri
2732m

Shivapuri Watershed &
Wildlife Reserve

Manichur Lekh
2030m

Bhimsen Temple

Budhanilkantha

Tokha

Sundarijal

Bagmati Nadi

Bajra Jogini

Nagarjun Reserved Forest

Jamacho
2096m

Kopan Monastery

Gokarna

Gokarna Reserved Forest

Sankhu

Tilkot Reserved Forest

Nagarjun

Bishnumati River

Dhobi Khola

Nagarkot

Ichangu Narayan

Balaju

Boudha

Changu Narayan

Swayambhunath

KATHMANDU

Chabahil

Pashupatinath

Manohara River

Nagarkot
2175m

TO POKHARA (200km)
& GORKHA (137km)

Tribhuvan Airport

Bageshwari Reserved Forest

Thankot

Thimi

BHAKTAPUR

Tribhuvan Hwy

Kirtipur

Panga

Jai Binayak

PATAN

Hanumante River

Arniko Rajmarg Hwy

Nala

Chobhar

Suryabinayak

Champa Devi
2247m

Lubhu

Sanga

TO JIRI
(186km)

Khokana

Harisiddhi

Banepa

Sesh Narayan

Bungamati

Bajra Barahi Temple

Bisankhu Narayan Temple

Dhulikhel

Bajra Jogini

TO NAMOBUDDHA
(5km)

Pharping

Chapagaon

Royal Botanical Gardens

Dakshinkali

Godawari

Bagmati River

Kodkhu Khola

PIA Memorial Park

Panauti

Tika Bhairav

Lele

Phulchowki
2762m

SEE KATHMANDU
AND PATAN MAP

0   3 miles

0   3 kilometers

N

The Kathmandu Valley

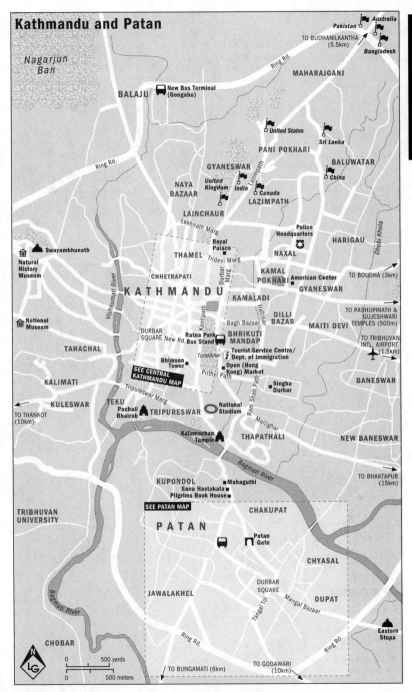

Kathmandu and Patan

NEPAL

Nagarjun Ban

Pakistan Australia
TO BUDHANILKANTHA
(5.5km) Bangladesh

New Bus Terminal
(Gongabu)

BALAJU

MAHARAJGANJ

Ring Rd.

United States

Ring Rd.

PANI POKHARI

Sri Lanka

GYANESWAR

BALUWATAR

NAYA
BAZAAR

United
Kingdom India

China

Canada

LAZIMPATH

LAINCHAUR

Lekhnath Marg

Swayambhunath

Police
Headquarters

Natural
History
Museum

THAMEL

Royal
Palace

Tridevi Marg

HARIGAU

Durbar Marg

NAXAL

CHHETRAPATI

KAMAL
POKHARI American Center

National
Museum

K A T H M A N D U

GYANESWAR

Vishnumati River

Kantipath

Hattisar

KAMALADI

KAMALADI

TO BOUDHA (3km)

Bagh Bazaar

DILLI
BAZAR

MAITI DEVI

TO PASHUPINATH &
GUJESHWARI
TEMPLES (500m)

DURBAR
SQUARE New Rd.

Ratna Park
Bus Stand

BHRIKUTI
MANDAP

TAHACHAL

Tundikhel

Tourist Service Centre/
Dept. of Immigration

TO TRIBHUVAN
INTL. AIRPORT
(1.5km)

Bhimsen
Tower

Prithvi Path

Open (Hong
Kong) Market

KALIMATI

SEE CENTRAL
KATHMANDU MAP

Singha
Durbar

BANESWAR

KULESWAR

Tripureswar Marg

TEKU

National
Stadium

Ram Shan Path

TO THANKOT
(10km)

Pachali
Bhairab TRIPURESWAR

Maitighar

Kalamochan
Temple THAPATHALI

NEW BANESWAR

Bagmati River

TO BHAKTAPUR
(15km)

KUPONDOL Mahaguthi

Sana Hastakala
Pilgrims Book House

TRIBHUVAN
UNIVERSITY

SEE PATAN MAP

CHAKUPAT

P A T A N

Patan
Gate

CHYASAL

Bagmati River

JAWALAKHEL

DURBAR
SQUARE

Tangal Tol

Mangal Bazaar

DUPAT

CHOBAR

Ring Rd.

Eastern
Stupa

Ring Rd.

0   500 yards

0   500 meters

TO BUNGAMATI (6km)

TO GODAWARI
(10km)

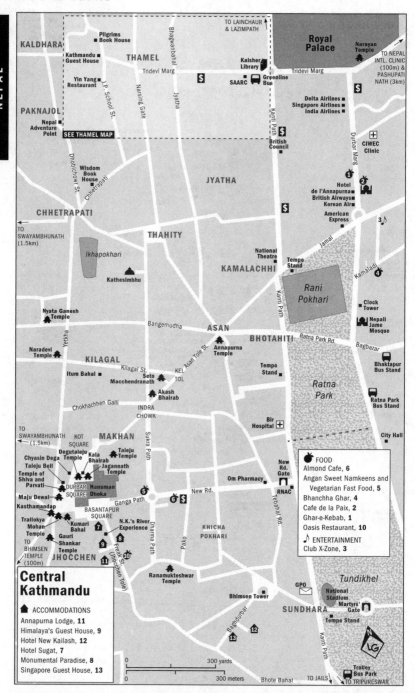

Central Kathmandu

🏠 ACCOMMODATIONS
Annapurna Lodge, 11
Himalaya's Guest House, 9
Hotel New Kailash, 12
Hotel Sugat, 7
Monumental Paradise, 8
Singapore Guest House, 13

🍴 FOOD
Almond Cafe, 6
Angan Sweet Namkeens and
    Vegetarian Fast Food, 5
Bhanchha Ghar, 4
Cafe de la Paix, 2
Ghar-e-Kebab, 1
Oasis Restaurant, 10

♪ ENTERTAINMENT
Club X-Zone, 3

NEPAL

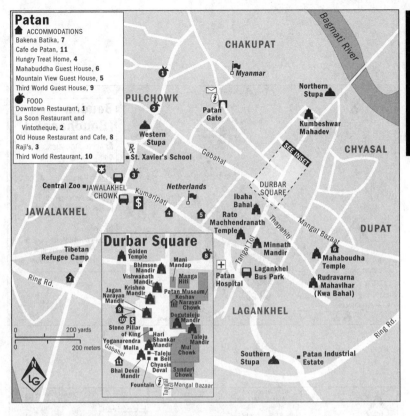

Patan

ACCOMMODATIONS
Bakena Batika, **7**
Cafe de Patan, **11**
Hungry Treat Home, **4**
Mahabuddha Guest House, **6**
Mountain View Guest House, **5**
Third World Guest House, **9**

FOOD
Downtown Restaurant, **1**
La Soon Restaurant and
   Vintotheque, **2**
Old House Restaurant and Cafe, **8**
Raji's, **3**
Third World Restaurant, **10**

Durbar Square

Golden Temple
Bhimsen Mandir
Vishwanath Mandir
Krishna Mandir
Jagan Narayan Mandir
Mani Mandap
Manga Hiti
Patan Museum
Keshav Narayan Chowk
Degutaleju Mandir
Stone Pillar of King Yoganarendra Malla
Hari Shankar Mandir
Taleju Bell
Chyasin Deval
Bhai Deval Mandir
Taleju Mandir
Mul Chowk
Sundari Chowk
Fountain

0   200 yards
0   200 meters

CHAKUPAT
Myanmar
Northern Stupa
Kumbeshwar Mahadev
CHYASAL
PULCHOWK
Patan Gate
Western Stupa
St. Xavier's School
Gabahal
SEE INSET
DURBAR SQUARE
Central Zoo
JAWALAKHEL CHOWK
Netherlands
Ibaha Bahal
Rato Machhendranath Temple
Mangal Bazaar
DUPAT
JAWALAKHEL
Kumaripati
Minnath Mandir
Mahaboudha Temple
Tibetan Refugee Camp
Patan Hospital
Lagankhel Bus Park
Rudravarna Mahavihar (Kwa Bahal)
Ring Rd.
Thapahiti
LAGANKHEL
Southern Stupa
Patan Industrial Estate
Ring Rd.
Tangal Tol
Mangal Bazaar
Bagmati River

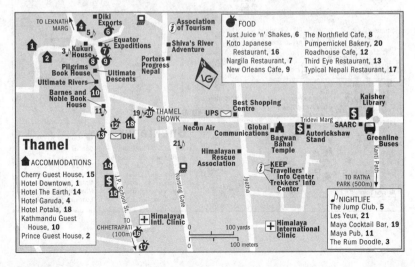

Thamel

ACCOMMODATIONS
Cherry Guest House, **15**
Hotel Downtown, **1**
Hotel The Earth, **14**
Hotel Garuda, **4**
Hotel Potala, **18**
Kathmandu Guest House, **10**
Prince Guest House, **2**

FOOD
Just Juice 'n' Shakes, **6**
Koto Japanese Restaurant, **16**
Nargila Restaurant, **7**
New Orleans Cafe, **9**
The Northfield Cafe, **8**
Pumpernickel Bakery, **20**
Roadhouse Cafe, **12**
Third Eye Restaurant, **13**
Typical Nepali Restaurant, **17**

NIGHTLIFE
The Jump Club, **5**
Les Yeux, **21**
Maya Cocktail Bar, **19**
Maya Pub, **11**
The Rum Doodle, **3**

TO LEKNATH MARG
Diki Exports
Association of Tourism
Shiva's River Adventure
Kukuri House
Equator Expeditions
Pilgrims Book House
Porters Progress Nepal
Ultimate Rivers
Ultimate Descents
Barnes and Noble Book House
THAMEL CHOWK
Best Shopping Centre
UPS
Kaisher Library
Necon Air
Global Communications
Tridevi Marg
SAARC
Bagwan Bahal Temple
Autorickshaw Stand
Greenline Buses
DHL
Himalayan Rescue Association
KEEP Travellers' Info Center
Trekkers' Info Center
Hotel The Earth
J.P. School St.
Narsing Gate
Jyatha
Kanti Path
TO RATNA PARK (500m)
TO CHHETRAPATI
Himalayan Intl. Clinic
Himalaya International Clinic

0   100 yards
0   100 meters

NEPAL

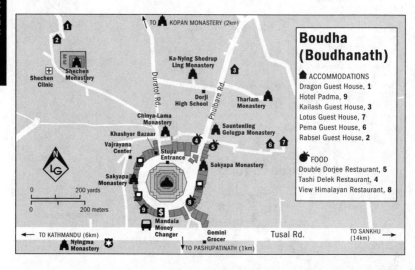

Boudha (Boudhanath)

🏠 ACCOMMODATIONS
Dragon Guest House, **1**
Hotel Padma, **9**
Kailash Guest House, **3**
Lotus Guest House, **7**
Pema Guest House, **6**
Rabsel Guest House, **2**

🍎 FOOD
Double Dorjee Restaurant, **5**
Tashi Delek Restaurant, **4**
View Himalayan Restaurant, **8**

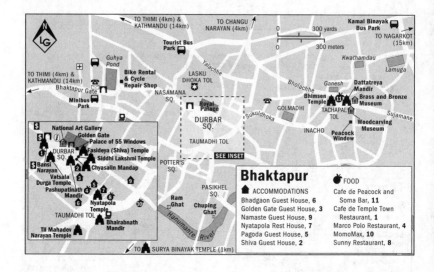

Bhaktapur

🏠 ACCOMMODATIONS
Bhadgaon Guest House, **6**
Golden Gate Guest House, **3**
Namaste Guest House, **9**
Nyatapola Rest House, **7**
Pagoda Guest House, **5**
Shiva Guest House, **2**

🍎 FOOD
Cafe de Peacock and
    Soma Bar, **11**
Cafe de Temple Town
    Restaurant, **1**
Marco Polo Restaurant, **4**
MomoMax, **10**
Sunny Restaurant, **8**

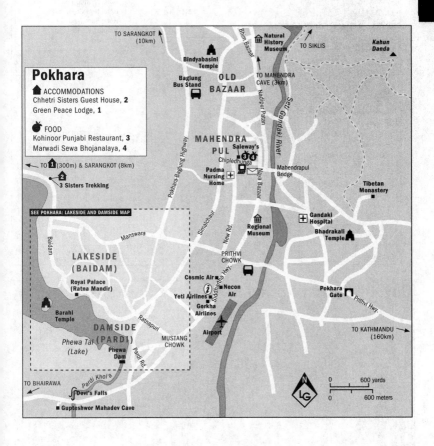

Pokhara

🏠 ACCOMMODATIONS
Chhetri Sisters Guest House, **2**
Green Peace Lodge, **1**

🍎 FOOD
Kohinoor Punjabi Restaurant, **3**
Marwadi Sewa Bhojanalaya, **4**

← TO ❶ (300m) & SARANGKOT (8km)

❷
3 Sisters Trekking

TO SARANGKOT (10km)

Bindyabasini Temple

Baglung Bus Stand

OLD BAZAAR

Bhim Bazaar

🏛 **Natural History Museum**

TO SIKLIS →

Kahun Danda ▲

TO MAHENDRA CAVE (3km)

Nadipur Patan

Seti Gandaki River

MAHENDRA PUL

Saleway's

Chipledhunga **3** **4**

Padma Nursing Home ✚

Naya Bazaar

Mahendrapul Bridge

Tibetan Monastery ■

SEE POKHARA: LAKESIDE AND DAMSIDE MAP

Pokhara-Baglung Highway

Manswara

Baidam

LAKESIDE (BAIDAM)

Royal Palace (Ratna Mandir) ■

Simalchaur

New Rd.

✚ **Gandaki Hospital**

🏛 **Regional Museum**

Bhadrakali Temple ▲

PRITHVI CHOWK

Siddhartha Hwy.

Cosmic Air ■

Yeti Airlines ■ 🅸 ■ **Necon Air**

Gorkha Airlines ■

Airport

Barahi Temple ▲

DAMSIDE (PARDI)

Ratnapuri

MUSTANG CHOWK

Phewa Tal (Lake)

Phewa Dam

Pardi Rd.

Pokhara Gate ⛩

Prithvi Hwy.

TO KATHMANDU (160km) →

TO BHAIRAWA ←

Pardi Khol

🏞 **Devi's Falls**

■ **Gupteshwor Mahadev Cave**

N

0   600 yards
0   600 meters

NEPAL

Pokhara: Lakeside and Damside

ACCOMMODATIONS

Butterfly Lodge, **5**
Camping Ground, **1**
Hotel Avocado, **10**
Hotel Fire on the Mountain, **16**
Hotel Gurung Resort, **22**
Hotel Himalayan, **21**
Hotel Jharna, **19**
Hotel New Cosmos, **20**
Hotel Snowland, **14**
Nature's Grace Lodge, **3**
Sacred Valley Inn, **17**

FOOD

Bistro Caroline, **13**
Boomerang, **11**
Little Tibetan Tea Garden, **2**
Monsoon, **18**
Moondance, **15**
Once Upon a Time, **6**
Tea Time, **9**

NIGHTLIFE

Club Amsterdam, **12**
Magic Club, **7**
Maya Pub, **8**
Old Blues Pub, **4**

Map labels: City Buses, Boat Hire, Equator Expeditions, Khampa Trek, Himalayan Encounters, ACAP and KEEP Offices, Sisne Rover Trekking, Barahi Medical Hall, Sunrise Paragliding, Ultimate Descents, UPS, MANSWARA, Manswara, MULTHOK, LAKESIDE (BAIDAM), Baidam, Boat Hire, City Buses, Royal Palace (Ratna Mandir), Barahi Temple, Phewa Tal (Lake), Green Line Buses, Encounter Destination, Sahid Chowk, Mountain Way Trekking, RATNAPURI, Simal Chaur, Ratnapuri, R. B. Chowk, Immigration Office, RNAC, DAMSIDE (PARDI), Buddha Air, Mustang Chowk, Phewa Dam, Pardi, Kholga, Manish Medical Hall, Birauta Chowk, TO DEVI'S FALLS & GUPTESHWOR MAHADEV CAVE

0   300 yards
0   300 meters

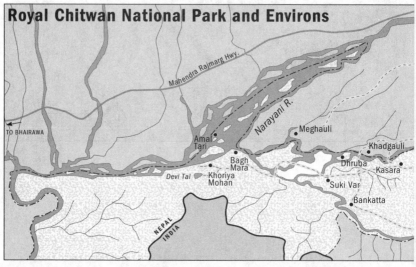

Royal Chitwan National Park and Environs

Map labels: Mahendra Rajmarg Hwy., Narayani R., Meghauli, Khadgauli, TO BHAIRAWA, Amal Tari, Dhruba, Kasara, Bagh Mara, Devi Tal, Khoriya Mohan, Suki Var, Bankatta, NEPAL, INDIA

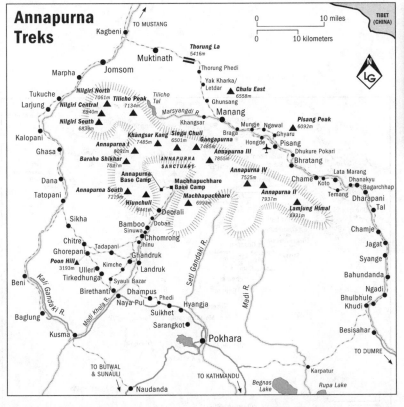

Annapurna Treks

TIBET (CHINA)

0   10 miles
0   10 kilometers

TO MUSTANG

Kagbeni

Thorung La 5416m

Muktinath

Thorung Phedi

Marpha   Jomsom

Yak Kharka/ Letdar

Chulu East 6558m

Tukuche

Nilgiri North 7061m   *Tilicho Peak* 7134m   Tilicho Tal

Ghunsang

Larjung   *Nilgiri Central* 6940m

Marsyangdi R.   Manang

Pisang Peak 6092m

Kalopani   *Nilgiri South* 6839m

Khangsar   Mungje Ngawal
Ghyaru

Ghasa   *Khangsar Kang* 6501m   *Singu Chuli* 7485m   *Gangapurna* 7485m

Braga   Hongde   Pisang

Annapurna I 8091m

Annapurna III 7855m   Dhukure Pokari

Dana   *Baraha Shikhar* 7647m

ANNAPURNA SANCTUARY   *Annapurna IV* 7525m   Bhratang

Tatopani   *Annapurna Base Camp*

Machhapuchhare Base Camp   Lata Marang   Dhanakyu

Sikha   *Annapurna South* 7219m   *Hiunchuli* 6441m   *Machhapuchhare* 6993m   Chame   Koto   Bagarchhap

Annapurna II 7937m   Temang   Dharapani

Deorali   *Lamjung Himal* 6931m   Tal

Bamboo   Doban

Sinuwa   Chhomrong

Chitre   Tadapani   Jhinu   Chamje

Ghorepani   Ghandruk   Jagat

Poon Hill 3193m   Kimche   Syange

Ulleri   Landruk   Bahundanda

Beni   Tirkhedhunga   Syauli Bazar   Ngadi

Birethanti   Dhampus   Bhulbhule
Khudi

Kali Gandaki R.   Naya-Pul   Phedi   Hyangja

Baglung   Modi Khola R.   Suikhet   Besisahar

Kusma   Sarangkot   Pokhara   TO DUMRE

TO BUTWAL & SUNAULI   TO KATHMANDU

Naudanda   Begnas Lake   Rupa Lake   Karpatur

Seti Gandaki R.   Madi R.

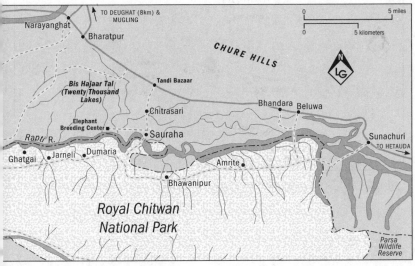

TO DEUGHAT (8km) & MUGLING

Narayanghat   Bharatpur

0   5 miles
0   5 kilometers

CHURE HILLS

Bis Hajaar Tal (Twenty Thousand Lakes)   Tandi Bazaar

Chitrasari   Bhandara   Beluwa

Elephant Breeding Center   Sauraha

Rapti R.   Sunachuri
TO HETAUDA

Ghatgai   Jarneli   Dumaria   Amrite

Bhawanipur

Royal Chitwan National Park

Parsa Wildlife Reserve

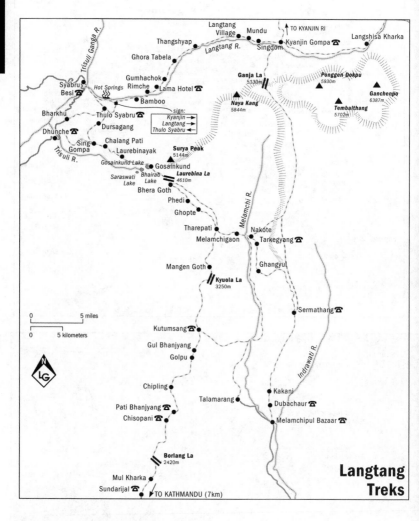

Langtang Treks

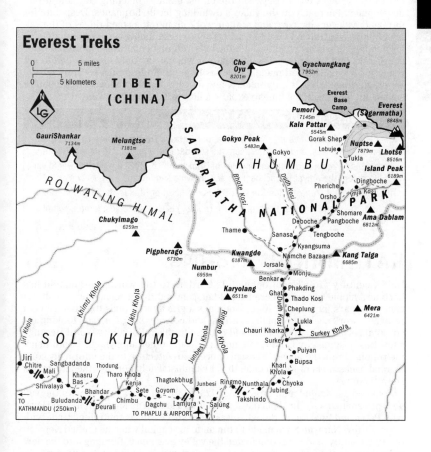

Everest Treks

0 — 5 miles
0 — 5 kilometers

N

TIBET
(CHINA)

Cho Oyu 8201m

Gyachungkang 7952m

Everest Base Camp

Everest (Sagarmatha) 8848m

GauriShankar 7134m

Melungtse 7181m

Pumori 7145m

Kala Pattar 5545m

Gokyo Peak 5483m

Gorak Shep

Nuptse 7879m

Lhotse 8516m

S A G A R M A T H A

Gokyo

Lobuje

Island Peak 6189m

K H U M B U

Tukla

ROLWALING HIMAL

Bhote Kosi

Dudh Kosi

Pheriche

Dingboche

Orsho

Imja Kosi

Chukyimago 6259m

N A T I O N A L   P A R K

Shomare

Ama Dablam 6812m

Pigpherago 6730m

Thame

Sanasa

Deboche

Pangboche

Numbur 6959m

Kwangde 6187m

Tengboche

Kyangsuma

Kang Taiga 6685m

Karyolang 6511m

Jorsale

Namche Bazaar

Benkar

Monju

Khimti Khola

Likhu Khola

Phakding

Thado Kosi

Mera 6421m

Ringmo Khola

Cheplung

Dudh Kosi

Lukla

Chauri Kharka

Surkey Khola

S O L U   K H U M B U

Jiri Khola

Surkey

Puiyan

Bupsa

Jiri
Chitre
Sangbadanda
Thodung
Khari Khola

Mali
Khasru Bas
Tharo Khola
Kenja
Thagtokbhug
Junbesi
Ringmo
Nunthala
Chyoka

Shivalaya
Bhandar
Sete
Goyom
Jubing

Buludanda
Chimbu
Dagchu
Lamjura
Salung
Takshindo

TO KATHMANDU (250km)
Deurali
Junbesi Khola

TO PHAPLU & AIRPORT

THE KATHMANDU VALLEY

Set against a backdrop of rolling green hills and the awe-inspiring peaks of the Himalayas, the Kathmandu Valley is the heart of Nepal and the focal point of any visit. Before Prithvi Narayan Shah's unifying conquest in 1768, the city-states of Kathmandu, Patan, and Bhaktapur vied for control of the valley. Today, Durbar (Palace) Squares, towering temples, *sindur*-covered shrines, and the unrivaled metal work of the indigenous Newari people provide glimpses of the former splendor of the valley's cities. Between the cities, exhaust-belching cars and urban development encroach on the valley's dwindling fertile farmlands. Desperate for farmland, villagers have expanded their work up into the steep ridges of the valley's hilltops—a truly remarkable sight. Trails with stunning views of both the valley and the Himalayas wind through the hills, offering countless opportunities for short treks and bike rides. Though many travelers stay only long enough to get ready for a trek, the Kathmandu Valley is home to no less than seven UNESCO World Heritage sites. It only takes a few days to see the valley's most popular sights, but those with the time to explore a little will be richly rewarded.

HIGHLIGHTS OF THE KATHMANDU VALLEY

Most cities in Nepal have a central square, but **Patan's Durbar Square** (p. 831), with its temples, palaces, and pavilions, sets the standard by which all others are judged.

The cobbled streets and restored temples of **Bhaktapur** (p. 843) are a window into valley life before the arrival of backpackers and brownie sundaes.

The monumental *stupa* at **Boudha** (p. 839) is the heart of Tibetan Buddhism in Nepal.

Far from the tourist crowds, **Pashupatinath** (p. 826) is Nepal's largest temple complex and holiest Hindu site.

KATHMANDU काठमाण्डु ☎ 01

Half a century after Nepal opened its borders to the world, Kathmandu has become a hippie haven, a mecca for trekkers, and a thriving cosmopolitan cultural center. Nepal's largest city, Kathmandu has a gravity that pulls together Tibetan refugees, work-seeking Nepalis, tourists, and cowboy *bodhisattvas* looking for spiritual salvation in linen shirts and endless hashish. For all its World Heritage sites, this bustling city is no fossil, nor is it just another anonymous South Asian metropolis. From the majestic design of urban architecture to the informally commercial backstreets of Kathmandu, the city unmistakably portrays the indigenous Newari culture.

Founded as Manju-Patan around AD 723, Kathmandu was not always the valley's pre-eminent city. In Malla days, when it was known as Kantipur, it stood level with Patan and Bhaktapur, though it was more successful at controlling trade with Tibet. Prithvi Narayan Shah made Kathmandu his capital when he unified Nepal in the 18th century, and it has dominated the valley ever since. Bursting into the new millennium as the fast-growing capital of a desperately poor country, present-day Kathmandu bears the imprint of rapid economic growth: an array of imported goods, arts, institutions, diplomatic missions and foreign aid agencies, and, of course, planeloads of tourists. Despite the optimism inspired by Nepal's movement toward democracy in the 1990s, Kathmandu faces plenty of problems. The city suffers from heavy pollution, chronic shortage of resources, and a crippling lack of infrastructure, as its government languishes under ineffective politicians.

For the tourist, Kathmandu is a fascinating city where pagodas crowd the traffic into narrow cobbled lanes and neighborhood boys kick soccer balls around dusty stone shrines. Unfortunately, many areas have been overcrowded with stores, endless Internet cafes, and aggressive vendors yelling at every tourist who walks by. Trekkers who come to Nepal for the tranquility of nature often feel frustrated by the oppressive tumult of downtown streetlife, but many admit that even the commercial bust grows on you. Even the most avid nature buffs often find themselves putting off expeditions to enjoy the tumult of Kathmandu's tourist life and the enchantment of its cultural character. In the end, the city is one where myth, religion, and history intertwine at every corner—time-worn shrines stand alongside ancient shops, while the buses careening through the streets bear murals of Shiva's joyful blue face.

■ INTERCITY TRANSPORTATION

FLIGHTS

If you're flying into Kathmandu from the east, try to sit on the right side of the plane to get a good view of the mountains. Flights land at **Tribhuvan International Airport** (☎4472256), 5km east of the center of town. Planes are small, seats are limited, and facilities are so basic that even slightly bad weather can delay flights. Bring a book. If you have a reasonable amount of baggage (i.e., just personal belongings, nothing to sell or give away), you can pass through the "Green Channel" almost instantly. If you find yourself in the "Red Channel," you will probably face extensive delay through searching. As you leave the airport, you will find yourself at the left edge of a large parking lot; to get to the bus stop, walk to the far right and follow the downhill road through the huge archway to Ring Rd., where you'll wait for a bus heading to your left. **Bus #1** goes to **Ratna Park** (30min., frequent, Rs8), but not all buses are numbered and not all buses heading this way go to Ratna Park, **so be sure to ask the driver or conductor.** Buses can be bewildering and excessively crowded, and they are often not equipped to carry travelers with lots of luggage. A better option is to take a **pre-paid taxi** from **Swoniga Services Pvt. Ltd.** (to Thamel Rs250; Freak St. Rs250), which can be arranged at a counter just before the airport exit or at a booth outside. The airport exit station accepts dollars, while the booth outside might not. With this taxi, a volunteer for the tourist sector of the government will climb in unasked in your taxi. Although his non-stop chatter will mostly consist of innocent promotion of Kathmandu's cultural offerings, this person might try to persuade you to choose a certain guest house (their own, or a friend or relative's). This is a common scam, so don't give in. Also, be aware that if someone carries your bag to the taxi, they will demand a tip.

Visas are issued upon arrival to anybody with a passport, photograph, and hard currency (payable only in US dollars, $30). There is a currency exchange booth next to the visa check-point. For more information, see **Visas: Nepal,** p. 11. There is a **departure tax** of Rs770 to South Asian countries and Rs1100 to all others.

INTERNATIONAL FLIGHTS. RNAC and **Indian Airlines,** Hattisar (☎4220757; fax 419649), east of Durbar Marg, fly to **India,** but flight schedules change frequently, so call around to find out current departure times. International flights to: **Bangalore** (2½hr., US$257); **Delhi** (1¼hr., US$142); **Mumbai** (2½hr., US$257). If you're under 30, both RNAC and Indian Airlines will give you a 25% discount on tickets to India purchased in Kathmandu.

DOMESTIC FLIGHTS. It is best to book domestic flights one week before and check for cancellations the evening before. Fares on domestic flights are virtually identical across airlines. **Royal Nepalese Airline Carrier (RNAC),** Kantipath (☎220757), at the corner of New Rd. and Kantipath. Open daily 9am-4pm during the winter, 9am-5pm summer. **Necon Air** has a branch near New Rd., just south of Nepal Bank of Ceylon (☎4480565; resv@necon.mos.com.np). To: **Bhadrapur** (45min., US$109); **Bhairawa** (1hr., US$79); **Biratnagar** (1hr., US$87); **Janakpur** (30min., US$67); **Jomsom** (1hr., US $50); **Lukla** (40min., US$93); **Nepalganj** (1hr., US$109); **Pokhara** (40 min., 4 per day, US$69). Mountain-viewing flights from Kathmandu cost US$109. The cost of these flights may be inflated if arranged through a travel agent. Other good airlines for domestic flights are **Buddha Airlines** (☎4437025; buddhaair@buddhaair.com) and **Cosmic Air** (☎4427150, soi@wlink.com.np), which has an office on Maharajyan.

BUSES

The cheapest way into town is by bus. To get to Thamel from Ratna Park, turn right after leaving the bus park, walk north along Durbar Marg all the way to the end, turn left, and walk three long blocks. The walk takes 20min. without heavy luggage. Most buses to destinations outside the Kathmandu Valley leave from the **New Bus Park** (also called **Gongabu**), Ring Rd., near Balaju. Almost all city buses make a stop at the New Bus Park. **Bus #23** from Ratna Park takes one of the most direct routes; it also stops along Kantipath, north of Rani Pokhari (30min., every 5min. 5am-8pm, Rs4-7). You can also take a **taxi** (Rs50-70 from Thamel, Rs60-80 from New Rd.). The departure bays are not labeled in English, but some of the ticket vendors speak English. Most buses that leave after noon are night buses—for these you should book 1-2 days in advance in season.

There are no express or deluxe distinctions here, and even tourist buses sometimes pick up locals along the way. Night buses are generally more expensive than morning buses.

PRIVATE BUSES. The **microbuses** are generally more comfortable and environmentally safe than their larger, clunkier alternatives. To: **Bhadrapur** (14hr., 4pm, Rs560); **Bhairawa** (every hr. 6:30am-8pm, Rs212-264); **Birganj** (8hr., every hr. 6am-7pm, Rs200-219); **Dharan** (12hr., 3-5pm, Rs440); **Gorkha** (6hr., every hr. 7-10am, Rs112); **Ilam** (20hr., 2pm, Rs630); **Janakpur** (11hr., 6 and 7am, Rs250/300); **Kakarbhitta** (16hr., 3-5pm, Rs135/260); **Pokhara** (7-8hr., frequent 6am-8:30pm, Rs190-260); **Tansen** and **Palpa** (11hr., 7am and 5:30pm, Rs216-408); **Tardi Bazaar** (frequent 7am-2:50pm, Rs137) for **Sauraha.**

GOVERNMENT BUSES. Sajha, the government bus corporation, is slightly cheaper and faster than private buses and runs mostly day buses; reserve two days in advance. To: **Bhairawa** (8hr., 7:15am and 7pm, Rs181-225); **Birganj** (8hr., 7am, Rs172); **Gorkha** (5hr., 6:30 and 7:45am, Rs94); **Lumbini** (9hr., 6:45am, Rs200); **Narayanghat** (4hr., 6:45am, Rs100); **Pokhara** (7hr., 7:30am and 7pm, Rs141-161); **Tansen** and **Palpa** (10hr., 7:30am, Rs200).

TOURIST BUSES. Tourist buses are slightly more expensive minibuses, with clear aisles and comfortable seats. Tickets for tourist buses to **Chitwan, Pokhara,** and **Nagarkot** can be booked through travel agencies in Thamel. Fares include a commission, but the stops are much more conveniently located on Kantipath at the intersection with Tridevi Marg. **Greenline Buses,** at the corner of Tridevi Marg and Kantipath, has A/C coaches to **Pokhara** (6hr., 8am, US$10) and **Chitwan** (4½ hr., 8am, US$8), with breakfast included. Tickets should be bought one day in advance. (☎4257544. Open daily 10am-6pm. AmEx/MC/V.)

✦ ORIENTATION

Kathmandu is a deceptively complex city to navigate. Streets are narrow, often look alike, and are almost never labeled. Most maps have agreed upon some standard street names, but in practice, these aren't useful for asking for directions. Locals (and police officers) will recognize names of shrines, squares, select hotels, and areas. However, they will usually not be able to give you directions based on a map or street names. The winding back roads of regions such as Thamel can be so confusing and circular that metered taxis can take you for quite a ride without you realizing it. The shrines of **Swayambhunath** and **Pashupatinath** are at the western and eastern edges of the city, respectively. Almost exactly halfway between them, the two main roads of **Kantipath** and **Durbar Marg** run parallel to each other, north to south. Kantipath has the post office and banks; Durbar Marg is home to many airline offices, trekking agencies, luxury hotels, and upscale restaurants, as well as the **Royal Palace** at its north end. Both of these streets are main arteries for vehicle traffic, and are hardly comfortable for pedestrians. Between the two streets farther south is the **Tundikhel** parade ground, around which Kantipath and Durbar Marg become one-way streets.

Kantipath and Durbar Marg divide Kathmandu into two halves—most of the older, more interesting parts of the city are to the west of Kantipath. The area east of Durbar Marg is mainly new neighborhoods. West of Kantipath, in the northwestern corner of town, is the year-round tourist carnival that is **Thamel.** Thamel can be the hardest part of the city to navigate because all of its narrow, nameless streets can look identical to a freshly arrived traveler. Thamel is joined to Kantipath and Durbar Marg by **Tridevi Marg.** Kathmandu's old center, **Durbar Square,** filled with magnificent architecture, is west of Kantipath, close to the banks of the **Vishnumati River. New Road,** built in 1934 out of the rubble left behind by an earthquake, runs east from Durbar Sq. to Kantipath. New Rd. is the city's commercial district, with rows of jewelers and electronics sellers. **Freak Street** runs north-south past the western end of New Rd., starting at the southern edge of **Basantapur Square.** A nameless narrow lane that sprouts northeast from Durbar Sq. used to be the main trading center. It cuts through **Indra Chowk,** one of Kathmandu's most interesting neighborhoods, and **Asan Tol,** the center of Kathmandu's main bazaar.

Tripureswar Marg is the biggest road in the southern half of town, running east-west and leading to the **Patan Bridge.** The capital's twin city, Patan, is across the **Bagmati River,** the southern limit of Kathmandu. **Ring Road** encircles Kathmandu and Patan, connecting them with the suburbs that have grown up around them.

⊡ LOCAL TRANSPORTATION

LOCAL BUSES

By far the cheapest means of getting around the Kathmandu Valley, the bus ensures that you rub shoulders with locals—just when you thought another wailing child couldn't possibly squeeze in, five more people and seven roosters climb on board. Though often overcrowded and maddeningly slow, Kathmandu buses do work. Since the route numbers are almost always only painted on in Nepalese numerals, it is a good idea to learn them when attempting to ride on a local bus. Buses will stop just about anywhere, though if the bus is ridiculously full, the driver might not bother. **Always confirm that the bus is going to your destination.** The valley bus station is known as **Ratna Park** (named for the park across the street); Nepalis also call it *purano* (old) bus park. Listen for bus drivers shouting *"ranapa ranapa"* to find a bus heading toward Ratna Park. Bus #7 (to Bhaktapur) leaves from **Bagh Bazaar,** one block north of the old bus park, still across the street from the natural park.

What the local bus system lacks in speed and efficiency it certainly makes up for in frequency. There will almost always be a bus leaving soon for your destination. Buses generally leave as soon as they're full.

#	DESTINATION	LENGTH	COST	#	DESTINATION	LENGTH	COST
1	Tribhuvan Airport	40min.	Rs6	12	Dhulikhel	2hr.	Rs20
2	Boudha (Boudhanath)	40min.	Rs6	14	Jawlakhel and Lagankhel	20min.	Rs6
2	Pashupatinath	30min.	Rs6	19	Swayambhu	45min.	Rs6
4	Sankhu	2hr.	Rs20	21	Kirtipur	1hr.	Rs6
5	Budhanilkantha	45min.	Rs6	22	Dakshinkali	1½hr.	Rs15
7	Bhaktapur	45min.	Rs10	23	New Bus Park	30min.	Rs6
9	Old Thimi	30min.	Rs7	23	Balaju	30min.	Rs6
9	Bahaka Bazaar	1hr.	Rs7	26	Patan	30min.	Rs6

TAXIS AND RICKSHAWS

Shiny new red, green, or yellow **taxis** are all metered, as are the older ones (identifiable by their black license plates). The meters typically start at Rs10 and increase Rs15 per kilometer. After 9pm rates should only go up to Rs20 per kilometer, but drivers are more likely to rip you off after hours. You might want to negotiate a price beforehand even with metered taxis, as long as you are willing to bargain hard and if there are several other taxis in site. Trips within the city should never cost more than Rs150: Rani Pokhari to Swayambhu or Pashupatinath costs around Rs75; shorter trips like Thamel to New Rd. will cost around Rs40. A 6hr. sight-seeing tour around the valley should cost about Rs1200, but be sure to negotiate the price beforehand and pay only when the tour is completed. Taxis queue on Tridevi Marg near the entrance to Thamel. **Auto-rickshaws** and **cycle-rickshaws** can be cheaper than taxis, but only if you bargain hard with often-aggressive drivers. In rush-hour traffic on crowded, narrow streets like those in Thamel, cycle-rickshaws are the fastest mode of transport. Fully aware of this advantage, cycle-rickshaws often charge more during these occasions. However, rickshaws are not allowed on some major streets (e.g. Durbar Marg), and are only useful for short trips in the western part of the city.

TEMPOS

Tempos, either sturdier versions of auto-rickshaws or minibuses, can be flagged down anywhere along their routes; to request a stop, bang on the metal ceiling and honk like a mongoose. Tempos use the same route numbers as buses but leave from different places. Some tempos are four-seaters, into which usually six will cram. Some eight-seaters will be made to fit 12. The motors are very weak, so expect to go up hills at a painfully slow place. Tempos leave from **Sundhara,** just outside the GPO: #2 to **Boudha** via **Pashupatinath** (30min., Rs10). Others depart from just north of **Rani Pokhari:** #5 to **Budhanilkantha** via **Lazimpath** (45min., Rs9); #23 to **Balaju** (40min., Rs6); #14 **Lagankhel** via **Jawalakhel** to **Patan** (20 min., Rs8).

BICYCLES AND MOTORCYCLES

Bicycles and motorcycles can be rented in Thamel, especially around Thamel Chowk and Chhetrapati. They are often a quicker way to get around the city, but be prepared to cycle within the flow of traffic. Mountain bikes (Rs400-600 per day) are better for trips outside the city; heavier, bell-equipped one-speeders (Rs100 per day) are fine for the city. Motorcycles Rs400 per day, not including a 10% tax.

☑ PRACTICAL INFORMATION

TOURIST AND FINANCIAL SERVICES

Tourist Office: The Nepal Tourism Board's main office, the **Tourist Service Center,** Bhrikuti Mandap (☎4256909; www.welcomenepal.com), south of Ratna Bus Park, just east of Durbar Marg. The office provides free brochures and information about the country. Open Su-F 9am-5pm. They also have an office at the **airport** (☎4470537), open daily 9am-5pm. The **Thamel Tourism Development Committee,** (☎4429750; ttdc@mail.com.np), is dedicated to improving the Thamel area and offers limited volunteer opportunities. Open Su-F 9am-4pm.

Trekking Information: Himalayan Rescue Association (HRA), P.O. Box 4944 (☎4440292; hra@mail.com.np). In Thamel Mall at Jyatha-Thamel, just south of Kilroy's. Focuses on mountain safety, providing info on altitude sickness and free safety talks in the spring and fall. If 4 people or more sign up, talks Su-F 2pm. HRA also runs 2 clinics in Manang (Annapurna circuit) and Pheriche (Everest trek); they appreciate donations of medicine and money. Open Su-F 10am-4pm. **Kathmandu Environmental Education Project (KEEP),** P.O. Box 9178 (☎4259567; www.keepnepal.org), Thamel Mall, in the same complex as HRA. Has slide show presentations on low-impact trekking twice a week. Both offices keep log books for trekkers to record their experiences and to read about those of their predecessors. They also have informative bulletin boards posted with trekking tips and up-to-date info. Fill out an embassy registration form at one of these offices (or at your embassy) before you go trekking. Open Su-F 10am-5pm.

Budget Travel: Choosing between the hundreds of budget travel associations located around Thamel, Durbar Marg, and Freak St. can be extremely challenging. Unfortunately, rip-offs are common and it is difficult to judge the companies for reliability. Make sure to shop around at multiple places for the same package. Feel free to use competitors' prices to bargain down the price of a trip. Do not purchase plane tickets from travel agents. **For plane tickets, go directly to the airline offices,** as travel agencies charge commission on flights, and your fee could be heavily inflated (see **Intercity Transportation,** p. 807). Most major airlines have offices on Durbar Marg, just south of the Hotel de l'Annapurna, or in Hattiswar, the area just east of Durbar Marg. For bus tickets to Pokhara and Chitwan, go directly to **Greenline Buses,** on the corner of Tridevi Marg and Kantipath. For bus tickets to Nagarkot or bus and train tickets to major Indian cities, your best bet is shopping among Thamel's small travel agencies. Get signed receipts for everything and maintain your skepticism. For more high-end trips try the well-established and more luxury-oriented agencies on Durbar Marg: **Annapurna Travels, Everest Express,** and **Yeti Travels.**

Adventure Travel: The following agencies are relatively well-established in the business. **Everest Trekking,** P.O. Box 19170, Thamel (☎4226358; www.ecotour.com.np), 150m south of Kathmandu Guest House. **Himalayan Journeys, Ltd.,** P.O. Box 989, on Kantipath (☎4226138 or 4226139; hjtrek@mos.com.np). **Snow Leopard Trek, Ltd.,** P.O. Box 1811, Naxal (☎4434619; www.snowleopardtreks.biz).

Immigration Office: The **Department of Immigration** (☎4222453 or 4223590; www.immi.gov.np) has recently moved to Bhrikuti Mandap, next to the Tourist Service Center. This is the place to get your **visa extended** or to purchase a **trekking permit.** Trekking permits can be bought in the white bldg. opposite the Dept. of Immigration just outside the Tourist Center's compound. Permits are no longer required for the major areas of Everest, Annapurna, Langtang, or Rara. For: **Humla** (US$90 for the 1st week, US$15 per day thereafter); **Lower Dolpa** and **Kanchenjunga** (US$10 per week for the 1st month; US$20 per week thereafter); **Manaslu** (US$90 per week Sept.-Nov.; US$75 for treks Dec.-Aug.); **Upper Mustang** and **Upper Dolpa** (US$700 for the 1st 10 days, US$70 per day thereafter). Treks to Dolpa, Kanchenjunga, Makalu, and Upper Mustang must be organized by a registered trekking agency. Visa extensions and trekking permits require a passport and two photos. Late fees for visa extensions is US$2 per day for the first 30 days, US$3 for the next 60 days, US$5 for each day thereafter. Tourist visas may be extended for up to 120 days upon request. Visa extension without reentry privileges US$30, with multiple reentries US$80. Allow at least 2hr. for processing. Apply M-F 9am-3pm (9am-2pm in winter); pickup before 5pm (4pm in winter). There is an additional fee of Rs1000 for treks through a national park or conservation area (Rs2000 for Kanchenjunga and Annapurna). To avoid hassles and often doubled prices during your trek, pay these entry fees in advance at the **Entry Fee Collection Centre** (☎4222406), in the basement of the Himalayan Bank Bldg., by Fire and Ice. Open M-F 9am-4pm, Su 9am-2pm.

Currency Exchange: Exchange Centers are plentiful in Thamel, and some don't charge a commission for exchanging traveler's checks. The **Himalayan Bank** (☎4250201) has a foreign exchange booth conveniently located on Kantipath, just south of the intersection at Tridevi Marg, but it only exchanges US dollars. Commission on traveler's checks Rs150 or 0.75%. **Moneygram** services are also available here for quick money transfers. Open M-F 8am-8pm. **Nepal Bank of Ceylon Ltd.,** New Rd. (☎4231713), takes a 1% commission on traveler's checks. Open M-F 9:30am-5pm (limited service 5pm-8pm) and Sa-Su 10am-2pm. Rs100 for currency exchange. **Standard Chartered Bank Nepal Ltd.,** Kantipath (☎4228474), just south of the intersection at Tridevi Marg. Sells AmEx traveler's checks and gives cash advances on MC and Visa. Commission on traveler's checks Rs200 or 1.5%. Rs 100 for currency exchange. Open 9:30am-3:30pm. **Western Union,** Durbar Marg (☎4223940; fax 4222966), in Annapurna Travel and Tours, on the east side of the street. Money can be wired here in 1min. Open daily 9am-1pm, 1:45-5pm. **American Express**: **Yeti Travels,** Hotel Mayalu, Jamal, P.O. Box 76 (☎4226172; fax 4226152). Sells traveler's checks with 1.5% commission. Open Su-F 10am-1pm and 2-5pm.

EMBASSIES

Australia, Bansbari (☎4371678; fax 4371533), just past Ring Rd, in Maharajgunj. Open M-F 8:30am-12:30pm, 1:30-4pm.

Bangladesh, on Chakrapath (☎4372843; fax 4373265), near Hotel Karnali, in Maharajgunj. 2 photos required for a 15-day tourist/transit visa, US$100. Open M-F 9:30am-5pm. Apply for a visa M-F 9:30am-noon, and pick it up the same day between 4:30 and 5pm or the next day 9:30am-noon depending on how busy they are.

Canada, Lazimpath (☎4415389; fax 4410422), down the lane opposite Navin Books stationery shop. Open M-F 8:30am-4:30pm.

China, Baluwatar (☎4411740, visa services ☎4419053). Visas US$30; bring your passport and 1 photo. Allow 7 days for processing. Visas to **Tibet** are available only to organized groups of 5 or more and obtainable only through a travel agency (see **Surrounding Countries,** p. 11). The border to Tibet may, however, be closed temporarily. Check before making extensive plans. Open M-F 9am-noon and 3-5pm. Visa dept. open M, W, F 9:30-11am.

India, Lainchaur (☎4410900; fax 4413132). Walk north up Lazimpath and veer left before the Hotel Ambassador. 15-day transit visas require 1 photo, a confirmed ticket, and Rs800 (Rs2350 for US citizens) and can be picked up the same day from 4:30-5:15pm. 6-month tourist visas require 1 photo and Rs3350 (Rs4900 for US citizens), and you must wait to be cleared by your home embassy, which can take up to a week. Apply for visas M-F 9:30am-noon. The rest of the embassy is open M-F 9am-5:30pm.

Myanmar (Burma), Chakupat, Patan (☎5524788; fax 5521788), near Patan Gate. 1-month tourist visa requires 4 photos and US$20. Apply M-F 9:30am-noon and 1-4pm; visas ready in 4-5 days. In case of emergencies, visas can be rushed in 24hr. Rush service may require an additional fee.

Sri Lanka, Baluwatar (☎ 4413623; fax 4419289). Visas require 2 photos. Australian citizens US$30, UK US$54, US US$190, but some nationalities do not require visas for travel in Sri Lanka. Allow 2 days for processing. Apply M-F 10am-noon. The rest of the office is open M-F 10am-5pm.

UK, Lainchaur (☎ 4411590; fax 411789). Visas to **Malaysia** are administered through the UK's consular services (☎ 410583). A 3-month tourist visa (Rs2300) requires 2 photos, traveler's checks, plane ticket, and occasionally a hotel reservation slip. Apply M and W 2-3pm; processing takes 2 days. Many nationalities do not require visas for travel to Malaysia. Open M-Th 8:15am-12:30pm, 1:30-5pm.

US, Pani Pokhari, Maharajgunj (☎ 4411179 or 4412718; fax 4419963). Open M-F 8am-5pm. For emergencies after hours involving US citizens: ☎ 4410531.

LOCAL SERVICES

Bookstores: Pilgrims Book House, Thamel (☎ 4424942 or 4436769, www.pilgrims-books.com). Just north of the Kathmandu Guest House. Browsing here is one of the joys of being in Kathmandu. An enormous place that not only has every book you never knew you wanted, but also CDs, local handicrafts, classical music concerts, yoga classes, and limited mail services with 10% delivery surcharge. Also check out the **Feed 'n' Read Restaurant and Bar** with Indian, Nepali, and Tibetan foods. Open daily 8am-10pm. AmEx/D/JCB/MC/V. A good choice for cheaper, mostly used English-language books is **Wisdom Book House** (☎ 4260663), Thamel. Everything from outdated travel guides to romance novels and 19th-century classics. Open daily 9am-8pm.

Market: At **Asan Tol,** in front of the Annapurna Temple, locals sell fruits, vegetables, spices, meats, and random commodities on blankets on the ground. Extremely crowded with Nepalis in the mornings, though rarely frequented by tourists (see p. 822). **Open Market** (also called Hong Kong Market), south of Ratna bus park, is a large tarpaulin congregation of food, clothing, and other products. This market is not targeted towards tourists. Snacks, toiletries, and trekking supplies are at the **Best Shopping Centre,** where Tridevi Marg narrows into Thamel. Open Su-F 8am-8pm, Sa 10am-8pm, or in the million retail stores around Thamel.

Laundry Service: Almost all guest houses have laundry service, but independent establishments sometimes charge less. All do pricing by item. **The 1 Hour Laundry,** next door to the Khukuri House, north of the Kathmandu Guest House, also does dry cleaning and has the quickest service around. Prices range from the pricey one-hour "express" service (slacks Rs55, shirts Rs50) to one- (Rs25, Rs25) and two-day service (Rs20, Rs20). Open daily 8am-8pm.

EMERGENCY AND COMMUNICATIONS

Emergency: Ambulance (☎ 4244121 or 4230213). **CIWEC** (☎ 4228531) is a clinic on Durbar Marg that has 24hr. emergency service. Another option is the **Himalaya International Clinic** in Thamel. Emergency house calls (☎ 4223197 or 4223818).

Police: The **Tourist Police** handles petty thefts and rip-offs and can be reached at any of the city's tourist offices: Bhrikuti Mandap (☎ 4247041 or 4256231), Tribhuvan Airport (☎ 4470537), and Thamel (☎ 4429750). Contact the **city police** (☎ 4226999) for more serious issues or emergencies (☎ 100).

Pharmacy: Om Pharmacy, New Rd. (☎ 4222644). Near RNAC. Open daily 8am-8pm. Many common prescription medicines can be bought over-the-counter at the street-front clinics around Bir Hospital on Kantipath and Thamel. **Himalaya International Clinic** has a pharmacy outside (☎ 4225455, fastwhn@wlink.com.np).

Hospital/Medical Services: Kathmandu has numerous reliable clinics geared toward Westerners. In case of illness, visit one of these first. **CIWEC Clinic** (☎ 4228531 or 4241732), off Durbar Marg, behind the Yak and Yeti sign, to the right. US$45 per consultation, US$65 after hours or on weekends. Open M-F 9am-noon and 1-4pm. On call

FROM THE ROAD

DOWNTOWN THAMEL: THE NEWEST FREAK OF KATHMANDU

Thamel, Kathmandu, over the years, has come to replace the aptly named "Freak Street" as the center of a tourism circus. In its prime, Freak Street was populated mainly by marijuana-smoking flower children, who ate simply and meditated in the dusty streets. However, the newest generation of Western travelers to Nepal has, in line with the times, acquired a different reputation within Kathmandu. They are assumed to be hyper-capitalists, on an unrelenting search for gratutous vehicle rides, imitation brand commodities, 'Nepali' memorabilia, and US dollars to throw into the air. Thamel has become so crowded with touts and hawkers that it can be difficult to find legitmate establishments within the simple four roads of the area. Shops alternate between faceless travel agencies, elaborate collections of burned CDs, Europeanstyle bakeries, and places pushing imitation brand-name trekking gear.

With the number of tourists far exceeding locals in the J.P. School Street area, foreigners might expect to go unnoticed. Unfortunately, the words "taxi," "rickshaw," "hashish," and "rupees," among others, follow travelers everywhere they go in an unending and dissonant chorus.

-Natalia Truszkowska, 2004

24hr. MC/V. **Nepal International Clinic** (☎4435357; fax 434713), opposite the Royal Palace, 3min. east of the main gates, down a lane to the right. Consultation US$35, after hours US$50. Open Su-F 9am-1pm and 2-5pm. On call 24hr. for emergencies. AmEx/MC/V. **Himalaya International Clinic,** Jyatha (☎4225455; fax 4226980). Consultations US$20, house calls US$40. Open daily 9am-5pm. **Patan Hospital,** Lagankhel, Patan (☎5522266 or 5522295). Has a better reputation than the government-run **Bir Hospital,** Kantipath (☎5221119, emergency ☎6223807), north of New Rd. **Himalayan International Clinic,** Chhetrapati-Thamel (☎4225455). 150m south of Kathmandu Guest House on the east side of the street. Consultations US$25, house calls US$50.

Internet: Internet cafes are everywhere around Thamel and Durbar Sq. Look for the ones advertising broadband connections. **Easy Link Cybercafe** (☎4416239), in Thamel. Walk north on Narsing Gate and take a left at the small Bhagwati temple. Has fast connections, A/C, low rates, and offers 10 free min. after your first visit. Rs40 per hr.

Post Office: General Post Office (GPO) (☎4227499), near Bhimsen Tower, entrance just off Kantipath, can be a bewildering experience. The post office is largely outdoors, with long lines and small windows labelled only in Nepali. Stamps sold Su-F 8am-7pm, Sa 11am-3pm. **Express Mail Service (EMS),** at the GPO, delivers within 3-7 days to pretty much anywhere in the world, but it's of dubious reliability. Open M-F 10:15am-3pm. To send a package abroad, visit the **Foreign Parcel Office,** around the corner on Kantipath, where it will be checked by customs. Open M-F 9:15am-2pm; in winter 9:15am-1:30pm. More reliable mail services are provided by the **FedEx** office on Kantipath (☎4269248; fax 4269249). Open daily 9am-7pm. You can also use **DHL** International, on JP School Rd. across from the Ying Yang Restaurant (☎4496248, 4496427, or 4495861; fax 4220215). Open daily 9am-7pm. A final option is **UPS,** along Tridevi Marg next to the Best Shopping Center (☎4780851 or 4780852; fax 4780535; nac@mos.com.np). Open daily 9:30am-6:30pm.

🏠 ACCOMMODATIONS

The majority of budget travelers head to Thamel, where increased competition has led to a general standardization of prices for similar accommodations. The prices listed are for in-season rates and do not include the 10% government tax. Rates are usually negotiable. **Beware of touts:** don't let anyone lead you to his friend's hotel; a hefty commission will appear on your bill.

Freak Street is Kathmandu's original tourist district. Ever since it hit its peak back in the 70s, Freak St. has been cheaper, less hectic, and less populated than

Thamel; most of its hotels have been around for almost 25 years, growing old and musty as lodges in Thamel steal all their business. Located just south of New Rd., **Sundhara** is popular with Indian tourists; its accommodations are less conveniently located and pricier than the bargains found in Thamel, but they are a good option if you want to "find" the city before it finds you. The places below, unless otherwise noted, have hot water, seat toilets, laundry service, luggage storage, and a noon check-out, but no towels or toilet paper. Many places list room rates in the more stable US dollar, but you can pay in rupees; the manager will do a more or less arbitrary conversion using the going exchange rate of the day.

THAMEL

Kathmandu Guest House (☎4413632; www.kathmanduguesthouse.com). Built out of a former Rana Palace, this guest house has stunning architecture and is excessively famous in Nepal. The old wing is darker but has the best access to the guest house's communication center, swanky lobby with satellite TV, ticket booking, bike rental, and barber shop. The new wing has beautifully furnished rooms overlooking a lush garden. With its own gate, grounds, and an extensive driveway, the KGH is exceptionally safe and quiet. Reservations recommended. Old wing: singles with common bath US$2-8; doubles US$4-8; with bath US$12. New wing: singles US$50; doubles US$60. 10% discount for stays of over 1 wk. and for HI/IYH members. AmEx/MC/V. ❷

Hotel Garuda (☎4416340 or 4414766; www.garuda-hotel.com), on the right side of JP School St. following a left curve, north of Kathmandu Guest House. Five-star service and 34 spotless rooms make Garuda popular with Himalayan expeditions. Has wall-to-wall carpeting and one of the few rooftop "gardens" in Thamel that is actually a garden. Attached baths with towels and toilet paper. Free luggage storage and safe deposit. Budget rooms (no phone or TV; singles US$10; doubles US$15), standard (phone, no TV; singles US$15; doubles US$20), hi-standard (phone and TV; singles US$25; doubles US$30), A/C room with heating and cooling (singles US$35; doubles US$40). Prices do not include 12.2% tax. 25% discount off-season. AmEx/MC/V. ❹

Hotel Downtown, Satghumti-Thamel (☎4430471; www.hoteldowntown-nepal.com), opposite the Prince Guest House, look for the small red sign. Spacious rooms and immaculate bathrooms somewhat sheltered from the noise of central Thamel. Generous single beds big enough to sleep 2. Common or attached bath. Reception closes 11pm, but you can ring the bell to get back in. Budget rooms: singles US$6; doubles US$10. Deluxe rooms include cordless telephone, small TV, nicer furniture, and sunny rooftop location. Deluxe singles US$12; doubles US$20. ❸

Hotel Potala (☎4419159; fax 4416680), opposite K.C.'s, at the center of Thamel; look for the big yellow smiley face. Well-managed by a friendly Tibetan family, Potala has comfortable rooms with common baths. Though its low prices make it one of the best budget places in Thamel, its central location next to several bars makes it a bit noisy at night. All day, backpackers congregate around the TV in the lobby. Singles Rs125; doubles Rs175, with fans Rs250. ❶

Hotel Vaishali, Thamel, on an alley between JP School St. and Narsing Gate St. (☎4414510; www.vaishalihotel.com). Luxuriate in elegantly furnished guest rooms at this centrally located hotel. Isolated from the rest of Thamel by guarded gate. Includes large outdoor swimming pool, a fitness center, and doting staff. Singles US$90; doubles US$110. Executive Suite US$145; Vaishali Suite US$160. Extra bed US$25. AmEx/MC/V. ❺

Cherry Guest House, 300m south of Kathmandu Guest House in JP School St. (☎4250675). Clean, with a great location and fewer crowds than other similar hostels. All rooms have private baths. Singles Rs700; doubles Rs400. ❹

Hotel The Earth, Chhetrapati-Thamel (☎4260312; fax 4260230), south of Kathmandu Guest House, on the west side of the street. Entrance through clothing store. Dark hallways, but bright, clean, and simply furnished rooms at economical prices. Singles Rs200, with bath Rs350; doubles Rs300, with bath and additional furniture Rs500. Negotiable deals for students and volunteers; 10% discount for stays over 1 week. ❷

Prince Guest House, Satghumti-Thamel (☎4414456; princeguesthouse@hotmail.com). North of Kathmandu Guest House—turn left at the bend in the road by The Jump Club and walk 200m on your left. Pink n' purple decor and wall-to-wall carpeting in clean but small rooms with fans, phones, and attached baths. Rooftop garden and the delicious attached **Delima Garden Cafe**. Singles US$7, US$6 off-season; doubles US$10-15. ❸

FREAK STREET

Himalaya's Guest House, Basantapur, Jhochhen (☎4246555; himalgst@hotmail.com). Take the 1st right off Freak St. as you walk from Basantapur Sq. Bright, clean rooms all have TV and fan. Attached baths with hot showers. Managed by a friendly, accommodating family. Reception closes at 10pm, but ring the bell if you arrive later. Singles Rs200; doubles Rs300-500. Higher floors cost more. ❷

Monumental Paradise, Freak St. (☎4240876; www.monumentalparadise.com), 50m from Basantapur Sq., on the east side of the street. Ambitious name, but this new kid on the block lives up to its title with large, spotless rooms and friendly service. Wall-to-wall carpets, tinted windows, hot showers, and seat toilets in all rooms. Somewhat upscale for Freak St., but the dorms are a good deal. Dorms Rs150; singles Rs250; doubles Rs300-400. One special room is perched above the terrace with a hammock and twin beds (Rs500). ❷

Hotel Sugat (☎4245824; maryman@mos.com.np), along the southern edge of Basantapur Sq., facing the royal palace. The rooftop garden has fantastic views of the square's temples, the palace, and the Himalayas. Spacious, carpeted rooms overlook Durbar Sq.; some have tubs and balconies. Fans, toilet paper, towels included. Singles Rs110, with bath Rs300; doubles Rs300, with bath Rs350, deluxe Rs400. Extra bed Rs100, extra person Rs75. ❶

Annapurna Lodge, Freak St. (☎4247684; fax 4281051), down the 2nd right as you walk from Basantapur Sq. Aging and simply furnished rooms are quiet and clean. Seat toilets in attached baths; squat and seat toilets in common bath. Common shower has hot water. Attached Diyalo Restaurant shows free movies at 5:30 and 7:30pm. Singles Rs125, with bath Rs225; doubles Rs200, with bath Rs300. ❶

SUNDHARA

Singapore Guest House, Baghdurbar (☎4243817; fax 4221703), south of Bhimsen Tower, on the left toward the end of the street. Large, comfy rooms with well-worn carpets, phones, TVs, fans, and attached bath with hot water and toilet paper. Attached restaurant (entrees Rs40-120). Singles Rs250-450; doubles Rs350-550. Negotiable discounts for students and groups. ❷

Hotel New Kailash, Baghdurbar (☎4268079), south of Bhimsen Tower. Take a left at the stone sign. Bright, spacious rooms all with phones, fans, and attached baths. Popular with South Asian travelers. Singles Rs200; doubles Rs400; triples Rs500. ❷

◖ FOOD

Beginning with the founding of Kathmandu's first luxury hotel in 1954 which featured fresh fish carried in by porters, to the advent of "Pie Alley," where 1960s overlanders gathered for apple pie and hash brownies, Kathmandu has achieved mythic status as an oasis of displaced delicacies. Today, Western favorites are *de rigueur* on tourist menus, but much of this food is bland, borrowing most of its flavor from the *ghee* (clarified butter) in which it has been ritually drowned. The Japanese, Thai, Tibetan, and Indian restaurants that elbow for room in neighborhoods frequented by foreigners and wealthy Nepalis generally offer more appetizing and less contrived fare. For a more regional experience, you can always dig into the undisputed national dish, *dahl bhat tarkari* (rice, lentils, and vegetable curry) available on nearly every menu as the "Nepali Set Meal." For a spicier version of Nepali food, try the more interesting specialties of Newari food. While

Hindu Nepalis are vegetarian, Newaris usually feature meaty dishes on their menus. Prices, especially in Thamel, can vary widely from one restaurant to the next, so be sure to check the menu before getting comfortable.

THAMEL

Typical Nepali Restaurant, JP School St., south of Kathmandu Guest House, down an alley on the left, 10m south of Koto Restaurant. The singing, dancing manager, who identifies himself as J.J. (for "John Joker") persistently refills clay bowls of endless, free *raksi* (rice wine) while live Nepali music plays in the background every evening. Ironically named "typical" restaurant because it has no specialty—Nepali, Indian, continental, Italian, and Chinese are all on the menu. Complimentary bananas and popcorn accompany the all-you-can eat regional plates (Rs110-175), including *dahl bhat tarkari, roti,* and *momos* (Rs45-80). Open daily 7am-10pm. ❷

The Northfield Cafe (☎4424884), a few doors north of Kathmandu Guest House. A great place for homesick *gringos* to down homemade chips and salsa (Rs120) and gnaw on spicy chicken wings (Rs135). Portions are huge. Burritos Rs185-210, quesadillas Rs170, fajitas 225-270, meat dishes up to Rs280, brownie sundaes Rs150. Brand new bar on beautiful gardened terrace, with stone bottom and palm trees. Classical, jazz, and blues music blares. The breakfast menu is one of the best around. Open daily 7am-10pm. MC/V. ❸

Just Juice 'n' Shakes, down a lane to the right, north of Kathmandu Guest House. Friendly place with quite a reputation for thick, frozen smoothies and shakes (Rs50-90), hot espresso (Rs50), cappuccino (Rs50), and fresh juices (Rs25-60). A good place for breakfast—the fruit muesli with yogurt is delicious (Rs55). Limited seating on low stools, but a fun hangout. Check out the amusing visitors' wall. Open daily 5:30am-10pm off-season, hours extended in-season. ❷

Roadhouse Cafe, JP School St. (☎4260187), 50m south from Kathmandu Guest House. Popular locale for specialty wood-fired pizzas (Rs195-295). Also a great place for a light meal, with its large selection of vegetarian sandwiches. Main courses Rs165-245, excellent espresso Rs50-85. Open daily noon-10pm. ❸

Pumpernickel Bakery, opposite K.C.'s. A Thamel institution. At breakfast time, the line to order freshly baked croissants, cakes, and cinnamon rolls (Rs20-40) spills into the street. Delicious cakes (Rs40), dairy treats (Rs35-45), and gelati (Rs50 per scoop) to satisfy any neglected sweet tooth. The pleasant garden patio and wicker furniture in the back make it a nice place to linger and people-watch. Open daily 6:30am-7pm. ❶

Koto Japanese Restaurant, JP School Rd., across the street from Tibet Enterprises, and near the Chhetrapati intersection (with another branch on Durbar Marg). Impeccable service, high-quality food, and simple bamboo furnishings. Tea refills and *yakis* (Rs190) will revive the pizza-weary. Noodles, soups, meat, fish, and Japanese curries (Rs180-380). 10% tax. Open daily 11:30am-3pm and 6-9pm. ❸

Third Eye Restaurant (☎4260289, bakery ☎4425510), 100m south of the Kathmandu Guest House, on the right. This quality Indian restaurant specializes in tandoori chicken (half-chicken Rs225, whole Rs375). The interior dining area is classy with enormous windows and elegant mirrors; the rooftop terrace has great views. Veg. dishes Rs120-180, *naan* Rs30-60. Attached bakery offers a wide variety of delicious Indian pastries. Open daily 8am-10pm. AmEx/MC/V. ❸

New Orleans Cafe (☎4425736), just north of the Kathmandu Guest House. Enjoy jambalaya, creole chicken, and other soul food, all with a generous helping of freshly baked, all-American Tibetan bread on a bustling but low-key candlelit patio. Try the highly acclaimed steak (Rs260-300). Veg. dishes Rs80-170, non-veg. Rs90-250. Live music M and F 7:30pm. Open daily 6:30am-11:30pm. ❸

Nargila Restaurant (☎ 4264781), 150m north of Kathmandu Guest House, on the right and up one flight by Hotel Nana. One of a few Middle Eastern restaurants around. Serves freshly made pita and hummus (Rs55), falafel sandwiches (Rs105), couscous (Rs80-110), and other treats (Rs60-150) with kind service and spacious seating. Open daily 8am-10pm. ❷

NEW ROAD AND FREAK STREET

▨ **Angan Sweet Namkeens and Vegetarian Fast Food,** at the intersection of New Rd. and Dharma Path. Serves ice cream (Rs30-40), samosas (Rs8), Indian sweets, *dosas* (Rs40-50), and other veg. treats (Rs20-65) on the go. Pay in front and shoulder your way into the back room for a table. Free mineral water. Open daily 9:30am-8:30pm. ❶

Almond Cafe, New Rd., is cheap and clean despite the fast-food feel. Several powerful fans keep Kathmandu's hippest high school students cool in the spacious indoor seating area. Over 20 kinds of ice cream Rs35. Chow mein Rs40-60, pizzas Rs60-120. ❷

Oasis Restaurant, Freak St. Big leafy plants and rainbow umbrellas shelter the outdoor dining area. Great place to pretend you went on a tropical vacation instead. Mexican dishes Rs95-145, pizza Rs95-145, burgers Rs95-115, Nepal set veg. meal Rs125, with meat Rs175. Open daily 8am-10pm peak-season, 9am-9pm off-season. ❷

DURBAR MARG

Bhanchha Ghar, Kamaladi. From Durbar Marg, walk east at the clock tower; it's on the right. The name is Nepali for "kitchen," but there's a lot more than *dahl bhat* on the menu here—this is Nepalese *haute cuisine*. Specialties (Rs170-290) include wild boar and curried high-altitude mushrooms. The enormous set menu is pricey (Rs1000) but includes a cultural show at night. 10% tax. Open daily 11am-10pm. AmEx/MC/V. ❸

Ghar-e-Kebab, next to Hotel Annapurna. Top-quality Indian restaurant, with delicious food, powerful A/C, and attentive service. Ravi Shankar impersonations nightly. Tandoori dishes Rs375-650. 8 course set meal US$12. 10% tax. Open daily noon-2:30pm and 7-10:30pm. AmEx/MC/V. ❺

Cafe de la Paix, across Durbar Marg from Hotel Annapurna and in front of Hotel Sherpa. Mixed menu of high quality, light foods with low-key service. Great breakfast sets including Continental (Rs210), American (Rs300), Indian (Rs200), and Sherpa (Rs200). For a special treat, try the fresh-squeezed fruit drinks (Rs45-95). Open daily 7am-10pm. AmEx/MC/V. ❸

◉ SIGHTS

There are so many temples in Kathmandu that the word "templescape" has been coined to describe the city's skyline. The city's main attractions are in **Durbar Square, Indra Chowk, Asan Tol,** and **Swayambhunath,** just west of the city. However, these areas are virtually unlabeled and can be hard to navigate (or appreciate) without some preparation or a hired guide. Fortunately, guides proffer themselves at wandering tourists every few meters in the entrances to sights. The guides can be a valuable source of interesting information—and hiring one will fend off the remaining swarms. Guides are paid based on your gift at the end of the tour, typically Rs50-200. However, if you ask them how much they charge, they will cite an exorbitant amount, which is by *no* means expected.

DURBAR SQUARE

Durbar (Palace) Sq. is the heart of the old city, and a famous cultural and religious center of the country. Formally known as Hanuman-dhoka Durbar Square, it was listed as World Heritage Site of UNESCO in 1979. Most of the square's architecture is in the 'pagoda' style and was built between the 12th and 18th centuries. Though the royal family, who used to be located here, moved about a hundred years ago to the north end of town, the square retains its religious, social, and commercial importance. Many of Kathmandu's most interesting temples and historic buildings are located here in this bustling, wide-open space. A good way to explore the sights is to start from Basantapur Sq., the large open plaza by Freak St., and head west and then north in a clockwise arc; the sights are organized below in this manner. Entrance booths (including one at Basantapur) charge Rs250, Rs25 for citizens of SAARC. The entrance fee is good for the length of your visa—so hold on to that stub! For more information about this site or to volunteer in the conservation effort, contact **Hanuman-dhoka Durbar Square Conservation Program** (☎ 1268969).

KUMARI BAHAL. The first building you'll see at the western edge of Basantapur Sq. is the Kumari Bahal, marked by the two painted stone lions that stand guard outside. A traditional 18th-century Newari palace built by the last Malla king, the Kumari Bahal sports beautifully-carved window frames—the central one is gilded. This is the home of the living, earthly, human goddess of Kathmandu, the **Kumari**. She once appeared at one of the windows in the courtyard to silently answer her devotees' questions with the look on her heavily made-up face (see **The Living Goddess: Kumari**, p. 819). However, her family has recently forbidden her appearance to non-Hindu tourists. *(No photography allowed.)*

TRAILOKYA MOHAN TEMPLE. Just to the left of the Kumari Bahal, this temple is a shrine to Vishnu, with a massive dusty-black statue of Garuda (Vishnu's man-bird vehicle) kneeling reverently before the image and clasping his palms together in the *namaste* position.

THE LIVING GODDESS: KUMARI

A Newari Buddhist girl considered to be the living incarnation of the Hindu goddess Durga, the Kumari, is a perfect example of the religious fusion of the Kathmandu Valley. Kathmandu's Kumari, the most important of the 11 in the valley, is selected at the age of four or five from the Buddhist clan of the Newari *shakya* (goldsmith) caste. The Kumari-to-be must satisfy 32 physical requirements, including having thighs like a deer's, a chest like a lion's, eyelashes like a cow's, and a body like a banyan tree. She must remain calm in a dark room full of buffalo heads, frightening masks, and loud noises. Finally, her astrological chart must not conflict with the king's. If all these conditions are met, the Kumari is installed in the Kumari Bahal in Durbar Sq., where she leads the privileged, secluded life of a goddess until she reaches puberty. Several times a year she is paraded about town on a palanquin (the Kumari's feet must not touch the ground). As soon as the Kumari menstruates, or sheds blood in any other way, her goddess-spirit leaves her body, and she must return to her parents' home, where the transition to mere mortality can be difficult. Former goddesses often have difficulty finding a husband, since men who marry them are said to die young. Nepal's newest Kumari was chosen on July 11, 2001, when Preeti Shakya, a four-year-old from Kathmandu, assumed the traditional top knot and painted third eye that signify the living goddess.

KASTHAMANDAP. Continuing west away from Basantapur Square past Trailokya Mohan, you will find the Kasthamandap, a gorgeous temple that (perhaps) gave Kathmandu its name. The wooden pavilion—built from the wood of a single tree—is Kathmandu's oldest existing building. Originally a *dharamsala* dating from the 14th century, it was eventually made into a temple and has been substantially altered over the centuries. Today, loitering porters contribute their share to the atmosphere of the temple. A central, *sindur*-smeared image of Gorakhnath, the deified Hindu saint who watches over the Shah dynasty, anchors this sacred space. Small Ganesh shrines sit in each corner and one of the idols' golden mouse-mounts points its nose at another Ganesh shrine, the **Maru Ganesh** (also known as **Ashok Binayak**). This shrine is enclosed in its own metal-flagged enclosure near the eastern corner of the temple. Worshippers flock here on Tuesdays and Saturdays, the sacred days of Ganesh. Travelers also visit the elephant god of fortune before undertaking major trips.

MAJU DEWAL. From the Kasthamandap, turn right and head north toward the main part of the square. The Maju Dewal Shiva Temple takes up the prime location, towering over everything on its 10-level step-pyramid. The temple was built in 1690 and makes a well-placed observation deck for Durbar Sq.—its height, however, does nothing to isolate it from the fray below. It is colloquially known as the "hippie temple" due to its popularity with 1960s American visitors. An imitation *sadhu* circles the temple with signature face paint and the beckoning call "photo." A white *shikara* dedicated to Kayu Dev sits at the foot of the steps.

TEMPLE OF SHIVA AND PARVATI. As you continue north, you'll come to the rectangular Shiva and Parvati Temple. Brightly painted statues of the divine couple lean out from a tiny window above the entrance, leering eerily at the visitors who dare disturb their conjugal bliss. The platform below was used for dance performances under the Malla reign.

TALEJU BELL. As you walk northeast past the Shiva and Parvati Temple, you'll see the Taleju (Great) Bell, put up by Rana Bahadur Shah in 1797. The bell, similar to the ones found in the other valley cities of Patan and Bhaktapur, rings for worship in the Degutaleju Temple. It sits below two massive stone podiums, with a stylized tile roof.

CHYASIN DEGA TEMPLE. The octagonal temple to Banasgopal (Krishna playing the flute), just past the Taleju bell, was built in 1648 by King Pratap Malla to mourn his two dead wives. The temple houses images of Krishna and two goddesses that bear a curious resemblance to Pratap Malla and his wives. Next to the temple, a small hut shelters two enormous drums. Twice a year, a goat and a buffalo are sacrificed here.

KING PRATAP MALLA'S COLUMN AND THE DEGUTALEJU TEMPLE. In the center of this part of the square stands a column topped by a statue of King Pratap Malla, the architect of many buildings in this area. He sits facing his personal prayer room, housed in the Degutaleju Temple. In contrast to Shah and Rana kings, Mall chose to be depicted in a religious and tranquil (rather than military) pose.

SWETA BHAIRAB. As you face the Degutaleju Temple, you'll see a large wooden screen just to the right that hides the figure of the scowling, fanged, golden face of an enormous Sweta Bhairab (White Bhairab). At the **Indra Jatra Festival** (Aug.-Sept.), the screen comes off and beer spouts from the mouth of this fearsome form of Shiva as devotees crowd in for a drink of the divine spittle.

JAGANNATH TEMPLE. Built in 1563, the Jagannath Temple (at Pratap Malla's left) is the oldest temple in this part of the square. Scandalously flexible couples are caught with their pants down in the carvings on the roof struts. This temple is familiarly known as the "Kama Sutra" temple.

KALA BHAIRAB. Behind Pratap Malla, facing north, is the huge, garish monolith of Kala Bhairab (Black Bhairab), trampling an unfortunate demon underfoot. The intimidation inspired by this figure is so great that the temple is also used as a place to swear in witnesses or government officials. It is said that anyone who dares to tell a lie in front of this raging destroyer of evil will vomit blood and die. Don't even think about it.

TALEJU MANDIR. At the north end of the royal palace, the Taleju Temple's three-tiered golden pagoda towers over everything else in this part of the square. King Mahendra Malla built the temple in 1564 to honor Taleju, his dynasty's patron goddess, a bloodthirsty form of Durga. Legend claims that human sacrifices were performed here. At 37m, the Taleju Temple was for a long time the tallest building in Kathmandu, a distinction preserved by building codes. But no more—the city, eager to modernize, has dispensed with this tradition. Ordinarily, the temple is open only to the king, a few priests, and the Kumari, but on the ninth day of the October Dassain festival, lay Hindus are allowed to enter.

HANUMAN DHOKA DURBAR. The old royal palace takes its name from the statue of Hanuman that stands guard at the entrance, to the left of the Pratap Malla. The monkey-god lounges under a parasol. No one has lived in the palace for over a century, but it is still used for royal ceremonies, including King Birendra's coronation in 1975. Although the building has been evolving steadily since the time of the Licchavi kings of the 13th century, its art and architecture were influenced mainly by the patronage of King Pratap Malla (r. 1641-74). No Licchavi buildings remain, and the palace now has plenty of Shah-era whitewashing. Just inside the palace entrance is **Nasal Chowk,** a courtyard where the nobles of the kingdom used to assemble. It was here in 1673 that Pratap Malla danced in a costume of Narasimha, Vishnu's man-lion incarnation. Afraid that Vishnu would be angry about the stunt, Pratap Malla installed a Narasimha statue, to your left as you enter the courtyard, coyly fingering the snaking entrails of the demon he has just disemboweled. The main section of the palace open to the public is the **Tribhuvan Memorial Museum.** King Tribhuvan (r. 1911-55), who overthrew the Ranas in 1951 and restored Nepal's monarchy, is remembered here in a display of personal belongings including ceremonial outfits, newspaper clippings, and his stuffed bird clamped into its original cage. At the southern end of Nasal Chowk stands **Basantapur Tower,** a nine-story lookout erected by Prithvi Narayan Shah after he conquered the valley. It has great views of Durbar Sq. from above. The circuit around Nasal Chowk then leads to the **Mahendra Memorial Museum,** which isn't quite as impressive as Tribhuvan's. Outside the palace, along the wall past the Hanuman statue, is a **stone inscription** put up by Pratap Malla, which uses words from 15 different languages (including English and French). It's said that if anyone manages to read the whole text—a poem dedicated to the goddess Kali—milk will gush from the spout. (☎ 4258034. Open Tu-Sa 9:30am-3pm. Rs250 for both museums. Cameras prohibited.)

NORTH OF DURBAR SQUARE

Kathmandu's most interesting street runs northeast from Durbar Sq. Without a name of its own, the street takes the title of whatever area it runs through. In earlier times, it was the beginning of the trade route from Kathmandu to Tibet, and it was Kathmandu's main commercial area until New Rd. was built after the earthquake of 1934. Today it is still a buzzing, temple-packed market area.

INDRA CHOWK. Marking the crowded meeting point of six Kathmandu streets, the second-story temple of **Akash Bhairab** is unmistakable. Just look up for the garish metal gargoyles. In the evening Indra Chowk is a site of informal musical performance of traditional "bhajan" singing. The ground floor of the temples is also filled with hectic stores. (The first crossroads on the diagonal street running northeast from Durbar Sq. is called Indra Chowk. Akash Bhairab is on the left side at this corner.)

SOUTH ASIAN SEDER With 95% of Nepal's 20 million citizens claiming Hinduism, Buddhism, or both, as their religion, you'd hardly expect Kathmandu to host the largest *seder* (ritual Jewish Passover meal) in the world. Each year the Israeli Embassy puts on a *seder* for the 1300 or so young Jews who find themselves in Nepal during the week of Passover. Most of them have come to roam the Nepali wilderness following completion of their national military service, but at the *seder*, the trekking diaspora ditches *chappatis* and *dahl bhat* in favor of *matzos* and *maror*, in remembrance of the ancient Israelite exodus from Egypt. If you don't have an Israeli passport, you'll have to get your background checked by resident rabbis. For more information, contact the Israeli Embassy (☎ 411811).

KEL TOL. The **Temple of Seto Machhendranath** is one of the most widely revered shrines in the valley. Both Hindus and Buddhists come here to pay homage to Machhendra, the valley's guardian, also considered to be an incarnation of Avalokitesvara, the *bodhisattva* of compassion. The white-faced image is paraded around town during the **Machhendranath Festival** in April, but the temple itself is covered by an unattractive iron fence to ward off thieves. *(Just off Kel Tol, down a passageway marked by a short pillar capped with a meditating Buddha.)* The pagoda in the middle of Kel Tol is dedicated to **Lunchun Lun Bun Ajima**. The road has been repaved so many times that this goddess' tiled sanctuary is now sunk beneath street level. *(Kel Tol is the 2nd crossing northeast of Durbar Sq.)*

ASAN TOL. This crossroads is one of the most perennially crowded locations in Kathmandu. Vegetable sellers crowd the ground of the six sidestreets that feed into Asan Tol. It's a great place to buy Nepalese spices and encounter street culture. The **Temple of Annapurna** is on the right, draped with broad brass ribbons. The goddess of plentiful food, Annapurna, is depicted here as a silver pot.

BANGEMUDHA. The name of the square west of Asan Tol, Bangemudha, literally means "Twisted Wood." In one of the southern corners is a twisted lump of wood stuck to the wall, with an armor of coins nailed into it. The wood is dedicated to the god of toothaches, **Vaisya Dev**, and nailing a coin here is supposed to relieve dental pain. On the road north from Bangemudha you'll be greeted by jawfuls of grinning teeth. This is the dentists' quarter, and their signs all bear this happy smiling symbol. On the left side of this road, a lane leads to **Kathesimbhu**, a miniature model of the Swayambhunath *stupa* west of Kathmandu. Kathesimbhu, said to have been built with leftover earth from Swayambhunath, shares some of Swayambhunath's power. The elderly and those too weak to climb the hill to Swayambhunath can obtain an equal blessing here. Children seem to be the most devoted visitors, however, holding endless soccer games around its *chaityas*. *(The Bangemudha crossing is about 150m due west of Asan Tol.)*

SOUTH OF DURBAR SQUARE

BHIMSEN TEMPLE. The Bhimsen Temple is dedicated to the hero-god of Newari craftsmen—its bottom floor has been entirely taken over by shops. Next to it is a *hiti* (water tap) in a cellar-like depression, where jugs are filled from an elephant-shaped spout. *(On the lane that runs southwest of the Kasthamandap in Durbar Sq.)*

JAISI DEWAL TEMPLE. The Jaisi Dewal Temple is a large, dilapidated, step-pyramid Shiva temple covered with four centuries of pigeon dung. Painted with flowers and leopard-skin patterns, the temple is graced by a smooth figure of Shiva's bull mount, Nandi, at the base of the steps. Across the street from the entrance, a 2m high, uncarved *linga* promises fertility to those who pray to it. *(Continue to the end of the road from the Bhimsen Temple, turn left, and go up the hill.)*

BHIMSEN TOWER. The 59m-high Bhimsen Tower, also called Sundhara or Dharahara, is a useful landmark if you get lost along Kathmandu's streets. It looks like a run-down lighthouse with portholes, though Bhimsen Thapa, the prime minister who built it in 1832, was probably trying to imitate the Ochterlony Monument in Kolkata—ironic, considering that the British erected that monument to commemorate the defeat of Nepal in 1816. *(Off Kautipath in southern Kathmandu, next to the GPO. The tower is closed to the public.)*

TEKU. The junction of the Bagmati and Vishnumati rivers at Teku is a sacred place often used for cremations. The wailing of the bereaved echoes around the temples and *chaityas*, and a tall brick *shikhara* stands over the confluence. The riverbanks might look like something out of a pastoral idyll, with buffalo munching hay in the shade, but the buffalo are in fact being slyly fattened for slaughter. *(In the southwest corner of the city. Be sensitive about photography.)*

PACHALI BHAIRAB. The area between Tripureswar Marg and the Bagmati might be wet and dirty and home to a big share of Kathmandu's slums, but its many temples make it an interesting part of town to explore. The shrine of Pachali Bhairab contains an image of Bhairab, decorated with coins under the spreading roots of a great pipal tree. Music from the nearby monastery jangles down into Bhairab's courtyard, where a golden human figure lies peacefully dead with its well-articulated golden toes morbidly sticking straight up. Don't fret; this is a *betal*, a representation of death meant to guard against the real thing. *(In a cluster of temples south of Tripureswar Marg, just east of the footbridge across the Bagmati.)*

KALAMOCHAN TEMPLE. The Kalamochan Temple is hard to miss, its architecture is a fusion of Mughal (onion domes), and Nepali (its dragons and doorways). On the exterior, Jung Bahadur Rana's beguilingly peaceful figure rises from a turtle's back. This Machiavellian prime minister built the temple in the mid-19th century. The ashes of the 32 noblemen he slaughtered in the Kot Massacre are supposed to be buried in the foundations. *(On Tripureswar Marg, close to the Patan Bridge.)*

TUNDIKHEL AND MARTYR'S GATE. The **Tundikhel,** or parade ground, is occasionally used for military marches and equestrian displays, such as the **Ghora Jatra Horse Festival** in late March, although you're more likely to find families picnicking here in Kathmandu's biggest open public space. *(East of Kantipath.)* Kathmandu's newer neighborhoods are to the east of the Tundikhel. **Martyrs' Gate** is a monument to four accused conspirators executed after a 1940 coup attempt. *(On a circle in the middle of the road, south of the Tundikhel.)*

SINGHA DURBAR. Until most of it burned down in a fire one night in July 1974, Singha Durbar was once the greatest of the Rana palaces. The off-white building, meant to rival the palaces of Europe, was built in three frantic years from 1901 to 1904 by Prime Minister Chandra Shamsher Jung Bahadur Rana—his monogram decorates the railings. The prime minister's household and entire administration fit into this complex, which, with 1700 rooms, claims to be the largest building in Asia. Ministries and departments are lodged in what's left of the palace, and their offices are off-limits to the public. *(East of Tundikhel.)*

WEST OF THE CITY

The west bank of the Vishnumati River is beyond Kathmandu's traditional city limits, but it has been brought into the metropolis by Ring Rd. Encircling the area, Ring Rd. makes the western part of Kathmandu easily accessible by vehicle.

SWAYAMBHUNATH. The most prominent feature of the west bank is the hilltop *stupa* of Swayambhunath. More than 2000 years old, Swayambhunath is the holiest place on earth for Newari Buddhists, and it is the focus of the Kathmandu Valley's creation myth. Swayambhunath is also known as the "Monkey Temple," for the dozens of rhesus monkeys that clamber over the shrines, staining their behinds with *sindur* as they gobble up the daily rice offerings.

At the base of the hill is a large rectangular gateway flanked with prayer wheels—from here, the long crooked steps wind through the trees and Buddha-icons to the top where an enormous *vajra* stands; behind it is the *stupa*. From the golden cube on top, the Buddha's all-seeing eyes gaze out in every direction, as do the crowds of tourists ogling at the splendid panoramic views. What looks like Buddha's nose is actually the number "1," representing the unity of all things.

Three hundred and sixty-five stone steps lead to the *stupa* at the top of the hill. Each element of the *stupa* depicts part of the Buddhist cosmology. The dome itself represents the creative womb, while the 13 discs on the spire represent the steps toward nirvana. The nine gold shrines surrounding the *stupa* enclose images of the *dhayani* Buddhas, who portray the different aspects of the Buddha through the elements of earth, water, fire, air, and space. The four Buddhas, who occupy the shrines at the secondary points, also have female elements *(taras)*. Buddhist pilgrims circle clockwise around the *stupa*, turning the prayer wheels and meditating on this towering Buddhist symbol.

In the evenings and early mornings the Vasupur shrine is the site of monastic prayers. A beautiful cacophony of traditional trumpets, drums, and clarinets, as well as singing, this service is an impressive experience. If you take off your shoes at the door and leave a small donation, the monks permit laypersons to walk clockwise around their ceremony. Photographs are permitted. *(2km from the city. A 30min. walk straight across the suspension bridge or bus #19 from Ratna Park leads you to Ring Rd., just west of Swayambhunath. It is a 5min. walk uphill from the bus stop to the foot of the stupa. Stupa Rs50. Open daily 7am-6pm.)*

NATIONAL MUSEUM. Nepal's National Museum has an art gallery with a good collection of wood, stone, and metalwork. While excellent carvings can be seen on the houses and temples of the Kathmandu Valley, the museum allows you to get a closer, cleaner look. The Historical Museum building is at least as interesting as the art gallery. Its natural history section features the pelt of a two-headed calf, a set of bones from a blue whale, and an unusual abundance of stuffed deer heads. Another section is wholly devoted to depicting Nepal's experiences of warfare, with a unique display of traditional weapons. Organized by geographical region of origin, the recently-renovated bright white Buddhist art gallery provides a decent introduction to different styles of Nepali Buddhist art. The most aesthetically interesting portion of this gallery is the metalwork. One metal sculpture is a 14th century depiction of Sukhavarna Samvara (the deity with dozens of legs and arms as well as 5 heads). *(1km south of Swayambhunath, on the road from the river. Open Tu-Sa 9:30am-4pm; in winter 9:30am-3pm. Rs50; camera fee Rs50.)*

🎵 🍴 ENTERTAINMENT AND NIGHTLIFE

When it comes to nightlife in Nepal, Kathmandu is ground zero, but it still isn't much in this early-to-bed country. Options include bars in tourist areas (which close by midnight), four casinos (the only ones on the Subcontinent), and a few nightclubs (which also close around midnight). Women travelers may feel uncomfortable in nightclubs. **Casino Royale** is in the Yak & Yeti, and **Casino Anna** in Hotel de l'Annapurna, both on Durbar Marg. **Casino Everest** is in The Everest Hotel in New Baneswar and **Casino Nepal** in the Soaltee Holiday Inn in Tanachal, at the western end of the city. All are open 24hr. For the latest news about gaming in Nepal visit www.casinosnepal.com. **Himachali Cultural Group,** Lazimpath, has daily performances; call for reservations. (☎4415280. 7pm. Rs350.) During high season, **Bhanchha Ghar,** Kamaladi (see p. 818) offers cultural shows to diners. At least half a dozen establishments around Thamel—among them the **Twa Dewa,** Yaju's free movie restaurant—hold Video Nights in Kathmandu, showing recent film releases throughout the day. On Freak St., **Diyalo Restuarant** shows free movies (daily 5:30 and 7:30pm). **Pilgrim's Book House** also has concerts of classical sitar music (Su, Tu, and F at 7:30pm, Rs300). In addition to the following pubs and discos, check out the **New Orleans Cafe** (see p. 817).

> **The Rum Doodle 40,000½-Feet Bar and Restaurant,** Thamel. Follow the turn in the road north of the Kathmandu Guest House; it's on the left. The bar's namesake is a 1956 literary spoof about a mountaineering expedition; the book is sold at the bar (Rs150). The walls are decorated with foot-shaped cut-outs signed and decorated by trekking and mountaineering parties. The bar boasts the worlds's largest collection of Everest summiteer's signatures, including Sir Edmund Hillary's and former US President Jimmy Carter's. Also, the locale offers free food to card-holding summiteers and 25% discount on drinks. Beer (Rs80 draft, Rs120-150 bottles), and cocktails (Rs120-200). Live music F nights. Draft beer Rs75-140. Open 10am-10pm.

The Jump Club, 100m north of the Kathmandu Guest House, next to Hotel Garuda. The latest favorite of the younger tourist crowd, this club/bar features snooker, black lights, and a small dance floor with the DJ spinning a schizophrenic mix of techno, R&B, rock, and reggae. Cocktails Rs100-160, beer Rs80-140. Open daily "6pm until you drop"; happy hour 5-9pm. Usually no cover for foreigners.

Maya Cocktail Bar and **Maya Pub,** Thamel. The cocktail bar is upstairs from the Pumpernickel Bakery; the pub is at the intersection 500m south of the Kathmandu Guest House. Both offer free popcorn and 2-for-1 cocktails 4-7pm. The dark pub is less crowded and has a mainstream pop music soundtrack; the funkier cocktail bar is trendier, bigger, and more raucous. Beer Rs80-140, cocktails Rs110-130. Pool and snooker at the bar Rs40 per game, Rs250 per hr. Both open daily 2 or 3pm to around midnight.

Les Yeux, Thamel, on Thahity, just south of the intersection. In season, this rooftop bar and restaurant features concerts on M, W, F, and Sa nights by local rock and blues bands. Bring a guitar down and you might just get to play. Chill atmosphere only rarely moves to dancing. Beer Rs75-140, cocktails Rs100-160. Concerts 7-10:30pm. Open 8:30am-10:30pm (and sometimes grooving later).

Club X-Zone, in Kasthamandap Plaza, Kamaladi. Groove on the black-lit dance floor or mellow out on the surrounding sofas. Beer Rs80-150. Open daily 9pm-1am. Cover charges Rs300-500, depending on who you are and whom you're with.

⌐ SHOPPING

In Thamel or Durbar Sq., roving merchants hawk everything from flutes and chess sets to hash pipes and Tiger Balm. Just about anything made in Nepal can be bought in Kathmandu, though most crafts are better bought in their places of origin. For woodcarving and pottery, head to Bhaktapur, while papier-mâché masks and puppets originate in Thimi. Patan is the best place for intricate metalwork and Boudha offers the greatest variety of Tibetan crafts. You can purchase the best quality pashminas at the **Cashmere House** in Basantapur Plaza, Basantapur (☎4230975; cashmerehouse@ifnti.com.np). They feature over 450 varieties of color and design of pashminas. Lower price (and quality) pashminas, saris, and other female attire are available in small shops and outdoor stands along Bag Bazaar. Bargain hard in those shops, but not in larger stores. Cloth and beads can be found north of Indra Chowk.

The **Khukuri House,** in Thamel, at the zig-zag north of the Kathmandu Guest House, next door to the 1hr. laundry, deserves special mention. This well-reputed knife shop is owned by a former Gorkha officer. (☎412314; www.khukurihouse.com. Open Su-F 9:30am-7:30pm. MC/V.) **Didi's Boutique** and **Didi-daju,** both on Chhetrapati, east of Everest Steak House, carry a wide selection of handicrafts, many of which are produced by the Janakpur Women's Development Centre. (Open daily 10am-9pm. MC/V.)

Perhaps the most useful shopping for a backpacker will happen along JP School St. and Narsing Gate. You can buy cheap knock-offs of all the big names in sporting goods, with almost every other retail store catering to adventure travelers. The Western knock-offs seem to be more expensive than Asian products of similar quality. Shop around and bargain hard—store owners often expect travelers to pay grossly inflated prices.

VOLUNTEER OPPORTUNITIES

Expat prisoners in the central jail near **Sundhara,** 200m south of the GPO, appreciate visitors who'll talk to them for a little while. Bring a little extra food or cash when you go—it's greatly appreciated. Walk south on Kantipath until you pass the Ministry of Finance and then a gas station on the right; the prisons are down the lane that forks south off Kantipath. Bulletin boards around backpacker hostels list expat prisoners and countries of origin. Visiting hours Su-F 10am-5pm. The **Sisters of Charity of Nazareth** (☎4426453 or 4419965), Navjyoti Center, Baluwatar, perform prison ministry, including assisting former women prisoners. **St. Francis Xavier's School** (☎4526732), Jawalakhel, and **The Missionaries of Charity** (☎471810), Mitra Park, work with impoverished families in the Kathmandu area. You may also contact **Thamel Development Center** for more information (see **Practical Information,** p. 811).

Trekkers interested in giving back to those who helped make their journeys possible can contact **Porters Progress Nepal** on the north end of Narsing Gate (☎4410020; porter@wlink.com.np). They accept donations of hiking clothing and equipment and offer a free screening daily at 4pm of the BBC documentary about Nepali porters "carrying the burden." They also help organize volunteer teaching of porters in English and first aid. This organization is run by and for Nepal's brave porters.

◢ DAYTRIPS FROM KATHMANDU

▨ PASHUPATINATH पशुपतीनाथ

Pashupatinath is only nominally outside of Kathmandu, and it's easy to get there by **bike***—follow Tridevi Marg away from Thamel, and turn right at the first road after Durbar Marg. At the Marco Polo Business Hotel, turn left and follow the zig-zagging road east across a bridge. Watch for signs showing maps of Pashupatinath.* **Bus #1** *from Ratna Park (25min., frequent, Rs6) stops along Ring Rd. at the turnoff to Pashupathinath; follow the signs from there. The* **#2 tempo** *from Sundhara (via Rani Pokhari) stops across the street, just inside Ring Rd. (30min., frequent, Rs8).* **Auto-rickshaws** *from Thamel cost about Rs100-150.* **Taxis** *cost Rs100-150.*

Dedicated to Shiva's incarnation as Pashupati, the gentle Lord of Animals and the guardian deity of Nepal, the temple complex of Pashupatinath, east of Kathmandu, is the holiest Hindu site in Nepal and the country's largest shrine complex. In addition to the bathers who dip in the Bagmati on auspicious full-moon nights and on the 11th day after them, thousands of *sadhus* and Hindu pilgrims descend upon Pashupatinath during the full moon of late February or early March for the **Shivaratri** festival, a celebration of Shiva's birthday. A full day of carnivalesque festivities—and one of the most boisterous festivals of its kind on the Indian Subcontinent—the celebration embraces marijuana-smoking and nudity on the part of the *sadhus*.

The **Pashupati Temple,** built in 1696, rests on the banks of the Bagmati. The brass backside of an enormous statue of Nandi can be seen from the entrance, but the rest of the temple is out-of-view and out-of-bounds for non-Hindus. Other viewpoints in the area afford over-the-wall glimpses of the gold-roofed pagoda. Away from the river and across from the main road is a cluster of five towering white cupolas known as **Panch Dewal,** whose compound has become a social welfare center. **Biddha Ashram,** operated by Mother Teresa's Missionaries of Charity, welcomes walk-in volunteers to help clients of the compound's hospice with basic domestic chores.

Two footbridges span the river. Between them on the near (west) bank is the 6th-century **Bacchareswari Temple,** reportedly once the site of human sacrifice during Shivaratri festivities. Eight *ghats* and precipitous stone walls line the river. Still frequently used for 15 or so daily cremations, the smouldering *ghats* are aligned in caste order. The northernmost *ghat* is reserved for royal cremations, and the next is for political and cultural figures. **Be sensitive about photographing the ghats during cremations.**

Across the footbridges, on the east bank of the Bagmati, is a row of 11 small Shiva shrines, each housing the familiar stone Shiva *linga* and *yoni* icons. Not every show-stopping *linga* is made of stone, however—one of the *sadhus* dwelling in the cliff-carved cave houses (just north of Pashupati Temple on the west bank) can reputedly lift 75kg of rock with a string tied to his penis. The steps up the hill on the east bank of the river eventually level out at a wooded village of over 200 small Shiva temples; Nandi figures crouch along the main street. At the end of the village is a ▨temple dedicated to **Gorakhnath,** an 11th-century saint revered as an avatar of Shiva. The steps continue downhill to the **Gujeshwari Temple,** locally considered to be the place where part of Sati's body fell when her flaming corpse was hacked to bits by Vishnu (the Kamakhya Temple in Guwahati, India, is more widely recognized as this site). According to Buddhist lore, the temple's sacred well is a bottomless hollow left by the root of the lotus that blossomed and inspired the creation of the Kathmandu Valley. Non-Hindus may not enter, so many lotus-spotting tourists can only see the disappointing, rusty roofs of the buildings surrounding the temple. The road downstream in front of the temple leads to a bridge; once you cross it, stone steps lead over the hill and back to the Pashupati Temple. The road on the right heads to **Boudha** (see p. 839), a 30min. walk north through fields and small villages. (Admission to complex Rs250.)

SANKHU साँरव

*Bus #4 (1½hr., frequent, Rs12) departs Ratna Park in Kathmandu for Sankhu and also stops east of Boudha. Sankhu is also accessible by **bicycle** (although the road to Boudha is heavily congested and then uneven and uphill beyond Boudha) or by **foot**, along a northwest trail from Nagarkot. It is also possible to walk between Sankhu and Changu Narayan in the dry season.*

A peaceful, isolated Newari village, Sankhu is an ideal change of pace from hectic Kathmandu. Once a prosperous stop along the Tibetan trade route and a site of architectural wonder in Nepal, the town now hosts only crumbling buildings and a few scattered foreign visitors. Nevertheless, the seventeenth-century **Vajrayogini Temple,** one of the valley's numerous sites of multi-faith convergence, remains a favorite pilgrimage site for both Hindu and Buddhist Nepalis. Hindus revere Vahrayogini as the fierce incarnation of the protector goddess Durga. Newari Buddhists have adopted her as a tantric goddess representative of the powerful female characteristics of the Buddha. The temple, built on an ancient Buddhist plot, has three main copper roofs and a beautifully carved door with images from the Buddhist pantheon. The smaller two-tiered temple enshrines a replica of the Swayambhunath *stupa*. The shrine's interior contains an ornately decorated statue of the goddess. Though you may be tempted to snap a picture, be aware that no photography is allowed when the doors to the goddess' sanctuary are open. A cement cave used for tantric rituals lies at the end of a short trail near the entrance. There are also small Buddhist sculptures, a fountain, and strings of Buddhist flags.

The 2km walk from town to the temple is one of the highlights of the trip. Enter through the light blue cement archway, bordered by small pools, to the left of the bus stop. Follow this road through Sankhu's center, winding right to the Dhunlia Tole, a small town plaza with a large trident as its centerpiece. The road will fork here and a sign will indicate that the left path leads to the temple. Leaving the town, you will pass through a small, faded yellow archway. Here you will pass ancient Newari brick houses and rice fields. After 500m straight along this path, you will be faced with another fork in the road. Both directions will ultimately lead to the temple. To the left, a stone path will lead into the woods and past several sacred fountains. To the right, the slightly-longer path will wind through the outskirts of the village and more rice fields. The two meet again at the base of the long, steep stone stairway to the top of the hill. From the base of the stairs, it's an arduous 15min. climb to the top.

PATAN पाटन ☎01

With only the Bagmati River lying between Kathmandu and its temple-dotted neighbor, Patan, the two cities have practically merged. Patan has two faces, however, which helps to keep the cities distinct. The outer edges of Patan, those reaching Kathmandu to the north and the rest of the Valley to the south, hum with the energy of a commercial center, dotted with factories and NGO offices. The crowds here may also seem younger by comparison, moving through the streets in jeans and in salwars and saris tailored to match the current western fashion. The other face of Patan, found in its central, narrow lines and time-stained stone buildings, moves with a different energy, an energy pulsing since the 17th century. The relics of that time remain in the form of small *stupas, shikharas*, and the ancient water tanks that dot even the industrial areas, many of which still host daily *puja*. Well-established as the valley's center for Newari handicraft production, Patan (also known as Lalitpur, or "City of Fine Arts") is a great place to observe metal smiths, woodworkers, thanka painters, and Tibetan carpet-weavers at work. Despite being the second-largest city in the valley, Patan manages to retain the small-town sincerity that eludes its over-touristed neighbor to the north.

▐ TRANSPORTATION

Tempos, buses, and minibuses are the most convenient way to travel between Patan and Kathmandu or between Patan and the rest of the valley. Auto-rickshaws and taxis between Patan and Kathmandu are expensive (Rs200-250), as Patan's main sites are far from the river. **Tempos** to Patan (20min., Rs6-7) leave frequently from Kathmandu's GPO and the tempo stand near the Rani Pokhari. Most head to Jawalakhel and then Lagankhel, but some go to Mangal Bazaar. **Bus #26** runs frequently from Kathmandu's Ratna Park to Patan Gate (25min., Rs6). **Bus #14,** also from Ratna Park, goes frequently to Lagankhel via Jawalakhel (30min., Rs6). Most tempos and buses, along with white, 15-passenger minibuses, eventually loop back around and return to Kathmandu from Patan Gate, Lagankhel, and Jawalakhel. All can be flagged down anywhere on the main roads between Lagankhel, Jawalakhel and the river (Rs5-10). Few however, can be found on Gabahal and Mangal Bazaar.

Local transportation within Patan is not usually necessary as most distances are walkable, sidewalks abound, and most roads have become pedestrian zones.

▐▐ ORIENTATION AND PRACTICAL INFORMATION

Patan is linked to Kathmandu by a bridge across the **Bagmati River** and bounded to the south by the same **Ring Road** that encircles Kathmandu. Patan's main road, which runs from Kathmandu, goes by the name of whatever neighborhood it's passing through: from the bridge to Ring Rd. it evolves from **Kopundol** to **Pulchowk**, and finally to **Jawalakhel.** Several roads split off from the main road as it moves away from Kathmandu and they form the city's main interior streets. In central Kopundol, at the roundabout, the left fork goes to **Patan Dhoka** (Patan Gate) and then becomes the boundary of **Durbar Square** closest to the river. At Pulchowk, **Gabahal** breaks away perpendicular to the main road and leads to the part of Durbar Square farthest from the river. It becomes **Mangal Bazaar** as it passes Durbar Square. Finally, at **Jawalakhel Chowk,** the road that splits off leads to **Lagankhel** and the **bus park. Tangal Tole** runs parallel to the main road, connecting Lagankhel and Durbar Square.

The **Old City,** which includes Durbar Square, Mangal Bazaar, and many other temples, is loosely bounded by four **stupas** (supposedly built by Ashoka in the 3rd century BC). The eastern *stupa* is beyond Ring Rd.; the western *stupa* is along the main road in Pulchowk, opposite the turn-off to Durbar Sq. The northern and southern *stupas* are both on the outer reaches of Tangal Tole. Overall, Patan is a maze of narrow streets, even narrower pedestrian-only alleys, and paths that dead-end at courtyards filled with unused temples. Unless you have an innate sense of direction, stick to the main roads.

Tourist Office: In order to keep the city's sites in good repair Patan has instituted an **entrance fee** of Rs200. The receipt is good for 1 week and is sometimes requested in Durbar Sq. Two convenient booths, one on the Kathmandu side of Patan Gate and the other at the corner of Mangal Bazaar and Tangal Tole to pay the fee and pick up a "free" map. Open daily 10am-5pm.

KATHMANDU VALLEY

Currency Exchange: Gorkha Money Exchange, next to the Third World Guest House in Durber Sq., changes cash with no commission and traveler's checks (1.5% or Rs150, whichever is more). Open daily 8:30am-7pm. **Standard Chartered,** just toward Lagankhel from Jawalakhel Chowk. Changes cash, traveler's checks, and gives cash advances on credit cards. Open M-F 9:30am-3:30pm.

Bookstore: Pilgrims Book House (☎ 5521159), has a huge branch on the main road in Kopundol at the roundabout. Open daily 9am-8pm. AmEx/MC/V.

Market: Patan is overflowing with things to buy. Fruit, fabric, and household items are sold in Lagankhel, along Tangal Tole from the bus stand to Durbar Square. Handmade crafts are best bought in Kopundol and Patan Industrial Estates (see **Shopping,** p. 835), but jewelry, thankas, and metalwork can also be found around Durbar Sq. The Square itself is the place to find beads and religious items. Plus everyone has a pashmina to sell. **Namaste Supermarket,** along the main road in Pulchowk, sells pre-packaged Western items. Open daily 9am-8pm.

Police: ☎ 5521350, in Jawalakhel, opposite the Central Zoo.

Pharmacy: There are many pharmacies in Mangal Bazaar, and along Tangal Tole. **Alka Pharmacy** (☎ 5535146) on the main road in Jawalakhel, 1 block from St. Xavier's school, can arrange house calls. Open daily 7am-10pm.

Hospital: Patan Hospital, Lagankhel (☎ 5522266), offers a Private Clinic daily 5-7:30pm. Appointments can be booked throughout the day (☎ 5548007). The best way to be seen is to go to the 24hr. emergency care because of the extended process to get seen at the regular clinic.

Internet Access: Since Patan is bursting at the seams with schools, academics, and computer education, centers, Internet access has been put into every available nook and cranny. Never pay more than Rs25 per hr. **Cyber Zone,** at Durbar Square and Mangal Bazaar, is centrally located and has Internet phone for Rs15 per min. Noon-3pm Rs20 per hr., other times Rs25 per hr.; open daily 8am-8pm.

Post Office: On the Kathmandu side of Patan Gate. Open M-F 9am-5pm. **DHL,** on Kumeripati, sends things quickly worldwide for a high fee. Open Su-F 9:30am-5:30pm.

■ ACCOMMODATIONS

Thamel's tourist explosion has put the squeeze on Patan's budget accommodations. Most people ride into Patan for the day and return to Kathmandu at night. Patan's budget accommodations are spread out across the walkable city so visitors can find an area they like and are almost always guaranteed a respite from the morning racket of Kathmandu. All with noon check out unless otherwise noted.

☒ **Mahabuddha Guest House,** Mahabuddha Mandir (☎ 5540575; mfosterm@wlink.com.np). The hidden gem of Patan's accommodations. Recently renovated, the rooms may be a few extra min. from the sights, but the cleanliness and quiet more than make up for it. The friendly proprietor arranges plane tickets and trekking. Laundry service and luggage storage available. Internet cafe in the lobby charges Rs20 per hr. Dorm beds Rs100; singles with bath Rs200; doubles with bath Rs300. ❶

Hungry Treat Home (☎ 5534792), two blocks from Jawalakhel Chowk toward Lagankhel. Clean, but drab rooms are amply sized with fans and carpeting. Tiny bathrooms with seat toilets and toilet paper. The complex includes an attached rooftop restaurant with entrees for Rs35-100. Doubles Rs220, with bath Rs330. ❷

Cafe de Patan, Mangal Bazaar (☎5537599; pcafe@ntc.net.np), just outside of Durbar Sq. Small quiet rooms are available above this restaurant, just steps away from the sights. Some rooms are nicer and better kept than others, but all have common bathroom with shower and seat toilets. Singles Rs300; doubles Rs400. ❷

Third World Guest House, Durbar Sq. (☎5522187; dsdp@wlink.com.np), just behind Krishna Temple, next to Gorkha Money Exchange. Despite the name, it is a classy place with spotless, well-furnished doubles and amazing views of the sq. The well-kept bathrooms are worth it. Rooms US$15, with bath US$20. ❺

Mountain View Guest House (☎5538168), just off Kumaripati, behind the Campion Academy. 10min. from either Lagankhel bus park or Jawalakhel Chowk. A bit outside the older part of town, these rooms are part of a friendly household. Though small, each room has several windows. All bathrooms have shower and seat toilet. Singles with common bath Rs200, with bath Rs350; doubles with common bath Rs250. ❷

Bakena Batika (☎5523998), at Ring Rd. and the main road in Jawalakhel. Set in a converted traditional Nepali house, the tastefully decorated rooms give the feeling that you never left home. The lush central garden with its own rice paddy adds to the natural and calm atmosphere. Living room restaurant serve wholesome Nepali and continental meals. Doubles with attached bath US$20. ❺

🍴 FOOD

Patan's food selection is less varied than Kathmandu's, but it's also less tourist-oriented, with more *tarkari* (veg. curry) than teriyaki. Fast-food tandoori joints line the roads between Pulchowk and Jawalakhel and Lagankhel. More expensive places serve the same menu in more pleasant settings with cloth napkins. For breakfast, **Hot Breads ❶**, just off Jawalakhel Chowk, offers a wide range of pastries, and the **German Bakery ❶**, on Jawalakhel Chowk opposite Raji's, has cake and loaves of bread to go. Both open at 8am; arrive early for good quality and selection.

🍴 **Raji's,** just outside Jawalakhel Chowk toward Pulchowk. Amazing Indian food at amazing prices set in an unassuming atmosphere. The locals recognize its quality as it is packed at lunch tine. *Masala paneer dosa* (Rs65) and *samosa chat* (Rs40) are excellent choices. The two brothers/owners' specialty is Indian sweets so don't forget dessert (Rs5-15). Open daily 7am-8:30pm. ❶

🍴 **La Soon Restaurant and Vinotheque,** just toward Kathmandu from the Pulchowk- Gabahal intersection. Catering to a sophisticated western appetite, this classy restaurant serves up concoctions at only moderately classy prices and blocks the sounds of traffic outside. Enjoy pumpkin ravioli with creamy tomato sauce (Rs175) or a feta wrap with chicken (Rs160). Even their beverages give a taste of the West. Sotto cafe with iced mint tea Rs35; real drip coffee Rs85. Open M-Sa 10:30am-10pm. ❸

Downtown Restaurant, Pulchowk, opposite the now defunct Sajha bus park. Lace curtains screen the sights but not the sounds of the busy street. Deservedly popular for its extensive menu and low prices. The locals order *momos* (Rs40-60) by the plateful and fish dinners (Rs105-145) are also available. Open Su-F 10am-9pm. ❷

Old House Restaurant and Cafe, behind Manga Hiti, away from Bhimsen Mandir. Besides the amazing views from the roof, it is most notable for its extensive use of vegetables. The menu has an unlikely mixture of Newari and Mexican food, to be served on any one of the many open-air levels. Newari set meals (Rs30-70), Mexican chicken burrito (Rs160), and breakfast veggie omelette (Rs105). Open daily 9am-9pm. ❷

Third World Restaurant, in Durbar Sq. behind Krishna Mandir, next to Third World Guest House, on the rooftop. Watch devotees set Krishna Mandir aglow with butter lamps over some of the best *dal bhat* and *thalis* (Rs150-190) in Nepal. Open daily 8am-9pm. ❸

Cafe de Patan, Mangal Bazaar, immediately outside Durbar Sq. toward Pulchowk. Chug the Square's safest lassis (Rs40-55; no water) in the ground floor dining area or the garden rooftop. A great place to try Newari lentil cakes (Rs40-60) or a mild veggie curry (Rs90). Open daily 8am-9pm. ❶

Bakena Batika, Jawalakhel, just inside Ring Rd. Though removed from the sights, this beautifully renovated Nepali house and tranquil courtyard make the perfect setting. Practically self-sustaining restaurant with mid-courtyard rice paddy serves set Nepali meals (Rs180) and off-beat Western dishes like polenta (Rs120). Service can be slow, however, because nothing is even thawed until you order. Open daily noon-8:30pm. ❸

👁 SIGHTS

In Patan, even an afternoon stroll can feel like a day's worth of temple hopping, but there are several areas of concentrated importance and interest.

DURBAR SQUARE

A good approach to exploring Durbar Sq. is to start at the end of the **Royal Palace,** closest to Magal Bazaar and Tangal Tole and continue toward the river, away from Gabahal, circling around counter-clockwise. The entire square, arguably one of the most beautiful in Nepal, was named a World Heritage Site in 1979. Although damaged during Prithvi Narayan Shah's 1768 conquest of the valley and the 1934 earthquake, the Royal Palace's three main courtyards have since been nearly restored to their 17th-century splendor.

THE ROYAL PALACE. The courtyard, **Sundari Chowk,** closest to Mangal Bazaar, is not open to the public, but **Mul Chowk,** the next courtyard towards the river Mul Chowk dates from the mid-18th century, can be entered between the two stone lions. On the right wall, gilded statues of the Indian river goddesses Ganga (on a tortoise) and Yamuna (on a *makara,* a mythical snouted sea creature) guard the locked doorway to the **Taleju Shrine.** Dedicated to the goddess of Nepal's royal families, the shrine is open to Hindus one day a year during the **Dasain** festival. Held on an auspiciously chosen date in the fall, the Dasain festival pays tribute to the goddess Kali, a reincarnation of Parvati, with animal sacrifices and the metal around the shrine and on the statues is dented and tarnished. The hand-carved wood buttresses depict a different god or goddess, many with far more arms than usual. Other pagodas that rise around Mul Chowk are the **Taleju Mandir,** an octagonal tower in the far left corner as you enter, and the **Degutaleju Mandir,** which as the square's tallest, dominates the Chowk's left side. *(Mul Chowk open daily 9am-5pm.)*

NO WORK, ALL PLAY

RATO MACHHENDRANATH FESTIVAL

Every April and May the citizens of Patan participate in one of the most involved festivals in all of Nepal. The Rato Machhendranath Festival is more than just making an offering.

In April the Machhendranath image is removed from its resting place in Lagankhel temple and brought to Pulchowk. Here, a towering chariot is constructed of wheels the height of a man, a yoke the girth and length of a tree trunk, and a central standard of pine bough stems of several meters high, balancing precariously upright above the platform. With thick hemp ropes attached and the image placed appropriately, the pulling begins. The men of Patan assemble each evening fueled by *rakshi* and *chang* for 2-3 hours to advance the chariot. However, these hours can be more waiting than pulling since the chariot can only move at auspicious times, as declared by a group of four priests. When the day's pulling is over, coconuts are thrown from the top of the central standard, blessing those who catch them with good luck.

The overall journey is from Pulchowk to Jawalakhel Chowk, though the route is a bit circuitous and is one of the main reasons the festival can last so long. Since Rato Machhendranath lasts for such an extended period of time, finding accommodation or the time to hop on a bus from Kathmandu isn't very difficult. Just ask a local where the chariot is currently located, then head over to try and catch a coconut.

The ▨**Patan Museum,** in **Keshav Narayan Chowk,** has been hailed as one of the best on the Subcontinent. Visitors enter through an elaborate golden doorway and a set of monkey-faced lions sporting fangs and smiles. With the help of the Austian government, the palace was restored to its 1737 splendor after being ravaged by conquest, monsoons, and earthquakes for nearly 300 years. The displays of metal, wood, and stone sculpture here provide an excellent introduction to Hindu and Buddhist iconography, including the stances, postures, clothing, and adornments of deities. The histories and legends of the *stupas* of Nepal are also catalogued. The 3rd-floor gallery proceeds step-by-step through the sculpting processes. Most of the palace's extensive gardens, including the Royal Bath, are off limits. *(Museum open 10:30am-5:30pm. Ticket booth and cafe open daily 10:30am-5pm. Rs250. Cameras free.)* Towards the river from the palace, in front of the Adarsha Kanya Niketan Higher Secondary School, is the water tank **Manga Hiti** whose mythical crocodile-like statues have been spouting water since the 6th century. The adjacent pavilion, **Mani Mandap,** was once used for coronations, but today many people use it for bathing and drinking water.

OTHER TEMPLES. Diagonal towards the river from Manga Hiti is the three-tiered **Bhimsen Mandir,** with a lion-topped pillar in front of its unfinished and decaying marble facade. The temple is dedicated to the strongest of the Pandavas and is still in use as Hindu merchants (non-HIndus are not allowed) toss coins onto the older, gilded first floor of this temple. In fact, most shop owners in Durbar Square have a personal statue of Bhima for when they can't make it to the temple. The next temple, exactly opposite the Manga Hiti, is the **Vishwanath Mandir,** a double-roofed temple guarded by two stone elephants. The original structure dates back to 1627, but it collapsed in 1990 and has since been restored. The presence of the interior *linga* and the Nanda, which faces the temple, is dedicated to Shiva. Offerings can be made only in the morning when the screens are open. Continuing toward Gabahal, the next temple is the stone, Indian *shikhara*-style **Krishna Mandir.** Supposedly the first all-stone *shikhara* specimen in Nepal, it is one of the few temples in Durbar Sq. still in active use. In the evenings, devotees set the building's balconies aglow with butter lamps. The upper floors, carved with friezes depicting scenes from the *Mahabharata* and *Ramayana*, are closed to non-Hindus.

Vishnu is the patron god of the square's oldest temple, the **Jagan Narayan Mandir.** The temple opposes the dominating Degutaleju Mandir, but is not open for use. Immediately toward Mangal Bazaar is a fenced complex of small shrines. To get to the next temple, head to the Third World Guest House, on the side of the square opposite the palace turn left and continue past Gorkha Money Exchange and the bead stalls. The squat **Bhai Deval Mandir** is in front of Cyber Zone, next to Gabahal. The nanda again means a temple dedicated to Shiva. Continuing along Gabahal, back toward the palace with a metal bust in the center, you'll pass a fountain. Between the fountain and the palace is the octagonal stone **Chyasin Deval,** which is like the other Krishna temple in the square, was built in an Indian style. After Patan built the enormous **Taleju Bell** in front of the Sundari Chowk, Bhaktapur and Kathmandu were quick to commission similarly oversized bells. The next temple away from Gabahal is the **Hari Shankar Mandir,** an elaborately carved, three-tiered pagoda from the 18th century. The temple is dedicated to Vishnu (called Har. here) and Shiva (Shankar) and its entrance is flanked with kneeling stone elephants. In the middle of the square is a stone pillar topped with a golden statue of **King Yoganarendra Malla,** which faces the palace. King Malla is the ruler who displaced a Buddhist monastery so he could take up residence in Patan's palace. To commemorate this, every year a Buddha image is submerged in water outside the entrance to the Patan Museum and is worshipped there for a month.

NORTH OF DURBAR SQUARE

GOLDEN TEMPLE. The Golden Temple, one of Patan's most famous buildings, is a 5min. walk north of Durbar Sq. Also known as **Hiranyavarna Mahavihar,** this ornate, gilded temple makes up the west side of the **Kwa Bahal,** a 12th-century Buddhist monastery still in operation that conducts daily morning *pujas.* The temple's central feature is the image of Shakya Muni Buddha, which is located opposite the entrance gate and is the only area where photographs are not allowed. In the center of the courtyard stands a small, but equally opulent, golden shrine. Named the Swayambhu Chaitya, it is the temple's most ancient structure and houses the holy text of Pragya Parmita, written in letters of gold. The temple's facade contains images of Buddhas and *taras* the mother of all Buddhas because she represents all the enlightened activities of Buddha. She is found here in the transformed bodies of Avalokiteshvara. In each corner of the courtyard stands a statue of Lokeshvara, all of which are renowned for their superb artistic value. Gods supposedly slide down the *patakas,* the golden belts that hang from the roofs, to answer their worshippers' prayers. The stairs, in the near right corner as you enter, lead to a collection of icons and Tibetan-style murals inside the monastery and the best spot to take pictures. *(Walk to the end of Durbar Sq. farthest from Gabahal, take a left at the Bhimsen Mandir, then take the next right. The temple is one and a half blocks down on the left just before the blue and yellow sign. Open daily 8:30am-6pm. Rs25 for foreigners. No leather shoes are allowed in the courtyard–either leave your Birkenstocks in the hotel or change into flip-flops available at the ticket counter.)*

KUMBESHWAR MAHADEV. A few minutes north of the Golden Temple, Kumbeshwar Mahadev is the oldest temple in Patan. Though it had only two tiers when it was built in 1392, three stories were added later to make it one of two free-standing, five-roofed pagodas in the Kathmandu Valley (the other is the Nyatapola Temple in Bhaktapur). The deity-in-residence is Shiva, as indicated by the Nandi outside the temple and the stone *linga* inside. The water tank next to the temple is believed to be connected to the holy Himalayan lake of Gosainkund. A pilgrim is said to have dropped a *kumbh* (pot) in the lake, which then emerged in the tank in Patan, giving the temple its name. Thousands of devotees come to bathe in the tank during the **Janai Purnima festival** (held in August), when high-caste Hindus change their *janais,* sacred threads that male Brahmins and Chhetris wear over their left shoulders. Every Thursday the enclosure becomes a sea of umbrellas and exquisitely colored cloth as the residents of Patan come to make offerings to Bungalamukhi, often waiting in line for hours to do so. Housed in the two-story building to the right of the temple as you enter, Bungalamukhi is a reincarnation of Kali, the goddess of success. Wishes made on Thursday are more likely to come true.

SOUTH OF DURBAR SQUARE

Continuing along Mangal Bazaar for 5min. away from Gabahal, you'll see signs for the **Mahaboudha Temple;** take the right hand turn off and then after 200m take another right turn into the shop-lined hallway leading to the cramped courtyard. The architect of this "temple of 1000 Buddhas" was inspired by the Mahabodhi Temple in Bodh Gaya, India, where the Buddha achieved enlightenment. The *shikhara*-style temple is covered with terra cotta tiles, each of which bears the same sculpted figure of Buddha in his most well-known pose. The temple was severely damaged in a 1934 earthquake, and the builders who reassembled it found themselves with so many bricks left over that they built a small shrine to the Buddha's mother Mayadevi, which stands in the back left corner of the courtyard. Out of the Mahaboudha's entrance, turn right, take the first left to reach **Uka Bahal (Rudravarna Mahavihar).** At 1400 years old, it is the oldest monastery in Patan. A pair of stone lions protects this former Newari Buddhist monastery, while the rest of the zoo watches from the courtyard currently under construction. Through the courtyard is the *stupa* Swoyambhu Bajrayana, a work of colorful mastery.

As you leave Uka Bahal, turn left onto **Thapahiti**. The sound of metal being hammered in unseen workshops fills the avenue, which ends at Tangal Tole as it runs from Durbar Sq. to Lagankhel. At the intersection of the two streets stands the **Ibaha Bahal,** a monastery dating from 1427 which was renovated in 1995 with the help of the Nippon Institute of Technology. Three-hundred meters toward Lagankhel on Tangal Tole on the left, is the **Minnath Mandir.** Surrounded by houses, the temple is well-used almost into disrepair, making its garish paint job hard to make out. Minnath is often called *sanno* ("little") Machhendranath, in reference to the deity who inhabits another temple down a short lane across the street. This temple, the **Rato Machhendranath Mandir,** is a three-roofed pagoda from the 17th-century standing in the center of a grassy courtyard. The courtyard is entered from behind the temple so circle around to find a collection of brass animals, each one representing a month of the Tibetan calendar, poses on posts facing the temple. The temple is one of the most colorful and well-kept in Patan, despite its heavy use, Machhendranath is a multi-purpose deity: he is an incarnation of Avalokiteshvara who is the *bodhisattva* of compassion, he is revered as the guru of a 7th-century saint, and he serves as the Newari god who controls the rains. In late May, the *rato* ("red") image of Machhendranath rides in a towering chariot that makes its rounds in Patan, followed by a smaller chariot carrying Minnath, who is considered to be his brother. Beginning in Pulchowk, the local residents tow the chariots to the next stop on the tour, having first fueled themselves with *raksi* and *chang*. The chariots are often halted along the way to wait for a suitably auspicious moment to move, and it can take them up to 60 days to reach Jawalakhel, their final destination. From here, the image of Machhendranath is removed from the chariot and carried to his temple in the nearby town of Bungamati. The enormous, rickety temple-chariots *(raths)* are destroyed and built anew every year, and the remnants remain around Jawalakhel Chowk, casually strewn between tempos and buses.

JAWALAKHEL

The Jawalakhel neighborhood is notable for its foreign residents and foreign aid organization offices. Most non-Nepalis are Tibetan refugees or South Asian expats with a few British ex-Gorkha soldiers mixed in.

TIBETAN REFUGEE CAMP. It was established by the Red Cross and the Nepalese government in 1960 after the Chinese takeover in 1959 drove large numbers of Tibetan refugees to the area. The booming carpet industry, centered here, provides jobs to over 1000 Tibetans in the area. Proceeds from the showrooms go to the workers and to a social welfare fund that supports children's educational programs and provides a stipend to elderly Tibetans. Visitors are free to wander and observe all stages of the carpet-making process. The weaving room is the busiest area, with over 40 huge looms. (☎ 5521305. 5-10min. walk toward Ring Rd. from Jawalakhel Chowk. Open Su-F 9am-5pm.)

CENTRAL ZOO. Just outside Jawalakhel Chowk is Nepal's only zoo. See that tiger that eluded you at Chitwan, dodge siamarg feces (they've been known to throw), and commune with flamingoes on a paddleboat ride in the pond. Or, spin yourself sick on the dilapidated merry-go-round, and queasily recover on an elephant ride around the zoo. Just don't visit in the early afternoon, as most animals retreat to the shade to avoid the heat. (Open Tu-Su 10am-6pm, tickets sold until 5pm. Rs100; camera fee Rs10; merry-go-round Rs20 per ride; paddleboat Rs40 per person; elephant ride Rs100.)

◖ SHOPPING

A lower-pressure sales atmosphere than Kathmandu make Patan an ideal place for souvenir shopping. Most of the items for sale are actually produced here, especially woodcarvings, metalworks, or Tibetan rugs. Therefore prices and selection tend to be even better than in Kathmandu. Aside from the markets and individual stores geared toward bargaining tourists (see **Markets**, p. 829). Patan is also full of non-profit outlets selling crafts from all over the country at fixed prices. Many benefit underprivileged workers—especially women—and ensure fair wages.

Jawalakhel Handicraft Center, part of the Tibetan Refugee Camp, in Jawalakhel near Ring Rd. All the carpets are made here, from the spinning to the dyeing and weaving, and are renowned on the international market for their superior quality. The lowest quality carpet, with 60 knots per sq. in., costs $80 per sq. m. All profits are used internally to subsidize housing, send children to school, or pay for elderly care. The workshops, open to visitors, and showrooms are open Su-F 9am-5pm. MC/V.

Mahaguthi, sponsored by Oxfam, carries everything from Nepalese paper to pottery to traditional cloth. Its Kopundol branch, two blocks toward Kathmandu from the Pilgrim Book House, is open M-F 10am-6:30pm, Sa 10am-5am. The Degutaleju Madir in Durbar Sq. has a branch open M-F 10am-5:30pm. MC/V.

Sana Hastakala, Kopundol, opposite Hotel Himalaya, focuses on fair wages for Nepali women and therefore stocks mostly women's items like dresses and jewelry. Open M-F 9:30am-6pm, Sa 10am-5pm. AmEx/V.

Patan Industrial Estate, in Lagankhel near Ring Road, houses showrooms catering to large tourist groups. Here the government has centralized factories and showrooms, It is a great place to find a wide variety of metalwork, wood carvings, and *thankas*. Prices are higher here, but it is worth it (free!) to come and watch the artisans at work. Most showrooms and workshops open daily 10am-5pm and accept a variety of credit cards.

◗ DAYTRIPS FROM PATAN

GODAVARI गोदावरी

From Lagankhel bus park, bus #14 continues up the hills to Godavari (25-30min., Rs10), with views of rice paddies and a wide variety of architectural styles along the way. Godavari bus park is the last stop.

If the dry, dusty city has you craving a return to nature, Godavari is the place to go. In this horticultural haven, on the valley's southeastern edge, you'll find the peaceful, expertly landscaped Royal Botanical Garden, the National Herbarium, and the nurseries that supply florists in Patan. In among the trees are Godavari Kunda and Pulchowki Mai, two local temples. The **Royal Botanical Garden** is a 15min. walk from the bus park, up the road to the left. Continue on the paved road past the Natual Herbarium and the Conservation and Educational Gardens as it curves around the outer edge of gardens and comes to a stop at the main gate. The garden, founded in 1962, has manicured terraces with greenhouses and path-filled woods. At 82 hectares, it is big enough to get lost in. Shady pavilions next to gurgling brooks are numerous so bring a lunch and picnic. *(Open daily 9am-5pm. Rs100; camera fee Rs10.)* The small dirt road that branches off to the right 200m before the entrance to the Botanical Garden leads for 100m to the **Godavari Kunda,** a pool shrouded with faded prayer flags. Clear mountain water collects in an interior pool (closed) which then flows through spouts to the outer pool, both filled with fish. Pilgrims come here every 12 years to purify themselves in the waters, but you might see kids swimming on any hot day. Occasionally, most likely in the morning, the pujari is present and will open the gates to the inner tank. Back at the bus park,

KATHMANDU VALLEY

the road to the right leads uphill for 10min. past St. Xavier's College to a marble quarry and **Pulchowki Mai,** a rather run-down temple. The temple houses images of Vishnu, Ganesh, and a tantric mother goddess, but most, even the *linga*, have been worn beyond recognition. Outside the temple is a pool fed by nine spouts, symbolizing the nine streams that flow off Pulchowki, the nearby mountain for which the temple is named. A trail behind the temple starts the 3hr. climb to the peak, which, at 2762m, offers panoramic views of the valley.

BUNGAMATI बुँगामथी

The bus to Bungamati departs frequently from Patan's Jawalakhel Chowk (15min., Rs6). Stay on until the last stop, which is Bungamati's bus park, called Jawalakhel. To get to the temple, take the path from the end of the bus park closest to Patan. At two adjacent pools, turn left and follow the path around to the temple's courtyard. For a less noticed entrance, continue through the bus park on the paved road and take the right fork. This leads to the rear of the temple's courtyard. The only evidence of tourists is a hand painted map at the bus stand, but if this is still too much, head to the untouristed town of Khokana. Take the path from the bus park towards the temple; at the two pools continue straight and then take the right fork. The last bus to Patan from Bungamati is at 6:30pm.

Few tourists ever venture to **Bungamati's** cobblestone alleys, which run between a jumble of red-roofed brick houses. With everything from baby goats and ducks munching on weeds to curious children greeting the village's rare visitors with wide-eyed stares, the visitor will experience life in a typical Newari village.

The town's main claim to fame is its tall, *shikhara*-style Rato Machhendranath temple. Although extremely well-used and surrounded by houses, the temple's white, red, and yellow paint job and ceremonial adornments are still very much intact, providing an excellent playground and field for the never-ending game of soccer played around its base. There are signs advertising a free cultural museum, but it's rarely open, and when it is, the museum is not much more than a collection of dusty pottery and statues in the attic. Bungamati is revered as the birthplace of Machhendranath, the patron god of the Kathmandu Valley, also believed to be an incarnation of Avalokiteshvara, the Bodhisattva of Compassion. Machhendranath's rainmaking prowess is vital to this self-sufficient agricultural community. The god's image is only here six months out of the year during the growing season, because it is moved by man-pulled chariot from a corresponding temple in Patan.

KIRTIPUR कितीपुर

Located on a southwestern ridge overlooking the valley, Kirtipur is known for its pluralistic religious community and its turbulent history. Simultaneously fighting off the encroaching development of nearby **Tribhuvan University** and inviting much-needed public funds for infrastructure within the town itself, Kirtipur, like Bungamati, remains largely ignored by tourists. Still, its ornate temples, hilltop views, and proximity to Chobar make Kirtipur a worthwhile daytrip from Kathmandu.

In the 18th century, the citizens of Kirtipur bravely fended off the Gorkha forces of Prithvi Narayan Shah twice (see **History,** p. 782). However, the Gorkhas' superior weaponry turned the tide two years later, when Kirtipur finally surrendered after a six-month siege. The Gorkhas violently punished the townsmen, slicing off their noses, ears, and lips so that people throughout the country would see them as the troublemakers from Kirtipur. Today, Kirtipur is an impoverished Newari town and supports itself largely through handmade cloth and carpets.

■ ▶ **ORIENTATION AND PRACTICAL INFORMATION.** To reach Kirtipur, take a **taxi** (Rs200) or **bus #21** (30min., frequent, Rs6) from **Kathmandu's** Ratna Park bus station. The bus follows **Dakshinkali Road,** passes the gates of **Tribhuvan University,** and finally climbs a steep hill into town before taking a sharp left. Get off at the top of the hill, where you'll see the sign "Hearty Welcome to our Historical Place: Kirtipur." A rusted, nearly unreadable town map is blocked by this newly painted sign. To your left, around the winding road into town, is the Shree Kirti Vihana. Up the stone steps to your right is the town district of **Gutepave.** The road to the left goes on past the temple to become the **Naya Bazaar,** home to several small shops offering **STD** and **Internet** services. On the right-hand side of this road, heading into town, is **RB Computer Concern and Cyber,** with a helpful university student staff and phone, Internet, and fax services. (☎4333150. Rs25 per hr. Open daily 7am-8pm.)

🞂 **SIGHTS.** A walking tour of Kirtipur's sights can be completed in under 2hr. The Buddhist temple is left from the welcome sign, down the stairs on the left side of the street 200m from the sign, while all other sites are up the staircase to the right of the sign. The Nagara Mandapa **Shree Kirti Vihara,** a Thai-style Theravada Buddhist temple built in 1989, is immaculately maintained by the resident monks. Its fusion of Newari and Thai sculpture, architecture, and landscaping is a gem of intercultural creativity. Often empty, this cliffside religious oasis makes a nice place to relax. A small four-door gallery, stamped with the Thai Airways logo, depicts the four major stages in Buddha's life: his birth in Lumbini, his enlightenment at Bodh Gaya, his first sermon at Sarnath, and his death in Kushinagar.

From the rusty city map, take the steep, stone stairs to your right. At the top, turn right after passing under a shrine gate, then left when you reach the pool with a solid green surface of moss. The steps up to the ancient **Chilandeo Stupa** (also called Chilancho Vihara) are to your right through a small gate, near a standard stone *shikhara.* This 1400-year-old *stupa* is surrounded by a number of stone shrines, some of which are relatively new. The prayer wheel, to the right as you enter, is only six years old, but it is the largest in Kirtipur. Along the left side of the *stupa* and down the steps is an abandoned 17th-century monastery, adorned with just one remaining *torano* arch on the center door, and guarded by a sturdy Newari-crafted lock.

Facing the monastery, turn right and then right again and walk behind the *stupa.* At the second corner, follow the small, bumpy stone path left out of the *stupa* area. From the path, take your first right into an open area dominated by a towering stone **shikhara.** The upper level of the temple features representations of the Buddha, while the lower level is devoted to Hindu deities. This half-Buddhist, half-Hindu temple was built during the 17th century as a gesture of goodwill during a period of religious tension.

From the *shikhara,* turn left and follow the slate path down to a large courtyard with another green pool. At the far end of the courtyard is the **Bagh Bhairab Mandir,** an 11th-century temple dedicated to Shiva the Destroyer *(Bhairab)* in the form of a tiger *(bagh).* Gorkhali swords and uniforms mounted along the three stories of the facade commemorate Kirtipur's defeat by the Gorkhas. These swords are original, offered to the god after the 18th-century massacre. Worshippers and musicians visit Bagh Bhairab every morning and evening; there are chicken or buffalo sacrifices on Tuesdays and Saturdays. Bagh Bhairab is also the center of Kirtipur's December **festival** for the goddess Indrani, an offshoot of Kathmandu's Indrani festival.

Facing the entrance to the Bagh Bhairab Mandir, take the road to the left, then turn right at the dead-end with a shrine. Next, take a quick left up steep stones to the **Uma-Maheshwar Mandir.** Built in 1575, the temple overlooks the valley from the highest point in Kirtipur (1440m). Two stone elephants guard the temple, which houses intricately carved images of Shiva and his consort Parvati. More noteworthy than the temple itself is its superb panoramic view. To the southwest looms one of the highest points of the Kathmandu Valley's rim, and to the northeast sprawls the city of Kathmandu. On a clear day, you can even see Everest.

CHOBAR चोभार

When Manjushri drained the Kathmandu valley with one legendary swing of his sword, the blow carved out the plunging cliffs of **Chobar Gorge.** A narrow Scottish-built **suspension bridge** spans the gorge, connecting the pine-covered hills with the lower portion of village. The choked, putrid Bagmati, the site of many local cremations, foams underfoot. From the bridge it is possible to see the cliffside steps leading to South Asia's third-longest cave, **Chobar Gupha** on the west bank. Next to the bridge is the three-tiered, brightly colored **Jal Binayak,** a 17th-century temple dedicated to Ganesh, who is represented here in the form of a large rock protruding from the back of the temple. Locals lean against this rock to harness its curative powers. The engravings at the base of the temple depict complicated, erotic positions. Around the temple, a stylized Shiva *linga* dances with Parvati before the statue of a rabbit. Chobar Village spreads across a small hill that overlooks the gorge. At its peak (reached by following the town's single uphill winding road) is the 14th-century **Adinath Lokeshwar Mandir,** a half-Hindu, half-Buddhist temple covered with hundreds of utensils, pots, and pans—contributing kitchenware to the temple is said to enhance the culinary skills of new brides as well as the strength of the marriage. The donation is also made by the children of newly-deceased parents, hoping for their good fortune in the next life. A series of photographs in the back left corner of the temple honors the massacred members of the royal family.

Bus #22 (30min., frequent, Rs6) heads to Chobar from Ratna Park in Kathmandu. Get off just before the bus turns west into the gates of Tribhuvan University, and continue along Dakshinkali Rd., the town's main road. Just after the **Himalayan Bee Concern** on the right, stone stairs lead uphill to Chobar. The gorge can be reached either by continuing on paved Dakshinkali Rd. or through the village of Chobar—turn right as you exit the temple and follow the dirt path steeply downhill. From the gorge, it's about 1hr. to Patan; cross the bridge, head straight along the uphill path, and turn left at the first intersection. Chobar is a 30min. walk away from Kirtipur. Follow the main road through the Naya Bazaar; with the Buddhist temple on your left, turn left at Ratna's **Beauty Parlor,** take another left at the cinema sign, and follow the street straight past the Snow Lion Carpet Factory to your left. When you reach a tree with tiny shrines encircling its trunk, veer left onto the main road and climb the stone staircase up to Chobar.

NAGARJUN नागार्जुन AND BALAJU बालाजु

Many believe that the Buddha once meditated on Nagarjun; others maintain that the first *bodhisattva*, Viswapa, stood on the peak to throw the lotus seed that would blossom into *swayambhu*. Crowned by an old *stupa* festooned with a canopy of aging prayer flags, Nagarjun (also called Jamacho) is the closest summit to Kathmandu and offers a breathtaking panoramic view of the valley. Camping is permitted, but not easy, since the hillside is steep and covered in thick brush. The area is a favorite among Tibetan weekend picnickers, but is rarely crowded during the week. Nagarjun sits in the **Rani Ban Forest Reserve** (also called Nagarjun Royal Forest), a well-preserved chunk of woods protected by the government that used to be a Rana hunting ground (Rs10). You might spot a leopard in this reserve, though wild boars and unherded bulls are far more common. After you enter Rani Ban, a well-marked trail (5km, 2hr.) on your right leads to the summit. At the top you'll find a lookout tower and the Buddhist shrine **Jamacho.** Jamacho is the center of April's full-moon festival, **Balju Jatra,** when worshippers hold an all-night vigil at the summit and descend to Balaju the next day for a ritual bath in Baais Dhara.

Pleasant outdoor recreation can also be found in **Balaju Water Garden** (Balaju Bashdhara) in nearby Balaju, the industrial suburb just south of Nagarjun. Balaju is an uncomplicated but unpleasant 40min. urban walk from Thamel. Walk north from Kathmandu Guesthouse, turn left at Lekhnath Marg, and follow the congested traffic northwest over the bridge and then straight past the rotary. Continue straight for another 500m past the "Welcome Balaju Industrial District" sign on your left and tiny Balaju shopping center on your right. The garden is on the left, approximately 50m later. **Bus #23** (30min., frequent, Rs5) leaves from Ratna Park and stops at the garden, one of the few well-maintained public spaces around. Nepali families relax around manicured rose gardens, shaded benches, and fantastically garish fountains spraying water in all directions. (☎4350111. Open daily 7am-7:30pm. Rs5; camera fee Rs5; video fee Rs15.) A former royal garden for the Malla queens, the park used to be closed to the public. During festival season, worshippers bathe in the water that courses from the 22 carved crocodiles of the **Baais Dhara**, to the right. The water is considered to have a holy connection with the waters of Trisoli and is now used for both daily bathing and laundry. Midway through the park is the **Bala Nilkantha**, a 7th-century contemporary of the more elaborate sleeping Vishnu in Budhanilkantha. Devotees crawl over the 3.65m long Vishnu and pour milk and honey over his face. Thamel-weary travellers can find respite in the noisy **swimming pool.** (Open daily 9am-12:30pm and 1-4pm. Rs40, students with ID Rs35. Women only on Th. To experience the pool without the crowds, you can buy a seasonal membership for Rs2500 and use the pool during the members-only slot, 4:30-7pm.) **Park Restaurant ❷,** on the left side of the garden, is a small food stand that serves samosas, ice cream, fried rice, tea, and coffee, while blaring Nepali and Indian pop.

BOUDHA (BOUDHANATH) बौद्धनाथ ☎01

The massive, whitewashed dome of Nepal's largest *stupa* draws Buddhists from far and wide to Boudha, east of Kathmandu. A cherished site of Tibetan pilgrims and refugees, here there is also a growing population of Westerners seeking academic and spiritual enlightenment in Buddhism. Circumambulation (or *Kora* in Tibetan, walking clockwise around and on the *stupa*) takes place *en masse* throughout the day at this holy center. Due to the town's popularity with tourists, the monks are accustomed to and welcome respectful foreign visitors. In Boudha, you can experience the serenity of monastic life, while still embracing its simple charms—local children clamoring on the *stupa*, the smell of incense drifting in every direction, and every few hours, horns and drums announcing the rituals of the nearby *gompas*.

✴ ⁊ ORIENTATION AND PRACTICAL INFORMATION

Boudha has expanded far beyond the confines of the **stupa compound,** but the *stupa* remains its symbolic center and the reference point for all other directions. The *stupa*, 5km east of Kathmandu, can be entered through a **gate** on the north side of **Tusal Road,** the main east-west road. The sprawling community north of the *stupa*, where you will find most of Boudha's monasteries, is accessible from two parallel lanes leading north out of the compound. The commercial area inside the *stupa* contains all the town's phones, banks, and Internet service. The area outside consists mainly of small craft shops and monasteries. Wide **Phulbare Road** runs from the eastern edge of the compound past Tashi Delek Restaurant and Kailash Guest House. **Duratol Road,** a narrow path lying just to the west, leaves the compound opposite the entrance to the *stupa* itself. Small east-west lanes beside Tusal Rd. connect these two roads. None of the roads are labelled, and only these three have been named by city officials. **Always walk clockwise around the stupa**.

Buses: Bus #2 from **Ratna Park** (30min., frequent, Rs7) drops people off a few yards before the gate. Blue **tempos** (#2, Rs8) leave from Jamal, the street running along the southern edge of Rani Pokhari. **Taxis** from **Thamel** cost around Rs100.

Currency Exchange: Mandala Money Changer (☎4478714), on the left, just inside the southern gates, changes traveler's checks and US, British, Australian, Japanese, and EU currency for a 10% fee. Open Su-F 9am-5pm, Sa 9-11am.

Market: Fruit-sellers gather on Tusal Rd. outside the entrance to the *stupa* compound and in the lanes north of the *stupa*. Across the east-west road, about 25m east of the gate (on your left and across the street coming out of the *stupa*), is the well-stocked **Gemini Grocer.** Imported wines, many varieties of hygienic products, and shelves of packaged foods. Open daily 7am-8pm. MC/V.

Police: Tusal Rd. (☎4470545). 100m west of the *stupa* on the south side of the road.

Hospital: There are numerous storefront pharmacies and clinics on the 2 northern lanes. The largest and most modern is the **Shechen Clinic** (☎4487924), on the road that branches left from Duratol. Upon leaving the *stupa*, follow signs to Rabsel Guest House, across the street on the left from the Shechen Monastery. This pleasant clinic provides services for Westerners and free care for the underprivileged. Homeopathy offered Su-Th 9am-2pm, F 11am-3pm. Tibetan Medicine consultations M-F 9am-4pm, Su 9am-1pm. Standard Western-style doctor consultations Rs500. Attached **pharmacy** sells condoms, as well as Western, homeopathic, and Tibetan medicines. Clinic and pharmacy open Su-F 9am-4pm.

Internet and Telephones: Internet cafes surround the *stupa*. One of the best is **Dharana Cyberspace** (☎/fax 4494178). Services include STD/ISD, fax, Internet phone, and Internet access (Rs1 per min., Rs30 per hr.). Open daily 6:30am-9:30pm.

▐ ACCOMMODATIONS

Boudha's clean and peaceful lodgings might make you want to stay a few extra nights. With the exception of Peace Guest House, all guest houses listed have seat toilets, hot water, and noon check-out. Those farther from the *stupa* tend to be quieter and many have private gardens.

Rabsel Guest House (☎4479009; www.rabselguesthouse.com), on the way to Dragon Guest House. Clean rooms with private bath. This not-for-profit guest house run by Shechen Monastery has an obliging staff and a landscaped central garden. Large, comfortable reception and common space on each floor. Free continental breakfast in attached veg. restaurant. Internet 8am-8:30pm. Reception 7am-9pm. Sept.-May 15 singles Rs620; doubles Rs840; triples Rs1260. May 16-July singles Rs520; doubles Rs720; triples Rs1120. ❹

Kailash Guest House, Phulbare Rd. (☎4480741), 2min. from the *stupa,* on the right, above the public clinic. Bare bones accommodations, but spacious with large common areas on each floor. Singles Rs200; doubles Rs250-300. ❷

Pema Guest House (☎4495662; fax 4487545). From Phulbare Rd., take the 1st right after exiting the *stupa* compound, then follow the winding road to the left. With elegant emerald decorations, plush carpeting, and immaculate bathrooms for only slightly more money than its competitors, Pema is certainly worth the splurge. Double bed with common bath Rs450; 2 beds with private bath Rs650; deluxe Rs950. ❸

Hotel Padma (☎4479052 or 4470957; hotelpadma@wlink.com.np), in the southwest corner of the *stupa* compound, on the left when entering from Tusal Rd. A luxurious oasis in the busy compound. Higher prices buy well-furnished, comfortable rooms overlooking the *stupa*. Large reception area with plush couches. Attached Chepangs Restaurant and Cheevry Bar are popular among Western visitors. 24hr. laundry, room service, and airport transfer. Discounts for longer stays. Singles US$18; doubles US$25; deluxe US$35; extra bed US$5. Add 2% tourist fee. JCB/MC/V. ❺

Dragon Guest House (☎/fax 4479562; dragon@ntc.net.np), 15min. from the *stupa*. From Duratol Rd. follow signs to Rabsel Guest House; continue walking past Rabsel and the Shecher monastery. A small, peaceful, well-priced guest house with a kind staff and a loyal Western clientele. Terraces on each floor. Used book library. Veg. restaurant. No meat or alcohol allowed. Breakfast Rs40-80, Tibetan, Nepalese, Chinese, and Japanese entrees Rs50-100. Open daily 7am-10pm. Singles Rs250; doubles Rs350. ❷

Lotus Guest House (☎ 4472432 or 4472320), beside the colorful Dobsang Monastery. From Phulbare Rd., take the 1st right after exiting the *stupa* compound. Follow the winding road left to the gated entrance of the courtyard. Motel-style layout, simple furniture, and an expansive, well-groomed garden courtyard. Reservations recommended Oct.-Nov. Singles Rs250-290; doubles Rs350-390; triples Rs490. Special Lotus Room double with bath Rs690. ❷

◻ FOOD

If you could build *stupas* from *momos*, Boudha would boast hundreds of delicious houses of worship. The town's chorus line of hole-in-the-wall restaurants serves quality Tibetan treats alongside the standard tourist fare. A few *stupa*-side eateries will let you exchange romantic glances with Buddha's blue eyes as you eat; the cheaper, smaller places line Duratol and Phulbare Rd.

Double Dorjee Restaurant, on the right, off Phulbare Rd., just past the Kamapa Service Society Nepal. A favorite with monks and ex-pats. Low tables, floral upholstery, and paper lanterns. Huge servings of mouth-watering Tibetan, Chinese, Japanese, and continental dishes listed on a blackboard menu (Rs40-120). The Tibetan family provides slow, friendly service, so you'll have plenty of time to chat. Open daily 7am-9pm. ❷

View Himalayan Restaurant, overlooking the *stupa* from the southeast side of the compound. Among loads of indiscernible Tibetan restaurants around the *stupa* with the word "view" in the title, this locale stands out for its popularity with tourists. *Momo G Kothey* Rs60-90, *thukpa* Rs60-90, *biryani* and *pulao* Rs80-110. ❷

Tashi Delek Restaurant, on the corner of the *stupa* compound, at Phulbare Rd. A curtain marks the entrance to this 3-table, low-profile eatery. Attentive, kind staff dishes up any local dish you may fancy (Rs25-90). Their veg. *thukpa* (Rs30-55) is hard to beat. Open 7am-9pm, but hours vary. ❶

◉ ◗ SIGHTS AND FESTIVALS

Boudha's *stupa* is one of the largest in the world. All kinds of legends surround its origins—the 5th-century date assigned by historians is really only a guess. A Tibetan myth tells of a poultry farmer's daughter who wanted to build a *stupa*. The king granted her permission to use an area the size of a buffalo skin. Not content to build such a small *stupa*, the girl sliced the skin into strips to trace the perimeter of the huge lot on which the *stupa* now stands. The Newari version tells the tale of a king who built taps from which no water would flow. Convinced that only the sacrifice of a great man would bring water, he ordered his son to go to the spouts and behead the shrouded man he found lying there. This, of course, turned out to be the king. Horrified by his deed, the prince built the *stupa* to redeem himself. The *stupa* has inspired awe and reverence since ancient times, when its location along the Kathmandu-Lhasa trade route made it a popular pilgrimage site—people still pray here for safe passage through the Himalayas.

Each segment of the *stupa's* structure corresponds to one of the five elements: the three-leveled *mandala*-shaped base represents earth; the dome, water; the spire (with its 13 steps corresponding to the 13 steps to nirvana), fire; the parasol, air; and the pinnacle, ether. The red-rimmed, blue Buddha eyes that gaze out from each of the four sides of the golden spire are unique to Nepali *stupas*, and the "nose" in between them is actually the number "1" in Nepali script. The white-washed *stupa* is splashed with stripes of rust-colored wash to resemble the lotus shape. Niches in the wall contain prayer wheels and 108 images of the Buddha. At the entrance to the *stupa* itself is a shrine to the Newari goddess Ajima, protectress of children and goddess of smallpox. Visitors can climb onto the first three tiers of the *stupa*, but may not ascend higher than the statues on the third level.

Monasteries typically welcome visitors as long as they observe the necessary etiquette (usually posted on signs outside). Dress modestly, take your shoes off before entering the *lhakang* (main hall), walk in a clockwise direction inside, and always ask before taking photos. As monasteries have traditionally relied on contributions from visitors and pilgrims, donations are greatly appreciated. If you visit a lama, present him with a white *khata* (prayer scarf). These are inexpensive and available at many shops around Boudha, where someone can show you how to fold them properly. In the *lhakang*, you'll find intricate wall paintings in overwhelmingly vivid colors and gold statues of notable Buddhist figures surrounded by offerings of food, incense, and butter-lamps.

The **Sakyapa** and **Sauntenling Gelugpa** *gompas* are right next to the *stupa* compound, and nearly 40 more *gompas* are spread out in the area to the north. The Shechen *gompa*, off Duratol Rd., features an immaculate and peaceful courtyard. A small building northwest of the Shechen *lhakang* has three gargantuan, 10 ft. prayer wheels, one of the most impressive sets in the area.

The year's largest celebrations happen in February when thousands come to meet friends and family for **Losar,** the Tibetan New Year. The festivities begin with February's new moon and last for two weeks. During the first three days of the festival, monks at the local monasteries perform celebratory dances. The holiday ends with the full moon on a day known as the **Festival of Lights,** or Day of Offerings (*Cho-trul Duechen* in Tibetan) when worshipers circle the *stupa* amidst prayers and chantings of penance and thanksgiving.

Shops surrounding the *stupa* sell souvenirs, religious emblems, and written information of varying quality. Tibetan antiques can be found in glass-covered display cases, but most are relatively expensive. Tibetan head-and-foot gear, incense, CDs of Buddhist prayer music, and Buddhist prayer flags can also be purchased in the complex, but are much more affordable elsewhere. The entry fee to the entire *stupa* compound is paid at the entrance from Tusal Rd. (Ticket office open daily 6:30am-6:30pm. Rs50.)

STUDY AND VOLUNTEER OPPORTUNITIES

Known as the white monastery or *seto gompa*, **Ka-Nying Shedrup Ling Monastery** (☎ 4470993; www.clos.edu.np or www.shedra.com.), between Phulbare and Duratol Rd., is one of the many monasteries in the area that welcome Westerners. To get there, follow Phulbare Rd., and take the left after you pass the Tashi Delek Restaurant. The monastery's leader meets visitors (daily 10am-noon) and holds a teaching session in English (Sa 10:30am-noon). Teaching sessions often get cancelled and rescheduled during low tourist season—confirm by calling the office (☎ 4479870) or Bu Chung on his mobile (☎ 98031530). This monastery also works in association with the Kathmandu University Center for Buddhist Studies and the Rangjung Yeshe Institute to host longer academic sessions. Courses offered include Buddhist philosophy, Tibetan, Nepali, Sanskrit, Buddhist rituals, and meditation. Sessions range from four months to four years.

Kopan Monastery (☎ 4481268; www.kopan-monastery.com), on a hill 2km north of Boudha, holds a short meditation course called "Discover Buddhism" throughout the year (7-day course Rs4600-7000), organizes longer retreats for Westerners seeking Buddhist instruction in a hilltop facility, and offers lodging when courses aren't being held. (Dorms Rs110, rooms with private bath Rs400. Breakfast included.) Offerings include a one-month meditation course in November, a three-month Vajrasattiva Retreat, the Nyung Nye Fasting Retreat during Chokar Duchen in August, and a prayer festival for Monlam. Nun Ani Karin leads meditations at Kopan and invites the public to attend free of charge. (M-F 10 and 11:30am. Videos on meditation Su 10am.) The facility also has a well-stocked library of Buddhist literature and a large meditation space for passing visitors. To get there from the *stupa*, follow Duratol Rd. for about 10min. until it meets a paved taxi road. Turn right, then turn left on the dirt path and continue for about 30min., veering to the left until it leads into Kopan; a map marks the entrance.

The **Vajrayana Center** is a non-formal venue for English-speaking visitors to teach English to recently-arrived Tibetan refugees and Nepalese from the Himalayas. You can teach for any length of time. The center also organizes free, ongoing Tibetan classes. To get to the center, follow Duratol Rd. from the *stupa* and take the first left onto a small road. Turn left at the first fork and again at the second; the center is on the left next to the Shakya Monastery and Kumari College. (☎ 4481108; vajrayana-centre@yahoo.com. Classes Su-F 7-9am and 1-5pm.)

BHAKTAPUR भक्तपुर ☎ 01

The gods of city planning decimated Bhaktapur in 1934 with a disastrous earthquake, which proved to be a backhanded gift—diligent restoration and preservation efforts since then have returned the city to its 15th-century splendor and have made Bhaktapur the cleanest city in the Kathmandu Valley. Forking over the hefty entrance fee (Rs750) to stroll along the neatly paved pedestrian zone might remind you of being at a theme park, but Bhaktapur is no Disneyland. Look between the magnificent temples and sacred landmarks of the Kathmandu Valley's third largest city and you might see scenes from a medieval Newari town—armies of clay pots left in the sun to dry, kids clambering for rides on the backs of ancient stone griffins, and wide brick lanes lined with street vendors hawking their colorful wares. The entry fee continues to finance restoration projects and civic programs such as trash collection. Though the fee is considerable, don't be deterred—the loveliness of the area in comparison to other Durbar Squares makes it worth the price.

▐ TRANSPORTATION

Buses: Bus #7 leaves from Kathmandu's Bagh Bazaar, just east of Durbar Marg and north of Ratna Park, and arrives at Bhaktapur's Minibus Park, near Guhya Pond (45min., frequent, Rs10). Unfortunately, this bus is very crowded and stops about a dozen times before even leaving Kathmandu city limits. Buses to **Nagarkot** (#7, 1hr., every 30min., Rs10) leave from **Kamal Binayak,** on the northeast edge of Bhaktapur, past Dattatraya Sq. You can also catch one heading from Kathmandu at the bus stop 50m north of the minibus park. Tourist buses arrive at the **Tourist Bus Park,** 5min. north of Durbar Sq. at the edge of town.

Local Transportation: To curb pollution, the city has banned heavy vehicles inside the gates; Bhaktapur is best explored on foot. **Bus #7** runs along the northern edge of town from the hospital to Kamal Binayak. **Taxis** wait just outside the main gate into Durbar Sq. and around the minibus park. **Bicycles** are available from the outdoor stand on the road that connects Guhya Pond and Durbar Sq. **Cycle Repair Center,** on the south side of the road, rents standard, one-speed bikes. Rs20 per hr.; Rs100 per day. Open daily 7am-7pm, though hours are flexible.

✷ ORIENTATION

Bhaktapur lies slightly north of the Arniko Highway, which leads 14km to Kathmandu to the west. The southern half of the city is filled with fields, residential streets, and the *ghats* that line the **Hanumante River.** About half of the city's residents derive their livelihood from agriculture in this area. If you don't have the time to travel to a village during your stay in Nepal, this area can give you a taste of rural life in the country. Bhaktapur's main sights are in the northern half of the city, in three squares strung together by a curving main street. **Durbar Square** is connected by a short lane at its southeastern corner to **Taumadhi Tol,** which, in turn, is connected to **Dattatraya Square** (also called **Tachapal Tol**) by a wide, shop-lined street known as **Sukuldhoka.** Minibuses from Kathmandu arrive near a large water tank called **Guhya Pond** to the west of Durbar Sq. Gate. Buses to Nagarkot stop north of the minibus park, or from Kamal Binayak Bus Park in the northeast corner of the city.

To enter the city, tourists must pay Rs750 or US$19 at the **Durbar Square Gate** or at the other check-points. If you sneak into town by another route and avoid these booths, you may still be asked inside for your ticket. The ticket can be used for multiple entries on different days as long as you notify the **Tourist Service Center.** If you plan to stay for more that a couple days, the center will issue a free long-term pass that lasts for the duration of your visa.

⁊ PRACTICAL INFORMATION

Tourist Office: Tourist Service Center and Information Hall, Durbar Sq. Gate (☎6610310; www.catmandu.com/bhaktapurmunicipality). Run by the Bhaktapur Municipality, this is the place to pay the entrance fee (see **Orientation,** above) and to get a brochure and useful map. Keep your ticket and have it certified to re-enter if you leave. Public toilets with toilet paper are available. Open daily 6am-7:30pm.

Currency Exchange: Several shops around Durbar Sq. Gate, including **Layaku Money Exchange Counter** (☎6613563). No commission. Open daily 8am-5pm.

Police: ☎6610284 or 6614821. Just outside Durbar Sq., down the small street between the Palace of 55 Windows and Fasidega Temple. Open 24hr. Handles everything from emergencies (☎100) to petty theft (Kathmandu's tourist police ☎4247041).

Pharmacy: Pharmacies line **Sukuldhoka,** the wide street connecting Taumadhi Tol and Tachapal Tol. There are also several opposite the hospital, including **Sewa Medicine Store** (☎6613773). Open daily 6am-9pm. Pharmacist on call 24hr.

Hospital: Bhaktapur Hospital (☎6610676), west of the Navpokhu Pokhari Minibus Park, on the north side of the street. Not the cleanest, most up-to-date of medical clinics—if you're really ill you should probably head to Kathmandu for treatment. Many of the **pharmacies** have doctors affiliated with them who will see patients there during the day. For a simple consultation and prescription, though, this is your best bet. **Siddhi Memorial Hospital** (☎6610570; fax 6612866), a charitable private hospital in Bhilukhel has both in-patient and out-patient care.

Ambulance: Local to Bhaktapur (☎6613200).

Internet: Many businesses in Bhaktapur now offer Internet services; most of them are of the one-computer-in-a-room variety. Cybertech Computers (☎6610581), west of the southwest corner of Taumadhi Sq. Rs2 per minute, Rs70 per hour. Open daily 6am-9pm.

Post Office: ☎6614153. Next to the minibus park by Guhya Pond. Open M-F 9am-5pm.

⌂ ACCOMMODATIONS

All the places listed below have hot showers, convenient temple-side locations, and ultra-accommodating owners. Deciding which temple you want outside your window might be the toughest decision you have to make. Rates are always negotiable, especially during the off season (May-Aug.). Reservations are recommended in season (Sept.-Dec.). Noon check-out is standard everywhere, and most places lock up at 10pm. Prices listed here are in-season.

Pagoda Guest House, Taumadhi Tol (☎6613248; ghpagoda@wlink.com.np), on the right behind the Nyatapola temple up a stone driveway. Bed and breakfast atmosphere and a unique location (practically on top of a 5-story temple) make this an inviting place. All rooms have different decorations and amenities; choose furnishings to your needs (desks, futons, TVs, chairs). Squat and seat toilets. Popular restaurant on terrace open 7am-9pm. Front door locked at 9pm. Singles US$6-25; doubles US$8-30. 20% discount for *Let's Go* readers. Off-season up to 50% discount. MC/V. ❸

Golden Gate Guest House, Bahatal (☎6610534; www.goldengateguesthouse.com), on the left side of the street as you approach Taumadhi Tol from Durbar Sq. Duck through the doorway on your left to reach the Golden Gate. Clean rooms have simple furniture and soft blankets. Try to get one with a balcony, to enjoy the view of both squares. Singles Rs250, with bath Rs400; doubles Rs350, with bath Rs750; top floor suites US$15. AmEx/MC/V. ❷

Bhadgaon Guest House, Taumadhi Tol (☎6610488; www.bhadgaon.com.np), on the right after Cafe Nyatapola, as you leave Taumadhi Tol for Potter's Sq. Lovely marble stairs and isolated garden courtyard, but mediocre rooms for the price. Clean and newly tiled bathrooms, and a rooftop restaurant with terrific views. 9 rooms, all with attached bath, TV, fan, toilet paper, towels, and slippers. Breakfast US$3, lunch and dinner US$4. Singles US$25-35; doubles US$30-50. 40-50% off-season discount. MC/V. ❺

Shiva Guest House (☎6613912 or 6610740; www.shivaguesthouse.com.np), opposite Pashupatinath Temple. Bhaktapur's first guest house, founded 20 years ago, has clean rooms, email (Rs2 per min.), an in-house travel agency, and attached restaurant, Cafe Corner (entrees Rs100-200). Most fresh-smelling rooms face the temple and have large wooden windows. Singles US$6, with bath US$15; doubles US$8, with bath US$20; triples US$30. 20% discount for off-season. Restaurant open daily 7am-9pm. MC/V. ❸

Namaste Guest House, Sakotha Tol (☎6610500; kumari@mail.com.np), on the corner of Tibukchhen and Sakotha, leading into the northeast corner of Durbar Sq. Less calm area with more traffic, though terrace still has extraordinary views of the temples. Sparsely-decorated rooms are more spacious than most. Kept clean with friendly service. Guests get 10% off at the **Sunny Restaurant** (see below). Singles Rs300, with bath Rs500; doubles Rs400-600. Special double suite with living room and spacious bath US$20. MC/V. ❷

Nyatapola Rest House, Taumadhi Tol (☎6612415), opposite Pagoda Guest House. Pink mosquito nets over all beds, foam mattresses on wood planks, rusted bars over windows, wallpaper covering cement ground, and views of a brick wall for the lowest of budgets. Attached restaurant with rooftop terrace (entrees Rs30-115). Singles Rs200; doubles Rs300. Prices extremely flexible. ❷

FOOD

Most of Bhaktapur's restaurants whip up the usual Nepali-continental-Indian-Chinese food, though there are some less touristy places in the older, more residential areas of town where you can find Nepalese cuisine that's twice as good but half the price. *Juju dhau* (king of curds), a creamy, sweet yogurt, is a local specialty that is sold everywhere. Newari set meals are commonly available, usually consisting of *wo, chatamari, aalutarkari,* and *juju dhau* (Rs130-160).

Sunny Restaurant, Taumadhi Tol. Near Nyatapola Temple. Glowing lanterns, sweet-smelling incense, engraved wood menus, knee-high tables, and a balcony with a splendid view of the square. The low ceilings and decorations are fashioned in the style of traditional Newari homes. Continental (Rs120-220), Newari (Rs75-150), and Nepali (Rs110-350) set meals. Open 7am-8:30pm. MC/V. ❷

MomoMax, Sakotha Tol, off an alley at the intersection of Kibukchhen and Sakotha near Namaste Guest House, turn at the sign for Lotus Guest House. A low-lit, low-ceilinged, hole-in-the-wall mostly frequented by budget tourists. Devastatingly good *momos* (Rs25-40). Also serves Chinese and Tibetan dishes (Rs30-50). The veggie *pakora* (Rs30) might make you declare Nepali citizenship. Open daily 10am-8:30pm. ❶

Cafe de Peacock and Soma Bar, Tachapal Tol, faces Dattatraya Temple, 2nd fl. on the left. Indoor and outdoor seating make for great people-watching. Mexican, Italian, and Nepali dishes Rs100-300. Open daily 9am-9pm. AmEx/MC/V. ❸

Marco Polo Restaurant, Taumadhi Tol, immediately to the left as you face Nyatapola Temple, on the corner. A marginally cheaper alternative to other tourist restaurants, but with fewer local dishes. Extensive menu includes burgers, pasta, pizza, and a "light meal" of fried chicken (Rs130). A couple of Indian offerings, but only one Nepali dish (Rs100). Open daily 7am-8pm, flexible hours. ❷

Cafe de Temple Town Restaurant, Durbar Sq. Turn right after entering the Durbar Sq. Gate. Pricey but ideally-located in between the Krishna and Shiva temples. Small garden with patio seating and rooftop terrace. Pizzas Rs175-215, Indian and Nepali set dishes Rs255-395. Open daily 9am-9pm. ❸

◔ SIGHTS

DURBAR SQUARE. Bhaktapur has the oldest and least cluttered Durbar Square in the valley, with a wide-open pedestrian area surrounded by just enough architectural wonders to be imposing without also being overwhelming. The **Royal Palace** encloses the north side of the square. The current buildings date from the 16th and 17th centuries when Bhaktapur was the heart of Kathmandu Valley culture. Paintings, statues, and tapestries from this era still decorate the west wing of the palace, which now houses the **National Art Gallery.** The gallery displays intricate Newari *paubha* and Tibetan *thanka* paintings; its oldest objects are stone sculptures from as early as the 11th century. The gallery affords the best view of the palace's courtyards, most of which are closed to visitors. (Museum open Tu-Sa 9:30am-4:30pm. Admission Rs20. No photography.) East of the palace is the famous Garuda-crested **Golden Gate,** built in AD 1754 by King Ranajit Malla. The king's image caps a stone pillar facing the gate. On the other side of the gate sits the three-storied **Palace of 55 Windows**—each one of the intricately carved windows took a craftsman about 100 days to construct. On the backside of the palace, to the right is the former royal bath of the Malla royalty. Here, you can see the Golden Spout (AD 1678) with water spurting out of a goat head statue.

Like the palace, the temples in Durbar Square exemplify the remarkable craftsmanship of the Malla era. The westernmost temple in the Square, **Bansi Narayan,** is dedicated to Krishna, and its roof struts depict various incarnations of Vishnu. Across from the Golden Gate is the elephant-flanked, stone-carved **Vatsala Durga Temple.** Built in the mid-18th century in the *shikhara* style, this temple contains an impressive display of metalwork and carvings in wood and stone. To the left is the **Chyasilin Mandap** (Eight-Cornered Pavilion), a 1990 reconstruction based on a 100-year-old photograph of the *mandap.* Disguising the earthquake-resistant steel reinforcements are fragments of the 18th-century original. Near the Chayasilin Mandap and opposite the Shiva Guest House, the **Pashupatinath Mandir,** the busiest of the Durbar Square temples, contains a 17th-century reproduction of the *linga* at Pashupatinath. Check out the especially creative erotic contortions of the couples on the roof struts. In the eastern section of the square, around the corner from the palace, are more temples and temple foundations. The most interesting of these is the 17th-century stone **Siddhi Lakshmi Temple,** with its procession of animals and people on either side of the stairs. Behind it is the larger, white, and somewhat unattractive **Fasideya Temple,** dedicated to Shiva. The two-story wood and brick buildings that surround this part of the square were once *dharamsalas.* The **big bell (Taleju Bell)** between the palace and the Pashupatinath, in the middle of the square, is rung twice a day to honor the goddess Taleju.

THANKAS FOR THE MEMORIES
Hanging in shop windows, peering out at you from glass frames with their gold-painted eyes, *thankas* are everywhere in the Kathmandu Valley. Traditional *thankas* (pronounced TONG-ka, and meaning "something rolled up") are religious scroll-paintings that serve as aids for meditation in temples or at family altars. Colorful and elaborate, they are painted to comply with strict rules that dictate style and subject matter. Most *thankas* depict one of three main themes: the lives of the Buddha, *bodhisattvas*, saints, or lamas; the wheel of life; or the *mandala*. In representations of the Buddha's life, pictures start in the top left-hand corner and continue counter-clockwise. The wheel of life *thanka* depicts the various spiritual states of humankind, from sin (at the bottom) to enlightenment (at the top). The *mandala*, which shows the steps to enlightenment, is the most popular. A *thanka* might take anywhere from a week to six months to create. A *thanka* cannot be used, however, until it has been consecrated by a *lama*, who makes an inscription on the back. Most *thankas* that are sold have not been consecrated properly, and many don't meet the prescribed guidelines. If you're interested in buying one, shop around first, as sizes, quality, and prices (Rs100-40,000) vary widely.

TAUMADHI SQUARE. Connected to Durbar Square by a short, bustling street, Taumadhi Tol, a place where architectural masterpieces and religious ceremony mingle with daily life, is Bhaktapur at its best. Musicians and daily worshippers converge on the square during the **Bisket Jatra,** Bhaktapur's renowned celebration of the new year in April. Nepal's tallest pagoda, **Nyatapola Temple,** dominates the square and can be seen from the outskirts of the city. A total of 108 intricately carved beams support the five roofs of this building. Built in AD 1702, this Hindi temple is guarded by elegant lions, griffins, and, on the top step, a lioness and tigress. On the bottom step sit massive human wrestlers, legends of the Malla dynasty. Each pair is said to be 10 times stronger than the one below. The image of **Siddhi Lakshmi,** the goddess to whom the temple is devoted, is locked inside and accessible only to priests. Visitors can still climb the steps for an unparalleled view of the square.

On the eastern side of the square is the bulky, three-story **Bhairabnath Mandir,** which was built as a single-story temple during the 18th century. A second floor was added later, but the 1934 earthquake leveled the structure and it was completely rebuilt with three stories. The tiny golden image over the entrance, often obscured by rice and dye offerings, is the frightful Lord Bhairab, God of Terror. Huge painted chariot wheels lean against the left side of the temple; Bhairab's head, which usually stays locked up in the temple, is carted around during Bisket Jawa celebrations. A doorway in the building at the south side of the square leads to a courtyard filled by the **Til Mahadev Narayan Mandir,** a 17th-century temple (on an 11th-century temple site) reminiscent of Changu Narayan, with its pillar-mounted painted Garuda, golden *chakra*, and *sankha*.

TACHAPAL TOL (DATTATRAYA SQUARE). A wide, curving street lined with shops links Taumadhi Tol to Bhaktapur's oldest square, Tachapal Tol. The wooden buildings that enclose the square were once *maths* (priests' residences), but they have all been converted for other uses. The ponderous **Dattatreya Mandir** presides over the eastern end of the square. Built in 1427, it is the oldest surviving building in Bhaktapur and was allegedly built from the trunk of a single gigantic tree. From the looks of it, that must have been quite a tree. Two hulking, eight-foot Malla wrestlers, gaudily painted during festivals, guard the entrance. Directly across from them, a stone cut Garuda figure kneels faithfully on a towering pillar, emphasizing the temple's connection to Vishnu. Dattatraya appeals to followers of Vishnu and Shiva as well as Buddhists, since he

THE INSIDER'S CITY

NEWARI WOODCARVING

The art of woodworking began in Nepal in the 14th century. Ranging from geometric designs to erotic engravings, these stunning carvings often serve a story-telling function. Carvings might depict, for example, the process by which Ganesh (one of Nepal's most beloved gods) came to have an elephant head.

Some of the best private carvings adorn the windows of the houses, which are considered holy and worthy of special decoration. The window lattices often have such brilliantly engineered structures that they do not need any nails to stay intact.

Woodcarvings are almost always covered with a gaudy layer of paint, a modern convention. Originally designed to conceal the wearing effects of time on the wood, slathering on a layer of paint has now become the norm. Some restoration projects are devoted to the painstaking task of removing the paint from Nepal's national treasures. You can see Newari woodcarving in villages, squares, and in Bhaktapur's **National Art Gallery Woodcarving Museum.**

is considered an avatar of Vishnu, a guru of Shiva, and a cousin of the Buddha. At the other end of the square is the rectangular **Bhimsen Temple,** honoring a favorite god of Newari merchants.

Inside the two *math* buildings that flank the temple are two museums. To the left, the **Brass and Bronze Museum** displays a collection of 300-year-old functional objects such as lamps, cooking pots, hubble-bubble hookahs, spittoons, and carved ritual paraphernalia. Opposite, in the **Pujari Math,** is the **National Art Gallery Woodcarving Museum,** worth visiting more for its magnificent, sun-drenched courtyard than for its collection. Set into the eastern wall of the *math*, around the corner from the museum, is the famous 17th century **Peacock Window,** often lauded as the paragon of Newari window-carving. It is surrounded on all sides by smaller, less ornate, and sometimes decapitated fowl-themed woodcuttings. *(Admission to any one of the 3 museums allows entry to the other 2. Rs20. Camera allowed only in Brass and Bronze museum for Rs20 fee. Open Tu-Sa 9am-5pm.)*

OTHER SIGHTS. Three-hundred meters southwest of Taumadhi Tol is **Potter's Square,** where you can see potters at work behind enormous homemade wheels and hundreds of pots lined up to dry in the sun. Since the craft of earthenware is a family trade in Nepal, the square is divided into clans of workers. Stroll south toward the river to see *ghats*, fields, and temples that, in contrast to those farther north, are more functional than decorative. The city also features numerous decorative ponds, some quite moldy, along the periphery of the main squares.

📷 SHOPPING

Bhaktapur is home to some of the finest **pottery** in the valley, and while similar items are also available in Kathmandu, it's much more satisfying to purchase directly from the artisans here in Bhaktapur. The best place to meet up with potters and their collections of bowls, masks, and icons is **Potter's Square.** If you are just looking for souvenir pottery, head instead to Dattatreya Square, a smaller version of Potter's Square, less expensive but less artistic. Bhaktapur also has a long-standing reputation for fine **wooden handicrafts,** which are sold in Durbar along the periphery of Dattatreya. In the many shops of downtown Bhaktapur you can also buy handmade paper, tea, pashminas, and *thanka* paintings.

CHANGU NARAYAN चाँगु नारायण

Home to Nepal's oldest dated temple and a much-adored Vishnu shrine, Changu Narayan remains virtually undiscovered by tourists. Popular with pilgrims, the town provides a welcome respite from overcrowded Durbar Squares. Legend has it that many years ago a valley brahmin noticed that one of his cows was no longer giving milk. Suspicious, he kept his eye on the cow until one day, he saw a small boy materialize from a nearby *champak* tree, drink all of the cow's milk, and then disappear inside the tree again. Convinced that this was the work of a demon, the brahmin cut the tree down immediately. No sooner had he done so, however, than the tree began to bleed and the face of Narayan appeared and reprimanded him for what he had done. Mortified by his sin, the brahmin built a temple to Narayan where the tree had stood. To this day, the secluded temple has remained one of Nepal's most sacred sites.

Since its construction in the 4th century, worshippers have visited, adorned, restored, and revered this Vishnu shrine. Patched together and built upon over the centuries, the temple is a living time capsule revealing more than a millennium's worth of stylistic and artistic developments. Equally impressive are the large sculptures and polished black relief panels that cluster around the temple; these are considered among Nepal's greatest treasures. The hilltop town that surrounds this marvelous site has breathtaking panoramic views of the whole valley. The town now charges a Rs60 **entrance fee**, payable at a small shack to the left of the city gates (open daily 7am-6:30pm). In return for the fee, you receive a brochure containing information on the temple area.

▛ TRANSPORTATION. The main road into Changu Narayan leads into the new bus park. **Bus #7** begins and ends at Bhaktapur's minibus park, near Guhya pond (45min., Rs8). There is no direct bus from Kathmandu to Changu Narayan. A **taxi** is the fastest way to reach Changu Narayan (Rs700 from Kathmandu; Rs400 from Bhaktapur). Otherwise, Changu Narayan is a strenuous, uphill, 45min. bike ride or 2hr. walk from Bhaktapur; follow the signs from the minibus park. Changu Narayan can also be reached via a 2hr. hike from the mountain viewpoint of Nagarkot to the east—not suggested during monsoon season. Getting off the **Nagarkot #7 bus** at Telkot (45min., Rs8) and walking straight along the ridge will get you there in about 1½hr. You can also begin from the north side, off the road between Boudha and Sankhu, but only in the dry season (Oct.-Apr.) when the Manohara River is low enough to be forded. The **temple** is up the steps from the city gates. Narayan is 13km east of Kathmandu and 4km north of Bhaktapur.

▛▟ ACCOMMODATIONS AND FOOD. A visit to Changu Narayan works best as a day trip from Kathmandu or Bhaktapur; if for some reason you need to spend an unplanned night here, options are basic and uninspiring. The rustic **Changu Narayan Bed and Breakfast ❷** is a harrowing 15min. hike from the temple; follow the steep set of stairs from the side of the temple farthest from town. The B&B offers stunning views of the valley and basic backpacker accommodations. (Rs200 per night.) At the back of the Changu Narayan bus park sits the **Binayak Restaurant ❸**. Offering standard continental (Rs70-380) and Indian (Rs50-160) food, as well as a range of drinks (Rs15-120), it's a good place to catch a light meal while waiting for your bus. Rooftop garden seating offers views of the temple. (Open daily 7am-8pm.) Just inside the main gate sits the **Valley View Restaurant ❷**, offering continental fare (Rs35-115) in a bamboo- and straw-roofed seating area that offers incredible views of the valley.

▣ SIGHTS. Coming from town, you will enter the courtyard of the **Changu Narayan Temple** at the rear, under the gaze of two stone griffins warning that the 4th-century golden image of Vishnu inside is open only to Hindus. A brass doorway embossed with flower designs frames the entrance, and on either side of the temple, **pillars** bear the symbols of Vishnu. The temple itself is an architectural masterpiece, a classic three-tiered pagoda. A life-wheel and a stone staff on the left represent brahmins and *chettris* respectively; a conch shell and lotus flower on the right represent the occupational and business castes. The inscription at the base of the pillar describes the victories of King Mahadeva. It is the oldest inscription in the valley, dating from AD 464. The **statue** of Vishnu's man-bird vehicle, Garuda, kneeling at the door with a cobra around his neck, was carved at about the same time. His face is said to be a likeness of King Manadeva himself, who reputedly said that he too was a vehicle for Vishnu. In the **birdcage** over Garuda's shoulder are two more recent figures, Bupathindra Malla and Bubana Lakshmi, the 17th-century king and queen of Bhaktapur who introduced metalwork to the temple by financing the ornate copper doorway.

The best sculptures are clustered around the **Lakshmi Narayan Temple,** past the pillar to the right of the main temple. In the central relief, Vishnu as Narasimha, half-man and half-lion, tears a hole in the chest of a demon. To its left, another relief shows the story of Vishnu as Vamana, the dwarf who grew to celestial size and crossed the earth and the heavens in three steps. On the **platform,** next to the Lakshmi Narayan Temple, is an image of Vishnu as Narayan, sleeping on a knotted snake. The ten-headed, ten-armed figure above Narayan depicts the universal face of Vishnu, showing each of his 10 avatars. Opposite the platform is an image of a ten-armed Vishnu, known as **Maha Vishnu,** with his consort Lakshmi sitting in his lap. Across the courtyard, near the temple's left pillar is the **sculpture of Vishnu** atop his *vahana*, Garuda. All of these sculptures date from the Licchavi period, before the Mallas took over in 1200 and when the art of stone sculpting in the valley was at its height (see **Malla Kingdoms,** p. 782).

DHULIKHEL धुलिखेल ☎ 011

From its lofty position at 1440m, Dhulikhel routinely delivers spectacular Himalayan sunrises. But in contrast to its more touristy neighbor Nagarkot, Dhulikhel is also a living, breathing Nepali town, a fact to which its lively streets and squadrons of schoolchildren attest. Hikers and bikers come to this eastern mountain town to explore the wilderness beyond. In the surrounding valleys there are a number of scenic villages, including the Buddhist *stupa* at **Namobuddha** and the endearing **Panauti**. Both make ideal one-day treks from town. Once an important stop on the trade route to Tibet, the town's former wealth can be glimpsed in the elaborate woodcarving of its older buildings. Dhulikhel's comfortable accommodations and natural beauty make for a pleasant stay—even when monsoon clouds obscure the snowy mountains.

■ ☑ **ORIENTATION AND PRACTICAL INFORMATION.** Dhulikhel is just off the Arniko Highway, 32km southeast of Kathmandu. From Ratna Park in Kathmandu, take **bus #14** (1½hr., frequent, Rs20), which also stops at Banepa's bus park. Past the Dhulikhel **bus park,** the road forks uphill. The right fork leads to the Rastriya Bunijya Bank and the hospital; the left fork leads to the **town center,** where a bust of King Mahendra stands next to a water tank. Facing the bust in the center of Dhulikhel, the road to the right leads to Dhulikhel's temples and the old part of town; the road to the left leads to the Nawarnuga Guest House, the post office, and the Kali Shrine. The **Rastriya Banijya Bank,** on the left 50m north from the bus park, exchanges currency. (☎661118. Open Su-Th 10:30am-5pm, F 10:30am-1:30pm.) The **hospital** (☎661497 or 661727) is 10min. away from the bus park—follow the signs to the right. (Clinic open Su-F 9am-4pm, Sa emergencies only.) There are several small pharmacies along the road to town, but the hospital's well-stocked **pharmacy** is the best place to get prescriptions filled (open daily 9am-9pm). **DCI and Communication Services,** just before the Nawaranga Guest House on the road to Kali, has **Internet, phone,** and **email** services. (☎661064; dcidhu@yahoo.com. Rs5 per min. Open daily 7am-7pm.) The **police station** (☎662020) is a 5min. walk from the center of town, just past Dhulikhel Technical School next to the **post office** (☎661170, open Su-Th 10am-5pm, F 10am-3pm), on the road to the Kali Shrine.

▌▐ ACCOMMODATIONS AND FOOD. Dhulikhel has a good selection of guest houses, all with attached restaurants. ▌**Nawaranga Guest House ❶,** a 5min. walk up the road to the right of King Mahendra's bust, is a backpacker's heaven. It makes up for what it lacks in luxury with an uncommonly friendly and hospitable atmosphere and small library of English language paperbacks. The superb restaurant serves Nepali dishes (entrees Rs15-90) and doubles as an art gallery exhibiting the works of local painter, Chiranjin Makajir. (☎661226. Dorms Rs100; singles Rs125, Rs200 with bath; doubles Rs200, Rs300 with bath. Restaurant open daily 6:30am-8:30pm.) If you've come to see mountains, **Panorama View Resort ❹,** is your best bet. Up the hill below the Kali shrine (3km from the bus park), this place has large doubles with balconies and clean bathrooms with hot showers and seat toilets. The restaurant offers unrestricted views of the Himalayas from east to west. (☎662085; rameshsarada75@hotmail.com. Doubles US$7, with attached bath US$10. Off-season 20% discount. Reservations recommended during the peak season. Restaurant open daily 6am-10pm.) On the main road just north of the bus park is the **Dhulikhel Royal Guest House ❸.** The rooms vary in size and amenities, but they're all clean and comfortable. The attached restaurant has a rooftop terrace and a TV parlor; treat yourself to any of the movies in the guest house's obscure collection, which includes such forgotten classics as "Lost in Siberia." (☎664010 or 260139. Singles US$6, with bath US$12; doubles US$10, with bath US$20. Prices negotiable during off season and for students.) **Dhulikhel Lodge ❷,** 100m south down the hill from the bus park, has 20 large rooms with common bath and seat or squat toilets. (☎661753 or 664382; dhulikhellodge@hotmail.com. Singles Rs250; doubles Rs300.) The restaurant serves Nepali, Chinese, and Italian meals (Rs55-160), with seating on floor cushions.

◙ SIGHTS AND SUNRISES. The spectacular sunrise over the mountains is the main draw in Dhulikhel, and the most popular place to watch is from the **Kali Shrine.** To reach the shrine, take a left at the king's bust and follow this road past Nawaranga Guest House, Dhulikhel Technical School, and, finally, the police station. 50m after the police station, you will come to a fork in the road. Turn right, as is indicated by the Panorama View Resort sign. At this point, you will have a choice of a rocky footpath to the left and a more manageable dirt road to the right. Both will lead you to the top of the hill. The steep ascent takes approximately 30min. The shrine is on the right, up 50m from Panorama View Resort. Dhulikhel's cobblestoned **main square** is also worth exploring. To see this area, take a right at the king's bust. The square's two temples honor two different forms of Vishnu: the triple-roofed temple surrounded by a metal fence is dedicated to Harisiddhi, while the brightly tiled one in the middle of the square honors Narayan. Stumble a few steps northwest, past the brick and lumber construction rubble, to the pagoda-like **Bhagwati Mandir,** which has more to offer as a lookout point than as a temple.

◪ NEAR DHULIKHEL. Dhulikhel is the popular starting point for a number of one-day treks, the most established of which is the **Namobuddha Circuit,** with the option of ending at **Panauti.** The Dhulikhel Lodge's helpful map can be purchased at most guest houses for Rs2. **Dhulikhel Royal Guest House** makes a smaller free version attached to its brochure. *Namobuddha* means "hail to the Buddha"—it is the place where he supposedly offered his body as food to a starving tigress. In addition to a small *stupa,* this area is also home to a number of monasteries and a small tea shop, making this an ideal place to take a break and respectfully observe the daily rituals of the local Buddhist monks. Namobuddha is 3hr. from Dhulikhel, 2hr. past the Kali Shrine along the same unpaved road. The walk is both uphill and downhill, past the villages of Kavre and Phulbari. It's possible to take an alternative path back in Dhulikhel, but the 1hr. hike to **Panauti,** a quiet Newari village famous for its wooden carvings, is equally rewarding. Its impressive array of temples and its idyllic setting at the junction of two streams make it a great daytrip. In the center of town is the **Indreshwar Mahadev Temple,** which, with its delicately carved roof struts and *toranos,* may be the oldest temple in Nepal. The triple-roofed **Krishna Narayan** temple sits at the junction of the town's two rivers. Across the river, by the suspension bridge, the 17th-century **Brahmayani Temple** honors the village's chief goddess. **Buses** run from Panauti to Banepa (25min., frequent, Rs5) and from there to Dhulikhel and Kathmandu, so a one-way trek is possible. The road along the hillside from Dhulikhel to Bhaktapur is ideal for **mountain biking.** From the bus park, follow the main highway away from town and then follow the signs to Bhaktapur. There are no bike rental facilities in Dhulikhel, so it is best to rent in Kathmandu or Bhaktopur. You can bring your bike on the bus (the driver will attach it to the roof for you) or put it in the back of a taxi.

NAGARKOT नगरकोट

Teetering 2175m above the eastern rim of the Kathmandu Valley, Nagarkot is the popular Himalayan viewpoint from which, in clear weather, you can see central and eastern parts of the range including the peaks of Everest, Lhotse, Cho Oyu, Makalu, and Manaslu. Tourism has spurred the development of Nagarkot beyond its origins as a military base. Today, hundreds descend upon the many guest houses, not to plot troop maneuvers, but to trace the path of the sun as it ascends over the Himalayas. During monsoon season, though, the views are completely blocked by a clouded haze and the town empties of tourists. The town's one road fills with deep mud and vehicles cannot make it up the ridge. There are several day treks down to neighboring villages. On the bus ride up, if you can bear to look out the window as the bus careens around hairpin turns, you'll see patterned rice and corn plots etched into the hillside next to uncultivated hills.

⊑ TRANSPORTATION. Local **bus #7** travels from **Kathmandu** to Nagarkot via **Bhaktapur.** In Kathmandu, catch it at Bagh Bazaar (2hr., every 30min., Rs20); sometimes an express to Nagarkot is not available from Kathmandu and you must change buses in Bhaktapur (total 3hrs., frequent, Rs23). In Bhaktapur, from the Kamal Binayak bus park in the northeast or from the bus stop one block northwest of Guhya Pond (1hr., frequent, Rs13). The last bus leaves Nagarkot at 6pm. In-season **Tourist buses** leave from Kantipath in Kathmandu (1½hr., 1:30pm, round-trip Rs200) and return from Nagarkot the next morning. Tickets can be bought at any agency in Thamel. The price is standardized, but like with any travel agency transaction in Nepal, be careful of rip-offs. **Taxis** from Kathmandu cost about Rs100, from Bhaktapur Rs500.

▉▐ ORIENTATION AND PRACTICAL INFORMATION. Nagarkot consists of an ever-growing cluster of guest houses grouped along a **ridge.** The road to Bhaktapur forks at the base of a hill, where the bus stops and a few small shops sell groceries. The road that curves to the right leads to **The Tea House, Club Himalaya,** and the **lookout tower.** The road that curves north around the left side of the hill leads to the bank, the rest of Nagarkot's guest houses, and the high point of the ridge marked by the tiny **Mahakal Shrine.** Winding north road leads to Himalayan bank, Hotel Galaxy, Hotel Naked Chef, Hotel at the end of the Universe, Hotel Madhuban, and then finally, at the top of the ridge on the right Mahakal Shrine. The road is covered with signs pointing the way to each guest house. With 15% or Rs150 commission, **Himalayan Bank Ltd.** exchanges currency and traveler's checks (☎6680049. Open M-F 9:30am-3:30pm.) The nearest hospital is in Bhaktapur. **Club Himalaya** on the left-side of right-curving road through a large metal gate and up a brick stairwell (☎6680083, fax 6680068) has Internet services for Rs5 per min., and international telephone services. The closest **police** is in Bhaktapur (☎6610284 or 6614821, 24hr.).

⌂☎ ACCOMMODATIONS AND FOOD. As the hotel strip above the clouds expands, true budget lodges are becoming something of an endangered species, though prices are negotiable, especially off season. The following hotels cling to the ridge below the Mahakal Shrine. **The Hotel Madhuban ❸**, has a collection of compact A-frame cottages perched atop a high point in the strip, as well as larger and more expensive "standard" rooms. (☎6680114. Rooms Rs500-1000; cottages Rs400, with bath Rs500) The glassed-in dining room (entrees Rs40-200) showcases the town's stunning views. **The Hotel at the End of the Universe ❷**, up the stairs on the right past Hotel Galaxy, is one of Nagarkot's originals. The brick and bamboo bungalows have large windows and cozy feel. Reservations recommended in season. (☎6680011; oasis@umpire.com. Bungalows sleep 2-8, Rs200-1500.) **The Hotel Galaxy View Tower ❷**, offers a number of musty, carpeted rooms with attached or common baths (☎6680122; hotelgalaxy@wlink.com; singles Rs300-800, doubles Rs400-1500) as does the **Sherpa Alpine Lodge ❷** (☎6680015; all rooms Rs350). The newly-opened **Naked Chef ❸**, boasts sparkling facilities (☎6680115; doubles with attached baths Rs500-1000) and the fully-clothed waiters at the adjacent restaurant serve decent but pricey continental/Indian food (entrees Rs165-275).

Most hotels have adjoining restaurants serving identical, mediocre tourist food; marginally better grub tends to carry exorbitant prices. **The Tea House ❸**, just below Club Himalaya, is Nagarkot's most elegant place to eat. The plate-glass windows offer terrific views to compliment continental (Rs175-225) and Indian and Nepalese dishes (Rs85-225). Attached bakery spoils your sweet tooth with a wide variety of cakes, pastries, and mousses (Rs75. Open daily 5:30am-8pm). The **Restaurant at the End of the Universe ❷**, attached to the similarly titled resort, serves hitchhikers from all over the galaxy a typical continental variety of entrees. Comfy pillow seating. (Burgers, chicken, and rice Rs50-200.) Open on demand.

◐ SIGHTS. The hip thing to do in Nagarkot is to watch the sun rise and set behind the valley as it washes the mountain peaks in pink light. While all the guest houses have great views, there are some

THE BIG SPLURGE

DHULIKHEL LODGE RESORT

Many travel to Dhulikhel to experi ence the popular sanctuary of moun tain views and fresh air without the crowds. However, you might make time here to indulge a little bit and enjoy the classiest hotel around.

The rooms at the lodge are spa cious and comfortable, and their large glass windows provide dazzling views of the Himalayan Range and the Panchkhal Valley. The entire resort is cushioned from the rest o the town by a thick forest, including everything from peach trees to bird watching huts. Most of the hotel's 26 guest rooms have private balconies facing the mountains. The rooms are divided into three Nepali-style bunga lows, with beautifully tiled private bathrooms, room heaters, and cable TV. Common areas are meticulously maintained, with beautiful furnish ings and fresh flowers. At dinnertime the hotel sometimes hosts barbeque festivities, and on most evenings guests gather near the circular open fireplace for drinks.

The hotel is a 10min. walk from the town center, along the road to Kathmandu. The entrance will be up a steep brick staircase to your left However, you can take full advan tage of your splurge by requesting the hotel's airport pickup.

(☎661114, 661494, 662042 www.dhulikhellodgeresort.com. Sin gles US$70, doubles US$80. Break fast US$8, lunch US$14, dinne US$16. All rates subject to 12% tax Reservations recommended, espe cially in high season. AmEx/MC/V.)

particularly fine lookout points in the area. You can walk up to the tiny **Mahakal Shrine,** on the right past Hotel Madhuban or sit at one of the benches in the brick-paved area between the Tea House and Club Himalaya. The best views are from the **lookout tower,** a leisurely 1hr. stroll south past Club Himalaya and the army base (ask around to make sure it's open). The tower sits at 2164m, Nagarkot's highest point. Alternatively, in-season, many hotels and stores along the main road sell tickets for a pre-dawn tourist bus to the tower (Rs100). Lodge owners enthusiastically offer directions for walks to **Changu Narayan** (2hr.), **Sankhu** (2hr.), **Dhulikel** (5hr.), and **Shivapuri** (2-3 days). However, hiking trails are steep and may be dangerous during monsoon season.

DAKSHINKALI दक्षिण काल्री

Most days of the week, "Southern Kali" looks pretty much like any other quiet little town on the fringes of the Kathmandu Valley. However, it takes on a very different personality on Tuesday and Saturday mornings (7-10am), when the town hosts the famous Dakshinkali **animal sacrifices,** bloody offerings to propitiate the patron goddess Durga (also known as Kali). Every year about 400,000 Hindus—brightly clad women and men with doomed roosters, goats, sheep, and ducks—queue up to offer their animals at the shrine, which is enclosed by a low metal railing and sits beneath a metal canopy suspended by four brass *nagas.* Inside the shrine, a small black image of Durga stands victorious atop a corpse, barely visible to tourists who are only allowed on the walkways above. If you would like to move closer, you must remove your shoes. The image was installed in the 17th century by King Pratap Malla, purportedly on the orders of the goddess herself, though Durga worship had taken place at the site long before that. Devotees wash their animal offerings in the stream behind the shrine before making the sacrifice. If the animals do not attempt to shake off the water poured over their heads, they cannot be sacrificed. It's believed that animals killed in sacrifice will enjoy the reward of higher incarnation. Those offered during the eighth and ninth days of the festival of **Dasain,** the October celebration of the triumph of good over evil, are relieved from burdensome animal life and reincarnated as humans. When it reaches the image of Durga, the animal's throat is cut, and its blood splatters onto the idols. The animal's head is given as payment to the butchers—the body is considered *prasad* (blessed) and becomes the main course at a family picnic in the surrounding hills. Signs from the Dakshinkali temple lead to the nearby **Mata Temple,** which is unremarkable except for its views.

Bus #22 runs from Ratna Park in Kathmandu to Dakshinkali (1½hr., Tu and Sa, Rs16). Huge crowds and few buses mean you'll have to get to the bus station very early if you want to see the sacrifices. Alternatively, the journey can be made by **taxi** (round-trip Rs400 plus Rs10 tourist tax along the road and Rs25 private vehicle entrance fee at the town gate). Either way, the torturous ride up through hillside homes and fields offers stunning valley views. Stay on the bus past Pharping, the deceptive Dakshinkali Cold Store, and the town gate with the "Welcome to Dakshinkali" sign, and get off when the bus pulls into a parking lot filled with of motorcycles, minibuses, and taxis. If you've left your sacrifice back in Thamel, don't worry: the stands lining the 500m walkway to the staircase down to the temple sell uncastrated roosters, the vegetables and spices that will later condiment them, and sacrificial accessories. Farther down the walkway, if you still have your appetite, countless stands sell buffalo-milk yogurt, *phuwa* (gelatin cream-milk), and deep-fried Indian desserts. Enter the shrine through the painted green stone gate on your left (look for the Nepali writing and "(In)" marked on its face) and walk downstairs to the sacrifices. To leave, use the stairs to the middle, right of the arena (if you are facing the dying animals). The stone steps up are lined with beggars and old men trying to make a tikka mark on your forehead. For more information about this site, visit www.dakshinkali.org.

MET A YETI YET? Some believe he's the brutish lovechild of a lusty primate dominatrix and a hapless village man; others claim he's the missing link, a naked Hindu ascetic, a maligned *bodhisattva* whose head glows with a curious light, or a man-eating monkey marauding around the Himalayas. No one's really sure, but the elusive, hairy Yeti has been keeping tabloids, folk storytellers, and conspiracy theorists in business for years. Yetis have been spotted as far away as Indonesia and Mongolia—perhaps on their way to family reunions with their Western wild-man cousins, the US Pacific Northwest's Bigfoot and Australia's Yowie—but they are most frequently spotted around Everest's Khumbu region by the Sherpa villagers who gave them their name. "Yeti" may be a corrupt form of *Yati*, the Hindi word for "hermit," but the mysterious critter goes by at least a dozen different names. Newari myth tells of the *Khya*, a furry mischief-maker who lurks in dark rooms and tickles people to death. Likely to be seen throwing and eating yaks, the Yeti is unnaturally fond of imitating humans, giving rise to folktales about villagers who have been tricked into lighting themselves on fire or hacking each other to death with *khukuri* knives. Because seeing a Yeti condemns the spotter to fatally bad luck, few first-hand sightings have been reported, despite efforts of the Yeti-search teams in the 1950s and 60s. In 1960, Sir Edmund Hillary brought a Yeti scalp to Western scientists, who promptly dismissed it as the rump of a Himalayan blue bear.

NEAR DAKSHINKALI: SEKH NARAYAN TEMPLE

Tucked beneath an overhanging limestone cliff and surrounded by clear pools, the Sekh Narayan Temple (also known as the Shikar Narayan Temple) is a roadside oasis just north from Dakshinkali. Built during the 17th century to honor Vamana (the dwarfish 5th incarnation of Vishnu), the temple has been dutifully maintained, and its bold, bright red and gold look particularly impressive pocketed between the pristine waters and rugged mountain rock. Unfortunately, the temple's prized icon of Vishnu was stolen a few years ago, so visitors have to make do with a black stone replica. Next door is a 20th-century Tibetan Buddhist Monastery of Iama Chatrol Rinpoche. To reach the Sekh Narayan Temple from Dakshinkali, walk on the main road straight out of the parking lot for 45min. A half-mile past Pharping, you'll reach a cluster of pools on your left, behind which are the stairs to the temple. You can catch the bus back to Kathmandu from Pharping, though it might be difficult to get a seat.

THE WESTERN HILLS

Modern-day Nepal was conceived in the hills west of Kathmandu, where, 250 years ago, King Prithvi Narayan Shah of Gorkha had a vision of a unified country. Several millions of years before that the central Himalayas, including Macchapuchare and the Annapurna massif, pushed their way upward, to form a spell-binding backdrop and terrain that would forever shape the region. Visitors come to the Western Hills, one of Nepal's most popular regions to explore the remnant of both these ages. Trekkers lose themselves in the hills and mountains that stretch from Kathmandu to Pokhara and north to the Tibetan border, and come to understand why the region's infamous Gorkha soldiers have so much physical stamina. Others head to the town of Gorkha itself and its ridge-top palace for a history lesson.

HIGHLIGHTS OF THE WESTERN HILLS

Nepal's second-most visited city, lakeside **Pokhara** (p. 864), lies in a beautiful subtropical valley overshadowed by the dazzling Annapurna massif.

The hill towns of **Tansen** (p. 860) and **Gorkha** (below) offer beautiful respite from Nepal's tourist mainstream.

Have your wishes fulfilled at the ridge-top temple of **Manakamana** (p. 859), now accessible by Nepal's first cable car.

GORKHA गोर्खा ☎064

A clutch of small residences scattered over a hillside, quiet and rural Gorkha seems an unlikely birthplace for modern Nepal. However, it was from here that Prithvi Narayan Shah initiated the military rampage that eventually unified the nation. Spectacularly positioned overlooking the valleys halfway between Pokhara and Kathmandu, Gorkha was ruled by a succession of small kingdom-states until Prithvi Narayan, a direct ancestor of the present king, left his home in Gorkha to conquer the Kathmandu Valley. After 24 bloody years of fighting, he finally succeeded. Shah's mighty soldiers were the first to be called "Gorkha," a name initially based solely on their origin. Eventually this name came to be used for all Nepalese soldiers. These fierce fighters were recruited by the British Army and now make up a significant minority in the Indian Army. Gorkha's history is enshrined in the hilltop Gorkha Durbar, birthplace of Prithvi Narayan.

At the end of a paved road to the Kathmandu-Pokhara highway, Gorkha forms a link between many sleepy mountain villages and the outside world, and is a starting point for Manaslu-Himalchuli treks. Still comfortably untouristed, Gorkha's historic palace and sweeping mountain views make it a great place to take a break from the hectic pace of Kathmandu and Pokhara.

▐ TRANSPORTATION

All **buses** from Gorkha go through **Anbu Khaireni**, a few kilometers toward Pokhara from Mugling. Anbu Khaireni is where the Gorkha road meets the Kathmandu-Pokhara highway. **Prithvi Rajmarg Bus Syndicate**, a private company, has buses that leave from its booth just outside the bus park on the side opposite the road from Kathmandu. (☎420323. Open daily 5:30am-5:30pm.) Buses to: **Anbu Khaireni** (1hr., frequent 6am-6pm, Rs30); **Bhairawa/Sunauli** (7hr., 7am, Rs180); **Birganj** (7hr., 4 per day 6:30-11am, Rs175); **Royal Chitwan National Park** via **Tandi** (3hr., Rs70); **Kath-**

mandu (5hr., 9 per day 6:15am-2:20pm, Rs100-120); **Narayanghat** (3hr., 7 per day 8:45am-3:30pm, Rs60-75); and **Pokhara** (4hr., 6 and 9:15am, Rs90). The departures are a mixture of minibuses and regular buses; the latter are almost always safer.

⚿ ℹ ORIENTATION AND PRACTICAL INFORMATION

Gorkha has evolved into three distinct sections. The newest part of town, only 15 years old, is centered on the **bus park**. It includes the asphalt road down the hill toward Kathmandu and on the other side of the bus park, away from Kathmandu. The second area, about a century old, winds uphill from the right fork at the bus park as the wide stone street. Most of it is a tangle of cobblestone roads and foot paths, but also includes the **Tallo Durbar** and some shops and services. A 1hr. walk up the hill is the third and oldest section, consisting of the majestic **Gorkha Durbar**.

Tourist Office: Up the crumbling stones on the right as you enter the bus park from the Kathmandu side. Open Su-F 10am-5pm. There is a hand-painted, but accurate, map of Gorkha available 10m up the stone street at the bus park.

Currency Exchange: Rastriya Banijya Bank (☎420155). Downhill from the bus park, between Hotel Gorkha Prince and Gurkha Inn, on the right. 4% commission on cash and 2% on traveler's checks. Open M-F 10am-3pm.

Police: (☎420199). From the bus park, walk downhill for 5min., turn right at the first paved road after Hotel Gorkha Bisauni, which is a switchback. Take the right fork and the police station is the white bldg. with the blue and yellow coat of arms.

Pharmacy: New Gorkha Medical Center (☎420116), opposite Hotel Gorkha Prince. Open Su-F 7am-8pm, Sa 7am-noon.

Hospital: (☎420208). From the bus park, go 5min. downhill on the main road; after the Hotel Gorkha Bisauni, turn left onto the 1st paved road and walk 5min. uphill. The hospital is yellow with red stripes. Clinic open daily 8am-2pm, 24hr. emergency care.

Telephone: The unnamed communications office under the tourist info office makes international calls for Rs65 per min. and callbacks for Rs3 per min.

Internet: Service is extremely variable in Gorkha. The most reliable is **Unique Computers,** at the intersection of the asphalt road leading to Kathmandu and the 2nd paved road after the Hotel Gorkha Bisauni. Su-F Rs12 per min. Sa Rs8 per min. Free to type email offline first. Open daily 6am-7pm.

Post Office: At the end of the older section of town; walk past the stone steps that lead to the palace, take the left fork and continue up the steep dirt road. Open Su-Th 10am-5pm, F 10am-3pm.

⌂ ACCOMMODATIONS

Gurkha Inn (☎420206), 120m downhill from the bus park, on the right. Set in a lush and manicured garden, the rooms are mid-sized and well-furnished. All with a view of the valley and serene rice paddies. Friendly staff and excellent garden restaurant only makes the experience better. Singles with bath Rs300; doubles Rs200-500. ❷

Hotel Gorkha Prince (☎420030), 100m downhill from the bus park; the hotel, marked by a red signboard, is on the left. Spacious but bare rooms surround dark, multi-story courtyard. Room prices are based on the number of windows and direction they face; the extra money is worth it. Rooftop restaurant, phone service, and common and attached baths. Dorms Rs50; singles Rs100-200; doubles Rs200-500. ❶

Milan Guest House, 100m outside the bus park, down the asphalt road, away from Kathmandu. Cleaner than the others around the bus park, offers concrete rooms with barred windows, common bath with squat toilets. Dorms Rs150; doubles Rs200. ❷

☐ FOOD

Twelve percent tax is added to all meals in every restaurant. Almost all menus in town have individual flair.

Fulpati Restaurant, at the Gurkha Inn, 120m down main road from bus park, on right. Great views, a lush garden, and tasty food make this Gorkha's best place to eat. Set breakfasts equivalent to feasts (Rs90-185), *pakoras* (Rs40-65 for 8 pieces), and continental dishes with meat (Rs135-160). Open daily 6am-9pm. ❷

Garden Restaurant, at the Hotel Gorkha Bisauni. The outside terrace is the perfect place to sit, enjoy chicken momos (Rs75), and watch the sun set over the rice paddies. *Pulaws* (Rs60-100) have interesting twist with raisins. Open daily 6am-10pm. ❷

Gorkha Prince Rooftop Restaurant, at the Hotel Gorkha Prince. Offers rooftop setting, friendly staff, and low prices. *Dahl bhat* set meal Rs95-150. Open daily 7am-10pm. ❷

◎ SIGHTS

GORKHA DURBAR. Straddling the high ridge above Gorkha, this grand palace is where Prithvi Narayan Shah was born in 1722 after his mother had a dream in which she swallowed the sun. The ambitious prince was crowned at the age of 21, and within two years had set out to conquer the Kathmandu Valley, never to return to his birthplace.

Though the exact date of its construction is uncertain, the palace is believed to have been built eight generations prior to Prithvi Narayan's birth, under the reign of Ram Shah (1606-1636), in a style similar to the Malla durbars in the valley. The city of Gorkha was ignored by the Shah Dynasty until King Mahendra returned here in 1958. However, the same families of Hindu priests had continued to perform religious functions at the temples in the Durbar. The palace's present priests are direct descendants of those who served during (and before) Prithvi Narayan's rule.

As you enter the palace complex, the first building on your left is the **Kalika Temple,** whose entrance is in the courtyard just after the temple. The doors are rarely open as only the Royal King, Queen, and Prince are allowed to enter. Before, 1978 commoners weren't even allowed to worship Kali, the goddess of valor, at the Gorkha Durbar; today they can, and do, on the few steps before the doorway. The cobblestones leading to the temple are often sticky with the blood from the boisterous bi-monthly sacrifices at the sacrificial post in the middle of the courtyard. Underneath the overhang, in front of the post, are two copper drums and a metal canon which date to the era of the palace's believed construction. Just past it is the **main palace,** which is closed to non-Hindus. The Shah dynasty's **eternal flame** burns inside, out of sight, but Prithvi Narayan's **throne** is visible through the second window on the right side of the building.

Past the main palace are several shrines off-limits to non-Hindus. However, going past the main palace on its right, out the back entrance, and down the stairs to the lower building can give a good idea of the architecture and woodcarving. A small shrine sits on the opposite side of the lower building from the main palace, and is notable for the turtle carved into the cobblestones at its entrance. For all their martial prowess, the Gorkhalis sacrificed architectural flair; the palace was designed and built by Newaris and carted in from Kathmandu. With so much of the palace closed off, wander the palace grounds along the ridge as the reward for climbing all those stairs. Back at the main entrance, to the left of the palace is a small **parade ground,** now a helipad, but once used for military training. Following the stairs down, first is another helipad and then **Siddhi Ganesh,** where there is a rare, standing image of Ganesh. Out the gate and down 5 more flights of stairs is **Ram Shah's Chautari** (open platform), which has great views of both valleys. Here the palace's builder, who was known for his justice, decided the people's cases.

On the opposite side of the palace, taking the right fork at the top of the stairs from Gorkha, is **Hanuman Bhanjyang.** This image of Hanuman, the monkey god, is exactly 52mi. from Kantipur Hanuman in Kathmandu's Durbar Square. For unblocked views of **Manasula** to the north, ascend several flights of stairs on the side of the ridge opposite Gorkha. It is said you can see more of the mountains from the palace than you can from Pokhara. There's an even better view from the top of Upallokot, another 30min. up the stone stairway past the Hanuman Bhanjyang. (Follow the main street through the older section of town and take the stone stairway on the left just before the fork. The road forks several times; stick to the right and you'll reach the palace in about 30-60min. At the top, follow the sign to the temple (left fork). Open daily 6am-6pm. Cameras and leather articles are not allowed inside the compound; lockers provided. You may want to bring a lock and flip flops for walking around on the sticky floor—neither are provided.)

OTHER SIGHTS. From the bus park, the wide, stone-paved street leads up to the **Rani Pokhari** (Queen's Pond), a terrace with a sunken, mossy pond. To the right and just uphill of the pond are three small **temples.** The white onion-domed temple closest to the pond is **Mahadev Mandir.** A statue of Prithvi Pati Shah, Prithvi Narayan's father, caps a stone pillar facing the temple, made under influence of King Malla of Patan. To the left is the two-tiered **Krishna Mandir.** On Krishna's birthday, in August, this temple's image is carried in a chariot to the Gorkha Durbar and back. Behind the Rani Pokhari, is the domed **Ganesh Mandir.** Continuing on the stone road uphill past the temples, you will come to an open square, **Thulo Aagan.** On the left is the **Bhimsen Mandir,** which draws crowds of pilgrims for the **Janai Purnima** festival in August. During the full-moon celebrations, Brahmin men change their sacred threads (called *janai*), stick-dance, and bathe at the communal water taps. The brown gateway on the right leads to the magnificent **Tallo Durbar Palace (Lower Palace),** built in the Mala style. It was planned as a residence-in-exile for Prince Surendra Bir Bikram Shah Dev whom the then current queen, his stepmother, tried, and failed, to banish him so she could enthrone her own son. A **museum park** honoring Prithvi Narayan and the Shah dynasty has been under construction for years. For now both the palace and the magnificent terraced and pathed gardens that cover the hillside between the two youngest parts of town are closed to the public. Sometimes a kind worker will let people in to wander the grounds and enjoy the exquisite woodcarvings.

The streets in the older part of the city are worth a wander. They're pleasantly clean, thanks to the Gorkha Youth Movement for the Environment. The area on the left fork at the intersection below Rani Pokhari is particularly nice. Other than that, a glance at the breathtaking night sky on a clear night is enough to make anyone happy about being away from the big city.

NEAR GORKHA

◪ MANAKAMANA मनकामना

It is claimed that the goddess Manakamana's choice of a remote, rugged hilltop for an earthly abode was her way of testing the resolve of her devotees. Her plan, however, has been foiled by the arrival of Nepal's first and only cable car system, US$6 million of Swiss engineering that runs from Cheres, 5km east of Mugling on the road to Kathmandu, to the top of the 1300m ridge where the temple stands.

WESTERN HILLS

The wife of Gorkha king Ram Shah (r. 1606-1636) had divine powers that she concealed from all but one of her devotees, Lakhan Thapa. Mr. Thapa was understandably distraught when she committed ritual *sati* on the funeral pyre of her husband, but she had promised him that she would reappear soon, in fulfillment of his wishes. When, months later, a farmer came across a stone oozing milk and blood, Lakhan Thapa took this to be the promised reappearance. The stone is in the shrine of the **Devi of Manakamana** temple (it has stopped oozing), and its current attendant is a 17th-generation descendant of Lakhan Thapa. Because Manakamana Devi is known as the wish-fulfilling goddess, it's not surprising that she is popular. Half a million visitors come here every year, sacrificing goats and chickens. (Shrine closed to non-Hindus.)

Before the cable car was in place pilgrims who made an offering had to first trek 4 hours from Gorkha. While this is still possible (ask at the Gorkha tourist info office for directions), short treks from Manakamana also exist. **Bakreshwar Temple** is 40-50mon. away, up the path to the right of the Devi. **Lakhan Thapa Gupha** (cave) is 15min. past it. Bakreshwar is the rock in which they found Thapa's staff, the last sign of him. The cave is where he disappeared after a 12 yr. pilgrimage.

The town itself is a sizable cluster of colorful shops along the bazaar, leading from the cable car to the temple and then forking left and right. Although many of the hilltop accommodations are geared towards locals, any guest house or restaurant with a sign in English is foreigner-friendly. **Hotel Moonlight ❷**, one minute from the temple towards the cable car, has airy doubles with huge beds and mosquito nets. (☎460054. Doubles with bath and both squat and seat toilet Rs200.) For something off the main bazaars, try **Hotel Alpine ❷**, in a courtyard off the left fork at the temple. Rooms here vary so be sure to look at your room first. (☎460102. Rooms with common bath Rs150-200, with attached bath Rs200-300.) **Hotel Satkar ❷**, on the left fork from the temple, has some of the best views in town of the valley opposite the cable car. Rooms are small, but clean, and there is a nice deck in the back. (☎460052. Doubles with squat toilet and no sink Rs200). High season is Sept.-Nov. and rates rise variably. Reservations or calls ahead are recommended during that time, especially for Friday and Saturday nights. The **Black and White Restaurant ❷** (no sign, but appropriately named) is by far the cleanest restaurant in town. Located 25m from the temple, on the left fork, it has no menu, but all the usual suspects. (Bottomless veg. *dal bhat* Rs65. Open daily 7am-7pm.)

A visit to Manakamana can be done as a daytrip on the way between Kathmandu and either Pokhara or Gorkha: just ask the bus driver to drop you off at the cable car (Round-trip Rs972). The ride takes about 3½-4hr. from Kathmandu or Pokhara and 1½-2hr. from Gorkha. Ascend the mountain in the cable car, which opened in November 1998. The 10min., 2.8km ride to the top is positively surreal, gliding over terraced greenery and small hamlets unchanged by, if not oblivious to, the space-age incursion overhead. On not-so-clear days you can ride right into the clouds. (Open daily 9am-noon and 1:30-5pm. US$10 plus 14% tax, payable in either US or Nepalese currency. Goats for sacrifice Rs110.) To return to Kathmandu, hop on any bus heading to the left as you leave the cable car complex's driveway.

TANSEN (PALPA) तानसेन ☎075

It is hard to believe that a jewel like Tansen, 1370m up in the Mahabarat range, has remained untouched by the traffic between Pokhara and Sunauli. In this bustling town, with its remarkable architecture, amazing scenery, near-perfect climate, and cobblestone streets, simply going for a walk is a pleasant adventure. Tansen was once the capital of the mighty kingdom of Palpa, which first prospered under the 16th-century Sen kings and eventually grew to encompass most of the area from Mustang to the Terai. From its assimilation into the kingdom of Nepal in the early

19th century until the fall of the Ranas in 1951, Tansen served as an honorable place of exile for troublesome, power-hungry members of the royal family. Now simply the central marketplace of the Palpa district, Tansen is still one of Nepal's tidiest and most endearing hill towns, with exquisite views of the Chure hills to the south and the Himalayas to the north.

TRANSPORTATION

A counter in the northeastern corner of the **bus park** sells tickets to: **Butwal** (1½hr., every 30min. 6am-5pm, Rs40); **Kathmandu** (9hr.; 6, 7:30am, 5:30pm; Rs203-280); **Pokhara** (7hr., 6 and 9am, Rs115).

ORIENTATION AND PRACTICAL INFORMATION

Tansen is built on the southern slope of Srinagar Hill. The **bus park** is at the southern (downhill) edge of town, while uphill (toward the pine-covered peak) is always north. From the bus park, the main road heads north and then west past the **tourist office** and the university campus. The main road comes to a junction 500m after the university. Gauri Shankar Guest House will be on the left. Continuing right, you pass Hotel the White Lake, before reaching an intersection marked by a **police post** and the **post office**. A steep, unmotorable road leads downhill from here to the bus park. The main road continues north, becoming **Bank Road**. At the end of Bank Rd., another lane leads downhill to **Amar Narayan Temple**. The main road curves left to **Shital Pati**, the town's central square, marked by a white gazebo-like structure.

Tourist Office: Tansen has two tourist offices. The **Tourist Information Centre and Cake Shop**, on the main road near Hotel the Bajra, was recently taken over by Nanglo West—hence the pastries. Open Su-F 7:15am-6pm. The other office, 50m down the side street leading west from Nanglo West, is run by **GETUP Palpa** (☎521341), an NGO recently founded to promote tourism in the region. Open Su-F 11am-6pm. Both offer maps of Tansen and useful brochures.

Currency Exchange: Nepal Bank, Bank Rd. (☎502130), near the post office, cashes traveler's checks for a 0.5% commission (Rs50 minimum) and an additional Rs45 service charge. Open Su-Th 10am-2pm, F 10am-noon.

Police: The main police station (☎520255 or 520215) is in Durbar Sq.

Pharmacy: Pradhan Medical Hall (☎520279) is 20m down the cobblestone path leading from Shital Pati to the Amar Narayan temple. Open daily 8am-7:30pm.

Hospital: Skip the district hospital west of Tansen in favor of the **United Mission to Nepal Hospital** (☎520111 or 520489), a 15min. walk northeast past the Amar Narayan Temple.

Internet: Internet access in Tansen is expensive and unreliable. Try **Tansen Communication** (☎520205) on the corner across the street from the post office, at a "cheap" Rs5 per min. Open daily 8am-7pm.

Post Office: At the southern end of Bank Rd. Open Su-Th 10am-5pm, F 10am-3pm. **Postal Code:** 32501.

ACCOMMODATIONS

Hotel options in Tansen are limited. There are a few good places in town and a lot of cheap hole-in-the-wall places around the bus park. As you move higher up the hill, the views improve and the prices rise accordingly.

WESTERN HILLS

Hotel the White Lake (☎520291; fax 520502). Carpets, fans, and warm beds with attached baths (seat toilets), towels, soap, and toilet paper. Cheaper rooms have shared bathrooms but the same comfort and cleanliness. Restaurant serves one of the broadest menus in town. Set breakfasts Rs50-150, pizzas Rs75-110, non-veg. dishes Rs100-140, and beer Rs75-90. Singles Rs200-900; doubles Rs300-1200. ❸

Gautam Siddhartha Guest House (☎520280). Take a left just before Hotel the White Lake and then left again at the square. This homey place has bare, basic rooms, but offers a magnificent view from the top floor. Doubles Rs150. ❶

Gauri Shankar Guest House (☎520150). Signs lead the way from the bus park. Follow the main road until it heads east uphill and instead go north downhill for 150m. Bright, well-maintained rooms with or without attached bathrooms. Good views from the roof-top terrace. Doubles Rs200-450. ❷

Hotel the Bajra (☎520443), 10m north of the bus park, is convenient for transportation but not as scenic as places higher uphill. The rooms are clean, the common spaces are big and beautiful, and the immaculate 8-bed dormitory is a good option for single travelers. Attached restaurant. Dorms Rs50; singles Rs100-150; doubles Rs150-250. ❶

 FOOD

The culinary scene in Tansen revolves around the magnificent Nanglo West. Other restaurants pale in comparison, both for atmosphere and food. There are plenty of cheaper options, particularly near the bus park, where simple meals are Rs25-40.

Nanglo West, Shital Pati. Comfortable dining in the shady courtyard or on cushions in the elegant dining room upstairs. The bakery has freshly made croissants (5 for Rs25) and cinnamon danishes (Rs13), and the restaurant offers local *sukuti* (dried buffalo meat with garlic and ginger, Rs60). Hamburgers Rs60. Bakery open daily 7:30am-7pm; restaurant open daily 9am-8:30pm. ❶

Hotel Srinagar, a 15min. walk northwest of town. The patio dining area, on the ridge just west of Srinagar peak, has excellent views. Veg. *biryani* Rs90, chicken chili Rs120, spaghetti Rs180. Open daily 6am-11pm. ❷

Bhattarai Restaurant, opposite the entrance to the Bhagwati temple, serves tasty Nepali meals popular with locals. *Dal bhat* Rs30. Open daily 6am-10pm. ❶

 SIGHTS

AMAR NARAYAN TEMPLE. One of the oldest buildings in Tansen, the 3-story Amar Narayan Temple serves as a stopover for pilgrims on their way to Muktinath. After annexing the city in 1804, Amar Singh Thapa imported Newari craftsmen and artisans and began to turn Tansen into a mini-Kathmandu. The Amar Narayan complex contains an image of Vishnu and exquisite often erotic woodcarvings. It is surrounded by the meter-wide **Great Wall of Palpa,** a water tank with spouts fed by a natural spring, and a garden as popular with bats as it is with worshippers. *(From Shital Pati, follow the steep flagstone lane downhill and east through the old bazaar.)*

DURBAR SQUARE. Durbar Sq., in the center of town, can be entered from Shital Pati through **Baggi Dhoka** ("Chariot Gate"), a large white-washed gate built by Palpa's first exile, Khadga Shumshere, who came here in 1891. One of the largest gates in Nepal, it was made to measure for Shumshere *and* his elephant—dismounting can be such a drag sometimes. Shumshere was also responsible for the

Square's first palace, but the present blue and orange **Tansen Durbar**, which currently houses Palpas's district secretariat, was built by General Pratap Shumshere in 1927. You can enter the square less grandly through a small gate off Bank Rd.

BHAGWATI TEMPLE. Before heading out to battle with the British in 1815, Rana Uji Singh Thapa promised the goddess Bhagwat that he would build her a new temple if she led him to victory. Bhagwati came through and so did Thapa, who erected the temple shortly after his military success. Though not much to look at, this little temple hosts Tansen's largest festival, the **Bhagwati Jatra,** held in late August. An all-night celebration precedes the festival. In the morning, a chariot holding an image of Bhagwati is led through town. *(From Shital Pati. take the 1st road clockwise from Baggi Dhoka. The temple is 30m down on your left.)*

SRINAGAR HILL. The pine-forested ridge above Tansen, known as Srinagar Hill, is one of the most peaceful spots within walking distance, and the hilltop park boasts one of the longest mountain views in Nepal. The brilliant sunrises and sunsets during the week usually dazzle only a few hardy hikers and Nepali youths out for their morning workout. If the pre-dawn hike up the hill isn't enough to send you bouncing out of bed in the morning, consider spending the night here—there's an open-sided shelter and water spigot. *(There are two ways to get to the park. The first is to follow the signs up toward Hotel Srinagar, but head east instead of west when you arrive at the ridge, and follow the wooded path up past the TV tower and back down to the park. The more straightforward, but less scenic alternative is to take the steps up to the park from behind the United Mission Hospital. It takes about 30min. to climb the hilltop from town and 20min. to traverse the ridge between the park and Hotel Srinagar.)*

OTHER SIGHTS. A few minutes south of Amar Narayan, the **Tundikhel,** a large field used for sports and big events, marks the southeastern edge of town. Next to it is the rose-filled **Birendra Park**, honoring the late king. The town also has several other temples—of special note are the **Mahachaitya Bihar,** a small Buddhist temple, and a **Ganesh Temple** with a beautiful brass door. *(Opposite each other, a 3min. walk west of Shital Pati. Follow the road past the Bhagwati Temple, and take a right up the cobblestone street when the road forks.)* The road directly north of Shital Pati leads to another **Ganesh Temple,** set into the hillside. A short, steep flagstone path leads past the Jama Masjid Mosque to the small red-and-white temple, which affords good views of the city below. *(Follow the road north of Shital Pati for 30m, but when the road curves left, just keep going straight up the narrow cobblestone street.)*

🗂 SHOPPING

A few locally produced goods deserve special mention. Tansen's Newari craftsmen employ the lost-wax method in their remarkable **metalwork.** The Tansen *karuwa*, a bronze water jar, is particularly well-known. There are a number of shops clustered around Taksar Tol, the area surrounding the Gauri Shankar Guest House, where you'll find most *karuwa* for Rs400-1200. However, if you're looking for something really special, ask the shopkeeper at "Palpali Karuwa" to show you his special stash, which contains a gleaming meter-high monster that he claims is Nepal's largest *karuwa* (Rs 80,000). The *dhaka*, woven by women in Tansen and the surrounding hills, is also noteworthy. Several handicraft associations in town, especially along Bank Rd., sell shawls (Rs300-1300), *topis* (hats, Rs25-225), and handbags (Rs25-250) produced from this cloth.

WESTERN HILLS

DAYTRIP FROM TANSEN

RANIGHAT

Follow the road up from Tansen toward Hotel Srinagar and then descend Srinagar Hill on the other side. The path is relatively easy to follow: there are newly posted signs at the confusing places, and when in doubt you can just follow the larger or more downhill path. It takes 2-3hr. to get to Ranighat and 3-4hr. to get back. The hike back uphill toward Tansen can be grueling.

Known as the "Taj Mahal of Nepal," Ranighat was built around the turn of the 20th century by Khadga Shumshere as a monument to his wife and was designed by British planners. These days the opulent mansion is in pretty poor shape: the walls are covered by graffiti scrawled by visiting Nepali students, and most of the rooms appear to have been overwhelmed by hordes of incontinent rodents. After a restoration attempt in 1997, the place seems to have been left to its fate once again, resulting in its half-crumbling, half-glistening white appearance. Locals talk of a foreign NGO's plan to take over the mansion and convert it into a hospital, but no visible steps have yet been taken. While the interior is mostly in disrepair, there are plenty of rooms, doors, and balconies which make for some fun exploration. If Ranighat itself, set by the pebbly white shore of the Kali Gandaki river, is not enough to get you excited, the walk there is even better than the destination. The energetic hike leads you through a sub-tropical valley surrounded on all sides by looming mountains and populated by hardy Magar subsistence farmers.

POKHARA पोखरा ☎ 061

The starting point for treks in the Annapurna region, the heart of the country's river-rafting industry, and a stunning part of the world in its own right, Pokhara is second only to Kathmandu as Nepal's most popular tourist destination. Over 300 hotels, countless souvenir shops and trekking agencies, and a multitude of Westerners make Pokhara's Lakeside district a strange little world all its own.

It is difficult to grow accustomed to Pokhara's impossible skyline. Behind the local hills (which would count as mountains anywhere else) loom the gargantuan white peaks of the Annapurna Massif. But Pokhara's natural scenery isn't limited to mountains: its name derives from the Nepali word for "pond," *pokhari*. Pokhara Valley, like the Kathmandu Valley, was once one huge lake. Today, only three lakes—Phewa, Begnas, and Rupa—remain. The Gurungs, the true "natives" of the region, used to live on the hilltops surrounding the valley. Only when Newari traders—traffickers of salt between Kathmandu, Bandipur, and Dhankuta—settled in Pokhara did a city begin to rise on the banks of the Seti River. The Newars built the Bindyabasini Temple in the 16th century, by far the oldest structure in Pokhara. More recent development began with the construction of two highways during the 1970s—one connecting Pokhara to Kathmandu, the other linking it to India. With the infrastructure in place, hotels, restaurants, and adventure-seeking tourists soon followed.

✈ INTERCITY TRANSPORTATION

Flights: The **airport** is on the Siddartha Hwy., between the bus park and the lake. Taxi fares from the airport to Lakeside are fixed (Rs100), but bargain for rides to the airport (Rs50-80). **Buddha Air** (☎534998; open daily 8am-6pm), and **RNAC** (☎521021; open daily 10am-5pm) both have offices near the airport, on the road leading to Lakeside. **Gorkha Airlines** (☎525971; open daily 8am-6pm), **Cosmic Air** (☎526680; open daily 7am-6pm), **Yeti Airlines** (☎530016; open daily 9am-

5:30pm), **Necon Air** (☎525311; open daily 8am-6pm), and **Skyline Airways** (☎536001; open daily 9am-6pm), are along the highway north of the airport. Private companies all fly to **Kathmandu** for about the same rate (30min., frequent 8:45am-4:20pm, US$65-69). RNAC flies to **Kathmandu** (US$65), **Jomsom** (25min., 2 or 3 per day, 6-10am, US$54), and **Manang** (22min, 8:30am, US$54; no flights July 15-Sept. 30). Gorkha and Cosmic also offer daily flights to Jomsom (6,7, and 8am, US$63). Many travel agencies on the main road in Lakeside sell tickets for these companies at no additional charge.

Buses: The **bus park** is a muddy hell-hole when it's wet and a dusty hell-hole when it's dry. Follow the highway 1.5km north from the airport the Prithvi Chowk rotary. Turn right and go 200m to the bus park (taxi Rs60). If you are coming from the bus station, walk to the road and take a left toward Prithvi Chowk. Local buses depart frequently from Prithvi Chowk for Lakeside. The **day bus office** (☎534757), in the center of the muck, has one blue and one red window. Open daily 4:50am-6pm. Day buses to: **Besisahar** (5hr., 6 per day 7:25am-1:25pm, Rs 100-120); **Bhairawa/ Sunawli** (8hr., 11 per day 5:15-10:55am, Rs195); **Birganj** (8hr., 7 per day 5:40-11:10am, Rs190); **Gorkha** (4hr.; 7, 9:30am, and 12:30pm; Rs90); **Janakpur** (9hr., 5:30am, Rs270); **Kakarbhitta** (13hr., 4:20am, Rs450); **Kathmandu** (6hr., 10 per day 5am-1:30pm, Rs155-235); **Narayanghat** (4hr., 11 per day 9:45am-3pm, Rs100); **Tansen** (7hr., 7am, Rs120). The **Night bus office** (☎523564) is on the right when facing the bus park, up a set of stairs. Open daily 7:30am-8:30pm. Night buses to: **Bhairawa/Sunawli** (10hr., 7 and 7:30pm, Rs225); **Dharan** (15hr., 3:30pm, Rs455); **Janakpur** (1hr., 4:20pm, Rs320); **Kakarbhitta** (15hr.; 3:55, 4:45, and 5:30pm; Rs525); **Kathmandu** (8-9 hr., every 15min. 6:30-8:30pm, Rs175). Buses heading out on the road to Baglung depart from the **Baglung Bus Stand,** at the far north end of town, north of **Mahendra Pul.** There is no such thing as a "tourist fare" no matter how much touts try to convince you. To: **Baglung** (3½hr., every hr. 5:15am-5:15pm, Rs70) via **Dhampus Phedi** (45min., Rs20) and **Naya Pul** (1½hr., Rs45); **Beni** (4½hr., 7 per day 6:05am-1:10pm, Rs110). Ticket counter open 5am-5:15pm. Travel agencies and hotels at Lakeside/Damside operate pricier and more comfortable coaches with morning departures (6:30-7:30am) from hotels. To: **Kathmandu** (Rs250); **Narayanghat** (Rs250); **Sunauli** (Rs250-300). Buses are added or canceled according to demand. **Green Line Tours** (☎531472), Lakeside, is open daily 10am-6pm and operates luxury A/C buses (with lunch and refreshments) to: **Kathmandu** (7hr., 7:30 and 8am, US$12) and **Chitwan** (5½hr., 8am, US$10).

■ ORIENTATION

For all its rustic feel, Pokhara is actually a huge, sprawling city. **Phewa Tal** (the lake) and **Pardi** (the dam) are the two major points of orientation—many travelers never get beyond **Lakeside (Baidam)** or **Damside (Pardi)**. The residential section of town is to the north, away from the lake. The **Siddhartha Highway,** linking Pokhara to India, arcs from north to south through the city. It meets the **Prithvi Highway** from Kathmandu at **Prithvi Chowk,** the city center, where you'll also find the **bus station.** Farther north, the main road leads to the **Mahendra Pul** area, the historic heart of the city and the center of the **Pokhara Bazaar.** Lakeside overshadows Damside both in size and popularity. Lakeside's two main sections extend south from the campground to the Hotel Hungry-Eye and east from the Royal Palace to Fish Tail Lodge. It's a 30min. walk from one end to the other. Damside reaches south along **Pardi Road** from the intersection with the main Lakeside thoroughfare. There are **maps** posted at several of Pokhara's *chowks* and intersections.

☐ LOCAL TRANSPORTATION

Bikes are the best way to get around when it isn't raining. Shops in Lakeside/Damside rent bikes (Rs10 per hr., Rs40-50 per day). Many of the same shops also rent **motorcycles** and don't require a license or permit (Rs300-350 per day plus fuel). **Taxi** fares rise in season. Fares are higher on Saturdays and double after 7pm. Drivers may be reluctant to turn on the meter, but be persistent. It's always cheaper to pay according to the taxi meter. **City buses** leave every 30min. from the boat docks nearest Barahi Temple and pass through Mahendra Pul (Rs8) on the way to Pritvi Narayan Campus (Rs9). More buses wait by the boat docks by the campground in northern Lakeside, and go to Prithvi Chowk (Rs6) before heading to Mahendra Pul (Rs8). Other buses run to most major locations in the city (5:30am-7pm).

☑ PRACTICAL INFORMATION

Tourist Office: Siddhartha Hwy. (☎520028), a short walk northeast from the airport entrance or a 20min. bike ride from Lakeside. One of the best sources of impartial information on trekking. Padma K.C., the office head, has lots of information on the Annapurnas and Nepal's other trekking routes. Free city maps. Open Feb. 13-Nov. 16 Su-Th 10am-5pm, F 10am-3pm; Nov. 17-Feb. 12 Su-Th 10am-4pm, F 10am-3pm.

Immigration Office: (☎521167). On the main road in Damside. Extends visas (US$30 for 1 month). Apply for visas Su-Th 10:30am-1pm, F 10am-noon.

Trekking Information: Annapurna Conservation Area Project (ACAP) Trekking Entry Permit Counter and Visitor Information, opposite the Standard Chartered Bank in Lakeside. **You must purchase an entry permit (Rs2000) before trekking in the Annapurna Conservation Area.** Bring 2 passport-sized photos. The office has a well-informed, impartial staff as well as a number of maps, free pamphlets, and displays. Open Feb. 15-Nov.15 Su-F 9am-4:30pm; Nov. 15-Feb. 15 Su-F 9am-3:30pm. Just next door is Pokhara's newly-established ■ **Kathmandu Environmental Education Project (KEEP)** office (☎531823), which among its many useful features has a trekker's bulletin board, logbooks for the major trekking areas, information on altitude sickness and water purification, and iodine tablets and anti-leech oil for sale. In addition, KEEP's "Green Cafe" serves tasty food and hosts a weekly trivia night (Th 6:30-9:30pm, Rs200). Proceeds support conservation efforts.

Passport Photos: A number of places near the Trekking Entry Permit Counter will do 4 black and white photos for Rs150.

Currency Exchange: There are many authorized currency exchange counters in Lakeside and Damside. Most accept major currencies and AmEx, Visa, and Thomas Cook traveler's checks. **Standard Chartered Bank** (☎520102), in northern Lakeside, just south of the campground, gives cash advances on MC and V (no commission) and cashes traveler's checks (Rs200 or 1.5% commission, whichever is greater). Open Su-Th 9:45am-4:15pm, F 9:45am-1:15pm.

ATM: Standard Chartered has two 24hr. ATMs in Lakeside. One is at the bank itself and another is just north of Moondance. Cirrus/MC/V.

Market: The markets in the Lakeside/Damside area sell clothes, groceries, trekking equipment, and pharmaceuticals. The **Mahendra Pul** area has less expensive local shops (taxi Rs60-80 one-way; bus from Lakeside Rs8; bike ride 20min.). **Saleway's,** in Mahendra Pul, has cheaper trekking food than Lakeside. Open daily 8am-8pm.

Police: The **police station** (☎521087) is a 10min. bike ride south from the center of Lakeside; on the right just before the road to Damside crosses a small river. In Lakeside, the **Community Police Service Centre** (☎534010) is next door to the campground. There is a frequently empty 24hr. **Tourist Police Booth** in front of Moondance.

Pharmacy: Dozens of small pharmacies in Lakeside and Damside carry first-aid supplies for trekking. Many have doctors on call. In Lakeside, the **Barahi Medical Hall** (☎522862) is well-stocked and has a nurse on call 24hr. Open daily 7am-9pm. In Damside, Dr. Prakash Mishra is on call 24hr. at **Manish Medical Hall** (☎525650), on the main road. Open daily 7am-9pm. 50m past the turn-off to Hotel New Cosmos.

Hospital: The **Padma Nursing Home,** New Rd. (☎523048), southwest of Mahendra Pul, has a large facility and many doctors. Open 24hr. for emergencies. The main regional hospital is **Gandaki Hospital** (☎520066; emergency 531954) east of Mahendra Pul, on the far side of the Seti Gandaki River.

Internet: Internet access providers in Pokhara have formed cartels to prevent competition. The going rate is Rs2 per min. In Mahendra Pul you'll find **OnyxB** (☎522920), just across the street from Saleway's, on the 1st floor. Rs40 per hr. Open daily 7:30am-8:30pm.

Post Office: The **main post office** (☎522014), is on the main street in Mahendra Pul. There is another post office nearer to Lakeside. Head out of Lakeside and turn left after passing the police station; it's on your left after 200m. Both open Su-Th 10am-5pm, F 10am-3pm. Most bookstores in Lakeside and Damside sell stamps and postcards. The **UPS Office** (☎527241), in Lakeside around the corner from Tea Time on the side road, sends packages quickly, safely, and expensively worldwide. Open Su-F 9am-7pm.

ACCOMMODATIONS

Lakeside bursts with travel agents, bookstores, money changers, supermarkets, and entertainment. Damside, a 15min. bike ride away, is quieter, smaller, cheaper, and has better mountain views. All hotels listed have luggage storage, laundry service, fans, phones, and noon check-out. Expect off-season discounts of up to 50%. In-season, you may want to phone 2-3 days ahead. There will always be a hotel available, but you might not get your first choice.

LAKESIDE

Butterfly Lodge (☎522892; butterfly@cnet.wlink.com.np). Heading north on the main road, turn right at Pyramid Restaurant; on the right after 100m. A friendly atmosphere, gorgeous garden, wide variety of rooms and meticulous cleanliness right down to the shared (seat!) toilet. Not only is it the best place to stay in Pokhara, but all profits go to the Child Welfare Scheme, which runs day-care and health care centers in the Annapurnas. Dorms Rs100; doubles Rs150-700. ❶

Chhetri Sisters Guest House (☎524066), on the right side of the road, 600m north of Grindlay's Bank as the town begins to thin out. With gorgeous hardwood floors, pristine furniture, and carefully-chosen artwork, the rooms at Chhetri Sisters have a stately elegance not to be found at even Lakeside's most expensive places. The hotel is run by Lucky, Dicky, and Nicky, the friendly and helpful women who also brought you 3 Sisters Adventure Trekking. Dorm beds US$3; doubles US$8-10. ❷

Nature's Grace Lodge (☎527220), 50m beyond the Butterfly. Clean and comfortable rooms are decorated with photographs, statuettes, and embroidered cushions. In addition to the rooftop terrace and bar, the hotel also has a garden next door for additional lounging. Run by the same organization as the Butterfly Lodge. All profits go the Child Welfare Scheme. Doubles Rs250-400. ❷

Sacred Valley Inn (☎531792), on the main road, 150m south of Moondance. Peaceful, convenient location and just a brief stroll to the heart of Lakeside. A slightly more upmarket option, but with big, airy rooms and rattan furniture on the balconies. Views improve (and prices rise) on the upper floors. Doubles with common bath Rs200; with attached bath US$4-12. ❷

Green Peace Lodge (☎532780; gplodge@bb.com.np) about a 15min. walk north of Lakeside. Built on a small outcropping jutting into the lake, Green Peace offers the kind of serene isolation absent from central Lakeside. The rooms aren't spectacular, but the price is right and the lake view is stunning. Singles Rs100; doubles Rs150. ❶

Hotel Snowland (☎520384; www.leisureplanet.com), in Central Lakeside, 50m north of Moondance. Those looking to trade their extra cash for a few nights of luxury should head to the Hotel Snowland, the most central of Lakeside's high-end hotels. Standard, deluxe, and super-deluxe rooms are all well-furnished, with carpets, TVs and telephones. Top rooms have A/C, mini-bar, private balconies, and bathtubs. Singles US$15-55; doubles US$20-65. AmEx/MC/V. ❺

Hotel Fire on the Mountain (☎531461). A short walk from the main road, 250m south of Moondance. Peaceful, but close to the action. Beautiful garden, spacious rooms, and soft beds. Doubles Rs200-500. ❷

Hotel Avocado (☎523617), in the heart of Lakeside, behind Once Upon a Time. Helpful management, sparkling clean rooms, an attractive little garden (no avocado tree), and hot water. Double with common bath Rs150; with attached bath Rs200-300. ❷

Camping Ground (☎524052 or 521688), on the north end of Lakeside; turn left at the intersection north of Standard Chartered Bank and go 100m down toward the lake. Bordering the lake, with unobstructed mountain views, Pokhara's only campground is ideal in dry weather but sloppy during the monsoon. Squat toilets. Check-out 6pm. Hot showers Rs50, cold showers Rs30. Tents Rs40; vehicles Rs60. ❶

DAMSIDE

Hotel Himalayan (☎521643), east off the main road in Damside, just past Manish Medical Hall. A meticulously well-kept garden, equally well-maintained rooms, and great mountain views from the balcony. Dorms Rs40; singles Rs100; doubles Rs150. ❶

Hotel New Cosmos (☎521964), behind the main road in Damside. Great views of the lake and mountains. Try to get one of the 3 rooms with a view. Friendly, familial feel. All rooms have attached bath. Doubles Rs200-300. ❷

Hotel Gurung Resort (☎532936), next door to Hotel Himalayan. Rooms are plush but reasonably priced, with carpets, fans, balconies and great mountain views. Attached bathrooms are brand-new, with sparkling seat toilets and bathtubs. Doubles Rs500. ❸

Hotel Jharna (☎521925), next door to Hotel New Cosmos. Carpeted doubles have big windows and attached bath. Several rooms overlook the lake. Common spaces are big and bright. The ivy-covered terrace on the second floor is a nice place to sit and relax. Singles Rs250-300; doubles Rs350-450. ❷

 FOOD

Most restaurants cluster around central Lakeside and offer similar menus. If, despite the cinnamon buns, Swiss chocolate, garlic pizza, and steak *au poivre* you still crave a hearty plate of *dal bhat*, there are a number of inconspicuous Nepali eateries tucked away down alleys or side streets. Of these, the **Yuriko Momo Restaurant ❶**, on the road leading to the Butterfly Lodge, is cheap, tasty, and convenient (*dal bhat* Rs60, *momos* Rs40). In Damside there are few restaurants to speak of outside of hotels, while Mahendra Pul is home to a number of places serving delicious and inexpensive Indian and Nepali food.

LAKESIDE

▨ **The Little Tibetan Tea Garden,** 50m east of the main road, on the road just north of Standard Chartered Bank. Tibetan food, a quiet bamboo garden, and reasonable prices put it leagues above the rooftop restaurants on the main road. Big, delicious *momos* Rs90-150, *thenthuk* Rs90-125. Open daily 7am-10pm. ❷

▨ **Moondance,** central Lakeside, on the main road. Moondance is the best of Lakeside's mega-places. Creative decor, good music, and board games contribute to the charm. The pub upstairs also wins top marks for after-dinner fun. Big menu ranges from pizza (from Rs120) to apple crumble (Rs80). Open daily 9am-10pm. ❷

Bistro Caroline, in central Lakeside, just north of Hotel Snowland. Though it's one of Lakeside's most expensive places, Bistro Caroline is worth a visit for its Mediterranean Cafe atmosphere and unique menu, which eschews the common crowd in favor of a few select dishes. Entrees include crepes, Rs190-290; *Tarte aux tomates et a la Mozzarelle,* Rs 260; and *Spaghettis aux trois fromages,* made with Parmesan, blue, and yak cheeses. For dessert try the *Ile Flottnate* (caramel almond mousse with vanilla sauce; Rs 160). Open 10am-9pm. ❹

Boomerang, just north of Club Amsterdam. The real attraction here is the giant lakeside garden with palm trees, shady gazebos and a wicker swing chair. Veg. burger and fries Rs115; chinese dishes Rs105-245. The attached bakery serves fantastic chocolate croissants (Rs20) and veg. pastries (Rs20). Cultural show every night 7pm-9pm. Open daily 8am-11pm. ❶

Monsoon, on the main road, 150m south of Moondance, next to the Sacred Valley Inn. A quiet cafe run by British expats and stocked with reading material (not to be confused with the oversized Monsoon Bar and Grill across from Hotel Snowland). Quiche Rs175. Only open for breakfast (Rs115-160) and lunch (Rs65-175) 6am-6pm. ❸

Tea Time, on the main road in central Lakeside. Very popular place where the staff follows its "Live the life you love, love the life you live" motto. The cheapest and most subdued of the central Lakeside spots. Movies in the evening and a pool table (Rs50 per game). Big salads Rs65-190, Indian dishes Rs70-95. Open daily 6am-midnight. ❷

Once Upon A Time, central Lakeside. Among the most popular restaurants in Lakeside. Bamboo motif pervades. Pleasant atmosphere and decent (if pricey) food. One of the few places to feature specialty Nepali dishes like *gundruk* (dried greens) and *dhedo* (millet paste). Nepali set meal Rs145-499; most entrees Rs99-270; beer Rs90-120. Movies shown nightly with dinner in a barefoot sitting area (around 7pm). Open daily 7am-10pm. ❷

MAHENDRA PUL

Marwadi Sewa Bhojanalaya, 50m east of Saleway's grocery store. Veg. Indian restaurant serving sublime *baingan bharta* (Rs35) and *masala dosa* (Rs50). Top it off with *ras malai* (Rs30) or *pera* (Rs5 per piece) for dessert. Open daily 6:30am-9pm. ❶

Kohinoor Punjabi Restaurant, down the alley behind Saleway's grocery. Look for the "Club Ten" sign. Just plain, good Indian food. The chicken butter *masala* (Rs110) will have you scrambling to buy a Punjabi cookbook. *Aloo gobi* Rs40. Open daily 7:30am-10pm. ❶

◉ SIGHTS AND ACTIVITIES

Much of Pokhara's old bazaar burned down in 1949 in a fire that spread from a *puja* at Bindyabasini Temple, so most of the architecture is new. Most lakeside agents (try **Encounter Destination,** ☎521963, just south of the Green Line bus office; open daily 8am-8pm) offer mini-bus tours of the valley. *(10am-5pm or 10am-1pm, both Rs250.)*

WESTERN HILLS

The tranquil **Barahi Temple** sits on an island in the middle of the lake. The **Peace Pagoda** (built by the same Japanese group who constructed the giant Peace Stupa in Lumbini) stands atop the ridge across the lake. The view is the best in Lakeside. To get there, row to the pink Hotel Fewa and take the trail in back to the top (a 45min. hike). Boat rental is available from a number of places in Lakeside. Largest and most convenient is the Barahi Ghat, down the road to the lake from Moon-dance. *(Rs140 per hr., Rs400 per day.)* The agency down the road to the lake from Tea Time also rents out pedal-boats *(Rs140 per hr., Rs 400 per day)* and sailboats *(Rs200-250 per hr., Rs 900-1200 per day).*

REGIONAL MUSEUM. The farmhouse-like Regional Museum showcases the cultural range of the Central Western region, with a number of excellent displays on Nepal's diverse ethnography and crafts traditions. The descriptions of the exhibits are both extensive and well-written. One of the exhibits features the Thakali **La Phewa** festival, in which the gods of each of the four Thakali clans are paraded from their respective temples while the clan history is recited. The festival is held only every 12 years in the Thak Khola—the next is scheduled for 2004. *(On the road between Prithvi Chowk and Mahendra Pul. Taxi from Lakeside Rs50-70. Bike ride 25min. ☎ 520413. Open Sa-M and W-Th 10am-4:30pm, F 10am-2:30pm. Rs10; camera fee Rs20.)*

DEVI'S FALLS. The lake flows out at its southern end into the Pardi Khola, a stream that slices its way through the soft sedimentary rock and suddenly shoots down into a surprisingly deep, narrow gorge at Devi's Falls (known locally as **Patale Chhango** or Hell's Fall), 1km out of Pokhara, down the road toward the Indian border. Locals agree that the falls were named after a woman who was swept away in a 1961 flash flood, but accounts vary as to whether it was a Swiss Mrs. Devi or an American Mrs. Davis. *(1km from Pokhara. Taxis from Lakeside Rs100 round-trip, 20min. by bike. Open daily 6am-7pm. Rs10.)*

GUPTESHWOR MAHADEV CAVE. Discovered in 1992, this cave extends 3km into the earth, and is dedicated to Shiva (Gupteshwor is one of his many names) for the natural *linga* that was found inside. The first 100m are well-lit, and paved with concrete steps, at the bottom of which stands a small Shiva temple. In the dry season, the narrow passage behind the temple, which after another loom leads to the base of Devi's falls, is also lit up. To explore any farther you'll need a flashlight; the ticket office also has an information sheet which gives descriptions of the caves three main branches. **Beware of falling rocks.** *(Across the street from Devi's Fall. Cave open daily 5:30am-6:30pm. Rs20.)*

BINDYABASINI TEMPLE. A long flight of steps leads up to Bindyabasini Temple, built during the 16th century by Newari traders who had just settled in the Pokhara Valley. The fire that engulfed Pokhara in 1949 started here. The main shrine, dedicated to Kali, is accompanied by a modern brick Shiva temple. There is a small Buddhist monastery at the base of the steps. *(In a park at the north end of town, on the highway to Baglung. Taxis from Lakeside Rs80-90; 35min. uphill bike ride from Lakeside.)*

NATURAL HISTORY MUSEUM. Originally founded in 1965 by an American Peace Corps Volunteer to educate and entertain the local townspeople, the Annapurna Natural History Museum is today divided into two sections. The museum's original exhibits include paintings and descriptions of wildlife the world over as well as well-preserved specimens of Nepal's birds. The highlight of the museum is unquestionably the vast collection of butterflies, in which nearly all of Nepal's 640 species are represented. The ACAP Visitors Information Center was added to the museum in 1988. The Center provides valuable ethnographic details of the Kathmandu Valley and also highlights the hazards of over-population and heavy tourist traffic. *(At the north end of Pokhara on the Prithvi Narayan Campus. Open Su-F 10am-12:30pm and 1:30-5pm; Sept.-Feb.: 10am-12:30pm and 1:30-4pm. Free.)*

OTHER SIGHTS. The hilltop **Tibetan Monastery** ("Madepani Gompa") has excellent views of the valley, and the monastery's paintings are brilliant and colorful. Nearby, on another hilltop, the **Bhadrakali Temple** is peaceful and shaded. *(To get to the Tibetan Monastery, cross the Seti Gandaki River at the Mahendra Pul Bridge and keep going until you reach the base of the hill, where a road and a staircase lead up to the monastery. To get to the Bhadrakali Temple, continue past the base of the monastery, heading away from Jahendra Pul, and turn right at 2 consecutive forks. Taxi from Lakeside Rs 100. 1hr. by bike.)* North of Pokhara, outside the city limits, is a cave, **Mahendra Gupha.** Tunnels inside allow for a good 30min. of exploration. Some parts of the cave have electricity, but take a flashlight anyway. *(City buses run to the cave from Bagar, about 250m north of the Natural History Museum; Rs7. Taxi Rs150. Cave Rs10. Open daily 7am-5pm.)* One kilometer up the dirt road from Mahendra Gupha is the more extensive **Bat Cave.** No batmobiles inside, but it makes for some fun climbing. A few locals know the cave well, and may offer to be your guide. *(Guides Rs100. Cave Rs10. Open daily 6:30am-6pm.)*

◪ RAFTING AND TREKKING

Most people are drawn to Pokhara by the natural attractions beyond the city limits. Pokhara is teeming with agencies that can help you enjoy the great outdoors in safety and comfort and under the supervision of experienced guides.

Rafting expeditions run from a couple of days to nearly two weeks and generally cost US$35-60 per person per day. Rates should include equipment rental, guides, instruction, food, and transportation. Be wary of cheap deals—you get what you pay for. Routes on the challenging **Kaligandaki** (Class 3-4 rapids; 3 days) and the manic **Marsyangdi** (Class 4-5 rapids; 5 days) run only in season as the monsoon rains make them unnavigable. The **Seti Khola** and **Trisuli** (Class 3-4 rapids; 2-3 days) are more fun during the high-water season from June to August. Some companies combine a Trisuli trip with a visit to **Chitwan National Park** (see p. 880). Others also do **kayaking** trips and offer beginner-level **kayak schools** (4 days, US$150-200) with food, transport, accommodations, and equipment included. Schools usually spend a day on Phewa Lake and then three days on the Seti Khola River.

Trekking agencies provide everything from equipment rental to guides to fully planned treks. Expect to pay US$12-15 per day for an English-speaking guide and US$6-9 per day for a porter. For more information see **Trekking in Nepal**, p. 894.

Equator Expeditions (☎520688; equator@mos.com.np), just north of Standard Chartered Bank. Honest and smart, Equator sends you rafting with safety kayakers and sends you trekking with knowledgeable guides. Kaligandaki US$100 for 3 days; Trisuli US$65 for 2 days. 4-day kayak clinics US$15-200. Office open daily 8am-8pm.

Himalayan Encounters (☎520873; rafting&trekking@himenco.wlink.com.np), 200m east of the main road from the intersection north of Standard Chartered Bank. A British-run rafting and trekking agency that charges a little more than most, but makes up for it with professionalism and experience. Rafting on the Kaligandaki US$165 for 4 days; Trisuli US$75 for 2 days. English-speaking trekking guide US$20 per day; guide-porter US$15 per day; porter US$11 per day. Office open daily 8am-9pm.

Ultimate Descents (☎523240; info@udnepal.com), in central Lakeside, just north of Maya Pub. Your best bet for rafting in Nepal, UD are pioneers in the field, with 15 years of international experience. Safety kayakers accompany every trip. Kaligandaki US$99 for 3 days; Marsyangdi US$250 for 5 days; Trisuli US$70 for 2 days. 4-day kayak clinic US$220. Office open daily 9am-8pm.

WESTERN HILLS

3 Sisters Adventure Trekking (☎524066; www.3sistersadventure.com), on the right side of the road, 600m north of Standard Chartered Bank as the town begins to thin out. Female trekkers will appreciate this unique woman-run company that provides female guides (US$12-20 per day) and porters (US$10 per day). Office open daily 8am-8pm.

Sunrise Paragliding (☎521174; www.nepal-paragliding.com), next door to Ultimate Descents. While any trekking company can take you up Nepal's mountains, only Sunrise can help take you off them. This British-Nepali partnership offers tandem flights of 15-90 minutes from the hills around Pokhara (US$75-120), as well as a 9-day paragliding course (US$300 for each 3-day segment) and combination gliding/trekking packages. Clients both fly and walk between remote villages in the Annapurna region. Sunrise's "Parahawking" trips follow a trained hawk which leads the glider's pilot to thermal air currents that can keep the glider aloft for hours. Office open daily 8am-7pm.

Mountain Way Trekking (☎520316; mountway@trekkin.mos.com.np), on the road with the median, that connects Lakeside and Damside. One of Pokhara's oldest trekking agencies with grizzled veteran sherpa guides. The office also has informative free pamphlets. Organized trek US$45-70 per day; guide US$8 per day; porter US$6 per day.

Sisne Rover Trekking (☎520893; sisne@mos.com.np), across the street and slightly south of Tea Time. Reliable and reasonably priced, Covers both rafting and trekking and sends a safety kayak for every 2 rafts. Kali Gandaki US$65 for 3 days; Seti Khola US$35 for 2 days; Trisuli US$15 for 1 day. 3-day kayak clinic US$150. Trekking guide US$10-15 per day; guide-porter US$9 per day. Office open daily 8am-9pm.

Khampa Trek (☎521520; www.khampatreks.com), next door to the ACAP office. One of the few exclusively guide-owned companies, Khampa Basudev, the manager, is a helpful source of information on trekking conditions, safety, and other practical matters such as embassy registration. Open daily 7am-7pm. Offers guides (US$10-15) and porters (US$6-8) with a range of skill and experience.

🎵 ENTERTAINMENT

Entertainment in Pokhara consists mostly of eating, drinking, listening to music, and taking in the views from Lakeside's restaurants. Many restaurants feature **Nepali cultural shows** (including **The Hungry-Eye** and **Boomerang**) or **movies** (see **Once Upon a Time, Tea Time, Moondance,** and **Maya**) during the evenings. Most movies start around 7pm and require that you have dinner. **Bars** are common along the main drags. In addition to those listed below, Moondance is one of the best. **Musical entertainment** runs the gamut from Nepali folk dance to classic-rock cover bands; there's even a piano bar. The **Maya Pub** is one of the most popular places in town with pool (Rs30 per game, Rs 100 per hr.) and movies downstairs. The colorfully-lit upstairs terrace has a powerfully mellow atmosphere. (Beer Rs 65-120; cocktails Rs150.) **Club Amsterdam** in central Lakeside has live music, food, booze, a pool table (Rs50 per game), a TV, an outdoor sitting area, and "the cleanest toilet in Lakeside." (Beer Rs80-130. Open daily noon-11pm. Live music W, F, Sa.) The **Old Blues Pub**, just off the main road in northern Lakeside, has recently brought in an excellent band from Darjeeling, "Mantra," as its house band, and the kitchen defiantly serves breakfast into the wee hours. (Soft drinks Rs20; beer Rs100-110; pool and darts free. Open daily from 10am.) If you're wondering what Nepali youths do after hours, check out the **Magic Club**, 100m away from the main road by Tea Time. This is Pokhara's only dance club and the closest thing to a hot local hang-out. (Beer Rs100; shots Rs45. Cover Rs200 for men, includes one free beer. Rs100 for women, includes one free Coke; no cover for women M and Th. Open daily 8pm-1am.)

⚡ DAYTRIPS FROM POKHARA

SARANGKOT. Sarangkot (1592m) has some of the best views around. If you're feeling lazy, take a **taxi** (Rs500-600 round-trip) up the road that runs most of the way to the top and walk up for another 30min. Or rent a **motorcycle** (See **Local Transportation,** p. 866) and head up the same road. You can also walk up the auto road. When heading north, turn left off the Baglung Rd. at the "Sarangkot" sign, 1km north of the Baglung bus park. The walk from Lakeside (3hr.) is much nicer. It's easy to lose your way on the trails that criss-cross the hillside. Guides will magically appear as soon as you start heading up the hill (Rs20-40). Dawn is the best time to come. To catch the morning light, it's easiest to stay at one of the places just below the hilltop. Many places are very cheap but expect (or require) you to eat your meals at the hotel. Water is also scarce, so make sure they have it and find out the cost of using it. The **Didi Lodge ❶** has simple, trekking-style rooms with great views. *(Doubles Rs50. Bucket of hot water Rs25.)* The small and cozy **Sarangkot View Point Lodge ❶,** along the steps just below the top of the hill, also has three very basic and cheap rooms. *(Doubles Rs50. Hot water bucket Rs50.)*

Nicer, though considerably more expensive, rooms are available at the **Lake View Lodge ❶,** near the bottom of the steps. Rooms have vinyl floors and surprisingly well-equipped and maintained attached bathrooms. *(Doubles Rs350. Hot water bucket Rs40.)* The hotel restaurant has an outdoor seating area with great views of the valley. *(Dal bhat Rs110-160. Pizzas Rs95-120. Breakfast Rs80-100.)*

BEGNAS AND RUPA LAKES. Phewa, Begnas, and Rupa Lakes were all part of the huge body of water that once filled the Pokhara Valley. Phewa bears the burden of tourist traffic while Begnas and Rupa remain untouched. **Begnas Bazaar,** 15km from Mahendra Pul, is serviced by **local buses,** which leave from the main Prithvi Chowk bus park in Pokhara (1hr., every 15min. 5am-7pm, Rs15). Alternatively, the 2hr. **bike ride** to Begnas will certainly loosen up your legs. (From Pokhara, head east out the Prithvi Narayan Hwy. toward Kathmandu and turn left at Tal Chowk, 12km from Pokhara.) **Taxis** charge Rs500-600 round-trip. You can rent a **boat** and row to the other end of Begnas. From there, it's a 20min. hike to Rupa over Panchabhaiya Danda, but at Rs250 per hour, it's hard to lose track of time and enjoy it. *(Entrance fee to Begnas Lake Rs10, camera fee Rs20.)*

WESTERN HILLS

THE TERAI तराई

The Terai is the flat bit of Nepal to the south that dips into the Gangetic plain. Its flatness means that the Terai has many of Nepal's best roads, but travelers continue to see the region as a sweaty, mosquito-infested purgatory between India and the mountains, meriting no more than a few hours of frustrated transit. For Nepalis, however, the Terai holds special significance as producer of the vast majority of the country's rice. It also hosts most of Nepal's industry, construction, and transportation infrastructure. The region was covered with impregnable malarial jungle until the 1950s and 60s, when eradication efforts prompted massive migrations from Nepal's hills and bordering Indian states. Large areas of land, such as the Royal Chitwan National Park, have been set aside to preserve some of the region's natural riches. The demands of a growing population, and now a burgeoning tourism industry, however, are at odds with these efforts. Despite the Terai's economic importance, the needs of the native population in this region remain largely ignored by Kathmandu elites, who regard them as a bit too closely tied to India for comfort. The neighboring towns of Narayanghat and Bharatpur are the main gateway from the hills. The Mahendra Rajmarg Highway, running east-west from one corner of Nepal to another, connects the entire Terai. Lumbini, in the west, and Janakpur, in the east, are two of Nepal's main religious sites.

HIGHLIGHTS OF THE TERAI

The jungles, swamps, and plains of **Chitwan National Park** (p. 880) are proof that even the flatter parts of Nepal can be beautiful.

Janakpur's temples (p. 886) offer a look at heavily Indian-influenced culture and architecture, without the headache of a border crossing.

Pilgrims flock to Buddha's birthplace, **Lumbini** (p. 875), home to temples and monasteries contributed by Buddhist communities from all over the world.

✺ BORDER CROSSING: BHAIRAWA भैरहवा

Just 5km north of the Indian border, Bhairawa (Siddharthanagar) has managed to avoid the nasty border-town grime that plagues its counterpart to the south, Sunauli. What the town lacks in sights, it makes up for in pleasant accommodations; it's a popular stop on the way to or from the border and for daytrips to Lumbini. If you're crossing the border from Nepal, you'll *have* to stop here, as buses don't run directly to Sunauli.

Bhairawa is spread along a north-south highway: as you stand with your back to the bus station, south (towards Sunauli) is to your left, and north (towards Lumbini) is to your right. A 10min. walk north of the bus station brings you to **Devkota Chowk**, with a number of hotels, shops, and services; another 10min. north sits **Lumbini Chowk,** from where there are frequent buses to Lumbini. Several carriers offer daily flights to **Kathmandu** (35min., 7 per day 8:50am-6pm, US$78-81). **Gorkha Air's** office is on the highway 150m north of the bus park. (☎526665. Open daily 7:30am-6:30pm.) **Buddha Air** (☎526893; open daily 7am-6pm) and **Skyline** (☎521115; open daily 8am-7pm) are in the Hotel Yeti building at Devkota Chowk, while **Necon Air** (☎521244; open daily 7:30am-6:30pm) is on the right side of the highway 150m north of the chowk. From the **bus counter,** at the southwest corner of Bus Chowk (☎520351; open daily 5am-8:30pm), tickets are available for day/night buses to: **Kathmandu** (7-9 hr., frequent 4:30am-8pm, Rs195/240); **Pokhara** (8hr.; frequent

4:50am-noon, 6:45, 8pm; Rs193/227); **Kakarbhitta** (13 hr., 4:30am and 6:15pm, Rs447/522); **Lumbini** (1½ hr., every 30 min. 6:25am-6:20pm, Rs20); **Tansen** (4hr., 6:15am, Rs60); **Gorkha** (6hr., 6:30am, Rs163). Many more connections are available at **Butwal.** Buses to **Lumbini** (1½hr., frequent 6:25am-7pm, Rs20) also depart from Lumbini Chowk. A **rickshaw** from Lumbini Chowk to Bus Chowk costs Rs20.

Shared jeeps make frequent departures from the bus station for **Sunauli** (10min., frequent 6am-8pm, Rs6) and **Butwal** (1hr., frequent 7am-7pm, Rs18). Private jeeps can be reserved at the bus station for trips to Sunauli (Rs100) or Lumbini (round-trip Rs700). Any Lumbini-bound vehicle can stop at the **airport.**

Reliable **Internet** is available at the UN Cyber Centre, Devkota Chowk. (Rs40 per hr. Open daily 7am-9pm.)

The best place to spend the night in Bhairawa is the **Hotel Moonlight ❷,** 80m north of Devkota Chowk, whose clean, carpeted rooms come with or without attached bath. The pleasant restaurant downstairs serves all your favorites at reasonable prices. (☎522808. Singles Rs150, with attached bath Rs250; doubles Rs250/350. Veg. chow mein Rs35, *dal bhat* Rs50.)

The **Hotel Ashoke International ❸,** overlooking the bus park, has some more luxurious options, and the terraces on every floor provide lots of natural light. (☎525986. Doubles Rs400, with attached bath Rs700; deluxe A/C suite Rs1000.)

✖ BORDER CROSSING: SUNAULI सुनौली

The second-most popular entry point to Nepal (after the airport in Kathmandu), Sunauli (technically called Belahiya on the Nepal side) has all the inevitable frontier grime but is much less of a hassle than Birganj and less dismal than Kakarbhitta. Don't get stuck here for long, though.

The **bus park** on the Indian side is about 500m south of the border. Purchase tickets on board the bus. Buses leave frequently for: **Allahabad** (10 hr., 7am and 2pm, IRs210); **Delhi** (23hr., every 30min. 4:30am-6:30pm, IRs393) via **Ayodhya** (5½hr., IRs122) and **Lucknow** (9-10hr., IRs170); **Varanasi** (10hr.; 4, 8am, 4, 7pm; IRs145); all buses go via **Gorakhpur** (2½hr., frequent, IRs47). There is also a tourist bus to Varansi that departs from the Indian Immigration office at 8:30am (IRs180). Touts on the Nepali side will tell you that they can get you on board luxury buses or that you can purchase tickets only *before* you cross the border; none of this is true. You'll have to go to Bhairawa first to get anywhere else in Nepal; shared **jeeps** leave frequently from the small lot 100m north of the border (10min., 5am-8pm, IRs6). You can take a **rickshaw** (NRs10) across the border, though it's probably easier just to walk.

The requisite stops at both Indian and Nepali **customs and immigration** should take less than an hour. Nepalese visas can be obtained on the spot, but citizens of countries other than India or Nepal need visas to enter India (available only in Kathmandu). The border is open 24hr., as are both Nepalese and Indian immigration offices. The Nepali **tourist office** (☎520304, open Su-Th 10am-5pm, F 10am-3pm) and **police outpost** are just south of the big Nepali entrance gate, opposite one another. The **UP government tourist office,** next door to Hotel Niranjana, is run by the amazingly resourceful Mr. Zaidi, who has a wealth of information about both UP and Nepal. (Open M-Sa 10am-5pm; closed every second Sa.) There are numerous **currency exchanges** on both sides of the border. (Most open 6am-6pm.)

LUMBINI लुम्बिनी   ☎071

Lumbini is a work in progress. Today's Lumbini is not a town, but a five sq. km plot of land set aside to honor the Buddha, who was reputedly born in the Sacred Garden at the south end. In ancient times, Lumbini saw its fair share of pilgrims and monuments, most notably the pillar erected in the 3rd century BC by the emperor Ashoka. By the 15th century AD, however, Lumbini's claim to fame had been forgotten, and it wasn't until 1896 that Ashoka's pillar was unearthed. The current halfhearted drive to raise the site's status from just an obscure spot in the Terai began in 1967 with a visit by U Thant of Burma, then Secretary General of the UN. It continues with the ambitious "Master Plan" of Japanese architect Kenzo Tange that envisions Lumbini as "an expression of Buddha's universal message of peace and compassion creating a sculpted landscape to make the teachings of Lord Buddha accessible to all humanity." While the principal elements of the Master Plan have recently been completed, construction of many individual monuments and monasteries still continues. If the heat isn't too bad, a visit to Lumbini can be a wonderful experience, consisting of pleasant walks through wetlands and *sal* forest to visit temples contributed by Buddhist cultures and communities from around the world.

▐ TRANSPORTATION

Frequent **buses** run between **Bhairawa** and **Mahilwar,** the small town adjacent to Lumbini. Buses leave from the main bus station and from Lumbini Chowk every 30min. between 6:30am and 7pm and make the return journey every 30min. between 6:30am and 5pm (Rs15). **Bikes** are a great way to get around; **Lumbini Village Lodge** (see **Accommodations and Food,** below) has a few decent ones for hire (Rs20 per hr., Rs100 per day).

▐▐ ORIENTATION AND PRACTICAL INFORMATION

While Lumbini is laid out in a very precise and orderly fashion, everything is extremely spread-out; the road to enlightenment is long, and the road from enlightenment back to the bus stop is longer still. If you don't have a ride, rickshaw-*wallahs* will be eager to give you one. Lumbini is a 1½km by 5km rectangle enclosed by **Ring Road** and divided into three equal 1½ sq. km segments. The southernmost segment contains the **Sacred Garden,** where the Buddha was born. The middle segment is the **Monastic Zone,** cut through the middle by a canal. Mahayana temples and monasteries line the west side and Theravada temples and monasteries line the east side. The northernmost segment is mostly empty wetlands, though it contains a museum, research institute, and the impressive **Peace Stupa.** The town of **Mahilwar,** home to most of the accommodations and services, is just off the eastern side of Ring Rd., a short walk from the Sacred Garden. **Tourist information** is available from the **Lumbini Development Trust** information booth, on the edge of the Sacred Garden opposite the Mayaderi Temple. (☎580189. Open daily 6am-6:30pm.) **Currency exchange** is available in Mahilwar at the **Nepal Credit and Commerce Bank,** right at the entrance to town. (☎580152. Open Su-Th 10am-3pm, F 10am-1pm.) The **police station** (☎580171) is 150m southwest of the Sacred Garden. **Tara Medical Center,** in Mahilwar, is a **pharmacy** run by Tara, a retired medical advisor. (☎580088. Open daily 8am-7pm.)

STUDY OPPORTUNITIES

There are two permanent centers for **Vipassana Meditation** in Lumbini. The **Panditarama** center (☎580118) offers year-round instruction in the Pandita technique. Courses are taught by Pandita's pupil, Sayada Vivekananda, though every February Pandita himself comes to lead a course.

Dhamma Janani, across the road from the Gautami Nun's Temple, runs 10-day courses starting on the 15th of every month, following S.N. Goenka's teachings. To book a place or get more information, contact the Dharmashringa center in Kathmandu (☎01 4250581). There is no charge for the courses, but a small donation is expected to defray food and lodging expenses.

⚑ ▢ ACCOMMODATIONS AND FOOD

Most people visit Lumbini for the day and return to Bhairawa to sleep. But there are a few good hotels in Mahilwar, a five-minute walk from the Sacred Garden, and there's usually space available, even in season. The cream of the crop is the **Lumbini Garden Lodge ❷**, on Mahilwar's main street. The rooms are clean and the prices are the lowest in town. (☎580146. Doubles Rs150-250.) Newer and slightly more upscale is the **Hotel Lumbini ❷**, with bright, spacious rooms and attached toilets. (☎580142. Singles Rs200; doubles Rs300; triples Rs450.) The best place to eat in Lumbini is the **Peace Land Restaurant ❷**, on Ring Rd. across from the turn-off to the Sacred Garden. The food is good, the prices are reasonable, and there are a variety of comfortable indoor and outdoor seating options. (Open daily 7am-9pm. Main dishes Rs40-120; veg. Nepali set Rs75.) Another option in Mahilwar is the cozy and familial restaurant in the courtyard of the **Lumbini Village Lodge ❶**. The hand-lettered menu is limited to the basics, but everything is tasty and carefully prepared. (Veg. chow mein Rs45, *dal bhat* Rs65, fried rice Rs30-80.) On the road leading west toward the Sacred Garden, is the **Lumbini Garden Restaurant ❹**, which serves decent Chinese, Indian, Nepali, and continental food at an exorbitant Rs70-225. (Open daily 7am-9:30pm.)

◉ SIGHTS

Lumbini's centerpiece is the **Sacred Garden,** which marks the birthplace of the Buddha. According to legend, Siddhartha Gautama, a prince in the Sakya royal family, was born in Lumbini in 623 BC, when the site was merely a forest grove near a water tank. Siddhartha's mother, Mayadevi, was on her way back from her husband's palace when she stopped to bathe in the water tank, took a few steps to the north, and then gave birth while holding on to the branch of a *sal* tree. The site of this event is now occupied by the newly-renovated **Mayadevi Temple.** Enter the temple via the lower ramp, and once inside follow the walkway clockwise, according to Buddhist tradition. At the center of the chamber, below the walkway, lies the **marker stone** that is said to mark the exact location of the Buddha's birth. Mounted in the shaft just above is the somewhat worn **Mayadevi sculpture** (3rd-4th century AD) which has long been worshipped by Hindus as a representation of a fertility goddess. The sculpture depicts Mayadevi as she holds on to the tree branch with one hand; below her the precocious infant Buddha has already taken his first steps, and all around them gods and goddesses gather to rejoice and pay tribute. Beside the Mayadevi Temple is Nepal's oldest monument, the **Ashokan Pillar,** erected in 249 BC when Ashoka came to town to throw himself a party for the 20th anniversary of his coronation. South of the Ashokan Pillar is the **water tank** where Mayadevi bathed before giving birth to Siddhartha. Surrounding the Mayadevi Temple are half-excavated remains of monasteries, temples, and *stupas* dating from Lumbini's glory days, the 3rd century BC to the 9th century AD. A minute's walk south is another pillar honoring Nepal's King Mahendra, who was the first to encourage Lumbini's renaissance.

Just east of the Sacred Garden is the large yellow Lumbini Buddha Vihar. Constructed by King Mahendra in 1953, it contains statues from Burma, Thailand, and Nepal—including a gold Buddha at the main altar whose meditation seems unperturbed by the halo of garish LED lights flashing around his head. Wall paintings depict the wheel of life, four *bodhisattvas*, the Buddha's life, and the major Hindu gods welcoming Siddhartha back to Nepal after his enlightenment. Immediately north of this complex is the **Tibetan Temple;** aside from the Buddha statue at its center, the most striking feature of the Temple is its well-kept rose garden. A 10min. walk north of the Sacred Garden, the **Eternal Flame** commemorates the 1986 International Year of Peace.

The **Monastic Zone** lies to the north of the eternal flame. The road forks here to flank the central canal. The first building on the west (Mahayana) side is the **Burmese Panditarama** center, which offers courses in **Vipassana meditation** (see **Study Opportunities,** above). The most impressive of the Mahayana temples is the **Chinese temple,** which cost a whopping 70 million rupees to build. The **Nepali Monastery** is also finished, while temples for Korea, Vietnam, and Japan are still under construction.

The first building on the east (Theravada) side of the canal is the **International Gautami Nun's Center,** with statues honoring Buddhism's first nun, the Buddha's stepmother Gautama. Across from it is another Vipassana Center, the Dhamma Janani, while the nearby side road leads to the future site of the Sri Lankan Temple, still in the early stages of construction. The real eye-catcher on the Theravada side is the **Myanmar Golden Temple,** which looks like an enormous bell. The adjacent **monastery** houses a large community of monks. **The Maha Bodhi Society of India** also has a completed temple. The **Thai Monastery** is still under construction but is already home to a monastic community. North of the Theravada Monastic Zone are the **Lumbini Museum** and the **Lumbini Research Institute.** The museum houses a few relics of interest, and the research center has a largely untouched library, but both buildings are most interesting for Kenzo Tange's architecture. (Research Institute ☎580175; liri@mos.com.np. Open Su-Th 10am-1:30pm and 2-5pm, F 10am-1pm and 1:30-3pm. Museum open M and W-Sa 10am-5pm. Free.)

At the far north end of Lumbini stands its largest monument: the colossal 41m high **Peace Stupa.** Facing the cardinal directions are golden statues honoring the four principal events in the life of the Buddha: on the south side, his birth at Lumbini, then in clockwise (not chronological) order, his death at Kusinagara, his enlightenment at Bodh Gaya and his first sermon at Sarnath. The Peace Stupa and the neighboring **Fuji Guruji Monastery** were built by Nipponzan Myohoji, a Buddhist order founded by the Japanese monk Nichidatsu Fuji and dedicated to world peace. Visitors are invited to participate in the monastery's twice-daily prayer sessions, which consist of drum-beating and chanting of the mantra "Na Mu Myo Ho Ren Ge Kyo" (prayers 5am-6:30am and 5pm-6:30pm).

NARAYANGHAT AND BHARATPUR ☎056

There are no two ways about it—Narayanghat is a big, noisy, smelly city. Most travelers will only pass through *en route* to Chitwan National Park, but if you're hoping to experience a taste of the urban Terai, you might actually like the place. The neighboring town of Bharatpur—which will interest you only if you need to go to a hospital or the airport—is quiet and refreshingly laid back. For most travelers, however, the only reason to spend any length of time amid Narayanghat's clogged chaos will be to visit the utterly peaceful *sadhu* community of Devghat, an hour's walk upriver, where the Kali Gandaki and Trisuli rivers merge to become the sacred Narayani.

⌐ TRANSPORTATION. Cosmic Air (☎524218), and **Gorkha Air** (☎521093), both with offices on the highway opposite the airstrip, offer daily flights from Bharatpur to **Kathmandu** (20min., 11:40am and 12:40am, US $63 plus a Rs138 airport tax).

Buses leave from the **Pulchowk Bus Park** to: **Birganj** (4hr., every 30min. 6am-1pm, Rs120); Bhairawa/Sunauli (4½hr., every 30min. 6am-6pm, Rs105); **Kakarbhitta** (9hr.; every hr. 5am-7pm; Rs309 for day buses, Rs422 for night buses); **Kathmandu** (4½hr., every 30min. 5am-6pm, Rs110); **Gorkha** (3hr., every hr. 6:30am-4:30pm, Rs86); **Pokhara** (4hr., every 30min. 5am-6pm, Rs110); **Tansen** (6hr.; 11am, noon, 11pm, and midnight; Rs142). The bus park is intimidatingly chaotic, but it's not hard to find your bus. As a general rule, buses for a particular destination congregate in the part of the bus park closest to that destination: Pokhara to the north, Birganj to the east, Sunauli to the west, etc. At the eastern extremity of the crowd of buses, Chitwan-bound travelers can catch the local service to **Tandi** (15 min., Rs15). From **Pokhara Bus Park,** buses and minibuses go to **Beni** (7hr., 8am, Rs270); **Besisahar** (6hr.; 7, 8, 9:30, 11am, and 1pm; Rs90/115); **Gorkha** (3hr., every 30min. 6am-4pm, Rs60/75); and **Pokhara** (5hr., every hr. 6am-4pm, Rs100). The privately-run **Tourist Information Centre** sells tickets for flights and tourist buses to **Kathmandu.** (☎521890; touristcent@hotmail.com. Open daily 7am-7pm. Buses 4hr.; 10:30am; regular Rs150, luxury Rs622.)

A **cycle-rickshaw** between Narayanghat and Bharatpur should cost Rs10-20; noisy blue **tempos** make the trip for Rs5.

▉◪ ORIENTATION AND PRACTICAL INFORMATION. Narayanghat and Bharatpur are on the east-west **Mahendra Rajmarg Highway.** Narayanghat sits on the east bank of the Narayani River, while Bharatpur is up the hill, 2km farther east. The center of Narayanghat is the **Pulchowk Bus Park,** at the chaotic intersection of the highway and the north-south road to Mugling. A 15min. walk north along this road leads to the **Pokhara Bus Park.** Bharatpur sprawls out along the highway; its two major landmarks are the hard-to-miss airport and the four-way rotary intersection on the highway farther west. **Nepal Bank,** on the road to Mugling, in the big, pink building 500m north of Pulchowk, changes currency and traveler's checks for a 3% commission. (☎520170. Open Su-Th 10am-3pm, F 10am-noon.) The **police** (☎520146) are in the red building off the dirt road two blocks south and one block west of Pulchowk Bus Park. There are decent private **hospitals** in Bharatpur, on the road leading north from the main intersection: Om Hospital (☎521066) is 80m north of the intersection, and Asha Hospital (☎52535) is another 20m farther on. There are a number of **pharmacies** along this road as well (most open 6am-9pm). **Hello Chitwan,** on the highway 200m east of the Pulchowk Bus Park, has 8 computers with sluggish but reliable **Internet.** (☎525524. Rs40 per hour. Open 7am-7pm.) The **post office** is 25m east of the Pokhara Bus Park, just off the road to Mugling. (Open Su-Th 10am-5pm, F 10am-3pm.)

▉◨ ACCOMMODATIONS AND FOOD. All accommodations listed below are in Narayanghat, near one of the bus parks. If you don't need to stay near Pulchowk, the best place to stay in town is the **Satanchuli Inn ❷,** behind the Pokhara Bus Park. It's cozy and clean, opens up onto a refreshingly green garden, and is just a stone's throw away from the river. (☎521151. Singles Rs150-300; doubles Rs300-500.) **Quality Guest House ❶,** 20m north and 20m east of Pulchowk Bus Park, is close to the action but far enough from the bus park to afford some peace and quiet. (☎523488. Singles Rs130-200; doubles Rs250-300.) A pricier and correspondingly more luxurious option is the **Hotel Gangotri ❺,** on the corner just 20m north of Pulchowk. While you'll pay a premium for A/C, all the rooms have carpets, TVs, bathrooms with seat toilets, and hot water. In addition, the garden below is immaculately well-kept. (☎524626. Doubles Rs800, with A/C Rs1600. V.) Narayanghat's finest eating establishment is unquestionably the well-advertised **Kitchen Cafe ❸,** on the north side of Pulchowk, with its garden, interior waterfall, bowtied waitstaff, and deliciously cold drinks. The extensive menu combines the usual array of Indian, Nepali, and continental dishes. (Pizzas Rs90-140, Nepali dishes Rs130-180, veg./non-veg. Indian *thali* Rs125/160. Open daily 8am-10pm.) For something cheaper and more laid-back, try the **Sangam Greentop Restaurant ❷,** on the south side of the highway, 200m east of Pulchowk Bus Park. There are performances of Nepali folk music every evening at 7pm, and the food is cooked over a *taas*—a large, clay barbecue pit. (Veg. *thukpa* Rs40; excellent *paneer chilly* Rs90. Open daily 8am-10pm.) For a quick meal, don't overlook the ramshackle **food stands** surrounding Pulchowk Bus Park. (Curries Rs20-30, chow mein Rs25-40. Most open daily 7am-9pm.)

■ **SIGHTS. Devghat,** 8km north of Narayanghat, honors the confluence of the Trisuli and Kali Gandaki rivers, and is a popular *sadhu* hangout. It's easy to see why: the triple rivers, expansive cornfields, and countless temples all contribute to an atmosphere of hushed serenity that is disturbed only by chirping birds and the occasional lectures of priests in nearby ashrams. Buses arrive in the small square on the east side of the river, where there is a shrine to the monkey god Hanuman, represented here by a large pink statue. Steps lead up and away from the river to a modest Buddhist temple, but most of Devghat's temples and ashrams are across the long suspension bridge, on the point of land between the two rivers. Devghat's three major ashrams, **Goleshwar, Harihar,** and **Mahesha,** house a total of roughly 150 students, all Nepali. The sandy beach at the holy **Triveni,** or point of confluence, is a nice spot for bathing or just cooling off; to get there, follow the path left from the suspension bridge, or ask for directions to the Goleshwar Ashram, which is located nearby. The real action comes around January 15, when thousands make the pilgrimage here. (A 1½hr. walk up the river from Narayanghat. Alternatively, buses from Pokhara Bus Park. 20min., every 30min. 7am-5pm, Rs6. Round-trip taxi ride plus 1hr. waiting time Rs250.)

Another option for a few hours excursion is the **Mauli Kalika Mandir,** poised on top of a ridge just west of Narayanghat. The temple itself is not particularly old or impressive, but on a clear day its expansive views of the entire Chitwan area make the steep 1½hr. walk worthwhile. (Cross the Narayani on the big bridge from Pulchowk, take the first right, and follow the road around to an intersection with a large concrete arch. Don't go through the arch; instead, take the road to its left, which leads to the foot of the hill and the steps up to the temple.)

ROYAL CHITWAN NATIONAL PARK
चितवान   ☎ 056

Royal Chitwan National Park is Nepal's largest and most touristed nature reserve. Its 932 sq. km—ranging from dense jungle to swampland and grassland—are home to hundreds of species of animals and birds, including 21 protected species. While you'll be lucky to see a tiger, leopard, or sloth bear, sightings of rhinos, crocodiles, deer, and monkeys are almost guaranteed.

Until recently, Chitwan was the playground for Nepal's elite, and the sport was hunting big game. Things have changed, however, and Royal Chitwan National Park is now the most protected wildlife reserve in Nepal. In fact, the greatest threat to the wildlife came not from aristocratic rifles but from the area's 1950s malaria eradication program. The program's success indirectly led to the destruction of the local habitat as people moved down from the hills to take advantage of the fertile flatlands. Resettlement of these people began in 1964, and the area was declared a national park in 1973. Eleven years later, UNESCO designated the Royal Chitwan National Park a Natural World Heritage Site.

The village of Sauraha, just north of the park on the bank of the dreamlike Rapti River, is the best base from which to explore the park. Sauraha now survives almost exclusively on tourism, and while there is something artificial about the rooftop restaurants and "safari" lodges, the place remains pleasantly tranquil.

☞ TRANSPORTATION

Buses: Buses depart from Chitrasari for Kathmandu (5½hr., 10am, Rs150); Pokhara (6hr., 10am, Rs150); Sunauli (5hr., 10am, Rs150). There are more destinations and departures from Tandi, which has buses to Birganj (5hr., frequent 5am-4pm, Rs120); Kathmandu (5½hr., frequent 5:40am-9am, Rs135); Pokhara (6hr.; 8, 9, 10am; Rs140); Kakarbhitta (13hr., 5:30pm, Rs471); Janakpur (7hr., 10:30am, Rs150); Sunauli (5hr., 10am, Rs150). The bus counter in Tandi is 15m east of the turn-off to Sauraha. You can also book tickets through your lodge in Sauraha or through one of Sauraha's many travel agents, but expect to pay a commission. To get to Narayanghat, where other connections are available, go to Tandi, and catch any westbound bus on the highway (15min., Rs15).

Local Transportation: You can get a rickshaw between Tandi and Chitrasari for Rs20. Your rickshaw driver will want an additional Rs30 to cross the rickety footbridge and carry you to Sauraha. Jeeps wait on the other side of that bridge and will take you to Sauraha for Rs30, though they may ask as much as Rs100. Unless you're exhausted or weighed down excessively, it's probably worth your while just to walk from Chitrasari to Sauraha. Follow the right fork after you cross the bridge, and you'll be in Sauraha in 15min. Sauraha has lots of **bike rental shops** along the main road (Rs70-100 per day). **Mona Lisa Guide Office** (☎580131), on the main road, just north of the Jungle View Restaurant, has good bikes. (Open daily 6:30am-9pm; Rs15 per hr., Rs80 per day.) A few places in Sauraha rent motorcycles, and, for better or worse, don't require any kind of driver's license. **Chitwan Motorbike on Hire and Repairing Center,** near the north end of town, rents for Rs140 per hr. or Rs500 per day, including a liter of petrol and a helmet. (☎580069. Open daily 6am-8:30pm.)

✦ ⓘ ORIENTATION AND PRACTICAL INFORMATION

Chitwan National Park is at the center of the Terai. Its southern boundary is the Indian border, its northern boundary the Rapti River, which meets the Narayani River further downstream. The Mahendra Rajmarg Hwy. runs almost parallel to the northern boundary of the park. The dirt road leading to the park entrance branches south off the highway in the town of **Tandi,** 20km east of Narayanghat. This dirt road heads south for 4km until it hits **Chitrasari,** a footbridge river-crossing that has developed into a little transportation hub. From there, it's 2½km farther south to **Sauraha,** the town that sits right at the park entrance. Sauraha is home to all the hotels, restaurants, and tour agencies that serve the park and its visitors. It's a small town and oriented almost entirely along the north-south **Main Road,** which runs all the way down to the river.

Tourist Office: The **Visitor Center** has a little museum with displays and information about the history and wildlife of the park (open daily 6am-9pm), as well as the park **ticket office** (open daily 6-8am and 1-2:30pm). The center sells elephant rides (7:30am and 4:30pm; Rs1000) and **permits** (Rs500 per day) for entering the park. **Steep fines** await those caught in the park without a valid permit. **No one may enter the park at night.** In season, the wait to get park entry permits can be 3-4hr. Most of the time, the permit is purchased by whatever guide service you are using, so you don't have to go to the office yourself. To get to the Visitor Center, head down the main road toward the river, take a left at the Jungle View Restaurant, take your first right after about 50m, and then turn right again at the end of the road. The Visitor Center is 20m ahead on your left.

Currency Exchange: A number of places in town change cash and traveler's checks for a 2% commission. The most central of these is **Sauraha Money Changer**, Main Rd. Open daily 7:30am-8pm.

Police: The **main police station** (☎580099) is a 20min. walk east of Sauraha along Tharu Village Rd., take a left at the Jungle View Restaurant. The police station in **Tandi** is on the main highway, 300m east from the turn to Sauraha.

Pharmacy: Raj Medical Hall (☎580133), opposite K.C.'s Restaurant, near the center of Sauraha. Open daily 7am-9pm. The nearest hospital (☎521066) is in Bharatpur.

Internet: Alisha Cyber Cafe (☎580054), south of the Jungle View Restaurant on the road toward the river, charges Rs4 per min. for slow and sporadic service.

VOLUNTEER OPPORTUNITY. The **Children and Women's Promotion Center,** which opened in February 2000, provides education for underprivileged children and vocational training for women. It also serves as a boarding school which houses and feeds 20 children from nearby villages. The center relies exclusively on private donations, and it is deeply in need of not only financial help but also English-language instructors. (*☎580158; cwpcenter@hotmail.com or childrenwpc@wlink.com.np. The center is a 10min. walk north of Sauraha, on the road to Chitrasari.*)

⛰ ACCOMMODATIONS

Many tourists come to Chitwan on pre-paid package deals arranged in Kathmandu or Pokhara. If you arrive in Tandi without a reservation, fight off the touts and head to Sauraha. Standard accommodations are free-standing cottages in garden compounds with solar-heated water. All hotels offer basically the same three-day, two-night package consisting of a jeep or elephant ride, half-day jungle walk, canoe trip, cultural program, lodgings, meals, and bus transportation from Kathmandu or Pokhara to any return city in Nepal. Be wary of bogus budget "deals," and ask to see a park permit. Also beware at cheaper hotels, as many are subsidized by their tour operations; if you opt to use a different tour company, you may find yourself harassed and even told to leave. Off-season (June-Sept., Dec.-Feb.) prices plummet; bargain hard, although some of the costs (park entry fee, government elephant ride) are fixed.

Rain Forest Guest House, Main Rd. (☎580007), near the north end of town. Friendly staff, clean grounds, and reasonable prices make it the best deal in Sauraha. The dining room serves tasty spaghetti bolognese (Rs100). Doubles Rs100-300. ●

Tiger Wildlife Camp, Main Rd. (☎580137), at the north end of town. Pleasant, tranquil, garden setting, large rooms, and the cheapest rates in town. They'll expect you to join their tours, but their prices are absurdly low and their guides are excellent. Doubles Rs60-200. ●

Travellers Jungle Camp, (☎580013), on Main Rd. 200m north of central Sauraha. One of Chitwan's oldest tourist lodges, the Jungle Camp has a wide range of accommodations and very clean, well-kept facilities. The restaurant is good, and there's a money changer next door. The mosquito nets are brand spanking new, and the affable owner speaks flawless English. Clean, bright doubles Rs350, with big bathtub Rs500. ❸

Hotel Wildlife Camp, Main Rd. (☎580023), just north of the town center. Don't be frightened off by the hotel's palatial, well-kept garden—it's not as expensive as you think. Rooms come in different sizes, but all are well-furnished and have fans, mosquito nets and attached bathrooms with seat toilets. Doubles Rs300-500. ❷

Riverside Hotel, Main Rd. (☎580008 or 580009), on the beach, at the south end of town. This upmarket hotel, under the same ownership as K.C.'s Restaurant, is simply luxurious. Lots of natural light in large, nicely decorated rooms that come with towels, soap, and toilet paper. Proceeds go toward the education of local children. Doubles Rs250-750. ❷

Jungle Tourist Camp, Main Rd. (☎580030), close to the center of town. Basic but clean, the Jungle Tourist Camp is another reliable budget option. The garden is dusty, but rooms are neat and well-priced, and all have attached bath. Email access available for Rs4 per min. Doubles Rs200-300. ❷

River View Jungle Camp, Main Rd. (☎580096), near the center of town. With one of the nicest gardens in Sauraha, this upmarket lodge offers some decent budget options. Gopal, the manager and resident guide, speaks excellent English and is a knowledgeable veteran of the field. Basic thatched-roof cottage singles Rs150; doubles Rs250. More plush double rooms with attached baths, toilet paper, soap, and balconies that look on to the garden Rs325-650. ❷

⬛ FOOD

Most lodges have attached restaurants, though the Chitwan culinary experience revolves around the **rooftop restaurants** in the center of town. A number of small establishments at street level offer Nepali fare. The rooftop places stay open well into the evening and join forces with the numerous beach bars on the riverbank to bring you Bob Marley and cocktails with ridiculous names (Monkey Gland Rs115). Baby don't worry: everything gonna be alright.

▨ Jungle View Restaurant and Bar, Main Rd., smack dab in the middle of town. The best food and the best service of the rooftop restaurants earns this place top marks. Chicken curry Rs105, veggie burger Rs110, delectable veg. mushroom enchilada Rs125. Happy hour 4-8pm. Open daily 6:30am-11pm. ❷

K.C.'s Restaurant and Bar, just around the corner from Jungle View Restaurant. The oldest and classiest of Chitwan's rooftop restaurants, with an experienced waitstaff. While the menu covers a little bit of everything, the chef's specialty is Mexican. Delicious veg. enchiladas Rs130, cheese and bean burrito Rs130. Happy hour 5-8:30pm. Open daily 6am-10:30pm. ❸

Sunset View Restaurant and Bar, the first beachside restaurant on your left as you follow Main Rd. to the river. Watch the sun set over the jungle from super-reclining beach chairs as you enjoy delicious pizzas (Rs120-150) lasagna (Rs110), or other items from Sunset View's vast menu. Open daily 6am-10:30pm. ❸

Moonlight Restaurant and Bar, Main Rd., just south of the Rain Forest Guest House. Conveniently located for those staying near the north end of town, this small establishment offers Nepali standards for a fraction of what the rooftop places charge. (*Dal bhat* Rs80, *momos* Rs30-45, *chow mein* Rs40-60.) Open daily 6am-9pm. ❶

⯅ THE PARK

The highlights of Chitwan National Park include the one-horned rhinoceros, the Bengal tiger, leopards, sloth bears, and wild bison. There are an estimated 56 mammalian species in the park and over 500 species of birds, nine species of amphibians, 126 species of fish, 150 species of butterflies, and 47 species of reptiles, as well as 107 of Nepal's 300 tigers. (*Park open daily sunrise-sunset. Rs500 per day.*)

TOURS AND GUIDES. Since visitors to the park must be accompanied by guides at all times, it's inevitable that you'll end up booking a tour. Many people book **package tours** from Kathmandu or Pokhara, which include lodging, activities, and

> **WARNING.** Due mainly to the risk of attack by a charging rhino, the government requires visitors to Chitwan National Park to be accompanied by at least two guides at all times. Let's Go does not recommend being bitten, gored, or trampled by a charging rhino.

transportation. These packages are generally convenient and hassle-free; most tours are 3-days 2-nights, and run US$55-65. In Sauraha, activities can also be booked *a la carte* through all hotels or independent tour operators. Hotels are generally slightly more expensive but are also more convenient since they can wake you up for early morning departures. Probably the best independent tour operator is the **United Jungle Guide Service,** under K.C.'s Restaurant, in the Jungle Guide Office. Guides are experienced and friendly, and tour prices are reasonable. (☎ 580008. Open daily 7am-6:30pm.) The **Mona Lisa Guide Office,** in the center of town, also gets enthusiastic reviews from its clients. (☎ 580131. Open daily 6:30am-9pm.) When looking for a guide, ask other tourists for referrals; the number of years of experience should also be on the guide's permit certificate. For any fixed-rate activities, service charges should run Rs50-200 regardless of where you book. Be sure to tip the guide at the end of a good trip.

ELEPHANT RIDES. Plodding along on a ponderous pachyderm is not only the classic way to see Chitwan, but it is also the most popular activity in the park. Elephant rides offer an opportunity to see the jungle animals at closer range than either walking or jeep tours allow—if you're lucky, you could end up just 2m away from a rhino. There are two kinds of elephant rides in Chitwan: government-run and private. **Government** elephant rides are the only ones that go into the park itself, across the Rapti River. These rides take 1hr. and leave from near the park ticket office at 7:30am and 4:30pm (see **Practical Information,** p. 881). You can book them directly from the park ticket office or through a tour operator. (Rs1000 fixed rate, plus variable service charges.) By far the better deal, **private** elephant rides stay on the near side of the Rapti River and traverse the still-wild **Buffer Zone,** a section of the park added in 1977. Park tickets are good for two days in the Buffer Zone, so if you purchase one the day before your ride (for a jungle walk, for example) you won't need to pay for another one. These rides last 2hr. and leave from Main Rd. in front of the Tharu Cultural Program Building at 7am and 3pm. Private rides must be booked through a tour operator or hotel. (Rs550-800.) Either way, be sure to wear long pants and sturdy shoes, as the elephants seem to enjoy walking straight through patches of thick vegetation and even whole trees.

JUNGLE WALK/CANOE RIDE. A jungle walk is certainly the most exciting way to see the national park. All walking groups are accompanied by at least two guides, and trips wander along the park's trails in search of a rhino, tiger, sloth bear, or crocodile. Because walking groups are unprotected and guides are unarmed (except for a long stick), the rhinos do pose a real threat—in the fall of 1999, a guide was attacked by a protective mother rhino and was lucky to survive the encounter. However, groups go out every day without incident. Jungle walks come in three basic lengths: half-day (4hr.), full-day (12hr.), and two-day. The half-day walk usually includes a **canoe ride:** an hour floating down river, then a 2-3hr. walk back. Both the half-day and full-day trips explore the jungle from Sauraha, while the increasingly popular two-day trips stay overnight in a local village on the park's border farther downstream. If you're up to it, the two-day walk is a great way to see the park; it covers a lot of ground and spends ample time inside the park's boundaries. Walks are privately operated and prices vary by season, tour operator, and number of people. *(Half-day walks Rs300-400 per person, full-day Rs500-700 per person, two-day Rs1200-1400 per person; canoe ride Rs250-350 per person.)*

JUNGLE DRIVE. At the time of publication, the park authorities had suspended jungle drives within the park proper, both as a result of flood damage to roads and bridges and because of the army's fears of Maoist activity inside the park. Jeeps are permitted in the Buffer Zone and 20,000 Lakes however, and in general offer longer (4-5hr.), more extensive, and more expensive tours of the jungle. The major drawback is that Jeeps, unlike elephants, can't leave the road to follow animals or go through tall grass. Still, rhino sightings are practically guaranteed on any jungle drive. As the grass grows tall from June to the annual grass-cutting in January or February, animal spotting becomes increasingly difficult. Each jeep should come with a driver and a separate wildlife spotter. *(7:30am and 1:30pm; Rs700-1000, depending on the number of people.)*

BIKE TO 20,000 LAKES. Because they're outside the park boundary, it's possible to visit the 20,000 Lakes without any tour guide supervision. While 20,000 is a bit of an exaggeration, there are a number of small watering holes in this peaceful wooded area. Bird-watching is the popular thing to do here, though if you're lucky, you may spot a gharial (long-snouted, non-dangerous crocodile) or a rhino. If nothing else, it's a pleasant place to sit back, relax, and watch the butterflies flutter by. The best way to reach this area is by bicycle, which you can rent from one of the many places in Sauraha. To get to the lakes, go north from Sauraha all the way to Tandi (6.5km). Head west along the main highway for 3km until you pass over a bridge. Immediately after the bridge, a dirt road branches to the left and follows alongside a small canal all the way to the lakes (5.5km). In all, the trip should take about an hour. *(Rs40 **entrance fee** for this community forest, payable at the small check-post on the road before the lakes. Rs300-500 per person including bike rental. Guided trips also available.)*

ELEPHANT BREEDING CENTRE. Although it is better known for its rhino and tiger denizens, Chitwan is also populated by elephants. Just about every elephant in Chitwan is from India, where elephants still roam wild despite a millennium-old trade of capturing and training them. With elephant stomping grounds receding fast, elephant prices have sky-rocketed—they can cost up to one million Indian rupees. Chitwan has responded with its Elephant Breeding Centre, established in 1987. Training begins when an elephant turns two; both a human and a "role model" senior elephant are teachers. Each elephant has 3 attendants: the *phanet* is the elephant's driver and principal companion; the *mahout* is the one who takes the elephant to bathe and forage; and the *pachhewa* makes the food and also has the enviable task of cleaning out the stable. Most of the elephants are chained to posts, which may be upsetting to some, though the animals are given daily exercise. For Rs30, you can buy a bunch of 12 bananas and enjoy the peculiar experience of having an elephant eat out of your hand. *(To reach the stables, take the road near the north end of the town, opposite the Rain Forest Guest House, and walk or bike west for 3km. The road ends at a shallow stream; the breeding center is on the far bank. Ferry across the river Rs10. Entrance fee Rs15, with park permit.)*

THARU VILLAGES. The **Tharu,** the indigenous people of Chitwan, have the dubious privilege of serving as one of its additional "attractions." A **guided walk** through the Tharu village along the road to the park entrance covers the culture, history, and religion of the people. *(2hr., Rs75 per person.)* The half-day walk to the village offers a more authentic introduction to Tharu culture. As the walk takes you through the park, a visit to the village can usually be tacked onto a regular half-day jungle walk. *(4hr., Rs250-300.)* **Tharu stick dances** exuberantly invite participation. Dance troupes perform regularly at hotels and every evening at the Tharu Cultural Program on Main Rd., north of Sauraha Bazaar. *(Program starts at 8pm. Rs60 per person.)*

JANAKPUR (JANAKPURDHAM) जनकपुर ☎ 041

The scorching heat, dust storms, and mounds of muck from the roaming bovine population of Janakpur don't seem to deter tourists, many of whom are Indians making pilgrimages to the birthplace of Sita, the famous *Ramayana* heroine. Janakpur was the capital of the mythical kingdom of Mithila, which was said to have flourished between the 10th and the 3rd centuries BC. According to the *Ramayana*, it was here that the Mithila king Janaka found the baby Sita lying in a field and adopted her as his daughter. Despite its ancient associations, most of Janakpur's temples are modern constructions. Still, the city's skyline shines with the constant devotion of pilgrims, dominated by the flaking onion domes and triangular roofs of its many pilgrim hostels, while the ground is pitted with *sagars* (artificial ponds) used for ritual baths. This quiet Terai city comes to life during its festivals, particularly **Vivaha Panchami** (Nov.-Dec.), which features a re-enactment of Rama and Sita's wedding, complete with elephant processions, chariots, horses, and traditional dancing. Another extremely important festival is **Ram Navami** (Mar.-Apr.), which commemorates the birth of Rama.

▮ TRANSPORTATION

Sita Air, Station Rd., 50m south of Bhanu Chowk, offers daily **flights** to **Kathmandu**. (☎ 525990; sita_air@wlink.com.np. Open daily 7am-7pm. Flights 25min., 11:25am, US$69.) **Buddha Air,** across the street from the tourist office, 50m northwest of Bhanu Chowk, also flies to Kathmandu (8:50am and 4:40pm) at the same price. (☎ 525022 or 252894. Open daily 7am-6pm.) **Buses** go to numerous destinations from the bus park, including: **Bhairawa/Sunauli** (8hr., 5:45am and 10:30pm, Rs230, night bus Rs285); **Biratnagar** (6hr., 4:30am-8pm, Rs220); **Birganj** (4hr., every 30min. 3:30am-4:20pm, Rs125); **Dharan** (7hr., 5:30am, Rs220); **Kakarbhitta** (8hr.; 4:30-11:15am and 5:30-8pm; Rs200, night bus Rs226); **Kathmandu** (11hr.; 6:15am and 8pm; Rs230, night bus Rs300); **Pokhara** (10hr.; 6am and 3:30pm; Rs330, night bus Rs350). However, catching a local bus from a major intersection—Itahari to Dharan, Hile, and other points north—is often the easiest way to get where you're going.

▮ ORIENTATION AND PRACTICAL INFORMATION

Janakpur's network of curving alleyways makes it easy to get disoriented, but the city is small enough that a recognizable landmark is never far away. The bus park is at the southwest end of town, across from the towering telecom tower. Both roads leading northeast out of the bus park eventually connect with **Station Road,** the main thoroughfare, at **Dhanush Sagar,** a large pool. From here, Station Rd. runs northeast past **Bhanu Chowk** (named for the Nepalese poet whose bust tops a pillar in the middle of the intersection) and continues to the **railway station,** at the northeast corner of town. Station Rd. also continues south of Dhanush Sagar to **Kuwa Village,** Janakpur's Women's Development Center, and the **airport,** 2km from town. Rickshaw is the only vehicle to take around town, since there are no taxis around. Essentially, Janakpur is a pedestrian's city.

The **tourist office** is on Station Rd., north of Bhanu Chowk. (☎ 520755. Open Su-Th 10am-5pm, F 10am-3pm.) The **NB Bank,** at Bhanu Chowk, exchanges Indian rupees and US dollars (☎ 521548. Open Su-Th 10am-2:30pm, F 10am-noon.) **Angljon**

Hospital (☎520033) is just northwest of the Janaki Mandir, and **pharmacies** on Station Rd. The **haat bazaar** (Su, Tu, W, F) is west of Ram Mandir. Stores along Station Rd. south of Bhanu Chowk offer **Internet** access. **Royal Cyber Cafe,** next door to Hotel Welcome, has helpful English-speaking staff and many services. (☎4125441; fax 4125442. Rs20 per ½hr. or Rs30 per hr. Open daily 6am-9pm.) The **post office,** southwest of Dhanush Sagar, is hard to find; ask for directions or take a rickshaw. (☎520162. Open Su-F 10am-4pm.)

ACCOMMODATIONS

Accommodations in Janakpur are plentiful but basic and crowded with boisterous Indian families. It's hard to find anything more luxurious than a foam mattress with an attached squat toilet. All rooms have tiny padlocks on the doors, so keep valuables at your side. Make sure that your room has a working fan and mosquito net, especially in the summer.

Hotel Welcome, Station Rd. (☎520646; fax 520922), northeast of Dhanush Sagar. Bright spacious rooms with kind, competent staff. The older rooms are basic; the more upscale ones are some of the nicest around. Five rooms have working A/C. Singles Rs75-600; doubles Rs300-1500. Bike rental Rs150 per day. ❶

Hotel Rama, Mills Area Chowk (☎520059). Heading from Dhanush Sagar, it is to your left at Bhanu Chowk. Hotel Rama is 300m from Bhanu on the left. Though slightly removed from the center, Hotel Rama has a wide range of comfortable rooms with bright blue walls, and is surrounded by a spacious, well-groomed garden. All have attached bath. Singles Rs150-800; doubles Rs350-1000. More expensive rooms have A/C, telephone, hot water, and TV. ❷

Kathmandu Guest House, Bhanu Chowk (☎521753; fax 523888). A friendly and simple place with open hallways, ceiling fans, mosquito nets, and some attached bathrooms with squat toilets. Singles Rs100, with bath Rs150; doubles Rs200, with bath Rs250, with TV and small couch Rs350. ❶

Hotel Namaskar (☎522192), at the northeast corner of the bus park. Though the constant traffic makes it a bit noisy, the rooms are simple and clean, all with fans and mosquito nets. Some with balconies overlooking the busy street. Singles Rs100, "fancy" singles with hot/cold shower, TV, and dubious A/C Rs250; doubles Rs200-400. ❷

FOOD

Janakpur offers diners little beyond north Indian dishes; some of it is so tasty that you'll hardly notice the limited selection. Most meals run at similar prices as well (Rs30-90 for veg. curry dishes, *naan* Rs15-50). Few places have menus, utensils, or hygiene enough for a Western stomach. You might want to indulge in the many Indian sweets sold throughout the plaza surrounding Janaki Mandir. The air-conditioned restaurant at the **Hotel Welcome** ❶ has a slightly wider selection, including a Western breakfast menu. (Omelette Rs30, pancake Rs55, main dishes Rs55-60. Open daily 7am-9pm.) **Ramailo Restaurant** ❶, just east of Bhanu Chowk, offers private bamboo booths, but standard Janakpur fare. (Open daily 8am-9pm.) **Rooftop Restaurant** ❶, 50m north of Dhanush Sagar, has a breezy and clean indoor dining area. It dares to extend its menu to include Chinese and south Indian dishes. (*Dosa* Rs25-90, Chinese Rs50-90, curries Rs40-70. Open daily 9am-9pm. Attached game club and bar open at the same time, with pool and snooker tables.)

T E R A I

IE LOCAL LEGEND

THE MURALS OF MITHILA

The former Mithila kingdom spanned southern Nepal and north-ern India. It was fenced in by the Himalayas in the north and by the Indian Ganga, Gandaki, and Kosi riv-ers in the south. The definition of Mithila now is a fluid one, preserved by women of the region who keep the ancient tradition of muraling.

The mural tradition began with women decorating the insides of their thatched-roof and bamboo homes. This ritual brightening of the floors and walls is usually done in preparation for festivities or religious ceremonies. Other occasions that warrant such painting include wed-dings, funerals, and the christening of a new home. A woman may create paintings for her future husband as part of their courtship.

The images in these murals have symbolic significance: pregnant ele-phants, parrots, bamboo, turtles, and fish represent fertility and mar-riage, while peacocks and non-preg-ant elephants are symbols of luck.

The palette for this artistic cre-ation includes mud, rice paste, and manure. The black coloring derives from soot, which is considered most holy if taken from an oil lamp that burns for 24hr. during a sacred time of year. The green is taken from plants, and the red from seeds.

Unfortunately, these murals—sym-bolic of the region's natural splendor and religious heritage—have been replaced and commercialized. Sold to tourists at high prices, they are now often more a source of revenue than a form of cultural expression.

◉ SIGHTS

TEMPLES. There are few other things to do in Janak-pur aside from temple-hopping. None of Janakpur's temples are very old, and all are still in use. A good walking tour begins at Station Rd. south of Bhanu Chowk at **Dhanush Sagar** and **Ganga Sagar,** Janakpur's largest and holiest ponds, and continues west and south through the city. The sights below are arranged in that order. On the west bank of Dhanush Sagar, through a faded yellow archway, is the **Ram Mandir,** Janakpur's oldest (built in 1882) Nepalese temple, hemmed in by a ring of small *lingas.* Built under a large banyan tree, the temple hosts the **Ram Navami Festival** to celebrate Ram's incarnation on earth. From the archway, turn left and walk north. After you pass a white, beehive-shaped shrine on the right, turn left and follow the road to the huge, white-and-primary-colored **Janaki Mandir.** The Janaki Mandir was built in 1911 on the spot where the infant Sita was discovered by King Janaka. Lending the spot further importance, a miraculous image of the leg-endary lady was said to have appeared there in 1657. Sita's silver image is unveiled twice a day, once in the early morning and once in the evening. *(No smoking or photography inside the temple gates.)* Next door is the more stately, glassed-in **Ram Janaki Vivaha Mandap,** built 17 years ago to mark the place where Rama and Sita tied the knot. The colorful statues inside the twin-roofed pagoda represent Rama, Sita, and the friends and pilgrims present at their marriage. At each corner of the white-tiled platform are smaller temples, dedicated to each of the four couples married that day: Rama and Sita, and Rama's three brothers and their brides. *(Entrance Rs5; camera fee Rs5.)* During the **Vivaha Pan-chami Festival** in December, *sadhus* and brahmin priests re-enact the wedding ceremony. Follow the wide street northwest from the Ram Janaki Vivaha Mandap, past the hospital, until it intersects with the main highway at Ramanand Chowk, marked by a rotary with towering, interlocking arches. Opposite Ramanand Chowk, a brick path leads to the peaceful and sacred **Bihara Kund,** a shady pond surrounded by dozens of Rama and Sita temples. A 20min. walk south of Ramanand Chowk on the main highway is the **Hanu-man Durbar.** This small temple housed, until recently, the world's fattest monkey (55 kg), thought to be an incarnation of Hanuman. The beloved rhesus, affection-ately called Bauwa Hanuman, died at the age of 22 after a lifetime of continuous eating. The temple now houses his slimmer son, Punya.

JANAKPUR WOMEN'S DEVELOPMENT CENTRE. For an alternative to temples, the **Janakpur Women's Development Centre** is a must for anyone interested in art or economic development. Almost an hour's walk south of Janakpur, the centre can also be reached by rickshaw (Rs100 roundtrip); ask to be taken to the "development store." From the main road that runs south along the west bank of Dhanush Sagar, the road to the airport, follow signs for a turn-off to the left. This will take you through a large gate with a sign "Mithila Painting," and then lead into the village of Kuwa. As you make your way through the village, you'll see Mithila paintings on the walls of the houses. Once in the village, take the first road to the right; when you come to a large temple, take a left, then an immediate right. Continue along the road until you come to open fields; the center is in a brick complex with a red metal gate to your right. The artists use traditional motifs on handmade paper, papier-mâché, ceramics, and textiles (see **Local Legend**, p. 888). The complex is designed so that visitors can observe art-making in progress, segregated by type, through the large windows facing the garden complex. The products are for sale here and at various non-profit outlets in Kathmandu and Patan. The center also trains women in literacy, mathematics, and business management. It is a grass roots NGO devoted to the empowerment of Mithili women through their artistic tradition. (☎ 421080; women@jnk.com.np. Open Su-Th 10am-5pm, F 10am-4pm. No entrance fee, but donations are warmly appreciated.)

STEAM RAILWAY. Janakpur is also the point of departure for Nepal's only **steam railway**, a slow and stately way of seeing the surrounding countryside. You can take the train to any of the villages between Janakpur and the Indian border and either walk back or wait for a return train. However, since there is no entry point here, be sure to **get off the train before the border; otherwise, you may not be able to re-enter Nepal.** Trains leave Janakpur at 7 and 11:55am, and 3:30pm, and stop at **Parbaha** (20min., Rs15), **Baidehi** (40min., Rs20), and **Khajuri** (1½hr., Rs30), the last stop in Nepal. The railway station can be reached by walking northeast along Station Rd. past Bhanu Chowk to the intersection with the major road to Jayanagar. The station is directly across the street. (Ticket office open 6am-5pm.)

DHARAN धरान ☎ 025

At the point where the hellish plains meet the heavenly hills is the bazaar town of Dharan, where people from miles around converge to buy everything from portable tapeplayers to squat toilet bowls. The few foreign visitors who come here tend not to stay for long, but Dharan is a far more pleasant place to spend the night than many of the Terai's transportation hubs. **Chatara,** where river-rafters pull out onto the Sun Kosi, is 15km west; the trekking trailheads of **Hile** (p. 892) and **Basantapur** (p. 892) are to the north. Once the site of one of the British Army's Gorkha training camps, Dharan still hosts a number of Nepal's *khukuri*-smiths, now producers of knives for tourists. Buses arrive and depart from **Bhanu Chowk,** a busy rotary marked by a statue of the poet for whom it was named. **Chata Chowk,** the other major intersection, is a 10min. walk north, uphill on the same main street—it's easy to miss, as there is no landmark, but keep your eyes peeled for helpful English road signs. The signs will tell you that in the walk to Chata Chowk from Bhanu, you will pass two streets on your left, College Rd. and Gatan Path, before arriving at Bhanu, the third intersection. To your left are the hotels and straight ahead on the right is the bank. The closest **airport** is in Biratnagar; **Necon Air** and **RNAC** have several daily flights to Kathmandu. **Buses** go to: **Basantapur** (5½hr., every 30 min. 4:30am-5:10pm, Rs140) via **Dhankuta** and **Hile** (4hr., Rs90); **Biratnagar** (2hr., every 30min. 5am-6:10pm, Rs35); **Kakarbhitta** (2½hr., every 30min. 4:30am-5pm, Rs95); **Kathmandu** (12hr.; 4:20am, and 3 and 5pm; Rs310, night bus Rs380). Other bus connections can be made at **Itahari** (30min., frequent 4:25am-3:30pm, Rs20), at the junction of the area's two highways. The **Nepal Bank Ltd.,** just north of Chata Chowk, has no English front. Look for the bright orange sign with a green disc at the top. Exchanges only Indian rupees. (☎520084. Open Su-Th 10am-4:30pm, F 12am-1pm.) **Internet Cafe** (☎/fax 23338), at Chata Chowk, has STD/ISD service, free callbacks, and Internet access. (Open daily 7am-8pm. Rs45 per hr.)

A number of hotels are along Chatara Line, the lane running west from Chata Chowk. **Dragon Hotel and Restaurant ❶**, 100m down on the right side, offers bare bulbs, common bath, and low prices. Restaurant upstairs has chow mein (Rs25-40), *thukpa* (Rs20-30), and *momos* (Rs20-30). (☎522220. Single Rs130; double Rs150. Restaurant open daily 7am-8pm.) The **Dharan Hotel ❸**, next door to Dragon, has slightly more comfortable rooms with attached baths at significantly higher prices. (☎522412. Doubles Rs400.) **Unique Restaurant and Bar ❶**, 100m south of Chata Chowk along the main road on your right, serves decent Continental, South Indian, and Tibetan veg. food at good prices. Veg. *momo* Rs25, pizzas Rs80-160, *dosas* Rs15-50, chow mein Rs35-70. (Open daily 8am-8pm. Live music F 6-8pm.) Three doors to the north is the airy, popular bakery, **The House of Sweets and Snacks ❶**, the *samosas* are plump and fresh (Rs5).

⚑ BORDER CROSSING: KAKARBHITTA काकरभित्त ☎ 023

At the border, Nepali visas are available to anybody with a passport photo (US$30 for 60 days). Nepali immigration (☎ 562054) at the border crossing, is open daily 6am-8pm. Indian immigration is open daily 6am-10pm. Indian visas, however, must be obtained from the Indian embassy in Kathmandu.

Kakarbhitta is a trading town on the India-Nepal border. Though not as oppressive as some of Nepal's other border towns, it is essentially a large, dusty mess of a bazaar centered around the bus station on the north side of the east-west highway.

Buses run to: **Birganj** (7hr.; 4 and 4:30am, and 6:45pm; NRs300); **Birtamod** (30min., frequent 4:30am-6pm, NRs13); **Dharan** (2½hr., frequent 4:30am-4pm, NRs90); **Janakpur** (8hr.; 7 per day 4am-7pm; NRs200, night bus NRs225); **Kathmandu** (16 hr.; 11 per day 4-6am and 4-5pm; NRs365, night bus NRs470); **Pokhara** (13-15hr.; 5 per day 4am, 2:30-5:30pm; NRs430). **Rickshaws** run from the border to **Panitanki** in India (IRs3 or NRs5), where there are buses to **Siliguri** (1½hr., frequent 5am-7pm, IRs10). Alternatively, you can take a **taxi** directly from Kakarbhitta to Siliguri (IRs40).

Most of the hotels and restaurants are in the market area, west of the bus park. Along the highway, east of the bus park, are the **banks** and the helpful **tourist office,** in a garden on the north side of the highway. It is surrounded by private travel companies—look for the sign for **Nepal Travel Service Government Authorised.** (☎562061 or 562005. Open daily 6am-8:30pm.) **Travel agencies** around the tourist office charge NRs30-40 commission, which you can avoid by buying tickets at the ticket counters along the east side of the bus park. **Nepal Rastra Bank,** across the highway, 50m south of the tourist office, buys foreign currency and traveler's checks (2% commission) and is one of the last places to get rid of your Nepalese rupees before you hop across the border. (☎562066. Open daily 7am-5pm for foreign exchange.) Kakarbhitta is packed with hotels, which surround the bus park. At the far left (northwest) corner of the bus park is the **Hotel Rajat ❷**. The spartan, older rooms have fans, mosquito nets, and common squat toilets. Rooms in the new building have clean attached baths with seat toilets, fans, TVs, phones, and mosquito nets. Some rooms have A/C. (☎562033, 562238, or 562433; hotelrajat@jhapa.info.com.np. Singles NRs150-1200; doubles NRs200-1600.) The attached garden restaurant—the only grassy patch in Kakarbhitta—serves an impressive array of dishes. (Chinese NRs40-125, Nepali NRs40-130, Continental NRs50-200, *paneer* NRs70-150. Open daily 7am-10pm.) Attached is the town's fastest **Internet** (under 15min. NRs30; up to 30min. NRs50, up to 1hr. NRs75. Open daily 7am-6pm). **Hotel Lumbini ❷** has cozy blankets and powerful fans in spacious though stuffy rooms. All have attached bath with squat toilet and shower. Friendly matron whips up *dal bhat* and curries downstairs. (☎562047. Singles NRs200; triples NRs350. No doubles. Restaurant open 6am-9pm. Dishes NRs35-90.)

THE EASTERN HILLS

Eastern Nepal is home to some of the world's most jagged and otherworldly peaks. Six of Nepal's eight 8000-meter peaks, including Everest, tower over this part of the country. They are a staggering prospect for even the most experienced mountaineers, who spend their lives polishing their ice picks and dreaming of lugging oxygen tanks to the top of the world. But you don't have to be a mountaineer to enjoy yourself here—the cool and misty foothills have a beauty all their own.

Eastern Nepal is home to an astonishing variety of ethnic groups, including the Limbu, Lepcha, Tharu, Rajbansi, and, of course, the famous Sherpa. All ethnicities have distinct dialects and customs, visible in everything from female jewelry to rural architecture. A journey to the Eastern hills rewards with views of the Himalayas, spectacular day treks, and friendly chats with lodge owners over *dahl bhat*, even if you don't have the time or the energy (or the ice pick) for a monster trek.

JIRI जीरी ☎ 049

Keep the prayer-wheels turning, for the grueling bus ride to the main trailhead of the Everest trek will shake whatever faith you had left in the Nepalese road system. However, the one-road town of Jiri (1905m) provides travelers with the rest, sustenance, and stable ground necessary for to recover from the bumpy ride and to prepare a successful trek. Buses to Jiri leave from Kathmandu's Ratna Park (11hr.; 5:30, 6:30, 7:30, 8:30, 10am; Rs210; express 8hr., 7am, Rs243). From Jiri's **bus park,** buses run to **Kathmandu** (11hr., 5 per day 5:30-10am, Rs210; express bus 8hr., 7am, Rs243). Purchase tickets in the bus park at the window (open 6am-6pm) opposite the Jiri Medical Hall. Tickets for the **express bus** to or from Jiri must be purchased a day in advance. Arrive at the bus park 30min. before departure.

Arriving buses drive through Jiri to get to the bus park at the far end of town, the last pavement before Everest. To reach most shops, backtrack up the road toward Kathmandu. **Naya Bazaar,** a market open Su-F, is a 30min. walk up the road away from Jiri. The **police station** is 4km away on the road to Kathmandu. **Jiri Medical Hall,** is a well-stocked pharmacy. (☎29149. Open daily 5am-8pm.) **International phone calls** can be made for Rs150 per min. Calls to Kathmandu Rs9 per min. The **hospital** is a 5min. walk from the bus park, along the cobblestone/dirt path 10m toward Jiri from the bus ticket window. (Open Su-F 10am-4pm; doctor on-call 24hr.) International medicine patients are taken to the **Jiri Helminth Project,** down the road toward Jiri from Naya Bazaar. Ambulance service to Kathmandu is available from the hospital, the Jiri Helminth Project, and Chedung Lodge.

Lodges line the road through Jiri. During the high season (Oct. to mid-May), beds are at a premium, prices are high, and reservations are highly recommended. Low-season (late May-Sept.) rates are much lower (Rs20-50) and ultimately flexible. All lodges offer hot water and trekking services. **Hotel Gaurihimal ❶,** on the right after the 2nd bridge from the bus park, is the cleanest and has the best lit rooms (☎29158; Rs100 per bed; doubles with bath US$15). **Sagarmatha Lodge ❶,** 50m from the bus park on the right, is the cheapest (☎29152; chhatra20@hotmail.com; singles Rs50, doubles Rs100). Both Sagarmatha and **Hotel Jimel Gabila ❶,** on the left after the 2nd bridge, have friendly staff (Camping Rs35-150; 2 single beds Rs150; double bed Rs200; double with attached bath Rs400). **Chedung Lodge ❶,** on the left before the 2nd bridge (dorms Rs20; singles Rs50; doubles Rs100), and **Hotel Jiri View ❶,** on the right after the 2nd bridge, both have cramped, dark rooms, but the most flexible rooming situation (singles Rs100; doubles Rs200; triples Rs250).

HILE हीले ☎026

A cool, misty 1900m above the Arun Valley, Hile has spectacular mountain views and is home to a unique cultural and ethnic mix of Bhotiyas, Rais, Newaris, Tibetans, and Indians. A trailhead for treks into the world's deepest valley, Hile hosts a colorful, bustling market, but the terraced villages below offset the bartering frenzy. Piles of *doka* (the conical, head-strapped baskets that porters use) wait to be filled and carried off into the hills. Most of Hile's visitors soon head for higher ground, but the town, with its several small *gompas* and tea estates on the way up to Basantapur, is worth a visit even for non-trekkers. A lovely *gompa* is 50m south along the main road from the bus park on the left. The Buddhist structure, Ugen Namochhoelinggumba, is decorated with the flair and color of a Hindu shrine, making it a fascinating demonstration of the area's cultural hybridity. The real attention-grabber is the Himalayan range itself; there are great views from the hilltop north of town, a 45-minute walk away.

The **bus stand** is at the northern end of the north-south road that runs downhill through town. Tickets are sold at a small unlabeled booth set back on the east side of the street. The **night bus** booking stand for Kathmandu is 200m south of the bus station, on your right hand side. There are **buses** to: **Basantapur** (1½hr., every 30min. 6am-6pm, Rs60); **Biratnagar** (5hr., 11am, Rs120); **Dharan** (4hr., every 30min. 4:30am-5:30pm, Rs90); **Kathmandu** (18hr.; 1 and 5pm; Rs420, night bus Rs460). **Global Telecommunication Service**, 300m south on the main road, has STD/ISD and fax. The **post office** is down the narrow alleyway and steep staircase winding left next to the Hotel Himali (☎40119; open Su-F 9am-4pm). South of the bus stop are several trekking-style lodges, which have restaurants, electricity, showers, and hot water on request. Run by a friendly Tibetan family, **Hotel Himali ❶**, 150m south of the bus stop on the left, is basic, but the common squat toilet is kept very clean. (☎40140. Singles Rs60; doubles Rs100.) **Taplejung Restaurant and Lodge ❶**, next door to Himali, has similar accommodations at slightly higher prices. (☎46178. Singles Rs70; doubles Rs120.) The more rustic **Gumba Hotel ❶**, opposite Himali, won't win any awards, but the dorms are the cheapest around. (Dorms Rs25; doubles Rs100.)

BASANTAPUR बसन्तपुर ☎026

At an elevation of 2200m, Basantapur is blessed with a beauty and peace spoiled only by insolent roosters intent on rousing slumberers at 4am. This is the end of the road for buses, but only the beginning for trekkers through the Eastern Hills. Whether or not you're planning a trek, if you've come as far as Dharan or Hile, it's worth making the trip to Basantapur to take in the cool atmosphere. The bumpy bus ride along an unpaved road from Hile terminates at Basantapur's southern tip, near the **police post**. A 5min. walk along the rutted road brings you to the other end of town, where the road continues east toward **Terhathum** (26km) and, in clear weather, has great mountain views. During monsoon season, however, an otherworldly fog shrouds most mountain views and leaves everything (and everyone) damp. Even summer days can get chilly, so bring your thickest socks. **Buses** run to **Biratnagar** (7hr., 8:30am, Rs185) and **Hile** (1½hr. or up to 3hr. in monsoon, every 30min. 4:30am-5pm, Rs60), continuing on to **Dharan** (5½hr., Rs150). Basantapur's **post office** is just past Hotel Yak (toward Terhathum); look for a red-and-white sign and stairs leading to a letter box. (Open Su-F 10am-5pm, Sa 10am-1pm.)

Basantapur's lodges all offer similar tea-house accommodations: beds in wooden rooms, common squat toilets, and restaurants where you can spend the evening sipping *tong-ba* (Rs10-20). **Hotel Yak ❶**, 200m past the bus park along the main road, offers some reprieve from the noise pollution of the buses and has clean rooms, showers, and a quality restaurant. (☎/fax 69047. Singles Rs65; doubles Rs100. Restaurant open 7am-9pm.) **Birat Hotel and Lodge ❶**, just past the bus park, has small rooms with heavy comforters. (☎69043. Singles Rs50; doubles Rs80.) The restaurant below is the only place around where you can devour *dahl bhat* under the watchful eyes of Lenin. The slightly cramped but clean rooms at the **Laxmi Hotel ❶**, across the street from the Birat are above the TV-equipped restaurant where you'll find most of Basantapur's after-hours fun. (☎69022. Singles Rs40; doubles Rs75. Restaurant open 6am-9pm.)

ILAM इलाम ☎027

Safely removed from the rest of civilization by a 20hr. bus ride, Ilam is one of Nepal's hidden gems. Its visitors are rewarded by crisp air, pleasant strolls, and amazing views of mountains and valleys. Ilam is a starting point for treks through the **Kanchenjunga** region, although daytrips through the countryside can be just as rewarding. The 4-5hr. walk to the pilgrimage site of **Mai Pokhari**, 12km to the north, winds past tea gardens and forests to the top of a ridge crowned by a temple and a sacred lake. To the northeast, a 3½hr. walk leads to the bazaar town of **Mangalbare** (**Mechitravels** also offers a one-way taxi into town, Rs80). The descent to **Mai Khola,** the river crossing on the road from **Birtamod,** is another breathtaking journey that takes only a few hours on foot. While recovering from long walks, you can join the mob at the **haat bazaar,** held near the post office every Sunday and Thursday, or stroll through Ilam's famous **tea estates,** which stretch across the hills above the bus park. Before they are drowned in a steamy cup of *chiya* (milk tea), Nepal's finest tea leaves are harvested and dried here. The estates have no regulations about visitors, so you can wander at will. With your back to the bus park, the road leading there will be on your left. Walk 300m down and you will reach the first one, with dozens to follow along for the next few kilometers.

Getting a seat on the **bus** that winds its way up to Ilam can be difficult. Your chances are best from Birtamod, accessible by **local bus** from Kakarbhitta (30min., frequent 4:30am-6pm, Rs15). Shared **taxis** from Birtamod, comfortable SUVs that cram in about 11 people at a time, are the best deal (across the street from the bus park; frequent 7am-3pm; Rs30). The even more cramped **bus** is another option (4hr., every 45min., Rs100). Most buses heading toward Kakarbhitta or Bhadrapus, the nearest airport, also stop in Birtamod. There are also direct night buses from Kathmandu's New Bus Park (20hr., 2pm, Rs550). From Ilam, there are frequent buses to: **Biratnagar** (5hr., 11:30am, Rs190); **Birtamod** and **Charali** (4hr., every hr. 6am-1:30pm, Rs100); **Dharan** (6hr., 6am, Rs190); **Kathmandu** (20hr., 12:30pm, Rs565); and **Phidim** (5hr., 6am, Rs140), north of Ilam. The bus park is at the bottom of the hill, at the south end of town. Lodges and **pharmacies** line the main street, which leads north from the bus park up to the **town square,** marked by a large bust of King Birendra in a plaster lotus flower. **Mechi Tours and Travels** arranges bus and domestic plane tickets, private vehicles and drivers, has **currency exchange** with 1% commission, as well as **phones** and fax service. The owner, Sunil Choudhari, is a good source of information about the surrounding areas. If no one in the office speaks English (a common case during low season), try calling the owner. (☎20458 or 20313. Open daily 9am-6pm.) Three lanes diverge from the square opposite the main street. The one to the right leads to the **post office** (open Su-F 10am-2pm) and the **haat bazaar** (Su and Th dawn to dusk). The rudimentary **hospital** (☎20036) is at the end of the path. **Tea Town Lodge ❶**, 250m north of the bus park on the west side of the main road, has bright, clean rooms with common squat toilets. It is a small step up on the price ladder—the lodges next to the noisy buspark are slightly cheaper—but to minimize the possibility of a roach encounter, it's probably worth it. (Singles Rs150; doubles Rs250.) The restaurants attached to the lodges all serve all-you-can-eat *dahl bhat* at pretty standard prices (Rs30-40).

TREKKING IN NEPAL

For many years, the Classic Three—the **Annapurna, Langtang,** and **Everest** regions—were the only zones open to foreign trekkers. Fabulous treks in their own right, these three also have the benefit of a good trekking infrastructure—you can stay in tea houses, eat locally prepared food, and not worry about the leaking tents and freeze-dried breakfasts that have blighted many a trekking expedition. While most trekkers still stick to the Classic Three, Nepal has seen an explosive growth in trekking routes as more and more trekkers have come to the country in search of fresh air, unadulterated mountain views, and unparalleled tranquility.

THE ANNAPURNA REGION अन्नपूरण

The Annapurna Conservation Area is Nepal's most popular, and arguably most spectacular, trekking region. The ecological and cultural diversity are remarkable, and the vistas—notably at Annapurna Base Camp, Poon Hill, and around Manang—are peerless. Trekkers follow three main routes in the Annapurna region: the Annapurna Circuit, the Jomsom trek, and the Annapurna Sanctuary. These can be done separately, or combined into a single three to four week mega-trek. If you've only got a few days, however, it's easy to get a good taste of trekking by connecting some of the routes out of Pokhara. A popular option is the 4-5 day loop from Pokhara to Ghorepani to Ghandruk and back. This route has fine views (from **Poon Hill** above Ghorepani) and provides the opportunity to spend some time in Gurung villages. Alternatively, you can trek through Birethanti, Ghandruk, Landruk, and Dhampus. Both of these routes involve cobbling together parts of the Jomsom (see p. 898) and Sanctuary (see p. 901) treks.

🗒 THE ANNAPURNA CIRCUIT

The Annapurna Circuit is a trekker's dream come true, with as rich a cross-section of Hindu and Buddhist culture, mountain landscapes, and exhilarating hikes as one could cram into a 16-21 day trek. You might find yourself knee-deep in snow one day, crossing wind-swept desert the next, and strolling through forests of rhododendrons a few days after that. The exhausting challenge of the Thorung La (5416m) is well-rewarded upon arrival in the holy town of Muktinath. Almost everybody walks it in the same direction, crossing the pass from Manang to Muktinath. The pass is easier to cross in this direction, and there are more accommodations high up on the Manang side than on the Muktinath side. The route also seems much less crowded without traffic coming toward you.

BESISAHAR TO CHAME. The circuit starts in **Besisahar,** at the end of a road heading north from Dumre on the Kathmandu-Pokhara road. Besisahar is a typical Nepali end-of-the-road town with plenty of accommodations, electricity, phone service, and the first of many ACAP offices where you'll have to register and get your permit stamped. If you're hoping to put off walking as long as possible, you might be able to catch a bus to Bhulbhule (Rs30), but service is unpredictable and the rough road is often under construction.

From Besisahar, the trail leads to **Khudi** and then heads north along the Marsyangdi, criss-crossing the river on suspension bridges. **Bhulbhule,** named after the sound of bubbling water, and **Ngadi** are next. The first real climb of the trek up to **Bahundanda** ("Brahman Hill"), at a notch in the ridge high above the river, is child's play compared to what you'll get later on. You'll still be high above the river after the steep descent beyond Bahundanda, following a mag-

TREKKING NEPAL

nificent trail hewn out of the valley's rock walls. Of the many waterfalls along this trip, the most scenic is the one that comes crashing down the west wall of the valley close to **Syange**, where a suspension bridge takes traffic across the river. Beyond **Chamje**, a steep climb up through the rubble of a huge landslide brings you to **Tal**, a paradise on the dry lakebed left behind when a landslide dammed the river. There's an ACAP office here as well as a number of hotels.

There are three river crossings between Tal and **Dharapani**, where you'll find a police check-point, post office, and several telephones. Beyond Dharapani, the route follows the river left and takes you to the north of the main Annapurna massif. The villages are more Tibetan in style from this point. Next, you'll pass through **Bagarchhap**, a town that has bounced back from a devastating landslide in 1995, and **Dhanakyu** shortly thereafter. Just after leaving Dhanakyu, the trail splits: the more commonly taken low route passes through **Lata Marang** before climbing up to **Koto**, while the upper route climbs steeply for about an hour to **Temang** before descending steadily to meet the low route of Koto. If you're up for the climb, Temang has pleasant accommodations and affords excellent mountain views, particularly in the morning. Whichever route you chose, you'll end up in **Koto**, a spread-out town with a police check-point at the far end. **Chame**, not far from Koto, serves as the seat of government for the Manang district. It's the closest thing to a real town since Besisahar. Chame has everything—a hospital, bank, post office, police headquarters, the last telephones before Manang, an information bureau, and stores where you can stock up on supplies and cold weather gear. The highlight of Chame lies cross the bridge, where there's a hot spring beloved by locals. **Beyond Chame, altitude sickness becomes a serious risk.**

ANNAPURNA CIRCUIT: BESISAHAR TO CHAME

TRANSPORTATION: Buses are the best way to get to the trailhead in Besisahar. From **Pokhara** to **Besisahar** (6hr.; daily 7:25am, 8:35am, and noon; Rs100); from **Kathmandu**, take a Pokhara-bound bus to Dumre; then from **Dumre** to **Besisahar** (3hr., frequent, Rs40).

SERVICES: Food and lodging are available in numerous villages along this section of the trek. There are also post offices, police stations, and check-points, some equipment stores (in Chame), and telephone booths along the way.

HIGHLIGHTS: Views of Himalchuli, Ngadi Chuli, Manaslu, Annapurna II and IV, and other snow-capped mountains. Various waterfalls surrounded by lush forest vegetation and rice terraces cut into the hillsides.

VILLAGE	ALTITUDE	TIME
Besisahar	820m	start
Khudi	790m	2hr.
Bhulbhule	840m	1hr.
Ngadi	920m	1hr.
Bahundanda	1310m	2hr.
Syange	1140m	2½hr.
Chamje	1410m	3hr.
Tal	1660m	2hr.
Dharapani	1880m	2½hr.
Bagarchhap	2100m	1hr.
Dhanakyu	2180m	30min.
Lata Marang (low route)	2350m	2hr.
Koto	2530m	2hr.
Chame	2620m	30min.

FEATURES: This portion of the hike leads first through verdant subtropical woods and rice paddies, then through rhododendron and pine forests and stands of bamboo. At higher elevations, rice cultivation gives way to corn, barley, and potato fields, while evergreens replace tropical vegetation in the woods. Along the route, Buddhist and Tibetan influences begin to dominate the local architecture and culture.

CHAME TO MANANG. The route from Chame to Manang, following the increasingly deep Marsyangdi River valley, provides the best mountain views on the circuit trek. You're liable to go through a lot of film here—you'll stop to capture the perfect panorama of alpine green and rugged, white peaks only to find one even more perfect 30min. down the road. Heading west from Chame to Manang, the major peaks are: Lamjung Himal (6932m), Annapurna II (7939m), Annapurna IV (7525m), Annapurna III (7555m), and Gangapurna (7454m). The road west of Chame is dominated to the north by the "Great Wall of Pisang," a huge, smooth slab of slate that rises 1200m above the valley floor—to the Gurung people, it is the gateway to the land of the dead. You'll pass through Thaleku and Bhratang before crossing the river and ascending to picturesque Dhukure Pokhari, a breathless climb that serves as a friendly reminder of how high up you've come. Pisang, a popular resting point one day from Manang, is divided in two: New Pisang, on the south side of the river, is full of enormous lodges; Old Pisang, up the hill on the north side, is a dense tangle of flat-roofed stone buildings clustered around a *gompa* that hasn't changed much in the past 500 years.

From Pisang, you have a choice of routes to Manang. The low route is a short day's hike; the high route is a couple of hours longer. The **low route,** or **main trail,** from Lower Pisang is the main drag along the valley floor. It passes the airstrip at **Hongde** and heads to **Braga** and **Manang.** While the low route doesn't disappoint, the **high route** rewards the extra exertion a hundred-fold. Climbing and then descending to sleep is also good for acclimatization. The high route begins with a short, sharp ascent to Old Pisang and continues for a relatively flat first few kilometers before ascending steeply to **Ghyaru** (3670m), where the views of the Annapurnas to the south are unbeatable. From Ghyaru, the road stays high, following the valley wall to a promontory just above the ruined fort at Tiwol Danda before arriving at **Ngawal**, where there is a *gompa* that was built in 1990.

From Ngawal, the route heads back down to join the low route in the main valley. Route-finding can be a little tricky here: pick up the trail dropping down the minor valley just beyond Ngawal, but avoid the major left fork (which leads to the airstrip). The high route follows the north bank of the river until the main trail crosses the river to join it at **Mungje** (3480m). **Braga,** 30min. further, is an extraordinary village crowned with the region's oldest *gompa*. It is well worth a visit. If it is not open, ask around and someone will chase down the key for you.

Manang, a medieval, Tibetan-style village, is the main destination of the Circuit trek. This is your last chance to make sure that your gloves are warm enough for the Thorung La. Manang's HRA clinic gives a free talk on altitude sickness at 3pm in-season (Sept.-Dec. and Mar.-May). The HRA shop sells iodine, vitamin C, diamox, and has a small book exchange. There's an ACAP office and a post office in town, and Manang's only telephone is in the small building behind the Hotel Himalayan Singi, near the entrance to town. Because Manang is a popular one- or two-day stopping point for acclimatization, the lodges and restaurants are excellent, and there is plenty to do. There are a number of *gompas* and other attractions in the vicinity that make for popular daytrips, and if AMS is holding you back, you can chill out and watch movies at a number of places in Manang. **Khangsar** (3710m), an easy 2hr. walk away, is a popular acclimatization point for people on day hikes out of Manang. There are lodges here that can serve as a first stop on the way to the great high-altitude lake, **Tilicho Tal** (5000m), first explored by Herzog's 1950 expedition; there's a seasonal lodge between Khansar and the lake.

MANANG TO MUKTINATH. Beyond Manang, thoughts turn to the **Thorung La Pass** (5416m). You'll want to spend 1-2 days acclimatizing in Manang and then 3 short days climbing to the foot of the pass to guard against altitude sickness. HRA recommends ascending no more than 450m in a day once you get above 3500m. Stops include **Tengi, Ghunsang,** and **Yak Kharka/Letdar.** There are plenty of opportunities for hikes up the flanks of **Chulu,** north of Ghunsang and Letdar.

Two routes go from Letdar to Thorong Phedi, neither of which is fully safe. The lower, easier route is prone to landslides and avalanches, which have proved fatal in the past. The higher route involves a steep, narrow descent into Thorung Phedi, which, when covered in snow or ice, can be quite dangerous.

Thorung Phedi, literally "foot of Thorung," is the last settlement before the pass, though there is a lodge at the **high camp** 350m higher up. Staying at high camp may save you an hour ascending to the pass, but the dramatic change in sleeping altitude may also cause difficulties with AMS. Set out from Thorung Phedi at first light. Severe conditions are common on the pass, and plenty of trekkers have left with frostbite. Come prepared, and be willing to sit out bad weather. There is a stone hut at 5100m and another one at the pass itself, inhabited by a hardy entrepreneur who sells soups (Rs130-140) and much-needed hot drinks (Rs60-70). If everything goes well, crossing the pass can be a marvelous experience. It's a long, steep descent to **Muktinath;** the only settlement along the way is the lodge at **Chatar Puk** (4120m), not far above it.

ANNAPURNA CIRCUIT: CHAME TO MUKTINATH

TRANSPORTATION: Flights leave from **Hongde** and head to **Pokhara** (Tu and Sa 8am, US$50). Check departure details at the RNAC office opposite the airstrip.

SERVICES: Food and lodging are not difficult to find, although the trail from Thorung Phedi to Muktinath is essentially barren, so be prepared. Manang contains a post office, an HRA clinic with pharmaceutical products for sale, several lodges, and some equipment shops. There is a police check-point at Hongde.

HIGHLIGHTS: Views of the Annapurnas. The icy, crystalline Tilicho Tal glacial lake. Tibetan-style villages with ancient *gompas* and herds of rugged animals, including yaks. Thorung La, a breath-takingly high pass with spectacular views of the surrounding ridges.

VILLAGE	ALTITUDE	TIME
Chame	2620m	start
Thaleku	2720m	45min.
Bhratang	2850m	1½hr.
Dhukure Pokhari	3060m	2hr.
Pisang	3130m	1hr.
Hongde (low route)	3320m	2½hr.
Braga	3480m	1½hr.
Manang	3500m	30min.
Tengi	3640m	30min.
Ghunsang	3880m	1hr.
Yak Kharka/Letdar	4100m	1hr.
Thorung Phedi	4470m	1hr.
Thorung La (pass)	5416m	5hr.
Muktinath	3800m	3½hr.

FEATURES: The trail ascends from Chame travels through deep woods and past enormous rock faces. Beyond Pisang, the trek enters the Nyesyang region, a dry area where locals grow hardy crops and herd horses, yaks, and goats. The trail to Thorung La has been used by herders for hundreds of years. This portion of the trek puts hikers at risk of **frostbite** and **altitude sickness**. Make sure that you have adequate clothing for cold conditions. Do not push yourself if you experience any symptoms of AMS (see p. 35).

TREKKING NEPAL

MUKTINATH TO POKHARA. The rest of the Annapurna circuit trek is the Jomsom trek done in reverse (see below). After Thorung La, this leg will be luxury. It's mostly downhill, rarely steep, and there is a lot of great apple pie along the way. Dig in—you've earned it.

JOMSOM TREK जोमसोम

This there-and-back route can be converted into a there-*or*-back route by flying one way between Jomsom (2710m) and Pokhara. Flying directly to high altitudes means spending one or two days acclimatizing upon arrival. Hiking up to Muktinath from Pokhara should take around **6-9 days.** For its spectacular scenery, high-quality accommodations, and relative ease, the trek up to (and past) Jomsom is the most popular stretch of trail in the Annapurnas.

BIRETHANTI TO GHOREPANI. Trekkers typically start at **Birethanti,** a town at the confluence of the Bhurungdi and Modi Khola Rivers and a picturesque spot with plenty of lodges, a bank, a post office, an art gallery, and an ACAP check-post.

The trail follows the Bhurungdi Khola to **Hille** and another dense cluster of lodges at **Tirkedhunga** (1580m). Now, the *real* climbing starts: it's basically uphill all the way to Ghorepani. The first, steepest section brings you through intricately terraced hillsides to the village of **Ulleri.** Beyond Ulleri, you move into increasingly dense forest. If you're trekking in the pre-monsoon season (Mar.-May), this area will probably reward you with spectacular floral displays of the arboreal rhododendrons of the Himalayas.

Ghorepani, or the pass **(Deorali)** just beyond it, is a major tourist center. The surrounding area bears the ugly scars of deforestation. Ghorepani itself, a creation of the trekking business, is a bizarre hybrid of resort and shanty-town. There's an ACAP office here and a phone in the Nice View Lodge. A couple of bookshops/exchanges can outfit you with reading material for your trek. There are a number of side trails through the nearby forests, and Ghorepani commands a magnificent panorama of Dhaulagiri and the entire Annapurna massif—the view is best seen at dawn from **Poon Hill** (3194m), 1hr. behind Ghorepani. It is possible to connect to **Ghandruk or Chhomrong** via a forest path from Ghorepani.

> ❗ **WARNING.** There have been several incidents of theft on the secluded forest trails around Ghorepani. Trekking in a group is recommended, particularly between Ghorepani and Tirkedhunga and between Ghorepani and Ghandruk.

GHOREPANI TO TUKCHE. From Ghorepani, the main trail heads gently downhill through Chitre, Phalate, Sikha, and Ghara to **Tatopani** and the Kali Gandaki Valley. From Chitre, there are trails via Tadapani to Ghandruk and Chomrong, on the way to the Annapurna Sanctuary. Trekking in the opposite direction, from Tatopani to Ghorepani, is 6-8hr. of blood, tears, toil, and sweat. Tatopani's famed **hot springs** (Rs10 entry fee) have been converted into two concrete, naturally heated hot tubs, flanked by a stand that serves soft drinks and beer (Rs120; Happy Hour 3-6pm offers beer and popcorn for Rs110). This luxury, plus a number of great lodges with delectable food, make Tatopani an ideal rest stop. You can find the essentials here, including a shoe-repair shop, post office, bank, phone, booksellers, and a police check-post. The quickest way to the hot springs by the river is to cut through the idyllic garden of the Trekker's Lodge.

While most people heading south through Tatopani choose to head up toward Ghorepani, an alternative low-level route along the river to **Beni** (820m) and **Baglung** is the quickest passage between Pokhara and Tatopani. Beni marks the endpoint of the road out of Pokhara, and is within a day's walk of Tatopani. Since part of the road is unfinished, you may need to take two buses from Beni to Pokhara (5hr., Rs70). A private vehicle will set you back Rs2500—contact the Yeti Hotel in Beni for jeep service.

Heading north out of Tatopani, start your journey through the Himalayas with Dhaulagiri to your left and the Annapurnas to your right. Houses range from the scattered, thatched homes of the Nepalese hinterland to the flat-roofed stone houses of the higher altitudes, which are often tightly clustered into dense, claustrophobic villages for protection against the brutal upland winds. Hindu shrines and iconography never disappear entirely, but prayer flags, wheels, and stones become the dominant religious motifs as you head north. Make sure to keep all shrines on your right as you pass them, in accordance with Buddhist custom.

The first major settlement north of Tatopani, **Dana** once thrived on salt trade taxation. From here to **Ghasa**, keep an eye open for langur monkeys. **Lete** and **Kalopani**, the next major settlements, have effectively fused into one and are linked by a flagstone trail. As you head north from Kalopani to **Tukuche,** you will be immediately below the immense eastern buttresses of Dhaulagiri. Its magnificent ice fall dominates the view; a trail out of the valley will take you on a daytrip to the base of the ice fall. Navigation south of Tukche can be tricky in the dry season because the route heads to the stony valley floor, crossing the river on wobbly temporary bridges. Don't attempt to ford the river. It's deep and the current is vicious.

TUKUCHE TO MUKTINATH. The next town north after Tukuche, **Marpha** is a trekker favorite, with its neatly-clustered stone houses and elegantly-paved main street. Marpha's highly-potent, locally produced **apple brandy** is exported throughout Nepal and appears in local shops and on restaurant menus throughout the region (Rs80-100 per bottle). Marpha has a **brandy factory**, in an unmarked building a few minutes south of town, where you can see the fermentation and distillation.

Beyond Marpha is the high altitude desert of the Trans-Himalaya. Every afternoon, this area (and everywhere north) is blasted by brutal winds that whip the grit of the river valley into a blinding, flesh-stinging frenzy. Plan on being indoors by midday, especially if you're heading south *into* the wind.

Jomsom, the regional administration center, is a mix of traditional highland trading town, trekking mecca, and unpopular bureaucratic post. Its airstrip is also the beginning or end of many treks. Don't be misled, however, by the Jomsom trek's name—Jomsom is not the highlight of the trek, it's merely the biggest town on the route. The town has all the facilities you'd expect of an administrative center, including a hospital, bank, and post office. Many of these services, as well as a small cluster of lodges, are on the east bank of the river across the new suspension bridge. The airport and airline offices, police check-post, and most of the lodges and trekking supply stores (some of which sell books as well as toilet paper and biscuits), are on the west bank of the river at the south end of town. At the south end of Jomsom is the **Mustang Eco-Museum,** with interesting, informative exhibits on the region's history, geology, and culture. (Rs50. Open daily 9am-5pm.)

Beyond Jomsom, the farther you go up the valley, the more you begin to feel that you are in Tibet. Keep going north (you'll need special and expensive permits to do this) and you will enter the ancient Buddhist kingdom of **Mustang,** a finger of Nepal that juts northward into Tibetan territory. It was this area that Kampa guerillas from western Tibet claimed as their own during the 1960s when they waged war against the occupying Chinese. A regular trekking permit will take you as far as **Kagbeni,** a dusty cluster of Tibetan houses around an ancient *gompa* set in its own patch of irrigated green.

The real goal of the Jomsom trek is **Muktinath,** at the head of a valley to the east of the main Kali Gandaki Gorge. It can be approached from Kagbeni or more directly from Jomsom. While following the stony riverbed of the Kali Gandaki north of Jomsom, keep an eye open for fossil ammonites, the distinctively coiled long-dead mollusks that symbolize Vishnu. They were thrust up from their sea-bed graves along with the rest of the Himalayas when the Indian Subcontinent collided with Asia. It's partly the abundance of these fossils, known locally as *shaligram,* that accounts for Muktinath's importance to Hindu and Buddhist pilgrims.

As you approach Muktinath, keep an eye out for the **Muktinath Traditional Tibetan Medical Center,** in the small village of Jharkot, less than an hour from Muktinath, which trains local youths in the practice of Tibetan medicine. If he's not out on a house-call, the resident *amchi* will even give you a free consultation.

The brown and ochre desert hills, the snow-capped peaks to the south, the deep blue sky, the little patches of irrigated green in the valley floor, and the Tibetan villages scattered about the valley make Muktinath worth every drop of sweat and every aching joint. The complex of temples that draw many pilgrims to Muktinath includes 108 spouts of holy water and a sacred spot where a jet of natural gas sustains a small flame in a pool of water. Less spectacular, but nonetheless useful, are Muktinath's ACAP office and police check-post. While only the very fit or masochistic will try to cross the Thorung La Pass from Muktinath (it's a very steep 7-8hr. climb), a daytrip part of the way up will reward you with great views and can help acclimatization. When the open road calls again, you can retrace your steps to Jomsom and then either fly or walk back to Pokhara.

JOMSOM TREK: BIRETHANTI TO MUKTINATH

TRANSPORTATION: RNAC, Cosmic, Shangri-La, and Skyline all **fly** out of **Jomsom** to **Pokhara** (20min.; all flights 7am, weather permitting; RNAC US$50, others US$61). Ask for a window seat and gawk at the closer-than-close mountain views. **Buses** run from Pokhara's Baglung Bus Stand to **Naya Pul** (2hr., every hr. 5:30am-6pm, Rs50). **Cars** will also make the trip for Rs600, 4 passenger max. **Birethanti** is a 20min. walk from Naya Pul.

SERVICES: Food and lodging options abound on the trail. Tatopani offers all the essential shops and services: a post office, a bank, public phones, shoe-repair, book shops, etc. There are several police check-points along the trail.

VILLAGE	ALTITUDE	TIME
Birethanti	1100m	start
Ulleri	2080m	3hr.
Ghorepani	2820m	3hr.
Sikha	1980m	2hr.
Tatopani	1190m	2hr.
Dana	1400m	2hr.
Ghasa	2040m	4½hr.
Kalopani	2530m	3½hr.
Tukche	2590m	3hr.
Marpha	2670m	2½hr.
Jomsom	2710m	1½hr.
Kagbeni	2800m	2½hr.
Muktinath	3800m	4hr.

JOMSOM TREK: BIRETHANTI TO MUKTINATH

HIGHLIGHTS: Amazing views of Himalayan giants, including Dhaulagiri and the Annapurnas. Deep canyons, graceful waterfalls, great lodges, and delicious grub. Fossilized mollusks, known as *shaligram*. The complex of temples in Muktinath.

FEATURES: The beginning of the trail passes through bamboo stands and runs next to streams and waterfalls. After Ulleri, hardwood and rhododendron forests surround the path. Beyond Tatopani and its hot springs, the trail heads through Kali Gandaki Gorge, which becomes landslide-prone and frighteningly narrow at points. Near Ghasa, the plants are mostly subtropical species and gradually change to pine woods towards Kalopani; at Marpha, the climate becomes arid as the winds of the Trans-Himalaya buffet the land. The rest of the way to Muktinath, the countryside is barren and rocky, although locals have managed to cultivate some fruit trees and other crops. Beyond Kagbeni, **altitude sickness** becomes a risk, and if you plan to cross Thorung La from this side, allot several days for acclimatization.

◼ THE ANNAPURNA SANCTUARY

Pioneered by British climbing expeditions during the late 1950s, the **7-12 day trek** into the Annapurna Sanctuary up the Modi Khola Valley is the quickest and easiest route from Pokhara up to the Himalayan giants. The sanctuary itself is a gargantuan natural amphitheater with a 360-degree panorama of looming white peaks.

BIRETHANTI TO DEORALI. The trek begins in **Birethanti** (also the starting point for the Jomsom trek) and goes north up the west bank of the Modi Khola. This pleasant riverside amble turns serious at the spread-out **Syauli Bazaar,** when the trail turns uphill to **Kimche,** and after many stone steps, leads to **Ghandruk.** For many years, the source of this well-heeled Gurung village's wealth was the British Army, which recruited heavily here for its famed Gorkha fighters. Now, however, the village is riding the crest of a major trekking wave, as its several grand concrete hotels suggest. As well as a police check-post, you'll find an ACAP office with a number of displays and two "Gurung Museums," both of which are rooms crammed with traditional Gurung tools, clothes, and wares (Rs30 entrance fee for each). A number of hotels have phones. Ignore the signs for Jhinu hot springs here—it's a 2-3hr. walk, and easier to visit on the return journey (see below).

From Ghandruk, the route heads up to **Kimrong Danda** before descending steeply to a river crossing at **Kimrong Khola** (1830m) and ascending painfully to **Upper Chhomrong** (2180m). There are plenty of lodges, but try to resist the temptation to call it a day here. Instead, go down to **Chhomrong** proper, another large, handsome Gurung village, with a beautifully engineered stone staircase. Chhomrong is your last chance to stock up on supplies for the sanctuary; you can buy and rent gear here for non-negotiable rates. A number of lodges have telephones. The ACAP check-point in Upper Chhomrong is the last on your way up toward the sanctuary. The ◼**Hiunchuli Guest House** wins the prize for "Best Food in the Annapurnas." The chocolate cake and pizzas are especially scrumptious. The staff is friendly and efficient, and the VCD player downstairs entertains with daily movie showings.

The road out of Chhomrong leads down across a river, and then steeply up to **Sinuwa,** which commands some impressive views of the surrounding countryside. From Sinuwa, a pleasant walk through the woods turns steeply downhill through a bamboo forest to the aptly-named **Bamboo,** a small collection of hotels. Beyond Bamboo, the path leads steadily upward, first to **Doban,** and then to **Himalaya,** which is nothing more than a couple of lodges. The last stop-off in the valley is at **Deorali,** just beyond **Hinko** (3140m); a huge over-hanging boulder here has provided shelter for many a weather-beset party. There are also a number of non-boulder lodges in Deorali. Note that your rate of **altitude gain** should now be a serious consideration, especially if you've come straight up from Pokhara.

DEORALI TO ANNAPURNA BASE CAMP. The section between Deorali and **Machhapuchhare Base Camp**, or **MBC**, on the edge of the sanctuary, can be dangerous. It basically serves as a repository for avalanches coming off the upper slopes of Hiunchuli to the west, making it a bad place to be after heavy snowfall. In March 2001, four trekkers were killed in an avalanche just beyond Deorali. Pay attention to conditions and seek local advice; **it's best to leave early in the morning and be past the avalanche tracks by 10am, before the sun and wind start unsettling heavy drifts of snow.** There is an alternate route beyond Deorali that bypasses the most dangerous stretch. Five to ten minutes out of town, a small path cuts across the river on a rickety footbridge. The trail leads along the east bank of the river for 45min. before rejoining the main path on the west bank. Beyond this point, you still have to cross a couple of avalanche tracks.

As you emerge from the gorge of the Modi Khola, the first cluster of lodges is at what is inaccurately called Machhapuchhare Base Camp—after one unsuccessful British expedition in the 1950s, the mountain was declared sacred and off-limits. The best views are farther into the sanctuary at the **Annapurna Base Camp**, or **ABC**. If you've come up from Pokhara and altitude sickness is a potential problem, consider spending two nights at MBC and doing an early there-and-back trip to ABC. Originally established by Chris Bonington's Annapurna South Face Expedition in 1970, ABC now consists of several lodges crouched in a very desolate, windblown spot (if you're trekking Jan.-Feb., check to see that the lodges are open). The view from ABC includes a whole series of Himalayan walls; clockwise from the south are: Hiunchuli, Annapurna South, Baraha Shikhar (Fang), Annapurna I, Singu Chuli (Fluted Peak), Tharpu Chuli (Tent Peak), Annapurna III, and Machhapuchhare. There are a couple of memorials dedicated to climbers who have died in the mountains, including one for Anatoli Boukreev, the Russian mountaineer made famous for his rescue efforts during the Everest disaster of 1996. He was killed in an avalanche the following winter while attempting to ascend Annapurna's South face. The snowy slopes around ABC are ideal for sledding. Bring snow pants or a plastic sheet and you can slide all the way back down to MBC.

ABC TO DHAMPUS. The return trip backtracks to Chhomrong, from which it's possible to take a different route back to Pokhara than the one that starts in Birethanti. To continue to Dhampus from Upper Chomrong, drop down to **Jhinu Danda** (1730m), which is a 15min. walk away from the idyllic **Jhinu Hot Springs**. Now a concrete-sided pool, the hot springs are located by the river in a cool, forested valley that is popular with both trekkers and langur monkeys. Continue across the Modi Khola on the not-so-new **New Bridge** (1650m), which also contains a small cluster of lodges. From here, follow the river and then ascend to the bustling village of **Landruk** (1630m). **Tolka** (1730m) is strung out over 2km. A final reminder of the rigors of uphill hiking brings you to **Bhichok Deorali** (2100m). It's then a pleasant walk along the ridge to **Pothana** (1970m). If you're heading from Pothana up toward Landruk, keep right at both of the forks that come up shortly after Potana. If you're heading down from Potana, keep left at the fork 10min. after Potana. **Dhampus** (1690m) is the final settlement along the route. A big village stretched out along a ridge for a couple of kilometers, Dhampus used to have something of a reputation among trekkers as a den of thieves, but that dubious claim to fame seems to have been based on only a handful of incidents that occurred 20 years ago. The final descent from Dhampus to **Dhampus Phedi** (1140m), where you visit your final

ANNAPURNA SANCTUARY: BIRETHANTI TO ANNAPURNA BASE CAMP

TRANSPORTATION: The trek begins in **Birethanti** (see directions for **Jomsom Trek**, above). A **bus** to the Baglung bus park in **Pokhara** leaves from **Dhampus Phedi** (2hr., every hr. 6am-6pm, Rs17), should you choose to end the trek here. **Taxis** make the trip to Lakeside, Pokhara, for Rs250, 4 passenger max.

LANDMARK	ALTITUDE	TIME
Birethanti	1100m	start
Syauli Bazar	1150m	2½hr.
Kimche	1760m	1hr.
Ghandruk	2010m	2hr.
Kimrong Danda	2260m	2hr.
Chhomrong	2050m	3½hr.
Sinuwa	2320m	2hr.
Bamboo	2350m	2hr.
Dovan	2610m	1hr.
Himalaya	2870m	1½hr.
Deorali	3230m	1½hr.
Machhapuchhare Base Camp	3700m	2½hr.
Annapurna Base Camp	4130m	2hr.

SERVICES: There are lodges all the way up to Annapurna Base Camp, but the luxuries (satellite TV, equipment stores, telephones) stop after Chhomrong. Ghandruk and Chhomrong are the largest villages on the trek, and most services are available in them. **Lodges in the sanctuary often close during the winter,** so ask around to find out if they are open.

HIGHLIGHTS: Friendly Gurung villages with luxurious accommodations. Incredible Himalayan panoramas, including Machhapuchhare, Hiunchuli, and the Annapurnas. Sledding on the snowy slopes around Annapurna Base Camp.

FEATURES: The trail moves uphill through forests and rice paddies. After Chhomrong, the last permanent settlement on the trek, the path passes through stands of bamboo and rhododendron. Beyond Deorali, the trail enters an avalanche-blasted gorge and emerges in the Annapurna Sanctuary, a windblown bowl enclosed by exquisite 7000-8000m peaks. **Avalanches** are a serious concern on portions of the trek. **Altitude sickness** is a risk around and after Deorali. If you are cooking your own food, be aware that **the use of firewood is not permitted beyond Ghandruk.**

check-post, is long, steep, hot, and dusty. An alternative route out of Chhomrong takes you via Tadapani to Ghorepani and Poon Hill (see above). From there, it's a steep descent to Birethanti and Naya Pul.

THE LANGTANG REGION लांगटांग

The black sheep of the Classic Three, the Langtang region is often passed over by trekkers drawn by name recognition to Annapurna and Everest. The relative obscurity of the Langtang trek means that its trails are relatively uncrowded, and with its majestic terrain and proximity to Kathmandu, Langtang is really quite an attractive trekking region. The general title "Langtang" actually covers three distinct but adjacent areas, the **Langtang Valley, Gosainkund,** and **Helambu.** Each of these areas can be visited alone, or they can be strung together into one longer trek. Individually, each area takes between 4-8 days to trek; collectively, the three regions can be hiked in **12-16 days.** In addition to the dramatic scenery of the valley itself, the Langtang Valley also offers the chance to explore some of the peaks and glaciers at its head. In Gosainkund, there is a series of frigid, high-altitude lakes, and plenty of alpine terrain. Helambu is lower and greener, winding through the jungled hills at the northern edge of the Kathmandu Valley.

TREKKING NEPAL

ANIMAL INSIGHT In a land devoid of almost everything but rock and ice, animals are necessary for survival—they carry supplies, provide food for villagers, and have also served as inspiration for proverbs that run the gamut from droll to bizarre to utterly revolting. So, before you head out on the trail tomorrow, contemplate these words of wisdom from ancient Himalayan cultures.

When pride rides a donkey, her dainty feet dangle on the ground... When the horse is on the move, don't goad it with the stirrup; when a man is humility itself, don't treat him with arrogance... Just as a horse with a long jaw appears old, a man of patience may also look a fool... When falsehood is a hill, truth is only a yak... The miraculous: butter without a cow; an egg without a bird. The ridiculous: to load cargo upon a frog; to get milk from a tadpole... When a man nourishes a baby conch on milk, he hopes to use it to fend off crocodiles... For the tortoise living in a well, just hearing of the ocean's greatness will kill it... Donkey's dung: a person who is smooth on the outside, coarse and rough on the inside... A pigeon's anus cannot excrete a gold earring (huh?)... A bigger yak doesn't mean bigger dung.

◪ THE LANGTANG VALLEY

According to legend, a lama first discovered the Langtang Valley when following a runaway yak; in Tibetan "lang" means yak, and "tank" means "to follow." After leading the lama to a high pasture for a glimpse of the holy peaks at the head of the valley, the sacred yak promptly died and the pasture, Langshisa Kharka, which means "the pasture where the yak died," was named to commemorate the event. For most people not in pursuit of yaks, a trek through the Langtang Valley takes 5-6 days round-trip from Syabru-Besi. The trail is straightforward, following the Langtang River up the Langtang Valley, passing through the village of Langtang, and on to the Langtang Lodge for a few hours of rest. The return trip plods back down the same trail, either heading back out to the roadhead at Syabri Besi or turning uphill towards Gosainkund and Helambu. The stunning views, as well as the numerous opportunities for exploration from Kyanjin Gompa at the head of the valley, make this the most popular of the Langtang treks.

SYABRU BESI TO LAMA HOTEL. Treks in Langtang used to start in the town of **Dhunche,** but the development of this area has made **Syabru Besi,** a bit farther along the road by bus, a more attractive and convenient base. The town has a number of decent hotels catering to trekkers, including the **Buddha Guest House** and the **Northland Tibetan Guest House.** Besides telephone services, Syabru Besi has few other facilities. If you really want to escape the crowds, cross the river, and stay in one of the quieter but more basic hotels on that side of town.

From Syabru Besi, the trail starts just north of town; there's a small yellow "To Langtang" sign to point the way. The path passes an army check-point where park permits are checked, crosses a steel bridge, winds through the other part of town, and heads east up the valley, along the northern (left) bank of the Langtang River. It soon crosses the river on a wood-and-stone bridge and continues along the southern bank. Within an hour, the trail passes a small tea shop, and on the opposite side of the river, a pleasant **hot spring** set up for a refreshing bath. Continuing along the south side of the river, the trail hits a **T-junction,** where a sign points the way to Thulo Syabru (left to Kyanjin Gompa and Langtang). The trail then passes through **Bamboo,** a small settlement that makes a good lunch stop and also contains several hotels, including the **Old Bamboo Riverside Lodge.** If you want a more relaxing first day, stick around Bamboo. From here, the trail continues along the lush south side of the river until it hits a large steel suspen-

LANGTANG VALLEY: SYABRU BESI TO KYANJIN GOMPA

TRANSPORTATION: Buses leave from the New Bus Stand in Kathmandu and head to **Syabru Besi** (10hr., 6:30 and 7am, Rs140) via **Dhunche** (8hr., Rs110). Buses return from Syabru Besi to **Kathmandu** (10hr., 6:30 and 7am, Rs140). There is an airstrip near Kyanjin Gompa, but you would be very lucky to get a flight out from here.

SERVICES: Lodges and tea houses dot most of the region, and several have satellite telephone service, but beyond Kyanjin Gompa, you will have to camp on your own. There are several national park check-points where you will have to prove that you paid the **national park entrance fee.** Because this is a less-traveled region, you should arrive with all necessary equipment; you will likely not be able to buy it on the trail.

VILLAGE	ALTITUDE	TIME
Syabru Besi	1460m	
Bamboo	1850m	4hr.
Rimche	2250m	2hr.
Lama Hotel	2380m	25min.
Ghora Tabela	3020m	1hr.
Thangshyap	3110m	1½hr.
Langtang Village	3430m	25min.
Mundu	3550m	15min.
Singdom	3680m	1¾hr.
Kyanjin Gompa	3850m	4hr.
Langshisa Kharka	4160m	3½hr.
Kyanjin Gompa	3850m	
Langshisa Kharka	4160m	

HIGHLIGHTS: Wildlife from various birds to red pandas, wild boar, monkeys, and black bears. Tamang and Sherpa villages. Views of Langtang Lirung (7245m), dramatic ice falls, and gargantuan glaciers.

FEATURES: The trail begins in terraced fields and hardwood and bamboo forests. Further along, there are many yak and cattle pastures, and yak dung is often used as a heating product in local houses. North of Kyanjin Gompa is a moraine whose higher reaches offer a spectacular vista of the surrounding mountains. Beware of **altitude sickness** beyond Ghora Tabela.

sion bridge. There are a couple of tea shops here that can provide lodging in a pinch. After the bridge the trail becomes steeper and drier, climbing up to the **Hotel Langtangview Lodge.** The trail continues up to the town of **Rimche,** home to a few lodges. The **Hotel Ganeshview Lodge** offers decent rooms and views. The **Sherpa Lodge** and the **Lama Guest House** are also good options in town. **Lama Hotel,** a 10-15min. walk from Rimche, is a pleasantly-sized tourist destination with more than six lodges and phone service.

LAMA HOTEL TO LANGTANG VILLAGE. From Lama Hotel, the trail climbs steeply through the forest on the north side of the river, and after an hour or two reaches the **Gumnachok Lodge,** in a small clearing. From here, the trail continues steeply until it reaches **Ghora Tabela,** home to a small tea shop and a national park check-post, where permits must be presented. After Ghora Tabela, the trail flattens somewhat and soon reaches **Thangshyap** and **Hotel Tibetan Lodge.** Langtang Village comes into view around this point, but it's still more than an hour's walk to town. The trail passes through several more settlements and tea shops before reaching **Langtang Village,** an attractive stone village with fantastic views of the mountains. The **Valleyview Lodge and Hotel** and the **Villageview Lodge and Hotel** are both fine places to stay. Authorities have fixed prices in town at a flat rate, so pick your favorite view. As Langtang Village is above 3000m, **altitude sickness** can be a problem. It is best to rest here before journeying on to Kyanjin Gompa.

LANGTANG VILLAGE TO KYANJIN GOMPA. The path from Langtang Village to Kyanjin Gompa is fairly flat and the total gain in altitude is only 400m. Passing through sparse alpine terrain, the trail follows the north side of the river past *mani* walls carved with Tibetan script. The first settlement after Langtang Village is tiny **Mundu,** home to the **Mundu Village Guest House.** After passing more *mani* walls, the trail leads to **Sindum,** where there are two lodges, including the **Sindum Village Hall and Lodge.** After Sindum, the terrain is dotted with increasing numbers of large boulders. These are the work of glaciers that hollowed out the upper part of the valley. From Sindum, the trail climbs through the boulder fields and soon reaches **Kyanjin Gompa,** the highlight of the trek. The best place to stay in town is the **Yeti Guest House,** which has phones and solar-powered showers. Another good option is **Yala Peak Guest House.** Check out the local **Yak cheese factory** where the employees are generally glad to give a quick tour. (Cheese Rs280 per kg. Open daily 7am-5pm.)

Kyanjin is a great place to take in the splendid views and unwind on a few day-trips. The most popular is the ascent of **Kyanjin Ri** (4773m), a hill to the north of town. The trail climbs up steeply from town to the prayer-flag-festooned first crest at 4350m and then continues up the ridge to the peak. The views of Langtang Lirung are incomparable, and the climb is fairly easy and generally free of snow. From here you can cross to the higher peak of **Tsergo Ri** (4984m). It's important to watch for signs of altitude sickness when attempting to climb either of these peaks. Another popular excursion is the hike up the valley to the pasture of **Langshisa Kharka,** which has glacier views. Some more difficult options include **Yala Peak** (5500m), which generally requires two days (including a high camp) and some equipment (ice axe, crampons, boots). The Ganja-La Pass (5130m) is another multiple-day affair that is an alternative way to reach Helambu from Kyanjin Gompa. The pass is difficult and requires several days of camping.

THE RETURN OR CONNECTING TO GOSAINKUND. To get back from Kyanjin Gompa, simply follow the same trail in reverse. People often go from Kyanjin Gompa to Lama Hotel in one day and from Lama Hotel to Syabru Besi the next.

If you're heading to Gosainkund from the Langtang Valley, make a detour after Bamboo and head to **Thulo Syabru** (2130m). Then take off the next day to **Sing Gompa** (see p. 907) or **Chalang Pati** (see below). There are two trails leading to Thulo Syabru from Langtang Valley. The first is marked by the yellow sign at the **T-junction** downhill from Bamboo. The second is farther down the trail just past the hot springs. The second trail is shorter and easier. In Thulo Syabru, the best places to stay are the **Yeti Restaurant and Hotel** and the **Eveningview Guest House.** The next day's hike connecting to the Gosainkund trail in Sing Gompa is steep but pleasant. The trail switchbacks uphill, passing the town of **Dursagang** (2720m), where accommodation is available at the **Himalay Hotel and Lodge.** The trail continues up the ridges to two tea shops at the crest (3210m) and then curves around the ridge to **Sing Gompa** (3250m), on the Gosainkund trail (see below).

▨ THE GOSAINKUND TREK गोसैनकुंड

The main connection between Langtang and Helambu, the Gosainkund trek is marked by a series of often-frozen high-altitude lakes. The approach to the lakes provides views from the Langtang Valley all the way west to Machhapuchare and the Annapurnas. According to Hindu legend, when the multitudes of Hindu gods churned the oceans in an ill-conceived search for the elixir of immortality, they uncovered instead a virulent poison which threatened to destroy the earth. Shiva stepped up and obligingly drank the poison, but it burned his throat so intensely that he rushed to the Himalaya, struck the earth with his trident, and quenched his thirst with the cool waters that came forth. The gushing torrents formed the Gosainkund Lake, which Shiva found so pleasant a watering hole that he remains there sleeping to this day. Each year the lake becomes a major pilgrimage site during **Janai Purnima,** which occurs around the July-August full moon. By itself, this is a short trek—it can be done round-trip in 3-4 days—but most people couple it with a trek up the Langtang Valley or continue on from the lakes down into Helambu.

GOSAINKUND TREK: DHUNCHE TO GOSAINKUND

TRANSPORTATION: Dhunche is the most convenient starting point for the Gosainkund trek, unless you are hiking in from another region (see **Langtang Valley,** above, for bus info).

SERVICES: There are several acceptable lodges along the path, though Dhunche is about the only place to stop for anything more than trail-side food and beds.

VILLAGE	ALTITUDE	TIME
Dhunche	2030m	
Sing Gompa	3250m	6hr.
Chalang Pati	3580m	1hr. 20min.
Laurebinayak	3900m	1hr.
Gosainkund	4380m	2hr.

HIGHLIGHTS: High-altitude lakes with dramatic scenery all around.

FEATURES: The trek passes through evergreen and rhododendron woods, brush, and eventually leads to rather barren, rocky territory where **heavy snow is a dangerous possibility.** If the path into Gosainkund is inundated with snow, do not attempt to hike through to the lake. Around and after Sing Gompa, beware of **altitude sickness.**

DHUNCHE TO SING GOMPA. While Syabru Besi is now the most convenient starting point for the Langtang Valley Trek, **Dhunche** remains the best access point for Gosainkund. Dhunche has a number of lodges; the length of the bus ride means spending the first night here. Both the **Hotel Tibet Mountain View** and the **Hotel Thakali** are decent. There's also a small **pharmacy** in town (open daily 8am-5pm).

The trail for Sing Gompa departs from the road just north of town and follows the southern bank of the Trisuli River. It's quite steep, and you gain altitude quickly as you ascend toward the ridge. The trail crosses to the north side of the Trisuli and continues to climb up, up, and away. Just before Sing Gompa, the trail reaches a junction. The left path leads down to Thulo Syabru and the Langtang Valley and the right path to Sing Gompa and then Gosainkund. **Sing Gompa** is not far beyond this junction. The **Green View Hotel and Lodge** and the slightly more secluded **Red Panda Hotel and Lodge** are good. There's another **cheese factory** in town, where you can savor the taste of excellent yak cheese and curd. Be careful of altitude sickness since the ascent is over 1200m from Dhunche to Sing Gompa.

SING GOMPA TO GOSAINKUND. This leg of the trek can be done in a single day, but if you've come directly from Dhunche the previous day, your best option is to spend the night part way up in Laurebinayak. The trail from Sing Gompa winds around to the southern side of the ridge and follows the Trisuli River up the valley. After detouring briefly around the northern side of a small hill, the trail reaches **Chalang Pati,** where there are two small lodges, including the acceptable **Chalang Pati Hotel and Lodge.** Chalang Pati marks the end of the evergreen forest; from here, the terrain becomes increasingly alpine. The trail switchbacks up to **Laurebinayak,** home to a number of lodges and some fantastic Himalayan views. The **Hotel Mount Rest** is a good place to stay. If the altitude is a problem, there's no need to push on all the way up to Gosainkund in one day. From here, the trail shoots straight uphill past a large *stupa,* and farther uphill, a series of roofless stone houses. Here, the trail rejoins the Trisuli River. The first lake you see is the

TREKKING NEPAL

Saraswati, far below the trail against the opposite ridge. The trail passes quite close to the next lake, Bhairab, where Gosainkund village comes into view. **Gosainkund** itself is a small windblown settlement on the shore of Gosainkund Lake. Both the **Peaceful Hotel and Lodge** and the **Lakeside Guest House** offer reliable, friendly accommodation. In town, there's not much to do except bundle up and drink tea; the more adventurous (and acclimatized) can walk around Gosainkund Lake or climb the surrounding hills. The 20-30 min. climb to the summit rising directly above the village rewards with particularly spectacular views of the peaks of Langtang and Ganesh Himal.

THE RETURN TRIP OR CONNECTING TO HELAMBU. The return trip to Dhunche can be done in one long day or two shorter, easier days; the route is the exact reverse of the one described above. If you're going from Gosainkund up to the Langtang Valley, take the right trail just below Sing Gompa and head downhill to Thulo Syabru (see p. 906).

If you're doing the popular trek from Gosainkund into Helambu, you can connect to the Helambu circuit at Tharepati in one very long day or in two average-length days. The trail from Gosainkund skirts the eastern edge of the lake before ascending up toward the pass. This section of the trail is often snow-covered and is impassable at certain times of year and in bad weather conditions. **Laurebina Pass** (4610m) is marked by prayer flags and a *chorten*. To the south you can see the green foothills of Helambu, which lead into the Kathmandu Valley. The south side of the pass (descending into Helambu) is generally drier and easier to hike through. The trail descends steeply from there to a small tea shop at **Bhera Goth**, where the path forks and a sign points downhill to Ghopte and Tharepeti. It is better to take the lower trail as the upper one is undeveloped, often snow-covered, and has no facilities until Tharepati. The lower trail continues down from the tea shop all the way to **Phedi** (3630m), home to two hotels and a tiny helipad. The **Taj Mel Lodge,** the lower of the two, is a pleasant, riverside accommodation. After Phedi, the restless trail indicates the up-and-down character of the Helambu area. It makes one steep ridge climb before reaching **Ghopte** (3430m), where there are another two lodges (both dorm-style). It is a fairly long day from Gosainkund to Ghopte, but some people push all the way to **Therapati,** on the Helambu circuit, to avoid the pile-up of pass-crossers in Ghopte (see p. 910).

◎ THE HELAMBU TREK हेलम्बू

Unlike the Langtang Valley or Gosainkund treks, both of which wind mainly through high alpine country, the Helambu Trek is relatively low-altitude, thick-forested, and hot. Also, unlike the other two, Helambu is criss-crossed by trails running between villages, and there is no one particular route that must be taken or sight that must be seen. The entire area can be visited via any number of different routes. The route described below, a horseshoe-shaped trek starting in Sundarijal and ending in Melamchipul Bazaar, is one of the most common, but the variations are infinite, and the crowds disappear the minute you get off the beaten path.

SUNDARIJAL TO CHISOPANI. Sundarijal, the starting point, is very close to Kathmandu. The trail from Sundarijal begins ascending directly from the bus stop and follows a concrete path alongside a large black metal pipe running water to Kathmandu. The concrete path becomes concrete steps, which climb past the Sundarijal Reservoir. The path crosses a dirt road after this and continues up the steep concrete steps to **Mul Kharka.** Above Mul Kharka is an army base where permits are sometimes checked. The trail climbs up **Borlang Pass,** the high point of the day, and then makes a short descent to **Chisopani,** home to numerous hotels. Both

HELAMBU TREK: SUNDARIJAL TO MELAMCHIPUL BAZAAR

TRANSPORTATION: Buses go from Ratna Park bus station in Kathmandu to **Sundarijal** (1hr., every 30min. 6am-8pm, Rs20). Taxis to and from **Thamel** cost Rs200-300. Buses return from Melamchipul Bazaar to **Kathmandu** (4hr., every hr. 7am-3pm, Rs40). Buses from Kathmandu also continue up the road from Melamchipul Bazaar to **Talamarang,** about 10km further.

SERVICES: Numerous food and lodging options are available on the trail, and a few hotels have telephone service. There are some police and national park checkposts along the way, so be ready to prove that you've obtained your permits and paid your entrance fees.

HIGHLIGHTS: Stunning panoramas of the Helambu hills and the monstrous peaks of the Langtang Himal. Large Buddhist monasteries tucked in among the mountains and valleys. Sherpa agricultural settlements and villages. Endless possibilities for side-trail exploration and connections to other hiking regions, such as the Langtang Valley and Gosainkund.

VILLAGE	ALTITUDE	TIME
Sundarijal	1460m	
Mul Kharka	1860m;	1¾ hr.
Borlang Pass	2420m;	1½hr.
Chisopani	2215m;	1 hr.
Pati Bhanjyang	1170m;	1½hr.
Chipling	2170m;	1¾hr.
Golpu	2130m;	1¾hr.
Gul Bhanjyang	2250m;	30min.
Kutumsang	2470m;	1½hr.
Kyuola Pass	3250m;	2½hr.
Mangen Goth	3220m;	20min.
Tharepati	3510m;	1½hr.
Melamchigaon	2530m;	4hr.
Nakote	2000m;	3hr.
Tarkegyang	2740m;	2½hr.
Ghangyul	2770m;	1¾hr.
Sermathang	2590m;	1¾hr.
Kakani	1996m;	5 hr.
Dubachaur	1440m;	30min.
Malamchipul Bazaar	870m	

FEATURES: The trail passes through several different types of vegetation and topographical areas. As it winds up and down the hills, the trek goes through bamboo, oak, and rhododendron forests, up steep canyons, over high ridges, and through terraced fields. Unlike many other Himalayan treks, the Helambu circuit does not ascend to some high point and then descend to the finish; it climbs and drops throughout the hike, arriving at the crest of a ridge only to descend into a valley and then head up the next ridge. The only place where altitude sickness should be a worry is around Tharepati.

the **New BBC Hotel,** and farther on, the **Hotel Manakamana,** offer good facilities. Some continue down the hill to Pati Bhanjyang the same day, but unless you're in a hurry, the views and pleasant atmosphere make Chisopani a better option.

CHISOPANI TO KUTUMSANG. From Chisopani, the trail runs briefly along the dirt road. At the first sharp turn, the trail splits and heads north. It drops down through a number of steep gullies and finally merges with the dirt road again just before **Pati Bhanjyang.** It is possible to walk the dirt road all the way to Pati Bhanjyang, though this takes longer. The **Valley View Lodge,** south of town, is a peaceful place to stay. From Pati Bhanjyang, one trail heads north to Kutumsang and another goes east to Talamarang. Continuing north to Kutumsang, the trail climbs steeply again to **Chipling** and the **Chipling Lodge Hotel and Restaurant.** Beyond the ridge, the trail arrives at the village of **Golpu** and the **Himalaya Lodge and Restaurant.** The trail leads north to the small settlement of **Gul Bhanjyang,** with a couple of lodges, including the **Hotel Dragon.** The trail ascends to the top of the ridge, and then makes a gentle dip into the saddle that holds **Kutumsang,** a pleasant village with good views on either side. The **Nama-**

TREKKING NEPAL

ste Hotel and Lodge and the Sherpa Lodge, at either end of town, are quiet accommodations. From Kutumsang, one trail heads east down the valley to **Mahankal** (1130m). The other heads north up the ridge to Tharepati, the highest point of the circuit.

KUTUMSANG TO THAREPATI. This is a relatively straightforward (though at times steep) trail, which follows the ridge all the way up from Kutumsang to Tharepati. Heading north from Kutumsang, the trail approaches **Kyuola Pass,** which is visible from town. This section of the trail is heavily forested, but there are plenty of mountain views, which improve throughout the day. After the pass, the trail soon reaches **Mangen Goth,** the only large settlement on the trail. A number of accommodations are available here. After Mangen Goth, the trail climbs steeply again, following the ridge all the way to **Tharepati.** High up on a crest, Tharepati shows off its spectacular views. To the east, west, and south are the staggered ridges and river valleys of Helambu. To the north are the snow-capped peaks of Gosainkund, and threading between them, the Laurebina Pass. In Tharepati are a number of lodges. On the very top is the **Gosainkund Hotel and Top Lodge.** Lower down the hill is the **Jimmy Lama Mountain Hostel.** To the north runs the trail to Gosainkund (p. 908). To the east the trail runs down to Melamchigaon and Helambu.

THAREPATI TO TARKEGYANG. From Tharepati, the trail drops steeply off the eastern side of the ridge. The vegetation becomes thick and lush once again and is dominated by bamboo and rhododendrons. Switchbacking down to the river valley, the trail crosses a small stream before leveling out somewhat. It drops down to a suspension bridge and then climbs briefly to **Melamchigaon,** a lovely agricultural Sherpa village with a large Buddhist monastery and more spectacular views down the valley. A short daytrip from Tharepati, this is also a good place to stay the night. Both the **Sun Lodge** and the **Wild View Hotel and Lodge** are friendly and have adequate facilities. The trail from here is unexciting and winds through the terraced fields in the lower part of town. It jumps sharply down to the Melamchi River and a suspension bridge. The **Riverside Lodge** lies just before the bridge. After the bridge, the trail climbs to the village of **Nakote,** where there's another sizeable monastery. Just after Nakote, there's a large fork in the trail. The right (lower) fork leads down to Thimbu while the left fork heads up to Tarkegyang. Climbing the hill, the trail passes several small farms. The **Sherpa Lodge** is about halfway between Nakote and Tarkegyang. The trail continues to ascend to **Tarkegyang,** a large settlement with numerous accommodations. The **Mountain View Hotel** is big and clean and has telephone service. A number of trails converge in Tarkegyang. To the north is the trail up to **Yangri Peak** (3771m), then to the **Ganja La** (5130m), and into the Langtang Valley. Two trails leave from the south—one follows the ridge to Sermathang, the other (lower) trail drops down to Kakanj and Kiul.

TARKEGYANG TO SERMATHANG. The trail to Sermathang follows the birds south from Tarkegyang. There are several forks, and the larger fork often leads downhill to Kakani, so be sure to ask along the way. The trail stays at roughly the same altitude, snaking along the ridge to the village of **Ghangyul.** There, the **Dolma Lodge** boasts clean, well-kept facilities. From Ghangyul, Sermathang is visible to the south—it's the cluster of houses in the notch at the top of the ridge. **Sermathang** is a pleasant place to stay. Although only a short day's hike from Tarkegyang, the accommodation options beyond Sermathang are much less pleasant, and it's a long walk to go all the way to Melamchipul Bazaar in a single day. In Sermathang, both the **Mountain View Lodge** and **Yangri Lodge** offer decent rooms. There's a **KEEP Office** in town that sells iodine tablets and also houses a tiny but lovely cultural

museum. Sermathang also contains a **national park check-post.** If you're coming from Melamchipul Bazaar, you can buy your park permit here. The town has several monasteries as well. Pay a visit to the *stupa* on the knoll to the south of town.

SERMATHANG TO MELAMCHIPUL BAZAAR. The trek down from Sermathang to the road at Melamchipul Bazaar is long but gentle and can easily be completed in one day. The trail follows the top of the ridge the entire way down, passing through increasingly developed settlements as it nears the road. In the reverse direction, this would be a lot of climbing to do in a single day, especially since the total change in altitude is 1720m. From Sermathang, the trail descends along the ridge to **Kakani,** where there are a couple of places to stay, including the **Himalayan Dorje Lakpa Guest House.** Kakani is a good overnight destination if you're coming up from Melamchipul Bazaar. After Kakani, the trail becomes a little harder to follow. It's a good idea to ask for directions. Continuing down the ridge, the trail comes to the dusty village of **Dubachaur** and the **Langtang Guest House.** From Dubachaur the trail crosses through more small settlements and farming terraces before dropping down and crossing the Melamchi River on a long suspension bridge to reach **Melamchipul Bazaar.** Melamchipul is not a particularly scenic place, but if you need to stay here for the night, the best option is to cross back over the suspension bridge to the north side of the Melamchi River and walk 5min. up the trail to the **Jugal Himal Resort,** a secluded lodge away from the bazaar. Up the road several kilometers from Melamchipul Bazaar, **Talamarang** (960m) is quieter and cleaner, and home to the tidy **Talamarang Guest House.**

◪ LANGTANG-GOSAINKUND-HELAMBU COMBINATIONS

Most often, treks in the Langtang region combine the separate treks into one longer trek. A Langtang-Gosainkund-Helambu trek is usually done in around 12-15 days and normally follows roughly this route: Syabru Besi—Lama Hotel—Langtang Village—Kyanjin Gompa—Lama Hotel—Thulo Syabru—Sing Gompa—Gosainkund—Ghopte—Kutumsang—Chisopani—Sundarijal. This direction is generally preferred over the others, as the Langtang Valley provides a better chance to acclimatize before crossing through Gosainkund and the Laurebina Pass (4610m). But the opposite route is also possible and is regularly done by trekking groups. The exit through Helambu is also flexible. From Tharapati, you can head south to Kutumsang and out to Sundarijal (the most common route), or from Kutumsang you can branch east down the less-traveled trail to Mahankal and then Talamarang. Or you can head east from Tharapati itself to Tarkegyang and to Melamchipul, a scenic three-day route. There are myriad other options too, so your best bet might be to let your feet and whims guide you around the trails.

THE EVEREST REGION

A trip to Everest used to involve setting out on foot from Kathmandu, several hundred kilometers to the west, and necessitated a sequence of arduous ascents and descents of up to 2000m at a time. Today, a road extends approximately half of the way to **Jiri,** connected by bus to Kathmandu. From Jiri, it still takes 10 days to walk to **Namche Bazaar,** the Sherpa capital, and 3-4 long days from Namche Bazaar to Everest. A trip to Everest by bus and on foot is a month-long undertaking. Most people save time by flying at least one way—there is an airstrip in Lukla, a two-day walk south of Namche Bazaar. If you decide to hike one way, rather than flying both in and out of Lukla, the logical choice is to walk in: you'll arrive in Namche already acclimatized. Many people do the reverse, walking from Namche to Jiri, because waiting for a flight out—particularly if you've got fixed international connections to make—can be extremely frustrating. Weather conditions have to be pretty good at Lukla before flights can take off and land.

Since trekking in the Everest region, especially on the approach to Namche Bazaar, involves steep ascents and descents, the trekking charts include a column on altitude gained and lost during each leg of the trek.

◢ JIRI TO NAMCHE BAZAAR

JIRI TO BHANDAR. With the introduction of plane service to Lukla, tourist traffic through Jiri has diminished sharply, and this stretch of the trek is much quieter than the areas above Lukla. Nepali porters carrying supplies to higher altitudes are the trail's most frequent users.

EVEREST TREK: JIRI TO NAMCHE BAZAAR

TRANSPORTATION: Buses run from Kathmandu's Ratna Park bus station to **Jiri** (11hr., 5 per day 5-10:30am, Rs210; express bus 8hr., 7am, Rs243) and from Jiri to **Kathmandu** (11hr., 5 per day 5-10:30am, Rs210; express 8hr., 7am, Rs243). Purchase tickets at the window opposite the Jiri Medical Hall (open daily 6am-6pm). Express bus tickets for either direction should be purchased the day before, and travelers are expected to arrive 30min. early. There are no roads after Jiri.

SERVICES: In villages, plenty of food and lodging options vie for hikers' attention. On this portion of the trail, low and high season accommodation prices often change day to day. Therefore most room prices are not listed. Also, there are not as many services (phone, pharmacy, police, etc.) available as in Namche Bazaar (see **Lukla to Everest Base Camp,** p. 915).

HIGHLIGHTS: Rhododendron and hardwood forests in steep valleys. Sherpa villages with many *mani* walls. Glimpses of Everest, Numbur, Mera, and other colossal peaks.

VILLAGE	ALTITUDE	TIME	GAIN/LOSS
Jiri	1905m	start	
Chitre	2330m	1¼hr.	
Mali	2220m	30min.	
Shivalaya	1767m	1½hr.	490m/-600m
Sangabadanda	2240m	1¼hr.	
Deorali	2705m	1¾hr.	
Bhandar	2194m	1hr.	900m/-510m
Kenja	1634m	3½hr.	
Sete	2575m	2¼hr.	1040m/-650m
Dagchu	2850m	1hr.	
Goyom	3155m	45min.	
Lamjura La Pass	3530m	1½hr.	
Thagtokbhug	2860m	1½hr.	
Junbesi	2710m	1¼hr.	990m/-860m
Salung	2960m	2hr.	
Ringmo	2700m	1½hr.	
Takshindo Pass	3070m	1hr.	
Takshindo	2930m	20min.	
Nunthala	2350m	1¼hr.	820m/-1340m
Jubing	1680m	1¾hr.	
Khari Khola	2070m	1½hr.	580m/-700m
Bupsa	2350m	1¼hr.	
Puiyan	2835m	3hr.	
Surke	2300m	2hr.	

FEATURES: The trail climbs up and down ridges, through valleys and forests, and past numerous rivers, creeks, monasteries, fields, and pastures. Watch for many species of birds along the way. **Altitude sickness** becomes a concern in the areas around Lamjura Pass.

The trail from Jiri begins at the end of the bus park away from the lodges. From the bus park, follow the dirt road past the end of the buildings for about 10min. Here, a trail branches left up the hill just after the waterfall passes under the road. This rocky trail climbs more or less straight up toward the ridge, passing small settlements and tea houses. The largest settlement before the ridge is **Chitre**, where you'll find the **Solu Khumbu Lodge**. The trail climbs gently to the first pass (2400m), then drops down the opposite side to **Mali**, a town that is sprinkled along the trail for 1km. Lodges include the **Sherpa Lodge and Restaurant** (dorm beds Rs15). After Mali, the descent becomes steeper as the trail drops down to meet the Khimti River, which is crossed by the suspension bridge. The trail continues on toward the juncture of the Shivalaya and Khimti rivers. A suspension bridge over the Shivalaya River leads to **Shivalaya**, a common stop for trekkers at the end of their first (short) day. The **Trekking Guide Hotel and Lodge** is a good option in town. Even if you don't stop here, you don't need to go all the way to Bhandar in one day—there are plenty of places to stay between Shivalaya and Bhandar. From Shivalaya the trail heads steeply uphill for about 600m to **Sangbadanda**, where it levels off a little. Be careful to stay on the most well-used trail because this is the direct route to Deurali and Bhandar; all locals know the way—ask them for directions. In Sangbadanda, the **Everest View Lodge**, at the farthest end of town, is the nicest place to stay. From here, the trail continues toward the ridge, passing a number of newer settlements along the way. In **Khasru Bas** is the new **Danfey Lodge and Restaurant**. Farther along is **Buludanda** and its **Hill View Sherpa Lodge**. The trail reaches its highest point at **Deurali**, a wind-swept pass where clouds float through at waist level. This is another good place to stop at the end of the first day, as it allows you to get acclimated to the higher altitude (2705m). The **Lama Guest House**, is the best of several good lodges in town (room with two beds: high-season Rs100, low-season Rs50). Right after the pass is a somewhat confusing junction. When the trail comes to a "T" at a completely wooden tea house, take the left trail to reach Bandar. This village is the most common stop at the end of the first day. The **Shangri La Guest House** is just uphill and outside of town, while **Ang Dawa Lodge** and **Shubha Lodge and Restaurant** are just past the monastery and *stupas*. The monastery can be opened on request except at 6pm. The trail from Jiri to Bhandar is rocky and dusty and therefore extremely slippery when wet.

BHANDAR TO JUNBESI. From Bhandar, the trail continues to drop down toward the Likhu River Valley. The path can be confusing at points; always take the trail that leads downward. After the footbridge over the narrow Bhandar River, the trail keeps descending and follows the valley's curve. As the trail nears the Likhu river, it crosses a stream on a wooden footbridge into the small village of **Tharo Khola** (1460m). From here the trail makes a sharp left and heads up the Likhu Valley along the left side of the river. A suspension bridge takes the trail to the right side of the river. After 250m another suspension bridge leads to **Kenja,** which is situated on a peninsula where the Likhu and Kenja Rivers meet. Kenja is blessed with a medical health unit (50m after the bridge, turn left before the corn field), the **New Everest Guest House,** and the **Sherpa Guest House**. Above Kenja, the trail gets very steep as it climbs up toward the Lamjura Pass. The first big town is **Chimbu** (2150m), where you can nurse your blisters at the **Hill Top Himalayan Lodge and Restaurant**. A short walk (30min.) uphill from Chimbu is **Sete,** where many trekkers spend the night to break the 2000m climb from Kenja to Lamjura. Another option is to spend the night in Kenja and climb the 2000m in one day. Spending the night in Lamjura (3380m) allows for better acclimation. In Sete, the **Sherpa Guide Lodge,** near the *stupa* at the far end of town, is well-kept. Sete is so popular, however, that those with the energy might want to go an hour farther to the **Maya Tamang Lodge,** in **Dagchu,** to escape the crowds.

Beyond Dagchu, the trail continues its steep climb toward the ridge, passing through the villages of **Goyom**, with its **Hotel Rhododendron**. Up next is **Lamjura** (3380m), the last town before the pass and home to the **Himalayan Lodge, Restaurant, and Bar**. Just before the pass, the trail levels off significantly and follows the ridge to the pass through a dense rhododendron forest. The **Lamjura Pass** (3530m) is the highest point between Jiri and Namche Bazaar. It is marked by a pile of stones and tangle of prayer flags that flap mercilessly in the wind. From the pass, the trail becomes very rocky and drops steeply into the Junbesi valley, passing through dense rhododendrons. Shortly after an all-wooden tea house, the forest clears and the trail descends more gently through groves and pastures. Ten minutes uphill of **Thagtokbhug's** center, **AM's Restaurant and Lodge**, which offers decent rooms for those who didn't end their day in Lamjura. At the heart of the village is a *stupa*, and next to it, an impressive *mani*-carved boulder. From here the trail runs along the left (northern) side of the valley and descends slowly toward **Junbesi**, a prosperous community full of *gompas*, *stupas*, and lodges. **Hotel Namaste**, 10min. uphill of Junbesi's center, has large private rooms with panoramic views of the valley, and cooking that features fresh, seasonal vegetables. On a clear day, usually the morning after a heavy rain, or most days Sept.-Nov., the peak of **Numbur Mountain** (6959m) can be seen. When in Junbesi, stand facing the river and then turn left (north); Numbur will peek over the small hill at the very top of the valley. Aside from its comfortable ledges, Junbesi has services and cultural activities that make it a good place to spend the night. A public telephone, healthpost, and post office are all found in town. Nearby monestaries—Stero (15min. uphill of Hotel Namaste; ask for directions), Thuptenchholing (1¼hr. north up the valley; follow the sign posts from the center of town), and Junbesi (in town)—all allow respectful visitors to attend the daily 5am meditation session. The large *stupa* on the edge of town nearest the river can be circled clockwise.

JUNBESI TO BUPSA. From Junbesi, the trail crosses the Junbesi River and gradually climbs up the next ridge. Just after the bridge is an important junction—the left (uphill) fork leads on to Namche Bazaar; the right (downhill) fork leads south to **Phaplu** where there's an airstrip (a half day's walk). Continuing on the left fork, the trail climbs through **Phurtyang**, home to the **Everest View Sherpa Lodge and Restaurant** and continues to the top of the ridge at **Salung**. On clear days, Salung is where you'll catch your first views of Everest. At the **Everest Panorama Lodge and Restaurant**, you can sit, sip tea, and take in the top of the world. After Salung, the trail drops down into the Ringmo Valley and moves in and out of shade. Crossing the footbridges and the Ringmo River by suspension bridge, the trail makes a short, steep climb up to **Ringmo**, a welcoming little village surrounded by apple orchards. The **Numbur Cheese Factory Lodge and Restaurant**, right next to the *stupa*, has a menu full of seasonal apples and *nak* (female yak) cheese and well-kept bathrooms with hot showers (Rs50). From Ringmo it's a short and at times steep and slippery ascent to the **Takshindo Pass**, but the hard work is rewarded by the spectacular views. Even on partly cloudy days the majestic Mera peaks (6100m) can be seen through the prayer flag-adorned gate at the top. On the far side of the pass, the trail passes through the village of **Takshindo**. Takshindo is home to an impressive monastery and a number of lodges, including the **Panorama Guest House**, overlooking the monastery. The trail drops steeply after Takshindo, down to the Dudh Kosi. This is a long descent, and many stop for the night halfway down in the village of **Nunthala**, also called Manidingma. The **Himalayan Trekkers Lodge** is centrally located. Try to get a room that faces the trail as it runs through town.

After Nunthala, the trail continues to drop, crossing the Dudh Kosi (1500m) via a long suspension bridge. Up a steep but short ascent is the Rai village of **Jubing;** not many people stay here, but if you do, the **Gorkhali Lodge** and the **Green Garden**

Lodge and Restaurant, with its extensive garden, are good choices. Beyond Jubing, the trail continues to climb, this time to **Chyoka.** Immediately past Chyoka is a series of forks in the trail—always take the right (uphill) fork, which should bring you directly over the top of the ridge rather than around it. This section of the trail is extremely rocky and steep at parts; after rains expect a slippery time, and on hotter days, take regular breaks and drink extra water as there is very little shade. On the far side of the ridge is **Khari Khola,** a large village with many lodges. The **Sagarmatha Khumbu Lodge and Restaurant** is run by a very friendly family and has decent rooms. Just downhill of the *stupa* is the Khari Khola market, held weekly on Tuesdays until 4:30pm. A new suspension bridge crosses the Khari Khola, after which the trail climbs very steeply up the next ridge to **Bupsa,** visible from below, a popular place to spend the night. During the high season, however, the town may be crowded and noisy. The **Hotel Yellow Top** and **Hotel International Trekker** both stand out for their friendly atmosphere and available amenities.

BUPSA TO NAMCHE BAZAAR. The trail from Bupsa climbs steadily upward, weaving in and out between ridges and valleys. After passing through Khari pass, a mere tea house on a rock outcropping, it begins to follow rolling terrain. The next major settlement is **Puiyan,** home to the **Bee Hive Lodge and Restaurant.** The chalet-style rooms here are extremely private. Charmingly, the restaurant offers popcorn as a side-dish for everything. An hour after Puiyan, the trail rounds another large ridge and Lukla comes into view two ridges over at the same altitude—you can sit here and watch the planes land. The trail drops steeply down toward the valley floor, crossing a small river at **Surkey.** The **Everest Trail Lodge** and **Yak and Yeti Cafe** are by far the best options in town. At the *mani* pile 15min. after Surkey, toward Namche, there's a fork in the trail; the right trail climbs steeply up to Lukla, the left one continues toward Namche Bazaar. Continuing along the left (lower) trail, the route climbs quickly up to **Chauri Kharka.** The **Danfe Lodge and Restaurant,** has a shower and some of the thickest mattresses on the trail. This is the last major settlement before the trail joins the crowded Lukla trail at **Cheplung.** To reach Namche, follow the directions for the "Lukla to Everest Base Camp" route. From Chauri Kharka and Cheplung, it usually takes two days to reach Namche Bazaar.

▩ LUKLA TO EVEREST BASE CAMP

LUKLA TO NAMCHE BAZAAR. Lukla, proud owner of Nepal's third-busiest airport, is a major tourist center with extensive facilities and equipment. Many people skip the Jiri-Lukla section of the trek and fly in and out of Lukla, making a (roughly) two-week trip up to Base Camp. If you do fly straight here from Kathmandu, it is important to take at least one day to acclimatize before heading out on the trail. All sorts of equipment are available for purchase or hire, and there are plenty of agencies competing to outfit trekkers with guides, porters, and woolen socks. The **health post** is up the hill from the airport, but it might be better just to wait for a flight to Kathmandu. All of the airlines flying between Lukla and Kathmandu (one-way US$91 plus tax) have ticketing offices in town. The **Economy Home** and **Himalaya Lodge** are just two of the many good lodges in town, with clean rooms, bathrooms, and hot showers. (Singles Rs50; doubles Rs100.) For those who are returning from the trail and want a quiet day, the **Lukla Monastery** is down the hill from the main path through town.

From Lukla, the trail drops steeply downhill from the end of town opposite the airport. The first big town on the trail is **Cheplung,** where the Jiri trail joins from below. The **Himalayan Rest House and Restaurant** is a large, clean place with western food, private rooms, and dorms. Most people opt to hike on to

EVEREST TREK: LUKLA TO EVEREST BASE CAMP

TRANSPORTATION: There is a very popular **airstrip** at **Lukla.** Unfortunately, flights depend solely on the weather, so reservations are sometimes cancelled and airline schedules change constantly. For the latest information and to make bookings, call RNAC in Kathmandu (☎220757); be sure to reserve well in advance of your intended departure; flights fill up quickly. If you are unsure about your return date, some airlines, including Gorkha Airlines, sell open-ended tickets that can be filled upon return to Lukla. However, don't assume you'll get a seat on the next flight out.

SERVICES: There are plenty of lodges and restaurants all the way to Gorak Shep. Namche Bazaar is a major administrative town and also the largest settlement on the way to Everest Base Camp. Anything you forgot to bring on the trek can be purchased here.

VILLAGE	ALTITUDE	TIME	GAIN/LOSS
Lukla	2860m	start	
Cheplung	2660m	45min.	-200m
Phakding	2650m	2hr.	
Benkar	2790m	45min.	
Chumoa	2780m	30min.	
Monju	2820m	20min.	320m/-160m
Jorsale	2810m	30min.	
Namche Bazaar	3450m	2½hr.	630m
Kyangsuma	3610m	1¼hr.	
Sanasa	3620m	15min.	
Tengboche	3860m	2¼hr.	760m/-350m
Deboche	3770m	20min.	
Pangboche	3860m	1¼hr.	
Shomare	3900m	45min.	
Orsho	3970m	30min.	
Pheriche	4220m	1¼hr.	450m/-90m
Tukla	4620m	1½hr.	
Lobuje	4940m	2hr.	720m
Gorak Shep	5160m	1¾hr.	220m
Everest Base Camp	5350m	2½hr.	190m

HIGHLIGHTS: Sherpa villages and high-altitude monasteries. Chances to rub elbows with world-class mountaineers as they prepare to tackle the world's highest mountain (Mar.-May). And, of course, the opportunity to gaze at some of the most rugged peaks on the planet: Mt. Everest, Lhotse, Makalu, Pumori, and Ama Dablam, among others.

FEATURES: The trek heads mainly through forested valleys until Pangboche, where the trail passes above tree line. Be aware that the trail out of Lukla goes through some areas where avalanches and floods have scarred the hillsides. Consequently, the location of the trail changes from time to time, mostly during the winter. Beyond Pangboche, the vegetation is mainly scrub brush and wildflowers until Tukla, where the trail climbs up the Khumbu glacier's terminal moraine and, at various points, onto the glacier itself. While on the trail, adhere to **leave-no-trace waste disposal practices** since almost no toilet facilities are available and human refuse has made many camping sights both unsightly and unsanitary. This means burning or carrying out any non-biodegradable waste, including toilet paper, and in the absence of toilet facilities, burying human waste away from water sources. **Altitude sickness** is a risk above 3000m, after Jorsale.

Ghat or Phakding on the first day. From Cheplung, the trail heads north up the valley, meandering to **Thado Kosi** (2500m), an attractive settlement on the river of the same name. Due to its prosperity, most lodges here are nice, but if you want to part ways with the crowds, stay for the night in **Saino Lodge and Restaurant.** You can still reach Namche the following day. Just around the next bend is the equally lovely (but more crowded) town of **Ghat** (2530m). Despite its decrepit sign in Thado Kosi, the **Lama Lodge and Restaurant,** at the far end of town, is clean and has a glass-walled restaurant. Next door is Ghat's active monastery and forest nursery, complete with *mani* boulders that rival the size of small houses. Here the trail threads in and out of boulder piles. Stay to the left of any stone with sacred adornment. Coming from either Lukla or Jiri, Ghat makes a good overnight stop: it's more pleasant and less crowded than Phakding, and still within a day's trek of Namche.

Phakding, 1hr. up the trail from Ghat, shows some of the first signs of increased tourist traffic on this part of the trail. Lodges are plentiful and large, offering western meals and various amenities. The town extends along the trail and across the river; if you do choose to stay here, the higher parts of town (across the river) are usually less crowded. One of the first buildings in town, the **See You Lodge and Restaurant** greets you with chocolate cake. The **Tashi Taki Lodge and Restaurant,** with seat toilets (Rs50 per bed), and the **Namaste Lodge** (Rs50 per bed) are both good options in central Phakding. To really escape the crowds, the **Kongde Peak Guest House and Restaurant** (Rs50-100 per bed) is a 10min. walk past Phakding on the opposite side of the bridge. The trail continues up the opposite (west) side of the river to **Benkar,** a small village with a small waterfall. To escape the crowds, stay directly above the waterfall at the **Waterfall View Lodge.** Otherwise, the **Benkar Gastehaus** and the **Yak and Yeti Lodge and Restaurant** are larger, comfortable options. A long suspension bridge leads to the east side of the Dudh Kosi and the village of Chumoa. The **Riverside Lodge and Restaurant,** at the far end of town, is one of the better lodges, but its real use is as a pit-stop for acclimatization. A short way up the trail is **Monju,** the liveliest of the villages between Phakding and Namche. It has a small monastery and a few good lodges, including the **Mount Kailash Lodge and Restaurant.** Make sure to get a room facing the Dudh Kosi for good valley views. Immediately past Monju, still on the river's east side, is the Jorsale entrance to **Sagarmatha National Park.** You must present your passport and pay (or prove you have already paid) the Rs1000 entrance fee, good for a single entry. **Jorsale** itself is located after a steep descent and another suspension bridge. Stop in at the **Everest Guest House** to rest before pushing up the steep ascent to Namche. Jorsale is the last settlement before Namche, so if you are feeling ill, consider spending the night here to recuperate. A temporary wooden footbridge that was put in place when work began on the new suspension bridge in 1998, leads out of Jorsale to the east bank of the Dudh Kosi. Trekkers must then pick their path between waterfall run-offs and water pools. Farther along, a high, wooden suspension bridge leads over the junction of

IN RECENT NEWS

50-YEAR EVEREST JUBILEE

In May of 2003, enormous festivities were held in Nepal to honor well-known climbers like Sir Edmund Hillary, the first non-Nepali to successfully summit Mount Everest. Sir Hillary, along with the late Tenzig Norgay Sherpa, reached the world's highest peak on May 29, 1953. His achievement was an amazing feat of sportsmanship that triggered a boom in trekking expeditions, currently a great source of wealth for Nepal. Each year, starry-eyed mountaineers—amateur and professional alike—generate millions in tourist-sector revenue as they endeavor to do as Hillary did so many years ago.

In honor of both his ground-breaking achievement and its subsequent effects on Nepal, Sir Hillary was granted Nepalese citizenship during the weekend festivities. In addition to Hillary, other famous mountaineers such as Junko Tabei and Reinhold Messner received the royal treatment. Tabei was the first woman to climb Mount Everest, while Messner was the first to successfully summit without the aid of bottled oxygen. The celebrations culminated in a parade from New Road to Durbar Square of bands, trekkers, students, and Nepali officials. Organized by Ang Tshering Sherpa, president of the Nepal Mountaineering Association (NMA), the festival was designed to celebrate both monumental heroes and the ordinary tourist to Nepal, both of whom the NMA maintains aid the country's development and bring it prosperity.

the Bhote Kosi and Dudh Kosi. The ascent to Namche from this point takes several hours. The trail gets much steeper as it switchbacks its way up the hill. Take this hill quite slowly, drink lots of water, and take multiple breaks.

Namche Bazaar is a sizable administrative center, offering more services than you're ever likely to need—currency exchange, bookstore, bakery, equipment shops, souvenirs, and a dentist. It also offers an excellent showcase of Sherpa culture, since it is their regional capital. The town itself sits between two ridges, taking a tiered, U-shaped form. The trail from Lukla enters town from one end of the U. The trail up the Bhote Kosi valley to Thame leaves Namche from the other end of the U, while the trail towards Everest Base Camp via Tengboche leaves from the mountain saddle to left of the U's curve, near the military compound. The interior of Namche is a relatively mysterious maze of paths and alleyways, but most shops and services are in the immediate center and can be found by following the numerous signs. Within the military compound is the **Saharmatha National Park Visitor's Center,** open daily except Saturday. The **bazaar** is held all day Saturday just above where the trail from Lukla enters town. Although there is a healthpost in Namche, for emergencies head to the **Khunde Hospital** (2-3hr. trek uphill, behind Namche Bazaar; open 6 days per week and 24hr. for emergencies). There are **police** and **military check-points,** both on the upper level of the left leg, and a **post office,** where you can finally send off those Everest postcards.

Internet cafes offer satellite email for Rs15 per min. and phone calls for Rs200 per min. **Laundry** is done menu-style (Rs80 per pair of pants, Rs50 per shirt) at most lodges and in numerous shops around town. The **Khumbu Lodge** (☎40054), in central Namche, and the **Moon Light Lodge** (☎40088), on the top level of the U's curve, stand out among the bevy of excellent lodges (Rs100 per bed). At the **Mt. Everest Bakery,** donuts can alleviate the monotony of breakfast *chapati*. Namche Bazaar is the usual place to spend a day getting acclimated. During this day, stop by the **Cafe Danphe Bar,** and read the walls, t-shirts, and occasional pair of underwear covered in messages from those who have come before. When not reading, play a game of pool (Rs50), check your email, or have a drink at the bar.

NAMCHE BAZAAR TO DINGBOCHE. The trail from Namche heads up (northeast) past the military compound and along the right side of the hill. On clear days, the area just around the first ridge outside of town provides the best views of Everest. Some of the first flat trail since Lukla leads to **Kyangsuma,** a tiny settlement with the **Ama Dablam Lodge and Restaurant,** (Rs50 per bed). The trail stays fairly level beyond Kyangsuma, leading to **Sanasa** a short distance away, where the souvenir stalls will tempt you to weigh yourself down with junk. Here the trail to Gokyo breaks away to the left. The **Khumbila Lodge and Restaurant,** in Sanasa, is the last lodge before Tengboche, so stop here if you feel unfit to make a long ascent. Beyond Sanasa, the trail heads downhill toward the Dudh Kosi, crossing the river on a suspension bridge at 3230m. From here it's a 1-2hr. climb up the ridge to **Tengboche,** which is much smaller than Namche and situated on a ledge in the midst of the Khumbu Valley. This ascent should be taken slowly, just like the one to Namche, especially if you have a headache or did not spend a day acclimating in Namche. The stately **Tengboche Monastery** dominates the Tengboche townscape, as well as its daily goings-on. Meditation takes place daily at 6am and 3pm, and is open to visitors; donations are highly recommended. At other times, visitors are allowed to quietly tour the monastery on their own and visit Sacred Land Information Center for a 30min. film on the monastery (Rs100 per person for the film; center open daily Sept.-May 7am-6pm with varying hours for lower season months). The **Tashi Delek Lodge,** run by an enthusiastic family, is clean and has hot showers (dorm Rs60; room Rs150; showers Rs150). While

Tengboche is a good place to stay for culture and acclimation, high-season tourists overcrowd the lodge and sanitation facilities. If this is the case when you arrive, continue on to Debourne.

Dropping off Tengboche's edge, the trail leads down through lush forest to **Deboche**, a quiet, attractive village away from the crowds of Tengboche. The **Ama Dablam Garden Lodge**, set back off the trail on the left, has large private rooms. A gradual descent leads to a high, fixed bridge that crosses the Imja Kosi. On the far side of the river the terrain is more arid, and as the trail climbs, the vegetation becomes increasingly sparse and more alpine. At the fork, the upper trail leads to upper Pangboche and the Pangboche Monastery. The lower trail leads shortly to lower **Pangboche**, a good (though long) first day's stop after Namche. The **Ama Dablam Lodge** has clean rooms and excellent views of its namesake.

Beyond lower Pangboche, the trail passes through **Shomare**, a small Sherpa settlement. The **Pasang Lodge and Restaurant** has decent accommodations, although most people either stay in Pangboche or continue on to Dingboche or Pheriche. Above Shomare, the trail follows the river to a large boulder-strewn meadow and the tiny "village" of **Orsho**. At a small *mani*-boulder roughly 200m after Orsho, the trail splits—the right fork drops down and crosses the river, then heads up to Dingboche; the left trail heads directly uphill to Pheriche. The split is hard to see. Both trails lead to base camp, but the right trail is more scenic (providing views of Amai Dablam and Island Park) and is a better way to get acclimatized. After crossing the river, the right fork becomes increasingly sandy and climbs steeply uphill to **Dingboche** (4410m). The town is spread across a wind-swept shelf immediately next to, and almost at the same height as, the Imja Kosi. Because of its altitude, Dingboche is a great place to spend a day acclimatizing, and there are a number of good short hikes to fill the time. Continuing on the trail from Tengboche, the village of Chukhung is a 2-3hr. trek and the Island Peak Base Camp is a 4-5hr. trek. The **Himalaya Hotel**, on the left halfway through the village, is open all year and has small, private rooms and dingy dorms. There are other lodges, but this far along the trail many close during the low season. If you prefer to head to Pheriche (4243m), take the left fork uphill along the ridge, crossing the Khumu Khola just before **Pheriche**, which stretches along the side of the river and is more protected than Dingboche. The **Himalayan Rescue Association** runs an altitude sickness clinic from Apr.-May and from Oct.-Nov. The clinic is the best medical facility in the area. The **Himalayan Lodge and Pumori Lodge** in Pheriche are good places to stay. From Pheriche, the trail continues up the valley, gradually getting steeper until it meets the trail (from Dingboche) just before Tukla.

DINGBOCHE TO GORAK SHEP. From central Dingboche, the trail doubles back along a ridge above the town, ascending to a medium-sized *stupa*. From there it follows the valley's wide, upper ridge and at one point goes through several abandoned pastures. At certain points you can look down at Pheriche and the lower valley. There's a short, steep descent to a glacial run-off stream just before **Tukla**, sometimes known as Duglha. Here, the lower trail from Pheriche joins the trail from Dingboche. Tukla, a two-building town, is at the bottom edge of the Khumbu glacier's enormous terminal moraine, the steep rocky hill looming over the settlement. This is a good place to stop for a while and check for altitude sickness—if you're feeling any symptoms, either stay here or descend. The **Yak Lodge** is the nicer of the two places to stay here, but it closes for the off-season. If rooms at the Yak Lodge are unavailable, try the **Pumori Lodge and Hotel Restaurant,** the other lodge and building in the settlement. Immediately past Tukla, the trail begins to climb the moraine. The going is steep and rocky, and is arguably some of the hardest trekking on this route. Many a trekker has had to give up after trying to take it too fast—breaks are absolutely necessary between Jiri and Base

Camp because of the altitude. Also, by this point, the trail is completely surrounded with the highest peaks on earth. Be sure to suspend concentrating on where the next footfall should go and take in Taweche, Lobuche, Ama Dablam, Nuptse, Cholotse, Pokalde, Kongma Tse, Chukhung, and Pumori. Just before the top of the moraine, the trail veers to the left and flattens out substantially. On this plateau are roughly 20 *mani*-piles for those, foreigner and sherpa alike, who have died on Everest and nearby summits. From here, the trail follows the left side of the glacier at a much flatter grade to **Lobuche** (4940m), a small town at the base of East Lobuche Peak. Although there is extensive development on several lodges, the **Alpine Inn** currently provides the nicest facilities. Only dorms are available at Rs60 per bed. Many people spend a miserable night adjusting to the altitude and then push on to Gorak Shep and Base Camp; toward the top, people tend to rush to see the sights in misery and then head back down as quickly as possible. Some people make this their highest overnight camp and make daytrips from here to Kala Pattar and Base Camp. This means a *very* early start if you plan to be on top of Kala Pattar in time for sunrise. However, with the proper acclimatization and rest days, trekking above 5000m does not have to be painful or hurried. If you are feeling well in Lobuche, one of the best ideas is to spend the night here, leaving early (perhaps 5:30am) to eat breakfast in Gorak Shep. Then make the round trip to Base Camp, taking only a daypack, and spend the night in Gorak Shep. The next morning leave early to be on Kala Pattar for sunrise and start descending immediately afterward. From Lobuche, the trail continues along the left side of the glacier. When the valley dead-ends, veer up toward the left valley wall to the flat but rocky edge of the glacier. After dodging in and out of boulder-fitted valleys, the trail descends to **Gorak Shep.** This tiny settlement on a sand flat next to the glacier is the highest point of the trek where you can spend the night. The **Snow Land Inn,** has the best food and lodging, as well as a choice of private (Rs250) or dormitory (Rs60) rooms.

GORAK SHEP TO EVEREST BASE CAMP/KALA PATTAR.

From Gorak Shep, most people continue either to Kala Pattar, the large brown hill that looms above the village with views of Everest and the Khumbu Glacier Valley, or to Everest Base Camp, the launching point for summit expeditions. It is possible to visit both in one very long day (10-12hr.).

The trail to **Kala Pattar** (5545m) is fairly straightforward, starting from the opposite side of the sand flat, and it can be seen switchbacking up the initial ascent. It takes 1-2hr. to reach the summit from Gorak Shep. The most popular time to visit Kala Pattar is at sunrise. This is when the sky is the clearest and the sun peaking out from behind Everest, Nuptse, and Lhotse, provides the best views.

The **Everest Base Camp** (5350m) trail is less well-defined. From the Snow Land Inn, follow the sand-flat up the glacial valley away from Lobuche. The trail begins at the memorial *mani*-pile. After several extremely rocky switchbacks, the trail stays on top of the glacier's immediate left ridge. When the ridge ends, descend the steep, loose rock slope to the glacier itself. Here is where the trail can sometimes be too faint to follow. In general, head up the valley away from Gorak Shep, aiming for the border between ice and rock. If possible, follow another group, be it porters or expedition members, rather than forging your own route across the glacier. The route is slippery from loose rocks and wet from glacial melt.

Despite the hype, Base Camp is less than overwhelming. From June to March, it consists of little more than stone chimneys, tangled prayer flags, and garbage. In fact, due to icy conditions and frequent avalanches, it is recommended that trekkers not go to Base Camp in Dec. and Jan. Furthermore, in July the glacier has melted too much to provide the necessary support for trekkers. It is only during the climbing season (Apr.-May) that Base Camp is in full bloom with huge tents and would-be summiteers. That is when a visit is most fruitful. Although Everest itself isn't visible from Base Camp, the chance to talk with expedition members (and see the spectacle) makes it worthwhile.

RETURNING FROM GORAK SHEP. Trekkers can get down from Gorak Shep very quickly. It's a 4hr. trek to Pheriche, 6½hr. to Tengboche, or 9hr. to Namche. Namche to Lukla is usually done in one 8hr. day, and most people try to arrive in Lukla in time for the airline offices' afternoon hours (3-4pm). Those going back to Jiri usually go down at about the same pace as they came up.

TREKKING IN OTHER REGIONS OF NEPAL

For information on treks through regions beyond the Classic Three, you'll have to go beyond this book. Consult a trekking company in Kathmandu (see p. 811) or in your home country. Some of the popular non-Classic Three treks include:

Lamjung. Starting in Dumre, this route takes trekkers up a minor peak, Rambrong (4400m), for fantastic views of the east end of the Annapurna massif.

Manaslu Circuit. The high point and highlight of this trip, starting in Gorkha, is the Larkya La Pass (5153m). Trekking permits cost US$90 per week Sept-.Nov. and US$75 per week Dec.-Aug.

Dhaulagiri Circuit. Starting from Beni, this trip around the world's seventh-highest peak takes you over two 5000m+ passes.

Dolpo and Mustang. An exploration of two remote and rugged regions north of Kagbeni where the awesome mountain scenery competes for attention with living vestiges of ancient cultures. Trekking permits cost US$70 per day, and you must be accompanied by an environmental officer and a registered trekking company.

Kanchenjunga Base Camp. Kanchenjunga's south face is the centerpiece of one of the planet's most awesome mountain vistas. Treks start from Tumlingtar or Taplejung. Trekking permits cost US$10 per week, and you must go with a registered trekking agency.

Simikhot to Kailash. Trek into the far northwest of Nepal, and cross the border into Tibet to join pilgrims paying their respects to holy Mt. Kailash and Manasarovar Lake.

RAFTING IN NEPAL

Whitewater rafting in Nepal presents a fantastic opportunity for ecotourism and athletic adventure. It is possible to cover tremendous distances while rafting, and traveling by water reveals spectacular views of Nepal's many gorges. Aside from the sightseeing benefits, whitewater rafting is also an excellent way to bond with fellow travelers and to engage in a challenging and thrilling form of teamwork.

The typical large group rafting schedule is quite rigorous. After a 7am wake up call and a quick breakfast, rafters help to pack up camp, inflate rafts, and sort safety equipment. Mornings and afternoons both consist of 3-4 hours of rafting, with a break around noon for lunch. Some rafting trips end with a social gathering at a camping site or at a nearby bar, but rafters typically hit the sack early. Beginning rafters can be easily integrated into rafting expeditions, although some expeditions may require a certain level of physical fitness.

Rafters may choose between two different kinds of rafting styles. In an oar frame raft, the guide does most of the rowing. In the more common paddle raft, guides navigate while calling out instructions to the entire crew. Paddle rafting requires extensive teamwork.

WHEN TO GO

The peak seasons for whitewater rafting in Nepal are from late September to late November and from March to late April. Rivers are full, but not as powerful as they are in summer, and the temperature is more pleasant.

During the monsoon, May to July, rivers swell and are at their most hazardous. In some places rivers expand to 10 times their regular size. When rivers reach flood levels, they are considered unnavigable and tour companies are not permitted to schedule trips. Since Nepal has fewer tourists during the summertime, organized trips may be canceled at the last minute. It is also likely that rafters will have to disembark and walk past a rapid rather than paddling through.

Rafting from December to February is unpleasant and can put rafters at risk of hypothermia. It is possible to rent a wet suit and attempt to raft during this period, but guides and tourist agencies are often unwilling to travel with anyone but the most experienced of rafters.

ORGANIZED TOURS

All rafting in Nepal must be done on organized tours. Among the dozens of companies in Kathmandu offering rafting expeditions, many are understaffed; try to stick with the major firms. Travel agencies that do not specialize in whitewater rafting often inflate prices and provide rafters with inadequate information about the trip. Companies that specialize exclusively in rafting tend to employ an experienced staff that can provide you with complete information about tours. Still, be sure to meet with your guide beforehand.

You can usually cancel your spot on a rafting trip for a small fee with a few days notice. Most companies do not provide refunds for missed trips, including oversleeping the early departure hour.

More extensive rafting trips have team meetings the night before departure that provide an overview of the trip. If you are going for a short trip, you can request such a debriefing at the time of payment. Most rafting companies provide a written statement of company policy and a list of suggested supplies for rafters.

SAFETY

All rafting trips should include at least two rafts and two rescue kayakers. Three rafts are ideal for the highest grade rapids. Inquire extensively about the quality of equipment aboard the raft and the quality of the raft itself. Rafts should have a self-bailing design and should not be loaded with more than 8 paddlers per 16ft. raft. Helmets and life jackets should be up to international standards, and every boat should carry first aid kits. Also inquire about the company's private transport to the rafting site itself. You are safer whitewater rafting than riding on a poorly-driven night bus. Food hygiene is also a major concern for the major rafting companies, who should cater their menus to foreign stomachs.

Perhaps the most important aspect of your safety hinges on the quality of your guide. Although you might feel more comfortable with a guide that speaks your language, Nepali guides can be just as qualified (if not more so) to navigate the rivers of their homeland. Ask to see training certifications for first aid and CPR.

PACKING AND EQUIPMENT

The rafting company should provide all specialized whitewater rafting equipment, including life jackets, helmets, water-proof undershirts, plastic and metal paddles, and waterproof containers. Be sure to consult with your guide on what to pack. During most months, only light clothing and waterproof sandals with heel straps are needed. Shorts and thermal tops for sleeping are also recommended. Some companies may require sleeping bags and tents, but these items are often provided. You may also wish to pack sunscreen, a flashlight (torch), a towel, toiletries, a swimsuit, and a water bottle.

Rafting expeditions provide few opportunities for spending, unless you stop to camp at a resort (where alcohol and culinary treats are available). Three meals a day are also often provided, along with occasional snacks on the river. Meals accommodate both vegetarians and non-vegetarians. Vegans should consult the travel agency ahead of time to research suitable alternatives.

For long trips, pack lightly as your belongings may have to travel in the raft with you. Longer rafting trips provide plastic bags to protect backpacks from moisture, but a certain amount of exposure is unavoidable. Keep necessary valuables in a waterproof cylinder. It is advisable to leave valuables and unnecessary items in storage in Kathmandu. Short trips usually have no limit on backpack size, because the pack travels in the bus alongside the rafts.

DIFFICULTY LEVELS

River grades are highly subjective and often manipulated by tourist guides to meet the desires of the travelers. However, the international grading scale is as follows:

Grade I: No rapids. Water has downstream currents, but is completely flat.

Grade II: Small rapids. Occasional white-caps.

Grade III: Sizable rapids. Average grade for a rafting trip.

Grade IV: Exhilarating for both experienced and non-experienced rafters. Almost always involves high decibel screaming, and multi-lingual cursing.

Grade V: Enormous, powerful rapids easily capable of capsizing a raft. The absolute limit for the non-professional.

Grade VI: Impassable. You will have to bank and walk around it.

Anything Grade III or above requires an experienced guide.

RAFTING NEPAL

RAFTING COMPANIES

Company specializing in rafting expeditions offer the fairest prices, the greatest availability of trips, and the highest safety standards. The following companies are the major rafting companies in Kathmandu; several have branches in Pokhara. Prices are comparable—although rates fluctuate based on the demand, season, and your bargaining skills. For trips to: **Karnali** (US$400); **Sun Kosi** (US$350); **Marsyangdi** (US$200); **Bhote Kosi** (US$70); **Kali Gandaki** (US$100). When negotiating a trip, make sure to ask about how many spots are left before the trip can run. Especially during low season, rafting trips are often cancelled due to insufficient passengers. There are usually several options for luxury accommodations, with simple, standard, and deluxe packages (of safari tenting). It is appropriate to ask about the nationality, credentials, and experience of the guides assigned to your trip. Try to book longer trips ahead of time by email or phone; shorter trips may be booked as late as 5pm on the evening before departure.

Ultimate Descents Nepal, J.P. School, Thamel (☎ 4419295 or 4426329; fax 4411933; www.udnepal.com), 100m north of Kathmandu Guest House next to Northfield Cafe. With dazzling brochures, photo gallery, and obliging staff, this company is a favorite among fun-loving, young rafters. Choose among Karnali, Kali Gandaki, Sun Kosi, Tamur, and Marsyangdi tours. Check out the board on the street for tentative departure dates. Current prices are always listed on the website. The company also runs a 4-day kayaking clinic on the Seti River. Open daily 9am-9pm.

Ultimate Rivers, J.P. School, Thamel (☎ 4439526 or 4429566; info@urnepal.wlink.com.np), next door to Kathmandu Guest House and Pilgrims Book Store. This premiere rafting company's talented and spirited Nepali guides contribute to its popularity. Ask to see their descriptions of each river and their extensive collection of photographs. Open daily 9am-7pm.

Shiva's River Adventure Ltd., J.P. School, Thamel (☎ 4417685, 4414167, or 4412972; fax 4414167), 150m north and down the curve to the left of Kathmandu Guest House; walk up the stairs on the right before Hotel Marsyangdi. This company is not as well-known nor as well-established as the others, but it offers a wide selection of trips (Trisuli, Buri Gandaki, Bhote Kosi, Sun Kosi, Kali Gandaki, Tamur, Karnali) for slightly lower prices. Open daily 9am-7pm.

N.K.'s River Experience Ltd., Freak Street (☎ 4223170, 4240318, or 4240876; www.nksriver.com), across the street from Monumental Paradise. Well-established and continually successful, despite its location in the languishing Freak Street area. Founded in 1991, its office provides extensive information and attentive assistance. Open daily 9am-7pm, flexible hours.

OTHER RESOURCES ON RAFTING IN NEPAL

www.udnepal.com
www.raftnepal.com
www.visitnepal.com/mountainriver
www.go2nepal.com
www.travel-nepal.com/rafting.html
www.raftingassociation.org.np
www.raftnepal.org
www.nepalvista.com/travel/rafting.html

A definitive resource (though out of print, with limited availability) for the white-water-rafter in Nepal is *Whitewater Nepal: A Rivers Guidebook for Rafting & Kayaking,* by Peter Knowles. Menasha Ridge Press, 1997.

RIVERS

BHOTE KOSI

AT A GLANCE	
LENGTH: 2 days **DEPARTURE POINT:** Kathmandu **GRADE:** Fall, III to V; Spring, III to IV	**RAPIDS:** Gerbil in the Plumbing, Frog in a Blender, ExLax, The Great Wall, Liquid Bliss, Dazed and Confused

By far the most popular trip among tourists, Bhote Kosi brings rafters through mountainside villages 30km from the border with Tibet. The trip begins with a 3hr. bus trip out of the Kathmandu Valley, where, on clear days, the Himalayas may be visible from high points on the road. The rafting route begins with almost 6km of non-stop rapid drops followed by an ominously calm flat 1km stretch towards a dam. Rafters face 50m of breathtaking rapids where the pressure built up in the dam is released. The second day of Bhote Kosi involves five hours of rigorous Grade III and IV rapids. Here guides bank boats to check out the conditions for the Frog in the Blender, the climax of the trip. After several jarring drops, rocky sides, and petrifying plummets, the rapid eventually finishes into an unruffled pool.

During the trip, villagers will line the banks and the suspension bridges above the river marveling at rafters. Many villages are built along the calmer parts of the river. In addition, several tent resorts in the area, such as the Bhote Kosi Riverside Resort, provide safari tents, toilets, showers, bar, and gorgeous views of the river. Another less lavish option is **The Last Resort,** home to the second-highest bungee jump in the world (160m) and Nepal's longest bridge. The resort also has offices in Thamel. (☎4439525; www.tlr-nepal.com. Bungee and canyoning US$115; bungee and rafting US$115; canyoning and rafting US$80; biking and rafting US$60; biking and canyoning US$60. First bungee jump US$70, 2nd jump US$20.)

KARNALI

AT A GLANCE	
LENGTH: 10-12 days **DEPARTURE POINT:** Kathmandu **GRADE:** Fall, III to IV; Spring, III	**RAPIDS:** Freight Train; Touching the Void; Snapshot; Flip 'n' Strip; Juicer; Inversion; Jailhouse Rock; Humans for Lunch; Shake, Rattle & Roll; Sweetness and Light

Karnali flows through Himalayan gorges, jungles, canyons, and the Bardiya National Park, in an area only recently opened up to the tourist industry. A combination of massive overland journey and over a week of rafting, this trip enables you to explore an immense portion of Nepal's wilderness-covered west. One part of Karnali involves a 7km stretch of rapids, plunging deep into a colossal gorge. Karnali flows through the least developed areas of Nepal and, thus, offers the best opportunity to encounter wild animals, including the Royal Bengal Tiger.

The trip begins with an 18hr. bus ride up through remote areas of Nepal to the mouth of the river. Rafters have a day to rest at the first forest campsite before heading out to some enormous rapids, often flooded by snow melt-off and jungle storms. The second half has no major rapids, and rafters will be able to enjoy the scenery, including freshwater dolphins and gharial crocodiles. Some companies also offer kayaks or canyon jumping. The trip ends at the town of Chisopani. Some Karnali trips including trekking in the Bardiya National Park and fishing.

KALI GANDAKI

AT A GLANCE

LENGTH: 3-4 days **DEPARTURE POINT:** Pokhara **GRADE:** Fall, III to IV+; Spring, III to IV	**RAPIDS:** Little Brother; Big Brother; Wake and Bake; Good Morning Cobra; Walk in the Dark

Featuring one of the deepest gorges in the world, Kali Gandaki races south between the Dhaulagiri and Annapurna ranges. Named after the Hindu goddess of death and destruction, this valley used to be a popular route for trade with Tibet. Now it is mainly a trekking region, with opportunities for magnificent whitewater rafting. It is the most popular mid-length trip among foreign tourists. The trip begins with a 3hr. bus ride West from Pokhara to Baglung. The river consists of a good amount of both calm water and intimidating rapids. In good weather, you may have an all-day view of the Annapurna Range. Wildlife, sandy beaches, and waterfalls are a constant treat. Many small temples have been constructed along the banks. You might pass sights of holy bathing and cremation.

TRISULI

AT A GLANCE

LENGTH: 1-2 days **DEPARTURE POINT:** Kathmandu **GRADE:** Year round, III+, except June-Sept., IV+	**RAPIDS:** Snell's Nose; Monkey; Teen Devi; Lady's Delight; Upset; Surprise; Pinball (Mugling)

Trisuli is a favorite beginner's river, with placid waters and scenic basins during all but monsoon season, when it is overwhelmed by powerful runoffs. The river starts in a narrow valley near Bhareni, and the gorges slowly expand over the hours until the river opens up near Gai Ghat into the lowlands surrounding Royal Chitwan National Park. The trip begins with a 2hr. bus ride to the rapids. The highlight of the overnight trip is the gorgeous campsite at Royal Beach, an Eden of white sand in the jungle. Many combine this trip with a day in the National Park.

SUN KOSI

AT A GLANCE

LENGTH: 8-9 days **DEPARTURE POINT:** Kathmandu **GRADE:** Fall, III+ to V-; Spring, III to IV+	**RAPIDS:** Meat Grinder; Punch & Judy; Valentino; High Anxiety; Jaws; El Wasto; Rakshi Roller; Dead Man's Eddy; Big Dipper

At 270km, Sun Kosi is the longest stretch of navigable water that Nepal has to offer. The river begins approximately 2hr. outside of Kathmandu in Dolalghat. Spanning from the Tibetan border to the lowlands of Northern India, this ride offers an impressive variety of remote ecological sights. The first days are calm, with Grade II and III waters making up most of the route. The most powerful rapids are mid-journey, with a final placid stretch through the largest river in Nepal, the Sapta Kosi. Highlights include speedy descents past majestic canyon rock formations. Some choose to end the trip with a long trek from the Arun Valley to Everest Base Camp. To return to Kathmandu, most companies offer either a 17hr. overnight bus or a 2hr. drive and 1hr. flight.

APPENDIX

TEMPERATURE CHART (LOW/HIGH)

CITY	JANUARY		APRIL		JULY		OCTOBER		MONSOON	BESTTIME
	°C	°F	°C	°F	°C	°F	°C	°F		
Calcutta	12/26	54/79	23/35	73/95	25/32	77/90	23/29	73/84	June-Sept.	Nov.-Mar.
Chennai	20/29	68/84	23/34	73/93	25/36	77/91	24/32	75/90	Oct.-Dec.	Dec.-Mar.
Cochin	23/31	73/88	26/31	78/88	24/29	75/84	24/29	75/84	May-Aug.	Dec.-Mar.
Darjeeling	3/9	37/48	9/17	48/63	15/19	59/66	11/19	52/66	June-Sept.	Apr.-June; Oct.-Nov.
Delhi	7/21	45/70	17/32	63/90	26/39	78/102	16/35	61/95	June-Sept.	Nov.-Mar.
Guwahati, Assam	10/23	50/73	18/32	64/90	25/32	77/90	22/27	72/80	Apr.-Sept.	Oct.-Mar.
Hyderabad	16/29	1/84	24/36	75/97	22/31	72/88	19/30	61/86	June.-Sept.	Nov.-Feb.
Jaipur	8/22	42/72	19/33	61/92	26/35	78/95	15/31	59/87	July-Aug.	Nov.-Mar.
Kathmandu	2/18	36/64	12/28	54/82	20/29	68/84	13/27	55/80	June-Aug.	Oct.-Nov.
Mumbai	16/31	61/87	23/32	73/90	25/29	77/84	23/32	73/90	June-Aug	Nov.-Mar.
Panjim, Goa	19/31	66/87	23/32	73/90	24/28	75/82	21/32	70/90	June-Aug.	Dec.-Mar.
Shimla	3/9	37/48	10/17	50/63	15/21	59/70	8/19	42/61	July-Sept.	Apr.-July; Oct.-Nov.
Srinagar, Kashmir	3/4	37/39	7/20	45/68	17/31	63/87	6/22	42/72	None	Mar.-Sept.

GLOSSARY

adivasi: indigenous peoples of India
Agni: Hindu god of fire, messenger of the gods
ahimsa: non-violence
AIADMK: All-India Anna Dravida Munnetra Kazhagam, regional party in Tamil Nadu
air-cooling: low-budget air-conditioning—a fan blows air over the surface of water
Allah: literally, "the God," to Muslims
AMS: Acute Mountain Sickness
arati: Hindu candlelight ritual ceremony
artha: material wealth, one of the four goals of a Hindu's life (and most other people's, too)
ashram: hermitage for Hindu sages and their students
ASI: Archaeological Survey of India
atman: Hindu concept of individual soul, the breath of Brahman
attar: alcohol-free perfume
auto-rickshaw: three-wheeled, fire-breathing vehicle with the engine of a scooter and the soul of a demon
Avalokitesvara: Bodhisattva of Compassion
avatar: incarnation of a Hindu god on earth
ayurveda: ancient Indian system of medicine
azan: Muslim call to prayer, usually given from a minaret; Islamic alarm-call
bahal: Newari houses or monasteries forming a quadrangle with a central courtyard
baksheesh: tip, donation, bribe, or all of these at once
bagh: garden
ban: forest
bandh: general strike, often involves shop closings and transportation difficulties
basti: Jain temple
bazaar: market area of a town, good place to buy plastic buckets and spare tires

Bhagavad Gita: "Song of the Lord," philosophical scripture sung to Arjuna by the god Krishna; part of the *Mahabharata*
bhajan: Hindu devotional song
bhakti: personal, emotional devotion to a Hindu deity
bhangra: Punjabi folk music
Bharat: the Sanskrit word for India
bhavan: office or building
bidi: small cigarette made from a rolled-up tobacco leaf
bindi: forehead mark, worn mostly by Hindu women; symbolizes the third, all-seeing eye
BJP: Bharatiya Janata Party (Indian People's Party), the major Hindu nationalist party, symbolized by a lotus
bodhisattva: would-be Buddha who postpones his own enlightenment to help others
Bon: pre-Buddhist, animist religion of Tibet
Brahma: the Creator in the Hindu trinity
Brahman: the universal soul or spirit, embodied by Brahma
brahmin: member of the hereditary priesthood; highest of the four Hindu *varnas*
Buddha: Enlightened One
bugyal: high meadow above the treeline
cantonment: former British military district
caste: Hindu group that practices a hereditary occupation, has a definite ritual status, and marries within the group
chador: shawl
chaitya: Buddhist prayer hall or miniature stupa
chakra: Wheel of the Law in Buddhism; Vishnu's discus weapon in Hinduism
chalo: let's go
chappals: leather sandals
charbagh: traditional Mughal garden form, used particularly in tombs.
chattri: cenotaph; cremation monument
chillum: mouthpiece of a *hookah*; a pipe use to smoke *ganja*
chorten: Tibetan Buddhist memorial shrine
chowk (chauk): market area or square
chowkidar: watchman
coir: woven coconut fibers
communalism: religious prejudice, especially between Hindus and Muslims
Congress (I): party that grew from the Indian National Congress that pushed for Indian Independence; party of Jawaharlal Nehru and Indira Gandhi; "I" is for "Indira"
crore: 10 million, written 1,00,00,000
dacoit: armed bandit
Dalit: currently preferred term for former "Untouchables"
darshan: "seeing" a Hindu deity through his or her image
deodar: tall Indian cedar tree
dhaba: roadside food stand
dham: place, often a sacred site
dharamsala: resthouse for Hindu pilgrims
dharma: system of morality and way of life or religion (Hindu or Buddhist); one's duty and station in life
dhobi: washerman or -woman
dhoti: *lungi* with folds of cloth between the wearer's legs
dhow: boat of Arab origins
diwan-i-am: hall of public audience
diwan-i-khas: hall of private audience
DMK: Dravida Munnetra Kazhagam, regional party in Tamil Nadu
dorje: Tibetan Buddhist thunderbolt symbol
dowry: money or gifts given by a bride's parents to the son-in-law's as part of a marriage agreement; officially illegal but still practiced
dun: valley
dupatta: scarf warn as part of a *salwar kameez.*
durbar: royal palace or court
Durga: Hindu goddess who slayed the buffalo demon Mahisha
eve-teasing: cat-calling, sexual harassment
fakir: Muslim ascetic
ganj: market
ganja: dried leaves and flowering tops of female cannabis plant—smoke it and see what happens
Garuda: Vishnu's half-man, half-bird vehicle
ghat: riverbank used for bathing, often paved with steps
Ghats: ranges of hills on the east and west coasts of the Indian peninsula
ghazal: Urdu love song
godown: factory warehouse
gompa: Tibetan Buddhist monastery

gopis: Krishna's flirtatious milkmaid friends
gopuram: entrance tower of a South Indian Hindu temple
GPO: General Post Office
guru: religious teacher; in Sikhism, one of the 10 founding leaders of the Sikh faith
Guru Granth Sahib: Sikh holy book
gurudwara: Sikh temple
Haj: the pilgrimage to Mecca that all Muslims are required to make once in their lifetime if physically and financially able
Hanuman: monkey god, helper of Rama in the *Ramayana*
harmonium: air-powered keyboard instrument
harijan: literally, "child of God," Mahatma Gandhi's name for the Untouchables
hartal: general strike
haveli: Rajasthani mansion, traditionally painted with murals
hijra: eunuch; transvestite
hookah: elaborate smoking apparatus in which the smoke is drawn through a long pipe and a container of water
howdah: seat for an elephant rider
imam: prayer leader of mosque, or Shi'a Muslim leader descended from Muhammad
imambara: tomb of a Shi'a Muslim imam, or a replica of one
Indo-Saracenic: architecture merging Indian style with Islamic style from the Middle East
Indra: early Hindu god of thunder, king of the Vedic gods
jagamohana: audience hall or "porch" of a Hindu temple
jali: geometric latticework pattern in Islamic architecture
Janata Dal: political party based in U.P. and Bihar, supported by low-caste Hindus, symbolized by a wheel
Jat: large North Indian agricultural caste
jati: sub-division within the four Hindu castes
jauhar: Rajput custom of mass *sati*
-ji: respectful suffix added to names
JKLF: Jammu and Kashmir Liberation Front
juggernaut: corruption of the deity Jagannath's name; refers to large ceremonial carts used to transport the deity
jyotirlinga: a self-erecting *linga;* there are 12 in India
Kali: black-skinned Hindu goddess with lolling tongue who wears snakes and skulls
kama: physical love, one of the four goals of a Hindu's life. Have you heard of the Kama Sutra?
kameez: loose-fitting woman's shirt
karma: what goes around comes around, man
kata: silk prayer shawl, usually presented to a lama when visiting a monastery
khadi: homespun, handwoven cotton cloth
Khalistan: "Land of the Pure, " name of independent Punjab desired by Sikh separatists
khalsa: Punjabi for "pure;" a "baptized" Sikh
khukuri: machete-like Nepalese "Gurkha" knife
Krishna: blue-skinned Hindu god, who plays the flute and frolics with milkmaids; Arjuna's charioteer in *Mahabharata* who sang *Bhagavad Gita;* considered an avatar of Vishnu
kshatriya: member of the warrior/ruler caste, second highest of the four *varnas* of the Hindu caste system
kumbh: pitcher or pot
kurta: long men's shirt
la: moutain pass in the Himalayas and surrounding ranges
lakh: one hundred thousand (usually rupees or people), written 1,00,000
Lakshmi: Goddess of fortune and wealth, often considered the consort of Vishnu
lama: Tibetan-Buddhist priest or holy man
lila: Hindu concept of divine "play:" a god (usually Krishna) sporting with human worshippers, or theatrical production depicting a myth (usually *Ramayana*).
linga: also *lingam;* stone phallus that symbolizes Shiva
Lok Sabha: lower house of Indian parliament
lungi: sarong tied around a man's waist
Macchendranath: Newari rain god
maha: great
Mahabharata: Sanskrit epic about the five Pandava brothers' struggle to regain their kingdom
mahal: palace
mahout: elephant trainer
mandala: circle symbolizing universe in Hindu and Buddhist art, used in meditation
mandapam: colonnaded hall leading up to a Hindu or Jain temple sanctum
mandir: temple
mani: stone wall with Tibetan inscriptions
mantra: sacred word or chant used by Hindus and Buddhists to aid in meditation
marg: road
masjid: mosque; Muslim place of worship

math: residence for Hindu priests or sadhus
maya: the illusory world of everyday life
mehendi: painting of intricate, semi-permanent henna designs on the hands or feet
mela: fair or festival
moksha: Hindu salvation; liberation from cycle of rebirth
monsoon: season of extremely heavy rains
muezzin: crier who calls Muslims to prayer from the minaret of a mosque
mullah: Muslim scholar or leader
nadi: river
naga: Hindu aquatic snake deity
nagar: city
Nandi: Shiva's bull vehicle
Narayan: Vishnu sleeping on the cosmic ocean
nawab: Muslim governor or landowner
NDP: National Democratic Party, right-wing party in Nepal
neem: plant product used as an insecticide
Nepali Congress: centrist party that led the movement for democracy in Nepal, symbolized by a tree
nirvana: nothingness, the snuffing out of the flame, the goal of Buddhists
Om: ॐ; sacred invocation; mantra used by Hindus and Buddhists.
paise: 1/100 of a rupee
pagoda: Nepalese Hindu temple with tiered roofs
palanquin: hand-carried carriage
panchayat: traditional 5-member village
pandit: honored or wise person; Hindu priest
Parsi: "Persian; " Zoroastrians who migrated to India after Muslim conversion of Iran
Partition: 1947 division of British India along religious lines to create India and Pakistan
Parvati: mountain goddess; consort of Shiva through whom his power is expressed
peon: low-level worker
pipal: the Buddha meditated his way to enlightenment under one of these.
prasad: food consecrated by a Hindu deity and given out to worshipers
puja: prayers and offerings of food and flowers to a Hindu deity
pujari: Hindu priest conducting ceremonies in a temple
pukka: finished, ripe, complete
Puranas: Hindu mythological poems
purdah: Muslim practice of secluding women
qawwali: Sufi devotional or love song
qila: fort
Qu'ran: Muslim holy book containing God's revelations as told to Mohammed
Radha: milkmaid consort of Krishna
raga: melodic structure, the base for lengthy musical improvisations
raj: government or sovereignty
Raj: the British Empire in India
raja: king
Rajputs: medieval Hindu warrior-princes of central India and Rajasthan
Rama: Hindu hero-god of the *Ramayana* who defeats the demon Ravana; avatar of Vishnu
Ramadan: holiest month in the Islamic calendar, when Muslims fast from dawn to dusk
Ramayana: epic "romance of Rama" telling of Rama's rescue of wife Sita from Ravana
rani: queen
rath: cart, particularly one used in Hindu religious festivals
Ravana: villain of the epic *Ramayana*
RSS: Rashtriya Swayamsevak Sangh (National Volunteer Corps), Hindu nationalist paramilitary organization
sadhu: ascetic Hindu holy man
sagar: sea or lake
sahib: "master," Raj-era title for Europeans
salwar: women's baggy pants worn with kameez
sambar: large, dark brown deer
samsara: the endless cycle of life, death, and rebirth in Buddhism and Hinduism
sangam: meeting point of two rivers; also name of early gatherings of Tamil poets
sankha: Vishnu's conch shell
sannyasin: "renouncer," Hindu ascetic wanderer who has given up worldly life
sant: saint, holy man
sari: six(sometimes nine) yards of cloth, usually silk or cotton, draped around a woman's body, worn with a matching blouse
sati: ritual whereby widows burned themselves on their husbands' funeral pyres
Sati: Hindu goddess who landed in pieces all over India, forming *shakti pithas;* considered Shiva's consort
satyagraha: "truth force," Mahatma Gandhi's protest by non-violent non-cooperation

scheduled castes: official name for the former "Untouchable" groups, whose castes are listed in a "schedule" in the constitution
scheduled tribes: aboriginal groups recognized under the Indian constitution
sepoy: Indian serving in British Indian army under the Raj
Shaivite: follower of Shiva
shakti: divine feminine power in Hinduism
shakti pitha: Hindu holy place associated with the goddess Sati
Shankara: another name for Shiva
shanti: peace
shekari: an Orissan architectural style
Shi'a: Muslim sect which split from the Sunnis in the 8th century AD in a succession dispute; Shi'as look to imams in Iran as their spiritual leaders
shikhara: pyramid-shaped spire on a Hindu temple
Shitala: "cool" goddess of smallpox and other fever diseases in North India
Shiva: great god of Hinduism, known as the Destroyer in the Hindu trinity; usually depicted as an ascetic holy man
Shiv Sena: regional Hindu nationalist party in Maharashtra
shudra: member of the laborer caste, lowest of the four Hindu castes
sindur: vermilion paste used as an offering to Hindu deities
Sita: Rama's wife in the *Ramayana,* kidnapped by Ravana
sitar: 20-stringed instrument made from a gourd with a teakwood bridge
Sri: title of respect and veneration
STD/ISD: standard trunk dialing/international subscriber dialing. Nothing to do with sex
stupa: large mound, traditionally containing a Buddhist relic
Sufi: member of Islamic devotional and mystical movement
Sunni: largest Muslim sect; believes in elected leaders for the Islamic community
swadeshi: domestic goods; the Indian freedom movement called for their use rather than British imports
swaraj: self-rule, as demanded by the Indian freedom movement
sweeper: low-caste or Untouchable Hindu whose vocation is sweeping streets (hence the name) or cleaning latrines
tabla: two-piece drum set
tal: lake
tara: Tantric female companion to a dhyani Buddha
Terai: foothills at the base of the Himalayas
tempo: Bee-colored three-wheelers that screech and stink their way through cities like mechanised elephants on speed
thanka: Tibetan scroll-painting of a *mandala,* used as an meditation aid
thukpa: Tibetan noodle soup
tirtha: "crossing" between earth and heaven
tirthankara: one of 24 Jain "crossing-makers," a series of saints culminating with Mahavira, the founder of Jainism
tonga: two-wheeled carriage drawn (slowly) by an old horse or maltreated pony
topi: cap
trishul: trident, symbol of Shiva and originally a symbol of the Goddess
Untouchables: casteless Hindus, formerly shunned by high-caste Hindus because their touch was considered polluting; now known as scheduled castes, Dalits, or Harijans
Upanishads: speculative, philosophical Sanskrit Hindu hymns composed around 800 BC
utthapam: thick dosa made with onion
Vaishnavite: follower of Vishnu
vaishya: member of the merchant caste, third-highest of the four Hindu castes
vajra: Nepalese Buddhist thunderbolt symbol
varna: broad group of Hindu castes; *brahmins, kshatriyas, vaishyas,* and *shudras* are the four *varnas*
Vedas: sacred Sanskrit hymns composed between 1500 and 800 BC, forming the basis of the Hindu religion
Vishnu: one of the Great Gods of Hinduism, known as the Preserver in the Hindu trinity; frequently appears on earth as an *avatar* to save earth from demons
VHP: Vishwa Hindu Parishad (World Hindu Society), Hindu nationalist organization
wallah: occupational suffix, e.g *rickshaw-wallah, Let's Go-wallah*
yaksha/yakshi: early Hindu nature deity
Yama: early Hindu god of death
yoni: circular base, often accompanying a *linga*
zakat: almsgiving required of Muslims
zamindar: tax collector or landlord in Mughal India

FOOD AND DRINK

aloo: potato
am: mango
appam: South Indian rice pancake
arrak: fermented mash of malted rice, serious headache juice
badam: almond
baingan: eggplant
barfi: milk- and sugar-based Indian sweet
betel: red nut with mild narcotic properties when chewed; key ingredient in *paan.*
bhaji: vegetables dipped in batter and fried
bhang: dried leaves and shoots of the male cannabis plant
bhat: cooked rice
bhindi: okra (lady's fingers)
bidi: small cigarette made from a rolled-up tobacco leaf
biryani: rice cooked with spices and vegetables or meat
capsicum: bell pepper
chaat: snack
chai (chiya): tea, generally boiled with milk and sugar
chang: Himalayan rice wine
channa: chickpeas
chappati: unleavened, griddle-cooked bread
cheeni: sugar
chikki: peanut brittle
cutlet: meat or vegetable patty
dahi: yogurt
dal: lentil soup, a staple dish eaten with rice
dhaba: roadside food stand
dosa: South Indian rice-flour pancake
dudh: milk
dum: steamed
feni: Goan drink made from fermented coconuts or cashews
ganja: dried leaves and flowering tops of female cannabis plant—smoke it and see what happens
garam: hot
ghee: clarified butter
gosht: mutton or goat
gulab jamun: dry milk balls in sweet syrup
halal: food prepared according to Islamic dietary rules
idli: South Indian steamed rice-flour cakes
jalebis: deep fried, orange, syrup-filled sweet
kaju: cashew nut
kheer: rice cooked in sweetened milk, raisins, and almonds
kofta: meat- or vegetable-balls
korma: creamy curry
kulfi: thick pistachio-flavored ice cream
kumb palak: spinach
lassi: yogurt and ice-water drink
machli: fish
masala: a mix of spices, usually containing cumin, coriander, and cardamom
mirch: hot pepper
momo: Tibetan stuffed pastry similar to wontons or ravioli
murgh: chicken
mutter: green peas
naan: unleavened bread cooked in a tandoor
naryal: coconut
paan: betel leaf stuffed with areca nut
pakoras: cheese or other foods deep-fried in chickpea batter
palak: spinach
paneer: fermented curd; cheesy comestibles
pani: water
papad: crispy lentil wafer
paratha: multi-layered, whole-wheat bread cooked on a griddle
phal: fruit
pongal: rice item garnished with black peppers and chilies, often sweet
pulao: fried rice with nuts or fruit
puri: small, deep-fried bread
raita: spicy salad of vegetables and yogurt

raksi: strong Himalayan liquor
roti: bread
saag: pureed spinach or other greens
sabji: vegetables
sambar: South Indian lentil soup
samosa: deep-fried vegetable or meat pastry
thali: complete meal served on steel plate with small dishes of condiments
thukpa: Tibetan noodle soup
tiffin: snack or light meal
toddy: unrefined coconut liquor
tong-ba: Nepali grain liquor
utthapam: thick dosa made with onion
vadai: doughnut-shaped rice cake dipped in curd or sambar
vindaloo: very hot South Indian curry

ENGLISH	HINDI	ENGLISH	HINDI
		Hindi is understood in most of North India.	
Hello.	Namaste.	**How are you?**	Kaise hain, aap?
Sorry/Forgive me.	Maaf kijiyega.	**Yes/No**	Ha/Nahin.
Thank you.	Shukriya.	**No thanks.**	Nahin, shukriya.
Good-bye.	Phir milenge.	**No problem.**	Koi baat nahin.
When (what time)?	Kub?	**What?**	Kyaa?
OK.	Thik hai.	**Why?**	Kyoonh?
Who?	Kaun?	**Help!**	Bachao!
How much does this cost?	Kyaa daam hai?	**Go away/Leave me alone.**	Chale jao/Mujhe akela chor do.
Stop/enough.	Bas.	**Is...available?**	Yahand...milta hai?
Please repeat.	Phir se kahiye.	**What's this called in Hindi?**	Hindi mein kaise kehte hain?
Please speak slowly.	Kripya, dhire boliye.	**I don't understand.**	Mein nahin samajhta.
What is your name?	Apkaa naam kyaa hai?	**My name is...**	Mera naam...hai.
I like...	Mujhe...achaa lagta hai.	**I don't like...**	Mujhe...achaa nahin lagta.
Directions			
turn right	dayne hath muro.	**turn left**	bayne hath muro.
How do I get to...?	...kaise jayen?	**How far is...?**	...kitna dur hai?
near	paas	**far**	dur
Where is...?	...kahan hai?	**out**	baahar
below	neeche	**at the back of**	peeche
above	oopar	**in front of**	saamne
Food and Drink			
bread	roti, chappaati, naan	**rice**	chaaval
meat	gosht	**water**	pani
vegetables	sabzi	**sweets**	mitthai
Times and Hours			
open	khula	**closed**	bandh
What time is it?	Kitne baje hain?	**morning**	subah
afternoon	dopaher	**evening**	shaam
night	raat	**yesterday**	kal
today	aaj	**tomorrow**	kal
Other Words			
alone	akela	**friend**	dost
good	achhaa	**bad**	bura
hot	garam	**cold**	thunda

ENGLISH	HINDI		ENGLISH	HINDI	
		Hindi is understood in most of North India.			
medicine	dawaii		alcohol	daru/sharaab	
Numbers					
one	ek	१	ten	dus	१०
two	do	२	eleven	gyaarah	११
three	teen	३	twelve	baarah	१२
four	char	४	fifteen	pandraah	१५
five	paanch	५	twenty	bees	२०
six	chey	६	twenty-five	pachis	२५
seven	saat	७	fifty	pachaas	५०
eight	aath	८	one hundred	ek sau	१००
nine	nau	९	one thousand	ek hazar	१०००

ENGLISH	BENGALI	ENGLISH	BENGALI
	Bengali is spoken in West Bengal and Bangladesh.		
Hello.	Nomoshkar.	How are you?	Kemon achen?
Sorry/Forgive me.	Maf korben.	No problem.	Hoye jabe.
Thank you.	Dhonyobad.	Yes/No.	Ha/Na.
Goodbye/ See you later.	Biday/Abar dekha hobe.	OK.	Achha/Thik.
Why?	Keno?	When?	Kathan?
Who?	Ke?	What?	Ki?
What is your name?	Apnar nam ki?	Stop/enough.	Bas.
How much does this cost?	Koto taka?	Go away/leave me alone.	Chere din/Birakto korben na.
Is...available?	...ache?	What's this called in Bengali?	Banglay eta ke ki bole?
Help!	Bachao!	Please repeat.	Aabar bolun.
My name is...	Amar nam...	Please speak slowly	Aste aste bolun.
I like...	Amar...bhalo lage.	I don't like...	Amar...bhalo lage na.
I don't understand.	Bujhi na.		
Directions			
(to the) right	dan dike	(to the) left	bam dike
How do I get to...?	...ki kore jabo?	How far is...?	...koto door?
near	kache	far	door
Where is...?	...kothai?	across	opar
Food			
bread	paoruti	rice	bhat
meat	mangsho	water	jol/pani
vegetables	shobji	fish	maachh
Times and Hours			
open	khola	closed	bandho
What time is it?	Koita baje?	morning	shokal
afternoon	bikel	evening	sondhya
night	raat	yesterday	gotokal

ENGLISH	BENGALI	ENGLISH	BENGALI
	Bengali is spoken in West Bengal and Bangladesh.		
today	aaj	tomorrow	agamikal
Other Words			
alone	aka	friend (M/F)	bondhu/bandhobi
good	bhalo	bad	kharap
happy	khushi	sad	dukhi, mon mora
hot	gorom	cold	thandha
office	doftor	backpack	bojha
condoms	nirodh	pain	byatha
Numbers			
one	ak	১	twenty	bish	২০
two	dui	২	thirty	tirish	৩০
three	tin	৩	forty	chollish	৪০
four	char	৪	fifty	ponchash	৫০
five	panch	৫	sixty	shaat	৬০
six	choi	৬	seventy	sattar	৭০
seven	saat	৭	eighty	aashi	৮০
eight	aat	৮	ninety	nabbai	৯০
nine	noi	৯	one hundred	ek sho	১০০
ten	dosh	১০	one thousand	ek hajar	১০০০

ENGLISH	TAMIL	ENGLISH	TAMIL
	Tamil is spoken in Tamil Nadu.		
Hello.	Namaskaram.	How are you?	Yep padi irukkai?
Sorry/Forgive me.	Mannikkavum.	No problem.	Kavalai illai.
Thank you.	Nanri.	No thanks.	Illai, véndam.
Yes/No.	Amam/Illai.	OK.	Se ri.
Good-bye.	Poittu Varén.	When (what time)?	Yéppo?
Why?	Yén?	What?	Yénna?
Who?	Yaru?	Is...available?	...irukka?
How much does this cost?	Yenna velai?	Go away/leave me alone.	Yenna vidu.
Please speak slowly.	Medhuva pésungo.	What's this called in Tamil?	...Tamilla yenna?
I don't understand.	Puriyalai.	Help!	Kapathu!
Please repeat.	Thiruppi.	Stop/enough.	Porum.
I like...	Ennakku...pidikkum.	I don't like...	Ennakku...pidikkaathu.
What is your name?	Ungal péyar ennai?	My name is...	En peyar...
Directions			
(to the) right	valadu pakkam	(to the) left	idadhu pakkam
How do I get to...?	...eppadi poradu?	How far is...?	...evvalavu dooram?
near	pakkam	far	dooram
above...	...kku melai	below...	...kku kirai
in front of...	...kku munnadi	at the back of...	...kku pinnadi
Food and Drink			
vegetables	kari kai	rice	saadam
meat	maamsam	water	thanni

ENGLISH	TAMIL	ENGLISH	TAMIL
		Tamil is spoken in Tamil Nadu.	
mango	maampazham	bread	roddi
Time and Hours			
open	tharandhu	closed	moodi
What time is it?	Yénna néram?	morning	kaathaalai
afternoon	madyaanam	evening	saayankaalam
night	raatri	yesterday	néthikku
today	innikki	tomorrow	nalai
Other Words			
alone	thaniya	friend	nanban
good	nalladhu	bad	kettadhu
hot	soodu	cold	aarinadhu
temple	kovil	doctor	maruthuvar
hospital	aaspathri	medicine	marunthu
Numbers			
one	onrru	1	twenty	iruvathu	20
two	eranndu	2	thirty	muppathu	30
three	moonrru	3	forty	naapathu	40
four	naanru	4	fifty	aiympathu	50
five	aiynthu	5	sixty	aruvathu	60
six	aarru	6	seventy	yerupathu	70
seven	yeru	7	eighty	yennpathu	80
eight	yettu	8	ninety	thonnoorru	90
nine	onpathu	9	one hundred	noorru	100
ten	paththu	10	one thousand	aayeram	1000

ENGLISH	NEPALI	ENGLISH	NEPALI
	Nepali is spoken in Nepal.		
Hello.	Namaste/ Namaskar.	How are you?	Kasto chha?
Sorry/Forgive me.	Sorry (maph garnus).	No problem./I'm fine.	Thik chha.
Thank you.	Danyabad.	No thanks.	Pardaina, danyabad.
Yes/No.	Ho/Hoina.	Good-bye.	Namaste.
When(what time)?	Kahile?	What?	Ke?
Who?	Ko?	Is...available?	...paincha?
Why?	Kina?	OK.	Huncha./La.
How much does this cost?	Kati ho?	Go away. (polite/ impolite)	Tapai januus ta./Jau!
I don't understand.	Bujina.	Please repeat.	Feri bhannus.
Please speak slowly.	Bistarai bolnus.	What's this called in Nepali?	Nepali ma ke bhanchha?
What is your name?	Tapai ko naam ke ho?	My name is...	Mero naam...ho.
Help!	Guhar!	My country is...	Mero desh...ho.
I like...	... man parcha.	I don't like...	... mar par dai na.
Stop/enough.	Pugyo.	Please give me..	Kripa garera malai...
Does anyone here speak English?	Yahan angreji bolne kohi chha?	I have a reservation.	Mero yahan reservation chha.

ENGLISH	NEPALI	ENGLISH	NEPALI
		Nepali is spoken in Nepal.	
Directions			
(to the) right	daya, dahurie.	**(to the) left**	baya, debre.
How do I get to...?	...kosari janne?	**How far is...?**	...kati tada cha?
near	najik	**far**	tada
east	purba	**west**	paschima
Food and Drink			
bread	pauroti	**rice**	bhat
meat	masu	**water**	pani
vegetables	tarkari	**food/meal**	khana
Time and Hours			
open	khulcha	**closed**	bandha
What time is it?	Kati bajyo?	**morning**	bihana
afternoon	diooso	**evening**	sanjha
night	rati	**yesterday**	hijo
today	aaja	**tomorrow**	bholi
Other Words			
alone	eklai	**friend**	sathi
good	ramro	**bad**	naramro
happy	kushi	**sad**	dukhi
hot	garmi (weather)/tato	**cold**	jaado (weather)/chiso
newspaper	akhbar	**magazine**	patrika

ENGLISH	NEPALI		ENGLISH	NEPALI	
Numbers					
one	ek	१	**twenty**	biss	२०
two	dui	२	**thirty**	tees	३०
three	teen	३	**forty**	chaliss	४०
four	char	४	**fifty**	pachass	५०
five	panch	५	**sixty**	saathi	६०
six	chha	६	**seventy**	sattari	७०
seven	saat	७	**eighty**	asi	८०
eight	aathh	८	**ninety**	nabbe	९०
nine	nau	९	**one hundred**	ek saya	१००

ENGLISH	GUJARATI	ENGLISH	GUJARATI
	Gujarati is spoken in Gujarat.		
Hello.	Namaste.	**How are you?**	Kem cho?
Sorry/Forgive me.	Maaf karo.	**Yes/No.**	Ha/Na.
Thank you.	Aabhar.	**I am fine.**	Hu majama chu.
Good-bye.	Avjo.	**No problem.**	Kaye vandhon nathi.
When?	Kyare?	**I like...**	Mane...gameche.
Is...available?	...maleche?	**Stop/enough.**	Bas.
What is your name?	Tamaru nam su che?	**Help!**	Bachao!
My name is...	Maru nam...che.	**My country is...**	Maro desh...che.
Go away/Leave me alone.	Jatore.	**I don't like...**	Mane...gamtu nathi.

ENGLISH	GUJARATI	ENGLISH	GUJARATI
	Gujarati is spoken in Gujarat.		
Directions			
to the right	jamani baju	to the left	dabi baju
How do I get to...?	...no rasto kayo che?	How far is...?	...ketlu dur che?
Time and Hours			
open	khulu	closed	band
night	raat	yesterday	kale (gay kale)
today	aaje	tomorrow	kale (avti kale)
Numbers			
one	ek	૧	six	chah	૬
two	be	૨	seven	sat	૭
three	tran	૩	eight	aath	૮
four	char	૪	nine	nav	૯
five	pach	૫	ten	das	૧૦

ENGLISH	KANNADA	ENGLISH	KANNADA
	Kannada is spoken in Karnataka.		
Hello.	Ain samachar.	Good-bye.	Namaskara.
What is your name?	Ni nna he sa ru?	My name is...	Na nna he sa ru...
Please excuse me.	Da ya ma di na nna ksha mi si ri.	How much is this?	...nsu he ge?
Give me...	Ardha...	newspaper	varthapatrike
room	kone	address	vilasa
Directions			
to the right	jamani baju	to the left	dabi baju
How do I get to...?	...no rasto kayo che?	How far is...?	...ketlu dur che?
front	munde	back	hinde
Time and Hours			
open	khulu	closed	band
evening	sayankala	night	rathri
noon	hagalu	early morning	...ketlu dur che?
Food and Drink			
bread	rotti	rice	akki
meat	mamsa	fruit	hannu
vegetables	tharakarl	water	niru
curd	mosaru	*dal*	thovve
Numbers			
one	ondu	೧	six	aru	೬
two	eradu	೨	seven	elu	೭
three	muru	೩	eight	entu	೮
four	nalku	೪	nine	ombathu	೯
five	aidu	೫	ten	haththu	೧೦

ENGLISH	MALAYALAM	ENGLISH	MALAYALAM
	Malayalam is spoken in Kerala.		
Hello.	Namaste.	How are you?	Enngane irikkunnu?
Sorry/Forgive me.	Kshemikkuga.	Yes/No	Ade/alla
Thank you.	Valara upakaram.	No thanks.	Véndá.
Good-bye.	Pogetté.	No problem.	Sárawilla.
When/What time?	Eppoyá/eppam?	OK.	Seri.
Who?	Árá?	I like...	Enikka ... istamá.
Go away/Leave me alone.	Pó, salyappadade.	Stop/enough.	Madi.
I don't understand.	Samajha nahin.	Use the meter!	Míteru kanakkáyitta!
What is your name?	Ninngade pér endá?	Help!	Onnu saháyikkámó?
My name is...	Enda péru ...	My country is...	Enda támassam ... ilá.
Directions			
How do I get to...?	... édu vazhiyá?	How far is...?	... ettara dúramá?
Where is...?	Ewidá?	above...	... ende molil
below...	... ende thara	in front of...	... munbil
behind...	... pinnil	inside	aahathe
outside	purethe		
Food and Drink			
bread	rotti	rice	córa
meat	eracci	water	vellam
meal	batchanam		
Time and Hours			
open	torannu	closed	adaccu
What time is it?	Ettara maniyá?	yesterday	innala
today	innu	tomorrow	nále
Numbers			
one	onnu	൧	six	aaru	൬
two	rendu	൨	seven	eru	൭
three	moonu	൩	eight	ettu	൮
four	naalu	൪	nine	onpathu	൯
five	anju	൫	ten	pathu	൰

ENGLISH	TELUGU	ENGLISH	TELUGU
	Telugu is spoken in Andhra Pradesh.		
Hello.	Emandi	How are you?	Meeru ela unnaru?
Sorry/Forgive me.	Kshaminchandi.	No problem.	Paravaledu.
Thank you.	Krithagnatalu	No thanks.	Vaddandi.
Yes/No.	Avunu/Kaadu	OK.	Sare.
Good-bye.	Poyesta.	When(what time)?	Eppudu (time entha)?
What is your name?	Mee peru emiti?	My name is...	Naa peru ...
Directions			
How do I get to...?	... ki poye daniki dari emiti?	How far is...?	... entha duramu?
near	daggara	far	dooramu

ENGLISH	TELUGU		ENGLISH	TELUGU	
Telugu is spoken in Andhra Pradesh.					
Food					
vegetables	kooragayalu		rice	annamu	
meat	mamsamu		water	neeru	
Numbers					
one	okati	1	six	aaru	6
two	rendu	2	seven	eedu	7
three	moodu	3	eight	enimidi	8
four	naalugu	4	nine	tommidi	9
five	aidu	5	ten	padi	10

INDEX

ABOUT LET'S GO

GUIDES FOR THE INDEPENDENT TRAVELER

Budget travel is more than a vacation. At *Let's Go*, we see every trip as the chance of a lifetime. If your dream is to grab a knapsack and a machete and forge through the jungles of Brazil, we can take you there. Or, if you'd rather enjoy the Riviera sun at a beachside cafe, we'll set you a table. If you know what you're doing, you can have any experience you want—whether it's camping among lions or sampling Tuscan desserts—without maxing out your credit card. We'll show you just how far your coins can go, and prove that the greatest limitation on your adventure is not your wallet, but your imagination. That said, we understand that you may want the occasional indulgence after a week of hostels and kebab stands, so we've added "Big Splurges" to let you know which establishments are worth those extra euros, as well as price ranges to help you quickly determine whether an accommodation or restaurant will break the bank. While we may have diversified, our emphasis will always be on finding the best values for your budget, giving you all the info you need to spend six days in London or six months in Tasmania.

BEYOND THE TOURIST EXPERIENCE

We write for travelers who know there's more to a vacation than riding double-deckers with tourists. Our researchers give you the heads-up on both world-renowned and lesser-known attractions, on the best local eats and the hottest nightclub beats. In our travels, we talk to everybody; we provide a snapshot of real life in the places you visit with our sidebars on topics like regional cuisine, local festivals, and hot political issues. We've opened our pages to respected writers and scholars to show you their take on a given destination, and turned to lifelong residents to learn the little things that make their city worth calling home. And we've even given you Alternatives to Tourism—ideas for how to give back to local communities through responsible travel and volunteering.

OVER FORTY YEARS OF WISDOM

When we started, way back in 1960, Let's Go consisted of a small group of well-traveled friends who compiled their budget travel tips into a 20-page packet for students on charter flights to Europe. Since then, we've expanded to suit all kinds of travelers, now publishing guides to six continents, including our newest guides: *Let's Go: Japan* and *Let's Go: Brazil*. Our guides are still annually researched and written entirely by students on shoe-string budgets, adventurous travelers who know that train strikes, stolen luggage, food poisoning, and marriage proposals are all part of a day's work. Even as you read this, work on next year's editions is well underway. Whether you're reading one of our new titles, like *Let's Go: Puerto Rico* or *Let's Go Adventure Guide: Alaska*, or our original best-seller, *Let's Go: Europe*, you'll find the same spirit of adventure that has made *Let's Go* the guide of choice for travelers the world over since 1960.

GETTING IN TOUCH

The best discoveries are often those you make yourself; on the road, when you find something worth sharing, please drop us a line. We're Let's Go Publications, 67 Mt. Auburn St., Cambridge, MA 02138, USA (feedback@letsgo.com).

For more info, visit our website: www.letsgo.com.

"no worries, mate."

"no worries" is exactly what you will get with contiki – a hassle-free vacation designed just for 18 to 35 year olds. make new friends, enjoy your free time and explore the sights in a convenient trip that gives you more bang for your buck...**from only $70/day** including accommodations, sightseeing, many meals and transportation. with contiki, you will never get bogged down downunder!

> 7 nights **great keppel island** from $439*
    exclusive contiki resort located off the queensland coast!

> 6 days **sydney to melbourne** getaway from $679*
    sydney opera house, sydney harbor, melbourne cricket gound, bells beach and other hot spots!

> 14 days **beaches and reefs** from $965*
    sydney, brisbane, noosa, townsville, cairns, port douglas, surfers paradise, great barrier reef and more!

    *prices subject to change, land only.

for more info on our trips...
see your travel agent
call 1-888-CONTIKI
visit www.contiki.com

contiki
VACATIONS for 18-35 year olds

CST# 1001728-20

> europe   > australia   > new zealand   > america   > canada

FOUR-STAR HOTEL PAID FOR WITH MONEY FOUND IN COUCH.

Save up to 70%
on great hotels
with OrbitzSaver rates.*

ORBITZ.com

©2003 Orbitz, LLC. CST# 2063530-50 *Savings based on comparison with published rack rates.

Travel to another country by volunteering internationally

"You will feel the heartbeat of the country."

~ Judy, India volunteer

Participate in a Cross-Cultural Solutions short-term international volunteer program and get to know a country from the inside-out. Connect with local people while working side-by-side on locally designed and driven projects, participating in educational and cultural programming and reflecting on your experience during your free time.

It's your experience.

Make the most of it by participating in a Cross-Cultural Solutions international volunteer program either in Brazil, China, Costa Rica, Ghana, Guatemala, India, Peru, Russia, Thailand, or Tanzania. Programs run year-round from 2-12 weeks and the 2003 program fees start at $1,985. Contact us today to learn more about participating in your international volunteer program.

Cross-Cultural Solutions
AN INTERNATIONAL
VOLUNTEER PROGRAM

WWW.CROSSCULTURALSOLUTIONS.ORG
1-800-380-4777 · INFO@CROSSCULTURALSOLUTIONS.ORG

MAP INDEX

MAP LEGEND

✈ Airport	🏠 Hotel/Hostel	∫ Waterfall	
✚ Hospital	🚌 Bus Station	⛺ Camping	Border Crossing
Police	🚆 Railway Station	🍎 Food	Ⓜ Subway Station
✉ Post Office	A Hindu Temple	♪ Entertainment	
ⓘ Tourist Office	Sikh Gurudwara	🍺 Bars/Pubs	Mountains
$ Bank	Buddhist Temple	Theater	Countour Lines
℞ Pharmacy	Church/Cathedral	🏛 Museum	
☎ Telephone	Mosque	Mountain Pass	Ferry Route
■ Site or Point of Interest	Ghat	Hot Springs	Pedestrian Zone
Embassy or Consulate	Capital City	Beach	Stairs
Library	Gate or Entrance	⚓ Ferry Terminal	Footpaths/Trails
Internet Cafe	TAXI Taxi Stand	Lighthouse	Railroads